Peasants and Religion

This study permits the authors to open new perspectives for the understanding of key features of Dominican culture. It is based on an impressive empirical investigation and a penetrating contribution with respect to popular religion and messianic movements.
Roberto Cassá, Universidad Autónoma de Santo Domingo

A remarkable and exhaustive study that should be required reading for anyone with a serious interest, not only in the island of Hispaniola, but in the Latin American peasantry and folk religion.
Bernard Diederich, ex *Time* magazine correspondent for Mexico,
Central America and the Carribbean

Peasants and Religion is a very rare example of a work of 'social science' in the true sense of the word, one that transcends the traditional divisions between economics, history, anthropology and political science. Its analytical depth and richness make it a remarkably integrated contribution in the tradition of Gunnar Myrdal.
Ronald Findlay, Columbia University

Its importance lies in the attempt to show how this microcosm might explain the continuing power of religion. It provides a laboratory 'experiment' which could also explain the origins of the world's great religions.
Deepak Lal, University of California, Los Angeles

The authors have given us a painstakingly detailed reconstruction of dramatic events. With a fine historical sense, they analyze the subject within the framework of economic and political change in the Dominican Republic.
Magnus Mörner, University of Göteborg

An ambitious and meticulous work, whose conceptual significance stretches well beyond the Dominican Republic.
Allan Pred, University of California, Berkeley

Peasants and Religion

Peasants and Religion examines the relationship between economics, politics and religion through the case of Olivorio Mateo and the religious movement he inspired from 1908 in the Dominican Republic. The authors explore how and why the new religion was formed, why it was so successful and why it was violently suppressed, considering such factors as the geographical and political context, changes in the international economic system and the arrival of modern capitalism in the country. Comparing this case with other peasant movements, they show ways in which folk religion serves as a response to particular problems which arise in peasant societies during times of stress.

This fascinating work will be of importance across the social sciences, offering new perspectives on the development and influence of religion and on the much-noted links between peasant rebellion and religious cults.

Jan Lundius is a research officer at the Department for Research Cooperation, Swedish International Development Cooperation Agency (SAREC/SIDA), Stockholm. He has worked as a consultant for several UN agencies.

Mats Lundahl is Professor of Development Economics at the Stockholm School of Economics. His previous publications with Routledge include *New Directions in Development Economics* (1996), *Economic Crisis in Africa* (1993), *Markets or Politics? Essays on Haitian Underdevelopment* (1992) and *Agrarian Society in History* (1990).

Routledge Studies in Development and Society

Peasants and Religion

A socioeconomic study of Dios Olivorio
and the Palma Sola Movement in the
Dominican Republic

Jan Lundius and Mats Lundahl

London and New York

First published 2000
by Routledge
11 New Fetter Lane, London EC4P 4EE

Simultaneously published in the USA and Canada
by Routledge
29 West 35th Street, New York, NY 10001

Routledge is an imprint of the Taylor and Francis Group

© 2000 Jan Lundius and Mats Lundahl

Typeset in Baskerville by Helen Skelton, London
Printed and bound in Great Britain by
St Edmundsbury Press, Bury St Edmunds, Suffolk

British Library Cataloguing in Publication Data
A catalogue record for this book is available from
the British Library

Library of Congress Cataloging in Publication Data
Lundius, Jan, 1954–
    Peasants and religion: a socioeconomic study of Dios Olivorio
and the Palma Sola movement in the Dominican Republic /
Jan Lundius and Mats Lundahl.
        p. cm.
    Includes bibliographical references and index.
    1. Mateo, Olivorio, 1908–1922. 2. Dominican Republic–
Religion–20th century. 3. Cults–Dominican Republic–History–
20th century. 4. Religion and sociology–Dominican Republic–
History–20th century. 5. Palma Sola (San Juan de la Maguana,
Dominican Republic)–Religion–20th century. 6. Cults–
Dominican Republic–Palma Sola (San Juan de la Maguana)–
History–20th century. 7. Religion and sociology–Dominican
Republic–Palma Sola (San Juan de la Maguana)–History–20th
century. I. Lundahl, Mats, 1946–   . II. Title.
BL2566.D65L86   2000
306.6'097293–dc21   99-24619
                                                      CIP

ISBN 0–415–17411–2

Contents

List of figures

Preface

The story of this book goes back to 1983 when one of us (Jan Lundius) was teaching history of religions at *Universidad Católica de Santo Domingo.* He then found out that the father of one of his students, Emigdio Garrido Puello, had written a biography of a mysterious 'messiah', Olivorio Mateo, who in the 1920s had been active in a valley close to the Haitian border. The story of Olivorio sounded like a medieval tale, but the events had taken place during the present century, and the cult was still active.

From there on it has been a long and winding road, both troublesome and tiresome, but constantly thrilling and rewarding: from our initial, vague and tentative discussion and identification of the problem, through innumerable drafts until the preparation of the final text. Our cooperation in writing this book has been sheer delight.

The book could never have been written without the unselfish and dedicated collaboration of a large number of people. First we want to thank all our interviewees, for opening both their homes and their hearts to us, and discussing highly personal and painful matters and events with two complete outsiders. We sincerely hope that we have been able to communicate their story in the same spirit as it was offered to us, conveying at least some of the love and respect that we feel for the people of the Dominican Republic.

Doña 'Tala' Cabral Ramírez shared her recollections of old San Juan with us and directed us to the person who was to become a constant conversation partner and source of information during a full decade, 'Mimicito' Ramírez, who in spite of his advanced age accompanied us into the countryside and introduced us to old *Olivoristas,* like the centenarian Julián Ramos, who had been a friend of Olivorio himself and who became one of our main informants. Very special thanks are due to one of the protagonists of our study, León Romilio Ventura, to the daughter of Delanoy Ventura, Juana María, and to the members of the vast Ventura family in Media Luna. Macario Lorenzo, the 'secretary' of Palma Sola, introduced us to the theology of the Palma Sola movement.

Leopoldo Figuereo brought us to Jínova and introduced us to Diego Cépeda, who gave us the opportunity to take part in genuine *Olivorista* ceremonies. Alina and David Alvarez put us in contact with several people in San Juan de la Maguana and Las Matas de Farfán. Alina's mother, Telma Dotel Matos, put us on the track of Olivorio's son and shared her recollections of her childhood in San Juan with us. José Garrido Ramírez introduced us to the subject of Olivorio, gave us access to his family's invaluable collection of *El Cable*, the newspaper which his father, Emigdio Garrido Puello, edited between 1921 and 1930, and introduced us to Víctor Garrido, Jr, who put us in touch with people from the old business community in San Juan and told us about his parents, Víctor Garrido and Tijides Ramírez de Garrido, both influential members of the San Juan elite. In San Juan we benefited from the wealth of information given to us by Mayobanex Rodríguez, ex-mayor of the city, and by Monseñor Thomas Reilly, who shared both his memories of the turbulent Trujillo decades and his rum with us.

The *Olivoristas* around the queen of Maguana Arriba, María Orfelia, were always generous and welcoming. Carlos Andújar, Juana López and Fradrique Lizardo took us to see voodoo ceremonies. The sons of General Miguel Rodríguez Reyes, Ramón Jesús and Miguel Antonio, gave us their trust and confidence in discussions of the very sensitive matter of the death of their father. 'Patoño' Bautista shared his manuscript of recollections of the Palma Sola movement with us and in addition gave us as many interviews as we requested. Jorge Feliz, Bryan Kennedy and 'Zita' Závala were helpful in providing information about the Palma Sola episode.

The second category of people who have been instrumental for our endeavor are our Dominican fellow researchers. Ana Marina Méndez collaborated actively in the project, sharing with us her unique collection of material surrounding the Palma Sola massacre, documented in her own book, *Palma Sola ... desde el sol hasta el ocaso: Un aporte bibliográfico a su estudio* (1986), an indispensable source for any future study of the Palma Sola movement, and in addition provided us with contacts to a large number of our interviewees, as well as inputs in the form of photos, articles, videos, etc. Without her the study would not have been carried out. Roberto Cassá also deserves more than just an honorary mention. Over the years we have bothered him with just about everything, ranging from material from his own investigations of the *Olivorista* movement, via specifics on Dominican currency history, to the significance of obscure Dominican terms and the spelling of names of people, places and institutions. Always a busy man, he has never failed to find the necessary answers for us.

Antonio Lluberes, of the *Sociedad de Jesús*, historian and good friend, both served as an intermediary when it came to establishing contacts with the Dominican clergy and published our first piece on Olivorio (Lundius and Lundahl (1989)), in *Estudios Sociales*. Segundo Vásquez, journalist at the *Hoy* newspaper, facilitated our access to the press archives and gave us useful inputs about Dominican history and folklore. Frank Moya Pons gave us access to the collections of the *Sociedad Dominicana de Bibliófilos* and helped us to establish our first base in Santo Domingo. Angel Moreta, himself a *Sanjuanero*, who at the time was working on his thesis about agriculture in the southwest, shared his knowledge about the San Juan Valley and its inhabitants with us. César Iván Feris gave us the foothold in the *Universidad Católica de Santo Domingo* which provided the initial idea for the book. Rubén Silié went out of his way to secure the necessary permissions for some very crucial material at the last moment. Michiel Baud, at the University of Leiden, who must count as a Dominican, if not in terms of nationality, definitely in terms of spirit and research orientation, gave us his findings about rural change in the Cibao during the nineteenth century and was a useful discussion partner in general.

We owe a special intellectual gratitude to our predecessors in the *Olivorista* field. Emigdio Garrido Puello's *Olivorio: Un ensayo histórico* (1963) remains the logical starting point for all research on both Olivorio and Palma Sola. Orlando Espín's doctoral dissertation, '*Evangelización y religiones negras: Propuesta de modelo de evangelización para el pastoral en la República Dominicana*' (1984), put *Olivorismo* in its wider social and religious context. Juan Manuel García's *La masacre de Palma Sola (Partidos, lucha política y el asesinato del general: 1961–1963)* (1986), pioneered the political analysis of the 1962 massacre and Lusitania Martínez' *Palma Sola (Su geografía mítica y social)* (1991) not only provides an account of the 1961–63 events, but also dissects the ideological and theological message of *Olivorismo*. Lusitania furthermore willingly shared and discussed her results and knowledge of the area with us.

Our interminable drafts have been read and improved upon by several friends and colleagues: Rosemary Vargas-Lundius, David Stoll, Tord Olsson, Arnim Geertz, Christina Rapp Lundahl, Kai Kaiser and Ronald Findlay. Michael Pretes not only had to suffer the contents but also the form. Together with Alan Harkess he is responsible for checking our English. Mats Lundahl enjoyed the privilege of spending the spring of 1991 in the congenial intellectual atmosphere of the Swedish Collegium for Advanced Study in the Social Sciences (SCASSS), in Uppsala. Bo Gustafsson, Ulf Hannertz, Hernán Horna, Jonas Pontusson, Tinne Vammen and Björn Wittrock all did their best to improve what was presented at the SCASSS seminar. The influence of Alan Pred, also at SCASSS in 1991, will be obvious to all readers. Some chapters have also been presented at the international economics seminar at the Stockholm School of Economics, to bewildered colleagues trying to figure out exactly what economics had to do with it all. At the postgraduate seminar at the Department of History of Religions at the University of Lund, Lundius experienced a similar problem: trying to explain why on earth he was working with an economist.

Mayra Ureña, Sagrada Bujosa and Carmen Rita Morera have assisted us with a large number of practical details, ranging from translations of some of our findings into Spanish, procurement of photos and publishing rights, transportation and contacts of all kinds. Carin Blomkvist has displayed unlimited patience keeping track of all our versions, emanating from such diverse places as Lund, Santo Domingo, Uppsala, Guatemala, Hanoi, New York, Stockholm and Rome. She has had to introduce a larger number of changes than we like to recall at this stage, chasing the most obscure bibliographical references, trying not to lose the vast amount of paper in circulation in any given moment. She is probably even happier than we that our work has finally come to an end. Siw Andersson has had a similarly traumatic experience attempting to draw maps from confused instructions, not necessarily written, having to correct them as soon as we have changed our minds about the courses of rivers, names of cities and the like.

Our research has been financed by the Swedish Agency for Research Cooperation with Developing Countries (SAREC). This support is gratefully acknowledged.

Last, but not least, we owe a debt of gratitude to those who for a lengthy period have had to suffer the direct consequences of our research activities: our wives, who may have had considerable doubts about the viability of the project and who at this point are completely fed up with both local religion and global economics, especially the never-ending mix of the two. Neither carrot nor stick has proved successful in speeding up the pace of our work, and local inputs, such as Brugal, have at times slowed it down. *Al fin, sin embargo, nos imaginamos que nos levantamos bien.* To the two involuntary claimants of the residual of our research process, Rosemary and Christina, this book is dedicated.

Jan Lundius and Mats Lundahl
Rome and Stockholm, June 1998

Acknowledgements

The authors would like to acknowledge the following permissions to reprint the figures used in the text:

Teresita Buonpensiere Cabral: 2.4

El Caribe: Figures 2.2, 2.7, 3.5, 3.10–11, 4.3, 4.5–9, 4.11, 4.14, 4.16–26, 6.4, 7.13–14, 8.5–6, 8.8–12, 9.4, 12.2–6, 12.8, 12.10

Roberto Cassá: 7.6–7

Fundación Peña Battle: 3.8

Juan Manuel García: 4.2, 4.15

Lusitania Martínez: 4.1, 4.12

Arturo Ramírez: 2.18

Carmen Rosalía Ramírez: 2.3, 2.5, 3.4, 3.6

Miguel Tomás Suzaña: 4.13

Time/Life Inc.: 8.7

United Press International: 8.4

United States Marine Corps: 2.16–19, 2.21

Bernardo Vega: 2.4, 2.8, 8.1–3, 9.1

The rest of the photographs either lie in the public domain or have been taken by the authors.

Some Spanish and Creole* words that appear in the text

aguardiente	raw sugar cane liquor
alcalde	mayor
alcaldía	mayors's office
audiencia	regional court
ayuntamiento	town council
La Bella Aurora	the Beautiful Dawn
blé (ble*)	blue denim
bohío	hut
bòkò*	sorcerer
brujo, f. bruja	sorcerer, voodoo priest
caballo	(horse), possessed person
cabildo	town council
cacique	chieftain
caco*	guerilla
caída	fall
calié, pl. calieses	thug, henchman
calvario	a group of three crosses
campesino	peasant
candomblé	Brazilian syncretic (African and Catholic) religion
caridad	charity
caudillismo	local strongman leadership
caudillo	local strongman leader
cayuco	trunk
cebollín	small onion
centinela	sentry
cerca	fence
chamarra	shirt
cimarrón	runaway slave
Cívico	member of the *Unión Cívica Nacional*
clientelismo	clientship
cocolo	immigrant from the English-speaking Caribbean

cofrade	brother, member of a *cofradía*
cofradía	religious brotherhood
comisaría	police station
compadrazgo	ritual coparenthood
componer	fix
común	see *provincia*
conjuro	spell
consejero	member of *El Consejo de Estado*
El Consejo de Estado	the State Council (the caretaker government that ruled the Dominican Republic in 1962)
conuco	agricultural garden plot
convite (konbit*)	communal work party
copla	popular song
cuenta	bill
curandero	healer
enramada	gathering place covered by a roof
ermita	rural chapel
esperanza	hope
El Espíritu Santo	the Holy Spirit
estancia	farm
evangélico	Protestant
falda	skirt
fanega	1 *fanega* = 55 liters
fe	faith
finca	farm
forastero	stranger
fucú	bad luck
gagá (rara*)	rural carnival band
ganadero	cattle rancher
gavillero	guerilla
gracia	(divine) grace
El Gran Poder de Dios	the Great Power of God
guayabo	guava tree
guïro	a musical instrument that is rasped
hatero	rancher
hato	cattle ranch
hermandad	brotherhood
Hispanidad	Spanishness, Spanish culture
holófrase	holy phrase
hungan (ougan*)	voodoo priest
indio claro	(light Indian), light-skinned
indio oscuro	(dark Indian), dark mulatto
ingenio	sugar estate, sugar factory
El Jefe	the Boss (Rafael Trujillo)

jefe comunal	local community leader
kleren*	a cheap, white rum
labranza	farm
luá (lwa*), pl. luases	voodoo god
El Maestro	Olivorio
Lo Malo	the Evil
maniel	runaway slave community
La Mano Poderosa	the Powerful Hand
mellizo (marasa*)	twin
minifundista	smallholder
misterio	(mystery), voodoo god
moreno	brown
novena	vigil
La Número Uno	Number One
ougan*	voodoo priest
padrino	godfather
palo	stick, big drum
palo de piñón	stick made from a branch of the *piñón* tree
pandero	tambourine
panyòl*	(Spaniard), Dominican
perico ripiao	small rural orchestra
peristil	peristyle
peso de posesión	title to a share in a *terreno comunero*
plasaj*	concubinage
ponerse chivo	(make oneself a goat), pretend not to understand
prieto	very dark
procurador	district attorney
promesa	vow
provincia	the Dominican Republic is divided into *provincias*, each provincia is divided into *comunes* (today *municipos* and *distritos municipales*) and each *común* into *secciones*
pulpería	small (rural) shop
quintal	1 *quintal* = 46 kilos
ranchero	rancher
rancho	hut
rayano	border dweller
recua	line of pack animals, usually mules
reina	queen
rezador	prayer man
rezo	prayer
romería	pilgrimage
rosario	rosary, procession of penitents

sabio, f. sabia	wise
sagrado	holy
salve	popular religious anthem
santería	Cuban syncretic (African and Catholic) religion
sección	see *provincia*
ser	voodoo god
sinvergüenza	(a person with no shame), scoundrel
soletas	rough peasant sandals
tarea	1 *tarea* = 0.1554 acres, or 0.063 hectares
terrenos comuneros	common land
trapiche	crushing mill
tronco	trunk
tronco del lugar	trunk of the place, patriarch
vela, velación, velorio	vigil
yagua	leaf base of certain palm trees
zafra	sugar harvest
zonbi*	zombie

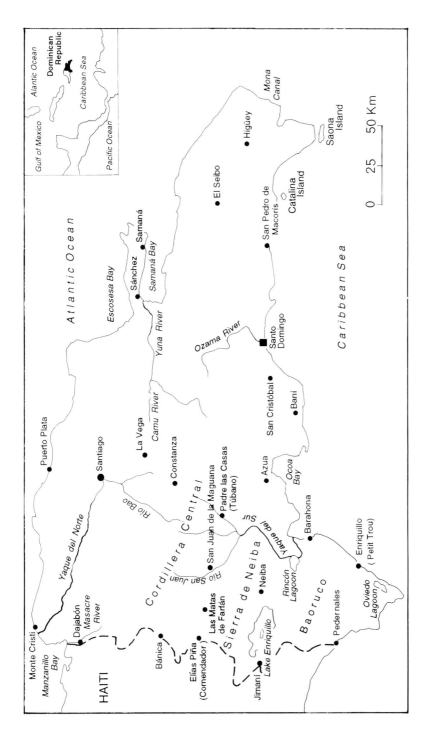

Map of the Dominican Republic.

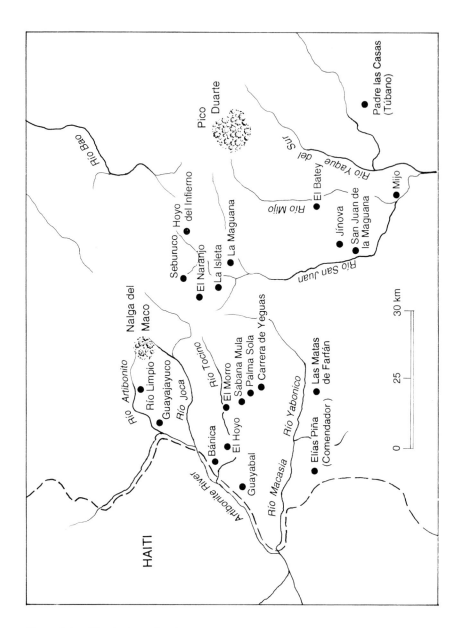

Map of the *Olivorista* heartland.

1   Introduction

The landscape of the southwestern part of the Dominican Republic is strange and varied. Sugar cane fields, rice paddies and fertile plains are set among inaccessible mountain ranges, deserts and salt marshes. This part of the country has been a place of refuge for many insurgents. Here runaway slaves established their own communities and many a fierce battle was fought between Haitian and Dominican armies. The border between Haiti and the Dominican Republic has always been vague and the exchange between the peoples on the two sides of the frontier has been very lively. The governments of both countries have repeatedly attempted to increase their control over the border area in order to obliterate the possibilities of using the remote mountain areas as a base for insurrections.

In these areas the population nourishes a well-founded suspicion of authorities. Most of the fertile areas are in the hands of a few big landowners and the majority of the peasants seek their meager livelihood in poor, insufficient plots. The southwest is the poorest and most neglected part of the Dominican Republic and has thus been an excellent hotbed for peasant movements of different kinds.

In the present work we analyze one such peasant movement that was quenched in blood – not only once, but twice. This movement is of a messianic type that has been observed elsewhere in poor rural areas of Latin America:

> All are built around one individual, who is held to have supernatural attributes and who prophesies catastrophes from which only his followers will escape. The followers seek either to release the spell from an enchanted Kingdom or to found a Holy City, thus carrying into practice the forms of behaviour counselled by their leader. All these messianic Kingdoms, moreover, have the same characteristics; they are envisaged as celestial kingdoms with miraculous qualities which shall come into being in this world. There will be no sickness, and men will not need to work; there will be universal happiness in the abode of the

saints. The communities formed in this spirit are almost invariably destroyed by the forces of global society.[1]

The movement discussed in the present work came into being during times of social and economic crisis. It can thus be analyzed with tools from the social sciences. We will view peasant religion as a strategy employed to meet particular problems and tensions that arise within peasant society during periods of stress. Religious movements may then serve as collective attempts to overcome the perceived threats to the community.

The subject

Some time around the year 1910, a fifty-year-old field hand from the San Juan Valley in the southwestern part of the Dominican Republic, named Olivorio Mateo, underwent a mystical experience that completely changed not only his own life, but also that of many others. He disappeared, was believed to be dead, and when he reappeared claimed that God had ordered him to preach and heal the sick. Olivorio thus initiated a career as faith healer, prophet and local leader. His followers – mainly illiterate peasants and farm hands – were inclined to believe that he was divine.

Others, however – particularly 'progressive' landowners, merchants and local authorities – considered Olivorio to be an obstacle to the wheel of progress and a representative of 'African obscurantism' and backwardness in general. When the Dominican Republic was occupied by the United States in 1916, Olivorio was put on the American list of suspect individuals, and after a turbulent career of slightly more than a decade, he was killed by the US marines, only to be converted into a spiritual presence which, almost forty years after his death, would serve as the main inspiration for another manifestation of the movement that eventually was to be quenched in blood as well.

In 1961, the members of a family named Ventura founded a holy city in Palma Sola, northwest of San Juan de la Maguana. At that time, one of the most notorious of all Latin American dictators, Rafael Trujillo, had held the Dominican Republic in his iron grip for more than thirty years, suppressing all popular movements, including religious ones. Trujillo was murdered at the end of May 1961 and it was then only a matter of weeks before the Palma Sola movement sprang into full bloom. The Venturas had stated that their mission would come to an end on 1 January 1963. On 28 December 1962, however, the Dominican military moved into Palma Sola and massacred its inhabitants.

---

1 Pereira de Queiroz (1965), p. 64.

The present study constitutes an investigation of how and why the *Olivorista* religion was formed, why the movement and its revival in Palma Sola were successful in attracting large numbers of followers and why on both occasions it was violently suppressed. Our analysis will combine tools and methods from various social sciences. In this chapter we provide an overview of the approach that we will follow in the book.

The local scene

Every person lives and acts within a particular environment. A social phenomenon, like a religious movement, must be analyzed in relation to the cultural means of expression that are at the disposal of the adherents to a particular faith. This leads to a study not only of the interaction between individuals, their sets of values and attitudes, their relationship to the ecosystem, their economic activities, etc., but also of the historical, economic and sociological roots of the society that generates the kind of faith which triggers messianic movements.

When, at the beginning of the twentieth century, Olivorio Mateo, an illiterate peasant, succeeded in gathering a large following around himself and for several years was able to challenge the power of landowners, merchants and foreign troops within an entire province, he could do so due to the particular conditions that prevailed within the area of his activities. The San Juan Valley constantly witnesses the rise and fall of soothsayers and faith healers, but none of them have achieved the almost instant success and strong influence of Olivorio Mateo (and the Ventura brothers several years later). Extraordinary circumstances underpinned the attraction of such personalities.

The majority of the believers in the message divulged by Olivorio and the Venturas have been peasants and as such they live and work within a production landscape, making use of their immediate physical environment. Any change affecting their surroundings is likely to influence their livelihood and consequently their view of the world. It is seemingly contradictory that even if the peasant world is highly dynamic, in the sense that slight climatological changes and political turbulence may have severe repercussions on the peasants' welfare and opinions, their traditions and beliefs still tend to reflect a kind of long-term stability in both the physical and social landscape.

In the case of the San Juan Valley this stability is provided by a production landscape to which a religious system has been adapted. A belief system has been constituted by ideas and traditions originating from both Europe and Africa: a unique blend which can be traced in all the aspects of the religious movements we will consider. Peasants' religious convictions tend to serve 'practical' ends and are accordingly influenced by changes in their material welfare and economic output – a pattern that becomes obvious when studying the *Olivorista* movement in the San Juan Valley.

As faith healers like Olivorio are always present in the San Juan Valley, the extraordinary attraction he exercised must be related not only to his particular personality, but also to structural changes that occured at the time of his appearance, i.e. the transformation of traditional life, primarily by the consolidation of agricultural holdings and the substitution of market-oriented production for subsistence farming and cattle raising.

Just as the *Olivorista* movement was an answer to sociopolitical changes that occured in the San Juan Valley in the 1910s and 1920s, its continuation initiated by the Ventura brothers in Palma Sola in 1961 was a local response to feelings of anomie that had taken hold of many Dominicans in the agitated aftermath of the murder of Trujillo. The Trujillo years had brought thorough structural change to Dominican society and the San Juan Valley had not escaped the dictator's ruthless rule. Several followers of Olivorio Mateo suffered severe persecution. With the dictator gone, however, the lid was lifted from the boiling pot of *Sanjuanero* discontent. As in Olivorio's times the actions and the speech of the peasants in the San Juan Valley were steeped in religious language and behavior. Their protest took the form of an *Olivorista* revival. In a highly volatile atmosphere of political tension, the official response to the movement in Palma Sola was fierce and meshed in political machinations. The result was a ruthless massacre of unarmed peasants and a heritage of unanswered questions which still haunt political debate in the Dominican Republic.

Religious beliefs and traditions in the San Juan Valley result from a symbiosis between economic and 'spiritual' factors. The valley has served as a melting pot for Indian, African and European creeds and only a long historical perspective can illuminate some essential components of the intricate 'ideology' which constitutes present-day *Olivorismo*. The same applies to the particular socioeconomic environment which emerged in the valley, and when stating that *Olivorista* religion is based on the economic reality of the *Sanjuanero* peasantry, it must also be said that the socioeconomic reality is influenced by religious notions.

The long and winding road leading up to present-day *Sanjuanero* religiosity passes through religious fraternities in medieval Europe and West Africa and beliefs in 'suprahuman' powers like the Holy Spirit in Europe and Ashé among African Yoruba. Fertility cults, processions, dancing, singing, drumming, possession beliefs, communal celebrations, etc., whose origins can be found in various geographical contexts, have been fused together by the people in San Juan Valley and adapted to their particular socioeconomic environment.

An account of the economic history of the San Juan Valley leads us back in time to the establishment of an economic system based on forced Indian labor which subsequently led to imports of African slaves and sugar production. When the importance of sugar dwindled and political considerations depopulated the area around San Juan de la Maguana, cattle breeding grew in importance, to be replaced by food production for the market only during the present century, a shift that influenced landownership structures and eventually triggered the rise of the *Olivorista* movement. In order to understand and analyze the socioeconomic situation which prevailed in the San Juan Valley at the time of Olivorio Mateo's emergence as a 'living god', a long historical perspective must be taken, and we must analyze the complicated process in which the political realities of the time and the ethnic composition of the *Sanjuaneros* interacted and created a peculiar culture which constituted a fertile breeding ground for a movement like *Olivorismo*.

However, a relatively isolated area like the San Juan Valley is not only subject to more or less impersonal influences from the natural environment, economic activities and ethnic traditions: the interaction between individuals is also of crucial importance. The character and forceful individuality of certain persons have always been important and must be related to local traditions like coparenthood, affiliation to powerful men and sociopsychological concepts like charisma – traits that come together and constitute important ingredients in an intricate political power play. Furthermore, politics in the San Juan Valley has often had a tendency to expose tensions between the center and the periphery, between the capital and the 'backlands' along the Haitian border. A pattern has thus been created which exposes the tensions between an 'urbanite', 'progressive' ideology, tainted by racial and cultural prejudices, and the 'conservative' traditions of a fairly close-knit and isolated peasantry. Such contradictory world visions frequently lead to violent conflicts, mainly due to a severe lack of communication and understanding.

From a global perspective, the San Juan Valley may appear as nothing but an insignificant speck on the world map. Accordingly, on one level, *Olivorismo* can be considered as an obscure movement without much influence or importance. However, the valley may just as well be considered as a microcosm illustrating how economic, political and cultural forces of diverse origins interact and clash with one another. Agrarian communities like the one in the San Juan Valley exist all over the world and all of them are subject to 'alien' influences and 'development' processes. Movements similar to *Olivorismo* have been constituted in many geographically dispersed places and a multifaceted study of an isolated and peculiar area like the San Juan Valley may therefore provide insights that may prove helpful in studies of local communities in other parts of the world.

A plausible story

The present work tells the story of Olivorio and *Olivorismo*. Storytelling calls for an approach that is partly 'literary', something that is often abhorred by economists, who often tend to argue that scholars 'had better be factual and logical'.[2] However, even 'theoretical' economists tell stories, even though they are not always aware of it. In three celebrated and controversial pieces on the methodology of economists, Donald McCloskey makes the point that in practice economists tend not to adhere to their official, rule-bound credo but instead engage in rhetoric of various kinds to persuade their readers that the points they make are valid ones.[3]

McCloskey's message is that rule-bound methodology is not good because it amounts to no less than the impossible. It claims that we know what makes for good science. In economics, the rulemaker has perfect knowledge not only of all present economics but of all future economics, too.[4] In practice, this may be less important, however, because economists do not adhere to the canon they have set up. Instead, they engage in conversation with their audience, and that is precisely what they should do. When doing so, they necessarily resort to rhetoric, i.e. 'the art of speaking'. They attempt to persuade those with whom they engage in conversation. However, as a rule they are either not aware of the fact that this is what they do or deny that they do so and make reference to the 'official' creed instead. This, McCloskey argues, should be changed. Not even mathematicians 'prove' theorems for good. 'They temporarily satisfy their interlocutors in a conversation.'[5]

The methodological implication of McCloskey's view is that scientists of all brands (natural, social, humanistic) are basically persuaders. Hence it become necessary to focus on the techniques of persuasion. Which are the best methods available? Quoting Wayne Booth, McCloskey points to the various contributions an informed use of rhetoric can make to the economic discourse. Rhetoric is

> 'the art of discovering good reasons, finding what really warrants assent, because any reasonable person ought to be persuaded'; it is 'careful weighing of more-or-less good reasons to arrive at more-or-less probable or plausible conclusions – none too secure but better than what would be arrived at by chance or unthinking impulse'; it is the 'art of discovering warrantable beliefs and improving these beliefs in shared discourse'; its purpose must not be 'to talk someone else into a preconceived view; rather it must be to engage in mutual inquiry'.[6]

2 McCloskey (1990), p. 1.
3 McCloskey (1986), (1990), (1994).
4 McCloskey (1986), p. 20.
5 Ibid., p. 34.
6 Ibid., p. 29. The quotations are from Booth (1974), pp. xiv, 59, xiii, 137.

Economists seldom realize that out of the rhetorical tetrad – fact, logic, metaphor[7] and story[8] – they need, and do in fact use, all four elements. Above all, modern, or modernist, economics lacks an awareness of the role of storytelling. Economists concentrate on making their metaphors – 'models' – meet rigorous standards of logic, and far less on making their stories – 'stylized facts' – meet equally rigorous standards of fact.[9] That is not a healthy state of things, since not even in scholarly writing is 'the content ... separable from the style and the arrangement'.[10] Facts, logic, metaphors and stories must complement each other. None of these elements is capable of standing on its own.

The present work should be read in the spirit of McCloskey. We are telling the story of *Olivorismo* in factual, logical and metaphorical terms that we feel have something to contribute to the understanding of the economic, social, religious and political roots of the movement, its contents and the historical events connected with it. The book in this sense represents an effort to persuade our readers that what you get is a plausible story, one which is more probable than those told about the movement hitherto. The focus is on the explanation of the individual case seen in its local context. Like McCloskey, we want to make 'sense out of ... [a determinate] economic [and social] experience'.[11]

In this we will draw on, among other things, well-established principles of economic theory – not in order to be 'rigorous', whatever that means,[12] but as a rhetorical device – i.e. we use these principles because we feel that their use adds to the plausibility of our story. Needless to say, the same goes for our use of other social science tools. Metaphors and stories should complement each other in the construction of a persuasive argument. 'Metaphors and stories, models and histories, subject to the discipline of fact and logic, are the two ways of answering "why."'[13] A story answers a model, if the model is offered first, but a model also answers a story, in the opposite case. The map is never the territory, but if it is well drawn it can help a great deal with the orientation on the ground.

---

7 'A metaphor brings "two separate domains into cognitive and emotional relation by using language directly appropriate to the one as a lens for seeing the other"' (Black (1962), p. 236, quoted by McCloskey (1990), p. 12).
8 'A story ... sets down in chronological order the raw experience of one domain. It is a "presentation of a time-ordered or time-related experience that ... supplements, re-orders, enhances, or interprets unnarrated life"' (Booth (1988), p. 14, quoted by McCloskey (1990), p. 12).
9 McCloskey (1990), p. 23.
10 McCloskey (1994), pp. 124–5.
11 McCloskey (1986), p. 175.
12 Cf. McCloskey (1994), p. 136.
13 McCloskey (1990), p. 10.

Peasants and outsiders

In most of the literature dealing with the Dominican Republic, the rural inhabitants are referred to as 'peasants' [*campesinos*].[14] This is a convenient term, although its use implies some difficulties – difficulties that pertain to the very definition of the word. Almost every scholarly work that makes use of the term 'peasants' dedicates a number of pages to a discussion of its definition.[15] Still, the definition and application often tend to be bewildering. An illustrative example – one which is highly pertinent in the present case – is given by the ongoing debate about the emergence of a Caribbean peasantry:

> After 'discovering' a Caribbean peasantry in the 1950s, stressing its uniqueness in the 1960s and 1970s, and denying that uniqueness in the 1970s and 1980s, scholars now tend to integrate the analysis of Caribbean peasantries into the wider peasant debate without ignoring the specific historical circumstances of the peasantries' origins.[16]

One of the most outspoken and frequent participants in this debate, anthropologist Sidney Mintz, draws attention to the fact that typologies are 'tools of analysis, not truth "on the ground". Their purpose must be to understand better what is on the ground, rather than to be reified, as if they somehow could transcend social and historical reality.'[17]

To describe the *Olivoristas* simply as 'peasants' would amount to a rather crude generalization. In the first place, not all of them are peasants in the sense of the term that will be employed in the present work. Indeed, some of them are not even agriculturalists. Nor do all of them live in the countryside. Second, it is also rather doubtful if all *Olivoristas* engaged in rural activities can be described as 'peasants'. Some are, or were, cattle owners, squatters, day laborers, 'proto-peasants', *pulpería* [a small rural shop] owners, truck drivers, school teachers, etc. Third, the use of the term 'peasant' delimits the object of study, but possibly in a biased way. Roy Wagner describes how a social anthropologist studying other people, relating them to what he delimits as a certain culture or society, himself in a way creates his object to be able to describe it: 'anthropology teaches us to objectify the thing we are adjusting to as "culture", much as the psycho-

---

14 Cf. e.g. the titles of three rather recent works: 'The Dominican peasantry and the market economy: the peasants of the Cibao, 1880–1960' (San Miguel (1987)), *Peasants in Distress: Poverty and Unemployment in the Dominican Republic* (Vargas-Lundius (1991)) and *Peasants and Tobacco in the Dominican Republic, 1870–1930* (Baud (1995)).
15 For the Dominican context, see Baud (1995), pp. 35–48.
16 Ibid., p. 37.
17 Mintz (1990), p. 37.

analyst or shaman exorcizes the patient's anxieties by objectifying their source.'[18] There is, however, no evidence that this process of objectification creates a 'true' picture of the 'culture' and its members, particularly when the analytical tools employed have been manufactured within the lecture rooms and studies of European and American universities:

> When modern anthropology began to construct its Other in terms of topoi implying distance, difference, and opposition, its intent was above all, but at least also, to construct ordered Space and Time – a cosmos – for Western society to inhabit, rather than 'understanding other cultures,' its ostensible vocation.[19]

Needless to say, the same goes for the employment of 'peasant' in the present context. Nevertheless, despite these reservations, we will use the term in our analysis of *Olivorismo*. The majority of the faithful may be described as people engaged in agrarian activities within an economic and social framework commonly referred to as a 'peasant society'. The intention is not to dispute the uniqueness of *Olivorismo* but to indicate certain traits and conditions that the rural inhabitants of the San Juan Valley may share with other people in other places and at other times so as to make it clear that *Olivorismo* is far from an isolated phenomenon.

Thus, the protagonists of this study are 'peasants' and our discussion concentrates to a large extent on the relations these 'peasants' have with non-peasant society. But what then is a 'peasant'? In economics and economic history 'peasants' are sometimes identified as a 'separate' analytical category.[20] Peasants live in rural areas and their main occupation is agriculture. They till their own land,[21] basically with the assistance of their families. Their plots are often small and cultivated with the aid of rudimentary tools in an uncertain and often outright niggard environment which tends to make them averse to risk.[22] As Arthur Lewis expressed it in a formulation that has become classic, 'Peasants ... know how near they live to the brink of disaster.'[23] Most of the uncertain income derived from the land goes to consumption and only lesser amounts are left for investment

---

18 Wagner (1981), p. 8.
19 Fabian (1983), pp. 111–12. *Topoi* derives from Greek *topos*, place, although Fabian employs the term in a broader context, indicating something like a 'mental image' or 'visualized object'.
20 Cf. e.g. Thorner (1965), Wolf (1966) and Shanin (1971), (1973), (1974), (1990). For a criticism of this type of approach, see e.g. Dalton (1972).
21 In addition to his own plot, he may lease land from other owners.
22 Lipton (1968), Roumasset (1976), Scott (1976).
23 Lewis (1955), p. 227.

in increased production possibilities. This, however, does not imply that peasants do not *want* to make investments:

> Although poor and close to the margin … there are still many occasions when peasants do have some surplus and do make risky investments: the fact that they are poor and risk averse does not imply, either logically or factually, that they do not make investments. Peasants make long-term as well as short-term investments, and therefore have long-term and short-term investment crises, and they make risky as well as secure investments. Peasants plan and invest throughout both the crop cycle and the life cycle, and they place a high priority on investment for old age. Furthermore, besides deciding between long-term and short-term investments, peasants must choose between public and private investments, both long and short run. Peasants do decide whether to invest in children, animals, land, and other individual or family goods, on the one hand, or on the other, whether to spend their surplus through the village, on insurance or welfare programs or village improvements.[24]

Peasants live in small communities, often far away from political decision centers. From an urban point of view, their education is frequently deficient, or even non-existent, and the possibility of their obtaining modern medical attention is remote. Compared with workers, peasants possess a certain degree of autonomy. Much of what they and their families consume comes from the family farm. Unlike modern farmers, peasants do not run agricultural enterprises. They run household units where production and consumption decisions are interdependent. This, on the other hand, does not preclude peasants from engaging in production for sale. Such activities complement subsistence production. Production for the market is always an option for peasants, since much of what they consume they may not be able to produce on their farms.

The relations between peasants and non-peasants are to a large extent antagonistic. Peasants are subordinate to and dependent on an 'outside' society that appropriates a surplus and controls part of their economy, e.g. through taxation. The outsiders in turn do not cultivate the soil themselves but are forced to live off what the peasants produce. For them, the peasant is thus not very much more than a supplier of products, and in addition an object of taxation and a potential worker who may be recruited into non-agricultural pursuits when there is a need for it. It has even been argued that no peasantry existed before the first city came into being, i.e. that it is the very dependence on outsiders that constitutes a peasant.[25] Conversely,

24 Popkin (1979), pp. 18–19.
25 Cf. Wolf (1966).

When outsiders tried to obtain a hold on peasant society and to interfere with its social and agricultural organization, their attempts often
failed. The evasiveness of peasant society has become proverbial. It
infuriated modernizing politicians and entrepreneurs and underlay
the myriad negative stereotypes of the cunning peasant or 'lazy native.'
Peasants defended that part of their life which they considered essential for their material and immaterial continuation. This statement
applies to social relations and productive techniques, as much as to
cultural institutions such as witchcraft, rituals of birth and death, and
popular religion. The results may be different in each peasant society.
What makes these societies comparable is their efforts to create niches
that outsiders cannot penetrate.[26]

Culturally, peasants and urban dwellers are different. The urbanite is a
member of a much more cosmopolitan community than the peasant.
New ideas and ways of thinking penetrate the cities with greater ease than
they reach peasants in their environment.[27] As a consequence, townspeople often have a tendency to regard the peasant as an anachronism.
The awkward peasant is a stock figure in urban literature and popular
humor, famous for his 'backward' manners. In the urban environment,
old traditions are made subject to attacks. Old beliefs are reformulated.
The future is viewed as being different from the past. Peasants, on the
other hand, as viewed by the urbanite, resist innovations and cling to their
antiquated ways.

Peasant societies have been described as 'long-established homogeneous, isolated and non-literate integral (self-contained)' communities.[28]
This view has, however, been harshly criticized from several quarters.
'Many theories ... depict the peasantry as an immobile class of agricultural
producers who are stuck to their land and possess an extremely local world
view', writes Michiel Baud. However, these theories 'tend to ignore or
disguise the fact that individual members of peasant society often are
extremely mobile and spend an important part of their lives in migratory
and off-farm activities'.[29] Peasant culture is not necessarily homogeneous,
nor is it particularly fixed or stable. Inhabitants of any village community
manifest a wide range of opinions and religious doubts. Accordingly, they
also interpret human and natural phenomena in different ways. Radical
transitions often take place in rural areas, and global changes which have

26 Baud (1995), p. 45.
27 On this point, cf. Redfield and Singer (1954).
28 Ibid., p. 58.
29 Baud (1995), p. 39.

affected the economy over the past 150 years have undoubtedly left their mark on almost every peasant's notion of the world.[30]

Still, peasants have their own view of the world, and this often differs sharply from the urban view. They work within a 'production landscape' where they make use of their immediate physical environment. They must develop an ability to interpret, classify and cultivate the ecological system that they live in. Changes in climate and vegetation are observed, registered and interpreted through a body of knowledge most of which has been inherited from older generations, and developed as a result of trial and error processes. The environment that peasants have come to know through their constant interaction with it makes a heavy imprint on their views. The local geography, the plot and the village determine what the peasants express when they make contact with an outside world which is to a large extent unknown and frequently regarded as hostile. Outsiders are 'different'. They are imbued with 'unknown' powers.

The peasants' view of life is to a large extent conditioned by the inputs they receive from their immediate surroundings. They are members of close-knit communities that influence their opinions heavily. The village and its traditions constitute their point of reference. The membership in the village community and the sense of belonging and security that this entails helps peasants to face a world governed by capricious forces that they cannot themselves control. The collective tradition of the community helps them to interpret their environment in a meaningful way.

The urbanites may innovate more easily than the peasants. This, however, does not mean that peasants can afford to ignore the future. We have already pointed to how they must make investment decisons, and in their production decisions they must plan ahead at all times. What is to be planted and sown during the coming year? Peasants are constantly involved in questions regarding survival. In a sense everything they do is forestalling. They must leave enough means for their children to survive. When peasants die their children will go on tilling their soil. Their existence is precarious. Nature is capricious. Drought and pests easily destroy their crops. The future is difficult to predict. Peasants live without much protection against unforeseen difficulties. It becomes natural to strive for order and security. Thus, they want to give meaning to the inconceivable and make the unpredictable predictable. Tradition provides a key to the future – to the way to avoid known and unknown dangers by the development of survival algorithms.[31] The village community means a great deal to the individual peasant: 'in a peasant community men must often depend

---

30 Christian (1987), pp. 371–2.
31 See e.g. Lipton (1968), Roumasset (1976) and Scott (1976), for discussions of such algorithms.

on each other if only for that sense of continuity which renders life predictable, and hence meaningful.'[32]

The difference in outlook between peasants and outsiders will loom large in the present work. The religious movements that we discuss arose in an environment characterized by a pronounced lack of communication between the urban authorities and the 'sectarians'. The latter created their own communities, designed to be independent of the former. This in turn triggered reactions from the authorities who ended up by resorting to violent action to destroy the rural 'utopias' built by the peasants. The incapability of the outsiders in understanding and accepting the peasant movements is evident, but so is the refusal of the peasants to mingle with outsiders.

The problem of oral transmission

Much of the material presented in the present work has been orally transmitted and hence tends to display the advantages and disadvantages of such material. We have made the selection and the interpretations and much of it must naturally be dependent on our own shortcomings as interviewers, observers and interpreters. The study of 'other cultures' is, after all, based on individual perceptions, what the so-called Realists of the nineteenth century called 'nature viewed through a temperament',[33] i.e. an interpretation limited by the observer's various qualifications, biases and conditions.

On the other hand, our reading of newspaper cuttings, US marines' reports, official correspondence and different scholarly works has convinced us that such sources are in no way superior to oral ones. Nothing guarantees that a written source is unprejudiced and correct. A US marine officer putting together a report about the persecution of *Olivoristas*, or a contemporary urban newspaperman condemning 'base superstitions' in Palma Sola are no more reliable than a legendary tale told by a hundred-year-old *Olivorista*. At best the accounts are complementary. All types of sources – written or oral – must be scrutinized with an open mind. The truth is not easy to find. What really happened is veiled by a shroud of contradictory voices and what remains for the researchers is approximations and guesses, made on the basis of their knowledge of the entire context of the happenings that they are investigating.

---

32 Wolf (1966), p. 98. This does not mean that peasants live in a state of constant harmony with their neighbors. As in all other societies, tensions are likely to erupt between individuals. Jealousy, competition, slander and fights over land and inheritance are endemic in peasant societies.

33 About this concept in the fine arts, see Nochlin (1971), pp. 235–8.

That the 'truth' is elusive is demonstrated by the interviews made with León Romilio Ventura, the only surviving leader from the massacre that ended the *Olivorista* revival in Palma Sola in 1962. It was not only dates and figures that changed from one occasion to another. Certain events were also related in new ways and songs, and dreams and visions were presented differently from time to time.

For example, on one occasion León Romilio stated that in 1961 a small child with blue eyes appeared and told him to go into the mountains and find his brother, because the two of them had to carry out a mission together.[34] When reminded that on another occasion[35] he had stated that it was 'a bearded, old man' who gave him the mission, he did not seem to care at all. Faced with the inconsistency León Romilio simply explained that appearances are not important in themselves. It is the presence of the power that counts. The old man and the child are both manifestations of the same force: the Holy Spirit or the Great Power of God [*El Gran Poder de Dios*].[36]

León Romilio is equally inconsistent when talking about Olivorio Mateo. On one occasion he maintained that Olivorio 'is the name of the soul of God',[37] while later on he stated that 'Olivorio is not God, and not Jesus either. He is not the Holy Spirit. He is a prophet who came to earth, sent by the Holy Spirit. We do not believe in him, but in his works.'[38] When it was once more pointed out that he had changed his version, León Romilio maintained that it is 'the work, not the appearance that counts'.[39]

This 'relativist attitude' towards what we are accustomed to call the 'truth' is apparently quite common in other cultural settings as well. To take but one example, in his studies of Moroccan folk culture Vincent Crapanzano states that 'truth' often has to be viewed in relation to 'determined contextual frameworks'. The way in which things are told is not so important as the message, open or concealed, that is conveyed.[40] According to Crapanzano, one may talk about both a 'personal' and a 'historical' truth and it is not always easy to judge which one is most 'correct'. We cannot always disqualify one 'truth' with the help of another.[41]

In the San Juan Valley, León Romilio Ventura is not unique in expressing himself ambiguously. Other 'missionaries' underline that the 'spiritual sphere' must be 'felt' or 'experienced'. When it was pointed out to them

34 Interview with León Romilio Ventura, Media Luna, 5 May 1986.
35 Interview with León Romilio Ventura, Media Luna, 17 January 1986.
36 Interview with León Romilio Ventura, Las Matas de Farfán, 14 May 1989.
37 Interview with León Romilio Ventura, Media Luna, 17 January 1986.
38 Interview with León Romilio Ventura, Media Luna, 5 May 1986.
39 Ibid.
40 Crapanzano (1985), pp. 80–1.
41 Ibid., p. 6.

that their own stories of personal encounters with the dwellers of the spiritual sphere differ from one occasion to another, they simply shrugged their shoulders and stated that this is not important, since the force and the message do not change. After talking to several people and learning some of the 'idiosyncrasies' of the valley, you soon realize that in most cases the discrepancies in their stories are not very large and not of any crucial importance. As the informants themselves state: 'We do not change the message or the truth.'[42]

The hidden transcript

Much of the Olivorio story consists of myths and folklore and the borderline between real and imagined events is often very difficult to draw. Olivorio is seen as a spiritual being and is worshiped as such. All religions have their sacred myths that serve to highlight the extraordinary, superhuman qualities of their gods, saints, spirits, etc., and around these a variety of folkloric tales are spun. *Olivorismo* is no exception to this rule.

The myths are interesting in their own right, as they provide us with the core ideas of each particular religion. We will therefore analyze the *Olivorista* ideas in the present work. The lore surrounding Olivorio, however, has more to offer. Myths, tales, songs, etc. tell us a great deal about how those who collectively created them viewed the world they lived in and its social and economic realities, i.e. they allow us to acquire a deeper understanding of their ideologies. These cannot always be freely or openly expressed because the worshipers are dominated by and dependent on other groups in society – the typical situation for peasants. Because ideologies, including religious beliefs, typically express wishes and hopes, not least for change, they are often considered rebellious or insubordinate and are hence viewed with suspicion by outsiders, and this, in turn, creates a tendency for the insiders to express themselves in ways not easily understood by others.

In this sense, James Scott's concept of the hidden transcript becomes relevant.[43] A *transcript* is defined as 'a complete record of what was said', a *public* transcript is 'a shorthand way of describing the open interaction between subordinates and those who dominate' and the term *hidden* transcript denotes the 'discourse that takes place "offstage," beyond direct observation by powerholders'.[44] The members of the latter group by and large define what is appropriate to reveal in public, and the extent to

---

42 Interview with Zita Závala, Paraje El Ranchito, Carrera de Yeguas, 10 April 1986.
43 Scott (1990). Cf. also Scott (1985), pp. 284–9.
44 Scott (1990), note, p. 2, p. 4. Note, however, that dominant groups also may have hidden transcripts.

which open communication of ideas is possible is very much a function of the inequality between them and the subordinate group.[45]

The underdogs create a 'social space' where they may give vent to their frustrations, hatred, aspirations and dreams:

> At its most elementary level the hidden transcript represents acting out in fantasy – and occasionally in secretive practice – of the anger and reciprocal aggression denied by the presence of domination. Without the sanctions imposed by power relations, subordinates would be tempted to return a blow with a blow, an insult with an insult, a whipping with a whipping, a humiliation with a humiliation. It is as if the 'voice,' to use Albert Hirschman's term,[46] they are refused in the public transcript finds its full-throated expression backstage.[47]
>
> An individual who is affronted may develop a personal fantasy of revenge and confrontation, but when the insult is but a variant of affronts suffered systematically by a whole race, class, or strata [sic], then the fantasy can become a collective cultural product. Whatever form it assumes – offstage parody, dreams of violent revenge, millennial visions of a world turned upside down – this hidden transcript is essential to any dynamic view of power relations.[48]

It is precisely the existence of domination that prevents an open exchange of earnest views and creates the hidden transcript, and the strength and extent of domination bear strongly on the contents of it. However, the transcript which has been formed behind the back of the powerholders 'is typically expressed openly – albeit in disguised form … rumors, gossip, folktales, songs, gestures, jokes and theater of the powerless …'.[49] The hidden transcript is always present in the public discourse of subordinate groups, but in 'a partly sanitized, ambiguous, and coded version' which is difficult to interpret,[50] and only under special circumstances does it come into the open and produce direct confrontation with the discourse of the dominant groups. Exactly what these circumstances are is very difficult to determine.

However, certain events are more likely than others to trigger eruptions of the hidden transcript into the open. To this category belong 'economic and political changes that result in an increase in the indignities and appropriations to which subordinate groups are subjected'. These will

---

45 Scott (1985), pp. 286–7.
46 See Hirschman (1970).
47 Scott (1990), pp. 37–8.
48 Ibid., p. 9.
49 Ibid., pp. xii–xiii.
50 Ibid., p. 19.

increase the probability that acts of open, 'both symbolic and material', defiance will occur.[51]

In the present work, we make an attempt to decipher the hidden transcript of *Olivorismo*, with the aid of the *Olivorista* lore as expressed in the songs, myths and tales that have sprung up around Olivorio's person. This is an important exercise because this transcript was to a large extent forced into the open when the movement had to confront the outsiders, and knowledge of its contents contributes to our understanding of why the latter took a hostile view of the *Olivoristas* and their behavior – to the point where this hostility was conducive to two massacres of Olivorio's followers.

The spiritual sphere

'Religion' is a word that is constantly encountered in studies of peasant society. On some occasions, religious matters take precedence above all else. This is the case in 'closed' or 'corporate' peasant communities in Latin America, i.e. communities that represent 'a bounded social system with clear-cut limits, in relations to both outsiders and insiders … [with] structural identity over time'.[52] In these communities, which attempt to seal off their members from the surrounding world and try to prevent outsiders from becoming community members,[53] it is the very right to participate in the religious affairs of the community that defines who is a member in the community and who is not. Those who are included in the circle of participation are members; those who are outside it are not members. Religious participation thus defines the boundary between the community and the outside. Those who participate belong; those who do not participate remain strangers.[54] Here, religion is the most important activity in the community, the one around which everything rotates.

Religion is also important in 'open' communities, which interact to a much larger degree with the outside world, although it is not the hub of things. Still, religious beliefs often constitute the core of peasant 'ideology' and are as such in turn strongly colored by the peasant way of life. Peasants live a life that is characterized by exposure to powers that they cannot control and which therefore predispose them to religious thinking and supernatural explanations. The vagaries of nature are of importance here. The size and quality of the harvest are never given, and peasants may easily find that a promising crop has failed and that their very existence is in peril. This type of experience tends to make the peasants explain events as

---

51 Ibid., p. 219.
52 Wolf (1955), p. 456.
53 Wolf (1957).
54 Wolf and Hansen (1972), p. 100.

a result of fate or supernatural causes,[55] and vice versa; peasant religion is practical and utilitarian. It deals, for example, with problems related to the yearly cycle of cultivation and problems of protecting crops and animals against natural hazards.[56]

Compared with the faiths found in urban areas, peasant religion exhibits some particular characteristics. The religion of peasants is intimately tailored to their needs and environment. It is a local phenomenon that can rarely be studied from a distance: 'The ways that it consecrates relationships with nature, society, and identity must be lived to be understood. Context is crucial, for it gives meaning, often of a particularly local variety, to religious behavior that might otherwise appear to be universal.'[57] If peasant religious beliefs are studied at close range, it soon becomes evident that these beliefs constitute a highly dynamic faith which adapts smoothly to changing local conditions and furthermore interacts with the developments that take place in urban areas. Rural worshipers share several religious beliefs with their urban counterparts. However, compared with the urban setting, there is an aspect of permanence in the peasant's life, 'a long-term stability in his physical and social landscape'.[58]

The peasants' religious beliefs perpetuate traditions that have become extinct in more dynamic urban settings. Traditional places of veneration are often situated on the same spot for thousands of years, and traditional acts, such as religious vows and offerings, are often the same acts that have been carried out during previous centuries. In essence, they have survived within the local landscape, been transmitted through use and kept alive for centuries in close-knit family communities.

Contrary to the opinion often held by outsiders, peasants tend to be practical-minded and think in terms of 'real' situations and realizable possibilities.[59] Economic considerations influence daily decisions. The peasants want to get something in return for their effort and this is also true in religious matters. Peasants often approach religion in a businesslike fashion, making 'deals' with the representatives of the 'other' world. They offer gifts that are believed to please their deities, such as candles, flowers and different types of other vows. In turn, they expect the recipients to favor them in other ways.

The peasant treats nature as analogous with society. According to Maurice Godelier, the human world consists of two spheres, one which is visible and which can be controlled and one which cannot. The latter – nature – is the realm of the invisible, spiritual forces and is more difficult

55 Ortiz (1971), pp. 330–1.
56 Wolf (1966), p. 99.
57 Christian (1987), p. 371.
58 Ibid., p. 372.
59 Cohn (1970), p. 245. Cf. Berger (1979), pp. 195–213.

to cope with. In peasant society, the forces of the invisible world are often conceived of in analogy with the visible world. In this way, they assume a shape that is understandable for the human mind. 'Impersonal' forces assume human qualities.[60] It then also becomes natural to communicate with the invisible beings. These spiritual entities may be deceased relatives, saints, any kind of supernatural forces, and they are more powerful than living beings, but at the same time they also display human characteristics. Just like your neighbors, they can be both vain and capricious, good or evil. Thus, religious ceremonies constitute important recurrent events in peasant everyday life and since the beings of the 'other' world are often dangerous the peasant needs expert assistance to communicate with them.

To these experts the peasant can turn in times of crisis. Often refuge is taken collectively, since peasants are members of collectives and their religion is partly based on social relations. According to Max Weber, the peasantry becomes a carrier of religion only when threatened by enslavement or proletarianization.[61] This is, however, not true. In one sense, the peasantry is *always* a carrier of religion, since religion is an important part of peasants' daily life. Most of the time this goes unnoticed by the outsider who only sees the 'superstitious' acts of the peasants without realizing that these acts are integrated in their universe. The spiritual sphere for peasants is as important a part of their universe as is the community in which they are living and the work that they perform. Their existence is multiplex, not specialized on a single activity.[62]

When the peasant's existence crumbles, he grasps for his ideology, turning to the religious specialists who then assume vastly increased importance in the community. His religion comes to the surface and becomes an explicit carrier of his hopes for a just world, and in this the community – the collective – is in the center. What is good for one peasant is good for all. The peasants adapt their lives to their religion and become what outsiders characterize as 'fanatics'.

Religion in peasant society: a local phenomenon

Even though most potential popular religious leaders do not attract large crowds, *Olivorismo*, of course, does not constitute an isolated success story. On the contrary, similar movements are common in tribal and peasant societies all over the world.[63] Peasant religiosity reflects the peasant view of the world, as locally conceived, and springs from the immediate

60 Godelier (1975), pp. 202–3.
61 Weber (1968a), p. 284.
62 Bailey (1966), p. 401.
63 See La Barre (1971) and Turner (1977), (1979).

environment. It forms part of local peasant ideology; the 'system of meanings through which [peasant] peoples interpret and understand the
world'.[64]

The local geography, the plot, the village and other similar factors to a
large extent determine how the peasant interprets 'the cycles of nature,
day and night, the human cycle, the life cycles of animals and plants – all
[of which] hold particular importance for cultivators'.[65] Peasants face a
world governed by forces over which they do not have full control.
Droughts, insects or plagues can easily mean ruin and death for themselves
and their families. Thus, they have to seek order in their lives; they try to
make events predictable. In this they are surrounded by others who find
themselves in exactly the same situation. The collective tradition of the
community thus helps peasants to interpret their environment in a meaningful way.

Religious rituals and routines assist peasants in shaping the time and the
landscape that surrounds them into something comprehensive. They
'sanctify' the calendar and the physical environment: 'peasants tend to
establish locally distinct sacred places, times and divinities. Whether it is at
a spring, cave, mountain-top, river-bank, or a special tree, peasants come
to pay homage to their divinities according to the calendar, and in times of
crisis.'[66]

Consequently, peasant religiosity, to a very large extent, is a local
phenomenon, and as such it can only rarely be studied from a distance,
detached from its immediate context. On the other hand, once this is realized, it becomes evident that peasant religion is dynamic: it adapts to
changing local conditions and it interacts with urban developments. As
long as the physical, economic and social landscape of the peasant remains
more or less unaltered, there is 'permanence' in peasant life. However, if
this apparent stability is shaken or altered in an abrupt way, the adaption
of the peasants to the new situation may be a difficult and painful process.
The threats to their traditional way of life may lead to desperate efforts to
save the old traditions and search for solutions with the aid of 'ideology' or
religion, i.e. 'nativistic' solutions are sought that represent conscious
attempts to revive or perpetuate certain aspects of peasant culture.[67]

At times, this type of behavior leads to a total repudiation of 'outside'
society – the society which appropriates part of what the peasants produce
because it controls an important part of the peasant economy. The
town dwellers who live off the peasants' produce are frequently those who

64 Harriss (1982), p. 215, quoted in Kahn (1985), p. 49.
65 Christian (1987), p. 371.
66 Ibid.
67 Linton (1943).

introduce the new ideas that are perceived as threats to the age-old way of life in rural areas. As a result, some peasants may refuse to have anything to do with changes signaled from the outside. They may even withdraw to form secluded – frequently religiously based – societies of their own, opting for self-sufficiency and turning their backs on society at large. Others may choose to take up arms against the intruders.

Olivorio's first biographer, Emigdio Garrido Puello, has stated that Olivorio was 'a product of his environment'.[68] We agree. In order to understand and interpret his movement and its relative success, we will therefore make use of a deliberately multidimensional approach which focuses precisely on the events that shaped and changed the particular community where he made his appearance.[69]

In a discussion of how to counteract the tendency that prevailed within geography in the 1970s, of splitting the analysis into limited, specialized fields, thereby losing the larger, synthesizing perspective, Torsten Hägerstrand cites Håkan Törnebohm and advocates a distinction between two main types of synthesis: compositional ones and contextual ones.[70] The former deals with 'how a certain whole is divided into a hierarchy of constituent parts and maps how the parts are joined so as to form the whole'.[71] It represents an 'anatomic' and 'static' way of arriving at the synthesis, but it conveys little insight into how coexisting phenomena influence each other when change is taking place. The contextual synthesis, on the other hand, concentrates on 'the contexts of which an object is part and the relations which exist between the characteristics of the object and its appearance in the different contexts'.[72] It emphasizes processes. Hägerstrand notes that the compositional approach has been the predominant one in geography.

Sciences of religion also tend to be somewhat limited in their approach. Common are hermeneutical and phenomenological research methods. The former fix the interest on a single interpretative key to reveal the mysteries of investigated phenomena. The latter tend to focus on the synchronic elements of religion, describing creed and rituals without reference to particular historical contexts. History of religions, on the other hand, intends to 'grasp religion in its concreteness, in its historical creativity, and its meaningfulness for the cultural, social and individual lives with which it is interwoven'.[73] The historian of religions 'is not concerned with facts isolated from their historical contexts and processes, but rather with

68 Garrido Puello (1963), p. 54.
69 Cf. Abrahams (1976), pp. 15–16.
70 Hägerstrand (1974), pp. 86–7.
71 Ibid., p. 87.
72 Ibid.
73 Bianchi (1987), p. 400.

these contexts and processes themselves'.[74] Religion cannot be isolated from its immediate environment and any analysis of the phenomenon ought to consider '[historical] processes as they actually developed, in their own *milieux* and it tries to take into consideration all the problems of historical influence, of convergence or divergence in relation to other processes or *milieux*'.[75]

In short, a principle of holism ought to serve as the final criterion of adequacy, thus avoiding the danger inherent in 'certain intellectualist rigidity of principles which, because it presumes to define or to presuppose too much on a theoretical basis, runs the risk of misunderstanding the phenomena in question, comparing them too arbitrarily with "patterns" or systematic formulae which are not always appropriate'.[76]

Religion must be studied as it is today and be seen in relation to the complex framework of the modern world. This means that not only themes, motives, details of creeds and cults, but the entire system of which they form an integral part must be studied, so that details may be illuminated by the light of the whole. Nevertheless, 'interest in today's events does not in any way deprive of their decisive importance problems of genesis and developments in past, or even in remote, times',[77] always keeping in mind that it is not only the modern world which is complex.

Hence, the phenomenon we are interested in cannot be analyzed within the framework of a single traditional academic discipline. We need building blocks both from the history of religions and from economics, and in addition from geography, sociology, anthropology, psychology and linguistics. The reason is the one pointed out above. Peasant religion is a multidimensional phenomenon about which it makes no sense to discuss other than in relation to its local context, because this very context has a decisive influence when it comes to shaping religion and its interaction with the surrounding society. 'Biographies should be carried out in the form of contextual syntheses', observes Hägerstrand.[78] We agree.[79]

Religion is a human phenomenon. Like other human activities it manifests itself within the environment of its practitioners. Accordingly, we will argue that religion is an integrated part of *Sanjuanero* peasant existence. Its threads run through the entire warp of traditional peasant life. If society changes, religion is doomed to follow suit. Such a shift may sometimes mean a complete break with old traditions and former ways of life.

74 Ibid., p. 402.
75 Bianchi (1975), p. 3.
76 Ibid., p. 34
77 Ibid., p. 163.
78 Hägerstrand (1974), p. 87.
79 In addition, 'To anyone who is not a blockhead, all the sciences are interesting ...' (Bloch (1953), p. 7), and scholars can be absorbed by more than one of them.

However, if the peasant remains within the same environment, the 'new' religion will probably become more adjusted to local traditions and develop other characteristics.

The backdrop for our analysis of *Olivorista* religion is the 'animated' landscape of the Dominican San Juan Valley and the Cordillera Central. Over the years the actors have changed and mingled. The valley has been a meeting place for different peoples and different faiths. We trace the possible origins of various beliefs and rituals, describing the process of their assimilation to local conditions. Even if historical, political and ecological factors have shaped the San Juan religion over time, the setting and the traditional way of life have maintained a certain kind of stability. *Sanjuanero* religion may be likened to a play performed by different actors, but acted out on the same stage, in front of unchanging side screens and in similar costumes. Beliefs were brought from Europe and Africa, but over the years they became adapted to the valley and the traditions that survived there. The 'play' has been updated and changed in response to the demands of viewers and participants. Even the set has been somewhat changed, but the 'message' stays essentially the same, and the *Olivoristas* would probably say that the director who manages the performance from behind the scenes has always been the same – the Great Power of God, who is eternally present within the landscape and animates everything.

We provide a description of the *Olivorista* environment and the changes that affected it at the time of Olivorio Mateo's appearance. We also present some local traditions and rituals which may have affected Olivorio and his cult. Within a limited space like the San Juan Valley, it is easy to discern the importance of certain individuals who exercise power over their fellow beings. The intricate web of power relations in the valley is conditioned by concepts like *caudillismo* [local strongman leadership], *compadrazgo* [ritual coparenthood] and *clientelismo* [clientship], and a phenomenon such as *Olivorismo* must be related to these Latin American 'institutions'. In order to explain the attraction of Olivorio, we have also touched on concepts like charisma and thaumaturgism, comparing his movement with similar phenomena from entirely different settings. The intention has been to see how general concepts have been 'acted out' within a particular 'habitat' like the San Juan Valley.

We present *Olivorismo* as a local agrarian religion which absorbs notions and rituals from different cultural settings and adapts them to a particular habitat. In this context, *Olivorismo* stands out as a practical creed which answers to the needs of its practitioners. It is not a 'pure' religion. It is a conglomerate, a syncretistic religion, which interacts and answers to the environment of its believers. A religion that is not adapted to its environment is like a play in an incomprehensible language. It does not tell its spectators anything and the spectators do not have any use for it. Social life and beliefs in the San Juan Valley offer an example of how changing socioeconomic conditions shape religious beliefs and how different creeds mix within a given setting, creating a religion that serves as an instrument for individual and communal interpretations of existence and thus becomes a tool for change and adoption to new ways of life.

Beliefs that have been adapted to *Olivorismo* appear to have undergone a process similar to what is nowadays promoted by a radical wing of the Catholic clergy. When Latin America in 1992 'celebrated' the 500th anniversary of the Spanish discovery of the 'New World', the Latin American Catholic bishops met in Santo Domingo and lamented the violent conversion of the Indians while indicating how the church had been instrumental in the destruction of their religions and often been guilty of treating the native inhabitants as second-class citizens in the conquerors' society. In order to make up for these sins, the concept of 'Theology of Inculturation' was introduced.

This concept was explained as a theological term which does not denote a relation between two cultures, but the relation between the Christian gospel and a determinate culture into which the Christian message enters. The beliefs, values, customs, symbols and institutions of that particular culture thus transform and perfect the Christian message.[80] According to the Latin American bishops, the message of the gospel is eternal and all-embracing, but in order to be properly understood it has to be translated into not only the language, but also the culture of the recipients of Christian doctrine.

The theological base for such a transformation is Chapter 1 in *John*: 'In the beginning was the Word, and the Word was with God, and the Word was God. [...] And the Word was made flesh, and dwelt among us ...'[81] The word of God is incarnated within a culture. Accordingly, Jesus was a Jew and he used the Jewish culture in order to divulge his message. Likewise, in order to fulfill his mission Paul had to be a 'Jew among Jews' and a 'Greek among Greeks'.[82] The Christian message is being adapted to Mayan culture among Guatemalan Indians and to voodoo among Haitian peasants (to give but two examples).

Unwittingly, the Catholic bishops have given an apt description of the workings of religion in the San Juan Valley. Religious notions from different corners of the world became 'inculturated' by the inhabitants of the valley and were adapted to the needs of the *Sanjuaneros*. A study of *Olivorismo* thus turns into a study of religion as a social force which reacts

80 Espeja (1993), p. 12. The concept of inculturation developed among the Jesuits. The first official mention of the word is found in the Decrees from the Jesuits' 31st General Congregation in September 1966 (Martin (1987), p. 386).
81 *John* 1:1, 14, *The Holy Bible: King James Version* (1991). All references to the Bible in the following are to the King James Version.
82 Celada (1993), p. 84.

to, and adapts itself to the 'development' of a certain area inhabited by persons who are mainly agriculturists. *Olivorismo* is accordingly but one example of a dynamic process which constantly has manifested itself throughout history and which, at this very moment, continues to unfold itself all over the world.

The socioeconomic context: the failure to inculturate capitalism

Two of the main tasks of the present investigation are to explain why the *Olivorista* movement was successful and why – twice – it was put down violently. The analysis of these interrelated problems will to a large extent be carried out with the aid of economic tools. The area in which *Olivorismo* developed was an agrarian society with a specific production system. With the aid of the theories of international trade and transaction costs, we will at some length investigate how this production structure evolved over the course of the centuries that elapsed since the first Europeans arrived in Hispaniola in 1492 and how this structure was destroyed in the course of a few decades around the time Olivorio was active in the San Juan Valley. What took place in Palma Sola almost half a century later from the economic point of view was a continuation of these events. Herein lies the clue both to the success of the *Olivorista* movement and to the tragedy that befell it.

Putting emphasis on economic factors means that we subscribe to a largely materialistic view of the process that we analyze. In this, we do not lack precedents. In a footnote in the first book of *Capital*, Karl Marx calls for a materialistic analysis of religion: 'Every history of religion … that fails to take account of [the] material basis, is uncritical.'[83] This call for a social science based analysis of religion was heeded by later generations of social scientists. One need only to think of the classic works of Max Weber and R. H. Tawney on the influence of the contents of creed on economic practice in European society and vice versa.[84] A modern variety is the one presented by anthropologist Marvin Harris and his attempts to found an entire theory of culture on materialist principles.[85]

---

83 Marx (1954), note, p. 352. Marx continues: 'It is, in reality, much easier to discover by analysis the earthly core of the misty creations of religion, than, conversely, it is, to develop from the actual relations of life the corresponding celestialised forms of those relations. The latter method is the only materialistic, and therefore the only scientific one' (ibid.). It is by no means evident what Marx meant by the latter statement. One is bound to agree with Eli Heckscher that when it comes to Marx' discussion of historical materialism, much of it was carried out as 'quite short remarks on the subject, and they are buried in layers of interpretation that are as deep as for any passage in the Bible' (Heckscher (1944), p. 9).
84 Weber (1930), Tawney (1947). Samuelsson (1965) provides a critical review.
85 Harris (1980).

Not surprisingly, the same strand of thought has been brought to bear in analyses of Third World communities, and in particular in discussions of cultural obstacles to economic and cultural change.[86] The present book deals with the interaction between religion and the economy among peasants in a remote corner of the Dominican Republic and their religious beliefs as manifested during periods of economic and social stress. It analyzes the kind of circumstances that gave rise to the *Olivorista* movement and the factors that led to the repression of it by the worldly authorities.

The theological concept of inculturation may be transferred to the socioeconomic sphere. As will be demonstrated during the course of the present investigation, one of the keys to the understanding of the *Olivorista* movement is the introduction of modern capitalism in the Dominican Republic towards the end of the nineteenth century and at the beginning of the twentieth century, and its resistance by the followers of Olivorio. In this confrontation, the 'modernizing' forces pulled the longer straw, destroying economic relations which had existed for almost four centuries. In the same way as the Catholic church failed to merge with the preexisting American cultures at the time of the European conquest, capitalism failed to merge with the economic order that existed in the San Juan Valley at the time when Olivorio appeared and founded his movement.

Thus, our analysis is concerned with what in Marxist geography is sometimes called restructuring.[87] In particular it will deal with how, when

> capitalist enterprises respond to changing competition by altering ... the way production and distribution are organized, [...] these changes result in consequential changes in the way economic activity is organized across geographical space, through the creation and destruction of spatial divisions of labour [... and] some of the links between the spatial division of labour and the geographical pattern of social relations.[88]

Our analysis will not be carried out within a Marxist framework. However, we share the conviction of those employing the reconstructing approach that both local and global circumstances must be taken into consideration:

> it is not sensible to focus on a town or region in isolation [...] But ... modest spatial zones – localities – may be meaningful units for

86 Cf. e.g. Lewis (1955), pp. 101–7, for an early summary, and Long (1977), and the works cited there, for a later discussion.
87 Cf. e.g. Lovering (1989).
88 Ibid., p. 199.

research. This is because most people live, work, and form their immediate social relationships within a restricted geographical area. The 'local community [involves] sets of relations which are multiplex (neighbours who are workmates, who are leisure-time companions etc), where "everybody knows everyone else"'… Its emphasis on social relations leads the restructuring approach to pay special attention to the locality. But at the same time, its emphasis on the capitalist character of the market (which is by no means local), means that this approach cannot be satisfied with a treatment of localities as autonomous units. No man, woman, no *place* is socially an island.[89]

We will argue that *Olivorismo* arose as a mixture of the same, local and foreign, ingredients that constitute Dominican popular religion in general: Catholicism, notably of the Spanish variety, Taino religion, African reminiscences and, to a minor extent, voodoo. Hence, the *Olivorista* movement represented successful religious inculturation. This to a large extent explains its creation and survival as a religion. On the other hand, it proved impossible for the preexisting economic structure in the San Juan Valley to absorb and transform modern capitalism – imposed from outside as a result of changes in the world economy – in a way which would have made it possible to preserve the traditional socioeconomic structure, values and lifestyle. The advent of modern capitalism implied an either/or choice for the inhabitants of the valley. The requirements of capitalism were not compatible with the structure of the economy of the San Juan Valley. Either this economy had to change – become 'modernized' – or capitalism had to be rejected. It is in this local context that we must seek both the attraction of the *Olivorista* movement to the peasants and the causes of its persecution and destruction as a major social movement.

The scene of modernization

The *Olivorista* story is a modernization drama. It deals with how a time-honored way of life constructed over several centuries was destroyed by exogenous, 'modernizing' events. Marshall Berman defines 'modernity' as

> a mode of vital experience – experience of space and time, of the self and others, of life's possibilities and perils – that is shared by men and women … To be modern is to find ourselves in an environment that promises us adventure, power, joy, growth, transformation of ourselves and the world – and at the same time, that threatens everything we have, everything we know, everything we are. […] But it is a

---

89 Ibid., pp. 199–200. The quotation is from Lash and Urry (1987), p. 91.

paradoxical unity, a unity of disunity: it pours us into a maelstrom of perpetual disintegration and renewal, of struggle and contradiction, of ambiguity and anguish. To be modern is to be part of a universe in which, as Marx said, 'all that is solid melts into air.'[90]

'Modernization', then, is 'the social processes that bring this maelstrom into being, and keep in a state of perpetual becoming'.[91] Most relevant in the present context, as stressed by Edward Soja, it

> is a continuous process of societal restructuring that is periodically accelerated to produce a significant recomposition of space-time being in their concrete forms, a change in the nature and experience of modernity that arises primarily from the historical and geographical dynamics of modes of production. For the past four hundred years, these dynamics have been predominantly capitalist, as has been the very nature and experience of modernity during that time. Modernization is, like all social processes, unevenly developed across time and space and thus inscribes quite different historical geographies across different social formations.[92]

Modernization may be conceived of as a general process. As such, it lends itself to theoretical analysis. However, theoretical work alone 'can never generate all the types of discovery necessary to give knowledge of specific spatial outcomes'.[93] General processes produce qualitatively different outcomes in different localities because the localities themselves differ qualitatively from each other. Thus, the mere use of social sciences theories will not make the *Olivorista* story intelligible. For a full understanding of the events, knowledge of the local context and of how this context has developed is indispensable:

> All histories are geographically specific,
> and their making is context dependent
> dependent on what is already present,
> already situated,
> is inseparable from the social production of spaces and places,
> from the place-specific conduct of everyday life
> and nonroutine activities

90 Berman (1983), p. 15.
91 Ibid., p. 16.
92 Soja (1989), p. 27.
93 Lovering (1989), p. 218.

states Alan Pred, in his characteristically emphatic way.[94] The homogenizing influences can be readily interpreted with the aid of theory alone, but

> Any homogenizing influences that may be produced by corporate capitalism, the State, and the mass media do not easily translate into the homogenization of resistance and conflict. Metaphorically, as well as physically, each place has its own sites of confrontation, its own spaces of struggle, its own arenas of contention, even if the contested issues are embedded in nonlocally based power relations and geographically extensive processes. Such conflicts cannot escape intersecting with unique local historical geographies, cannot avoid the bringing into play of locally sedimented, practice-based knowledge and experience, cannot but come up against the singular ways in which interests locally cross-cut one another and in which local agendas are set.[95]

Where do we begin to disentangle this web? This is no simple task. In one sense, our study of Olivorio and *Olivorismo* represents an attempt to write biography. However, biographies are not formed in a vacuum. On the one hand, their formation is affected by historical events, by institutions that already exist as a result of human action in the past, by economic and social power constellations that have been created before, by behavioral patterns that have been set and handed down by previous generations. On the other hand, the presence of the *Olivorista* movement and the events that took place in the San Juan Valley in connection with it had a definite influence on the course of history in the valley. For both reasons, a historical approach is indispensable if we are to gain any insight into why events took the course they did, and, for the same reasons, we need to anchor the analysis in the local context. Events were shaped by the unique local mixture of institutions, power constellations and behavioral patterns, and events, past and contemporary, in their turn, made an imprint on the local geography, transforming it profoundly. All this has to be taken into account in the analysis. The constituent parts are all what Pred calls 'elements of the same geographically and historically specific process of becoming'.[96]

Nevertheless, we must start somewhere. Our beginning will be a 'traditional' one. In Part I we will try to reconstruct the events as they took place, with the aid of written sources and oral information extracted from

94 Pred (1990), p. 1.
95 Ibid., p. 232.
96 Pred (1986), p. 21.

interviewees who were either present themselves or had privileged access to people who were present.

In the single chapter of Part II we turn from the actual events to legend, by examining some of the *Olivorista* lore. We make an attempt to map some of the mythical universe of which *Olivorismo* forms an integral part, and decipher the hidden transcript of the movement. The difference between 'urban' and 'rural' ideologies will become apparent here.

Part III presents the interpretation of the events with the aid of the framework sketched in the present chapter. Our interpretative chapters will be explicitly historical. In the first, the roots of the *Olivorista* religion is traced. In the second, the economic history of the San Juan Valley is sketched against the backdrop of events in the larger national and international economy, notably its continuity during four centuries and the disruptive events that took place at the end of the nineteenth and the beginning of the twentieth century.

In the chapter that follows, our analysis of local economic events in the San Juan Valley is continued until 1963 and the rise and fall of the *Olivorista* movement in Palma Sola. The political power play within the valley and at a national level is brought to the forefront, because the persecution of the movement in Palma Sola was intimately connected with the political discourse prevalent in the Dominican Republic at the time. The political language used in the persecution of the *Olivoristas* in Palma Sola cannot be understood without a description of its ideological background, something that is provided in the chapter that comes after our account of local economic and political developments in San Juan.

In Part IV the perspective is widened. Some aspects of *Olivorismo* are compared with similar phenomena within religious movements in other parts of the world. We argue that the official justification of the massacre in Palma Sola as an annihilation of a superstitious anomaly imported from Haiti had little foundation in reality. A movement like *Olivorismo* is an often logical and not uncommon answer to social anomie. In a concluding chapter we provide an interpretation of the *Olivorista* episode as a story with many bottoms – a historically contingent process unfolding in a local context. Finally, the epilogue briefly describes the *Olivorismo* of today and the fate of some of the actors in the tragic drama of Palma Sola.

Part I

The events

2 Olivorio Mateo

The life and death of a peasant god, 1908–22

A strange savior

In the summer of 1908, a storm ravaged large areas of the district of San Juan de la Maguana. The storm triggered violent rains that lasted for many days. People and animals were killed, the San Juan River rose and overflowed its banks, and the harvest was destroyed. The authorities were powerless. Nothing was done to alleviate the situation for those who had been affected by the catastrophe. In those days of hopelessness a strange savior appeared in a village called La Maguana: Olivorio Mateo, commonly known as 'Olivorio' or 'Liborio', an illiterate former field laborer.[1]

Olivorio was considered to be 'an odd character', possibly bordering on the insane. He often went away on wanderings for many days. He had disappeared during the violent storm and was thought to be dead, but reappeared on the last day of the funeral ceremonies that were held for him. 'I come from far away',[2] he said, and told that he had been taken to heaven by an angel on a horse. There he had met God who had given him his 'divine seal' and ordered him to return to earth to preach and cure the sick. 'I am not crazy', Olivorio told the villagers. 'I am sent by God on a mission that will last for 33 years. Everyone who believes in me will be saved.'[3]

The above constitutes the standard account of how Olivorio Mateo, the founder of a religious peasant movement in the Dominican Republic at the beginning of the century, started his activities. Olivorio was shot by the police in 1922, after a five-year hunt by the American occupation forces and the Dominican authorities. His movement, however, did not die. During the Trujillo years it was forced underground, but once *El Benefactor*

---

1 Garrido Puello (1963), p. 7.
2 Ibid., p. 8.
3 Quoted in op. cit., p. 55.

had been killed, it surfaced again – in Palma Sola.[4] By this time, Olivorio was already a deity himself: the subject of religious worship.

Who was Olivorio? Unfortunately, the standard account offered above is not very reliable. In fact, most of the events contained therein never took place. Olivorio shares the fate of most founders of religious movements, in that facts and myth have been spun into a web that is difficult to disentangle. Nevertheless, in the present work, an effort will be made to separate reality from fiction, to construct a picture of the person Olivorio and his activities during a critical decade in Dominican history.

The source material: myth and reality

Many peasants in the Dominican Republic consider Dios Olivorio to be a living god. The believers frequently state that the person Olivorio Mateo means nothing. It is the 'living god' who bestows grace upon them: 'He himself lived many years ago. I did not know him. Now, his spirit is with us, and that is all that matters.'[5] The former field laborer Olivorio Mateo has turned into a legend, and the real person caught in the web of myth is hard to discern – in spite of the fact that people who knew him personally are still alive and can be interviewed.

A friend of his may start a description of Olivorio with what appears as a convincing matter-of-fact statement: 'He was a very calm man, even taciturn. He was of medium height, and when he grew older he became robust. He ate a lot and was fond of all sorts of fish.'[6] Thereafter, however, the same person may confess that Olivorio 'is the one and only God, the only one who knows everything', and continue his memories with a tale of how *El Maestro* resurrected a girl from the dead in the Cibao – told in the same colloquial manner.[7]

The fabrication of legends about Olivorio has been diffused across the

---

4 The initiators of the Palma Sola movement were two brothers, Plinio and Romilio Ventura. They were smallholders, anti-Trujillistas and sons of former *Olivoristas*. They founded a cultic center at a place called Palma Sola, close to Carrera de Yeguas, some kilometers north of Las Matas de Farfán. The movement was initiated a few months before the murder of Trujillo (30 May 1961). Rafael Leonidas Trujillo had been the leader of the Dominican Republic for more than thirty years and often ruthlessly attacked all opposition, among them members of the Ventura family. Thousands of poor peasants were attracted to Palma Sola, seeking hope and security in the tumultuous times that followed after the death of the dictator. Political intrigues and religious intolerance put an end to the sanctuary of Palma Sola, which was completely destroyed on 28 December 1962. Hundreds of peasants were massacred by the authorities. (See García (1986) and Martínez (1991).)

5 Interview with María Orfelia, Maguana Arriba, 18 January 1986.

6 Interview with Julián Ramos, Higüerito, 16 January 1986.

7 Ibid. Julián Ramos does not say that he witnessed such a miracle, but he apparently believes that it occurred.

entire area where he lived and the stories often differ from place to place. Some are connected with well-known localities and people, whereas others give the impression of having been copied from events in the Bible. It is thus a delicate task to construct a biography of the 'real' Olivorio Mateo. The oral tradition is both contradictory and infused with myths and legends. Nevertheless, there is little doubt that the oral tradition contains an essence of truth which can be confirmed by the scant information that is to be found in written sources.

From time to time, short articles and notes concerning Olivorio have appeared in the Dominican press and in such publications as autobiographies, anthropological texts and collections of poems or anecdotes. Some of these are based on eyewitness accounts, but the majority of them fall back on a chapter in Horacio Blanco Fombona's book *Crímenes del imperialismo norteamericano*, published in 1927,[8] and/or Emigdio Garrido Puello's biography of Olivorio, from 1963.[9]

Blanco Fombona was a political refugee from Venezuela who for some years lived in Neiba, a town south of the San Juan Valley. Later, he moved to the capital, where he published a weekly, called *Letras*. Blanco Fombona was a fervent opponent of the American occupation of the Dominican Republic (1916–24) and when, in 1920, his paper published a photograph of a Dominican peasant who had been brutally tortured by American troops, the American military governor had him expelled from the island.[10] His book, which was published in Mexico, is a sharp attack on the American administration of the Dominican Republic.

This hatred towards the Americans also characterizes his story about Olivorio. As he lived in Neiba he probably picked up local traditions related to Olivorio, who at that time was active in the mountains north of San Juan de la Maguana. Many years later when he wrote down an account of his experiences, they were heavily tinged with pure legend. Blanco Fombona makes Olivorio a powerful peasant leader who controlled the whole southwestern area of the country as his own personal jurisdiction and negotiated on an equal footing with the Dominican presidents who preceded the American occupation. When the Americans arrived, they had Olivorio and many of his followers poisoned by contaminated water.[11]

---

8 Blanco Fombona (1927).

9 Garrido Puello (1963).

10 See Blanco Fombona (1927), pp. 117–37 and Mejía (1976), p. 173.

11 Blanco Fombona (1927), pp. 59–61. Such statements seem to be unfounded, and even if Blanco Fombona's account occasionally contains plausible observations, most of it is contradicted by sources from the time when the events occurred. For example, such documents as notes in the Dominican press and American military reports clearly state that Olivorio was shot in an ambush, and all *Olivoristas* we have met so far agree on this. Strangely enough a standard work like the widely used *Diccionario enciclopédico dominicano, Volumen I* (1988), p. 282, uncritically repeats Blanco Fombona's story.

Figure 2.1 Olivorio Mateo (Liborio), probably in 1909.

Even though Blanco Fombona's account is more or less fictitious, it has been very influential and some Dominican writers have retold it as the true story of Olivorio Mateo.[12] For example, his description of Olivorio's appearance turns up in nearly every subsequent account:

> Negro, evidently of pure race, without being contaminated with either White, or Indian; ugly like an Aztec idol; rather tall, broad chest, well developed muscles; skinny; very wide mouth; fleshy lips; the eyes, filled with magnetic current, displayed big patches of red in the white parts.[13]

This completely negative description of Olivorio ought to be complemented by the more accurate description given by Manuel de Jesús Rodríguez Varona, who served as Public Notary in San Juan de la Maguana at the time and met with Olivorio several times:

> Olivorio was of short stature, dark-skinned and always conversed in an animated and jovial manner, attentive to people; he had a liking for alcoholic beverages but did not get drunk, liked music and dancing;

12 A recent example is Ferreras (1983), pp. 307–16.
13 Blanco Fombona (1927), p. 59.

Figure 2.2 Emigdio Garrido Puello.

but hardly danced himself. [...] Olivorio was always a rustic man, poor-minded, simple and humble and profoundly religious, ephemeral and contemplative.[14]

A more reliable source than Blanco Fombona is Garrido Puello's book on Olivorio. Emigdio Osvaldo Garrido Puello, 'Badín' (1893–1983), was one of the most prominent citizens in San Juan de la Maguana[15] during the first quarter of the century. The descendant of famous military leaders of the district and the son-in-law of 'Carmito' Ramírez, the most influential *caudillo* of the San Juan Valley, he was a member of the economic and cultural elite. He served as a teacher in his youth and in 1921 he founded a newspaper, *El Cable*, which the new president, Rafael Trujillo, forced him to close in 1930. During the 1920s he served various periods as *Presidente del Ayuntamiento* [chairman of the town council] of San Juan de la Maguana.

14 Rodríguez Varona (1947), p. 4. Even if this account is sometimes mentioned in the literature concerning Olivorio and the original is readily available at the National Archives in Santo Domingo, we have not seen it cited anywhere.
15 Interview with José Garrido Ramírez, Santo Domingo, 21 April 1986. Emigdio Osvaldo Garrido Puello has described his own views and personal development in various books (Garrido Puello (1963), (1972), (1977), (1981) and (n.d.)).

As a relative of influential landowners and a retail dealer of modern agri-cultural implements, Garrido Puello was heavily involved in the change and modernization of the traditional peasant way of life. Having been an educator, deeply engaged in politics and interested in culture, he also saw it as his mission to fight superstition and 'Haitian' influences. His personal convictions have quite probably influenced the rather harsh judgement that he passes on Olivorio and his followers. The book on Olivorio was written more than forty years after the events took place, but it must be deemed to be fairly well informed, due to Garrido Puello's familiarity with the scene of the actions. In spite of this, it is imbued with the 'urban' conceptions formed among the economic elite of San Juan de la Maguana: Olivorio and his movement are viewed from the 'outside' and Garrido Puello presents many vague rumors and biased judgements as if they were proven facts.

Additional information concerning Olivorio can be found in scant reports in the Dominican press of the time, many of them written by Garrido Puello, who not only reported events in his own *El Cable*, but also served as a correspondent for other periodicals. The American occupation forces that hunted Olivorio in the mountains for many years also wrote occasional reports on the hunt. Unfortunately, subsequent political distur-bances have led to the destruction of valuable archives in San Juan de la Maguana, Santo Domingo and Azua, where material concerning Olivorio was deposited. No copies seem to exist of these lost documents.[16]

To this day legends are spun around Olivorio and fantastic stories occa-sionally appear in the press. Certain time periods have fostered particular interpretations of his person. In the early 1960s, during the persecution of the sect in Palma Sola, he was depicted as a charlatan or an evil witch doctor.[17] During the United States intervention in 1965 he was turned into an anti-imperialist freedom fighter and the religious traits of his movement were toned down.[18] These examples both come from the capital. In the

16 Some examples: The parish archives of San Juan de la Maguana were burned to ashes in 1961 by hooligans in the service of Trujillo, who was furious with the bishop there at the time (Reyes (n.d.), pp. 185–6). The dictator's own huge personal archive was looted and dispersed in the disturbances that occurred after his death (Garrido Puello (1977), p. 142). However, quite a lot of this valuable material was rescued and is presently kept in the National Palace. Unfortunately we have not had the opportunity to see these archives, but bits and pieces have been published by Bernardo Vega (1981), (1982a), (1982b), (1984), (1985a), (1985b), (1986a), (1986b), (1986c), (1986d), (1986e), (1987), (1988a), (1988c), (1989), (1990), (1991a), (1991b), (1992), (1993), (1995a) and (1995b). Scattered fragments from the dispersed archives in Azua may be found in the National Archives in Santo Domingo, but the majority of their contents seem to have disappeared forever. (Between 1844 and 1930, Azua was the capital of a province that also included the San Juan Valley.)

17 Many examples exist. Paniagua (1962), can be taken as a representative for the tone that is apparent in all of them.

countryside, on the other hand, the peasants have completely different views – views that vary from community to community and from individual to individual.

To construct a credible biography out of this patchwork of divergent legendary and often biased information is a delicate task indeed. What will be offered in the following should be regarded as a mere sketch that traces the lifespan of Olivorio and points to some aspects of his teachings and the religious behavior that evolved around his person. It must be read bearing in mind that nothing definite can be said about him:

> Biography, like autobiography, is of necessity a fiction, that is, a construct arranged by an interpreter following examination and analysis of available evidence, published and unpublished writings, the works of critics and biographers, as well as the social, political, and artistic history of the age. The collected materials are shaped on the basis of the biographer's insights, empathy, and assumptions; the materials are inevitably incomplete, particularly for the formative years; the opinions of contemporaries are distorted by prejudices and limited knowledge; and the subject's carefully fabricated veils block insight and render judgments problematical. For these and other reasons no biography can be definitive or wholly truthful: it is only fitting that all individuals should have an inalienable right to their mysteries.[19]

The field laborer

Olivorio was born to a peasant woman called Zacaría Mateo in a small village called Maguana Arriba, a few kilometers north of San Juan de la Maguana.[20] Zacaría, who was light skinned, originally came from the fertile plains of the Cibao, on the other side of the Cordillera Central.[21] The year of Olivorio's birth is not known, but he was around fifty years when he initiated his mission some time before 1910.[22] He had several brothers and sisters and they all owned land around La Maguana.[23] Olivorio had some

---

18 *Patria*, No. 58, 7 July 1965. A more recent example of a homage to Olivorio as a Dominican patriot is found in a collection of poems written by Conde Pausas (1983).

19 Miller (1991), pp. xvii–xviii.

20 Interview with Julián Ramos, Higüerito, 16 January 1986.

21 Interview with Arquímedes Valdez, son of Olivorio Mateo. Maguana Abajo, 31 May 1989. Arquímedes never met his grandfather, who was not around when he was born. He does not remember hearing anything about Olivorio's father. Zacaría died when she was 89 years old and accordingly outlived her son (ibid.).

22 Rodríguez Varona (1947), p. 4.

23 Arquímedes mentions seven uncles and aunts: Carlitos, Juanico, José Lucía, Eugenio, Zindín, Catalina and Juana.

Figure 2.3 Wenceslao Ramírez.

plots in the village, but not enough to support himself, his wife Eusebia and what eventually became eight children.[24] He thus had to get odd jobs whenever he could find them, to supplement what his various plots brought. His specialty was to construct *cercas* – fences made out of hurdle poles – and this profession took him all over the San Juan Valley.

Olivorio often worked on the lands of Wenceslao Ramírez. 'They were good friends since long ago and when the general needed the help of my father he sent for him.'[25] Wenceslao was the most influential *caudillo* in the southwestern part of the Dominican Republic around the turn of the century. He was an old soldier, general, 'Superior Chief of the Borders' and 'Communal Chief of Bánica and San Juan de la Maguana'. He was a

---

24 Cordero Regalado (1981), p. 6 b. Olivorio's son, Arquímedes, states that 'the Mateos were never really poor, they were better off than most of their neighbors and food was never lacking' (interview with Arquímedes Valdez, Maguana Abajo, 31 May 1989).

25 Interview with Arquímedes Valdez, Maguana Abajo, 31 May 1989. According to Arquímedes, Olivorio had served as a soldier under Wenceslao Ramírez (cf. Rodríguez Varona (1947), p. 2). Ramírez' grandson, 'Mimicito' Ramírez, stated that Olivorio had received a rifle from the authorities and served in the militia of La Maguana: 'Under Lilís nearly every man belonged to the rural militia, which served as some kind of reinforcement to the regular army. Each section of the Municipality of la Maguana could muster a group of militia men, who were under the command of a 'captain' from the municipal police. In those days the Municipality of la Maguana consisted of no less than 39 sections' (interview with Mimicito Ramírez, San Juan de la Maguana, 1 June 1989).

Figure 2.4 Wenceslao Ramírez with three of his sons at the beginning of the 1920s. *l. to r.* José del Carmen (Carmito), Juan de Dios (Juanico) and Octavio.

big landowner with various vast *hatos* [cattle ranches], all over the San Juan Valley. The largest one, Guayabal, just south of the border town of Bánica, extended into Haitian territory.

Wenceslao Ramírez established his residence on the Mijo *hacienda*, in the vicinity of San Juan de la Maguana. There he lived as a patriarch, a man of enormous physical proportions, feared by some and respected by everyone, a personal friend of most Dominican presidents of his time. He died in 1927.[26]

26 Wenceslao Ramírez, commonly known as Don Lao, was born in Azua in 1843 and spent his youth in Bánica, where he became *Jefe Comunal* in 1880. In 1887, he obtained the same position in San Juan de la Maguana. Wenceslao Ramírez obtained the confidence of the dictator Ulises Heureaux, 'Lilís', who controlled Dominican politics from 1880 to 1899. (Lilís did not serve as president during the entire period, but the political power all the time rested in his hands.) Heureaux, who had important interests in the San Juan Valley, where he had concubines, children and land, counted on the loyal support of Wenceslao whom he promoted to general in 1884, and 'Superior Chief of the Borders' in 1895.

Wenceslao maintained all his titles and obligations under the presidents that succeeded Lilís. He served on various occasions as a principal member on the commissions that negotiated the exact position of the Haitian-Dominican borderline. Until his death, in 1927, he was unrivaled as the most influential man in the San Juan Valley, and much of his importance was transferred to his son 'Carmito' Ramírez (Garrido (1972), pp. 261–8, cf. Martínez (1971), pp. 414–15).

Some old people state that they saw Olivorio at Mijo when they were children. 'Mimicito' Ramírez, one of Wenceslao's grandchildren, describes
Olivorio as a 'strong, but rather thin, man of average stature. He was a dark
mulatto [*indio oscuro*] and had curly hair. He was not crazy at all and knew
very well how to express himself. He was a peaceful man and never made
fuss about anything.'[27] Another of Wenceslao's grandchildren, Atala Cabral
Ramírez, often heard people talk about Olivorio in her grandfather's
house. It was said that Olivorio considered himself to be 'a great friend of
the Ramírez family' and he 'never did anything bad to anyone'.[28]

Even before Olivorio disappeared and returned with his divine mission,
he was considered to be something of a clairvoyant. He was frequently
asked by other people to find runaway donkeys 'through his revelations'.[29]
Evidently he was a dreamer. Some days 'he was lost in his own thoughts'.
Others, 'he could wake up singing and work hard the whole day'. The over-
seer at Mijo used to complain to his *patrón* that Olivorio was a manic
depressive, a very uneven character, but Wenceslao Ramírez did not care,
since he was inoffensive and always pleasant in his speech and manners.[30]

Around 1907, Olivorio worked on the lands of María Olegario Carrasco,
the ex-wife of Wenceslao Ramírez, who from time to time sent someone to
help with her garden plot. María Olegario had a *pulpería*, where the peasants bought things that they did not produce themselves, sold some of
their produce, obtained credit or simply had a chat over a shot of rum.
María Olegario's *pulpería* was situated on the main road to Azua, some 70
kilometers further south, and its busy seaport Puerto Tortuguero. Since it
was the last *pulpería* a stranger would encounter before coming to San Juan
de la Maguana, it was natural for wayfarers to make a stop there in order
to inform themselves about the latest events in town before they entered it.

27 Interview with Mimicito Ramírez, San Juan de la Maguana, 14 December 1985.
28 Interview with Tala Cabral Ramírez, Santo Domingo, 21 November 1985. Doña Tala
    never met Olivorio personally, but states that she was 'very close' to her grandfather
    during his last years, and that he often told her stories about Olivorio. She used to read
    for Wenceslao and help him with his correspondence. Don Lao was illiterate and could
    neither read nor write. Nevertheless, he maintained a vast correspondence and never
    failed to indicate where the punctuation marks were to be put when he dictated his
    letters. Other members of the Ramírez family have stated that Doña Tala was Don Lao's
    favorite among his grandchildren. She subsequently became a very respected teacher in
    San Juan de la Maguana.
29 Ibid.
30 Interview with Víctor Garrido, Jr, Santo Domingo, 22 April 1986. Víctor Garrido has his
    information about Olivorio from his mother, Tijides Ramírez de Garrido, one of Wences-
    lao Ramírez' daughters, who met Olivorio various times while he worked on her father's
    land. She was married to Emigdio Garrido Puello's brother Víctor and died in 1976, at
    eighty-nine years of age. Concerning Olivorio's manners there exists a tradition among
    peasants that he was 'a quiet person who did not talk much' (Mateo Pérez and Mateo
    Comas (1980), p. 45).

Figure 2.5 María Olegario Carrasco.

One day, Olivorio was planting *cebollines* [small onions] in María Olegario's backyard. When he finished his work, he took a drink at the *pulpería* counter. He had been attracted by a mysterious character who had come from Azua: a certain Juan Samuel – a traveling salesman who carried different kinds of trinkets and textiles, but who also sold *panaceas*, Catholic prayers and popular religious literature. Juan Samuel was an intelligent man who knew how to read and write and how to impress those he met. Olivorio's new acquaintance was one of those who 'lived on others'.[31] He knew several tricks with which to fool people, combining the roles of magician, quack and preacher. Olivorio was fascinated by the man, and when Juan Samuel bought some land in Acerito – a village just a few kilometers from Olivorio's own home in Maguana Arriba – Olivorio offered his services and helped Juan Samuel to cultivate his plots.[32]

Some people state that Juan Samuel was a very dark-skinned person. Others contend that he was a light-skinned mulatto. There is also disagreement regarding his origin. Some observers claim that it was Guadeloupe, others that he came from the British Virgin Islands. Most call him a *cocolo*, something that indicates that he spoke Spanish with an English accent,[33]

---

31 Interview with Mimicito Ramírez, San Juan de la Maguana, 14 December 1985. Cf. Garrido Puello (1963), pp. 11 and 13–14.

32 Interview with Mimicito Ramírez, San Juan de la Maguana, 14 December 1985.

33 The word probably originates from a mispronunciation of the name of the island of Tortola, one of the British Virgin Islands (Mota Acosta (1977), p. 2). It was used in order to denominate the English-speaking canecutters who came from the British West Indies to participate in the Dominican *zafra* [sugar harvest]. (Cf. Bryan (1979).)

Figure 2.6 A rural *pulpería*.

and the only American report which mentions him describes him as 'an English negro named Juan Samuel who had a knowledge of hypnotism and sleight-of-hand work'.[34] Most likely, Juan Samuel came from the Danish colony of St Thomas.[35]

In Acerito, Juan Samuel organized religious gatherings, where he preached and the attendants became possessed. He spoke of strange and marvelous things and performed faith healings. The exact contents of his religion are not very clear. 'Maybe it was something like the teachings of Jehova's Witnesses',[36] because Juan Samuel spoke of the end of the world. Quite probably, the preaching of Juan Samuel taught Olivorio a great deal

34 McLean (1921).
35 One of the oldest sources mentioning the nationality of Juan Samuel is a report written in 1922 by Emigdio Garrido Puello's brother, Víctor Garrido, where it is stated that Juan Samuel was a *Santomero*, a man from St Thomas (Garrido (1922), p. 233). There are various other indications of Juan Samuel's possible nationality. He could read and write and was English speaking, he came walking either from Azua or Baní, both towns connected with St Thomas through trade. Furthermore, he seems to have been familiar with Catholicism. At the turn of the century, the Danish Virgin Islands had the most advanced schooling for the black population in the entire Caribbean. No less than 90 percent were literate. Most of the population of the islands spoke English and the Catholics constituted the second largest congregation there. (Cf. Larsen (1950).)
36 Interview with Mimicito Ramírez, San Juan de la Maguana, 14 December 1985. It is impossible to pinpoint the importance Juan Samuel had for Olivorio Mateo. It is clear that he was with Olivorio when the latter initiated his 'mission'. In a photo presented in one of the first articles dealing with Olivorio, Juan Samuel appears by the side of *El Maestro* and is presented as his 'apostle' (*Blanco y Negro*, No. 42, 4 July 1909).

that was to be of use later on.[37] Possibly he also caught up with some of the teachings of another odd character that moved within the circles of Juan Samuel: a certain Pasute (Pasoute?) who was known to be a Haitian *ougan* [voodoo priest].[38]

One of Olivorio's sons, however, strongly denies that his father was under the influence of Juan Samuel:

The further fate of Juan Samuel is veiled in obscurity. Garrido Puello states that when 'Olivorio saw himself entangled in the nets of justice, he [Juan Samuel] disappeared as a passing shadow, leaving only a vague rumor behind' (Garrido Puello (1963), p. 14). Garrido Puello's statement seems to be confirmed by the fact that Juan Samuel's name does not appear in a list of wanted persons presented by a marine officer who led a search party chasing Olivorio and his men in the Cordillera Central during the American occupation (Feeley (1919)). When Olivorio and his men were attacked in July 1910, Juan Samuel, described as the *compañero del loco* [friend of the madman], was captured by government troops (Díaz (1910b)) and it is possible that he never returned to his friend and disciple. Nevertheless, some contemporaries hold that Juan Samuel was together with his 'apprentice' to the bitter end. According to Mayobanex Rodríguez, whose father was in charge of the San Juan police force for many years, Juan Samuel was murdered a short time after the death of Olivorio. Lieutenant Esteban Luna, who had been in charge of the *Olivorista* hunt for several years, ordered the death of Juan Samuel since 'the man who initiated the *Olivorista* movement would be able to do the same thing again' (interview with Mayobanex Rodríguez, San Juan de la Maguana, 12 December 1985).

It appears that the religious behavior and teachings of Juan Samuel bear some resemblance to the different Protestant millenarian sects, originating from the United States, that started to make their appearance in the Caribbean around the turn of the century. During Olivorio's lifetime, the San Juan Valley had only been reached by a couple of Protestant lay preachers from the American Bible Society who did not stay long and whose influence was probably negligible (Lockward (1982), pp. 340–1).

On the other hand, if Juan Samuel came from the Danish West Indies he was probably well acquainted with various Protestant sects. The Moravian Brethren had established their secluded agricultural communities all over the islands and American sects were gaining a foothold in the towns. Reports to the Danish archbishop in Copenhagen mention various 'extreme' sects like the Adventists. Reports concerning a sect called 'Church of Emanuel' are of particular interest. A priest in Christiansted on the island of St Croix describes its gatherings as occasions where the preachers induced the adherents into 'a strange state of half hysterical excitement' (Nygaard (1903)). Furthermore, he writes that the church leaders made aggressive attacks on the priests of other congregations and that their behavior caused indignation 'among the more thoughtful and self-conscious class' (ibid.). The police had to post an officer on guard in order to calm the unruly crowds that gathered in connection with the meetings (Hørlyk (1903)).

In a petition for 'acceptance' that the 'Church of Emanuel' sent to the archbishop of Denmark, the name of James Samuel appears among the fifty-three signatures (Gibson and Crocker (1903)). Is James Samuel the same man as the Juan Samuel who appeared in the San Juan Valley four years after the incidents in Christiansted? The thought is appealing, perhaps even probable, but unfortunately impossible to prove.

37 '[I]t may be deduced that it was this gentleman [Juan Samuel] who instructed him [Olivorio] in the practice of healing and necromancy' (Rodríguez Varona (1947)).

38 All Creole words have been transcribed with the aid of *Haitian Creole–English–French Dictionary* (1981).

Figure 2.7 Juan Samuel and Olivorio.

It was the other way around. It was Juan Samuel who tried to use the influence of my father. My father already had his thing when Juan Samuel appeared. He put himself in his [Olivorio's] shadow. Juan Samuel was a fucking trouble-maker [*hombre jodón*]. He came with his magic in the head. He had money, but he did not sell anything. I do not know where he came from. He talked with some kind of accent, but I do not believe he was a *cocolo*. Maybe he came from San Pedro de Macorís [the eastern sugar districts]. He was light skinned, long, but not very fat. He stayed here for 10 to 12 years, he did not till the land and had no children, but he ran after women and used his magic to get what he wanted. He gathered people around himself and made them fall to the ground, as if they were dying. They said he killed and resurrected them. It was also said that he made improper advances to the wives of the men he succeeded in 'killing' with his powers. My father used to resurrect the people Juan Samuel had 'killed'. People used to say that Juan Samuel killed, while Olivorio resurrected [*Juan Samuel mató, Olivorio levantó*].[39]

39 Interview with Arquímedes Valdez, Maguana Abajo, 31 May 1989. The *Olivorista* Julián Ramos, who stated that he knew both Juan Samuel and Pasute personally, also denies that Olivorio had anything to do with them (interview with Julián Ramos, Higüerito, 16 January 1986).

The great storm

Most students of the life of Olivorio agree upon the fact that it was a great storm that changed the illiterate farmhand Olivorio Mateo into Dios Olivorio. His biographer, Garrido Puello, provides an account of a storm in the summer of 1908 – the account presented in the opening paragraph of this chapter.[40] However, no contemporary newspaper that we have seen mentions the devastating natural catastrophe that constitutes the alleged beginning of *Olivorismo*. Nevertheless, a violent storm is recalled by old peasants: 'It was a cyclone, and it rained incessantly for eight days: water and water all the time. There was no wind, because it is very seldom that strong winds manage to climb the huge mountains that surround the valley.'[41]

Quite probably, eighty years later, the memories of the violent storm are confused. It may not have been in the year 1908 that the San Juan Valley was struck by the floods. A year later, the famous San Severo hurricane swept across the country. The newspapers of that year are filled with descriptions of the sufferings that followed in its tracks. In the Cibao area it rained for twenty-one days. The rivers rose, thousands of cattle were drowned and plagues and fevers of various kinds ravaged the countryside. A civil war was avoided, as a huge insurgent army marching on the capital had to be disbanded and return home because of the hurricane.[42]

If the legend is true, it was not San Severo that initiated Olivorio's religious activities, since San Severo hit the Dominican Republic only at the end of 1909, and the first newspaper article that deals with Olivorio's activities that we have been able to find appeared in *La Voz del Sur*, published in San Cristóbal, on 19 June 1909.[43] However, this is not likely to be the case. In retrospect, two unrelated events have merged into a spectacular legend according to which Olivorio disappeared during a storm.[44]

40 Garrido Puello (1963), pp. 7–8.
41 Interview with Julián Ramos, Higüerito, 16 January 1986.
42 Troncoso Sánchez (1964), pp. 326–7. Cf. Mejía (1976), p. 71. Both Mejía and Troncoso Sánchez call the hurricane San Severo and state that it hit the Dominican Republic by the end of 1909. Fray Cipriano de Utrera, who came to the country in 1910, fails to mention San Severo in an elaborate list of hurricanes that he presented in 1927. Instead he lists a hurricane called San Zacarías which hit the island on 6 September 1910, and 'a strong storm' [*fuerte temporal*] called San Wenceslao that hit 'the south coast of the island' on 27 September 1910 (Utrera (1978), p. 362).
43 Hoepelman (1909).
44 However, one of our interviewees, Víctor Garrido, Jr, insisted that the current dating of Olivorio's first appearance as thaumaturge and prophet is erroneous. Víctor Garrido states that his mother said to him that Garrido Puello was wrong. It was not in a storm in 1908 that Olivorio disappeared, but on an earlier occasion, '1898 or 1899' (interview with Víctor Garrido, Jr, Santo Domingo, 22 April 1986). If Víctor Garrido is right, Olivorio's disappearance could be put in relation to a hurricane called San Ciriaco, which hit the country on 8 August 1899 (Utrera (1978), p. 362).

At first, the legend continues, no one was worried, since Olivorio was known to be away regularly for many days without leaving any traces behind, presumably because of his profession as an itinerant laborer and fence builder. However, as the rivers had risen, Olivorio's brother Carlitos, who was the head of the Mateo family, started searching for him, fearing that he had drowned in the torrents of some mountain river.[45]

The search produced no results. Olivorio could not be found anywhere. The family took for granted that he had fallen victim to the storm and celebrated a vigil in his honor.[46] It was on the ninth and last day of this *velorio* that Olivorio made his reappearance, announcing the divine mission referred to in the opening paragraph.[47]

Arquímedes Valdez, Olivorio's son, however, emphatically denies the existence of any storm: 'There was no storm. I never saw this storm. I was ten years old when he disappeared. He disappeared for seven days and they searched for him up in the hills. He came back with this knowledge in his head.'[48]

The three signs

Olivorio established himself as a thaumaturge[49] (faith healer) in his native village, where people quickly started to gather around him: 'It did not take long. If someone came here with pain and ailments, he put his hands over

---

45 Garrido Puello (1963) p. 8.
46 The Dominican term for a vigil is *velorio*. A certain confusion reigns concerning the terminology. Some mean that the *velorio*, in other places of the Republic also called *velación* or *vela*, is a ceremony celebrated in order to honor a patron saint and prefer to denominate the act of celebrating vigils *hacer los nueve días*, do the nine days. Accordingly, a *velorio* may also be called *novena*, a term which is also in common usage among English-speaking Catholics.
   The ninth day of mourning is the most important one, and on this occasion friends and relatives of the deceased gather in the room where an *altar de los acompañamientos* [altar of accompaniment; the term *acompañamientos* is also used to denominate funeral processions] has been erected in honor of the deceased. A *rezador* [prayer man] summons the spirit of the dead person and begs it to leave the house. When the ceremony has ended, some of the altar decorations are usually burned and a communal meal is offered to all participants in the ritual. In the San Juan Valley, the *novena* often takes the form of a *rincón*, a ceremony that includes dancing and the playing of the *palos*, big drums made out of hollow trunks (Lemus and Marty (1975), pp. 117–20 and Deive (1979), pp. 353–7).
47 Garrido Puello (1963), p. 55. Carlitos Mateo, the brother of Olivorio who organized both the search and the vigil, became a loyal *Olivorista* and was an influential leader for the remaining followers of Olivorio when *El Maestro* had been killed. (Cf. *El Cable*, 31 July and 20 November 1923.)
48 Interview with Arquímedes Valdez, Maguana Abajo, 31 May 1989.
49 From Greek *thaumatourgos*, miracle working.

them. Soon they came from all over the Dominican Republic. All the time people came.'[50] The times were favorable indeed for wonder makers. An apocalyptic mood prevailed among the peasants of the San Juan Valley. Strange forebodings were interpreted as announcing the arrival of Doomsday. The weather behaved oddly. Floods and droughts made their appearance in uncommon intervals. The imminence of Halley's comet spread fear among the rural population.

Possibly under the influence of Juan Samuel, who stayed with his disciple after the latter's marvelous conversion into divine messenger and prophet, Olivorio grasped the sentiments of the peasants: the world might come to an end. He professed a strong conviction that his own days were numbered and frequently predicted his own death: 'Live the faith in Jesus Christ and Holy Mary. I am going, because Olivorio is tired. Help me to take my drink, because I am going. But pay good attention to me, because you will remember me.'[51] 'They will kill me in the end.'[52] 'You will all denounce me.'[53] He also predicted that 'many signs will convince the non-believers of the truth of my mission.'[54] And there were signs. The *Olivoristas* refer to 'the three misfortunes' predicted by Olivorio, following actions taken against him by the authorities of San Juan de la Maguana or Azua, the provincial capital: the arrival of Halley's comet in 1910, the San Bruno earthquake in 1911 and the civil war of 1912.

The comet

The first trial that befell the people of the San Juan Valley was the coming of Halley's comet. The comet was clearly visible for more than five months. *La Voz del Sur* reported how it could be seen at its closest on the morning of 18 May 1910, around 4.30 a.m., illuminating the northeastern part of the sky.[55] This ill-fated omen caused fear and despair among the peasants. Rumors circulated that the earth would pass through the tail of the comet and that all life would be annihilated. The fear of the comet was quite probably to some extent a distant echo of a possibility indicated by the contemporary scientific community. Natural scientists had identified a matter called *cyanogen* in the coda of Halley's comet which, if combined with certain salts, would turn into deadly poisonous cyanide. The Earth could be engulfed in a cloud of this poison. As the celebrated French

50 Interview with Arquímedes Valdez, Maguana Abajo, 31 May 1989.
51 Interview with Julián Ramos, Higüerito, 16 January 1986.
52 Interview with Javier Jovino, Río Limpio, 30 April 1986.
53 Interview with León Romilio Ventura, Media Luna, 17 January 1986.
54 Interview with Julián Ramos, Higüerito, 16 January 1986.
55 Hoepelman (1910).

astronomer Camille Flammarion put it, 'the *cyanogen* gas would probably impregnate the atmosphere and possibly snuff out all life on the planet.'[56]

The peasants organized *rosarios* [processions of penitents] all over the countryside. They confessed their sins openly and awaited the end. The dreadful night when the comet passed at its closest distance to earth, states an eyewitness,

> we observed ... a very big explosion in the infinite. Everybody knelt down and started to yell: The earth is coming to an end!!! The earth is coming to an end!!! But the old women went on singing: Virgin of Mercy, Sovereign Mother, take us to Heaven, Sovereign Mother! After that night the comet grew smaller and smaller, and smaller, until it vanished.[57]

The fear of the comet was great also in Maguana Arriba. 'Everybody was afraid' of it and 'a woman ... died when it came'.[58] Olivorio had predicted its arrival and an old *décima*[59] gives an impression of the tension and expectations that prevailed around Olivorio in those days:

Si mentamos el Santo	If we mention the Saint
nos prende la Ley.	the Law gets us.
Líbranos, Señor,	Save us, Lord,
del Cometa Halley.	from Halley's Comet.
Ya Papá Olivorio	Right away Papa Olivorio
compró su escopeta	bought his shotgun
apuntó pa' el cielo	aimed at the sky
Y tumbó el Cometa.[60]	And knocked the Comet down.

To the followers of Olivorio, the comet was a sign of divine wrath, since Olivorio had been summoned to appear in court the year before. The first reports of his activities appear in the Dominican press in 1909. A physician in San Juan de la Maguana, Dr Alejandro Cabral, who attended Wenceslao Ramírez and accordingly knew Olivorio personally,[61] sent a photograph of Olivorio and Juan Samuel to several Dominican newspapers, accompanied by a warning of the possible consequences of illegal medical practice.[62]

---

56   Sagan and Druyan (1985), p. 126.
57   Emeterio Valdez Gómez, ninety-one years of age, cited by Montánd (1986).
58   Interview with Julián Ramos, Higüerito, 16 January 1986.
59   Strictly speaking, a *décima* is a stanza of ten octosyllabic lines, but in practice this convention is far from always observed. The composition of *décimas* used to be common among Dominican peasants. The *décimas* deal with politics and news that are the talk of the day. They often have a satirical twist to them.
60   Cited by Garrido Puello (1963), pp. 59–61.
61   Interview with Tala Cabral Ramírez, Santo Domingo, 21 November 1985.
62   The photograph reproduced as Figure 2.7.

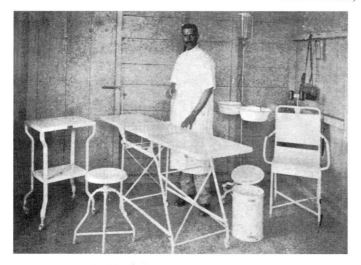

Figure 2.8 Dr Alejandro Cabral in his operating room.

One of these articles mentions that 'last week more than 2,500 souls made the pilgrimage to La Maguana'.[63] Olivorio's fame was spreading rapidly and it appears as if Dr Cabral's action was triggered by the attention that Olivorio's summons to court had attracted the same year. Olivorio had been accused of practicing medicine illegally. However, he had been acquitted in court since he did not charge anything for his services. The decision to set him free was also based on his personal statement that he did not administer any beverages or herbs to his patients, but simply used his hands to cure them.[64] A contemporary witness of the trial, at the time 'around twelve years of age', recalls:

> They brought Olivorio down from the mountains because the *alcalde* [mayor] wanted to interrogate him. The *alcaldía* [mayor's office] was just in front of our house, so it was easy to run across and look. Chichí Batista, who was *alcalde* at the time, asked Olivorio: 'Who are you?', and he answered: 'I am nobody. I am a man to whom people come, but I am nobody myself.' He talked like a peasant, full of reservation. Chichí was convinced of Olivorio's inoffensiveness and let him go.[65]

After his successful trial, people started to gather around Olivorio in huge flocks.

---

63 Hoepelman (1909). Cf. *Blanco y Negro*, 4 July 1909.
64 Hoepelman (1909).
65 Interview with Maximiliano Rodríguez Piña, Santo Domingo, 23 April 1986. However it appears as if Olivorio indeed was brought down to the provincial capital, Azua, to stand

The earthquake

On St Bruno's Day, 6 October 1911, around 5.30 a.m., a local earthquake hit the San Juan Valley. The ground moved every ten minutes. The movements continued intermittently for three days. Many trees died since their root systems were damaged beyond remedy.[66] Panic seized the inhabitants of San Juan de la Maguana. The church and the house of a certain 'Juan Jáquez' (Juan Rodríguez), the only two stone buildings in town, collapsed completely and gave rise to a cloud of dust that hovered over the city.[67]

The earth continued to move occasionally for the rest of the year. The slightest movement made people rush into the street, beating their chests, begging the Lord for mercy. Tales about the imminent end of the world filled the *Sanjuaneros* with terror, and the intensity of the fear increased when the waters of the San Juan River suddenly turned white as milk, probably as a result of earthslides on the mountainsides.[68]

Among the *Olivoristas*, the San Bruno earthquake was interpreted as God's answer to the trials and tribulations that *El Maestro* had to undergo during the year of grace 1910. When Olivorio had been acquitted from the charges raised against him in 1909, the authorities started to prosecute his followers and discredit his movement. The Dominican press mentions various incidents, the most famous of which is 'The nudist parties in Las Matas de Palmas'. A man by the name of Pedro Sánchez, who called himself 'the envoy of Olivorio' was alleged to have enticed a group of *Olivoristas* to take off all their clothes during a ceremony. All participants in the act were prosecuted.[69] Two months earlier, the newspaper *El Tiempo* in Santo Domingo carried a story of how a lady had been advised to unearth one of her dead sons and carry a piece of his cloth to Olivorio in order to cure herself from sickness. The article ends with a warning that new 'barbaric acts' could be expected from Olivorio's quarters, 'where people from every village in the Republic, as well as numerous leprous Haitians, are to be found'.[70]

The presidency of Ramón Cáceres (1906–11) was characterized by a policy intending to limit the powers of local strongmen. To that end huge sums of money were invested in the modernization of the army, converting it into a loyal and effective constabulary force in the service of

---

trial. Nevertheless, he was almost immediately released due to lack of evidence (Díaz (1909)). The scene appears to bear more than casual resemblance to the one of Jesus and Pontius Pilate.

66 Interview with Julián Ramos, Higüerito, 16 January 1986.
67 Garrido Puello (1972), pp. 100–1. Cf. Utrera (1978), p. 292.
68 Garrido Puello (1972), p. 101.
69 *Listín Diario*, 11 June, 13 June and 27 June 1910. Cf. *El Tiempo*, 11 June 1910.
70 *El Tiempo*, 2 April 1910.

Figure 2.9 General Ramón Cáceres Vásquez, president, 1906–11.

the president of the Republic. All attempts at rebellion were ruthlessly nipped in the bud. Cáceres initiated his term in office by instructing the inhabitants of the notoriously rebellious northwestern parts of the country to move themselves and their cattle to specially designated areas. When the given respite had expired, he ordered his troops to 'comb' the entire district, killing all cattle found outside designated areas, thus intending to deprive the *guerrilleros* of their main source of nourishment. The entire economy of the so-called Línea Noroeste (the lowland area around Monte Cristi) was thoroughly destroyed. However, Cáceres succeeded in 'pacifying' the area for several years ahead.[71]

In other parts of the country well-equipped army units went after 'bandits' and other armed groups opposed to the central government. In March 1910, a local *caudillo* named Cabo Millo surrendered himself to government troops just north of Azua, and in June the same year another 'small boss', Neno de la Cruz, came out of hiding in San Juan de la Maguana.[72] However, armed skirmishes continued to occur all over the district and a number of 'law-abiding citizens' actively supported the government in its struggle against anarchy and disorder.

The authorities of San Juan de la Maguana came under pressure from public opinion to take action against the 'shameful acts' supposedly taking place in La Maguana. The *jefe comunal* [local community leader], Juan de

71 Moya Pons (1980), p. 449.
72 Cassá (1994a).

Dios Ramírez, 'Juanico', a son of Wenceslao Ramírez, ordered that Olivorio be captured. A group of armed men was sent to La Maguana and Olivorio followed them without any resistance. On their way down to San Juan de la Maguana, however, the men were suddenly attacked by a great number of armed *Olivoristas*. A fierce battle ensued: 'The head of the county constabulary in San Juan reports that Olivorio was captured along with some of his confidants and guards. However, shortly afterwards, in rugged terrain, approximately two hundred of his armed worshipers succeeded in liberating him.'[73]

One of the representatives of the authorities was injured, and two *Olivoristas* were killed when Juanico's men went after their attackers.[74] The following day, armed expeditions went into the mountains in pursuit of Olivorio and his men. Little more than a week after the attack, *El Diario* in Santiago de los Caballeros reported that one hundred of the 'fanatics of San Juan that rescued Dios Liborio' had submitted themselves to the authorities, but that 'the remaining one hundred' stayed along 'by the side of their idol'.[75]

A unit of forty men from the *Guardia Republicana* was sent after the remaining *Olivoristas*. Under the command of a certain Colonel Vargas they attacked Olivorio and his men in La Maguana. The fighting was very fierce:

> Before [the troops] reached the place, partisans from Liborio's group opened fire, with the result that one of our men was wounded while one of theirs was killed and another wounded [whom] they left behind in the flight. The place we had to advance upon was the 'Cerro de San Juan', situated one hour's [walk] before reaching the place where Liborio was [...]. After having been evicted [from their position on the hill] they [the *Olivoristas*] tried to reoccupy their initial position, but they were driven back again.[76]

When the fighting had died down the *Olivoristas* fled in various directions. Colonel Vargas and his men were unable to pursue them. Nevertheless, the authorities convinced themselves that a fatal blow had been delivered to Olivorio and this was established by the Azuan governor: 'This thing has been cleared up, it does not have any political implications, it is just fanaticism, and I believe it will cease.'[77]

---

73 Díaz (1910a).
74 *Listín Diario*, 25 July 1910.
75 *El Diario*, 4 August 1910.
76 Díaz (1910c).
77 Díaz (1910d).

Harsh measures were taken to eradicate the cult at its core. All 'outsiders' were forced to leave La Maguana and told that any *forastero* [stranger] who roamed the section of La Maguana would be severely punished by the authorities.[78] The *Olivoristas* soon reunited in a place called Viajaca, not far from Sabana Mula, a village further to the west, not so far from the Haitian border. However, they were not given any rest. Just a week after the attack at La Maguana the *Olivoristas* were attacked by a detachment of Dominican frontier guards under the command of a Lieutenant Sánchez. A short fight ensued and the *Olivoristas* dispersed after leaving two wounded members of their group behind.[79]

The skirmishes which resulted from Juanico Ramírez' unsuccessful attempt to capture Olivorio turned out to be embarrassing for the Ramírez family. Everyone in the neighborhood knew of Olivorio's old connections with the powerful family and rumors of foul tactics on the part of Juanico Ramírez were in swing. Had he let the loyal friend of the family go deliberately? The Ramírezes had to guard their position as the most important *caudillos* in the San Juan Valley and it was a blow to their prestige that 'outsiders' like government troops were chasing a former client of theirs within their 'own' territory. Things got to the point where Wenceslao Ramírez' most brilliant and dashing son, General José del Carmen, 'Carmito', Ramírez, land surveyor, warrior and university graduate, *caballero de los caballeros* [gentleman's gentleman],[80] had to save the family honor by promising to capture Olivorio: 'If he escapes me, I will believe in the divinity of Olivorio.'[81] With the help of a party disguised as common peasants, he infiltrated one of Olivorio's strongholds and lured him to San Juan de la Maguana, where Olivorio was seized by his brother Juanico. Before the next day had dawned, Olivorio had been brought in forced march to Azua, the provincial capital, which was reached the very same night, before the *Olivoristas* had realized that their leader had been captured again.[82]

Olivorio quickly became a celebrity in Azua as well. A great deal of political tension existed between the prosperous port of Azua and the powerful *rancheros* [ranchers] of the San Juan Valley. The latter objected strongly to being subjected by the provincial authorities of Azua who, in turn, saw nothing wrong with humiliating the leading *Sanjuaneros*. The governor of the province of Azua, Túbano Mesa, was quite unpopular in San Juan. Thus, since Olivorio had been captured and prosecuted by the *Sanjuaneros*,

78 Ibid.
79 Cabral (1910).
80 Interview with Tala Cabral Ramírez, Santo Domingo, 21 November 1985.
81 Garrido Puello (1963), p. 26.
82 Interview with Víctor Garrido, Jr, Santo Domingo, 22 April 1986.

it was natural that the *Azuanos* should treat him gently. The counsel for the defense, Manuel de Jesús Bidó, had Olivorio released without difficulty. Nevertheless, he stayed for some time in Azua, receiving both supplicants and curious townspeople.[83]

Subsequently, Olivorio decided to return to San Juan de la Maguana. He arrived there as a victor. On the outskirts he was greeted by a joyous crowd. More than one thousand men, women and children, many of them on horseback, bade him welcome and escorted him up to La Maguana.[84] The acquittal in Azua – which after all was the provincial capital – increased his respectability, and for the poor peasants he became a hero: *El Maestro* and Dios Olivorio.

Not everyone approved of his success, however. Olivorio felt himself counteracted from various quarters and went on to condemn his enemies. Legends are told of how he caused the earthquake of San Bruno in order to punish the unbelievers: the priests of San Juan de la Maguana sometimes went up to La Maguana in order to celebrate the mass in the *ermita* [rural chapel] that the *Olivoristas* had erected there. Such visits apparently proved to be beneficial for the church dignitaries, since the *Olivoristas* were keen givers. Thus, when one of the priests, a certain Padre Rodríguez, came to celebrate the mass, Olivorio ordered his followers to put their offerings on kerchiefs which he spread over the ground. The kerchiefs were filled with gifts, tied up and delivered to the priest after mass. While Padre Rodríguez rejoiced at the offerings, Olivorio entered the *ermita*, returned with a picture of Christ in his hands and said to the bystanders: 'May my enemies come forth.' After this utterance the earth trembled. Likewise, when the earthquake of San Bruno took place, people remembered his words to another priest, Canónigo Benito Piña: 'Father, your house will fall', and put them in connection with the destruction of the church of San Juan de la Maguana, which was caused by the unchecked forces of nature.[85]

83 Ibid. Cf. Garrido Puello (1963), p. 27. It appears as if the judicial system of Azua at the time of the process against Olivorio left a great deal to be desired. A report from the *Secretario de Estado en los Despachos de lo Interior y Policía* [Secretary of State of Domestic Affairs and Police] complained in 1912 that the Court of Azua 'does not possess any reference books'. Its archives are described as 'very incomplete', and the town 'has no suitable premises, or even the furniture necessary for maintaining the dignity of a judicial establishment'. The report finishes with the complaint that Azuan justice 'has not shown the impartiality which is required for the welfare of the people who have been associated with it' (Soler (1912), pp. 5–6).

84 Garrido Puello (1963), pp. 57–8.

85 Ibid. A *canónigo* is a member of a religious group living according to a certain canon or religious rule.

The civil war of 1912

Olivorio's position had been strengthened to a considerable degree, but he was still met with a great deal of disdain and skepticism among the oligarchy in San Juan and the central government in Santo Domingo did not tolerate the existence of armed, independent groups like the one that had developed around Olivorio. The officially sanctioned persecution of the *Olivoristas* was intensified in 1911 and occasional reports in the newspapers mention arrests of followers of Olivorio.[86]

But time was working for Olivorio. The third calamity that came upon the San Juan Valley, the civil war of 1912, forced the oligarchy not only to make a truce with him but to turn him into an ally as well. This acceptance was the final proof for Olivorio's followers that he really was a divine person with a God-given mission to fulfill.

The causes of the war are far too complicated to be dealt with in any detail in the present work.[87] In short, however, a number of local *caudillos* saw their power circumscribed by the actions of the government of Eladio Victoria, who was in reality totally controlled by his young nephew, General Alfredo Victoria, commander in chief of the army. The situation was further complicated by old party strifes that had come to life with the murder of the strong and authoritative president Ramón Cáceres on 19 November 1911. Moreover, the United States had gained an ever increasing influence on Dominican affairs during the Cáceres regime and was now reluctant to lose it. Many of the more or less independent *caudillos* felt the unpopular presence of US dictates behind the back of the central government and were eager to get rid of it.

In an attempt to overthrow the government, the influential Ramírez family joined forces with 'General' Luis Felipe Vidal[88] and started a rebellion in the San Juan Valley. In an operation involving, in addition, the *caudillos* of the fertile plains north of the Cordillera Central, the insurgents whipped up support among the peasants, creating large armies to march on the capital. However, the resistance offered by the government troops

---

86 *Listín Diario*, 17 May 1911, reports that a certain 'Azuan criminal' and follower of Olivorio, named Moreno Bueno, had been captured by the authorities, and *El Diario*, 16 October 1911, names ten persons known to be 'walking with Dios Olivorio' that had been taken prisoners in San Juan de la Maguana.

87 See Mejía (1976), pp. 79–112, Garrido (1970), pp. 29–57 and Garrido Puello (1977), pp. 17–70.

88 Luis Felipe Vidal was born in Azua and had a past as school teacher and administrator of an *ingenio* [sugar factory]. He had participated in the bloody disputes between different political factions that fought for political power after the murder of Lilís in 1899. He had also served in some of the short-lived administrations that preceded the presidency of Ramón Cáceres (1906–11). His title as 'General' was not officially granted. When the rebellion began he lived in exile in Haiti, probably due to his alleged involvement in the murder of Cáceres (Garrido (1970), pp. 49–53).

Figure 2.10 Fortification in the Puerta del Conde, Santo Domingo during one of the civil wars.

turned out to be far harder than the rebels had calculated with. The result of this miscalculation was one of the most violent civil wars that the country had hitherto known. The fighting extended across the entire country. Imprisoned political opponents were executed in large numbers by the government. Blood was shed in the San Juan Valley as well, and many lives were lost.[89]

Olivorio and his followers soon became involved in the fighting. Manuel de Jesús Rodríguez Varona, the commander of the government troops stationed in San Juan de la Maguana, was loyal to the central government. Already before the war broke out he rode into the mountains to secure the support of Olivorio and his men. To his astonishment he found that the Ramírez family had already begun to plot against the government and had been there before him. 'I am sorry', replied Olivorio, 'but you come too late. I have already given my word to General Wenceslao Ramírez and I remain loyal to him and his people.'[90]

Throughout the civil war, Olivorio increased his prestige and power. It was a well-known fact that he had been at ends with the governmental troops already before the war broke out or, rather, the troops had harassed Olivorio and his men, who were not in the habit of starting unprovoked skirmishes. The strong regime of President Ramón Cáceres, that immediately preceded the one of Victoria, whose perceived misrule provoked the civil war of 1912, had not tolerated Olivorio and his cult. The provincial governor of Azua was thus forced to take armed action.

89 Moya Pons (1980), p. 458.
90 Interview with Mayobanex Rodríguez, San Juan de la Maguana, 12 December 1985.

Contrary to the advice given by the Ramírezes, Olivorio's sanctuary in La Maguana was assaulted and destroyed. Olivorio and his followers fled to El Naranjo, a place higher up in the mountains, to which it was more difficult to gain access and easier to defend. The hard core of his movement remained with *El Maestro* and started to arm themselves to a larger extent than before.[91]

In July 1912, Olivorio suddenly appeared in San Juan de la Maguana, seeking to negotiate with the authorities. The event was reported in the press:

> For more than two years, Dios Olivorio and his men have been roaming across the countryside of San Juan, and on the fourth [of this month] he presented himself, together with 80 men, to the governmental authorities. Dios Olivorio manifested his desire to contribute to the definite establishment of peace.[92]

However, Olivorio did not join forces with the authorities and it is possible that he fought side by side with the Ramírezes and the other insurgents when they took San Juan de la Maguana on 24 August.[93]

The rebel generals supplied Olivorio with arms and provisions, but seemingly received little in return. The *Olivoristas* proved to be a highly inferior fighting unit. They showed up in the camps with flying colors and picturesque clothing but preferred to stay far behind the lines when it came to actual fighting:[94]

> He was smart. He just wanted the firearms: the only security a man like Olivorio could have in those days. If he got the arms, people would leave him in peace. He was a peaceful man and never behaved badly towards the rest of the community.[95]

> In 1912 I was 12 years old. A certain General Ampalle came and tried to convince my father to join his forces and march on the Capital. 'Olivorio', he said, 'I am going to the revolution, please follow me.' 'Don't go', said Olivorio and he was right, General Ampalle was killed. Olivorio never went.[96]

When the civil war came to an end, Olivorio was left to himself. He seized the opportunity to create a community that was almost totally self-

91 Garrido Puello (1963), pp. 30–1.
92 *El Diario*, 9 July 1912.
93 Garrido (1970), p. 40.
94 Ibid., pp. 32–3.
95 Interview with Mayobanex Rodríguez, San Juan de la Maguana, 12 December 1985.
96 Interview with Arquímedes Valdez, Maguana Abajo, 31 May 1989.

sufficient. Masses of poor peasants once more flocked around him, in search of security, advice or relief from their pains and ailments. It was not until the United States marines occupied the Dominican Republic in 1916 that Olivorio took to arms again – this time living the insecure life of a hunted guerilla warrior in the isolated mountain valleys and caves of the Cordillera Central.

The cult site

La Maguana, or more exactly, Maguana Arriba, has always been the spiritual center of *Olivorismo*. Even though Olivorio did not live there permanently after his conversion, he was forced to leave the place on many occasions, he probably returned there as often as he could. When people in the San Juan Valley are asked about Olivorio today, the more or less standard answer is: 'Go to La Maguana … where his people live.'[97] This statement should not simply be taken to mean that many of Olivorio's relatives still live in Maguana Arriba but, more importantly, that his most ardent worshipers are to be found there.

La Maguana was probably a cult center before the birth of Olivorio. The Spring of San Juan is not far from Olivorio's alleged birthplace. According to local tradition, St John appeared there long before Olivorio was born.[98] Hence the spring was a place for worship not only of Olivorio but also of St John and in addition of various Indian chiefs. Its history as a cult site could thus go far back in time.

The connection between Olivorio and St John the Baptist is apparent in various distinctive features of *Olivorismo*. Among the peasants of the San Juan Valley, St John the Baptist, like the Indians, is connected with water and fertility. He removes sin and sickness, he cleanses the soul and he offers sprouting power to seeds and offspring to barren women. As a voodoo *luá* he may possess people and like his Haitian[99] equivalent Jean

---

97 Interviews with Zita Závala, Paraje El Ranchito, 10 April 1986, Javier Jovino, Río Limpio, 30 April 1986, Mayobanex Rodríguez, San Juan de la Maguana, 12 December 1986 and Arsidé Gardés, El Batey, 11 April 1986.

98 Interview with Bartolo de Jiménez, Maguana Arriba, 13 December 1985.

99 Simpson (1971), p. 510. *Lwa*, in Spanish *luá*, is the most common denomination of a Haitian voodoo deity. Voodoo, in the Dominican Republic generally spelled *vodú*, is the common name given to a wide range of religious phenomena that are to be found in both Haiti and the Dominican Republic. (Cf. Deive (1979) on Dominican *vodú*.) Simpson calls Jean Baptiste a *loa* [*lwa*], even if he carries the name of a saint. If he has an equivalent in the voodoo pantheon it could be Shango, a relative to the West African thunder god, but Shango is commonly equated with the Catholic Saint Barbara (Deive (1979), p. 240). There are various Haitian *lwa* carrying the name of Jan [Jean]. Famous are, for example, the various 'Ti Jan' [Ti Jean], Small Johns, like Ti Jan Kento [Ti Jean Quinto] who appears as an insolent policeman (Simpson (1971), p. 511), or Ti Jan Petwo

Figure 2.11 A *calvario* in the road.

Baptiste he is the guardian of thunder. He may also cause earthquakes. It is thus obvious that the earthquake of 1911 was seen as a sign of divine wrath directed against Olivorio's persecutors.

Close to the place where Olivorio is said to have been born, a *calvario* [calvary, a group of three crosses] has been erected.[100] A feast is held there every year in honor of San Juan Bautista, who as 'Master of the Source', is celebrated by 'playing the drums'. People eat and drink and some become possessed. An *hermandad* [brotherhood], composed of supporters of the *calvario*, organizes the feast. All this indicates the existence of an old cult of St John – before the appearance of Olivorio. According to María Orfelia, the actual guardian of the *calvario*, the latter has 'always been at this holy place', and the crosses were erected in order to 'purify the people'.[101]

[Ti Jean Pétro] and Ti Jan Rada, called Tinyó in the Dominican Republic. Tinyó is connected with water and Indians, but is considered to have his Catholic equivalent in Saint Rafael (Jiménez Lambertus (1980), p. 182).

100 The *calvarios*, which play an important role in the popular piety of the Dominican Republic, consist of a group of three crosses. They are often found at the entrance of villages or in in places 'with a spiritual presence'. *Calvarios* are thought to be imbued with divine power. They sanctify and clean the places where they are erected and protect from all evil. People often make pilgrimages to particular places that are sanctified by the presence of these crosses. They kneel in front of them and dispose of the burdens that they have brought with them, often heavy stones, and shrug their shoulders in order to 'rid themselves of the weight of sins'. (On the importance of crosses in the Dominican Republic, see Lemus and Marty (1975), p. 162. Cf. Nolasco (1956), pp. 46–99.)

101 Interview with María Orfelia, Maguana Arriba, 18 January 1986.

Thus, when Olivorio started to preach and cure the people he was in a place that for a long time had been considered holy and was the scene of various miraculous cures. Olivorio's success seems to have been more or less immediate. As early as July 1909 the epithet Dios Olivorio appeared in a newspaper article. It is also mentioned in the same article that a *cofradía* [religious brotherhood] had been formed around him.[102]

The thaumaturge

Olivorio established himself as a thaumaturge (faith healer) in La Maguana. It seems that most people came to him to be cured from various diseases. He employed different techniques to this end. His use of the *palo de piñón*, a stick made from a branch of a tree, became famous.[103] The stick was placed on the sick person. Thereafter the formula '*Salga el mal y entre el bien*' ['May the bad leave and the good enter'] or '*Carajo, ven a tu Dios*' ['Damned, come to your God'] was employed, and if it was felt that the cure had been successful, Olivorio concluded the session with '*Ya está curado*' ['Now, he is cured'].[104]

102 *Blanco y Negro*, No. 42, 4 July 1909.
103 The word *piñón* carries different meanings in different parts of the Caribbean. The Dominican linguist Pedro Henríquez Ureña assumes that *piñón* is the same as *Erythrina corallodendron*, coral tree (Henríquez Ureña (1978), p. 218). He is possibly correct about Cuba, where the common name of the *Erythrina corallodendron* is *piñón de pito*, while it is called *piñón espinoso* in Puerto Rico. However, in the Dominican Republic the most common denomination of this particular plant seems to be *amapola* (Marcano Fondeur (1977), p. 146). It is more probable that Olivorio's *piñón* was a specimen of a bush, or small tree, which carries the scientific name of *Jatropha curcas*, a plant with magical and curative qualities.

   The *Jatropha*, or *piñón*, contains a very active poison called *curcina*. Twelve drops of the content of the seeds are sufficient to poison a cow. The sap is viscose, milky or reddish. It is in common use in Dominican popular medicine (ibid., p. 97 and Liogier (1986), p. 166). Tea, made out of the leaves, is sometimes administered in order to cure intestinal problems and the sap may be used as treatment of open wounds and eye infections (Lemus and Marty (1976), p. 53).

   When the *piñón* loses its leaves in the months of February, March and April, the sap undergoes a process of oxidation and becomes red. According to the traditions of Dominican popular religion, the *piñón* bleeds on Good Friday, the day of Jesus' crucifixion and death; as a matter of fact the *piñón* 'bleeds' during all the months of its defoliation, but people associate the 'blood' of the *piñón* with the blood of Jesus and only notice it on Good Friday (interview with Eugenio de Jesús Marcano Fondeur, Santo Domingo, 27 January 1989). Since the strong branches of the *piñón* are also used in order to make fences (Liogier (1986), p. 167 and Schiffino (1945), p. 92) we are also reminded of the fact that Olivorio was known as an able fence maker.
104 Garrido Puello (1963), p. 19. The formulas used by Olivorio are typical examples of magical utterances that are commonly called *holófrases* [holy phrases] in the Dominican Republic (Deive (1979), p. 204). The words and his use of the stick indicate that Olivorio shared a view that is common among many faith healers in the Caribbean, and many

The use of the *palo de piñón* was not the only method of healing employed by Olivorio.[105] During the inquiry in San Juan de la Maguana in 1909, he mentioned that he used his hands to cure people.[106] Garrido Puello describes yet another cure:

> With his hands stretched out, with the studied attitude of a magician, he tried to suggest the patients with penetrating glances and the gestures of an actor. He talked to them in a soothing, or bullying, manner, adorning his speech with cabbalistic signs, turning the act into a ritual. He walked, turned around, shook cords and scapulars,[107] made lines on the ground with the stick, that served him as staff. He always ended these superstitious practices with the ... expression *salga el mal y entre el bien.*[108]

In order to drive away the 'evil spirits' believed to cause sickness and ailments it happened that Olivorio ordered afflicted persons to be immersed in certain watercourses. One such place was situated by Los Manaclares, outside the village of Yacahueque,[109] and another one was the Spring of San Juan outside La Maguana.

Olivorio is also reported to have made the sign of the cross over those parts of the body that were afflicted by pain or sickness, after having dipped his finger in his own urine.[110] People were also baptized with 'holy' water, but this was not done as a curative measure. That particular ritual was probably considered to be a way to purge sins. Bottles with 'holy' water

other parts of the world as well, namely that the body of the sick person has been invaded by malevolent spirits that have to be driven out (Laguerre (1987), p. 75). The words used by Olivorio are almost identical to utterances reported from Haitian voodoo rituals: 'All that is bad has to come out, all that is good has to go in' (Métraux (1974), p. 276). Vetilio Alfau Durán (1940) cites an article that appeared in *El Imparcial* (7 March 1914) issued in the eastern town of Higüey, where Olivorio is stated to have visited the district and healed people by hitting them on the head with his *palo de piñón*. If a flow of blood appeared he said that it happened in order to 'get rid of the bad'.

105 Pimpina Luciano, probably around eighty-eight years old, states that she witnessed Olivorio curing people, but never saw him use any *palo de piñón* (interview by Roberto Cassá, Mao, 22 January 1995).

106 Hoepelman (1909). Cf. Alfau Durán (1940).

107 A scapular worn by laymen consists of textile badges worn over the chest and the back, connected with cords over the shoulders. They are often decorated with holy symbols and indicate that the carrier is devoted to a particular saint and/or is member of a certain *cofradía* (Hilgers (1912), pp. 508–9).

108 Garrido Puello (1963), p. 19.

109 Interview with Pimpina Luciano by Roberto Cassá, Mao, 22 January 1995. Pimpina comes from Yacahueque, a village situated by a creek with the same name, between Las Matas de Farfán and Carrera de Yeguas.

110 Interview with Mayobanex Rodríguez, San Juan de la Maguana, 12 December 1985.

were also given away by Olivorio.[111] Sometimes he touched or rubbed the sick part with his bare hands or with a cloth – a method often used by voodoo practitioners.[112] Carmito Ramírez' son, José del Carmen, 'Mimic-ito', recalls witnessing an act of healing performed by Olivorio in his father's house:

> Olivorio was dining in our house when my brother Danilo, who was two years old, the youngest of twelve brothers and sisters, got hold of nitric acid that was kept above the door to keep the cockroaches away. Danilo fell to the floor and the acid burned him on his belly. The people around the table rose and my mother ran up to Danilo. Olivorio rose as well and said, with a calm voice: 'What happened, Lady?' Danilo was crying and Olivorio approached him, knelt by his side, passed a kerchief across his belly and apparently cured him in this way.[113]

Olivorio also gave away *pabilos* [cords made out of raveled cotton] which were tied around the head in order to cure severe headaches.[114] It is also commonly testified that he cured through dreams as well. As a matter of fact, he is still believed to cure people in their sleep, through their dreams. He appears to the sick and tells him that his pains will disappear. Next morning the sick person rises from his bed, cured of his disease. Any wounds that the person may have had are completely healed.[115]

Garrido Puello states that Olivorio offered different kinds of herbal concoctions,[116] and some interviewees remember that Olivorio gave away

111 Interview with Pimpina Luciano by Roberto Cassá, Mao, 22 January 1995.
112 This behavior is common in voodoo sessions in both Puerto Rico and the Dominican Republic. Moving the hands over the sick parts of the body is called *hacer pases* (cf. Lemus and Marty (1976), pp. 41–2). Kerchiefs are often used by voodoo practitioners and different *luases* prefer different colors. While putting themselves into a state of trance some voodoo practitioners hold a cloth in their hands, tying various knots in it, wringing it in their hands and putting it around their head. The kerchief may be seen as a symbol of the *luá* and accordingly is imbued with its powers. It can be used in acts of healing (visit to Doña Nieves, *bruja* [sorcerer and fortune teller] in the slum district of Buenos Aires in Santo Domingo, 6 January 1986; cf. Lemus and Marty (1975) p. 154). Many *brujas* are found in the slums of Santo Domingo. They give advice and tell the future, often in a state of possession. Most of them are devotees to one or more *luases* but nearly all of them would probably object to the epithet 'voodoo practitioner', partly because they consider themselves to be devout 'Dominican Catholics' who do not want to be mixed up with 'Haitian voodooists', and partly because the practice of voodoo is forbidden by the Dominican penal law.
113 Interview with Mimicito Ramírez, San Juan de la Maguana, 16 January 1986. Cf. Garrido Puello (1963), pp. 56–7.
114 Interview with Pimpina Luciano by Roberto Cassá, Mao, 22 January 1995.
115 Interview with Julián Ramos, Higüerito, 16 January 1986.
116 Garrido Puello (1963), p. 20.

decoctions of herbs, which were taken for different ailments.[117] This is a common practice among *curanderos* [healers], but it is not completely clear whether Olivorio actually did so. After all, he was cleared of the accusation of illegal practice of medicine, among other things because he was reported not to have administered any drugs or beverages.

Another reason for Olivorio's acquittal was that he did not request any fee for the services rendered to the people who came to see him. Olivorio '*curaba y no cobraba*' [healed without demanding any payment].[118] It is still considered a virtue among *Olivoristas* to offer food to visitors without demanding any reward. When this is done, reference is often made to the example of *El Maestro*.[119]

Promiscuity?

Many different people gathered around Olivorio in La Maguana. Some sought his help for ailments. Others saw the community of Olivorio as a sanctuary where they could avoid the persecution of the legal authorities. Some came simply because they were curious. Olivorio welcomed them all – even the hecklers.

Rumors quickly started to spread of what took place within the supposedly religious community. La Maguana was a spot where 'easy and cheap pleasures that made it easy to forget the hard daily toil'[120] could be obtained. The place was 'like a cabaret'.[121] Olivorio had a 'harem' and unrestrained free love was practiced.[122] The young men from San Juan came up to La Maguana to feast, drink and have fun with the peasant girls.[123] Even somebody as respected as Carmito Ramírez could think of some excuse to go there, because he was 'attracted by *faldas* [skirts]'.[124]

The urban tales of the 'licentious' ceremonies in La Maguana often contain ingredients that are more or less literally the same – word for word. Garrido Puello's description may stand for them all:

> Saturdays and Sundays were holidays for the brotherhood. The reunion was celebrated with dances and songs. A circle was formed, the line was kept and then, from a corner, *El Maestro* said: up with the robe and *cayuco* [trunk] in hand. With these licentious words,

117 Interview with Pimpina Luciano by Roberto Cassá, Mao, 22 January 1995.
118 Interview with Telma Odeida Dotel Matos, Santo Domingo, 2 November 1985.
119 Cf. Cordero Regalado (1981), p. 6b. Various personal experiences verify this statement.
120 Garrido Puello (1963), p. 22.
121 Interview with Mayobanex Rodríguez, San Juan de la Maguana, 12 December 1985.
122 Interview with Telma Odeida Dotel Matos, Santo Domingo, 2 November 1985.
123 Interview with Mayobanex Rodríguez, San Juan de la Maguana, 12 December 1985.
124 Interview with Tala Cabral Ramírez, Santo Domingo, 21 November 1985.

pronounced as an overture to the participants to engage in free love, the ceremony began. The women fell into some kind of paroxysms, the men chose their occasional consort and the Bacchanal continued far into the night.[125]

Does this mean that La Maguana was a place where the moral rules otherwise prevailing in Dominican society had given way to lascivious sex orgies with men and women copulating right and left? The probable answer is: 'No'. Garrido Puello's account is hardly a credible one. 'Promiscuity' is a label used by outsiders in many accounts of 'strangers' and marginal groups. Thus, for example, the descriptions of the rituals and 'free love orgies' of Olivorio correspond very well to the wealth of stereotype accounts of heretic sects that Norman Cohn exemplifies and unmasks as false in his book *Europe's Inner Demons*.[126] In the Dominican context similar tales are told about Haitian voodooists and of the Olivorio-inspired cult of Palma Sola at the beginning of the 1960s.[127]

125 Garrido Puello (1963), p. 21. Doña Tala gave us an almost identical description of the ceremonies, but in a rather different wording. For example she cited Olivorio saying: '*Sable en mano y falda alzá*' ['sabre in hand and skirt up'] (interview with Tala Cabral Ramírez, Santo Domingo, 21 November 1985). According to Garrido Puello, he said: '*Manto arriba y cayuco en mano*'. *Cayuco* is a word of Taino (Indian) origin designating a kind of canoe made out of a hollowed-out tree trunk. *Cayucos* were still in common use during Olivorio's life time (Vega (1981), pp. 19–28).

126 Particularly the description of Italian Waldensians during the Middle Ages provides an almost direct parallel to the present case (Cohn (1975), p. 38).

127 Descriptions of voodoo sessions performed by Haitians that turn into 'orgies' sometimes appear in Dominican novels (for example José Jasd's *Beliná* from 1973) or collections of anecdotes like Manuel Tomás Rodríguez (1975) *Papá Legbá*. (*La crónica del voudú o pacto con el diablo y algo más* ...). Such descriptions have their equivalents in books by American or European authors, like William Seabrook's *The Magic Island* (1929) and Richard Loederer's *Voodoo Fire in Haiti* (1935). The latter, like the book by Rodríguez, is full of drawings of half naked, exotic and sensuous 'voodoo priestesses'. Books like these have formed a lot of popular misconceptions about voodoo, ideas that still prevail in cheap movies and miserable horror tales like the ones fabricated by Dennis Wheatley, who in an introduction to Métraux's excellent book on voodoo, complains that the French anthropologist fails to mention that 'men consider it an honor to be allowed to kiss the vagina of a woman while she is possessed and in convulsions' (Wheatley (1974), p. 10).

　Vulgar ideas about voodoo promiscuity also played an important part in the press campaign that was waged against the cult in Palma Sola, which was described as a place where 'virgins are raped' and 'women legally and honestly married are induced to adultery' (Paniagua (1962)), where young 'victims' were brought to the leader of the cult, who involved them in 'cynical' acts 'offending the chastity' (*La Nación*, 6 December 1962), where 'more than 50 women became pregnant after the celebrations of certain cults' (Gómez Pepín (1962a)), celebrations that terminated with 'men chasing women' (Gómez Pepín (1962b)), etc. It is striking that a large part of the campaign was concentrated on accusations of promiscuity.

Then, why did the rumor arise that La Maguana was a place of *gente de mal vivir*, i.e. of people whose standards of decency left a lot to be desired? Matrimonial fidelity apparently was not a characteristic of life in the San Juan Valley. Emigdio Garrido Puello's brother, Víctor Garrido, describes the morals in a report to the *Superintendente General de Enseñanza* in 1922: 'There exist rural Don Juans who distribute their love to up to a dozen mistresses and count an illegitimate offspring of forty, or more, children. To tell the truth, polygamy actually exists in this country.'[128]

Víctor Garrido did not have to go very far to find examples. His own brother-in-law, Carmito Ramírez,[129] had various children 'outside the canons of the law',[130] and a second brother-in-law, Juanico Ramírez, had no less than some hundred children with different women, even though he lived in a seemingly happy marriage.[131]

Olivorio was no exception. He also had various women and begot many children.[132] After his initial revelation, he left his first wife, Eusebia Valdez. Some of Olivorio's children with her are still alive and it is sometimes stated that they do not want to recognize the alleged divinity of their father, expressing bitterness because he left their mother.[133] Many *Olivoristas*, on the other hand, maintain that he did not forget his duties towards her and, in fact, a woman named Eusebia is mentioned as one of his *compañeras* [female companions]. Also, the fact that Olivorio left his family may have been due to completely different reasons:

> When they started to persecute him he left the family. My mother [Eusebia] was 117 years old when she died. She always accepted what he [Olivorio] had. He walked from hill to hill, from mountain to mountain and never came back to live with us here. But, we knew where he was and one of my brothers, Eleuterio, died together with him when he was killed.[134]

---

128 Garrido (1922), p. 230.
129 Brother of Víctor Garrido's wife Tijides Ramírez de Garrido, one of Wenceslao Ramírez' daughters.
130 Garrido Puello (1981), p. 52.
131 Interview with Thomas Reilly, San Juan de la Maguana, 12 December 1985.
132 'My father had eight kids with my mother, Eusebia Valdez, three with a lady called Felipa, who lived in San Juan de la Maguana and three kids in Cibao, with Petronila Domínguez, who lived there' (interview with Arquímedes Valdez, Maguana Abajo, 31 May 1989).
133 Cordero Regalado (1981), p. 17 a. It is, however, possible that the people Cordero Regalado talked to were a bit suspicious of the Dominican newspaperman. An example: Cordero Regalado states in his article that Arquímedes Valdez did not approve of his father's actions. The two interviews carried out with Arquímedes for the present work conveyed a totally different impression. He appeared as a firm believer in his father's spiritual powers and was very proud of being his son.
134 Interview with Arquímedes Valdez, Maguana Abajo, 31 May 1989.

Garrido Puello also mentions two other women: Felipa Encarnación and a certain Matilde Contreras, who lived in Bánica, close to the Haitian border. With these two women Olivorio had various children.[135] There were others as well, but Matilde Contreras was his favorite, with whom he spent most time.[136] 'No girls were handed over to Liborio. He never had any girls [lovers] following him. He had a woman whose name was Matilde.'[137]

In principle, many Dominicans would presumably not consider Olivorio's rather complicated family life to be a sign of promiscuity. It is not uncommon that Dominican men support more than one family. The sexual pattern in the San Juan Valley can maybe be compared with the moral values that used to be upheld in rural Mediterranean societies. In Andalusia, for example, as well as in Latin American societies, an honorable man is often described as somebody who possesses manliness, *hombría*. This expression is connected with his physical valor, i.e. his sexual quintessence. A man with honor is a man with *cojones* – balls.[138] A man without honor, on the other hand, is *manso*, a word which means 'tame', and by implication 'castrated'.[139] A real man lacks the physiological basis of sexual purity or monogamy. He runs the risk of putting his masculinity and virility in doubt should he insist on remaining 'chaste'.

The entire complex of honor and shame revolves around such notions as sexual potency and purity. The weaker sex lacks *cojones*. Hence, the manifestation of the sexual drive does not form any part of the demands on female honor. A man has to defend the virtue of his mother, wife, daughters and sisters, but this does not mean that he has to watch his own sexual purity.[140] On the contrary, taking a mistress, or supporting more than one family may be a demonstration of superior masculinity, even if in theory it is condemned by both the community and the church. The moral verdict very much depends on who the transgressor is. A wealthy man who is able to maintain various households, both those of his mistress and lawful wife, may do so without losing any prestige, while a poorer man who takes a mistress and forgets about his obligations towards his wife is said to 'desecrate' his family.[141]

135 Garrido Puello (1963), p.14. Felipa Encarnación is the lady mentioned by Arquímedes as the mother of three in San Juan de la Maguana.
136 Interview with Julián Ramos, Higüerito, 16 January 1986.
137 Interview with Pimpina Luciano by Roberto Cassá, Mao, 22 January 1995.
138 The overwhelming importance of male virility and central position of the *cojones* in the popular culture of Spain is well illustrated by Camilo José Cela (1969) in his *Diccionario secreto, 1*, which is entirely dedicated to words, expressions and conceptions related to *cojones*.
139 Pitt-Rivers (1971), p. 90.
140 Pitt-Rivers (1977), p. 23.
141 Ibid., pp. 27–8.

Such views may help to explain the difference between the views of the urban elite of San Juan of what took place in La Maguana and those of the *Olivoristas*.[142] To the elite, Olivorio was a simple *sinvergüenza* [a man with no shame, i.e. a scoundrel] – a view reflected by Garrido Puello who writes that Olivorio used his 'licentious religion' to satisfy his vile desires and that orgies were performed in his honor so that he could 'amuse himself with the best and most appetizing little lamb of the flock'.[143] The latter-day *Olivoristas*, on the other hand, vehemently deny that sex orgies took place. In their opinion, sex had no part in the religion of *El Maestro*. They also stress that women played an important role within Olivorio's *hermandad*. Rafaela Pérez, for example, described by Garrido Puello as an amazon who used to ride at the head of Olivorio's cavalry, adorned with colored bands and scapulars, carrying a knife by her side, became famous.[144]

Life within Olivorio's community

There is at least one more reason why moral accusations were advanced against the *Olivoristas*. The mixture of the profane and the sacred that characterizes Dominican folk religion may have struck the outsiders as a violation of taste and good manners. Popular dances are performed to the accompaniment of tunes with religious lyrics. Rum is drunk by both men and women and some of the 'sacred' songs are filled with allusions to fertility and sexual potency. During a *velación*[145] a festive mood often prevails, spirits are high as a result of singing and dancing,[146] and 'the rural youngsters long for these ceremonies since flirtations are permitted'.[147]

Music and dance played an important role within the community of La Maguana. A vast repertoire of *salves* – popular religious anthems – still exist among the *Olivoristas*. Some of these appear to be from the period when Olivorio was alive and allude to the conditions that prevailed at the time.

---

142 'There were both men and women. The men were with their women, but never in public' (Interview with Julián Ramos, Higüerito, 16 January 1986). Zita Závala, (interview, Paraje El Ranchito, 10 April 1986) stated the same thing. Then one has to keep in mind that Zita is an orthodox Mennonite who considers *Olivorismo* to be a 'grave superstition'.

143 Garrido Puello (1963), p. 29.

144 Ibid., pp. 27–8. When Olivorio came on his rare visits to San Juan de la Maguana he was sometimes accompanied by a *caballería* composed of riders that carried flying banners and were clad in strange clothes (interview with Maximiliano Rodríguez Piña, Santo Domingo, 23 April 1986). An article in *El Cable* mentions how the brother of Olivorio, Carlitos Mateo, after his brother's death came with such a company to San Juan de la Maguana (*El Cable*, 20 November 1923).

145 Regarding *velaciones*, see Jiménez Herrera (1975), p. 196, Lemus and Marty (1975), pp. 120–2 and Jiménez (1927), pp. 152–7.

146 Garrido (1922), p. 231.

147 Ibid.

The *salves* can be said to constitute the core of *Olivorista* religious beliefs and activities. Every *Olivorista* knows a number of *salves* in honor of Olivorio. Their singing is a communal activity. The participants are often standing or sitting close together and move their bodies rhythmically. Food and rum are usually distributed during the act. Today, after spilling a few drops on the ground, to feed the spirit of Olivorio, the rum bottle is passed around to all participants. Only small sips are taken. The intention is not to get drunk. Even the children are given their share. Rum is simply the liturgical drink of *Olivorismo*.

During the singing of *salves* it may happen that a singer *se sube* [rises]. He or she reaches an inspired state through singing. This state of mind may develop further yet – into possession. Today it is frequently the spirit of Olivorio who descends on the possessed. People who are old enough to remember how Olivorio acted in real life are able to verify whether the 'horses' are ridden by *El Maestro* or not. (Possessed people are often described as 'horses', since their behavior is controlled by descending spirits who 'ride' them.) If they are, they speak with a calm, slightly drawling voice and put emphasis on certain words. They often tend to forecast the future and it is common that they repeat the words Olivorio is stated to have employed when he greeted the curious skeptics who appeared in La Maguana: 'You say you don't believe in me, but now you are here.'[148] However, it is far from always that the singing of salves is accompanied by drinks or leads to possession. Frequently the ritual is just a simple way to be together and share a certain feeling.[149]

The singing of *salves* is often followed by dancing, and that was the custom among Olivorio and his followers as well. The dances were accompanied by music from concertina, drums and *güiro*.[150] One of Olivorio's most well-known disciples was Benjamín García, whose name appears in a report issued by the American occupation forces in 1919.[151] He was called *El Músico del Maestro* and was skilled in his art.[152]

148 Interview with Telma Odeida Dotel Matos, Santo Domingo, 2 November 1985. Some *Olivoristas* deny that people can be possessed by Olivorio, since 'God and Jesus do not possess people' (interview with Julián Ramos, Higüerito, 16 January 1986).

149 We have witnessed several sessions of *salve* singing. *Salves* are not a distinct feature of *Olivorismo* alone. They are sung all over the country. For the importance of *salves* in Dominican folk religion, see Davis (1981). Espín del Prado (1984), p. 600, considers the importance of communal drinking and eating among the *Olivoristas* to be the most salient feature of this particular cult.

150 This is an instrument which is rasped. If it is made out of a calabash it is called *güiro* in the Dominican Republic. In other Spanish-speaking countries it is more commonly referred to as *güira*. Nowadays the calabash is often replaced by a metallic cylinder and the instrument is then sometimes called *guayo* (Lizardo (1988), pp. 248–9).

151 Feeley (1919). Cf. Garrido Puello (1963), pp. 18 and 42. Benjamín was killed in an ambush on 19 May 1922, a week before the death of Olivorio (Morse (1922a)). Benjamín

Garrido Puello mentions that one of the central rituals of the *Olivoristas* consisted of a kind of dance, or ritual, called *conrueda*. The devotees apparently danced in circles while Olivorio placed himself in the middle and directed their movements. The dance was accompanied by alternating singing, genuflections and praises unto the Virgin and Olivorio.[153]

Communal dances directed by a leader were very popular in the San Juan Valley during Olivorio's time. Very common was the *carabiné*, which was danced both in the rural areas and in the salons of merchants and major landowners in San Juan de la Maguana. This particular dance was directed by a *bastonero* who told the couples, who moved around in circles in accordance with a strict scheme, in what direction they had to turn.[154]

Presumably the dances described by Garrido Puello were related to the *carabiné*. Another possible source of inspiration can be traced from the fact that Garrido Puello mentions that the *Olivoristas* adorned themselves with 'flashy kerchiefs'.[155] This may indicate that the rituals of the *Olivoristas* have been influenced by Haitian *rara*. By the time of Olivorio's appearance, *rara* was already known in Dominican territory. Whether it was brought there by Haitians or if it was an age-old local custom is hard to tell. *Rara* is a Lenten phenomenon, intimately related to old fertility rites. Its most salient feature is the various *rara* bands moving through town and villages on Good Friday week. Male stick dancers, known as *batonni*, dressed in women's clothing or with layers of multicolored kerchiefs round their waists, crouch in circles and perform baton-tapping dances to the accompaniment of drums and songs. The *rara* processions move from village to village and dance day and night.[156] The movements of the dancers are very sensual and many of the songs are 'boldly ribald or licentious'.[157]

In the Dominican Republic, the *rara* groups are called *gagá* and are often

was a key figure among the *Olivoristas* and served as a contact between Olivorio's warriors and the peasants in La Maguana during the final stages of the pursuit of Olivorio (*El Cable*, 1 July 1922).

152 Interview with Julián Ramos, Higüerito, 16 January 1986.
153 Garrido Puello (1963), p. 22 and interview with Tala Cabral Ramírez, Santo Domingo, 21 November 1985.
154 Garrido (1922), pp. 228–9. Cf. Lizardo (1975), pp. 177–203. Some of the words of a *bastonero* who in 1947 directed a *carabiné* in Estebanía, Azua, are cited by the anthropologist Edna Garrido de Boggs (1961), p. 14: 'That's good, ladies in their place and the men walking, to the left, leaving your lady by your back and turning her half around; that's good, my arm, little dancing girl, I love you, take me with you to the glory.' For a musical example, see e.g. Angel Viloria and his Conjunto Típico Cibaeño, 'El Carabiné', *Merengues*, Vol. 3, Ansonia Records, HGCD 1208. In Haiti the *carabienne* (or *crabienne*) often forms a part of voodoo ceremonies, during the so-called Arada rites it intersperses into long drawn-out rituals as some kind of 'rest dance' (Courlander (1966), pp. 134–5).
155 Garrido Puello (1963), p. 32.
156 Courlander (1960), p. 106.
157 Ibid.

Figure 2.12 Rara scene, by Haitian painter André Normil.

organized as kind of religious fraternities where the members are bound together by different kinds of vows.[158] The groups are directed by an 'owner' who is in charge of organizing the rituals.[159] Today, the Dominican *gagá* is concentrated to the sugar districts and to the San Juan Valley, along the Haitian border.[160] The same appears to have been the case during the 1920s. An article in *El Cable* from 1924 laments the presence of *gagá* on Dominican soil: 'The loathsome and repugnant dance of Gagá, which is an attack on morals and decency, in spite of being forbidden by our laws, is danced in different parts of the commune [...] We notify the Government of the case. It is a practice that discredits us.'[161]

Some facets of *Olivorismo* remind us of the *gagá*, e.g. the accusations of immorality in connection with *Olivorista* dances, the kerchiefs, the role of the leader. The central part played by sticks in the *gagá* rituals could indicate a connection with the importance that has been given to Olivorio's *palo de piñón*.

Olivorio used to rise at seven o'clock in the morning. Then a group of disciples would be waiting outside his house, greeting him with music played on the concertina, *güiro* and *pandero* [a kind of tambourine].[162] Olivorio gave those who waited for him his blessing.[163] Those who came to see him were invited to eat and drink. Everybody was welcome: 'He never

158 *Rara* and *gagá* music may be compared by listening to *Caribbean Revels: Haitian Rara and Dominican Gagá*, Smithsonian Folkways, CD SF 40402.
159 Rosenberg (1979), pp. 67–71.
160 Ibid., p. 37.
161 'Baile inmoral', *El Cable*, 26 April 1924.
162 On Dominican folk instruments, see Lizardo (1988).
163 Rodríguez Varona (1947).

threw anybody out. God himself does not do that either. He gave goodness to all.'[164]

On Mondays, Olivorio received gifts from his admirers: cloth, shoes, foodstuffs and money – all of which he divided among the faithful. Everything in La Maguana was done on a communal basis.[165] In La Maguana, El Palmar, El Naranjo and other places where Olivorio founded religious communities, the communal principle of distribution ranked supreme. Everything was shared among the members who lived there.[166] This was true not only of goods and money. Work was shared as well. Fields were planted around the dwellings of the believers and all the work on these fields was carried out in the form of *convites*, a type of communal work parties frequently employed in the southwest during Olivorio's times.[167] The second economic guiding principle was that of self-sufficiency. It was not often that Olivorio procured any goods from the merchants of San Juan de la Maguana.[168]

Olivorio and his followers often organized a *recua* – a line of pack animals. Long before he was chased by the Americans Olivorio led long marches all over the southwest.[169] Either he traveled fast with a small group of men and women, using horses and mules, or he walked between two lines of followers who sang hymns along the way.[170] When the persecution was intensified he walked surrounded by armed bodyguards, particularly Benjamín García, Eleuterio, Perdomo, Liborio Prieto and Máquina. It was

---

164 Interview with Julián Ramos, Higüerito, 16 January 1986.
165 Garrido Puello (1963), pp. 56–7.
166 The number of people who chose to live close to Olivorio varied from time to time and dwindled considerably when the American occupation forces started an intense persecution of the *Olivoristas*. (Cf. below.)
167 Garrido Puello (1963), p. 34.
168 Interview with Maximiliano Rodríguez Piña, Santo Domingo, 23 April 1986.
169 Interview with Julián Ramos, Higüerito, 16 January 1986. Cf. Rodríguez Varona (1947). It is still an open question whether Olivorio visited the eastern parts of the country. Vetilio Alfau Durán (1940), cites two articles that appeared in *El Imparcial* (21 February and 7 March 1914), an Higüey newspaper, that relate a visit by Olivorio and many of his followers in great detail. The articles mention a lot of particular traits of the *Olivorismo*, such as *El Maestro*'s method of healing people only by the use of his hands, or with the help of the *palo de piñón*. Members of his group are listed, together with the names they had been given by Olivorio. It also appears that *El Maestro* had a huge following in the eastern provinces, since Olivorio's particular patron saint was *La Virgen de la Altagracia*, who has her sanctuary in Higüey, the most important pilgrimage site in the Dominican Republic. Olivorio's alleged visit to Higüey is, however, fervently opposed by Garrido Puello (1963), pp. 64–5, who states that he never visited the eastern provinces. There exists a possibility that the man described in the *Imparcial* articles was not Olivorio himself because it occasionally happened that members of his group were caught in Higüey (*El Diario*, 5 July 1912).
170 Garrido Puello, (1963), p. 56.

only Olivorio's closest followers, the so-called *principales* [the main ones], who were armed. Most of their firearms were pistols they carried exposed, tucked into their belts.[171] The *principales* were then followed by a group of men and women with horses carrying food.[172] These caravans could be quite extensive, including 'women who had just given birth, the elderly, children'.[173]

When Olivorio arrived with a big retinue they often camped outside the villages they visited and people came out to see *El Maestro*. At such occasions he often stayed fourteen days or more.[174] Some of Olivorio's followers had set aside various plots for him in the mountains, and people along the road used to offer him food, which he always distributed to the poor, without demanding any payment for it.[175]

On their wanderings, Olivorio and his people came to many remote corners in the southwestern Dominican Republic:

> He often came to Río Limpio. Sometimes he brought lots of people with him, but he could also arrive in the company of just three or four [...] When he came, people crowded around him. He cured people with a stick in the form of a cross; he touched people with it. He also prophesied. All that is happening, he foretold. There were dances as well. To the accompaniment of drums and concertina people danced the *carabiné*, the *mangulina* and the *merengue*. They sang *salves*, never common songs. Just as suddenly as he appeared, he disappeared. You never knew where he went. He did not want people to know.[176]

Olivorio obviously built shelter and lodgings and even planted small *conucos* [garden plots] in inaccessible areas in the Cordillera Central. He was frequently on the move and stayed for longer or shorter periods in those places.[177]

---

171 Interview with Pimpina Luciano by Roberto Cassá, Mao, 22 January 1995. Most names are nicknames and it is no longer possible to identify all the men. Eleuterio was Olivorio's son and Liborio Prieto [the black Olivorio] was a man who looked like *El Maestro*. Máquina, who was said to be wanted by the police for a murder committed in La Vega, has been described as 'a small and crazed [*alocaíto*] man' (ibid.).
172 Garrido Puello (1963), p. 56.
173 Interview with Pimpina Luciano by Roberto Cassá, Mao, 22 January 1995.
174 Ibid.
175 Interview with Julián Ramos, Higüerito, 16 January 1986.
176 Interview with Javier Jovino, Río Limpio, 30 April 1986.
177 Garrido Puello (1963), p. 34. 'Up in the hills they planted yucca, sweet potatoes, bananas and corn, just for their own consumption. They did not sell anything. They got guns and revolvers from Haiti and the Cibao. They did not need cooking-oil, if they came down it was in order to get clothing and pepper' (interview with Arquímedes Valdez, Maguana Abajo, 31 May 1989).

In spite of Olivorio's nomadic habits, La Maguana remained the spiritual center of his movement. In the *salves*, the place appears as a Jerusalem for the *Olivoristas*. The pilgrims came to meet Olivorio at the *ermita* in Maguana Arriba. When they came there, many carried stones on their heads to be deposited in front of the *calvario* that was erected there, in order to liberate themselves from their sins – as the custom is in other rural *calvarios*, all over the Dominican Republic. Olivorio blessed the stones before they were placed in front of the crosses and made the sign of the cross on the forehead of all visitors before they left the place.[178]

Besides seeking the advice and cures of Olivorio, the visitors, exactly like today, quite probably visited the Spring of St John the Baptist and paid homage to the saints in the *ermita*. Olivorio's own favorite saint was the patron saint of the Dominican Republic, *La Virgen de la Altagracia*, and vigils in her honor were often held in La Maguana,[179] sometimes even in the presence of invited priests from the church of San Juan de la Maguana.[180] The participation of the latter was not viewed with gentle eyes by some of their colleagues, one of whom, Padre Esteban Rojas in Baní, even wrote a letter of protest to the archbishop in Santo Domingo.[181]

Olivorio's teachings

Olivorio made speeches to the people who came to see him. Emigdio Garrido Puello maintains that his language was foul,[182] but this statement appears to lack factual foundation. Contemporary witnesses emphasize instead that he expressed himself well, speaking softly. His sermons were not phrased in terms of everyday language. Olivorio spoke 'in a strange way up there [in La Maguana] but normally down here [in San Juan de la Maguana]'.[183] A stream of words came over his lips, which made a strange and rather incomprehensible impression on the listener. These words constituted an 'inspired' speech, where proverbs, personal testimony, fragments of hymns and biblical texts, as well as impressive descriptions of extraordinary visions mingled with scattered bits of invented words and expressions borrowed from the worldly authorities:[184] 'this fellow had the habit of using the phrase "*Justo y Bento*" [just and *bendito*, blessed] in his

---

178 Garrido Puello (1963), pp. 24–5.
179 Interview with Tala Cabral Ramírez, Santo Domingo, 21 November 1985.
180 Garrido Puello (1963), pp. 56–8.
181 González (1983), p. 34.
182 Garrido Puello (1963), p. 34.
183 Interview with Mimicito Ramírez, San Juan de la Maguana, 14 December 1985.
184 Ibid. Mimicito Ramírez referred to the particular way of expressing themselves that the cult functionaries of the *ermita* in Maguana Arriba still use today. We have witnessed this phenomenon on various visits to Maguana Arriba. (Cf. also Martínez (1980), pp. 152–3.)

conversations; and also "*Apotemos*" [*apostemos*, let us bet] when he wanted
to underline his sayings or judgements about what was discussed.'[185]

Present-day *Olivoristas* like to stress that Olivorio's preaching was not
dogmatic, that his acts were of greater importance than his words:

> Liborio did not teach anything. He gave advice: 'Unite with one
> another. All of you, eat together from one *paila* [frying pan]. Become
> twins. If you find a sweet potato, share it between you. You have to
> unite. Do not wish evil for others.' Not everyone cared for Liborio's
> words. He never spoke against the people of the cities. The people of
> Yacahueque did not perceive the people from San Juan de la Maguana
> or Las Matas de Farfán as enemies. We are all friends.[186]

It is rather difficult to arrive at a clear idea of the contents of Olivorio's
message, except that he apparently preached tolerance, compassion and
solidarity. What is still very much alive in the oral tradition are his different
predictions. 'The three inflictions' that befell the San Juan Valley
augmented his fame as a soothsayer and were almost immediately accepted
as proof of his divinity. A questionnaire employed in an investigation of
popular religion carried out in the area of San Juan de la Maguana in 1977
contained the question: 'Is there a famous soothsayer in the place where
you live; or do people remember one who is already dead?' Most of the
respondents answered 'Olivorio' and many of them added that he knew
'all the truth'.[187] In everyday conversation, people sometimes sponta-
neously allude to predictions which they connect with Olivorio. Thus, a
peasant in Río Limpio stated that Olivorio had predicted that the village
would fall into decay if electricity were introduced.[188] A cab driver maintained that Olivorio, 'who was a man for the poor', would soon return and
call the poor to power.[189] It is also common to hear that Olivorio foresaw
technical inventions: '[Olivorio said] that people would fly through the
air.'[190] In his own days he was also known to come up with various predictions. Some were of a rather general character: 'My father often predicted

185 Rodríguez Varona (1947), p. 4.
186 Interview with Pimpina Luciano by Roberto Cassá, Mao, 22 January 1995.
187 Lemus and Oleo (1977), pp. 52, 69, 77, 110, 113, 117–19.
188 Interview with Aquilino, Río Limpio, 1 May 1986.
189 Interview with Niño Gómez, Restauración, 3 May 1986.
190 Woman, twenty years old, interviewed in Jaquimelle by Lemus and Oleo (1977), p. 52.
    The examples of this type could easily be multiplied. It is said Olivorio predicted that
    certain villages would disappear in the future, by saying that 'the river will run over
    them', thereby indicating that they would end up at the bottom of the reservoir of the
    Sabaneta dam. He indicated where future roads would run by hitting the earth with his
    palo de piñón and saying: 'Here a road will pass by.' He showed where future canals would
    be dug, by saying: 'The river San Juan will run here too.' He also predicted the invention

that a time will come when fathers will have no children and children no fathers. And, see, it has all come true nowadays when families are splitting up all around us.'[191]

> There will come a time when there will be no sons for the fathers and no fathers for the sons [...] the capital will be filled, everyone will go to the capital. The parents will come after their children, mothers will leave their children to go to the capital. However, a time will come when a ball will be given and then people will know what will happen.[192]

Other predictions, and 'miracles', were more matter-of-fact and of current interest: 'When the United States cruiser *Memphis* went ashore and the news filtered back into his remote valley, Olivario [sic] let it be known in Gath that he had put her on the rocks, thus acquiring great merit with his people.'[193]

During Olivorio's times, a presentiment that Doomsday was imminent permeated the community of La Maguana. Olivorio reputedly knew the end of the world: 'The prophecy will be fulfilled. Everything will perish. He did not tell the exact date, but every year is worse. No one knows himself and does not know his neighbor either [*nadie se conoce y no conoce al otro*].'[194] However, he also delivered a message of hope for future generations: 'For

of the telephone and radio by saying that: 'In a not too distant future, you will be able to sit in San Juan de la Maguana and listen to what is being said in the capital. Yes, you would even be able to talk to them' (interview with Juan José Medina Mesa, San Juan de la Maguana, 18 January 1989).

It appears as if this type of prediction belongs to a certain kind of legend which grows around charismatic leaders that have alleged prophetic gifts. Another well-known Dominican example is the cycle of legends which have evolved around Bibiana de la Rosa, who founded a cult in Baní at the beginning of the century. She was contemporary with Olivorio and the predictions attributed to her are almost identical with the ones connected with Olivorio (Medina (1989)).

191 Interview with Arquímedes Valdez, Maguana Abajo, 31 May 1989.

192 Interview with Pimpina Luciano by Roberto Cassá, Mao, 22 January 1995. The last prediction may be seen in relation with the massacre in Palma Sola. It is a common practice that 'prophecies' are constantly changed and adapted to new situations and upcoming needs.

193 Marvin (1917). On 29 August 1916, the United States armored cruiser *Memphis* was washed ashore in Santo Domingo by a hurricane. The vessel was totally destroyed and forty men were killed, while 204 were injured. The losses would have been far greater if the Dominicans on the shore had not made a heroic effort to save the Americans' lives (Musicant (1990), pp. 265–7). What Marvin means with 'Gath' remains obscure. Maybe the newspaperman wanted to display his Bible knowledge by alluding to the Palestinian town of Gath, the birthplace of Goliath (1 *Sam.*, 17:4), thus indicating that Olivorio saw himself as a Dominican David battling the imperialist giants of the United States.

194 Interview with Julián Ramos, Higüerito, 16 January 1986. Cf. Ekman (1970), p. 374.

God nothing is difficult. We are the imperfect ones. Just now, we do not know where to seek, but we – the poor ones – will move upwards.'[195]

It is commonly agreed among the *Olivoristas* that Olivorio 'was for the poor',[196] 'for the people who work'[197] and that he preached that 'everybody had to work together and seek means for the poor ones, so that they can improve their existence.'[198] *Olivorismo* is seen as a faith that 'brings a hope that one day Olivorio will get the power of the Universe and all things in the world will change in such a way that life will be better for everybody.'[199]

The most tangible program attributed to Olivorio was that of a just distribution of land. Most peasants agree on this point,[200] even though no hard evidence is available that Olivorio intended to take land from the rich landowners or even that he mentioned nurturing such a plan during his lifetime. The peasants mean that through his way of life – the communal tending of the plots and the egalitarian distribution of food – he indicated how things had to be and that in this he only predicted the future.[201] Garrido Puello claims that Olivorio disapproved of violence and that he even punished a group of his followers when these robbed a wealthy *ganadero* [cattle rancher] who lived in the vicinity of his community.[202] Both adversaries and supporters of Olivorio agree that it was not because of any revolutionary action taken by him against the well-to-do that he was repudiated and persecuted by the established society, but rather because he was 'a god apart' – a man who turned his back on the existing society.[203]

At any rate, through what has been preserved of Olivorio's teachings via the oral tradition runs his strong conviction that he was a chosen man: 'I am on a mission that will last until I come to the trunk of the cross.'[204] 'The word has been hidden, but people who seek Olivorio will stay alive.'[205] However, even though he was obviously considered as a divine being by his followers, who sang *salves*[206] in his honor during his lifetime, his present-

195 Interview with Julián Ramos, Higüerito, 16 January 1986.
196 Interview with León Romilio Ventura, Media Luna, 5 May 1986.
197 Interview with Julián Ramos, Higüerito, 16 January 1986.
198 Interview with León Romilio Ventura, Media Luna, 17 January 1986.
199 Interview with Patoño Bautista Mejía, Distrito de Haina, 5 March 1986.
200 Cf. Mateo Pérez and Mateo Comas (1980), p. 46.
201 Interview with Julián Ramos, Higüerito, 16 January 1986. Cf. Sosa (1982a), p. 18.
202 Garrido Puello (1963), p. 24.
203 Interview with Julián Ramos, Higüerito, 16 January 1986. Cf. interview with Tala Cabral
       Ramírez, Santo Domingo, 21 November 1985 and interview with Mayobanex Rodríguez,
       San Juan de la Maguana, 12 December 1985.
204 Garrido Puello (1963), p. 17.
205 Interview with Julián Ramos, Higüerito, 16 January 1986.
206 Garrido Puello (1963), p. 22. Cf. interview with Julián Ramos, Higüerito, 16 January 1986.

day followers indicate that he considered himself to be a 'nobody' – a mere vehicle of the Great Power of God. Nevertheless, such expressions do not detract from the fact that he considered himself a 'different being' – a fact that was apparent in the way he greeted his visitors: being assured that a divine power had led them to him.[207] Olivorio was obviously an unusual personality, endowed with strong charisma. Even today, a ninety-eight-year-old *ganadero* who lives in San Juan de la Maguana may state that although he does not believe in the 'divinity' of Olivorio, he is convinced that 'the man had an inner light that illuminated him'.[208]

The followers of Olivorio

Most *Olivoristas* came from the province of Azua, particularly from La Maguana, San Juan de la Maguana, Jínova, Sabana Mula and Bánica, but many also came from places spread all over the Republic. After a murderous assault on Olivorio's group in 1922, the marine officer in charge listed dead and living members from various parts of the island: José Adame, 'ex-guardia from Moca and San Francisco de Macorís', Conrada Jerronemo [sic] from the sugar estate of Ansonia in Azua, Lucas Ledesma from La Vega, José Prieto from El Seybo, Manuel Vásquez from Moca, Marciunliano Pérez from Azua, Saturina Bautista from Pedro Corto, and 'a person known as Maquina [sic] from around Santo Domingo City', etc.[209]

Olivorio organized his closest collaborators in an *hermandad*. The inner circle of this *hermandad* was known as *La Jerarquía*, whose members carried mythological and biblical names. His allegedly favorite wife, Matilde Contreras, was *La Número Uno* [Number One] and another lady was called *Santa Clara*.[210] Some of the men carried apostolic names that were sometimes changed. Thus, Enerio Romero, one of the men who would eventually betray Olivorio, was also *San José*.[211] Some other names that obviously were used by members of the community were *Santa Mariquita, San Manuel de Jesús, Virgen María* and *San Pedro*.[212]

207 Interview with Telma Odeida Dotel Matos, Santo Domingo, 2 November 1985. Cf. interview with Enrique Figueroa, Hato Nuevo, 18 January 1986.
208 Interview with Manuel Emilio Mesa, San Juan de la Maguana, 20 January 1989.
209 Morse (1922a). The spelling of the names is probably very tentative. Morse's Spanish was very limited and he often spelled the same name differently in the same report. According to Conrado Mateo, who lives in Maguana en Medio and states that he visted Olivorio's band when he was a child, 'Máquina' was an ex-criminal from La Vega, who wanted to hide his identity. Another *Vegano* called himself 'Pañero' for the same reason. Both Máquina and Pañero were killed shortly after Olivorio (Conrado Mateo quoted in Cassá (1994b)).
210 Deive (1978), p. 192. Cf. Garrido Puello (1963), p. 23.
211 Interview with Víctor Garrido, Jr, Santo Domingo, 22 April 1986.
212 Alfau Durán (1940).

Olivorio's community became a sanctuary, not only for poor peasants and landless day laborers, but people who one way or another had got into trouble with the legal authorities also found a haven in La Maguana.[213] Old *Olivoristas* confirm the fact that Olivorio had law breakers within his ranks. He was tolerant and accepted everybody. Besides, 'crimes in those days were not the same as they are today'.[214] The first two decades of the twentieth century constitute an insecure period in Dominican history. Weak governments contributed to a state of anarchy throughout the country. Under these circumstances, a poor peasant could easily become a criminal, even a murderer.

To carry arms was a sign of prestige among Dominican peasants: 'He who wants to be a man must possess a good horse, his revolver, a saddle and his woman.'[215] Revolvers were expensive. In order to get a Colt or Smith and Wesson, most peasants had to 'throw in a year' of work, and when they finally obtained it, the revolver became their most precious possession.[216] An American traveler who visited the country in the 1910s offers the following description of Dominican peasants:

> the country folk are literally armed to the teeth [...] Men are often seen with two machetes – one is the ordinary working tool, the other a long keen-bladed, carven handled, scimitar-like weapon slung from the shoulder – a heavy Colt's or Smith and Wesson revolver, a dagger-like knife and a shotgun or a musket.[217]

All these arms were not carried for display purposes only. They were likely to be used when sentiments ran high during cockfights or bar brawls.

The tension in the San Juan Valley was also high for political reasons. The smouldering discontent which exploded in the revolutionary upheavals in the early 1910s was kept alive among the people of the valley afterwards as well, and the revolutionaries were not disarmed until the US gained control of the area in 1917. A *Sanjuanero* laments the situation in 1915 in a letter to the editor of the newspaper *El Radical* in Santo Domingo. A police force whose arrival from the capital failed to show up:

> They have been on their way for a year now but the guards have not yet shown up. In the meantime, the undisturbed thieves break locks

---

213 Garrido Puello (1963), pp. 16 and 18.
214 Interview with Julián Ramos, Higüerito, 16 January 1986.
215 Dominican contemporary saying cited by Jiménez (1927), p. 6. Regarding arms and Dominican peasants, see Cruz Díaz (1965), pp. 127–8 and Rodríguez Demorizi (1975a), pp. 62–3 and 301–2.
216 Rodríguez Demorizi (1975a), p. 302.
217 Verrill (1914), p. 268.

and destroy houses without being hindered. When the night comes and you must go out, you walk out with a revolver in your hand, since the shooting goes on from when the sun sets until it rises.[218]

Another reason for bloody skirmishes between the people of the San Juan Valley and the authorities was the control which the Americans had over the Haitian border, beginning in 1907. The formerly open roads to the neighboring country were blocked and tariffs were charged on products crossing the border. In the late nineteenth century, the Dominican Republic had taken a series of loans from both Europe and the United States. When several European governments pressed for the payment of debts due to their nationals, the United States, the biggest claimant, more or less forced the Dominican government to agree to a plan which the US government had worked out for the adjustment of the debts. As a result, the US was granted a general receivership of the proceeds from foreign trade and the border was controlled by American customs officials.[219] The *Sanjuaneros* reacted violently when they found that this meant that their traditional trade with Haiti had become illegal contraband in the eyes of the Americans. During the first twenty-eight months of American general receivership, a total of eighteen American customs officials were killed or wounded in gunfights with 'contraband agents'.[220]

The constabulary that had been created in order to exercise control over the Haitian-Dominican border was led by an American sergeant named James McLean. McLean married the sister of a wealthy businessman in San Juan de la Maguana and lived in the area for most of the remainder of his life.[221] An American reporter visited McLean in 1920, and his description of the man reflects the views many Americans had of life on the border:

218 *El Radical*, 5 January 1915.
219 Clausner (1973), p. 142.
220 A treaty signed in 1907 provided that an American receivership of customs revenue that had begun in 1905 should continue until the retirement of the bonds issued under the plan. An American-trained constabulary was formed to 'maintain order' along the borders and a general receiver of Dominican customs, as well as other employees of the receivership, were appointed by the president of the United States. A minimum of US$ 1,200,000 per year had to be deposited in a New York bank for the creditors and it was determined that at least 45 percent of the customs revenue belonged to the Dominican Republic (Knight (1928), pp. 38–9; ibid. pp. 6–66 deals with the whole complicated history of the various Dominican foreign loans). We will return to the issue below, in Chapter 7.
221 Interview with Maximiliano Rodríguez Piña, Santo Domingo, 23 April 1986. Maximiliano is the son of Domingo Rodríguez, brother-in-law of James McLean. McLean arrived in the country in 1907 (Burke (1935), p. 181). During the US occupation of the Dominican Republic (1916–24), he held various offices. In 1918–19, he commanded a section of the *Guardia Nacional Dominicana* (GND) in the eastern parts of the country. The GND was the constabulary force formed by the American occupation forces in 1917 (Calder

The top sergeant Mac [...] was the first of our fellow-countrymen to accept the dangerous task of patrolling the Haitian-Dominican frontier. Many a party of smugglers did he rout out single handed; times without number he was surrounded by bandits, or threatened with such fate as only the outlaws of savage Haiti and their Dominican confederates can inflict upon helpless white men falling into their hands.[222]

(1984), p. 120). In 1920–21, McLean was director of the Southern Department of the GND and was stationed in Santo Domingo (McLean (1921), cf. *Libro azul de Santo Domingo* (1920), p. 27). Hicks (1946), p. 29, states that McLean lost this position due to excessive drinking and Burke (1935), p. 181, specifies that McLean was court-martialed and dismissed in 1922, after 'talking too freely about his superior officers'.

McLean always maintained close contacts with San Juan de la Maguana. Sometimes he served as the most important representative for the Americans in the area. After his appointments as officer in San Pedro de Macorís and Santo Domingo, he visited San Juan various times, often as guide to other American officers and as an expert on all matters related to the San Juan Valley and the Dominican-Haitian frontier. He was known to be a practical joker of the rude type and liked to be funny at other persons' expense: 'He got worse with power' and was never really liked by the majority of the *Sanjuaneros* (interview with Mayobanex Rodríguez, San Juan de la Maguana, 18 January 1989; cf. Garrido Puello (n.d), pp. 138–9).

His friend and fellow-toper, William Burke, characterizes McLean as 'too happy-go-lucky and independent to work well in harness, and should have moved out when the country became civilized and tame' (Burke (1935), p. 181). A 'respectable citizen' of Las Matas de Farfán described his behavior in the following way: 'the famous McKlean [sic], even if he was married to a distinguished Dominican lady and had lived together with us even before the intervention [...] did not behave as before, when he was a humble and cordial friend, but when he felt the support of these troops [the US marines] all that he had carried within himself came forth and he started to throw around his habitual Godenme [God damn it?] and give his kicks, turning himself into an ass' (Rodríguez Pereyra (1978), pp. 239–40).

McLean was murdered under mysterious circumstances in 1925 (*El Cable*, 16 and 23 June 1925 and Burke (1935), p. 181). There are some indications that his death was ordered by Trujillo, who on his way to his future dictatorship (1930–61), had been in McLean's service for a time. Trujillo ran a lot of shady errands for McLean ('The colonel, when sufficiently sober, found a profound satisfaction in the company of harlots') and was known as McLean's 'pimp' (Hicks (1946), p. 28, cf. Burke (1935), pp. 197–211). Trujillo went to such extremes that he abducted 'and tied up black women so McLean could satisfy his eroticism with them' (Morales (1930), p. 750).

McLean befriended Trujillo while the latter was commander in chief over the rural guards in service of the private sugar companies in Boca Chica and San Isidro. During this time McLean was Inspector of the GND in San Pedro de Macorís. When McLean, in December 1918, was consulted concerning an application Trujillo had made in order to be enrolled in the GND he answered: 'I have no objections to this applicant' (McLean (1918)). With these words McLean probably initiated the political career of the future dictator. McLean was also the personal friend of one of Trujillo's uncles, with whom he wrote a book about the Dominican-Haitian frontier (McLean and Pina Chevalier (1921), cf. Vega (1986a), pp. 749–50).

222 Franck (1921), p. 208.

Figure 2.13 James McLean.

Due to his long stay in the country, McLean's knowledge was highly appreciated by several American officers. For some years he was considered to be one of the few Americans who really 'understood the people and the language'[223] and his services were used while organizing a constabulary force consisting of Dominican nationals: the *Guardia Nacional Dominicana* (GND). In a report from 1921 McLean describes Olivorio's followers as 'mostly criminals who are fugitives from justice'.[224] Their crimes are listed in another American document: carrying firearms, escaping from prison, smuggling rum, homicide.[225] The 'criminals' that these reports refer to probably constituted the 'hard core' of Olivorio's followers, easily identified persons who could not leave the band since they were well known to have 'broken the law'.

223 Burke (1935), p. 178. His 'understanding' of the Dominicans did not prevent McLean from being prejudiced. When William Burke (Inspector General of Sanitation during the American occupation) told McLean that he nearly had killed a Dominican by mistake, McLean simply laughed and told his friend: 'It would have meant one nigger less, and there's a million of them on this island. So forget it, and have another rum' (quoted in ibid., p. 181).

224 McLean (1921).

225 Feeley (1919). The group of Olivorio was always well armed. After an attack in 1922 the marines listed the weapons the fleeing *Olivoristas* had left behind: 'Nineteen revolvers, all of the Smith and Wesson type, 38's and 44's, eleven of which are in very good condition and the other eight in serviceable condition, two rifles of the 55-90 type in serviceable condition and 484 rounds of ammunition were captured. The ammunition consisted of 30-30's for Springfields and Kreg-Jergensens [sic], 38's, 44's, 55-90's, 7 mm's and 45's of the automatic pistol type' (Morse (1922a)). (The correct name of the rifle is Krag-Jorgensen (Musicant (1990), p. 276).)

It is, however, wrong to label the *Olivoristas* indiscriminately a 'bunch of criminals'. The majority had no criminal record whatsoever and they numbered several hundred before the Americans started to persecute *El Maestro*.[226] Furthermore, the Americans themselves reported that 'every countryman in this común looks upon Livorio as a saint. People from half the Republic come to him to get medicine.'[227] Few records have been found of complaints that the *Olivoristas* molested peasants or authorities unprovoked. The only exception we have come across can be found in a report by a marine officer, Lieutenant Colonel George Thorpe:

> Certainly Olivorio is a great curse to the people of the whole part of Azua Province northwest of San Juan. Most of the people know it and would be glad to be rid of him but fear to oppose him or give information. The people at El Morro and Pesquero, where we bivouaced [sic], were delighted with our treatment of them, paying for what we got, and I heard them talking among themselves, saying, 'The Americans pay for what they take, but Olivorio just takes what he wants and never pays.'[228]

Thorpe is contradicted by various sources, which stress that Olivorio and his men were far from being a menacing presence.[229] He gave rather than took away and tried to make his group as self-sufficient as possible. Even people who were no supporters of his have agreed upon the fact that Olivorio was a rather harmless character, 'humble', even 'contemplative'. The words are Manuel de Jesús Rodríguez Varona's, who also passes a somewhat harsher judgement on Olivorio:

> I knew him and and had dealings with him personally for many years; he was not courageous and astute in the real sense of the words; he was rather a dark and insignificant man with pretensions of being a soothsayer and healer, a person who the environment turned into a

---

226 McLean (1921).
227 Bales (1920).
228 Thorpe (1918a). Thorpe prided himself with his ability of coming on friendly terms with Dominicans. In a speech he gave in the United States in 1920 he stated: 'I always find people the most promising objects of interest, it was natural that wherever I went I made friends with the natives and talked to them on intimate terms. In riding up to a mountain hut with my escort, we would dismount and exchange ceremoniously polite greetings with the family [...] By the time I had asked the names and ages of children coming from every window and corner and had told them I had little ones at home myself [...] the ice was broken and they saw nothing terrible about the foreigner who knew that children liked sweetmeats' (Thorpe (1920), p. 63).
229 Cf. Cassá (1993a), p. 4.

deceptive and tricky healer and a rural politician of a semi-African, medieval type.[230]

It appears that Olivorio's companions were also rather peaceful. As McLean wrote in 1921, 'they invariably refuse to fight as a band, even when attacked.'[231]

In spite of their inoffensive behavior, the *Olivoristas* could still make a rather imposing and threatening sight. An American reporter named George Marvin described Olivorio and his followers in the following way:

> At San Juan they naïvely told you not to go to Palmar, you were sure to get hurt there. This demesne had established and generally respected boundary lines not printed on any map, and the people who inhabited and cultivated it were not citizens of Santo Domingo; they were 'la gente (hen-ty) de Olivario [sic]', Olivario's sub-subjects. Olivario made Napoleon Cha-cha look like a piker. He did not have to cache his wives around in isolated *casitas*, they herded with him. He did not have to blow a whistle to summon his janizaries, they hived at headquarters in Palmar, 328 of them with rifles and bandoliers of ammunition. When emissaries arrived from other states on official business, Olivario was wont to receive them seated in the midst of all 328 of his standing army, nearly every one of whom was a fugitive from justice, whatever in Santo Domingo that may have meant.[232]

The *Olivorista* dress

The *Olivoristas* dressed in a peculiar way and it is often told that Olivorio paid special attention to the way he dressed. All his clothes were made by one of 'his' women, called Comay Bona, who lived with her husband Vale Domingo de Oca in San Juan de la Maguana.[233] On the two existing photos,[234] Olivorio wears cotton threads around his head, adorned with

230 Rodríguez Varona (1947).

231 McLean (1921).

232 Marvin (1917). Salustiano Goicoechea (sometimes spelled Goicochea) (Chachá) was a *gavillero* [guerilla] leader in the southeastern districts. Marvin's description of Olivorio and his men probably refers to the situation prior to Bearss' attack (see below). It is possible that Marvin got his information from Bearss himself. For example, Bearss and Marvin are the only ones we have found who spell Olivorio's name as Olivario.

233 Rodríguez Varona (1947). Comay Bona lived for various periods with Olivorio, something which apparently was accepted by her husband, who also was a firm believer in the powers of Olivorio.

234 The photographs were probably taken in 1909 by a San Juan photographer named Julián Suazo (interview with Mimicito Ramírez, San Juan de la Maguana, 14 December 1985).

Figure 2.14 Painting of Olivorio by Príamo Morel.

various knots. One is placed right over his forehead and ends in a fringe that hangs down over his nose. He has an open *chamarra* [shirt] and a kerchief around his neck. On a large painting, made by Príamo Morel,[235] the *chamarra* is blue and the kerchief red. In his right hand he holds a cross – perhaps indicating either his *palo de piñón*, or the cross-hilted sword he always wore.[236]

It was of the utmost importance that the male *Olivorista* dress had to be made out of blue denim, a material called *blé* in the San Juan Valley[237] and considered to be the material favored by all peasants, but blue and white are also the colors of the Virgin as well as the Spanish warrior saint, Santiago (St James the Major), also known as Ogún Balenyo, the voodoo deity who stands for justice and represents all military and knightly virtues.[238] On festive occasions, present-day *Olivoristas* still dress in blue and white and carry banners in the same colors.

235 The painting can be seen in the house of Enemencio Mora in Maguana Arriba. It is made by an artist from Santiago de los Caballeros, named Príamo Morel and was a personal gift from President Joaquín Balaguer to Enemencio, delivered to his house by local representatives of *El Partido Reformista*.

236 Upon his death, the sword of Olivorio was confiscated by the Americans (*El Cable*, 1 July 1922) but later it came in the possession of one of his disciples, José Popa. A sword of the same appearance, venerated as the original one, is still kept by an old *Olivorista*, who wants to remain anonymous.

237 This comes from Haitian Creole. In Haiti the same material is called '*blé*'.

238 Miniño (1980).

Olivorio wanted the people who came to his *calvario* in La Maguana to wear cords around their heads or across their chests.[239] The number of knots on the cotton threads appear to have been important to the *Olivoristas*. Garrido Puello mentions that there had to be twelve of them – one for each month. Three of these knots had a particular significance – that of 'dangerous' months when the danger of being hit by gunfire was higher than otherwise.[240]

The particular looks of the *Olivoristas*, and the teachings and behavior of their leader, may also be connected with the descriptions of the Apocalypse that are found in the Bible. Such accounts could have been transmitted to Olivorio by Juan Samuel. The description of a rider on a white horse that is offered in *Revelation* 19 is reminiscent of both Olivorio's tale of how he was brought to heaven and of his particular head gear:

> And I saw heaven opened, and behold a white horse; and he that sat upon him was called Faithful and True, and in righteousness he doth judge and make war. His eyes were as a flame of fire, and on his head were many crowns; and he had a name written, that no man knew, but he himself.[241]

Another indication that Olivorio was familiar with this particular text was the fact that he is reported to have preached that 'there were two words: one in heaven and another one on earth, but he never explained the mystery and meaning of these two unknown words'.[242]

To dress in a particular way is often a sign of penitence, or indicates membership in a certain religious group. This custom is as common in the Dominican Republic as in other Catholic countries. Thus, many of the

239 Garrido Puello (1963), p. 24.
240 Ibid., p. 32. Amulets and different safeguards against gunfire were common among Dominican peasants. The equipment of some *Olivoristas* can be seen in relation to notions held by other Dominicans who have been persecuted by the authorities. When Enrique Blanco, a famous Dominican bandit, was shot in 1937, the police found a vast assortment of magical devices on the corpse. Tied around his waist he had a string with seven knots, one for every day in the week. He wore two pairs of trousers. One pair was turned inside out, the other was worn back to front. He carried various trinkets, two amulets, made out of pieces of a crucifix, and seven *cadenitas* [small chains] 'of small material value, but doubly and invaluably priced when used in the esoteric rites where they are employed'. In his pockets he carried sheets of paper, imprinted with various prayers (Arzeno Rodríguez (1980), pp. 33–4; quotation from p. 33). Enrique Blanco had been hunted like a lonely animal for several years and most of his magical equipment could probably be interpreted as safeguards against bullets.
241 *Revelation* 19:11–12.
242 Garrido Puello (1963), p. 57. Cf. *Revelation* 2:17: 'To him that overcometh will I give to eat of the hidden manna, and will give him a white stone, and in the stone a new name written, which no man knoweth saving he that receiveth it.'

'peculiarities' in the *Olivorista* outfit – like the scapulars[243] – can be explained as indications of belonging to a particular *hermandad*, i.e. a religious organization constituted by laymen.

The large scapular (from Latin *scapula*, shoulder) forms the most important part of the habit of the Catholic monastic orders. It consists of a piece of cloth, about the width of the chest and is worn over the habit so that it almost reaches the feet both in front and behind. There are also smaller scapulars, consisting of textile badges worn over the chest and the back connected with cords across the shoulders. These originated during the late Middle Ages when monastic orders attached laymen to their communities and gave them small scapulars as a sign of their commitment. Later on, independent fraternities were founded and often composed scapulars of their own. Scapulars were often worn as a sign of their bearers' devotion to certain saints, particularly the various manifestations of the Virgin.[244] As previously mentioned, Olivorio was particularly devoted to *La Virgen de la Altagracia*, who has her sanctuary in Higüey. It is possible that the scapulars worn by the *Olivoristas* were the ones which were worn in order to show devotion to her. It is also feasible to consider the cords the *Olivoristas* obviously wore cross-wise over the chest[245] as a form of scapulars, or at least as signs that they considered themselves to belong to an *hermandad*.

Olivorio and the Americans

On 15 May, 1916, the United States marines landed in Santo Domingo without meeting any resistance. The prelude to this intervention was long and complicated, and the reasons were various. A proclamation that was issued by the Americans, after they had taken control over the country, declared that the Dominicans themselves had caused the intervention by violating Article 3 of the 1907 US-Dominican treaty concerning the American receivership of customs revenues. The crime of the Dominican government was that, contrary to the agreement, it had increased the public debt without the required prior agreement of Washington officials.[246] This accusation, however, appears to have been a mere pretext. The decision to intervene was based mainly on other considerations. The US intervention in the Dominican Republic was just one of many other military actions carried out by the Americans all over the Caribbean,[247] and

243 Garrido Puello (1963), p. 56.
244 Hilgers (1912), pp. 508–9.
245 Interview with Olimpia Almonte, Río Limpio, 30 April 1986. She stated that *Olivoristas*, until the authorities started to persecute members of the cult in Palma Sola, often wore cords cross-wise over their chests, around the left upper arm and around the waist.
246 Calder (1984), p. 21.
247 The most important US interventions in Central America and the Caribbean during the

Figure 2.15 Juan Isidro Jimenes Pereyra, president 1899–1902 and 1914–16.

may be connected with the desire to keep the Western Hemisphere free of European control and to consolidate the United States' political and military control over the Caribbean area.

What forced the Americans to intervene was their fear that the Dominican Congress would choose a president who was hostile to them, namely General Desiderio Arias. The Dominican president, Juan Isidro Jimenes (elected in 1914) and his government had been under constant pressure from the US government demanding increased power for the American 'financial adviser' that had been forced upon the Dominicans. In 1915, the Americans also required that the Dominican government should disband its armed forces and replace them with a constabulary to be controlled by a nominee of the president of the United States.[248] President Jimenes did not trust his anti-American minister of war, Desiderio Arias, fearing that the latter was preparing a coup against him. In April 1916, Jimenes tried to prevent the anticipated coup attempt by imprisoning the commander in the fortress in Santo Domingo. This was an unconstitutional act and immediately aroused the anger of the opposition who sided with Arias, who

1910s were Nicaragua in 1912, Mexico in 1914 and Haiti in 1915. Cuba was affected various times during the period. (See e.g. Munro (1964), Langley (1980) and Perkins (1981).)
248 Calder (1984), p. 7.

eventually occupied the fortress in the capital. President Jimenes, who at that moment was at his country residence, marched on the capital with an improvised army. The Americans saw their chance to intervene and landed some of their troops, ostensibly to protect the US legation.

On 13 May, the American admiral William Caperton delivered an ultimatum to General Arias to disarm the Dominican forces and warned that the city would be bombarded if any resistance was offered. During the night of 14 May, the Dominican army marched off to the north, bringing all its equipment with it.[249] Desiderio Arias set up his headquarters in the fort of Santiago and some of his men offered scattered resistance to the advancing American troops in the north.[250]

In June and July, American troops were disembarked in various Dominican ports. Successively, the Americans gained control over the entire country. Only in the north did they meet any organized resistance worth mentioning. On 1 June, the marines landed in Monte Cristi from where they had to fight their way down to Santiago, the 'stronghold' of General Arias, which was reached on 6 July. The hardest fighting took place at La Barranquita, a few miles north of the town of Mao, where forty out of eighty Dominicans were killed or wounded and one American lost his life. The marines were well armed and the Dominicans could not do much against their heavy machine gun fire.[251]

The hero of the entire operation was Major 'Hike 'em' Hiram Bearss,[252] 'a noted extrovert' with 'a reputation among contemporaries as one of the best storytellers in the Marine Corps'.[253] While the main column of 1,100 soldiers marched along the road to Santiago, Bearss and his men secured the railroad from Santiago to the busy port of Puerto Plata. In Altamira, halfway between Santiago and Puerto Plata, the American advance was halted by a group of Dominican peasant fighters. Bearss made a frontal attack with sixty men and in a 'spectacular style of personal command',[254] charged through a railroad tunnel, killing and wounding some fifty 'insurgents' who had taken up positions there.

---

249 Knight (1928), pp. 70–3.
250 González Canalda (1985a), pp. 43–4.
251 González Canalda (1985b), pp. 23–46.
252 Hiram Iddings Bearss (1875–1938) had attended the universities of Notre Dame, Purdue, De Pauw and Norwich. He was commissioned as second lieutenant in the marine corps in 1898 and served in the Spanish-American and Philippine-American wars. Before he arrived in the Dominican Republic he had been stationed in Panama (Shavit (1992), p. 23). Hiram Bearss was nicknamed 'Hike 'em Hiram' because he 'habitually force-marched his men during the day and amused them at night with wild stories about his exploits' (Langley (1985), p. 148).
253 Fuller and Cosmas (1974), p. 22.
254 Ibid., p. 21.

Figure 2.16 Hiram Bearss.

While Fortson directed the fire, Bearss, furiously pumping a handcar, dashed forward at the head of his men into the tunnel mouth. It was 300 yards long, pitch-black [...] But, without casualty or mishap they burst through, only to see the rebels in high flight down the tracks. As one marine noted, 'it was the most fun Hiram had enjoyed in a long time.'[255]

By this action, the railroad line was finally 'secured'. Colonel Joseph Pendleton, commander in chief of the troops in the north, wrote in his report that the work of Bearss had been performed so well that it was beyond praise.[256]

255 Musicant (1990), p. 262. Cf. Fuller and Cosmas (1974), pp. 20–2. However, the operation was not entirely without casualties on the American side. A second lieutenant and a trumpeter were wounded by Dominican fire just before the attack on the tunnel (McClellan (1921), p. 242). This was not the first time Bearss performed dashing feats. His bravery was already legendary within the marine corps. In 1934 he was awarded the Congressional Medal of Honor because in 1900, under extremely difficult circumstances, he had led a patrol through the jungles on the Philippine island of Samar and wiped out an enemy stronghold (Metcalf (1939), pp. 273–4). In 1914 he had landed incognito in Vera Cruz, Mexico, several days before American forces took over that city. It was information that Bearss had obtained from his reconnaissance which made it possible for the marines to seize that city without many casualties (Shavit (1992), p. 23).
256 González Canalda (1985b), p. 65.

Figure 2.17 Marine railway patrol, on the Puerto Plata-Navarrete line, 1916.

Early in July 1916, General Arias surrendered to the Americans in Santiago and disbanded his army. This act brought an end to the formal, organized resistance to the US occupation. Yet, throughout the presence of the marines in the Dominican Republic hardly a month went by without an armed clash between the US troops and Dominican armed units that were usually lumped together by the Americans under the label of 'bandits'.[257] The first battle of this irregular war was delivered in the San Pedro de Macorís area, where Bearss[258] tried to subdue a local *caudillo* named Salustiano Goicoechea, 'Chachá'.[259] Chachá and his 100–200 men eluded Bearss' detachment completely, but the Americans succeeded in getting the situation in the east 'under control' after five days.[260] His methods were harsh, Bearss reported: 'Found natives [...] unfriendly and almost uncivilized and unwilling to give least information about anything [...] By threats of force and by other threats made prisoners act as guides.'[261]

257 Fuller and Cosmas (1974), p. 33. These fights are commonly known as the '*gavillero*' uprising. The Dominican term *gavillero* is used to denote rural bandits, but the meaning of the word has changed and *gavillero* has become synonymous with any man belonging to any group of Dominican peasants making armed resistance against the Americans (see Calder (1984), pp. 115–32).

258 Bearss had assumed command over what came to be called the southern district of the Dominican Republic, including, among other sections, the capital, the San Juan Valley and the eastern sugar districts (Musicant (1990), p. 273).

259 Goicoechea's rebellion, which started in 1917, was a reaction to the marines' entry in San Pedro de Macorís.

260 Calder (1984), p. 134.

Bearss left the area after offering a reward of 300 dollars for Chachá, dead or alive.[262] However, the situation did not calm down, and in August in the same year, Bearss was back, now chasing a 'bandit' called Calcano. After arresting Calcano and bringing him to Santo Domingo for confinement,[263] Bearss went to deal with Olivorio and his men in the southwest.

In December 1916, another US marine officer, William Freden, had visited Olivorio's stronghold in El Palmar. Together with Carmito Ramírez and the chief of the San Juan police force, Manuel de Jesús Rodríguez Varona, he had met Olivorio and asked him if he would be willing to hand over his arms. Olivorio received them personally in La Maguana.[264] After a lengthy discussion, they convinced the *Olivoristas* to hand over their weapons in spite of the fact that Olivorio's men greatly outnumbered the followers of Freden and Rodríguez Varona. However, even though Freden is reported to have been both 'a nice person and a good psychologist',[265] it was quite probably the presence of Carmito Ramírez that made Olivorio favorably disposed towards the Americans. The day after the encounter, sixty to seventy men came down from La Maguana and deposited their weapons with the police in San Juan.[266] The monthly intelligence report of the US marine corps in Santo Domingo mentioned: 'The well known revolutionist OLIVORIO in the Valley of San Juan de la Maguana is turning in his arms. The town of San Juan is quiet.'[267]

But, Olivorio never turned in all his weapons, after all: 'You carried a revolver in order to gain respect, so my father really needed all his arms.'[268] When Freden had left their town the *Sanjuaneros* themselves made an

---

261 Bearss, quoted in Musicant (1990), p. 277.

262 Calder (1984), p. 134.

263 Fuller and Cosmas (1974), p. 22.

264 Rodríguez Varona (1947).

265 Interview with Mayobanex Rodríguez, San Juan de la Maguana, 12 December 1985. Mayobanex Rodríguez was an eyewitness to the event in La Maguana, being with his father, Manuel de Jesús Rodríguez Varona. However, he says it was not Freden, but Bearss, who met with Olivorio on that particular occasion. But he is contradicted by his father's memoir. Mayobanex mentioned that Bearss stayed over night in his parents' house before he went to meet with Olivorio, something Rodríguez Varona in 1947 wrote that Freden did. In his personal report about his encounter with Olivorio, Bearss does not mention anything about any verbal negotiations with Olivorio. He went into armed action immediately (Bearss (1917)). Strangely enough Mimicito Ramírez coincides with Mayobanex in stating that it was Bearss who convinced Olivorio of turning in his weapons (interview with Mimicito Ramírez, San Juan de la Maguana, 14 December 1985).

266 Interview with Mayobanex Rodríguez, San Juan de la Maguana, 12 December 1985. Garrido (1922), p. 233, writes that the *Olivoristas* refused to cooperate in turning in their weapons, but an almost contemporary source states that Olivorio 'handed over his 328 standing rifles together with small arms and ammunition and promised to be good' (Marvin (1917)).

267 Ramsey (1917).

268 Interview with Arquímedes Valdez, Maguana Abajo, 31 May 1989.

attempt to convince Olivorio that he, for the safety of the whole community, had to give up all his weapons. A 'commission' headed by Carmito Ramírez failed to come to terms with Olivorio. The dignified members of the commission felt that they had been treated with disrespect. Olivorio had received them surrounded by his armed men and had behaved as if they were 'uninvited spies'.[269]

The mission to Olivorio's stronghold can be seen as an effort to ease the tensions which were growing within the community of San Juan de la Maguana. The old party strife from the civil war of 1912 was still alive and former adversaries resumed the hostilities by accusing one another in front of the Americans. Powerful enemies of the Ramírez clan tried to link with Olivorio, and the Ramírezes, in their turn, tried to appease their old ally. Nevertheless, their efforts turned out to be in vain, as increasingly frantic reports, fabricated by Ramírez' enemies, reached the marine headquarters in Santo Domingo:

> For the past week, the people there [in the San Juan Valley] have been representing that there was a serious uprising in the vicinity of San Juan [...] The leader is Labori [sic] a religious and medical fanatic, seriously self-styled a saint. The mountainous country that he has chosen for operations is very favorable to a long defensive [sic]. As I was finishing the last sentence reliable reports came in that this Labori force has been joined by General Ramírez, probably is [sic] a concentration of General Vidal's followers, and has two hundred entrenched near San Juan in same position, in which insurgents have, in times past, defeated Dominican Government forces.[270]

Upon his arrival in San Juan, Bearss summoned all the men living in town to a meeting and informed them of his intentions of making a direct armed attack on Olivorio and his men. Bearss was well aware of the fact that Olivorio had old contacts with the influential Ramírez family and Carmito Ramírez thus saw himself forced to offer his services as a guide for the American troops, probably in order to free himself and his family from the accusations of being supporters of the 'bandit' Olivorio.[271] Carmito did not only guide the marines to Olivorio's stronghold, he also drew an excellent map, which still can be seen in the National Archives in Washington, DC.[272]

---

269 Garrido Puello (1963), pp. 35–6. Cf. Rodríguez Varona (1947).
270 Chief of Staff (1917).
271 Garrido (1970), pp. 103–4.
272 Interview with Mimicito Ramírez, San Juan de la Maguana, 14 December 1985. See appendix to Bearss (1917). Bearss mentions in his report that a marine was sent out 'to execute a panoramic sketch of the topography' of the area for the planned action and it

The action began at dawn on 6 April. Bearss and his sixty-six marines had the support of units from the former Dominican army, at least seventy men under the command of Lieutenant Buenaventura Cabral, among them a mounted group of eleven men from Monte Cristi. The other Dominicans were apparently soldiers from San Juan de la Maguana and Azua. With pack animals, horses and heavy machine guns, the troops advanced through La Maguana and camped at La Isleta, just where Cordillera Central rises steeply above the narrow valley of the San Juan River.

At 7.00 a.m. the next day the soldiers started their ascent up towards the hill of El Palmar, where Olivorio had previously maintained a stronghold. Informed beforehand about the advance of his enemies, he had moved his center a little further into the mountains, to an almost inaccessible place called El Naranjo. When they followed a narrow path in between the hillocks, the troops were ambushed. Protected by huge boulders, maybe a thousand *Olivoristas* opened fire from the surrounding cliffs and hurled rocks and turned loose big boulders upon their pursuers. A Dominican officer was killed, two Dominican guardsmen were severely wounded, and three marines received slight wounds. The *Olivoristas* fought bravely for several hours but were finally forced to retreat into the mountains, leaving their dead and wounded behind. The Americans counted nine dead and twenty-four wounded *Olivoristas*. The next day the *Olivoristas* were hunted down in El Palmar and El Naranjo, and the Dominican soldiers killed five more *Olivoristas* in a place called El Corozol. Olivorio disappeared into the Cordillera.[273]

Bearss stayed for a while in San Juan de la Maguana and succeeded in making himself popular among several *Sanjuaneros* and he is still, several years later, remembered as a jovial and nice man.[274] Carmito Ramírez

was maybe that man who made the map, though the blueprint which is kept at the National Archives is rather detailed and does not give the impression of being a mere 'sketch'.

273 Garrido Puello (1963), pp. 40–1 and Bearss (1917). In his report Bearss writes 'Sleta' instead of 'La Isleta'. Some confusion exists around the incident. Dominican sources, both written and oral, agree on the presence of Carmito and even Wenceslao, but the name of the Americans in charge, as well as the place of the ambush, differ a lot. It probably occured close to a place called Arroyo Limón, where Olivorio and his men used to camp on the lands belonging to an Antonio Peguero, who remained loyal to Olivorio all his life (interview with Mimicito Ramírez, San Juan de la Maguana, 14 December 1985). Arroyo Limón was a key position because the place constituted the point of departure for a mule track that led over the Cordillera Central to the town of San José de las Matas, situated on the fertile plains on the other side of the huge mountain massif (cf. Ekman (1970), p. 372). Garrido Puello (1963), p. 41, claims that the place was called Cercadillo, situated higher up in the mountains.

274 Interviews with Mayobanex Rodríguez, San Juan de la Maguana, 12 December 1985 and Mimicito Ramírez, San Juan de la Maguana, 14 December 1985. Not all sources agree. Through the clashes he had with representatives of the press in Santo Domingo, upon

Figure 2.18 Carmito Ramírez in the 1920s.

became a very good friend of Bearss, but as soon as the American left Carmito's troubles started again. He was imprisoned for nine months accused of plotting against the invaders and planning to start a revolution like the one in 1912. Carmito's son-in-law, Víctor Garrido, writes that the imprisonment was due to false accusations from Carmito's enemies, who were envious of his position as 'Master of the South'. Finally the old Wenceslao Ramírez succeeded in arranging the release of his son through a direct appeal to the US military governor who, at that moment, probably realized the decisive influence of the Ramírez family in the area.[275] An American reporter, who visited the Republic in 1917, even called the San Juan Valley 'the principality of the Ramírez[es]'.[276] Wenceslao Ramírez

whom he tried to impose severe censorship, Bearss obtained a reputation of being both crude and inconsiderate. On one occasion he called upon the Dominican provincial governor in Santo Domingo to stop the 'attacks' that Dominican papers made on the behavior of the marines. When the governor answered that such a move was not among his legal functions, Bearss shouted that 'the laws have never been obeyed in this country!' (Knight (1928), p. 79, cf. Blanco Fombona (1927), pp. 17–18). At the same time Bearss himself was accused of disorderly behavior. An open letter to a newspaper in Cuba stated that 'the invading horde [i.e. the American soldiers] staggers drunk through streets and parks, raising scandals and disorders [...] Major Bearss who is the Major Bacchus of this horde answers the protests of the papers by ordering the Governor of the City-Capital, to muzzle the press and menaces him with a personal punishment if he fails to carry into effect his orders' (López (1916)).

275 Garrido (1970), pp. 109–10.
276 Marvin (1917).

Figure 2.19 Marine corps instructors train the *Guardia Nacional Dominicana.*

afterwards maintained very good connections with the American military governors, who even visited him on his *hacienda*, El Mijo.[277]

Bearss was followed by various American officers, most of them with the rank of captain, who were successively in charge of a Dominican military force: the *Guardia Nacional Dominicana* (GND), after 1921 called the *Policía Nacional Dominicana* (PND). Those Dominicans who entered the ranks of the GND became very unpopular with their compatriots. The Americans themselves were dissatisfied with the members of this force, complaining about the problems of recruiting apt members among the Dominicans: 'the recruiting was carried on ... apparently more with a desire for numbers than for quality.'[278] To be a member of the GND was considered a disgrace and it was reported that only very unscrupulous – or very poor – individuals were enticed by the promise of fifteen dollars per month and free room, board, clothing, and medical care.[279] The acronym PND, used after 1921, was quickly reinterpreted to mean *Pobres Negros Descalzos* [Poor Shoeless Negroes].[280]

The American reporter Harry Franck, who visited the Dominican Republic during the occupation, quotes a priest in El Seibo who stated that the GND 'included some of the worst rascals, thieves, and assassins in the

277 León (1972), p. 131.
278 A marine officer quoted in Calder (1984), p. 55.
279 Ibid., p. 56.
280 Interview with Mimicito Ramírez, San Juan de la Maguana, 14 December 1985.

country [...] and these often egged the naïve Americans on to vent their own private hates'.[281] The complaints against the 'lawlessness of the *Guardia*' were many and some acts committed by its members were despicable, but one also has to keep in mind that the marines themselves often used *Guardia* soldiers for unpopular tasks and sometimes even used them as scapegoats to cover up for guilty marines.[282] Like in the rest of the country, however, some members of the GND in San Juan de la Maguana were known to use their authority to harass the local population and extract favors and money under the threat of violence, a type of behavior that was facilitated by the fact that many of the men recruited to the GND came from other parts of the Dominican Republic.[283]

There is some confusion as to who was the leader of the operations against Olivorio that took place after Bearss' heavy onslaught on his group. The immediate successor of Major Bearss[284] was a Captain James, who made great efforts in securing information about Olivorio.[285] After the devastating battles of 7 and 8 April 1917, it appears as if Olivorio disbanded his large group, keeping some twenty armed men and women around him, while he constantly moved around in the Cordillera Central.[286]

The Americans lost track of Olivorio and his men for at least eight months, but in January 1918 Captain James suddenly received information that he was hiding on a hillock called El Colorao (Monte Colorado), not far from a little village called El Morro, behind high mountains four kilometers north of Sabana Mula. The place could be reached with extreme difficulties from the border town of Bánica by following the glen of a small creek, El Tocino:[287]

> The place is about two days March WNW from Joca which is eastward from Banica [sic]. He has about forty bad criminals with him all well armed, and has taken up a strong position in the mountains where he

281 Franck (1921), p. 235.
282 Calder (1984), p. 58.
283 Cf. Garrido Puello (n.d.), pp. 138–45, and *El Cable*, 24 June 1922.
284 Bearss was drafted to the European battlefields. He wrote various letters to Carmito Ramírez, both from Europe and the United States (interview with Mimicito Ramírez, San Juan de la Maguana, 14 December 1985).
285 Interview with Mimicito Ramírez, San Juan de la Maguana, 14 December 1985, who referred to him as 'Major Fields', but his name was probably William C. James. Garrido Puello (n.d.), p. 139, just calls him Capitán James, but he is mentioned as Captain Wm. C. James in Thorpe (1918d). It is of course also possible that Captain James and Major Fields were two different persons.
286 Garrido Puello (1963), pp. 41–2.
287 See US Army Map Service, sheet 5873 II, series E733, edition 2: Bánica, Dominican Republic.

has planted a crop of foodstuffs; every indication that he has settled there with intention of staying as long as possible.[288]

Position: On top of high steep mountain […] Condition: Ground around his camp cultivated with food crops. Extending from foot of mountain several fertile valleys inhabited by a few ignorant natives who probably furnish food to him.[289]

An armed expedition against the 'Old Man' was organized in strictest secrecy. On 15 January, the troops left San Juan. They consisted of one company of Dominican guards, under the command of a US marine captain, accompanied by eighteen marines under the command of two other US marine captains and a lieutenant colonel, George C. Thorpe.[290] The Americans did not trust any *Sanjuaneros* and strict orders were given to cover up the real purpose of the expedition:

I am telling people that we are going to map the country west of here. The Guardias will leave here on the Azua trail and then swing around to the Bánica trail. We will go out displaying sheets of paper (large ones that I am getting from the stores in town) etc. […] people here are extremely curious and hang around our quarters looking in the windows, and I have a surveyor's transit that I am working with to give the impression of surveying expedition. Of course it is hard to fool all the people all the time, but we may keep suspicions down. None of the Guardias or Marines know anything about an expedition, except the officers. […] If I have to wire I shall speak of the Old Man as 'Simpson' and of his followers as 'Simpson's men', and of our own people as 'map makers' and our expedition as 'map making expedition', furthermore I may use slang or obscure sentences, with confidence that you will discern the meaning. I don't like to use the code if possible to avoid it because it excites suspicion.[291]

However, all precautions were in vain. After much hardship the big expeditionary force finally reached Olivorio's camp,[292] only to find that it was

---

288 Thorpe (1918b).
289 Thorpe (1918c).
290 Thorpe (1918d).
291 Thorpe (1918b).
292 Olivorio and his followers had apparently lived in this secluded place for almost ten months. Close to a small creek within a dense forest, the *Olivoristas* had constructed two villages. They tended small fields, dispersed in the surroundings. With him Olivorio had approximately forty armed men and an unspecified number of women and children (Cassá (1993b), p. 5).

deserted. *El Maestro* had been warned in good time. The troops burned down Olivorio's hideout and after an exhausting week they returned to San Juan de la Maguana bringing with them three prisoners that they had picked up along their trail. One of them refused to tell his name, but had been caught 'stealing up on' the marine camp, carrying 'the usual Olivorio tokens and a bottle of "medicated" water from Olivorio'.[293] The other prisoner had been pointed out by an informer as an *Olivorista* and the third one was a man who in 1916 had murdered one woman and two children, and who was known to have been given a haven by Olivorio.[294]

Even if the expedition of Lieutenant Thorpe had been unsuccessful, Olivorio's band received a very hard blow a month later when Olivorio's 'commander-in-chief', Colén Cuevas was killed in Sabana Mula, by members of the PND.[295]

Olivorio once again disappeared for some time,[296] but by the end of 1918 he apparently was back in Naranjo Dulce, close to his home district, La Maguana. Here he was attacked by the marines and an associate of his, José de los Santos, was severely wounded and brought down to San Juan de la Maguana, where he later died of gangrene.[297] Olivorio had to return to his nomadic ways once more.

A small group of Dominicans from the GND, under the command of a Dominican officer from San Juan de la Maguana, Lieutenant Esteban Luna, were soon given a special assignment: to track Olivorio down.[298] In spite of being a member of the despised GND, Luna was respected by the *Sanjuaneros* and at times acted as a mediator between them and the Americans.[299]

The man who probably ordered this special mission was a certain Captain George H. Morse, Jr. Among both *Sanjuaneros* and *Olivoristas* Captain Morse became the symbol of American stupidity and oppression. People who remember him refer to him as a 'brute', a 'soldier fresh from the barracks', without 'manners',[300] who succeeded in intimidating the

293 Thorpe (1918a).
294 Ibid.
295 McLean (1919). Colén Cuevas was gunned down on 19 February 1918. The report mentioning his death states that Colén had been in Olivorio's service for seven years, that he was influential among rural dwellers and his reasons for joining Olivorio had mainly been 'political' (Cassá (1993b), p. 6).
296 The *Olivoristas* probably moved to places not so far from La Maguana (Cassá (1993b), p. 6).
297 Rodríguez Varona (1947).
298 Interview with Mayobanex Rodríguez, San Juan de la Maguana, 12 December 1985.
299 Ibid. and Garrido Puello (1973), p. 51.
300 Interview with Mayobanex Rodríguez, San Juan de la Maguana, 12 December 1985. Cf. Garrido (1970), p. 123, Garrido Puello (1977), p. 79 and (n.d.), p. 145. George H. Morse, Jr was in reality a lieutenant in the US marines, but served as a captain in the

Sanjuaneros in various ways. Popular legend ascribes all the subsequent fierce persecution of Olivorio to this man, even though various US officers were involved in the act. He is rumored to have initiated brutal actions against Olivorio's supporters, 'even if Olivorio did not bother anyone'.[301]

The coarse manners of American officers like Morse can easily be explained. Many of them bore particular personal grudges against Dominicans. Morse, for example, suffered from severe difficulties in expressing himself: 'even his English sounded as if it came from the harbors',[302] and the deep wound he had in the groin, given to him by a peasant in the east, did not make him any friendlier towards the *Sanjuaneros*.[303] But other factors influenced his behavior as well. When the United States entered World War I in Europe, the best men who were active in the Dominican Republic were drafted to the European battlefields and those left behind were disappointed and disgruntled because they had to serve in Santo Domingo instead of fighting in Germany.[304] Neither officers nor enlisted men knew much about Dominican culture and few of them could speak any Spanish.[305] Some lived isolated in small towns like San Juan de la Maguana, surrounded by uncooperative and often outright hostile Dominicans.[306]

Making matters worse, many marines were accustomed to patterns of white superiority in both the northern and the southern United States.[307] A sense of disdain for the 'colored races', often combined with the 'jingoistic nationalism prevalent in the early twentieth century United States',[308]

GND. The US military government gave temporary commisions as first lieutenants and captains to marine-enlisted men. In the GND, all ranks above lieutenant were reserved for Americans, something which meant that even corporals and privates gained a quick promotion if they entered the ranks of GND (Calder (1984), p. 56).

301 Interview with Mayobanex Rodríguez, San Juan de la Maguana, 12 December 1985.

302 Interview with Mimicito Ramírez, San Juan de la Maguana, 16 January 1986.

303 Ibid.

304 Fuller and Cosmas (1974), p. 31.

305 Calder (1984), p. 123.

306 Fuller and Cosmas (1974), pp. 31–2. San Juan was particularly inaccessible. Coming from the capital by land could take several days and the travel along the coast in leaking, small vessels was also uncomfortable. No American was happy to go there, or as Lieutenant Colonel Henry C. Davis wrote on a small paper slip attached to a telegram about a mission to San Juan de la Maguana: 'My dear Lake [Lieutenant][...] [the trip to San Juan] holds no charms or allurements for me, bo [sic], take it from me!' (Rines (1921)).

307 Calder (1984), p. 124.

308 Ibid., p. 123. 'Racial nativism' was in vogue in the United States at the time. Both among 'intellectuals' and within the 'popular stratum' of the population, racist ideas concerning Anglo-Saxon superiority were in full swing. The idea that the most 'civilized' persons of the United States belonged to the Anglo-Saxon 'race' had crystallized in the nineteenth century as a way of defining American nationality in a positive sense. By the turn of the century these ideas had been influenced by vulgar Darwinism and imperialistic endeavors that implemented notions about 'the white man's burden', etc., as well as a

was promoted by an American press that described the occupation of Santo Domingo as an 'Anglo-Saxon crusade', carried out in order to keep the Latin Americans 'harmless against the ultimate consequences of their own misbehavior'.[309] The racially mixed composition of the Dominican people was pointed to as a mixture that explained 'their abomination of work, their inability to learn, and their inferiority to Southern Negroes'. The Dominicans were even described as 'a horde of naked niggers'.[310]

The racial question is occasionally raised in the reports marine officers sent into headquarters, and often American morals are described as being entirely different from Dominican ones, such as in a report submitted by Lieutenant Colonel Thorpe, who sometimes led marine detachments in pursuit of Olivorio:

> No one in any of these groups [Dominican opposition groups] really cares for Americans because: (a) Every Dominican is conscious of the instinctive antagonism between white and colored races; (b) No white nationality has less sympathy with colored races than the American; i.e. the American goes farther than any other people in its race prejudice; (c) American manners are antithetical to Dominican at almost every point: where the former is frank the latter is adroit; where the latter is frank the former is reserved; where the Dominican is gentle the American is rough and where he is coarse we are fine. For example, about the practical affairs of life – business and governmental – the Dominican is instinctively sly whereas we are instinctively severely accurate, for with us a man's credit ordinarily is the keystone of his capital. It is difficult to find points of contact in typical Dominican tastes and manners. Sociologists and psychologists frequently observe that it is natural mental trait to distrust and dislike what is strange or foreign and that inclination for the exotic is unnatural and cultivated.[311]

Thorpe agreed with the paternalistic attitudes many Americans applied to 'less developed' areas of the world:

> As to the propriety of American occupation there is the same necessity to protect a whole population of helpless people against a few exploiters and criminals that there would be for you to [...] step between a villain and a helpless little girl about to be ravished.[312]

growing hostility towards certain immigrants and the rising demands of the black population. The result was that a large part of the national debate at the time reflected a rather distasteful racism (cf. Higham (1981)).
309 American press voices cited in Blassingame (1969), p. 29.
310 Ibid.
311 Thorpe (1918e).
312 Thorpe (1920), p. 85.

The Haitian connection

Around 1919, the American persecution of Olivorio and his men was intensified considerably. Lieutenant Luna and his Dominican soldiers in the GND were often joined in their hunt by well-equipped search parties consisting of American marines. This increased interest in Olivorio can probably be seen in connection with the events that simultaneously took place in neighboring Haiti.

One year before the Americans occupied the Dominican Republic, they had landed in Haiti. The background was more or less the same. For several decades, Haiti had been torn by a series of coups, uprisings and civil wars among cliques contending for political power. These cliques had not hesitated to mortgage the Haitian treasury abroad, taking a series of foreign loans on scandalous conditions – loans that were used for political purposes and not for strengthening the economy. During the same period, foreign investments, mainly American, but also, for example, French and German, had begun to be made in the country. In the political turmoil that mounted towards the end of the nineteenth century, and in particular during the one-and-a-half decades immediately preceding World War I, the foreign powers felt their interests being threatened. However, the trigger-ing event behind the occupation was the outbreak of the war and the appearance of German submarines in the Caribbean waters. In particular, the Americans had an interest in securing Môle Saint-Nicolas opposite Guantánamo in Cuba and the control of the Windward passage.[313]

By 1918, the Americans were involved in a fierce guerilla war in Haiti, trying to crush the so-called *caco* uprising led by Charlemagne Péralte. *Cacos* were bands of peasant mercenaries who had taken part in the fights for political power towards the end of the nineteenth century and the start of the twentieth. The name had been transferred to an uprising that began on 15 October 1918, when a hundred *cacos* under the command of Péralte attacked the town of Hinche. It was the second time he attacked that particular town. After the first attempt, made on 11 October 1917, he had been caught and condemned to five years of forced labor. On 3 September 1918, he escaped and succeeded in collecting a group of peasant fighters in order to begin a fierce struggle against the American invaders.[314]

The Americans had attempted to make use of an old law paragraph which allowed for forced labor in road works – a *corvée* law. Both the term

313 The intervention in Haiti is dealt with e.g. in Millspaugh (1931), Schmidt (1971), Castor (1971) and the still unfinished series by Gaillard (1984), (1988), (1992), (1993), (1995), (1973), (1981a), (1981b), (1982a), (1982b), (1983). For comparative aspects of the occu-pations of Haiti and the Dominican Republic, cf. also Munro (1964), (1974) and Perkins (1981).
314 Gaillard (1982b), p. 11. Cf. Heinl and Heinl (1978), p. 452.

Figure 2.20 Charlemagne Péralte.

– with connotations of the colonial slave gangs – and the circumstances under which the work was carried out were such as to make the Haitians resist. The uprising finally engaged some 40,000 insufficiently armed men who fought the occupation forces under the supreme command of Charlemagne Péralte, a member of the local *élite* of the town of Hinche. The uprising lasted for three years. Péralte was betrayed by one of his own officers and shot by an American marine in November 1919.[315] The date of the end of the uprising can be set to 19 May 1920 when Péralte's successor, Benoît Batraville, was killed by the marines.[316]

The *caco* uprising involved not only Haitians but to some extent Dominicans who took part as well. The Americans had put harsh penalties on the carrying of contraband across the Haitian-Dominican border. The citizens of both countries were often harassed by the occupation forces for transporting small quantities of Haitian rum or Dominican cigarettes.[317] This was perceived as meddling by outsiders with the traditional way of life. Before the occupation, the borderline had not had much practical importance for the people living on either side of it. 'Haiti and the Dominican Republic were the same thing in those days.'[318] Commerce had always been

315 For an account of Péralte's uprising, see Gaillard (1982b).
316 For Batraville's guerilla war, see Gaillard (1983).
317 Moral (1961), pp. 65–6.
318 Interview with Sarni Ramírez, Bánica, 2 June 1989. Sarni Ramírez enlisted in the Dominican border patrol in 1921. *Guardia de Aduanas y Fronteras*, the Dominican frontier guard which had been created by American customs authorities in 1905, was in February 1918, absorbed into the *Guardia Nacional* (McLean (1919)).

intense in the border areas. Most of those living there were bilingual, intermarriage was common and so were political liaisons. In times of political unrest, the vicinity of the border had often meant a strength for various groups engaged in political fights in their respective countries:

> It appears as if the proximity of the border that separates Haiti from the Dominican Republic has for a long time been the mainspring of political combinations used by the Haitian or Dominican revolutionaries to provoke attempts at insurrection against this or that established government in this or that country.[319]

During the various wars that the people of the San Juan Valley had waged on the central government in Santo Domingo they had counted on help from friends in Haiti, and vice versa. During the civil war of 1912, the insurgents under the command of Carmito Ramírez had obtained support from the Haitian generals Charles and Oreste Zamor, who gave Carmito's troops a haven within their districts. When the Zamor brothers later on, in 1914, took part in a tumultuous Haitian civil war, which ultimately led Oreste to a short and extremely chaotic presidency (8 February–29 October 1914), the Ramírezes returned the help.[320] Charlemagne Péralte, brother-in-law of Oreste Zamor,[321] was probably not unaware of the old ties that existed between the Haitian Zamor family and the Ramírezes in the valley.

Olivorio must have also had connections with Haiti. Wenceslao Ramírez owned vast grazing lands on both sides of the border.[322] Particularly the Guayabal *hato* close to Bánica extended far into Haitian territory. Olivorio is reported to have frequently worked there and his favorite female companion lived in Bánica. Accordingly, Olivorio was well acquainted with the area and American search parties often covered the Bánica district.[323]

Olivorio had, and still has, many of his most fervent followers in a village called Sabana Mula, sometimes referred to as 'the village of Olivorio'

319 Price-Mars (1953), p. 242.
320 Garrido Puello (1977), p. 26. The father of Garrido Puello served various years as Dominican consul in Haiti and Charles Zamor had been Haitian consul in Comendador (present-day Elías Piña), an important Dominican border town. Charles Zamor had a son with a woman in San Juan de la Maguana (ibid.). 'The Zamors often crossed the border and contracted a lot of Dominicans around here to help them with the fighting in Haiti' (interview with Sarni Ramírez, Bánica, 2 June 1989). For a relation of Oreste Zamor's time as president in Haiti, see Heinl and Heinl (1978), pp. 371–9.
321 Heinl and Heinl (1978), p. 451.
322 'Wenceslao was the owner of vast lands in Guayabal, Sabana Mula and Cercadillo on this side of the border. On the other side he owned land all the way up to Hinche, mostly grazing land, but also mahogany forests' (interview with Sarni Ramírez, Bánica, 2 June 1989).
323 Interview with Narciso Serrano, Bánica, 3 May 1986. Cf. Feeley (1919) and Vidal (1972) (written in 1925), pp. 101 and 107.

and he often camped outside it. The most famous *Olivorista* in Sabana Mula was Nicolás 'Colén' Cuevas, a man who sometimes was pointed to as the 'real leader' of Olivorio's band.[324] Halfway between Sabana Mula and the Haitian border is a place called Rincón Grande where Domingo Contreras was an influential landowner. Domingo was a follower of Olivorio and the head of the Contreras clan which dominated many villages along the border,[325] particularly the area around Guayajayuco, further to the north.

When the Americans sealed off the border to control the movement of goods between Haiti and the Dominican Republic, the smugglers frequently made use of the narrow paths that crossed the border in the vicinity of Bánica. The Dominican center of this illegal trade was the secluded village of Guayajayuco, situated some 25 kilometers north of Bánica. The village was surrounded by fertile land and excellent pastures but it was accessible only through a narrow and inconvenient path, difficult to negotiate. In 1925, an estimated 80 percent of its inhabitants were of Haitian origin, although most of them were born in the Dominican Republic.[326] When a search party of thirty-five GND soldiers commanded by Major Feeley tried to capture Olivorio they concentrated their efforts to the area around Guayajayuco and Río Joca.[327]

Further to the northeast, behind huge mountains, lies the village of Río Limpio, also mainly populated by Haitians at the time. People wanting to cross the border or get information about the situation on the other side often sought the assistance of the inhabitants of these two villages.[328] There, the traditions about Olivorio and his men remain strong. It is thus quite probable that he lived in the area for long periods and that he upheld close contacts with Haiti.[329]

---

324 McLean (1919). Colén Cuevas was paternal grandfather of the *Mellizos* who were to revive Olivorio's cult in Palma Sola in 1961 (interview with Sarni Ramírez, Bánica, 2 June 1989).
325 Interview with Sarni Ramírez, Bánica, 2 June 1989. Rincón Grande is situated 5 kilometers from Bánica. Two Contreras, Ambrosio and Heraldo, appear in a list of Olivorio's followers made up by the Americans (Feeley (1919)).
326 *El Cable*, 7 March 1925. An inspector of public schools at the time, José Aristy, gave the following description of Guayajayuco in a report that was submitted to the authorities in 1919: '[It is situated] in a very fertile, but under-cultivated, little valley which offers a splendid view and is sparsely populated [...] The elevated part, situated to the northwest of this section is said, and its aspect confirms it, to be of an extraordinary exuberance. It is inhabited, almost completely, by Haitians who exploit their lands for their own benefit, selling the fruits from their cultivations in their own country without being subjected to any kind of taxation, this according to one piece of information' (Aristy (1919), p. 393). Guayajayuco is still an important marketplace, frequented by both Haitians and Dominicans (Ducoudray h. (1980)).
327 Feeley (1919).
328 Arzeno Rodríguez (1980), pp. 182–3.
329 Interview with Marcelina Ovando, Río Limpio, 1 May 1986. In the census carried out by José Aristy in 1919, in order to find out the number of children of school age living in

If one checks maps of the Cordillera Central and look for the place names mentioned in the different American reports which were submitted by various search parties, it becomes clear that Olivorio moved in a particular way. Apparently he followed the valleys of various mountain streams. From La Maguana he could follow the stream of the San Juan River, and its tributary Los Gajitos, until he came to the mountain tributaries to Río Artibonito (which passes close to Río Limpio and Guayajayuco), Río Tocino (which passes El Morro, El Hoyo and Bánica), Río Joca (which runs close to Nalga del Maco, Monte Colorao, Los Cercadillos and Las Cuevas), or Río Yacahueque (which runs by Sabana Mula and Carrera de Yeguas). Many of Olivorio's strongholds were situated close to the sources of these rivers, high up in the heartland of Cordillera Central.[330]

On the other side of the border Charlemagne Péralte and his troops also moved around in a similar manner, engaged in constant skirmishes with various search parties and maintaining intimate connections with Dominicans. He had a Dominican mistress who was well versed in magical arts, whom he had met when he was making his trips over the border in search of provisions. Furthermore, one of his most important followers was his spiritual adviser, Pèdre.[331] This man was called his disciple *panyòl*, to indicate that he spoke Spanish, i.e. that he came from the Dominican Republic. Pèdre reputedly knew about the future and was able to distinguish between God's will and chance.[332] As we know, Olivorio also predicted the future. Furthermore, when Péralte was killed, among his belongings was found a prayer in Spanish, 'to the Great Power of God', printed in Higüey.[333] This prayer, which exists in various versions, is one of the most common among the *Olivoristas* who claim that Olivorio was in possession of this power. The Great Power of God is seen as a divine force that comes forth either in places like springs and caves or in humans like Olivorio.[334]

Guayajayuco, it appears that the majority of the families living there were named Contreras (Aristy (1919), p. 405). This is reminiscent of the fact that Olivorio's favorite consort was named Matilde Contreras and was said to have her home in Bánica. Guayajayuco is a section of the commune of Bánica. Arquímedes Valdez (interview, Maguana Abajo, 31 May 1989) denies that his father ever went into Haiti, and so does Sarni Ramírez (interview, Bánica, 2 June 1989) from the Dominican border guards: 'He often passed along the border with his *recuas*. I never heard that he crossed it, though the youngsters of his band frequently did so.'
330 Cf. US Army Map Service, sheets 5873 I, II, III and IV, 5973, I, II, III and IV. The report of Major Feeley is particularly revealing since he apparently used the same trails as Olivorio (Feeley (1919)).
331 Gaillard (1982b), pp. 331 and 291.
332 Ibid. p. 291.
333 Ibid., pp. 292–3.
334 For example, when asked who Olivorio really was, one interviewee stated that 'he is the name of the rosary', i.e. he is a denomination of the divine (interview with Julián Ramos, Higüerito, 16 January 1986). Another interviewee, who had been accused of saying that

During the first half of 1919, various American reports from Haiti mention two Dominican leaders, Tabo and Gregorio, fighting US troops side by side with Péralte, Tabo with fifty men under his command, and Gregorio with 700. Gregorio's men received ammunition from Las Matas de Farfán.[335] Quite probably, 'Gregorio' is simply a mis-spelling of Olivorio, or Liborio.[336] Various facts appear to indicate this. In the first place, no guerilla leader named 'Gregorio' is known to have existed on the Dominican side of the border.[337] Second, 'Gregorio's' lines of supply led straight into Olivorio's territory. He had many followers in Las Matas de Farfán.[338]

In April 1919, 800 Haitian *cacos* had been cornered just south of the Dominican border town of Comendador (Elías Piña). They were apparently operating on both sides of the border and the US marines on the Haitian side of the frontier asked permission from their headquarters in Santo Domingo to cross into Dominican territory in order to get them.[339]

Already in January 1918, Major Joseph Feeley, in a summary of the activities of the Ninth Company of the *Guardia Nacional Dominicana* during December 1918, reported that he had received reports from Haiti that

he himself was the new Olivorio, explained that he felt the presence of the Great Power of God in himself, just like it had manifested itself in Olivorio. In that way he could be said to be identical with *El Maestro*, since both of them had been struck by the same divine power (interview with Enrique Figueroa, Hato Nuevo, 18 January 1986).

335 Gaillard (1982b), pp. 177–80.

336 It is possible that the marines in Haiti mixed up Olivorio's name with that of Gregorio Urbano Gilbert, who for a long time was the most wanted 'criminal' in the Dominican Republic. In January 1917, while shouting: '*Viva la República Dominicana*' the seventeen-year-old Gregorio had shot and killed an American marine in San Pedro de Macorís. After that deed, he was hunted all over the country until he was caught in Monte Cristi on 2 February 1918. He was sentenced to life imprisonment, but was released in 1924. He later joined Sandino, fighting the marines in Nicaragua.

While in prison Gregorio was impressed by a man who had been arrested as an Olivorio supporter. In his autobiography Gregorio pays homage to Olivorio as a hero 'who through his political-bellicose-religious activities is the most interesting man the municipality of San Juan de la Maguana has produced; he is the most influential, the most admired and venerated Dominican who has ever come from the people of the central and western districts [of the Dominican Republic]. In spite of the very high natural barriers created by the Cordillera Central [...] his power reaches many inhabitants in the Southwestern Cibao' (Urbano Gilbert (1975), p. 148).

337 This is clear from the interviews we have made in the area. None of our interviewees knew of any 'Gregorio'. It could be argued that the large number of people reported to have been with 'Gregorio' – no less than 700 – could indicate that 'Gregorio' and Olivorio are not identical. However, Gaillard (1982b), p. 180, reports that 'Gregorio' in June 1919 had three Haitian generals under his command. Thus, the majority of the 700 could easily have been Haitians. Olivorio himself, six months before, was stated to have some 125 men in his force (cf. the quotation below).

338 Cano y Fortuna (n.d.), pp. 158–9.

339 Catlin (1919).

groups of bandits which have been operating in Haiti during the last two months, being hard pressed for provisions and supplies, intended to enter the Dominican Republic to secure some, also that 'Olivorio' was becoming active again: that he was reported in the mountains close to Joca and had about 125 followers, and in all probability was connected with the movement in Haiti.[340]

In *Primitive Rebels*, Eric Hobsbawm discusses the size of the units usually led by 'social bandits'. His main finding is that social bandit groups tend to be very small, as large groups pose problems both in terms of economic support and in terms of leadership: 'One may guess that a band of thirty [...] represents about the limit which can be dominated by an average leader without organization and discipline such as few brigand chieftains were capable of maintaining, larger units leading to secessions.'[341]

Bands of up to sixty people must be considered 'extremely large' and they cannot be sustained without special means of support. Olivorio is reported to have had no less than 125 men which may indicate that he was involved in guerilla warfare at the time: 'In periods of revolution, when bands become virtual guerilla units, even larger groups of some hundreds' may be formed.[342]

The reports of Olivorio's activities made the Americans launch a special investigation. For more than two weeks they tried to track him down in the area where he had last been seen. However, they had immense difficulties getting information from the local inhabitants. Many were imprisoned on charges of 'vagrancy' or 'protecting criminals'. Detachments searched the houses of families known to be *Olivoristas*, but all in vain. Native guides who were forced to lead the troops to Olivorio's hideouts obviously exposed themselves in such a way that lookouts were able to spot them in time, so that the band was able to escape before the arrival of its pursuers. They also saw signs of other kinds of 'trickery': 'On the night we arrived at El Morro a big fire was built on top of the highest mountain just to the eastward and another fire on top of mountain far to westward [sic] that intervened between El Morro and Olivorio's mountain. This was probably a signal of our approach.'[343]

The Americans were convinced that they were cheated by their unwilling scouts, since time and again they found deserted camp sites, sometimes with the ashes still warm from the camp fires. Cattle and provisions that were suspected to be intended for Olivorio and his men were seized, and deserted huts and fields that were presumed to have been occupied by

340 Feeley (1919).
341 Hobsbawm (1959), pp. 18–19.
342 Ibid., p. 18.
343 Thorpe (1918a).

Figure 2.21 Marines searching a house for weapons, 1916.

Olivoristas were destroyed and burned down.[344] The cult site in Maguana Arriba was completely destroyed.[345]

> The Guardia [GND] entered [Yacahueque] with the blancos [whites]. They came mounted on mules which they let loose to graze in the planted fields. They killed the animals of those living there, including the pregnant cows. They ate only the yearling calves and threw away the rest of the beef. The whites did not burn down the houses. They did not take the men prisoners, since these had all fled up into the mountains. They [the US marines] never saw them. [...] No man stayed behind in Yacahueque. The whites destroyed Yacahueque. This attack they launched because they knew Liborio was there, and because a guard [a member of the GND] had been killed there.[346]
>
> People did not like the Americans, they were not known [to people]. When they came to Yacahueque it was to kill the animals. They did that several times while they were searching for Liborio. Always abusive, doing bad things. The men ran away, but the women stayed behind in the houses. [...] They [the US marines] caused a lot of damage, but never raped women.[347]

344 Feeley (1919).
345 Interview with Julián Ramos, Higüerito, 18 January 1986.
346 Interview with Pimpina Luciano by Roberto Cassá, Mao, 22 January 1995.
347 Ibid.

Exactly a year after these extensive operations, on 5 January 1920, a certain Lieutenant Lassiter finally came upon Olivorio and his men at Yacahueque, north of Las Matas de Farfán. A kind of celebration was apparently in progress and many people had assembled. Lassiter was accompanied only by three men, and the *Olivoristas* 'numbered over 50'. Nevertheless, the unequal numbers did not prevent Lassiter and his men from firing into the crowd, killing three 'bandits' and wounding several others, but when one of Lassiter's men became severely wounded, the party was 'forced to retire'.[348]

Late in July 1920, a marine detachment went into a place located north of Sabana Mula where one of Olivorio's camps had been discovered. 'Every precaution' was used to get in before being discovered but when the place was finally reached, the band had 'apparently been gone about twenty minutes'.[349] Later the same year a US marine captain named Robertson moved around in the 'country sections [...] north of San Juan', trying to secure information with the help of a Puerto Rican interpreter. This trip was interpreted by the 'natives' around San Juan as an unsuccessful American effort to secure the surrender of Olivorio.[350] Even if small patrols continued to chase him, this operation was the last 'officially sanctioned' effort to catch Olivorio for more than a year. He and his band moved around in his mountainous 'territory' that stretched along the Cordillera Central, from Bánica by the Haitian border, to the town of Constanza,[351] situated in a fertile valley, northeast of San Juan de la Maguana. Sometimes he probably went further to the north, crossed the Cordillera and reached the vast plain of La Vega,[352] where he had many followers, or crossed the border into Haiti.[353]

---

348 Bales (1920) and Breckenridge (1920).
349 Bales (1920).
350 McLean (1921). A letter from Robertson to Olivorio was found among the belongings of a member of his band who was shot in 1922 (Morse (1922a)).
351 Bales (1920).
352 Ibid. Two of the *Olivoristas* that were killed together with Olivorio in the final battle of 27 June 1922, came from La Vega (*El Cable*, 1 July 1922). Mimicito Ramírez remembered the 'slender and beautiful *Cibaeñas*' he saw in Olivorio's camp when he was young (interview with Mimicito Ramírez, San Juan de la Maguana, 14 December 1985). El Cibao is the name of the fertile agricultural district northeast of the Cordillera Central.
353 Garrido Puello (1963), p. 63, claims that Olivorio was never outside 'the northern part of the Municipio of San Juan de La Maguana', but this claim is made to refute reports that Olivorio had been seen in Higüey in the easternmost part of the country (cf. Alfau Durán (1940)). He never deals with the question of whether Olivorio may have crossed the border into Haiti, a far simpler venture. However, in the discussion of Olivorio's death, Garrido Puello states that Olivorio was caught at the moment when he and his followers were about to leave their hideout, 'presumably to go into the mountains of Haiti or of Manabao, on the other side of the Cordillera' (Garrido Puello (1963), p. 43).

Even after the death of Péralte in 1919, the close contacts between Dominicans and the Haitian *cacos* continued. American troops constantly patrolled the border on both sides, dedicating themselves to the task of sealing off the 'Dominican sanctuary' for the *cacos*. The Haitians received money, ammunition, provisions and guns from the Dominican *rayanos* [border dwellers] in exchange for meat and hides.[354] Patrols of marines sometimes came across camps on the Dominican side of the border, where both Haitian *cacos* and Dominican 'bandits' were caught.[355]

On the run

The report of Major Feeley sheds some light on the kind of life Olivorio and his men led during the years of persecution. When not involved in guerilla activities, they were by and large able to feed themselves without much aid from the outside, even if it is reported that peasant women occasionally carried provisions to them.[356] In 1940, Mimicito Ramírez guided one British and two American scientists in the mountain areas close to the Haitian border. There, traces of a series of *conucos* were found, extending towards the Haitian border. At that time, the fields were deserted, but local traditions told that they had originally been cleared by Olivorio and his followers.[357] American reports also mentioned that small plots with various crops used to be found around deserted *Olivorista* hideouts: 'The trail from Olivorio's camp showed fresh tracks. All the plants around his camp were stripped of food and no buds had had time to develop, showing that the crop had just been gathered thoroughly.'[358]

The Feeley report describes how a Lieutenant Williams together with a detachment of the GND found one of Olivorio's camps. The place lay secluded in a small plain in the mountains,

> completely surrounded by high hills [...] he found 8 deserted *bohíos* [huts], a large shed with benches fixed to the wall for sleeping, and a dance hall or meeting place. Musical instruments (native) and other paraphernalia were scattered around. There were several conucos [fields] close by; a stream of water ran from one of the hills and disappeared into the ground a few yards below the camp [...] The camp was located in the underbrush and its roofs ran close [to the] ground. It was invisible at 50 yards.[359]

354 Gaillard (1983), pp. 124–5.
355 Ibid., p. 123.
356 Feeley (1919).
357 Interview with Mimicito Ramírez, San Juan de la Maguana, 14 December 1985.
358 Thorpe (1918a).
359 Feeley (1919).

One year earlier the marines had come across another of Olivorio's hide-outs. Great efforts had been made in order to hide this place as well:

> His place was never permitted camp fires (as they might reveal posi-tion); fires allowed only inside huts and barracks; all the timber had been dragged to the edge of the clearing (at expense of great effort) to avoid making smoke incidental to burning it. The building consisted of two separate huts and one long barrack with one side of roof running to the ground. A mountain spring or brook ran along one edge of camp. The whole mountain is dense forest and as seen from southern approach, the locality [sic] of Olivorio's camp is [on] a saddle and in hazy shadow.[360]

An American report from December 1920 described how Olivorio 'with a small group' constantly moved around in the mountain range north of San Juan de la Maguana, as well as in other parts of the country.[361] Ameri-can reports from the second half of 1920 and most of 1921 dealing with Olivorio have a calmer tone than those issued before:

> He [Olivorio] is supposed to have about 8 men with him continually. Never carries arms of any kind and discourages fighting. He is a reli-gious fanatic whose main tenet seems to be free-love. His greatest offense is that he offers refuge to criminals. At present he is supposed to be in the mountains between Jarabacoa and Constanza, La Vega.[362]

> Olivorio, alias Dios Olivorio, operating in the province of Azua. (Not at present active.)[363]

> In the Southern District, a band of armed men were reported by the Sindico of La Victoria [...] as passing through that section on Novem-ber 11, 1921, where they committed minor depredations. The group led by Dios Olivorio (religious fanatic) in the province of Azua still remain quiescent [sic].[364]

Even if occasional search parties from the GND went after them, and the *Olivoristas* were sometimes forced to go into hiding among the mountains,

360 Thorpe (1918a).
361 Bales (1920). Bales mentions that Olivorio was known to visit the northern provinces of La Vega and Santiago, and popular legends tell about miracles he performed both there and in the southern province of Barahona.
362 Breckenridge (1920).
363 Maguire (1921).
364 McNamee (1921).

Olivorio and his followers were apparently able to stay for longer periods in Maguana Arriba, or in the two strongholds further north: El Palmar and El Naranjo.

Olivorio and urban residents

Olivorio obviously maintained close contacts with people living in San Juan de la Maguana and even the local police force, the *Policía Municipal*, aroused the Americans' suspicions. In 1921, the generally disliked Captain Morse stirred a lot of indignation among the *Sanjuaneros* when he ordered the disarmament of the entire *Policía Municipal*. He defended his move by stating that he had received information from his 'secret agents' that a kind of 'surprise was to be given to the PND', and that this expected action 'was connected with Liborio and Haiti and that it was going to be supported by the *Policía Municipal*'.[365]

Morse caused a similar stir during Lent in 1922 when he confiscated the holy and much venerated *palos* [big drums] of the *Cofradía del Espíritu Santo* in San Juan de la Maguana. This action was interpreted as an ugly provocation since the religious brotherhood only used the drums during Lent and when one of their members died. The leaders of the *cofradía* directed a letter to the US military governor in Santo Domingo, lamenting that the *palos* were kept by the guards 'just for fun'. The governor ordered the return of the drums, Morse obeyed but commented that the drums had been confiscated because dances accompanied by the *palos* were carried out 'next door to the cuartel' and that he thought that the celebrations could be seen in connection with information he had received that 'a group of Olivorio's people would be in town for the purpose of attacking the Policia [sic] Barracks'.[366]

Captain Morse's preoccupations about the imminent danger coming from Olivorio and his men were, however, not shared by all his colleagues. A document in the National Archives in Santo Domingo, written in 1921, gives Sergeant McLean's view of Olivorio. McLean considered him to be harmless and inoffensive after the marines had dealt him a 'crushing blow' a few years before. The sergeant reported that Olivorio and other leaders of his group 'were either killed or captured during [the] engagement and cleaning up' that followed the attack. According to McLean, Olivorio's band consisted of no more than fifteen to twenty-five 'depending upon [which] section he is hiding in', and they were never hostile. The remaining followers were 'mostly criminals who are fugitives from justice'.[367]

---

365 *El Cable*, 15 July 1921. In June 1921, the GND had been renamed *Policía Nacional Dominicana* (PND) (Moya Pons (1980), p. 478).

366 Morse (1922b).

Olivorio got nearly all his support from the peasants. In the eastern provinces of the Dominican Republic, other armed peasant groups, the so-called *gavilleros*, waged a desperate war against the US, and some could count on support from various Dominican intellectuals in the towns.[368] But Olivorio was considered to be far too odd a character to be of any use in the patriotic propaganda. A young urban patriot of those days recalls:

I remember that we had a newspaper called *La Pluma de la Juventud* [*The Quill of the Youth*], that was edited in the town of Santiago de los Caballeros and, in those days of patriotic ardor, any sign of rebellion was for us youngsters an object of praise and eulogies and the Yankis called this 'Dios Alivorio' [sic] *gavillero*, and we called him, and any other man who harassed them, patriot. In this newspaper we published a photograph of this agitator, although without comments for the time being, but in reality we thought he was a real patriot.[369]

367 McLean (1921). Another American marine, William Bales, in a report written a month before the one of McLean, states that he does 'not believe that the Común of San Juan is suffering from Livorio or his group' (Bales (1920)). McLean was apparently well informed about the activities of Olivorio. He was a good friend of the mayor of San Juan de la Maguana, Félix Valoy de los Santos Herrera, who in homage to his old friend McLean gave the same name as a nickname to a son who was born the same year as McLean left for Petit Trou (Enriquillo). Valoy de los Santos was also a very good friend of Olivorio and was in constant contact with him (interview with Jesús Antonio Mario Santos (Maclín), San Juan de la Maguana 19 January 1986). McLean went to Petit Trou, situated south of Barahona, in order to supervise a plantation for an American friend of his. He stayed there until his own death in 1925.

James McLean always tried to belittle the importance the marines used to attach to Olivorio's alleged contacts with the Haitian insurgents on the other side of border. In a book about the frontier that he wrote in 1921, McLean states: 'An insignificant group of Dominicans who are better termed as robbers or *gavilleros*, in parties of two or three, altogether some thirty marauders, left secretly from various places along the border to enter Haiti and take advantage of the situation created by the revolutionaries. The acts committed by these malefactors made the Haitian government exaggerate the issue and formulate severe accusations against the Dominicans, creating suspicions that they [the Dominicans] are the accomplices of the Haitian revolutionaries' (McLean and Pina Chevalier (1921), p. 174).

368 The resistance shown by urban intellectuals to the American intervention was mostly a war of words, which was waged in the press, books and letters, from the lecture platforms and in the theaters (Calder (1984), p. 13). It was the peasants in the eastern regions who stood for the greater part of the armed resistance. They had taken to arms for various reasons, both personal and political. Many of them were desperate after losing their land to big sugar companies. (On the reasons for the *gavillero* uprising, see Calder (1984), pp. 115–32, Baud (1988a) and Ducoudray h. (1976).) Many of these *gavilleros* fervently opposed the label of 'bandits' which the marines had foisted on them and insisted on the ideological nature of their struggle (Baud (1988a), cf. Calder (1984), pp. 121–2). They were supported by a large part of the Dominican press and some intellectuals even joined forces with them (Calder (1984), pp. 19–20).

369 Cruz Díaz (1965), p. 151.

Apparently the young patriots changed their minds when they were reached by rumors that Olivorio was a faith healer who occupied himself with 'amorous games with his unhappy sect members'.[370] '*Olivorio era un dios aparte.*' Olivorio was a god apart, and people did not like him because of that.[371]

Olivorio's status as an outsider from the point of view of established society is apparent in a few articles that appeared in the newspaper of San Juan de la Maguana, *El Cable*, in June and July 1922. The paper reports that a band of thugs from the PND, among them the notorious Vence and Colorado, who have been immortalized as peasant torturers in *salves* that are still sung by *Olivoristas*, came to La Maguana, extorted money, sacked houses, assaulted some peasants, and even tied two of them to a tree and raped their women in front of them. A group of the maltreated people from La Maguana came down to San Juan in order to report the occurrences to the police. A reporter from *El Cable* met them, and the next day an indignant article appeared in the paper.[372] The owner of *El Cable*, Emigdio Garrido Puello, later stated that he had to report to Captain Williams, the local commander of the PND, who threatened him by saying: 'You have slandered the Police. If you do not deny the published lies, I will communicate to the policemen maltreated by you that they may reclaim their injuries in any way they wish.'[373]

Garrido Puello returned to his office, loaded his revolver, put it in a drawer of his desk and waited for the worst to happen. Dominican members of the PND tried to intervene in the conflict. Garrido Puello obviously listened to them and finally surrendered to the demands of Captain Williams.[374] A week later an 'Explanation of the Accusations against the P.N.D.' appeared in *El Cable*. In this article it was stated that Captain Williams had explained to the director of *El Cable* that the complaining 'individuals' had been working for Olivorio's cause, and that they had been accused of procuring provisions for Olivorio.[375] An assertion that the victims of the police violence were *Olivoristas* apparently served as an excuse for the brutal behavior of the thugs. Nothing else was mentioned about the incident.[376]

---

370 Ibid.
371 Interview with Julián Ramos, Higüerito, 16 January 1986.
372 *El Cable*, 24 June 1922.
373 Garrido Puello (1973), p. 50.
374 The angered Garrido Puello called the marine officer a 'troglodyte', while the latter's fellow Americans apparently held another opinion about his character: 'He [Captain Williams] was a quiet, efficient little officer who did not drink' (Burke (1935), p. 173).
375 *El Cable*, 1 July 1922.
376 In a book about his newspaper that Garrido Puello published in 1954, this particular incident plays an important part. However, he fails to mention that the victims were *Olivoristas*. He depicts himself as a man who did not yield in front of the oppressor (Garrido

The death of Olivorio

When the 'explanation' appeared in *El Cable*, Olivorio was already dead. He had been shot at a place called Arroyo Diablo [Devil's Creek] on 27 June 1922.

In May, the persecution of Olivorio had been intensified while units of the US marines and the PND went into villages known to be *Olivorista* strongholds, trying to extract information from their inhabitants. People tended to be extremely unwilling to disclose anything about the whereabouts of *El Maestro* and his men:

> There was an old mayor in Yacahueque, Mimín de la Rosa, who once stayed behind [when the troops entered the village], believing that they were not going to do anything against him. The whites tied up his arms and hanged him from a dry pine tree. They began shooting at him, aiming into the air, in order to frighten him. The women cried out: 'Ay! They are killing Mimín. They are killing Mimín!' After a while they took him down. The old man answered their questions by saying: 'I am telling you that I do not know where this Liborio is. It is better that you kill me. What do I know about this damned Liborio?' They could not get anything out of him and he returned to Liborio, bringing coffee with him.[377]

On 19 May, forces from the PND had made a surprise attack on Olivorio and his followers near La Loma de la Cotorra. What took place was a cold-blooded massacre. It was Morse himself who organized the attack and he wrote a lengthy report about it. Captain Morse, three marines and Lieutenant Luna, together with twenty enlisted men from the GND, left San Juan de la Maguana after sunset on 17 May, and protected by the night they passed through La Maguana, where they succeeded in capturing a certain Pedro del Carmen, who was bringing foodstuffs to Olivorio's camp and at gunpoint they forced him to show the way to *El Maestro*'s hideout: 'To describe the trail is beyond my powers. Darkness, steep ascents and descents, vines to climb the faces of waterfalls, thru gardens, over ledges and treachous [sic] cliffs.'[378]

When they finally reached Olivorio's camp, at 5.20 a.m., they found that it was unprotected. Four people were awake, three men and a girl, who did

Puello (1973), pp. 49–52), a version that probably is not wholly in agreement with the truth. However, we do not want to imply that Garrido Puello was not a brave man. On the contrary, *El Cable* was fervently opposed to Trujillo's machinations and was subsequently closed down by the dictator. Garrido Puello maintained his anti-*Trujillista* position during most of the long dictatorship of *El Jefe* [the Boss].

377 Interview with Pimpina Luciano by Roberto Cassá, Mao, 22 January 1995.
378 Morse (1922a).

not notice the assailants until they opened fire. Lieutenant Luna, with ten men, rushed down to the camp, while Morse, with the remaining force, opened fire on the defenseless people: 'the surprise was so complete that the people scrambled from their shacks, climbing in all directions to get out of our range which was about 100 to 150 feet, leaving their arms, ammunition, and clothing.'[379]

The indiscriminate fire went straight through the shacks. The attack

> resulted in the death of twenty-two members of his band, including twelve men, eight women and two small children. The women and the children were killed in their beds due to the concentrated fire into the shacks. [...] The number of men and women wounded is not known, however the sides of the mountain were covered with bloody trails, indicating that a large number of the band was wounded.[380]

No remorse was felt for the bloody deed. Instead the 'sub-human status' of the victims was stressed:

> Needless to say, the camp of Olivorio cannot be compared even with a pig-pen. In searching the shacks, large quantities of food stuffs were found, many empty bottles, showing that a large amount of the Haitian rum smuggled across the border reached Olivorio's camp. All kinds of letters and papers were found, the contents of which would disgust anyone. They show that Olivorio and his band are of the lowest order of human beings and that debauchery and prostitution were the only modes of living. People from all over the republic either visited his camp or received instructions how to cure ailments, which was paid for by rum, tobacco, foodstuffs and money. There are no letters to show that Olivorio was or is in any way connected or in communications with any of the former revolutionary leaders on the island.[381]

Olivorio lost several of his closest collaborators, among them his 'musician', Benjamín Gómez, whom Morse described as 'the real leader and chief of the Olivorio band'.[382] Morse had concentrated his fire to Olivorio's shack and he had seen him flee into the mountains, assisted by two of his sons, Eleuterio[383] and Cecilio. *El Maestro*'s bunk, which consisted of two

379 Ibid.
380 Ibid.
381 Ibid.
382 Ibid. Apparently, Olivorio's 'favorite wife', Matilde Contreras, was among the victims of the massacre (cf. Conrado Mateo, quoted by Cassá (1994b)).
383 Arquímedes Valdez calls him 'Lauterio'. The marine report of the final encounter with Olivorio calls him 'Elauterio'. It is probable that his proper name was Eleuterio, which is more common in the Spanish-speaking world.

white sheep skins, was found covered with blood. Since Olivorio was assumed to be wounded, Morse and his men hunted him for several days, but had to give up in the end. They had however taken some prisoners, among them Enerio Romero, Olivorio's nephew, who together with his brother Lalín subsequently would lead the Americans to Olivorio. Lalín had been in the camp with Olivorio but escaped his pursuers twice. The second time was a few days after the assault when he was attacked together with another important man of Olivorio's group, Rafael Perdomo Díaz. Díaz was shot to death, but Lalín was able to run away.[384]

Enerio Romero finally succeeded in bringing Lieutenant Luna and Sergeant Dotel in contact with his brother, 'the former *Alcalde Pedáneo* [justice of the peace] of the section of La Maguana [...] This person for over five years has been the go-between for anyone wishing to see Olivorio.'[385] It was these two brothers who were paid by the police[386] and during the night between 26 and 27 May finally guided Captain Williams, Lieutenant Luna and twelve enlisted men along the narrow mountain trails to *El Maestro*'s last hideout close to a deep gorge called Arroyo Diablo. The troops attacked at dawn, when Olivorio and twelve of his followers celebrated their morning rituals, with their rucksacks packed, about to leave for the vicinity of Constanza, further into the Cordillera. In the crossfire most of his men fled, but Olivorio, one of his sons, Eleuterio, and two other men fought until they were killed. Olivorio's first and third fingers were shot from his right hand and he was hit fifteen times before he fell.[387]

384 Ibid. Garrido Puello (1963), pp. 42–3, also mentions the attack briefly, stating that the victims were '23 women'.
385 Morse (1922a).
386 Garrido Puello (1963), p. 43. Cf. Rodríguez Varona (1947). One has to keep in mind that the two Dominican officers of the PND – Lieutenant Esteban Luna and Sergeant Félix Dotel – both came from the area where Olivorio's influence was the strongest. Both had relatives and friends among the *Olivoristas*, and were not considered to be such brutes as Colorado and Vencé. Dotel even had two brothers in the ranks of Olivorio. One of these, Feliciano Romero y Dotel, died in the ambush of 19 May (*El Cable*, 20 May 1922). Accordingly neither Dotel nor Luna were fervent anti-*Olivoristas*. They saw themselves obliged to persecute Olivorio due to their commitment to their superiors, and it is possible that the chase after Olivorio took so long time due to these two officers' reluctance to catch him (interview with Telma Odeida Matos, Santo Domingo, 2 November 1985). The case of Lalín Romero may have been different: 'Lalín was able to kill anyone for a penny [*chele*]' (interview with Arquímedes Valdez, Maguana Abajo, 31 May 1989). Enerio Romero's name figured together with those of the PND members who were accused of robbing and raping peasants in La Maguana during the prosecutions that occurred in connection with Olivorio's death (*El Cable*, 24 June 1922).
387 Williams (1922). Arroyo Diablo is situated high up in the Cordillera, not far from Pico Duarte (called La Pelona in the times of Olivorio), the highest mountain in the Dominican Republic. This place is one of the stopovers along the trail to the town of Constanza and the plains of La Vega and the Cibao.

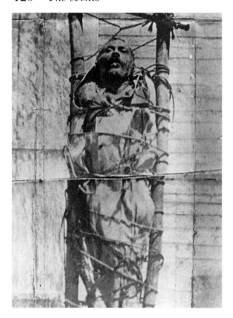

Figure 2.22 The corpse of Olivorio while exposed in the central square of San Juan de la Maguana. The photo was taken by Julián Suazo, 28 June 1922.

The corpse of Olivorio was tied to a *parihuela* [litter] and was brought down to San Juan de la Maguana.[388]

The patrol arrived in San Juan de la Maguana at noon the next day.[389] The litter, with the corpse still tied to it, was placed under a huge tree in front of the *Comandancia de Armas*, the PND headquarters, on one side of the main square. The litter leaned against the trunk of the tree and people say it looked as if Olivorio had been crucified. The schools closed, the school children and their teachers joined the crowd of peasants and towns-folk that formed a half-circle around the dead Olivorio. The photographer, Julián Suazo, was fetched from his studio by the Americans and put his huge camera in front of the corpse taking various photographs.[390] The

388 *El Cable*, 1 July 1922 and *Listín Diario*, 29 June 1922, reported the death of Olivorio. *Listín Diario*, issued in Santo Domingo, quoted parts of Captain Williams' report. That the newspaper was able to do that was probably due to the fact that its offices were placed on the first floor of a building that housed the American consulate on the second one (Vega (1981), plate 35). Furthermore, *Listín Diario* was on good terms with the Americans since it had deserted the nationalist camp in 1922 and from that moment came out in support of the different actions of the Americans (Calder (1984), p. 227).

389 *Listín Diario*, 1 July 1922.

390 To get the right light for the photograph the corpse was put against the wall of the *Comandancia*.

dead Olivorio was placed under the tree until the sun set, the flies were crawling all over him. The Americans and the members of the PND kept out of the way, staying close to their office. The spectators were quiet and composed. In the evening Olivorio was finally buried at the cemetery in San Juan de la Maguana.[391] *El Cable* wrote: 'With the death of Olivorio we consider his coarse religion to be finished forever. It constituted a disgrace for this municipality, particularly since the majority of his disciples were alien elements.'[392]

The heritage of Olivorio

Some of Olivorio's 'apostles' took up his fallen banner. They continued to spread the message of *El Maestro* and practiced his healing methods. Many of them were persecuted by the authorities, but still, *Olivorismo* survived. A fatal blow appeared to have been delivered when Olivorio's most important successor, José Popa, was murdered in Guayabal in 1930.[393] Shortly after that incident, two other famous Olivoristas, Domingo Valeria and Manuel Ventura, were killed in an exchange of shots in Los Copeyes.[394] Behind the killings was a certain 'Popoyo' Hernández, a thug in the service of Trujillo,[395] who was at that time about to start a thirty-year period as unmatched sovereign of the Dominican Republic. *El Jefe* 'did not like any competition and under his reign you could not even light a candle in honor of Olivorio'.[396]

But *Olivorismo* was aglow in the shadow of the dictator and after Trujillo's death in 1961 the old beliefs were revived by a group of brothers who were nephews to Manuel Ventura. They founded the cultic center of Palma Sola, which was finally ruthlessly eradicated by governmental troops on 28 December 1962. Once more the *Olivoristas* were forced into hiding, but

391 Interviews with Mimicito Ramírez, San Juan de La Maguana, 14 December 1985, Julián Ramos, Higüerito, 16 January 1986 and Maximiliano Rodríguez Piña, Santo Domingo, 23 April 1986.
392 *El Cable*, 1 July 1922.
393 Guayabal is situated a few miles east of the town of Padre las Casas. There exist several places with the name 'Guayabal' (literally meaning 'a place with *guayabos* [guava trees]').
394 We have not yet been able to identify this place. Since *copey*, just like *guayabo*, is the name of a tree, there exist many places that include the word *copeyes* in their names.
395 Interviews with Mimicito Ramírez, San Juan de la Maguana, 11 April 1986 and León Romilio Ventura, Media Luna, 5 May 1986. León Romilio stated that the name of Trujillo's henchman was José Solís.
396 Interview with Julián Ramos, Higüerito, 16 January 1986. *El Jefe* [the Boss] was the popular epithet given to Trujillo. His megalomania has become legendary even outside the borders of the Dominican Republic. The capital and the highest mountain peak were renamed after him and he has succeeded in getting an entry in the *Guinness Book of World Records* as the man who had most statues erected in his honor during his own lifetime (McWhirter (1985) p. 481). On Trujillo's megalomania, see Galíndez (1962), pp. 181–4.

soon the *salves* were heard again in remote corners of the Cordillera Central and *Olivoristas* are still to be found all over the southwestern part of the Dominican Republic. They are not organized and their beliefs and convictions differ from village to village. They all know about other *Olivorista* groups, but they do not consider that their specific beliefs belong to a particular sect or religion. For most of them *Olivorismo* is the same as 'true' Catholicism, wholly in line with the teachings of the church. All *Olivoristas* preserve the memory of *El Maestro* and maintain that his soul is present in this world, but they deplore the fact that this presence is not acknowledged by everyone:

Son muchos los convidados	Many are the invited
y pocos los escogidos.	and few are the chosen.
Somos pocos los que llegan	We are few who come
a los pies del Rey Olivó.[397]	to the feet of King Olivó.

---

397 *Salve* recorded in Maguana en Medio, 16 January 1986.

3 Interlude

The survival of *Olivorismo*, 1922–61

El Cable proved to be wrong. Olivorio was dead, but his religion was not. During the weeks that followed Olivorio's death, the newspaper reported that Cecilio Mateo, one of the most influential leaders of the *Olivorista* group, had turned himself in to the forces of the PND in San Juan de la Maguana,[1] and an American report written in July 1922 states that firearms were being collected from former members of Olivorio's group.[2] Most townsfolk presumably thought that the movement had been stamped out, but in the mountains surrounding San Juan de la Maguana some of Olivorio's old followers were gathering strength. They did not consider themselves beaten because their leader had been killed. The mountains began to reverberate with legends about the miraculous life and death of Olivorio. His *salves* were heard, and new ones were sung in his honor:

Dicen que Olivorio es muerto.	They say that Olivorio is dead.
Olivorio no es muerto ná.	Olivorio is not dead at all.
Lo que pasa es que Olivorio	What happens is that Olivorio
Nunca comió pendejá.[3]	Never took any shit.

Olivorio had drawn his power from *El Gran Poder de Dios*, which was inherent in the very soil of the San Juan Valley, and a force like that could not be annihilated. It was soon to show up again in other religious leaders who came forth to continue where Olivorio had left off.

---

1 *El Cable*, 1 July 1922. Cecilio was probably Olivorio's son (see Chapter 2). Many of Olivorio's relatives also became his followers. His brother Carlitos, who was the head of the Mateo clan, became an important *Olivorista* leader after Olivorio's death. Also, as noted in Chapter 2, one of Olivorio's sons, Eleuterio, was killed with his father in Arroyo Diablo and his first wife, Eusebia Valdez, 'always accepted his mission' (interview with Arquímedes Valdez, Maguana Abajo, 31 May 1989).

2 Williams (1922).

3 Different versions of this song are known in the southwestern parts of the Dominican Republic. A modern interpretation recorded by Luis 'Terror' Días became a national hit in 1984 (*Liborio*, Pareja Records, pr. 2297, Santo Domingo).

The occupation and the San Juan elite: resistance and collaboration

In the meantime, life continued in the San Juan Valley. Within three months after the death of Olivorio, the marines would leave San Juan de la Maguana. The occupation would enter a period of Dominicanization and, on 12 July 1924, Horacio Vásquez was sworn into office as constitutional president of the Dominican Republic.[4]

The impact of the occupation had been strong. *El Cable* constantly complained about the behavior of the marines in the San Juan Valley. Its editor, Emigdio Garrido Puello, like most other leading *Sanjuaneros*, was known to be a fervent patriot. When the leaders of the Dominican 'intellectual' resistance movement against the American occupation arrived in San Juan de la Maguana in December 1921, they were enthusiastically received by the 'prominent' citizens of the town. Patriotic speeches were delivered in the Teatro Anacaona and in the evening a sumptuous feast and ball were offered them in the house of Alberto Gómez, one of the most influential businessmen in the town. The notorious Captain Morse tried to interfere in the celebrations 'treating the present persons like a herd of cattle', but he was effectively silenced by the anger of the old *caudillo* Wenceslao Ramírez.[5]

In spite of all this patriotic fervor, however, a large number of *Sanjuaneros* secretly approved of many of the results of the occupation:

> What the people suffered from was the disorder, the lawlessness. We got fed up with it. Here were many bandits, but all that changed with the Americans. They forced people to work, to clean up the streets and paint their houses. They did not like when people gathered in order to sit and talk, or just play a game of dominoes. The Americans were obsessed with activity. Oh, how those *gringos* beat up people! But it was only the troublemakers who got beaten. Common people, more or less, accepted their presence. They liked the order they brought about.[6]

4 Calder (1984), p. 237.
5 Garrido Puello (1977), pp. 78–9. Cf. Garrido (1970), pp. 122–3. One of the visitors was Dr Francisco Henríquez y Carvajal, who had been elected provisional president by the Dominican Congress immediately after the arrival of the US troops. Humiliated, unrecognized and overpowered by the occupants, he left the country in December 1916 and began to direct a fierce campaign against the invasion both in Cuba and in the United States. He even presented his views at the peace conference in Versailles. Also with him in San Juan de la Maguana were the Republic's foremost novelist, Tulio Cestero, and one of its most famous poets, Fabio Fiallo, who had spent various terms in prison for his protests against the US military presence. Among other things, Fiallo had referred to the United States as 'this cruel civilization which came to us through the back door with fixed bayonets in a dark night of deceit, surprise and cowardice' (Knight (1928), p. 115).
6 Interview with Manuel Emilio Mesa, San Juan de la Maguana, 20 January 1989.

Most town dwellers benefited from the presence of the Americans. The American troops left a healthier town behind them. All latrines were inspected by them and people were forced to throw creolin over the feces in order to take away the smell. The backyards also had to be cleaned up and disinfected; almost everyone had animals in those days: hens, pigs, horses and even cows. The American officers were very demanding in everything that had to do with hygiene. They were probably afraid of epidemics. Smallpox came to the valley with Haitian workers who were brought into the Republic in order to work on the roadworks and in the new *ingenio* in Barahona. Everyone had to be vaccinated. I have been told that most American officers were decent people. They used to be invited to our feasts. They wanted everything to look nice and tidy and forced people to paint their houses.[7]

Even the Ramírezes, who sometimes expressed open disdain in front of the occupants, frequently offered their services to them, presumably as a matter of practical politics. Carmito served as their guide and interpreter at various times, he drew maps for them and was employed as land surveyor within the national land surveying program that the US military government initiated. He was also on friendly terms with some of their officers.

Wenceslao Ramírez knew and corresponded with the US military governors and they appear to have appreciated him, like Rear Admiral Harry S. Knapp, who wrote about him:

> a man of considerable prominence in the San Juan province, who has at one time or another been of great assistance to the Military Government, and who is, I think, sincere in his attitude. He is not an educated man, but is a man of great force of character and I think his influence is large and good at the present time.[8]

The governors always visited Wenceslao Ramírez if they passed through the valley and the Ramírezes returned these visits when they came to the capital. The successor of Knapp, Rear Admiral Thomas Snowden, wrote to Wenceslao after such a visit: 'It has been very pleasant to have had you here with me and I always appreciate your opinions about public affairs, because they are the children of your long experience and your knowledge of the country.'[9]

Another influential member of the San Juan elite who was on friendly terms with the Americans was Domingo Rodríguez, San Juan's wealthiest

---

7 Interview with Carlos Peguero Matos, San Juan de la Maguana, 4 July 1990.
8 Knapp (1918).
9 Snowden (1919).

Figure 3.1 Interior of the store of Domingo Rodríguez, San Juan de la Maguana.

businessman and a representative of the 'progressive' forces in the valley. He owned 2,120 hectares devoted to cattle-breeding and the cultivation of rice and beans. His agricultural lands were all artificially irrigated, since he, together with the Ramírez family, was the first one who constructed irrigation canals in the valley. He also introduced electricity to San Juan de la Maguana when he installed a generator by a small stream in order to generate power to his store and ice factory. He was an agent for various banks and insurance agencies. His store was large and well equipped with imported goods, such as hardware, china and textiles. It was an important meeting place for the *Sanjuaneros* and many went there to have a drink and a chat. He also ran a small hotel, where foreigners would stay when they came to San Juan. James McLean, who was in charge of the constabulary force which protected the US-controlled custom houses along the border, took up his living quarters there after 1907 and, as we mentioned in Chapter 2, later married a sister of Domingo Rodríguez. As brother-in-law to McLean, Rodríguez was put in charge of all disbursements to the customs personnel along the border.[10] Mr Stout, another American active within the US-Dominican custom system, also married a sister of Rodríguez.[11]

When representatives for the US military government came to San Juan de la Maguana, they stayed with the Rodríguezes and Don Domingo used to present the needs and worries of the *Sanjuaneros* to them, something

10 Interview with Maximiliano Rodríguez Piña, Santo Domingo, 23 April 1986. Cf. *Libro azul de Santo Domingo* (1920), p. 106.
11 Interview with Sarni Ramírez, Bánica, 2 June 1989.

which is evident from his correspondence with various American governors, as in a letter to Rear Admiral Snowden:

> Your visit to these regions left a pleasant impression in the hearts of their most prominent inhabitants and they are all convinced of your good intentions for the well-being and progress of this country, which needs so much, and it is only to be lamented that the confusion of the world economy, which also affects this country, impedes the opening up of the sources of wealth and does not permit the Government to do all that it, without doubt, wishes to do within the different branches of the Public Administration.
>
> I am one of those convinced of the good intentions you nourish for this country, and because of that I wish you the utmost success in your governmental endeavors.[12]

The *Yanquis* and the *Olivoristas*

In his memoirs Víctor Garrido writes that the *Yanquis* in the San Juan Valley

> did not drag anyone from a horse's tail as in Hato Mayor, nor did they put red-hot irons on the body of any man, as they did with Cayo Báez in Salcedo […] but I saw how they forced men, appreciated for their nice qualities and social position, like José Alfonso Lagranje and Abigail Díaz, to sweep the streets and carry cans with water on their heads […] for the simple reason of having a shotgun in their house …[13]

Had Garrido chosen to include the *Olivoristas* in the San Juan community, the list of sufferings could easily have been made longer. In May and June 1922 many of Olivorio's followers were made to witness how their fields and homes were burned down, their belongings stolen and their women raped during the ruthless campaign the marines initiated just a few months before they left the valley. At least twenty-seven *Olivoristas* were killed in cold blood – among them eight women and two children. An unknown number of them were seriously wounded.[14]

This fierce persecution obviously took place with the tacit approval of the majority of the San Juan elite, who in their dealings with the occupation authorities appeared eager to disassociate themselves from the *Olivoristas*.

12 Rodríguez (1920).
13 Garrido (1970), p. 109.
14 Morse (1922a) and Williams (1922).

As expressed in a letter from Wenceslao Ramírez to Rear Admiral Snowden, 'the inhabitants, with the exception of Olivorio and his party, are always prepared to accomplish the orders of the legal authority'.[15] For many of the 'progressive minded' people of San Juan de la Maguana and Las Matas de Farfán the *Olivorista* community constituted an anomalous remnant of backward times – one which preserved the worst aspects of the 'traditional' way of life, such as the maintenance of age-old contacts with the poor and despised Haitian peasants, the drinking of *kleren* [a cheap white rum] and the preservation of old 'superstitions'.

As a matter of fact, it was members of the San Juan elite, who, from the beginning of 1917, repeatedly urged the American occupants to do something about Olivorio. At the beginning of the occupation, the marines hoped that the 'native lieutenant' of the *Guardia Republicana* in San Juan would 'handle the situation', but as his calls for reinforcements became more and more 'frantic', the US military governor took the decision to send Colonel Bearss to San Juan at the head of a detachment of marines to deal with the *Olivoristas*, thereby complying with the repeated requests of San Juan petitioners.[16] After that at least one US officer always remained in charge of the local troops in San Juan de la Maguana.

This attitude on the part of the San Juan elite, reflected for example in Garrido Puello's editorials in *El Cable*, has its mirror image in the attitude of Olivorio's followers. The *Olivoristas* of today see their predecessors as the only true patriots during the occupation. 'My father was the only Dominican man who dared to take up arms against the Americans', states Arquímedes Valdez.[17] Even though most *Sanjuaneros* prided themselves for having assumed an upright and uncompromising position vis-à-vis the American occupants, often having supported the Dominican opposition against the occupation, as we have already seen, this position by no means excluded collaboration with the occupation forces. No member of the elite ever raised arms against the marines and the American persecution of the *Olivoristas* definitely gives the impression of having the full approval of the majority of the 'progressive' forces in the valley.

Departure of the Americans and return of the *caudillos*

On 20 October 1922, a little less than four months after the death of Olivorio, the *Sanjuaneros* could witness how the last US marine, Captain Charles F. Williams, left their town in an airplane, which came to bring him to

---

15 Ramírez (1921). Of course Ramírez' caution may also have been a result of earlier problems his family had had with the US occupation forces.
16 Chief of Staff (1917).
17 Interview with Arquímedes Valdez, Maguana Abajo, 31 May 1989.

Santo Domingo. In the morning he had formally handed over the command of the local PND forces to the Dominican lieutenant Juan Esteban Luna, and given Emigdio Garrido Puello a 'treaty of evacuation', to be published in the local newspaper.[18] A week before this event all other US marine officers stationed in the southern district of the Dominican Republic had been replaced by Dominicans who had graduated from the military academy in Santo Domingo, and on the following day, 21 October, Garrido Puello, relieved by the fact that he would have no further disputes with the resigning captain, wrote in his editorial in *El Cable* that he rejoiced now when the *Sanjuaneros* were at last 'free from Yankees and the arrogance of these exotic officers'.[19]

Garrido Puello's feelings were not unique. The vast majority of Dominicans felt that the American withdrawal was long overdue. Resistance had been mounting on several levels and by 1922 it was clear to the US State Department that the occupation could not continue.

In the eastern part of the country the marines had been fighting a guerilla war since the beginning of 1917.[20] This war had been only partially successful. The outbreak of hostilities during the first six months of that year was followed by what, to the Americans, appeared as a return to pacific conditions, as the major guerilla leaders, notably Vincentico and Tolete, surrendered. In 1918, however, the situation once more exploded and at the beginning of 1919 the number of marines stationed in the eastern provinces had to be trebled:

> fighting this irregular war was extremely frustrating. The guerillas seemed to know every marine move, despite elaborate and tiring efforts to deceive them with feints and night or secret movements, while the marines' information was almost always outdated or inaccurate. Most people refused to confide in the marines [...] because they feared the guerrillas or sympathized with them. Moreover, the nature of the countryside made operations both dangerous and unproductive. Flank protection was impossible and concealment was easy, so ambushes were common.[21]

The marines who had been stationed in the east since the beginning of 1917 were replaced by a three times larger but completely inexperienced unit. 'Years of accumulated field experience were lost.'[22] The war

18 Garrido Puello (1973), pp. 51–2.
19 *El Cable*, 21 October 1922.
20 See Calder (1984), Chapters 5–7, for details.
21 Ibid., p. 153.
22 Ibid.

continued and developed into a stalemate until 1921, when the guerillas again increased their activity. Marine efforts to 'cordon off' large areas to arrest people suspected of having relations with the insurgents failed to produce the desired results, and, in the spring of 1922, marine tactics changed again. By then the marine corps had finally realized that the *gavillero* guerillas were not 'bandits', but political opponents of the American occupation of the Dominican Republic. This made the Americans grant amnesty to the guerillas who surrendered voluntarily, on much more generous terms, including suspended sentences, than at any time hitherto. To increase the appeal of this offer, paramilitary, basically Dominican, 'civil guard' anti-guerilla units consisting of people experienced both in guerilla warfare and the local area were employed to track the *gavilleros* down. This combination of carrot and stick turned out to be effective, and by May 1922 organized guerilla warfare had come to an end.

The occupation forces had to face a more pacific, but equally effective, form of resistance as well.[23] From the very first moment Dominican nationalists had launched a campaign against the foreign intrusion – a campaign that had continued thereafter. The first two years, 1916–18, had not been very successful. Dominican opinion with respect to the occupation was divided and as the United States entered World War I in 1917, the Dominican issue tended to be forgotten by the world. Once the war was over, however, it was easier for the Dominicans to make their voice heard and present the legal and moral case against the occupation, not only in the United States, but in Europe and Latin America as well. Protests started to pour into the State Department regarding censorship and treatment of Dominican citizens.

Towards the end of 1919 the protest movement, although still divided, had been considerably strengthened, partly due to the effort already made, but also as a result of military governor Snowden's publicly made remark that the occupation ought to continue for a generation. The following year, the nationalist movement was radicalized by the founding of the *Unión Nacional Dominicana*, led by Fabio Fiallo and fellow writer Américo Lugo. This union, which demanded the immediate reestablishment of national sovereignty and condemned all collaboration with the US military government, quickly developed into the most important protest organization in the country.

The increase in vocal opposition eventually resulted in the arrest of more than twenty publishers and intellectuals, including Fiallo and Lugo. The initial sentences were hard, in Fiallo's case five years of hard labor, and eloquently indicated that American justice in the Dominican Republic was of questionable quality. These sentences were eventually overturned by the

---

23 Ibid., Chapter 8.

Figure 3.2 Fabio Fiallo in prison clothes, 1920.

Department of the Navy and, more importantly, paved the way for what amounted to a *de facto* abolition of censorship.[24]

The protests were also brought into US politics via the American press and labor movement (American Federation of Labor), and, once the 1920 presidential elections were over, the new president, former Republican senator Warren G. Harding, reversed the Caribbean policy of the Wilson administration.

The door had finally been opened for American withdrawal, which, however, saw a couple of false starts before the so-called Hughes-Peynado Agreement could be signed in 1922.[25] Both the 1920 Wilson Plan and the 1921 Harding Plan were rejected by the Dominican nationalists because the scheduled withdrawal in both cases was not unconditional enough. It would take the first half of 1922 and the private diplomacy of lawyer and former cabinet minister Francisco Peynado to set the terms, very different from the *Unión Nacional Dominicana* formula of a withdrawal *pura y simple*.

The Hughes-Peynado Agreement was signed in Washington, DC, on 30 June 1922.[26] Among other things, it included the setting up of a provisional

24 Both Fiallo and Lugo were honest men who later attempted to avoid getting involved with Trujillo, who, needless to say, crushed both of them. See Ornes (1958), pp. 187–8.
25 See Calder (1984), Chapters 8–9.
26 The agreement was negotiated by leaders of various Dominican political parties: Federico Velázquez for the *Partido Progresista*, Horacio Vásquez for the *Partido Nacional* and Elías Brache for the *Partido Liberal*. Francisco Peynado, the originator of the whole process, was considered to be apolitical, but he later ran for president as leader of a party mostly constituted by followers of the then recently deceased *caudillo* Jimenes. The church was represented by the Catholic archbishop, Adolfo Nouel (Knight (1928), p. 124, Welles (1928), 853–65, cf. Mejía (1976), pp. 181–8).

Dominican government. The Dominican signatories of the accord chose the sugar tycoon Juan Bautista Vicini Burgos as provisional president. The Vicini Burgos government was installed in the cathedral of Santo Domingo on 21 October 1922, and the date for free Dominican elections and concomitant American complete withdrawal was set for March 1924.[27] By the beginning of September 1922 the military government had begun concentrating the marines in a few specific locations, such as Santo Domingo, Puerto Plata, Santiago and San Pedro de Macorís, leaving it to the local PND forces to 'keep the peace' in the the rest of the country. This was a preparation for the final withdrawal, but it was also a part of a program intended to create more 'harmonious relations' with the Dominican population.[28] The Americans did not want to leave any sore feelings behind, which could preclude them from further interference in Dominican politics, at a time when they were finally going to leave the Dominicans 'on their own'.

The fierce Dominican agitation against the occupation gradually subsided: it was being superseded by the traditional, internal, political battles between various *caudillos*. The factions that had fought bloody civil wars before the US intervention were activated once more. One of the old *caudillos*, Juan Isidro Jimenes, had died in 1919 and the only remaining strong man on a national level who still lingered on was Jimenes' eternal adversary, Horacio Vásquez. Vásquez' main opponent in the upcoming elections was Jacinto Peynado, the Dominican architect of the American withdrawal plan. Peynado was respected and popular, but lacked the charisma and attraction of a 'real' Dominican *caudillo*. People still preferred the personal attachment to a strong man who could offer them personal benefits, and thus Vásquez won over many former adversaries to his cause by promising them support and various kinds of treats. He traveled around the country seeking out other *caudillos* who were able to whip up support for the experienced old arch-*caudillo*. Under the circumstances the existence or non-existence of any specific political program was of secondary importance.

At this time the most influential leader of the San Juan Valley was Carmito Ramírez, who, however, was highly unwilling to get involved in politics once more. During the occupation he had spent several months in jail due to the crucial part he had played in the revolutions prior to the

---

27 Calder (1984), pp. 231–2. Vicini Burgos had no political experience whatsoever. He was a wealthy businessman, known for his administrative abilities, and he had a solid background in economics. The *caudillos* who chose him felt secure that such a man would be an excellent leader of a transitional government and that he would not nourish any ambitions of prolonging his political power (Welles (1928), pp. 874–5 and Mejía (1976), p. 189).

28 Calder (1984), pp. 230–1.

Figure 3.3 General Horacio Vásquez Lajara, president 1899, 1902–3, 1924–30.

coming of the marines, and he was more inclined to go on with his work as land surveyor, busying himself with the 'modernization' of agriculture in the valley. It took the persuasion of his father, the aging Wenceslao Ramírez, to convince him that if he did not act then, the San Juan Valley would soon end up as a backwater of the 'New Republic'. If the old *Partido Legalista* of Carmito and Luis Felipe Vidal were not resurrected and united with Horacio Vásquez' *Partido Nacional,* the *caudillos* of the San Juan Valley would be rendered powerless under the new regime. Carmito gave in, sought out his old party companions, started negotiations with Vásquez, and the *Legalista* and *Nacional* parties were finally merged into a new political entity called *Coalición Patriótica de Ciudadanos.*[29]

Carmito and the people of the new party traveled back and forth across the vast territory of the province of Azua drumming up support for Vásquez in the forthcoming elections,[30] and the *Horacistas* won an over-

29 Garrido (1970), pp. 127–34. The *Legalista* party was originally an offspring of Vásquez' party and most people still considered the *Legalistas* to come from the same mold as the *Horacistas.* The *Legalista* party was not the only political entity that merged with the *Horacista* fraction. The party of the old political fox Federico Velázquez also joined forces with Vásquez. Velázquez had served under several Dominican presidents and knew how to land on his feet. He was known to be fervently pro-American and had been a keen supporter of the American interference in Dominican politics even before the final takeover in 1916 (Martínez (1971), pp. 514–18). With the support of the *Legalistas* and the *Velazquistas* Vásquez turned out to be invincible.
30 Garrido (1970), p. 134.

whelming victory on 15 March 1924.[31] For the Ramírez fraction, however, the joy at the election results soon turned into bitter disappointment. Víctor Garrido relates how Carmito came back on horseback to San Juan de la Maguana after negotiations with Vásquez in the capital. He stopped in front of Garrido's porch:

> All is lost. I have not even been able to negotiate a single post of importance for any of you in Azua, because all have been given to old Horacistas. It has been insinuated to Don Horacio that I wouldn't be able to occupy a position in the Government since I am not acceptable to the Americans, and it is a miracle that I am not in prison.[32]

Emigdio Garrido Puello lamented that Vásquez, who came from Moca in the Cibao Valley, did not take any advice from *Sanjuaneros* and only favored people from his own district, 'putting his confidence and faith in men who did not deserve it, just because they were flatterers and courtiers'.[33] Still, a few governmental posts were given to people close to the Ramírezes. The position of senator for the province of Azua went to Dr Alejandro Cabral, who was a *Sanjuanero* and a close friend of the Ramírez family, though the Ramírezes had expected Carmito to have that post.[34] Víctor Garrido was appointed to the influential position as secretary of the land tribunal and thus initiated a long and successful political career.[35]

The San Juan Valley under President Vásquez: 'The principality of the Ramírezes'

The government of Horacio Vásquez (1924–30) was in many ways an ideal one for the *caudillos* of the San Juan Valley. The local political leaders, notably the powerful Ramírez clan, had always been favorably inclined towards the *Horacista* party. At the same time, they had been careful to maintain their independence. This state of affairs was reflected in the representation of the *Sanjuaneros* within the Vásquez government. This representation was not strong. Nevertheless, in return, the president *dejaba hacer y dejaba pasar* [allowed people to do things and let things happen].[36]

---

31 Campillo Pérez (1986), pp. 172–5. In the province of Azua, 9,374 out of 13,942 inscribed voters voted for Vásquez and 3,291 abstained from voting (ibid., pp. 466–8).
32 Garrido (1970), p. 136.
33 Garrido Puello (1977), pp. 115–16.
34 Garrido (1970), p. 134.
35 Ibid. p. 137. Víctor Garrido (1886–1972) held various administrative posts under Vásquez. Under Trujillo he held various portfolios. He was also Secretary of State and served as ambassador to Brazil.
36 Peguero and de los Santos (1983), p. 320.

Figure 3.4 Carmito Ramírez in the 1930s.

The leading men of the valley were given a free hand in local affairs by the central government.

During the Vásquez era, Carmito Ramírez became the most influential member of his family. As such, he commanded great respect among the *Sanjuaneros* – respect which, judging from the flowery language of contemporary newspaper articles, often came close to idolizing:

> This illustrious Sanjuanero, one of the most prestigious and solid men to be found in the South, is a pleasant character, appreciated for the nobility of his soul, for the unselfishness and impartiality of his political activities, always carried out with the good of the Mother Country as their luminous goal, for his intensive culture and for his frank spirit, open to all manifestations of good and his chivalrous generosity, and accordingly a favorable motive power for redeeming initiatives. He is Bachelor of Science and Arts, Public Surveyor and was Commanding General: [the battlefields of] Sombrero, San Juan and Boca Canasta all proclaim the magnanimity of his soul and his courage, like that of a new Bayard. His sound strategic judgements always gave him victory in thousands of battles, and, a rare thing in our vicious environment, he never executed or showed any disrespect towards other citizens, and he never abandoned his honorable convictions [etc.].[37]

37 *Renacimiento*, 15 September 1915.

This was written in 1915, and during and after the American occupation Carmito's influence was to increase even further. The Americans soon realized the importance of the Ramírez family. The first contacts were hostile. Presumably under the influence of advice given by enemies of the Ramírezes, Carmito was imprisoned and the Americans attempted to curb the influence of the family in the valley. Their views were reflected in a contemporary article in an American magazine:

> Up in that country lived – still live, for all I know – some compelling and romantic personalities, too. At San Juan de Azua [sic], four days' hard riding from Santo Domingo city, the Ramírez family were the law and the prophets within a radius of fifty agriculturally productive miles south, east, and west. At the head of this local paternal government, which by several years anticipated our own, old 'General' Wenzeslao [sic] Ramírez laid down the law and did most of the prophesying; Octavio, Juan de Dios, Carmito, and Juan Bautista Ramírez, his sons, and his son-in-law, 'Doctor' Cabral, carried out his ukases and harvested the tribute. About 287 animated rifles and plenty of smuggled ammunition added punch to their league to enforce peace.
>
> In the San Juan Valley there was a lot of independence, but it was of the Ramírez brand.[38]

Yet, as we found in Chapter 2, with time, the Americans changed their views. The Ramírez clan emerged from the US occupation as powerful as ever and continued to control what the American journalist had labeled 'the principality of the Ramírezes', i.e. the San Juan Valley and the borderland between Comendador [Elías Piña] and Bánica.

An impressive manifestation of the admiration some of the leading *Sanjuaneros* felt for the Ramírez family was when Carmito, in 1928, returned to the valley after medical treatment in Cuba. The inhabitants of the towns of Comendador, Las Matas de Farfán, San Juan de la Maguana and Azua erected triumphal arches in honor of their *caudillo*, who returned as a victorious emperor, accompanied by a huge mounted escort and thousands of people who followed him all the way from Comendador to Azua, where he embarked for the capital. In every town sumptuous banquets were held in his honor, complete with laudatory speeches and poems, cannon salutes, dances and champagne toasts. *El Cable* dedicated four of its issues to detailed descriptions of the festivities and reproductions of the most important speeches and poems.[39] This was the pinnacle of Carmito's career and many *Sanjuaneros* nurtured hopes that he would run for the presidency of the Republic:

38 Marvin (1917), p. 213.
39 *El Cable*, 6 June, 10 June, 14 June, and 18 June 1928. Cf. Garrido Puello (1977), pp. 94–8.

an event whose significance was decisive for the aspirations of the South and the success of the aspirations of its thinking men: to present General Ramírez as a national figure of high relief, as someone with prominence within the political panorama. [...] General Ramírez was not only the banner of the South, but the hope for all those who believed in a great and prosperous Fatherland.[40]

For most members of the Ramírez clan, the 1920s stood out as good times:

The Vásquez regime was corrupt, but there was no oppression and he respected free speech. My father and other influential persons were free to carry out much work for the common good. My relatives held various important posts in the valley and were also rather influential in the politics of the Republic.[41]

It was one of the best governments this country has had. We have to judge it taking into consideration the epoch in which it existed and the resources which were available.[42]

However, dark clouds had started to gather and soon political fragmentation, chaos and violence struck the valley once more. The Ramírez' hope of bringing Carmito into the presidential saddle vanished. In the words of Emigdio Garrido Puello, Carmito had represented

a political force that the blows of destiny shattered when it could have been useful to the grandeur of the Fatherland. The disastrous events of 1930 swamped this prestige and also the political liberty that the country enjoyed, creating the abominable and corrupt tyranny of Trujillo.[43]

The survival of the cult

The *Olivorista* movement survived the Vásquez years, but not without difficulties. The year 1923 began with a terrible drought in the San Juan Valley. The situation worsened, to the point where, finally, 'the fields, yellowish and languid', bore testimony 'about ruin and misery'.[44] In such circumstances, the Dominican peasants often get together and, through

40 Garrido Puello (1977), p. 98.
41 Interview with Mimicito Ramírez, San Juan de la Maguana, 11 April 1986.
42 Garrido Puello (1977), p. 121.
43 Ibid., p. 56.
44 *El Cable*, 13 February and 3 March 1923.

communal religious rituals, attempt to obtain help from the heavenly powers. In the San Juan Valley, groups of peasants thus marched through the barren lands in long files, preceded by crosses and wooden statues of saints, chanting rosaries and beating their chests as acts of penitence.[45] Some groups marched all the way to Higüey, in the easternmost part of the country, in order to attend to the feast in the temple of *Nuestra Señora de la Altagracia*, the patroness of the Dominican Republic.[46]

One of these groups was led by José Popa, an old friend and disciple of Olivorio, who had been with *El Maestro* just before the latter was killed.[47] As a sign of his status as Olivorio's successor José Popa carried *El Maestro's* cross-hilted sword and a scar on one of his legs. The scar, which had the appearance of a 'Chinese character', was said to be identical with one that Olivorio also had.[48]

With five companions, José Popa had made the Virgin a solemn vow to visit some of the most holy places of the *Olivoristas* on their way back. First they went to the cave of San Francisco close to the border town of Bánica,[49] and after paying their respects to the saints at that place they continued to La Agüita, the spring close to Olivorio's birthplace. Their arrival caused great commotion among the surviving *Olivoristas*.

Soon a huge crowd gathered around José Popa and his men and a rumor spread that they heralded the immediate arrival of *El Maestro*. As a result the *Policía Nacional* were informed by some troubled citizens, and, by means of a surprise attack on the *Olivoristas* by the spring who at the

---

45 In Dominican popular religion the word *rosario* not only denotes the recitation of the Catholic prayers of the rosary but also the big processions that are occasionally staged, especially during the dry season between December and May. The rites are often very elaborate. Cf. Valverde (1975).

46 The feast of *Nuestra Señora de la Altagracia* takes place on 21 January and huge crowds of pilgrims still gather every year in Higüey in order to pay the Virgin their homage.

47 Morse (1922a). Morse writes his name as 'Jose Paupa'. José Popa was a smallholder from Bartolo, a small village in the Cordillera Central, situated northeast of Sabaneta. Popa had met Olivorio just before the latter's mission was coming to an end (Cassá (1994b)).

48 Cassá (1994b).

49 The Cerro de San Francisco is a huge cave close to the top of a hill, just outside the town of Bánica. It is reached after a one-hour climb. It is very spacious and the ceiling of its main chamber is around 20 meters high with small holes which let in sunlight, thereby providing impressive illumination. Peasants often refer to the cave as a 'cathedral'. Crosses, altars and traces of sacrificed chickens are found inside the cave. A fraternity, the *Cofradía de San Francisco*, conducts ceremonies there on 1–4 October in order to honor San Francisco (personal visit to Cerro de San Francisco, 2 June 1989). It is a common belief among *Olivoristas* that the Cerro de San Francisco is connected with Seboruco through a secret passage that runs several miles under the ground. Seboruco is a cave situated close to the dam of Sabana Alta not far from San Juan de la Maguana. *Olivoristas* conduct rituals there in honor of the *Virgen de Altagracia* on 21 January (interview with Leopoldo Figuereo, San Juan de la Maguana, 4 June 1989).

moment were 'engaged in their prayers', the police succeeded in capturing forty-seven persons, who were brought to San Juan de la Maguana
where they aroused a 'spectacular curiosity among the residents, who
crowded the streets and the park, eager to obtain details concerning the
events'.[50] The prisoners were, however, released after one week in custody
as the *Juez Alcalde* [town judge] did not find them guilty of any crime.
According to his opinion they were 'just simple peasants who returned
from Bánica fulfilling a *promesa*' [vow].[51]

Apparently José Popa was not frightened by the rude intervention of the
authorities. He established himself in La Maguana[52] and crowds of people
from the neighboring communes once more came to the old cult site in
search of remedies and spiritual counseling. By his side Popa now had
Carlitos Mateo, Olivorio's older brother and head of the Mateo clan in La
Maguana.[53]

Both Popa and Carlitos were old men. Some people state that José Popa
was over seventy years old when he appeared as Olivorio's successor in La
Maguana, but he was probably somewhat younger than that. He was of
small stature, rather stout and had a bushy beard. He was not as charismatic as Olivorio and never considered himself to be his master's equal.
His following was not as large either. Popa wandered all over the district
living like a simple and poor man, sleeping on the floor by peasants who
took him in for a night or two, and subsisting on the food they offered him.
He was always clad in a *chamarra*, the typical blue shirt of Dominican peasants, and wore a piece of red cloth wrapped around his forehead.[54] Sometimes he used it while curing people, making mystical signs over the
affected parts with it. José Popa was a peaceful man, walked unarmed and
was cautious not to stir up the feelings of people who came to see him.[55]

The editor of *El Cable* became worried at these signs of a resurrected
Olivorismo. In an editorial he warned the authorities of the possible consequences of too much laxity when dealing with this 'delicate matter':

> Around this topic versions and accusations circulate which are of such
> a serious nature that we will ignore them for the moment, in order not

50 *El Cable*, 20 March 1923.
51 *El Cable*, 27 March 1923.
52 *El Cable*, 31 July 1923.
53 *El Cable*, 20 March 1923.
54 However, some people remember that Popa, in spite of his poverty, dressed in a flashy
way: in a huge hat with three feathers and in clothes made out of *rompe-tocón*, a more
expensive type of *blé*. He rode on a fine horse and was even adorned with some jewelry,
as well as the ropes and scapulars common among the *Olivoristas* (Cassá (1994b)).
55 Interview with Zita Závala, Paraje El Ranchito, 10 April 1986. Cf. interview with Pirindín
Solís, El Batey, 11 April 1986, and interview with Javier Jovino, Río Limpio, 30 April 1986.

to pronounce judgements on circumstances which are unknown to us. The moral health of this municipality, still bleeding after the humilia- tions and tortures suffered during the recent epoch, caused by this stupid cult, demand immediate action by the authorities. The past is still fresh. The lenience of those times caused a lot of damage. There is still time to put an end to the growth of Olivorismo, a cult which serves no other purpose than to protect corruption in all its stages. The best means to give it a deadly blow would, in our opinion, be by expelling from the municipality all those persons who at the moment are administering this attack on morals and civilization. It is now up to the Ministry of Interior to act. We will be back.[56]

To the great despair of Emigdio Garrido Puello, however, the authorities did not act against this *fermento de salvajismo* [ferment of savagery] and in November he found proof of their 'tolerance and indifference', when José Popa, with a small group of followers, entered San Juan de la Maguana triumphantly. The 'new Olivorio' walked at the head, followed by Carlitos Mateo and three 'strong and sturdy' men who acted as the *Olivorista* leaders' bodyguards. Two young women and two children also followed the leaders. They all carried crosses and images and above them a white banner fluttered in the breeze. A curious crowd accompanied them to the church where the small group kneeled in front of the altar dedicated to *Nuestra Señora de la Altagracia*. After a short prayer they then made a cour- tesy call to the *comisaría* [police station], 'not because they were molested by the police, but because they felt like doing so'. They told the police that they were on their way to pay homage to the Virgin in Higüey. Garrido Puello states somewhat sourly that the authorities acted as accomplices in this crime against the public morals instead of eradicating the 'ridiculous' cult, as was their duty.[57]

The views of indignant citizens, like Garrido Puello, apparently had some effect on the reluctant authorities, and in December 1923 the latter dealt a crushing blow to a community of *Olivoristas* that had grown up around a new cultic center that Popa had established at a place called La Florida, west of San Juan de la Maguana, not far from El Batey.[58] In La Florida the

---

56 *El Cable*, 31 July 1923.
57 *El Cable*, 20 November 1923.
58 El Batey is an old spiritual center for the *Cofradía del Espíritu Santo*. In a church, the frater- nity keeps a miraculous small wooden statuette of 'The Holy Spirit', depicting a child around ten years of age, clad in red robes and carrying two small drums in a string around his neck and a white pigeon in one of his hands. It was said that a peasant found the statuette in one of his fields around the middle of the nineteenth century. It is still venerated by the constantly growing *cofradía* in a newly (1985) erected church. Many members of the *cofradía* consider themselves to be *Olivoristas* (interviews with Pirindín Solís and Arsidé Gardés, El Batey, 11 April 1986).

Olivoristas had constructed various houses and planted fields around their new village. When the *Policía Municipal* attacked, they burned down the houses and captured fifty-eight persons, mainly 'women with numerous families and newborn babies'. The prisoners were brought down to San Juan and sentenced to five days in prison and ordered to pay fines of five pesos each.[59] It was apparently after this event that José Popa began his life as a solitary wandering preacher and *curandero*.[60]

The *Olivoristas* were persecuted in other municipalities as well. They were still found in many places along the Haitian frontier and within the Cordillera Central. True to the habits of their master some of the *Olivoristas* kept moving from one place to another. One group, led by a certain Zenón Adamés, was tailed by Lieutenant Rosario of the PND in Comendador,[61] and was finally attacked at a place called Cerro Mico, not far from the Haitian border. There the *Olivoristas* had constructed 'various small huts and enclosures'. The group members were taken by surprise when they were 'preparing their altars and raising their banners'. Five men and nine women were caught, the place was burned down and different objects were confiscated, among them '2 banners, 7 saints, 8 wooden crosses, 3 rosaries with glass beads, 1 candle, 1 pipe, 1 packet of incense, 1 book "No.1", 1 booklet, 1 morrito [small earthenware pot], 1 packet of Haitian matches, one bottle of sanctified water'.[62] A month before this incident *El Cable* had reported that it was common that smugglers were caught by surprise in places not far from Comendador while they were drinking their illegally purchased rum by altars erected in honor of the Virgin or Santa Teresa, the patron saint of Comendador.[63]

In July 1923, a *curandero* called Mundo Bocío was captured together with three followers in the *sección* of Juan de la Cruz. They were brought to the nearby town of El Cercado[64] and were formally accused of practicing illegal medicine and 'the rites of Olivorismo'.[65] They were apparently acquitted and soon Bocío was well established just outside Juan de la Cruz, by a creek called El Soñador. People from all over the district came to see him, and a small village with around forty inhabitants grew up around the place (which Garrido Puello called the 'Holy Mecca' of Bocío).[66] Even if Bocío was accused of being an *Olivorista* his methods differed from those of *El*

---

59 *El Cable*, 25 December 1923.
60 Interview with Zita Závala, Paraje El Ranchito, 10 April 1986.
61 In 1930 the town was renamed Elías Piña (Tolentino Rojas (1944), p. 245).
62 *El Cable*, 26 April 1924.
63 *El Cable*, 1 March 1924. Of course it is possible that these groups were not *Olivoristas*, but their behavior was apparently akin to that of the members of the *Olivorista* groups.
64 These places were situated on the western slopes of Sierra de Neiba, the most fertile part of the San Juan Valley (*El Cable*, 22 November 1924).
65 *El Cable*, 10 July 1923.
66 *El Cable*, 16 January 1926.

Maestro. He charged compensation for his services – ten or twenty pesos depending of the kind of treatment he offered – and, contrary to the methods of Olivorio, he mostly cured his patients with the help of various decoctions and herbal baths. Like La Maguana, El Soñador became the target of various rumors suggesting that it was a place to which some people came 'in order to be cured, some in order to politicize; some in pursuit of easy love making'.[67]

The *Olivoristas* continued to be active in and around La Maguana. In 1926, an old *Olivorista* named Jesús M. Ledesma returned from years of exile in Cuba. He originally came from Hato Viejo, a few kilometers from the sanctuary in La Maguana. On his return from Cuba he established himself in the old spiritual center of *El Maestro* where he cured his patients after he had put himself into a state of possession. Jesús Ledesma also impressed people with ventriloquistic tricks. Together with some forty faithful followers (men, women and children) he was brought to prison in San Juan de la Maguana and finally sentenced in accordance with the *Código Sanitario* [sanitary law].[68]

The *Olivorista* movement also survived within towns and villages, mainly among families known to have been keen followers of *El Maestro*. A well-known family, which for many years made a cult to the deceased Olivorio, was the family of Severo Colón, who lived in the village of Olivero, not far from Las Matas de Farfán.[69] In San Juan de la Maguana there also existed families who remained loyal to the teachings of Olivorio. One of these families held healing sessions in their house and many people went to see what occured during those. Apparently the family members used Olivorio's famous method of administering blows with a *palo de piñón*, hitting the patient on the neck, while they repeated the words: 'Let the bad leave!' If they considered the treatment to have been successful they commanded the bystanders, who crowded the little room, to open a passage to the front door, saying: 'Open up! Open up! Let the spirit leave!'[70]

Pockets of old *Olivoristas* also existed high up in the Cordillera Central, where former members of his band maintained small, self-supporting communities. One of these was led by José Vargas, also called the 'second Olivorio'. In 1930, the Swedish botanist Erik Ekman came across one of his abandoned strongholds, Los Vallecitos, 2,500 meters up in the Cordillera Central. It consisted of a small settlement with five rather well-constructed

---

67 Ibid. Cf. *El Cable*, 15 January 1927; this is the last mention of El Soñador and we do not know anything about the final fate of Mundo Bocío and his community.

68 *El Cable*, 18 September 1926.

69 Cano y Fortuna (n.d.), pp. 158–9. One of the most outstanding members of Olivorio's band was a certain Felipe Colón (Feeley (1919)).

70 Interview with Maximiliano Rodríguez Piña, Santo Domingo, 23 April 1986. Maximiliano would not name the family, since many of its members are still alive.

ranchos [huts]. Ekman was told by his guide that the hamlet had been abandoned when José Vargas and his men left for Haiti.[71]

Other preachers and healers also roamed the San Juan Valley, claiming allegiance to Olivorio, even stating that the spiritual presence they felt within themselves made them equal to, or even identical with, Olivorio. One of them was called '*Einoé*', because if asked if he was the resurrected Olivorio, he used to answer that he 'is and isn't', *es y no es*, the real Olivorio Mateo.[72] Another famous *curandero*, who was sometimes hailed as the new Olivorio, was a man named Ramón Mora, who still lives close to Hato Nuevo, not far from La Maguana.[73]

The rise of Trujillo and the subjugation of the Ramírezes

By the end of the 1920s, the weakness of the Vásquez government had become apparent.[74] The ruling *Partido Nacional* was nothing but a loosely formed composite of various small factions, each of which consisted of the followers of some local *caudillo* or power-hungry individual who had entered politics simply to have his own piece of the cake. As long as the president remained his own powerful self he was able to keep the party together with the aid of his old *caudillo* charisma, but when the worldwide

---

71 Ekman (1970), pp. 374–5. It is possible that José Vargas is identical with José Popa. Los Vallecitos is situated close to the summit of La Pelona (Pico Duarte), a mountain situated about a mile from La Florida, the spiritual center of José Popa. Los Vallecitos would be an ideal hideout for the people of La Florida (to avoid persecution). One former follower of Popa, Pío Rosado, remembered that José Popa had established cultic centers in Los Vallecitos and La Pelona (Cassá (1994b)). Accordingly, if José Vargas is not identical with José Popa, he would at least have been in contact with him and his followers.

    Various *brujos* with the name Vargas are known to have been active in the Dominican countryside. In 1896 the Santiago-based newspaper *La Prensa* reported that a certain Carlos de Vargas had gathered a huge 'crowd of curious and sick people' around himself and that he 'kept the nerves of the general public in a state of constant commotion' (*La Prensa*, 18 October, 1896). He was said to have cured many persons and to have created a community around him that gave the visitors the sensation of 'being in the heart of Africa' (*La Prensa*, 19 November 1896).

72 Interview with Mayobanex Rodríguez, San Juan de la Maguana, 12 December 1985. *Es y no es* is pronounced *e y no e* in the valley. The utterance may be seen in relation to the notion of the 'Great Power of God', which in the San Juan Valley is considered to be a kind of spiritual force granted to certain individuals and places. Since this force is the most prominent feature in the personality of a person afflicted with it, he may accordingly state that his individual characteristics are of a limited importance when you compare him with other individuals who had the same gift – like Olivorio.

73 Interview with Mayobanex Rodríguez, San Juan de la Maguana, 12 December 1985, and Enrique Figueroa, Hato Nuevo, 18 January 1986.

74 A detailed account of the Vásquez presidency is given in Medina Benet (1986). Víctor Medina Benet was a Puerto Rican who worked at the US legation in Santo Domingo during the 1920s.

economic crisis of 1929 spread to the Dominican Republic and Vásquez' personal health began deserting him, a free-for-all broke out among his subordinates.

Horacio Vásquez was himself an uncorrupted person, but the people with whom he surrounded himself were known as *botellas*, i.e. bottles who filled themselves with the illegal profits they gained from their political positions. As the control of the president gradually weakened, money from the treasury was wasted on the creation and maintenance of obscure administrative posts, created with the sole purpose of pleasing the many 'friends' of the presidential *caudillo*. Such 'friends' convinced Horacio Vásquez that the only way of avoiding political anarchy was to postpone until 1930 the elections scheduled to be held in 1928 and he was furthermore advised to change the constitution so as to allow for his reelection. These maneuvers were primarily carried out in order to prevent the vice president, Federico Velázquez, who came from another party, from attaining the presidency.[75] To that end a paragraph was added to the new constitution, stating that the vice president could only succeed the sitting president if the latter died in office. Otherwise the president's successor would be elected by the Supreme Court.

As Vásquez was rather sick at the time, several candidates for the presidency saw in this particular paragraph a chance to come to power before the elections in 1930, and when Vásquez had to leave the country in 1929 in order to undergo a kidney operation in the United States, all kinds of political intriguing began in the Dominican capital. The Supreme Court elected a faithful *Horacista* as president in Vásquez' absence, but when the president came back from abroad no one was able to cool off the overheated political activity which had flourished during the months he had been away. Nearly all politicians of any standing tried to form a support group around themselves, and most of them were ready to use any means, legal or illegal, to come to power.[76]

Discreetly biding his time was the commander of the army, Rafael Leonidas Trujillo Molina. He was quietly watching the political jugglery,

---

75 Campillo Pérez (1986), p. 178. Medina Benet (1986), p. 98, claims that the idea of prolonging Vásquez' term came in 1926 from the adversaries of Dr José Dolores Alfonseca, a member of Vásquez' *Partido Nacional*. According to Medina Benet, it was fairly certain that Alfonseca would become the next president because of the patronage he enjoyed from Vásquez. 'The most faithful acolytes of the Doctor belonged to the group of undesirables and reactionaries within the party. Among this group the generals Cipriano Bencosme, Augusto Chottín and José del Carmen (Carmito) Ramírez stood out ...' (ibid., p. 99).

In August 1928, Alfonseca decided that he would not run for the presidency and that he supported the reelection of Vásquez (ibid., p. 219). One of those applauding and supporting this decision was Víctor Garrido (ibid., p. 224).

76 Campillo Pérez (1986), pp. 176–80.

making secret plans of his own, using the political actors in his own coldly calculated power game. At his disposal he had a formidable weapon, put in his hands by the American occupation:

> The army of the old days has developed into the Policía Nacional Dominicana, a national constabulary, to which is entrusted the maintenance of local order outside those cities or towns where municipal police forces are established, as well as the patrol of the boundary between the Dominican Republic and Haiti. At present, the constabulary is a well trained, well organized, well disciplined body, commanded by officers trained for their functions, and in theory, at least, is a corps solely concerned with the laws and removed from politics. Because of its efficiency the Policía Nacional is a body far more potent than the old army ever was. The elements of danger therefore, are ever present. Should those who compose this force ever become convinced that their promotion or their well-being depends more upon political favour than upon their own efficiency and their individual excellence, the safety of the Republic itself will be jeopardized. It is only through the settled conviction of the governors of the country that their own interest as well as the safety of the nation lies in the maintenance of this branch of the service completely apart from politics, that the national security of the Dominican Republic may be assured.[77]

These prophetic words by Sumner Welles, American commissioner to the Dominican Republic in 1922–25, were published in 1928. Nobody understood their significance better than the commander of the armed forces.

Trujillo, who was born in 1891 and came from a middle-class family, had started out as a petty criminal in his home town, San Cristóbal. Later he appeared first as a weigher and later as *guarda campestre*[78] on the great sugar estates in the Southeast. 'Trujillo's duty was to reveal labor discontent and to help stifle it.'[79] At that time he became acquainted with the notorious James McLean, who had then been transferred from San Juan de la Maguana to the eastern sugar districts. In 1918 McLean recommended Trujillo to the US-controlled PND forces[80] and the following year Trujillo

---

77 Welles (1928), pp. 908–9.
78 A *guarda campestre* was 'a combination of watchman, troubleshooter, and private policeman' (Crassweller (1966), p. 36).
79 Ornes (1958), p. 33.
80 Protected by McLean and wearing the uniform of the PND, Trujillo went on a rampage in the eastern districts of the Dominican Republic, committing himself to extortion, rape and even murder, everything described with malicious detail by Angel Morales, in a letter he wrote to Sumner Welles (Morales (1930), pp. 749–51). Angel Morales had been a

Figure 3.5 Rafael Trujillo, 1930.

began a meteoric career within the military ranks, which in 1928 brought him to the position as commander of the national army.[81] His astonishing career was aided by a natural talent for playacting, a shrewd intelligence and an extreme ruthlessness.[82]

The Ramírez family was well known to Trujillo and he apparently had some respect for its members (i.e. if a man like Trujillo was at all capable of cherishing such a feeling). He had surely heard about them from his uncle Teódulo Pina Chevalier, who posed as an expert on all matters concerning the Haitian frontier, and from his American mentor James McLean, who knew the Ramírez family from his time in the valley. In his youth Trujillo must also have witnessed how the revolutionary forces of Felipe Vidal and Carmito Ramírez moved through San Cristóbal on their

protégé of Horacio Vásquez and dared to lead a coalition against Trujillo in the elections of 1930. After that he lived in exile in the United States, as an important leader of the Dominican opposition and a perpetual object of several attempted murders by the infuriated Trujillo (Crassweller (1966), pp. 69, 72, 213, 238 and 311).

81 Captain in 1922, major and lieutenant colonel in 1924, colonel and commander of the PND in 1925, brigadier general in 1927 (Vega y Pagán (1956)). A 1927 law had turned the PND into the *Ejército Nacional* [National Army] (Galíndez (1962), p. 11).

82 For an analysis of Trujillo's strange personality, see Ornes (1958), pp. 70–85, Crassweller (1966), Chapter 7, and Galíndez (1962), Chapter 7.

Figure 3.6 Carmito Ramírez in the 1940s.

way to the capital. He had also met the son of Carmito, José del Carmen (Mimicito), who once had turned down a job application presented by the young Trujillo, who wanted employment at the Archives of the Land Court where Mimicito was an employee.[83]

Since Carmito Ramírez was one of the key figures in political life at the time and since it was known that he was not on completely good terms with Horacio Vásquez, Trujillo cautiously approached him in order to find out if he would be willing to participate in an overthrow of the government. Carmito adopted a wait-and-see policy and declined Trujillo's offer of weapons to arm a revolutionary army of southerners. The influential *Sanjuanero* did not trust Trujillo. He suspected that the army commander was acting on behalf of Horacio Vásquez and that the offer was a trap set up in order to test his loyalty to the president.[84] According to the confidential reports which the US minister Charles B. Curtis sent from the embassy to the US secretary of state, Carmito constantly tried to find out which faction he ought to side with. Curtis, however, suspected that he mainly sought the support of the powerful commander of the army and wrote that 'General Ramírez is flirting with General Trujillo …'[85] The

83 Interview with Mimicito Ramírez, San Juan de la Maguana, 14 December 1985.
84 Garrido (1970), pp. 149–50.
85 Curtis, quoted in Vega (1986a), p. 389.

Americans had never trusted Carmito Ramírez and they kept him under close watch.

It took some time before Horacio Vásquez realized that his army commander was plotting against him. During his entire military career, Trujillo had stayed out of politics, gaining the confidence of President Vásquez. When the latter was told to watch out for the greedy general he used to state: 'That is not true, I have created Trujillo.'[86] As the situation grew progressively more precarious for Vásquez and he finally realized that the gravest danger came from Trujillo's quarters, he turned to Carmito for help and made him defense minister, perhaps with the hope that this experienced and authoritative politician[87] would be able to curb the ambitions of the army commander. Vásquez probably did not realize that Carmito already had judged the president's cause to be hopelessly lost and that he had been intriguing with Trujillo for some time. Carmito soon openly deserted the Vásquez faction and left his post after less than two weeks.[88]

By then Trujillo had found a more manageable and willing instrument than Carmito – a young politician named Rafael Estrella Ureña, a popular man, idealistic and eloquent but totally incapable of recognizing the sinister game of Trujillo. With the consent of Trujillo, Estrella Ureña staged a fake revolution in Santiago; 'defending' army troops were 'attacked' and 'capitulated' after some volleys in the air. Afterwards the revolutionaries moved down to the capital where Trujillo acted as if he were loyal to the government and tried to convince Vásquez that he was going to put up a fight. In the end Vásquez realized that he had been tricked and stepped down, letting the Supreme Court offer the presidency to Estrella Ureña.

Elections were scheduled for 16 August 1930, and now Trujillo was free to show his true face in the open. He intimidated Estrella Ureña and forced the latter to confine himself to the post of vice president, while he himself was going to run as candidate for the presidency. Carmito was alarmed, but decided to side with Trujillo in order to keep up his position as an influential politician. Trujillo was grateful for his support and offered him the post of secretary of state for industry and public works within the provisional government of Estrella Ureña, and the Ramírezes started campaigning in the south, trying to persuade their *Horacista* associates to back Trujillo in the upcoming elections.[89]

Meanwhile, Trujillo unleashed a band of thugs and gangsters called '*La 42*', former associates of his in the criminal acts committed in his youth.

86 Garrido (1970), p. 147.
87 'a southern caudillo with the reputation of being a hard-fisted man' (Franco Pichardo (1993), p. 483).
88 Garrido Puello (1977), pp. 116–17.
89 Garrido (1970), 159–60.

In a red Packard, the so-called *carro de la muerte* [death car], they roamed the towns and countryside and sprinkled the political meetings of Trujillo's adversaries with machine-gun fire. Several assassinations of important politicians took place all over the country. Most notorious was the death of Virgilio Martínez Reyna, a military man opposed to Trujillo, who together with his pregnant wife was gunned down in his own home.[90] The automobile of his main opponent, Federico Velázquez, was riddled with bullets outside Santiago and Velázquez, who was thrown into jail immediately after the elections, eventually had to flee the country. Without opposition Trujillo gained an easy victory.[91] Before that the Ramírezes had withdrawn from the campaign. Carmito resigned from his post as secretary of state after Trujillo had declared that he would become president even if he had to pass through a river of blood.[92]

After Trujillo had been inaugurated as president things got even worse. The old *caudillos* who had supported him scrambled away in all directions when they realized that Trujillo intended to govern on his own terms, and that he was ready to violate all old agreements if they did not suit him. Some of them tried to put up a fight. Among them was Carmito's old friend, Cipriano Bencosme,[93] who opposed the new president with a small band of armed supporters, but he was finally gunned down near Moca, where his mutilated corpse was exposed after his troops had capitulated.[94]

In the San Juan Valley, *El Cable* reported several threats against the Ramírez family, as well as killings and beatings of ordinary citizens.[95] Its owner, Emigdio Garrido Puello, and one of Carmito's brothers, Juan de Dios, left for the mountains with 300 men. They tried to get weapons and establish contacts with resistance groups in other parts of the country. The group camped several kilometers outside of San Juan de la Maguana while

90 Crassweller (1966), p. 71.
91 Campillo Pérez (1986), p. 187. Officially, 45 percent of the electorate abstained from voting. However, the real figure was probably even higher because the counting of the votes was highly irregular (ibid.). *El Cable*, 17 May 1930, lists dead people, children, foreigners and unknown people whose names had been put up on the election lists in San Juan de la Maguana. According to the first counts, Trujillo received 223,851 votes, which far exceeded the total number of registered voters in the country (Curtis, quoted in Vega (1986a), p. 597). Presumably, fewer than 25 percent of the voters showed up (Crassweller (1966), p. 70).
92 Garrido Puello (1977), p. 122.
93 Bencosme was the most important *caudillo* in the districts of Espaillat and Puerto Plata. Carmito had once surveyed his vast territories around Moca and had cooperated with Bencosme in both revolutionary fighting and political intrigues (interview with Tala Cabral Ramírez, Santo Domingo, 21 November 1985). The terror that struck the country after Trujillo's victory was appalling. Mejía (1976), pp. 310–11, lists some of the victims of the new president's capricious blood thirst.
94 Vega (1986a), pp. 934–5. Cf. Martínez (1971), pp. 63–4.
95 *El Cable*, 30 July 1930 and 23 August 1930.

Figure 3.7 Juan de Dios Ramírez.

new men enlisted all the time. They planned an attack on the government troops stationed in San Juan, but before they were able to put their plans into action Carmito appeared from the capital and convinced them that armed resistance was useless.[96] He pointed to the tragedy of Bencosme and his men and said that the same would happen to them if they attacked Trujillo.[97] The troops were disbanded and Garrido Puello was imprisoned and brought to Santo Domingo where he was jailed, together with his brother Víctor Garrido and many others of their influential friends.[98]

Ramírez' old enemies in the valley were active once again. They had sided with Trujillo in their efforts to wrench power from *los dueños del Sur* [the owners of the South]. The governor in Azua, Miguel Angel Roca, was Trujillo's most important representative in the valley and his thugs made various attempts on Carmito's life.[99] Carmito attempted to strengthen his position in San Juan, but when drastic changes took place in the administrative ranks and many posts were occupied by his enemies he was forced to escape to Haiti.[100] He left the country, after resigning from his post as

96 Garrido Puello (1977), pp. 124–5.
97 Interview with Mimicito Ramírez, San Juan de la Maguana, 11 April 1986.
98 Garrido Puello (1977), p. 126 and Garrido (1970), p. 161.
99 Interview with Mimicito Ramírez. San Juan de la Maguana, 4 July 1990.
100 The American minister Charles Curtis quoted in Vega (1986a), p. 418. Curtis mentioned that the conditions in the province of Azua, where San Juan de la Maguana is situated, seemed to be 'a little worse than in other districts' (ibid.).

secretary of state on 20 March 1930. The American minister to the Dominican Republic suspected that Carmito's move had something to do with the procurement of arms for the resistance movement.[101]

Carmito was soon followed by Juan de Dios Ramírez. The two brothers lived on a Ramírez estate close to Croix-des-Bouquets, not far from Port-au-Prince. In Haiti they were protected and supported by General Charles Zamor, a Haitian senator who the Ramírezes had once protected when he had run into problems in Haiti.[102]

The Ramírezes could apparently cross the frontier without much difficulty and visited the San Juan Valley at various times during their exile. They even visited people known to be close to Trujillo, like Leoncio Blanco, who in October 1930 reported to the new president:

> yesterday, General José del Carmen Ramírez was in my office, talking to me about certain specific questions favorable to your government, but I understand … that one can have no confidence in these people, only treat them with respect without believing in any way that they may have good intentions.[103]

Trujillo immediately answered the letter: 'I have noted all you tell me about General Ramírez and the political situation there; I have paid good attention to it all.'[104]

The greatest worry of the *Trujillistas* was whether Carmito was supporting the troops of Desiderio Arias from his base in Haiti. Desiderio Arias, an old *caudillo* who had been commander of the army when the Americans invaded the Dominican Republic in 1916, had recovered politically under Horacio Vásquez and later on sided with Trujillo. When he realized that Trujillo was unwilling to share his power with any local *caudillo*, he returned to his northern stronghold, Monte Cristi, by the Haitian border, and initiated a fierce guerilla struggle against the *Trujillistas*, who finally killed him on 21 June 1931. His head was chopped off and brought to Trujillo.[105] With the capitulation of Arias' troops all organized resistance against Trujillo was crushed.

---

101 Ibid.

102 Interview with Mimicito Ramírez, San Juan de la Maguana, 11 April 1986.

103 Blanco (1930), pp. 901–2. Leoncio Blanco later on rose to the position of Commanding Officer of the Military Department of the South. He gathered much authority and gained wide popularity. When he felt mistreated by Trujillo he worked up a conspiracy which was exposed in 1933. Blanco was tortured for months until he was finally hanged in prison. More than a hundred of his fellow conspirators were shot (Crassweller (1966), p. 97).

104 Trujillo (1930), p. 902.

105 Crassweller (1966), p. 94.

The personal archives of Desiderio Arias were ransacked and among his correspondence a letter from Carmito Ramírez was found, in which the *Sanjuanero* advised him to make truce with Trujillo and declined to procure Haitian weapons for him.[106] Armed with this proof of Carmito's loyalty Trujillo urged him to return to the Dominican Republic. He gave him guarantees that he would remove all Ramírez' enemies from administrative posts in the valley and he even offered Carmito a post in his government. In July 1931, Carmito returned and the Haitian press paid much attention to this move by the Dominican *caudillo*: the final acceptance of the rule of Trujillo by one of the most important politicians in the Dominican Republic. Carmito declined the offer of participating in Trujillo's government, but later on he served for various periods as a senator for the Southern province.[107]

Thus, even if the Ramírezes finally succumbed to Trujillo's power, their capitulation meant that they were able to keep a great deal of their influence and independence. (Many people state that the Ramírez influence made Trujillo unwilling to interfere too much in the local politics of the valley and that his tyranny was never felt as much there as it was in other places.)[108]

Like all other Dominicans, the Ramírezes had to pay homage to Trujillo when he reached the pinnacle of his power and was intoxicated by his own megalomania. He demanded to be adored by everyone, and one way of showing loyalty to him was to praise him in the press. In 1933 a long contribution to this strange genre was presented by Carmito Ramírez in *Listín Diario*, the largest newspaper in the Dominican Republic. In his laudatory article Carmito wrote, among other things:

> He has imposed order where ambition without nobility wanted chaos and he has created respect for the law where unrestricted liberties led to tumult [...] President Trujillo has demonstrated strength in his work and capacity to govern in a country where the eminence of power always was nothing other than a gift from illiterate caudillos, a favor granted from above to presumptuous camarillas alienated from any strict observance of the duties imposed by public functions ...[109]

---

106 Interview with Mimicito Ramírez, San Juan de la Maguana, 11 April 1986.
107 Vega (1988c), p. 58.
108 Interviews with Mimicito Ramírez, San Juan de la Maguana, 4 April 1986 and Mayobanex Rodríguez, San Juan de la Maguana, 18 January 1989.
109 *Listín Diario*, 21 December 1933. Such articles were often written after some discreet sign had been given that it would be appropriate to write them if one would like to avoid any problems with the government.

Trujillo's initial attacks on the *Olivoristas*

Trujillo was probably familiar with *Olivorismo* before he came to power. As a military man he must have seen reports concerning the hunting of *Olivoristas* and as a commanding officer he probably had to pay some visits to the border and the southern districts. Some contemporary *Olivoristas* even maintain that *El Maestro* once met with Trujillo long before the latter became 'the most important man in the Republic'. According to Julián Ramos, 'Trujillo was just a simple errand boy for McLean when he first came up to La Maguana and met with Olivorio'.[110]

Through his various informants and supporters Trujillo knew that *Olivorismo* was far from dead and that it could easily be turned into a political force. The relative laxness of the Vásquez government had apparently fostered the growth of José Popa's movement. During the last years of the 1920s Popa and his followers made their presence felt in a more spectacular way than before. It happened that caravans of *Olivoristas* showed up in different villages, headed by Popa, mounted on a beautiful horse, followed by banner-waving disciples. Popa appears to have found his most dedicated followers among the inhabitants of small villages in the fertile terrain along the river Las Cuevas, twenty kilometers east of Túbano (presently called Padre las Casas).[111] This district was known as Guayabal, and the people living in its villages, La Siembra and La Laguna, were described as fervent believers in Olivorio.[112]

Trujillo considered it best to strike hard at the *Olivorista* leaders. One of his accomplices in this struggle was Leopoldo Fernández, alias Popoyo, a ruthless common soldier, extremely feared by everyone because it was commonly known that he was the most influential of all Trujillo's *paleros* [henchmen].[113] Popoyo was put in charge of the elimination of the old José Popa, who roamed the countryside, curing the sick and preaching the gospel of Olivorio. In November 1930 Popoyo arranged that Popa be invited to a 'Feast of the Cross' in Guayabal. José Popa came alone, riding on a horse. Just outside Padre las Casas, while crossing the river Las Cuevas, he was shot to death by Popoyo and his accomplice, Rafael Luca, another thug with credentials from the old PND.[114] The place of the murder is still called Paso de Popa [the Passage of Popa].[115]

---

110 Interview with Julián Ramos, Higüerito, 16 January 1986.
111 The name was changed on 19 April 1928 (Tolentino Rojas (1944), p.222).
112 Cassá (1994b).
113 Interview with Mimicito Ramírez, San Juan de la Maguana, 11 April 1986.
114 Interview with Mayobanex Rodríguez, San Juan de la Maguana, 18 January 1989. Other versions of the episode state that Popa came accompanied by people from various sections of San Juan. Among them was a group from Padre las Casas, who finally turned out to be the perpetrators of the crime, feigning friendship before they struck.
115 Cassá (1994b).

The bloody persecution of the *Olivoristas* at the beginning of the 1930s rested entirely with Trujillo's thugs. Lieutenant Juan Esteban Luna, who had been instrumental in the final hunt for Olivorio and his men, had fled to Haiti together with his friend Juanico Ramírez, the brother of Carmito.[116] The friends and associates of Lieutenant Luna were harassed by soldiers loyal to Trujillo and the old forces of law and order in the valley were paralyzed.[117] Luna was widely known as an able and correct soldier. Under his command, during the Vásquez government, the *Olivoristas* were both pursued and persecuted, but none of them was killed and if they were imprisoned or fined this was done according to the law and after open legal proceedings. Most of them were also acquitted for lack of proof against them.

Under Trujillo, on the other hand, the terror was in full swing and at least two bloody deeds proved to have serious consequences. In 1932, two men, Domingo Valeria and Manuel Ventura, were shot in an ambush close to the village of Los Copeyes, not far from Las Matas de Farfán. Both had been close associates of Olivorio and had even been at his side when he fought the Americans. They were considered to be important *Olivoristas* and had continued to preach the message of *El Maestro* after his death. Valeria and Ventura were killed by a certain José Solís, a *calié* [thug], in the service of Trujillo.[118]

A brother of Manuel Ventura named León[119] ran into trouble a few months later. Shaken by the death of his brother he picked a fight with Trujillo's military and had to escape to Haiti. This incident took place near Guayacanes, where one of León's sons, Delanoy, served as second *alcalde*, a kind of magistrate on the village level, in the district of Carrera de Yeguas. Delanoy Ventura, who was in charge of law and order within his territory, had captured a band of smugglers, and two men from the *Guardia Fronteriza* came to bring the prisoners down to Las Matas de Farfán. Both guardsmen were drunk and one of them had a certain grudge against Delanoy since both of them were courting the same girl. Accordingly, this guardsman treated both Delanoy and the old León, the well-known *Olivorista*, with disdain.

---

116 Vega (1986a), p. 902.
117 Jovine Soto (1978), pp. 115–16.
118 Interview with León Romilio Ventura, Media Luna, 5 May 1986. Interviewed by the anthropologist Lusitania Martínez, León Romilio said that the year of the murder of his uncle was 1935, i.e. three years after his father had been forced to flee to Haiti (Martínez (1991), p. 129).
119 Manuel and León were half-brothers (interview with Telma Odeida Dotel Matos, Santo Domingo, 2 November 1985). Their father Nicolás Colén Cuevas, who came from Sabana Mula in the district of Bánica, had been a very close friend of Olivorio. American reports had even pointed to him as the real leader of Olivorio's band. He was shot down by Dominican soldiers in American service on 19 February 1918 (McLean (1919)).

Delanoy had to accompany his prisoners to the district court in Las Matas, and according to custom the captives had to walk while their guards were riding. When the small group was preparing to leave the village the guardsmen demanded that Delanoy go on foot. The *alcalde* got terribly upset and shouted that both the horse and the mule on which the guards were mounted were his property and that he would not accept walking together with his own prisoners while the guardsmen were sitting on his animals. His rival got angry and hit Delanoy over the ribs with the butt of his rifle. Meanwhile, the father of Delanoy, the old León, flung himself on the other guard. In the tumult that followed Delanoy ran his knife through the guard who had attacked him.

After that, both father and son had to flee across the border into Haiti. Delanoy took his fiancée with him, raised a family with her and ended up as a rather wealthy man in the Haitian town of Hinche. León Ventura left a large family behind and in order to save the children from the rage of Trujillo's military they were dispersed and brought up by various relatives. Some of the Ventura land was seized on the order of Trujillo and distributed to people loyal to the dictator. The Ventura children grew up within a strong *Olivorista* tradition, nurturing a hope of reviving the cult of their father and avenging themselves on Trujillo and his associates.[120]

After a while the killing subsided. The Ramírezes returned, Trujillo's thugs cooled down and more moderate men handled the valley's affairs. Nevertheless, throughout the entire reign of Trujillo (1930–61) the practice of *Olivorismo* was forbidden and many *Olivoristas* were put in prison, accused of practicing witchcraft. Prior to 1943 a law enacted in 1908 was used against the *Olivoristas*. The law stated that all 'non-Christian cults' were simple pretexts for vagrancy and different forms of corruption. Many expressions of popular Catholicism were labeled 'forbidden cults'. Vigils in front of the saints, rites in honor of the dead, puberty rituals and other religious, 'unauthorized' acts were considered to be 'nothing else than extremely profane behavior, acts of savagery that constitute occasions for getting drunk, criminal diversions directed against good customs'. Accordingly, all such celebrations were strictly forbidden.[121] This law was supplemented in 1943 with a law against *vodú* and witchcraft, which was also used against the *Olivoristas*.[122] 'In those days you could not even light a candle in honor of Olivorio. Trujillo could not stand any kind of competition.'[123]

120 García (1986), pp. 49–51. Cf. Martínez (1991), pp. 128–9.
121 *Mandato al Jefe de la Guardia Republicana*, cited in Bryan (1979), p. 73.
122 'The spectacles known by the name "voudou" or "lua", or any others of the same, or similar, character ... are considered to be a violation of good manners and as such they will be punished with correctional punishments' (*Ley Núm. 391, G.O. Núm. 5976*, cited in Cruz Díaz (1965), p. 18).
123 Interview with Julián Ramos, Higüerito, 16 January 1986.

Still the movement survived. It was impossible to supervise the vast and inaccessible territory where the cult had its most fervent adherents and, over time, most *Sanjuaneros* gradually formed the opinion that the teachings and rituals of the *Olivoristas* were harmless and inoffensive.

In 1940, the son of Carmito Ramírez, Mimicito, was called to Trujillo in Barahona and ordered to go on horseback all along the Haitian border, from Pedernales in the south to Monte Cristi in the north. He was going to act as an 'agricultural inspector' and present a report to the president:

> My mission was not very well defined. The journey took two and a half months and I wrote an extensive report afterwards. What surprised me most on that journey was that *Olivorismo* was so strong on both sides of the border. And I met *Olivoristas* nearly all along the entire frontier.[124]

The Dominicanization of the San Juan Valley

A recurrent theme in *El Cable* during the 1920s was the constant 'penetration' of Haitians into Dominican territory. The establishment of the huge sugar plantations around Barahona, as well as the roadworks, had brought many Haitian workers to the southeastern regions of the Dominican Republic. The *caco* wars against the American invaders had created a sense of insecurity all along the Haitian side of the border. The recurrent fighting often interrupted the agricultural cycles and many cattle were slaughtered in order to feed the Haitian irregulars. Many Haitian peasants sought the peace and modest prosperity on the Dominican side of the border, where virgin land was still plentiful. This was not a new phenomenon. Both Haitians and Dominicans had passed unprovoked back and forth across the border for centuries and there were many Dominicans who owned land on the Haitian side of the border:

> In those days Haiti and Santo Domingo [the Dominican Republic] were the same thing. A lot of Haitians lived here and my grandfather, who was a Dominican, was raised in Alonceano, which is on the Haitian side [...] Wenceslao Ramírez was the owner of Guayabal, Sabana Mula and Cercadillo, but he also owned land from here [Bánica] all the way up to Hinche [...] The Americans had their customs houses in Comendador, Descubierta, Neiba and Dajabón, and sent their patrols along the frontier, but that did not interfere too much with the intense commerce between the countries. This went on until Trujillo evicted the Haitians from the Republic in 1937.[125]

124 Interview with Mimicito Ramírez, San Juan de la Maguana, 4 July 1990.
125 Interview with Sarni Ramírez, Bánica, 2 June 1989.

Haitian gourdes were the means of payment as far as Azua, and through the 1920s thousands of cattle from the San Juan Valley were brought to Haiti and sold in Port-au-Prince. Many Haitians established themselves as tailors, bricklayers and farmers in and around the southern towns and many more lived in small, isolated communities up in the Cordillera, or along the frontier.[126] Several editorials in *El Cable* objected to this Haitian presence, as, for example, the following four from 1925:

> This black people is not just a horde, it is the most grave danger to the happy life of every Dominican family.[127]

> The government has to use a firm hand along the frontier in order to uplift its morals. This demand stems both from patriotism and decency.[128]

> The Haitians are in their majority miserable and ruinous people. Still they are treated in this country with a consideration that their condition does not make them worthy of.[129]

> [...] the local authorities are incapable of halting the wave [of Haitian immigrants] not only due to their lack of arms but also because they find no support when they want to apply the law.[130]

Through these articles Emigdio Garrido Puello found an avid reader in Rafael Trujillo who in 1935 approached him with a proposal. By then, a long time had passed since Emigdio had been released from prison and a pact had been concluded between the dictator and the old leaders of San Juan. Emigdio then lived as a businessman in Santo Domingo. (*El Cable* had been closed down by Trujillo in 1930.)

The search for a 'Dominican identity' was an old theme within Dominican politics and intellectual debate. The nation was relatively new. It was composed of an original mixture of people from different countries and races, who for more than a century had suffered all kinds of hardships, wars and occupations. The island was shared with the Haitians, who for a hundred years had been viewed as a constant threat to the survival of the Dominican Republic. The border between the two countries had never been definitely settled and in 1935 it remained a mere line on the map. The Dominican governments kept stressing the Spanish roots of the

---

126 Interview with Carlos Peguero Matos, San Juan de la Maguana, 4 July 1990.
127 *El Cable*, 18 July 1925.
128 *El Cable*, 28 July 1925.
129 *El Cable*, 22 September 1925.
130 *El Cable*, 7 March 1925.

Figure 3.8 Manuel Arturo Peña Batlle.

population in order to strengthen its patriotic feelings in the face of the dark-skinned Creole-speaking Haitians. Being Dominican became synonymous with being 'white' or 'Indian', i.e. a preserver of Spanish cultural values, like Catholicism and 'chivalry', as opposed to the alleged 'Africanism' and 'barbaric voodooism' of their 'Negroid' Haitian neighbors – in spite of the fact that most Dominicans were mulattos and adherents to religious beliefs which did not have very much in common with officially sanctioned Catholicism.[131]

Trujillo strengthened the central power in the Dominican Republic. Hence he sought support in such views, attempting to turn them into what amounted to a state ideology. His efforts were backed by an impressive cohort of intellectuals. The most eloquent was Manuel Arturo Peña Batlle:

> Let us not forget that this Spanish nation, Christian and Catholic as we Dominicans are, arose pure and homogeneous in the geographic unity of the island and that it would have remained like that until today if it were not for the scion that, from the end of the seventeenth century [i.e. the establishment of the French colony of Saint-Domingue], was grafted onto the original trunk to infest its sap with elements profoundly and fatally distinct from those that originally grew on the island of La Española.[132]

131 See Lundius (1990).
132 Peña Batlle (1943a), p. 12.

The main target for most of all these writings was Haiti, which was considered a mortal enemy of Dominican morals and cultural identity:

> There are no human feelings, or political reason, or any occasional agreement whatsoever that could force us to contemplate the picture of Haitian penetration with indifference [...] the Haitian who invades us ... lives infected by numerous and capital vices, and he is nearly without exception deformed by diseases and physiological deficiencies, endemic among the low strata of that society.[133]

The reasons for all this mistrust and disdain expressed towards the neighboring nation were partly political in the sense that Trujillo wanted to protect the border, since enemies to the central government had for centuries used the Haitian side of it as a base for their armed attacks on the Dominican state. He wanted to have the border securely sealed off to minimize all contact between the inhabitants on either side of the frontier. This policy also entailed getting rid of all Haitians living on the Dominican side. It was precisely while pondering these issues that he contacted Garrido Puello through his secretary of state:

> Trujillo had read my articles about the Dominicanization of the frontiers published in *El Cable* and he had liked my ideas and showed interest in their application and he now wanted to put me in charge of some kind of organization suggested by me, and I could count on whatever support from the government and hierarchy that I considered convenient for the carrying out of my official activities.[134]

However, Garrido Puello, who still nurtured a grudge against Trujillo and did not want to be identified with his regime, turned down the offer.

His obsession with the frontier and his hatred of the Haitians continued to influence the politics of Trujillo until, in the autumn of 1937 he ordered thousands of Haitian men, women and children living in Dominican territory to be butchered with machetes, knives, clubs and bayonets. The massacre was carried out by soldiers dressed in civilian clothes. Quite probably firearms were not used because Trujillo wanted it all to look like a desperate act carried out by peasants.[135]

When the news leaked out the international reaction was violent and, in 1938, Trujillo delivered, as an indemnity, a check of US$250,000 to the

133 Ibid., p. 12. Note the metaphor of 'penetration', with its obvious sexual connotations, especially when associated with the perceived sexual licence of the Haitians.
134 Garrido Puello (1977), p. 135.
135 Cf. Gardiner (1979), pp. 11–33, García (1983), Castor (1987) and Vega (1988c), (1995a).

Haitian government,[136] still maintaining that it was Dominican peasants
who had carried out the massacre and showing no remorse whatsoever.
The true extent of the crimes was never revealed to the Dominican people.
Instead, a flood of books and articles defending the massacre was released.
Every author seemed to try to outdo the others in gilding the picture of the
Benefactor, as Trujillo was now called, painting the Haitians in the blackest
possible shade. Trujillo was depicted as a defender of Dominican, Hispanic
and Catholic values against the 'uncivilized, black hordes' who constantly
threatened the peace-loving Dominican nation on its western border.

In order to fit into this picture of a 'civilizing father' of the Dominican
Republic Trujillo embarked on a huge program conceived to 'Dominicanize' the frontier.[137] In 1938, the old province of Azua was divided and the
communes of San Juan de la Maguana, Las Matas de Farfán, El Cercado,
Bánica and Elías Piña (formerly Comendador) were combined into a new
province called El Benefactor, with San Juan de la Maguana as its provincial capital.[138] In San Juan a huge fortress was constructed as the headquarters of the army. Visitors had to enter the city through a huge
triumphal arch, erected in Trujillo's honor, followed by a long paved
avenue, lined with several huge and sumptuous official buildings – a luxury
hotel, a 'palace' for the local government, another for the district department of justice, a third for the administration of public works and a fourth
for the administration of education along the frontier. A convent and two
hospitals were also founded.[139]

A series of military posts was constructed along the Haitian border and
land was distributed, in a system of agricultural colonies, to Dominican
families that were willing to settle on the frontier. Elías Piña was converted
into a model town – a showpiece for the program – with modern infrastructure. Roads were built or repaired and irrigation facilities were greatly
improved.[140] The speaking of Creole was declared illegal and Haitian-style
houses were forbidden.[141]

136 Cuello (1985), pp. 34 and 171–6.
137 *La frontera de la República Dominicana con Haití* (1946) gives the details as well as some of
the official reasons behind the program.
138 Tolentino Rojas (1944), pp. 281–2.
139 Machado Báez (1955), pp. 243–4.
140 Lundahl and Vargas (1983), pp. 123–5.
141 Palmer (1976), p. 90. Somewhat later, Haiti's president, Dumarsais Estimé, decided to
convert Belladère, which is situated opposite Elías Piña on the Haitian side of the border,
into a model town as well: 'Belladère was on the main road from Port-au-Prince to the
Dominican Republic. At a cost of $600,000 Estimé paved the main street, put in a new
hotel and new houses, supplied them with electricity and drinking water. It apparently
made Trujillo unhappy to see such progress next door. In opposition he rerouted
Dominican traffic through the town of Jimaní, a more southern border exit and
Belladère was left isolated' (Diederich and Burt (1972), p. 62).

Figure 3.9 The model town of Elías Piña.

Many of the large landowners prospered, land prices rose and agricultural production became more diversified. Particularly the large-scale production of peanuts and rice gained importance and two influential landowners and businessmen, Miguel Paniagua and Pedro Heyaime, built the first grain silos of the Dominican Republic.[142] Heyaime became the wealthiest man in the valley and erected a huge theater house in the center of San Juan.[143]

The Ramírezes under Trujillo

Trujillo was very keen on enriching himself and the members of his family. One way of doing this was buying or confiscating land. Many landowners were threatened and intimidated until they sold their land for ridiculous prices – some even to the point of leaving their land behind them as they were forced to leave the country. When the Trujillo regime fell, in 1961, the Dominican government confiscated all 'Trujillo land', i.e. land owned by the former dictator, his heirs, family and satellites. The total came to almost three-and-a-quarter million *tareas*.[144] In the San Juan Valley

---

142 Garrido Puello (1972), p. 50.
143 Interview with Víctor Garrido Ramírez, Santo Domingo, 22 April 1986.
144 1 *tarea* equals 0.1554 acres, or 0.063 hectares.

Trujillo owned more than twice as much land as he did in any other place: 1,110,250.83 *tareas.*[145] This land, however, was mostly forest land in the mountains and he did not interfere much in the business of the wealthy landowners, leaving their property in peace.[146]

Many poor people in the San Juan Valley state that they did not particularly suffer under Trujillo. Today you may find many Dominican peasants who speak favorably about the dictator, maintaining that they were better off under his reign. You may even come across his portrait on some family altars in remote areas. By some *Olivoristas* and voodooists he is considered to be a powerful, spiritual force which still looms in the Dominican landscape. Few consider him to have been a totally benign ruler. It is rather his forceful character, his power, that attracts his devotees.[147] What still lingers in the mind of many of those who talk of his brutality is the treatment Trujillo gave the Haitians, but they still often state that his influence was not too bad: 'We, the Dominicans who lived along the frontier, never had any problems with Trujillo in spite of the fact that he did not do anything for free.'[148]

Some of Trujillo's lands in the Cordillera Central were set up as a National Park, named after Carmito Ramírez. Trujillo was careful in maintaining the cordial relations with the influential Ramírez family and if problems occured he always tried to appease them.

Still, the attitude taken by Miguel Angel Ramírez Alcántara, one of Juanico Ramírez' many sons, constituted a constant tension in the relationship between Trujillo and the Ramírezes. In the early 1920s Miguel Angel had left for the United States to become a land surveyor. When Horacio Vásquez was elected president in 1924 he started to work for the Dominican consulate in New York as a vice-consul, renouncing this position after the election of Trujillo in 1930, and making a living as a wholesale commission banana merchant. His extroverted and adventure-loving character gained him many friends among numerous Dominican exiles who had fled from Trujillo's tyranny. Soon he became one of the leading representatives of Dominican resistance abroad. He earned the title of general when, together with several other Dominican exiles, he had participated with the rank of colonel in the rebellion of José Figueres in Costa

---

145 Clausner (1973), p. 235. After the death of Trujillo the Benefactor province was divided into the provinces of San Juan and Elías Piña.
146 Interview with Mimicito Ramírez, San Juan de la Maguana, 11 April 1986.
147 Interview with a *bruja* in a Dominican border town. She had several pictures of *El Benefactor* on her altar and wanted to remain anonymous. It must be stated that all kinds of political affiliations may be found among the *Olivoristas*. Some were fervent anti-*Trujillistas*, while others supported him and today one may find *Olivoristas* who state that they are communists, just as one will find supporters of various right-wing groups.
148 Interview with Sarni Ramírez, Bánica, 2 June 1989.

Figure 3.10 Miguel Angel Ramírez Alcántara.

Rica in 1948, as his chief of staff.[149] The year before he had participated in an aborted attempt to invade the Dominican Republic from the Cuban Cayo Confites shore,[150] and after the Costa Rican war he was involved in planning an armed expedition against Anastasio Somoza in Nicaragua.[151]

The Dominican participation in the Costa Rican civil war was due to the hopes of obtaining a new, more secure, base for their operations in Central America. This, however, proved difficult. In 1949, after a provocation staged by Somoza, the members of the Caribbean Legion, as the exiles called themselves,[152] were given a hint by Figueres that they should leave Costa Rica.[153] They, however, found a haven in Guatemala. From there they launched an airborne attack on the Dominican Republic, which was easily repelled by Trujillo's loyal forces. Before that, however, the majority of the

---

149 Figueres Ferrer (1987), pp. 155, 182–3, 201–6, 221, 227, 320, Ameringer (1996), pp. 44, 48, 66–7, 70–4, 84. Interview with Mimicito Ramírez, San Juan de la Maguana, 4 July 1990.
150 For the Cayo Confites episode, see Grullón (1989).
151 Ameringer (1996), pp. 77, 80.
152 'Although sometimes called a Communist movement, the Legion was apparently principally composed of exiles from various dictator-ridden nations of the Caribbean and Central America, plus the usual number of Caribbean adventurers' (Martin (1966), p. 46). The history of the Caribbean Legion is told in Ameringer (1996).
153 Ameringer (1996), pp. 87–92.

members of the expedition – including Ramírez – had been arrested in Mexico where they had been forced to land by bad weather.[154]

Having been released by the Mexican authorities, later in 1949, Ramírez made it to Cuba.[155] Five years later, he was once more in Guatemala, for when the Arbenz government of Guatemala was toppled by troops supported by the CIA and Trujillo, Miguel Angel Ramírez was seized and jailed by Arbenz' successor, General Castillo Armas, who, however, refused to extradite him. Castillo Armas' refusal to hand over Ramírez to Trujillo may have been an important reason why Trujillo had the Guatemalan president assassinated in 1957.[156] In 1958 we find Miguel Angel Ramírez with Fidel Castro in the Sierra Maestra. Later he, however, quarreled with his Cuban brother-in-arms and was jailed, to be released in 1960,[157] restoring his friendship with Castro. Still, he never became a communist.

This colorful character was profoundly hated by Trujillo, but the dictator was careful not to let the Ramírez family feel any of this hatred. Still, whenever a member of the numerous family ran into trouble with Trujillo they had to abjure any connections with the notorious Miguel Angel. This, for example, was the case when Carmito Ramírez attempted to obtain amnesty for a brother of Miguel Angel who had been jailed in Ciudad Trujillo:

> [The widow of Juanico Ramírez] came together with Senator José del C. Ramírez, her brother-in-law.
>
> She says that her son Porfirio Ramírez (a) Prim, is imprisoned: but she as well as Senator Ramírez assures that he [Porfirio Ramírez] is a loyal Trujillista and even if it is true that he is a brother of Mr. Miguel Angel Ramírez, she wants it to be known that this man left this country 25 years ago and that he never cared for his family, which is why she does not have any relations whatsoever with her son.[158]

What Juanico's widow told was not wholly in accordance with the truth, since the Ramírez family always kept close, clandestine, contact with its Prodigal Son.[159]

Porfirio Ramírez had ended up in jail due to the machinations of Lieutenant General Federico Fiallo, one of Trujillo's most feared and loyal henchmen, a very ruthless and corrupt man. With Trujillo's tacit consent he controlled the commerce in gasoline in the south. Porfirio, who

154 Crassweller (1966), pp. 237–42, Ameringer (1996), pp. 95–116. Ramírez was to land in the vicinity of San Juan de la Maguana with twenty-five men (Ameringer (1996), p. 100).
155 Ameringer (1996), p. 116.
156 Crassweller (1966), p. 336.
157 Martin (1966), p. 318.
158 Secretaría Particular del Presidente de la República (1948), p. 147.
159 Interview with Mimicito Ramírez, San Juan de la Maguana, 4 July 1990.

transported gasoline to San Juan, refused to pay Fiallo the customary bribes and therefore ran into constant trouble.

On 2 June 1950, Porfirio's truck was found smashed and burning in a ravine by the southern highway from San Cristóbal to Baní. In the wreck were the incinerated bodies of five men and a woman. The driver was missing. Badly hurt, he had crawled all the way to Baní, where, by pure coincidence, he was treated by Dr Víctor Manuel Ramírez, a brother of Porfirio Ramírez. Before he expired the driver told the terrified doctor that Lieutenant General Fiallo and some of his thugs, armed with clubs, had stopped Porfirio's truck. The sturdy *Sanjuanero* had got angry and had knocked down the lieutenant general, who shot him in the chest. Afterwards, Porfirio's three helpers, as well as a hitchhiking man and an old lady, were clubbed to death, soaked in gasoline and put into the truck, which finally was pushed over into a deep ravine. The thugs also clubbed the driver until they thought he was dead and dumped him in the ravine as well. After a while, however, the almost mortally wounded man succeeded in climbing back on the road again. The corpse of Porfirio was simply left by the roadside.

This bloody deed became an international scandal when Miguel Angel alerted the Dominican exiles and a formal UN investigation was demanded. The act was interpreted as a reprisal for Miguel Angel Ramírez' political activities. Trujillo put Fiallo at the disposal of the attorney general for indictment and quietly let some of the lesser executioners disappear.[160] He feared that the wrath of the Ramírezes would make things get out of hand in the San Juan Valley and thus tried to do everything in order to appease them. He sent a personal letter to the son of Carmito, Mimicito Ramírez, who was a congressman at the time. In this letter Trujillo wrote:

> Look Ramírez, I am not the guilty party and in order to prove my confidence in all of you I will make a governor out of you. This deed was not directed against the Ramírezes. If I had wanted to harm your family I could just as well have killed anyone of you instead, but I have not touched you.[161]

Mimicito was made governor twice for the Benefactor province and once for Monte Cristi:[162] 'Trujillo was always cautious in treating our family with due respect.'[163]

---

160 Ornes (1958), pp. 125–7.
161 Interview with Mimicito Ramírez, San Juan de la Maguana, 4 July 1990. The same story was told by various persons in San Juan, among them Thomas Reilly (interview, San Juan de la Maguana, 12 December 1985).
162 1946–50 in the Benefactor province and 1950–53 in Monte Cristi (interview with Mimicito Ramírez, San Juan de la Maguana, 11 April 1986).
163 Interview with Mimicito Ramírez, San Juan de la Maguana, 4 July 1990. Fiallo was soon

Trujillo and the *Olivoristas*

Trujillo engaged the Catholic church in his struggle against 'superstition and other Haitian influences'. Churches were erected in every important town along the border and a year before the massacre on the Haitians the Jesuits had been granted the province of Dajabón as their field of mission. The Jesuits were engaged in missionary work along the frontier and in the build-up of a center for vocational training in the town of Dajabón.[164]

In 1935 the Redemptorists had been granted the San Juan Valley as their missionary field.[165] The Redemptorists are a missionary order founded in 1732 by Alphonsus Maria Ligouri at Scala, close to Amalfi in southern Italy. The main task of the brethren was to work among the neglected country people, and their sermons and instructions should be 'solid, simple and persuasive'.[166] They were very solicitous in providing well-equipped parochial schools and the order soon spread all over the world, concentrating its efforts in teaching poor peasants and trying to convert them to the true teachings of the church. Their center is in Boston.[167]

The Redemptorists became very influential in the valley, particularly since the energetic Thomas Reilly arrived there in 1948 and later became bishop with residence in San Juan de la Maguana. He had been with the US troops in the Pacific during World War II and had afterwards worked with the Redemptorist mission in Japan. Reilly was a man of action. During the war he had followed the troops and he was a trained parachutist. He became popular among many peasants even though he was a sworn enemy of all kinds of 'superstitions'. Still, he avoided 'excessive' harshness in his dealings with the *Olivoristas*, whom he characterized as people suffering from 'grave superstitions':

---

pardoned and ended up as chief of the national police. When the Ramírezes brought legal action against him after the death of Trujillo he killed himself in his cell (ibid.).

164 López de Santa Anna (1957), pp. 19–21. Cf. Sáez (1988a), pp. 59–110. The Jesuits of the frontier mission were well aware of the atrocities that had been committed against the Haitians. The majority of the Jesuit fathers' parish members had been Haitians: 'Of the thirty-four thousand inhabitants of this mission remain only some four thousand; just the Dominicans. The mass of Haitians that filled the chapels and came to the *Padre* in order to confess their sins, the caravans that crossed the fields with children on their hips to have them baptized when the *Pater* came by, are not to be seen any more. Abandoned villages, barren fields, stray dogs howling in search of their masters, desolation and solitude in our countryside and an intense pain in our souls for those disappeared and for the responsibility of those who had made them disappear was what we felt when we passed by the human remains that appear along the roads' (Gallego (1943), p. 293). Still, the Jesuits kept quiet due to the constant threats of Trujillo, choosing instead to carry on their missionary work among their remaining parishioners.

165 Balaguer (1983), pp. 86–7.

166 Wuest (1911), p. 683.

167 Ibid., pp. 683–7.

Figure 3.11 Bishop Thomas Reilly.

I had an assistant who had worked with the Haitian mission where the converted voodooists had been forced to burn all their drums and other voodoo stuff on huge bonfires. But I told him not to be too hard on superstition here, since it is not organized as in Haiti. If you give the peasants proper attention, they will eventually turn into good Catholics.[168]

Yet Reilly considered that indulgence could not be allowed to go too far:

During my time we had seven or eight outbreaks of fanaticism here. Such incidents created tensions among the peasants and could even end in bloodshed. I used to identify the leaders and have them sent to prison in the capital, just for a week or so in order to cool them down. I got the word of the police that nothing was going to happen to them and when they came back the commotion would have ebbed out.[169]

Such proceedings were common even before the arrival of Reilly. Trujillo had ordered that all activities of the *Olivoristas* had to be duly reported and dealt with:

168 Interview with Thomas Reilly, San Juan de la Maguana, 12 December 1985.
169 Ibid.

In accordance with the instructions of His Excellency, the President of the Republic I would like to make it known to you that Father Lorenzo Ms. de Ubrique, Parish Priest of Las Matas de Farfán, Bánica and El Cercado has informed this presidency that numerous persons within the regions of his jurisdiction are dedicating themselves to *Liborista* practices, conducted by an individual named Nicolás Montero, alias 'Siné', who lives in the section of Rancha (Guamal), in the commune of El Cercado. [...] In accordance with the given instructions it is recommended that this State Secretariat [Secretariat of Interior and Police] impart the necessary orders to the National Police so they may put a stop to the denounced immoral practices.[170]

Ten years later another document in the personal archives of President Trujillo mentions other *Olivorista* activities:

we were informed about the appearance of a group of lazybones, tramps or thieves, catechized by perverts or persons who are badly informed about the order of things, dedicating themselves to a kind of *Olivorismo*, ill-fated and prejudicial. People are missing from their jobs and the lives of the ignorant who let themselves be dominated by these persons are in danger. This may lead to some kind of outbreak of disguised communism, which makes it urgent to bring an end to all this. Some of these persons have been taken prisoner and brought to justice. They were acquitted in default of proof of guilt; the proceedings were handled in a bad way. The centers of their actions are the sections of El Hoyo, La Jagua and El Naranjo, within the commune of Las Matas de Farfán.[171]

We have not come across any of the verdicts which were delivered in those cases. It is, however, suggested that some of the *Olivoristas* that were sent to the capital even gained the favor of Trujillo himself:

The bishop of San Juan de la Maguana, Tomás O. Raily [sic], raised his voice to heaven and was supported by his flock in his struggle to expose the ignorance and obscurantism that undermined the collective of the region.

Facing this situation the Governor of the province asked the Commander of the National Army to imprison the said sorcerer [a man who had established himself as thaumaturge in La Maguana] and those who participated in his demonic acts and erase this African custom [i.e. *Olivorismo*] that hurts the principles of the society.

170 Bonnetti Burgos (1938). *Liborista* underlined in the original.
171 Calderón (1948). *Olivorismo* underlined in the original.

One morning the sorcerer and all those who came to consult him were taken prisoners. The sorcerer was quickly brought to the capital to be judged according to the law, etc. After three days the sorcerer returned in a sumptuous official car, with revolver by his waist and with a lot of money.

Proud of his triumph he divulged the rumor that he had been brought into the presence of Trujillo as soon as he came to the capital and from the moment he met with *El Jefe* the latter started to suffer from contortions and he [the sorcerer] succeeded in conjuring the evil spell which had been cast upon Trujillo and made it leave his body.[172]

The anecdote concludes by telling that Trujillo, in gratitude, constructed a new road to La Maguana, but the *brujo* could not enjoy his good fortune for a long time, since he became insane and was taken to the lunatic asylum in Nigua.[173] When asked whether he believed this story was true or not Reilly stated that he did not recall the incident, but that it might be true since Trujillo was a very superstitious man who at times entertained *brujos* at his estates.[174]

> He frequently consulted those whom he believed to hold the power of divination. He used spells on occasion. […] A medicine man would be summoned and would report his findings. The men possessing these powers, the *brujos*, were used for general information rather than for specific decisions on particular policies of state. These decisions Trujillo would share with no man, however exalted or depraved the source of his powers.[175]

After the death of Trujillo the Dominican press was filled with speculations about his alleged addiction to sorcery and 'superstition'. The *Olivorista* movement was sometimes mentioned in these articles:

> Trujillo, according to the confident revelations which form the basis of this article, gave on one occasion various stud animals to the Liboristas who lived within an agricultural colony by the frontier.

---

172 Arzeno Rodríguez (n.d.), pp. 162–3.
173 Ibid.
174 Interview with Thomas Reilly, San Juan de la Maguana, 12 March 1986. In Santo Domingo we have personally participated in voodoo sessions conducted by a famous *bruja*, who was known to have been, and according to her own testimonies was, the lover of Trujillo and who has a daughter with him. She stated that 'Trujillo was very interested in all things concerning the spiritual sphere' (interview with 'Doña Blanca', Santo Domingo, 4 November 1985).
175 Crassweller (1966), p. 85.

Then, just like now, the 'sanctuary' of the Liboristas had been turned into a refugee camp for bandits and other criminals who were on the run from the justice, people who united themselves with the naive fanatics of the sect, apparently accepting their beliefs in order to escape persecution from the justice.

One of these 'brujos' was living for a long time on a farm belonging to Nieves Luisa Trujillo, close to Villa Mella, where ceremonies similar to those in Palma Sola were staged.[176]

The majority of these articles were mere speculations which surfaced after the massacre in Palma Sola, where hundreds of *Olivoristas* were killed in December 1962. Still, it is evident that Rafael Trujillo was a superstitious man. In his personal archives one finds the very elaborate astrological charts which where made for him on a regular basis by his 'court astrologer' Henry Gazó.[177] What his astrologers probably failed to do was to pinpoint the day of his assassination in 1961 and all the commotion which followed.

However, a correct forecast is said to have been made in the remote San Juan Valley where new leaders had appeared among the *Olivoristas*, prophesying the death of the dictator and declaring that the spirit of Olivorio was still alive in his old home district. When Trujillo was dead, Miguel Angel Ramírez came back to claim the principality of his family and in the mountains the *Olivoristas* were now asserting that the dawn had come for the establishment of a new world order under the auspices of the spirit of Olivorio Mateo. The stage was set for a new and tragic act in the *Olivorista* drama.

176 Bobea Bellini (1963).
177 Vega (1986c), pp. 133–7.

4 Palma Sola

The revival of *Olivorismo*, 1961–62

To many peasants in the San Juan Valley the Great Power of God is always present. The force of this spiritual sphere is always with them, ready to spring forth in the landscape or through some human being:

> These things are always around here. People are very idolatrous, very believing. If some prophet appears people gather from all directions, eager to receive benefits of various kinds. Just as an example: three months ago crowds of people went to Bánica in order to see a half-buried man who was predicting the future. It turned out to be just another rumor but it shows how interested people are in spiritual things.[1]

> They all say '*Soy católico de cuerpo y alma*' ['I am Catholic to body and soul'] but many of them are attached to a '*religión popular*', an exaggerated belief in healing saints and something they call 'the Great Power of God'. When some 'healer' comes along he will always find followers.[2]

Many *Sanjuaneros* are convinced that Indian spirits live in caves and springs and that these spirits, together with the *misterios* [voodoo gods], are able to communicate with human beings through powerful mediums who serve as intermediaries between the world of the living and the spiritual sphere. That sphere is considered to be just as real as the one we call 'reality'. The realm of the spirits is always present and can never disappear. It remains around us even if people are forbidden to worship its invisible forces.

---

1 Interview with Eugenio Fernández Durán, San Juan de la Maguana, 4 July 1990.
2 Interview with Thomas Reilly, San Juan de la Maguana, 12 December 1985.

Olivorio resurrected: the twins of Palma Sola

After his death in 1922, Olivorio had passed into the spiritual sphere. He was no longer a medium, an intermediary between the human and the spiritual world, but he was worshiped in his own right. His soul had retreated into the spiritual abode after the disappearance of its worldly receptacle.

Thus, Olivorio continued to be present in the San Juan Valley. Many peasant dwellings contained altars dedicated to both saints and *misterios*, and often these altars were decorated with his blue and white flag[3] and the photo of his corpse taken by photographer Suazo in 1922. Not even Trujillo was able to wipe out the family cult of Olivorio, which was carried out mainly in the privacy of the *Olivorista* homes. It was only when the cult went public that problems arose. This happened with certain intervals. Bishop Reilly recalled that 'we had at least seven or eight outbreaks of fanaticism during the time I served in the valley'.[4]

One of these 'outbreaks' completely overshadowed all the others. Eight kilometers north of Las Matas de Farfán lies the *sección* of Carrera de Yeguas, named after the village with the same name. At the time Trujillo was assassinated, in and around Carrera de Yeguas lived the sons and daughters of León Ventura, the man who more than thirty years before had been forced to flee to Haiti after his son Delanoy had killed a *Trujillista* guard. His other children had been brought up with different relatives, as the Ventura family wanted to have them spread out in the event that the *Trujillistas* were to take vengeance on the children of the rebellious peasant.

León and his wife, Paulina del Rosario Rodríguez de Ventura, had seven children together.[5] Of these, four boys and one girl are mentioned in the Book of Baptisms of the parish of Santa Lucía in Las Matas de Farfán. Delanoy was the oldest one, born in 1907. After him came Nicolás, called 'Barraco', born in 1918, Plinio, born in 1921 and León Romilio, born in 1924. The girl, Bonifacia, was born in 1927.[6]

---

3 The appearance of this banner differs, but it usually consists of three white crosses against a blue background.

4 Interview with Thomas Reilly, San Juan de la Maguana, 12 December 1985.

5 León Ventura had seven more children with a woman named Carmelita Beltré and one with Juliana Rodríguez (Martínez (1991), p. 126). The sons and daughters of these different unions were in constant contact with one another and many of them participated in the activities in Palma Sola.

6 *Libros de bautismos de la Parroquia de Santa Lucía de las Matas de Farfán*. The books mention two more children of León Ventura and Paulina del Rosario. The first is Hilario, who is entered as a 'legitimate' son of theirs, but who was actually the child of a brother of León. Another entry mentions a certain Manuel, who could not be identified by the Venturas interviewed. The parish priest explained that this may be due to the fact that children are sometimes inscribed in the books with names that are often forgotten by their

Paulina had several twin births and due to this phenomenon many neighbors treated the children of Paulina with special respect. In the western districts of the Dominican Republic, *mellizos*, twins, are sometimes considered to have special links with the spiritual world. This may be due to the strong presence of voodooistic beliefs in these areas. Within the voodooistic belief system, *mellizos*, or *marasas* as they also are called along the Haitian border,[7] are venerated as powerful beings. Not only the actual twins but also the child born before them, called *soquete*, or the one born after them, called *dosú*, are believed to be endowed with spiritual powers.[8]

The Ventura family was particularly favored by powers endowed by twin births. Paulina bore twins no fewer than three times: León Romilio was born together with a twin sister who died after a week.[9] Another child, Tulio, was born together with a brother who expired after some hours. Paulina also begot two still-born twin sisters.[10] Thus, even though no pair of twins survived, many of the Ventura children were still considered to be *soquetes*, *dosús* or *jimos*[11] [another denomination used on a twin], and all of them were frequently referred to as the *Mellizos*.

Olivorista traditions were strong within the Ventura family. Both the children's grandfather, Colén Cuevas, and their own father had been personal friends of Olivorio and firm believers in his heavenly mandate. Furthermore, the Venturas owned somewhat more land than the average peasant in Carrera de Yeguas. They were far from being wealthy landowners but by Carrera de Yeguas standards they could be classified as 'middle-holders', i.e. they did not belong to the huge majority of *minifundistas*

relatives, who prefer to use different names instead (interview with Bryan Kennedy, Las Matas de Farfán, 4 May 1986).
7 The Creole word for twin is *marasa*.
8 Cf. Peñolguín (1940), pp. 110–12, Labourt (1979), pp. 73–6, Deive (1979), pp. 139–41 and Davis (1987), pp. 129–31. The *marasa* cult is very prominent in Haitian voodoo. Twins, both dead and living, are served in an annual, very elaborate ritual, and every fifth year an even more sumptous feast – the *gran sèvis* – is offered to them. Twin spirits are personified by a *lwa*, also named *Marasa*, who is believed to be exceptionally powerful as he is considered to be the spirit of the first of all human children who have died, 'and as the child precedes the man. Marassa [sic] is the first and foremost of all loa' (Courlander (1960), p. 34).
    The prominence of the twin cult in voodoo may be an inheritance from Dahomean religion, where twin gods like Mawu-Lisa, Aido-Hwedo and Hoho are very important (Herskovits and Herskovits (1933), pp. 11–14, 56–7 and 59). For a comparative study of twin cults all over the world, see Harris (1906).
9 León Romilio Ventura was always considered to be endowed with special spiritual gifts, and so was his *soquete*, Plinio, who became the leader of the cult they founded together, and Bonifacia, his *dosú*, who was considered to be a gifted spiritual medium.
10 Espín del Prado (1980), p. 66.
11 The word *jimos* probably has the same origin as *jimaguas*, the denomination of twins within Cuban *santería* (Deive (1979), p. 138).

Figure 4.1 Plinio Ventura.　　　　　*Figure 4.2* León Romilio Ventura.

[smallholders].[12] All these facts made them a rather powerful influence in the daily life of Carrera de Yeguas and its surrounding hamlets. 'They were all able workers and people of good habits.'[13]

The most eloquent members of the family were Plinio and León Romilio. Plinio was a good-looking, short, thin man, with impressive, sharp features. He was serious, endowed with a contemplative nature, and even though he was illiterate he was eloquent in his manner of speech. According to one of his daughters 'he spoke more elegantly and beautifully than any man of letters',[14] and one of his followers stated that Plinio 'always spoke very eloquently because he was constantly carrying the Holy Spirit within himself'.[15] Plinio was forty in 1961. His younger brother, León Romilio, who was born three years later, was more educated. He could read and write and had served as a teacher in one of Trujillo's 'emergency

12　León Romilio Ventura, the only surviving male of the Ventura children, presently owns between 10,000 and 20,000 *tareas* in *Sección de Carrera de Yeguas* (García (1986), p. 35), and his older brother, Plinio, owned approximately 20,000 *tareas* (1,250 hectares) in 1962 (Sosa (1982b)).

13　Interview with Mimicito Ramírez, San Juan de la Maguana, 14 December 1985.

14　Marina Rodríguez, quoted in Martínez (1980), p. 148. Marina is forty-one years old (in 1991). She owns an elaborate altar in honor of Olivorio in Carrera de Yeguas and is considered to be one of the leaders of his cult there (cf. de la Mota (1980), pp. 216–17). For Plinio and León Romilio, see Martínez (1991), p. 130.

15　Interview with an *Olivorista*, Las Matas de Farfán, 5 July 1990. This man wanted to remain anonymous since he stated that 'I have been suffering so much from my participation in all that'.

schools'.[16] León Romilio was the most extroverted of the brothers. He was considered to be a practical man and the most able organizer of the two.[17] When dealing with authorities and other 'outsiders' it was mostly León Romilio who pleaded Plinio's cause, because Plinio 'did not always know how to behave in front of such people and he could easily get annoyed'.[18]

When their father escaped to Haiti, Plinio and Romilio stayed with their mother while their brothers and sisters went to the homes of other relatives. When their mother died in 1953, they went to live with with an older half-sister named Adela.[19] Plinio and Romilio were brought up within the traditional *Olivorista* faith and like most of their neighbors were convinced of the presence of a powerful spiritual sphere surrounding them:

> I have always been in contact with the spiritual world. It has never abandoned me. Those who speak with me are persons. They appear when they want to give me a message or advice, but I may also search for them myself. Wherever I am, they are around me. They appear as persons. I have met with the Eternal, Almighty Father, the Holy Ghost, Jesus, Olivorio, St John the Baptist and the Queen of the Earth. I have been talking to all the *misterios*.[20]

At the beginning of 1961[21] the powers of the spiritual realm began to make their presence felt in a more urgent manner. Plinio was afflicted by

---

16 In 1941 it was decreed that 5,000 'emergency schools' would be established in the rural areas of the Dominican Republic. Two years were considered enough to qualify the rural youngsters as 'literate' (Clausner (1973), pp. 220–1). The first-year students ranged from eight to eleven years in age and the second-year ones from eleven to fourteen. The first year was dedicated to elementary reading and writing, the second included arithmetic, history and geography. The education was very elementary and the teaching staff inferior. In 1952 the monthly salary of an emergency teacher was less than half that of a teacher in a regular rural primary school (ibid., p. 221). León Romilio Ventura had eight years of formal schooling and had attended primary school in Las Matas de Farfán. For seven years he served as emergency teacher in Rincón Grande, Las Cañitas (Bánica) and Los Limones (Carrera de Yeguas). At the age of thirty he quit his teaching position and got part-time employment as 'inspector' for the peanut company *La Manicera* (Martínez (1991), p. 131). The inspectors of *La Manicera* provide peasants with peanuts for seeding and after harvest the peasants have to return the 'given' amount of peanuts and sell the surplus to the company representatives (Vargas-Lundius (1991), p. 7).

17 Espín del Prado (1980), p. 67.

18 Interview with León Romilio Ventura, Media Luna, 5 May 1986.

19 Interview with Juana María Ventura, Media Luna, 5 May 1986. Adela Ventura died at the age of eighty-three in 1983. She was the eldest of León Ventura's children.

20 Interview with León Romilio Ventura, Media Luna, 5 May 1986.

21 The date differs from source to source. León Romilio himself has stated on several occasions that the strange occurrences began some months before the death of Trujillo (30 May 1961) (interviews with León Romilio Ventura, Media Luna, 17 January 1986 and Las Matas de Farfán, 14 May 1989).

strange dreams, and, as many *Sanjuanero* visionaries had done before him, he went to the caves and other holy places in the Cordillera Central in order to make contact with the powers he felt were trying to reach him. Later on he claimed that there, high up in the mountains, a vision of an old bearded man clad in white robes had appeared in front of him. He did not know the meaning of the apparition but he knew for sure that it had something to do with a kind of 'divine mission'.

Meanwhile, his brother, León Romilio, while working in one of his fields in Sabana Larga, had another vision. He claimed that he had seen a small child with blue eyes. The child was dressed in golden clothes and short trousers. The child told León Romilio that he had to go into the mountains and find his brother, because the two of them had to carry out a mission together.[22] León Romilio saddled his mule and went in search of his brother, to tell him about his revelation. He searched for him for a long time and finally found him in a place called Palma Sola, were he had been some fifteen to twenty days.[23] It then became clear to the two brothers that the same spiritual force – the Great Power of God, or Olivorio, had chosen that particular place 'because a great work had to be carried out there'.[24] 'We left everything, cattle, land. Everything was lost, but we gained God.'[25]

Still, Plinio and León Romilio were not sure of the exact meaning of 'great'. The two brothers set out together on a kind of spiritual search. They figured out that the message had to do with Olivorio[26] and they visited many of the sites where cults were carried out in honor of *El Maestro*, collecting information about his life and 'works'.[27] During these wanderings it frequently happened that the brothers became possessed by the spirit of Olivorio and preached and cured people under his influence.[28]

---

22 Espín del Prado (1980), p. 54.
23 Interview with León Romilio Ventura, Media Luna, 5 May 1986. Palma Sola was a piece of dry land belonging to Tibo de los Santos, the father-in-law of Adela, the older half-sister of León Romilio and Plinio. It was fit only for goat-breeding. When the movement in Palma Sola grew the *Mellizos* were granted land from other neighboring landowners (Martínez (1991), pp. 133–4).
24 Interview with León Romilio Ventura, Media Luna, 17 January 1986.
25 León Romilio Ventura, quoted in Martínez (1991), p. 132.
26 Among many *Olivoristas* there seems to be a very close connection between the Holy Spirit, who introduced the Ventura brothers to their mission, and Olivorio. It appear as if Olivorio is seen either as identical with the Spirit, or considered to be a kind of transmitter of its force (interview with Leopoldo Figuereo, San Juan de la Maguana, 4 June 1989).
27 Ibid.
28 Bautista Mejía (1988), pp. 12 and 14–16. Possession by the spirit of Olivorio is a rather common phenomenon among *Olivoristas* in the San Juan Valley. For example, on a feast carried out in Olivorio's honor in Jínova (4 June 1989) we witnessed how a woman was possessed by Olivorio while she was sitting quietly on the floor by his altar. She was very calm and with a voice that had a slightly 'masculine' tone she gave the bystanders several

Just like *El Maestro* had done before them, Plinio and León Romilio prophesied and touched on political issues. Their most coherent, and dangerous, prophetic statement was that Trujillo would be killed in the not too distant future.[29]

The Ventura brothers were not the only *Olivorista* visionaries who were active in those days. People like that were always around in the San Juan Valley, and in days of need and political tensions they seemed to multiply. The Venturas were not even alone in predicting the imminent death of Trujillo. On their wanderings they met with a certain Mauro Medina, who acted in a fashion similar to their own.[30] Mauro used to foretell the death of Trujillo in the following manner: 'in the Dominican country there is a very big trunk and this trunk is going to be cut down with wood from the same trunk. Tell it to the whole world.'[31] However, Mauro recognized the stronger power of the Ventura brothers and soon joined them on their wanderings.[32]

After the death of Trujillo it was as if the lid had been lifted from the boiling pot of *Olivorismo*. A wave of religious emotions swept through the old *Olivorista* districts. Old believers came forth and new visions appeared to several people. Among the new visionaries was another Ventura brother, Barraco, who five months after the death of Trujillo stated that he had had an encounter with the *El Padre Externo* [the External Father], or more likely, *El Padre Eterno* [the Eternal Father].[33] The Ventura brothers interpreted this as the ultimate sign that the day had come to found the mission in Palma Sola. But before they agreed upon Palma Sola, they made a long trip together through the Cordillera Central, visiting the holy places within

pieces of advice. She constantly repeated that 'community' was the most important thing of all: 'People have to be united in work for the common good.'

    Bautista Mejía states that Olivorio often possessed León Romilio and Plinio by turns. When he spoke through the mouth of Plinio, León Romilio was quiet. The informant contended that the phenomenon could even be observed when the brothers were far from one another. When León Romilio fell silent, Plinio started to talk even if he was out of earshot (interview with Patoño Bautista Mejía, Distrito de Haina, 5 March 1986).

29 Bautista Mejía (1988), pp. 16–19.

30 Ibid., p. 20.

31 Manuel Caamaño, quoted in Martínez (1980), p. 165.

32 Bautista Mejía (1988), p. 20.

33 Ibid. At the beginning of the 1960s, few Dominican peasants had any first-hand knowledge of biblical texts. Their religious terminology was often based on hearsay: a mixture of disconnected phrases taken from the Catholic mass, the Bible and various prayer books. Many popular preachers pride themselves on not having read the Bible, such as Bartolo, a 'missionary' by the Spring of San Juan in Maguana Arriba, who stated that 'I got my message directly from *los misterios* and Olivorio. I do not know how to read the Bible, but people who know say that I preach the same message and that proves that I am right' (interview with Bartolo de Jiménez, La Agüita, Maguana Arriba, 13 December 1985).

the huge mountain massif. At their return they finally settled in Palma Sola. From there they went in search of assistants. They visited many well-known *Olivoristas*, inviting them to join forces with them in Palma Sola. One of them was Diego Cépeda, who is still an important *Olivorista* leader in Jínova:

> I am not familiar with *seres* [voodoo gods] and all that, but I have a commitment with God and his mother. I am all alone with that. [...] I did not know the *Mellizos*, and before they came to me I did not know that there existed a place called Palma Sola. They came searching for me because they knew I was a religious man. They searched for people like me.[34]

Diego followed the *Mellizos* up to Palma Sola, was impressed by what he and stayed there for several long periods. Meanwhile, in a place called La Palma, not far from the border town of Bánica, a young widow, Inés Rosario Alcántara, was possessed by the *seres* Belié Belcán and Ogún Balenyó. After that experience she felt that the 'powers' stayed with her and that she was able to cure people with the help of 'her' *seres*. Her fame grew rapidly in the neighboring villages and finally the *Mellizos* came to her and brought her with them to Palma Sola where they crowned her as a 'virgin'.[35]

Still, not all *Olivoristas* accepted the *Mellizos* and their mission: 'Palma Sola was nothing but a fraud. We did not go there, they were in politics and I did not believe in them. I told them: "I believe in another one, not in you. [...] I never saw any Ventura when I was with Olivorio".'[36]

However, many others came, even some of the leaders of the powerful *Cofradía del Espíritu Santo* in El Batey, the largest religious brotherhood in the San Juan Valley, with local branches in almost every village and town within the area:

---

34 Interview with Diego Cépeda, Jínova, 4 June 1989.
35 Interview with Inés Rosario Alcántara, Bánica, 2 June 1989. Doña Inés is still practicing a variety of Dominican *vodú*. Belié Belcán is one of the most popular *seres* within the Dominican voodoo cult. On the altars he is depicted by a chromolithograph of St Michael. People possessed by him like to dress in red and green and talk with a harsh, guttural voice. Belié Belcán is known to be rude, but wise and sincere. An enemy of witchcraft, a seducer and merrymaker, Ogún Balenyó is also a warrior, his color is red and he likes gin. People possessed by him move rapidly and talk with much intensity. This *ser* is considered to be the champion of justice and represents all military and knightly virtues. On altars he is represented by St James the Greater, the Catholic warrior saint. Like Olivorio he is clad in blue and white and he is often identified with *El Maestro*. In *vodú* sessions Belcán and Balenyó frequently appear together. For a description of the characteristics of these *seres* see Miniño (1980) and Jiménez Lambertus (1980), p.182.
36 Interview with Julián Ramos, Higüerito, 16 January 1986.

I myself was there at least 12 times. [...] It was a strange experience coming up there. Everything was shared; nothing was lost or stolen. [...] Some leaders directed the word, but it was Olivorio who was in charge of the mystery. He could not be seen, but he was there all right.[37]

The first group of peasants who settled in Palma Sola came from the village of Cocinera. Most of them belonged to an extended family named Bautista, whose members became very influential in Palma Sola, particularly in the practical organization of the place. The first visitors lived in the house of Adela, the *Mellizos'* older sister, and her husband later stated: 'Never again did I sleep in my own bed. Sometimes I wanted to go to bed, but when I tried to, I [always] found a group of people sleeping in it.'[38]

The foundation and organization of Palma Sola

The place

The construction of houses and huts started almost immediately in Palma Sola. Today it is a desolate, god-forsaken place. Among the thorny brushwood one may still discern the stone-lined procession roads and small mounds of white stones that were once piled up around ceremonial crosses. Various simple house foundations, not more than stones laid out in rectangles, are found all over the terrain, confirming that it was once inhabited by many people. Today there are no houses, no people. The only living beings are some ravens, a few stray goats, and perhaps a lonesome cow. Among *cambrones*, *guazumas*, *candelones* and other dry and spiny plant species, carbonized bits of wood litter the ground, bearing silent but eloquent testimony to the tragedy that once took place in Palma Sola.

In 1962, however, the scene was completely different. Palma Sola was then a cult center bustling with activity. The terrain consisted of about 100 *tareas* (6.3 hectares)[39] with at least 200 houses.[40] On 11 December, *El Caribe* reported that more than 3,000 people were arriving every day,[41] and between 1,500 and 2,000 lived there on a more or less permanent basis.[42]

---

37 Interview with Arsidé Gardés, El Batey, 11 April 1986.
38 Gaspar Mora, quoted in Martínez (1991), p. 134.
39 Interview with León Romilio Ventura, Media Luna, 5 May 1986.
40 When the community was destroyed the military counted 184 occupied houses and 203 more in the process of being constructed (Bodden (1962), p. 10). León Romilio claims that Palma Sola had as many as 800 houses, and that 500 more were under construction (interview, Media Luna, 5 May 1986).
41 Gómez Pepín (1962b).
42 Interview with Thomas Reilly, San Juan de la Maguana, 12 December 1985.

Figure 4.3 Fording the Yacahueque River on the road to Palma Sola.

The men who frequented the bars of San Juan de la Maguana or Las Matas de Farfán used to count the overcrowded buses, jeeps and trucks that constantly poured in from all over the country on their way to Palma Sola. They soon discovered that many came from such far away places as Samaná and Cotuí. The rumors about miracles in Palma Sola had spread rapidly.[43]

The vehicles parked by a ford on the Yacahueque River just north of Carrera de Yeguas. From there the pilgrims had to walk about 4 kilometers, through the rice paddies of La Colonia, up to the small hillock of Palma Sola. The walk was hot and tiring, and many visitors obtained food and drink from the many stalls that lined the road by the ford. There was no water in Palma Sola and all commerce was banned from the holy place, but by the ford business was thriving to such a degree that some people came there only to trade, without bothering to go to Palma Sola. Items from both Haiti and the easternmost parts of the Dominican Republic were available.[44] Some of the stalls were furnished and controlled by a member of the inner circle of the leaders in Palma Sola, Patoño Bautista, who later stated that he received a good income from his business:

43 Interview with Radhamés Gómez Pepín, Santo Domingo, 18 March 1986.
44 Interview with Bolívar Ventura Rodríguez, Palma Sola, 5 May 1986. Bolívar guided us through the deserted cult site of Palma Sola. He lives in the 'new' Palma Sola, a small village constructed a few kilometers from the old one. It was erected when the original site was destroyed. Most of the inhabitants of the new Palma Sola are survivors from the massacre in 1962.

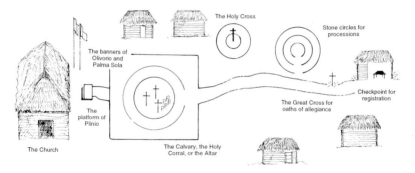

Figure 4.4 The center of Palma Sola.

Note: This is a reconstruction and it is not to scale. The sketch was drawn in Media Luna, with the help of some members of the Ventura family, after visiting the site of the massacre (5 May 1986). An elaborate and probably more accurate plan is presented in Martínez (1991), p. 151.

without doubt, the *Mellizos* detested those things. Sometimes, when some of my friends noticed that this business was mine they considered me a false Liborista and they even told me that if I did not fall into line I would be lost, because, for them, anyone who did something secret or contrary to the orders of the *Mellizos* would not live until 1963.[45]

Arriving at Palma Sola (see Figure 4.4) all visitors had to stop by a checkpoint at one of the entrances. There were three entrances to the holy compound. Most important was the main entrance in the south which was directed towards Carrera de Yeguas. The one in the north was situated by a path which led all the way to the border town of Bánica. All checkpoints, or *centinelas* [sentries], were manned by at least five members of Palma Sola's own guard: volunteers dressed in blue denim pants, white shirts and black ties. By their side the guards carried white-painted wooden truncheons. No one was allowed to carry any kind of weapon – except Plinio, who always had a dagger stuck into his belt.[46] The sentry houses were large enough to house several guards, who were on duty day and night. On

---

45 Bautista Mejía (1988), p. 29. The irritation the *Olivoristas* felt when they heard about Patoño's business was quite natural. It is still considered to be very rude to offer food for money to any visitor who comes to take part in an *Olivorista* ceremony.

46 The dagger, a long one with colored stripes around its handle, was of a kind which is still very common around Carrera de Yeguas. Like the famous sword of Olivorio, it was probably some kind of insignium, as were the spurs Plinio always wore and which he told people would not be removed until he was dead (cf. García (1986), p. 169). To one of his disciples he explained: 'I am involved in a struggle and he who takes my spurs away from me has disarmed me and a disarmed rooster never wins the battle' (quoted by Bautista Mejía (1988), p. 34).

Figure 4.5 The checkpoint at the entrance to Palma Sola.

certain hours during the night they checked that nothing 'improper took place'. It was, for example, totally forbidden for men and women to sleep together within the sacred grounds. Most visitors slept in the open air, but some stayed with relatives who had established themselves in Palma Sola.[47]

All pistols, machetes and knives had to be checked at the entrance. By a table sat Macario Lorenzo, or one of his assistants, who was responsible for Palma Sola's book of register, called *Libro de la Unión Cristiana Mundial* [Book of the Worldwide Christian Union]. From its first entry on 12 November 1961, until the last name was written on 28 December 1962, 43,000 names were inscribed in it. Every entry carried the name of the visitor, the number of his or her identity card, the year of birth, as well as the profession and the place of residence. The book, 'authorized by the Holy Spirit',[48] was kept 'as an outward sign of the visitors' willingness to confess their sins before entering the holy corral and that by their inscription they gave testimony to the world that they were abiding by the rules of Palma Sola. Only persons older than eighteen years were inscribed.'[49]

47 Interview with Patoño Bautista Mejía, Distrito de Haina, 5 March 1986. In the beginning this force counted 300 men, working in shifts (Bautista Mejía (1988), p. 23). Later on, when more and more people crowded in to Palma Sola, its size was increased. Patoño himself mentioned a figure of 600 men. Other sources estimate the guards to have had around 400 members (*Santomé*, 30 November 1962).

48 Interview with León Romilio Ventura, Media Luna, 17 January 1986.

49 Interview with Macario Lorenzo, Las Matas de Farfán, 14 May 1989. The inscriptions were at first made in common notebooks, but later huge bound books were acquired. The military seized the last one of these books which was found to contain 477 pages with some 10,000 names (Estrella Veloz (1962a)).

Figure 4.6 The book of the *Unión Cristiana Mundial.*

Figure 4.7 The great cross for oaths of allegiance at Palma Sola.

After going through the formalities at the checkpoint the visitors proceeded to *La Cruz Grande de Juramento* [Great Cross for Oaths of Allegiance]. One of the Ventura brothers was always posted beside it and administered the oath to the visitors, who had to kneel in front of the black-painted cross.[50] The Ventura brother who was in charge of the oaths was Tulio, even if he sometimes had one of his brothers stand in for him. Since Tulio was a *mellizo*, he was thought to be imbued with special spiritual powers.[51] The oath that every visitor had to repeat was the following:

Juro por Dios, el Padre, el Hijo
y el Espíritu Santo y por
Olivorio Mateo cumplir la
misión que se me ponga para
que Dios me sane de todos
mis quebrantos.[52]

I swear by God, the Father, the Son
and the Holy Spirit and by
Olivorio Mateo to carry out the
mission imposed on me so
that God may deliver me from
all my afflictions.

---

50 All crossbeams of the crosses in Palma Sola were tied to their trunks with ropes, since 'the Holy Spirit forbade nails to be used while making them'. The Cross of Allegiance was black because 'it took the sins of the people upon itself' (interview with Patoño Bautista Mejía, Distrito de Haina, 5 March 1986).

51 Cf. above: Tulio's twin brother had died just a few hours after birth.

52 Quoted by Patoño Bautista Mejía, interview, Distrito de Haina, 5 March 1986.

Another oath used was:

Usted jura ser fiel a Cristo	You swear to be true to Christ
y al Maestro Olivorio.	and to Master Olivorio.
Las tres niñas Santa y Bendita [sic]	The three Holy and Blessed girls
y a mi Madre María Santísima.	and to my Most Holy Mother Mary.
'Yo juro', contestaban.[53]	'I swear', they answered.

After pronouncing the oath the visitors often continued to some stone circles, which were circled three times. This was not necessary, but everyone had to make a halt in front of the Holy Cross, which carried several other names: the Black Cross, Cross of Reverence or *Cruz del Paso* [Cross of the Step], probably because it was erected at the entrance to the Holy Corral, the center of Palma Sola. By this cross the visitor encountered a man named Manuel Tapia. He was possessed by a personal *misterio* of his called Componte. This spirit had revealed itself to Manuel stating: 'I am Componte. I have come to fix this world [*componer a este mundo*]. I come from Heaven and I am going to Palma Sola because there are my brothers.'[54] Inspired by Componte, Manuel Tapia spoke to the multitude kneeling in front of the Holy Cross.[55]

After the halt by the Holy Cross the pilgrims proceeded to the spiritual center of Palma Sola – the calvary. Many approached these three crosses on their knees, others carried stones on their heads as an act of penitence. The procession road which led up to the crosses was lined with white stones. The crosses were circled three times and afterwards the pilgrims kneeled in front of them, making the sign of the cross and shrugging their shoulders in order to deliver themselves from their sins.[56]

A guard was always on duty beside the crosses in order to ensure that no one entered the inner circle around them, where there were flags and pictures of saints and *misterios,* as well as the candles the visitors burned in front of the images. Transgressors who violated the strict rules were caught and brought into custody by the entrances until their company left. If they had come without companions they were simply thrown out of the holy

---

53 Quoted in Martínez (1991), p. 140. The meaning of the three 'Holy and Blessed girls' remains obscure to us, although the worship of various 'divine' children is common in the San Juan Valley, both in the form of the Holy Spirit and twin saints like Cosmas and Damian. See Turner and Turner (1978), p. 73, on the role of child saints in agrarian societies.

54 Bautista Mejía (1988), pp. 26–7.

55 It is somewhat unclear if Manuel Tapia was placed beside this cross. Lusitania Martínez states that Manuel was to be found close to the Cross of Allegiance and that León Romilio used to stand by the Great Cross (Martínez (1991), p. 141).

56 This behavior was not unique for Palma Sola. It is repeated in front of calvaries which are found in many rural areas of the Dominican Republic.

Figure 4.8 The calvary of Palma Sola.

grounds. The force of the sacred place was said to be so strong that sinners and evildoers fell to the ground in convulsions in front of the crosses. Many others were gripped by more benevolent spiritual forces who possessed them and made them prophesy.

Communal rituals took place by the calvary at 7 a.m. and 5 p.m., when one of the *Mellizos* administered an oath to all those present. On Tuesdays and Fridays,[57] Plinio entered the rostrum behind the calvary and delivered a lengthy sermon to the multitude. He used to touch on various subjects, but his central theme was always 'the union of all Christians, the work for the common good and justice for all. Only healthy advice, all of it.'[58] The visitors often brought with them pieces of wood called *palos de cruz* [sticks of the cross], small wooden sticks from some aromatic tree. These *palos* were blessed by the *Mellizos* and brought home to the family altars.[59]

The preaching and blessing of the *palos* were followed by the communal singing of *salves*,[60] and dancing. Sometimes the dancing had an ecstatic

---

57 As Fridays and Tuesdays are associated with the crucifixion and resurrection, they are, across Latin America, the days for rites of sorcery and its reversal (Taussig (1980), pp. 107 and 148).

58 Interview with León Romilio Ventura, Media Luna, 17 January 1986.

59 Bautista Mejía (1988), p. 39. Such *palos* may still be seen on the altars in the southwestern regions of the Dominican Republic.

60 The singing of *salves* is a communal activity and an important ingredient in most popular religious acts in the San Juan Valley. New *salves* are constantly being composed and they differ from community to community. There are several hundred honoring Olivorio and many new ones were made in Palma Sola. On Dominican *salves* see Davis (1981).

Figure 4.9 Kneeling at the calvary at Palma Sola.

character; people raised their hands and shook their bodies violently. Some participants fell to the ground and rolled back and forth. It was even said that some dancers started to 'fly' in their moments of ecstasy. They jumped up and made swirling movements in the air.[61] Often traditional peasant dances, like the *mangulina,* the *carbiné* and the *merengue,* were performed to the accompaniment of a *perico ripiao,* the customary rural orchestra consisting of an accordion, a *güiro,* and a *balcié,* a small drum. The dance of the *palos,* the big drums of the *Cofradía del Espíritu Santo,* was also performed.

The practice of these dances in the cult of Palma Sola did not differ from what was common in other religious ceremonies within the vast spectrum of Dominican popular religion. The only difference may be the many instances of *caídas* [falls], related above. These were apparently not unlike similar phenomena which may occur in sectarian prayer meetings. Exactly as in *vodú* sessions, 'fallen' people were often taken aside and treated by the *Mellizos,* who tried to calm the persons afflicted by such fits by driving out the spirits believed to be attacking them.[62] When the communal

61 Interview with Radhamés Gómez Pepín, Santo Domingo, 18 March 1986 and interview with Marina Bautista, Las Matas de Farfán, 5 July 1990. Marina came with her widowed father to Palma Sola, where he served as one of the guards. Her father was later killed in the massacre. In Palma Sola, Marina lived with a 'woman of Plinio'.

62 As some young ladies were carried into the 'church' during their attacks, this may have been one of the reasons for the rumors which soon developed, suggesting that the *Mellizos* took sexual advantage of some of their female followers (interview with Radhamés Gómez Pepín, Santo Domingo, 18 March 1986).

dancing had finished, usually after an hour, the pilgrims would walk up to a nearby hill where they kneeled in the light of candles, torches and *faroles*,[63] singing *salves* and praying to God, the Virgin and Olivorio.[64]

The church: healings, virgins and promiscuity

The center of religious life in Palma Sola was the calvary and the 'church'. Like the rest of the houses in Palma Sola, the blue-painted walls of the church were made of intertwined twigs, called *tejemaní*, and the roof was done with *yaguas* or *pencas de cana*, i.e. the leaf-base from certain palm trees.[65] Outside, the banners of Olivorio and Palma Sola fluttered in the breeze. According to Juana María Rodríguez Ventura, who made the banner of Palma Sola, against a white background it carried the appliqués of a royal palm and the Virgin together with the embroidered text of *Unión Cristiana Mundial*, made with blue letters.[66] Lusitania Martínez offers a more elaborate description. According to this, the banner carried a picture of the palm, but instead of the Virgin it was embroidered with an elaborate coat of arms in the form of a heart. Fernando Lorenzo, one of the people close to León Romilio, presents a drawing of the coat of arms of Palma Sola in handwritten testimony he compiled in 1967.[67] This drawing is reproduced in Figure 4.10.

The flag was hoisted at 8 a.m. and lowered at 6 p.m. A rather long hymn was then sung in honor of the banner, mentioning Christ, the Virgin and

---

63 Lamps made out of cut-out, colored paper, arranged around candles and carried on long poles.

64 Interview with Juana María Ventura, Media Luna, 17 January 1986.

65 A few houses were made of planks and had zinc sheets roofs. All building material had to be carried up to Palma Sola. The work was carried out communally and the houses were erected very rapidly (Bautista Mejía (1988), pp. 28–9).

66 Interview with Juana María Ventura, Media Luna, 17 January 1986.

67 Martínez (1991) reproduces various pages of what she calls 'written literature from Palma Sola', consisting of four handwritten notebooks. Unfortunately she does not state which is which when she presents the facsimiles in her book. Judging from the hand-writing, the coat of arms from Palma Sola appears to come from a notebook entitled *¡Buenos días, Cristo! Un sencillo memorandum sobre La Bella Aurora, Misionera, cuna de la Unión Cristiana Mundial, cuya lema inmortal es 'Fe, Esperanza y Caridad' que infunde Amor y Perservancia. Relatado por Fernando Lorenzo, un testigo presencial* [How Do You Do, Christ: A Simple Memorandum Concerning the Mission of the Beautiful Dawn, Cradle of the Worldwide Christian Union, Whose Immortal Motto is 'Faith, Hope and Charity', Which Inspire Love and Perseverance. Told by Fernando Lorenzo, an Eyewitness] (title page reproduced in Martínez (1991), p. 139). The coat of arms is reproduced in op. cit., p. 153.

68 Such inscriptions are common on many crosses erected in the San Juan Valley. For example, close to the Spring of St John in Maguana Arriba is a cross whose crossbeam is inscribed with the word *Maestro* (i.e. Olivorio). The trunk carries the words *La Fe*, while the ends of the crossbeam are inscribed with *Esperansa* [sic] and *Caridad*, respectively.

Figure 4.10 The coat of arms of Palma Sola.

Note: The letters stand for *Fe* [Faith], *Esperanza* [Hope] and *Caridad* [Charity].[68] The arrow cross is called the 'Holy Sword of the Four Winds' and the initials under the 'southern' arrow stand for *Unión Cristiana Mundial*, the 'political party' of Palma Sola. The outer heart, formed by palm leaves, is said to symbolize both Palma Sola, *Santa Palma Libertadora* [the Holy Liberating Palm Tree] and 'World Liberty'. The crowning cross symbolizes Christ, and also the healing and purifying force of Palma Sola. The royal palm tree placed by the coat of arms on the banner was flanked by a big number 1, said to symbolize the Great Power of God (Martínez (1991), pp. 141–2).

Olivorio.[69] A wooden sign was also placed close to the banners, carrying the inscription: '*Unión Cristiana Mundial: Escuela del Cristo*' ['The Worldwide Christian Union: School of Christ'].[70]

The church consisted of two rooms. One of them was kept empty, except for a few chairs. People who were familiar with the setting of Dominican popular religion always marveled at this empty space, since everyone expected to see one of the elaborate altars which are so common in the Dominican countryside. 'Nothing was there, except our own living faith and the presence of the spirit of Olivorio.'[71] The empty room served as the 'office' of Plinio and León Romilio and prominent visitors were received there. One of the Ventura brothers was always present in the room, usually Plinio:

69 Martínez (1991), p. 142. Elaborate ceremonies in connection with the hoisting of the flag are common all over the Dominican Republic. While the flag on public buildings is hoisted or lowered, everyone, including car drivers, must stop in veneration and all people must face the flag. At Olivorio's cult site in Maguana Arriba, the caretaking 'queen' hoists and lowers the banners of Olivorio and the Republic while she sings the national anthem by herself, after delivering a somewhat incomprehensible discourse.
70 Martínez (1991), p. 140.
71 Interview with León Romilio Ventura, Media Luna, 17 January 1986.

Figure 4.11 Patoño Bautista Mejía and León Romilio Ventura.

It was always Romilio who went out and made contacts with people outside of Palma Sola. It was he who talked to the authorities and the press. Plinio always stayed in Palma Sola. It was his powers which cured the people; it was he who was the real boss. Many of the things Romilio did were not approved of by Plinio.[72]

Guards were posted by the entrance to the church in order to calm the visitors, who came in hundreds every day to talk to the *Mellizos* and receive their blessings. Even if the force of the place was said to be enough in order to cure people it appears as if the *Mellizos* also practiced various forms of faith healing, mainly by simply putting their hands on the suppliants, or making the sign of the cross over them, invoking the names of 'God, Olivorio and the Holy Cross'. They also gave away various decoctions, probably of the same composition as the ones León Romilio still makes: 'he cures colds, the evil eye, the liver, intestinal worms, etc., with roots that are commonly known as "*damajuana*".'[73]

The church was surrounded with much mystery, mainly due to the presence of the virgins:

---

72 Interview with Marina Bautista, Las Matas de Farfán, 5 July 1990.
73 Martínez (1991), p. 215. *Damajuana*, or *Mama Juana*, is the popular name given to all mixtures made with rum and certain roots or leaves. A distinction is usually made between medicinal *Mama Juanas* and aphrodisiac ones (Lemus and Marty (1976), pp. 45–6). The *Mellizos* were well aware of the fact that Dominican laws concerning 'illegal medicinal practices' could be used against them and accordingly they did not give away their 'medicines' in the open.

Figure 4.12 Inés Aquino, '*La Virgen Purísima de Palma Sola*'.

It was all very strange. When I visited that house during the election campaign for Miguel Angel [Alcántara Ramírez] we met with Plinio, who all alone on a chair in the middle of the room. When I left I opened another door and came into a room where a woman was sitting; she was all dressed in white. Plinio rose to his feet immediately and shouted: 'That is not the exit. You cannot go out there!' So I had to go out through the other door. I did not see any altars in the house and I could not understand why they called it the 'church'.[74]

The white-clad lady was probably Inés Aquino, a relative of the Venturas who came from Sabana Mula, the birthplace of the *Mellizos*' father and a well-known *Olivorista* stronghold. Her husband, Nonito Cuevas, was related to the Ventura family and had been a prominent member of Olivorio's group. Later on he became known as a medium for *El Maestro*, and was occasionally 'mounted' by Olivorio, speaking like him and carrying his banner. It was said that Nonito could easily be 'confounded with the Messiah'.[75] Inés Aquino was called *La Virgen Purísima* [the Most Pure Virgin] or *La Madre Piadosa* [the Pious Mother]. She was a lady of impressive stature and 'really looked like a saint or a virgin'. She seldom raised her head and was always dressed 'in a dress which covered her to the tips

---

74 Interview with Mimicito Ramírez, San Juan de la Maguana, 14 December 1985.
75 Martínez (1991), p. 160.

of her toes and her voice was like that of a nun surrendered to religion'.[76] She stated that she had come in January 1962, obeying orders that had been given to her by Olivorio and that her mission consisted in taking care of the children of Palma Sola. Thousands of children were brought to her to be baptized in the name of 'the Father, the Son and Olivorio'.[77] The children were given water and *malta morena*[78] by Doña Inés.

The women of Palma Sola, especially, sought the help of *La Madre* and asked for her blessing in order to be cured from their afflictions, and to have their sins forgiven. She also took care of pregnant women, stating that 'Every woman who gives birth is a Virgin, and the children are angels'.[79] At night young women used to sleep in the church. 'Even if all fornication was forbidden and the place was guarded by Palma Sola's own guard, many women still preferred to sleep close to *La Madre*.'[80] Much speculation was triggered when León Romilio Ventura, in a newspaper interview, stated that *La Purísima* was 'only a person who is carrying out a mission, and who almost always is lying on the floor'. He explained that she remained concealed, because to see her 'one has to become Christian, and not think of any sin of the World'.[81]

It is not perfectly clear whether León Romilio was referring to *La Madre Piadosa*. It appears as if there were various women carrying out different ritual functions in Palma Sola. One was called the Virgin of Palma Sola and was apparently a lady named Inés Rosario Alcántara: 'The *Mellizos* put me on a throne and an altar was erected in front of me. Many people were brought in front of me and they all believed in the Virgin Inés. All was done in the glory of God. […] I lived in the church and slept on the floor.'[82]

León Romilio has at various times been accused of impersonating a 'virgin' himself, and the secrecy that surrounded 'the Virgin' and '*La Madre*' has been used as a justification for all the rumors concerning lewdness which evolved around Palma Sola:

---

76 Bautista Mejía (1988), p.28.
77 Ibid. See also Martínez (1962), in which the district attorney of Las Matas de Farfán states that 'there circulate rumors that the ceremony of Christian baptism is carried out there [in Palma Sola]'.
78 A sweetened beer, very popular all over the Dominican Republic.
79 Inés Aquino, quoted in Martínez (1991), p. 147.
80 Interview with Juana María Ventura, Media Luna, 17 January 1986. Otherwise most of the visitors to Palma Sola slept on plaited grass mats in the open air. Some big *enramadas* [gathering places covered by roofs on poles] were reserved for female visitors (García (1986), p. 189).
81 León Romilio Ventura, quoted in Gómez Pepín (1962d).
82 Interview with Inés Rosario Alcántara, Bánica, 2 June 1989. Gómez Pepín, who wrote the first newspaper reports on Palma Sola, probably mixed up this Inés with Inés Aquino, since he mentions that Inés Aquino came from 'La Palma, the district of Cueva, Bánica' (García (1986), p. 155), a place which was the home of Inés Rosario Alcántara.

All fornication was prohibited up there. Men and women slept apart, the only ones who sinned were the *Mellizos* themselves.[83]

El Mellizo was '*La Madre*', he is a beast when it comes to women. He has at least 50 children.[84]

'*La Madre*' was a man dressed as a woman, and when he gave advice to the women it was interpreted that he made love to them, because every time he chose a woman in order to counsel her, the only door which normally stayed opened was closed. The women who were chosen were those who were accustomed to 'be possessed'.[85]

Such rumors were repeated and exaggerated by the press, but it appears that some tension even appeared between the two most important leaders of the cult, due to their different views on sexuality. Both agreed that no sexual intercourse could be allowed on the premises, but León Romilio apparently made an exception for himself:

Plinio did not like that people had sexual contacts in Palma Sola and he ordered that all transgressions be punished. That León Romilio indulged in some orgies is not true, but he had at least three women.[86]

It was said that Plinio and León Romilio had many women: '72 and 75', respectively. They lived there with their ex-wives and the current women, but they did not have any sexual relations with any of them since the *misterios* prohibited it.[87]

83 Interview with Zita Závala, Paraje El Ranchito, 10 April 1986.
84 'The woman of the *Mellizo*, mother of Francisco [Ventura]', quoted in Martínez (1980), p. 151. The rancor of this lady may be due to the fact that she no longer lives with León Romilio Ventura.
85 Zenón Made, quoted in ibid., pp. 146–7. It is not at all clear whether these accusations are based on truth. People who knew Inés Aquino and Inés Alcántara state that they were the 'Virgin' and the 'Mother' and that León Romilio never acted as one of them. They also confirm that these women were surround by much secrecy and veneration. That a 'queen' or a 'virgin' is chosen in order to manage a 'mystery' is a very common practice in the Dominican Republic, where cult communities like those that grow up around rural *ermitas* are almost always headed by women with such titles. The same is true of communities practicing *vodú* and *gagá*. Deceased and famous female cult functionaries, like Bibiana de la Rosa from Baní and Vetilia Peña from Samaná, are still venerated all over the Republic.
86 Interview with Marina Bautista, Las Matas de Farfán, 5 July 1990. 'In that place, in Palma Sola, I did not have [sexual] relations, not even once, not even with my women, who slept there by my side' (León Romilio Ventura, interviewed by *Rahintel*, 25 August 1990).
87 Martínez (1991), p. 145.

The road to the massacre

According to León Romilio Ventura, Palma Sola grew automatically and things and miracles happened without any conscious efforts on the part of the Ventura brothers. People brought their own beliefs to Palma Sola and the life and cultic behavior within the community evolved into a sample of the religious behavior found in different parts of the San Juan Valley: the calvaries, the *salves*, the communal dances to the rhythms of *palos* and *perico ripiao*, the vigils, the processions, the banners, the queens, *Olivorismo*, the spiritual possessions, etc. Palma Sola was almost like a theme park for Dominican popular religion. No entrance fee was charged. The only demand was that all visitors repented their sins and vowed that they were going to respect the rules of the place and symbolically join the community by having their names recorded in the register book, thus becoming members in the *Unión Cristiana Mundial*.

Palma Sola was a 'sacred' place, in the original sense of the Latin word, *sacrare* – to set apart. It was not like the rest of the world, which was believed to be under the dominion of the devil, called Luis or Bello [the Beautiful]. On the sacred grounds of *Bella Aurora* [the Beautiful Dawn], another name for Palma Sola, arms, money and fornication were all banned, and everything was done communally. Everybody was considered to be equal, except the *Mellizos* and the queens, who were, however, seen as mere vehicles for the divine powers, just like the crosses. The powers of the place were so strong that it was believed that all transgressors were punished by them. The fear of this tremendous force was so intense that many of the survivors believed the massacre that finally ended Palma Sola to be some kind of infliction, a punishment because some of the visitors had been unable to observe all the strict rules of the place.[88]

Palma Sola was an organized place, guided by both spiritual and worldly forces, the latter in the form of the army of Palma Sola. It was an oasis of peace and harmony in a world governed by the powers of darkness. If the evil forces dared to enter the holy compound they were smitten to the ground by the might of the crosses in Palma Sola. Sinners and evildoers fell to the ground and the 'witches' were forced to 'fly'. The blasphemers and the hecklers had to lick the dust, as in a *salve* giving praise to the power of the place:

Yo me llamo tumba coco	My name is Knocking Down Coconuts
ay, ay, ay	Ay, ay, ay.
que tumbo los mangos ...	I knock down the mangoes.
los maduros van cayendo ...	The ripe ones are falling

---

88 Cárdenas Fontecha (1964), p. 53.

y los verdes van quedando …	and the green ones remain.
ay, María …	Oh, Mary!
ay, María …	Oh, Mary!
yo me llamo tumba coco …	My name is Knocking Down Coconuts
y tumbo cocos de verdad …	and I really knock down the coconuts.
los tumbo esta noche …	I knock them down tonight,
los tumbo de madrugá …	I knock them down in the morning.
ay, María …	Oh, Mary!
ay, María …	Oh, Mary!
del cielo vienen bajando …	From Heaven come descending,
tres piedrecitas secretas …	three secret pebbles.
ellos [sic] *vienen reclamando …*	They are claiming
el partido liborista.[89]	the *Liborista* party.

Everyone was welcome in Palma Sola, but according to León Romilio: 'The success of the place created envy among the politicians, the church and the medical doctors. They closed their minds and never accepted the good things that were to be found up there. For that reason they finally turned against us.'[90]

Like so many sectarians before them, some of the people in Palma Sola began to consider the persons who did not join them as mere slanderers and repudiators, but it took a long time before the disagreements were transformed into open conflicts. At an early stage the Catholic church forbade its followers to visit Palma Sola and the priests stayed out of the place. Some *Olivoristas* and neighbors of the establishment did not go there either, maintaining a wait-and-see attitude:

> I knew the Venturas personally and I could never understand the attraction of Palma Sola. How could it come about so suddenly? I did not believe in it, because I knew the people. We never went there, but we saw all the people who came by here and on the last day we felt the panic around us and saw how the airplanes flew in over the place. It was a terrible tragedy.[91]

In the beginning, the people of Palma Sola were confronted only by the Mennonites, who at that time constituted the largest evangelical congregation in the area. The Mennonites had come to San Juan de la Maguana

---

89 Quoted in García (1986), pp. 185–6. In Palma Sola, *tumba cocos* was the name given to the spiritual forces that forced sinners to fall down to the ground: 'everywhere there were *tumba cocos*' (Palma Sola visitor, quoted in Vásquez and Fermín (1980), p. 76).
90 Interview with León Romilio Ventura, Las Matas de Farfán, 14 May 1989.
91 Interview with Milita Alcántara, Carrera de Yeguas, 17 January 1986.

in 1946 and by 1962 their missions were spread all over the valley. They had united their missionary efforts with the only evangelical church of some importance in the valley, the *Iglesia Evangélica Dominicana*, and even succeeded with a spectacular conversion of a Catholic nun. In San Juan de la Maguana the Mennonites had an active center with both a school and a bookshop. They were very active around Palma Sola as well, where they offered technical assistance to various peasant communities.

In charge of these operations were two young and efficient pastors, Jay Spring and Bruce Sommers, who had come to the valley in 1953 as conscientious objectors to the war in Korea:[92]

> Pastor Bruce was against it [the Palma Sola movement]. We believed like him: 'The Holy Spirit cannot be in a dove made out of plaster.' With them it was different. They did not believe in God, only in Olivorio and Plinio, and the *Mellizos* were like gods to them. They threatened us and told us that we had to repent because the *Mellizos* would become *jefes en todas las partes* [bosses all over the place]. They came in thousands and we stood by the road singing our hymns. They were many and we were few. When we sang, they sang their *salves*, shouted and beat on things in order to drown our voices. They never attacked us, but told us that if we, the *evangélicos* [Protestants], did not ask for forgiveness, the villages up here would start to burn. Some even threw gravel on us when they saw us.[93]

> In those days I lived in Sabana de la Cruz, close to Bánica, not far from Palma Sola. I am a Mennonite, and Pastor Jerry Bruklor [sic] told us that the mission in Palma Sola was diabolical. The faith of the Mennonites was strong and we went out to combat the doctrine of Palma Sola. The discussions were fierce, but it never came to any fighting. [...] Things got more and more complicated. The *Mellizos* lost all their self-control, they became self-magnified through their success and their abuse of women and their envolement in politics came as a result of that.[94]

By August 1962, the pressure on the Palma Sola community became stronger. Both the worldly authorities and the Catholic church were

---

92 Lockward (1982), pp. 407–8.
93 Interview with Zita Závala, Paraje El Ranchito, 10 April 1986. In El Batey, the Holy Spirit is venerated by the *Cofradía del Espíritu Santo* in the form of a child and two plaster doves. Many *Sanjuaneros* associated the *Cofradía* with Palma Sola since some of its most influential *cofrades* [brothers] went there and the drums of the brotherhood were played during various *Palmasolista* rituals.
94 Interview with Eugenio Fernandéz Durán, San Juan de la Maguana, 4 July 1990.

beginning to react. It is possible that these growing threats to Palma Sola changed the teachings of the *Mellizos*. What from the beginning had been seen as a manifestation of divine powers, giving strength and hope to their believers, gradually started to turn apocalyptic:

> They excited the people by saying that there would be an earthquake that would finish the world.[95]

> They said you had to be inscribed in the book because when Christ would call you he had to recognize you.[96]

> While swearing the oath they were told to believe in Christ and Mary and be like brothers, because the time would come when God would look upon the world and separate the pure ones from the impure and purify them through his counsels. The mission ... would finish by 1 January, irrespective of whether the world would tremble or not.[97]

The second half of 1962 had taken a bad turn for the community of Palma Sola and alien forces were moving in closer and closer, seeking its total annihilation.

The reaction of the local authorities

Among the first of the authorities to react were some teachers in the rural schools of the valley. In May 1962, a report which stated that the peasants took their children with them up to Palma Sola reached the Ministry of Education in Santo Domingo. Since the principal reunions at Palma Sola took place on both Tuesdays and Fridays, not much of the week was left for other activities, which meant that many children did not show up in school at all. Most schools in the district had around fifty inscribed children per classroom, but in some of them only three pupils appeared on certain days. The document concluded that 'the situation has reached an alarming level among the pupils of the district',[98] and the Regional Board of Education stated that 'official action has to make this anomaly disappear. All this is unbelievable in an epoch of scientific excellence like the one we live in.'[99]

On 28 May, the governor of San Juan de la Maguana directed himself to the mayor of San Juan, Demóstenes Remigio Valenzuela, and ordered the

95 Silvano Montero, quoted in García (1986), p. 344.
96 Manuel Amador, quoted in ibid., p. 344.
97 Nazario Lorenzo, quoted in ibid., pp. 346–7. The testimonies quoted by García were taken from tapes recorded by the police after the massacre.
98 Quoted in García (1986), p. 38.
99 Ibid.

Figure 4.13 Miguel Tomás Suzaña, 1962.

latter to 'take all measures which are appropriate in order to correct the situation'.[100] The *procurador* [district attorney] of San Juan de la Maguana, Miguel Tomás Suzaña, had already been put in charge of an investigation of the activities in Palma Sola and in April he had sent one of his employees, Baldemar Santil Pérez, up to the cult site, in order to find out if any legal measures could be taken against its leaders. After his visit, Santil consulted his law books and finally reported to Dr Suzaña: 'in this place no medicines are given, no concoctions, nor any other thing, noxious or not. No prescriptions are given and no fees are taken from any of the visitors. Therefore I understand that I do not have any juridical pretext to take action against these persons.'[101]

The authorities in the capital were not satisfied with the results of the investigation but stated that, until further notice, they had to confine themselves to the judgement of District Attorney Suzaña, which he repeated on various occasions: 'The public which attends to this superstition is disconcerting [*el público que asiste a esta superstición es desconcertante*] [...] but you already know the obstacles pointed out by Public Prosecutor Santil Pérez ...'[102]

Still, Suzaña recommended that some kind of action should be taken. If it was not possible to pursue a judiciary solution, some kind of agreement with the cult leaders could perhaps be worked out. A final solution ought to be based on a thorough investigation. The problem was that 'these people lived apart. [...] Up there reigned a mortal superstition. They

100 Ibid.
101 Quoted in ibid., p. 39.
102 Suzaña, quoted in ibid., p. 40.

believed themselves to be superior to the religion which is practiced by others and only responded to and worshiped their own *Olivorista* beliefs.'[103]

While time passed Suzaña grew more and more desperate and wrote to the attorney general in Santo Domingo: 'I am just waiting for orders so the business of the *Mellizos* of Palma Sola can be solved.'[104] In the meantime he had received a denunciation from the public prosecutor of Las Matas de Farfán, Altagracia Martínez García, where she listed some of the accusations directed against Palma Sola. In her letter she lamented that no legal actions could be taken against Palma Sola and wrote that although denunciations came to her office on a daily basis she could not use them to start a legal case since they were all anonymous and came from persons who persisted in citing 'one person (without identity) from an X place'. Still, she forwarded some of these denunciations to Suzaña. According to Altagracia Martínez García, one witness stated that

> he would not return to the place of the *Mellizos*, because he saw how a young lady was locked up 'for observation' while her mother stayed on the outside. When the daughter after a while shouted: 'Mum, they are raping me', the mother answered from the outside: 'No, my daughter, they are injecting you with the blood of our Lord Jesus Christ.' This is apparently a rape and has to be viewed in relation to many others committed earlier. They say that in Neiba there are two minors in a state of pregnancy (hidden by their mothers when they discovered the grave error committed). We are also informed that within our jurisdiction, in Los Jobos (section), there is a similar case and on Saturday we are going to make investigations there. [...] We are also informed that they write down the visitors' personal history and keep their identity cards, and they say they are being inscribed in the Party of Christ, and that they will die if they venture to inscribe themselves in another party. [...] The thousands of parents who bring with them their starving and sick children, to a place where one has to bring in the water because none is to be found there, return to their homes in order to find that they go back to bury them, if they don't die on the road.[105]

103 Interview with Miguel Tomás Suzaña, San Juan de la Maguana, 7 May 1986.
104 Suzaña, quoted in García (1986), p. 39.
105 Martínez García (1962). In spite of some efforts to find it, no evidence of actual rape could be presented against the *Mellizos*. In *El Caribe* a named lady confronted León Romilio Ventura, accusing him of intended rape, but it appeared that she did not know him personally and had never been actually violated, only warned about the *Mellizo's* intentions (Gómez Pepín (1962d)). We will deal with politics in Palma Sola in Chapter 8. It appears as if Suzaña did not take the accusations of political propagandists in Palma Sola seriously: 'They kept a list of their supporters, but they never talked about politics, only about their beliefs' (interview with Miguel Tomás Suzaña, San Juan de la Maguana, 7 May 1986).

As always, Suzaña forwarded the information to Attorney General Vásquez in the capital, but still no action was taken and when the authorities in Santo Domingo finally acted, according to Suzaña, it was too late and too improvised: 'What happened in the end was the worst thing imaginable. They were the people who had to decide what to do. García Vásquez was my superior and I could not understand what prevented him from acting in time.'[106]

In the meantime, the government was put under pressure from other quarters as well. On 31 July 1962, Palma Sola is first mentioned in the House Annals of the Parish of Santa Lucía. It appears as if the general chaos that reigned in the district after the death of Trujillo had diverted the attention of the American Redemptorist clergy in Las Matas de Farfán. The constant threats to which their bishop in San Juan de la Maguana had been subjected under the faltering Trujillo regime, and the local political struggles which followed in the wake of the fall of the dictator fill the pages of the House Annals until the name of Palma Sola suddenly appears:

> Should be mentioned here that in one of our campos [sic] – Palma Sola – a new sect has begun. It is being run by campesinos from Carrera de Yeguas. They are called Los Mellizos. The group claims that there is a 'god' in P. Sola and that all must go there. They have a woman there whom they call the '*Virgin*'. They send out word to all the campos that all must go to Palma Sola: quite a few of our people have gone out, many out of curiosity. Large crowds pass through town every day from El Cercado, S. Juan, Vallejuelo, H. Valle, Neiba, going to Palma Sola. Fr. Forrest considers it not as an ordinary 'brujería' but as a *real false* religion – Those who go to Palma Sola need *not* go to Church mass, etc. – They are 'justified' by their assistance at Palma Sola, more will be said about P. Sola at end of the year. Our masses have *not* fallen off as a result of Palma Sola. People from C. de Yeguas scoff at the idea that they have to go to Palma Sola – for all campo masses we are preaching against P. Sola so that the people know just what the position of the Church is in regard to the superstition.[107]

The bishop of San Juan de la Maguana became worried and pressed the authorities in order to stop the spread of the Palma Sola cult:

106 Interview with Miguel Tomás Suzaña, San Juan de la Maguana, 7 May 1986.
107 *House Annals* (1959–1962), 31 July 1962. Italics underlined in the original. Considering that it was written in July and knowing what we know today, the phrase 'more will be said about P. Sola at end of the year' appears as both strange and prophetic. Had the priests in Las Matas prior knowledge about any action against Palma Sola, planned to take place by the end of the year?

Sucursales [subsidiaries] sprang up in new places. The authorities did not react in time, because we had a very weak government in those days. Palma Sola was a new thing. It was something like organized voodoo. [...] I told my priests not to go up there, I did not want people to think that we supported the place. Several times I told García Vásquez, the Attorney General in Santo Domingo, that this thing could not go on and suggested to him that he ought to follow the old procedure by picking up the leaders and let the place die down by itself. The District Attorney of San Juan sent up three men, but they returned and said that nothing could be done. Anyhow, I continued with my warnings, but I felt it was more or less in vain.[108]

'Call in the police!'

On 25 September 1962, Attorney General García Vásquez decided to act and contacted General Belisario Peguero, chief of the national police force, requesting that fifty policemen be sent to San Juan de la Maguana in order to 'exorcize' the situation that had been created by the 'witchcraft' installed by the *Mellizos*.[109]

The Dominican police force was growing during this time and under its new commander, General Belisario Peguero Guerrero, it became an extremely important factor in the political life of the country. This was in accordance with US interests in the Dominican Republic. The Americans felt that they were unable to control the huge *Trujillista* 'war machine'.[110] They needed a more manageable counterforce.

John F. Kennedy had a somewhat 'romantic view of the possibilities of diplomacy', and in the early 1960s the Americans wanted US foreign personnel to be 'reform-minded missionaries', spreading the gospel of democracy and involving themselves in local struggles against communism and 'ignorance'. This new concept was called 'action diplomacy' and meant that the Americans got involved in almost every aspect of Dominican life.[111] Kennedy wanted to create a 'showcase for democracy' next door to Castro's Cuba.[112] When John Bartlow Martin[113] was appointed US

---

108 Interview with Thomas Reilly, San Juan de la Maguana, 12 December 1985.
109 García (1986), p. 57.
110 Trujillo had built up the most powerful army in the Caribbean, a force which was far out of proportion to the security needs of his tiny nation. 'It included 17,000 troops; 12,000 policemen; light-, medium-, and heavy-tank battalions; and squadrons of fighters, bombers, destroyers, and frigates. The armed forces simply occupied their own nation' (Lieuwen (1964), p. 55).
111 Schlesinger (1978), p. 440.
112 Martin (1978), p. 75.
113 A freelance journalist, Martin had worked as a 'key speech writer' in the presidential

ambassador to Santo Domingo in March 1962, he was told that he would function there 'as would the authoritative coach of a rather backward football team'.[114]

One of the American instruments for getting the Dominicans 'fit for democracy', and for exercising their power over the Dominican armed forces, was a US military assistance and advisory group (MAAG), which assisted 'in the training and economic rehabilitation of the Dominican armed services'.[115] The US ambassador stated: 'Perhaps MAAG's most successful program was the counter-insurgency training [...] By the end of the year [1962], despite Castro/Communist outcry, we had trained three companies of counter-insurgency troops ...'[116]

The build-up of these forces began in May 1962. As part of the national police force they were more or less independent from both the army and, to a certain degree, the government. The chief of police, General Peguero, had the exclusive right to choose his own employees and the government could replace him only if he was sentenced for a criminal offense.[117] This independence was 'inspired' by the Americans, who did not trust the old army men and feared the new radical opposition groups, whom they lumped together as 'Castro communists'. The Dominican police would become the true guardians of 'public security' by keeping the 'reactionaries' in check and limiting the influence of the 'Castro communists' by 'neutralizing popular mobilizations'.[118] Ambassador Martin later stated:

> Under President Kennedy our diplomats generally were activists (or in the view of more traditional diplomats, outrageously interventionist) and nowhere were they more so than in the Dominican Republic. We went well beyond giving the Republic money [...] The Republic contained a number of trained communist agents financed by the Soviet Union or Cuba. They organized and paid thieves and thugs to riot; we organized counter-riots. They infiltrated the nascent Dominican labor movement; we also infiltrated it. They tried to subvert

campaigns of Adlai Stevenson. He had also worked on John F. Kennedy's campaign staff and helped Robert Kennedy in his 'get Hoffa campaigns'. He had visited the Dominican Republic for three weeks in 1961, written a report about his experiences to the president and later proposed himself to Robert Kennedy as ambassador to that country (Martin (1986), pp. 201–11).

114 Schlesinger (1978), p. 440.
115 Hermann (1983), p. 69.
116 Martin (1966), p. 145.
117 Alcántara (1963).
118 Hermann (1983), p. 71. In 1962, the police force grew from 3,000 to 10,000 men (Atkins (1981), p. 15).

political parties; so did we. But we did more than match the communist moves. We trained the Dominican police to control rioters.[119]

The spearhead of this 'reformed' police force would be the newly
created special task force, *La Tropa Anti-Motines* [the Anti-Riot Troops],
commonly called *Los Cascos Blancos* [the White Helmets]. Even if the
members of this exclusive group were chosen by Belisario Peguero himself,
the Americans nevertheless had a voice in the matter. After all, it was all
their idea and the US ambassador noted that 'we wanted them carefully
selected – they would be the crack troops of the Republic, and we didn't
want them shooting in the wrong direction'.[120]

The White Helmets became the darlings of the American military advisers, who armed them and trained them with the help of Spanish-speaking
police officers from Los Angeles. This idea also came from Ambassador
Martin. He had gone directly to President Kennedy with his proposal, who
in front of Martin had told one of his aides: '"Ask Bobby [Kennedy, the
attorney general] if he can get him [Martin] some help." Shortly two excellent Spanish-speaking Los Angeles detectives arrived in Santo Domingo,
and in a few weeks the council rewon the streets.'[121] A young US-educated
Dominican major, Francisco Caamaño Deñó,[122] was chosen as commander
for the White Helmets and was, together with various other officers, on
2 July 1962, sent on a three-month training course at the Interamerican
Military Academy at Fort Davis in Panama.[123]

In September the Dominican attorney general had asked the chief of
police to send fifty policemen, i.e. White Helmets, to deal with the Palma
Sola problem, but it appears as if both men had some second thoughts
about how the action should be carried out, so the troops were not sent
after all. By the end of October, Attorney General Vásquez wrote to the
secretary of the interior and the police, Tabaré Alvarez Pereyra: 'on various
occasions I have discussed the matter with the Chief of Police, General
Belisario Peguero [...] it is urgent to take action and send the policemen
to San Juan.'[124]

Before the troops were sent, however, the authorities in the capital
apparently wanted to test the methods proposed by Bishop Reilly, i.e. 'to
pick up the leaders and let the place die down by itself', something which
had also been suggested by the public prosecutor of Las Matas de Farfán:

119 Martin (1978), p. 76.
120 Martin (1966), p. 141.
121 Martin (1986), p. 219.
122 During 1954 and 1955 Caamaño Deñó had received military training at the US marine
    facilities in Coronado, California and Quantico, Virginia (Hermann (1983), pp. 32–3).
123 Ibid., p. 77.
124 Quoted in García (1986), p. 66.

Figure 4.14 Major Francisco Caamaño Deñó, commander of the White Helmets.

if we, day by day, stubbornly continue to try to find a way of solving this social evil, we think that it can only be overcome (forgive us the boldness of the suggestion) by drastic and unexpected action, taking the said gentlemen '*Mellizos*' as prisoners for 'Investigation purposes' and placing policemen by the entrance of the said place, who will turn back the caravans of stupid believers. When these find the entrance closed and the *Mellizos* in custody they will after a short time decline to visit this center of depravation ...[125]

To this end the commander of the White Helmets, Major Francisco Caamaño Deñó, who had recently returned from Panama, was ordered to infiltrate Palma Sola and obtain information that could serve as the basis for further actions. Caamaño was a natural choice for this kind of operation. He was the son of General Fausto Caamaño, one of Trujillo's most dreaded henchmen. Fausto had been secretary of state for the armed forces under *El Benefactor*, and he had been one of the very few persons who could be considered as Trujillo's friend.[126]

As part of his career, Fausto Caamaño, nicknamed *El Carnicero* [the Butcher], had been been chief of Trujillo's secret police and organized the dreaded killing unit of '*La 42*'.[127] He had been entrusted with such delicate operations as killing all people found on the estate of the dictator's

125 Martínez García (1962).
126 Crassweller (1966), p. 225.
127 Mallín (1965), p. 29. Cf. Balaguer (1989), p. 254.

Figure 4.15 Plutarco Caamaño.

brother Aníbal Trujillo, when the head of state had an argument with his relative,[128] and it was under the command of Fausto Caamaño that units of the Dominican army, in 1937, carried out the massacre of all Haitians found on Dominican soil.[129]

Fausto Caamaño was born in San Juan de la Maguana and maintained close contacts with many of its citizens, among them his old school teacher Emigdio Garrido Puello.[130] The father of Fausto Caamaño had been a big landowner in Mogollón, just outside San Juan de la Maguana, and his sons had inherited and extended his properties. Wealthiest among the Caamaños in the San Juan Valley was Fausto's older brother, Plutarco. In his youth Plutarco Caamaño had been a personal friend of Olivorio. He was a San Juan *caudillo* of the old stock, father of no less than eighty-four children. Even after he had become a big landowner and an influential politician (he served a term as mayor of San Juan de la Maguana) Plutarco Caamaño maintained his *Olivorista* creed.[131] He knew the Ventura brothers well and had a house constructed in Palma Sola.[132] 'He [Plutarco

---

128 Crassweller (1966), p. 228. Apparently Fausto Caamaño was ordered to kill the brother of Trujillo as well, but he saw to it that Aníbal was given an opportunity to escape. Fausto knew that *El Benefactor* had a somewhat capricious temper and would probably change his mind and regret that he had caused the death of his own brother (Hicks (1946), p. 151).
129 Castor (1987), p. 30.
130 Garrido Puello (1977), p. 137.
131 García (1986), pp. 177–9.
132 Interview with Mimicito Ramírez, San Juan de la la Maguana, 4 July 1990.

Caamaño] was a true believer. When I was with him up in Palma Sola and heard Plinio [Ventura] speak I told Plutarco that "this man must be crazy". But, Plutarco answered me: "Listen carefully, this man is right."'[133]

The *Mellizos* were proud of their connections with Plutarco Caamaño and considered him to be a confirmed *Olivorista*: 'He was a good servant and a loyal friend. We all respected him and he did not lie to us.'[134] Other *Olivoristas* and visitors to Palma Sola, however, had a lower opinion of Plutarco Caamaño: 'That Plutarco was a crazy guy. He was mayor around here. How he could become that I never understood. Maybe because his brother was a general. He had a lot of land. Later Balaguer's government bought most of it.'[135]

At any rate, the new commander of the White Helmets, Francisco Caamaño, had spent many of his vacations with his uncle Plutarco and his relatives' connections with the people of Palma Sola were of much use to him. In the fall of 1962, Francisco Caamaño visited Palma Sola no fewer than five times. He went disguised as a common pilgrim in the company of his cousin Félix Caamaño, one of Plutarco's many sons:[136] 'He participated spontaneously in the rituals, probably to learn what took place and to avoid unnecessary antipathy.'[137]

Francisco reported his findings to his superior Belisario Peguero, who in consultation with Attorney General Vásquez finally decided to act in accordance with the advice given by Bishop Reilly: 'to pick up the leaders and let the thing die down'.

On 4 December 1962, forty-two organizations from the towns of San Juan de la Maguana and Las Matas de Farfán sent a joint letter to the government in the capital demanding that the state put an end to 'that humiliating abnormality', as Palma Sola was called. The letter gave the authorities eight days to change the situation, and in the event that no remedy was obtained the organizations threatened to paralyze San Juan and Las Matas completely. The document ended with an allusion to the fate of Olivorio:

> the extension [of the cult in Palma Sola] is due to the passivity the governments have shown in confronting it, and we have to confess, even if it is painful in these days when nationalism is acclaimed from all the political platforms, that the humiliating Yankee intervention of 1916 was necessary in order to let us rest in peace from the cretinous and voodooistic empire of Liborio.[138]

133 Interview with Mimicito Ramírez, San Juan de la Maguana, 14 December 1985.
134 Interview with León Romilio Ventura, Las Matas de Farfán, 14 May 1989.
135 Interview with Arsidé Gardés, El Batey, 11 April 1986.
136 García (1986), p. 75.
137 León Romilio Ventura quoted in Martínez (1991), pp. 237–8.

A week later Attorney General Vásquez visited San Juan de la Maguana in order to calm the worried citizens, promising that determinate action would be taken after the elections on 20 December 1962. Meanwhile, Major Francisco Caamaño went to Palma Sola to get Plinio Ventura. As usual he went with his cousin, but this time he carried a doctor's coat in order to gain the Venturas' confidence and he was also accompanied by three policemen dressed as peasants. Caamaño succeeded in convincing Plinio to follow him to San Juan de la Maguana and meet Attorney General Vásquez and the press.[139] Since Plinio went, León Romilio could also be persuaded to come to the meeting in the provincial capital. Caamaño had given his word of honor to Plinio that León Romilio was going to be released after the interview with García Vásquez, and Plinio was also free to go after the meeting. But despite Camaaño's protests, León Romilio was kept in custody in San Juan de la Maguana.[140] Caamaño was later ordered by Belisario Peguero to accompany the *Mellizo* to the capital, where León Romilio was questioned and brutally beaten. Caamaño later stated that he had felt 'ridiculed' by the behavior of his superiors, who made him break his promise to his prisoner.[141]

> I considered Francis Caamaño to be a friend of ours. His uncle, Plutarco, was a very good friend of mine, who knew what Palma Sola was all about. He had told me that the meeting was for the best of all of us. I was received as a visitor, not as a prisoner, but they fooled me. It was not Vásquez who gave the order for my imprisonment; I think it came from the president himself, Bonnelly. As an excuse they used the false testimony of a woman who said I had tried to rape her. In the beginning they were very rude to me. They kept me in custody for thirty-five days.[142]

138 Quoted in García (1986), p. 161. Cf. Hermann (1983), p. 84 and Gómez Pepín (1962c). The letter was signed by all prominent leaders of social clubs and institutions in the two towns, as well as medical doctors, lawyers and businessmen. It is worth noting that no church functionaries signed the document (García (1986), pp. 161–3).
139 Hermann (1983), p. 85. Cf. Bautista Mejía (1988), p. 40. León Romilio Ventura denies that Caamaño was dressed as a medical doctor and also states that Plinio was never taken into custody (Martínez (1991), p. 238). It was always León Romilio who spoke with Caamaño and other representatives for the authorities.
140 Hermann (1983), p. 85. León Romilio Ventura has offered a somewhat different version, stating that Plinio at this time refused to leave Palma Sola and that he, himself, went instead, because he did not want Palma Sola to be left without its real leader [Plinio], 'for the military and the State Council [...] I [León Romilio Ventura] was the leader of Palma Sola' (quoted in Martínez (1980), p.183).
141 Sáenz Padrón and Rius Blein (1984), p. 81. Cf. Cárdenas Fontecha (1964), p. 57, and Martínez (1980), p. 184.
142 Interview with León Romilio Ventura, Media Luna, 17 January 1986.

León Romilio was the most eloquent of the *Mellizos* and it is possible that the authorities were reluctant to release him since they considered him to be the most influential of the Palma Sola leaders: 'Plinio was owner of it all, but it was I who was the twin [*mellizo*]. I think it was because of that they believed I was the most important one.'[143]

The press campaign

It was probably the press that eventually forced the government to take action in the delicate matter of Palma Sola. Even if Palma Sola had been hot news for quite some time in the San Juan Valley, it took a very long time before news about the cult appeared in the Dominican press. The San Juan Valley remained a rather isolated corner of the country, but that is not a valid explanation for the press silence. The Dominican Republic is not a big country and all means of communication had been fairly well developed under the Trujillo regime. Both Las Matas de Farfán and San Juan de la Maguana had local newspapers, but it was not until 30 November 1962 that news about Palma Sola appeared in the largest of them, *Santomé*,[144] and this was ten days after the first newspaper articles concerning Palma Sola had appeared in the press of the capital.[145]

These articles, published in one of Santo Domingo's largest newspapers, *El Caribe*, opened the floodgates and until the end of December 1962, all Dominican papers published daily reports about Palma Sola, all of them making frequent use of words like superstition, witchcraft, ignorance and debauchery.

In August 1962 *El Caribe* had published a series of articles dealing with the state of abandonment and poverty which reigned in the southwestern Dominican Republic: 'The zone appears as if it has been taken out of one of the descriptions of Dante, and to tell the truth, it could have served as an example for the immortal poet.'[146] The articles touched on the issue of peasant religiosity, but strangely enough they did not mention the cult of Palma Sola. It was stated that most rural inhabitants in the area 'nurture a profound religious faith which neither the events nor the abandonment have been able to change'.[147]

El Caribe was owned by Germán Ornes Coiscou – one of the most controversial persons in the Dominican Republic. The paper had been founded in 1948 by an American promoter, Stanley Ross, who had persuaded

143 Ibid.
144 *Santomé*, 15 December 1962.
145 Gómez Pepín (1962a).
146 *El Caribe*, 4 August 1962, p. 1. The articles appeared on 4, 5, 6 and 7 August.
147 *El Caribe*, 9 December 1962, p. 2.

Figure 4.16 Germán Ornes, editor of *El Caribe*, around 1961.

Trujillo that his international prestige would increase if an 'independent' newspaper was founded, beside the ones which were known to be the government's loyal mouthpieces. Thus, *El Caribe* was established with Ross as its editor-in-chief. A timid 'criticism' of the government was allowed and even if Trujillo often edited certain pieces himself and the government provided some of its funds, *El Caribe* was officially 'totally independent'.[148]

After Ross' resignation in 1949, Germán Ornes joined the staff of *El Caribe* as editor-in-chief. In his youth Ornes had been a member of an organization called *Juventud Revolucionaria* [Revolutionary Youth], and he had even spent a short time in jail. Nevertheless, he soon learned how to flatter *El Jefe* in writing, and as a technical assistant in the Labor Department he had drafted the new labor code of the Dominican Republic. When Ornes' brother Horacio Julio was captured while commanding an armed invasion in 1949, Trujillo was very careful to stress his own unfaltering friendship with Germán Ornes, and the favors which were bestowed on Germán by *El Benefactor* were used in the propaganda as proof of the 'understanding, open-mindedness and good-heartedness' of *El Jefe*.[149]

In 1954 Germán Ornes bought *El Caribe* and for some years the old policy of cautious criticism of governmental measures and limitless ovations to the dictator was continued. As in the rest of the Dominican press, Trujillo was likened to God. He restored health to dying patients and, in 1955, 'like God, created from nothing on the seventh day a splendid Fair of the Peace

---

148 Ornes (1958), pp. 194–6.
149 Ibid., p. 79.

and Brotherhood of the Free World'.[150] However, the Damocles sword of Trujillo fell on the head of Ornes when *El Caribe*, in 1955, through an error, put the wrong text under a picture which showed children putting flowers under one of the 1,800 busts of Trujillo. The caption read that the children were putting their blossoms on the 'tomb of the Benefactor',[151] and thus Ornes had to flee the country, joining the fierce opposition against Trujillo. He became one of the most eloquent mouthpieces of the anti-*Trujillistas* and the object of the dictatorship's frenzied verbal attacks and various death threats.[152]

When he came back to the country in 1961, Ornes was greeted as a hero and President Balaguer returned his newspaper in December of the same year. During most of 1962 *El Caribe* was promoting the presidential candidacy of Horacio Julio Ornes, who had returned to the country together with his brother and formed a political party called *Partido Vanguardia Revolucionaria Dominicana* (VRD). By the end of the year, however, the policy of the paper suddenly changed and instead of backing the VRD it started to support another party, the *Unión Cívica Nacional* (UCN), which was considered to have a greater chance of winning.[153]

On 15 November 1962, the reporter Radhamés Gómez Pepín was called into Germán Ornes' office and ordered to go to San Juan de la Maguana 'to do a thing about Palma Sola'. Gómez assumed that Ornes had 'heard something' from his friends within the government, since the director of *El Caribe* 'was allied to the *Consejo*'.[154] The direct reason for Ornes' sudden interest in Palma Sola seems to be a letter from a certain Teódulo De Oleo Matero. He was the local representative of the UCN in Hondo Valle, a village south of Elías Piña. Hondo Valle is situated approximately 60 kilometers from Palma Sola, but the impact of the cultic center was felt even there. Oleo Matero was president of an organization called the *Junta Protectora de Agricultura* [Assembly for Agricultural Protection] and was concerned about the harvest losses which might occur if huge crowds of peasants and agricultural workers preferred to go to Palma Sola instead of tending their fields.[155] With the approval of his party superiors, Oleo

---

150 Ibid., p. 182 and 81.
151 Ibid., p. 197.
152 See e.g. *The Betrayal of Germán Ornes* (1956) and *Germán Ornes, a Self Portrait* (1958).
153 Interview with Radhamés Gómez Pepín, Santo Domingo, 18 March 1986.
154 Ibid. *El Consejo de Estado* [State Council] was an 'apolitical' caretaker government with six members who, under the presidency of Rafael Bonnelly, governed the country from the renunciation of President Balaguer on 17 January 1962, until the elections on 20 December of the same year. The father of Ornes, also named Germán, was secretary of education of the *Consejo* (García (1986), p.149).
155 This is a concern that appears several times in the correspondence received by the government representatives. Thus, the administrator of the agricultural colony in Vallejuelo, where the Venturas had established an offshot of Palma Sola, urged the secretary

Figure 4.17 Radhamés Gómez Pepín, around 1961.

Matero sent his letter directly to Rafael Bonnelly, the president of the Republic. Matero did not limit himself to notifying the government, but also wrote to the radio and TV stations in the capital, as well as to the two largest newspapers in the country, *El Caribe* and *La Nación.*[156]

As soon as he arrived in San Juan de la Maguana, Radhamés Gómez went straight to District Attorney Suzaña, who was happy to brief the reporter from *El Caribe* on everything concerning Palma Sola. The district attorney hoped that pressure from the mass media would finally compel the government to act. Together with *El Caribe*'s representative in San Juan de la Maguana, Antonio Paulino, Radhamés Gómez was the only Dominican journalist who actually visited Palma Sola. He went there in the company of Antonio Paulino, *El Caribe* photographer Rafael Emilio Bidó and a medical doctor from San Juan de la Maguana, José Rodríguez Soldevilla,[157] who had treated one of Plinio's sons for a dagger wound in the stomach.[158]

The appearance of Radhamés Gómez in Palma Sola caused some commotion and Rafael Bidó was taken into custody by the guards at the

---

of agriculture that immediate measures be taken in order to 'eradicate Palma Sola' (García (1986), p. 78), and in one of his reports to García Vásquez (13 November 1962) District Attorney Suzaña laments that the harvest of more than 375 hectares of beans was in danger because 'there are no men to harvest them' (ibid., p. 158).

156 Ibid., p. 76.
157 Interview with Radhamés Gómez Pepín, Santo Domingo, 18 March 1986.
158 This son had been sent to the capital for medical treatment and Plinio once went to see him there (Dr Julio Méndez Puello, quoted in Martínez (1980), p. 159).

entrance. When it became clear that the group would not be allowed to enter, Doctor Soldevilla suddenly spotted Plinio in the crowd and shouted: '*Mellizo*, how is your son?' This eased the tension and both Gómez and his group were finally allowed to enter and walk freely within the compound, even if they had to to be very discreet while taking their photographs. They stayed overnight and witnessed the ceremonies by the calvary:

> They took place close to their 'temple', around three crosses placed within stone circles. A huge crowd of people stood outside the circles. By the crosses were two *Mellizos* and a woman. Drums were played and people jumped and danced to the rhythm. Two women fell to the ground and were brought into a shack. I never witnessed what happened in there, if someone made love to them or if they just were treated with herbs or something like that. I don't know. I wrote some harsh things, but I made it totally clear that some of my statements were based on rumors.[159]

The Gómez articles, which appeared by the end of November,[160] centered on the 'fraud' committed by the *Mellizos* against thousands of illiterate peasants, making use of their superstition. According to Gómez more than fifty women had become pregnant after participating in the rites connected with the cult. The women themselves explained this as a result of the presence of the Holy Ghost. The articles alleged that many of the pregnancies were the result of rapes, committed when the entrance gates had been closed after 5.30 p.m. Among those raped, ten- and eleven-year-old-girls were stated to be found.

Gómez also reported that the *Mellizos* had prohibited their followers to work on two days a week and that on 19 December a meeting would be held where the leaders would announce for whom the devotees should cast their votes in the upcoming presidential elections.

The articles indicated that Palma Sola seemed to be a lucrative operation for its founders. No money was charged to those attending the cults or those who came for healing, but gifts, e.g. of food, were gladly accepted, and Gómez suspected that these gifts went into some of the ten little shops that had been established on the road from Las Matas to Palma Sola. He thought that the proceeds from these shops were pocketed by members of the Ventura family. As a consequence, the commercial activity that was not controlled by the Venturas had decreased considerably. It was not only the food sales which had decreased in Las Matas and San Juan, but the

---

159 Interview with Radhamés Gómez Pepín, Santo Domingo, 18 March 1986. Cf. Bautista Mejía (1988), pp. 42–3. They never revealed that they had been sent by *El Caribe*. Instead they posed as Puerto Rican tourists.
160 Gómez Pepín (1962a), (1962b).

Mellizos had declared that all female visitors to Palma Sola had to dress in simple, flowered or white dresses, while the men should wear blue denim.

Other competitors to the *Mellizos* were affected as well. The director of the Santomé hospital in San Juan de la Maguana was quoted as saying that the number of people coming in for treatment had fallen drastically since the beginning of the thaumaturgical activities in Palma Sola. School attendance was also reported to be down. Finally, there were rumors that on 2 or 3 December the *Mellizos* were to bless some 500 daggers, to be distributed among their men of confidence. As usual, the authorities were taken to task for their passivity with respect to the events in Palma Sola. The articles ended with the recommendation that 'what is to be done, has to be done as soon as possible'.

The exaggerations and misinterpretations apparent in the Gómez articles may be due to a failure to understand a religious movement like the one of Palma Sola. Gómez later acknowledged that he came unprepared in his initial confrontation with the cult and that the experience proved to be quite frightening:

> The environment instilled fear, there is no doubt about it. I would like to say this: 'I am from Santiago and I have never seen anything like it, either in Santiago, or in any other place in the Cibao. I know the Cibao very well.' When I saw what took place there [in Palma Sola] I said to myself: 'Come on! Good God, is this really the Dominican Republic? What is this?' To me it was a tremendous spectacle. Tremendous and unbelievable. It was not possible. What frightened me was the mixed crowd of people. [...] What that crowd said about people. There were sick people, there were healthy people, there were anguished people, something you noticed because they had come to solve, or to try to solve, explicit problems typical for anguished people. Due to this fact, people became frightened by anything and everything made them excited in no time at all.[161]

The Gómez articles triggered a flood of protests against the *Mellizos*. Attorney General Vásquez became alarmed by the sudden attention and asked Belisario Peguero to send seventy policemen as a reinforcement to San Juan de la Maguana, '*because the case was publicly denounced in El Caribe*'.[162] Other Dominican journalists quickly picked up the thread and Gómez himself developed his original argument.[163] Thus, the *Mellizos* at various times were accused of exploiting the credulity and illiteracy of the

---

161 Radhamés Gómez Pepín, interviewed by *Rahintel*, 25 August 1990.
162 A note from García Vásquez, quoted in García (1986), p. 157. Italics in the original.
163 For a list of some of the most representative articles, see Espín del Prado (1980), pp. 64–5.

peasants, of practicing sorcery and fetishism, of reviving the cult of Olivo-rio, of prostitution, of rape, not least of underage girls, of defloration of virgins, of sex orgies and free love, of keeping children away from school, of preventing their followers from working, of destroying the local economy, of not accepting food from CARE (Cooperative for American Relief Everywhere), of prohibiting their followers from voting in the pres-idential elections, of housing fugitives from justice, notably one of Trujillo's henchmen, of being supporters of Trujillo, of distributing weapons among their followers, of training these militarily, of planning to overthrow the government, making Plinio Ventura president, of plotting against François Duvalier in Haiti, and, finally, of having received orders from the communists in Cuba.

It was a fantastic brew of fears and rumors. The peasants were depicted as absent-minded zombies, totally subjected to the will of the *Mellizos*, who were said to govern them through their diabolical powers:

> in the cult of Liborio the legally and honestly married women are induced to practice adultery. And all this without remorse. […] Opposed to the Sacred is the sinful, the carnal and the diabolical, etc. And precisely because of these things the name of Holy is manipulated within the insane practices of Palma Sola, to mock holiness […] The authorities have the word when it comes to the extermination of this fetishist and immoral barbarity.[164]

Much attention has been given to the leaders within the *Olivorista* cults in the San Juan Valley. Of course, they had great importance in Palma Sola, but it is still conspicuous that very few people who visited Palma Sola, when interviewed, mention the *Mellizos* with reverence or talk much about their influence. Almost unanimously they speak about the power of the place and how this power influenced everyone there. The *Mellizos* were just a part of all this. Nowadays, in a place like La Maguana one still finds power-ful cult leaders who preach and carry out ceremonies. Many of them are also politically organized, but still most pilgrims see them as simple care-takers of the holy places and even if they listen to their preaching they do not submit unreservedly to them.

It is possible that many of the fears exposed in the articles concerning Palma Sola and its masses of 'brain-washed' peasants reflected memories of the Trujillo period, when *El Benefactor* consciously bred a cult of his own person and all Dominicans were relegated to secondary positions. The descriptions also echo popular descriptions of the state of affairs in communist countries whose citizens used to be described as herds submit-ting to the will of 'Big Brother'.

164 Paniagua O. (1962).

It is not without interest to note that Radhamés Gómez, whose articles in those days reflected the view that portrayed the leaders in Palma Sola as all-powerful, has today changed his opinion:

> In those days, before the the elections, everybody's interest was fixed on politics and thus the manipulative powers of the *Mellizos* were stressed. However, in the San Juan Valley, religion has always been more important than politics. People did not seek political advice from the *Mellizos*, they got that from other quarters. It was religion they sought in Palma Sola. The political and manipulative influence of the *Mellizos* was a second-hand thing; religion came first. When it comes to voting, most Dominican peasants make a distinction between religion and politics. For example, the UCN carried out a very fierce campaign directed against Juan Bosch, depicting him as an atheist, and he did not really deny that particular accusation. Still, it was Bosch who won the elections and it was the peasant votes that brought him to the presidency.[165]

The countdown

In Palma Sola itself, tension rose when people started to feel the bite of the press and the campaigns carried out by influential citizens in Las Matas and San Juan. The faithful became even more worried when they found out that León Romilio Ventura, the *Mellizo*, had been arrested. Even before the authorities took León Romilio into custody the leaders of Palma Sola had preached that their mission had a 'limited character' and that it probably would end by the beginning of 1963, and, while he was imprisoned, León Romilio repeated at various times that 'God' had told Plinio that the mission would be completed on 1 January 1963: that day all would come to an end with the last oath of allegiance. He stated that the mission to be carried out in Palma Sola was commended to him by an old, white and bearded man, and that the pilgrims should pray to Christ to forgive the sinners.[166]

The authorities did not take any notice of the words of León Romilio and the fierce press campaign against Palma Sola continued, promoting more and more fantastic rumors. Fear was aroused concerning the presence of 'white foreigners' working in close contact with the *Mellizos*, and it was speculated that these people could be anything from fugitive *Trujillistas* who had crossed the border from Haiti to *guerrilleros* trained by Castro in Cuba.

---

165 Interview with Radhamés Gómez Pepín, Santo Domingo, 18 March 1986.
166 Gómez Pepín (1962f). Cf. Espín del Prado (1980), p. 67.

The origin of these rumors could be the presence of Delanoy Ventura and his family, who on 23 May had arrived in Palma Sola from Hinche in Haiti. Delanoy had became quite a wealthy man in Haiti where he had married a 'white and beautiful lady' named Carmelita Quevedo Medina. Around Hinche and Thomassique he owned several hectares of good land and he had several tenants. When he came to his brothers in Palma Sola Delanoy did not sell any of his Haitian land, but his tenants crossed the border to pay rent. Among them was a Haitian landowner, named Gabriel Wilson, who leased some of his land from Delanoy. Wilson was an educated engineer, who had been active in Haitian politics and he was known to oppose Duvalier. He lived for a while with Delanoy's family in Palma Sola and was arrested by the military when the massacre took place.[167]

Delanoy and his family had brought several trunks with clothes, other personal belongings and quite a lot of money to Palma Sola: 'We were not poor and had both dollars and beautiful things with us. Among the things my dad brought was my entire marriage outfit, because I was getting married in the Dominican Republic. The soldiers took it all when they sacked Palma Sola.'[168]

Some peasants living around Palma Sola still remember the impression Delanoy Ventura and his family made when they came to the cult site: 'Delanoy was married to a very beautiful Haitian lady. She looked like an Indian. They had three lovely daughters. They brought with them a suit-case filled with silver, gold and things like that.'[169]

Possibly Delanoy, his family and their visitors were the mysterious strangers that appear in some rumors concerning Palma Sola, like the ones in a report delivered to the Dominican chief of police, Belisario Peguero, on 28 December 1962, where a certain Policarpio Vicente declared that

> in Palma Sola there is a zinc [roofed] house where three men and three white women live. They appear to be elegant and wealthy people, because they have a lot of nice clothes and do not have any occupation, nor do they participate in the Liboristic rituals. Only a man called Poché is allowed to enter this zinc [roofed] house; he is a

---

167 Interview with Juana María Ventura, Media Luna, 5 May 1986 and Bautista Mejía (1988), p. 74. Gabriel Wilson was referred to as a 'Haitian engineer' when his wife Yuliana Basili de Wilson was authorized by García Vásquez to visit her husband in the prison of Santo Domingo. The authorization is the only official mention of this man (García (1986), p. 318). Even if Wilson is mentioned as being an 'engineer' both by Juana Ventura and García Vásquez, it is not quite certain that he was one, since the word *enjényè* (*ingénieur*) in Haiti may be used as a title on anyone who has some kind of education.
168 Interview with Juana María Ventura, Media Luna, 5 May 1986.
169 Interview with Zita Závala, Paraje El Ranchito, 10 April 1986. Being an *India* is taken as a sign of beauty in the San Juan Valley and the epithet is applied to ladies with long, straight black hair and light skin.

school teacher and receives instructions from these people [...] I saw on 25 December, in the mentioned zinc house, another strange man, whom I had never seen before during my eight days in Palma Sola. He is a light-skinned [*indio claro*] man, half bald and with gold teeth; he is dressed in an olive-green jacket, like the one used by the officers of the National Army [...] In Palma Sola there is also a white-painted house with a room which has all its doors padlocked. No one may come close to it. It has special guards. There live the strange people. They have special guards day and night.[170]

Vicente continued to state that there existed a shooting range in Palma Sola. He had not seen it but had heard the shots. He believed that 'unknown' forces were arming the guard of Palma Sola and supporting the place: 'There they sacrificed two bulls on a daily basis and cooked seven *fanegas* of rice: I do not know who provides the money to buy all this.'[171]

Another document submitted by 'A Good *Sanjuanero*', found among the papers of García Vásquez, accuses Plutarco Caamaño of being an accomplice in the shady activities in Palma Sola and informs the attorney general that he has to ask Plutarco about 'a certain Mario and about a certain Luis Reynoso, a certain Tuto, who together with two high-ranking Haitian bosses passed the border to go to Palma Sola and locked themselves up in a house they have there, spending hours and hours consulting with him [Plutarco Caamaño]'.[172]

The Haitian connection was also stressed in the testimony given by Policarpio Vicente, who stated that people were trained in Palma Sola in order to attack the forces of the Haitian dictator François Duvalier on 29 December 1962. Vicente also indicated that Haitian rebels were prepared to help the people in Palma Sola if they were attacked by the Dominican police and military.[173]

The mentioning of white people in connection with Haiti reflects fears of the return of old *Trujillista* forces. Most of Trujillo's feared relatives had fled to Miami after his death, but some of them had friendly relations with the Haitian dictator. Among these was the feared José Arismendi (Petán) Trujillo. The relations between the Trujillos and Duvalier had always been strained, but, as villains and gangsters sometimes do, the two

---

170 Policarpio Vicente, quoted in García (1986), pp. 202–3. According to Juana, one of Delanoy's daughters, her family did not believe in the divinity of Olivorio and their participation in the rituals was very limited (quoted in ibid., p. 212).

171 Ibid., p. 203. A *fanega* is a unit of measurement. In San Juan de la Maguana it contains around 55 liters. (Its size varies between districts.)

172 Ibid., p. 206.

173 A facsimile of a police interrogation of Policarpio Vicente is presented in Martínez (1991), pp. 290–9.

dictator families also, occasionally, joined forces. In March 1962, the US ambassador to the Dominican Republic had received reports from the CIA that Petán was negotiating with Duvalier and planned a visit to Haiti.[174] That the suspicions of contacts were not unfounded was proved in April of the following year when Duvalier received four nephews of the deceased dictator as unofficial guests.[175] Several of Trujillo's old henchmen also found a haven in Haiti.[176]

The *Mellizos* were not only accused of being in contact with conservative forces like the Trujillos. At the same time they were depicted as communists, and Policarpio Vicente finishes his testimony in the following way:

Quest: Do you have anything else to declare?

Answ: Sir, I would like to declare that some days ago there were some people there in Palma Sola, they could be the same as in Sierra Maestra de Cuba.

Quest: Could you inform us a bit more about this?

Answ: No, sir.[177]

This new tinge to the complaints against Palma Sola was a reflection of the nervousness that grew around the religious community after the general elections of 20 December. Several *Olivoristas* had abstained from voting, something which according to the new constitution was a crime.[178] Furthermore, everyone knew that the government had promised to 'do something about Palma Sola' after the elections. The people from Palma Sola were agitated and afraid. The *Mellizos* had told them that the 'mission' would be ended on 1 January 1963, and many of them received constant threats from people who did not belong to the cult. The preaching of Plinio Ventura had also become more uncompromising and violent after a petition for the release of León Romilio had been turned down by the government. Together with his brothers he had sent a telegram directly to

---

174 Martin (1966), p. 87.

175 Diederich and Burt (1972), pp. 207–8.

176 Most famous was the sinister Johnny Abbes García, Trujillo's number one spy and hitman, who, however, did not arrive to offer his services to Papa Doc until 1966. One year later Duvalier had him, his wife and their two children murdered (ibid., p. 363).

177 Quoted in Martínez (1991), p. 299. Sierra Maestra is the mountain range in the south-eastern part of Cuba where Fidel Castro and his revolutionaries first established themselves.

178 The fact that some 12,000–15,000 refused to vote in the region where Palma Sola is situated, i.e. the municipality of San Juan de la Maguana, was blamed on the 'propaganda' of the *Mellizos*. Paulino (1962b), p. 2, states that the figure was 12,000, while Hermann (1983), p. 86, mentions a figure of 15,000.

Figure 4.18 Procession of pilgrims going from Carrera de Yeguas to Palma Sola.

President Bonnelly. It was signed 'The Missionaries of Palma Sola' and stated that 'the Mellizo' is 'imprisoned and has no contact with his family and friends. A solution has to be given to this imprisonment, if it is not a crime to advise respect and obedience to Christ.'[179]

The leaders of Palma Sola wrote that they assumed that the persecution of León Romilio Ventura was due to the fact that they had declined to cooperate with any political party. They stated that they had done so because their mission was 'apolitical' and that they believed that everyone 'is free to vote as he likes to do'.[180] When the authorities did not respond to their plea and things started to look worse, Plinio Ventura preached defiance and firmness to the people in Palma Sola:

> I have information that you are worried because the mellizo is imprisoned, but this is no reason for alarm, because nothing will happen to him. What is going to happen will take place here, because it is here that the word of Liborio has to be signed and this word will be signed with blood and it is with blessed blood at the base of this calvary.[181]

The tensions had first exploded on 21 December. The versions of the incident which then took place are full of contradictions. According to Lieutenant Colonel Francisco Alvarez Guzmán, chief of the southern police district, the disturbances took place when some policemen from Las

179 Quoted in García (1986), p. 185.
180 Ibid.
181 Quoted in Bautista Mejía (1988), p. 41.

Matas de Farfán, 'for reasons of inspection', stopped trucks coming down from Palma Sola. The vehicles carried some 200 passengers 'armed' with 'sticks and machetes', and one man was shot when some of the pilgrims obstructed the registration. While 'hearing the firing, reinforcements of policemen and civilians came to the place and captures took place'.[182]

In a letter to the president of the Republic the 'Missionaries of Palma Sola' gave another version: 'The president of the Municipal Committee of the Unión Cívica Nacional in Las Matas de Farfán formed a mob together with the police of this place [Las Matas], attacking the missionaries of Palma Sola who were on their way to their homes.'[183] Patoño, the man in charge of the guard of Palma Sola, relates how pilgrims on their way from Palma Sola were provoked by a group of people active within the UCN. These were irritated over the electoral defeat of their party and started to provoke the people from Palma Sola. The arguments ran hot between the two groups and the UCN activists hurried to the police quarters of Las Matas de Farfán telling the agents that thousands of *Olivoristas* were coming down from Palma Sola, armed with machetes and sticks, in order to attack the town. The police panicked and using loudspeakers ordered the inhabitants of the town to stay inside and close their doors. Accompanied by various civilians the police went up to meet the people from Palma Sola and when they saw the *Olivoristas* coming down the road, carrying the pieces of wood that had been blessed by Plinio,[184] they thought that the worst rumors had all been true and attacked the innocent pilgrims, who started to defend themselves with their sticks and machetes. A young man from El Cercado was shot in the chest and died immediately.[185] The result of the clash was that 168 persons were jailed, three policemen and twenty civilians were wounded and one person was killed.[186]

The incident was to have great importance for the further development of the Palma Sola affair. Colonel Guzmán's report included some remarks

---

182 Francisco Guzmán, quoted in García (1986), pp. 199–200.
183 Quoted in ibid., p. 199.
184 The pieces of wood blessed by the *Mellizos* and carried as mementos by pilgrims returning from Palma Sola, frequently figured in the press, and the rumors about 'blessings of the sticks' were soon changed and interpreted as signs that the *Mellizos* were arming their followers: 'In this town [Las Matas de Farfán] rumors are spreading stating that the Mellizos of Palma Sola have started the distribution of 500 daggers, previously blessed by them' (*La Nación*, 11 December 1962).
185 Bautista Mejía (1988), pp. 40–1.
186 Paulino (1962a), p. 2. Radhamés Gómez, who earlier had been in charge of the reporting from Las Matas de Farfán, was at that time suddenly withdrawn from his mission by Germán Ornes. 'I said I wanted to stay but for some reason the paper called me back' (interview with Radhamés Gómez Pepín, Santo Domingo, 18 March 1986). The reporting was continued by Antonio Paulino, *El Caribe*'s correspondent in San Juan de la Maguana.

that would be used to justify the massacre that followed. Among other things, the report mentions that one of the individuals taken into custody carried with him leaflets that read: 'Since I am member of the *Partido Dominicano*, I will do my duty and vote on 15 December.'[187] The colonel stated that the leaflet carried the picture of the deceased dictator and a palm tree, which was the symbol of the forbidden *Trujillista* party, and that 'sources which deserve total credit' had told him that Palma Sola sheltered 'fugitives from justice'.[188] In a newspaper article based on the colonel's report the accusations were elaborated further and it was stated that suspicions existed that a feared *Trujillista* thug, José Antonio Jiménez (Balá), was in hiding in Palma Sola, as well as some 'supposed' Cubans who were 'giving instructions' to the criminal 'fugitives' who were believed to live in Palma Sola.[189]

The article, which was written by Antonio Paulino and published in *El Caribe* on 23 December, shows that Paulino had been given access to the 'testimony' of Policarpio Vicente and the internal communication of several government agencies. This has led to the suspicion that the campaign in *El Caribe* was controlled by the government itself, that the following attack on Palma Sola was already planned by the authorities and that many of the 'proofs' of clandestine revolutionary activities in Palma Sola were fabricated by government agents.[190] It is furthermore probable that the key witness for the police, Policarpo Vicente, was an informant contracted by Attorney General García Vásquez in order to infiltrate Palma Sola.[191] At any rate, the last 'revelations' in the press made García Vásquez issue an official denouncement of the activities in Palma Sola and on 27 December he finally announced that the government would 'attack the fraudulent activities in Palma Sola with firmness'.[192]

187 Quoted in García (1986), p. 200.
188 Ibid. The leaflet was worthless as proof that any political activity linked to the forbidden *Trujillista* party had taken place in Palma Sola. During the last elections under Trujillo, which took place on 15 December 1960, such leaflets were distributed in their hundreds of thousands all over the country and it was not unusual that such a scrap of paper appeared among the belongings of some peasant or at the police station in Las Matas (cf. Campillo Pérez (1986), p. 204).
189 Paulino (1962a). Jiménez had been in charge of Trujillo's vast sugar estates and ended up as boss of the Santo Domingo branch of Trujillo's feared secret police, the SIM (military intelligence service), whose victims often were tortured by him personally (Javier García (1986), p. 381). Neither Balá nor any Cubans were present in Palma Sola, however.
190 García (1986), p. 208.
191 Ibid. p. 211. In the witness report, Policarpio Vicente is described as a nineteen-year-old agriculturalist from La Villa in the southern district of Neiba, rather far from Palma Sola. He did not carry any identification documents and stated that he had been in Palma Sola during eight days (Martínez (1991), p. 294).
192 Quoted in Paulino (1962b).

The massacre

On 26 December, the police chief, General Belisario Peguero, came to Fort Ozama in Santo Domingo, the headquarters of the White Helmets. All officers of the 'anti-riot troops' were assembled and informed by the general that the operation against Palma Sola would soon be initiated. No date was given, but Peguero stated that the mission had to be carried out very soon. It had been proved that the sect had been used for political ends and strong suspicions existed that arms had been provided by *Trujillistas* and smuggled across the Haitian border in order to arm the 'guards' of Palma Sola.[193]

Belisario Peguero had the same morning flown over Palma Sola in a helicopter, together with Attorney General Vásquez and Antonio Imbert Barrera, one of Trujillo's murderers and an influential member of the governing State Council.[194] The captured *Mellizo*, León Romilio, had been with them in the helicopter:

> The helicopter circled over Palma Sola and people ran out to see it. We could see Romilio, he had a loudspeaker in his hand, but no one could hear what he said due to the noise of the propeller. Romilio started to make signs with his arms. He tried to make it understood that we had to leave the place, but Plinio, who stood in the middle of the crowd, misunderstood what his brother tried to say and told us that we had to disperse so the helicopter would be able to land.[195]

> The helicopter left and some people got worried. We had not understood what the *Mellizo* wanted, but most of us said there would be no danger in Palma Sola. It was a thing of God and nothing could threaten us. But I know now that Plinio knew what was going to happen – a letter had been thrown from the helicopter and it had been given to Plinio.[196]

That same evening the chief of the US military assistance and advisory group, Colonel Wolfe, had been summoned to the government palace in Santo Domingo and asked for four helicopters 'to airlift troops into the hills', 500 2.7 inch rockets and sixty napalm tanks. The Americans were told that Palma Sola was a subversive center where the cultists carried out paramilitary training. Harry Schlaudeman, who was in charge of the CIA

193 Interview with Darío Jiménez Reynoso, Santo Domingo, 10 March 1986.
194 Martin (1966), p. 303.
195 Interview with Marina Bautista, Las Matas de Farfán, 5 July 1990.
196 Interview with an *Olivorista* who wants to remain anonymous, Las Matas de Farfán, 5 July 1990. Cf. García (1986), p. 239.

in the Dominican Republic, had visited one of Palma Sola's offshoots on election day, however, and seen 'much that was strange but nothing subversive'. The American embassy had also received information from some of the American Peace Corps volunteers who were active in the area and the US diplomats were accordingly unwilling to support the Dominican government in an action directed against the cultic center: 'We certainly did not want United States napalm dropped on religious pilgrims.'[197]

Belisario Peguero decided to carry out the mission without US support and on the morning of 27 December 1962 the White Helmets were provided with gas masks and equipment for the administration of tear gas.[198] They arrived in San Juan de la Maguana in the afternoon. The men were briefed in the evening; their task consisted of encircling Palma Sola early the next morning, and by peaceful means trying to capture as many of the sect members as possible. They knew that army personnel was on its way from both Santo Domingo and Bánica in order to help the police carry out the mission, but on the morning of 28 December became somewhat confused upon learning that an army general, Miguel Félix Rodríguez Reyes, had already left for Palma Sola, accompanied by twelve men.[199]

General Rodríguez Reyes was a prestigious officer. US ambassador Martin described him as 'an older man, gray-haired, intelligent, giving an impression of strength and decency. I had had my eye on him against the day when a shuffle of the high command might take place.'[200] The general was inspector of the armed forces. Accordingly he did not have any direct command over the troops and some authors have pointed out the singularity of sending Rodríguez Reyes to Palma Sola.[201] It is possible that the general volunteered for the mission, since he knew the district around the cultic center very well. He owned some land not far from the place and used to joke with his friends telling them that he was a witch doctor from Palma Sola.[202] From 1956 to 1958, Rodríguez Reyes had served as a commanding officer in the area.[203] During these years he made many

---

197 Martin (1966), p. 304.
198 Apart from their personal equipment, the troops carried with them a heavy tear-gas thrower with gas projectiles, as well as a Thompson gun (Manuel Valentín Despradel Brache, interviewed by *Rahintel*, 11 September 1990). The Thompson, also called Tommy gun, is the trademark of a .45 calibre submachine gun.
199 Interview with Darío Jiménez Reynoso, Santo Domingo, 10 March 1986.
200 Martin (1966), p. 302.
201 Cf. Kurzman (1965), p. 90.
202 Interview with Miguel Antonio Rodríguez Landestoy, Santo Domingo, 29 April 1986.
203 28 October 1956 – 21 March 1957, he was Assistant to the Commander of the Second Brigade, San Juan de la Maguana; 22 March 1957 – 25 July 1957, Commander of the Second Regiment of the Second Brigade, Barahona; 25 July 1957 – 29 March 1958, Commander of the First Regiment of the Second Brigade, Elías Piña (from the Military Records of General Miguel Félix Rodríguez Reyes).

Figure 4.19 General Miguel Rodríguez Reyes.

friends. 'He always had a keen interest in knowing different places, and liked moving around in the districts, trying to get to know how the people really are [*por su forma*].'[204] He was a personal friend of Attorney General Vásquez and various members of the governing State Council, particularly Luis Amiama Tió, whose personal bodyguard he had commanded for a short time.[205]

Juan Sully Bonnelly, son of the Dominican president of the time, Rafael Bonnelly, relates how he 'happened to pass by' the office of Antonio Imbert Barrera.[206] There he found Imbert involved in a discussion with Francisco Caamaño, Tavares Alvarez (secretary of state for domestic policy and police) and several 'other state functionaries'. Imbert Barrera was organizing a mission which was supposed to go to Palma Sola the next day. After having decided on what strategy to follow and the composition of the accompanying troops, those present were making themselves ready to leave when General Miguel Rodríguez Reyes, quite unexpectedly, appeared in the room. Rodríguez Reyes directed himself to Antonio Imbert Barrera and made the following proposition:

> Don Antonio, this is nothing for you. For a mission like this you need someone who is familiar with the frontier and I know the frontier like

---

204 Interview with Ramón Jesús Rodríguez Landestoy, Boca Chica, 15 June 1989.
205 Ibid., Amiama Tió had been involved in the assassination of Trujillo. Cf. Chapter 8.
206 It remains unclear if the related meeting took place on 26 or 27 December. Caamaño's presence, however, seems to indicate that it occured on 26 December.

the palm of my hand. It is necessary to go there [to Palma Sola] in order to establish a dialogue, but it would be stupid to send someone who does not truly and competently understand the mentality of the people over there. I am the right person to head this mission.[207]

The Catholic priest Oscar Robles Toledano, who was a close friend of Rafael Bonnelly, related the same incident in an article written twenty-two years later.[208]

On the evening of 27 December, Attorney General García Vásquez had a social gathering in his house, and among the invited guests was General Rodríguez Reyes.[209] Over drinks they agreed to go together to San Juan de la Maguana in Rodríguez Reyes' car and, in the words of García Vásquez' son, Eduardo García,

> Reyes, as well as my father, were both convinced that together they would be able to work out a satisfactory and peaceful solution, avoiding bloodshed in Palma Sola, a conviction that was based on Reyes' knowledge of the mentality of the peasantry, and, when it came to García Vásquez, his elevated, civic spirit and firm belief in persuasion as a way to reach a peaceful solution to a conflict which, he believed, had arisen from backwardness, ignorance and lack of education, and thus had to be confronted in a humanitarian spirit and with justice.[210]

At 5 a.m. on 28 December, Attorney General García Vásquez came to the house of General Rodríguez Reyes in order to accompany him to Palma Sola. One of the general's sons, who was a lieutenant at the time, wanted to go with them, but his father said it was better he stayed at home, and, while drinking a cup of coffee before they left, Attorney General Vásquez told the general's family that 'there will be no problems, no dangers. The general can go by himself.' They went and Rodríguez Reyes brought his

---

207 Rodríguez Reyes, quoted by Juan Sully Bonnelly Valle in an interview by *Rahintel*, 1 September 1990.
208 Robles Toledano quotes Rodríguez Reyes as saying: 'It is not you who ought to go, it's I who knows the region and its inhabitants and I would be able to talk to them, make them listen to reason and bring them to their senses' (Thompson (1985)). P. R. Thompson is the pen-name Robles Toledano uses when he writes a column in the Dominican daily *Hoy*. Imbert Barrera has confirmed the incident with the sole objection that it took place in Amiama Tió's office (*Rahintel*, 1 September 1990).
209 García Vásquez and Rodríguez Reyes had known one another for several years. When Rodríguez Reyes was placed in the San Juan Valley (1956–58), one of his closest friends had been a brother of Antonio García Vásquez, Bienvenido García Vásquez, who was a dentist in San Juan de la Maguana (Eduardo García Michel, interviewed by *Rahintel*, 1 September 1990).
210 Ibid.

rifle with him since he planned to shoot some pigeons after the mission had been fulfilled.[211]

Lieutenant Colonel Manuel Valentín Despradel Brache, who was second in command of the White Helmets, recalls that he met General Rodríguez Reyes on the morning of 28 December, while he was having breakfast at the Hotel La Maguana. Colonel Caamaño, who had spent the night with relatives, was not around yet. Rodríguez Reyes entered the dining room quite suddenly and the surprised Despradel Brache, who earlier had served under the general,[212] got up and greeted his superior officer. In a casual way, Rodríguez Reyes told Despradel Brache to sit down again and share his breakfast with him. After a while Despradel Brache asked: 'And where are you going, sir?' The general answered: 'I am going with you and I am telling you, taking the opportunity of Caamaño not being here yet, that I have come because I fear that Caamaño, violent as he is, will be unable to come to terms with this people. I know them quite well because when I was a captain I used to go to that place [Palma Sola] to cut *guayacán* [guaiacum] in order to export it.'[213]

Despradel Brache offered to drive the general to Palma Sola in his jeep.[214] Rodríguez Reyes agreed and told Despradel Brache that they would leave as soon as he had visited a friend in town. Despradel Brache left to prepare his troops for the trip to Palma Sola, but while he was entering the fort of San Juan, where the White Helmets were lodged, he was amazed to learn from the sentry that the general had already passed by in a jeep on his way to Palma Sola. In haste, Despradel Brache organized the enlisted men and ordered them up on the trucks, but, before the troops were ready to go and Caamaño had joined them, valuable time was lost and they were thus unable to catch up with the general.[215]

Despradel Brache is partly contradicted by Miguel Tomás Suzaña, who states that on the morning of 28 December he received a telephone call from his superior, Attorney General García Vásquez, who told him that he was waiting for him at the Hotel La Maguana. When Suzaña arrived he found García Vasquez, Rodríguez Reyes, and 'some other people', having breakfast in the dining room. They invited him to join them, and he sat

211 Interview with Ramón Jesús Rodríguez Landestoy, Boca Chica, 15 June 1989.
212 Despradel Brache had served under Rodríguez Reyes when the latter was in charge of the weapon factory of the Dominican army (Manuel Valentín Despradel Brache, interviewed by *Rahintel*, 11 September 1990).
213 Guaiacum, also called lignum vitae, is a tree with heavy resinous wood that is used in machine bearings, casters, etc. Its resin is used medicinally, mainly as an expectorant and to make varnishes.
214 Rodríguez Reyes' car, a Chevrolet Impala, could not negotiate the dirt road up to Carrera de Yeguas, where the path to Palma Sola began.
215 Manuel Valentín Despradel Brache, interviewed by *Rahintel*, 11 September 1990.

down, declining the breakfast since he had already eaten. While they were discussing the plans for the trip, Miguel Angel Ramírez Alcántara appeared at the scene and offered his services. Everyone knew that this famous San Juan *caudillo* maintained good relations with the people of Palma Sola, but strangely enough he stressed that he was experienced in guerilla warfare from his time in Costa Rica.[216] They thanked Ramírez Alcántara for his offer, but told him that they believed they were able to handle the situation without his help.

When the breakfast was over, Rodríguez Reyes called for a friend in whose care he left his hunting rifle until he had finished his mission in Palma Sola. Before the group left for Palma Sola they passed by Suzaña's house, where he told his family to prepare a goat for the evening so that García Vásquez, Suzaña and Rodríguez Reyes could have a little celebration in the evening, eating, drinking and playing dominoes, as it was Suzaña's birthday on 29 December.[217]

Before they left San Juan de la Maguana, they apparently also stopped for Rodríguez Reyes' old friend Bishop Reilly:

> No one had informed me about the operation. Reyes wanted me to accompany him to Palma Sola. Everyone knew I was against the thing, but I did not want any bloodshed. When Reyes came over to my house he discovered that I was not there. I had stayed over in the capital on my way from Boston, where I had gone for the funeral of my mother.[218]

They also picked up a relative of the *Mellizos*, who served as a private in San Juan de la Maguana. Rodríguez Reyes' small group left San Juan de la Maguana around 9 a.m. When it arrived in Palma Sola, around 12 noon, most of the inhabitants were eating or relaxing, taking their siesta. Some of them had just returned from the calvary where Plinio had mounted his tribune exactly at the same time as the general and his company had left San Juan. He had told the people of Palma Sola that the military intended to destroy the place and that they all had better leave for their home villages. Even if he talked very well and 'carried the spirit within himself', most of his listeners remained calm. A few prepared to leave. There were also many who had not been present to hear Plinio's message.[219]

The general and his escort were stopped at the entrance and one of the Ventura brothers, Nicolás (Barraco), asked them about their mission. The

216 Miguel Tomás Suzaña, interviewed by *Rahintel*, 6 October 1990.
217 Miguel Tomás Suzaña, interviewed by *Rahintel*, 11 September 1990.
218 Interview with Thomas Reilly, San Juan de la Maguana, 12 December 1985.
219 Interview with an *Olivorista* who wants to remain anonymous, Las Matas de Farfán, 5 July 1990.

general explained that the authorities were prepared to construct better housing for the people in Palma Sola and wanted to offer them a school and a medical clinic. All he wanted to do was to talk to their leaders and tell them that they had to abide by the law, respect the authorities and not pretend that they belonged to a different world. Not for a moment had he thought of coming there in order to fight and he did not intend to take any of them prisoner. The courteous manners of the general and the respectful way in which he talked to the guards of Palma Sola made them willing to let all the visitors pass and they even let them keep their weapons.[220]

The general had expressed his desire to meet all the leaders and Barraco accompanied him up to the church by the calvary, where Tulio Ventura was in charge, sitting in for Plinio. Rodríguez Reyes asked Tulio if he would be able to assemble all the Ventura brothers in order to plan for the future. Tulio answered that on that particular day he represented them all and it was enough if the general talked to him. Both Plinio and Delanoy Ventura were in the crowd that had started to gather around Tulio and the general, but only Delanoy disclosed who he was and joined Tulio in the discussion. The bystanders heard the general say that 'we have come to put an end to all this; the annoyance you are causing me with this disorder is already too great'.[221] After a while Tulio and the general went into the church, followed by District Attorney Suzaña, in order to meet with *La Madre Piadosa*. Suddenly they heard firing just outside the church and Suzaña ran out closely followed by the general. 'The confusion was total.'[222]

While the general was inside the church the soldiers who were posted outside got more and more nervous as the surrounding crowd closed in on them, trying to find out what was happening inside the church. One of the soldiers started to threaten the bystanders, which angered a certain Avelino Bautista (or, according to other witnesses, another man called Anselmo), who interceded and tried to stop one of the soldiers from hitting a bystander. According to the official reports Avelino attacked the soldier with a machete. Other witnesses state that the soldiers wanted to take a knife away from him.[223] Plinio, who had appeared at the scene, joined the quarrel with the soldiers and some say he drew the knife he always carried by his side. Another soldier fired right into his chest, and

---

220 Interview with Miguel Tomás Suzaña, San Juan de la Maguana, 7 May 1986.

221 Bautista Mejía (1988), p.45.

222 Interview with Miguel Tomás Suzaña, San Juan de la Maguana, 7 May 1986. In another interview with Suzaña, quoted by García (1986), p. 340, the reader gets the impression that the district attorney had followed the general into the church, but according to our own interview with Suzaña it appears as if he was outside the church when the shots sounded.

223 García (1986), pp. 251–2.

Plinio died immediately, falling to the ground, face up. As he hit the ground, Avelino was shot in the belly. People started to run in all directions while the general, together with Tulio, appeared in the doorway shouting: 'Cease fire! Cease fire! Stop this killing!'[224] These were his last words. Immediately afterwards he fell to the side and hit the ground. According to Tulio and most of the cultists he was shot in the neck by one of his own soldiers. According to the official reports he was clubbed and hacked to death by the cultists.[225] An *Olivorista* who wants to remain anonymous told us: 'I am sure it was not people from Palma Sola who killed the general. Several persons told me later that the corpse of the general was beaten with sticks, and it was the military who did it. They had their plans.'[226]

In the meantime, the troops of Caamaño, fifty-three men[227] who had arrived at the ford in three trucks, had moved up to Palma Sola. When they were half a kilometer from the place they heard firing – isolated, intermittent shots. They rushed up the hill and tried to surround the place, but it was too big and they had to divide themselves into groups of eight.[228] The three commanding officers, Colonel Francisco Caamaño Deñó, Lieutenant Colonel Manuel Valentín Despradel Brache and Major Rafael Guillermo Guzmán Acosta, went to the entrance where they were met by a soldier who came running from the religious compound and told the officers that the general had been shot. Colonel Despradel became angry and shouted at the messenger: 'You do not mean that you opened fire with all these people inside?' Caamaño decided to go in, accompanied by Major Guzmán and left the command of his troops to Colonel Despradel.[229]

Caamaño and Guzmán ran into Palma Sola and were met by fleeing people and gunshots. Guzmán was hit by a bullet in the chest and fell to the ground. When Caamaño stopped and tried to help his wounded comrade he was struck down by a pole and fell over Guzmán's body.

---

224 Cárdenas Fontecha (1964), p. 57. Cf. García (1986), p. 221. According to León Romilio Ventura and some of his relatives it was Caamaño Deñó who accidentally fired the lethal shot at Plinio (Martínez (1991), p. 241).

225 See for example Bodden (1962) and Nidio Ventura, quoted in García (1986), pp. 336–7.

226 Interview with an *Olivorista* who wants to remain anonymous, Las Matas de Farfán, 5 July 1990.

227 Despradel Brache states that the troops consisted of forty-eight enlisted men and five officers (interview by *Rahintel*, 11 September 1990). Darío Jiménez Reynoso, who served as a sergeant, estimated their number to be 200 (interview, Santo Domingo, 10 March 1986).

228 Interview with Darío Jiménez Reynoso, Santo Domingo, 10 March 1986. According to Despradel Brache the troops were divided into five groups, four which advanced on Palma Sola and one which stayed behind as a reserve (interview by *Rahintel*, 11 September 1990).

229 Interview with Darío Jiménez Reynoso, Santo Domingo, 10 March 1986. The man who contacted Caamaño was probably Colonel Méndez Lara, who had accompanied General Rodríguez Reyes in the morning (García (1986), p. 247).

Someone wrenched the rifle from Caamaño and hit him over the head
once more, but before he was hit a third time the colonel was able to fire
his pistol straight into the face of his adversary.[230] When Lieutenant
Colonel Despradel learned that Caamaño and Guzmán had fallen he
ordered his troops to attack, and after firing their tear gas grenades the
White Helmets rushed into Palma Sola.[231]

> They had some kind of machine which fired the grenades into the
> village. I remember the sound. It said 'tut, tut, tut' and suddenly the
> soldiers were over us. Many flung themselves to the ground, but we
> had to protect the children, so we ran towards the church. Shots flew
> through the air and the gas was all over.[232]

Enveloped in a cloud of tear gas Suzaña and García Vásquez tried to run
towards the entering troops:

> I heard the shots, but I do not know who fired them. When the general
> fell I was far away from him. We were talking at different places. We
> had parted in order to do so. He was already on the ground when the
> tear gas was thrown.[233]

> Some armed peasants were following me as well. And later, when it was
> all over, an army sergeant told me he saved me by pure chance,
> because with his weapon he had shot the one who followed me with a
> dagger.[234]

230 Sáenz Padrón and Rius Blein (1984), p. 82. Hermann (1983), p. 88, offers a slightly
different version. A third, and quite different, version is offered by Despradel Brache
who states that he came into the compound of Palma Sola just after Caamaño and that
he helped the wounded Major 'Maracota' [Guzmán Acosta] into a house. While
Despradel Brache was inside he heard Caamaño shouting: '*Compadre, compadre*, come and
help me! They are killing me!' Despradel rushed out of the house, and saw himself
forced to 'eleminate' a 'very big man' who had been hitting Camaaño over the head with
the latter's rifle. When Despradel Brache was trying to get the wounded Camaaño into
the relative safety of the house, he was himself attacked by a man carrying a huge stone.
Despradel Brache succeeded in killing his adversary, but only after having four of his ribs
crushed by the stone (Despradel Brache, interviewed by *Rahintel*, 11 September 1990).
In an interview with us, Marina Bautista (Las Matas de Farfán, 5 July 1990) stated that the
man who attacked Caamaño was a relative of hers, Dionisio Lebrón, and that he was
killed, not by Caamaño, but by other members of the White Helmets.
231 Interview with Darío Jiménez Reynoso, Santo Domingo, 10 March 1986. The official
reports of the time do not say anything about Despradel being wounded in the attack,
but Hermann (1983), p. 220, mentions that Despradel and Caamaño received medical
attention in Miami right after the massacre.
232 Interview with Juana María Ventura, Media Luna, 17 January 1986.
233 Interview with Miguel Tomás Suzaña, San Juan de la Maguana, 7 May 1986.
234 Suzaña, quoted by García (1986), p. 340.

I stayed close to Tulio Ventura who rushed to attack me with a blank weapon at the same time as I lost sight of General Rodríguez Reyes and District Attorney Suzaña. I retreated to a ditch where I met with a group of policemen. There we also found District Attorney Suzaña and Colonel Méndez Lara.[235]

By the church various men were crawling among corpses and wounded people. Both Delanoy and Onilio Ventura had been killed in front of the sanctuary. The machine-gun fire was concentrated on the church, which was encircled by the police and military. Women and children, who had fled to what they thought would be safety by *La Madre Piadosa*, were caught in the middle of the crossfire.[236] One of the *Olivoristas* had got hold of one of the soldiers' machine guns and was firing into the group of approaching policemen.[237] This infuriated the White Helmets even more:

> We had a guide with us and we ran towards a house in which he said the *Mellizos* were. We had orders to catch them and tried to reach that house. They were firing at us. They did not have many weapons, it must have been pistols. We did not find any rifles afterwards. Many of the fanatics did not care about our presence and ignored the bullets. They did not attack the military. It was the guards of order, those dressed in blue. I think it was they who were the ones firing at us. There were many children around, entire families.[238]

The chaos increased with the sudden arrival of soldiers from Bánica and Elías Piña:

> Those who came from Bánica and Piña and those [the White Helmets] who were already there did not recognize one another in the chaos and started to shoot. Everyone was caught in a crossfire. The disaster took place because of the behavior of the two army fractions which were there. There were not many of the civilians who fired. There were

235 Antonio García Vásquez, quoted by García (1986), p. 248.
236 Interview with Juana María Ventura, Media Luna, 17 January 1986.
237 Bautista Mejía (1988), pp. 46–7.
238 Interview with Darío Jiménez Reynoso. Santo Domingo, 10 March 1986. The arming of the *Olivoristas* was very meager. Most of the people who opposed the soldiers were throwing stones; only a few had daggers. Some members of Palma Sola's guard had tied their knives to long bamboo poles (Despradel Brache, interviewed by *Rahintel*, 11 September 1990). Macario Lorenzo suggests that the sounds of 'gunshots' reported by several soldiers came from lumps of salt that exploded in the heat of burning houses. The inhabitants of Palma Sola used *sal de peña* or *gema*, which was extracted from plants and kept in big lumps within the huts and houses (interview by *Rahintel*, 11 September 1990).

no arms around, you could not get in there with arms. The troops were not commanded by the general. They came later. I never understood why. Maybe it was some sort of power demonstration.[239]

General Rodríguez Reyes had not asked for any of them. He was the first one to be surprised by the presence of soldiers and policemen in the place where he was with us negotiating to bring these people out of Palma Sola.[240]

Two attack planes, 'enormous yellow machines with black letters painted on them strafed over Palma Sola in an aggressive manner'[241] and shortly after a loudspeaker bellowed: 'Cease fire, do not shoot any more, now it's enough!'[242] Soldiers and White Helmets were running back and forth through the village, banging on the closed doors with their rifle butts shouting: 'Everybody outside! Everybody outside!' All men had to leave their homes and the soldiers ordered them: 'Form lines! Line up!' Women and children were left in peace. Occasional shots were still ringing out and people continued to be shot.[243] One of Delanoy's sons found the corpse of his father lying outside the church. A soldier spotted him and ordered him to rise up, and when the boy did not obey immediately the soldier shot him straight in the face.[244]

Already before the firing the White Helmets had started to drag people from their houses. They shouted: 'To the corral! To the corral! All of you!' I was already there when the shouting started. I did not see anything because I lay with my head in the dirt, like everyone else around me. The lead was flying through the air and the cross stood in the middle of it all, like a Christ in the fire. When the firing had ceased they tied our hands behind our backs, while we still were lying down. They were constantly asking for the Venturas and two brothers rose. They were Tulio and Barraco.[245]

The principal order given to the White Helmets was to capture all of the Ventura brothers. Plinio, Onilio and Delanoy had already been killed, León Romilio was imprisoned in the capital, Tulio and Barraco were the only ones still alive in Palma Sola:

239 Interview with Miguel Tomás Suzaña, San Juan de la Maguana, 7 May 1986.
240 Suzaña quoted by García (1986), p. 340.
241 Interview with Marina Bautista, Las Matas de Farfán, 5 July 1990.
242 Bautista Mejía (1988), p. 48.
243 Interview with Marina Bautista, Las Matas de Farfán, 5 July 1990.
244 Interview with Juana María Ventura, Media Luna, 17 January 1986.
245 Interview with Diego Cépeda, Jínova, 4 June 1989.

Figure 4.20 After the massacre: the calvary.

Many of them continued to dance and sing after we had captured them. The army was cleaning up the place. We [the White Helmets] were searching for the *Mellizos*. The prisoners had to lay face down and their hands were tied to their back.

When everything had calmed down we identified the twin [Tulio?]. I do not remember their names. We took him 300 meters away from the prisoners; Despradel, I, Cío and others. Despradel was in command. He said that since General Rodríguez Reyes was dead this *Mellizo* could not be kept alive either. He took him apart for five to ten minutes. Then he said that we had to execute this *Mellizo* and that we had to do it all together. And we did it all of us – shot him.[246]

Barraco and Tulio were tied to a pole and shot. Afterwards their bodies were thrown into a hut which was soaked with gasoline and set on fire. Tulio, who already had been shot in the shoulder, miraculously survived. He succeeded in saving his own life, crawling out of the burning hut. His back, which had been seriously burned, became infected by worms, and he suffered greatly before he finally died in 1968, after six years of constant torment.

Tulio told his story to his brother León Romilio and his family. He stated that he had seen a 'policeman' behind the general when they came out of the church together. He had warned Rodríguez Reyes, saying: 'Take care

246 Interview with Darío Jiménez Reynoso, Santo Domingo, 10 March 1986.

Figure 4.21 Major Francisco Caamaño wounded and bandaged, after the massacre at Palma Sola. On the right, Attorney General Antonio García Vásquez.

General, there is a policeman behind you', but it was too late, the general had already been shot in the back of the neck.[247]

Meanwhile, the wounded officers, Caamaño Deñó and Guzmán Acosta, were brought down to Suzaña's car and driven to the hospital of San Juan de la Maguana. Suzaña stayed behind because he did not want to leave Palma Sola before Rodríguez Reyes had been found. In the commotion everyone had lost track of him and no one could tell if the general was dead or alive.[248]

An enlisted man from the White Helmets, Aristóteles Matos Herasme, found Rodríguez Reyes' dead body:

> I had never seen General Rodríguez Reyes, and after the incident, when I saw this person dressed in khaki and with yellow shoes, lying, thrown to the side, outside a simple house in the lower part [of Palma Sola], I said to a friend of mine, named Javier, who walked together with me: 'Look, Javier, that man who is lying dead there, he is not one of us. Who is it?' [...] He was lying on a ground that was dusty and dry, and there was no blood on it. I assumed he had been killed by a rock

---

247 Interview with León Romilio Ventura, Media Luna, 5 May 1986. Cf. García (1986), pp. 336–7 and Bautista Mejía (1988), pp. 63–7.
248 Miguel Tomás Suzaña interviewed by *Rahintel*, 29 September 1990.

Figure 4.22 Corpse being removed from Palma Sola to be put in the mass grave.

dropped on his chest. Close by was a huge stone which had been moved from its place.[249]

Suzaña, who brought the body down to the fort in San Juan de la Maguana, saw only a deep scar in the neck, which he assumed had caused the death of Rodríguez Reyes. It was not a gunshot wound. As far as he could see the body had no other visible injuries.[250]

The 'cleaning-up' began immediately. Corpses were carried on sheets of zinc and in hammocks and thrown into a deep ditch which had been used as a communal latrine. Some of the prisoners were forced to help the soldiers in this grisly occupation, while the majority still lay on the ground waiting for the trucks to arrive at the ford some thirty minutes away. Soldiers plundered the houses of their meager contents: 'They stole everything we brought with us from Haiti, all our money, the things I was going to have at my wedding.'[251] The houses and huts were burned down, many with corpses and wounded people inside. The planes swooped down and dropped napalm on some of them.

Strangely enough, two military attachés from the US embassy had entered Palma Sola together with the troops that had arrived from Bánica

---

249 Aristóteles Matos Herasme interviewed by *Rahintel*, 29 September 1990.
250 Miguel Tomás Suzaña interviewed by *Rahintel*, 29 September 1990.
251 Interview with Juana María Ventura, Media Luna, 17 January 1986.

Figure 4.23 Two of the victims.

and Elías Piña. It is not quite clear whether the two American army observers, Bevan Cass and Luther Long, had appeared at the moment of the massacre or just after it had all taken place. The report they presented to the US ambassador seems to indicate the latter:

> What had happened after that [the death of the general] was not a battle but a massacre. Cass and Long had counted forty-four cultists' bodies. Some had been killed inside their huts. Some lay alongside the trail on the way out – taken prisoners, then shot in vengeance. Many of the dead were old men, two were women, one was a child. Cass and Long felt certain that many more had been hunted down and killed in the hills. The huts had been burned to the ground, bodies inciner- ated. Troops were mopping up now. Worst of all, Cass and Long were absolutely certain the *Mellizos* had had no guns. No fire fight had occurred. Cass said flatly, 'It was wanton killing'.[252]

The suffering continued when the columns of prisoners moved over the rice paddies on their way to the waiting trucks. Several people were shot along the trail, some for the simple reason that they fell behind, others because they opposed some guard when he wanted to take their

---

252 Martin (1966), pp. 304–5. Lieutenant Colonel Bevan Cass was a US marine and Lieu- tenant Colonel Luther F. Long came from the regular US army.

Figure 4.24 Victim covered with propaganda leaflets for the *Unión Cívica Nacional.*

possessions;[253] 673 prisoners were loaded onto the trucks and taken to San Juan de la Maguana for questioning and further transport to Santo Domingo.[254]

The press was not allowed to enter the scene of the massacre until late in the afternoon, when most of the clean-up had already taken place. By then, the White Helmets had left for the capital and only army personnel were around when the journalists were shown what was left of the cultic center:

> We came in several hours after the massacre. Six kilometers before Palma Sola I saw how two pigs devoured a corpse which lay in a ditch. Up in Palma Sola most of the houses had already been burned down and most corpses had been buried. Only a few dead bodies were lying around. It was a strange sight. I remember a corpse littered with propaganda from the UCN. It appeared as if all had been arranged in a certain way. It was a total disaster. The Dominican military is probably the most imbecile you can find in the world. When you take them out of their routine they become crazy, because here routine is the same thing as doing nothing and learning nothing.[255]

253 Bautista Mejía (1988), pp. 49–52. Patoño Bautista Mejía stated that he witnessed four people being shot on the trail to the waiting trucks (interview with Patoño Bautista Mejía, Distrito de Haina, 5 March 1986).
254 *House Annals,* 28 December 1962.
255 Interview with Radhamés Gómez Pepín, Santo Domingo, 18 March 1986.

After the massacre

Official reports and explanations

After the massacre the Dominican press continued to reflect the official reports and few, if any, voices were heard questioning the behavior of the authorities. Several articles pretended to explain the phenomenon of *Olivorismo*, but almost unanimously they showed an amazing lack of insight and just repeated the same old gruesome voodoo lore found in pulp magazines all over the world.[256] Others repeated the accusations of connections between Trujillo and the *Olivoristas*. The latter articles were mostly based on prevalent anecdotes about superstitions cherished by Trujillo and unwarranted rumors about his voodoo beliefs. In short, these writings had nothing, or very little, to do with either the beliefs that flourished in Palma Sola or the ones that are customary among the *Olivoristas* in the Dominican southwest.[257]

Nevertheless, one of the results of both types of articles was the strengthening of a common opinion that Palma Sola was merely another, particularly eerie, example of base superstitions. For most people the *Olivorista* peasants in Palma Sola continued to be devoid of human qualities. They were seen as one-dimensional caricatures who had leapt out of the pages of some cheap horror magazine. This denial of the human value of the people from Palma Sola is perhaps one explanation of why the press and most people in the capital were willing to accept the unreliable explanations of the massacre offered by the authorities, mainly Antonio García Vásquez and Antonio Imbert Barrera.

On 29 December 1962, two days after the massacre, García Vásquez and Imbert Barrera called a press conference. Agents of the world press and other mass media were invited together with local journalists: representatives for *Time* magazine, *Paris Match* and Radio Luxemburg and various international press agencies were present. García Vásquez stated that many questions concerning Palma Sola remained unanswered, for example: Where did the '*Liboristas*' get the means to buy the 'uniforms, shoes and various arms' which were found by the police after the massacre?[258] What

---

256 See for example Caro (1963). This article, written by a *Sanjuanero* who ought to have been better informed, is 'based' on books by Fernando Ortiz and Raymundo Niña Rodríguez concerning Cuban *santería* and Brazilian *candomblé*. Caro presented anthropological research concerning totally different cultural settings just as if they also dealt with Palma Sola. He also cites a prejudiced anecdote by Freddy Prestol Castillo concerning a voodoo-related incident by the Haitian frontier, which apparently took place long before the emergence of the cult in Palma Sola.

257 See for example Bobea Bellini (1963).

258 The 'arms' found and listed by the military were '43 machetes, one military plate, two hatchets, and one canteen, also of a military type' (Bodden (1962)).

Figure 4.25 Press conference after the Palma Sola massacre. *l. to r.* Antonio Imbert
Barrera, Attorney General Antonio García Vásquez, General Belisario
Peguero, Dr Tabaré Alvarez Pereyra.

'mission' was to be carried out on 1 January, 1963? Why was the 'house of
zinc' taboo for the 'fanatics' of Palma Sola and why did its inhabitants occasionally travel to Haiti? According to García Vásquez none of these questions could be properly answered. However, he indicated that maybe a clue
was that the Dominican government 'has knowledge of the fact that Petán
Trujillo and his companions are in Haiti fomenting pogroms intended to
sow uneasiness and anxiety in the Dominican Republic'.[259] The attorney
general linked Palma Sola directly to this 'knowledge' stating that

> The motto of the fanatical followers of Liborio was 'Trujillo and the
> Fatherland', but their leader would be the one mentioned in ... [a]
> *copla* [popular song], that is, Plinio Ventura, after having taken power
> [after the reign of the Trujillo brothers].
>
> He [García Vásquez] said that various detainees have affirmed
> having seen on the 20th [of December] Luis Trujillo Reynoso, and
> from this it could be deduced that the movement of Palma Sola hid a
> Trujillo type conspiration.[260]

259 García Vásquez quoted by Bodden (1963).
260 García Vásquez, quoted by Estrella Veloz (1962a). The *copla* García Vásquez mentions
   was a *salve* sung in Palma Sola which stated that Plinio was going to be a leader on a
   'universal level' and that he was prepared for this 'by the mandate of God and Mary'. The
   'various' witnesses were in reality only one, and a very dubious one for that matter: Policarpio Vicente, a man who apparently had been planted in Palma Sola as a spy for the
   authorities (García (1986), pp. 211 and 201–8).

These unconvincing, and inaccurate, attempts to link the *Olivoristas* with
Trujillista machinations were uncritically accepted by the local journals,
but were largely ignored by the international media representatives. *Time*
magazine stated that Palma Sola evidently 'had little to do with politics',[261]
while the London *Times* preferred to quote a source other than García
Vásquez, stating that 'The [Dominican] Government denied early reports
that the rebellion had a political motive'.[262] An article in *Le Monde*
mentioned that the case of Palma Sola was the first time since the death of
Trujillo that civil unrest had been reported from a 'rural environment',[263]
but declined to disclose any political, or religious reasons for the Dominican *émeute paysanne* [peasant uprising].[264] However, the *New York Times*
published a divergent, dramatic and partly imaginative article which
labeled the massacre an 'uprising', stating that 'several thousand peasants'
had staged an attack on Palma Sola and taken 'over the city [sic]. They
killed Gen. Miguel Rodríguez, and an undisclosed number of federal
troops sent to put down the revolt. About 30 rebels were killed. The insurgents partially burned Palma Sola before about 400 guerillas pulled out for
the hills.'[265]

In his personal report, filed at the Archives of the Attorney General's
Office in Santo Domingo,[266] García Vásquez states that he did not see the
general being killed. The deed took place at a chaotic moment when the
whole area was covered with clouds of tear gas. Still, he implies that
Rodríguez Reyes was killed by some 'fanatics' among the Palma Sola
Liboristas, reporting that he saw the general's corpse surrounded by the
'zealots', after he himself had found protection in a ditch. He stated that
he had been forced to dash to security when Tulio Ventura attacked him
with a dagger. The attorney general declared that the burning down of the

261 *Time*, 4 January 1963. *La Nación* 12 January 1963, cites an article said to have been printed
in *Time*, 11 January 1963. This article must have been taken from another source,
however, since it never appeared in *Time*. 'We have no reference to a TIME story similar
to the one described in your letter' (*Time* (1993), Letter from 'The Editors' to Jan
Lundius, New York, 27 July). In the article quoted by *La Nación* it is stated that: 'In Santo
Domingo, the government received information that the Liboristas have been receiving
arms smuggled from Haiti and administered them to 5 thousand peasant guerillas in
order to start a rebellion, telling them that "within a few days we will be the government."' Still, this rather extensive article does not stress the political motivation for the
movement and does not mention the *Trujillista* connection García Vásquez hinted at.
262 *The Times*, 31 December 1962, p. 7.
263 *Le Monde*, 30–1 December 1962, p. 2. 'After the assassination of the dictator Trujillo, 30
May 1962, the only significant incidents had taken place in the towns. They were always
directed against former supporters of the dictatorship, who have stayed behind after the
death of the Benefactor' (ibid.).
264 Ibid.
265 *New York Times*, 31 December 1962 .
266 Document No. 10491-13, quoted in García (1986), pp. 247–9.

village was undertaken as a tactical operation in order to force its inhabitants out into an open space in the middle of the encampment, where a shallow depression in the ground ran across the open terrain. By burning down the houses the military and the police succeeded in gathering the peasants by the hollow, tied them up and rescued the corpse of the general.

In his report, García Vásquez is careful not to accuse anyone of killing the general,[267] and he tries to depict the behavior of the military as rational by offering a fairly plausible explanation as to why the village was burned to the ground. It is revealing that all through his report García Vásquez does not show any remorse about the tragic fate of all the innocent peasants who were mistreated, wounded and killed during the incident. Instead he explicitly writes: 'the only thing that hurts is the death of General Rodríguez Reyes.'[268] The press and most Dominicans apparently accepted the guilt by implication of the *Mellizos*, who could easily be used as scapegoats, since all the Ventura brothers who had been in Palma Sola were assumed to be dead. As one peasant living in the area stated: 'In those days everything was so chaotic that people did not have any time to think for themselves. They let the journalists and the authorities do the thinking for them and many accepted what they told them.'[269]

One of the official versions which was offered to the press stressed that Palma Sola 'was no longer a simple case of a fetishist cult, but the actual creation of groups training for rebellion'. The document continues to describe the occurrences in the following manner:

> While General Miguel F. Rodríguez Reyes, the Attorney General of the Republic, Dr. Antonio García Vásquez, and the District Attorney of the Court of Appeal of San Juan de la Maguana, Dr. Tomás Suzaña, and various officers and privates of the Army and the National Police tried to discuss with the '*Mellizos*' Tulio, Nicolás and Plinio Ventura, they

267 It was only in a sworn statement made on 24 January 1963, that García Vásquez explicitly stated that General Rodríguez Reyes was killed by the people of Palma Sola. At that occasion he stated that the general was found with the 'base of the skull fractured'. García Vásquez himself had not seen the actual killing of the general since at the moment he had been running for cover, but 'before, during or after that, the superstitious people had taken advantage of his [Reyes] unprotected position, giving him blows with sticks and stones, since he was unable to get protection from the accompanying group, because members of the National Police, without noticing the situation, had thrown tear gas in order to disperse the aggressive crowd.' (The document is reproduced in García (1986), pp. 307–8.)

268 From a report given by Attorney General García Vásquez, Expediente No. 10491-13, Procuraduría General de la República, Santo Domingo, quoted in García (1986), pp. 247–9.

269 Interview with Pirindín Solís, El Batey, 11 April 1986.

were attacked by a resolute [*calculada*] crowd consisting of more than a thousand persons, who had hidden themselves within various houses of the village.

In the action that followed, and while he tried to pacify the fanatics in order to avoid a bloodbath, General Rodríguez Reyes was killed with sticks. Eye witnesses have declared that, due to the fear that reigned in the place, the courage General Rodríguez Reyes showed in his efforts to evade the use of force was demonstrated in vain.

In order to save the beleaguered authorities, forces of the National Police and the National Army went into action to suffocate the riot. When this took place Colonel Francis Caamaño, of the National Police, and Major Guzmán, of the National Police, as well as four privates from the National Police and two from the National Army, received grave injuries. Furthermore, among the military forces several men received various small wounds, among the latter, Colonel Manuel Valentín Despradel, of the National Police.

Among the rebels 22 to 25 persons died, among them the '*Mellizos*' Nicolás and Tulio Ventura. More than 30 were wounded. Around 500 prisoners were taken. The village of Palma Sola was burned down as a result of the action.

The other '*Mellizo*', Plinio Ventura, succeeded in fleeing to the mountains followed by 400 to 500 persons. At the moment they are being pursued by units from the Armed Forces, specialists in anti-guerilla warfare.[270]

As we know, Plinio did not flee to the hills but was killed in the massacre. The report gives the impression that some people fled in Plinio's company from Palma Sola and apparently planned to put up some kind of armed resistance. Hence the call for anti-guerilla units.

The reality was totally different. Wounded and dying people fled in terror from infuriated police and military units. Many died from their injuries along the paths in fields and mountains. The House Annals of the priests in Las Matas de Farfán mentioned that 'A number of the wounded have fled, and are bleeding to death'.[271] Many died because they did not dare to come down to Las Matas and San Juan to have their wounds attended to.[272] Recollections of peasants living around the destroyed cultic center reflect the panic and terror which struck the survivors of the massacre:

---

270 Quoted by Alvarez Castellanos and Atanay Cruz (1962). The wounds of the mentioned officers were not particularly grave. Still they all received special medical treatment in Miami (Hermann (1983), p. 220).
271 *House Annals*, 30 December 1962.
272 Interview with Thomas Reilly, San Juan de la Maguana, 12 December 1985.

I was on my way up there [to Palma Sola]. But I met the fugitives and saw the airplanes sweeping down from the sky. I ran into two terrified small boys. They were almost naked and had only their shorts on. They told me they had seen all the soldiers: 'Everything is burning!' they shouted. I borrowed a horse and rode until I ended up some twenty kilometers from the place.[273]

It was terrible. They were all terrified. They knew we were Mennonites and before they had disliked us, just because we were Protestants. But after the killings many of them fled to us and sought our protection. They felt betrayed and many of their friends and relatives had been killed, wounded or taken prisoners. Dead bodies were found all over the area. They [the army] forced the survivors to pick up the corpses in and around Palma Sola. Many repented and became Mennonites. It began almost immediately and I think maybe eighty people converted to the Mennonite faith in the days that followed after the massacre. Many did so out of fear.[274]

The 'clean-up'

Palma Sola had various offshoots, all of them with their own independent spiritual leaders but endowed with similar calvaries, stone circles, and throngs of pilgrims demonstrating the same fervent beliefs in a spiritual presence. Most of these 'branches' were older cultic centers, which previously had developed around holy places or had been inspired by the teachings of cultic leaders, who later on had confessed their allegiance to the *Mellizos* of Palma Sola.

The authorities and the press described them all as nuclei of armed resistance, or dens of vile superstition, and after Palma Sola had been annihilated, military units continued to demolish all siblings originating from the fallen trunk of Palma Sola. García Vásquez ended his first report by stating:

I think it is necessary to continue the operations in Vallejuelo and Jínova in order to eradicate this evil which has caused so much tragedy. This demand is raised by all inhabitants of San Juan. I want it to be known that all the residents along the road and the paths applauded the measures taken by the government and lamented the loss of General Rodríguez Reyes.[275]

273 Interview with Arsidé Gardés, El Batey, 11 April 1986.
274 Interview with Zita Závala, Paraje El Ranchito, 10 April 1986.
275 From a report given by Attorney General García Vásquez, Expediente No. 10491-13, Procuraduría General de la República, Santo Domingo, quoted in García (1986), pp. 247–9.

The day after the massacre the army continued with its actions directed against the '*Liborista*' centers in the San Juan Valley. The priests of Las Matas de Farfán reported that 'A special group of soldiers, experts in guerilla warfare, are in the area looking for the fugitives – Heliocopters [sic] fly over the area all day long.'[276]

In La Sábila, not far from Neiba, an army force, accompanied by the district attorney of Barahona, moved in and destroyed 158 huts and houses, tearing down the crosses and banners which had been erected in this cultic center. Various prisoners were taken, among them Vetilio Medina, alias Octaviano, the leader of the 'mission', who confessed he had 'been instructed by the *Mellizo* Plinio'.[277]

> They had many branches all over the valley. *Sucursales* they called them. They were all the same. The three crosses and circles made with white stones. No women with dresses without long sleeves were allowed, etc. They wore skirts down to their ankles and purified themselves with water and sand. Holy places like that have always existed. The peasants around here have always had this business. When the *Mellizos* came about many of them turned into *sucursales* of Palma Sola. After the attack at Palma Sola the army tried to close all of them down.[278]

Monseñor Reilly, the bishop of San Juan de la Maguana, approved of the action and in a report to the government he listed the various places where *sucursales* to Palma Sola were functioning: Duvergé, Neyba, Tamayo, Valle-juelo, Batista, El Cercado, Jínova, San Juan de la Maguana and some rural places around Padre las Casas, Bánica and Pedro Santana. He noted that in his opinion the origin of the fervent activity that lately had grown among 'superstitious people' and '*vodúists*' was due to the recent 'war' the late Trujillo regime had waged against the Catholic church: thirteen priests had been expelled from the southern districts, Catholic schools had been shut down and economic support to the small parishes along the frontier had been cut. Reilly thus asked for renewed economic support for the church and the erection of chapels on places which had been affected by the '*Liborismo*'.[279]

In a press release issued on 30 December 1962, García Vásquez reported that cultic centers had been destroyed in 'La Sávila, where there existed 153 houses; in Vallejuelo, 60 houses; the encampment in Las Yajas, where

---

276 *House Annals*, 30 December 1962.
277 García (1986), pp. 315–16.
278 Interview with Thomas Reilly, San Juan de la Maguana, 12 December 1985.
279 Reilly quoted in García (1986), pp. 285–6.

the number of houses is unknown; the one in Batista; the one in Ginova [sic], jurisdiction of San Juan de la Maguana, and others'.[280]

When the army moved out, the priests came in, bringing the holy places within the folds of the Catholic church. Close to a place called San José, in the northwestern district of Dajabón, two 'dignified and wise' Jesuit priests, Antonio Sánchez and Francisco Guzmán, at the head of a group of Catholic devotees, consecrated a former *Olivorista* sanctuary. When they arrived their ceremony was disturbed by 'five youngsters', but

> due to the serenity and patience of the Missionaries, the Police and even the assisting public, the only result of all this [the incident with the heckling youngsters] was that of proving the low level reached by the enemies of religion and civilization. Valuable work was carried out and precious results were obtained by the Missionary Fathers, who with real tenderness enlightened the leaders and devotees about the *Liborista* superstitions in the villages of San José and Vengan a Ver. On the Santo Cerro de San José, after walking the Vía Crucis doing penitence, Father Sánchez, in front of an ardent multitude, had a provisional cross planted where a Palma Sola branch had functioned with its roaring fanaticism.[281]

The 'anti-superstition' campaign

In the official reports the survivors from Palma Sola were treated like children who had been led astray by their own innocence, illiteracy and adherence to 'superstitious' beliefs. Not much was said about improving their physical welfare. It was their souls that were going to be saved, at least according to the official discourse. At one of his press conferences García Vásquez declared that 'It is necessary that the Government carries out an educational campaign in the South, so that civilization may enter the most humble and isolated Dominican homes'.[282]

On 31 December 1962, the editorial page of *El Caribe* carried a lurid political caricature. Emerging from the distant horizon rose a skeleton-man garbed in a white robe, his elongated arm reaching to the foreground where the scrawny hand drove an enormous dagger, inscribed with the word 'tragedy', into a barren place which carried the inscription 'Palma Sola'. Contrary to the impression given by the drawing it was apparently not intended as a criticism of the State Council, or the behavior of the

280 Estrella Veloz (1962a).
281 Pérez (1963).
282 García Vásquez, quoted in Estrella Veloz (1962b).

—…Ahora, a combatir la ignorancia!

Figure 4.26 … Ahora, a combatir la ignorancia [Now, let's fight ignorance]. *El Caribe*, 31 December 1962.

army and the police, because the title of the artwork was a boisterous: 'Now, let's fight ignorance!'[283]

The peasants who had gone to Palma Sola were constantly depicted as innocent victims, lured into trouble by unscrupulous manipulators. According to most commentators the tragedy would not have taken place if the victims had been educated properly:

> The problem of Palma Sola should not have gotten the dramatic ending that everybody knows. The deaths of General Rodríguez Reyes and all the unfortunate, whose only sin was ignorance, could have been avoided if dabbling in politics had not been a priority during the confused days before the electoral process. Result: the fugitives from justice, the cattle thieves and adventurers, who made use of the fanatism of the followers of 'dios Liborio' – with their existentialist philosophy of free love and no work – have escaped in the main while the peasants [*guajiros*] were swept up with their blue trousers – a sign of their fanatism – and their lack of culture.[284]

283 *El Caribe*, 31 December 1962.
284 *Bohemia Libre*, 20 January 1963.

The Dominican press applauded the intentions of the government. They suggested that it was neither the government, nor the police, nor the army which was guilty of the massacre. It was 'ignorance': the 'ignorance' of the victims, not of the perpetrators of the crime. The people of Palma Sola were depicted as the actual aggressors, wishing to unearth the bad old times of Trujillo, anathema at the time:

> It is inconceivable that such an insulting spectacle is permitted as the one set up by the twins of Palma Sola that serves as a retaining wall against progress and the necessary mental restructuration of the citizens.
>
> [...] The twins of Palma Sola foment vices because they instill sexual perversions in those who consult them. They increase ignorance because they lock into the denseness of their illogical sermons the unfortunate who approach them. The twins of Palma Sola are, in short, a threat to the moral and educational recovery of the Dominican people.
>
> An entire history of political cannibalism that ended with thirty-two years of the darkest general obscurantism demands a regeneration of our mentality.[285]

After massacring the people of Palma Sola, no remorse for the violence was shown and the only consolation offered the survivors was that they were going to be given the opportunity to be 'educated':

> This phase of Palma Sola ended with lead and blood. But the fetishism, the absurd beliefs of the Liboristas, will survive in those minds lost in superstition since the times of their ancestors, and only an intense re-educative labor will transform these brains which are worthy of harboring better ideas.[286]

The intended 'education' had a 'spiritual' rather than practical character. After all, the whole business was blamed on the *Olivoristas*' presumed denial of 'Christian values' and 'decent moral behavior':

> The authorities have the [last] word concerning the physical extermination of this immoral fetishist barbarity. We pass judgement on those, who dedicate themselves to that [the *Olivoristas*] and stress the spiritual significance of it. But there is still another judgement left for them to face: that of God.

285 *La Nación*, 7 December 1962.
286 Bobea Bellini (1963).

It is to be wished that a Christian educative effort is directed to the zones affected by this evil. And that those who have fallen into this captivity [the *Olivoristas*] will return to the spiritual reality: the reality of God.[287]

The Catholic church approved of this interpretation and after visiting the afflicted zone the Vatican nuncio to the Dominican Republic, Monseñor Clarizio, presented the State Council with a report which stated: 'The Apostolic Nunciature is eager to confirm the intentions of the Church to continue to contribute to the re-establishment of tranquility in this region and eliminate the possibilities for new disorders ...'[288]

With the exception of some limited efforts by the Catholic church, the intended education program came to nothing, however, and most things remained as before in the areas surrounding Palma Sola: no apologies, no explanations, and no pecuniary compensation were offered to the survivors of the tragic event. The victims of the occurrences in Palma Sola continued to feel either harassed or neglected by the authorities.[289]

Nevertheless, the government and the press made a rather big deal of the 'spiritual education' that was given by the prison chaplain, Ernesto Montás, for several hours every day to the multitude of prisoners from Palma Sola. The priest used a megaphone to address his listeners, who participated in his 'spiritual guidance' in a fairly passive way, answering in unison, but without enthusiasm, to questions he flung at them.[290] Still, these meager 'instructions in the Christian faith' were applauded by the authorities and the press:

'At the moment important progress is obtained in what concerns the religious instruction and life circumstances of the persons who were taken prisoners after the tragic events in Palma Sola', declared this morning General Belisario Peguero Guerrero, chief of the National Police.

[...] Conversing with several of those arrested, we could clearly perceive the progress which has been made with respect to their religious education.[291]

For the majority of the prisoners this was probably not true. Most of them were shocked and numbed by their terrible experiences. They had all lost

287 Paniagua O. (1962).
288 From Oficio No. 2030, in the Archives of the *Cancillería de la República*, quoted in García (1986), p. 287.
289 Interview with León Romilio Ventura, Media Luna, 5 May 1986.
290 The scene is described in the *Time* article quoted by *La Nación*, 12 January 1963.
291 *La Nación*, 5 January 1963.

friends and family members. Since they had been brought directly from the place of the massacre to the damp and overcrowded cells in the capital, many of them did not know what had happened to their families. They wondered if wives and children were still alive, they felt that their future was utterly insecure and all of them found themselves in a new and strange environment. They were now entirely at the mercy of the authorities, an entity which had shown itself to be both distant and hostile in the immediate past. All prisoners had been subject to violent and intensive interrogations.

The majority of them believed that their safest strategy consisted in '*ponerse chivo*' [make oneself a goat], the traditional expression for a rural technique used to trick inquisitive strangers: being nice and seemingly cooperative while at the same time putting up a blank front in order to convince the outsiders that you are a bit dumb and have not seen, smelled or heard anything. Perhaps the priests and the journalists who visited them in the police precincts in Santo Domingo believed that the *Olivoristas* had repented of their 'sins' and eventually had come 'to grip with reality'. The truth, however, was that most prisoners suffered in silence and in reality felt deeply hurt by the treatment they had been given and were thus unable to understand the need of the 'Christian instruction' offered to them by people whom they considered the brutal murderers of their kin. After all, the *Olivoristas* had always considered themselves to be ardent believers in the God of the Catholic church and in the Christian mysteries. It was this belief that had brought them up to Palma Sola in the first place. If the official representatives of law and order, of God and civilization, had behaved like beasts in Palma Sola, why did the *Olivoristas* then have to believe their lessons about God and the mysteries?

> I do not think that a priest would be able to talk to human beings in such a way. I do not think he was a real priest. He was just a common chaplain [*padre capellán*]. We left indignant, feeling ashamed for his part in it all. He was tossing dirt around himself. He was only preoccupied with the fate of the general and was accusing all of us of his death.[292]

When the prisoners from Palma Sola were finally released on 20 January 1963 the authorities declared that the former detainees would be taken to an 'appropriate place' where 'they will receive education, work and food in abundance [...] with a view to raise their social and cultural level and ... adapt them to the progressive phase that the Republic is experiencing'.[293]

292 Interview with Patoño Bautista Mejía, Distrito de Haina, 5 March 1986.
293 Belisario Peguero quoted in *El Caribe*, 11 January 1963.

All this came to almost nothing. The former prisoners were given food and clothes and were taken to their respective villages, but after they had been dropped there nothing more was heard from the authorities, with the exception of the Catholic church, which initiated some limited assistance programs in the area.[294]

The helpers

After the massacre, General Miguel Angel Ramírez Alcántara, who had become senator in the 1962 elections, used his newly won influence in order to liberate some of the prisoners. He personally directed several petitions to both the police and the army, and ordered his co-workers to prepare lists of imprisoned members of his political party, *Partido Nacionalista Revolucionario Democrático* (PNRD). He succeeded in obtaining the liberty of several persons before the official amnesty came about and he constantly pressed the authorities to drop the charges against the people of Palma Sola.[295]

> Miguel Angel was truly upset and personally contacted President Bonnelly, telling him that 'Not only I, but the entire province will make you responsible if anything bad happens to the prisoners.' He also called on the attorney general and the chief of police in Santo Domingo, making several efforts to release persons who trusted in him.[296]

As a part of their 'educational effort', the authorities contacted the department of sociology at the *Universidad Autónoma de Santo Domingo* (UASD) to conduct interviews with all the prisoners from Palma Sola. The sociologists were going to carry out a 'socioeconomic investigation'[297] – which meant gathering as much information as possible about the lives and beliefs of the *Olivoristas*. The results would serve as guidelines for future policy. Possibly the authorities hoped that the detainees would be more willing to talk to the students than to the police interrogators.

In charge of the investigation was the Chilean sociologist Florángel Cárdenas Fontecha.[298] In the beginning she was reluctant to accept the offer because she feared that the investigation was going to be carried out simply to calm public opinion and that it would become part of some

---

294 Interview with Patoño Bautista Mejía, Distrito de Haina, 5 March 1986.
295 García (1986), p. 178. Cf. Bautista Mejía (1988), p. 61.
296 Interview with Wenceslao Ramírez, Las Matas de Farfán, 17 January 1986.
297 Cárdenas Fontecha (1964).
298 *La Nación*, 5 January 1963. Florángel Cárdenas also traveled to the area around Palma Sola in order to gather information.

cover-up planned by the authorities, but when she visited the cells at the *Palacio de Policia* [Police Palace] and saw the deplorable situation of the prisoners she changed her mind and declared that she was willing to do the job.[299] As her assistants she selected several young students, among them Rafael Sanabia and Ramón Tapia Espinal, who both later became lawyers, and Juan Dagoberto Tejeda Ortiz, who became one of the Dominican Republic's most influential anthropologists.[300]

Radicalization of the Dominican universities had begun during the clandestine struggle against Trujillo and was in full bloom in the aftermath of his fall. Florángel Cárdenas, who had come to the country in order to study agrarian reform, was a representative of this new wave of critical thinking and was an inspiration to her students, teaching a Marxist blend of sociology, something that is reflected in a rather sentimental book on Dominican poverty which she published shortly before her investigation of the Palma Sola affair.[301] Many of the prisoners trusted the university students and appreciated their work:

> I am very grateful to Florángel Cárdenas and Rafael Sanabia. When the students appeared things started to change for the better and I am sure that it was their pressure on the authorities which finally made our release possible.[302]

> We were taken directly to the capital, to the Police Palace, it was a big building, but in the beginning we were forced to live in small cells, very small, with water on the floor. We were 725 prisoners there, all of us from Palma Sola. We lived together, several persons in every cell, ate together and used to listen to a priest who preached with a megaphone. The guards threatened us and made fun of us, it was a hard time. We suffered there for fifteen days, but it became better when they brought us to Nigua, where we stayed for another fifteen days. There we met with students. Some of them came from Chile. They divided us into small groups and we sat talking to them on the lawn there in Nigua. There were fifty-two boys, supervised by a lady named Florángel Cárdenas. I particularly remember one of them, Rafael Sanabia. They were kind to us, our fear left us and we started to talk to them.[303]

299 Cárdenas Fontecha (1964).
300 Interview with Walter Cordero, Santo Domingo, 27 September 1985.
301 Ibid.
302 Interview with Patoño Bautista Mejía, Distrito de Haina, 5 March 1986.
303 Interview with an *Olivorista* who wants to remain anonymous, Las Matas de Farfán, 5 July 1990.

Florángel Cárdenas later stated that the preliminary results of her investigation were suppressed by her employers and not a word from the report of the UASD sociologists was published in the Dominican Republic. When Cárdenas left the country, she published a highly critical and very controversial article in a popular Venezuelan magazine, putting all the blame for the blood bath on the government, depicting García Vásquez as the sinister organizer of the crime.[304]

It was Thomas Reilly, the bishop of San Juan de la Maguana, who had arranged the transfer of the prisoners from the wretched cells of the police headquarters to the more comfortable and spacious lunatic asylum in Nigua. He followed them on their short trip to the hospital, situated just outside the town of San Cristóbal.[305] In Nigua the prisoners finally received proper medical care and decent food.[306] Reilly acted on behalf of the victims in spite of the fact that he was known to be a fervent opponent of all kinds of 'superstition', and he had originally urged the authorities to put an end to the movement in Palma Sola as soon as possible:

That thing [superstition] has always been strong here and people's feelings get easily upset when you try to do something about it. One time I was nearly killed when I tried to take down the crosses of one of their calvaries. Sometimes very weird things occurred, in a house in the *campo* [countryside]. I remember it was constructed on stilts. They used to carry out strange ceremonies. Suddenly a woman runs out after a fight with a man and got an axe through her back by the one who chased her. The police emptied that place. I used to tell the government that if they kept the stupid individuals who directed that kind of cult in prison for a while it would easily quench all attempts to new outbreaks of fanaticism. I also remember one time when I had to intervene in a brawl between religious fanatics and *galleros* [people attending the cockfights]. They were all armed with knives and it was a rather nasty business. Anyhow, they soon calmed down.

The peasants around here are essentially very nice people and easily convinced about their wrongdoings. I remember how I walked around among the wounded people from Palma Sola at the hospital here in San Juan. It was the day after the massacre and I had recently arrived from Boston. I still walked around in my priestly outfit and talked to at least seventy-five of them. They were all agreeable and nice. They said they felt deceived, a very common reaction. These people are easily inspired with enthusiasm. The attack was a shock to them. They did

304 Cárdenas Fontecha (1964).
305 Interview with Diego Cépeda, Jínova, 4 June 1989.
306 Bautista Mejía (1988), p. 62.

not defend themselves, they felt deceived. The poor people had the story that no bullets could hurt them, that this superstitious thing would protect them.[307]

After the former prisoners had been taken on trucks borrowed from the state-owned sugar companies and dumped in their respective home villages, the government hoped that the terrible occurrences in Palma Sola would be part of history and soon be forgotten by most people. However, too many riddles have remained, and too many questions have been left unanswered, so the Palma Sola massacre is likely to continue to crop up in the public mind as long as the mysteries remain unresolved, and as long as some of the actors in the tragedy are still alive. With Florángel Cárdenas' Venezuelan article in 1964 as a starting point, the Dominican press has, with a certain regularity, taken up the matter and has thus insured that the questions around 'the Palma Sola affair' will not evaporate until they are solved.

307 Interview with Thomas Reilly, San Juan de la Maguana, 12 December 1985.

Part II

The myth

5   *Olivorista* lore

In Chapter 2 we stressed the difficulty of distinguishing between fact and fiction – between real and imagined events – in the history of *Olivorismo* and the problems encountered when using often unreliable and biased written and oral sources of information to construct the most probable sequence. Chapters 2–4 were devoted to an attempt to find out *wie es eigentlich gewesen* from the first appearance of Olivorio some time around 1910 to the massacre at Palma Sola in 1962 and some of its aftermath.

We have not yet discussed the legendary side of *Olivorismo* – a theme that is well worth a book in itself. Thus, the present chapter will be devoted to an analysis of the folklore connected with Olivorio and Palma Sola. We will explore the myth that was created out of the real events by the *Olivoristas* and how this relates to a larger mystical universe of which it forms part. Such an analysis is warranted for several interconnected reasons.

On a general level, myths play an important role in all religions and, as we will demonstrate, *Olivorismo* does not constitute any exception to this rule. Other reasons are even more compelling, however. First, their lore provides an idea of how the *Olivoristas* themselves interpret the world they live in, mixing real and mythical elements, blurring the borderline between the two spheres. Second, an analysis of the myths reveals what the *Olivoristas* perceive as the main message of the founder of their religion and hence contributes towards the understanding of the appeal of Olivorio (and the Palma Sola movement) to his followers. (This exercise will be carried further in the chapters that follow.)

Third, the examination of *Olivorista* lore also serves to contrast the views of the outsiders, as expressed in Chapters 2–4, with those of the *Olivoristas* themselves, and hence documents some of the sources of conflict between the two groups. In particular, the myths and *salves* are the prime expression of a critique by a socially and economically subordinate group in Dominican society of prevailing power relations – the hidden transcript of this group – which in turn sheds some light on how *Olivoristas* face and resist their real or imaginary enemies.

We will begin the chapter with some general observations on the meaning of 'folklore' and its functions, stressing the importance of viewing it in the context of local cultural ecology. *Olivorista* myths and legends form part of a larger cultural complex. Thereafter the general magical environment prevailing in the San Juan Valley is explored. In the next section some examples of *Olivorista salves* are presented and their contents are interpreted.

The *salves* form an essential part of our analysis of how the *Olivorista* movement in Palma Sola came to view the prevailing social and political situation of the day as an indication of how the world was 'falling apart' in anticipation of an upcoming and decisive battle between the forces of good and evil. Such a view was fueled by an ever-increasing feeling of being encroached upon by hostile and evil forces, a state of mind which is not uncommon among other sectarians either.

The mythical material surrounding Olivorio also makes it possible to construct a 'legendary' biography of him, from the cradle to the grave and beyond. This occupies the main part of this chapter. We then move on to the *salves* of Palma Sola and their reflection of the situation of the worshipers of Olivorio, their worries and their dreams. What the outsiders perceived as a violent message is singled out for scrutiny. Finally, an effort is made to distill, interpret and summarize the hidden transcript of the *Olivorista* doctrine. In an appendix the view, sometimes advanced, that the Palma Sola movement had many traits in common with Jim Jones' People's Temple in Guyana, is refuted.

Folklore

In the Dominican Republic, *Olivorismo* has traditionally been studied together with other expressions of 'popular religion' as part of what is usually termed 'folklore' studies.[1] As early as the 1880s, folklore studies became a respected occupation in the Dominican Republic and a familiarity with certain aspects of Dominican folk traditions were considered a way of promoting a general feeling of national pride and patriotic loyalty.[2] Collections of anecdotes like César Nicolás Penson's *Cosas añejas* (1891),[3] or descriptions of rural life such as Ramón Emilio Jiménez' *Al amor del bohío* (1927 and 1929)[4] became very popular and inspired several

1 León Romilio Ventura, one of the leading *Olivoristas*, has accordingly been called 'one of the most relevant popular personalities of Dominican folklore' (Domínguez, Castillo and Tejeda Ortiz (1978), p. 45).
2 For ideological reasons the African roots of Dominican folklore were repressed. See Chapter 3.
3 Penson (1951).
4 Jiménez (1927), (1929).

books,[5] as well as poems and novels in a similar vein.[6] Scientific folklore studies were later carried out by both national and international researchers,[7] and the study of folklore is now an integrated part of the curriculum at several Dominican universities. The Ministry of Tourism has a department studying the subject, as well as exploring ways of using its findings commercially. However, in the Dominican Republic, as in many other places, it remains somewhat unclear what the term 'folklore' really means.

The folk

The word 'folklore' originates from two Old English words, *lore* and *folc*, meaning wisdom and folk respectively, and has come to denominate the 'spiritual tradition of the folk, particularly oral tradition, as well as the science which studies this tradition'.[8] Such a definition raises new questions: Who are the 'folk'? What does 'oral tradition' imply?

In ethnology,[9] the word 'folk' first appeared as a prefix in German compounds like *Volkslied*, *Volksglaube*, etc., and was then used 'in the sense of a small group, backward people, a group bound together by common interests, common people, peasants'.[10] 'Folk' was often defined in relation to other groups of people and was understood to constitute the lower stratum within a complex class society. In scientific discussions, the 'folk' contrasted with so-called 'savage' or 'primitive' peoples, who were considered to live 'outside' of civilization. While the 'folk' were understood to be an illiterate stratum within a literate society, the primitive societies were described as 'isolates, complete in themselves', and labeled as 'preliterate', a denomination which implied that 'savages' could probably achieve literacy if they were able to climb the ladder of cultural evolution.[11]

In the United States, the exclusion of so-called primitive peoples from consideration by folklorists came under fervent attack from several researchers, among them Ralph Steele Boggs,[12] who maintained that folklore studies ought to be extended into studies of regional cultures all

5 Rodríguez Demorizi (1975b), pp. 57–8.
6 For example Moscoso Puello (1936), Marrero Aristy (1939) and Cabral (1943).
7 For example Andrade (1948), Garrido de Boggs (1955), Nolasco (1956), Rueda (1970), Lemus and Marty (1975), Lizardo (1975), (1988), Deive (1979) and Davis (1981), (1987).
8 Hultkrantz (1960), p. 135.
9 The science of man as a cultural being (from the Greek *ethnos* [race], a word which later has also come to indicate people, or culture).
10 Hultkrantz (1960), p. 126.
11 Dundes (1980), pp. 2 and 6.
12 Ibid., p. 5. Ralph Steele Boggs, who had lectured and carried out fieldwork in the Dominican Republic, was married to Edna Garrido de Boggs. She was born in San Juan

over the world and thereby include 'primitive' societies.[13] However, anthropologists like George Foster maintained that folklore studies had to concentrate on what he called the 'folk stratum', defined as 'a part of a pre-industrial society characterized by social classes. In the rural setting, the folk stratum is coterminous with the entire community; in the urban setting the folk stratum is merely a part of the community.'[14]

Foster's view was further developed by Robert Redfield, who analyzed the rural folk society in relation to urban society and what he called the 'great tradition' of the latter,[15] a view which appears to reflect older notions, like those of William John Thoms, who in 1846 defined folklore as 'the traditional beliefs, legends and customs, current among the common people' and as 'the manners, customs, observances, superstitions, ballads, proverbs etc. of the olden time'.[16] Such conceptions are reflected by the general notion that folklore is constituted by the remains of an old, pre-urban culture. The old traditions of rural societies have accordingly been labeled as *survivals*, 'ancient popular beliefs, customs and traditions, which have survived among the less educated elements of civilized societies'.[17] The tendency to view folk beliefs as 'survivals' led several folklorists to consider them as remnants of a 'degenerated religion'[18] that would soon disappear in the name of progress. Such a view is present in the treatment several Dominican authors and journalists have given *Olivorismo* and other expressions of popular religion in the Dominican Republic.[19]

Views like the ones expressed above give folklore, and, accordingly, peasant culture, an ethnocentristic simplicity, which, however, is present

---

de la Maguana, where she spent her youth. Later she became one of the first *Sanjuanero* ladies who went to Santo Domingo in order to obtain higher education (Garrido Puello (1973), p. 57). She graduated as an anthropologist in Florida. For a summary of Edna Garrido de Boggs' research, see Garrido de Boggs (1961).

13 Steele Boggs was inspired by the research of the German-born anthropolgist Franz Boas (1858–1942), who has been very influential in American anthropology. Boas had in his youth worked together with the ethnologist Adolf Bastian (1826–1903), who stressed the 'psychic unity of mankind' and believed that all cultures could ultimately be reduced to the same basic mental principles – *Elementargedanken* (Kuper (1988), p. 127). Boas was influenced by Bastian, but at the same time he tended to emphasize individual cultures, rather than specific traits, and variance rather than stability.

14 Foster (1953b), quoted in Hultkrantz (1960), p. 143.

15 Redfield and Singer (1954), p. 341.

16 Thoms (1846), quoted in Hultkrantz (1960), p. 135.

17 Mish (1949), p. 401, quoted in Hultkrantz (1960), p. 136.

18 Hultkrantz (1960), pp. 136–7.

19 In the Dominican Republic popular religion, particularly the varieties which seem to present African influences, generally was termed 'superstition', a word derived from the Latin *superstitio*, dread of the supernatural, originally from *superstare*, to stand still by something (as in amazement). The word later came to mean an irrational belief, usually founded on ignorance or fear and characterized by obsessive reverence for omens, charms, etc., as well as notions, acts and rituals derived from such beliefs.

only in the eyes of an alien beholder.[20] A peasant society is far from being
a fixed or stable entity: it changes over time and is composed of a great
variety of different individuals. Before general conclusions can be applied,
it will have to be studied as a singular case.

The oral tradition

An essential part of most definitions of the science of 'folklore' is that it
mainly deals with 'oral transmission'. However, this is nothing more than a
statement about a particular form of communication, and most modern
folklore researchers pay attention not only to what the oral transmission
contains, but also to the communicative event itself.

Earlier folklore studies were generally divided into *historical research*,
focusing upon similarities across time periods, *comparative studies* examining equivalences across cultural boundaries, and *contextual descriptions*,
analyzing the integration of folklore performances into a system of artistic
communication in a particular society.[21] Later studies tend to be more
descriptive and instead of focusing on a single text, or genre, they intend
to describe the entire scope of communication within a particular society.[22]
Consequently, folklore is usually analyzed in relation to culture, often
defined as 'the sum total of ideological premises, learned behaviour and
transmitted mental, social and material traits characterizing a human
social group'.[23]

The trend towards the study of the function of folklore at given
moments, within specific environments, is partly related to studies of
different 'genres' contained in the Bible.[24] While studying what he
assumed to be traces of prescriptural oral traditions in the Old Testament,
the German Bible exegete Hermann Gunkel coined the phrase *Sitz im
Leben* [place in life] in order to relate the position that these traditions
had in the lives of the people who adhered to them. By implying their functions in the religious ceremonies and daily lives of the old Israelites, he

20 Ben-Amos (1982), p. 27.
21 Ibid., pp. 9–10 and 20–1.
22 Ibid., p. 21.
23 Hultkrantz (1960), p. 69. Cf. Honko (1981), p. 12. The concept of 'culture' in folklore
    studies became popular in Germany in the 1860s when the influential Adolf Bastian
    introduced the concept of *Völkergedanken* [folk ideas], certain elementary ideas that
    human beings had in common and which had been modified by a particular environ-
    ment. Researchers began to draw maps depicting the expansion of certain traditions and
    thus identified the resulting clusters as *Kulturkreise* [culture-circles] (Bronner (1986), p.
    66).
24 By the end of the last century, folklorists had began to study the Bible in the light of their
    findings. Worth mentioning is James G. Frazer's *Folk-lore in the Old Testament* (1919),
    which later served as inspiration for Claude Lévi-Strauss (Kuper (1988), pp. 210–16).

identified distinct prose and poetry genres.[25] Gunkel's findings inspired several other researchers to study the functions of oral traditions in the particular environment and situations where they were at hand.

Bronislaw Malinowski, one of the founders of the functionalist school of anthropology, also stressed the social function of myth and language. He wrote widely on 'primitive' language and collected enormous quantities of linguistic material for anthropological analysis. As a functionalist, he believed that traditions, as well as oral expressions, do not survive due to the interest they arise as poetry or history, but due to their function, their usefulness, within a specific setting:

> It is culture in its entirety that concerns the anthropologist [...] We must [...] refer social traditions to the physical environments in which they occur, but this concern to anchor functionalism in a wider determinism does not in itself contradict the concern to define a culture as an integrated ensemble. [...] [Malinowski's] notion of 'culture', whilst it may respond to needs, is no longer composed of 'cultural features' (features that circulate at the mercy of a diffusion whose scientific interest, and even whose reality, he denies), but of more complex ensembles, and of institutions orientated towards practice.[26]

As a part of an ethnographic theory of language, Malinowski formulated the concept of 'context', stressing that it is the context of a certain situation which gives meaning to particular utterances.[27] Context (i.e. the conditions and circumstances that are relevant to an event, a fact, etc.) has in folklore studies come to signify the social and cultural framework for oral representation.[28] The study of folklore in relation to certain contexts has changed the meaning of the word 'folk', which no longer denotes 'illiterate, backward peasants', but may refer to any group of people

> who share at least one common factor. It does not matter what the linking factor is – it could be a common occupation, language or

25 Ben-Amos (1982), p. 32. Gunkel's two most influential essays were *Genesis* (1901) and *Die israelitische Literatur* (1906).
26 Augé (1982), pp. 34–5.
27 It is interesting to note that Malinowski, as a person, illustrates the dilemma inherent in 'multifaceted' studies of a certain culture. He considered himself to be a 'participant observer' and thus believed himself able to study a particular environment as if he were 'a multifaceted entity who participates, observes and writes from multiple, constantly shifting positions. Such are the reflective capacities of this versatile, larger-than-life subject that it can absorb and transmit the richness of the whole culture' (Pratt (1986), p. 39). However, such a posture attracted criticism and Malinowski tended to 'provoke irritation' from different quarters (Augé (1982), p. 17). He was 'anything but the self-effaced, passive subject of scientific discourse' (Pratt (1986), p. 39).
28 Ben-Amos (1982), pp. 28 and 33.

religion – but what is important is that a group formed for whatever reason will have some tradition which it calls its own. In theory a group must consist of at least two persons, but generally most groups consist of many individuals. A member of a group must not know all other members, but he will probably know the common core of traditions belonging to the group, traditions which help the group have a sense of group identity.[29]

Cultural ecology: space and being

The science of folklore reflects the ongoing debate within other social sciences, and several folklorists participate in the reaction against certain received points of view. Marx, Weber and Durkheim, often described as the 'fathers of sociology', all stressed the primacy of time over space.[30] Marx taught a historical materialism and his portrayal of capitalist development gave only marginal treatment of its impact on space. Likewise, geographically specific circumstances were not of any great importance to the historical-oriented Weber, who turned to the past in order to unlock the meaning of the present.[31] Durkheim concentrated his analytical efforts on a metaphorical 'social sphere' and only dealt marginally with what he called a society's *morphologie sociale* – the material, terrestrial, social aspects of life, i.e. concrete, humanely created spaces.[32] However, the importance of space has increasingly been stressed, for example by historians such as Fernand Braudel, who, quoting the turn-of-the-century French geographer Vidal de la Blache, states that 'the social sciences must make room "for an increasingly geographical conception of mankind"',[33] and several folklorists now examine what they denote as the 'cultural ecology of human societies'.

Ecology is the study of different sets of relationships that living organisms have with their environment. The dwelling place of an organism is called 'habitat' and consists of both organic and inorganic surroundings. If applied to human beings, the term 'habitat' refers to their spatial organization, the place or territory they occupy within nature. The term 'niche' expresses an organism's relations to other living beings and the

29 Dundes (1980), pp. 6–7. This definition neatly describes the *Olivoristas*, who share a common belief, language and occupation (most of them are peasants who live on their own land). They do not know all other *Olivoristas*, but they share a common core of tradition and have a sense of group identity.
30 Pred (1990), p. 7.
31 Ibid., p. 8.
32 Ibid.
33 Braudel (1980), p. 52. The quotation is from Vidal de la Blache (1903), p. 239.

opportunities that are available to it for making use of existent natural resources. New niches are opened up through dominant or symbiotic behavior. In doing so human beings have an advantage compared with other organisms, since they are not limited by DNA information or the laws of the ecosystem. Humans have thus been able to build up technological systems within different ecosystems and create their own standards and rules, shaping cultural patterns of their own by exploiting their environment according to rules that are not only biological, but cultural as well.[34]

In order to study a human habitat, or niche, a social entity has to be delimited and then analyzed as a microenvironment (or microhabitat). The observer focuses on certain characteristics, like the interaction between individuals, their set of values and attitudes, etc., in short – the cultural means of expression which are at the group members' disposal and how these resources are applied to concrete situations.[35] The socio-cultural behavior of a human group finds itself in a process of constant change. Human transactions within a habitat are always reflected by the whole ecosystem, the flow of energy is constantly affected by human behavior and people have to adapt themselves to new situations which incessantly are created by their presence in the niche they occupy.[36]

Elements like language and traditions have to be considered in relation to their specific habitat. An observer may formulate questions like: 'Why has this particular cultural characteristic gained entrance into this kind of society? Why was it so readily accepted?' Or, on the contrary: 'What was the reason for its rejection, or why was it not entirely integrated in the culture?' A thorough study of the lore of a certain human group may offer a multi-faceted knowledge of how its members interpret their particular habitat and how they relate themselves to it.

The lore of people is not limited to tangible phenomena. It offers insights into that other dimension of reality which is constituted by what is usually called 'supranormal' reality, the unseen domain that *Olivoristas* often refer to as the 'other world' or the 'realm of spirits'.

While studying a certain body of folklore, one will detect notions and traditions that are common to several other human habitats. Certain themes and structures appear over and over again and are interpreted in similar ways. What is of interest when studying a limited habitat is not only the kind of lore, the general genres and themes which are present, but also to examine how these genres and themes have been adapted to a particular environment. Stories and legends which travel across the world undergo adaptations in different environments. In cold climates lions and

34 Honko (1981), p. 20.
35 Ibid., pp. 22–3.
36 Ibid., p. 27.

jackals become bears or foxes, in Sweden jokes about Irishmen or Poles are changed into jokes about Norwegians. Places are changed and times altered. The world of folklore thus finds itself in a state of constant change, incessantly reacting to the needs of the people who make use of it. Living folklore immediately becomes a part of the environment, which in turn may also change due to peoples' altered apprehension of it. Changing socioeconomic structures, modified role patterns, and different systems of values and standards are constantly at work in every society. New cultural elements are adjusted to already existent collective traditions.[37]

In the case of the San Juan Valley, notions related to *El Gran Poder de Dios*, certain holy places, the Indians and the 'realm of the spirits' stay more or less intact while alien influences are transformed and adapted to them. Folklore, the wisdom of the folk, is thus both a reflection of a certain habitat and a factor of change.

> The knowledge and other forms of consciousness held by people are not passive attributes or static possessions existing in a body-less vacuum. They are, instead, in a constant state of becoming as a part of active social being in particular historical and geographical contexts, in contexts that are themselves reproduced and transformed through that very same being.[38]

The tension between the center and the periphery

Another way of determining and denominating human habitats and niches is to consider them as 'locales'. A locale is a 'physically bounded area that provides a setting for institutionally embedded social encounters and practices'.[39] A locale can be anything from a street corner, a room in a house, a club, a bar, a village or a nation. Locales are social constructs which come into being when an observer obtains the knowledge needed for a recognition of the particularity of the attributes of a social entity.[40] A locale is an area which is delimited in order to recognize the characteristics that are inherent in a chosen section of human life.

Frequently one locale is contrasted with another. Observers may, for example, compare 'front' regions with 'back' regions. A 'front region' is usually defined as a zone in which some degree of norm-conforming behavior is expected, in which rule-following and 'correct performances' are required from citizens who are subject to some form of surveillance

37 Ibid., pp. 31, 34–5.
38 Pred (1990), p. 18.
39 Ibid., p. 22.
40 Ibid.

and control, feeling compelled to cover up certain aspects of self. On the contrary, 'back regions' are usually unobserved areas where norms are flouted, leaving space for a high degree of autonomy and the opportunity for inhabitants to sustain a psychological distance between their own inter-pretations of social processes and the official norms of the front regions.[41]

In back regions may be found largely illiterate, village-centered societies that have face-to-face interaction and direct communication with power holders. In contrast, front regions are often synonymous with industrial-ized societies, characterized by an intermingling of the local and the global, with activities and transactions that frequently involve people who are physically absent, where remote sources of power are sustained by impersonally defined rules and surveillance via information gathering and retrieval.[42]

Since front and back regions differ they naturally develop different sets of lore and norms. When members from a front region are confronted with inhabitants of the 'backlands', communication may often be difficult, as they do not have many cultural traits in common. Socioeconomic devel-opments tend to strengthen front regions and expand their influence into back regions, where the pressure becomes greater to replace customary practices of everyday life with new and different forms of behavior. Tradi-tional folklore is gradually transformed and adjusted to the new situation, and a new habitat takes form. The greater the differences between back region and front region, the more violent is the process. If the back region has developed more or less independently, the behavior and reactions of its inhabitants will appear as strange and incongruous to people who have been raised in front areas.

When back regions are confronted with modernizing forces from front regions, messianic and millenarian cults are prone to develop. All parts of the world present examples of such cultural clashes. Three examples from entirely different cultural settings are the Korpela movement which in the 1930s developed in the Torne Valley along the Finnish border in northern Sweden,[43] the Buu Son Ky Huong and Hoa Hao sects which developed during the nineteenth and twentieth centuries in the isolated and only partly settled areas along the Cambodian border in southern Vietnam[44] and the Conselheiro movement of the Brazilian backlands in the 1890s.[45]

41 Ibid., p. 23.
42 Ibid., p. 23–4.
43 See Lundmark (1985).
44 See Hue Tam (1983). It is interesting to note that both the Korpela movement and Buu Son Ky Huong developed in border regions where most of the population were bilingual and shared a 'mixed' culture; Finnish and Swedish in Sweden, Chinese, Cambodian and Vietnamese in Vietnam. Compare the Haitian connections of the *Olivoristas* in the Dominican border areas.

The following presentation of some examples of *Olivorista* lore does not intend to offer an exhaustive analysis of genres and contexts. The aim is simply to situate some of the songs and legends to their particular habitat and examine how they reflect the particular world view and ideology of the *Olivoristas*. We will also analyze how themes and stories found in other areas of the world have been adopted to a specific *Olivorista* environment and consider how the conflict between *Olivoristas* and their foes is reflected in their lore.

A magical environment

The undulating heights of the Cordillera Central rise diagonally across the Dominican Republic. Covered by slender pine trees, this imposing mountain range hovers above fertile plains, dotted with royal palms and huge mango trees, or the grey and thorny bushes of drier areas. Following sudden tropical rains, the pine forests on the slopes emit thin veils of mist, which spread a fresh fragrance over the surrounding lowlands. A wanderer who ventures into this huge mountain massif will encounter range after range of gently rounded hills and mountains, sometimes reaching heights of up to 3,000 meters, the highest in the Caribbean. The vegetation changes close to the summits, where meadows and forest edges display flowers reminiscent of the flora found in Northern Europe. Up there, nights may be piercingly cold and in the early mornings glittering frost sometimes covers the grass. The Cordillera harbors unexplored caves and deep gorges. Streams carry crystal-clear water and the occasional wild pigs and fowl stir in the bushes. The area is sparsely populated and only the valleys in the vicinity of San José de Ocoa, Jarabacoa, Jánico, Loma de Cabrera and Constanza have clusters of small villages. Before the initiation of Olivorio's 'mission', large lumber companies and enterprising individuals had made intrusions into the virgin forests, indiscriminately cutting down huge numbers of trees, laying waste several extensive forests, a practice that still continues to denude mountain after mountain.

A traveler in these areas may cover mile after mile without encountering a human being, but this does not mean that the *Sanjuaneros* living on the southern slopes of the towering Cordillera consider it to be an uninhabited place. On the contrary, it is considered to be a dwelling place of strange creatures, the domain of powerful spiritual forces. After days of hard work in the fields and garden plots, when peasants gather on the porches of their brightly painted houses, or ramshackle huts, to chat and play dominoes with their neighbors, or when the families meet around the kerosene lamps in their tiny lodgings, stories are told about the strange

---

45 Cunha (1944), Levine (1992).

inhabitants of the mountains, who hide themselves deep within caves and ravines, mystical tribes of savage *biembienes*, dark-skinned creatures who look like humans. Since they are unable to speak, they painstakingly avoid all contacts with humans. No one has ever caught a *biembién*, but people know they are harmless and no one fears them.

It is possible that the *ciguapa* belongs to the same family as the *biembienes*. She is a beautiful, extremely shy being who is endowed with raven black hair and a smooth, golden complexion. Many people say that they have seen her when she moves, swiftly like a hind, among the shadows of a deep forest or when she climbs among tree canopies in isolated areas, with the ease of a monkey. She survives on fish in the rivers and sleeps up in the trees. The *ciguapa* is not entirely human because her feet are turned backwards and she is dumb and mute, just like the primitive *biembienes*. People state they have seen *ciguapas* caught in places of difficult access, though these lovely and extremely sensitive creatures have to be turned loose the moment after they are seized. They cannot survive long in captivity and unavoidably die a few hours after their capture.

The mountains were, and still are for many people, a realm of the unknown, inhabited by dangerous and demonic forces, whose harmful influences can easily be conjured and brought down among humans, causing severe damage to villages and fields. The Cordillera is the traditional meeting place between evildoers and *El Malo* [the Bad One], also called *El Demonio* [the Demon], *El Viejo* [the Old Man] or Luis, i.e. the devil himself.

Anyone who aspires to purchase a *bacá* or *tuntún*[46] wanders off to a mountain peak where the devil is invoked at midnight. The leader of the hosts of Hell appears in any guise he considers fitting for the occasion, but preferably as a black dog, or an old man with golden teeth and luminous eyes. A pact is concluded in which the supplicant offers 'a loved one' in exchange for the services of a *bacá*. On his way back to the village, the successful supplicant finds that a violent storm is brewing, a sure sign that he has received the approbation of the Evil One. In the middle of the path, a straw-sack containing an egg is found. The lonely evildoer takes it with him and when he passes the fields that surround the village he throws the devilish egg onto a piece of his own land. After some time the 'loved one' which had been promised to Satan dies. The 'pigeon' of the *bacá* hatches in the field and slowly grows, fed by other victims offered to the devil by its proud owner. One night, after twelve o'clock, the evildoer is awakened by an inhuman whisper and when he unlatches the door of the house the *bacá* is waiting in the dark. During this first night of the fatal acquaintance, the

---

46 Both are names for evil entities which an evildoer uses to rob others of their wealth. Cf. Bretón and González Abercio (n.d.).

bacá shows itself in human shape, red-eyed and with a body of skin and bones. The demonic creature reveals its name and offers its services, putting on any guise it considers to be suitable for the various commissions it executes for its master, whether it is the killing of someone or amassing riches at the expense of neighbors. Having a *bacá* means wealth and success for its owner. The villagers whisper, indicating their knowledge of the real source of the sudden luck and success which have befallen a neighbor known to be unscrupulous and selfish. Sudden deaths are connected with strange creatures said to have been seen roaming the vicinity during dark nights. In the end, the *bacá* demands its final award – the soul of its owner – and during a stormy night it turns against its master, kills him and his soul is brought down to Hell.

Bacás are not the only terrifying creatures haunting Dominican nights. Children huddle up in their beds listening to the sounds of the night and imagine that they hear shrill, piercing shrieks, or muffled sounds of 'fo-fo-fo'. These are the alleged cries of flying witches, wicked ladies who have taken the devil as their lover and now spend their nights in search of unchristened children. Their speciality is to suck the life force out of the navels of innocent and helpless victims, prolonging their own lifetime and maintaining their ability to fly. A witch may turn herself into any kind of animal, even a mosquito, but most of them prefer to keep their human form. On moonlit nights, they sneak up in the deep shadows behind the cooking sheds, calling out the names of children sleeping in the house. If the children, or their parents, answer, the small ones end up in the power of the evil hags. The same method is used by the dead who walk in the night, trying to drag their loved ones with them to the other world. 'Never answer a dead person who calls your name, never turn around in the dead of the night, if you hear someone whispering your name.' However, not all the dead are dangerous; several are benevolent and may appear in dreams telling their relatives about winning numbers in the state lottery or where to find hidden treasure.

Nevertheless, most of the creatures who move around at night are considered to be malevolent and often extremely dangerous. *Zánganos*, male witches who are obsessed by female succuba and have become sexual perverts, stalk the neighborhood in search of victims. *Lugarús*, immense werewolves, lurk in ambush at the crossroads, hideous creatures that are immune to bullets or pointed weapons and ready to devour anyone who might stumble in their way. *El Anima Sola*, a solitary, roving, female soul, tries to alleviate her loneliness by abducting young males, doomed to die in her presence. *La Pesadilla* [the Nightmare] goes from house to house and upsets the dreams of people. She does not want to be disturbed while she does her chores and the senses of any unfortunate night wanderer who happens to meet her are irretrievably lost. *Dundunés, marimantas, espantos* and several other spirits and demons busy themselves with mischief all night long and some even dare to show themselves during daytime.

On moonless nights, *zonbis* [zombies] are driven along in chain gangs, perhaps on their way back from Alcagé in Haiti, a mythical place where 'people sell people' under the auspices of an all-powerful grand wizard, the master of all *bòkò* [sorcerers] and *ougan* in the neighboring republic and main purveyor of zombies to the entire island. Zombies are corpses that are unburied, sold into bondage and kept busy on plots of evil and unscrupulous landowners, after being robbed of their souls and willpower. A zombie is dangerous because it is like a machine controlled by an evil will and may thus maim and kill without remorse. Other night stalkers are more harmless, like *galipotes* and *dundunés*, people who change guise during the night, turning into cats, birds or butterflies.

At night, the other world comes forth and appears in the midst of what we are accustomed to call 'reality'. Discreet and gentle Indian spirits rise up from springs, caves and streams to dance in the moonlight. Old people telling their stories in the starlit darkness of the Dominican countryside whisper and say:

> Listen to the dog howling out there. I tell you, that is no dog. Oh no, it is a human who has turned himself into a dog. The butterfly you saw in your room last night, that was no butterfly, it was your beloved who dreamt about you and her dream turned her into a butterfly. The fire-flies over there are no flies, they are the souls of our dead ancestors. All around us; up in the air, in the earth down below us, in the springs and the trees live the *misterios*, the *luases*. All around us are things and creatures we do not know, we cannot see, cannot understand. What we believe to be our world is only a fraction of something else, something much, much bigger.[47]

Many rural *Sanjuaneros* consider themselves to be living in a world into which the forces from the 'other sphere' make damaging intrusions. Evil-doers in their midst use alien forces for their own egoistical gains. They make deals with *Belcebú* or *Barón del Cementerio* [the Baron of the Grave-yard], the voodoo god of the dead. Dark forces are helpful in empowering the *guanguás*, magical instruments used to hurt a fellow human being. A *guanguá* may be anything, organic or inorganic, but most common is the *enviación* [consignment], a magically prepared parcel buried in the path of the one you intend to hurt.

An envious neighbor might also seek the help of evil forces to identify a fellow peasant's *buena flor* [good flower], the plant which gives fertility and abundance to his fields, steal it and plant it on his own lands, thus destroying the neighbor's harvest while the malefactor benefits from the theft.

---

47 Interview with Julián Ramos, Higüerito, 16 January 1986.

Envy is dangerous, no matter if it is shown or hidden, it may cause *mal de ojo* [the evil eye], a deadly danger for every child. If anyone praises your offspring by saying: 'Such a nice and beautiful child', you must answer immediately: 'And may God bless him', otherwise the little one may be struck by *mal de ojo* and die prematurely. You must be on guard at all times and protect your child with different kinds of amulets, like the *azabache*, a cord tied to the arm of an infant. When you go to bed you have to cross your sandals to ward off evil. In the children's room a light must be left during the night. A broom cannot be left in the kitchen, or outside the house. Crosses guard private houses and entire villages, they are even laid out on the floors and put under pillows. In the south such 'pillow crosses' are often made from the *piñón* tree.[48]

The *Olivoristas* find themselves within a vast universe, where the frontiers between the concrete and the 'spiritual sphere' are blurred. Both realms interact, sharing the universe on almost equal terms. To safeguard himself, his family, village and livelihood, the *Olivorista* peasant has to confide in the community, its traditions, 'the path of our ancestors' and religious experts, *curanderos* or *brujos*, who are able to inform him about the customs and tastes of the inhabitants of the 'other sphere'. The religious experts in his midst also assist the *Olivorista* in his defense against evil influences which may emanate from unseen quarters, threatening himself, his income and his family. In *Olivorista* lore, we discern how believers in Olivorio's divinity view their world, how they interpret it, how they confront their enemies, both imagined and real, and how they go about claiming their own place in the universe.

Olivorista salves

An important part of the *Olivorista* message is conveyed through *salves* which are sung all over the San Juan Valley and in isolated villages in the Cordillera Central. Most *salves* are improvised and their content may change from day to day. Nevertheless, some get a fixed wording and are repeated year after year and it is possible that some may still have the original form they received during the lifetime of *El Maestro*.

The inspired circumstances in which most *salves* are created, when the lead singer often *se sube* [rises], and enters in a state of 'semi-possession' in which he improvises new texts and melodies, are often interpreted as a

---

48 Stories about strange creatures and dangerous forces which surround people living in the rural areas of the Dominican Republic are told in almost every village and we have presented just a small fraction of what any visitor might be told if he asks about such matters. Of course, the stories differ from place to place, from storyteller to storyteller. Cf. Lemus and Marty (1975), Domínguez, Castillo and Tejeda Ortiz (1978), pp. 127–42, Deive (1979), pp. 146–270, Labourt (1979) and Avila Suero (1988), pp. 71–5.

sign of divine intervention, or as a method that Olivorio's spirit uses to
come into contact with his worshipers. Accordingly the lead singer's words
vary from occasion to occasion, while the refrain, sung by a chorus, often
stays the same.

Below we offer some examples of *salves* recorded in Higüerito, the
dwelling place of Julián Ramos, once a personal friend of Olivorio, later in
life a venerated *Olivorista* patriarch and important transmitter of *Olivorista*
lore. The *salves* were recorded on 16 January 1986. The comments made
by Julián Ramos, which are quoted below, were given on the same occasion. It must be noted that almost every *salve* differs from place to place
and from informant to informant.

Salves are always sung collectively and in a festive mood. 'You need rum
to sing *salves*.'[49] *Salve* sessions are often preceded by dancing and eating.
The dances tend to have a certain *Olivorista* flavor, musicians sing short
refrains connected with *El Maestro*, like: '*Baile Olivorito, baile, baile*' [dance
little Olivorio, dance, dance]. Since *salve* singing is a communal ritual it is
natural that *salves* tend to stress the unity of the group and often foster an
impression that *Olivoristas* belong to a 'chosen people'.[50]

The *Olivoristas* pride themselves on being inhabitants of an area where *El
Maestro* was active. They have been given the privilege of knowing who
Olivorio really is and it is only they who are able to spread his message. The
'outsiders', those who were responsible for his death, did not realize who
Olivorio Mateo really was – God, the creator and owner of everything:

Ninguno sabe si no lo dicen	No one knows, if you do not tell them
como el Eterno hubo de venir	how the Eternal One will come
y están al menos como lo tienen	and it is wrong the way they have him:
siendo el dueño de su país.	he who is the owner of his country.

This *salve* hints at some kind of esoteric knowledge,[51] a feature that is
common to several *Olivorista salves*, and this kind of secrecy was particularly
pronounced in Palma Sola. The 'secret' messages in some *salves* often
make them hard to decipher and even if the *Olivoristas* who sing them may
know their real meaning, they are sometimes reluctant to convey it to an

49 Interview with Julián Ramos, Higüerito, 16 January 1986. The rum is served in a glass
   which is passed from person to person and even the children get a small sip. The alcohol
   is used more as a kind of liturgical drink than a way to get drunk. Before the glass is
   passed around a small amount of the rum is spilled on the floor in order to 'feed the
   spirit of Olivorio'. (When Julián Ramos is quoted in the text and no reference is given it
   means that the quotations are taken from the session of 16 January.)
50 Cf. the *salve* quoted in the last lines of Chapter 2.
51 A knowledge which is restricted to, or intended for an enlightened or initiated minority
   (from Greek *esotero* [inner]).

'outsider'. This tradition involves Olivorio as well. He used to stress that he was in possession of secret knowledge. 'There were two words: one in heaven and another one on earth, but he never explained the mystery and meaning of these two unknown words.'[52]

Hidden messages are common to many religions. Among the people living in the southwestern parts of the Dominican Republic it is quite common that certain individuals, out of fear of witchcraft, do not reveal their real names during their entire lifetime.[53] Both Haitian and Dominican voodoo contain esoteric teachings that the *ougan* or *brujo* are ready to reveal only to their closest confidants. Likewise voodoo initiates are often presented with secret knowledge and told not to reveal certain aspects of the initiation rituals.[54] 'Secrets' were of great importance in the religions of classical times. The Greek word for secret, *mystérion*, had religious connotations and is often used in such a way in the New Testament. The common *Olivorista* claim to know the hidden message of Olivorio echoes St Paul, when he writes that the *mystérion* of God's plans for the salvation of humanity, which had earlier been hidden from man, finally had been revealed to him, so he could give this knowledge to the Gentiles.[55] According to the Gospels, on several occasions Jesus limited certain aspects of his teaching to his disciples: 'And he said, Unto you it is given to know the mysteries of the kingdom of God: but to others in parables; that seeing they might not see, and hearing they might not understand.'[56] Occasionally Jesus forbade his disciples to reveal parts of his teachings: 'And he saith unto them, But whom say ye that I am? And Peter answereth and saith unto him, Thou art the Christ. And he charged them that they should tell no man of him.'[57]

Liborio tenía un secreto	Liborio had a secret
como un santo en el altar,	like a saint upon the altar,
que vive en la luz divina	who lives in the divine light
que ya llegó al terrenal.[58]	which has already come to earth.

---

52 Garrido Puello (1963), p. 57.

53 Avila Suero (1988), p. 74.

54 '"And don't tell nobody what go on when you in there. That your secret. Even they give you money, don't say nothing!" "I'm not going to tell the secrets," Karen said defensively. "That's right!" said Alourdes, sitting back in her chair. "You do that – you going die"' (Brown (1991), p. 321).

55 'by revelation he made known unto me the mystery [...] Which in other ages was not made known unto the sons of men, as it is now revealed unto his holy apostles and prophets by the Spirit' (*Ephesians* 3:4–5).

56 *Luke* 8:10.

57 *Mark* 8:29–30.

58 *Salve* recorded in Media Luna, 5 May 1986. Olivorio sometimes made hints about hidden words and objects, which were unknown to everyone but himself (cf. Garrido Puello

Judging from the *salves* Olivorio, or at least his spirit, is still alive. Whether or not he will come back in the flesh is not entirely clear. The *salve* quoted above seems to indicate that his spirit has already returned to earth, but other *salves* often allude to some kind of future judgement day when Olivorio will return and present some kind of a 'bill', listing his services to mankind, asking for payment for all help he has rendered. In Palma Sola it was often stated that Olivorio's 'bill' is already prepared, but older *Olivorista salves* claim that it has not been written yet:

Si Olivorio trajera una cuenta	If Olivorio had brought a bill
pá toda la humanidad	to all mankind
le anduviera todo el mundo atrás	everyone would have followed him
por tan buen amigo te da.	for he is such a good friend.

In such *salves*, it is often stated that Olivorio intends to offer his salvation to each and everyone. However, other *salves* state that Olivorio's message is particularly directed to 'the ones who work' and his adversaries will suffer some kind of punishment:

Cuando Olivorio caminaba	When Olivorio wandered about
sufría de hambre y mucho frío.	he suffered from hunger and much cold.
Está hundiendo la paciencia;	The patience is diminishing;
cobre del Padre al judío.	pass the bill from the Father to the Jew.

Olivoristas brand *El Maestro*'s enemies as 'Jews'. When asked who these 'Jews' really are, Julián Ramos answered: 'The enemies of Jesus, the people who killed God.' Like most other *Olivoristas* Julián does not consider 'Jews' to be a certain ethnic or religious group, they are only 'Christ killers' and thus identical with the *Americanos*, i.e. the US marines who were responsible for Olivorio's death, or the *banda de Vence y Colorao* [the gang of Vence and Colorao], i.e. the Dominican soldiers of the *Policía Nacional Dominicana* (PND), who under the command of Lieutenant Luna and Sergeant Dotel tried to track down Olivorio.[59]

(1963), p. 57 and *El Imparcial*, 21 February 1914). The 'secret' of both people and holy paraphernalia is often identified with *El Gran Poder de Dios*. One of the songs that is sung in honor of the drums of the *Cofradía del Espíritu Santo* in San Juan de la Maguana states that drums are recipients for the divine power: 'Under the great drum [*Palo Grande*] is a secret, lift the great drum and you will see it' (Davis (1987), p. 101).

59 The names of Vence and Colorao may be nicknames. Julián Ramos states that they were PND soldiers. A *salve* from the village of Cabeza de Toro on the southern slopes of Sierra de Neiba, also mentions *La Banda Colorá* (Vásquez and Fermín (1980), p. 75).

Se acabó la tiranía	The Red Gang's tyranny
de La Banda Colorá.	has come to an end.
Lo que le hicieron a Liborio	His son will settle
su hijo lo va a cobrar.	what they did to Liborio.

Julián Ramos was a bit uncertain of who 'the son of Olivorio' was, but stated after a while that 'the son' mentioned in the *salve* must be identical with Olivorio, 'since the Father and the Son are one'. It is also possible that 'the son' of this particular *salve* may be an allusion to one of Olivorio's own sons, maybe Cecilio Mateo, who escaped the attack in which his father was killed, only to give himself up to the authorities a few days later.[60]

It is possible that substantive information from the days of Olivorio has survived embedded in some of the *salves* that are still sung today. For example, in the following, which Julián Ramos described as 'a very popular one, one which everyone knows':

La Nalga del Maco sabe una cosa:	The Bottom of the Frog knows something:
cuidado quien dice que es profecía	beware of who says it is a prophecy,
cuando Colón lleve a Olivorio	when Columbus will take Olivorio
a La Maguana de romería.[61]	to La Maguana on pilgrimage.

Even if Julián explained that *La Nalga del Maco* was the same as a 'frog's behind' and Colón was identical with the 'famous explorer', Christopher Columbus (Cristóbal Colón in Spanish), La Nalga del Maco is the name of a mountain behind the village of Río Limpio, situated in the northern part of the Cordillera Central. This rather secluded village, which even today harbors an important group of *Olivoristas*, apparently served as one of Olivorio's hideouts. Río Limpio is connected with La Maguana, *El Maestro's* birthplace and heartland of the *Olivorista* cult, by a mule track which cuts through the center of the Cordillera. During Olivorio's lifetime, Río Limpio had a considerable Haitian population and was an important point of departure for illegal trade with Haiti. In a gorge behind La Nalga del Maco lies La Cueva [the Cave] which is one of the holiest places in the entire Cordillera, a goal of pilgrims from the entire southwest and an object of intense veneration by *Olivoristas* and other religious groups.[62]

If La Nalga del Maco is a place within the 'habitat' of the *Olivoristas* it is also highly plausible that the Colón mentioned in the *salve* does not allude to the 'famous explorer', but to Colén Cuevas, who in several American

60 *El Cable*, 1 July 1922.
61 Martínez (1991), p. 169, quotes a variant of this *salve* which was sung in Palma Sola.
62 Personal visit to Río Limpio, 30 April–2 May 1986.

documents is mentioned as the right-hand man of Olivorio, if not the 'real leader of Olivorio's band'.[63] If that is the case, this *salve* may have been contemporary to Olivorio and contained some kind of coded message for Olivorio's group in La Maguana, indicating that *El Maestro* would soon come out of hiding and could, together with his 'commander in chief', Colén Cuevas, be expected to come down in order to carry out a religious ceremony in the original center of his operations: La Maguana.

However, the *salve* can also be interpreted as an expression of messianic hopes. Several *Olivoristas* believe that Olivorio's spirit still dwells somewhere in the deep caves up in the Cordillera and might someday arrive from there to establish *El Maestro's* kingdom in La Maguana.[64] If the first interpretation is correct it would be strange if Julián Ramos, who was after all an active supporter of Olivorio's group and spent his entire life close to La Maguana, would be ignorant of the original meaning of the *salve*. By giving an alternative interpretation of an already equivocal message Julián Ramos maybe only followed the force of habit and *se puso chivo*, i.e. played ignorant while confronting inquisitive strangers – a method which often proved to be of decisive importance during other decades when American marines or *Trujillista* thugs were hunting down *Olivoristas*.

It is very difficult to discern what kind of existence Olivorio is believed to have – who he really is. Judging from several *salves* he is 'alive' and actively involved in the doings of this world:

Arriba el águila negra	Above the black eagle
abajo el contorno arriando.	below the spinning world.
Lo que hicieron a Olivorio	What they did to Olivorio
Olivó esta cobrando ahora.	Olivó is settling now.

Julián Ramos explained the 'eagle' as a revenging Olivorio attacking his enemies. Olivó and Olivorio are identical. Asked if Olivorio still exists in this world the old *Olivorista* explained that 'of course he exists. The things [*las cosas*] of Olivorio still exist and will always exist in the entire world. There is something more than ourselves and he is there.' After Julián had made this statement, he and his relatives sang the following *salve*:

Bajó la Reina Mora,	The Dark Queen descended,
bajó al terrenal.	she came down to Earth.
Vino a Olivorio	She came to Olivorio
y al Padre Celestial.	and the Heavenly Father.

63 McLean (1919).
64 Interview with Jamín Medina Mora, Maguana Arriba, 13 December 1985.

Julián Ramos explained that Olivorio and the Heavenly Father are identical, but after that statement he hurried to add: 'We do not know. We do not know if he will be back. We have to leave the future to God, he knows. All we have to do is to work hard and keep our faith in God.'

The Dark Queen referred to in the *salve* may be identical with *La Virgen de la Altagracia*, the patroness of the Dominican Republic, to whom Olivorio was particularly devoted. She can also be one of the many voodoo deities who on chromolithographs adorning peasant altars are represented by 'black Madonnas'. The Dominicans call such images 'Indian Queens'. If that is the case, the *salve* may allude to Olivorio's connection with the Spring of San Juan and the Indian queens believed to dwell there.

Different kinds of Virgins are mentioned in connection with Olivorio. He himself is often compared with Jesus and it is possible that some visitors to Palma Sola believed the queens of Palma Sola – *La Madre Piadosa* and *La Virgen* – to be the representatives, if not actual reincarnations, of the Holy Virgin. This view is in accordance with older *Olivorista* traditions. *El Maestro* himself apparently discovered some divine traits in his female consorts and named some of them after different saints. One was actually called *Virgen María* and his favorite, Matilde Contreras, was called *La Número Uno*, thus indicating that she was the Virgin.[65] Also, in the village of Los Mosquitos, situated on the other side of the mountain range of Sierra de Neiba, just south of the San Juan Valley, exists a thriving cult of Olivorio where the *Virgen de los Dolores* [Our Virgin of Sorrows] is venerated as Olivorio's wife and thus forms a divine couple together with him.[66]

Julián Ramos stresses that Olivorio, the Father and the Son are one entity. 'Olivorio's mother was Zacaría Mateo, but in another sense she was also the Virgin':

Yo no debo promesa	I do not owe any vow
ni a San Pedro, ni a su madre.	either to St Peter or to his mother.
Solo debo promesa	I owe a vow
al Hijo y al Eterno Padre.	only to the Son and the Eternal Father.

After his death and alleged resurrection Olivorio has by several *Olivoristas* become identified with Jesus Christ. Accordingly he is often envisaged as a celestial being who will soon come back to earth, pass his judgement on humankind and wage a final cosmic battle with the forces of evil:

---

65 Lundius and Lundahl (1989), p. 29.
66 Espín del Prado (1984), p. 609.

Diga a Olivorio Mateo	Tell Olivorio Mateo
que ponga su cuenta clara.	to make out his bill.
Que estoy peleando con Luis,	I am fighting with Luis [Lucifer],
ni se aguanta, ni se para.[67]	he can neither stand it, nor does he stop.

The great code

A photograph taken when Olivorio's corpse was put on display outside the *Comandancia de Armas* in San Juan de la Maguana now adorns several peasant altars in the San Juan Valley. This picture is alluded to by many *Olivoristas* as *Olivorio Crucificado* [Crucified Olivorio]. In spite of the fact that most *Olivoristas* traditionally have little knowledge of the Scriptures and seldom go to church, several of the stories told about *El Maestro* appear to have been patterned after the Bible. In the following pages, a number of episodes commonly told about Olivorio will be related. Some of them probably refer to actual occurrences, but the majority have a legendary character. Before doing so, however, some theories must be mentioned which may explain why such narratives are structured in a similar way.

Projections and bricolages

In psychology 'projection' refers to a tendency to attribute to one's environment, or to another person, what is actually within oneself. The term is mostly used to describe pathological conditions, as when a patient ascribes painful or unacceptable feelings to the external world, which is thus perceived as possessing a threatening character or appearance. Such patients are unable to recognize that the source of their perception of the world around is to be found within themselves. This condition often manifests itself in a much milder form – one may talk about projections when a lover sees 'everything in a new light' or when a superstitious person who has broken a mirror, or got up on the wrong side of bed, feels that nothing works and everyone and everything are against him or her.

Sigmund Freud introduced the concept of projection into the realm of religion when he stated that 'As a matter of fact I believe that a large portion of the mythological conception of the world which reaches far into the most modern religions is *nothing but psychology projected to the outer world*'.[68] Freud himself may have been guilty of projections; for example it has been indicated that his patients dreamed in a 'Freudian' manner, while

---

67 *Salve* recorded in Media Luna, 5 May 1986.
68 Freud (1938), p. 293, quoted in Dundes (1980), p. 37.

Jung's patients dreamed like Jung. Psychoanalysts who interpret folklorist materials, such as fairy tales, in accordance with certain theories,[69] may also come under the suspicion of being victims of more or less conscious projections.

Folklore can be considered as a kind of projection as well in the sense that it 'provides a socially sanctioned outlet for the expression of what cannot be articulated in the more usual, direct way. It is precisely in jokes, folktales, folksongs, proverbs, children's games, gestures, etc. that anxieties can be vented.'[70]

If folklore has a 'projective' capacity, it is not only individual attitudes which are reflected through it. Folklore is a communal entity, it has been created, passed on and enjoyed by members of certain groups living within particular habitats. Folklore alludes to something which is known to persons living within the environment where it is expressed. It can accordingly be said that it is founded upon a common 'code'.

Ferdinand de Saussure distinguished between *langue* [language] and *parole* [speech], where *langue* can be explained as the entire system of word conventions and usages which are available to the speakers of a certain language. *Parole* is the selection individuals make from the *langue* – the grammatical conventions, words, word order, tones and accents they use while they communicate with others. Accordingly the *langue* is a code individuals make use of when they want to formulate a message [*parole*].[71] This code is culturally determined and may include several features unknown to its users. Religious traditions, myths and legends constitute an important part of the cultural code of a society:

> Man lives, not directly or nakedly in nature like the animals, but within a mythological universe, a body of assumptions and beliefs developed from his existential concerns. Most of this is held unconsciously, which means that our imaginations may recognize elements of it, when presented in art or literature, without consciously understanding what it is that we recognize. Practically all that we can see of this body of concern is socially conditioned and culturally inherited.[72]

The Bible, its stories and to a certain degree its language, clearly constitutes a major element in the imaginative tradition of societies that contain features from European traditions. Without any conscious knowledge of

---

69 See, for example, Fromm (1951), for a peculiar Freudian interpretation of Little Red Riding Hood, and von Franz (1970), for Jungian interpretations of several different fairy tales.

70 Dundes (1980), p. 36.

71 Leach (1985), pp. 45–6 and Sturrock (1982), pp. 6–9.

72 Frye (1982), p. xviii.

what they are doing, members of such societies often use biblical 'codes' while interpreting their environment and communicating with other members of the same community. This behavior may be an explanation of why *Olivoristas* tend to reconstruct the life of Olivorio in relation to the life of Jesus and are able to do so even if their biblical knowledge is very limited.[73]

The *Olivoristas* thus project the interpretation of their environment onto a folklore which is constructed within a code containing aspects from the life of Christ, other popular Christian notions, as well as voodoo and European and African folklore. The use of such codes is mostly unconscious and individuals may even pattern their own lives in accordance with them.[74]

Olivorista legends are created within the communities in the San Juan Valley, probably in the manner that Claude Lévi-Strauss would call *bricolage*, a putting together of bits and pieces out of whatever comes to hand. A *bricoleur* has no precise equivalent in English, but may be described as a man who is a jack of all trades, a professional 'do-it-yourself man', who in his activities uses 'whatever is at hand'.[75]

Bartolo de Jiménez, the 'missionary' and keeper of the Spring of St John close to Olivorio's birthplace in Maguana Arriba, may be described as a *bricoleur* in the realm of mythmaking. He identifies objects in his vicinity and relates them to Olivorio; fissures and scratches on a rock beside him are said to depict *El Maestro*, a stone which makes a hollow sound if it is hit, is called the 'Trunk of the Cross' and another small formation is *La Mano Poderosa* [the Powerful Hand], a hollow tree trunk 'carries the face of Christ', and the palm of Bartolo's hand is 'inscribed with the sign of the cross'. Other cult functionaries and legend makers in the San Juan Valley behave in a similar way – stories about Olivorio and incidents in their own lives are interpreted in the light of myths and legends which together make up the code of *Sanjuanero* culture. The 'bits and pieces' are already there, but they are constantly rearranged into new patterns and

73 The vast biblical tradition, which, more or less consciously, is present in almost every aspect of Western culture has been called 'The Great Code' by Northrop Frye, a Canadian literary historian.

74 Dundes (1980), pp. 42–4, describes the American lunar landing as if it was patterned after an unconscious code, reflecting traditions prevalent within 'Occidental culture'. Dundes also examines the life of Jesus in relation to so-called 'hero patterns' used by folklorists when they interpret the genre of hero legends. The life of Jesus fits well into such patterns. Among the characteristics of hero legends applicable to Jesus, are for example: a virgin mother, unusual conception, being a son of a god, reared by foster parents, no particular details are given about his childhood, he lost favor with one of his followers, was driven from his city, met a mysterious death on a mountain, his body was not buried in a common way, etc. (ibid., pp. 223–61).

75 Lévi-Strauss (1972), p. 17.

related to the storyteller's personal conceptions of *El Maestro* and his message.

> The 'bricoleur' may not ever complete his purpose but he always puts something of himself into it. […] the characteristic feature of mythical thought, as of 'bricolage' on the practical plane, is that it builds up structured sets, not directly with other structured sets but by using the remains and debris of events.[76]

> the scientist [is] creating events (changing the world) by means of structures and the 'bricoleur' [is] creating structures by means of events.[77]

We now turn to analyzing some *Olivorista* legends by using the 'bits and pieces' which have probably been stored up in the minds of *Olivoristas* – goods borrowed from voodoo, Christian and Spanish folklore, etc., and reused in the making of new *Olivorista* legends.

A legendary life of Olivorio

Birth and youth

God decided it was time to give 'grace for grace' to just people. The imperfect plants of mankind would be nurtured to perfection and the weed of the bad ones would be taken away and thrown into the fire. To that end, St Anthony was ordered to find the most perfect woman in this world and the saint wandered in search of her. However, he did not find many worthy women. Finally he ended up in La Maguana where he decided that Zacaría Mateo was the woman he was looking for. St Anthony found the *matrona* [matron] in labor and waited until she gave birth. When the people had left Zacaría alone with her newborn, St Anthony put her to sleep and when she woke up Zacaría found to her astonishment that her child looked different. It had grown and appeared to be older than before. While she slept St Anthony had changed her child and she woke up with Olivorio, the Son of God, by her breast.[78]

The St Anthony often alluded to in *Olivorista* legends and *salves* is probably identical with the St Anthony seen on chromolithographs found on Dominican peasant altars. The saint is then depicted either as *San Antonio el Ermitaño* [St Anthony the Hermit] or as *San Antonio Abad* [St Anthony the

---

76 Ibid, pp. 21–2.
77 Ibid., p. 22.
78 Interview with Julián Ramos, Higüerito, 16 January 1986.

Abbot, i.e. St Anthony of Padua].[79] The latter, who holds the child Jesus and a lily, is considered to bring fertility to barren women, an association which makes him a natural choice for the saint who brought Olivorio down to earth.

In his shape as *San Antonio el Ermitaño*, the saint is more complex. In voodoo beliefs he is then associated with Legba, a god considered to be the ultimate ruler of all the twenty-one divisions of the Dominican voodoo pantheon.[80] According to voodoo theology, the sun was one of God's first creations and it is often identified with the creative power of Legba.[81] As a matter of fact, all powers exercised by any of the multitude of *misterios* who inhabit the spiritual realm are controlled by Legba, who is invoked at the beginning of all voodoo ceremonies.[82] He is called upon by sprinkling water on the ground,[83] just as the spirit of Olivorio is invoked at the beginning of *Olivorista* ceremonies by sprinkling the ground with rum. For *Olivoristas*, who consider Olivorio to be an incarnation of *El Gran Poder de Dios*, St Anthony/Legba is the exclusive promoter and guardian of that power. Accordingly, it must have been St Anthony who brought the spirit of Olivorio to earth.

St Anthony/Legba serves as a contact between this world and the world of spirits. Like Olivorio he carries a stick, which serves as both a symbol of his fertility aspect and as a visual sign of his connection with the two worlds, a kind of *axis mundi*. Legba's identification with St Anthony the Hermit is probably due to the fact that this particular saint on the chromolithographs is depicted with a stick and a bell. In voodoo ceremonies, a bell is used to 'open up the barriers' that separate mortals from the world of the *misterios*.[84] The sticks of both St Anthony/Legba and Olivorio are called *palos*, a word which also is used to denominate the holy drums used in *Olivorista* ceremonies and the crosses used to sanctify certain places. Furthermore, St Anthony the Hermit is depicted as an old man and it is in this guise he appears in dreams of neophytes who are going to be initiated in the voodoo mysteries.[85] In other words, St Anthony/Legba upholds the

79 Cf. Deive (1979), pp. 227–9. The Catholic St Anthony the Hermit, who is venerated as one of the so-called desert fathers, lived in Egypt 251–356. St Anthony of Padua was a Franciscan friar, born in Lisbon 1195 and died near Padua 1231 (Attwater (1965), pp. 49–51).
80 Davis (1987), p. 124.
81 Desmangles (1992), p. 108. Invocations to the sun, the 'Lifebringer', apparently opened several ceremonies in Palma Sola and hymns and prayers honoring the 'Sun' are still carried out during ceremonies celebrated by León Romilio in Media Luna (see for example the TV special produced by *Rahintel*, 'Somos así y así somos: Programa No. 48', presented 13 October 1990).
82 Rigaud (1985), p. 69 and Courlander (1960), pp. 76–7.
83 Ibid., p. 45.
84 Deive (1979), p. 227.

connection between God and his creation, he is the instrument which transmits *El Gran Poder de Dios* to God's creation. The identification of Olivorio with *El Gran Poder de Dios* guarantees *El Maestro's* eternal presence in heaven and earth, a state of affairs indicated in the following *salve*:

Que Liborio está en el cielo	That Liborio is in Heaven,
quién puede decir que no	who could deny it?
Pregúntenle a San Antonio	Ask St Anthony,
que fue quien lo llevó.[86]	who was the one that brought him.

Christ spoke through the mouth of Olivorio,[87] but it was not until Olivorio was an old man that *San Antonio Esclarecido* [St Anthony the Enlightened][88] was ordered by God to choose him to be the man who would represent all mankind. Even though Olivorio had proved himself to be a just and compassionate man, St Anthony was reluctant to consider him as the Chosen One, because the saint believed Olivorio was too old to carry out the mission, but God answered that for him old age did not exist. St Anthony did not know that God had already appointed Olivorio as his mouthpiece when he was born.[89] The midwife who delivered Olivorio had found a small golden crucifix [*un pequeño Cristo de oro*] in the mouth of the newborn, but when she washed the child and tried to get hold of the 'Christ', it was not to be found anymore. The little Olivorio had probably swallowed the cross.[90]

The spiritual powers of an *Olivorista* are not inherited; a religious leader must be chosen by *El Gran Poder de Dios* to serve as its receptacle. The signs of being chosen are the same as those which are common for voodoo practitioners: the unborn child cries in the belly of his mother, or is born with a caul. The more extraordinary the signs of birth are, the more powerful will the person be.[91] The crucifix found in the mouth of Olivorio indicated

85 Interview with Juana López, Santo Domingo, 24 July 1983. Olivorio, sometimes referred to as *El Viejo* [the Old One], was around fifty years when he began his mission.
86 *Salve* from Palma Sola quoted in Martínez (1991), pp. 173 and 179.
87 Interview with León Romilio Ventura, Media Luna, 17 January 1986.
88 Probably Legba in his aspect as the sun.
89 Contrary to Julián Ramos and several other *Olivoristas*, León Romilio Ventura does not believe that Olivorio was brought to earth by St Anthony as a child. 'Olivorio was chosen for his mission when he was an adult. Just like I and Plinio received our mission when we were mature men' (interview with León Romilio Ventura, Media Luna, 17 January 1986). It is not quite clear for whom old age did not exist. When talking to *Olivoristas*, one has to keep in mind that, from time to time, they talk about God and Olivorio as identical. At other times they may consider Olivorio to be God's son, not entirely identical with the Father.
90 Ibid.
91 Cf. Deive (1979), pp. 191–200 and Davis (1987), p. 267.

that he was going to be extremely powerful and he would achieve this through the power of his word, granted to him through *El Gran Poder de Dios*. *Olivoristas* consider the cross to be a tangible sign of divine presence, and gold, which is still found in streams or in the earth, is connected with the Indians, the 'owners of the land', who guard the fertility and richness of the earth.

A sign given by the birth is an indication that a person has been granted the gift of *videncia* [clairvoyance], a kind of extrasensory perception, which in the case of Olivorio manifested itself in his ability to find strayed animals.[92] What was still to come was the gift of *gracia* [divine grace] leading to *incorporación*, which in voodoo terminology means that a person has obtained the ability to be possessed by the *misterios*.[93] In the case of Olivorio the *incorporación* probably meant that he was accepted by and taken up into *El Gran Poder de Dios*.

Before Olivorio experienced this *incorporación* with *El Gran Poder de Dios* he spent his childhood and youth 'free like a sheep and nobody cared about him'.[94] He was, however, considered to be a special man. He had land of his own, but not enough to support his growing family. Like Jesus he was a dexterous man, able to lend a hand almost everywhere. His specialty was constructing fences, but he was good at just about anything. He often worked on the lands of Wenceslao Ramírez, who liked him and sometimes even invited him to eat with the Ramírez family.[95] Wenceslao did not care when his farm-bailiff complained that Olivorio could not be trusted with any work, since he was too much 'up and down'. Certain days Olivorio came to work in very good moods and sang while he worked, but other days he did not work at all and seemed to 'be lost in his own thoughts'. However, Olivorio always treated the Ramírezes with respect and Wenceslao, who could not stand violent and abusive people, always accepted the presence of Olivorio.[96]

92 Interview with Tala Cabral Ramírez, Santo Domingo, 21 November 1985.
93 Davis (1987), p. 267.
94 Interview with León Romilio Ventura, Media Luna, 17 January 1986.
95 Interview with Mimicito Ramírez, San Juan de la Maguana, 14 December 1985. That Olivorio was allowed to eat with the powerful Ramírez family greatly surprised one of Wenceslao's grandsons, Víctor Garrido Jr, who stated that: 'Of course my mother, Tijides, knew Olivorio, but not personally. The social distance between a daughter of General Ramírez and a man like Olivorio was too great and it was of course out of the question that Olivorio could be invited to eat in the house' (interview, Santo Domingo, 22 April 1986). However, Mimicito Ramírez maintains that when he was a child he several times saw Olivorio as a dinner guest both in the house of his father, Carmito Ramírez, and in that of his grandfather, Wenceslao Ramírez (interview, San Juan de la Maguana, 4 July 1990). Another of Wenceslao's grandchildren, Tala Cabral Ramírez, also states that Olivorio 'often ate at El Mijo, Wenceslao's ranch outside San Juan de la Maguana' (interview, Santo Domingo, 21 November 1985).
96 Interview with Víctor Garrido Jr, Santo Domingo, 22 April 1986.

Long before his conversion Olivorio was known to be endowed with a certain degree of clairvoyance. People often came asking for his help when their donkeys had disappeared and he was always able to locate the runaway animals through his 'revelations'.[97] Even though he was completely illiterate, Olivorio knew a lot of things. He often disappeared and could be away for days, wandering about in the Cordillera on his own. When he noticed that people were searching for him he often ran away. Some persons maintained they had seen him in the mountains reading a book, even if it was known that Olivorio could not read. He also appeared and disappeared in a peculiar way. It happened that when people were looking for him he could at one moment not be seen anywhere, the next second he was right beside the searchers, telling them: 'You are really fools, searching all over the place for me and here I am, right in front of you, looking at you.'[98] Many persons believed Olivorio to be somewhat peculiar, if not outright crazy. However, he knew how to express himself in a polite manner and he was never aggressive.[99]

The divine warrior

It took a long time before Olivorio received his *incorporación* with *El Gran Poder de Dios*. It happened quite suddenly during a violent storm. He was taken up to heaven by an angel on a white horse. There he met God, was given a 'divine seal' and ordered to return to earth to preach and cure the sick. The mission was going to last for thirty-three years, the life span of Jesus Christ.[100]

The episode with an angel on a white horse[101] is reminiscent of similar images in the *Book of Revelation*, but may allude to other myths as well. Horses are frequent actors in many different mythologies and legends. Various religions have considered them to be celestial beings and imagined them as carriers of sun and sky gods. Folklore often endows them with divinatory abilities and countless stories are told about their instinctive alliance with the 'spiritual sphere'. Considering all these traditions it does not appear strange that Olivorio is said to have gone to heaven on the back of a horse, and to deal with this detail in the biography of Olivorio may lead us astray into a forest of pure speculation. Nevertheless, it could prove

---

97 Interview with Tala Cabral Ramírez, Santo Domingo, 21 November 1985.
98 Interview with León Romilio Ventura, Media Luna, 17 January 1986.
99 Interviews with Víctor Garrido Jr, Santo Domingo, 22 April 1986 and Mimicito Ramírez, San Juan de la Maguana, 14 December 1985.
100 Garrido Puello (1963), p. 55. In reality, Olivorio's 'mission' lasted a maximum of fourteen years.
101 Garrido (1972), p. 232, states that the horse was 'yellow like gold'.

to be revealing to touch on a few notions connected with mounted celestial warriors within the immediate surroundings of Olivorio.

Heavenly messengers and just warriors mounted on horses are common within the Catholic folklore of the Mediterranean and Latin America. Such popular saints and heroes belong to a long tradition which includes the Greek *Dioscuri* and other celestial warriors from classical antiquity. Among Christian equestrian saints we find St George, St Martin, St Mauritius, St James the Greater and many more. In the Dominican Republic, they share ranks with other sword-brandishing 'saints' like the Archangel Michael and the Prophet Elijah. Several of these saints are in Latin America considered to be champions of the poor and they often play an important role in popular, messianic movements. For example, Sebastianism has played an important role in almost every millenarian movement which has taken place in Brazil during the last two centuries.

Sebastião (1557–78) was king of Portugal, but a vow of chastity made him refuse to marry. When this led to his loss of the Portuguese crown, he directed two crusades against the Muslims of North Africa, until he was finally killed at the battle of Al-Kasr al-Kebir. Many Portuguese refused to accept the fact that he was dead and he became a 'hidden king' who awaits a second advent on an enchanted island. Romances about King Sebastião are still sung in Portugal and Brazil, and many poor Brazilians expect him to return as kind of Messiah for the poor.[102]

A Spanish hero of almost the same proportions as King Sebastião was Rodrigo Díaz de Vivar (1043–99), better known as 'El Cid'.[103] In popular Castilian legends El Cid has became something of an embodiment of the Spanish crusades waged against the 'infidel Moors'. El Cid's central position as *the* hero of the Spanish *Reconquista* was immortalized in an epic poem from the thirteenth century, *El cantar de Mío Cid*, a book of which few Spanish schoolchildren are ignorant. Already by the end of the thirteenth century the tomb of El Cid in Cardeña became a destination for pilgrimages, and his legend soon merged with the legends spun around Santiago [St James the Greater].

In AD 834 a Christian king named Ramiro I blundered into a Moorish ambush. His army was cut to pieces and only a small group of surviving Spaniards escaped to a place called Clavijo. A wonderful thing happened there – St James appeared to the sleeping king in a dream and told him that Jesus Christ had ordered him to take Spain under his saintly

102 Pereira de Queiroz (1977), pp. 101–2 and 217–20. King Sebastião is imagined as an 'Emperor of the Last Days' believed to become the future founder of 'the fifth [...] monarchy that will precede the Last Judgement' (ibid. p. 102). Deive (1978), p. 187, indicates the similarities between *Olivorismo* and popular notions related to King Sebastião and Santiago Matamoros (St James the Moor Slayer).
103 For El Cid, see e.g. Fletcher (1989).

protection. The next day a miracle proved the saint's words to be true. The Moors attacked, but they could not vanquish the Christians since St James appeared in person at the head of the Spanish army, visible to all. Under his inspiring command, the outnumbered Spaniards killed around 70,000 of the 'infidels'. At the sight of the saint, according to this amazing story, the Christian warriors came out with the battle-cry of '*Adjuva nos Deus et Sancte Jacobe*' [Help us God and St James] and since that day the name of St James has been on the lips of Spanish warriors through the centuries.[104]

This fantastic story appears to originate from a forged diploma that was manufactured around 1150 (nearly fifty years after the death of El Cid) intended to support a tax levied to procure cash for the wars the Leonese empire waged on the Moors.[105] The forgery was a complete success and Santiago Matamoros soon became the patron saint of Christian Spain. When Spain expanded its empire over the world, St James became a highly esteemed protector of the conquering Spanish knights. The saint was said to make recurrent appearances on the battlefields and thus helped empire builders like Albuquerque, Cortés and de Orite. The knightly Brethren of Santiago became the spearhead of the *Reconquista* of the Iberian Peninsula and afterwards they carried their fervor over the ocean to the Americas. Their ferocious motto was: 'May the sword be red with Arab blood' and their battle cry was: 'With St James and close in Spain [*Santiago y cierra España*].'[106]

The second largest city in the Dominican Republic, Santiago de los Caballeros [Santiago of the Knights] was named after the Brethren of Santiago and an equestrian statue of Santiago Matamoros greets the visitor at the entrance to that town.

In many parts of Spain and Latin America, the battles between Christians and Moors are commemorated in the form of dances or mock battles, particularly during carnival times.[107] In the San Juan Valley, the Dominican Independence Day, 27 February, was celebrated through the enactment of

---

104 Kendrick (1960), pp. 21–4. According to Spanish tradition (dating from the seventh century) St James the Greater visited Spain and preached the gospel there. After his martyrdom in Jerusalem the body of the apostle was said to have been brought to Santiago de Compostela, which in due time became one of the greatest centers of pilgrimage in Christendom.

105 Ibid., pp. 198–9.

106 Ibid., p. 63 and Seward (1974), pp. 18 and 146–8.

107 Most common is a dance called *morisca* [Moorish dance] or, as it is called in Spain, *Los Moros y Cristianos* [the Moors and Christians]. Two factions dance and perform a dramatic recreation of a battle between the evil Moors and good Christians. These types of dances are, with the exception of Scandinavia, known all over Europe and they may originally have had something to do with fertility rites. In eastern Europe the Moors' role is usually replaced by that of the 'Turks' (Kurath (1950a), p.747; cf. Foster (1960), pp. 221–3).

Figure 5.1 Santiago Matamoros, by Haitian artist Manno Paul.

a mock battle between Dominicans and Haitians,[108] probably a local variant of the old Spanish tradition. The most obvious presence of Santiago Matamoros in the Dominican Republic are the chromolithographs depicting the battle of Clavijo. They are found on almost every *Olivorista* altar. There are various versions of this print, but they are all essentially the same: St James clad in a blue tunic and mounted on a white stallion, fights off the Moors. Some of his fallen enemies litter the ground around him, while others are trampled underfoot by his horse. The saint carries a sword and a shield and is surrounded by iron-clad knights, one of them holds the banner of Santiago, it is either red or blue, with a white cross.

The high esteem Santiago Matamoros enjoys among many Dominicans may not only be due to his importance as the patron saint of Spain. In Dominican voodoo his equivalent is Ogún Balenyó, champion of justice and patron of everyone who possesses manly and military virtues. He is a defender of the weak and people without legal knowledge or protection. He is invoked as an advocate in legal disputes and is even considered to be a procurer of United States visas. The saint has a taste for rum, tobacco and women. People possessed by Ogún Balenyó may demand these things and are also apt to brandish a sword, or a machete, while they wave multicolored kerchiefs like banners over their heads. They are also expected to adorn themselves with red, the color of Ogún Balenyó.[109]

Olivorio shares several characteristics with St James in his guise as Ogún Balenyó and *salves* are sung to honor both the warrior saint and Olivorio:

---

108 Cano y Fortuna (n.d.), p. 21.
109 Lizardo (1982), p. 24, Jiménez Lambertus (1980), p. 182, Miniño (1980), and Deive

Yo vengo de la montaña	I come from the mountain
vengo montando a caballo	I come riding on a horse
me llaman 'El Guerrillero'	they call me 'The Warrior'
y mi nombre es San Santiago.[110]	and my name is St James.

This *salve* gives the impression that it is Olivorio who is the warrior coming down from the mountains. Several *salves* indicate that the mountains are the dwelling place of *El Maestro* and when he 'returns' he will enter La Maguana from the Cordillera Central.

Like Santiago/Ogún, Olivorio was fond of rum, tobacco and women. He was always dressed in blue, carried a sword and used to have a red kerchief tied around his waist. Olivorio used the kerchief in his thaumaturgical activities. When he entered San Juan de la Maguana, he did so mounted on a horse, surrounded by armed followers and with banners fluttering around him. His personal standard, which still can be seen on *Olivorista* altars, was exactly like the one of Santiago, blue with a white cross. Olivorio's supporters saw him as a champion of justice, a righteous warrior always ready to defend his flock against 'godless' invaders – traits he shared with Santiago.

Fatal encounters

As soon as Olivorio had returned from the mountains and told his neighbors about his mission, people demanded miracles and he performed several. It even happened that he raised people from the dead. This scared the devil, who is the master of this world and does not want to lose his powers to anyone else. The devil, who felt threatened, tried to take more souls than he usually did and even took several that did not belong to him. This angered Olivorio and when he tried to resurrect a girl from the dead only to find that her soul was not there, he went into the mountains to meet with the devil. Olivorio said: 'This one belonged to me', whereupon the devil appeared, apologizing for himself by saying: 'I am sorry *Maestro*, I made a mistake. I was confused. Let us divide the humans between ourselves and if you respect my part, I will respect yours.' Olivorio agreed to this, but told the devil: 'In the end I will prohibit death.'[111]

The notion that the devil rules the earth has its foundations in the Bible, particularly in the Gospel of John:

(1979), p 185. Concerning the Haitian *lwa* Ogoun, see Deren (1953), pp. 130–7 and Thompson (1984), pp. 167–72.
110 *Salve* quoted in Martínez (1991), p. 173. The Castilian name of the saint was originally Sancte Jacobe, but changed over time to Sancte Yago, until it became Santiago, thus merging the word 'saint' with the proper name. Actually, the *salve* says Saint St James.
111 Interview with Julián Ramos, Higüerito, 16 January 1986.

Now is the judgement of this world: now shall the prince of this world
be cast out.[112]

Hereafter I will not talk much with you: for the prince of this world
cometh, and hath nothing in me.[113]

And we know that we are of God, and the whole world lieth in wicked-
ness.[114]

We have already mentioned that the devil is considered by many *Sanjuaneros* to have a tangible presence. Living in the mountains he occasionally
comes down to inspect his domains, riding a donkey or a goat. The presence of the devil in Latin American rural settings has been noted by several
researchers and pacts with the devil have been reported from different
peasant settings all over the continent. The most common explanation for
such devil-beliefs is that they delegitimize 'those persons who gain more
money and success than the rest of the social group',[115] a theory which
must be seen in relation to the concept of the 'limited good' said to be
common within peasant communities.

According to this theory, peasants consider that the resources of their
environment, not only tangible things such as land and water, but also spiritual 'gifts' such as luck and knowledge, are limited. From the beginning
of times they were more or less equally distributed, something which
indicates that if someone owns more than his neighbor the 'surplus' has
in reality 'been taken away' from someone else, a notion which apparently
fits well with the *Sanjuanero* belief in *bacás*. However, this view has lately
been contested by several authors, among them Michael Taussig, who has
pointed out that Latin American peasants are often well aware of the fact
'the economic pie is expandable and is expanding'. They know that the
'good' is not limited and most peasants are in reality opposed to *how* it
expands, not to the fact that it expands.[116]

Even if the devil is considered by many *Sanjuaneros* to move around in
person up in the Cordillera, it is possible that he has undergone a change.
In the Palma Sola *salves*, the Evil One appears to have gained force since
his personal encounters with Olivorio. The devil is no longer the rather
meek demon up in the mountains, but has been transformed into a more
magnificent creature. It is possible that he now represents the forces of
change and modernization that transformed the San Juan Valley since

112 *John*, 12:31.
113 *John*, 14:30.
114 First Epistle of *John*, 5:19.
115 Taussig (1980), p. 15.
116 Ibid., p. 16.

the days of Olivorio and, at least according to many of the *Palmasolistas*, succeeded in changing it into an evil place that had to be *compuesto* [fixed] by the people and spiritual powers in Palma Sola. In the Palma Sola *salves*, Olivorio is depicted as carrying out a cosmic battle with his foe, Old Luis, who 'cannot stand it' but still refuses to give up. However, Olivorio's first appearance on earth signaled the end of the devil's rule:

Que salgan los guapos	May the bullies depart
que Liborio llegó.	because Olivorio has come.
Recojan los 'lemas'	Pick up the watchwords [signs]
vamos a ver si no hay Dios.[117]	we will find out if God does not exist.

According to the *Olivoristas* the world is filled with 'signs' that can be interpreted by the *sabios* [the wise]. A *sabio* is someone who has been given the gift of *incorporación* and is thus able to recognize the most important sign of all, namely the fact that Olivorio is divine:

Si el Padre Eterno no hubiera salido	If the Eternal Father had not gone
a andar el mundo particular	out to wander in the strange world,
los hijos de Cristo se hubieran perdido	the children of Christ would have been lost
Viva Liborio y se acabó el mal.[118]	Hail to Liborio and the Evil is finished.

Lo dice San Simeón	St Simeon says so
y lo dice en alta voz:	and he says it in a loud voice:
Por la palabra de Liborio	Through the word of Liborio
vamos a conocer a Dios.[119]	we will know God.

It has not been possible to identify the 'St Simeon' of this *salve*, but it is possible that he is the same celestial being as St Peter, who was called Simon before Jesus named him Peter. If that is the case he is identical with St Anthony/Legba, who in the voodoo pantheon may also be represented by St Peter.[120]

Olivorio was initially sent down to earth in order to 'reveal his message' and liberate the world from the clutches of *Lo Malo* [the Evil]. Olivorio's message is believed to be contained in the *salves*, his miracles and his acts, like his armed struggle against the Americans and the stress he laid on doing work in the community and distributing its results. However, the

---

117 *Salve* quoted in Martínez (1991), p. 170.
118 Ibid.
119 Ibid.
120 Desmangles (1992), p. 113.

final victory over the devil lies in the future; the world, and even Heaven, still live in his shadow:

Levanta María tu pureza	Raise your purity, Mary
y ataca [sic] Liborio ese rezo	and Olivorio, heed this prayer
que repollen los reinos del cielo	that the kingdoms of Heaven enclose
y por eso que el mundo está preso.[121]	and that is why the world is imprisoned.

In Palma Sola, it was preached that on his forthcoming return to earth, Olivorio will bring his 'bill' with him. And like an authoritative bureaucrat, or judge, he will then administer justice and assure his people that the devil has finally been vanquished:

Cuando ese Maestro llegue	When that Master comes,
que pase para el aposento	let him come into the room
reuniendo a toda su gente	and gather all his people
y procurándole su cuenta.[122]	and present them with his bill.

Atención viene la Reina	Look out, the Queen is coming
diciendo que viva Dios	saying: Hail to God,
firmando los documentos	signing the documents
y jurando que el mal cayó.[123]	and swearing that the Evil has fallen.

Olivorista legends do not only relate Olivorio's meeting and dealings with the Prince of This World, they also offer a description of another important meeting with a different, worldly ruler, namely Rafael Trujillo, the future, omnipotent dictator of the Dominican Republic.

When Trujillo was just a simple *gavillero* [bandit] he ran into trouble with his *padrino* [godfather] Horacio Vásquez.[124] He had to run away from the capital and ended up in San Juan de la Maguana. Trujillo knew about Olivorio and came up to La Maguana to greet him. Olivorio looked at Trujillo and asked him what he wanted. 'I want to rule the world', answered Trujillo. 'I am the ruler', asserted Olivorio. Trujillo, who knew about Olivorio's limitless powers, said: '*Maestro*, I

---

121 *Salve* quoted in Martínez (1991), p. 170. The word *ataca* appears to be a mis-spelling of *acata*.
122 Ibid., p. 169.
123 Ibid.
124 Horacio Vásquez (president 1924–30) was not Trujillo's *compadre*, but he favored his rise through the military ranks, until Trujillo succeeded in becoming head of the army and finally ousted his benefactor from the presidency.

would like to have a *carta blanca* [carte blanche, a free hand].' 'For what?' 'For the capital.' 'I will give it to you,' promised Olivorio. 'You will rule for over thirty years and you will become the richest man in the world.' What Olivorio had decided came true. Trujillo was a nobody, he came running, but he became the richest and most power-ful man in the world. No one knows why Olivorio did it. Trujillo knew perfectly well what he owed to Olivorio. Nevertheless, when *El Maestro* had been shot, Trujillo began to persecute the *Olivoristas*. You could not even light a candle to Olivorio. Trujillo could not stand competi-tion. As soon as you paid homage to Olivorio you were arrested. But Trujillo was punished for his behavior and was finally shot to death.[125]

There is a small possibility that Trujillo met Olivorio. As a young sergeant, the future dictator used to hang about in the company of the notorious Major James McLean, who was married to a woman from San Juan de la Maguana and for a time served as commander in chief of the southern district of the PND. McLean, who knew several friends of Olivo-rio, had probably met *El Maestro* in person and it is not entirely unlikely that McLean had been able to arrange a meeting between Trujillo and Olivorio.

However, it is more plausible that the meeting between Olivorio and Trujillo belongs to a common legendary genre of encounters between worldly rulers and famous sages or fortune tellers, something which ever since Alexander met with Diogenes has been a standard feature in many biographies of the rich and famous.

Moreover, a meeting between Trujillo and Olivorio's contemporary, the prophetess Bibiana de la Rosa from Baní, is also recorded:

> On one occasion, when Trujillo was a soldier in San Cristóbal he passed by the church with a group of other men, pursuing some bandits. They went to ask Bibiana for water. She looked at him for a long time, while he was drinking water, and finally told him: 'Return, do not search for them. Within a short time you will govern the Repub-lic for many years.'
>
> Trujillo did so and returned with all his men. Years later Trujillo was elected president of the country and governed for more than 30 years. He returned to Mana and declared this zone as holy territory.[126]

125 Interview with Julián Ramos, Higüerito, 16 January 1986.
126 Tejeda Ortiz (1978), p. 81.

Olivorio and the outsiders

Olivorio was several times delivered into the hands of the law and several of these occasions have been preserved in people's memories:

> I believe it was around 1911, in La Maguana, a region up in the mountains. It was rumored that up there was a man called Liborio who cured people. It was mainly persons from the Cibao who came to him. I remember they brought Olivorio down from the mountains because the *alcalde* wanted to interrogate him. [...]
>
> [The *alcalde*] asked Olivorio: 'Who are you?' and he answered: 'I am nobody. I am a man to whom people come, but I am nobody myself.' He talked like a peasant, full of reservation.[127]

Olivorio was released, but he was soon recaptured. This time it was his old friends, the Ramírezes, who were involved in the apprehension of *El Maestro*. It was Juanico Ramírez, who together with his brother Carmito, had summoned the force that succeeded in capturing Olivorio. While they brought their prisoner down to San Juan de la Maguana, they were ambushed by some of Olivorio's followers, who were, however, unable to liberate their leader. Juanico wanted to bring down his captive to Azua, the provincial capital, as soon as possible, and when the levy entered San Juan de la Maguana, long before dawn, they took Olivorio directly to the house of Juanico. The town was full of Olivorio sympathizers and Juanico did not want anyone to know that the miracle worker had been taken prisoner. While he kept his prisoner under guard in his patio, Juanico went into the house to fetch his wife and his sister, Tijides, who stayed with Juanico's family at the time:

> 'Concha, come and see who I brought. It is a surprise.' The women went out into the patio, but due to the darkness they could not identify the prisoner. Olivorio stood by a wall with his hands tied behind him. Juanico went in and came back with a lantern. 'Concha, is it really true that you cannot recognize this fellow?' 'Juanico, I do not know who this *sinvergüenza* is.' At that moment Olivorio looked at my mother [Tijides Ramírez, Juanico's sister] and said: 'Tijín, do you not recognize me? I am Olivorio.' Even if she had met him several times before, Tijides could not recognize him because he had changed a lot, he looked stronger, more robust. 'Please, Tijín, ask Doña Concha if she cannot bring me some food. I have not eaten for two days.' When Concha came with the food she told Olivorio: 'Look, you scoundrel,

---

127 Interview with Maximiliano Rodríguez Piña, Santo Domingo, 23 April 1986.

have you become Jesus Christ just because you do not like to work? Before you were a simple idler [*haragán*] and now you have become a god.'[128]

This story reflects a quite common urban view of Olivorio: he was simply an imposter who invented his 'divinity' in order to have a pleasant time. It is also interesting to note the quite brutal treatment that Olivorio receives from Juanico, who after all was the son of Wenceslao Ramírez, considered to be the *caudillo* of Olivorio, who often was referred to as Wenceslao's client. In spite of the fact that a slight animosity sometimes shines through, *Olivorista* legends still stress the continuously good relationship between Juanico's brother Carmito and Olivorio. Carmito Ramírez often visited Olivorio and on one of those occasions, according to the urban legend, Olivorio confessed to him: 'Carmen [Carmito] it is much better to be a god up here, than to clean General Wenceslao's horses.'[129]

After receiving food and refreshments in the house of Juanico, Olivorio was brought down in a forced march to Azua, where he received a lot of attention. He was treated in a benevolent manner and was soon released for a triumphant return to San Juan de la Maguana. Since Olivorio's trip to Azua is considered to be an important stage by several *Olivoristas* to his way to future glories, it has in their legends been endowed with several miraculous happenings. It is, for example, stated that on his way back to San Juan de la Maguana, Olivorio ordered the rivers to open up a path for his retinue. Olivorio simply said: 'To your center!' and the waters parted.[130]

After Olivorio's return to La Maguana, his fame grew constantly and people came to him asking for advice:

Pedro Heyaime, one of the Turkish [i.e. Christian Lebanese] businessmen in San Juan, was having an affair with the wife of a peasant. The deceived husband went to Heyaime and told him he was going up to La Maguana to ask Olivorio what to do. Heyaime just laughed at him. After some time the peasant returned to Heyaime and told him that Dios Liborio had a message for him. Heyaime laughingly asked what the god might tell him, whereupon the peasant answered that Dios Liborio saluted Heyaime and just wanted to offer him a piece of advice. 'And what is that?' asked Heyaime. 'Only that if you cut off your own instrument, you will eventually become the richest man in the valley.' No one knew whether Heyaime did it or not, but the truth

---

128 Interview with Víctor Garrido Jr, Santo Domingo, 22 April 1986.
129 Ibid.
130 Martínez (1991), p. 77.

is that Heyaime did not get any more children of his own and eventually became the richest man in the valley.[131]

This story was told by Víctor Garrido Jr, whose parents had been influential members of the San Juan elite. Other slightly different versions of what seems to be a very popular *Olivorista* legend also exist. What is apparent is not only the humor of the tale, but also the cunning of Olivorio, who is able to appeal to the alleged greed of the businessman and by doing so succeeds in rendering the rich, urban seducer harmless to the *Olivorista* women.

Legends often describe Olivorio as a practical and good-humored man. His preaching is said to have been very 'down to earth' and was often intercepted by parables of a tangible kind:

> Olivorio knew he was going to be killed and this was a constant concern of his followers. Adolfo de los Santos, whom *El Maestro* had cured from a machete wound in an arm, once asked Olivorio what would happen after his death. Olivorio answered that he would never die. 'What do you mean?', asked Adolfo. 'I will show you', said Olivorio and together they went out into the sunshine and Olivorio handed Adolfo the sword he always carried with him: 'Take this and plunge it into my shadow.' Adolfo did as *El Maestro* had told him to do. 'What happened? Could you kill the shadow?' 'Of course not', answered Adolfo, 'you cannot do anything against a shadow.' 'If you cannot kill my shadow you cannot kill me either. Olivorio will never die, the shadow I cast will be with you as long as you remember me and thus Olivorio will never die.'[132]

During his later years, Olivorio constantly felt threatened by his persistent pursuers. He moved from place to place, but never stopped preaching and continued to perform miracles:

> Here in Bánica Olivorio came to a ball and invited a paralyzed girl to a dance. She said she was not able to dance but Olivorio insisted and when she rose she was healed and danced with him.[133]

> In the Cibao, Olivorio came across a funeral procession on its way to the graveyard. He stopped the mourners and ordered them to open the coffin. He said he wanted to see the face of the corpse. They told him it was a young girl and he told them that he already knew it. They

131 Interview with Víctor Garrido Jr, Santo Domingo, 22 April 1986.
132 Interview with Pirindín Solís, El Batey, 11 April 1986.
133 Interview with Narciso Serrano, Bánica, 3 May 1986.

opened the lid and put it on the ground and Olivorio said: 'Rise, it is not time yet. You are too young.' The girl came to life and she woke up with a terrible hunger.[134]

He was here in El Batey and once he resurrected a dead mule. It was a poor man who had lost his only animal and Olivorio asked: 'Where is the mule?' It lay by the roadside and he walked around it three times and then he kicked it hard three times. The mule came to life at once.[135]

He often came to Río Limpio. Sometimes he brought lots of people with him, but he could also arrive in company of just three or four [...] When he came, people crowded around him. He cured people with a stick in the form of a cross; he touched people with it. He also prophesied. [...] You never knew where he went. He did not want people to know. He could disappear at will. The troops sometimes passed him by and he was as close to them as you are to me now, but they could not see him. It happened that he was talking to someone and one of his enemies appeared. They could not see him, but his friends saw him just as clearly as you can see me now.[136]

Sudden disappearances and the faculty of making oneself invisible is a common ingredient in many legends, particularly in the lore dealing with 'bandits'.[137] The ability to disappear at will is in Dominican folklore sometimes applied to different *gavilleros* and a legendary, lone fugitive from justice called Enrique Blanco.[138]

Olivorio predicted his approaching end and often used images akin to the Gospels: 'I am on a mission that will last until I come to the trunk of the cross.'[139]

They persecuted him without mercy. They said he was a communist and a sorcerer. In the end, he told his people. 'Go away all of you.

134 Interview with Julián Ramos, Higüerito, 16 January 1986.
135 Interview with Pirindín Solís, El Batey, 11 April 1986.
136 Interview with Javier Jovino, Río Limpio, 30 April 1986.
137 In folklore the bandit is often a trickster-like figure using cunning, deceptions and disguises to achieve his ends (Austen (1986), p. 97). A common trait among tricksters is particularly shape shifting and the faculty of obtaining invisibility at will. Almost every legend about bandits contains this ingredient, two examples from different parts of the world may suffice: Kwame Abe, the most notorious bandit of the Gold Coast, 'could appear in an instant, and disappear at will if danger threatened' (Kea (1986), p. 125) and the Colombian bandit Cenecio Mina 'could transform himself into an animal or plant when pursued' (Taussig (1980), p. 65).
138 Arzeno Rodríguez (1980), p. 71.
139 Garrido Puello (1963), p. 17.

Today they will kill me. I will give myself up just as Christ gave himself to the Jews when he was betrayed.' He was killed the same day.[140]

Olivorio knew that someone was going to betray him. He often said: 'They will betray me. They will betray me!' In the end two of his own men did it for money. He was on a horse when they killed him and he had predicted that nothing was going to happen to that horse. When the bullets hit Olivorio, he fell like this, backwards from the horse. The horse stood still and did not move from the place where its master had fallen.[141]

When the soldiers came upon the corpse of Olivorio, he had already been dead for a while. They tied *yaguas* around the body and carried him down from the mountains on a bier that looked like a ladder. When they had placed Olivorio's corpse by the central square in San Juan de la Maguana, the soldiers found that Olivorio carried white flowers in his hand. They were unable to remove them from the dead man's grip and let him keep them when they finally lowered him into his grave. The soldiers were shocked when they saw the flowers, because Olivorio's hands had been empty when they had wrapped him in *yaguas* up in the mountains.[142]

These are all common *Olivorista* versions of the death of Olivorio. However, there also exists an urban variant in which Carmito Ramírez is present at the scene of Olivorio's death:

Olivorio always surrounded himself with guards and all his men had names of saints he had given to them. Sometimes he changed those names and they served as some kind of secret code. He also used names of saints as passwords. One of his men informed on him and told Juanico [Ramírez] that San José was the password of a certain day. Juanico revealed the secret password to his good friend José Esteban Luna, who was in charge of hunting down Olivorio, and he also told Luna where Olivorio could be found. Luna and his men killed Olivorio and soon after Juanico and Carmito arrived at the scene. Olivorio was not dead yet and Carmito, who liked him, kneeled by his side and told him: 'Look this is what comes out of living without God.' The dying Olivorio answered: 'Carmen, people die for what they believe in.'[143]

140 Interview with León Romilio Ventura, Media Luna, 17 January 1986.
141 Interview with Javier Jovino, Río Limpio, 30 April 1986.
142 Interview with León Romilio Ventura, Media Luna, 17 January 1986.
143 Interview with Víctor Garrido, Jr, Santo Domingo, 22 April 1986.

Resurrection

León Romilio Ventura states that before he and his brother Plinio initiated their 'mission' in Palma Sola, they had sought out all the *Olivoristas* they could find throughout the San Juan Valley and Cordillera Central and collected stories about *El Maestro*:

> I am very careful when I inquire about these things. I do not know if everything I am telling you is true or not, but one thing is certain – and that is that I only tell people what I have been told myself. I talked to an old lady who used to sit by the entrance to the graveyard where Olivorio was buried and she showed me the dried flowers Olivorio had kept in his hand when they buried him. She took these flowers when she saw them lying by the *yaguas* and ropes that had been left by Olivorio's open grave. They said he disappeared three days after his burial, only the hole in the earth remained and the things the old lady found. [...] The Americans and the Dominican commander saw the *yaguas* and the ropes. They accused the *Olivoristas* of taking the corpse. But, what use could they have of a corpse?[144]

One legendary item was missing at the burial ground and it was the kerchief of Carmito Ramírez. Several informants have stated that they were present when Olivorio's corpse was put on display in San Juan de la Maguana and that they saw how Carmito put his kerchief over the face of the dead Olivorio.[145]

> They were already there: the townsfolk, the soldiers and even schoolchildren. Everyone had to see the corpse. Carmito came, all dressed in white. For a while he stood quietly in front of Olivorio. The flies were crawling all over Olivorio's face and when Carmito saw it he took out his kerchief and wiped them away. Then he turned to the soldiers who stood in the shadow and told them: 'I knew this man. He was my friend and now you treat him like this. It is a shame.' Then he covered the face of Olivorio with his kerchief. Olivorio was buried at night and when the Americans and the soldiers had left, people walked through San Juan with lit candles and sang. When they came to the grave no one was there. Only the *yaguas* and the ropes. Carmito's kerchief was not there. Carmito walked by himself in another part of the town. No one was around and the moon was up. He thought about Olivorio.

---

144 Interview with León Romilio Ventura, Media Luna, 17 January 1986.
145 Interviews with Mimicito Ramírez, San Juan de La Maguana, 14 December 1985, Julián Ramos, Higüerito, 16 January 1986 and Maximiliano Rodríguez Piña, Santo Domingo, 23 April 1986.

Suddenly he heard someone whispering behind him and when he turned around he saw Olivorio coming towards him. Olivorio held out the kerchief and said: '*Compadre*, I wanted to give you this and thank you for your compassion.' When Carmito wanted to say something to Olivorio he had already disappeared.[146]

The story seems to show affinities with the Christian legend about St Veronica, a woman who, filled with compassion at the sight of Jesus' suffering on his way to Golgotha, wiped his face with a cloth.[147] One is also reminded of the kerchief Olivorio used to have around his waist and which he frequently used during his thaumaturgical activities. Kerchiefs, called *fulás* [*foulards* in French, *foula* in Haitian Creole] or *pañuelos*, play an important role in voodoo ceremonies. They are baptized and used to invoke the *misterios*. They are said to 'give force' to the possessed mediums. Kerchiefs are also considered to constitute a kind of link with the 'spiritual sphere' and each color corresponds to a certain *misterio*. As mentioned above Olivorio's red kerchief was thus probably related to Santiago/ Ogún.[148]

In the story, Carmito's kerchief may also be considered as a symbolical link between Olivorio and his urban counterparts, the Ramírez family, who often had a somewhat strained relationship with him, sometimes acting as friends, sometimes as foes. The exchange of kerchiefs seems to indicate some kind of truce beyond the grave between the two major forces of the San Juan Valley: the mundane one of the Ramírezes and the spiritual one of Olivorio. When Olivorio ceased to be a living being here on earth, he once again merged with the spiritual force of *El Gran Poder de Dios* and as such he continues to exist in the valley. 'He himself lived many years ago. I did not know him. Now, his spirit is with us, and that is all that matters.'[149]

The *salves* and the theology of Palma Sola

The singing of *salves* was essential to all rituals in Palma Sola and León Romilio Ventura has repeatedly stated that the *salves* are 'gospels which

---

146 Interview with Julián Ramos, Higüerito, 16 January 1986. At this occasion Carmito's son, Mimicito Ramírez, was present and he helped Julián to tell the legend. Mimicito stated it was a very common story, but he could not tell if it was true or not. Personally, Mimicito believes that the *Olivoristas* dug up Olivorio's corpse and buried it by *El Maestro*'s sanctuary in Maguana Arriba: 'When we offered to put cement on the floor up there, they got very upset. They had no reason to behave like that so I have come to the conclusion that they had him buried under the *enramada* by the *calvario*' (interview with Mimicito Ramírez, San Juan de la Maguana, 14 December 1985).
147 Attwater (1965), pp. 334–5.
148 Davis (1987), pp. 313–14.
149 Interview with María Orfelia, Maguana Arriba, 18 January 1986.

Christ and the Holy Spirit send for spiritual communication'.[150] If compared with the *salves* sung in Higüerito, which probably represent an earlier development of *Olivorista salve* singing, it appears as if the *salves* sung in Palma Sola were constructed on the firm base of older *Olivorista* traditions. Several older notions and turns of phrase reappear in *salve* variants sung and composed in Palma Sola.

When asked which was the most important *salve* in Palma Sola the relatives of León Romilio sang the following tune – the *Salve de la centena* [Salve of the Hundred]:

Unidad, decena y centena	Unity, ten and hundred
de centena y decena unidad.	between hundred and ten, unity.
Le sacamos la cuenta al setenta	We made out the bill to seventy
y ya la cuenta está entregá.[151]	and the bill is already delivered.

According to the Venturas, the 'hundred' stands for the 'gospel': 'The gospel comes from there. It is *lo sagrado* [the holy].'[152] *La cuenta* is Olivorio's judgement of this world, a concept also encountered in older *Olivorista salves*. The *Palmasolistas*, when being exposed to the influence of the spiritual presence of the holy place, were gradually converted into new beings, into something sacred. This transformation of the *Palmasolistas* is symbolized by the word *centena*, a holy number designating a harmonious multitude. Olivorio, or his spirit, was constantly present in Palma Sola, considered to be a sacred enclave where dramatic struggles for the salvation of the world took place. In order to contribute to this cosmic fight between the forces of good and evil, the *Palmasolistas* had to work in unity and share their belongings and their food.[153] Through such behavior they were assisting Olivorio in putting things in order. The 'seventy' mentioned in the *Salve de la centena* is a holy number, representing *lo sagrado*, i.e. all that belongs to the spiritual sphere.[154]

---

150 León Romilio Ventura, quoted in Martínez (1991), p. 166.
151 Recorded in Media Luna, 5 May 1986. Martínez (1991), p. 167, presents a variant of this *salve* with the rather amazing commentary that it may be 'anti-American'.
152 Media Luna, 5 May 1986.
153 The *Olivoristas* in Media Luna stressed the fact that the word *decena* also could mean *de cena* [of supper], the wording of the *Salve de la centena* would thus be: 'Unity of the supper and the hundred', indicating the common meals in Palma Sola which fostered a feeling of unity and generosity among the *Palmasolistas* (ibid.). Possibly, *de cena* also alludes to the Last Supper.
154 It is quite common among the peasants in the San Juan Valley to let the part stand for the entirety and let *lo sagrado* be symbolized by numbers or things. Martínez (1991), p. 167, puts sixty in the place of seventy in the *Salve de la centena*. Since time is counted in units of sixty, sixty is in religious symbolism often considered as a symbol of harmony and totality. Seventy may also be correct; it is considered to be a holy number for many

León Romilio has stated various times that the principal message preached in Palma Sola was 'not to hurt one another, part our daily bread, and the work to obtain it; to respect and not betray one another; only seek the good in other people'.[155] The guidelines for such behavior were found in the teachings of Olivorio, which, according to León Romilio, became 'public' in Palma Sola. He preached that *El Maestro* used to state that 'everyone has to work in communion in order to seek means for the *infeliz* [the unfortunate] so he might change his life for the better'.[156]

In the San Juan Valley a common belief exists that *El Gran Poder de Dios* manifests itself in the landscape and several cult sites are found by 'holy' springs and caves. It appears as if many of the pilgrims to Palma Sola thought it was a site where *lo sagrado* sprang forth. 'They went there because they believed a divine power was present, some kind of force related to the *Gran Poder de Dios*.'[157] The *Mellizos* apparently shared the same conviction:

> The most important thing was not the words we said. The message manifested itself through our customs, through the way of life in Palma Sola, through the rhythm and melody of the *salves*. We just acted in accordance with the work of Christ. We did not use the Bible, but we did the same things it preaches. We just followed the counsels of the Holy Spirit, which are all true. God wanted to test the capacity of the Dominican man. We had no fear. It was the *misterio*[158] that made everything happen. The influence of the place. The crosses cured people. The crosses were identical with the Holy Spirit. The people who came were all guided by the Spirit. They began to cure themselves, without our interference. Each and everyone acted in

reasons, one being that the normal lifespan of a man is commonly supposed to be seventy years. To determine the 'holiness' of a number is very tricky, if not impossible. Dominican folklore presents a wide range of numbers that are extremely important in magical practices (cf. Davis (1987), pp. 103–4). Elaborate numerology was present in many rituals carried out in Palma Sola, for example, the prayers directed to a spirit called *Componte* constructed as peculiar riddles, where numbers played an important role: 'One is God, he died; in two is God; three is God; four, I took my place' (quoted in Martínez (1991), p. 143). An anonymous text written by an *Olivorista* in 1971 lists various numbers related to the martyrdom of Christ, like Jesus received 6,666 lashes, lost 38,725 drops of blood, 118 soldiers took him to the calvary, he was spat 180 times in the face, etc. (reproduced in ibid., p. 225).

155 León Romilio Ventura, quoted in Espín del Prado (1980), p. 55.
156 Interview with León Romilio Ventura, Media Luna, 5 May 1986.
157 Interview with Eugenio Fernández Durán, San Juan de la Maguana, 4 July 1990.
158 Among the *Olivoristas* the word *misterio* can mean several things; it may be a secret, or something unexplainable, but it can also signify a sacred entity; a saint or a voodoo deity. Olivorio is often referred to as a *misterio*, as well as his message and the actual site of Palma Sola.

accordance with the criterion he had. No one understands the mystery which reigned there. But, one day the Dominicans will learn the true meaning of Palma Sola.[159]

Visitors to Palma Sola were asked to confess their sins and deliver their souls from evil influences, thus would they be able to open their hearts to *El Gran Poder de Dios* and partake of the powerful spiritual force emanating from the place. By such acts the benevolent force would increase its dominion and power until finally 'things would be put together again' and accordingly the whole world would change:

Aquí hemos venido	We have come here
a rezar a Palma Sola	to pray in Palma Sola
a darle luz al mundo	to bring light to the world
y a dejarle mucha gloria.[160]	and leave it much glory.

'If Palma Sola had continued there would be no bad people, because we were already seeing each other. The sorcerers and the bacás were coming to an end, all evil was killed ...'[161]

The force of Palma Sola, *El Gran Poder de Dios*, was identical with the Holy Spirit, but it was transmitted to the people through the intercession of the spirit of Olivorio. Here we once more encounter the often-mentioned secret, or *misterio*, of Olivorio. Several *Olivoristas* state that the secret lies in his divine nature. Older *Olivoristas* like Julián Ramos consider Olivorio Mateo to have been identical with the 'life force' in nature, *El Gran Poder de Dios*, and thus he is also the same entity as the Father and the Son. The Venturas who presided over Palma Sola probably considered Olivorio as a reincarnation of *El Gran Poder de Dios*. Thus, they identified him with Jesus. Plinio Ventura apparently revealed such an opinion:

What is in us, is the word of Liborio. Liborio is the same person as Christ. He never dies. Sometimes they say they have killed him, and what they killed was the body in which he was incarnated, but this time the same thing will not happen. Now he came to end all evil on this earth and he will unite the entire world for always ...[162]

This misterio does not have to do any specific tricks, he does everything he wants to do, because he is Christ himself. This reincarnation

159 Interview with León Romilio Ventura, Las Matas de Farfán, 5 May 1986.
160 Salve quoted in Cárdenas Fontecha (1964), p. 5.
161 Palma Sola visitor quoted in Vásquez and Fermín (1980), p. 76.
162 Plinio Ventura quoted in Bautista Mejía (1988), p. 30.

has not come in order to cure anyone. He came specifically to purge all evil from this world and they plant his own kingdom on earth. He [...] is purifying everyone, but he who thinks that this is a farce [*mojiganga*] and makes evil things in this holy corral [Palma Sola] will be erased from the holy book in which people are inscribed, because he who talks to me has said to me: 'You may not cast away anyone from here, because I bring them here myself without their knowledge and I will take them away myself, and then I will end it all.'[163]

Together with Olivorio the Virgin was the most venerated deity in Palma Sola. The following was considered to be one of the most popular *salves*:

No hay palo como la Cruz,	There is no trunk like the Cross,
ni luz como la del día.	nor light like that of the day.
No hay hombre como Jesús,	There is no man like Jesus,
ni mujer como María.[164]	nor a woman like Mary.

In *Olivorismo*, as in most other agrarian religions, earthly manifestations of abstract concepts are of utmost importance. One of these was the presence of the Holy Spirit, *El Gran Poder de Dios*, in Palma Sola represented by numerous wooden crosses. Jesus in the guise of Olivorio manifested himself through the words of the Venturas, particularly in Plinio's preaching, while the Virgin was represented by *La Virgen Purísima*, Inés Aquino, or the Virgin of Palma Sola, Inés Rosario Alcántara. The presence of the crosses and different impersonators of religious characters gave a sense of everyday reality to mysterious forces believed to be inherent in Palma Sola. Their presence created a sense of tangible stability in a crumbling, chaotic world.

Both Plinio and the *mellizo* considered the world to be evil and chaotic – a shattered place. In Palma Sola there was much talk about *componiendo el Mundo*:

Aeee componte	Aeee, fix yourself
Aeee componte	Aeee, fix yourself
que componte tá en la tierra	the fixer is on the earth
que no viene a componer.[165]	but he has not come to fix it.

The way to *componer* [fix] the world was to repent and change oneself in order to be able to act in harmony with the powerful, spiritual force believed to be present in Palma Sola. The *salves* stressed the fact that the

163 Ibid, p. 33.
164 Quoted by Patoño Bautista Mejía, in an interview in Distrito de Haina, 5 March 1986.
165 Quoted in Vásquez and Fermín (1980), p.75.

'power' of Palma Sola could not help people if they did not change their own minds first. If the *Palmasolistas* were able to do so they would be 'saved' and life would thus be much easier than before. Palma Sola was a kind of threshold, the entrance to a better world:

Suban los escalones	Walk up the stairs
y después sigan bajando	and then continue to descend
estamos en mundo nuevo	we are in a new world
y nos estamos perdonando.[166]	and we are forgiving ourselves.

It was commonly believed that in Palma Sola *El Gran Poder de Dios* mani-fested itself in a direct way. This peculiar force could be felt by everyone who opened up their hearts to the 'spiritual' sensation. Palma Sola was a place were 'actions spoke louder than words' in the sense that the message did not have to be transmitted through any priest or written text. To partic-ipate in the communal rituals was considered to be the same thing as 'reading the Bible':

Las hojas del libro nuevo	The pages of the new book,
quien es que las va a leer	he who is going read them,
es el mismo Jesucristo	is Jesus Christ himself
que nos viene a componer.[167]	who is coming to fix us up.

The religion which was acted out and preached in Palma Sola was founded on a message said to be delivered by the poor to the poor, the 'forgotten ones', i.e. uneducated peasants who knew what real truth was: the very same people who had shown faith in the murdered and despised Olivorio:

Dios es un hombre justo	God is a just man
hombre justo y verdadero	a just and real man
pero lo tenían botado	but they had him thrown away
como yagua en basurero.[168]	like *yagua* on the rubbish-heap.

The leaders of Palma Sola repeatedly pointed out that they and their followers all were poor and simple people, just like Olivorio had been when he walked upon the earth:

---

166 Quoted in Martínez (1991), p. 172.

167 Ibid.

168 Ibid., p. 168. That 'God' in this *salve* is identical with Olivorio is evident to any *Olivorista* since in all *Olivorista* lore the dead body of *El Maestro* is carried down from the mountains *envuelto* [wrapped] *en yaguas, yaguas* which were later found in the cemetery close to the empty grave of Olivorio. (This is of course very similar to the story of how Jesus' garments were found after the resurrection.)

Como me ven caminando	Like you see me walking through the
por el mundo	world
como los hombres vestido de	like the humans, dressed as a peasant,
paisano	
pero le voy a hacer ver a la gente	but I will make the people see
que Dios es grande, divino y	that God is great, divine and human.
humano.[169]	

The chosen ones are the poor ones, the gift of Christ is to the humble ones, those who need a piece of bread, a shirt, a pair of shoes [...] the rich ones only believe in their money: they do not care if a poor fellow dies of hunger ... or dies from exhaustion.[170]

It was probably his self-reliance and steadfast conviction that he represented the poor people of the Dominican countryside which convinced Plinio Ventura that he, a man wearing *soletas* [rough peasant sandals], could win the presidency of the Republic.[171] Still, it was not personal initiatives which were stressed in Palma Sola. It was the union between all people and work done in community:

Trabajemos la unidad	Let us work for the unity
trabajemos la unión	let us work for the union
que Dios tiene para todos	that God has for everyone
pero no para el porfión.[172]	except for the wrangler.

Most *Olivoristas* consider themselves to be practical people. They do not need any Bible or priest to tell them the truth.[173] They find *El Gran Poder de Dios* around and in themselves. They feel its presence in the nature. According to them, 'true' Christianity is as practical as they themselves, it has to be experienced and acted out, not read and studied: 'The science of Christ is neither with the men who have read so much, nor with the ministers of the Church, but in the depth of the mountains. In the depth of the mountains is the secret of Christ, the truths.'[174]

---

169 Quoted in Martínez (1991), p.169.
170 León Romilio Ventura quoted in ibid., p. 217.
171 Interview with Mimicito Ramírez, San Juan de la la Maguana, 14 December 1985.
172 Quoted in Martínez (1991), p. 171.
173 Besides, in the Catholic church the reading of the Bible by laymen has often been discouraged.
174 León Romilio Ventura, quoted in Martínez (1991), p. 191. León Romilio on various occasions told us that God can be found in the caves of the Cordillera Central and he also stated that he is able to visit these places both 'with the body and in the spirit' (interview with León Romilio Ventura, Media Luna, 17 January 1986).

The violent message: sectarians and outsiders

The hostility of 'outsiders' probably stressed the already strong feeling of unity which reigned within Palma Sola. Many *Palmasolistas* considered themselves to be 'the chosen ones'. They believed they were going to be saved from the different calamities which were expected to strike the entire world, that final disaster in which their adversaries would finally perish:

En Las Matas nos tienen odio	In Las Matas they hate us
y en San Juan también.	and in San Juan as well.
Cuando venga papá Liborio,	When father Liborio comes,
ellos van a ver.[175]	they will see.

La mata [sic] *sirve para leña*	Las Matas serves as firewood
san juan [sic] *para fogón*	San Juan as hearth.
baní [sic] *sirve para ceniza*	Baní serves as ashes,
la capital para carbón.[176]	The capital as charcoal.

Están mirando que tiembla la tierra	They are watching the earth tremble,
están mirando que estamos en peligro	They are seeing that we are in danger,
están mirando que dice el eterno	They are perceiving that what the Eternal says
que dice Liborio es lo mismo	and what Liborio says is the same:

No se apuren mis ovejas	Do not worry, my sheep,
porque la gente esté hablando	because people are talking
y se llegará el momento	and the moment will come
que los cogerán temblando.[177]	that will catch them trembling.

Already from the start Olivorio Mateo's teachings had been endowed with an apocalyptic tremor and *El Maestro* occasionally threatened his adversaries that various scourges would afflict them all if they did not repent and decide to follow him. It appears as if this particular *Olivorista* creed was an essential part of the teachings of Palma Sola as well: 'the pilgrims continue to march praising Liborio, carrying white and blue flags. Sometimes their songs carry with them threats concerning an

---

175 *Salve* quoted in Gómez Pepín (1962b).
176 *Salve* quoted in García (1986), p. 190.
177 *Salve* quoted in ibid. p. 191.

unpredictable future.'[178] The more threatened the *Palmasolistas* felt, the more violent and agitated was the message carried by their *salves*.

After the massacre, the violent content of some *salves* was used as evidence against surviving *Palmasolistas*, and the authorities presented them to the press as vivid proofs of the 'violent and revolutionary' character of the cult. It remains an open question whether this 'violent' message ever represented a central part of the *Olivorista* creed. León Romilio vehemently denies all accusations that the preaching in Palma Sola was violent or aggressive in any way. He states that all commonly known facts prove him right, particularly stressing that all arms had to be left outside the compound, that no visitors were denied access, and that the 'guardsmen' of Palma Sola only were allowed to carry a truncheon.[179]

People who opposed Palma Sola mention recurrent clashes between *Palmasolistas* and 'outsiders', but, with the exception of the chaotic happenings that took place in Las Matas de Farfán eight days before the massacre,[180] such quarrels were limited to verbal abuse and the occasional throwing of dirt or gravel.[181] However, several 'outsiders' felt threatened when they encountered huge crowds of people within Palma Sola and were confronted with what they interpreted as their fanaticism: 'The environment instilled fear; there is no doubt about it.'[182]

The hidden transcript of *Olivorismo*

Most religious movements reflect the view of their adherents of the world that they live in. Naturally, this is also the case with *Olivorismo*. The analysis of the myths and *salves* carried out in the present chapter should have made that clear. Much of the *Olivorista* message – and in particular the part that may be considered as the hidden transcript – deals with the place of the faithful in this world and their hopes for a change in this respect. Pulling some of the strands of the preceding sections together[183] allows us some insight into the core socioeconomic and political ideas of the movement – ideas which should be contrasted with the views of the outsiders and which, when inserted into the specific historic context, in Chapters 7 and 8, contribute to our understanding both of why *Olivorismo* was successful and of why it was put down violently on two occasions.

The *Olivoristas* regard themselves as a chosen people whom the outsiders have done wrong, as they did to Olivorio himself. In their public transcript

178 Gómez Pepín (1962b).
179 Interview with León Romilio Ventura, Media Luna, 5 May 1986.
180 Paulino (1962b), p. 2.
181 Interview with Zita Závala, Paraje El Ranchito, 10 April 1986.
182 Radhamés Gómez Pepín, interviewed by *Rahintel*, 25 August 1990.
183 In this we will also make use of the material presented in Chapters 2 and 4.

they are careful to point out that Olivorio never did harm to anybody, but was careful to maintain good relations with the outsiders, and all those who wanted could join the movement. Tolerance was a central part of his message. Thus, strong emphasis is put on the absence of any desire for insubordination – natually enough, since public manifestations of such a desire would have provoked a strong public response from the dominant outsiders.[184] This expressed intention, however, appears to be a genuinely felt desire, as confirmed by the events related in Chapters 2–4. At the very least, the *Olivoristas*, in the interest of survival, safety and possibly also success, have carefully avoided open confrontation and disguised their resistance to the powers that be.

Still, the outsiders did Olivorio harm and eventually killed him. With the death of Olivorio, the world in which the faithful lived was transformed into an evil and chaotic place which needed to be changed, and change was to be achieved through the Palma Sola movement. The world must be put together again, but for this to be possible, people's minds must be changed. '[P]eace, equality, harmony, unity', summarizes Lusitania Martínez the ideology of the *Palmasolistas*.[185] Just as Olivorio had done, the *Mellizos* and their followers withdrew from public scrutiny. Palma Sola was the place where the transformation would take place, the place of entrance to a better world for the repentant ones. This, however, required not only words but deeds. Mere words do not indicate repentance. Action was necessary, and this action took place in the secluded place of worship. Unfortunately, however, as James Scott has pointed out, unauthorized gatherings of subordinate people are seen as potentially threatening by the dominant strata in society.[186] Hence, they moved in to wipe out Palma Sola.

The end of Palma Sola did not put an end to *Olivorismo*. The movement survived the massacre and continues to look to the future, as it has done in the past. Olivorio's spirit is already here, for those who care to receive the message and live according to his principles. However, his final victory, i.e. the victory of the *Olivorista* movement, lies in the future. He will come back himself as a warrior to fight the devil (the symbol of the evil forces) and punish the wrongdoers. The bill will be presented to his foes. Salvation is mainly for 'those who work', i.e. for his own people, and those who oppose Olivorio will sooner or later pay for this. Not even Trujillo, who controlled everything in the Dominican Republic, and who persecuted the *Olivoristas* relentlessly, could escape the consequences of his acts, but in the end had to settle the bill for them with his life. The outsiders hate the *Olivoristas* and treat them accordingly, but upon Olivorio's return, the tables will be

184 Cf. Scott (1990), pp. 55–8.
185 Martínez (1991), p, 221.
186 Scott (1990), pp. 58–66.

turned and their places will be wiped out. Until then, the faithful will simply have to wait, but when their moment arrives, they will take their revenge.

Olivorio represents the poor people. His message to the world was delivered through them and it is the poor who are the chosen ones. The rich do not care about what happens to them. The poor have to fend for themselves and work together. Herein lies their strength. Olivorio stressed communal work and equal distribution of the fruits of the common efforts. In their struggle to save the world from evil, the *Palmasolistas* worked together for the common good and shared their material goods, not least their daily bread, on land that the Ventura family had put at the disposal of everybody. Working and sharing together is what men should do. They should eat and stay together. Their reward will eventually arrive: 'In the Millennium there will be no more maledictions, attacks, drug addiction or diseases. All the existing riches will be finished. But our riches will never end because from them will sprout the mines of the hills of the plain land, and wherever there is a treasure, it will be for everybody.'[187] This is the central economic message of *Olivorismo*.

Communal distribution of goods reigned supreme both in Olivorio's various communities (e.g. La Maguana, El Palmar and El Naranjo) and in Palma Sola.[188] Neither Olivorio nor the *Mellizos* ever charged for their services. Instead, they showed compassion with the poor. To strive for individual riches and wealth does no good:

Yo no quiero nada si Dios no me dá	I don't want anything if God does not give it to me
yo sólo quiero lo que Dios me dé	I only want what God gives me
¡ay!, Dios mío no quiero lo ajeno	Oh, my God, I don't want what belongs to others
porque me acusan de mala fe.[189]	Because they accuse me of bad faith.

In fact, it is altogether wrong and success in this respect can be obtained only by entering into pacts with the evil forces, and only by paying a price which is far too high. Pedro Heyaime became successful only by sacrificing the most cherished item in *macho* society.[190] In the end, however, it is

---

187 León Romilio Ventura, quoted by Martínez (1991), p. 216.

188 As we found in Chapter 2, it is sometimes argued that Olivorio was in favor of a just distribution of land and that he intended a redistribution. Whether this was actually the case, however, is impossible to tell. In any case, it appears clear that many *Olivoristas* are in favor of the idea.

189 Martínez (1991), p. 169.

190 The Heyaime story constitutes a good example of the use of rumor as a technique for voicing criticism behind the shield of anonymity. Cf. Scott (1990), pp. 144–8.

the poor – the *Olivoristas* – that will be saved and reign, and in his realm riches will not be sought, nor will goods be sold dearly.[191] The hidden transcript of *Olivorismo* provides a good example of what Scott means when he states that 'Most traditional utopian beliefs can, in fact, be understood as a more or less systematic negation of an existing pattern of exploitation and status degradation as it is experienced by subordinate groups.'[192] Dominance, and its ideology, produces its own negation in the form of hidden transcripts.

To conclude, the hidden *Olivorista* transcript, as expressed in lore and *salves*, is a simple, egalitarian one, a 'classical' message conceived by poor people living in a world which they consider unjust and brutal. The *Olivoristas* are peaceful people who simply do their best to help each other and who work for a common good, based on Olivorio's teachings. They want to live in peace and mutual respect with others. Against this, they set the behavior of the evil outside world which has never accepted them, or even listened to their message, but has always persecuted and killed them, as it did with Olivorio. In the end, however, Olivorio will return to settle the bill with his opponents and only the faithful will then be saved.

Conclusions

The *salves* sung in Olivorio's honor and the legends told about him form an integrated part of the environment, or habitat, where *Olivoristas* live and act. *Olivorista* lore is not frozen in time; it changes from place to place, reacts to different surroundings and adapts itself to the needs of performers, listeners and participants in rituals. This adaptability and flexibility proves that *Olivorismo* is a living religion and as such it is extremely meaningful to all of its adherents, constituting a practical creed which reflects their thoughts and aspirations.

While we have tried to trace some of the feasible sources to parts of the intricate conglomerate which constitutes the *Olivorista* lore, the intention has not been to determine whether *Olivorismo* is a typical example of an 'Afro-American religion', or whether it shows closer affinities to traditional European peasant beliefs. The 'code', or *langue*, forming the basis for *Olivorismo* is vast and difficult to map. However, the message, the functional core, of the *Olivorismo* is steeped in local conditions and only makes sense if studied in relation to them. As it seems, it can adequately be described as a *bricolage* in the Lévi-Straussian sense of the word. *Olivoristas* have picked up the useful 'bits and pieces' which were already existent in their immediate environment. They have rearranged them into new patterns

---

191 Cf. Martínez (1991), pp. 218–19.
192 Scott (1990), p. 81.

and thus created a partly hidden transcript which makes sense to them and helps them to perceive their world and situation in a meaningful way.

Like his followers, Olivorio lived in an animated world, where what we often perceive as 'the reality' is just a tiny fraction of a vast universe, which is only partly known and perceived. Every *Olivorista* uses his particular creed as a 'code' to understand the universe. It is an essential part of their 'language' in the sense that it is a system which is used to express thoughts, feelings, etc. – a means of communication – and since it is adapted to their needs and immediate environment, it may appear to be strange if perceived by 'outsiders' whose way of thinking has been molded by other sets of codes, other 'languages'.

In the following chapters we will see how the hidden *Olivorista* transcript was forced into the open by a series of powerful historical events, how it then had to confront the views of the dominant forces in the San Juan Valley and how this on two occasions led to disaster. Before the time comes to do so, however, we must arrive at an understanding of why *Olivorismo* was attractive to so many people on these two occasions. For this, two more building blocks are needed. First, we will make an attempt to account for the creation of the *Olivorista* religion, by tracing its roots in popular Dominican religion in general, and, second, we will embark on a sketch of the economic history of the San Juan Valley, its remarkable constancy during several centuries and the drastic changes it underwent around the time that Olivorio made his appearance. Together with the *Olivorista* message, these two blocks will provide an understanding both of the appeal of the movement to its followers and of the reasons why it was twice quenched in blood. Part III thus analyzes on the one hand the causes behind the rise and success of the *Olivorista* movement and on the other hand the reasons why it was perceived as such a serious threat by the outsiders that extraordinary measures had to be resorted to in order to stem its spread.

Appendix: Jonestown and Palma Sola

Tensions between cultists and 'outsiders' are common in many places of the world, and when, as in Palma Sola, the message preached by the believers has a certain apocalyptic tinge to it, the probability is high that the notion of a final struggle between good and evil will gain importance among cultists who feel beleaguered by hostile forces. This is a pattern that has been repeated from Classical times to the present day.

Some years ago, Palma Sola was compared with the so-called People's Temple of Jim Jones, a sectarian group which, in November 1978, gained international notoriety when more than 900 of its members committed mass 'suicide' in a remote area of Guyana. A TV movie which was released a few years after the event[193] induced several Dominican newspapers to compare the two movements, stressing that the majority of the members of both 'cults' were 'poor, black' people, described as being particularly susceptible to spiritual messages from 'fringe cults'. It was also pointed out that the leaders of both movements abused their faithful, isolated them from the surrounding world, terrified them with talk about an imminent end of the world, at the same time that they provoked clashes with political authorities.

Jim Jones is nowadays considered as an almost archetypical, paranoiac sect leader. He settled the hard core of his followers in a remote jungle strip in Guyana, where they built up an 'agricultural project' which was depicted by the omnipotent sect leader as a safe, but threatened, haven from a wicked world. Jim Jones constantly frightened his followers and himself with imaginary threats from 'racists', 'fascists', the CIA, and the American and Guyanese governments: 'The rivers are blocked to the rest of us! [...] The oceans are blocked to the rest of us! But our goddam land – we fought to build it, so we'll fight to die for it.'[194] Crazed by drugs and mental and physical sickness, Jim Jones kept his believers on the alert through recurrent war exercises and mock mass suicides. Most of the inhabitants in the remote Jonestown ended up in a nightmarish world, where they felt enclosed, threatened from all sides and with no escape roads open to them.[195]

When the Dominican press compared the People's Temple with Palma Sola the act may easily be interpreted as just another example of blaming the victims for the violence of the aggressors. In reality the two 'sects' do not have much in common. We have already mentioned that the leadership in Palma Sola was far from being as all-powerful and dictatorial as that of Jim Jones, whose slightest whim or frenzy had immediate and often severe repercussions on all members of the community surrounding him. The people of Palma Sola never submitted to any demanding daily regimen or any imposed, inadequate diet, something which was common in Jonestown and tends to be a widespread practice in several isolated, 'other-worldly' sects.[196] Nor was Palma Sola cut off from the world in the same sense as Jim Jones' Jonestown. On the contrary: until the bitter end every visitor was welcome. Even if the leaders of both movements preached that some kind of commotion was going to occur in a not too distant

193 *Guyana Tragedy: The Story of Jim Jones*, directed by William A. Graham and released by CBS in April 1980. The movie, which is excellent, obtained a great deal of attention all over the world and Powers Booth, the actor who interpreted Jim Jones, won the prestigious Emmy award for his achievement. The same year a poor, commercial movie premiered in Santo Domingo: a Mexican-Spanish-Panamanian co-production called *Guyana: Cult of the Damned*.
194 Jim Jones quoted in Wright (1993), p. 76.
195 See Kilduff and Javers (1978), Naipaul (1980), Hall (1990) and Wright (1993).
196 Hall (1990), p. 278.

future, the teachings of Jim Jones were much more explicit about how the world was going to end – it was going to be destroyed by a 'nuclear holocaust'.[197]

Jonestown had its particular folklore, but it was entirely different from the one which prevailed in Palma Sola and this fact may serve as an illustration of how religious movements, as well as other social entities, respond to and reflect their distinctive environments, their 'habitat'. In the case of Palma Sola it was the *Olivorista* traditions of the San Juan Valley which constituted the foundations of the cult, while the 'ideology' of the People's Temple was an odd mixture of fundamentalist traditions from the 'Bible Belt' and social upheavals the United States experienced in the 1960s and early 1970s.

> [The] Peoples Temple borrowed profusely – in matters of organization, social control, public relations, and politics – from the contemporary culture that surrounded it.[198]

> Jim Jones built his movement on the debris of the sixties; on its frustrations, failures and apostasies.[199]

> Jim Jones was as much a Protestant fundamentalist as he was a 'Marxist'. The traditions, atmosphere and techniques of Protestant Fundamentalism were all present in the People's Temple ...[200]

197 One of the reasons why Guyana was chosen as a center for the cult was Jones' conviction that it was situated in an area which would be one of the safest in the world in the case of a global nuclear war (Naipaul (1980), p. 118–19).
198 Hall (1990), p. 291.
199 Naipaul (1980), p. 200.
200 Ibid., pp. 200–1. From his childhood in Indiana, Jim Jones carried with him religious inclinations which found their breeding ground among Pentecostalists like 'Holy Rollers' and Southern Methodists. In 1956 he established his 'People's Temple', which provided scholarships for impoverished students, nursing homes for the elderly, soup kitchens for the old, job-rehabilitation programs for the unemployed, combined with a message of racial equality, ecstatic faith healing and a demand for unquestioning personal loyalty to an omnipotent leader – Jim Jones. The radicalism of Jones led him to contact the liberal, political establishment. He served for a while as chairman of San Francisco's Housing Authority and nurtured contacts with extremely radical black groups like the Black Panthers. He visited Cuba, his social work was praised by people like Jane Fonda, Rosalynn Carter, Walter Mondale, Angela Davis and several other well-known public figures. His move to Guyana was inspired by his close contacts with its president, Forbes Burnham, who demanded to be called called 'Comrade Leader' and posed as a 'Marxist-Leninist' and promoter of 'Black Power'. When Jones' mental disarray grew worse he sometimes raved through the jungles of Guyana, imagining himself to be 'Lenin fighting off the Trotskyites' (Wright (1993), p. 78).

In short, it is difficult to compare different religious movements without taking into consideration the 'habitat' they evolve in. However, similar patterns of behavior are easily discerned while comparing the *Palmasolistas* with members of the People's Temple, for example how downtrodden, marginalized and alienated people seek the authority of certain traditions and the guidance of charismatic leaders. We also discover the presence of down-to-earth preaching and 'miracles' which seem to prove the paranormal powers of the leaders. The importance of charity was stressed in both movements, as well as the carrying out of communal work. But when we enter into particulars, differences become more apparent than similarities. The People's Temple was a unique blend of the interaction of very particular circumstances found within the American society of the time, just as the Palma Sola movement received its own specific character when it grew out of the fertile ground of anomie and political chaos found in the San Juan Valley by the beginning of the 1960s.[201]

201 If Jones' movement got its particular flavor from American radicalism of the 1960s and 1970s, a recent and equally disastrous and controversial movement, the Branch Davidians of David Koresh (originally Vernon Wayne Howell) also mirrored tensions within American society. Koresh (born in 1959) started out as a Southern Baptist and a Seventh-Day Adventist and finally came to exercise the same lethal and omnipotent authority over his sect members as Jim Jones had done over his flock, but even if Koresh's message also stressed the coming of an Armageddon it was not steeped in political radicalism but appeared to reflect more recent phenomena within American mass culture. Koresh showed a great interest in sex, heavy metal rock music, violent videos and sophisticated weaponry, something which apparently was central to his preaching and the way of life he created within his secluded community of Mount Carmel (or Ranch Apocalypse) in Waco, Texas. The place was burned to the ground during an attack by the FBI in 1993 and more than seventy people perished in the flames (see Breault and King (1993) and Wright (1995)).

Part III

The causes

6 Popular religion in the Dominican Republic and its influence on *Olivorismo*

The *Olivoristas* were persecuted by authorities and other outsiders in the name of progress and nationalism. Their religion was branded as an anomaly in times of science and enlightenment and was depicted as a superstitious mishmash conjuring up 'primitive' beliefs based on 'animism' and witchcraft. Since the *Olivorista* creed developed in districts close to the Haitian border it was commonly assumed that 'singularities' found in the *Olivorista* cult were the result of influences from neighboring Haiti, which in Dominican political discourse was depicted as a hotbed of black magic and voodoo 'depravities'. Dominicans were told to be on the lookout for harmful superstitions which could sneak across the border and infect the minds of uneducated peasants living in small isolated villages in the backwaters of the southwestern part of the Republic.

While commenting on *Sanjuanero* popular religiosity, the former bishop of San Juan de la Maguana, Thomas Reilly, emphasized the Haitian presence in his parishes:

> Much of the superstition found here in the valley is of Haitian origin. After the massacres in 1937 many Haitians who still lived here changed their names. Many pockets of superstition that exist in the countryside often coincide with settlements of families of Haitian extraction. As an example of the persistence of Haitian customs one may take all the women one finds tending the fields here in the valley. That is a Haitian custom. Dominican women do not like to work in the fields.[1]

Reilly's view is probably in line with reality, but such an opinion can easily create a situation in which the researcher is induced to be on the outlook for traces of Haitian voodoo in almost every manifestation of *Sanjuanero*

---

1 Interview with Thomas Reilly, San Juan de la Maguana, 12 December 1985.

popular religion.[2] An example is given in the article by Ana Maritza de la Mota, 'Palma Sola: 1962', where she argues that the Palma Sola movement was 'a manifestation of voodoo in the Dominican Republic'.[3] Lusitania Martínez, who carried out field work together with de la Mota, later criticized her colleague stating that it was quite inappropriate to label the Palma Sola movement a pure voodoo cult:

> Strictly speaking vodú does not exist here [in the Dominican Republic]. Vodú is the syncretism between the African cults and the Catholic religion of Haiti. Our popular animism displays traces from African religion, either brought directly from Africa, or acculturated from Haiti, *but this process has taken place on our own cultural platform.* Because of this we believe that there are many differences between Afro-Haitian syncretism and the syncretism with African cults (from Africa or Haiti) which has taken place in our own country.[4]

Lusitania Martínez is of the opinion that religious beliefs in the San Juan Valley should be studied in relation to their unique cultural and economic context. That will make it possible to verify how popular Catholicism and African beliefs have 'adopted themselves to the particular environment in the valley through a process of acculturation'.[5] Such processes are common in several Latin American countries, where the rural population traditionally consider themselves to be fervent Catholics, even if they adhere to a religion that is adapted to their own special needs and therefore tends to differ from what is commonly understood as Catholicism. A description of popular religion among Colombian peasants might be used to describe rural religion in the Dominican Republic as well:

> There developed an integrated complex of Spanish Catholics and African usage, believed by the people themselves to be completely Catholic and therefore particularly immune to the efforts of priests who desire to banish the 'pagan' elements. This complex is a fundamental, functional aspect of their total way of life, and the adjustment

2 We use the term 'popular religion' for want of a better denomination for the regional peasant religiosity found in the Dominican Republic. While doing so, we are well aware that 'popular religion', like so many other terms describing religious phenomena, has proved to be an arbitrary term. 'Dario Rei, in an incisive article has pointed out that *popular* for some scholars has come to connote *rural* as opposed to *urban, primitive* as opposed to *civilized, traditional* as opposed to *modern*, and *proletarian* as opposed to *capitalist* (not to mention *better* as opposed to *worse*, or the reverse)' (Christian (1981), p. 178, referring to Rei (1974)).

3 Mota (1980), p. 218.

4 Martínez (1980), p. 177. Italics in the original.

5 Interview with Lusitania Martínez, Santo Domingo, 5 August 1985.

they have made to their spiritual and practical needs is an adjustment unshakable by Catholic and Protestant missionaries alike.[6]

Olivorista beliefs are firmly rooted in the district of San Juan.[7] What Olivorio did was to offer a personal interpretation of beliefs and traditions that had been present in the Dominican countryside for hundreds of years. Accordingly, *Olivorismo* should not be seen as an 'anomaly'. It is more correct to consider it as a regional variant of Dominican popular religion.

This is an important conclusion because it provides us with a clue as to why the *Olivorista* message was so eagerly received by the peasants. The message built on traditions that were well established on the local scene – traditions that had evolved gradually over time. *Olivorismo* represented continuity, not a break with the past or something alien to the local environment. Thus, it may be argued that Olivorio's followers were favorably predisposed to his preachings as he made his appearance. They could easily relate to what he had to say and make his message an integral part of their own *Weltanschauung*. The seeds of Olivorio's teachings fell on good ground and not stony places, simply because the ground was well prepared.

In this chapter we will trace Dominican religiosity through the centuries and by so doing indicate a number of possible influences on *Olivorismo*. We are conscious of the fact that any effort to analyze syncretistic beliefs is a highly speculative and troublesome activity. What we intend to achieve is not an exhaustive analysis, but a sketch suggesting that *Sanjuanero* popular religion in general and *Olivorismo* in particular is not a simple blend of voodoo and universal superstitions, but a sophisticated hybrid compiled from a vast and intricate spectrum of religious traditions, answering to the needs of people living within a particular environment.

The Indian presence in Dominican popular religion

Taino religiosity and some of its modern equivalents

After his first encounter with the Taino inhabitants of Hispaniola Christopher Columbus wrote: 'I think that they could easily be turned into Christians ... since it appeared to me that they did not have any sect.'[8] However,

---

6 Price (1955), p. 7.
7 The *Olivorista* faith tends to become weaker among former *Olivoristas* who migrate to the capital, where they often attend Catholic mass on a more regular basis than before, or are attracted by the Protestant sects that flourish in Santo Domingo (interview with Jorge Feliz, Santo Domingo, 5 January 1986).
8 Colón (1988), p. 110. Columbus' original diaries are lost, and what has been passed down to us are copies made by Bartolomé de las Casas (1484–1566), discovered in Madrid and originally published 1825, 1829 and 1837.

he soon learned that the Tainos had a religion of their own, particularly after he had taken part of a report submitted to him by a certain Fray Ramón Pané, a monk who on Columbus' orders had learned the language of the Tainos and lived with them for more than two years.[9] Pané's interesting, but somewhat muddled,[10] report describes a Taino pantheon of 'spirits' called *cemíes*, immortal entities which were said to be invisible, even if some of them were represented by idols placed in particular huts. Some were said to live in the sky, while others were connected with particularly holy places. Certain *cemíes* were venerated by all Tainos of the island, while others were worshiped only locally. The majority were connected with ancestor worship. Not all *cemíes* were benevolent, a few were described by Pané as 'demonical'.[11] Cult functionaries called *behiques* acted as intermediaries between the Tainos and their *cemíes*. The *behiques* were able to communicate with the deities with the help of *cohoba*, a narcotic snuff mixed with tobacco.[12]

Even if the Tainos were rapidly annihilated,[13] it is possible that a few traces of their religion may have survived within the syncretistic, religious conglomerate of the island of Hispaniola.[14] Among the most valued objects found on the altars that Dominican and Haitian peasants keep in their huts are the so-called *piedras de rayo* [thunder stones],[15] Taino celts, said to have been found where lightning has struck and identified as magical by their ability to pass certain tests. Their owners often declare that the stones are able to 'whistle', to perspire, or even 'talk'. Thunder stones are ordinarily passed on from one generation to another and kept in water or oil.[16] They are believed to promote fertility and are also used to cure indigestion

---

9 Pané (1980), p. 21.

10 'Because I wrote in a hurry, and did not have enough paper, I could not put in its right place what, by mistake, I moved elsewhere. Still, considering all this, I have not failed, because all their beliefs are as I have written down' (ibid., p. 28).

11 Ibid., p. 21 and Columbus, quoted in ibid., p. 89.

12 Pané (1980), pp. 33–40. The snuff, which was inhaled through the nostrils, apparently came from a tree, *Piptadenia* (or *Anadenanthera*) *peregrina*, commonly known in the Dominican Republic as *tamarindo teta* (ibid., pp. 68–9). The Indians living in the Orinoco basin still prepare a hallucinatory snuff called *yopo* from the *Piptadenia* tree (Schultes and Hofmann (1987), pp. 116–19).

13 Modern approximations of the number of Tainos at the arrival of the Spaniards vary considerably. See the literature referred to in Bethell (1984). At any rate, in 1548 Oviedo estimated that only 500 Tainos remained alive on the island (Vicioso (1979), p. 14). Their kin had been vanquished not only by intermarriage, starvation and measles, but also by forced labor and outright extermination.

14 Cf. Vega (1988b) and Deren (1953), pp. 63–70 and 82–4. Deren's assumptions are, however, quite speculative.

15 The literal translation is 'lightning stones', but since the term is commonly used on the English-speaking islands in the Caribbean, we will employ the latter term.

16 Courlander (1960), p. 21 and Deive (1979), p. 285.

and stomach pains.[17] *Salves* sung in Palma Sola mention 'secret *piedrecitas* [pebbles]' descending from heaven inscribed with messages to the *Olivoristas*.[18] White limestones were used in Palma Sola to delimit holy sites and indicate procession roads. Piles of stones also surrounded the crosses venerated by Olivorio and his followers:

> It was a general rule that both visitors [to La Maguana] and followers [of Olivorio] ought to carry a cord and when they came in Olivorio's presence they had to be adorned with stones on their heads. These stones, blessed by Olivorio's hand, were deposited by the calvary.[19]

Thunder stones, as well as other Taino artefacts, could until recently be found in caves that exist all over the mountainous island.[20] Many of these caves have probably served as Taino cult sites, and several still have their walls covered with rock paintings.[21] Various Taino myths were connected with caves, imagined to be endowed with procreative faculties. It was believed that the Tainos themselves, as well as the sun and the moon, had once appeared from caves.[22] Several caves within the mountain massif of Cordillera Central are still worshiped as abodes of life-giving forces. Most famous is the one close to a mountain called La Nalga del Maco. Since it is very spacious it is often referred to as La Catedral. A channel, which may be man-made, runs through the entire cave system and human-shaped stalactites are worshiped as saints. A visit to the huge cave, which is extremely inaccessible, is appreciated as a profound religious experience. Some *Olivoristas* state that one is able to 'encounter God' there. Crosses and chromolithographs depicting various saints are found inside and on

17 Affected parts are touched with the stones. Patients may also drink the liquid in which the *piedras de rayo* have been submerged. Cults of sacred stones are common in many different parts of the world and the concept of stones left by lightning appears in both Europe and Africa. Similarly, the connection between stones and fertility is often encountered, as well as the practice of submerging sacred stones in oil, or water. (A survey of conceptions connected with sacred stones is presented in Eliade (1976), pp. 216–38.) On Taino stone cults, see Pané (1980), pp. 26, 37 and 42–3, and Columbus, quoted in Pané, p. 89.

18 Cf. the *salve* quoted in García (1986), p. 186.

19 Garrido Puello (1963), p. 24. It is not clear whether the *Olivoristas* had the stones attached to the cords around their foreheads, or whether they simply carried them on their heads. The latter is most likely since it is still the custom at several *calvarios* that exist in Maguana Arriba, the present center of the *Olivorista* cult.

20 An increasing demand from tourists has made them rare and expensive, something which is compensated by an ever-expanding manufacturing of fakes.

21 For an interpretation of these rock paintings as indicators of religious beliefs and rituals, see Pagán Perdomo (1982).

22 Pané (1980), pp. 22–31.

certain occasions people go on pilgrimages to the cave in order to carry out nocturnal ceremonies.[23] According to León Romilio Ventura,

> It is like a town beneath the earth. It must be the biggest cave in the world [...] He who has not been to the cave does not know the secrets of the world. There is a spiritual presence. If God is on the earth, he is there. The *misterios* have taken me there several times. We, the sinners, know nothing.[24]

On 28 December of each year, while commemorating the massacre in Palma Sola, a group of *Olivoristas* gather for a ceremony in the cave of Seburuco, situated not far from the dam of Sabaneta, some 25 kilometers north of San Juan de la Maguana. According to local traditions, a subterranean pathway connects the Seburuco cave with another cave, the famous cave of San Francisco, situated outside Bánica, hundreds of kilometers from Seburuco.[25] Like other sacred caves in the Dominican Republic the cave of San Francisco houses altars, crosses and other religious paraphernalia. It is taken care of by a religious brotherhood, which carries out a feast in honor of its patron saint from the first to the fourth of October. The brotherhood of San Francisco has recently been allowed to keep its ceremonial drums close to the altar in the church of Bánica, and during the feast of San Francisco they play the drums inside the church. However, they are not allowed to dance there: 'They drink a lot of rum and their dances are rather tumultuous. They dance in circles with handkerchiefs in their hands. It happens that the women fall to the ground, shaking in violent convulsions.'[26]

Worship in caves is not exclusive to the *Olivoristas* but common to several other Dominican cults as well. Among the most famous is La Iglesia de Mana [the Church of Mana] a syncretistic cult founded by a Bibiana de la Rosa, a charismatic woman active at the same time as Olivorio. This cult evolves around a system of caves outside the town of Baní.[27]

23 Interview with Bryan Kennedy, Las Matas de Farfán, 4 May 1986.
24 Interview with León Romilio Ventura, Media Luna, 5 May 1986.
25 Interview with Leopoldo Figuereo, San Juan de la Maguana, 4 June 1989.
26 Interview with Lilian Corriveau, Bánica, 12 April 1986. Corriveau (who, together with two other 'school sisters' from the Order of Notre Dame, was in charge of Catholic instruction in Bánica) mentioned that the cult of Indians is very common along several streams in the district.
27 Cf. Tejeda Ortiz (1978). Even if the Church of Mana developed independently from *Olivorismo*, the two cults present several affinities, not least in the legend which has evolved around their founders. Olivorio and Bibiana are often accredited with similar, sometimes identical, healing miracles and prophecies.

Since our early childhood we have, on several occasions, listened to how adults have assured us that in them [the caves] live Indians who have hidden themselves there, fleeing from the persecution of Spanish conquerors. In order to prove this assumed presence of natives they [the elders] assured us that if some leftovers were thrown or small twigs were spread on the floor somewhere in these subterranean cavities, on the following day, the place would be found completely clean and with signs of being swept.[28]

In Dominican voodoo[29] the Indians have a division of their own. Voodoo is a possession religion, which means that humans during nocturnal ceremonies are believed to be possessed by certain deities, who at that particular moment control the behavior and actions of their *caballos* [horses, i.e. possessed persons].[30] The voodoo pantheon is divided into twenty-one divisions,[31] each headed by a specific deity. Each division belongs to one of the four elements and the behavior of each of the *misterios* is predisposed by its identification with air, earth, fire or water. Matters are further complicated by the fact that any *misterio* may manifest itself within a hierarchical pattern of several dimensions, called *puntos*.[32]

Leader of the Indian division is Tinyó, who on voodoo sessions introduces himself with the following words: 'I am Indian under the water, I am Tinyó', or most commonly, Gamao, also called *Le Gran Solei* [the Big Sun], who on voodoo altars is represented by a chromolithograph depicting

28 Colombino Perelló (1972), quoted in ibid., p. 79. No page given.
29 The use of the term 'voodoo' while describing a common special branch of Dominican religiosity has traditionally been very controversial, not least since the practice of voodoo is still, in theory, outlawed in the Dominican Republic. Recent books, initiated by a pioneering work by Patín Veloz (1975), have firmly established that voodoo is not only thriving in the Dominican Republic, but also presents several characteristics of its own. Enrique Patín Veloz had already in 1946 published a series of five articles on Dominican voodoo in the newspaper *La Nación* (Patín Veloz (1946)), but it was not until the 1970s that Dominican voodoo became the subject of serious investigation and Patín Veloz' work received proper attention. Carlos Esteban Deive published an extensive and well-researched volume on Dominican voodoo in 1979 (Deive (1979)). Other recent studies are Jiménez Lambertus (1980), Lizardo (1982), Miniño (1980) (1985), and Davis (1987).
30 'The essential factor in possession is the belief that a person has been invaded by a super-natural being and is thus temporarily beyond self-control, his ego being subordinated to that of the intruder' (Lewis (1975), p. 65).
31 Even if most voodoo practitioners are able to list twenty-one divisions, their names tend to vary from cult group to cult group. No group carries out ceremonies to all divisions and some divisions appear to be purely theoretical (cf. Deive (1979), pp. 178–81).
32 Eight *puntos* are usually listed; astral, sidereal, spiritual, radá (which also constitutes a division), Indian (also a division), Petró (also a division), material and abyssal (Davis (1987), p. 141).

St Nicholas of Bari.[33] Voodoo practicioners often reserve a separate place for their Indian *misterios*, mostly a corner on the floor where chromolithographs depicting Indians are placed on a small pile of stones. The Indians may also be represented by small earthenware and clay figures. Some voodooists dig a hole in the ground and line it with cement, painted blue and green. A number of objects are then placed in the basin which is filled with water: stones, shiny objects, bottle caps, fake pearls and coins, shells and bottles of soft drinks, the favorite drink of all Indian queens.[34]

The Indians 'manifest themselves through water', a clear and 'purifying' element.[35] People possessed by Indians move with a certain grace and do not talk in vain. The Indians are believed to be dignified and fair. They are 'innocent', never harmful, and do not approve of 'black magic'.[36] They are believed to be naked, or at least half-naked, adorned with feathers and jewelry. Noble and gracious, but sad and reclusive, they are the invisible keepers of hidden treasures and reward their devotees with wealth in the form of gold and diamonds or by granting them sexual prowess and fertility.[37]

Being *india* is a flattering epithet given to Dominican beauties with soft, brown skin and long, straight and raven-black hair. The notion of gracious Indian ladies living in springs and rivers has its equivalent in European folklore, which connects nymphs and other lovely maidens with water.[38] It

33 The French denomination of this deity may indicate Haitian influences. However, we have been unable to trace him to the Haitian voodoo pantheon. The identification of Gamao with the sun is probably due to the fact that Indians are considered to provide long life and fertility. St Nicholas of Bari is identical with St Nicholas of Myra (Santa Claus). The confusion is due to the fact that Italian merchants stole his reputed relics in Myra (present-day Turkey) and brought them to Bari, in Italy. On the chromolithographs, St Nicholas is depicted a dark-brown man dressed in priestly garb, studded with pearls and diamonds. He is associated with the Indians because they are believed to be chocolate brown and to be the keepers of the earth's treasures, such as gold and diamonds. Other chromolithographs showing dark-skinned Madonnas in pearl-studded 'Byzantine' garb are accordingly believed to depict Indian queens, like Anacaona and Hacuaí Dantó. One reason for the identification of Indians with these 'Byzantine' Madonnas, like *Mater Salvatoris*, may be that they are all depicted with large halos resembling the sun, a sign applicable to all Indians.
34 The description is based on several visits to *brujas* in and around Santo Domingo.
35 Davis (1987), p. 143.
36 Ibid., p. 138. Nevertheless, some people fear the Indians and assure that they are 'aggressive, ferocious, robust and have beautiful faces' (anonymous peasant, quoted in Lemus and Marty (1975), p. 184).
37 Cf. Lizardo (1982), p. 16, Miniño (1980) and Deive (1979), p. 179.
38 Emmanuel Le Roy Ladurie writes about the 'quasi-religious concepts of fertility-fecundity' connected with the 'immense popularity of the Melusine theme' (Le Roy Ladurie (1979), p. 101). Melusine was a creature with the body of a woman and the tail of a serpent, believed to inhabit wells and springs. She was considered to guarantee the fruitfulness of the harvests and the prosperity of the house (in the sense of both lineage and building), in her personality mixing the agriculturalist's interests of agriculture and the

is possible that the Dominican concept of Indian queens is reminiscent of Spanish legends related to *xanas*, water nymphs who, like their Dominican counterparts, offer riches to people who please them. *Xanas* are connected with fertility rituals which evolve around the summer solstice.[39] African slaves may also have contributed to Dominican notions connected with the Indians. Fon- and Ewe-speaking people in Dahomey have traditions relating to the *toxosu* [kings of the water], who were originally children born with defects or anomalies. Such children were believed to belong to the water and were thus sacrificed by drowning in lakes or rivers. *Toxosu* were visualized as powerful deities who dwelled under the water. Fierce and bellicose, they were able to bring their worshipers victory in armed battle.[40]

The cult of the Indians in the San Juan Valley

It is in their capacity as water deities and guardians of fertility that Indians are still important in the San Juan Valley, and their presence is acknowledged in several places: 'The Indians were just and discreet. When the Spaniards came and conquered the country, they withdrew to the waters and people say they still live in certain wells and springs.'[41]

Bryan Kennedy, a Redemptorist pastor in Las Matas de Farfán, who worked in close cooperation with the peasants, stated that the cult of the Indians is of great importance for many agriculturists in the area:

> We wanted to dig a well close to a spring, but people tried to stop us, saying that we could not do it because the Indians who lived there would be offended. We dug the well anyway and covered the spring, but the man who owned the premises got sick and people later blamed us, saying we had caused the anger of the Indians.[42]

Alleged Indian dwellings abound in the *Olivorista* heartland and offerings to Indians, commonly called 'owners of the land', are placed in caves or thrown into streams. The Indian food consists of rice, bread, cinnamon

family, with sexual desire and obsessions (cf. ibid., pp 203–20, and Le Goff (1980), pp. 205–22). European folklore abounds with similar ladies, like the Lady of the Lake of the Arthurian legends, the *Rusalki* of Slavonic countries and the Rhinemaidens in Germany. Scandinavian countries have traditions related to the *sjörå* [Ruler of the Lake] or *sjöfru* [Lady of the Lake], a beautiful lady who gives fishermen good luck and was apt to cajole men into sexual intercourse (Klintberg (1987), pp. 22, 92–9 and 296–9). She is also able to bestow magical powers on people (Klintberg (1980), p. 32).

39 Espinosa (1950), p. 1068.
40 Herskovits and Herskovits (1933), pp. 30–1.
41 Interview with Zita Závala, Paraje El Ranchito, 10 April 1986.
42 Interview with Bryan Kennedy, Las Matas de Farfán, 4 May 1986.

and honey. During ceremonies devotees are often possessed by Indian spirits and throw themselves into the water.[43]

The cult of Indians has always formed an important part of *Olivorista* religiosity. León Romilio Ventura presides over sacrifices to the Indians by the stream of Yacahueque, just behind his home in Media Luna.[44] On annual celebrations commemorating the massacre in Palma Sola, he leads a ceremony by the watercourse and invokes the sun in hymns and prayers.[45] The sun is probably invoked in its guise as Gamao, or St Nicholas the Sun, Indian owner of all land in the valley and harbinger of hope and prosperity.

The San Juan Valley is the entire island's center for Indian worship. It appears as if there are several historical reasons behind its elevated status. Bartolomé de las Casas tells that the island of Hispaniola was divided into five Taino 'kingdoms'. Of these, La Maguana was the biggest, and most influential, 'a country, very temperate and fertile'. When Columbus arrived, La Maguana was governed by Caonabo, the most powerful *cacique* [chieftain] of the entire island, 'who for power, dignity, gravity, and the ceremonies which were used towards him, far exceeded the rest'.[46]

A plausible center of the *cacicazgo* of La Maguana, situated a few kilometers north of San Juan de la Maguana, is El Corral de los Indios [the Indian Enclosure], the largest structure left by Indians in the Caribbean:

> The huge circular ring of stones at San Juan de la Maguana [...] is 2270 feet in circumference and made up of heavy granite boulders, in whose center is found a large block [...] on which a human face is carved [...] A road, paved with stone and ending at a brook, leads to this sanctuary. It is likely that the village itself was located here by this brook ...[47]

Few *Sanjuaneros* fail to mention this monument to the occasional tourist and most of them proudly state that El Corral de los Indios was once located at the center of the town of Anacaona, the wife of Caonabo. The legends surrounding the gallant warrior Caonabo, who fought the Spaniards and died as a prisoner on a ship bound for Spain, and the likewise tragic fate of his wife, Anacaona, who was hanged by the treacherous invaders, are known to every schoolchild in San Juan de la Maguana.

43 Interview with Zita Závala, Paraje El Ranchito, 10 April 1986.
44 Espín del Prado (1984), p. 695.
45 *Rahintel* (1990), 'Somos así y así somos: Programa No. 48', 13 October.
46 Las Casas (1972), p. 9. Our knowledge of the political structure of the Taino society is limited. *Caciques* were political and religious leaders of *cacicazgos*, 'federations' consisting of smaller political units, governed by less powerful chieftains (see Cassá (1974), pp. 120–34 and Lovén (1935), pp. 503–19).
47 Lovén (1935), pp. 86–7.

Olivoristas tend to relate the fate of Olivorio with that of Caonabo. The alleged birthplace of Olivorio is called La Maguana, just like the 'kingdom' of Caonabo, and like the Indian chieftain *El Maestro* was delivered to his enemies through a treacherous act by one of his followers. The spirits of both Olivorio and Caonabo are believed to have an invisible presence in the valley.

Several *Olivoristas* associate the Indian queen, Anacaona, with La Virgen de la Altagracia, patron saint of the Dominican Republic and Olivorio's special protectress. On her day, 21 January, people connected with Olivorio's sanctuary in La Maguana gather and carry out ceremonies around the large central stone of El Corral de los Indios. The megalith, the throne of Anacaona, is crowned with a garland of flowers by the *reina* [queen] of Olivorio's *ermita*.[48]

La Agüita: fertility and syncretism

The Indians are also worshiped in La Agüita, also known as the Spring of St John or La Fuente del Naranjal [the Spring of the Orange Grove].[49] From the *ermita*, which has been erected at Olivorio's birthplace in Maguana Arriba, a narrow path leads to a lush grove where St John's spring gushes forth. A spray of water emerges from a mound of stones, runs through a chute made of corrugated sheet metal and falls into a shallow pond. The water is considered to have healing powers and people come from all over the Dominican Republic to submerge themselves in the pool formed under the jet of water. It is sometimes called the Spring of Olivorio, but it is St John the Baptist who is the 'master' of the spring. He is believed to be the ruler of various Indian spirits said to dwell in the water of La Agüita. The spring has been the object of intense worship long before the birth of Olivorio and the popular appeal of Olivorio's message was probably supported by the fact that *El Maestro* was born in a dwelling close to the powerful Spring of St John.

Every day the spring is visited by a steady stream of pilgrims. This reached its peak in 1962 when the *Mellizos* of Palma Sola used to send people to La Agüita[50] and the multitude of bathers frightened several inhabitants in San Juan de la Maguana:

> In La Maguana (subsidiary No. 1 of Palma Sola), is a spring (La fuente del naranjar [sic]) today called the Spring of Liborio; this spring has clean and crystalline waters but not even these waters have been able

48 Interview with Leopoldo Figuereo, San Juan de la Maguana, 4 June 1989.
49 Eutasio L. (1962).
50 Interview with Bartolo de Jiménez, Maguana Arriba, 13 December 1985.

to escape the superstition of the Mellizos, because they have indicated to their followers that they ought to go to the Spring of Liborio and bathe to rid themselves of their sins and their diseases.

An average of 2,000 persons bathe there on Tuesdays and Fridays, most of them sick. One may see an army of cancerous, tubercular, scabby and leprous people, persons with syphilitic fluids, etc. bathe there. The prudent reader can imagine the damage this barbarity has already done to our health and to that of all other persons to whom the San Juan River administers water.[51]

A close study of notions surrounding La Agüita indicates that they present an interesting blend of fertility beliefs common to Europe, West Africa and the pre-Columbian Caribbean.[52] A study of concepts connected with La Agüita can shed some light on Olivorio's place within the religious traditions of his immediate surroundings. Being an agriculturist, Olivorio was firmly rooted in his own environment and his message must be considered in relation to the place where he was born and lived most of his life – a landscape sanctified by the presence of invisible forces believed to have existed in the same area for thousands of years. People have come and gone, but the life-promoting forces stayed behind in the soil, in caves and springs. New settlers offered new interpretations of the nature of this spiritual presence, notions which blended with those held by their predecessors.

Pilgrims walk along the narrow path to St John's spring carrying bottles and cans to bring the holy water back home. As an act of penitence some carry stones on their heads and deposit them in front of the crosses at the entrance to the holy compound. The spring is situated in a gorge not far from the rapid current of the La Maguana stream, whose course Olivorio and his men used to follow into the heartland of the Cordillera Central. The sound of running water is heard all the time. A cross standing in the midst of a pile of stones is reached after a steep descent. Stones are even piled on the beam of the blue-painted cross. Two oval discs are attached to the ends of the crossbeam. The words *La Fe* are written in big letters on the trunk, the crossbeam reads *El Maestro*, the left disc is inscribed with the word *Esperansa* [sic], the right one reads *Caridad*. Visitors to La Agüita pause in front of the cross, those who carry stones deposit them on the pile in front of it. Everyone makes the sign of the cross. Some shrug their shoulders to 'liberate themselves from their load of sins'.[53] Others stroke the cross with their fingertips before they let them touch their forehead. After

51 Eutasio L. (1962).
52 Several examples will be presented below.
53 Interview with María Orfelia, Maguana Arriba, 13 December 1985.

Figure 6.1 Bartolo de Jiménez, keeper of the Spring of St John, at La Agüita.

passing through an *enramada* visitors find themselves in front of El Monte Santo [the Sacred Mountain], a shallow opening in the side of the slope, surrounded by stones and boulders, adorned with burning candles, small crosses and a portrait of the Pope. It is hard to tell if the small cave is natural or man-made.

Bartolo de Jiménez, missionary and keeper of the Spring of St John, greets the visitors by the Monte Santo, sprinkles them with blessed water, makes the sign of the cross and delivers long and rather incomprehensible speeches. After preaching for some twenty minutes he presents the miracles of the small cave. Some fissures and scratches are said to depict *El Maestro*, a stone which makes a hollow sound if one hits it with the palm of one's hand is presented as the 'Trunk of the Cross' and another small formation is called *La Mano Poderosa*. Bartolo points to a hollow tree trunk which he declares 'carries the face of Christ'. He holds up the palm of his hand and demonstrates how it is possible to discern the sign of the cross upon it, explaining that the image was 'burned in one night when I touched the wall of the cave'.[54] In his search for signs of another reality in commonplace things Bartolo is quite typical of other cult functionaries active in the San Juan area.

Visitors place themselves on big tree trunks and listen to Bartolo's preaching with a kind of amused respect. After the speech several listeners come up to the 'missionary' and in low voices tell him about their different ailments. Others undress, preparing themselves for a dip in the healing water.

54 Interview with Bartolo de Jiménez, Maguana Arriba, 13 December 1985.

The spring is situated further up the slope, hidden behind corrugated sheet metal. At a visit to La Agüita, three women, who had come all the way from the capital, threw sweets and toasted bread in a cavity close to the place where the water emerges from the rock. The ladies were all naked. One of them was possessed by Anacaona, the Indian queen, and flung herself into the water, searching for 'signs'. When she found a glittering bottle cap it was kept as a lucky charm and interpreted as a message from the Indian ladies beneath the water, 'who are fond of glittering things'.[55]

In La Agüita we encounter an intricate web of syncretism. Presumably the concepts are composed of traits from Taino traditions,[56] but also from African and European ones. Anacaona, who dwells in the waters of La Agüita, appears to have much in common with Oshun, a water and fertility goddess among the West African Yoruba. Anacaona was a historical person, married to a fierce Indian chief. When her husband died, she became the leader of her people, until the Spaniards burned down her villages and hanged her.[57] Now she lives beneath the water and bestows on her believers gifts of wealth and fecundity. Oshun, the Yoruban goddess, is also believed to have been a queen who killed herself and took her wealth with her to the sacred, watery depths. From her abode beneath the water, she brings children to those 'seeking and longing for them'. She also supports her worshipers with 'other aspects of the "good life", such as money and wealth'.[58] Just like her Dominican counterpart, she is symbolized by feathers and considered to be lovely and calm, but like the Indian queen she is also eager for battle.[59]

In La Agüita, Anacaona serves under St John the Baptist. Among Haitian and Dominican voodooists, St John the Baptist is considered to be the master of earthquakes and thunder[60] and is sometimes said to be related to Metré Silí, the voodoo love goddess,[61] associated with water.[62] Such

55 Visit to La Agüita, 18 January 1986. Since men are not allowed to enter while women are immersing themselves in the water, it was a female companion of ours who witnessed and recorded the incident.

56 It is difficult to pinpoint direct Taino influences and it is possible that the entire subterranean tribe of 'Indians' guarding the fertility in the San Juan Valley only mirrors African and European traditions which have been adapted to the area. However, since La Maguana was one of the most thriving Taino settlements on the island and runaway Taino and African slaves for several years lived together in the southwestern parts of what is now the Dominican Republic (Deive (1980), p. 442), it is likely that certain Taino traditions may have survived after being incorporated with other thought patterns at a place like La Agüita.

57 Peguero and de los Santos (1983), p. 51.

58 Hallgren (1988), pp. 34–5.

59 Thompson (1984), pp. 79–80.

60 Simpson (1971), p. 510.

61 Ezili in Haitian Creole. As *lwa* of love, Ezili is believed to establish liaisons with male *lwa*, as well as with humans. Her main partners in spiritual *plasaj* [concubinage] are the *lwa*

associations link St John with the Yoruban god Shangó (Ṣòngó), master of lightning and fertility, and his three wives, who all dwell under water and are fond of feathers and glittering things. The most important of Shangó's wives is Oshun (Òsun). In the same way as Shangó governs his wives dwelling in springs and beneath water courses, St John the Baptist governs the Indian ladies in La Agüita and another Indian water spirit who is believed to dwell in a stream outside of El Batey.[63]

But how can Indian chieftains and West African fertility deities be connected with St John the Baptist? The connection with water is of course apparent, but there are several intricate points of contact between the European and African traditions enmeshed in the religious conglomerate of La Agüita. Several *Olivoristas* state that St John the Baptist is identical with *El Gran Poder de Dios*, or *El Espíritu Santo*, the incarnation of this power. In El Batey, a cult site much venerated by *Olivoristas*, *El Espíritu Santo* is kept in the guise of a small statuette, not more than 45 centimeters high. It looks like a doll; a white, black-haired, chubby-cheeked little boy, holding his hand in a gesture of benediction. The piece cannot be more than 150 years old. The 'saint' is dressed in a purple, gold-fringed mantle, with a cross embroidered on the chest.

Legba, Danbala, Gede, Ogoun and Agwe, to name a few. She is furthermore capable of marrying humans in ceremonies. Her *plasaj* with different *lwa* reflects Ezili's various roles as cosmic mother (together with Legba), guarantee for the flow of human generations (with Danbala), fertility (with Gede in his phallic aspect), the junction of female sexuality with male virility (with Ogoun) and the life-giving force of water (with Agwe) (Desmangles (1992) pp. 131–45). In the Dominican Republic Ezili is called Metré Silí (Metrès Ezili in Haiti) and even if she is believed to be married to the warrior Iva Ogún Balenyó, she is just as unbound and promiscuous as her Haitian counterpart (cf. Jiménez Lambertus (1980), p. 182). As the most prominent manifestation of female fecundity it becomes natural to regard Ezili as related to St John the Baptist, who is considered to be a main provider of fertility. While accounting for voodoo beliefs one has to keep in mind that voodoo constitutes a highly flexible belief system with many local, and even individual, variants.

62 Desmangles (1992), pp. 10, 135–6, 145, 155, 159, and Hurbon (1995), pp. 74, 142.

63 Some authors indicate that the Afro-American cult of Shangó (St John the Baptist) was replaced by that of Kalunga (the Holy Spirit). Kalunga, lord over death and water, is supreme god of several Congo-Angolan peoples. The shift is said to have been caused by increasing imports of slaves from areas of Kalunga worship (Espín del Prado (1984), p. 608 and Davis (1987), p. 203). In *santería*, a syncretistic religion common in Cuba and Puerto Rico, Kalunga is a water goddess worshiped by the *mayomberos* (*santería* worshipers considered to practice a 'Congolese' variant of the cult). *Mayomberos* consider Kalunga to be the mother of Shangó (González-Wippler (1992), p. 115). In Haitian voodoo, St John the Baptist is also associated with Zaka (or Azaka), a deity connected with agriculture. It is possible that Zaka's name derives from the Taino word for corn – *zada*, or maize [*maza*]. In northern Haiti, Zaka is known as Mazaka. Even if his name may be of Taino origin, the cult of Zaka shows many equivalents to the cult African Fon-speaking peoples render a deity called Yalóde (Desmangles (1992), p. 121).

The tiny statuette of *El Espíritu Santo*, carved with baroque flavor, fits well with European depictions of St John the Baptist.[64] Baroque art became the universal style of the Spanish colonies, with its guidelines determined by the demands of the Counter-Reformation. It was expressive and extroverted, a popular art form that aimed to win over as many souls as possible for the 'right cause'. Baroque art appeals to the senses in a high degree and sometimes appears to overwhelm the viewer with its luxury and opulence. Its symbols and allegories tend to be comprehensible and its iconography soon became popular all over the world – not least in the American colonies. It was a realistic art form, sensual rather than intellectual. Like Murillo's sweet and youthful Madonnas, faithful interpretations of popular fertility notions, akin to May queens, who presided over Spanish summer solstice festivals, they rise up to heaven, standing on the crescent moon, surrounded by lovely, plump and naked children, carrying roses and ears of corn in their hands. In the same hall of the Prado Museum in Madrid where we can admire Murillo's Virgins, we also find his depictions of St John the Baptist, a healthy, chubby-cheeked child who plays with lambs in lush meadows or is offered a drink of water by an equally sweet and childlike Jesus.[65]

Why is such a powerful saint depicted as a child? St John the Baptist is the only saint whose birth, not death, is celebrated in the Christian calendar. He is, together with Jesus, one of the few Christian deities who is worshiped in the guise of a child,[66] and both children are connected with the most important dates in the agricultural calendar – Jesus with the winter solstice, which takes place around Christmas, the principal feast of rejuvenation for all of Christendom, and St John the Baptist with the summer solstice, which takes place around his day (24 June) and serves as an occasion for feasts celebrating rejuvenation and fecundity.

In European iconography children incarnate possibilities that lie ahead. The New Year and the different seasons formerly were depicted as children. Children symbolize innocence, growth and fertility and they are often connected with water.[67]

64 Cf. Davis (1987), pp.186–7.
65 The French historian Philippe Ariès (1979), pp, 31–47, offers a historical description of how European art has depicted children.
66 Other examples are the Virgin Mary as a child, the Holy Innocents (the children of Bethlehem murdered by Herod) and the children of the Marys of Salome and Zebedee (two women believed to have been present at the crucifixion, around whom several legends were created) (cf. ibid., p. 35 and Warner (1983), pp. 344–5).
67 Compare legends of how small children are saved from water by fishermen or gardeners, or stories about newborn children who are brought to their parents by water animals such as storks or frogs. In a book written together with C. G. Jung, the Hungarian classicist Karl Kerényi interprets several myths connected with child deities, and in doing so stresses their connections with water and fertility (Jung and Kerényi (1993), pp. 46–51

Images representing human littleness inevitably became associated with the general good, the total community's welfare as opposed to selfish or sectional interests [...] and thus with the fertility of men, animals and crops, as well as with their preconditions: peace in the cultural order and rain (not excess rain, only 'little rain') in the natural realm.[68]

In La Agüita fertility notions from different corners of the world have been blended together and new notions have developed and been adapted to the local environment. Such syncretism may be observed in many other places in the Dominican Republic and researchers habitually label them as 'Afro-American syncretistic cults'. However, this term has a serious limitation, since it leaves out the rich European tradition which appears to have had a crucial impact on the conglomerate of rural religion in the Dominican Republic.

To sum up, to the extent that Dominican popular religion reflects Taino traits and customs, so does *Olivorismo*. The symbolism of stones, caves, the worship of and possession by 'Indian' spirits, the importance of water, streams and springs, not least in the physical location of sites of worship, the possible relation between Olivorio's birthplace and one of the traditional Indian 'kingdoms' of Hispaniola all point towards a connection between *Olivorismo* and what is usually considered 'Indian' in Dominican folk religion, although the latter is profoundly steeped in the syncretistic mold.

The religion of the *conquistadores*

Syncretism and nationalism

The religion of Latin American peasants is regularly stamped as 'syncretistic',[69] a term which often has a disdainful ring to it, much like the term

and 62–3). Kerényi points to the child god Eros and his connection with fertility (ibid., pp. 53–6), while Ariès (1979), pp. 41–3, demonstrates how Eros, through the Renaissance enthusiasm for classical antiquity, reenters European consciousness in the form of *putti*, the naked children who adorn so many European paintings from the fifteenth century onwards. Both Jesus and St John the Baptist were soon depicted as *putti* and thus inherited some of the classical love god's connotations.

68 Turner and Turner (1978), p. 73. The Turners' description is inspired by the baroque statuettes of the Jesus child that are the center of intense veneration in Mexico and Central America, particularly among Indian devotees.

69 From Greek *synkretizein*, meaning 'to join forces against a common enemy'. Later it came to mean 'in confusion with'. 'The process of fusing two different religious ideas or systems which are usually analogous' (Hultkrantz (1960), p. 228). The phenomenon has been much discussed among historians of religions. Early works include Hartman (1969) and Dietrich (1975).

'primitive'. Using 'syncretistic' to describe a religious practice often implies that it is not a full and worthy member of the league of 'Great World Religions', such as Christianity, Islam and Buddhism. Still, syncretism might just as well indicate a living and practical faith. Syncretistic believers pick up elements from a religious complex which have a direct meaning for them, in the same way as a peasant picks up a new tool and throws away an old one when he finds that the new one serves him better.

Through the Spanish conquest of America, Indians and Africans came in contact with a new and often aggressive faith. After years of struggle, they succeeded in combining Christianity with certain elements of their own beliefs. This process may be described as syncretistic in the sense of a fusion of analogous notions, but it was not an adaptation of 'primitive' beliefs to more 'sophisticated Christian notions'. The faith that was brought overseas to America was not exactly the Catholicism preached from the pulpits of Latin America today. Still, many Catholics like to imagine that the beliefs planted in the Indian and African soul were of a higher order than the traditional notions of these 'unfortunate peoples'.

The island of Hispaniola was chosen by Christopher Columbus to be the site of the first Spanish settlement in the New World and since that time many Dominicans have prided themselves on being the inhabitants of the 'island that Columbus loved'. At times the official veneration of Columbus has come close to idolization. The day on which the 'discovery' was formerly celebrated (12 October) was, until very recently, called *El Día de la Raza* [the Day of the Race] and eulogies presented to the great discoverer were without limit:[70]

> Those who put Columbus in the place second to Christ are right. Christ is the greatest of all reformers, philosophers and moralists [...] Columbus is the greatest of all discoverers, foremost in the bravery and daring feats in the service of science. He is also the most tormented and offended of all heroes. Christ immortalized the cross as a symbol of sacrifice, Columbus immortalized the chains as a synthesis of his martyrdom [etc.][71]

In 1992, a huge 'Columbus Memorial Lighthouse' was erected in Santo Domingo. An enormous marble building constructed in the form of a giant cross sits above the tomb of Columbus. It is crowned by powerful searchlights which cast beams of light into the sky, forming a luminous cross in the clouds. On clear nights the beams project to a height of 3,000 feet. The walls of this strange construction are engraved with the words of Columbus: 'You shall set up Crosses on all roads and pathways, for as God

---

70 For a capsule history of the celebration of Columbus, see Trouillot (1995), Chapter 4.
71 Jiménez (1938), p. 87.

be praised, this land belongs to Christians, and the remembrance of it must be preserved for all times.'

Such euphoria conjures up images of benevolent missionaries and valiant conquerors spreading the word of the Lord. Many Latin American regimes have used similar notions to unite their nations around the 'moral strength' of Catholicism. This was the case in the Dominican Republic under the dictatorship of Trujillo. The Spanish conquerors were then described as 'gentlemen of true *Hispanidad*', who came to America as messengers of God, implanting civilization and morals among primitive savages. Culture was made synonymous with Spanish Catholicism.[72]

Such rhetoric has convinced many that America was Christianized by erudite and outstanding personalities such as Bartolomé de Las Casas or Bernardino de Sahagún, reluctantly admitting that a few greedy fellows and unpleasant fanatics might have participated as well. However, a culture is not vanquished and transformed by a few missionaries and conquerors. It was primarily uneducated people who came to the Americas and it was 'popular European culture' which merged with the beliefs of Indians and Africans. The faith that was brought to Latin America was not so much the beliefs of dedicated scholars or fervent mystics, but rather something that had been fostered by the ancient, practical religion of European peasants and poorly educated parish priests – a faith with roots deep in the past, nurtured by ancient beliefs in magic and fertility. Cults and rituals found their expression in lascivious May-games, or coarse and merry carnivals[73] – a kind of religious merrymaking which came under heavy fire during the Catholic Counter-Reformation. The starting shot for that great event came with the Council of Trent in 1545,[74] but long before then European popular religion had traveled to the colonies on the far side of the Atlantic. While Europe was engaged in modernizing the medieval church, the existence of traditional beliefs and rituals was prolonged overseas.[75]

---

72 *Hispanidad* was a term often used by Dominican ideologists under the Trujillo dictatorship (1930–61). It implied that in order to adapt itself to an imaginary Spanish culture epitomized in the literal and artistic achievements of the 'Spanish Golden Age', the culture of the Dominicans had to be delivered from all African and Haitian traits (cf. Cassá (1976)).

73 Cf. Bakhtin (1984). The Basque anthropologist Julio Caro Baroja has stated that the celebration of carnivals was the 'local community's' way of insuring its continued existence by driving away evil (social, biological and anti-Christian) forces from its midst in anticipation of the cleansing Lent. This was done by donning grotesque masks and making noise, but also through the enactment of rituals that interpreted the normal course of human life – procreation, birth, death and resurrection (Caro Baroja (1965), p. 277).

74 The Council met on three occasions, 1545–48, 1551–52 and 1562–63. The last occasion was dedicated to matters of 'disciplinary regulation and correction' (Chadwick (1982), p. 274).

75 Ibid., p. 334.

Rural religion in medieval Europe

Since medieval Europe was agrarian to a very high degree, the most common expression of medieval religion was that of peasant society. Medieval agriculturalists lived close to the earth and were totally dependent on its fruits. It was only natural that they were interested in all aspects of fecundity. They assumed that a powerful force of germination was imbedded in the land and their universe was inhabited by a vast number of invisible forces. In their permanent struggle to achieve fecundity for barren fields and wombs, the peasants needed help from what was considered to be a 'suprahuman' world:

> agriculture, like all basic activities, is no merely profane skill. Because it deals with life, and its object is the marvellous growth of that life, dwelling in seed, furrow, rain and the spirits of vegetation, it is therefore first and foremost a ritual. It was so from the beginning and has always remained so in farming communities, even in the most highly civilized areas of Europe. The husbandman enters and becomes part of a sphere of abundant holiness. His actions and labours have solemn consequences because they are performed within a cosmic cycle and because the year, the seasons, summer and winter, seed-time and harvest-time build up their own essential forms, each taking on its own autonomous significance.[76]

The medieval church was unable to take action against the peasants' ancient traditions. It was obliged to incorporate pagan fertility festivals and turn pagan sites of nature worship into Christian ones by associating them with saints and virgins.[77]

The driving force behind the vast peasant universe was fertility and almost all agricultural rituals were connected with it.[78] Most of these rural fertility rites included common meals. Particularly important were the big communal feasts around the winter and summer solstices. In the summer, festivities were staged under the auspices of St John the Baptist, imagined to be a bringer of water and fecundity. St John cleansed with water, and rituals connected with the purification by fire and water are common in peasant communities all over Europe. Huge bonfires are lighted and people bathe in lakes and springs. Fields, animals and humans are anointed with blessed water. Amatory rites and activities of various types abound, as well as common meals and ritual dancing.[79]

---

76 Eliade (1976), p. 331.
77 Thomas (1984), p. 54.
78 Cf. Eliade (1976), pp. 331–66, for an interesting description of various European myths and rituals connected with fertility.
79 Foster (1960), p. 198. The celebration of the night of St John is the main event for the

Pictures and statues of saints in medieval rural churches and small village chapels were familiar and lifelike. They even looked and dressed like their believers. Paupers, monks, artisans, former prostitutes, children and lovely maidens could be found among the saints. No service was too small to ask of them. They shared the everyday problems of their worshipers, who endowed them with distinguished fancies and tastes. The statues were even dressed and washed. The saints became well-known members of the village community and did not inspire any fear or terror.

The saints had lived on earth as human beings and, accordingly, were closer to their devotees than God, the ultimate life force, who was imagined as aloof from mankind, both inaccessible and incomprehensible. In order to communicate with God, supplicants needed intermediaries, other divinities who were able to render warmth and compassion to the inconceivable power underlying everything. Most religions distinguish in practice, if not in strict theory, between a higher god and lesser divine beings. If the higher god tends to be remote, the lesser ones are in closer touch with mortals and concern themselves with such mundane matters as the wellbeing of the village and family, and the fertility of fields and beasts.[80]

Saints were worshiped in the parish churches, but also at altars kept in private homes, or in small chapels, known as *ermitas* in Spain. Most *ermitas* had been erected close to holy places that had been venerated for centuries, often due to their connection with fertility beliefs.[81] In such places a group of people often maintained the site and kept it holy by helping to distribute the powers of the spiritual powers believed to be present there.[82] Such keepers of holy places would be committed to their task through a personal vow[83] given to the force they believed to be at hand in the place they tended. The groups that formed around such sites would support a woman, *beata*, or a man, *santero*, whose task it was to take care of the place.[84] These guardians lived close to their *ermita*, separated from the other villagers, and they sometimes dressed in homemade habits. The supporting group helped the *beata* or *santero* by maintaining the *ermita* and provided economic support for the yearly feasts arranged on the guardian saint's day. Feasts meant vigils, processions and penance, but also music,

fraternity that supports Olivorio's sanctuary in Maguana Arriba and the spring by La Agüita.
80 Wilson (1983), p. 1.
81 Christian (1972), pp. 60–1.
82 Christian (1981), p. 177.
83 A religious vow, *votum* in Latin, is 'a solemn promise made to God or to any deity or saint, to perform some act, or make some gift or sacrifice, in return for some special favour' (*Oxford English Dictionary* (1961), p. 319. Cf. Christian (1972), pp. 119–20).
84 Christian (1972), p. 31. In Maguana Arriba we find María Orfelia who takes care of Olivorio's sanctuary, while her brother, Bartolo de Jiménez, looks after the Spring of St John: La Agüita.

dance, food, drink and merrymaking, particularly if the cults had grown up around sites of traditional worship believed to support fertility.[85]

The differences between the rural clergy and their parishioners were not great. The church formed an integral part of the village community and was considered a receptacle for life-giving powers. The devil was allergic to holy water which was taken as medicine or sprinkled over home, fields and domestic animals.[86] No ritual festivity was complete without the participation of a member of the clergy. Most rural priests did not care much about sermons or confessions and shared the peasants' view of the church as a provider of magic power. For many parishioners the priest was something of a master magician and his services were used to exorcize storms, drive away swarms of locusts and bless the fields and their fruits.[87] The church was far from ruling out supernatural intervention in human affairs, but taught that magic could emanate from only two sources: God or the devil.[88] Since the church and its clergy were God's representatives in this world, any layman's dabbling in the magical arts was highly suspicious.

Humble friars and poor parish priests dealt with the peasants on a daily basis, while members of the higher clergy tended to be hostile to rural dwellers. The spiritual centers of the church were concentrated in the towns, where a wealthy clergy served its well-to-do benefactors. In order to secure blessedness for themselves at the time of their death, it was customary among rich citizens to bequeath some of their wealth to the church. In the medieval economy, most wealth was simply hoarded and reinvestment on a grand scale was not introduced until the advent of the industrial revolution.[89]

Many bishops and abbots were simply politicians, courtiers and businessmen in ecclesiastic garb. Several monasteries were luxurious establishments, and bishops and popes lived in huge palaces. In short, members of the church hierarchy found themselves far away from the simple tillers of the soil. Few peasant saints are found in the calendars, and clerical writers often emphasized the bestiality and avarice of the peasants.[90] Until the coming of the Counter-Reformation, rural unorthodox beliefs were generally ignored and the peasants were left in peace with their 'superstitions'.

Whether or not the peasants received due attention from their parish

---

85 Caro Baroja (1974), pp. 31–76, describes strange rural festivals in the Spanish villages of Talavera and San Pedro Manrique which show compelling affinities with fertility rituals that during classical antiquity were carried out in honor of Ceres, the Roman goddess of agriculture and fertility.

86 Thomas (1984) pp. 33–4. In certain places in Russia, the priest himself was taken out of the church and rolled by women over the newly sown ground (Eliade (1976), p. 355).

87 Johnson (1980), p. 229. Cf. Christian (1981), pp. 29–31.

88 Thomas (1984), p. 303.

89 Ariès (1978), pp. 81–94.

90 Johnson (1980), p. 228.

priest depended much on the quality of the soil they tilled. Well-educated clergymen focused their efforts on wealthy country districts. Furthermore, most parish churches were privately owned and expected to generate a profit.[91] As long as the peasants attended mass and paid their levy, the parish priest accepted cultic transgressions without much objection. Clerics lived a fairly secularized life. In Spain, for example, many lived in open concubinage, and in Castile, until the end of the fifteenth century, a child of a priest could inherit from his father if the latter died intestate.[92]

The religion of the *conquistadores* – and hence what survives of it in present-day Dominican popular religion – was not of the exalted, sophisticated kind. Rather, it corresponded to the background of the average man taking part in the conquest: uneducated and with his roots in rural society and peasant religion. This religion displayed a number of 'pagan' features connected with the fact that peasants are agriculturalists and as such concerned with fertility. To this end rites had developed over the centuries which formed part of the Christian religion in Spain as well. A second trait in Dominican folk religion inherited from medieval Christian practice (but not exclusively from there) is the need for intermediation between God and men by the saints, who were close to men in the sense that they had themselves once lived on earth, as human beings. Third, the Spanish practice of building *ermitas* carried over to Dominican folk religion as well – to the point where many private houses have family altars. Finally, we should note the presence of the devil or evil – a force that needs to be exorcized by the priest from time to time – exactly as Olivorio would do.[93]

This was, generally speaking, the kind of religion the Spaniards brought with them to their western dominions – a down-to-earth Christianity, tinged by age-old fertility beliefs and relatively untouched by the new and radical doctrines of a modern clergy steeped in the new mold of the Counter-Reformation. On the island of Hispaniola isolated Spanish settlers soon blended their faith with that of their African slaves and the few Indian concepts which had survived the ruthless extermination of the Tainos.

The *cofradías*: an Afro-European fusion

African slaves

From an early date thousands of black slaves were brought into Hispaniola from West Africa. It was not because of any imagined 'inferiority' that black

---

91 Ibid., p. 228.
92 Elliott (1970), p. 103.
93 A fifth practice derived from medieval Spain – the establishment of *cofradías* – will be dealt with below.

slaves were preferred by the Spanish slave-owners. As a matter of fact, the first slaves brought to Santo Domingo were both white and black and all were nominally Christians.[94] However, white slaves could not stand the climate and the Indians died in their thousands. Thus, the use of African slaves was determined by their ability to work within plantation systems of tropical agriculture.

Many Africans had been serfs in their own countries as well. Some West African nations were powerful feudal states largely resembling the medieval European ones. Internal fighting was as endemic among the West Africans as it was in Europe. Strong states shook and changed the old framework of tribal equality and mass subjugation of one people by another was not an uncommon feature. Some African kingdoms also had masses of commoners, living in a form of vassalship under a limited class of rulers.[95] As in Europe, the religion of the ruling class differed from that of the practical-minded agriculturists among their subjects,[96] and West Africans also moved about, mixing their religious beliefs, although a traditional, practical, locally bound, fertility religion persisted.[97]

Black slaves were preferred to Tainos in the gold mines, which from the beginning constituted the backbone of Hispaniola's economy, because the Indians were considered to be 'very thin and endowed with little strength'.[98] After 1520, however, the profits from the mining enterprises declined steadily, as did the Indian population. Gold was no longer found

---

94 Christian black slaves proved to be 'ungovernable', apt to run off to the mountains and teach Indians 'bad manners' (Larrazábal Blanco (1975), pp. 13–14). When a devastating measles epidemic killed off vast numbers of the remaining Indians in 1518–19, large-scale import of black slaves began (ibid., p. 20). In 1568 it was estimated that some 20,000 black slaves were working in the Dominican sugar industry (Moya Pons (1973), pp. 6–7 and 15).

95 Davidson (1980), pp. 30–9.

96 'in Dahomey the worship of the pantheons which compromise these spiritual kingdoms (formed around particular deities) is as much specialized in belief and ritual as is that of the various religious sects of our civilization' (Herskovits and Herskovits (1933), p. 10). 'The position and prestige of the Mawu-Lisa cult in Dahomey may be considered analogous to the state religion of a European nation. The principal complex of temples for the gods of this pantheon and the cult-houses where the initiates are secluded during their period of training, are within the palace of Tegbesu. This does not mean, however, that the Mawu-Lisa cult is the popular religion [of Dahomey]' (ibid., p. 15). On the importance of fertility and the practical view on religion as a means of obtaining wealth and security among the West African Yoruba, see Hallgren (1988). The Fon (in Dahomey) and Yoruba of West Africa are (together with people from the Bakongo region) considered to be the main African contributors to Haitian (and Dominican) voodoo beliefs and practices (cf. Deive (1979), pp. 132–54 and Desmangles (1992), p. 95). Dahomey is the former name of present-day Benin. Oyo and Ife, the most important Yoruba kingdoms, were situated in what is now the southwestern part of Nigeria.

97 Cf. Hurbon (1995), pp. 14–18.

98 Quoted in Deive (1980), p. 29.

in the rivers and the superficial veins had disappeared. Wells and tunnels had to be dug and this resulted in higher production costs. More slaves were needed while at the same time the Indian population dwindled at an alarming speed. Spanish colonists left the island in ever-growing numbers. In order to exploit the gold mines, the governors demanded more African slaves, and workers were also required for the expanding sugar industry.

This forced the Spanish crown to put aside all restrictions on the imports of *bozales*. A *bozal* was a heathen slave imported directly from West Africa. Previously, the crown, fearful of 'harmful' influences from 'Moors' and other infidels (many Africans were Muslims), had put a ban on the import of all unbaptized slaves. *Bozales* were welcomed by the Spanish colonists since they were both cheaper and more submissive than *ladinos* [Christian slaves] and free from the 'contamination of the vices and bad customs of the Occidental world'.[99]

Sugar soon replaced gold as the most important product of the island. Since a great number of workers were needed to plant, grow and harvest this particular crop the *ingenios* [sugar estates] soon became important population centers. It was stipulated that every *ingenio* had to keep a church and a priest for the religious instruction of the slaves. The number of slaves working on an *ingenio* varied between 60 and 900, and in 1568 it was estimated that 20,000 slaves were working in the sugar industry.[100] It was hard to exercise control over so many slaves and escapes continually took place. *Cimarrones* [runaway slaves] created communities of their own in remote areas of the island.[101] In particular the mountainous area around the San Juan Valley was notorious for its communities of such slaves.

The maroons

When the town of San Juan de la Maguana was founded in 1503,[102] the surrounding Taino settlements were forced to work for the Spanish settlers. Already in 1519, however, a Taino *cacique* named Enriquillo, who came from an area close to San Juan de la Maguana, revolted against Spanish rule. He and his Indian warriors soon joined forces with runaway black slaves. The rebellion lasted for fourteen years and created a state of war within the entire district of La Maguana.[103]

Enriquillo's rebellion initiated a long, and almost unbroken, chain of revolts and internal fighting in the San Juan Valley. The town of San Juan de la Maguana was often the center of the fighting and it was burned down

---

99 Ibid., p. 35.
100 Moya Pons (1973), pp. 6–7 and 15.
101 Ibid., p. 9.
102 Garrido (1972), p. 330.
103 Peña Batlle (1970), pp. 74 and 93.

on many occasions. During the sixteenth century slaves from the surrounding sugar plantations revolted over and over again. Lemba – a slave from a plantation close to San Juan – with his group of *cimarrones* kept the San Juan Valley in constant terror during most of the 1540s. He was killed in 1547,[104] after having sacked San Juan de la Maguana thoroughly.[105] Diego de Ocampo,[106] another runaway slave, with a huge following, harassed the valley for several years around the same time.[107] The life of Spanish settlers in the San Juan Valley was almost constantly threatened by the inhabitants of several *manieles* [runaway slave communities] that had been established in the surrounding mountains. By the end of the sixteenth century, San Juan de la Maguana lay deserted, while groups of *cimarrones* lived in surrounding villages.

The culture of the maroons was probably quite meager and no clergy came to the valley. The *Sanjuaneros*' religion was probably akin to the one which had existed in the *manieles*: 'Some of them know how to pray Padre Nuestro and Ave Maria, but they all have some slips of idolatry.'[108] Their creed was 'neither completely Catholic, nor pagan, but a mixture of both beliefs'.[109]

Depopulation and tolerance

An epidemic in the 1580s killed half the slave population, with the result that in 1606, when an official census was taken, fewer than 10,000 were left.[110] Four years earlier, in 1602, peace had been made with some scattered groups of *cimarrones* who were persuaded to resettle in San Juan de la Maguana, which in the same year was once again granted the status of town by the Royal Council in Santo Domingo. This state of affairs quickly came to an end, however, because around this time ships from Holland, England and France made frequent stops along the coasts, offering slaves and luxury goods for prices far below the monopoly prices offered by the Spanish crown to its colonies. The foreigners also brought dangerous ideas and forbidden books, spreading messages from European protestants and humanists. In order to wipe out the contraband trade, the Spanish governor ordered a forced abandonment of the western districts of the island.

---

104 Moya Pons (1980), p. 37.
105 Deive (1980), pp. 449–51.
106 Utrera (1973), p. 482.
107 Deive (1980), pp. 447–8.
108 Archbishop Francisco de la Cueva Maldonado in a letter from 1663, quoted in Deive (1980), p. 491.
109 Deive (1980), p. 498.
110 Moya Pons (1974a), p. 21.

More than half of the island of Hispaniola was deserted between 1605 and 1606. Towns were set on fire and herds of cattle were brought into districts which were easier to control and protect.[111] San Juan de la Maguana was burned down once more, but many of its inhabitants refused to leave the district and returned to their former *manieles*.[112] For more than a century the San Juan district was a vast 'no man's land' where former *cimarrones* made a living by subsistence farming and the hunting of undomesticated cattle. The devastated parts of the island were turned into a wilderness where large numbers of cattle hunted by *cimarrones* roamed free after the *hatos* had been abandoned.[113]

The abandonment of western Hispaniola by the Spanish at the beginning of the seventeenth century signaled the beginning of a more-or-less constant depopulation of the present-day Haitian border area, especially in the interior of the island, for more than a century. As we will see in the next chapter, the French managed to establish a colony in the western third of Hispaniola, and after the treaty signed in Ryswick, in 1697, the island was officially divided into French Saint-Domingue, and Spanish Santo Domingo.[114]

Saint-Domingue developed into a highly lucrative colony for France. Its economy was based on a labor-intensive sugar industry which rested on vast numbers of African slaves.[115] Meanwhile the situation on the Spanish part of the island deteriorated. The entire Spanish empire sank into a deep economic crisis, and Santo Domingo was in addition struck by earthquakes, hurricanes and a shrinking population. Spanish settlers left continuously and the black population recovered only slowly from epidemics of measles, which in the 1660s had killed more than 2,000 slaves. 'It is the Negroes who cultivate the land and tend the cattle, but we lack them now because many are dying and these days they don't come from Guinea anymore.'[116] By that time, sugar cultivation had dwindled to the point where it was next to insignificant[117] and extensive cattle breeding and hunting of undomesticated cattle for hides had become the main economic activities. These were generally carried out by an *hatero* [rancher], his

---

111 Moya Pons (1977), pp. 109–29.
112 Utrera (1924).
113 Exquemelin (1969), pp. 49–50.
114 Moya Pons (1977), 255–61
115 During the second half of the eighteenth century 3,000–6,000 African slaves were imported to Saint-Domingue every year. These figures rose during the decade of the 1780s to 20,000–30,000 a year (Cassá (1985), p. 156).
116 From a letter written in 1650 by Luis Jerónimo de Alcocer, quoted in Rodríguez Demorizi (1942), p. 209. Guinea was the name given to the African coastline from the Senegal River to the town of Moçâmedes in southern Angola.
117 This was already the case at the beginning of the seventeenth century. Cf. Chapter 7, below.

family and three or four slaves, who often had families of their own. Some ranches were even run by the slaves themselves, while their masters lived in the city of Santo Domingo.[118]

On the human level, the general poverty and isolation which character-ized this system led to a high degree of equality and personal relationships between masters and slaves. Few priests found their way to the isolated ranches and whatever religion that was practiced was an intimate and private affair in front of a saint in a rural chapel. In this environment the beliefs of slaves and masters could easily mingle. Religious instruction was extremely defective in colonial Santo Domingo, and educated clergy were as good as non-existent outside the capital.[119] If a priest could be found in the countryside he had probably not been officially ordained for his office. Thus, in 1716, a French visitor found that the Spanish colony had a mere eleven parishes altogether, one in Santo Domingo and

> ten more in the rest of the colony: that is to say one in Altagracia, one in Santiago, one in La Vega, one in Cotuí, one in Seibo, one in Monte Plata, whose vicar also serves the Indian village of Boyá, and that of Bayaguana; one in Gohavá, one in Bánica, and the tenth in Azua, whose parish priest [*cura*] from time to time goes to say mass in the districts of San Juan de la Maguana and Neiva, where there are neither priests nor churches.[120]

Over time the differences between white masters and black slaves became less pronounced. A French visitor to the Spanish part of the island, Moreau de Saint-Méry, wrote in 1783:

> The prejudice of color, so powerful in other nations where a barrier has been established between the whites and the freedmen and their descendants almost does not exist in the Spanish part [...] It is also rigorously certain that the great majority of the Spanish colonists are mestizos [mulattos], who still have more than a touch of African which betrays them immediately [...] With regard to the clergy, men of color are admitted to it without problems, in accordance with the principles of equality which are the basis of Christianity, and only the Negroes are refused [...]
>
> The result of this [the white master's] opinion is a kindness that is consequently extended to the slaves. They are fed, generally, like their

118 Deive (1980), pp. 341, 344 and 349. *Hato* slaves tended their own *conucos* and seldom ran away since they lived more securely on the *hatos* than in the wilderness where they always ran the risk of being hunted down and shot (ibid.).

119 Wipfler (1978), p. 36.

120 Charlevoix (1977), p. 383.

masters and tended with a gentleness that is unknown among other nations that have colonies. Furthermore, since every slave can free himself, paying the [going] price to his master, who cannot refuse, it is very natural that the idea of seeing them make the move to the free class all the time, forbids treating them [the slaves] with the superiority which ordinarily exists between master and slave.[121]

The slaves had been treated harsher on the big *ingenios*, but there the former Africans were often able to join people from the areas where they had been born, creating cult groups of their own, reviving traditions from 'Guinea', a place which soon lost its geographic connotations and turned into some kind of dreamscape where gods and spirits had their home. The masters soon realized that relaxation was crucial if their slaves were to endure the hardships they were submitted to. On holidays the workers were allowed to dance. Dancing and drumming have always formed an integral part of African religion and what to some whites appeared as a harmless pastime for the slaves was meaningful, religious ceremony.[122] Funerals, or *bancos*, as they were called by the slaves, also provided an opportunity for praying, singing, dancing and practicing traditional African rituals.[123] Dancing and funerals soon became organized within *cofradías*, religious brotherhoods, which in some parts of the Dominican Republic still constitute an important feature of popular religion.[124]

The origin of cofradías

A *cofradía* is a religious brotherhood common in Europe during the Middle Ages. They still exist, particularly in Spanish towns, but differ from rural *cofradías* found in Latin America today. In the Dominican Republic some *cofradías* have obviously safeguarded various aspects of old European fertility rituals. Dominican *cofradías* have succeeded in preserving ideas and rituals which disappeared in Europe during the great reformatory movements of the sixteenth and seventeenth centuries. These features have been combined with similar notions from Africa, transmitted by black slaves, and the result is a particular expression of Dominican peasant religion, well adapted to its local environment.

---

121 Moreau de Saint-Méry (1944), pp. 93–4. Moreau, who visited Santo Domingo at the end of a short period of relative prosperity, saw the 'easy' life of the Spanish slaves in comparison with the harsh treatment of their peers on the French side of the border. However, in Santo Domingo the activities of both slaves and freedmen were circumscribed by severe laws, excluding them from several trades and offices, as well as restricting their use of weapons and certain tools (Deive (1980), pp. 309 and 314).
122 Deive (1980), pp. 333–4.
123 Ibid., p. 337.
124 See Lundius (1993).

Cofradías have been called 'the most characteristic expression of late medieval Christianity'.[125] They emerged in the twelfth century and soon became a familiar feature in both towns and countryside. They originated in Italian towns, where groups of people, often from particular guilds, gathered under the auspices of certain saints.[126]

Most urban *cofradías* were founded as associations intended to help their members with matters relating to death. Many people living during the late Middle Ages were obsessed with the thought of death. This could be explained by the fears aroused by recurrent plagues and wars. A general shortage of grain struck the whole of Europe around 1300, to be followed by social insecurity and the devastating Black Death, which ravaged the continent in the mid-fourteenth century.[127]

Teachings about purgatory took hold of people. The Middle Ages were insecure times, and, as part of an academic debate concerning the state of souls between death and the Final Judgment, the doctrine of purgatory was developed systematically. Christ's words on the sin against the Holy Spirit which will be forgiven 'neither in this world nor in that which is to come'[128] seemed to imply a state beyond the grave where expiation was still possible. Purgatory was related to that statement and was imagined as a place or state of temporal punishment, where those who had died in the grace of God were enabled to expiate their sins before being admitted to the vision of the Divine Being, which was believed to be the final destiny of the redeemed. The sufferings of the souls in purgatory could be alleviated through intercessions of the living and the saints. The official teaching concerning purgatory was developed at the Council of Lyons in 1274 and soon reached most strata of the population, and the doctrine was gradually transformed into a popular cult.[129]

Generous donations were given to the clergy and the friars by wealthy people so they could rest in peace after death, knowing that intercession was granted for their souls, thus avoiding the torments of purgatory. Masses and funeral processions for the wealthy became costlier and more elaborate, probably due to the fact that the clergy wanted to do their full share and attract new customers. Poorer urbanites probably wished for something similar and many longed for the communal rites of rural villages. They could not afford to pay for elaborate funeral rituals alone.

Soon laymen formed associations to take care of their own funeral services, as well as masses, common meals, processions, burials, graves, support of widows and orphans and recurrent intercessions for the souls in

125 Bossy (1985), p. 58.
126 Rojas Lima (1988), pp. 45–6.
127 Rothkrug (1979), p. 33. About the Black Death, see Ziegler (1989).
128 *Matthew* 12:32.
129 Livingstone (1977), p. 423. Cf. also Rothkrug (1979), pp. 32–3.

purgatory. Such societies were modeled after mendicant orders or town councils, and if they were dedicated to a saint they turned into *cofradías*.[130]

The *cofradías* came to constitute a form of devotion in which groups of people, through ritual acts, sought to establish collective security both on earth and in heaven. The *cofrades* formed corporate families, or 'artificial kinship groups', composed of living and dead members, each bound by local patterns of ritual.[131] People who moved into towns from the country-side often joined *cofradías*, which could be considered as urban copies of village communities. By guarding age-old village traditions they embodied kinship and communal solidarity. Members acquired a sense of belonging and since all *cofrades* were treated as equals, they acquired a strong sense of belonging and participation.[132] Men and women found breathing space in a society that assigned almost everyone determined roles and positions. *Cofradías* were voluntary associations and their members were recruited from specific professional groups, or from certain areas of a given town. A *cofradía* chose its own governing body, which handled the economy and governed the activities in accordance with an established constitution. Membership was for life and members who could not support themselves were helped by common means. Wealthy *cofradías* could even maintain a salaried clergy and independent chapels. Still, most funds were spent on feasts and processions.[133]

The highlights of the *cofradía* activities were communal meals called *convivium*, generally followed by dances and other entertainment.[134] Such merrymaking often reflected rural fertility festivities. Extremely important were the major annual processions in honor of the fraternity's patron saint, the care of its effigy, and the decoration and cleaning of the chapel where it was lodged.[135] The patron saint of a *cofradía* was considered its principal member and was endowed with a character and will of its own. When *cofrades* mentioned their saint they referred to it as a living being. In the countryside *cofradías* were founded around rural *ermitas* and age-old cult-sites. The worship carried out in such places was often far from the kind of religiosity acceptable to the official church.

130 Ariès (1978), pp. 75–88.
131 Rothkrug (1979), p. 34.
132 Bossy (1985), p. 58.
133 Bossy (1970), p. 59.
134 Bossy (1985), pp. 58–9. During the Reformation, the festivities of several *cofradías* were described as lewd and unfit for Christians. In medieval times, popular, festive banquets had nothing in common with static private life or individual wellbeing. Popular images of food and drink were active and triumphant. Religious banquets concluded a process of labor and struggle and thus stressed happiness, community and abundance. The *convivia* of the *cofradías* can be seen in connection with ancient traditions related to fecundity in rural societies.
135 Bossy (1985), pp. 58–9.

Over time, *cofradías* tended to be controlled entirely by laymen. The influence of the clergy was often limited to just a supportive role, embellishing the ceremonies with the celebration of mass. 'Indeed, in the fourteenth century the confraternity, not the church, may have appeared to ordinary folk as the institution outside of which there was no salvation.'[136]

The coming of the Counter-Reformation meant the beginning of the end for most *cofradías*. What exposed them to the wrath of church authorities was their independence and apparent flaws in their understanding of Christianity. Reformers thundered against them, demanding order and dogmatism.[137] However, several *cofradías* prolonged their existence in Spanish and Portuguese colonies, where for several reasons they attracted a huge following among black slaves.

Black cofradías

The governors of Spanish and Portuguese colonies saw *cofradías* as a useful means of social control. Blacks and mulattos were excluded from white fraternities, but they were allowed to govern and organize their own.[138] As a matter of fact, *cofradías* were often the only kind of organization permitted to operate among the non-white population in Spanish America.[139] The reasons why slave-owners accepted black *cofradías* were various. Most important was the discovery that the slaves' involvement in *cofradías* provided an outlet for tensions and frustrations. Through the communal life within the *cofradías* slaves regained some of their self-reliance and were able to turn their interests inward – towards their own group – instead of pondering too much about their personal alienation, and possibly directing their anger towards the slave-owners. Within the *cofradías*, slaves and freedmen competed for various positions and planned the communal feasts, dances and processions which took place on the feast days of the patron saints. The blacks were free to gossip and associate beyond the vision of the masters' scrutinizing eyes. In short, for a moment, they were able to live as independent human beings.

The attitude of the clergy was to accept those African customs which could be adapted to Catholicism. It was better to have 'Africans' organized around a Catholic saint and let them choose their own leaders than to have them live outside the realm of the church, apt to rebel under the leadership of some heir to old African kingdoms, maintaining pagan rituals in

---

136 Rothkrug (1979), p. 40.
137 Bossy (1970), p. 59.
138 Gray (1987), p. 54.
139 Davis (1987), p. 198.
140 Bastide (1978), pp. 53–4.

the bush. Black *cofradías* were modeled after white ones and the *cofradía* leaders often served as intermediaries between masters and slaves.[140]

West African slaves were not unfamiliar with associations similar to *cofradías*. Various regions in West Africa were homes of cult groups reminiscent of Christian *cofradías* – divinities such as Shangó, Omolí, Ogún, etc., had their own priests, fraternities, monasteries and sanctuaries.[141] In Dahomey the Fon envisaged groups of deities forming pantheons ruled by a pantheon head. Every such pantheon had a cult that was specialized in beliefs and rituals. Each Fon belonged to a particular cult group. As in medieval Europe, the most important godlings were the deified dead (like the saints), the *vodús*,[142] who changed into saints or *misterios* in Santo Domingo. Several *vodús* had the same intimate character as medieval saints. They had distinct tastes and personalities and their devotees considered them to be as close as kin.

A wide variety of different black *cofradías* emerged in colonial Santo Domingo. Many had chapels of their own in the cathedral of the capital and most of them safeguarded old African traditions, such as the *cofradía* dedicated to St Cosmas and St Damian, attended by *Araras*,[143] or the one dedicated to St John the Baptist – the most popular saint of all.[144] The *cofradía* of St John the Baptist was known to exercise various acts of charity and assumed at least half the costs of its members' funerals. Its chapel in the cathedral was very sumptuous and its feasts in honor of St John were popular among both blacks and whites.[145]

Black *cofradías* reached the Dominican countryside through the sugar plantations, which were large enough for a sufficient number of blacks to gather and form independent *cofradías*. By the time these *cofradías* finally reached isolated parts of the Spanish colony, they had already lost their exclusively 'black' character and attracted agriculturists of no particular racial denomination. In this new setting, the *cofradías* were transformed and adapted to the local environment.

141 Ibid., p.62.
142 Herskovits and Herskovits (1933), pp. 9–10, Hurbon (1995), pp. 14–15.
143 Larrazábal Blanco (1975), p. 136. The *Araras* were former members of the Ewe-Fon people of Dahomey. Cosmas and Damian are twin saints, often called 'the holy moneyless ones' and considered to be the patron saints of physicians. Their help is usually invoked by poor people afflicted with disease. Finding Fon as their devotees is not surprising, since much of the Fon religion concerns twins (Herskovits and Herskovits (1933), pp. 11–12, 56–7 and 59). Traces of African twin-cults may be found in Dominican concepts tied to the *Marasas* (Deive (1979), pp. 139–41 and Davis (1987), pp. 129–30).
144 Larrazábal Blanco (1975), pp. 137–8. San Juan is the fertility deity above all others, both in rural Spain and in Santo Domingo. Connected with water and fecundity he has his European feasts around the night of the summer solstice (15–24 June).
145 Nolasco (1982), pp. 354–5.

La Cofradía del Espíritu Santo *in the San Juan Valley*

It is not known when the *Cofradía del Espíritu Santo* came to the San Juan Valley. When Olivorio lived in the area it was already well established in the towns of Las Matas de Farfán, Bánica and San Juan de la Maguana, and had branches in several other places as well. Originally it probably came from the sugar-producing areas around the southern towns of San Cristóbal and Baní.[146] If this assumption is correct it is likely that the *Cofradía del Espíritu Santo* in El Batey is an offspring of a *cofradía* which bore the same name in Baní. Reference to this particular *cofradía* can be found in the eighteenth century. It was founded by black African slaves and was famous for its serious efforts in assisting sick plantation-slaves. It has been described as a '*cofradía* with "strong" rules. It was not only a manifestation of Afro-Catholic syncretism, but it often tended towards spiritism.'[147]

The main characteristic of the cult is a dance, called *El Baile del Espíritu Santo*. The three drums used in the ceremony are baptized, endowed with *compadres* and given names.[148] Every drum has a personality of its own and they are all connected in some way with *El Gran Poder de Dios*.[149]

El Baile del Espíritu Santo is an expressive and fascinating couple dance. It has been described as having a 'taste of the jungle',[150] giving an impression as if 'a savage tribe from the heart of Africa had set up its camp in the secluded house'.[151] However, other descriptions refer to it as 'expressive, gallant and entertaining if the couple knows to bring to it all the taste and enchantment of good dancers'.[152]

A small statuette of the Holy Spirit is kept in a church erected by the *cofradía* in El Batey (18 kilometers northeast of San Juan de La Maguana), the spiritual center of the organization. The effigy is the focal point of sumptuous ceremonies which take place around Pentecost. On Whit Saturday the statuette is carried down to a chapel in San Juan de la Maguana and kept there until the following Monday when it is returned to El Batey. Thousands of persons of all ages gather in San Juan de la Maguana for the weekend. Judging from their torn – but clean and tidy – clothes, most of them are poor peasants from rural districts. Some of the older women are

---

146 Cano y Fortuna (n.d.), p. 148. The *Cofradía del Espíritu Santo* in Las Matas de Farfán, which is independent from the big *cofradía* in El Batey, outside San Juan de la Maguana, is said to have been brought from Bánica by the Haitian border (Garrido Puello (1973), p. 72).
147 Larrazábal Blanco (1975), p. 136. 'Spiritism' is a term used by many Dominican authors to denominate Dominican voodoo.
148 Davis (1987), pp. 316–17.
149 Ibid., p. 101.
150 Jovine Soto (1965), p. 17.
151 Ibid.
152 Garrido Puello (1973), p. 72.

Figure 6.2 La Cofradía del Espíritu Santo in San Juan de la Maguana during Whit
Week 1989.

dressed according to their *promesas*,[153] in red and yellow dresses, the colors
of *El Espíritu Santo*, the patron 'saint' of the *cofradía*. Others wear the colors
of the Virgin – blue and white.

During its time in San Juan de la Maguana *El Espíritu Santo*, in its guise of
a child, is carried in processions through the town of San Juan de la
Maguana, visiting hospitals and private houses. When the statuette is taken
in and out of houses the devotees kneel in front of it and in a palanquin
the saint is carried over their heads. The same procedure is repeated in the
countryside, where the palanquin is also either lowered in front of domestic animals or carried above them, a ritual with obvious fertility connotations.[154] People become possessed, either by *El Espíritu Santo* or the
misterios. It even happens that the spirit of Olivorio invades the mind of
some *cofrades*. When the statuette is returned to the church in El Batey, the
dancing and feasting continue for another night. Before the 'saint' is
brought to rest he is also carried down to a small stream in El Batey to visit
his 'bride', an Indian 'queen' believed to live under the water.[155]

153 There exist various kinds of religious *promesas*. A *promesa* often implies the carrying out
of certain acts, performed as personal penitence, or as outward signs of earnest devotion.
In the rural Dominican Republic a very common *promesa* consists of dressing oneself in
a certain way for a limited time, sometimes for several years.
154 Statues of saints are still carried over fields or placed beside sick people as a part of
popular Catholic rituals in other parts of the world as well.
155 We witnessed some of the ceremonies of *La Cofradía del Espíritu Santo* during Whit Week
in 1989. Cf. Lemus and Oleo (1977), pp. 299–303.

Figure 6.3 Drums (*palos*) from an *Olivorista* sanctuary.

Several leading *Olivoristas* are members[156] of the *Cofradía del Espíritu Santo* and play an important part in its ceremonies, something which has led some people to the erroneous assumption that the *cofradía* emerged out of *Olivorista* beliefs.[157] As pointed out above, it is much older than *Olivorismo*, and members of its leadership are rarely self-confessed *Olivoristas*, even if most of them are familiar with *Olivorismo* and several visited and supported the movement in Palma Sola.[158]

The rituals carried out by Olivorio and his group, as well as the ones celebrated in Palma Sola, show many affinities to cultic behavior within a *cofradía* like the one of *El Espíritu Santo*. Most *Olivorista* sanctuaries keep three *palos*, of exactly the same type as the ones used by the *cofrades* of *El Espíritu Santo*. The dance of *El Espíritu Santo* was performed in La Maguana as well as in Palma Sola. Like *cofrades* both the people of Olivorio and the

156 In 1986, every member of the *cofradía* paid a minimum of five centavos a year for seven
    years in order to be a life member, but most devotees pay much more. A book with the
    names of all the members is kept in El Batey. *La Cofradía del Espíritu Santo* has local
    branches all across the southwestern part of the Dominican Republic. Its income is
    'rather impressive' and it owns 'some land' administered by a directorate, which is
    chosen and changed every year (interview with Arsidé Gardés, El Batey, 11 April 1986).
157 Cf. Jiménez de León (1974).
158 Interview with Arsidé Gardés, El Batey, 11 April 1986. Other *cofrades* were fervently
    opposed to the Ventura brothers. As a rule popular cults in the Dominican Republic are
    apolitical in the sense that some members may be supporters of certain political groups
    and factions, while others have totally different views and opinions. We have talked to
    several persons who believed in 'the mysteries of Palma Sola' while they disliked the views
    and behavior of the *Mellizos*.

people in Palma Sola dressed themselves in accordance with certain *promesas*. Dancing and communal feasting are given utmost importance in all *Olivorista* rituals. Just like the *cofrades* of *El Espíritu Santo* the *Olivoristas* are also convinced of the fact that the ultimate force behind everything in the valley is *El Gran Poder de Dios*, of which the effigy in El Batey is the visual symbol. Furthermore, both Olivorio's group and the people in Palma Sola were organized like a *cofradía*, headed by a group of leaders and 'queens'. Rituals and ceremonies were carried out on certain dates and both groups are often referred to as *logias* [lodges], *hermandades* or *fraternidades* [fraternities] – all common denominations of *cofradías*.

Other expressions of popular religion in the Dominican Republic reflected in *Olivorismo*

Crosses and calvarios

One outstanding feature of *Olivorismo* is the veneration of the cross and the elaborate cult which has been rendered by various types of crosses, both by Olivorio and in Palma Sola. Most *Olivoristas* consider crosses to be endowed with a personality of their own. They give them different names and equate them with Christ or Olivorio. The most lasting impression of an *Olivorista* who lay wounded in the dust of Palma Sola was the sight of one of the crosses in the central calvary: 'The lead was flying through the air and the cross stood in the middle of it all, like a Christ in the fire.'[159]

Olivorio erected crosses wherever he stayed for a long time and his cult in La Maguana is still centered around various calvaries, the most important of which is the one close to his alleged birthplace near the path to La Agüita. The cross was always present in Olivorio's preaching. He made the sign of the cross over the people he tried to heal and stated repeatedly: 'I am on a mission that will last until I come to the trunk of the cross.'[160] *Olivoristas* often call the cross *palo* or *tronco* [trunk], words that also are used to denominate the venerated big drums used in certain ceremonies, as well as respected village patriarchs, *troncos del lugar* [trunks of the place]. We have already mentioned how Olivorio's *palo de piñón*, formed like a cross,[161] played a very important part in his cult. Another of Olivorio's insignia was a cross-hilted sword.[162] In an oil painting, which can be seen at Enemencio Mora's *ermita* in Maguana Arriba, Olivorio is depicted holding a cross in his right hand, indicating either the *palo de piñón* or his sword.

---

159 Interview with Diego Cépeda, Jínova, 4 June 1989.
160 Garrido Puello (1963), p. 17.
161 For example an interview with Javier Jovino, Río Limpio, 30 April 1986.
162 Cf. *El Cable*, 1 July 1922.

Figure 6.4 Soldiers in the calvary of Palma Sola after the massacre.

Worship of the cross was also paramount in Palma Sola. 'God, Olivorio and the Holy Cross' were constantly invoked and the holy compound contained several *calvarios*,[163] each one the subject of complicated rituals. Some of the most popular *salves* sung by the *Palmasolistas* mention the cross: 'There is no trunk like the cross, nor light like that of the day.'[164] Visitors to Palma Sola returned home with *palos de cruz*, small wooden sticks from some aromatic tree which had been blessed by the *Mellizos*, as holy mementos.[165]

Erecting crosses in certain places in order to sanctify them is an old custom among European Christians, possibly dating back to the times when crosses were erected on old pagan sites, like banners being hoisted over occupied territory. The medieval warriors who tried to conquer Palestine from the Muslims carried crosses with them and were accordingly called crusaders, probably relating themselves to a legend about Constantine the Great which relates how the day before the decisive battle of Saxa Rubra he saw the sign of the cross in the sky together with the words: '*In hoc signo vinces*' ['in this sign you shall conquer']. The Castilian conquerors of Moorish lands in Spain were also called crusaders and carried crosses in front of their armies. When the Spanish *Reconquista* was completed it was

163 The three crosses are of course alluding to the calvary of Mount Golgotha, but they also symbolize the Trinity: Father, Son and Holy Spirit, as well as the three 'divine persons' in their manifestations as Faith, Hope and Charity. A single cross is used to represent the Holy Spirit (cf. Davis (1987), pp. 99–100).
164 Cited by Patoño Bautista Mejía, interview, Distrito de Haina, 5 March 1986.
165 Bautista Mejía (1988), p. 39.

celebrated by the erection of a huge cross on the heights of the Alhambra – the ultimate sign that the whole of Spain had been won for Christianity.[166] That same year Columbus planted the first Christian cross on the island of Hispaniola, 'as a sign that Your Highnesses have the land as your own, and above all as a symbol for Jesus Christ Our Lord and in honor of Christianity'.[167]

The tradition initiated by Columbus has continued to this very day. For example, the Jesuits of the so-called frontier missions initiated by Trujillo erected *calvarios* all over their districts along the Haitian border, 'sanctifying the land' by 'following the example of Columbus'.[168] The missionary district of the Jesuits partly covered areas where many *Olivoristas* lived and several of the latter must have been present at sumptuous inauguration ceremonies which often drew crowds of more than a thousand persons.

In medieval piety the cross was venerated as a sign endowed with immense powers, an effective weapon against the devil and all inflictions he was believed to bring about. It was used against locusts and hailbearing clouds and was dipped into streams and oceans in order to bring rain. During the plagues in the fourteenth century the adoration of the cross was more fervent than ever. The official name of the Flagellants, who in huge crowds moved across Europe scourging themselves, was 'Brethren of the Cross'.[169] In several places, Flagellants incited people to slay Jews '*en masse*', accusing them of being enemies of God and of poisoning wells. Such pogroms were carried out in the name of the cross while the Flagellants preached that 'if the Black Death was caused by the enemy, then the crucifix would keep them at bay'.[170] After the *Reconquista* of Spain the cross retained its popularity as a weapon against 'infidels' like Moors, Jews and Protestants. All kinds of legends were spun to demonstrate the contempt that 'enemies of Christ' showed the cross. Most of these stories intended to show how Jews and other enemies of the 'true faith' were finally subdued and injured by the immense powers inherent in the cross.[171] A reflection of such views may be discerned in Palma Sola where sorcerers and liars were said to fall to the ground in violent convulsions as soon as they approached the holy crosses.[172] Many *Olivoristas* believe that calvarios are

---

166 Christian (1981), p. 184. In the same vein Catholic priests 'sanctified' the sites of former Palma Sola subsidiaries by planting crosses on them (Pérez (1963)).
167 Colón (1988), p. 162.
168 From 1936 to 1956 they erected more than fifty *calvarios*, most of them quite imposing structures, made by stone or cement (López de Santa Anna (1957), pp. 65–6).
169 Ziegler (1989), p. 89.
170 Christian (1981), p. 184.
171 Trachtenberg (1945), pp. 118–23.
172 Interview with León Romilio Ventura, Media Luna, 17 January 1986. Cf. García (1986), pp. 185–6 and 188–9.

'witnesses' which by *El Gran Poder de Dios* have been given the faculty to punish every liar in an 'impeccable way'.[173]

It is quite common for Dominican peasants to state that *Lo Malo* fears the cross.[174] To that end crosses are placed in front of houses and by the entrances to villages, in order to ban access to 'the devil and all witches'. In order to protect oneself from nightmares, open scissors or small sticks tied together crosswise are placed under the pillow. Small crosses are placed in cots of newborn babies. In order to liberate themselves from *Lo Malo,* which may mean a variety of things – the devil himself, sickness, sin, or simply bad luck – people accede to the *calvarios* because the power of crosses exorcizes sorrows and problems[175] and offers protection from all evil.

On special occasions the crosses found in the Dominican countryside are completely covered with small strips of multicolored paper. This is particularly the case during the month of May,[176] when *fiestas de cruz* [celebrations of the cross] are carried out in commemoration of the recovery of the 'True Cross' by St Helen,[177] although this is merely a pretext for ancient spring rites promoting fertility. Celebrations take place in the vicinity of the adorned crosses where small altars are erected and decorated by the youngsters of the village. The Feast of the Cross is above all a celebration of youth. These feasts, which were more common fifty years ago than they are today, begin on the night preceding 3 May and often continue during evenings all through the month of May. In villages around San Juan de la Maguana it was common to elect a girl to be the May Queen and a boy to be May King and the sumptuous feasts, with food, singing and dancing, were considered suitable occasions for *conquistas amorosas* [amorous conquests].[178] The 'bawdy' character of some *fiestas de cruz* caused authorities to legislate against them.[179]

The May festivals form part of a cycle of festivities celebrating germination and fertility, culminating with the feast of St John the Baptist.[180] The

---

173 Cf. Espín del Prado (1980), p. 57.
174 Anyone who is familiar with vampire or other horror movies is well aware of the role asssigned to the cross as an exorcizer of evil (cf. Thomas (1984), pp. 570 and 589–90).
175 Lemus and Marty (1975), p. 162.
176 In several places, particularly around Azua and Peravia in the south, crosses are dressed like queens, complete with crowns, necklaces and cloaks (Davis (1987), p. 92).
177 St Helen (AD 255–330) was the mother of Constantine the Great and is connected with the alleged finding of the true cross close to the hillock of Calvary (Attwater (1965), p. 166).
178 Garrido (1922), p. 232 and Cano y Fortuna (n.d), pp. 126–7 and 149–50.
179 One example is a *Reglamento de Gobierno* from 1857 which stated that: 'by the altars of the Cross [...] dances are forbidden under the penalty of 15 *francos*' (quoted in Nolasco (1956), p. 93).
180 Cf. ibid., pp. 46–98.

intense veneration of the cross as a fertility symbol can be seen in connection with the tradition of the erection of maypoles, something which takes place around the time of the summer solstice in several European regions.[181] In Spain we find stick dances called *moriscas*, in Portugal *danças dos paulitos* (sometimes these dances are carried out by men dressed like women), and equivalents can also be found in countries like England (Morris dances), Denmark, Germany, Italy, Hungary and Lithuania.[182]

We have already mentioned the possible connections between *Olivorista* dances and those carried out by *gagá* societies in the Dominican Republic and *rara* groups in Haiti, where the *baton* wielded by men, often dressed as women, is related to fertility beliefs.[183] Legba, the *lwa* invoked at the beginning of every voodoo ceremony, also carries a stick, often in the form of a cane. Legba is believed to be the patron of the universe. Voodooists state that it was *Bondye* [God] who created the universe, but Legba sustains and nurtures it; he is related to an 'umbilical cord' which runs through all worlds in the universe. His cane also represents his phallus, the source of human life, a sign of virility and a link between human generations, and the central column in a voodoo sanctuary, the *poto mitan*, seen as a connection between the human and spiritual spheres. Legba is called the 'Lord of the Crossroads'[184] because he controls the various meeting points between different worlds.[185]

Legba is often identified with Jesus and some voodooists state that like Jesus he once sacrificed himself on a cross, *l'arbre-sec* [the dry tree] [*pyebwa chèch* or *sèk* in Creole].[186] The cross was already in Africa a symbol of Legba. As a matter of fact, the cross is extremely important in voodoo cosmology. It is considered as the metaphysical axis around which the world was constructed, the skeleton giving structure to the universe, connecting the four cardinal points and the four elements. The *peristil* [peristyle] where

181 Crosses are also 'erected'.
182 Cf. Kurath (1950b), p. 1082.
183 Similar dances are carried out by the Ewe people of Togo in West Africa and just as in Haitan *rara* and Dominican *gagá* the batons are wielded by men attired in women's clothing (Courlander (1960), p. 133).
184 Desmangles (1992), pp. 108–9.
185 Crossroads play an important role in European folklore as well. They are places where one is most likely to meet demons, evil spirits, ghosts and witches. As a 'no man's land', they were used as burial grounds for outcasts, considered as meeting places with forces from the 'spiritual sphere', ideal locations for divinations, sacrifices and magical rites (Smith (1949), p. 66.). In Dominican voodoo the crossroads and the cross are connected with the *guedés* [spirits of the dead] (*Gede* in Haitian Creole) and their leader Barón del Cementerio (in Haiti called *Bawon Samdi*, or *Gede*). He is the shameless and bawdy lord of death, churchyards and witchcraft, but also a protector of children, life-giver, purveyor of sexual prowess and custodian of fertility – a god without respect or limitations, lord of both life and death (cf. Deren (1953), pp. 102–14).
186 Rigaud (1985), pp. 17 and 164.

voodoo ceremonies are carried out are constructed in relation to the cruci-
form and the *vèvè* [geometric figures symbolizing *lwa*] are also traced in
the form of crosses with the *poto mitan* as a center. The importance of the
cross within voodoo rituals may be connected with African traditions,
particularly Fon and Bambara beliefs. Instead of adapting themselves to
Catholic beliefs, Africans probably reinterpreted the Christian cross in the
light of their own notions and customs.[187] However, although *Olivorismo* has
probably received some stimulus to its intense cross cult from voodoo and
African beliefs, the most obvious roots of this cult are to be found in old
European rural traditions.

Velaciones

When speaking about popular religion in the Dominican Republic one has
to keep in mind that it differs from place to place. General concepts and
specific rituals like *velaciones, velorios, rosarios*, the singing of *salves*, etc. are
found almost everywhere, but details and explanations differ substantially
from community to community. The reasons are varied. One is the lack of
good roads and adequate means of transportation which prevailed far into
the present century. Another is that local religious customs are subject to
constant changes and reinterpretations, at the same time as particular
rituals and traditions tend to be concentrated in certain villages, cult-sites,
or even families.

   An outward sign of Dominican peasant piety is the altar found in rural
dwellings. It usually consists of a cloth-covered table tucked away in a
corner of a bedroom. On the wall above the altar the owner has pinned up
chromolithographs. The tabletop is generally covered with disparate
objects such as vases with flowers, candles, lamps consisting of small plates
with wicks floating in oil, bottles with 'holy' water, bells decorated with
multicolored ribbons, bottles with rum, eau-de-cologne or soft drinks,
plaster doves, rosaries, open bibles and prayer books, framed pictures of
saints and plates with offerings like honey, sweet bread and cinnamon
sticks. Most of these objects are more or less 'standard', although the vari-
ations are innumerable. If the bedroom is very small, the holy objects are
placed on a shelf attached to the wall. If that is the case, the altar is seldom
covered with cloth. These rural altars constitute the center of peasant families' religious life and prayers are said in front of them at least once a day
– prayers which may be the ones currently used by Catholics, like the
rosario, novenas, Ave Maria and *Padre Nuestro*, or have been taken from
missals and devotional manuals. Several, however, are 'invented' or taken
from unorthodox sources and sold at any Dominican marketplace, either

---

187 Desmangles (1992), pp. 99–108.

Figure 6.5 Altar from an *Olivorista* sanctuary. Note the picture of the dead Olivorio.

in the form of booklets or on loose sheets. The content of many of these prayers is purely magical.[188]

As an act of devotion, token of gratitude, or as a kind of 'instalment payment' for expected favors it happens that a devotee makes a *promesa* to his patron saint. A *promesa* is a religious vow which constitutes a link joining the believer to a saint. During the Middle Ages vows were given to feudal lords as well, and several researchers consider them as typical of societies where a form of clientship prevails between influential people and their dependents.[189] This description fits well with the situation that traditionally

---

188 They may be directed to the 'Magnetic Stone', 'San Juan the Madman', the 'Four Winds', the 'Wandering Jew', the 'Lonely Soul' or the 'Tobacco and the Beneficent Spirits.' Sometimes they are not prayers at all, but magical recipes like the following example, dedicated to the 'Seven African Powers': 'If you want to obtain attractive powers and means of seduction, and want to be safe and sound in body and soul, as well as being relieved from the bad shadows pursuing you, then you have to give yourself a bath with petals from white roses spread in the water. Do this every Friday during 9 weeks, do this at noon, take another bath in the evening with the following ingredients: one leaf of rosemary, jasmine flowers, Eau-de-Cologne, 7 poplar leaves, 7 sage leaves, 7 rue leaves, 7 basil twigs. After the bath you light an oil-lamp and pray: "Our Father who art in heaven" to the saint you prefer' (from *Oración de Las 7 Potencias Africanas*, issued by 'santería Chencho, Santo Domingo). 'The Seven African Powers' are originally Yoruba *orishas* [deities]: Ọbatalá [Obàtá'lá], Eshu [Èṣù], Shango [Ṣòngó], Ogún [Ògun'], Orúnla (or Orún mila [Ọrun' mìlà], Yemonjá [Yẹmọnja] and Oshún [Òsun] (cf. González-Wippler (1992), pp. 107–25).
189 Sallmann (1979), p. 871.

prevailed in the San Juan Valley, where the *compadrazgo* system[190] has been strong for centuries. Both Olivorio and the Ventura brothers considered themselves bound to certain deities for a fixed amount of time, when talking about their 'missions'. Olivorio used to repeat: 'I am sent by God on a mission that will last for 33 years. Everyone who believes in me will be saved.'[191] The oath taken by visitors to Palma Sola contained the following statement: 'I swear by God, the Son and the Holy Spirit and by Olivorio Mateo to carry out the mission imposed upon me.'[192]

Giving a *promesa* often implies wearing a certain kind of dress. Olivorio and his followers wore blue denim adorned with cotton cords and scapulars. They also wore cords tied around their forefronts. Plinio Ventura did not take off his spurs, he ordered his followers to dress in blue denim and women had to wear long skirts. Common *promesas* are also pledges to offer a vigil by an altar on the day dedicated to a certain patron saint. Such vigils have several different names.[193] They are occasions for communal worship and merrymaking and are, as a rule, considered to be *divertidísimas* [very entertaining].[194]

A *velación* can be described as a multileveled ritual with many different aspects. It is a means of communication between this world and the spiritual sphere, and an occasion when the 'otherworldly' merges with the commonplace, when holy things are treated in what may appear as a rather casual manner, thus rendering presence and credibility to spiritual matters. Young and old join in the festivities, barriers are torn down at the same time as links with age-old traditions are revived, strengthening the unity between participants. This does not mean that 'outsiders' are excluded: on the contrary, everyone is free to join a *velación* on equal terms with the devotees. A *velación* is a feast, a moment to have a good time together with 'the other side of existence'. Some *Olivoristas* assert that during a 'successful' *velación* 'two worlds merge into one'.[195] When that happens the participants forget their individual selves, obtaining relief from their daily toil and tension, merging with the group.[196]

190 A person puts himself in relation to influential persons by choosing them as godparents for his children, thus creating 'a complex of formalized friendships and fictional kinship' (Foster (1948)).

191 Olivorio, quoted in Garrido Puello (1963), p. 55.

192 Quoted in an interview with Patoño Bautista Mejía, Distrito de Haina, 5 March 1986.

193 Among them are *velación, vela de canto, noche de vela, vela, velorio de santo,* and *fiesta de promesas.*

194 Jiménez (1927), p. 152.

195 Interview with Julián Ramos, Higüerito, 16 January 1986. What Julián probably means is that the 'spiritual sphere', which is inhabited by *misterios* and spirits, reveals itself to the participants in the ritual and that the borderline between the 'living' and the 'other side' thus becomes blurred.

196 Rodríguez Vélez (1982), pp. 295–6.

A *velación* may be prepared and carried out in several different ways. If it is scheduled for the particular day of a patron saint, preparations will begin several weeks in advance with *rezos* [prayers] in front of the altar. Such *rezos* are carried out on certain days in the week, often Tuesdays and Fridays. They are frequently directed by a 'professional' *rezador* or *rezadora*. The prayer leader places himself in front of the altar and reads, or sings, long prayers, which sometimes may be of his own invention, but which generally are taken from Catholic prayer books. At certain intervals he rings a small bell and sprinkles the surrounding devotees with holy water. Prayer sessions often take more than one hour.[197]

These ceremonies are repeated week after week until the *noche de vela* [vigil night] takes place. The *noche de vela* begins with *rezos* in the afternoon. Around seven o'clock the musicians arrive and, as a sign that the second part of the *velación* has begun, they 'warm up' their instruments.[198] People now start to sing their *rezos* to the accompaniment of an accordion, a small drum called *barcié*, or *bongo*, held between the knees of the drummer, and a *güiro*, a rasped instrument. The songs may be *plenas*, *tonadas* or *salves*. *Plenas* and *tonadas* are sung in a slow rhythm, frequently without the accompaniment of instruments. A lead singer improvises the stanza and the listeners answer with modulations sounding like 'AAeee' or 'OOooo'. The contents of a *tonada* are less formalized than those of a *pleno*. The *tonada* may be quite trivial and the singer often makes allusions to the manners and character of people who are present at the ceremony. These allusions may be quite outspoken and even frivolous.[199] Compared with *plenas* and *tonadas* the rhythm of *salves* is rapid and merry. Among *Olivoristas* *salves* are by far the most common songs during a *velación*. Prayers and *salves* are performed in intervals during the night, interspersed with dancing and eating. At midnight a *sancocho* is served, a thick, tasty stew which is considered to be the national dish of the Dominican Republic. Coffee and rum are served on a regular basis, a festive atmosphere prevails and people are relaxed and in a good mood.

In Olivorio's time, *Sanjuaneros* stated that 'rural youngsters long for these ceremonies since infatuations are permitted'.[200] Such a remark reminds one of similar gatherings in other cultures. Roger Bastide writes of Brazilian *novenas*:

At such times, when people exchange their customary isolation for closeness, a collective spirit may spring to life and forge the kind of

---

197 Lemus and Marty (1975), p. 121. In the southwestern parts of the Dominican Republic such sessions are often accompanied by *palo* drumming and the singing of *salves*.
198 Jiménez (1927), p. 155.
199 Lemus and Marty (1975), pp. 126–30.
200 Garrido (1922), p. 231.

bonds that distance destroys. That explains why 'novenas' end with a meal accompanied by brandy and with singing and dancing. The sound of a rustic guitar in the warm darkness creates a climate for love; couples form.[201]

When the *palos*, the big drums made out of hollow logs, are substituted for the accordion and the *barcié*, the intensity of a *velación* changes. A *fiesta de palos* generally implies a ritual that may lead to possession. *Gente se montan*: people become possessed by *misterios*, Indians, the Holy Spirit, Olivorio or other spiritual entities.

Velaciones are carried out in *ermitas*, as well is in private houses. Most *ermitas* have a *hermandad* or *cofradía* organized around them. The core of a small *hermandad* consists of nine persons and each of them represents a particular area in the vicinity of the *ermita*. These persons are responsible for the fund-raising which is necessary to pay for the elaborate *velaciones* held in honor of the *ermita's* patron saint; it is also their task to invite people for the upcoming feast. *Ermita velaciones* are generally preceded by a *reina* who may be the woman who takes care of the place, or someone elected especially for the occasion. When the queen enters the *ermita*, dressed in elaborate clothes, this is the signal for the feast to begin. The music starts to sound and *salves* are struck up.[202]

A *velación* organized by an *ermita* is usually concluded with a procession on the afternoon of the following day. The image of the patron saint is carried by devotees waving banners and ringing bells followed by the musicians. If a *calvario* is close at hand, it is circled several times during *salve* singing. After leaving the grounds of the *ermita* the image is carried through the neighborhood and stops are made at certain houses, or by specially erected *paradas* or *descansos*, decorated altars which have been placed along the procession route. Here the blessings of the saint are offered to bystanders while musicians play and *salves* are sung.[203]

Many of the rituals performed by Olivorio and his group, as well as the *Palmasolistas*, were related to the traditional pattern of rural *velaciones*. Thus, the *Mellizos* and their co-workers may be seen as a kind of *hermandad* which took care of the mission in Palma Sola, and the heavenly mandate given to them has the same character as the connection with the 'spiritual sphere' established through a traditional *promesa*. In Palma Sola we find the queens and processions typical of rural *velaciones*, as well as *salve* singing, dancing and communal sharing of food. What differs is the

---

201 Bastide (1978), p. 353.
202 Lemus and Marty (1975), p. 121.
203 Ibid., pp. 121–2. It is common that *velaciones* begin with processions more or less like the one described above.

absence of altars in Palma Sola, where the importance of crosses and *calvarios* was stressed instead.

The traditions continue to be upheld among present-day *Olivoristas*. Witness, for example, the following episode: the blessing of a house on an ordinary day in Jínova, a village just north of San Juan de la Maguana.[204] In the afternoon, the homeowner went to Diego Cépeda, a well-known *Olivorista* patriarch, to borrow his crucifix. Diego received the visitors in his courtyard. Among them was a small elderly man who played the *tambora*[205] and another musician who played the accordion. Together with Diego they went into his bedroom where one corner of the ceiling is covered with blue sheets arranged like a canopy over a large altar, covered by a blue and white cloth. The altar is flanked by two banners. One is white, i.e. the flag of the Virgin. The other one is blue with a white cross: Olivorio's flag. On the altar, Diego has various framed chromolithographs depicting different saints, among them photos of the dead Olivorio. To his visitors Diego handed over a picture of La Virgen de la Altagracia and another picture showing St Michael the Archangel fighting the devil,[206] the two banners and a small white-painted wooden cross. Finally he placed a small photo of the dead Olivorio above a big crucifix he had been given by Senator Mesa's wife[207] and handed it over to the man who was going to be in charge of the ceremony. Don Diego also lit a candle from one of the ones he kept burning on the altar and gave it to the man who carried the crucifix. He finally took a small bell and together with his guests went into the court-yard where Diego has three concentric stone circles laid out around three crosses – a white one flanked by two smaller blue-painted ones.

Diego Cépeda and his visitors formed a small procession and circled the crosses three times. First came a man waving the white flag. He was

204 Based on notes taken in Jínova, 4 June 1989.
205 A small drum with the drumheads covering both sides of a hollowed-out trunk. It is played with both hands while the drummer carries it in a cord slung over the left shoulder. Contrary to the three big blue *palos*, the *tambora* is not consecrated and has no particular liturgical meaning. The *palos* are usually baptized and are venerated as receptacles for spiritual powers (Lizardo (1988), pp. 349–52).
206 This saint is thought to ward off evil. He is identified with Belié Belcán, a *misterio* who is venerated as a powerful anti-witchcraft entity, but also a 'seducer and merry-maker who pretty well represents the psychological traits of our Spanish-African nature' (Miniño (1980)).
207 Interview with Diego Cépeda, Jínova, 4 June 1989. Juan Mesa, a respected physician and the *Reformista* party's most important representative in San Juan de la Maguana, has an *Olivorista* altar in his house, and the *Reformistas* support a peasant collective in Jínova called Papá Liborio (interview with Leopoldo Figuereo, San Juan de la Maguana, 4 June 1989). Dr Mesa does not consider himself to be a fervent *Olivorista*. He is, however, well informed of *Olivorista* beliefs and knows many stories about Olivorio and his alleged prophecies and miracles (interview with Juan José Medina Mesa, San Juan de la Maguana, 18 January 1989).

followed by Diego who rang his little bell, by a woman who waved Olivorio's banner and two women who walked side by side carrying the two framed chromolithographs of the saints. Then came the man with the crucifix, followed by a woman with the small white cross and, finally, the musicians playing the *tambora* and the accordion. All sang *salves* in honor of Olivorio. After this little ceremony, the paraphernalia were carried rather unceremoniously along dusty roads up to the house of the man who wanted to sanctify his house. Diego stayed home, but in his absence the man with the *tambora* acted as master of ceremonies. When the small procession came up to the house they were greeted by many people who had been waiting for them, and everybody walked around the house three times. Afterwards the procession entered the biggest room of the house, where all of the furniture had been taken out and an altar prepared for the crucifix with Olivorio's picture.

Two palm branches had been bent down to form an arcade over the altar. Both the altar and the branches were decorated with pink flowers called *flores del Perú* and the altar was covered with a white cloth. Under the palm branches, the chromolithograph, the bell, the candle, the small cross and the crucifix were now placed. The *salves* and the music ceased and the little man with the drum appeared calling for the housewife. In front of the altar, he held her by the hand while he read several prayers and sprinkled her with holy water from a green branch that he wet in a jar standing on the altar. The ceremony was repeated with her husband and the bystanders explained that the owners of the house were being 'bound' to the spirit of Olivorio. After this, three chairs were brought in for the musicians, who had by now been joined by a man who played a big blue-painted *palo* consecrated to Olivorio, and the dancing began.

The music was fast and merry, mainly *pri-pri* [rural *merengue*]. The songs were simple, not as elaborate as the *salves*. One just repeated: '*Baile Olivorito! Baile Olivorito!*' The room was filled with dancing couples. No one seemed to care about with whom they danced. Old ladies danced with much younger partners, boys with boys and girls with girls. All seemed to enjoy themselves, and it was amazing to see how many youngsters took part.

A bystander pointed to a young lady dressed in white and said: 'She is soon going to be possessed. Look at her. She is good.' The woman started to swirl around faster and faster and soon fell to the floor in violent convulsions. She was carried into an adjacent room. After a while the housewife also became possessed, but in a much gentler way. She was also brought into the other room, which was a bedroom with a small altar. Sitting on the floor together with two ladies, who kneeled by her side, she talked in a gentle and rather quiet voice. She seemed to be a bit dazed and tired while she gave advice to the bystanders: 'Be good to one another! Work and share the fruits of the earth. Most important of all is unity and the work done in common', etc. She was said to be possessed by the spirit of

Olivorio. Not many people entered the room. The majority had joined the dancing or were preparing food in the courtyard.

Outside the house, several fires were burning and plates with *chivo* and *moro* [goat meat and rice with black beans] were passed around. The music was silent for a while when the musicians joined in the eating and the housewife came out from the house. Later on, the feast continued as before, with singing and dancing, and now rum bottles began to be passed around. No one got drunk, however, and the feast ended around nine, because the next day was a working day.

Rosarios

An outstanding feature of the rituals in both La Maguana and Palma Sola was the recurrent processions through the holy compound, recalling rural *rosarios*. As in many other Catholic countries, popular piety in the Dominican Republic is very much attached to the Virgin Mary and the general impression is that her importance seems to surpass even that of the Father and the Son. Many peasants consider her to be the principal divine protector of humans, livestock and the fertility of the soil.[208] She is the compassionate face of a divine power which otherwise appears as impersonal as destiny.

Devotion to the Virgin is intimately connected with the veneration of the rosary. Just as the cross is equated with Jesus or *El Espíritu Santo*, the rosary tends to stand for everything included in concepts like 'holy' and 'divine'. An *Olivorista* who wanted to point out that Olivorio is divine expressed it in the following way: 'Olivorio is the true God, he is identical with the rosary.'[209]

Saying the rosary has been an integral part of Catholic culture for several centuries. The rosary originates from the Archangel Gabriel's greeting to Mary, as quoted by Luke: 'Hail, thou who art highly favoured, the Lord is with thee: blessed art thou among women'[210] combined with St Elisabeth's words in the same chapter: 'Blessed art thou among women, and blessed is the fruit of thy womb.'[211] During the late Middle Ages the rosary was spread among the Catholic laity by the preaching orders. During the fifteenth century the prayer was combined with the handling of a bead circlet, which also became known as the rosary.[212]

208 Cf. Lundius (1993).
209 For example in an interview with Julián Ramos, Higüerito, 16 January 1986.
210 *Luke*, 1:28.
211 *Luke*, 1:42.
212 The chain of beads originated in Brahminic India and the medieval crusaders are generally credited with spreading the habit to Europe, after having picked it up from the Muslims (Warner (1983), pp. 305–6). According to pious legend the founder of the

In Dominican popular religion the word *rosario* not only denotes a prayer and a bead circlet, but is also the name for processions organized in times of distress.[213] Such ceremonies are seen as the acting out of the rosary prayer and the processions are considered to be the equivalent of the rosary circlet, a communal, material manifestation of the prayer. The processions are carried out as an act of penance and the Virgin and the saints are invoked in order to save the faithful from misfortune and misery.

The devotees gather in the evening and the march begins after dark. A large cross is carried ahead of the people and it often rests in the hand of a *rezador*, heading the communal worship, singing and improvising the stanzas of the rosary, while the multitude answers in chorus:

Rezador: nosotros caminando buscando entre las flores	Prayer: We are walking searching among the flowers
Chorus: A ver si encontramos la Virgen de Dolores.[214]	Chorus: To see if we find the Virgin of Sorrows.

It is not an orthodox *rosario* which is sung during these processions. Dominican peasants have an extensive repertoire of *rosarios* of their own invention, varying from district to district, although they all follow the traditional order of orthodox *rosarios*, i.e. they are sung in groups of *tercios*,

Dominican order, the Castilian Santo Domingo de Guzmán (1170–1221), in a heavenly vision received the rosary from the hands of the Virgin herself. Since the capital of the Dominican Republic was named after this particular saint and its first chapel and *cofradía* were founded by sailors who had Our Lady of the Rosary as their patroness, the rosary has traditionally been very important in the Dominican Republic. Today a full cycle of prayers is composed as fifteen 'decades'. Each decade consists of ten Hail Marys, each one represented by a bead in the bead circlet, and a group of one Glory Be to the Father, one Our Father and another Glory (in the Dominican Republic often replaced by a 'Glory to the Virgin' saying: 'Mary, Mother of Grace and Mercy in life and death, protect us, Our Lady'). The glories are represented by the chains holding a single, larger bead, representing Our Father. The bead circled only contains five decades and hence has to be run three times (in the morning, at noon and in the evening) to be completed. Each session is dedicated to a 'mystery' divided into five groups. The mysteries the penitent has to concentrate on are the Mystery of Joy (the Annunciation, the Visitation, the birth of Christ, his presentation in the temple and his visit to the temple at the age of 12), the Mystery of Glory (the Resurrection, the Assumption of Christ, the Pentecost, the Assumption of the Virgin and the coronation of the Virgin) and the Mystery of Pain (the prayer in Gethsemane, the flagellation, the coronation with spines, the carrying of the cross and the crucifixion). (We are grateful to César Iván Feris for explaining to us the subtleties surrounding the handling of the rosary.)

213 In the San Juan Valley the term *rosario* is often used as an equivalent of *Lo Sagrado*, a kind of visible presence symbolizing the 'other sphere'. 'To do the rosary' is to engage in something holy (interview with Enrique Figueroa, Hato Nuevo, 18 January 1986).

214 Valverde (1975), p. 51.

meaning that the songs are sung during three sessions, each constituted by a repetition of the song fifty times.

Following the cross and heading the procession are framed pictures and statuettes of various virgins and saints, carried by women adorned with white scarves. They are flanked by *faroles* [lanterns], made of colored paper, containing lighted candles, carried on top of long poles that are often more than two meters high. After the images and the *faroles* come devotees who carry *rosarios* and bells in their hands. Along the route several participants pick up boulders by the roadside and carry them on their heads as an act of penance. Halts are made by crosses and by *calvarios*, which are often dressed in colored paper for the occasion. In front of the crosses, the penitents lay down the stones, shrugging their shoulders to 'rid themselves of sin'. The crosses are saluted with stanzas like:

Saludándote Cruz	I greet you Cross
con gran reverencia	with great reverence
Hoy vengo, Jesús	I come today, Jesus
a hacer penitencia.[215]	to do penitence.

In the southwestern parts of the Dominican Republic the participants in a *rosario* make three turns around every *calvario*, and if a house, or an *ermita*, is close by, this building is also circled three times. *Salves* are sung and the procession takes leave of the crosses with a song containing words like:

Madre del Verbo Divino	Mother of the Divine Word
madre de consagración	mother of consecration
Echanos la bendición	Give us the benediction
que ya vamos de camino.[216]	because we are now on our way.

When one *rosario* meets another, elaborate rituals are carried out. The banners are lowered, and while the multitude kneels around them the crossbearers approach each other. When the crosses are nearly touching each other, all spectators come to their feet and burst out singing, praising the Virgin Mary. After such a greeting ceremony, the two *rosarios* resume the march together. In times of drought, the most common occasion for organizing *rosarios*, the final destination is generally a riverbed where images, crosses and banners are dipped in the water, if the course is not entirely dried up.

---

215 Ibid., p. 54.
216 Ibid.

Even if all *rosarios* do not explicitly address drought, they are usually organized during dry seasons. Most rural rituals that demand a high degree of
communal participation tend to take place during dry seasons, when agriculturists have some spare time since they are not busy with planting and
harvesting.[217] In the San Juan Valley the driest period of the year is between
December and May.[218] The national celebration in honor of La Virgen de
la Altagracia takes place on 21 January and huge multitudes gather in her
sanctuary in Higüey, in the eastern part of the island. Formerly the
pilgrims walked in processions similar to *rosarios*, coming all the way from
the San Juan Valley and even Haiti.[219]

The physical landscape of the Dominican Republic is covered by a
network of places with 'spiritual' significance, where the 'other' reality
comes forth. We have already mentioned caves, springs, *calvarios* and
ermitas where the divine is believed to manifest itself.[220] Many of these sites
are final destinations for pilgrimages and *rosarios*. There are several shrines
on a national level, similar to the one in Higüey. However, every Dominican district counts several holy places which attracts the local population,
while being adapted to a particular cycle of events. Most important in and
around the San Juan Valley are La Agüita, La Maguana, El Batey, El Corral
de los Indios, the caves of San Francisco, the ones in Seburuco and under
La Nalga del Maco. La Zurza is a place with pools of water close to a small
stream outside Las Matas de Farfán where an Indian spirit called *Rey del
Agua* [King of the Water] is worshiped[221] and El Limón at the Haitian
border, where a piece of a tree trunk is venerated, is said to show the face
of the Virgin 'like a shadow'. The image is believed to have appeared when
a palm tree was hit by lightning sometime during the last century.[222]

The *Olivoristas* are firmly incorporated in this network of holy places.
Olivorio is known to have moved from one holy place to another in and
around the San Juan Valley, and before Plinio and León Romilio Ventura
began their mission in Palma Sola they went on *romerías* [pilgrimages] all

217 Interview with Bryan Kennedy, Las Matas de Farfán, 4 May 1986.
218 The most important holidays for the *Olivoristas* are: 13 December, the Feast of St Lucia,
    patroness of Las Matas de Farfán; 28 December, which commemorates the massacre in
    Palma Sola; 21 January, the Day of La Virgen de la Altagracia; 3 May, the Day of the Holy
    Cross. The feasts in connection with the Holy Spirit are carried out during Pentecost (in
    May or June) and finally we have the Feasts of San Juan at the summer solstice in June.
219 After the death of Olivorio it is recorded that several of his devotees went on *romería*
    [pilgrimage] to Higüey, and some newspaper articles mentioned that he himself went
    there on pilgrimage. Several songs and *salves* in Olivorio's honor also mention his visits
    to Higüey.
220 Davis (1987), pp. 88–98, accounts for what she calls the mystical geography and mystical
    calendar of the Dominican Republic.
221 Ibid., pp. 24–5.
222 Pérez (1985), pp. 23–8.

over the district, visiting holy places and searching out prominent *Olivoris-tas* and famous cult functionaries:

> I wanted to know everything and we went from place to place. We visited several different places putting questions to old people who had known Olivorio. I asked them about his miracles. I was very careful when I asked those questions and I remember all the answers.[223]

In times of crisis peasants are often prone to give in to an urge to obtain support and consolation from the invisible forces that they believe are hidden in the landscape which surrounds them. Since they are powerful expressions of the shared distress of an entire community, *rosarios* have traditionally been considered as powerful tools when it comes to invoking the life-supporting forces in nature. In that sense the community that grew up around Olivorio, and, even more, around the cult in Palma Sola, can be considered in relation to *rosarios*. The rituals and preaching of both Olivorio and the Ventura brothers were tinged with apocalyptic fears, feelings which also tend to stimulate *rosarios* in the San Juan Valley. For example, old people have vivid memories of the *rosarios* that were carried out due to the fears of an imminent end to the earth which were triggered by the appearance of Halley's Comet in 1910.[224] The cult that developed around Olivorio had several distinctive features typical of 'crisis cults'. Accordingly many of the ceremonies performed in La Maguana were conceived within the structural framework of traditional *rosarios*.

El Gran Poder de Dios – Lo Malo

We have already mentioned that many *Sanjuaneros*, and *Olivoristas* in particular, believe in a supreme power behind all spiritual forces that exist in nature – *El Gran Poder de Dios* – a force which is inherent in the soil, but also in certain individuals, like Olivorio. *El Gran Poder de Dios* is considered to be identical with cosmic order. It is the source behind all life; it creates life and it preserves life. All human actions, as well as the germination of the crops, depend on *El Gran Poder de Dios*. It is the vital principle of life and is as such identical with God, *El Espíritu Santo* and Jesus, but since *El Gran Poder de Dios* often is considered to be identical with life itself it is sometimes assumed that the Holy Trinity is just another aspect of this force, which generally is imagined to be just as 'impersonal' as fate.

---

223 Interview with León Romilio Ventura, Media Luna, 17 January 1986. The wanderings of Plinio and León Romilio have been compared with a custom connected with the initiation of *hungans* [voodoo priests], called *recorrer los portales* [touring the gates], i.e. visiting other cult functionaries in order to learn the trade (Mota (1980), pp. 209–10).
224 Interview with Julián Ramos, Higüerito, 16 January 1986.

However, *El Gran Poder de Dios* assumes various shapes and is also represented by chromolithographs,[225] such as one depicting the bust of a white-
bearded man, radiating beams of light running through the darkness.
From a cloud under him appears a hand holding th˙ scales of justice.[226]
The hand coming out of the clouds is interpreted as *La Mano Poderosa*: the
most common symbol of *El Gran Poder de Dios*. It is also depicted as a huge
hand exposing its palm to the viewer, pierced through and resting on
clouds, while over each fingertip there is a saint,[227] and over the thumb
Jesus stands in his guise as a child. Among most *Olivoristas* the inclusion of
the Jesus child in the picture is an indication that one of the most important manifestations of *El Gran Poder de Dios* is *El Espíritu Santo*, represented
by the statuette in El Batey. *La Mano Poderosa* is also represented by mark-
ings on rocks or tree trunks, like the ones found by the Spring of St John
in La Agüita, or it may be placed on altars in the form of paper cut-outs.
Some *curanderos* cut out white sheets of paper in the form of hands and
place healing herbs between them in order that they may gain power from
La Mano Poderosa.[228] The powerful hand is considered to be a beneficent
force and dreaming about hands is interpreted as a sign that one is under
divine protection.[229]

Several printed prayers directed to *El Gran Poder de Dios* exist and several
can be bought printed on paper sheets. One such *panacea* was found
among the belongings of the Haitian *caco* leader Charlemagne Péralte
after he had been shot by American marines in 1919. It was printed in
Higüey and had probably been given to him by his Dominican 'spiritual
adviser', Pèdre.[230] The prayers to *El Gran Poder de Dios* are intended to act
as a protection against evil: 'May the Council of the Most Holy Trinity
brake the power of my enemies, so they cannot do any evil, not against me,

---

225 Chromolithographs on altars all over the Dominican Republic are generally printed in
   Colombia or Mexico. Exactly the same type of prints have now been in existence for
   almost a hundred years and they were used by Olivorio and his followers in the same way
   as they are used today. Each print is normally filled with vivid details and various symbols,
   each of them interpreted in a certain way. Sometimes the owner of the prints interprets
   them in a very personal way, but more often similar interpretations are found in most
   parts of the country (cf. Deive (1979) pp. 224–41, and Desmangles (1992)).
226 See Desmangles (1992), pp. 164–5.
227 St Joachim and St Anna (the parents of the Virgin Mary) together with St Joseph and the
   Virgin herself.
228 Personal visit to a *bruja* in Santo Domingo, 14 October 1985.
229 Ibid. Dreams about old bearded men are also considered to be beneficent. León Romilio
   Ventura states that Plinio was ordered to carry out the mission in Palma Sola by a
   bearded man, while he himself was visited by a child. Both beings are interpreted as
   manifestations of *El Gran Poder de Dios* (interview with León Romilio Ventura, Media
   Luna, 17 January 1986). Another name of Olivorio is *El Viejo* [the Old Man], and some
   American reports refer to him thus (cf. Thorpe (1918a)).
230 Gaillard (1982b), pp. 331, 291–3.

nor against my sons and daughters, nor against my beneficent relatives. Amen.'[231] Some prayers are purely magical, written in a strange language which seems to be a fanciful, and quite incomprehensible, mixture of Spanish, Latin and Haitian Creole: '*Jesús magnífica ánima dómine salutario que repite maleciate Esili azul Elsonia vea tu medisis cofe puisi paien mano que apetenza su Santo espíritu*' [etc.].[232]

The more comprehensible parts of this particular 'prayer' are purely magical:

> I commit myself to the Great Power of God and the arms of the Most Holy Mary and the Most Holy Trinity – Father, Son and the Holy Spirit. I commit myself to the 3 ropes, which the Jews used in order to tie up Our Lord Jesus Christ to the Most Holy Cross; with these same ropes all my enemies will be tied up, from hands to feet.
>
> Jesus, deliver me from all diabolical arts; Jesus, liberate me from a vigorous bullet and any cutting weapon and liberate me as well from all temptations caused by the Demon [etc.][233]

Prayers are also printed to be addressed to *La Mano Poderosa*: 'Powerful hand of Divine Jesus: Today my soul is overburdened with a sorrow, I tear my chest in despair, coming to you, since you by the sublime virtue of your superiority are able to penetrate all hearts' [etc.].[234]

Even if prayers are directed to *El Gran Poder de Dios* and some people are also possessed by it, this power is believed to be quite remote from common people and considered to be just as capricious and indifferent to human suffering as heaven or earth. Many *Olivoristas* are of the opinion that it is of no use to seek direct contact with the ultimate power behind everything. They prefer to turn their attention to places where the power manifests itself through mediums like the Indian dwellers of caves and springs, or by persons who are believed to incarnate the power. Such a person is commonly known as a *sabio*, or *sabia*. A *sabio* is an individual who possesses power to heal and communicate with the 'spiritual sphere', someone who has been granted divine *gracia*, which in a Spanish context

---

231 From an *Oración al Gran Poder de Dios* [Prayer to the Great Power of God], bought at the Central Market in Santo Domingo.

232 From an *Ensalmo y Resguardo Real al Gran Poder de Dios* [Incantation and Royal Protection to the Great Power of God], bought at the Central Market in Las Matas de Fárfan. The Esili, mentioned in the text, is probably the voodoo goddess of love, Metré Silí.

233 From an *Ensalmo y Resguardo Real al Gran Poder de Dios*, bought at the Central Market in Las Matas de Fárfan.

234 From an *Oración a la Mano Poderosa* [Prayer to the Powerful Hand], bought at the Central Market in Santo Domingo. Among *Olivoristas* hands are considered to be the foremost vehicle of divine grace. It was primarily with his hands that Olivorio is said to have cured afflicted persons.

has been explained as 'a divinely ordained privilege, a power which is a free gift, which demands no rational justification and no payment'.[235] The San Juan Valley has always had its *sabios*, known under several different names like *brujos, divinos, curanderos, troncos, religiosos*, etc., and most of them believe that divine *gracia* makes them able to contact the 'spiritual sphere' and that their ability to heal people emanates from *El Gran Poder de Dios*.

However, not all *brujos*, or *brujas*, are considered to be vehicles of *El Gran Poder de Dios*. People also believe in *brujos* and *brujas malos*, who have obtained their powers by making deals with *Lo Malo*, a force which often is considered to be just as impersonal as *El Gran Poder de Dios*. Like the latter, the evil force may also come forth in certain places, exercising bad influences on visitors – sites imbued with *aire malo* [bad air]. As *El Gran Poder de Dios* manifests itself as the Holy Spirit, *Lo Malo* manifests itself as the devil who may also be referred to as *El Viejo*. He is then considered to be the lord of this world, given to him so he might test the faith of humans. As helpers in his evil deeds the devil counts on the Jews, an evil entity which has nothing to do with real Jews, but which is used to designate any kind of 'Christ-slayer', i.e. persecutor of righteous believers. Thus *Olivoristas* often refer to the American marines who killed Olivorio as the 'Jews',[236] and several *salves* in Palma Sola label adversaries such as Catholic clergy and politicians Jews as well.

Lo Malo is believed to come about through selfishness and it is quite common that people are accused of introducing *Lo Malo* in the midst of a community. Persons capable of doing so are referred to as *brujos* (*brujas*) *malos* (*malas*) and their speciality is to *chupar niños* [suck children]. In the spiritual war which is waged against *Lo Malo*, the foremost weapons are prayers and *conjuros*. A prayer is an act in which the supplicant asks for a favor. A prayer is a petition, not a demand. A *conjuro* [spell], on the other hand, is believed to be charged with some kind of power which, if properly executed, forces 'spiritual' entities to work for the conjurer. If a *conjuro* is sent against somebody the victim may defend himself or herself with the help of a *contra*, a kind of countermagic which will ward off the attack and hurt the conjuror with his own weapon. Persons and places connected with *El Gran Poder de Dios*, like Olivorio and La Maguana, are natural sources for such *contras* and the Ventura brothers prided themselves with the power of Palma Sola to subdue the evil might of witches and other 'Jews'.

> They [the press and the authorities] accused us of being sorcerers and evildoers. The truth was the other way around. The place subdued all

235 Pitt-Rivers (1971), p. 189.
236 Interview with Julián Ramos, Higüerito, 16 January 1986.

sorcerers and evildoers. They [the sorcerers] tried to enter. They hid themselves among us, but no one could resist the power. The sorcerers were vanquished and fell to the ground in convulsions.[237]

Several *Olivoristas* considered Palma Sola to be unique in the sense that it was a place exempted from the rule of the devil, lord of this world. After the original sin in Paradise the world had fallen into the hands of the evil one and after that fatal incident *El Gran Poder de Dios* can only emerge in certain places, through 'cracks' in the fallen world.

Apart from the machinations of the devil and his entourage *Lo Malo* expresses itself in a way similar to the *gracia* provided by *El Gran Poder de Dios*. People may attract noxious powers through no fault of their own. Any individual, be he good or bad from birth, may come under the evil spell of *fucú*.[238] Persons affected by *fucú* are avoided by others and it even happens that people are afraid of mentioning the names of persons stigmatized by *fucú*. *Fucú* is considered to be contagious and may lead to anything from bad luck to the death of the person believed to have been infected by it. However, an individual who has caught *fucú* may also simply be a carrier of the malign force, transmitting it to others while being unaffected himself. As is the case with *gracia*, not only people may be infected with *fucú*, but also animals and things.[239]

Thus, believed to be repositories of forces emanating from *El Gran Poder de Dios*, Palma Sola and La Maguana served as bulwarks against evil in a world which the *Olivoristas* believed to be dominated by *Lo Malo*. Many peasants came to Palma Sola in a quest for security and several believed themselves to have ended up within the confines of a spiritual presence which safeguarded them from the influences of a world lost in the lethal grip of *Lo Malo*.

Voodoo

Some analysts of *Olivorismo* consider voodoo to be one of the prime influences on the movement.[240] This is, however by no means an established fact. It is difficult to determine to what extent Olivorio himself and the cult

237 Interview with León Romilio Ventura, Las Matas de Farfán, 14 May 1989.
238 The word *fucú* is probably derived from *fufu*, a word which among Ewe-speaking peoples in West Africa means 'dust'. In the Americas the word came to mean 'witchcraft', 'being bewitched' or simply 'bad luck'. The connection between the different concepts is explained by a related word, *gullah*, which among black people living in South Carolina and Georgia denotes 'a dust used to bewitch or cause damaged to someone' (Deive (1988), p. 16). Among *santeros*, *fula* is the name of a gun powder used in certain ceremonies related to black magic (González-Wippler (1992), p. 131).
239 Vásquez (1986).
240 Notably Mota (1980).

that evolved around him adopted practices which have their roots in voodoo. León Romilio Ventura, on the other hand, is well versed in voodoo practices and even if he often states that he is a sworn enemy to the *misterios*, the name he uses to designate voodoo deities, he serves several related spirits:

> My revelations come like persons. They come with messages and sometimes they even come when I call for them. There are several: the Eternal Superior Father, Manuel Jesús, the Holy Spirit, St Olivorio, St John the Baptist, the King and Queen of the Earth. They appear in human shape and when I call them I use the rosary. I always succeed in communicating with them, one way or another. Most powerful of them all is the Holy Spirit, who appears as an old man, or as a child.[241]

Some of the cult functionaries present in Palma Sola, like Diego Cépeda, were repelled by anything which had to do with voodoo,[242] while others, like Inés Rosario Alcántara, were initiated voodoo practicioners.[243] Most Dominican cult functionaries make a clear distinction between serving the 'saints' and serving the *misterios*. In order to become a servant of the *misterios*, i.e. a voodoo practitioner in the strict sense of the word, the neophyte has to receive a special calling[244] from the *misterios*. Such a call is often followed by complicated initiation rituals and baptisms.[245] Most voodoo ceremonies are quite complicated and follow a relatively strict pattern, demanding an extensive knowledge of the tastes and behavior of a vast number of different spiritual entities.

The majority of the cult functionaries active in the San Juan Valley are not initiated voodooists and are accordingly not considered as servants of the *misterios*. This does not mean that they are ignorant of concepts related to voodoo, or that they are reluctant to incorporate certain aspects of voodoo in their own blend of religion. Even Olivorio is likely to have been influenced by his friend Pasute (Pasoute?), a Haitian *ougan* who lived in Maguana Abajo around the time when *El Maestro* received his 'calling'.

---

241 Interview with León Romilio Ventura, Media Luna, 5 May 1986.
242 Interview with Diego Cépeda, Jínova, 4 June 1989.
243 Interview with Inés Rosario Alcántara, Bánica, 2 June 1989.
244 The faculty of contacting *misterios* is often hereditary, but this is not an absolute requirement. That a child is chosen can be proved by several 'facts'; if it is a twin, cries in the belly before it is born, or carries a caul at birth. When a 'chosen' child grows older it is told to wait for its calling, something which may occur through dreams and visions, through different kinds of inflictions like serious illness, psychological disorders, fits and convulsions or through some extraordinarily strange incident. The most appropriate time to look out for these 'signs of acceptance' is when the child is around seven years old (Deive (1979), pp. 191–7 and Davis (1987), pp. 267–79).
245 Deive (1979), pp. 197–200 and Davis (1987), pp. 279–90.

However, even if few *Olivoristas* would deny knowledge of voodoo or dispute the powers of the *misterios*, the majority consider themselves good Catholics, and, in spite of the fact that voodoo concepts have contributed a certain flavor to their faith, the *Olivoristas* have far more in common with other aspects of Dominican peasant religion, like *cofradías*, *velaciones* and *rosarios*. Nevertheless, a short characterization of Dominican voodoo complements the picture of *Olivorismo*.[246]

The word 'voodoo' is of African origin. Among the Fon- and Ewe-speaking peoples in West Africa it denotes a god, or a spirit, but it can also mean a sacred object: in short 'all those things the European understands by the word fetish'.[247] The word 'voodoo' is seldom used in the Dominican Republic, especially not by people who are considered to be practitioners of that particular cult. Since its practice is forbidden there by penal law, voodoo has been forced into a kind of shadow existence.[248] Nevertheless, it is thriving all over the country and it is quite easy to get in contact with its practitioners.

Most Dominican voodooists consider Haiti to be the Mecca and birthplace of voodoo, and several famous *brujos* have gone to Haiti in order to learn more about their trade.[249] Popular traditions tell about a feared *jefe brujo* [boss sorcerer] living in L'Arcahaie, in central Haiti, from which place his spiritual powers extend over the whole island.[250] However, even if the Haitian influences are strong in Dominican voodoo it appears as if the development of voodoo beliefs in the Dominican Republic has taken a 'parallel path'. Different historical and social factors have contributed to the development of a distinct Dominican voodoo variety. Furthermore, while voodoo permeates the entire society in Haiti and constitutes a vital part of the peasants' concept of life in the countryside,[251] it only represents a part of the complex Dominican religious conglomerate.

The fundamental doctrine of voodoo is that the *misterios* are able to take possession of human beings. They are said to mount their 'horses', meaning that they take total control over the bodies of human beings,

246 For more exhaustive presentations of Dominican voodoo, cf. Patín Veloz (1975), Deive (1979), Jiménez Lambertus (1980), Miniño (1980), (1985), Lizardo (1982), Ripley (1985), and Davis (1987).
247 Métraux (1974), p. 31.
248 Cruz Díaz (1965), pp. 18–19 and Rosell (1983), pp. 279–82.
249 Interview with Doña Blanca, Santo Domingo, 4 November 1985. Despite being rather well known, several voodoo practicers wanted to remain anonymous.
250 Lemus and Marty (1975), p. 151. There is no foundation for these beliefs, something which is demonstrated by the fact that the informants tend to give different names to the place where *El Jefe Brujo* is supposed to live. The widespread notion does, however, demonstrate a fear of Haitian 'witchcraft' that is very common among the rural population of the Dominican Republic.
251 Courlander (1966), p. 21.

causing a kind of soul loss for the person who has been chosen as the instrument of their manifestations in this world. A *caballo* has temporarily lost his personality which is believed to have been substituted by that of a *misterio*, a spiritual entity which uses the body of a human being for communication with other humans. The spiritual sphere reveals itself in front of the very eyes of the worshipers, putting them in direct contact with the divine.

The *misterios* all belong to a complicated pantheon, divided into various divisions and spheres of activities and manifestations. Every voodoo deity is endowed with certain psychological traits, and their voices, clothing, movements, expressions and tastes vary accordingly. The behavior and looks of a *misterio*, i.e. the behavior of his *caballo*, depends not only on the division to which the spiritual entity belongs, but is also related to 'individual' preferences, depending on the *misterio's* particular field of activity, and its distinguishing personality. Every *misterio* is served with special music and special phrases and offered particular drinks and dishes.[252]

Each voodooist maintains special relations with one or several *misterios*, either due to personal preferences, or because he or she has been betrothed to his or her other *misterio* through special rituals. A devotee has certain obligations to the *misterio*. Most important are the daily offerings of food on the altar of the *misterio* known as *incruentes*, small dishes which do not contain any meat, served with soft drinks, or rum. Each *misterio* has its own favorite dishes, drinks and color. *Guedés* [*misterios* of the dead], for example, prefer black food and rum.[253]

Most *brujos* and *brujas* who 'work with the *misterios*' organize cult groups around themselves, very similar to the ones that develop around rural *ermitas*. Their clients often come to them for advice or private sessions, meaning that the *brujo* or *bruja* induces him or herself in a state of trance, allowing a *misterio* to take control over their bodies and minds and, through the 'voice' of the *misterio*, offer advice and remedies.[254]

On the day of their *misterios*, voodoo practitioners, or one of their clients, may arrange a big celebration called *prille* or *maní*.[255] Since they are communal celebrations carried out within the elaborate framework of great voodoo rituals, much preparation is needed; musicians have to be hired and a huge variety of food has to be prepared for both *misterios* and guests. The possessions, which are essential to the ceremonies, occur after

---

252 Cf. Davis (1987), pp. 124–49.
253 Interview with Doña Blanca, Santo Domingo, 4 November 1985.
254 We have participated in several such sessions.
255 A sense of the importance of voodoo in Santo Domingo can be grasped if a visit is made to certain bakeries around the day of Belié Balcán, a very popular Dominican *misterio*, whose day is 29 September. A large number of the displayed birthday cakes will then be green and red, the favorite colors of Belié Belcán.

elaborate rituals and offerings have been performed. When the *misterios* appear in the guise of their *caballos*, the ceremony turns into a fascinating and entertaining spectacle with several *misterios* acting and communicating between themselves and with the public. The days of the *misterios* are related to the Catholic calendar, i.e. every *misterio* has an equivalent among the saints. The relationships between saints and *misterios* are complicated and subtle and many studies have been carried out in order to disentangle the correspondences between the two. However, no voodooist considers a saint and a *misterio* to be identical:

> Belié Belcán is not San Miguel. Belié is a worker who works within the force of that saint, within his section [*entidad*]. This is the reason why Belié worships. And people say: 'Here is Belié, here is San Miguel'. It is not San Miguel; it is Belié who is here: the *misterio* who is working with the force of San Miguel. It is as if a president had an exclusive minister, a special one, who represents him in all places. When San Miguel is unable to visit a place, Belié comes instead.[256]

Either a cult functionary 'works with the saints' in the form of *velaciones* and *rosarios,* or he or she works with *misterios* through *prilles* or *maníes.* This does not mean that certain *brujos* are not able to 'work with both hands', i.e. to serve both saints and *misterios.* Some *Olivoristas*, like Emencio Mota in Maguana Arriba and León Romilio Ventura in Media Luna, are rumored to be able to do so.

Rural prophets in the Dominican Republic

Ermitas and similar cult-sites are found all over the Dominican Republic. Some, like that of the family Morenos a few kilometers outside Villa Mella, a small town situated just north of Santo Domingo, have enjoyed a thriving existence for a very long time, while others have fallen into decay. New ones are founded almost every year. The popularity of these rural sanctuaries depends not only on the liveliness of the traditions associated with them, but is also influenced by the vigor of their guardians.

Alejandro Mercedes Moreno, *El Mayor* [the Elder], leader of the cult of *Los Morenos,* is typical of cult functionaries who also serve as *troncos del lugar.* He is a venerated patriarch who upholds old family traditions. In Los Morenos (the place carries the same name as the family which lives there) the cult evolves around a small statue of a Virgin, which has been in the possession of the family for more than a hundred years. The complicated cult that centers on this effigy is complete with its own *salves,* dances and

---

256 A voodooist quoted in Davis (1987), p. 128.

processions. The leaders of the cult have always been members of the Moreno family, on whose land a church and several calvaries have been erected.

Under the leadership of Don Alejandro the cult has thrived as never before, attracting more pilgrims every year, and it has even obtained national fame through press, television and anthropological studies. Don Alejandro received his position through dreams and revelations and when his mother, the former leader of the cult, died, he was accepted by other family members as worthy of assuming the role of *El Mayor*.[257] Don Alejandro is now the head of the Moreno family and the undisputed leader of the cult. Both family members and other devotees are assured that he is 'like the Father for all of us; we have him like a father [*papá*] here'.[258] Don Alejandro's own firm conviction of the divine source of his authority is the ultimate proof of his power. As long as he feels that he is chosen for his position he emanates a 'natural' sovereignty, his judgement is respected and no one dares to challenge him:

> Look, here, I have never seen anyone who has put my mission in doubt. I believe this is due to the Virgin and also to my habits. People come to this place, even soldiers, because they have heard that in Los Morenos lives a man who dominates the whole community, even if he isn't an *alcalde* and does not have any other authority. Here the *alcalde* is *alcalde*, but he does not dominate in the same manner [as I do].[259]

Like La Maguana and Palma Sola, Los Morenos has its own 'holy geography', and the cult includes similar rituals: dances, *salves, toques de palos* [drum beating] and processions around *calvarios* and altars.[260] Olivorio was also considered to be like a father within his own community and was affectionately called Papá Olivorio. His former brother-in-arms, Julián Ramos, who died in 1991 at the age of 107, was likewise a venerated *tronco del lugar* among his relatives in Higüerito, where he headed a cult dedicated to Olivorio. León Romilio upholds a similar position in Media Luna, the village of the Ventura family.

Ermitas are still erected and cults founded in the Dominican Republic. In Jibaná, a small village 15 kilometers from the southern town of San Cristóbal, Julio Paniagua had a dream that described how he had to find a

---

257 He had, however, to share the role as *cabeza* [head] of the family and the cult with the older sons of his uncle. It was only when they died that he became the sole leader of both the cult and the family (Rodríguez Vélez (1982), p. 104).

258 Ibid., p. 106.

259 Alejandro Mercedes Moreno quoted in ibid., p. 105. The Virgin Don Alejandro speaks about is *La Dolorita*, the wooden effigy venerated by the *Morenos*.

260 See Figure 2 in Davis (1987), p. 153.

place to plant a cross. While walking around the countryside with a cross that he had made himself, the Virgin finally indicated the proper place to him. Julio erected a church and soon a community had grown around him. A cult was established with the cross and Julio at its center. This cult follows a pattern common to rural *ermitas*, supplemented with some of Julio's own inventions, among these the handling of a *cruz de hierro* [iron cross], a number of steel wires joined together which Julio manipulates in such a way that they convey messages from the spiritual sphere.[261]

Veneration of deceased cult leaders flourishes in various parts of the Dominican Republic. In Sabana de la Mar a cult is centered around the grave of Elupina Cordero, a blind lady who lived like a nun and died in 1939. It is said that her mortal remains cannot decay.[262]

Since the power of God is believed to penetrate every 'sanctified' human being, and never perishes, rural religious leaders are often believed to continue their existence 'on the other side of the grave', and several, like Olivorio, are venerated as 'independent' spiritual presences. Others are included in a voodoo division, an honor that is granted not only to religious persons but also to politicians and other forceful personalities, such as the opponents of the dictator Trujillo (like the *caudillo* Cipriano Bencosme and the bandit Enrique Blanco); these have been incorporated in the pantheon of certain voodoo societies.[263] Pictures of Trujillo himself can be found on several rural altars in the southwestern part of the country.

Ten kilometers from Iguana, a village north of the southern town of Baní, a cult thrives around a church constructed by Bibiana de la Rosa, who was almost a contemporary of Olivorio's. Her life story indicates that the case of Olivorio is far from exclusive and that cults similar to that of the *Olivoristas* have sprung up in several places. Like the *Olivoristas* the devotees of Bibiana de la Rosa state that their spiritual leader is not really dead. According to them La Bibiana is just resting for a while and 'when we need her the most she will return'.[264] Like Olivorio she is rendered divine status as 'the only goddess descended from heaven here on earth'.[265]

Bibiana de la Rosa was an illiterate peasant women of unknown origin. For several years she lived together with a *curandero* named Zacarías Arias, who probably taught her about the use of herbs and methods of magical healing. After Bibiana had separated from Zacarías she dedicated herself to helping others and constructed a small *ermita* where one night she

261 Puig (1975).
262 Davis (1987), p. 192.
263 Deive (1979), p. 171.
264 Quoted in Tejeda Ortiz (1978), p. 60.
265 Ibid., p. 59.

dreamt of God coming to her, giving her a 'mission' on earth. She had to prepare herself for the quest for a holy place. Bibiana confided in Padre Marcelino Borbón, the Catholic priest in Baní, who recommended that she seek a certain Florencio Bautista Isabel, who served as the priest's layman helper in the rural district of Iguana. Bibiana made a strong impression on Florencio and together they wandered through the mountain areas in order to find the holy place designated by God. Finally the exact location was revealed in a dream, and together with Florencio Bibiana planted a cross in a desolate place she named Mana.[266]

Soon people gathered in Mana, seeking healing and advice from Bibiana.[267] A church was built through unpaid *junta* work, finished in 1911. A special ritual was established with the church and a newly discovered spring at its center. The ritual baths in the 'Spring of the Virgin' were similar to the ones in La Agüita; men and women took turns bathing and undressed completely before they had water poured over them.[268] Devotees kneeled in front of a cross planted in a little dam by the spring, while other devotees poured water over them, washing away their sins. In 1916 a system of caves was discovered and incorporated in the cult, which by then had developed its own particular blend of the rituals and processions so typical of Dominican rural cults. The three big *palos* were played and the *sarandunga*,[269] a dance in honor of St John the Baptist, was performed.

Like Olivorio, Bibiana never charged anything for her services.[270] Legends grew around her and many miracles and prophecies connected with Bibiana are also told about Olivorio. Contrary to Olivorio, Bibiana maintained good contacts with both the authorities and the Catholic

---

266 Ibid., pp. 356. *Mana* [*manantial*] means source, but may also allude to the biblical manna, the miraculous food which sustained the Israelites in the wilderness; in that sense it may mean 'godsend'. Bibiana often talked about Moses: 'I have the history of Moses, I have been given the history of Moses, which is the ten commandments' (quoted in ibid., p. 37). The rather muddled way of expressing herself is something Bibiana had in common with many other rural prophets of the Dominican Republic, who when they are under the spell of 'inspired speech', tend to make use of strange associations and a partly incoherent syntax.

267 The 'push' factors for the almost immediate success of Bibiana's cult were probably similar to the ones at hand in the San Juan Valley: the fear of Halley's Comet, civil wars and sudden socioeconomic changes.

268 It appears as if the cult of Indians was of some prominence in Mana, as in La Agüita.

269 The *sarandunga* is probably related to the *zarabanda*, a couple dance which was introduced in Spain in the 1560s. It apparently came from Cuba, but like most couple dances it probably originated from Africa where such dances, as a rule, were connected with fertility rites (Jahn (1960), p. 85). *Zarabanda* was categorized as 'impious and obscene' and forbidden in Cuba in 1583. Even if offenders were punished with 200 lashes of the whip, the dance survived and finally became popular all over Europe and the Americas (ibid., p. 86).

270 Tejeda Ortiz (1978), p. 48.

church.[271] Bibiana de la Rosa died in 1925, but like Olivorio her soul is still believed to be present and her alleged last words were: 'My children, I do not leave any riches behind, but the shadow of this trunk [i.e. herself].'[272]

Conclusions

In this chapter we have argued that *Olivorismo* was born as a result of the historical factors that formed the life of the San Juan Valley. Fertile ground was created for a mixture of Taino beliefs with European and African ones. The agricultural activities of the *Sanjuaneros* constituted the most essential part of their lives and as agriculturists they seized upon fertility beliefs and similar notions found in the cultural composition of the people from different environments who ended up in the San Juan Valley. Thus, European fertility rituals became the trunk to which Indian and African beliefs were grafted, resulting in religious traditions and beliefs that were intimately related to the particular nature, social, economic and cultural environment of the valley, answering to the needs of its inhabitants.

The San Juan peasants' view of the spiritual sphere can thus be described as a mirror of their own society. The forces and deities in which they believe share their physical space. Accordingly, if their environment changes, the spiritual sphere changes with it. Since they are practical human beings, peasants also have a practical view of the suprahuman world. If old beliefs and traditions become antiquated they have to be renewed and adapted to the new situation. Hence, the peasant's religion is highly dynamic. *Olivorismo* was constituted as a response to the needs of its devotees; otherwise it would never have been successful. Its sudden impact, as well as the immediate success of the cult of Palma Sola, proves that it was intimately connected with local traditions and thus easily understood by everyone living in the particular areas affected by the 'new' cults. Accordingly, *Olivorismo* is far from being an 'exotic faith' imported from Haiti, or any other place for that matter. On the contrary, it is a natural growth from the fertile, spiritual soil which for centuries has nurtured popular religion in the Dominican Republic and constantly gives rise to new, religious interpretations of the needs and expectations of its rural population.

In other words, *Olivorismo* is a typical example of a regional agrarian cult:

> Regional cults are found in many parts of the world. They are cults at the middle range – more far reaching than any parochial cult of the little community, yet less inclusive in belief and membership than a world religion in its most universal form. Their central places are

---

271 Ibid., p. 56.
272 Quoted in ibid., p. 60.

shrines in towns and villages, by crossroads or even in the wild, apart from human habitation, where great populations from various communities or their representatives come to supplicate, sacrifice or simply make pilgrimage. They are cults which have a topography of their own, conceptually defined by people themselves and marked apart from other features of cultural landscapes by ritual activities.[273]

This definition seems to be applicable to *Olivorismo*, with the addition that it is also a peasant cult, where 'peasants' are understood as people with an existence which differs from that of the town dwellers – an existence char- acterized by agricultural activities, something which naturally influences their view of the world.

273 Werbner (1977), p. ix.

7 Economic and political change in the San Juan Valley, 1503–1922

Olivorio's biographer, Emigdio Garrido Puello, painted the standard picture of the *Olivorista* movement, the one that has been handed down to later researchers.[1] According to Garrido Puello, Olivorio was a foul-mouthed madman and opportunist who liked to get drunk.[2] His religious and thaumaturgical activities were pure cheating of simple-minded peasants. All Olivorio and his morally perverted followers were after was a life of cheap pleasures, sex and drinking, and honest work was shunned completely. His headquarters in El Palmar became a corrupt spot that constituted an imminent danger for the peace of the region:

> The pacific vicinity was shaken up and underwent a metamorphosis through the new religion. Criminals, vagrants, delinquents and fugitives from justice, coming from different parts of the Republic, moved under Olivorio's protection. It was a safe refuge at no cost to which all those who had unsettled accounts with the law fled.[3]

It was only due to the political and social chaos of the period, with intense *caudillo* fighting, that Olivorio could work successfully.

Views like these are of no help when it comes to understanding *Olivorismo*. In particular, they make the movement appear as a completely irrational phenomenon. This, however, is not the case. As Eric Hobsbawm has pointed out, 'rationalist' or 'modernist' historians have a tendency to underestimate the importance of the type of movements represented by Olivorio and his followers because 'being mainly educated and townsmen', they 'have until recently simply not made sufficient effort to understand

---

1 See Garrido Puello (1963), passim, especially pp. 8, 13–14, 16–24, 27 and 29.
2 Blanco Fombona (1927), p. 62, on the other hand, reports that 'Liborio drank little because he was not fond of liquor. His vices were different.'
3 Garrido Puello (1963), pp. 23–4.

people who are unlike themselves.'[4] Garrido Puello constitutes an excellent case in point and we will later come back to why he chose to propagate the views he did.

What Olivorio's biographer chooses *not* to deal with is the wider question regarding the circumstances that permitted Olivorio to become a successful founder of a new cult and the reasons why his movement was put down. We began such a discussion in Chapter 6, by examining the circumstances that made the rural inhabitants of the San Juan Valley susceptible to the religious message of Olivorio. We will continue our analysis with an interpretation of the rise of the movement and the reactions of the outside world that argues that the social roots of both the success of *Olivorismo* and the violent outside reaction are to be found in the changing economic, social and political conditions in the San Juan area during the time under consideration.

In this we are inspired by materialist interpretations of history ranging from the dialectical materialism of Marx to the cultural materialism of Marvin Harris,[5] without necessarily sharing the particular emphasis of these authors. Rather, it is the economic approach to history in a wide sense that is of relevance:

> The existence of man depends on his ability to sustain himself; the economic life is therefore the fundamental condition of all life. Since human life, however, is the life of man in society, individual existence moves within the framework of the social structure and is modified by it. What the conditions of maintenance are to the individual, the similar relations of production are to the community. To economic causes, therefore, must be traced in the last instance those transformations of society which themselves condition the relations of social classes and the various manifestations of social life.[6]

In this spirit, let us begin with a look at the region: the San Juan Valley.

The San Juan Valley

The San Juan Valley is located in the southwestern part of the Dominican Republic (see Figure 7.1). It lies principally in the province of San Juan, one of the seven provinces in the region (see Figure 7.2). The valley is located between two mountain ranges, south of the Cordillera Central and north of the Sierra de Neiba. In the west it extends towards Elías Piña and

---

4 Hobsbawm (1959), p. 2.
5 Harris (1980).
6 Seligman (1907), p. 3.

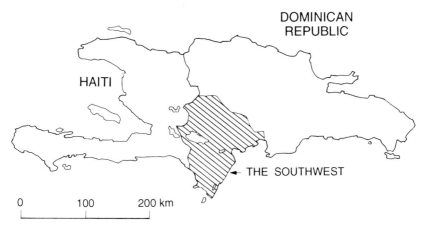

Figure 7.1 The southwestern Dominican Republic.

Figure 7.2 Provinces of the Southwest.

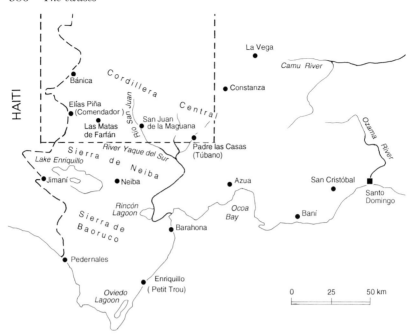

Figure 7.3 The location of the San Juan Valley.

the Haitian border and in the east towards the Azua Valley (cf. Figure 7.3).[7] The San Juan Valley, which is the second largest valley in the country after the Cibao, with its close to 632,000 *tareas* [40,000 hectares],[8] constitutes a continuation of the Plateau Central in Haiti.

Geographer Ernest Palmer, who has studied the border area between Haiti and the Dominican Republic, distinguishes three different natural subregions within the valley (cf. Figure 7.4). Subregion I, covering above all the San Juan area in the east and parts of the border area around Elías Piña and El Llano, consists of 'alluvial plains and terraces' with 'deep, dark brown calcareous soils of high potential productivity. An impermeable strat[um] … underlying the soils near San Juan de la Maguana provides the pedalogic conditions suitable for irrigated rice production.'[9] In the west, near El Llano, the reduced water retention and the increased soil permeability make the terrain less suited for rice.

Subregion III extends through most of the valley. This is 'an area of ridge and terrace topography' that becomes increasingly rugged in the area

---

7 A detailed map of the *Olivorista* heartland is found at the beginning of the book.
8 Moreta (1986), p. 50.
9 Palmer (1976), pp. 25, 27.

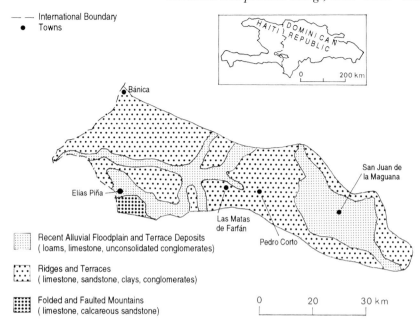

Figure 7.4 Natural subregions in the San Juan Valley.

Source: After Palmer (1976), p. 26.

around the Artibonite River.[10] The soils are generally clayey and their color varies from light to dark brown. They are not as fertile as those of Subregion I, due to deforestation and cultivation:

> The steeper slopes and summits have been denuded of their forest cover and soils have been eroded in many places exposing the underlaying rocks. Subsistence farming is [today] the principal land use on the gentler slopes and on the colluvial slopewash of the gullies and depressions. As a rule, lack of soil moisture is the primary limitation to agricultural productivity in this subregion.[11]

South of Elías Piña, near the Haitian border, the valley contains a small part of Subregion IV, which consists of 'folded and faulted mountains'. The shallow soils, deriving from permeable limestone, are fertile when not disturbed but as soon as the vegetative cover is removed, they become subject to rapid erosion.[12]

10 Ibid., p. 27.
11 Ibid., pp. 27–8.
12 Ibid., p. 28. Palmer also distinguishes a Subregion II, but only on the Haitian side of the border.

In the north and east, the valley is surrounded by mountains and 'dry' forest, with poor soil. In the south, desertlike areas take over. The overall rainfall in the region is unreliable and varies greatly between years. The Cordillera Central acts as a barrier to precipitation in the area. Droughts are frequent and have been so at least since the colonial period.[13]

The San Juan Valley was once known as *La Barriga Verde* [the Green Belly] of the Dominican Republic. Lush pastures surrounding the sleepy little towns of San Juan de la Maguana, Las Matas de Farfán and Bánica nourished large herds of free-roaming cattle, and the entire economy of the valley was built on cattle. The idyllic appearance of the valley seems to have remained unchanged for centuries.[14] In 1908, the very year when Olivorio began his activities, the municipality of San Juan was described in the following terms:

> It has 20,000 inhabitants generally occupied with cattle breeding or agriculture. Nearly the entire municipality consists of an immense plain covered with natural pastures and watered by various important rivers and innumerable little creeks.[15]

The San Juan Valley stretches into Haitian territory, where it merges with the Plateau Central. Thus, the current border is nothing but a line on a map and not a natural border at all:

> The ... region consists of the San Juan Valley in the Dominican Republic and its westward extension, the Central Plain [Plateau Central] of Haiti. This northwest-southwest trending physiographic region, one of the largest interior plains of Hispaniola, covers about 2,000 square kilometers on each side of the border. The northern limit of the Valley-Plain is the south-facing escarpment of the Cordillera Central (Massif du Nord), the island's principal mountain range, while its southern boundary is the north-facing escarpment of the Sierra de Neiba (Montagnes Noires). To the east, the region narrows near the confluence of the San Juan and Yaque del Sur rivers where spurs from the Sierra de Neiba and the Cordillera Central extend out onto the valley floor. The western limit is defined by outliers from the Massif du

13 Ibid., pp. 18–20. Garrido (1970), pp. 17–18 and (1922), p. 227, points to a deterioration of the climate after the turn of the century, with less rainfall and less water in the rivers, and so does Cano y Fortuna (n.d.), p. 57. The rainfall part, however, may be exaggerated. As it appears, precipitation in the area follows a cyclical rhythm, where plentiful years regularly follow relatively dry ones (cf. Palmer (1976), pp. 198–9, and Isa (1985)).

14 For descriptions of the valley from the beginning of the sixteenth century to the end of the nineteenth, see Garrido (1972), pp. 329–39.

15 Deschamps (1908), p. 54.

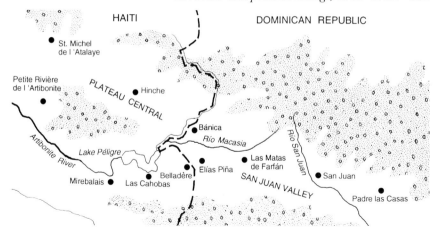

Figure 7.5 The San Juan Valley and the Plateau Central.

Nord and Montagnes Noires. As a whole, the ... region varies in width from sixteen kilometers at Hinche to forty kilometers along the international border; it measures approximately 150 kilometers from east to west. Elevation above sea level ranges between 300 and 400 meters with a slight downward slope from east to west.[16]

The fact that the San Juan Valley and the Plateau Central constitute a continuous natural region is eloquently demonstrated by Figure 7.5, which shows the area and the surrounding mountains.

The history of the secluded but vast San Juan Valley up to the beginning of the twentieth century is simultaneously one of economic continuity and turbulent politics, filled with wars and uprisings. This history constitutes an essential building block in any serious attempt to understand the *Olivorista* movement. During the course of four centuries, the economy was based on cattle ranching and trade with the western part of the island of Hispaniola. By the time Olivorio made his appearance, however, this economy was under severe stress, being threatened by outside, 'modernizing' forces. Olivorio entered the stage precisely when these forces were struggling to change what had been built during virtually the entire post-discovery history of Santo Domingo and the Dominican Republic. It was inevitable that he was to be drawn into this struggle.

16 Palmer (1976), pp. 17–18. Cf. Cooke (1983), p. 40: 'That part of the valley which is found within the borders of the Dominican Republic extends toward the northwest, a distance of approximately 80 kilometers and its width varies from 15 to 20 kilometers. The said valley contains low hills, undulating plains and large portions of almost plain savanna or pasture lands.'

The economy: the early years

In 1503, the town of San Juan de la Maguana was founded by the Spaniards on the orders of Governor Nicolás de Ovando.[17] It proved to be an attractive place for Europeans. The climate was considered healthy, the soil fertile and well watered. San Juan de la Maguana was among the *villas* [towns] founded upon royal request and the choice of location for San Juan was clearly influenced by the fertility of the valley.[18] Already at the beginning of the sixteenth century San Juan was known for its commercial production of fruit,[19] and gold was mined in the nearby mountains.

As gold mining declined in Hispaniola,[20] the European population started to decline as well and, following the news of gold in Mexico and Peru the process accelerated, in spite of the promulgation of royal decrees in 1525 and 1526 prohibiting emigration from the island. In 1526 capital punishment was instituted to curb the exodus.[21] In 1516, there remained fewer than 4,000 out of the 10,000 Europeans registered after the end of Nicolás de Ovando's term as governor in 1510.[22] However, San Juan de la Maguana remained populated.[23] The gold mines were already exhausted and the Indian population was dying out. The island of Hispaniola was in plain decadence.[24] Twelve years later, in 1528, the white population still remained a low 4,000, 3,000 of whom lived in the capital and only 1,000 in the nine villages or towns in the interior.[25] This concentration of people in the capital was to continue until the mid-eighteenth century.[26]

In order to increase the profitability of the colony and maintain its population the Spanish crown opted for sugar plantations.[27] The first attempts to grow sugar had been made in 1505 and 1506.[28] In 1515, the first horse-powered *trapiche* [crushing mill] was constructed;[29] two years later, the first

---

17 Peña Pérez (1980), p. 203.
18 See Sauer (1966), pp. 151–5.
19 Moreau de Saint-Méry (1944), p. 258.
20 For an account of the island during the first two and a half decades after the European conquest, when gold mining was the most important activity, see Moya Pons (1978b).
21 Peña Pérez (1980), p. 58.
22 Moya Pons (1974a), p. 21.
23 Utrera (1982), p. 336.
24 Peña Pérez (1980), p. 53.
25 Ibid., p. 58, and Moya Pons (1977), p. 75. Clausner (1973) p. 38, quotes a letter from the Hieronimite fathers to the Spanish crown stating that in 1519 the Spanish population was 53,000, but this appears to be on the high side and does not fit the overall picture of an exodus from the island.
26 Moya Pons (1974a), p. 5. Possibly the exodus also had to do with the monetary problems experienced from around 1530 to 1580. See Serrano Mangas (1992) for a discussion.
27 The early history of sugar is dealt with in Moya Pons (1973).
28 Incháustegui (1955), p. 72.
29 Báez Evertsz (1986), p. 49.

samples were shipped to Spain,[30] and in 1520 commercial exports took place.[31] By this time twelve sugar mills were in operation, but in spite of imports of black slaves, at least since 1502,[32] manpower was a severe problem, which was to make expansion difficult. Twelve mills projected for 1521 could not be put into operation for lack of hands.[33]

In the mid-sixteenth century, Hispaniola possessed some twenty-five to thirty-five *ingenios* and *trapiches*, two of which were located in San Juan de la Maguana,[34] where 'the best-quality sugar in the entire Island' was produced.[35] However, by 1555 the industry was heading for decline due to a lack of hands.[36] In 1546, the island counted some 12,000 blacks and no more than 5,000 whites,[37] and in 1568 the number of black slaves had increased with a mere 8,000.[38] Sugar was simply requiring too much labor.[39] Its production remained high at least until the years following the invasion of Santo Domingo by Francis Drake in 1586, but as the price of ginger increased towards the end of the sixteenth century, and sugar in addition suffered from Mexican competition,[40] the available slaves were employed almost exclusively in the cultivation of that product, plus maize and cassava, leaving less than 900 slaves for sugar production at the beginning of the seventeenth century.[41]

The colonial authorities were concerned about limiting the number of slaves in isolated parts of the island, like the districts around San Juan de

30 Peña Pérez (1980), p. 54.
31 Clausner (1973), p. 30.
32 Incháustegui (1955), p. 114. The year of the first arrival is not known with certainty. Deive (1980), pp. 18–22, claims it was before 1502.
33 Clausner (1973), p. 30.
34 Gonzalo Fernández de Oviedo mentions twenty-one *ingenios* and five *trapiches* in 1546 (quoted by Báez Evertsz (1986), pp. 51–2 and Moscoso (1993), pp. 14–15. Moya Pons (1977), p. 79, gives the number as thirty-five for 1548, and Peña Pérez (1980), p. 60, mentions twenty-five for 'the mid-sixteenth century'.
35 Mejía Ricart (1951), p. 20. At least, states Moreau de Saint-Méry 'it was considered to be equal to that of Azua' (Moreau de Saint-Méry (1944), pp. 257–8).
36 Peña Pérez (1980), p. 63 and Deive (1991), p. 16.
37 Moya Pons (1977), p. 80.
38 Ibid., p. 88.
39 Ibid., pp. 78–80, Incháustegui (1955), p. 73. As a result of smallpox epidemics the number of slaves declined in the 1580s (Moya Pons (1974a), p. 6, Cassá (1985), p, 75). According to a census taken in 1606 the slave population then fell short of 10,000 (Moya Pons (1977), p. 89).
40 Moya Pons (1973), pp. 14–15, Deive (1980), pp. 93–4.
41 Moya Pons (1977), p. 89. Ginger, the main use of which was to alleviate indigestion, was introduced to the island in 1577 and the good prices it fetched in Spain caused something of a frenzy among Dominican agriculturists. While witnessing the sudden shift from sugar to ginger and fearing that the ginger boom would come to an end, the authorities tried to restrict the land area permitted for ginger cultivation (Sánchez Valverde (1988), pp. 125–6).

la Maguana. They needed Spanish settlers not only for economic reasons, but also for defense. In 1533 the authorities in Santo Domingo voiced concern about the future of the settlement in San Juan. That same year the port of La Yaguana [present-day Léogâne in Haiti] had been sacked and burned to the ground by French pirates. San Juan de la Maguana, which was situated in the middle of the island, was strategically important because the capital counted on its habitants for the defense of La Yaguana, which was the island's point of departure for commerce with Cuba and the American mainland. San Juan de la Maguana also served as a bulwark against invasions from the west.[42] However, white settlers were continually abandoning San Juan, giving rebellious Indians and black slaves free hands to do what they wanted. In 1545 the *cabildo* [town council] of Santo Domingo received the following complaint from San Juan:

> since the town is so weakened [*enflaquezida* (sic)] and with so few Spaniards, the Negroes become shameless and do not want to work, they rebel and run off to the mountains and are not content with being runaways, but turn up along the roads and attack those who pass along them and they [the runaway slaves] do not do that on foot, but on horses and they have killed some Spaniards, cowboys [*baqueros* (sic)] and ranchers [*estancieros*].[43]

Repeatedly the authorities in Santo Domingo pleaded to the Spanish crown that 'white' settlers and laborers had to be sent to the areas around San Juan. Black slaves could not be trusted for their defense. After 1558 every Spanish settler was granted between 600 and 700 hectares of land upon arrival, and one-quarter of this area could be dedicated to cattle grazing.[44] However, this policy was often fervently opposed by large landowners and *ingenio* owners, who wanted to limit the numbers of settlers and were reluctant to pay wages to Spanish laborers. They preferred large, undivided land tracts for their cattle and slave labor at their *ingenios*. The authorities complained that the few settlers who ended up in the countryside soon sold their land to large landowners and illegally escaped to other parts of the empire. The authorities in Santo Domingo claimed that 'the fat ones are eating the small ones, buying their farms at low prices, this is the reason why the land is depopulated'.[45] Recently

---

42 Deive (1991), p. 15.

43 Ibid. The use of black cowboys mounted on horses was forbidden by law. However, the ranchers of San Juan de la Maguana did not act in accordance with laws and regulations delimiting the rights of blacks, stating that: 'it is impossible to suffer this [the laws] due to the lack of Spaniards and the effort it takes to follow them' (ibid.).

44 Ibid., p. 19.

45 From a letter from the *fiscal* [treasury official] of the *audiencia* [regional court] in Santo Domingo to the Spanish king, written in 1554 and quoted in ibid. It was not only

arrived settlers 'escaped en masse' to the mainland or other islands. In order to come away from the poverty and problems of Hispaniola they were willing to go 'to any part of the Indies, even if it is to the most wretched little island'.[46]

The solution to the 'chronic' labor shortage throughout the sixteenth century[47] did not lie in ginger cultivation but in an eminently land-intensive activity that required little labor: cattle raising. This was also the case in the San Juan Valley. In 1568, San Juan de la Maguana was more or less depopulated. Only the church and the people working in the two sugar *ingenios* were left.[48] Freely roaming cattle were allowed to move across large, unfenced *hatos*. The *hato* system had several advantages:

> The hatos were units which from the point of view of the land were worth nothing. The investment in slaves was small; the hatos with several thousand head [of cattle] normally had 3 or 4 slaves, and cattle wealth was much less subject to the imperatives of the market than all other forms, since it could be maintained forever without causing any important outlays.[49]

The cattle multiplied easily, and hides were exported,[50] but not without difficulties. Only those *ganaderos* who lived either in the neighborhood of Santo Domingo or close to the sugar mills in the southern part of the island, and who could rely on the barges transporting sugar to handle their produce as well, were in a position where they could easily employ the legal outlets. The remainder in principle had to drive their cattle over long distances, all the way to the capital, across a a country with no roads, risking the loss of their slaves and attacks by bands of *cimarrones* that roamed the interior. Only very irregularly did Spanish ships call on any island ports other than the one in the capital.[51]

The reason for this was the increasing pressure of Dutch, French and English privateers in the Caribbean waters, notably around the sparsely populated Hispaniola. Faced with this dilemma the few inhabitants of the interior of the island did not hesitate to approach the foreigners and trade

Spaniards who left the island. During one year alone (1559), more than 800 slaves originating from Hispaniola had been sold at various slave markets on the mainland (letter to the king from the *alguacil mayor* [governor] of Santo Domingo, quoted in ibid.).
46 From a letter from the *fiscal* of the *audiencia* in Santo Domingo to the Spanish king, quoted in Deive (1991), p. 19.
47 Clausner (1973), p. 51.
48 Garrido (1972), p. 331.
49 Cassá (1985), p. 80.
50 Peña Pérez (1980), p. 64, claims that as the second half of the sixteenth century began as many as 100,000 cow hides were exported to Spain every year.
51 Moya Pons (1977), pp. 110–12.

clandestinely with them, not least with the Portuguese, who had a very attractive commodity – slaves – to offer, and later increasingly with other European nations, which could supply badly needed manufactured goods. The contraband trade grew rapidly, in spite of Spanish efforts to put an end to it. On the western and northern (the so-called Banda del Norte) coasts of Hispaniola,[52] a tradition of trade was established that was to dominate the economic life of the island – including the San Juan Valley – all the way up to the first decades of the present century.

In the 1570s, contraband trade dominated the picture completely.[53] Foreign ships, breaking the Spanish commercial monopoly, utilized the natural and even the constructed harbors to bring in 'flour, wine, cloth, silk, work tools, arms, ceramics and black slaves'.[54]

> La Yaguana was the crucial point, the crossroads, of this entire maritime enterprise. The harbor of the settlement did not offer any great advantages for anchorage because it was neither safe nor protected; however, foreign ships came there to notify their arrival so traffickers would become aware of the occasion and then withdraw to Guanahibes [...] close to Cabo San Nicolás [Môle Saint-Nicolas in present-day Haiti], where the fair was opened. The latter was always a [...] secure harbor, 'tough to all winds', offering all the advantages to a commerce which never was properly controlled. When it appeared in the harbor the enemy fleet discharged one or two cannons, in order to make its presence known, and the message went from hato to hato until it reached Puerto Real and Monte Christi [sic] in the banda [sic] del Norte and San Juan de la Maguana in the interior.[55]

In the late 1580s, perhaps as many as 200,000 animals were slaughtered every year and left the colony on non-Spanish ships.[56] Smuggling was by far the most important commercial activity in Hispaniola.[57]

There were good reasons for this. Hispaniola was during the latter half of the sixteenth century an economy in decay, with a virtually extinct European population. The causes were mainly to be found outside the colony. Neither Charles V or Philip II had managed to put the finances of the Spanish crown in order. A long series of costly wars had been fought, revolts had broken out at home and the conquest of the New World had its costs as well. During the reign of Philip II, government debt payments

---

52 Ibid. pp. 112–13.
53 Cassá (1985), p. 87, Moya Pons (1977), p. 113.
54 Cassá (1985), p. 90.
55 Peña Batlle (1951), p. 45.
56 Peña Pérez (1980), p. 88.
57 Ibid., p. 90.

were suspended no less than four times.[58] This situation was to continue after the death of Philip II in 1598 as well, when Spain entered a period of economic decline that was not to come to an end until around 1660 when a period of stability and recovery set in.[59]

The effects of the bad finances in Spain were felt also in the colonies; not least in Hispaniola. One patent result of the lack of funds was that Spain could ill afford to protect not only its trade monopoly in the Americas but also the Spanish ships and possessions in the New World. The immediate result of this was that it was risky to trade, e.g. with Santo Domingo, so that comparatively few ships called on the island. The danger of running into pirates kept increasing as the sixteenth century advanced, culminating in the occupation of Santo Domingo by Francis Drake in 1586.[60]

The problem of defending its American trade made the Spanish crown determine, in 1543, that maritime traffic to the Americas was to be carried out by means of fleets that left Spain twice a year for Vera Cruz and Nombre de Dios, on the Panama isthmus. This system, which, however, did not operate on a regular basis until 1566, left Santo Domingo a complete backwater. It was no longer natural to land in Hispaniola. Havana was the only port to be called upon on the way back to Seville and the ships that were destined for Hispaniola had to negotiate the last part of their voyage alone – easy prey for ships from hostile foreign nations.[61] As could be expected, this shifted Spanish trade away from Santo Domingo to Havana. For all practical purposes, the Spanish crown had deserted Hispaniola during the latter half of the sixteenth century. Between 1548 and 1555 a mere eighty-one cargo ships were sent from Seville to Hispaniola.[62] From 1557 to 1588, in more than thirty years, the island received only 109 Spanish immigrants, the majority of whom had some official or religious position which he or she had to take up upon arrival.[63] A *Relación de la isla Española* written in 1568 concluded that the island would be empty in just a few years and commerce with Spain had all but ground to a halt.[64]

The only lifeline was contraband trade, but not everywhere. In 1574, San Juan de la Maguana was still listed as a depopulated town.[65] Only the people who worked in the two sugar mills lived there.[66] Life had become increasingly insecure as a result of a number of Indian uprisings and slave

58 See Lundahl (1993), pp. 46–9.
59 See e.g. Davis (1973), Chapter 9, and Kamen (1983), Chapters 4 and 5, for details.
60 Cf. e.g. Moya Pons (1977), pp. 98–104, for an account.
61 Ibid., pp. 99–100.
62 Peña Pérez (1980), p. 62.
63 Ibid., p. 65.
64 Ibid., pp. 66–7.
65 Palmer (1976), p. 41.
66 Peña Pérez (1980), p. 203.

rebellions during the course of the sixteenth century. *Cimarrones* roamed in the mountains in its vicinity, living in *manieles* – small, independent communities.

At the end of the sixteenth century, things appeared to take a turn for the better as peace was made with various groups of *cimarrones* who were resettled in San Juan. In 1602, Antonio de Ovalle, the man who negotiated the treaty, was installed as *corregidor* of San Juan de la Maguana by royal decree and the former *cimarrones* were ordered to spend their lifetime under his jurisdiction.[67] The recovery, however, turned out to be nothing but temporary, for soon the *Sanjuaneros* were to feel the impact of Spanish colonial policy. Towards the turn of the century, legal exports had almost ceased while at the same time the inhabitants of the Banda del Norte were selling a million ducats' worth of goods to foreigners.[68] The island had fallen into a state of misery.[69] The European population was hovering at somewhere around 5,000 people and, as a result of an epidemic in the 1580s, the slave population had been reduced to less than 10,000.[70]

The only way out of this situation was by breaking the law:

> For example, by far the greater part of what was produced in the large hatos close to Santo Domingo, which generally belonged to the colonial bureaucrat aristocracy, was earmarked for smuggling, to the point where in many a season the city of Santo Domingo and some ingenios that did not have hatos could not provide themselves with the meat they needed to consume. [...] the entire population in the western regions were accomplices in smuggling. Hence, nobody denounced anybody and it was very difficult to establish proven responsibilities ...[71]

The population in the northern and western parts of Hispaniola had reached the stage where it was coming very close to being in open rebellion against the Spanish king and this was, of course, something the Spanish crown and its representatives could not tolerate. The decision was taken to evacuate the western and northern parts of the island.

The evacuation took place in 1605 and 1606. As seen in Figure 7.6, all the settlements west of a line extending from Azua in the south to

---

67 Utrera (1978), p. 227, Deive (1980), pp. 458–9. The *corregidor* was a remunerated government administrator who had jurisdiction over a certain area, *corregimiento*, and the people living there (Deive (1980), p. 459).
68 Peña Batlle (1989), p. 59.
69 Peña Pérez (1980), pp. 99–108.
70 Moya Pons (1974a), p. 21, gives a figure of 5,000 Europeans for 1546, and when a census was taken in October, 1606, this yielded a non-slave community of 5,960 and a slave population of 9,648 (ibid., pp. 6, 21).
71 Cassá (1985), p. 92.

Figure 7.6 The evacuation of Western Hispaniola, 1605–06.

Source: Cassá (1985), p. 103.

Santiago de los Caballeros in the north were emptied: La Yaguana, Bayajá, Monte Cristi, Puerto Plata and San Juan de la Maguana, the latter during the first half of 1606:[72]

> The 21st of February [Governor Antonio] Osorio decreed that the hatos of San Juan should be moved towards the surroundings of the capital. It seems as if the inhabitants of the said town did not obey the orders of the governor, since Osorio, three months later, that is on the 19th of May, drew up another decree to allow that San Juan de la Maguana be destroyed. The excuse given by Osorio in the decree to move the people of San Juan was that the entire West was depopulated and without judicial courts and, hence, under the circumstances, the ranchers could bring their hides to the part of Guanahibes to do illicit trade with foreigners without any fear at all.[73]

All houses were to be burnt down in three days. San Juan de la Maguana was to be refounded in Buenaventura, close to Santo Domingo, and 'whoever ventured back to the valley ... risked the loss of his life and material goods'.[74] The *hatos* between San Juan and Neiba were vacated. (By this time, there were eleven *hatos* in the San Juan area.)[75] In the process the *hateros* stopped sending any cattle to Santo Domingo, with the result that the capital lacked meat.[76]

72 Peña Pérez (1980), Chapter 7, gives the details.
73 Ibid., p. 163.
74 Ibid., p. 164.
75 Garrido (1972), p. 332.
76 Mejía Ricart (1952), p. 544, Moya Pons (1977), pp. 127–8.

In the apparent chaos related to the forced evacuations, several slaves escaped to the northern and western districts. Fearing that these *cimarrones* would constitute a future threat to the Spaniards, Osorio ordered them to be hunted down, something Antonio de Ovalle, the former *corregidor* of San Juan de la Maguana had to do together with other Spanish officers and troops. Several *cimarrones* were captured and sent to the eastern part while others, mainly suspected leaders of bands of runaway slaves, were hanged. Still it was impossible to capture all who fled into the abandoned territories.[77]

The evacuation of the western part of Hispaniola hardly had the effects that the crown had hoped for. Instead it contributed to depressing the economy of the island ever more. Cattle were lost in great quantities, people left the island, the most important sugar mills, including those in San Juan de la Maguana, were destroyed.[78] Sugar production was on its way out. In the mid-seventeenth century only a few *trapiches* would remain and these only produced molasses and *aguardiente* [raw sugar cane liquor].[79]

Both the evacuated *Sanjuaneros* and that part of the population of the capital who claimed that it was from San Juan de la Maguana that they obtained 'cheese, butter and tallow' protested against the evacuations.[80] The *Sanjuaneros* were allowed back in 1608,[81] as the population in the capital could not survive without the meat produced in the valley.[82] However, virtually all the cattle had been lost in the meantime,[83] having disappeared with the wild animals in the interior of the island.

In the doldrums

After the evacuations of the western part of Hispaniola the Spanish colony entered a period of 'general crisis, which encompassed all aspects of society, like the economy, demography, education, religion, etc.'.[84] This crisis to a large extent reflected developments in Spain itself.[85] The financial situation of the Spanish crown had been precarious during the reign of Philip II and after his death in 1598 it grew even worse.

77 Deive (1980), pp. 460–2.
78 Cassá (1985), p. 95.
79 Ibid., p. 100.
80 Moya Pons (1977), p. 127.
81 Utrera (1979), p. 16.
82 Peña Pérez (1980), p. 1.
83 Moya Pons (1980), p. 127.
84 Peña Pérez (n.d.), p. 134.
85 For the Spanish crisis see e.g. Elliott (1970), Chapters 8–9, Kamen (1983), Chapter 4, and Elliott (1989), Chapters 6, 10 and 11.

The country was involved in a series of wars abroad and at home. Revolutions broke out which had to be put down and all this cost money which had to be raised through increased taxation. The currency was debased and suspension of debt payment became frequent. The domestic economic foundations were weak. Spanish manufacturing could not compete with goods of foreign origin, either at home or in the colonies – despite the Spanish trade monopoly. Agriculture suffered from harvest failures and plagues, which in turn caused repeated famines. The population declined to the point where at the beginning of the seventeenth century large parts of the Castilian countryside lay deserted.

With Spain itself in decline, the hardship that the colonies had to undergo comes as no surprise. The decline was especially felt in the smaller colonies – the least important ones.[86] When Diego Gómez de Sandoval arrived in Santo Domingo in 1608 to replace Antonio Osorio as governor, what he found was 'hunger, misery and affliction'.[87] Between 1606 and 1609 more than one-third of the population of Bayaguana, which had been founded in the neighborhood of Santo Domingo to house the former inhabitants of Bayajá and La Yaguana,[88] died of hunger and disease.[89] Meat was in short supply. Of the 110,000 head of tame cattle found in the western part of the island before the evacuations, a mere 8,000 were brought to the new settlements and of these only 2,000 ever made it there.[90] The new government ordered that extraordinary measures be taken. The slaughtering of cows and calves was prohibited and the *hateros* were ordered to go to the Banda del Norte with a certain regularity to hunt wild cattle.[91]

The general poverty caused a reduction of imports. The years 1607 and 1608 saw a serious lack of clothes and fabrics. A letter to the Spanish king from a group of concerned upper-class citizens written in 1608 indicated that the majority of the Dominicans appeared in the streets 'naked, impoverished and dishonored'.[92] Sugar production was down since the horses and slaves necessary for cutting and processing were lacking (and so was the meat necessary to feed the slaves).[93] Henceforth, sugar was reduced to 'a discreet survival'.[94]

86 Peña Pérez (n.d.), p. 134.
87 Moya Pons (1977), p. 135.
88 Peña Pérez (1980), p. 156.
89 Moya Pons (1977), p. 135.
90 Peña Pérez (n.d.), p. 151.
91 Moya Pons (1977), p. 136, Peña Pérez (n.d.), p. 154.
92 Peña Pérez (n.d.), p. 154.
93 Ibid., p. 155, Gil-Bermejo García (1983), pp. 63–5.
94 Gil-Bermejo García (1983), p. 65.

The most important export product of the time was ginger, cultivated mainly around Santo Domingo.[95] In 1606, the colony counted 102 middle-sized *estancias* [farms] dedicated exclusively to ginger production and another 328 produced ginger in combination with other crops, such as maize or cassava, employing altogether 6,790 of the 9,648 slaves.[96] Gradually, however, the importance of ginger was to decline. Even though the existing figures are sometimes of doubtful quality there is no question about the trend. For 1611 a harvest of 30,000 *quintales*[97] is reported. Two years later 18,395 *quintales* are known to have been shipped. For the early 1630s, arrivals of 10,000–12,000 *quintales* are reported from Seville. In 1639 9,544 *quintales* left Hispaniola and the following year an 'exceptional' 16,545. Eight years later, in 1648, a mere 4,754 *quintales* were reported.[98] By this time, Brazil and the non-Spanish Antilles had emerged as superior competitors on the European market.[99]

During the years that had passed from the evacuations in 1605–06 to the mid-seventeenth century the economic decline of the Spanish colony in Hispaniola had accelerated. The political and economic situation of *La Madre Patria* [the Mother Country] was a sad one, after half a century of stagnation and retrogression:

> An important part of the explanation of Spanish decline lies outside the material plane, outside the failure of rewards in the new conditions of the seventeenth century; it is derived from the prolongation of the military-feudal dream, and the exaltation of extreme religious attitudes sometimes at the expense of sanity. Failure in war – the Armada disaster of 1588, the surrender to the Dutch in 1609 and 1648 and to the French in 1659 – shattered the dream; the momentum of effort so long thrusting through these channels could not easily be turned back in its old strength to humdrum productive pursuits. Goals of achievement were changing. By the middle of the seventeenth century Spain was a tired nation, and those who could sought quiet lives as rentiers, sinecurists, landlords or monks. Many of the best incomes that were still to be had by work went to foreigners, especially those controlling overseas trade. There was too much parasitism, too many people whose ambition was to be parasites.[100]

95 Ibid., p. 66.
96 Peña Pérez (1980), p. 176.
97 1 *quintal* = 46 kilos.
98 Gil-Bermejo García (1983), pp. 66–8.
99 Ibid., p. 69.
100 Davis (1973), p. 155.

This tired nation was gradually losing the contact with its colony in Hispaniola. Complaints with respect to the lack of merchant ships arriving in and leaving Santo Domingo became a recurrent theme during the first half of the seventeenth century.[101] Imports were difficult and the tonnage available for exports was too irregular and too small and in addition not available on competitive terms:

> The majority of the producers in the [sixteen] thirties began to experience a serious impediment with respect to the export trade. Since few ships arrived regularly from Spain, a small group of traders, very closely connected with the official sector, came to exercise a monopoly in the business of sending merchandise outside the island.[102]

As a result, at the beginning of the 1640s the crown resolved that half the available space in the ships leaving Hispaniola had to be reserved for 'private persons' and the rest for the traders.[103]

The lack of transport was to a large extent a result of the weakened military position of Spain. The Caribbean waters were full of English, French and Dutch privateers. Drake's capture of Santo Domingo on New Year's Day 1586 was followed by the capture of Cartagena in February. These attacks revealed the vulnerability of the Spanish possessions in the Caribbean: 'in Spain the news seemed disastrous. It spurred preparations for retaliation, either in the West Indies or in European waters. Probably even more than the subsequent capture of Cartagena, the fall of Santo Domingo was a stinging blow to the King of Spain.'[104]

The Spanish Armada failed to break the English in 1588.[105] In 1595 another large English fleet, under the joint command of Drake and John Hawkins, was back in the West Indies, destroying Nombre de Dios and the Panama isthmus so thoroughly that the Spanish moved from there to the more easily defended Portobelo.[106] The English were not alone, but were joined in their efforts to break the Spanish trade monopoly and territorial power by the Dutch and the French, and they were successful in their efforts: 'The damage done to the Spanish Empire ... the exhaustion

---

101 Cf. Peña Pérez (n.d.) Chapter 11, Gil-Bermejo García (1983), p. 114, and Moya Pons (1977), pp. 143–4, 147. The available statistics are found in Chaunu and Chaunu (1956), pp. 496–516. However, great care has to be taken when interpreting these. (Sources and methodology are discussed in Chaunu and Chaunu (1955). Cf. also Gil-Bermejo García (1983), Chapter 4.)
102 Peña Pérez (n.d.), p. 167.
103 Ibid.
104 Keeler (1981), p. 33.
105 See e.g. Fernández-Armesto (1988), for details.
106 Parry (1966), p. 256.

caused by a military effort beyond the power of Spain to support, the depletion of resources in men, ships and money, the contraction of influence and commercial opportunity, were to have lasting and irreparable consequences.'[107]

The extent of Spanish misfortunes did not end here, however. The Dutch had become very efficient contraband traders in Caribbean waters at the beginning of the seventeenth century,[108] and thus were also involved in repeated attacks on Spanish ships and towns. After a twelve-year truce between 1609 and 1621, these activities culminated in the seizure of the entire Spanish homebound fleet outside Matanzas, by Admiral Piet Heyn, in 1628.[109] The Matanzas catastrophe had severe consequences:

> It was followed by several years of systematic pillaging by smaller fleets, which drove local Spanish shipping from the sea. The armed convoys, by a miracle of determination, continued their sailings; but an *armada* of at least twenty warships was now considered to escort a merchant fleet of, at most, the same number.[110]

The threats were real. The years between 1620 and the 1680s constituted the great age of Caribbean piracy, of European naval attacks on Spain's possessions, of 'no peace beyond the line'.[111] It was impossible to be everywhere at the same time:

> There is scarcely an account of a local Caribbean sea voyage after 1630 until nearly the end of the seventeenth century which does not tell of at least a chase by a pirate ship. The *armada de barlovento*, a fleet of warships which was supposed to protect the Spanish Caribbean, proved worse than useless. It could not cover such a vast area and was undermanned, made up of aged hulks and never around when needed.[112]

Spanish resources had to be concentrated on the protection of the most valuable possessions and transports, but this in turn opened the possibility both of non-Spanish settlement in uninhabited islands and of attacks on weak Spanish possessions. Thus, the Dutch managed to wrest Curaçao out of Spanish hands in 1634. In 1655, Oliver Cromwell sent off a major expedition with the purpose of capturing Santo Domingo and, with the latter

107 Ibid., p. 257.
108 Ibid., p. 258.
109 Parry (1966), pp. 259–61, MacLeod (1984), pp. 377–8.
110 Parry (1966), p. 261.
111 MacLeod (1984), p. 376.
112 Ibid., p. 374.

as the base, the rest of the Spanish possessions in the Americas. The attack – a singularly ill-planned and badly executed one – failed, but resulted in the subsequent English acquisition of Jamaica the same year.[113]

More important from the view of the present work is that Spanish weakness left the road open for the French to move first onto the island of Tortuga, north of Hispaniola, and from there onto the major island itself. In both cases they were able to move into empty lands. The French had first established themselves in the island of Saint Christopher (present-day Saint Kitts), which they shared with the English in 1625,[114] and as they were driven out from there by a Spanish expedition in 1630, a group of French ended up in Tortuga.

The Spanish never managed to drive the French permanently out of Tortuga.[115] After 1630, attacks were launched in 1635, 1638, 1643 (a failure) and 1654, but the French always came back.[116] Gradually they began to penetrate Hispaniola as well. By 1652 around 2,000 people were already living in the non-Spanish territories.[117] Two years later, in January 1654, the Spaniards conquered Tortuga, only to leave the island in August the following year. After a short English interval, the French were back in command in 1659.[118]

Five years later *La Compagnie des Indes Occidentales*, a joint venture between the crown and private interests, was formed in France and was given a monopoly on the West Indian trade. The company named a governor of Tortuga and the western part of Hispaniola. The French colony began to be organized and the French population, which in 1665 was some 1,100, had six or seven years later increased to 8,000 souls.[119] This consolidation continued for the next twenty years under renewed tension and friction with the Spanish, culminating in the battle of Sabana Real (Limonade) at the beginning of 1691, where a French army was effectively destroyed. Cap Français, by then the capital of the French colony, was sacked and the surrounding areas were left in total disorganization.[120]

However, the rest of the French colony remained intact. Tortuga had been more or less depopulated and the center of gravity had been transferred to Hispaniola, where the population had continued to grow up to

---

113 See Sutton (1990).

114 Cf. e.g. Crouse (1940), Chapter 2, for details.

115 For details on Tortuga during the period from the first French settlement until the Treaty of Ryswick in 1697, see e.g. Crouse (1940), Chapter 5, (1943), Chapter 5, Peña Batlle (1951), Moya Pons (1977), Chapters 8–9, Funck-Brentano (1979), and Peña Pérez (n.d.), Chapters 1–9.

116 Peña Pérez (n.d.), p. 28.

117 Ibid., p. 40.

118 Ibid., p. 53.

119 Ibid., pp. 57–64.

120 Ibid., pp. 67–92, Moya Pons (1977), pp. 179–96.

1691, when it suffered a decline as a result of the Spanish attack in combination with the emigration that took place in the aftermath of the battle.[121] The tension between the two colonies continued until 1697, when peace was signed in Europe after almost a decade of warfare between France and the League of Augsburg, involving, among other nations, Spain. The Treaty of Ryswick, even though it does not mention the French and Spanish colonies in Hispaniola explicitly,[122] effectively put an end to further Spanish claims to the western part of the island.

The creation of a trade pattern

The increasing isolation of Santo Domingo had strong consequences for life within the Spanish colony. The census taken in 1606, immediately after the evacuation of the western part, revealed that the capital was the only urban agglomeration of importance, with a total free population of 3,240. The second town, Santiago de los Caballeros, had a mere 775, Bayaguana had 575, Monte Plata 435 and Azua 230. The other five towns or villages that appear in the census all had 200 people or less – down to thirty-five in the case of Seibo.[123] Only Santo Domingo possessed any number of traders and artisans to be reckoned with and the smaller towns had none.[124] Some thirty years later, in 1634, Santo Domingo was in a state of decay as well, with a mere six *pulperías* functioning. By this time, domestic commerce had virtually ceased to operate for lack of goods[125] and whatever transactions that were carried out were virtually always barter transactions, for lack of money.[126]

The foreign trade of the colony was gradually reduced to smuggling as Spain proved increasingly incapable of satisfying the demand for manufactured articles on the one hand and of serving as an outlet for Dominican goods on the other.[127] The scarcity of imported goods reached such a severe state that the Archbishop of Santo Domingo complained that in 1656 and 1657 not only the poor but also some rich families hardly had any clothes and hence spent most of their time in the countryside where they could not be seen. People went to mass before the break of dawn so as not to have to expose themselves clad in rags.[128]

121 Peña Pérez (n.d.), p. 92.
122 See e.g. Peña Batlle (1946), pp. 81–3, Mejía Ricart (1953), pp. 299–302, Incháustegui (1955), p. 204, Peña Pérez (n.d.), pp. 96–7.
123 Peña Pérez (1980), pp. 172–6.
124 Cassá (1985), pp. 96–7.
125 Peña Pérez (n.d.), pp. 166–7.
126 Ibid., p. 173.
127 Ibid., p. 178.
128 Ibid., Cassá (1985), p. 107.

In the interior of the island the larger farms almost disappeared from the mid-seventeenth century and the *hatos* fell into a state of more or less complete disorganization. Hunting cattle that had run wild was substituted for raising domesticated animals and the pastures gradually reverted to forest.[129] This was definitely the case with the San Juan Valley. Luis Jerónimo de Alcocer in the 1640s described the valley as having 'a beautiful temperature, fresh and salutary, and sometimes it gets very cold. There, lots of cattle [*ganado mayor*] are bred and lots of small stock [*ganado menor* – goats and sheep] could be bred because they breed well [there]. There are some and a lot could be bred were it not for the lack of funds [*caudal*].'[130] Alcocer also mentions that the valley had some 20,000–30,000 wild horses around the same time.[131]

Alexandre-Olivier Oexmelin (alias Alexander Exquemelin or John Esquemeling), who came to Tortuga in 1666 as an indentured servant and who lived among the buccaneers and pirates of the island until 1674,[132] provides a similar description of the situation around the time he arrived:

> West of San Domingo lies another handsome village called Azua. The people here trade with another village named San Juan de Goave [San Juan de la Maguana], situated right in the middle of the island at the edge of a great prairie, at least twenty leagues in perimeter, full of wild cattle. No one lives in this village but cowskinners or hunters. Most of them are of mixed blood – people of Negro and white parentage, known as mulattoes, or of Indian and white descent, called mestizos. Those of mixed Negro and Indian blood are nicknamed *alcatraces*. There is a great mingling of races, for the Spaniards are extremely fond of Negro women, more so than their own. From this village comes a great quantity of hides and tallow, but nothing else is produced there on account of the great dryness of the soil.[133]

Quite probably, some of the trade of the San Juan Valley, however small, took place with the French colony. At the end of the 1660s the economy in the western part of the island developed a strong demand for the animal products of the eastern part. After the first French penetration of Tortuga, a social division was established encompassing three different economic groups.

---

129 Ibid., Peña Pérez (n.d.), p. 180.
130 Quoted by Garrido (1972), pp. 330–1.
131 Quoted in ibid., p. 331.
132 Beeching (1969), pp. 18–19. In 1697, he returned to the Caribbean and served as a surgeon when Cartagena was attacked, a battle which has been called the 'buccaneers' swan-song' (ibid., p. 19).
133 Exquemelin (1969), p. 36.

The first of these, the buccaneers, hunted animals: wild cattle for hides, and pigs and wild boar for meat. The second, the freebooters, attacked (mainly) Spanish ships and towns; the third consisted of agriculturalists cultivating mainly tobacco.[134] At the beginning of the French penetration, however, hunting was the main activity:

> They began cultivation on Tortuga about the year 1598, and the first crop they planted was tobacco. This did very well, but they were unable to make many plantations as the island is so small, with little agricultural land. [...] Consequently, as I said, most folk took to hunting or privateering ...[135]

In the early years hunting in Hispaniola was a profitable business for the French settlers, but the Spaniards were determined to put an end to the hunting endeavors of the French :

> There used to be huge numbers of wild bulls and cows, but nowadays they are beginning to become scarce, being rapaciously preyed from every side. The Spaniards destroy as many as they can, to grieve the French; the wild dogs devour many of their calves; and the French hunters slaughter them in great quantity. [...] It is a wonder there still remains a single bull or wild boar on Hispaniola. For the past eighty-one years, more than 1,500 wild swine have been destroyed every day, both by the Spaniards and the French. Indeed, from my own experience, I would say the French alone slaughter more than this every day ...[136]

However, this wholesale slaughter could not go on much longer, and after some years of hunting most French settlers

> turned to agriculture again, choosing the best place they could find for planting tobacco in the whole of Hispaniola. The first places they settled were in Cul de Sac, in the north-west of the island, and in time their numbers grew, so that they are now [at the beginning of the 1670s] a good two thousand strong. They are safe from the Spaniards, who cannot reach them.[137]

By this time a mere 300 full-time hunters were left, and in 1664 a petition was made by some buccaneers that their number be limited to 200.[138]

---

134 Ibid. p. 53, Peña Pérez (n.d.), pp. 25–7.
135 Exquemelin (1969), p. 59.
136 Ibid, pp. 49–50.
137 Ibid., pp. 59–60.
138 Moya Pons (1977), p. 183.

In spite of political tension, trade with the Spanish was becoming a necessity. In the early 1680s, the hostilities between Spanish and French receded and peaceful exchange of commodities came instead. Horses, salted meat and hides were bartered for manufactured goods which had arrived in Saint-Domingue in French boats.[139] This commerce continued in spite of the declarations made by the Spanish governor of Santo Domingo that such trade was 'totally and indispensably prohibited'.[140] Towards the end of the decade, the contraband had reached such proportions that in 1688 the governor thought it necessary to post infantry guards in the southern ports to prevent such transactions.[141]

The trade that was established in the 1680s was irregular and unstable. The Spaniards feared that the French planned to take over the entire island. In 1681, there were as many French (7,580) as Spanish (7,500) on the island,[142] and in spite of the somewhat more peaceful conditions that began to prevail around this time, the hostilities never ceased completely. To strengthen the Spanish presence on the island, immigration from the Canary Islands was encouraged during the 1680s.[143] One of the main objectives was to settle the border area in order to prevent further penetration of the French into the eastern part. To this end, in 1690 a request was sent to the Spanish crown for a hundred families, fifty for Santiago and the rest to be divided between Azua and San Juan de la Maguana.[144]

Irregularity notwithstanding, contraband trade increased to 'unimagined levels' between 1685 and 1690.[145] Without it, the Spaniards would have had severe problems surviving. As the seventeenth century advanced, and especially as it was drawing to an end, the overall economic situation worsened. Hands to work the land were lacking. Consecutive outbreaks of diseases had reduced the slave population,[146] and Portugal, hitherto the main supplier of slaves to the Spanish colonies, had broken away from

---

139 Ibid., p. 189. Deive (1991), p. 43, gives the figures of 4,000 free Frenchmen, 1,565 indentured laborers and 1,063 black slaves in the French colony and 7,500 'persons' in the Spanish one, of which 300 were soldiers.

140 Quoted in Moya Pons (1977), p. 191.

141 Peña Pérez (n.d.), p. 197.

142 Moya Pons (1977), p. 216, and (1974), p. 21.

143 The first embarkation of Canarians (540 persons) arrived in 1684 (Deive (1991), p. 47). The Canarians were willing to move to the Indies due to the wretched situation on the islands of Fuerteventura and Gran Canaria, where several years of bad harvests and a plague of locusts had caused diseases and an alarming decline in agriculture. The Spanish authorities were promoting emigration to the Indies, not only due to the need of labor in places like Santo Domingo, but also in order to prevent the Canarians from settling in the territories of hostile nations (ibid., p. 59).

144 Moya Pons (1977), pp. 217–21.

145 Peña Pérez (n.d.), p. 21.

146 Deive (1980), pp. 135–7.

Spain in 1640.[147] That year, the Spanish king excluded the Portuguese from all trade with the Americas with the result that the supply of slaves was drastically reduced.[148]

When slaves were actually available the colonists could not always afford to buy them. Thus, in 1669 a boat arrived with some 400 slaves on board, but in spite of remaining in Hispaniola for five months the captain was able to sell only 140, in a situation where there was an acute lack of workers.[149] The only solution to this dilemma was to trade with the French. In Saint-Domingue a plantation economy was rapidly being constructed. Indigo and then sugar were substituted for tobacco.[150] Little by little, Saint-Domingue was becoming the most profitable of all French colonies, exporting sugar and indigo to France in exchange for manufactures. The rise of the plantation economy, in turn, put pressure on the supply of meat.

To make up for the dwindling supply of cattle in the west the French resorted to trading with the Spanish. Some of the the French manufactures made their way into the Spanish colony, as Spain was unable to supply these goods except at extremely irregular intervals and high prices.[151] However unreliable the commerce with the French may have been, it constituted the only positive feature of the Spanish economy of Hispaniola at the end of the seventeenth century:

> During the last three years of the seventeenth century the economic situation of Española was a veritable disaster, and the two means most commonly employed for survival were contraband and eating wild fruits and animals. According to the report of 28 March 1699, sent to the king by Juan Nieto Valcárcel, the population got no 'benefit' from ginger, indigo, cocoa, etc., because 'in this Island are found no persons who want to work on a daily wage basis' to make the mines and estates [*haciendas*] produce, and the majority was content to be alive.[152]

Consolidation of the pattern

In the aftermath of the Treaty of Ryswick, the trade pattern established during the course of the seventeenth century was consolidated. The start of the War of the Spanish Succession, in 1702, cut Santo Domingo off from Spain even more efficiently than before. 'If in 1701 it was pointed out that

147 Kamen (1980), pp. 57–9, 350–1.
148 Ibid., pp. 136–7.
149 Ibid., p. 137.
150 Peña Pérez (n.d.), Chapter 9.
151 Ibid., p. 203.
152 Ibid., p. 217.

there would only be a ship every two or three years, in 1710 more than a decade had passed since the last embarkation', notes Antonio Gutiérrez Escudero.[153] The seaborne trade of the colony could take place only with Spain's other American colonies and those of other European powers.

In Hispaniola itself, the trade between the French and the Spanish colonies continued. Construction of sugar mills had begun in the northern part of Saint-Domingue by the 1690s, and after 1697 this process accelerated.[154] In September 1701, thirty-five mills were in operation on the French side of the border, twenty were almost ready to be put into production and construction had begun on another ninety.[155] Sugar cane cultivation was extended at the expense of cattle raising.

In 1700, the last Habsburg king of Spain, Charles II, died without having left any heir, and Philip V, Duke of Anjou and grandson of Louis XIV, was crowned king.[156] With a Bourbon on the Spanish throne, the disposition towards trade with the French increased. The Spanish colonists were now freer than before to supply cattle, hides and horses to the *colons* of Saint-Domingue:

> Clearly the sugar mills were not the only centers of demand for cattle that existed in the French colony. All the rest of the colony needed the cattle from the Spanish part to feed itself and it was known that the wild cattle of the western part of the island was a thing of the past with only a few wild animals appearing in the forests of the zone. Hence, the meat business was converted into one of the most important of the entire French colony and the leasing of abattoirs became one of the most handsome revenue providers for their owners, who turned this business into one of the most productive income sources.[157]

In 1711, the French authorities decreed that the entire northern territory between Limonade and the Rebouc River should be dedicated to agriculture.[158] Five years later the number of *ingenios* in operation far exceeded one hundred, all of which demanded a steady supply of meat and draught animals.[159] Protests from Spanish officials in Santo Domingo could not stem the rising tide, and the objections were at best half-hearted. At least three of the Spanish governors between 1691 and 1724 were themselves more or less actively involved in contraband trade with the French side.[160]

153 Gutiérrez Escudero (1985), p. 27.
154 Moya Pons (1977), pp. 229–30.
155 Ibid., p. 230.
156 Kamen (1983), p. 261.
157 Moya Pons (1977), p. 230–1.
158 Moreau de Saint-Méry (1944), p. 365.
159 Moya Pons (1977), p. 232.
160 Ibid., pp. 233–4.

For the general population, this trade was a matter of life or death. Xavier de Charlevoix quotes a contemporary French official traveling to the Spanish side in 1717:

> nothing is poorer than those colonists: except for the capital, where there are still various palaces and mansions that really retain their former splendor; everywhere else only huts and cabins are seen where one is hardly under shelter. For the time being no new construction is undertaken in Santo Domingo when the old houses are crumbling, either because of age or some other accident, and everywhere the furniture responds to the rusticity of the lodging. Therefore there is no longer either commerce or manufacture in most places; their large herds feed them; and it is from these that the French colony gets all its slaughtered meat. In exchange, we provide them with the means for satisfying the most indispensable necessities in life; because from Spain hardly anything is being sent to them anymore and they do not want to take the trouble to procure their necessities through their own industriousness and labor.[161]

Still, trade with the French continued to be formally prohibited until the end of the 1730s.[162] Formal prohibitions were of little avail, however, in a situation where it paid handsomely for both contracting parties to exchange commodities. Smuggling was a regular feature of the economic life of both the border area and the southern parts of the Spanish colony.[163] From those regions French (and other non-Spanish) manufactured goods were transported to the capital.

The volume of trade between the two colonies grew rapidly during the first three decades of the eighteenth century. A letter from some French officials describes the ambiguous situation of the Spanish officials in 1729:

> all the Spanish presidents [of the *audiencia* of Santo Domingo], who only govern in their own personal interest, do not cease to publish, from time to time, the prohibitions by the King of Spain for the Spaniards to maintain commerce with the French and, consequently, under severe penalties, to prohibit them from introducing any animals into the French storehouses. But that is only to make them buy the right to do so.[164]

161 Charlevoix (1977), p. 385.
162 Cassá (1985), p. 114.
163 Moya Pons (1977), pp. 237–8, 242–3.
164 Quoted by Moya Pons (1977), pp. 251–2.

At any rate, the intercolonial trade was firmly entrenched. Neither party could do without it[165] and more was yet to come. The lack of commercial contacts with Spain continued. In the 1730s a single ship left Hispaniola for Spain and in the 1740s the figure was the same.[166] Three and two ships, respectively, arrived from Spain.[167] The colony was completely dependent on trade with Spain's colonies and with other nations.

Fortunately, this trade was strong enough to lift Santo Domingo's economy out of the depression from which it had suffered for over a century.[168] From 1732, the colony benefited from governors whose views on trade were quite liberal:

> The new governors coming to the island, Alfonso de Castro y Mazo (1732–1740) and Pedro Zorilla de San Martín (1740–1750) acted in a different way. They wanted to do whatever possible to improve the situation for its inhabitants, sometimes by maintaining a certain liberalism with respect to contraband trade, sometimes through cattle traffic with the French colony or by opening the ports to trade with neutral states. Especially as far as Zorilla is concerned, one could speak of an economic 'takeoff' for Spanish Santo Domingo.[169]

In addition, during the second half of the eighteenth century, the Spain's trade with its colonies was gradually liberalized. The convoy system had been abolished in 1735.[170] In 1755 the *Real Compañía de Comercio de Barcelona* was created, which began its trade with Hispaniola two years later. This company was given certain privileges, but not any exclusive trading rights, and little by little these privileges were eroded. In 1765, a number of Spanish ports (hitherto only Cádiz) were granted the right to trade with the Antilles and the taxation of this trade was reduced considerably. In 1778, the *Reglamento del Libre Comercio* was promulgated, which authorized free trade among all the Spanish colonies in the New World, with the exception of Nueva España and Venezuela (which were incorporated a year later), and further tax reductions took place. This policy continued in

---

165 Ibid., pp. 252–3.
166 Gutiérrez Escudero (1985), p. 209. The figures for the preceding decades were 1700–09: three, 1710–19: none and 1720–29: none (ibid.).
167 Ibid., p. 213. Between 1700 and 1709 three ships had arrived, between 1710 and 1719 none and from 1720 to 1729, four (ibid.).
168 Moya Pons (1977), p. 249.
169 Gutiérrez Escudero (1985), pp. 42–3.
170 Sevilla Soler (1980), p. 174. The convoys to Nueva España were reintroduced in 1754 and continued on and off until 1789, when the system was finally abolished: 'It had long outlived its usefulness; in war it had become inadequate, in peace unnecessary' (Parry (1966), p. 286).

the 1780s, as a more liberal view of trade policy began to supplant the old mercantilistic doctrines.[171]

The gradual liberalization of trade, however, did not lead to the abandonment of trade between the Spanish and French in Hispaniola. The terms of trade when dealing with the peninsula remained unfavorable, relatively speaking, and goods were slow in arriving at the island. The increase in the trade between Spain and Santo Domingo was only marginal, and after 1778, when not only the Antilles but also the mainland were opened to trade, the latter turned out to be a superior competitor for the favors of the Iberian merchants.[172] The exchange that took place with Saint-Domingue, as well as some other foreign colonies, continued to supply the Spanish colony with most of its manufactures.[173]

At the same time, pressure from the prosperous French colony on the Spanish territory was felt. The border was only vaguely defined, and hence disputed, at the beginning of the eighteenth century. In 1731, the Dajabón (Masacre) River in the north and the Pedernales river in the south were agreed upon as demarcation lines, which, however, still left a great deal of disputed territory in the center.[174] French incursions into what in Santo Domingo was considered Spanish territory were common,[175] and in order to establish their presence and authority in the border zone the Spaniards founded or reformed a number of towns: San Juan de la Maguana (1733), Neiba (1735), Puerto Plata (1737), Dajabón (1740), Monte Cristi (1751), San Rafael (1761), San Miguel de la Atalaya (1768)[176] and Las Caobas (1768).[177] Immigrants from the Canary Islands were brought in to populate them, as well as Bánica (refounded in 1664) and Hincha (Guaba, founded in 1704). (The location of these towns is shown in Figure 7.7.)

Ever since the evacuations of the western part of Hispaniola in 1605 and 1606, the necessity of repopulating the San Juan Valley constantly figured in the correspondence between the authorities of Santo Domingo and the Spanish crown. The correspondence insisted that a resettlement was crucial for defense and it was repeatedly stressed that the valley was a 'healthy and fertile territory', rich in undomesticated cattle. A royal decree in 1693 finally ordered the settlement of the region. However, the project was not realized to its full extent until 1733, when San Juan de la Maguana was resettled.[178]

---

171 For details, see Sevilla Soler (1980), pp. 173–89.
172 See ibid., pp. 189–209, for details.
173 Ibid., pp. 209–19.
174 Tolentino Rojas (1944), pp. 40–1, Peña Batlle (1946), pp. 89–90.
175 See Moya Pons (1977), Chapter 12, for details.
176 Ibid., pp. 286–90.
177 Mejía Ricart (1953), p. 391, Gutiérrez Escudero (1985), p. 75.
178 Deive (1991), p. 101.

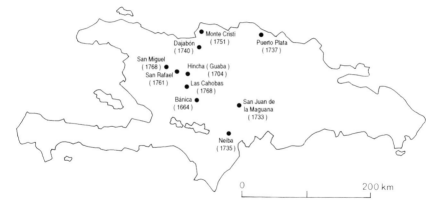

Figure 7.7 The border towns of Santo Domingo, around 1770.
Source: Cassá (1985), p. 119.

When Hincha was founded in 1704 it constituted the Spanish outpost closest to the French colony and it was decided that the population of Bánica had to be reinforced and San Juan de la Maguana repopulated in order to create a strong chain of military posts and settlements from Azua up to Hincha. Canarians were settled in all four towns, while ranchers who lived dispersed in the area were forced to move into the towns.[179]

Initially the Canarians concentrated on traditional agricultural products, such as plantains, sweet potatoes, manioc, maize, beans and yams. However, the majority soon turned to cattle grazing. The influx of Canarians did not interrupt the occupational structure of the colony. As small proprietors and free laborers the colonists maintained traditional social relations without 'changing them in any degree'.[180]

The immigration of Canarians to Hispaniola started on a regular basis in 1735, when every settler was provided with cash amounting to 1,602 *pesos*, together with axes, plows, steel and iron bars, as well as seeds, cattle and land. Single settlers were not encouraged; to enjoy the benefits provided by the state Canarians had to arrive with families. In 1764 this immigration policy was officially abandoned. Counting the embarkation of 1683, it is estimated that 4,035 Canarians, in groups of 781 families, reached the colony from 1683 to 1780.[181]

The formally refounded San Juan de la Maguana became a center for the surrounding ranching population.[182] However, the effects of the de-

179 Ibid. p. 102.
180 Ibid., p. 157.
181 Ibid., p. 168.
182 Moreau de Saint-Méry (1944), p. 256.

population in 1606 continued to be felt. In 1740, a mere 550 people lived in the town. Twenty years later, this figure had increased to 1,386.[183] Moreau de Saint-Méry reports that San Juan 'in 1764 still was considered new. It then had few houses …'[184] In 1751 the town was hit by an earthquake, which opened 'enormous ditches in the San Juan Valley into which men and cattle disappeared'.[185] A *censo parroquial* [parish census] for 1769 gave a figure of 1,838[186] and, according to another estimate, which may, however, be on the low side,[187] in 1777 the town and the surrounding *hatos* could still not boast more than 252 families with 1,851 members.[188] Another *censo parroquial*, carried out in 1782, gives a population of 4,900.[189]

By this time, Las Matas de Farfán and Pedro Corto had also been formally founded, further to the west of the valley, as ecclesiastical dependencies of Bánica,[190] whose population in 1782 was around 7,000.[191] Altogether, the total population in the plains from San Miguel de la Atalaya and San Rafael in the west to the eastern border of San Juan de la Maguana, on the Río Yaque del Sur, amounted to no more than some 25,000 at this time.[192] In spite of the population increase, the valley remained sparsely populated.

The economy that developed in the San Juan Valley during the course of the eighteenth century was built entirely on cattle raising. A 1744 cattle census indicated that there were in the San Juan area close to 8,700

---

183 Gutiérrez Escudero (1985), p. 51.

184 Moreau de Saint-Méry (1944), p. 256.

185 Gutiérrez Escudero (1985), p. 78.

186 Moya Pons (1974a), p. 24.

187 Moreau de Saint-Méry (1944), p. 256, gives a figure of 3,600 for the *parroquia* of San Juan in 1764.

188 Nouel (1970), p. 338.

189 Moya Pons (1974a), p. 24. Cf. Moreau de Saint-Méry (1944), p. 256, who visited the Spanish colony in 1783 and gives a contemporary figure for the population of San Juan of 'close to five thousand inhabitants'. These figures all appear to be somewhat shaky, possibly due to different ways of delimiting the areas where people were counted. Thus the *padrones vigentes* [the census in force] of the *audiencia* of Santo Domingo, stated that San Juan de la Maguana in 1784 had 219 families consisting of 1,598 *almas* [souls] (Nouel (1970), p. 339). Yet other figures for 'La Maguana', presumably referring to a smaller area, came from a 1785 *código* 'for the economic, political and moral government of the Negroes of Santo Domingo': 1740, 440; 1772, 1,600; 1782–83, 1,451 (Sevilla Soler (1980), p. 35).

190 Las Matas de Farfán was founded in 1779 (Tolentino Rojas (1944), pp. 63 and 396). See also Moreau de Saint-Méry (1944), p. 253, Mejía Ricart (1953), p. 442, Palmer (1976), p. 42.

191 Moreau de Saint-Méry (1944), p. 253, Moya Pons (1974a), p. 24. According to the *padrones vigentes* of the *audiencia* of Santo Domingo, Bánica had in 1784 '406 families with 2,689 souls' (Nouel (1970), p. 339).

192 Moreau de Saint-Méry (1944), pp. 257, 117, Moya Pons (1974a), p. 24 (a figure of 23,900 is given).

animals,[193] which, however, presumably amounts to an underestimation, since the purpose of the census was to establish how many animals each *ganadero* had to sell at a fixed price (far lower than what could be obtained on the French side) to the capital.[194]

The reports of other contemporary visitors also bear clear testimony. In 1764, the French engineer Daniel Lescallier reported a figure of no less than 18,000 cows and more than 10,000 horses:

> The soil of San Juan is very good but its inhabitants are idlers and do not dedicate themselves to any form of cultivation [...] Everywhere we found savannas where immense numbers of cattle graze.
>
> The air is healthy and fresh, but very often long dry spells occur which are extremely costly for the inhabitants. By the same token large numbers of animals perish.
>
> From this stem the enormous herds of oxen and horses in all the areas, from the necessity of each individual to breed many in order to secure sufficient numbers of them for their own use and for sale in case of some misfortune.
>
> The plain of San Juan is singularly cool and it can even be said that its nights are cold even during the hot period.[195]

In 1772, it was estimated that San Juan had no less than 25,000 head of cattle.[196] Moreau de Saint-Méry, who traveled through the area in 1783, described it in the following way:

> All that we have traveled through and described from San Rafael to the Yaquecillo [Río Yaque del Sur], which is divided into various plains that constitute two hundred square leguas,[197] is presently for no other use whatsoever than for breeding animals intended mainly for the provisioning of the French colony ...[198]

Another French traveler, a certain Albert, around 1795 reported: 'Very far into the interior of the land we find San Juan de la Maguana, a rather important town. Its plains are the most abundant ones of the entire island in terms of animals, like oxen, horses, mules.'[199]

During the eighteenth century, the eastern part of the San Juan Valley was covered with grass, without any evidence of cultivation. Further west-

193 Sevilla Soler (1980). p. 133, Gutiérrez Escudero (1985), p. 143.
194 Sevilla Soler (1980), pp. 134–8.
195 Lescallier (1979), p. 27.
196 Sevilla Soler (1980), p. 133, Gutiérrez Escudero (1985), p. 147.
197 1 square *legua* = 3,105.5 hectares.
198 Moreau de Saint-Méry (1944), p. 257.
199 Albert (1979), p. 82.

wards, from Pedro Corto towards Las Matas de Farfán and Bánica, and extending all the way to the border in the northwest, scrubland gradually took over and the aridity of the landscape increased, while the southwestern part of the valley remained forested.[200]

The economic development of the San Juan Valley constitutes an almost textbook example of specialization according to comparative advantage of the Heckscher-Ohlin type.[201] Given the low population density, the valley was eminently land-abundant, and one should expect it to be a net seller of land-intensive goods, like cattle, meat and hides, and that is precisely what took place:

> In general nuanced terms Santiago and its *hinterland* (La Vega, Hincha, Bánica, San Juan, Cotuí) would become essentially cattle raising during the first fifty years of the [eighteenth] century. Of course, the land would be cultivated and agricultural products would be harvested, but rather for internal consumption than for exports. Its real source of wealth, the activity that would bring large incomes, consisted in selling cattle to the neighboring French colony. Obliged, as [these towns] ... were, to sell the products through the only port that was authorized and permitted since 1605–06, that of Santo Domingo, the rebellion against this imposition materialized in an increase in the number of cattle which when sold in Saint Domingue permitted them to obtain all kinds of merchandise in exchange.[202]

Transport costs, however, may also have had to do with the decision to trade westwards instead of eastwards. In 1796, Moreau de Saint-Méry offered the following description of the road network in the eastern part of Hispaniola: 'Pointing out the nature of the roads amounts to saying that the Spanish part of Santo Domingo hardly carries on any trade at all; for trade needs good means of communications ...'[203] When he traveled from San Rafael to Santo Domingo in 1783, it took him eleven days on horseback from San Juan de la Maguana to the capital.[204]

> There are no more roads, than paths which are impossible to negotiate without difficulty and slowness. It is only possible to travel on

---

200 Palmer (1976), pp. 52–4.
201 See Södersten and Reed (1994), Chapter 3, for an exposition.
202 Gutiérrez Escudero (1985), p. 78.
203 Moreau de Saint-Méry (1944), p. 96.
204 Ibid., pp. 268–70. Moreau remarks that it would be impossible to cover the distance between San Rafael and Santo Domingo in less than ten days on horseback because of the distance, the terrain and the necessity to find food and lodging in the evening (ibid., p. 268). Cf. also Lescallier (1979), pp. 47–54.

horseback or by foot and it is indispensable to take the precaution of bringing along all that is necessary to feed and lodge oneself. Only eight leagues a day may be covered with much work and often without encountering one single dwelling.[205]

Westward communications were far easier, as the San Juan Valley extends into the Plateau Central on the French side.[206] Finally, the price on the French side was several times higher than the fixed price received in the capital.[207] No wonder that, around 1757, it was reported that even cattle from *hatos* fairly close to the capital found their way to the French side.[208] Altogether, Moreau – a French citizen – pointed out, not without pride, that 'the three million [*pesos fuertes*][209] that the Spaniards receive from us, make up three-quarters of the value of the production of their colony ...'[210] In the 1770s and the 1780s perhaps as many as 4,500–5,500 animals were brought to Santo Domingo each year, while perhaps three or four times as many were sold to the French side.[211]

Land tenure: the rise of the *terrenos comuneros*

The concentration on cattle raising had an impact on the property rights system as well. During the course of the sixteenth century the Spanish crown had become increasingly concerned with the land title situation in the colonies.[212] Evidence was accumulating that Indian land was being seized illegally by the colonists. According to a papal bull of 1493, all newly discovered land in principle belonged to the king personally. Hence, land seizure was viewed an encroachment on royal property.

To remedy this, a number of royal *cédulas* [letters] were issued beginning in 1591, with, however, the crown increasingly as the losing party. The cornerstone in the attempted legislation was the *amparo real* [royal protection] codified in 1591, which granted possession to those with good title or lawful continued possession. The *amparo real* did not grant title. That had to be obtained through *real confirmación* [royal confirmation] of already existing documents.

---

205 Moreau de Saint-Méry (1944), p. 96. 'Leagues' vary in length according to area and epoch. Moreau de Saint Méry uses a league that is probably equivalent to approximately five kilometers (cf. ibid., p. 112).

206 Lescallier (1979), p. 42. Cf. also Sevilla Soler (1980), pp. 145–7.

207 Sevilla Soler (1980), pp. 137–8.

208 Ibid., p 158.

209 A *peso fuerte* contained 25.563 grams of silver (Clausner (1973), p. 61).

210 Moreau de Saint-Méry (1944), pp. 390–1. Cf. Sevilla Soler (1980), p. 152.

211 Sevilla Soler (1980), pp. 139, 148, 171.

212 Clausner (1973), Chapter 7.

New efforts were made to straighten out the land title situation in 1631, 1694, 1741 and 1754, mainly for fiscal reasons.[213] In 1754, all those who possessed some sort of title or who could prove lengthy occupation were afforded absolute protection of their rights. Finally, in 1780, the crown gave up its efforts to regulate the land titles from Spain, as preceding efforts had had little effect. Spain remained too distant from its colonies, and the issue was left to the local colonial authorities.

However, one important piece of legislation was yet to follow. Charles IV issued a *cédula* which sternly prohibited the creation of any further *mayorazgos* [entails] without his personal permission in an attempt to limit the extent of absentee landownership with its concomitant underutilization of the land. This piece of legislation was hardly any more effective than the rest of the *cédulas* bearing on the land issues, especially not after 1801, when the crown began a policy of selling the rights to establish and confirm *mayorazgos*. It did, however, have the important effect that it clearly established the division of the land among heirs as the normal procedure.

This, plus the fact that cattle raising required vast tracts of land, determined the system of property rights in land that gradually evolved during the eighteenth century. With the gradual surrender of the crown in matters concerning agricultural land, the road lay open for privatization of the land, with or without explicit title, and, with the passage of time, possession came to constitute the basis for legally founded claims to the land in question. Thus, little by little, the most productive land passed from the crown into the hands of private individuals.

In some areas, notably around the capital, all the land was taken during the first or second decade after 1750. Daniel Lescallier, who traveled in the area in 1764, noted the scarcity:

> Who would think that no [land] concessions would be available any longer in a colony which is so vast and has so few inhabitants!
>
> For quite some time not a single inch of land remains without owner, so that all this vast land is distributed among the leading gentlemen in the capital who exploit and own it.
>
> In this way, an individual who wants to establish himself here has to buy a plot which will be sold to him very dearly or to lease the plot in question, the lessee becoming in the process a mere [tenant] farmer for the owner or lord.[214]

213 Ibid., pp. 57–8, Gutiérrez Escudero (1985), pp. 89–92. Alcibíades Alburquerque, a Dominican lawyer who analyzed the avalanche of false titles that hit the Dominican land tribunals after a land registration law had been passed in 1920, states that a law regulating the *amparos reales* was issued on 10 November 1578 (Alburquerque (1961), p. 12).
214 Lescallier (1979), p. 16.

The alternative to buying land was to acquire it through inheritance. This meant that the *hatos* somehow had to be subdivided, which, in turn, posed a very special problem,

> because the extensive cattle raising practiced in the colony required enormous extensions of pastures and forests and well distributed water supplies. If the division had continued, the divided areas frequently would have lacked rivers, grazing lands that were sufficiently extensive to feed a given number of cattle, or necessary forests.[215]

In other words, the smaller the size of the *hato*, the less useful it was to its owner, since the less likely it was that the cattle would survive, thrive and produce.

The practical solution to this problem, and the problem of allocating equal shares of equal quality, was not to subdivide the *hatos* in terms of *use*, but only in terms of *ownership*. In the seventeenth century the property rights system known as *terrenos comuneros* [common lands] made its appearance.[216] The origin of the custom is not clear. Marlin Clausner lists four different possibilities.[217] One has to do with land granted to an individual by the crown, defined only in terms of natural landmarks (rivers, roads, watercourses, etc.). If the individual wanted to sell this land he did so by putting a value on his entire property, thereafter selling an imprecisely defined share of it, i.e. the buyer would purchase a certain value rather than an area.

The second explanation builds on land originally granted in common for water, threshing and other activities defined as communal, or for wood-cutting. With time, individual rights to such lands became defined in terms of shares so as to preserve the land physically intact. A third possible mechanism is that private owners of land tracts sold them in terms of shares rather than in terms of physically delimited areas in order to avoid the costs of having the land surveyed. Finally, inheritance could cause problems, not only when the heirs were to share the usufruct rights to some already common property, but also when the costs connected with surveying and assessing lands of varying quality were high.

Regardless of the precise origin – probably a combination of all the mechanisms suggested by Clausner as well as the technological requirements of cattle raising – property rights in *terrenos comuneros* in time became defined with the aid of *pesos de posesión* or *acciones*, i.e. in terms of

215 Cassá (1985), p. 134.
216 Hoetink (1982), p. 3.
217 Clausner (1973), pp. 121–3.

each holder's share of the *value* of the land.[218] The possession of *pesos* gave their holders a vaguely defined usufruct right *to the* hato *as a whole*: grazing lands, forests, water, etc., a right which was in no way exclusive but which was shared with all other *peso* holders. This meant that it was not possible to set aside any of the *hato* area for *exclusive* use by one or more owners, with the exception of plots that were fenced in for agriculture or, in some cases, for breaking horses.[219]

In the mid-eighteenth century the *terrenos comuneros* system was widespread. More than fifty such entities existed in the eastern part of the country and some also in the south, while in the Cibao, for example, the tendency was to divide the land physically.[220] The *peso* titles had also begun to be sold commercially – to buyers outside the circle of heirs to properties, in a manner resembling the sale of modern shares.[221] As time went by it became increasingly difficult to get a clear picture of who owned what and of which rights were vested in a particular piece of land. The property rights system was becoming chaotic as the eighteenth century was drawing to an end. The system had its advantages, however, for the common man. We will come back to these below, since they are essential for arriving at a proper understanding of the *Olivorista* movement, its success and failure.

Destruction of the cattle economy

Without the trade with Saint-Domingue, notably the contraband, the Spanish colony in Santo Domingo would hardly have survived the eighteenth century. However, as we have seen in the foregoing, the proximity of the French colony was a mixed blessing for the Spaniards, because of the territorial rivalry and the largely undefined border between the colonies. The more prosperous French colonists pressed eastwards in contested areas and it proved difficult for the Spaniards to resist them, despite the establishment of the border towns from the 1730s to the 1770s. Provisional border treaties in 1773 and 1775 and above all the Treaty of Aranjuez in 1777 fixed the demarcation line, more to the satisfaction of the Spanish colonists than to that of the French.[222]

Soon a different type of influence was to extend from the French to the Spanish colony. In 1791, the slaves of Saint-Domingue rose in revolution against their French masters. A series of wars of liberation began that was

---

218 Ibid., p. 121, Gutiérrez Escudero (1985), p. 96, Cassá (1985), p. 134, Alburquerque (1961), p. 21.
219 Cassá (1985), p. 134.
220 Gutiérrez Escudero (1985), p. 96.
221 Ibid.
222 Sevilla Soler (1980), Chapter 9.

not to end until 1803, with the final expulsion of the French from the western part of the island.[223]

The wars of liberation had a tremendous effect on the eastern part of Hispaniola as well. When the French Jacobins declared war upon the enemies of the French Republic in 1793, Spain, together with England, among others, was to be found in the latter camp. This war involved the island of Hispaniola as well, and not least the border areas. Black troops under the ex-slave Toussaint L'Ouverture, who had sided with the French, captured Hincha, Las Caobas, Bánica, San Rafael and San Miguel de la Atalaya, i.e. all the border towns in the central region of the island. The war went badly for Spain in Europe as well. French troops penetrated the Iberian Peninsula and in 1795 Spain was forced to make peace with France under the Treaty of Basle and then had to cede the Santo Domingo colony to France.

This, however, did not mean that the hostilities came to an end. The war in Hispaniola was a reflection of the European wars which meant that English troops were also involved, and these did not leave until 1798 after having been active, among other things, in the San Juan and Neiba areas.[224] It was not until 1801 that Toussaint, who by this point had managed to become the supreme commander of the French army in Hispaniola, could enter the city of Santo Domingo. The island had been united under French supremacy.[225]

At the same time, however, the French were involved in an effort to put an end to the revolution that had broken out in 1791 but which had partly been overshadowed by the international war. In 1799 Napoleon had staged his Brumaire coup and made himself First Consul and, given his ambitions in Europe, he badly needed what had been the most profitable of the French colonies. The last phase of the wars of liberation in Hispaniola began in 1802, with the arrival of Napoleon's brother-in-law, General Leclerc, at the head of a French invasion army that captured Toussaint and sent him off to die in a French prison, before it fell victim to the combined efforts of the ex-slaves and yellow fever. On 1 January 1804, the sovereign state of Haiti was proclaimed.[226]

The Haitian wars of liberation and the international conflict ravaging Hispaniola during the same period had devastating consequences for the

223 The literature on the wars of liberation is extensive. The best-known work is that of James (1963). Ott (1973) provides a balanced overview. Heinl and Heinl (1978), Chapters 2–5, may also be consulted. Lepkowski (1968), (1969) deals not least with the economic consequences. Geggus (1987) concentrates on the British involvement. Brutus (1969) is a Haitian work on the period. Stoddard (1914) is an old classic. Contemporary accounts are given in Edwards (1797), Barskett (1818) and Lacroix (1819).
224 Moya Pons (1977), pp. 329–30.
225 Ibid., p. 333.
226 Ibid., pp. 333–5.

economy of Santo Domingo, not least for the border areas. With the outbreak of the Haitian revolution, the commerce between the two parts of the island suffered a severe setback. As Frank Moya Pons has observed: 'Everything that took place in the island of Santo Domingo during … [the] twenty years [between 1791 and the Spanish reconquest in 1809] was marked by violence.'[227] This fact had an impact on all aspects of life in the border areas.

In the first place, the territory at the center of the island, just a little to the west and northwest of San Juan de la Maguana, was in dispute, and both sides did their best to be in physical command over the zone in order to be able to claim it in future settlements. This involved troop movements and occupations precisely in the area through which the trade of the San Juan Valley with Haiti had taken place.

Secondly, neither the Treaty of Basle, nor the subsequent presence of French and Haitians on the soil of Santo Domingo, promised any good for the Spanish inhabitants. The invading armies lived off the towns and villages when they passed through them during their expeditions into the eastern part, and more permanently when they occupied them, like when San Juan was taken by English troops in March 1797 and by the French troops under Toussaint the following month.[228] This, in turn, had serious consequences for cattle ranching – wholesale slaughter of animals and the retreat of those ranchers who could move further to the east.[229]

Many *ganaderos* prepared themselves to leave Santo Domingo and sold as many animals as they could, thus lowering the price and increasing the demand for meat, which was already in short supply as a result of the wars. In the end the cattle economy broke down, as the herds were no longer able to reproduce. The scarcity of meat on the Spanish side increased drastically and trade with the French side (which was cut off anyway because of the war) became impossible.[230]

The inhabitants of San Juan de La Maguana suffered badly between 1797 and the turn of the century:

> every day they resented the French occupation of the towns of Bánica, Neiba and the other border towns more, because the military commanders at Toussaint's service continuously demanded to be given livestock for the maintenance and transportation of their troops, and the consignments that they delivered were normally paid at a very low price. The moment came when the inhabitants of San Juan

227 Ibid., pp. 339–40.
228 Ibid., pp. 355–6.
229 Lundahl and Vargas (1983), p. 115.
230 Moya Pons (1977), pp. 355–6.

complained that they hardly had some two hundred horses left for their own use and that it was hence impossible to part with them.[231]

Worse was, however, yet to come. Toussaint had stayed a mere six months in Santo Domingo in 1801.[232] The following year the French took over, immediately after their landing at Samaná. Three years later, the Haitian ruler, Jean-Jacques Dessalines, swept into the east in a two-pronged attack at the head of 30,000 men,[233] with devastating consequences for the towns on the way to Santo Domingo.[234] The attack failed, however, for lack of artillery. Dessalines could not take the city of Santo Domingo and had to return west, leaving the French to administer the eastern part until the Spanish rose in 1808, drove them out and rejoined the Spanish empire.[235]

By this time Santo Domingo's economy lay in ruins. Toussaint had attempted to introduce a plantation-based agricultural export economy along the lines that had proved relatively successful in the west.[236] The French administrator, General Louis Ferrand, had made a similar effort.[237] Both had failed, not understanding that the factor proportions were wrong. Santo Domingo was a colony with a small population and much land, i.e. a colony not suited for labor-intensive agricultural pursuits, and during the years that elapsed between the two Haitian invasions in 1801 and 1805–09 this fact became even more accentuated. Slavery had been abolished by Toussaint in 1801,[238] and the Spaniards did what they could to emigrate. 'All of the Spanish population decided to emigrate to other lands, and the only ones who did not leave were those who absolutely could not do so', noted a contemporary observer.[239] Venezuela, Colombia, Puerto Rico and (mainly) Cuba received a steady stream of refugees,[240] and Ferrand's efforts to stem the tide were in vain.[241]

The declining man/land ratio posed a tremendous problem in Santo Domingo – a problem which could not be solved for several decades and

231 Ibid., pp. 367–8. Cf. Deive (1989), p. 83.
232 Clausner (1973), p. 75.
233 Lundahl (1984), p. 82.
234 Mejía Ricart (1954), pp. 144–9, 157–9.
235 Clausner (1973), pp. 79–80.
236 Toussaint's agricultural system is analyzed in Lundahl (1985).
237 Moya Pons (1977), p. 392.
238 Deive (1980), p. 220. Slavery was, however, restored in 1805 by the French, who had invaded Hispaniola in 1802 (Clausner (1973), p. 77). It was abolished for the second time by Jean-Pierre Boyer after the Haitian invasion in 1822 (Moya Pons (1974b)).
239 Heredia y Mieses (1955), p. 162. However, this claim appears to be wildly exaggerated. No more than 10,000, at most, emigrated (see Moya Pons (1974a), for details).
240 Lundahl and Vargas (1983), p. 116. The emigration to Cuba (some 4,000 between 1795 and 1808) is dealt with in some detail in Deive (1989). (The figure is from p. 132.)
241 Clausner (1973), pp. 78–9.

which put the eastern part of the island back into a state of misery. The only activity that suited the prevailing factor proportions – cattle raising – had also been ruined. By the time San Juan de la Maguana was invaded by the English and French armies in 1797, the situation had not yet become critical. The herds had been decimated by the increased offtake as a result of the wars. Nevertheless, knowledgeable observers still thought that enough animals remained to make it possible to recreate the old stock over a fifteen-year period.[242] Four years later, the herds had been severely decimated by the indiscriminate slaughter by the armies and nobody cared about reproduction.[243] This was to continue in subsequent years. The remaining herds had to suffer both the consequences of Dessalines' invasion and the war of reconquest in 1808–09.[244] The latter consumed 30,000 animals in the south alone.[245] Nevertheless, the cattle trade with Haiti was restored, but only for a few years before it was prohibited by Governor Ferrand in 1808.[246]

When Spain got its colony back in 1809, it was worth very little in economic terms. The population in the capital was reported to eat donkeys, horses, cats and mice.[247] The workforce had left by the thousands, and the capital stock (the cattle) had been severely reduced. Under these circumstances abundant land had little to offer. Incomes had been reduced substantially. Again, Santo Domingo was a poor colony exporting a little tobacco, some hides from the remaining animals and a few years later also mahogany. During the years to come, the first and the last of these products took the lead over hides.[248] However, transportation possibilities remained miserable.[249]

> Economic breakdown was total. The cattle on which Santo Domingo's eighteenth-century prosperity had been founded had been eaten by the clashing armies. In spite of the many efforts made to revive it, at no time in the nineteenth century did stock-rearing succeed in regaining the volume of exports it had attained in the eighteenth century. Subsistence agriculture now accounted for most visible activity, and the only surviving money-producing occupations were the cutting and

242 Moya Pons (1977), pp. 374–5.
243 Ibid., p. 375, Rodríguez Jiménez and Vélez Canelo (1980), p. 76.
244 One of the causes of the uprising against the French was that Ferrand in 1808 had prohibited commerce with Haiti, and in particular sales of livestock (Deive (1989), p. 118).
245 Moya Pons (1977), p. 399.
246 Moya Pons (1985), p. 247.
247 Guerrero Cano (1986), p. 45.
248 Ibid., pp. 402–3.
249 Rodríguez Jiménez and Vélez Canelo (1980), pp. 80–1.

exportation of caoba [mahogany] wood from the south, and the growing and exportation of tobacco from the north of the country. Exports consisted of a few dozen tons of tobacco yearly, some thousands of hides and a little molasses rum. Imports were solely what was strictly necessary for an impoverished population amounting to no more than some 75,000 souls ...[250]

Cattle ranching did not recover for half a century. The price of cattle was down for lack of demand,[251] since the size of the population had fallen from an estimated 119,000 in 1782, and maybe as much as 180,000 in 1795, to 71,000 in 1819, when a census was taken, i.e. altogether by 35–60 percent.[252] In Haiti as well the population had declined as a result of the wars of liberation and it was not until the 1820s that it had recovered its pre-revolutionary size,[253] though, at a very low per capita income level. As a result the demand for cattle had decreased.

The Haitian occupation: the rise of a peasantry

Chaos and decline continued. In November 1821, the Dominicans again rebeled against the Spanish authorities and declared independence. However, the latter was to last for a mere nine weeks. In February 1822, the Haitian president, Jean-Pierre Boyer, gained control of the entire island of Hispaniola without resistance, at the head of a 12,000-man invading army.[254] The Haitians were to stay until 1844, when the Spanish-speaking population which had revolted the year before proclaimed the free and independent Dominican Republic.[255]

During the occupation years, Boyer made an effort to reshape the economy of the eastern part along the same lines as those simultaneously attempted on the Haitian side. During the long wars of liberation, 1791–1803, the French plantation system began to break down. The liberated slaves preferred to cultivate food crops on small plots instead of growing export crops on large estates. To prevent the breakdown of the export economy (exports were necessary for purchases of arms and ammunition) the early rulers – Toussaint, Dessalines and Henry Christophe – went back

250 Moya Pons (1985), p. 248.
251 Ibid., pp. 102–3.
252 Moya Pons (1974a), pp. 10–12, 25. Elsewhere, however, Moya Pons, (1985), p. 245, claims that the population on the Spanish side fell by two-thirds (125,000) between 1795 and 1810.
253 Lundahl (1979), p. 190.
254 Moya Pons (1978a), p. 35.
255 See ibid. for details with respect to the Haitian occupation. Cf. also García (1982), *Sexta parte*. The political events are also treated e.g. in Guerrero Cano (1986), Chapter 1.

to the plantation system and put the nominally free Haitians back on the land as serfs working under military supervision.[256] However, beginning in 1809, Alexandre Pétion, president of the southern half of the country, began to redistribute the land and let the agricultural laborers leave the plantations, and ten years later Christophe did the same in his northern kingdom.[257]

These changes were inevitable. The necessary conditions for maintaining *la grande culture* were simply not present. Above all, sugar – the most important export crop during the French colony – required large concentrations of both capital and labor at harvest time. However, as a result of the wars, the Haitian population had fallen by some 150,000 people between 1790 and 1805.[258] At the same time much of the plantation capital had been physically destroyed. Supply conditions had changed completely. So had demand. After independence from France, the demand for Haitian sugar was weakened by increased competition from Cuba, and also the Dutch and British Antilles and European beet sugar. To this came the disruptions of trade produced by the Napoleonic Wars. Thus, Haitian exports were squeezed both from the supply and from the demand side. The old export economy could be maintained only temporarily and only with the aid of exceptional devices: tying the laborers to the estates working under military supervision.

The redistribution of land by Pétion in 1809 was the beginning of a process which would end by converting Haiti into a nation of peasant smallholders. Once set in motion, this process proved impossible to stop. Nevertheless, in 1826, Jean-Pierre Boyer – for the same reasons as Toussaint, Dessalines and Christophe before him – made an effort to go back to the system with large estates, by issuing a new *code rural*. This legislation failed. Too much land had already been distributed, and the peasants simply chose to forget the new decree. Even the large estates that continued to exist proved to be impossible to administer. Strict military supervision was necessary, but even so the laborers escaped.

Boyer also made an effort to introduce the Haitian system in the east, but with as little, or less, success as in the west. His administration proved too weak to have the desired impact and labor and capital turned out to be as scarce on the Dominican side as on the Haitian. Around this time the total population of the former Spanish colony amounted to fewer than 70,000[259] and a great deal of capital had left with the emigrants.[260] Finally,

---

256 This is analyzed in Lundahl (1984), (1985) and Hedlund *et al.* (1989).
257 See Lundahl (1979), Chapter 6, and Lundahl and Vedovato (1991), for an analysis of the land reform process.
258 Lundahl (1979), p. 272.
259 Clausner (1973), p. 85.
260 Machín (1973), p. 26, Palmer (1976), p. 66.

the imposition of a plantation system would have required tying a majority of the Dominican population to large estates as virtual serfs – a condition that the population (with the exception of the slaves) had never experienced.

Nevertheless, Boyer was to have a profound influence on the Dominican countryside. By 1822 he had started to confiscate church and emigrant lands, declaring it state property.[261] Two years later, an attack was also made on the system of *terrenos comuneros*.[262] Communal ownership of land was declared illegal, and as a consequence many farmers had to abandon livestock raising.[263] Boyer also sought to stimulate agriculture during the years that elapsed between the beginning of the Haitian occupation and the introduction of the 1826 *code rural*. To this end he prohibited landholdings of less than 5 *carreaux*,[264] which amounted to only one-fifth of what was required for livestock raising to be profitable.[265] Instead, the farming population was to concentrate its efforts on export crops (coffee, cocoa, sugar cane, cotton, etc.) and on foodstuffs.[266]

These efforts failed. The Cibao region continued to concentrate on tobacco, and mahogany continued to be the most important export product in the southern part of the country. Boyer's main contribution to Dominican agriculture was rather that of accelerating the creation of a peasantry – a process that had already begun during the eighteenth century as the owners of large undivided *hatos* began to rent their land to sharecroppers, a common procedure by 1800.[267] During the Haitian occupation, peasant cultivation received a further impetus as Boyer proceeded to redistribute the land he had confiscated:

> Compounding the confusion caused by his prohibition of the traditional form of ownership, Boyer assigned these lands to the state, then under Haitian titles redistributed portions to landless farm workers, to Haitians who occupied farms, or to sponsored immigrants who came in later. The consequences of this policy, aggravated by the loss or destruction of earlier land records, were important because that led to a defective land title system, illegal occupation of land, an inadequate land tax system, and widespread frauds in connection with ownership of rural land.[268]

261 Clausner (1973), p. 84, Rodríguez Jiménez and Vélez Canelo (1980), pp. 117–18.
262 Moya Pons (1978a), p. 59.
263 Clausner (1973), p. 83.
264 1 *carreau* = 1.29 hectares.
265 Moya Pons (1978a), pp. 58–9.
266 Ibid., pp. 46–7.
267 Machín (1973).
268 Clausner (1973), pp. 114–15.

Thus a *minifundio* peasant society was being created in the east as well.[269] As early as 1839–40 there were indications that, numerically, small peasant holdings were the most common units in the Dominican countryside.[270] According to the systematic information presented to President Boyer by the commanding officer of the department of San Juan de la Maguana, at the beginning of 1840, the *común* of San Juan counted 557 *labranzas* [farms] and 141 *hatos*, Las Matas de Farfán 806 and 188, respectively, and Bánica, 90 and 54.[271]

During the Haitian occupation, the emigration of Dominicans continued, although not on a large scale and not for very long, being mainly limited to 'the most hispanified members of the creole bureaucratic elite'.[272] Nevertheless, over a somewhat longer time period, the population had declined substantially, by as much as 35–60 percent. This vacuum was now being filled by Haitian immigrants, and by the last four or five years of the occupation the population in the east had risen to some 125,000–130,000.[273]

This migration was a very gradual process. By the late eighteenth century Haitians dominated in places like Hincha, Las Caobas, San Miguel and parts of Las Matas de Farfán. At least from 1808 Haiti governed the central part of the island.[274] This domination was cemented during the occupation, and when the Haitians withdrew from the Dominican Republic in 1844, they retained large areas in the central part, including the four above-mentioned towns. The political chaos prevailing in the east prevented the Dominicans from establishing garrisons in the border area, and the Dominican population there was too small and too thinly spread to prevent the Haitians from settling.[275]

The creation of a Dominican nation did not mark the end of hostilities. Various Haitian invasions took place after the Dominican proclamation of independence,[276] and during these invasions the towns in the San Juan Valley were regularly captured, sacked and burned – San Juan de la Maguana in 1844 and 1849 and Las Matas de Farfán in 1849[277] – until the

---

269 Cf. Cassá (1985), pp. 174–80, for a discussion.
270 García (1982), pp. 174–80. García's figures are consolidated in Cassá (1985), p. 179.
271 García (1982), pp. 170–1. The total number of *labranzas* for San Juan is given as 553, but this is a misprint, as can easily be seen by adding the figures for the individual *secciones*.
272 Moya Pons (1974a), p. 12.
273 The lower figure, given by Moya Pons (1974a), p. 12, for 1844, comes from an interpolation of the census figures of 1819, 1863 and 1887. The higher one is given by Candler (1842), p. 132, for 1841.
274 Mejía Ricart (1954), pp. 339–40.
275 García (1982), p. 246.
276 Cf. Rodríguez Demorizi (1957), for details.
277 Ibid., pp. 14, 403, Palmer (1976), pp. 62–3.

Haitian army was finally defeated in the decisive battle of Santomé, a plain just outside Las Matas de Farfán, in 1855.[278]

At this time, the San Juan Valley was more or less completely abandoned by the Dominicans,[279] and with 'the abandonment of the *hatos*, frontier cattle ranching had reverted to a state only slightly more refined than the cattle hunting of the buccaneers. In overall terms, the borderlands had retrogressed.'[280] In the 1820s, the cattle trade was apparently dead. James Franklin, a British businessman who had made several lengthy visits to Haiti in the 1820s, reported in 1828 that following 'the union with the west … the [international] intercourse was restricted, and, consequently, the breeding of cattle has not been so much attended to as formerly, as they have only their internal consumption to take them off. Many are now killed for the skin and the tallow …'[281]

This continued to be the case after independence from Haiti, in the 1840s. Frank Moya Pons summarizes the situation:

> In San Juan de la Maguana, the inhabitants were occupied mainly in cattle raising, which was in crisis at the beginning of the Republic as a result of the war with Haiti and the lack of commercial exchange with that country. The border area was almost completely vacated, converted into a kind of no man's land.[282]

The few residents of the area had little to occupy them. An American physician who traveled in the area in 1833 or 1834 has left the following description of what was largely a state of autarchy, with exchange taking place only when the purpose was to obtain small quantities of imported goods:

> Crossing into the Spanish territory the same condition [of idleness] is described in a different language [Spanish] – for if it is demanded of these blacks what is the nature of their employments, the answer is readily forthcoming – 'nada, senor [sic].' […] These blacks assume the manners of Spanish hidalgos, forever smoking and forever lounging in their hammocks. A few of them are herdsmen or mahogany cutters. In the vast solitudes of the interior the former reside continually on horseback, with a lasso at their side, and a small case of cigars and a bottle of aquadente [sic] at their saddle-bow. The flesh of their

278 Garrido (1974), pp. 123–35.
279 Palmer (1976), pp. 62–3.
280 Ibid., p. 64.
281 Franklin (1828), p. 297.
282 Moya Pons (1980), p. 362.

cattle serves them for food, and the hides are sent to the different towns upon the coast to be exchanged for their favorite luxuries.[283]

Following the liberation from Haiti in 1844, exports of live animals had been prohibited. Once it was resumed, the scale was small indeed. In 1856, cattle sales to the British and Dutch Antilles accounted for less than 0.1 percent of the total export value, while that of hides amounted to 4 percent of the total. Thus, the formerly important role of animal products in the international trade of the Dominican Republic had been reduced to insignificance.[284]

Most of the exports of hides and cattle presumably came from the eastern part of the country.[285] The San Juan Valley had suffered severely from the hostilities. By the 1860s, however, it was again in the process of being populated.[286] The Dominicans moved back, but part of the population vacuum had also been filled from the west, which in turn served to strengthen the Haitian cultural and linguistic influence in the area. Also, the old trade patterns, which had been virtually eliminated during the period of Haitian invasions from 1801 to 1855,[287] were revitalized. Cattle herds had once more grown to the size where larger sales were possible. 'The district of San Juan ... is famous for its pastures and a large quantity of horses and cattle are bred. The hides are here the main export article', reported the American journalist Randolph Keim, who visited the Dominican Republic in 1869.[288]

Once more, the low man/land ratio, combined with the chaotic land tenure situation which had become even more complicated during the Haitian occupation, had established a cattle economy in the border area:

> Summarizing the panorama of agriculture in the seventh decade of the last century ... we can say that in an underpopulated country – the 1871 population was estimated at between 150,000 and 207,000[289] – a superabundance of land for farming led to the continuation of chaotic conditions with regard to the ownership of land. The deficient infrastructure, political instability, and scarcity of workers led to the

---

283 Brown (1837), p. 288.
284 Boin and Serulle Ramia (1979), p. 66.
285 Ibid., pp. 67, 84, Cassá (1983), p. 24.
286 Ibid., pp. 66–7.
287 Palmer (1976), p. 62.
288 Keim (1978), p. 242. Keim had been sent out by the *New York Herald* to find facts that would make annexation of the Dominican Republic to the United States (cf. below) appear in a favorable light to its readers (Sang (1991), p. 130).
289 Presumably more. The 207,000 figure refers to 1863 (207,700) and in 1887, the figure was 382,000 (Moya Pons (1974a), pp. 13, 21).

predominance of cattle enterprises, which required a minimum of personnel, in the East and in the West [...]

In comparison with the more flourishing colonial period, during which a stable pseudo-feudal structure was, if not attained, at least pursued with considerable success, there had been a regression to more diffuse, confused forms of land ownership; to relatively more primitive agrarian techniques; and, accordingly, to the diminished importance of land possession as a criterion for social stratification.

This regression, which in its social aspects could be called 'democratization' or 'levelling,' was caused by the economic and demographic decline that resulted from numerous wars and internal disturbances. It is also appropriate to recall that the Haitian occupier had carried out an enormous confiscation of property, not only ecclesiastical but private as well, and that this increase in state ownership had not been reversed by the governments of an independent Santo Domingo.[290]

The Haitian occupation had thus contributed to making the land tenure situation in the eastern part of Hispaniola even less transparent than it was before.[291] By 1871, up to 25 percent of all land was held 'under questionable title or with no written title at all'.[292] In due time, this was to have severe consequences for the Dominican peasantry.

The late nineteenth century

The last four decades of the nineteenth century constituted a turbulent period in Dominican history. Between 1861 and 1865, the Dominican Republic had once more been annexed by Spain. In 1863, however, the Dominicans rose against the Spanish and the so-called War of Restoration began. This ended in 1865 with the triumph of the rebels.[293]

The war left a very unfortunate heritage – one which was to plague the Dominican Republic all the way up to the beginning of the presidency of Rafael Trujillo in 1930. The war against the Spanish had been carried out by a large number of guerilla units, each one under the command of some local strongman. Once the war was over, the latter constituted an important element of power. Before the reannexation to Spain, political power was held by a few *caudillos* only, but after 1865, dozens of new actors – who had managed to make temporary peace by uniting against the Spanish –

---

290 Hoetink (1982), pp. 5–6.
291 Baud (1986), p. 26.
292 Clausner (1973), p. 121.
293 For details, see Archambault (1938) and Domínguez (1979). A condensed view is given in Moya Pons (1980), Chapter 26.

were added to the political scene and immediately began to dispute and fight among themselves, backing different candidates for the presidency. At this time, the army, which had been reorganized according to the Spanish model between 1861 and 1863, had ceased to exist and almost all its war material was gone.[294] This left the field wide open for the various contending factions: between 1865 and 1879, the Dominican Republic experienced twenty-one governments and more than fifty upheavals.[295] Political life had become incredibly fragmented and the military structure had turned into a marketplace where services were sold to the highest bidder.[296] When the Dominican Republic was annexed to Spain, in 1861, the country had perhaps seventy generals. During Buenaventura Báez' fourth term in the presidency (1868–74), this number had increased to almost one thousand, 'logically, virtually all of them fervent Baecistas'.[297]

From 1869 to 1874, the whole of the San Juan Valley found itself in a state of war due to a violent power struggle between two Dominican *caudillos*, José María Cabral and Buenaventura Báez. Cabral had for several years been one of the leading Dominican generals. It was he who had commanded the Dominican army when it defeated the Haitians in the battle of Santomé. Cabral served as Dominican president from 1866 to 1868, and in order to strengthen his government and defeat the various *caudillos* who opposed him, he offered to sell the Samaná bay and peninsula, considered to be one of the best sites for a Caribbean naval base, to the United States. However, before the deal could be concluded, Cabral – an ally of former Haitian president Fabre Geffrard[298] – was ousted by the forces of Buenaventura Báez, who were supported by the sitting Haitian president, Sylvain Salnave.[299]

Báez pursued the initiative of Cabral, and the US government, under President Ulysses S. Grant, showed a great interest in the Dominican offer. The Americans even expressed their desire not only to buy the Samaná peninsula, but to annex the entire Dominican Republic. Buenaventura Báez became a strong supporter of the US plan. However, in the meantime Cabral had entered the Republic from Haiti. In his effort to overthrow Báez, he had obtained strong support from the new Haitian president, Nissage-Saget.[300] Accompanied by Haitian troops under the command of

---

294 Hoetink (1982), p. 95.
295 See Moya Pons (1980), pp. 359–66.
296 Hoetink (1982), p. 96.
297 Cassá (1983), p. 103.
298 Sang (1991), p. 107.
299 Moya Pons (1980), pp. 368–9. For the Sylvain Salnave presidency, see Adam (1982). Cf. also Heinl and Heinl (1978), pp. 235–48.
300 See Sang (1991), Chapter 5, for details. Cabral had captured Salnave, who had fled to the Dominican Republic when he was toppled in 1869, and had handed him over to the Haitian rebels who executed him (ibid., p. 110).

several Haitian generals, Cabral succeeded in occupying the entire San Juan Valley. He established his headquarters in San Juan de la Maguana and for several years, with an army that occasionally numbered 3,000 men,[301] he put Báez' troops, the majority of which were stationed in Azua, under constant pressure. Since so many Haitians had sided with Cabral in the campaign, all members of his army were called *cacos*,[302] a term which originally denoted peasant irregulars from the northern regions of Haiti, but over the years obtained a derogatory meaning, indicating that *cacos* were either bandits or mercenaries.[303]

President Grant's initiative was defeated in the US Senate in 1871, but he continued his efforts to annex the Dominican Republic and the same year an American commission was sent to the island in order to prepare a report highlighting the benefits of annexation. The American commissioners were unable to enter the San Juan Valley and could only offer descriptions by quoting interviewees they encountered in the districts bordering the valley, but they all depicted the land and soil as excellent:

> The climate here [at El Maniel, between Baní and Azua] is very fresh for being in the tropics and it is also quite uniform. Generally people are in excellent health. I think this is the most healthy region I have ever known. [...] The [fertile and fresh] region is not limited to the valley you see here, not even to this district, but it extends for a long distance, all the way to the valley of Bánica, the valley of San Juan and even to the regions which are behind them [the Artibonite Valley in Haiti]. There you find many beautiful and very fertile valleys, among them the ones I just mentioned [around Bánica and San Juan de la Maguana]. They are just as fresh and fertile as this one [the valley of El Maniel]. I have lived in both places. San Juan is particularly fertile by nature and adapts itself well to cattle breeding and cultivation of tropical plants.[304]

---

301 It is very difficult to obtain clear figures about the strength of Cabral's army. It appears as if 3,000 is quite high, but it may be plausible as Báez' Dominican government had 2,000 men under arms in Azua. Prisoners stated that the majority of Cabral's men had been recruited among the local population around San Juan de la Maguana. Others were 'mercenaries' from the border regions, and several were professional soldiers from Haiti. Provisions, weapons and ammunition were brought in from Haiti (cf. the quotations from Juan Santana, Eugenio Ramírez, Flerimo Louis and Pedro Altagracia Cuello in *Informe* (1960), pp. 594, 596, 597 and 598). Cabral even printed a Spanish newspaper, *El Pabellón Dominicano: Boletín de la Revolución*, in Port-au-Prince and had it distributed in the Dominican Republic (Hazard (1873), p. 454).

302 *Informe* (1960), pp. 236 and 394. For a contemporary description of the situation in Haiti, see St. John (1889). Cf. also Heinl and Heinl (1978), pp. 249–58.

303 The term was later applied to the peasant warriors who resisted the US occupation of Haiti (1915–34).

304 Juan Cheri Victoria, quoted in *Informe* (1960), p. 580.

The warfare in the San Juan Valley kept people away in the early 1870s and several *Sanjuaneros* fled to other parts of the Republic. The US commissioners stated that, considering the excellent climate and great fertility of the San Juan Valley, it was underpopulated:

> The communes of San Juan, Las Matas, Bánica, Neyba and others have been estimated to have 22,000 inhabitants; but these communes have been depopulated due to the revolutions and the invasion and their actual numbers are by local residents and other competent witnesses estimated to be between 5,000 and 8,000.[305]

Buenaventura Báez had to resign at the beginning of 1874 and the new, patriotic administration formally regained possession of Samaná Bay and annulled former deals with US citizens concerning the acquisition of Samaná and a future annexation of the Republic.[306] The same year José María Cabral laid down his weapons and 'reintegrated himself with the Fatherland'. He no longer sought the presidency, but accepted some ministerial portfolios in the new government before he retired to private life.[307] Several of the Haitians who had followed him into Dominican territory settled in the San Juan Valley and the intimate contacts between Haiti and the valley continued.[308]

In the contacts between Haiti and the inhabitants of the San Juan Valley, not only the cultural influence played a role, but the state of communications was of at least equal importance. Santo Domingo was from five to six days away, whereas Port-au-Prince was less than two days on horseback from the western end of the valley. Consequently, the products of the valley, based on cattle raising, flowed westwards.[309] The Dominicans in the area bought and sold in Haiti. The Haitian *gourde* was acceptable tender in San Juan and the Dominican peso on the Haitian side of the border. Everybody knew enough 'commerce and agriculture *patois*' to do the trade.[310] Life was back to normal in the San Juan Valley.

In 1874 the border was officially reopened for trade,[311] and in 1897 a

---

305 *Informe* (1960), p. 75. The US commissioners estimated that the entire population of the Dominican Republic did not exceed 150,000 (ibid.).

306 Ibid., pp. 43–4.

307 Martínez (1971), p. 89.

308 After his retirement José María Cabral lived in the San Juan Valley until his death in 1899. He owned several rural properties, which were inherited by his son, Alejandro Cabral, who married Rosita Ramírez, one of Wenceslao Ramírez' daughters. Alejandro Cabral was Wenceslao's private physician and an influential man within the powerful Ramírez clan (interview with Tala Cabral Ramírez, Santo Domingo, 21 November 1985, cf. *Libro azul de Santo Domingo* (1920), p. 100).

309 Palmer (1976), p. 70.

310 Interview with Mimicito Ramírez, San Juan de la Maguana, 15 January 1986.

311 Fuente (1976), p. 17.

customs control was established at Comendador (present Elías Piña). However, duties were levied only on luxury articles imported from France into either of the two countries. Besides, the control was capricious and did not become efficient until the Dominican customs houses were put into American hands in 1907.[312]

Trading with Azua and Barahona in the south, let alone with the capital, was a difficult task, given the communications of the day. 'Truly, the barrier erected against all agricultural transactions by the complete absence of roads for transporting the products of agriculture is so [formidable] that it leads to a lack of initiative which borders on the apathetic', commented one of the members of the 1871 American commission to the Dominican Republic.[313] Two years later, Samuel Hazard sarcastically remarked that 'The roads [from Santo Domingo city westward to the Haitian border], like those in the rest of the island, are hardly worthy of the name ...'[314] Thirty-five years later, little had changed. In 1909, Francisco Peynado claimed that it was impossible for producers to grow fruits further than five *leguas* (25–30 kilometers) away from the urban centers if they were not to be faced with losses. Concentration on only a few products did not pay, as these products could not be transported in great quantities to the centers of demand. Thus, the peasants stuck to a subsistence orientation among their crops, preferring animals for the westbound trade with Haiti.[315] 'the non-existent communication routes made ... [the] existence [of the San Juan Valley] more autarchic than [that of] other regions and it continued with grazing and animal breeding until the beginning of the twentieth century', summarizes Angel Moreta.[316]

Communications continued to be bad for many years. A foreign traveler described the situation during the years preceding the US occupation:

> Throughout the Republic there is scarcely a thoroughfare suitable for wheeled vehicles save in the immediate vicinity of the towns and practically all travel and transportation is by horseback, donkey-back or on the long-legged riding bulls peculiar to the country. [...]
> In many ... places the 'roads' are simply narrow bridle paths barely wide enough to accommodate a single horse and so overgrown with

312 Interview with Mayobanex Rodríguez, San Juan de la Maguana, 12 December 1985. For the background to the American customs receivership, see e.g. Moya Pons (1980), Chapters 32–3. Even the Americans had great trouble controlling contraband trade. During the first twenty-eight months following the establishment of the American customs receivership (3 May 1907), eighteen American customs officers were killed or wounded in battles with smugglers (Clausner (1973), p. 142).
313 Ward (1960), p. 295.
314 Hazard (1873), p. 241.
315 Peynado (1909), pp. 60–1.
316 Moreta (1986), pp. 57–8.

vines, creepers and trees that one is compelled to couch forward on the saddle to avoid being swept from the horse by the overhanging boughs. In numerous places these trails are worn so deep that they become filled with mud and water and I have frequently travelled over trails where for miles the horses were actually up to their bellies in mud. ...

In the interior there are no bridges, and as the roads run fairly direct from one spot to another, and as the streams meander across the landscape in a serpentine course the traveller not infrequently crosses the same river half a dozen times in a distance of a few miles.[317]

The road from San Juan de la Maguana to Azua was not easy to travel, especially at the point where the Yaque River had to be crossed, since that river at the time was large, with plenty of often very rapid water. Mayobanex Rodríguez remembered the hardships connected with transportation from San Juan de la Maguana to Azua. Oxen or mules had to be used to pull the carts and on the road

there were slopes that made it necessary to unload half the load in order to make it possible to bring up the other half. You had to leave it there and go back down with the cart and then come back again with the load that had been left. After that you had to load again the load that had been left at the top. This was done in Los Bancos; there, where the bridge is that the Americans made, the river was a beach. That was the best ford, even though the river had lots of water.[318]

During the 83 kilometers that separated San Juan de la Maguana from Azua, travelers could count on food and lodging as well as fodder for their horses in a few places, but facilities were usually kept to a bare minimum: 'for rest, if one did not travel equipped with a hammock, the hard ground, wicker baskets under your head [*por cabecera*], the valises, the heroic recourse as an urgent necessity during a night of expectations ... in which waiting for the new day was a light in the darkness of despair.'[319]

It was a lot easier to get to Haiti, following the San Juan Valley westwards, than to go southwards, or to the capital. Those travelers who went to Santo Domingo seldom traveled overland but waited, often for more than a week, in Azua for a steamer that operated along the coast, frequently with detours to other islands.[320]

317 Verril (1914), pp. 251 and 252.
318 Interview with Mayobanex Rodríguez by Angel Moreta, cited in Moreta (1986), p. 103.
319 Garrido Puello (1972), p. 64.
320 Interview with Mimicito Ramírez, San Juan de la Maguana, 14 December 1985.

Property rights in land

During the late nineteenth century the open range dominated the San Juan Valley. The ownership pattern which had crystallized over the centuries was a complex one. The original *hatos* had been passed on from generation to generation without having been physically divided. Instead, as early as the seventeenth century[321] they were held as *terrenos comuneros* and each heir held *pesos de posesión* or *acciones* securing his or her share of the commonly owned land. The high costs of surveying the land, in combination with differences in quality between land areas, made the transaction costs involved in physical subdivision of the land so high that in most cases the communal system was preferred,[322] although some *hatos* obviously remained, as in the San Juan Valley, where, in 1885, the priest Carlos Nouel, noted the existence of thirty units in the San Juan area that were not close to the town.[323]

According to Harry Hoetink, 'the number of private *latifundistas* was considered small' in the 1860s, and the penetration of the modern sugar *ingenios* had not yet started, but '[a] well-cared-for plantation was, then, a great exception'.[324] The disorder caused by the repeated Haitian invasions in combination with the general political disorder following the second Spanish annexation (1861–65) made for confusion of land titles on the one hand and for a lack of well-managed, large, undivided *hatos* on the other.

> So turbulent were the early years of the nineteenth century that as of 1845 there was no land law in effect and no public office charged with direct or indirect intervention on supervision of acts involving the transmission of property rights. Public notaries in all parts of the country performed limited formalities in recording written documents, but … these acts were legally inadequate, if not defective.[325]

Attempts by President Pedro Santana to clarify the land title situation by legislation in 1845 and 1847 were partially effective in identifying and preserving state patrimony but did little to resolve 'the ownership of public lands which had been occupied without title, or the serious problems of defective titles, partition of communal lands, and fraud'.[326] The documentation of ownership, especially, was in a hopeless state of disarray:

---

321 Hoetink (1982), p. 3.
322 Hazard (1873), pp. 481–4, gives a contemporary account of the system. Cf. also Hoetink (1982), p. 3.
323 Nouel (1970), p. 338.
324 Hoetink (1982), p. 5.
325 Clausner (1973), p. 115.
326 Ibid., pp 115–18; quotation from p. 118.

One of the most confusing and disorganized aspects of Dominican public administration throughout this period concerned the documentation of landownership, even of private, noncommunal land. As has been mentioned frequently, public records in many towns had been destroyed or were not available. Nor was there a central office which maintained the record of titles, transfer of property, or any other legal act involving land. Particularly vexing was the existence of extensive communal lands and the traditional manner in which these lands were occupied without title or were inherited and passed on. The flaws in the system were an open invitation to fraud. Despite the fact that the government passed corrective legislation in 1885 and again in 1907, 1911, 1912, and 1916, the system retained its defects until 1920.[327]

Anyone could buy some *pesos de posesión* and thus become the co-proprietor of a *terreno comunero*. This meant that he or she was also free to use grass and water for the cattle and it was even possible for any owner to exploit other resources, such as forests or minerals. However, the holdings could not be legally enclosed and used for agriculture as the communal property rights system did not confer any exclusive rights to particular parts of each *terreno comunero*: 'In practice, every co-owner of a communal property had the right to use the resources of the property. He could take water and wood, cultivate the land, and pasture his cattle, so long as there was no infringement on the rights of other owners.'[328]

For enclosure, the land would have to be surveyed and divided, but this in turn was very costly.[329] In order to enclose a given area with n shareholders,

$$C = \sum_{m=1}^{n-1} (n-m)$$

contracts would have to be concluded, and as n increased to $n+1$, the number of contracts would increase with n. Thus, contract costs loomed large in the communal system, and they tended to increase over time as the number of shareholders increased.

Still, at the beginning of the 1870s, attempts were being made to break the old rules. In 1871, in El Maniel, a village situated in a small fertile valley between Baní and Azua to the southeast of the San Juan Valley, the *alcalde*

327 Ibid., pp. 118–19.
328 Baud (1995), p. 61.
329 Boin and Serulle Ramia (1979), pp. 121–2.

explained to a US inquiry commission how the *terreno comunero* system worked in that particular valley:

> The right to fell mahogany on the common land and the right to the land on these territories are different. I sold to a businessman from Santo Domingo for 2,000 pesos [...] [in my function as *alcalde*] a mahogany cutting [*corte*] close to this place. Afterwards he asked me to sell him 50 pesos worth of property, that is to say the land itself, something I call right or title of property or ownership. The 2,000 pesos gave him the right to the mahogany, but the 50 pesos gave him access to land on the communal terrain, or from the parish; he could choose whatever part he found unoccupied and make himself a farm or use the land in any way and to whatever extent he needed. The land is not measured here, because measuring it would cost more than what the land is worth.[330]

However, there was a strict requirement that the purchasing party justify the need for taking the land for his personal needs by occupying and using it.[331] Pedro San Miguel offers the following summary of the situation:

> The common lands ... permitted the development of agriculture. Once a patch of land was cleared and occupied by one of the *accionistas* [shareholders], the other occupants honored his/her claim to that plot. A sort of common law defined the rights of the *accionistas*. If the *accionista* wanted to heep his/her rights to the land, he/she had to continue using it either in the cultivation of crops or in grazing. If, however,
>
> ... a person leaves his home and abandons his land for more than a year, and the house burns down and the improvements disappear, another person may occupy [the land] and consider it his own. This is not a [written] law, but it has become custom in this country ...[332]
>
> According to the same source, a share-holder might occupy any part of the land, and even all the unoccupied land, regardless of the size, provided that he/she did not interfere with the land that was already under exploitation.[333]

Even though several authors have stated that communal land could not be enclosed it appears that this was done in several districts, and fencing often served as a sign that the land had been claimed:

---

330 Juan Cheri Victoria, quoted in *Informe* (1960), p. 583. In this period the Dominican peso was at par with the US dollar.
331 Clausner (1973), p. 122.
332 This paragraph quotes Juan Cheri Victoria, taken from *Informe* (1960), p. 583.
333 San Miguel (1987), p. 213.

Here the land is not measured the way that you do. That is not the tradition around here. Here is enough land for everyone. You can buy a title for 50 pesos, and if the land is not in other hands you may occupy as much land as you can cultivate: but as soon as you do not use the land for cultivation anymore you have to use it as pasture for animals or in any other way, or fence it in in order to secure further possession of it. My property measures more than five hundred square yards, by now cleared and cleaned. A person cannot come here and claim uncultivated land if he does not have a deed, a land title, for which he has to pay. I paid 25 pesos for this title. With the improvements I have made this property is now worth much more. The best places around here are now occupied; the ones which are still unoccupied are further away from the river and other water sources. Different places have different prices, from 3 pesos up to 25 pesos. A man had bought this title before me and had cultivated the land, planting some coffee and plantains, and later I bought it from him.[334]

It is difficult to know how common practices like the one just described were during the last three decades of the nineteenth century. Presumably protests were mild, especially in sparsely populated areas. In most parts of the country, land values were low,[335] and violations of written or unwritten law should hence have appeared as a minor nuisance only. Besides, peasant agriculture was largely based on shifting, slash-and-burn cultivation, which implied that the vaguely defined property rights of the *terrenos comuneros* suited the peasantry well.[336]

What the landholding and land-use situation was like in the San Juan region towards the end of the nineteenth century is not known in any detail.[337] It is obvious that some minor changes had been introduced:

Owing to political problems and frequent border incidents along the frontier during the late nineteenth century, there are relatively few detailed descriptions of land use and settlement during that period. [...] Contemporary Dominican geographers treated the region very

---

334 Augusto Gautier, born in Cherbourg, quoted in *Informe* (1960), p. 578. Gautier cultivated 'sugar cane ... coffee, tobacco, cocoa, all kinds of beans, chick-peas, cauliflower, celery, chicory, cabbage, lemons, tomatoes, maize, oranges, carrots, pineapples, sweet potatoes, yams, bananas, potatoes, plantains, radish, watercress, onions, and many tropical fruits and plants ...' (ibid. pp. 577–8).
335 Hoetink (1982), p. 5, Clausner (1973), p. 119, Cassá (1983), p. 127.
336 San Miguel (1987), p. 214, Baud (1995), pp. 163–5.
337 Hazard (1873) makes only a brief mention of the valley, 'comprising some of the finest parts of the island' (p. 242), 'noted for its great fertility in all time and the salubrity of its climate' (p. 245).

briefly and described it as used primarily for livestock raising. […] it is known that subsistence farming had been introduced to the region changing the principal land use from simply grazing to mixed grazing and agriculture.[338]

However, not more than 5–10 hectares of all the lands in the valley were used for *conucos*[339] and few people sold their agricultural products.[340] Extensive cattle ranching still dominated and no evidence exists of significant changes in the patterns of land cover between 1789 and 1899.[341] In 1893, open range cattle breeding still dominated in San Juan de la Maguana, Las Matas de Farfán and Bánica.[342] Most peasants in the valley in fact lived like that until the 1920s.[343] 'As was the case with the other villages of the Maguana [San Juan] Valley, … [the] main industry [of las Matas de Farfán] was cattle raising', wrote Otto Schoenrich in 1918.[344]

> The Sanjuanero, stupefied by the spontaneous growth of free breeding, had not yet thought of the convenience of breeding behind fences, which offers protection and security for the ranches, nor had he acquired the love of the cultivation of the soil. His main occupation was rounding up cattle for milking and branding.[345]

The cattle strayed freely in large herds grazing on both sides of the border.[346] At the beginning of the present century land was plentiful and questions of ownership did not seem to be of vital importance.[347] All important families owned cattle and the peasants held both cows and pigs.[348] The large landowners lived in their *hatos*:

338 Palmer (1976), pp. 75–6.
339 Interview with Mimicito Ramírez, San Juan de la Maguana, 15 January 1986.
340 Palmer (1976), pp. 76–7. Cf. also Deschamps (1908), who points out that the main occupation around Las Matas de Farfán was cattle raising (p. 213) and with respect to San Juan de la Maguana remarks that 'Almost the entire Común is an immense plain covered with excellent natural pasture and crossed by various important rivers and innumerable streams' (p. 211).
341 Palmer (1976), pp. 76–7. Cf. also Deschamps (1908), pp. 211, 213.
342 Boin and Serulle Ramia (1981), p. 252.
343 Interview with Mimicito Ramírez, San Juan de la Maguana, 11 April 1986.
344 Schoenrich (1977), p. 241.
345 Garrido (1970), p. 18.
346 The large landowners owned property on both sides of the border. Thus Wenceslao Ramírez had an *hato* close to Bánica which extended across the Artibonite River into Haiti and which was 'legal and measured there' (interview with Mimicito Ramírez, San Juan de la Maguana, 14 December 1985).
347 Ibid.
348 Interview with Tala Cabral Ramírez, Santo Domingo, 21 November 1985.

General Wenceslao Ramírez in his Mijo hacienda or in his Guayabal hato in Bánica; don Zolio Mesa in Gínova [sic]; don Rubio Ramírez and doña Aurelia de los Santos, widow Fernández, in the Charcas de Garabito; don Valoy de los Santos, don Leonardo Herrera, doña Nicomedes de los Santos, widow Herrera, in Hato del Padre; don Rosendo Prevost, don Manuel María de los Santos and the numerous members of the Santos family in Punta Caña; don Manuel Tejeda in the Prado; don Isaías Batista in Córvano; General Julián Roa Moreta in Tres Mangas; but some of them also had houses in town where they spent longer and shorter periods.[349]

Thus, *hatos* and *terrenos comuneros* dominated the valley.

Socioeconomic changes: the sugar industry

Little had changed in the economy of the San Juan Valley from the mid-seventeenth century to the year 1900. Yet changes were imminent. In the Dominican Republic in general the end of the nineteenth and the beginning of the twentieth century were to witness important economic changes. As we have already seen, the importance of cattle ranching had declined on a national scale. With the exception of the eastern part of the country and the San Juan Valley and the surrounding areas, animal husbandry displayed an 'agonizing persistence throughout the nineteenth century'.[350] It developed into an integral part of the subsistence activities taking place in the countryside, together with farming on small *conucos*, and exports of wood (especially mahogany) and tobacco (from the Cibao area)[351] came to dominate foreign trade until the 1870s.[352]

During the latter decade, however, a factor which was to have an enormous impact on the Dominican economy and society made its appearance in the country: the large-scale sugar industry. As we know, sugar cane was not a new product in the Dominican Republic. What was revolutionary was the scale on which its cultivation and processing were to take place. The immediate cause behind the expansion of sugar production in the Dominican Republic was the political situation prevailing in Cuba. There are records of sugar exports already in 1852,[353] and in 1870 more than 1.3 million pounds of sugar were exported from the province of Santo Domingo. The following year more than 1.5 million pounds were exported from Baní and Azua, where sugar was produced with the aid of

349 Garrido (1970), pp. 17–18.
350 Cassá (1983), p. 24.
351 See e.g. Lluberes (1973), San Miguel (1987), and Baud (1995).
352 For details, see Cassá (1983), pp. 13–27.
353 Báez Evertsz (1986), pp. 178–9.

family labor and some 200–300 *trapiches*,[354] but the first modern, steam-driven sugar factory was not set up until 1875, by a Cuban immigrant.[355] The Ten-Year War in Cuba (1868–78), when the Cubans fought the Spanish for independence,[356] triggered an exodus of Cubans (and others) from that island who possessed both the necessary technological knowledge and the capital to replicate abroad the expansion which Cuban sugar production had undergone a few decades earlier.[357] The modern *ingenio* replaced the old, smaller, *trapiche* technology.[358] Until 1882, over thirty *ingenios* were built in the Dominican Republic by Cubans and other foreigners, mainly in the southern part of the country.[359]

The expansion was not without problems. In 1884, sugar prices suddenly dropped as a result of subsidization of beet sugar production in Europe, and the Dominican sugar producers found themselves faced with an acute crisis which was compounded by the protectionist policy of the United States and the preferences which the country accorded its own interests in Hawaii, Puerto Rico, the Philippines and Cuba, and which lasted until 1902.[360] Many of the new *ingenios* disappeared during the following decade, the degree of concentration (mainly in foreign hands) increased in the industry and the average size of the remaining establishments, which were forced to modernize, increased.[361] During the same period, the American interest in the Dominican Republic was reawakened. American companies invested in the sugar sector until, in 1925, they dominated the latter completely, acounting for no less than 81 percent of the total area under sugar cultivation.[362]

In the areas penetrated by the sugar interests, large economic and social changes were instituted. One such change is of special significance. The cattle ranching activities had built on the system of communal ownership of the land. Due to its inherently high contract costs, however, this system acted as a brake on the development of large-scale sugar production. Investing in the Dominican Republic under these circumstances was considered too insecure a venture. Accordingly, the sugar companies pressed for a 'clarification' of land titles. The issue is clearly presented (with special reference to the San Juan Valley, where cattle

---

354 Baud (1986), p. 25
355 Cassá (1983), p. 130, Moya Pons (1980), p. 409.
356 For the war itself, see Thomas (1971), Chapters 20–2. The impact of the war on the Cuban economy is dealt with e.g. in Le Riverend (1985), Chapter 26.
357 Cf. Bonó (1980), pp. 253–5.
358 Baud (1987), p. 142.
359 Moya Pons (1980), p. 409, Hoetink (1982), p. 6. For details, see Cassá (1982), p. 130, and Rodríguez (1985), especially pp. 59–64.
360 For an account of the crisis, see Lluberes (1990).
361 Báez Evertsz (1986), p. 210.
362 Knight (1928), p. 139.

raising continued to be strong) in a pamphlet from 1893 advocating a switch to sugar production:

> SAN JUAN, LAS MATAS and BANICA, which, drowsy from pastoral life, do not come to our aid with their contributions to shoulder the burdens of the State. It is a duty to make these towns understand that free breeding is counterproductive; that 'this system, even though it may be relatively advantageous for a while, contains in itself that always sad idea of a backward state of civilization' and 'that grazing as a system of land utilization is an obstacle to progress and an enemy of all its manifestations ...'[363]

The land-use question received special attention during the American occupation of the Dominican Republic. By the time the American military government took over in 1916, sugar had become the leading export crop. The shortages in the international market caused by the world war made the value of sugar exports increase almost fourfold from that year to 1920, when an all-time high was reached.[364] Behind the rise of sugar to this paramount position in Dominican life was a massive transfer of land from the peasants to the sugar companies. '[B]ecause one of the sugar growers' greatest concerns was land tenure ... sugar became the focus of a major legislative endeavor of the military government.'[365]

Legislation which aimed to put the chaotic land-title system in order had already begun before the occupation. In 1910, a government decree prohibited freely straying animals.[366] In 1907, the execution of sales acts for land by notaries without prior measurement by a public surveyor had been made illegal.[367] Four years later, in 1911, the *Ley sobre División de Terrenos Comuneros* [Law Concerning the Division of Common Lands] 'attempted to facilitate the division of communal land and to establish clear titles by allowing any coproprietor of such land to demand that it be surveyed and permanently divided by a court, each coproprietor receiving title to a specific piece of property'.[368] The same year, the *Ley sobre Franquicias Agrarias* [Law Concerning Agrarian Concessions] conferred a number of privileges on modern agricultural enterprises, facilitating the expansion of the latter. Finally, in 1912, a law calling for the inscription of all rural land titles within a period of one year – the *Ley sobre Inscripción de la Propiedad Territorial* [Law Concerning the Inscription of Landed

363 Quoted in Sánchez (1976), pp. 9–10.
364 Calder (1984), p. 93.
365 Ibid., p. 91.
366 Decreto 4043. Cf. Crouch (1979), p. 16.
367 Clausner (1973), p. 124.
368 Calder (1984), p. 103.

Property] – further paved the way for surveying and registering all land in the country.[369]

The land reform efforts were continued by the US military authorities. The practical application of the previous legislation left a lot to be desired and the surveying and the speed of the registration process was slow indeed. The occupation government had to extend the deadline for registration of titles a number of times. A topographic survey, to be followed by a cadastral survey, was ordered to facilitate reform.[370] Finally, in 1920, the *Ley de Registro de Tierras* [Land Registration Law] superseded most of the former legislation, calling for immediate registration of titles and the demarcation, survey and partition of the *terrenos comuneros*.[371]

The 1920 legislation provided the legal landowner with a secure title to this land. He could be sure that this title, once registered, would stand against all bodies, including the state and any of its political subdivisions.[372] The road to this security, however, had been a long and winding one. The most immediate effect of the actual implementation of all the legislation enacted since the beginning of the twentieth century had been to create *more*, not less uncertainty – especially for the small landholders. As early as 1915, the sugar companies controlled some 350,000 *tareas*[373] and by 1923 the figure had risen to 1 million *tareas*.[374] Sugar exports increased rapidly as well, from 7,000 tons in 1880 to over 24,000 in 1980, 48,000 in 1905, 87,000 in 1913, 145,000 in 1916 and over 331,000 tons in 1925.[375]

The counterpart to this expansion was to be seen in the land market, where the price of lands suitable for sugar cultivation began to rise. This tendency was manifest already at the beginning of the 1910s, and in the chaotic situation which prevailed with respect to land titles, 'the fabrication of titles became a big business, especially for the communal lands of the east where sugar cultivation was spreading. And forgery was simple, so many records had been lost or destroyed over the years that verification of documents was often impossible.'[376] The sugar companies took advantage of the chaotic situation and turned the small peasants off their land with the aid of the new legislation. This was not particularly difficult, because when the latter had to face the new laws they were often cheated by unfair execution of the laws, or they found that the cost of hiring somebody to defend their legal interests was too high for them.[377]

---

369 Ibid., pp. 103–4.
370 Clausner (1973), Chapter 19.
371 Ibid., Chapter 20, deals with this legislation in some detail.
372 Ibid., pp. 206–7.
373 21,875 hectares (Schoenrich (1977), p. 361).
374 Muto (1976), p. 36.
375 Cassá (1983), p. 436.
376 Calder (1984), p. 104.
377 Ibid., p. 105.

Thus, the introduction of large-scale sugar cultivation largely clashed with the interests of the peasants who were unfortunate enough to live in the areas wanted by the *ingenios*. As Michiel Baud has pointed out, the confused situation with respect to land titles had conferred certain advantages on the peasant community:

> The advantage of the confusing system of land ownership for the peasant producers was that it enabled them also to usurp land on a small scale. Many cultivators did not possess land titles and took possession of lands of which the ownership was unclear. The *comunero* system enabled them, in this way, to maintain access to land and continue their agricultural production.[378]

With the new legislation, this changed drastically. Bruce Calder describes the situation of those who were turned off their lands:

> As cane fields replaced their homes and *conucos*, the farmers either had to leave the area, probably migrating to a town or northward into hillier country, or they had to accept jobs with the sugar companies which had taken over their lands. Of those displaced persons who stayed, only a few were able to obtain year-round employment in the mills. The fate of most was to work as cane cutters, a physically demanding but low-paid job which lasted only three to six months a year. [...] The conditions which the average sugar worker faced were appalling.[379]

As if that were not enough, hand in hand with the introduction of the *ingenios* went the introduction of foreign labor.[380] To begin with, the majority of the sugar workers were Dominicans. Only 500 of a total of 6,000 sugar workers in 1884 were foreigners. The year before the governor of Azua complained bitterly about the exodus of the peasants to the sugar areas at the price of a complete neglect of their own *conucos*.[381] This would, however, soon change. In 1922, an American sociologist remarked:

> The Dominican is reputed a rather capable but rather unreliable laborer. In considerable measure this is said to be due to the prevalence of land ownership. Having his own land he does not care to work regularly for others. He likes to take contracts, if not of too long

---

378 Baud (1995), p. 156.
379 Calder (1984), p. 94.
380 Cf. e.g. Baud (1988b), for details.
381 Baud (1987), p. 143.

duration, but cannot be relied on for steady performance. It has long been necessary to bring in outside laborers for the sugar plantations because of these conditions and the roads are today being constructed by Haitian labor.[382]

The scarce population in the sugar-producing areas put an upward pressure on the wage level. As a result, from the 1890s, foreigners dominated among the harvest workers.[383] *Cocolos* and Haitians were brought in to work on the new plantations. In 1884 some 500 foreigners were used by the *ingenios*, and in 1920 there were around 28,000 Haitians legally residing in the Dominican Republic, and many more staying in the country illegally.[384]

During the half-century that followed the introduction of modern sugar production in the Dominican Republic around 1875, the economy of the country underwent a profound transformation. This was the case not least as far as property rights and land tenure were concerned. The time-honored system of *terrenos comuneros* had to yield to one of exclusively individual ownership. In many areas, sugar production put an effective end to cattle raising and this would not have been possible without the change in property rights.

However, economic change did not produce the same effects everywhere. In particular, largely as a result of its geographical location, the San Juan Valley in many respects turned out to constitute an exception to the general pattern of change. Nevertheless, changes took place in the San Juan area as well: changes of a very drastic nature. These changes go a long way towards explaining both why the *Olivorista* movement was successful and why it was put down so violently by the authorities. To these changes we must now turn.

Changes in the Southwest

At the beginning of the twentieth century, when the vast majority of the population of the San Juan Valley made their living mainly from cattle raising, the most severe threat to their existence was recurrent drought. When creeks and rivers dried up and emaciated cattle strayed aimlessly across the dying savanna grassland, bellowing out their hunger and anguish, a fervent stage of activity took hold of their owners. They had to work day and night on the mountain slopes surrounding the valley in

---

382 Kelsey (1922), p. 170. Professor Carl Kelsey had been sent by the American Academy of Political and Social Science in 1921 to the Dominican Republic in order to study the social impact of the American occupation.

383 Baud (1987), p. 145. For details, see Baud (1988b).

384 Lundahl and Vargas (1983), pp. 118–19.

order to cut the canopy of the still-green *guásima* trees and collect *tinajos*, a parasitic plant much liked by the cattle. When these concerted efforts proved to be useless, the greatly feared eventuality, slaughter, had to begin. Decomposing carcasses would litter the brown, dead grasslands in the plains, after the hides had been removed and sold to Haiti.[385]

Quite probably the climate in the San Juan Valley underwent a change for the worse after the turn of the century, with less precipitation and less water in the rivers.[386] Possibly, the contemporary eyewitnesses exaggerate the changes in rainfall, as the precipitation pattern in the area tends to follow a cycle in which plentiful years alternate with relatively dry ones.[387] Nevertheless, there remains a real possibility that indiscriminate tree felling on the mountainsides may have affected the water content of the rivers. In 1924, the local San Juan newspaper, *El Cable*, wrote: 'Perhaps the lack of rain in all these regions and the decrease of the volume of water carried by our rivers have their origin in the irreverent clearing of the woods.'[388]

The quotation comes from an article that mentions that a big company, *La Habanero Lumber*, 'years ago' carried out extensive tree felling close to creeks and rivers in the Cordillera Central and that these fellings had been widespread. *La Habanero* was not alone. Some four to six lumber companies, exporting from Azua or Barahona, hired local peasants to cut trees in remote mountain districts. Since roads and paths were either non-existent or in very bad condition, the trees were felled close to creeks and rivers and the lumber was dragged along these until it could be brought down to the ports with the help of oxen. In this way, the forest close to the sources of the rivers of the Cordillera Central was destroyed completely.[389]

The lumber companies had moved into the mountains around the San Juan Valley because most of the forests around Azua had already been cropped beyond repair. In 1887 the governor of Azua complained that the deforestation had been excessive. Forestry became unprofitable and it was time to search for new sources of income.[390]

As the lumber and cattle industries were declining, commercial production of sugar, coffee and kidney beans assumed increased importance.[391] At the beginning of the century, the sugar industry in Barahona started to grow and Barahona and Azua were turned into relatively important

385 Jovine Soto (1978), p. 12.
386 Garrido (1970), pp. 17–18; Garrido (1922), p. 227; and Cano y Fortuna (n.d.) p. 57.
387 Cf. Isa (1985).
388 *El Cable*, 19 August 1924.
389 Interview with Tala Cabral Ramírez, Santo Domingo, 21 November 1985.
390 Cross Beras (1984), p. 75.
391 Boin and Serulle Ramia (1979), p. 82.

Figure 7.8 The Central Ansonia, around 1920.

ports.[392] By the same token, the areas around these towns developed into important markets for local products consumed by the growing labor force in the sugar *ingenios*, like the Azuano, Ocoa and Ansonia *centrales*.[393] The *Libro azul de Santo Domingo*, an investment guide printed in 1920, describes the latter:

> The original founder, owner and promoter of the 'Central Ansonia' sugar mills and plantations was the famous West Indian trader-captain, John Hardy, one of the old-time 'Yankee' sea traders, who became interested in the wonderful Azua Valley and succeeded in interesting capital and installing the mills and making the plantations, some 25 years ago. [...] At present the mills grind 600 tons of cane per day, which gives them 300 bags of sugar (220 pounds to the bag), or a total daily output of 66,000 pounds of finest raw sugar. The mills give employment to 1,500 laborers during the grinding season and about half that number during the growing or cultivating season. The Central Ansonia property is conveniently situated in the famous Azua Valley, some seven miles from the city of Azua.[394]

Transport companies and merchant houses were established in both Barahona and Azua, often with branch offices in San Juan de la Maguana and Las Matas de Farfán. In Azua, for example, the firm of Choisne & Risk

392 Ibid.
393 Cf. Muto (1976), p. 35, for a list of the main sugar mills.
394 *Libro azul de Santo Domingo* (1920), pp. 104–5.

was to be found, the former partner a Puerto Rican and the latter a Syrian, employing 'ten clerks and two traveling salesmen. They import direct from Europe and the United States.'[395] Three other Risk family members had their own businesses in Azua. There was also N. N. Ciccone,

> 'a very reputable and high-class merchant who engages in the liquor business, selling first-class wines and provisions in general'. [...] Mr. Ciccone owns a large amount of city real estate, as well as farms which are adequately situated for the cultivation of all kinds of products and the raising of animals.[396]

Similar trades were exercised by Rocco Capano, Liberato Marranzini and Vespasiano Ciaccio, whose relatives were found in San Juan de la Maguana.[397] Goods imported via the Azua port were thereafter marketed across the entire province.

Barahona was growing rapidly as well. In 1890, an Italian immigrant, Pedro Callo, had started to develop coffee growing in the area, introducing new methods both in cultivation and preparation.[398] Around the turn of the century, a number of infrastructural investments were carried out in the town: street lights, telegraph, a park and a wharf to boost coastal shipping, in particular of coffee.[399] During the 1880–1921 period, the sugar industry in the area around Barahona was concentrated mainly on producing *guarapo, aguardiente* and other sugar cane liquors.[400] In 1917, however, the Barahona Company Inc. started to clear and prepare a large area around Barahona for production of refined sugar which began in 1921.

The gradual conversion of Barahona and Azua into sugar-producing regions in turn created a large demand for food at the same time as some of the food-producing areas had been converted into sugar cane fields.[401] Food had to be obtained from further away. On the one hand, imports increased, but locally grown products had to meet large part of the increased demand.[402] Thus, Padre Suazo in Azua in 1899 observed that 'Here, on Sundays, a lot of people come from San Juan and Neyba to the

---

395 Ibid., p. 93.
396 Ibid., p. 97.
397 Ibid.
398 López Reyes (1983), p. 78.
399 Ibid., p. 87.
400 Ibid., p. 78.
401 This was true in other regions as well. Thus, Frank Moya Pons observes: 'A notable effect of the sugar industry within a few years of its establishment was the scarcity of fruit and provisions in the city of Santo Domingo as a result of the conversion into cane fields of all the surrounding lands and the disappearence of the few conucos and ranches [*estancias*] that existed before' (Moya Pons (1980), p. 411).
402 Cf. Muto (1976), p. 77.

[markets] of the ingenio Vicini and that of the Hardys; bringing eggs, onions [*cebollines*], beans etc.'[403]

During this period, there was an inflow of immigrant Italians (e.g. the Marranzini family) and Lebanese (the Michelén and Heyaime families) who settled in Las Matas de Farfán and San Juan de la Maguana.[404] The new immigrants together with some large landowners began cultivating the valley to a larger extent than previously with the aid of labor coming in via Azua and Barahona ports.[405] Food crops were sold to these two centers and to the large sugar complexes in the south. The Italians and Lebanese, together with some merchants of Spanish and Puerto Rican origin,[406] acted as intermediaries in this commercialization process, simultaneously selling imported goods and Dominican rum in the other direction.[407] Around 1905, San Juan de la Maguana began to experience increased trading:

> That movement was developed with the arrival of the Italians and the entry of don Domingo Rodríguez in the merchandise trade. Don Felipe Callado and don Domingo prepared skins for export and began the bean business with Santo Domingo. The westward-looking business turned eastwards when the creation of the Guardia Fronteriza made smuggling impossible or difficult. But it was from the year 1920 that the Sanjuanero conscience really began to wake up and the village converted itself into a village with pretensions of becoming a town.[408]

Las Matas de Farfán during the 1910s was a place with relatively well-developed trade, due in part to an Arab colony consisting of twenty-nine families (Bera, Arbaje, Yunes, Hauley, Hachaá, Sarraff).[409]

Many of the promoters of the new trade and production activities were immigrants, the majority coming from Italy and the Ottoman Empire; the

---

403 Quoted by Baud (1993b), note, p. 15.
404 At the beginning of the present century the *común* of San Juan de la Maguana numbered some 20,000 (Deschamps (1908), p. 211).
405 They continued to raise cattle as well, however. Cf. *Libro azul de Santo Domingo* (1920), pp. 102–3, 106–7, 126.
406 Moreta (1986), p. 21.
407 Interview with Angel Moreta, Santo Domingo, 25 July 1985.
408 Garrido Puello (1981), p. 102. A directory from 1907 mentions fifteen 'businessmen' in San Juan de la Maguana. Four of them were recently arrived Italians: Flor and Antonio Marra, as well as Horacio and Liberato Marranzini (Deschamps (1908), p. 212). They owned different stores, but were all related; the mother of the two Marras was a certain María Josefa Marranzini (*Libro azul de Santo Domingo* (1920), p. 102). Judging from the directory, commercial activity in San Juan was quite modest in 1907. Excluding the fifteen 'businessmen' it lists six carpenters, one barber, one distiller, two blacksmiths, four *plateros* [probably vendors of various trinkets], five shoemakers, four saddlers, one tailor and three *modistas* [dressmakers] (Deschamps (1908), pp. 212–13).
409 Cano y Fortuna (n.d.), pp. 15–16.

Figure 7.9 The interior of the Marranzini store, Las Matas de Farfán, around 1920.

latter, although known as *Turcos*, were mainly Christians from Lebanon, Syria or Palestine.[410] Most of the Italians settled in Barahona or Azua, but a few moved to the San Juan Valley, notably the Marranzini and Marra families, who soon began to carry out important trade, via Azua, in such things as textiles, medicine, German pottery, French wines, Italian luxury articles, and hardware from the United States and Germany. They also engaged in the production of beans and the raising of beef cattle, selling cowhides, honey and beeswax to Azua, and transporting goods between Azua and San Juan de la Maguana and Las Matas de Farfán on donkey and muleback.[411]

The first *Turcos* arrived in the Dominican Republic in the mid-1880s.[412] Many made their living as traveling salesmen or as small retail dealers in provincial towns. However, as a result of hard and incessant work, some of them rapidly prospered and their startling success and new business methods often made the locals envious. The same development took place in Haiti, where the *Syriens*, as they were called, were ordered to close all their businesses and were deported in 1905.[413] As a result, many of them ended up in Las Matas de Farfán, which is situated close to the Haitian border, continuing their trade with Haiti but also establishing contacts with the large import firms in Azua and Barahona. In the 1910s Las Matas had

---

410 For a general picture of the Arabs in the Dominican Republic, see Inoa (1991).
411 Interviews with Américo Marra, San Juan de la Maguana, 19 January 1989, and Maximiliano Rodríguez Piña, Santo Domingo, 23 April 1986.
412 Inoa (1991), pp. 35–6.
413 Heinl and Heinl (1978), pp. 333–4. For details on the Levantine immigration to Haiti, see Plummer (1981). Cf. also Nicholls (1981).

a total population of some 900 people, the twenty-nine *Turco* families accounting for more than 150.[414] Others settled in San Juan, where they established prosperous firms and bought land.[415]

Old *Sanjuaneros*[416] agree that it was the immigrants who brought change to the valley when they made their appearance at the turn of the century, turning the traditional westward-looking business eastwards:[417]

> In those days, the best business was carried out in Port-au-Prince. It was easy to get there and you could buy everything over there. People sent their children to the French schools in that city and you saw a lot of French merchandise here: fashion magazines and luxury textiles. The Cubans bought our cattle and hides in Port-au-Prince. The Italians changed all that. Their goods were more expensive but they brought the things right to us and it was easier and more practical to do business with them particularly since the supervision of the border became stricter under Mon Cáceres[418] and the Americans. Before that there were virtually no customs duties and no control.[419]

The network of the merchants also extended into rural areas, during the 1910s, when agents began to buy agricultural products from the peasants, transporting them via mule *recuas* to town. According to Angel Moreta, the first transactions were made by a Spanish immigrant, Felipe Collado, with Pedro Heyaime, Miguel Paniagua, Liberato Marranzini, Antonio Marra and José Paniagua following suit. This commerce soon developed into a network of agents working for the San Juan merchants in rural areas.[420]

The border problem

The above quotation points to another fundamental change which took place after the turn of the century. The conversion of the westward trade with Haiti into an eastward one, with Santo Domingo as the ultimate destination, was not only a result of the immigrants. An even more important cause was the introduction of border control measures beginning in 1907.

---

414 Cano y Fortuna (n.d.), p. 102.
415 For example, the Michelén, Paniagua and Heyaime families (*Libro azul de Santo Domingo* (1920), pp. 106–7).
416 Like Maximiliano Rodríguez Piña, interviewed in Santo Domingo, 23 April 1986, and Manuel Emilio Mesa, interviewed in San Juan de la Maguana, 20 January 1989.
417 Garrido Puello (1981), p. 102.
418 Ramón Cáceres, Dominican president 1905–11. For his biography, see Troncoso Sánchez (1964).
419 Interview with Manuel Emilio Mesa, San Juan de la Maguana, 20 January 1989.
420 Moreta (1986), pp 79–86.

At that time the border with Haiti, for all practical purposes, was non-existent. The Dominican *hateros* allowed their cattle to graze on the Haitian side and both Haitians and Dominicans participated in trade on both sides of the border. A treaty formalizing free trade had been signed in 1874.[421]

The border had been extremely permeable ever since the end of the hostilities between the two countries. The free trade agreement only served to codify what had been practiced clandestinely for several years. At the end of the nineteenth and the beginning of the twentieth century, the San Juan Valley was one of the few remaining cattle-raising areas in the Dominican Republic. The area had remained sparsely populated and had retained its comparative advantage in land-intensive products. Essentially, the valley remained grassland,[422] i.e. the base for trade remained unchanged:

> Towards the end of the nineteenth century, the depression in the Dominican frontier [caused by the repeated warfare between the beginning of the century and 1874] was compounded when US-owned sugar plantations developed in the southeast, causing yet another wave of emigration from the border.[423] In response, the frontier economy once again turned towards Haiti. Cattle production again became the basis of the border provincial economies, in part as the result of the new availability of land and the necessity of returning to more extensive methods of production due to labor shortages. Furthermore, the national economic shift towards the eastern regions encouraged the deepening of border trade networks with Haiti, a logical shift due to the region's proximity to the major Haitian cities of Cap-Haïtien in the north and Port-au-Prince in the south. Because much of this new commercial activity was in contraband, municipal authorities complained about the extent of trade with Haiti, couching their statements in nationalist terms (although free commerce with Haiti had been established in 1874). Probably these authorities were alarmed by the provincial governments' inability to capture the profits of the new bustling commerce.[424]

The main export article was hides, some 30,000 being exported every year, on average, between 1880 and 1885. However, live animals also constituted an important commodity. In 1889, the governor of the province of

---

421 The text of the treaty can be found e.g. in Peña Batlle (1946), pp. 396–402.
422 Palmer (1976), p. 77.
423 Michiel Baud (1993a), p. 46, even maintains that '[the] San Juan Valley was one of the main sources of labor for the nascent sugar sector'. This of course reinforced the land intensity of the production pattern in the valley.
424 Derby (1994), p. 498.

Azua (which contained the San Juan Valley) estimated that some 6,000 head of cattle had been exported from the territory of his jurisdiction to the other side of the border.[425] Three years later the figure was 8,000.[426] The cattle price was increasing as a result of Haitian demand, and the Haitian buyers paid with gold coins instead of the debased silver coins received in domestic transactions.[427]

Most of these animals were brought to some market in the neighborhood of Port-au-Prince (e.g. Verrettes or Croix-des-Bouquets). Víctor Garrido remembered his boyhood days just before 1900: 'Everybody traveled to Haiti to sell their cattle ...'[428] Going back, 'they brought all they needed of articles of foreign origin.'[429] The established way for the *Sanjuaneros* to obtain imported goods (mainly French manufactures) was across the Haitian border. Some of these goods were also brought by Dominican retailers, known as *buhoneros* [itinerant salesmen], who sold tobacco, wax and cotton on the Haitian side. The Haitian *machann* (mainly women), in turn, brought a variety of imported trinkets and textiles to the Dominican countryside; *marchande* (in the feminine) became the designation for 'salesman' in the border area and Haitian money was employed in the transactions.[430] In short, the Dominican and Haitian sides of the border constituted a well-integrated economic zone. 'We know little about the organization of the border trade, but there is no doubt that a large majority depended on the latter for their survival', concludes Michiel Baud in an investigation of the role of the border between the two countries.[431]

The first signals that changes might be imminent came in the 1880s after the sugar crisis had set in. When, as a result, the demand for consumer goods fell off, the members of the new Dominican merchant class began to lobby for stricter controls on the border trade, complaining that they were not in a position to compete with goods being brought in from Haiti free of import duties. The Haitian market was described as 'exorbitantly monopolistic and onerous' in a series of confused attacks in *El Eco de la Opinión*, the periodical of the sugar interests, the wealthy merchants and other big business.[432]

San Juan de la Maguana was caught in the middle of the battle between eastward and westward trade:

---

425 Baud (1993b), p. 10. The figure for live cattle is probably an underestimate, which does not take into account that most of the commerce did not go via official channels. Baud puts the probable figure for the entire country at 15,000 (ibid.).
426 Ibid., p. 12.
427 Domínguez (1986), pp. 196–9.
428 Garrido (1970), p. 17.
429 Ibid.
430 Baud (1993a), pp. 43–4, and (1993b), p. 2.
431 Baud (1993b), p. 11.
432 Quoted in ibid., p. 18.

there existed since the end of the nineteenth century an urban market – one which functioned on Wednesdays and Saturdays. This was attended by informal compradores and traders who carried their products on donkey and mule back from the places where they were stored. Some traders were representatives of companies established in Azua, like that of Julio Coean and Company, that of José Lench, the Recios, etc. These Azuan traders functioned as links; they received merchandise (wax, honey, hides, etc.) and foodstuffs (beans) that came with mule droves [*recuas*] from San Juan de la Maguana and provided, in their turn, merchandise that came from the capital (fabrics, matches, etc.) and which were transported to the San Juan Valley.

This movement also had to do with Haiti, across the border. San Juan was a zone traditionally linked to exchange with Haiti. Groups of small traders were busying themselves, almost always in the form of contraband, with disposing in the neighboring country of goods like hides, wax, etc., in addition to cattle. The merchants came back from Haiti with all kinds of articles and trifles: silk, blue denim, ... handkerchiefs, perfumes, porcelain, clairin, garlic, sisal and other things. Some of these articles crossed the border legally, across the terrestrial customs. Others did so in the form of contraband, 'which was the standard border practice, with a productive trade taking shape under the umbrella of this illegitimate manipulation'.[433]

In 1890 a conflict ensued between Haiti and the Dominican Republic with respect to the implementation of the 1874 treaty, and after territorial incidents in 1892 and 1893,[434] as well as a complete failure when establishing, in 1895, so-called *mercados fronterizos* [border markets] in Bánica, Las Matas de Farfán and Comendador where the *rayanos* [border dwellers] could sell to Dominican buyers in a government-controlled setting which, besides, would allow the financially hard-pressed Heureaux government (cf. below) to increase its revenue,[435] the Dominican government annulled the 1874 treaty and began to erect customs houses along the border. Surveillance, however, never managed to become effective and trade continued as before. It was not until ten years later that drastic changes that antagonized the *rayanos* began to take place.[436]

These changes were a result of the precarious situation of Dominican government finances. During the second half of the nineteenth century the governments of Buenaventura Báez and Ulises Heureaux had taken a

433 Moreta (1986), pp. 76–7. The quotation at the end is from Garrido Puello (1972), p. 47.
434 Peña Batlle (1946), Chapters 19–21.
435 Baud (1993b), pp. 47–8.
436 Knight (1928), pp. 32–3.

series of scandalous loans, both abroad and domestically.[437] The exact amount of the national debt, which was accumulated under somewhat chaotic circumstances, is not known with certainty. However, in 1905 the American economist Jacob Hollander, whom President Theodore Roosevelt had sent to the Dominican Republic to make an inquiry into the country's finances, estimated it at more than US$40 million.[438]

As the foreign debt accumulated, European governments began to press for repayment on behalf of their bondholder citizens, and in 1906, the United States, the biggest claimant, forced an adjustment plan on the Dominicans in order to reduce the debt to no more than US$20 million. In the previous year the Dominican president had authorized his American counterpart to name a representative who was to collect Dominican customs revenue, to be deposited in a New York bank on behalf of foreign and domestic creditors, and in 1907 the United States was granted a general customs receivership in the Dominican Republic and the customs houses were put under the control of American customs officials.[439]

To this the *rayanos* reacted violently. They now had to pay customs duties on every hide or head of cattle brought across the border. Both Dominicans and Haitians also felt harassed by the American customs officials when they confiscated the small quantities of Haitian rum or Dominican cigarettes that the peasants carried back and forth, and they were infuriated when high fines were demanded for these attempts at running an illegal trade.[440] It was inevitable that a clash would come. Just a few months after its construction, a customs house was blown up at a place called El Fondo, and during the first two years of American general receivership several American customs officials were killed or wounded in gunfights with 'contraband gangs'.[441]

In the San Juan Valley skirmishes had taken place even before 1907. In 1905, a *modus vivendi* agreement had been worked out with the United States, and small detachments of Dominican militia under American command had started to patrol the border. On 5 August 1906 a group of young peasants were caught by the militia, in the process of introducing smuggled goods into the Dominican Republic. The youngsters were released and the confiscated goods were brought to Las Matas de Farfán. The incident, however, set the Dominicans' teeth on edge and at dawn the following day the customs office in Las Matas was attacked. Two Americans

---

437 For Báez, see e.g. Sang (1991), Chapter 6. The details of Heureaux' borrowing policy are given in Domínguez (1986), Sang (1987) and Rosa (1987), pp. 32–74.
438 Rosa (1987), p. 158.
439 Moya Pons (1980), pp. 440–5, Cassá (1983), p. 195. The 1907 convention is treated in detail in Clausner (1973), Chapter 15.
440 Moral (1961), pp. 65–6.
441 Clausner (1973), p. 142.

were killed and a Dominican border guard was wounded. The attackers
were punished with long prison terms.[442]

During the 1910s, other similar armed encounters were reported in the
Dominican press,[443] especially after the establishment of a *Guardia de Fron-*
tera [border guard] in 1911 and the formal prohibition the same year of
imports of non-Haitian goods.[444] Despite the increased difficulties,
however, the coexistence and trade between Haitians and Dominicans
continued. It was simply impossible to control efficiently the long border,
which in some places cut through high mountain ranges and rough, uninhabited terrain. Nor was it always the case that those who were put in
charge of the control did their utmost to exercise it:

> national and municipal authorities did not necessarily agree on what
> was regarded as the problem of Haitian-Dominican contraband. This
> was understandable because the same customs inspectors who strug-
> gled to control this prosperous trade in public also benefited from it
> in private. The problem for northern Dominican border officials was
> not the existence of contraband per se, but the higher tariff rates of
> the Haitian border customs houses which, they argued, prohibited
> Dominicans from crossing the border to sell their cattle, produce,
> tobacco, sugar, and rice in Ouanaminthe, the neighboring Haitian
> town. There was variety of opinion over how to cope with the problem
> of contraband: Not all ... municipal authorities thought that strict
> control of border transit was the optimal policy option. In 1920, the
> municipal government of Monte Cristi, a northern Dominican coastal
> town, petitioned for 'the free passage of Haitians through this part of
> the border' on the grounds that this was absolutely 'indispensable for
> commerce.' For the most part, local officials saw their interests in
> league with, not opposed to, Haiti.[445]

Large landowners, like Wenceslao Ramírez, maintained close relations
with Haitian strongmen such as the Zamor family, and owned vast lands on
both sides of the border.

It appears as if most of the inhabitants of the San Juan Valley were irritated with the American-run customs houses. It was therefore only natural
that the revolutionaries of 1912 (cf. below), under the command of the

---

442 Jovine Soto (1978), pp. 31–6, and Cano y Fortuna (n.d.), p. 27. The presumed leaders of
   the attack were sentenced to twenty-five years of forced labor – later changed to ten years
   (*Revista Judicial*, 15 February 1909, No. 26, p. 532).
443 E.g. *Listín Diario*, 19 January 1912.
444 Baud (1993a), p. 50. These goods were reexported to the Dominican Republic.
445 Derby (1994), pp. 500–1.

landowning elite of the valley, burned the customs houses along the border and proceeded to an uninhibited sale of cattle to Haiti.[446] However, this attitude would gradually change. Once the American occupation forces had taken over the administration in both Haiti (in 1915) and the Dominican Republic (in 1916), border control was strengthened and the export-import trade more and more assumed the character of contraband. Its scale decreased and it increasingly became the exclusive pursuit of groups who operated on both sides of the border and who could count on the protection of powerful political patrons.[447] In addition, as southeastern trade gained importance with the coming of the immigrants and the growing market, the majority of the 'progressive' elite seem to have come to accept the presence of the Americans and their constant struggle against contraband trade. Smugglers were frequently condemned in the press and trade with Haiti was increasingly considered a thing of the past.

This change of attitude, however, was not shared by everybody in the valley. The Haitian *gourde* continued to circulate in the border areas until 1947,[448] and smuggling continued in spite of the American efforts, and it would appear that Olivorio was directly involved. The most common crime attributed to the followers of Olivorio, at least according to a list published in an American document,[449] was that of 'smuggling rum', something that indicates close contacts with Haiti. As mentioned above, Olivorio made frequent use of the narrow paths that cross the border in the vicinity of Bánica and he also resided for longer periods in villages like Guayajayuco, Río Limpio and Sabana Mula, all famous haunts for both Dominican and Haitian smugglers.

One of Olivorio's hideouts, El Palmar, was situated not very far from Hato Nuevo, where a battle between soldiers and smugglers took place in 1912. There Olivorio and his people apparently continued to trade with the Haitians: 'The flow of people, more numerous every day, favored the commerce of the place [El Palmar] and the establishment of a market

446 Soler (1913), p. 5.
447 Baud (1993b), pp. 19–20.
448 Derby (1994), p. 516. From 1900, the US dollar (known as the peso in the Dominican Republic) was introduced as official currency when the country adopted the gold standard (Domínguez (1994), pp. 37–8), but in the border areas Haitian currency was far more common (Derby (1994), p 516). In San Juan de la Maguana, the José Paniagua merchant house served as a clearinghouse (Moreta (1986), p. 78). *Clavaos*, domestic coins made of copper and silver, minted in 1897, and in circulation until 1937, were accepted as the equivalent of 20 American cents (Cassá (1983), p. 188, personal communication from Roberto Cassá, 29 May 1996), and the *gourde*, whose value in terms of dollars had been fixed at the same level in 1919, circulated at par with the *clavao* (Moreta (1986), p. 78).
449 Feeley (1919).

with a nearby cockfight arena in La Sigua, Hato Nuevo, in the same jurisdiction.'[450]

Thus, it seems that Olivorio had a direct interest in maintaining the old
trade routes to Haiti.

Surveying the land

During the first two decades of the twentieth century, and very much as a
result of the above developments, an effort was begun to reorganize
production in the San Juan Valley. Attempts were made to force the peasants to enclose their cattle herds and start food production (rice, beans,
pigeon peas) on a larger scale than hitherto, or to forego use of the land.
It was not difficult to come up with a rationale. Open-range ranching
meant that farmers had to

> take precaution against animals that belong to people without respon-
> sibility – to maintain one's land well closed behind fences whose
> construction is very costly, but whose conservation costs much more if
> it is desired to maintain them in such condition that they can resist,
> both day and night, the voracious attacks of pigs, goats and cows while
> the owners of these harmful beings have, in most parts of the Repub-
> lic, the power not to erect any fences and let their animals freely seek
> their nourishment wherever they want.
>
> If this anomaly is highly harmful to the agriculturalists, it is much
> more so to the very same pseudo-breeders because it keeps them igno-
> rant of the great benefit that breeding yields when the animals are
> made subject to a regular feeding and daily attention, behind fences,
> by their owners; and even more so to the country in general because it
> stimulates negligence in the legions of peasants that dedicate them-
> selves to free breeding and foments a spirit of idleness, vagrancy,
> gambling and revolutions.[451]

We have dealt with how in the first two decades of the twentieth century
a series of laws and decrees were passed which all served to facilitate the
conversion of *terrenos comuneros*. These measures also had an impact in the
San Juan Valley as well, especially since they were reinforced by other
developments.

Thus the land began to be surveyed and fences would soon block the free
passage of cattle across the vast savannas. In the 1890s, Wenceslao Ramírez,
at the time the most powerful man in the valley, started to experiment with

---

450 Aristy (1919), p. 393.
451 Peynado (1909), p. 57.

new methods of cultivation. Until then, the land had been considered suitable only for cattle breeding, but the recurrent droughts that had killed off some of his animals made Ramírez consider that traditional breeding was much too vulnerable in times of crisis. The remedy he suggested was artificial irrigation, and in 1895 he dug the first large irrigation canals on the lands that his friend, the Dominican dictator Ulises Heureaux, owned close to El Cercado in the valley. Beans and other vegetables were grown, as well as grass for the cattle, and the cultivated areas were fenced in. (Possibly, this was done by Olivorio, among others, whose specialty was to construct *cercas* [fences], and who often worked on the lands of Wenceslao Ramírez before turning to his religious activities.)

Wenceslao's experiment was an immediate success. Realizing what the future might have in store, he sent his son José del Carmen (Carmito) to the capital to study and become the first land surveyor in the valley.[452] This was a decision that would have important consequences:

> In that period the public surveyors were the key figures in the process of formal recognition of property rights, for they had the authority 'to judge the validity and adequacy of the titles that were presented by their claimants,' as the Surveyor's Law of 1882 put it, echoing the law of 1848. According to this 1882 law, 'students of the Instituto Profesional who had passed the second-year mathematics examination' could be surveyors. Often the surveyors received good lands in payment for their work.[453]

In 1902, Carmito was busy surveying land in the San Juan Valley. Some old *Sanjuaneros* are of the opinion that this took place mainly on Ramírez family lands but this is contradicted by other sources. Thus an old school friend, Heriberto Pieter, visited Carmito in 1905:

> In this town [San Juan de la Maguana] I was lucky to meet the land surveyor, my good school friend, Carmito Ramírez. Above his chamarra he carried a revolver, a cartridge belt filled with bullets and a luxurious dagger. Seeing him armed in such a way, I asked for the reasons for carrying so many instruments of death. He answered me calmly: 'It is not in order to kill anyone, rather for people to respect me and not interfere in my carrying out of my work while I am surveying the land, something that is nearly always subject to discussions, sometimes bloody ones. I have never had to use these arms, calming down the threatening turmoils by recommending my adversaries to

452 Interview with Mimicito Ramírez, San Juan de la Maguana, 11 April 1986.
453 Hoetink (1982), p. 11.

wait until we have time to discuss the results of my measurements in court.'[454]

Wenceslao Ramírez was not the only one who had land surveyed. Other landowners followed suit, not least those among the immigrants who had managed to amass some funds that could be used for buying *pesos de posesión*.[455] The *terrenos comuneros* began to be divided, a painful process that provoked fierce disputes from the very beginning. By 1912 the Ministry of Justice was receiving complaints regarding disorderly behavior of the legal authorities in San Juan de la Maguana.[456]

These land surveys brought about change. The progressive landowners still used most of their surveyed land for cattle-raising purposes, but made use of imported beef cattle and fencing on their pastures. However, slowly but steadily the cultivation of beans, plantains, rice, manioc, potatoes and coffee gained importance.[457] The former food-producing areas around Azua and Barahona gradually became converted into sugar cane fields or were used for coffee production. As more and more workers moved in, food had to be procured from localities further away. Imports increased, but most of the increased demand had to be met by domestic producers. This was not easy:

> migration to the sugar plantation had a disastrous effect on the food supply. Food production, now in the hands of the families of sugar workers who stayed behind on the *conucos* (foodplots), fell short of the growing demand. This shortfall resulted in high food prices in the urban areas and frequent shortages of basic foodstuffs. The problem became serious when wages in the sugar sector were no longer high enough to satisfy the sugar workers' basic needs. Here one finds an interesting aspect of capitalist penetration of a largely self-sustaining agrarian system. To attract labor for cane cutting, the sugar industry initially paid relatively high wages. As a result, thousands of men flocked to the sugar *fincas* [farms], rapidly forming a class of wage laborers who (at least during the *zafra* [sugar harvest] season) depended completely on wage income. Thus a relatively large market for foodstuffs and consumer goods was suddenly created in a region that hitherto had provisioned only small urban populations. Just when a substantial portion of the productive population had been drawn away from the agricultural sector, the demand for foodstuffs rose

454 Pieter (1972), p. 81.
455 See *Libro azul de Santo Domingo* (1920).
456 Soler (1912), p. 9.
457 Interview with Mimicito Ramírez, San Juan de la Maguana, 11 April 1986.

enormously. The money suddenly pumped into the small Dominican economy also helps explain the tremendous rise in food prices.[458]

In the urban centers of the Dominican Republic, food prices soared sky high from the 1890s onward. Crops that had been abundant for centuries were virtually disappearing. The governors of Azua and Santiago wrote worried letters to President Heureaux about the demoralization and apathy of the rural population in their districts.[459]

The importance of the southern market grew during the next two decades and the area dedicated to food crops expanded in the San Juan Valley. However, it was not until 1918, when a persistent drought killed thousands of cattle, that commercial agriculture in the area took a decisive leap forward.

This development generally favored the large landowners, those who were able to innovate and who could have their land surveyed. Many of the peasants who clung to their traditional way of life suffered in the process. The gradual closure of the Haitian border after 1907 led to a shrinking market for their hides and cattle and the recurrent droughts in the 1910s decimated their cattle herds. Still, many peasants refused to plant crops for the market because they could not pay for the costs of having *terrenos comuneros* surveyed and divided, or because they could not get a loan for cultivation:

> The farmer who owns an acción with an equivalent to two caballerías [150 hectares] of land cannot now, if he does not have large savings, and even though he is the owner of these two caballerías, obtain a loan of the capital required to start cultivation. If, on the other hand, he accepts ruinous interest rates, due to the risk that the lender is taking, the possible failure of the first harvest to correspond to the expectations that he and his debtor had in it, may prevent any effective guarantee that the loaned capital will be paid back. For such reasons, the common practice is, as is natural, that the farmer in such conditions, i.e. the Dominican peasant in general, since he cannot get any profit out of his land, nor out of his intentions to work it, finds himself forced to sell his acción, at a despicable price, to somebody who is easily fooled, or to a monopolist, and then become a farmhand, later a vagrant and thereafter a bandit.[460]

---

458 Baud (1987), pp. 143–4.
459 Ibid., p. 146.
460 Peynado (1919), pp. 2–3.

The buyers were mostly the larger landowners. The Ramírez family, for example, constantly bought land.[461] Not all land changed hands through regular sales, however. Other methods existed. Surveying was greatly facilitated by the fact that there were few legal deeds that could stand up in court. All lands to which no deeds existed in principle had to be surveyed. In addition, the field was left open for fraudulent practices:

> Basing themselves on the disorder and incompleteness of the archives of San Juan de la Maguana, Neyba and Azua, where it is impossible to find many originals of property titles that were conceded before the year 1882, as well as on that Article 1335 of our Civil Code that establishes that if the original is missing, first-hand copies are as valid as the original, there are persons in the said municipalities who have dedicated themselves to the task of forging first-hand copies of titles of which originals never existed, making use of special ink and the practice of putting their forgeries into hot ovens in order to make the paper and the ink appear old; and in this way they make great expertise necessary if these titles are not to be accepted as genuine. Many of them have been the subject of large-scale negotiation.[462]

To make things even worse for those who stuck to the old system, the landowning elite of the San Juan Valley carried on a constant struggle to make the authorities apply the existing laws restricting the free breeding of animals.[463] In 1846, a law had been passed which prohibited this practice within areas designated as 'agricultural zones', but this law had remained a dead letter for several decades, largely as a result of the weak development of commercial agriculture. From the end of the 1850s, however, and in particular after 1875, when the modern sugar industry began to spread across the Dominican Republic, calls for implementation were heard.[464]

In 1895, a *Ley sobre Crianza de Animales Domésticos de Pasto* [Law Concerning Raising Domestic Animals in Pasture] was passed which allowed cattle raising only when it was based on the possession of land and made breeders responsible for avoiding damage by animals to agriculture.[465] The implementation of this law, however, was half-hearted. Free breeding continued on *terrenos comuneros*, whose extent was unknown anyway, and agricultural interests were protected only in specially designated *zonas agrícolas* [agricultural zones] – land tracts in excess of 750 hectares which were

461 Interview with Tala Cabral Ramírez, Santo Domingo, 21 November 1985.
462 Peynado (1919), p. 7.
463 Decreto 4043; cf. Crouch (1979), p. 260.
464 Boin and Serulle Ramia (1981), p. 50.
465 Domínguez (1986), p. 209, Baud (1995), p. 161.

held by a single individual in regions not zoned for cattle raising and which had been declared agricultural land by a municipal council upon the request of the owner.[466] This law enabled large landowners to obtain government protection against inroads by peasant cattle on their property. In San Juan de la Maguana, however, the law was vigorously resisted by the breeders who simply thought that it was too costly to construct fences in the instances where the law required it, and in La Vega the law provoked an armed insurrection which made President Heureaux postpone its implementation.[467]

In February 1900, the year after the assassination of Heureaux, the 1895 law was abrogated,[468] but later the same year new legislation with a similar content was passed.[469] This was complemented in 1907 by a law that restricted the freedom of cattle raising, a law which, however, had little practical importance.[470] Finally, in 1911 a *Ley de Policía* [Police Law] was passed which contained clauses regulating and restricting free breeding.[471] A legal solution to the conflict between agriculture and cattle breeding was long overdue. From 1906 to 1910 between 40 and 50 percent of all cases heard in Dominican courts were the result of clashes between cattle breeders and farmers.[472]

Around this time cattle walked aimlessly along the streets of Las Matas and San Juan and rested in the shade of the trees in the central parks. Pigs and goats tore down fences and ravaged the cultivations of beans and vegetables.[473] Many irritated cultivators repeated the old saying that '*labranza mata crianza y viceversa*' [farming kills breeding and vice versa].[474] For a short while, the *Guardia Municipal* kept animals that had been caught and advertised the catches in the monthly issue of the *Gaceta Oficial*, which was printed in the capital and which could be read in the *alcaldía* in San Juan de la Maguana. Between 1911 and 1913 there is no lack of reports regarding the appearance of bulls and horses that have been taken into custody by the local police in the various towns of the San Juan Valley.[475] However, this service apparently disappeared gradually during the turbulent times following the civil war of 1912.

466 Baud (1995), pp 161–2.
467 Domínguez (1986), p. 209.
468 Domínguez (1994), p. 298.
469 Ibid., Baud (1995), p. 162.
470 Baud (1995), p. 162.
471 Troncoso Sánchez (1964), pp. 361–2, Boin and Serulle Ramia (1981), pp. 50–2, Castillo and Cordero (1982), p 108.
472 Bryan (1979), p. 54.
473 Interview with Mimicito Ramírez, San Juan de la Maguana, 11 April 1986.
474 Cf. Abad (1888), pp. 187–8.
475 *Gaceta Oficial* (1911–1913).

In 1918 the American occupation forces attempted to end the [free breeding], but failed:

> When the U.S. Military Government decided to put a definitive end to free cattle raising in 1918, it became clear how widespread this practice was, especially in the western regions of the country. Hundreds of petitions were sent by peasants in the northern and western parts of the country to the responsible U.S. official, Holger Johansen. Although the initial reaction of the military authorities was strict and uncompromising, eventually they had to budge. Johansen wrote to his superiors in September 1918: 'In our opinion, there are reasons, in the places where free cattle raising is most abundant, to concede some delay so as not to harm the cattle raising. We have on various occasions advised proceeding cautiously in this matter.'[476]

The land surveying continued during the American occupation. One of the first activities undertaken by the powerful San Juan families once the marines had landed was to write a letter to the American military governor demanding that the peasants enclose their cattle so that conditions favorable for cultivation could be established.[477]

New cadastral surveys took place. It was stated that the previous survey documents had been lost in the San Juan Valley. These new surveys were also carried out by Carmito Ramírez,[478] who apparently was the only surveyor in the valley until at least 1920,[479] and they made it possible for the powerful families (e.g. Ramírez, La Mesa, Rodríguez, Michelén) to appropriate yet more land. During this period the large landowners enclosed their properties, continuing to raise animals which still were sold in Haiti, while at the same time turning to agriculture aimed at the expanding market.

Virtually all the important immigrant traders also owned land. The *Libro azul* provides a few examples:

> La Flor de Italia. … Mr. Liberato Marranzini is the founder of this well-known establishment that has been in existence for twenty-two years. [...] 'La Flor de Italia' has twenty employees to execute the orders of their customers. Their goods are imported direct [sic] from the United States.

476 Baud (1995), pp. 162–3.
477 Interview with Angel Moreta, Santo Domingo, 25 July 1985.
478 Garrido Puello (1981), p. 49.
479 Moreta (1986), p. 116. According to the census taken that year, there were fewer than sixty surveyors in the entire country (ibid., p. 117).

Figure 7.10 Liberato Marranzini.

This firm has branches of the highest standard and splendid supply houses in Tubano [sic] and Azua. Mr. Marranzini is the owner of several houses and a valuable estate containing cattle ranches. The speciality of the firm is coffee, live stock and native products. […]

'La Linda' […] was founded in 1903. … Mr. Marra […] [is] the son of Samuel Marra and María Josefa Marranzini. […]

This house makes a speciality of fine cloth and odd designs. It imports directly from Europe and the United States. Five clerks are employed.

Mr. Marra is the owner of various properties among which are four houses and four lots; a ranch situated in Gavilan [sic] with 200 head of cattle, and a house for his laborers. […]

He does a large business in buying and exporting all kinds of country produce such as coffee, hides, honey, wax, etc., etc. […]

Don Domingo Rodríguez. … This is a general store selling merchandise and a special line of hardware. It has been established for twenty-two years by its owner […]

He also owns two country estates devoted to breeding cattle, cultivating rice and grass for feed. These estates contain 5,230 acres […]

'La Venus'. … This is the name of a well known general store established for eight years by its thriving proprietor, Juan J. Michelen [sic]. […] The house also buys and sells native products, especially kidney beans, … coffee, hides etc., etc.

Figure 7.11 Flor Marra.

> Mr. Michelen is the owner of a completely equipped tannery with one hundred mules to transport the orders that are constantly flowing in [...] In addition he is the proprietor of several cattle ranches.[480]

The enumeration of similar circumstances continues over several pages: Paniagua, Lama, Heyaime, two more Marranzini brothers, with 10,000 acres of property with cattle and beans, etc. All were engaged in imports via the port in Azua and in buying peasant produce. As early as 1911 it was reported that to the *común* of Azua, where the Azuano and Ansonia sugar *ingenios* were located, agricultural foodstuffs were brought 'on a large scale' from the countryside surrounding San Juan de la Maguana.[481] This was to become much easier as the state of communications improved during the American occupation. In 1918, the Americans had improved the road from San Juan de la Maguana to Azua to the point where it was possible to negotiate the distance between the two towns in five days by car, but only during the dry season.[482] The following year, an American geological expedition reported that the road from San Juan to Azua was in a good, and improving, state: 'San Juan de la Maguana ... communicates with Azua through a road which can virtually always be traveled by automobile and which, once the reparations, which are now being carried out are finished, can be used to go to Azua without difficulties.'[483] Commercial

480 *Libro azul de Santo Domingo* (1920), pp. 101, 102, 106, 107.
481 Boin and Serulle Ramia (1981), p. 251.
482 Acevedo (1918), p. 41.
483 Cooke (1983), p. 40.

agriculture had begun to drive cattle out of the San Juan Valley, and in this process the peasants were fighting a losing battle when it came to keeping to their land. As we will see in Chapter 8, this was a process that would continue and accelerate during the next few decades.

Once they started to lose their land, life became much more difficult for the San Juan peasants, since with increased land concentration among the larger landowners, they became more and more dependent on the latter for their existence. Thus, for example, Wenceslao Ramírez was considered to be a 'dangerous' man, a 'godfather', in the sense that the common peasants could not turn down an offer to take part as workers in his *convites* [communal work parties].[484] ('He was the friend of all the principal men of the country and all the governments wanted his friendship and services', and he 'had friendly relations with the most prominent personalities of Haitian politics, especially with the authorities of the border provinces and when necessary he extended his own [authority] to the other side of the Artibonite', summarizes Víctor Garrido, in a portrait of the old general.[485]) Patterns such as these were to be even more emphasized during the 1920s, after the death of Olivorio.

Political chaos and anarchy: the crisis of *caudillismo*

By the time Olivorio made his appearance as a founder of a new religious sect, the San Juan Valley, as we have seen, was experiencing socioeconomic changes that were putting an end to the traditional way of life. The 1910s were also a time of violence. Even nature itself behaved strangely. Halley's Comet, the recurring droughts and the San Bruno earthquake were interpreted as forebodings of an approaching doomsday. These strange events increased the fame and prestige of Olivorio. People claimed that he had foretold these catastrophes and interpreted them as signs of other-worldly wrath against those who denied Olivorio's divinity. His community in the mountains turned into a Utopia for the peasants of the San Juan Valley. Everything there was done on a communal basis. Food and drink were shared, the traditional rituals of a vanishing peasant society were celebrated and the powers of Olivorio were manifested through the miracles he worked on the sick. La Maguana appeared as a safe spot, a fixed point in a world that seemed to be crumbling.

Economic changes and natural catastrophes were, however, not the only events threatening the equilibrium of traditional life in the San Juan Valley. There was yet another factor that played into the hands of Olivorio: the turbulent political situation and the concomitant lack of law and order.

484 Interview with Julián Ramos, Higüerito, 16 January 1986.
485 Garrido (1972), pp. 267, 264.

In those days, people helped one another. You lived in a community. I do not think it was because of the loss of the land that people came to Olivorio. That was later. No one starved either. It was probably curiosity and because they believed in his healing powers that made them go up there. What the people suffered from was the disorder, the lawlessness. Here were many bandits.[486]

Apparently, life in the San Juan Valley displayed some features close to the stereotypes of the American 'Wild West'. The valley was a rough frontier area, to a great extent inhabited by cattlemen who prided themselves on their recklessness and *macho* courage – qualities they had plenty of opportunity to demonstrate during the upheavals and fights that regularly shook the valley.

During the nineteenth century the most important force in Dominican life was *caudillismo*, with power wielded by local strongmen 'who could combine military skills, economic resources, personal strength, charisma, friendship, family ties, and the ability to manipulate followers'.[487] The central authority in Santo Domingo was seldom strong enough to control all the remote areas of the country. A *caudillo* could thus undisturbed build a power base of loyal people around himself, all tied to him through an intricate web of promises and obligations, and who sought his attachment as a means for political advancement, participation in the power machinery, or simply as a way of finding security in an unruly environment.

The relationship between a 'client' and his *caudillo* was usually strengthened by factual and fictitious kinship. The latter mainly took the form of *compadrazgo*, a kind of coparenthood whereby a person becomes the godparent of a friend's child, thus binding the adults through promises and socioeconomic and religious obligations.[488] A powerful *caudillo* was thus often considered to be some kind of patriarch and was supposed to act like a severe but benevolent father.

It was quite common that the ranks of the *caudillos* swelled because young peasants who had been compulsorily recruited to the army often fled from military service and sought the protection of powerful local *caudillos*, forming part of their armed retinues:

the bad food, the slavery in our dirty military quarters; the carelessness with which he [the soldier] is sent into battle, without field ambulances, or medical doctors; the exposure to a life of corporeal punishments and confinements in filthy prison cells; being assured of the fact

---

486 Interview with Manuel Emilio Mesa, San Juan de la Maguana, 20 January 1989.
487 Calder (1984), p. 116.
488 See Foster (1953a).

that if he is mutilated he will not receive any pension, but has to turn to begging; and much more: because everything is black on the horizon of his life, even the hope that he will be dismissed after serving his term, which depends on whether he is able to find a compassionate protector from the higher spheres of the political power, or if he is able to sell his body and soul to some rapacious little boss [i.e. a *caudillo*].[489]

Caudillos usually surrounded themselves with armed men and throughout Dominican history they had repeatedly taken up arms against Haitian or Spanish invaders, or fought bloody civil wars with competitors among their fellow countrymen. Traditionally they had a very strong influence on national policies. The sitting president had to rely on at least some of them and their private armies in order to retain power while other *caudillos* were easily persuaded to join forces with the adversaries of the government. In such power struggles the strongmen of the San Juan Valley had a great comparative advantage: their proximity to the Haitian border. The neighboring country had traditionally served as the basis of insurrections against the central government and the Dominican *caudillos* cultivated an intense acquaintance with their equals across the border.[490]

On the other side of the border, revolutionaries could always find protection and supplies. The natural base for launching a revolt in the Dominican Republic was Haiti and vice versa. Revolutionary bands moved to and from the San Juan Valley and foreigners and casual visitors tended to avoid the valley because of its reputation as a rough country, populated by bandits and freely roaming cattle. As Samuel Hazard put it in the 1870s: '[The] country west of Azua [finds itself] in a state of suspense similar to that of our Indian frontier.'[491] This state of affairs continued when Olivorio came on stage.

Even if a *caudillo* in the San Juan Valley was considered to be a powerful fellow and habitually referred to his retinue as *his* men, he was in reality a *primus inter pares*, a first among equals. By the beginning of the twentieth century most rural inhabitants of the valley considered themselves to be members of one or another of the *caudillo* clans found in the area, but their apparent loyalty did not mean they felt themselves to be totally at the mercy of 'their' *caudillos*.

Most *Sanjuaneros* denied that they were submitted to any kind of authority and prided themselves on being independent peasants or cattle breeders. Work in the fields of a wealthy landowner like Wenceslao Ramírez was

---

489 Peynado (1909), p. 24.
490 Price-Mars (1953), p. 242.
491 Hazard (1873), p. 243.

Figure 7.12 Ulises Heureaux, president 1882–84, 1887–99.

carried out in the form of *convites*.[492] A San Juan *caudillo* always had to compete with his fellow *caudillos*. It was essential that he had something to offer his clients, e.g. in the form of protection, prestige etc.; otherwise he might easily lose their support.[493]

The 'justice' that was administered by the *caudillos* was swift and merciless, and did not leave much room for deliberations. Thus President Ulises Heureaux in 1898 sent the following instructions to his representative in the valley, Wenceslao Ramírez: 'What is to be done to the burglars who infest these municipalities is to execute them all [...] Give the adequate orders to the Jefes Comunales to be carried out rigorously.'[494]

After Heureaux was murdered in 1899, his decade of *orden y paz* [order and peace] was followed by several years of internal fights between the *caudillos* and their respective bands. Once more, political factions became involved in fierce battles, fought all over the Dominican countryside, and *caudillos* replaced each other as presidents at regular intervals.

Political unrest and fighting frequently created unbearable situations for law-abiding citizens in the San Juan Valley. Thus in 1913 a letter to the editor of a newspaper in Santo Domingo laments the state of anarchy that reigned in San Juan de la Maguana after a period of civil wars. The

492 Probably from *convidar* [invite]. Neighbors and friends are invited in order to clear a field or gather a harvest. After the collective work, which is carried out to the accompaniment of songs and music, the inviting farmer provides food, drinks and entertainment. In the San Juan Valley, *convite* (or *junta*) is still a common denomination for all kinds of unpaid cooperative work (Eusebio Pol (1980), p. 22, and Labourt (1979), pp. 113–19).
493 Cf. Wolf (1966), p. 87.
494 Letter from Heureaux to Ramírez, 14 December, 1898, quoted by Sang (1987), p. 89.

insurgents had not yet been disarmed and the police force promised by the government had failed to arrive:

> They have been on their way for a year now, but the guards have not yet shown up. In the meantime, the undisturbed thieves break locks and destroy houses without being hindered. When the night comes and you must go outside, you walk out with a revolver in your hand, since the shooting goes on from when the sun sets until it rises.[495]

For most of his life Olivorio considered himself a client of Wenceslao Ramírez, but when he formed his own group he began to behave independently. The members of the San Juan elite continued to appeal to the Ramírezes when they wanted to restrict Olivorio's influence, probably considering him to be a Ramírez 'client'. Even if Olivorio, most of the time, treated the Ramírezes with due respect he apparently considered himself to be on an equal footing with them, and it could happen that he behaved somewhat irreverently when they tried to interfere with his mission.[496]

When turmoil and disorder shook the world outside Olivorio's community, people gathered around him. His self-sufficient community was not as vulnerable to the political and socioeconomic changes in the San Juan Valley. Moreover, La Maguana was a holy place where all violence between community members was banned and Olivorio was the undisputed master. He was 'a God apart'[497] and he ruled over a world which was 'apart' as well. If anybody from the outside wanted to deal with him, he had to come in person. His prestige received its final confirmation when the powerful Wenceslao Ramírez, his old employer, accompanied by his son Carmito, came to La Maguana in 1912 to ask for his support in the war they were to wage against the central government.[498] This formal approach by the respected Ramírezes was the final proof that the 'God' and leader of the *Olivoristas*, the former field-hand, had risen to the ranks of the most revered and feared leaders of the valley. Olivorio had become a *caudillo* in his own right.[499]

---

495 *El Radical*, 5 January 1915.
496 Garrido Puello (1963), pp. 35–6. Cf. Rodríguez Varona (1947).
497 Interview with Julián Ramos, Higüerito, 16 January 1989.
498 Interview with Mayobanex Rodríguez, San Juan de la Maguana, 12 December 1985.
499 Such a view may be traced in the way old *Olivoristas* tenderly refer to Olivorio as Papá Olivorio, Daddy Olivorio, or simply *El Viejo*. Several *Olivorista salves* reflect the attraction exercised by Olivorio and his group:

Yo no voy a la montaña.	I am not going to the mountain.
No me vuelvo al cantón ná.	I will never return to the garrison (cantonment).
Yo me voy pa La Maguana,	I am going to La Maguana,
por allá está mi Papá.	because my Father is there.

(*Salve* recorded in Higüerito, Maguana en Medio, 16 January 1986.)

One of the most significant changes that took place in the San Juan Valley of the 1910s was the breakdown of the traditional *caudillo* system. Wenceslao Ramírez had for almost two decades acted as a local enforcer of the politics of the ruthless dictator Heureaux and had later, under the weaker governments that followed the Lilís regime, behaved as an almost sovereign *caudillo*. However, with the arrival of enterprising immigrants of Italian and Syrian descent he experienced how his power and influence declined.

The participation of the Ramírezes in the revolution of 1912 can be interpreted as a last bid for power on both a local and a national level. The attempt was not wholly successful. The Ramírezes felt they were being outmaneuvered by other political forces and Wenceslao Ramírez soon realized that the old ways of life were changing fast. He had already forced his son and heir, Carmito, to become a land surveyor and successively he turned himself into one of the most 'progressive' landowners in the district. Still, just before the arrival of the US troops, a power vacuum existed in the valley. The Ramírezes had difficulties maintaining their authority. Olivorio was not the only local leader who had turned his back on them: several political adversaries smelled future power changes and opposed the Ramírezes openly. A state of anomie took hold of the entire province of Azua.

Such a state of lawlessness constitutes an ideal breeding ground for a movement like *Olivorismo*, which may be interpreted as a flight from anomie. The peasants turned their backs on the chaotic times and sought refuge in the community that was formed around Olivorio, who acted as a charismatic *caudillo* endowed with a heavenly mandate. In his mountain refuge he recreated the 'good old times' when people worked in communion and shared the fruits of their work, while they venerated the lifegiving force of nature through communal feasting, song and dance.

When the occupying US marines arrived in the San Juan Valley the position of the Ramírez family was ambivalent. Several of their opponents believed the Ramírezes were going to fight the invaders in order to safeguard their old privileges. Some anti-Ramírez groups even succeeded in convincing the Americans that Wenceslao and his sons were likely to join forces with Olivorio and offer armed resistance to the marines. However, being a stout and practical politician, the old Wenceslao had already realized where the real power was and to the great astonishment of his enemies he promptly sided with the Americans. This saved the Ramírez position and favored the family when the Americans finally left the San Juan Valley, enabling the Ramírez clan to become the most influential power in the valley once more. However, the traditional ties of the Ramírezes with Olivorio and his band had been damaged, if not entirely severed, in the process.

War and occupation

In the Dominican Republic at the time of Olivorio the possibilities for economic and social advancement within the traditional society were extremely limited. One of the few ways open for social advancement and higher income was by means of association with powerful leaders, with a hope of a reward should they come to power:

> I joined the revolution out of compromise. Nearly everybody did. Esteban Mesa sided with the Ramírezes. He was an old friend of mine and if he went I had to go too. The Ramírezes were the politicians. They always were fervent *Horacistas*.[500] We fought our way to the capital in order to form a government. We were more than 200 youngsters from San Juan de la Maguana and many of us died in Azua, Baní and San Cristóbal.[501]

The attraction of both Ramírez and Olivorio for their respective followers can probably to a large extent be explained by the type of *clientelismo político*[502] to which reference is made in the quotation. They both represented, in different ways, a source of security in a changing and uncertain world and they could, each one in his fashion, reward their followers.

The civil war of 1912 was lost by the *Horacistas*. At the national level it turned out to be disastrous. The United States increased its influence, government finances became even more chaotic than before and the losses in terms of lives and agricultural production were large. The San Juan Valley was greatly affected. Herds of cattle were slaughtered and sold to Haiti to finance the war effort and the economy began to suffer from the lack of labor, since many young men were away from their daily tasks for almost a year.[503] An unknown number of them never returned.

The civil war also served to enhance the power and prestige of Olivorio, whose men came out relatively unharmed. They could return to their isolated *conucos* in the mountains, which had not been touched by the war events – in contrast to the San Juan Valley. The alliance between the peasant god, Olivorio, and the Ramírezes was, however, a very fragile one. Carmito Ramírez served as the main intermediary between the *Olivoristas* and the urban population of the San Juan Valley. He was known to visit Olivorio's community and take part in the festivities. Once he headed a 'commission' set up by businessmen from San Juan de la Maguana who worried about the presence of Olivorio and his armed men in the area. The effort failed, Olivorio treating the commission as 'uninvited spies'.

---

500 Supporters of Horacio Vásquez, president three times between 1899 and 1930.
501 Interview with Manuel Emilio Mesa, Santo Domingo, 20 January 1989.
502 González Canalda (1985a), p. 34.
503 Soler (1913), p. 5.

At other times, Carmito was more successful. In 1912, he managed to win Olivorio's support in the oncoming civil war and in 1916, during the American occupation, he convinced Olivorio that he had to turn his weapons over to the marines. Yet at other times we find Carmito on the side of Olivorio's adversaries. In 1910, he lured Olivorio into a trap set up by his brother Juanico Ramírez, then chief of police, to bring Olivorio to trial in Azua,[504] and when a marine contingent under Major Bearss' command arrived in San Juan de la Maguana in 1917, it was Carmito who served to guide the marines into Olivorio's hideout.[505]

It is not difficult to find a plausible explanation for this inconsistent behavior: 'When judging the contacts between the Ramírezes and Olivorio, one has to keep in mind that the Ramírezes were politicians. Olivorio sometimes proved to be useful to them in various ways [...] they needed his support in order to win the presidency for Horacio Vásquez.'[506]

When the Americans occupied the Dominican Republic, the Ramírezes ran into trouble and one of the charges was their connection with Olivorio. Their political foes plotted against them, the main target being the dashing and vigorous Carmito, the heir of the aging Wenceslao. The American authorities became convinced that Carmito was a potential troublemaker and intriguer and had him thrown in jail. It was Wenceslao's efforts to release his son which presumably convinced the occupation authorities that advantages could be gained from cooperating with the powerful Ramírez family. The governor began to show up as a guest on Wenceslao's hacienda. After helping the marines with Olivorio, Carmito took to surveying the land again and gave the Americans a hand in implementing the law that they had passed concerning the final subdivision of the *terrenos comuneros*. A modern road was then built to Azua and the thorough modernization of agriculture was begun, with strong support from the Ramírezes and other agents of change in the valley.

The political chaos connected with the 1912 civil war provides one of the clues to the attraction of Olivorio. This war to a large extent may be analyzed as a war between rival *caudillo* factions – along nineteenth-century lines. The *caudillo* system, in turn, built on patron–client relations established by the *caudillos* and their men. Olivorio sided with the most powerful *caudillo* in his area, Wenceslao Ramírez, becoming his client. However, at the same time, Olivorio may be viewed as a *caudillo* in his own right – albeit a lesser one than, and subordinate to, Ramírez – a *caudillo* with a very strong appeal to the peasant masses of the San Juan Valley

504 Garrido Puello (1963), p. 26; interview with Víctor Garrido Jr., Santo Domingo, 22 April 1986.
505 Garrido (1970), pp. 103–4.
506 Interview with Mayobanex Rodríguez, San Juan de la Maguana, 18 January 1989.

during a period of economic threats and changes, natural catastrophes and political anarchy, as he represented a return to the way of life that had crystallized itself in principle over the entire period since the Spanish discovery of Hispaniola and which hitherto had survived all attacks from hostile economic and political forces. Olivorio became a fixed point in a time when everything else seemed to be in a state of flux.

Olivorio's relation with the Ramírezes, however, also had a second dimension to it – one which is critical when it comes to understanding why Olivorio was turned into an outlaw by 'established' society. The Ramírezes were some of the principal agents of change in the San Juan Valley during the time of Olivorio, i.e. the fundamental relation with him was an antagonistic one of change versus continuity. Hence the alliance was a precarious one, building almost exclusively on temporary interests, and when it did not suit the Ramírezes to preserve the alliance with Olivorio he was sacrificed in the political game they played. He became a hunted animal who was fair game since he stood in the way of the desired change.

The *gavilleros*

The fate of Olivorio was not unique. During the period when Olivorio appeared and had an impact on life in the San Juan Valley other movements which resisted change appeared in other parts of the country.[507] The most important of these was the so-called *gavillero* uprising, which took place between 1917 and 1922.[508] We will not go into any detailed account of this movement here, but what deserves to be highlighted is the official view of this movement, because it constitutes a very close parallel to the Olivorio case and hence contributes to understanding its fate.

Soon after the US officials had assumed dictatorial powers in the Dominican Republic they had to face fierce opposition from small bands of armed peasants. The fighting was most intense in the east, where the peasants resisted being pushed off their lands by the rapidly expanding sugar companies.[509] However (and for the same reasons), the Americans also met armed opposition in the southwestern districts of Barahona and Azua. Most important among these southern resistance leaders were Andrés Cueva, with his hideouts in the mountain range of Neiba, and, a bit further to the north, Olivorio.

US marine patrols and local police detachments waged an undeclared war against these forces. Most marines were 'unprepared for what soon

---

507 For an overview, see Baud (1988a).
508 Calder (1984), Chapters 5–7, offers a good summary of this uprising. Ducoudray h. (1976) presents a selection of original documents and oral testimonies, while Cassá (1994c), (1994d) and (1994e) discusses the origins of *gavillerismo*.
509 Baud (1988a), p. 131.

degenerated into a brutal and debilitating guerilla war. Much of the onus for this can be placed on the American military's lack of a cohesive, centralized operational command.'[510]

When the fighting ceased in 1922 the commanding general of the US forces in the Dominican Republic summed up the events: 'since the date of occupation the Brigade has had four hundred and sixty seven contacts (467) with bandits, which have resulted in the killing and wounding of eleven hundred and thirty seven bandits (1137) while the Brigade has suffered twenty killed and sixty seven wounded.'[511]

The body count was one of the few measures of success the marines were able to obtain in a war without territorial gains, waged against an enemy who was invisible most of the time. The US estimates of dead and wounded have been called 'fanciful' since they were at best inspired guesses, such as a report which stated: 'The [ammo] pouch was cut by a bullet and blood stains were found nearby. Also a shattered belt buckle was found and from that, I believe, two or three bandits were wounded or killed.'[512]

However, the uncertainty of the figures is no indication that excessive violence was not used during this undeclared war. One gruesome example of this is when twenty-two people from Olivorio's group were relentlessly massacred in less than an hour, eight women and two children being among the victims.[513]

The indiscriminate use of violence clearly has to do with the view that the US authorities held of the resistance movements. 'Bandits' was the common label the marines put on all Dominican peasant fighters and in the monthly intelligence reports Olivorio Mateo often figures among persons listed under the headings of 'bandits'[514] or 'leaders of organized bandit groups'.[515] The word 'bandit', used in such reports, was a direct translation of the Spanish *gavillero*, from *gavillo*,[516] meaning band or gang. This term had earlier been reserved for common outlaws:

510 Musicant (1990), p. 276. 'The men on the ground have been left to their own devices. Admiral Knapp decided to interfere as little as possible and Washington was satisfied. Admiral Snowden who is reported to have said, that he "would be damned if he did anything and damned if he didn't," decided on the former course and Washington was just satisfied' (Kelsey (1922), p. 178). Harry S. Knapp served as US military governor 1916–18, and Thomas Snowden served 1918–21.
511 Lee (1922).
512 Quoted in Calder (1984), p. 158.
513 Morse (1922a).
514 See, for example, Breckenridge (1920) and Maguire (1921). Other groups of 'suspect' individuals were listed under the heading of 'politicians', a category which included former *caudillos*, like members of the Ramírez clan in San Juan de la Maguana.
515 Lee (1922).
516 The original meaning of the term *gavilla* is sheaf (of grain, hay, etc.). From this the figurative meaning of a 'band of many persons and usually of low category' [*junta de muchas personas y comúnmente de baja suerte*] is derived (Real Academia Española (1984), p. 683).

Most were outright professional criminals, full-time highwaymen called *gavilleros*; others were 'peaceful' tillers who worked the soil by day and robbed and killed at night. The *gavilleros* and their cohorts coalesced around some dynamic personality or minor *caudillo* and operated in bands that generally numbered less than fifty men.[517]

Some of these *gavilleros* were outlaws before the US occupation and had been known to terrorize rural communities, extorting money from wealthy people. Still, most *gavilleros* who fought the marines came from a somewhat different background.

Rapidly changing social and economic structures had in certain areas of the Republic deprived formerly independent peasants or cattle breeders of the land they had lived on for centuries and forced several of them to become part of a seasonally employed rural proletariat.[518] When the Americans speeded up the process of land concentration by supporting the claims of big sugar estates and wealthy landowners, the ranks of the *gavilleros* were prone to swell, particularly in the eastern sugar districts but also around the newly developed sugar estates outside Azua and Barahona in the southwest:

> A number of the bandits were displaced smallholders, thrown off their land in complicated deals by [sic] the foreign-owned sugar companies [...] Once a poor peasant became a wage-earner, he was reluctant to return to farming, especially as the roving bandits made that living unprofitable.[519]

Several of the *gavilleros* were also uprooted clients of former *caudillos* and had been active in the series of civil wars beginning in 1912, exactly like Olivorio, and who had learned their trade in these wars.[520] When the US marines arrived in 1916, the *caudillo* system was still thriving in several parts of the Dominican Republic. Desiderio Arias, the only Dominican politician who was able to muster any organized armed resistance to the invading forces, was a full-fledged *caudillo* of the old school, with his stronghold in Santiago de los Caballeros. His life story is typical of a Dominican *caudillo*, with the sole exception that he was of humbler stock than most *caudillos*.

The example given by the Real Academia to illustrate the meaning is a band of rascals [*GAVILLA de pícaros*] (ibid.). The term *gavillero* had been in use in the Dominican Republic since the nineteenth century, but it was not until 1902 that *gavillerismo* came to be used as a term for politically inspired guerilla activities, often in the borderland between politics and outright criminality (Cassá (1994c), p. 13).

517 Musicant (1990), p. 276.
518 Calder (1984), p. 119.
519 Musicant (1990), p. 276.
520 Cf. Cassá (1994d).

Figure 7.13 Desiderio Arias.

Like his father before him, he had been attached to the Jimenes clan in the northwestern part of the Dominican Republic. He had participated in the complicated revolutionary struggles which dominated Dominican politics at the beginning of the twentieth century, and in these wars he had learned to master all the tactics which later became commonplace for *gavilleros* fighting the US marines: i.e. to fight with great mobility, breaking camp as often as possible, attacking only when he was sure to win and preferably from ambushes, using Haitian territory for regrouping and as a haven, trying to win over the local population through gifts and services, and letting periods of intense activity be followed by times of complete rest and inactivity, periods during which the fighters went back to the carrying out of their daily chores as common peasants.[521] Olivorio Mateo and his men later used identical tactics.

As Arias gradually rose to power he made use of the traditional *caudillo* sources of income, such as holding concessions from custom houses and the state-owned railway company. When he finally obtained a ministerial portfolio he demanded that his followers would be given the customary 30 to 40 percent of the appointments to official posts, as well as other benefits[522] – a natural consequence of the *clientelismo* system. Arias' behavior led the Americans to brand him as a 'bandit', a term which offended several Dominicans.[523] After all, Arias had only displayed the standard behavior of

521 González Canalda (1985a), p. 33.
522 Ibid., p. 35.
523 González (1984), pp. 210–11.

any Dominican *caudillo*, or president for that matter. Furthermore, he was a strict follower of the unwritten, moral code of all 'honest' *caudillos*: He was opposed to dictatorship and censorship, supported direct elections, did not violate the constitution and never forgot to instruct his soldiers to treat the rural population with decency and respect.[524] Moreover, he was a great patriot and a fierce opponent to all US meddling in Dominican domestic affairs.

Arias was the last leader on a national level who was defeated by the Americans, but most *gavilleros* who continued the fight against the foreign invaders had either been local *caudillos* themselves or members of former *caudillo* retinues. Whether they were 'bandits', in the sense of regular criminals, as the Americans and the interests related to them thought, appears doubtful indeed. Even if most Dominican guerilla fighters were moved more by personal than purely political considerations,[525] several incidents indicate that they considered their struggle to be a political one. When one *gavillero* group in Las Pajas in the eastern part of the Republic was taunted for being bandits by their pursuers, several angered *gavilleros* cried out from their hideouts: '[We] are not gavilleros; we are revolutionists!'[526] Accordingly, it is difficult to draw a straight line between 'banditry' and what may be called politicized and organized guerilla resistance. In this, the *gavillero* fighting in the Dominican Republic resembled several other contemporary Latin American resistance movements, particularly the Cuban *Chambelona* movement.[527]

Even if *gavilleros* occasionally robbed small company shops on the sugar estates or even molested Dominicans in outlying areas or killed 'traitors' within their own ranks, it is evident that they enjoyed strong popular support and that they were 'something other than the "bandits" born of military propaganda and accepted by subsequent writers – they were peasant guerrillas fighting for principles and a way of life'.[528]

---

524 González Canalda (1985a), p. 37.
525 Unemployment, loss of land or hurt patriotic feelings were not the only reasons for people to join the guerillas. Piques, due to racist gibes from American soldiers, also served as an incentive to take up arms, as well as the unnecessary violence the Americans were inclined to use when they hunted down the guerilla fighters (Calder (1984), pp. 123–7).
526 Ibid., p. 121. 'All resistance was "banditry" to the Marines, even when it was organized, using flags and uniforms' (Knight (1928), p. 110). Among the *gavillero* leaders was the old *caudillo*, General 'Chachá' Goicochea (Cassá (1983), p. 230).
527 Pérez (1987). As in the Dominican Republic, many of the 'bandits' connected with the *Chambelona* movement, which was concentrated in the Cuban sugar districts, were uprooted peasants who disliked the big sugar estates and the US presence in their country. Some of them had earlier been followers of both local and national political leaders.
528 Calder (1984), p. 132.

They shared this quality with Olivorio, although not in the eyes of the 'modernizing' forces and the occupation authorities.

A social bandit

For many of his contemporaries Olivorio and the *gavilleros* were 'bandits', but not for all of them. Several Dominicans considered the label utterly unjust and objected to its use, thinking instead in terms of 'peasant compatriots' or 'resistance movements' and the like. In one sense the choice of terminology is trivial, since it all depends on whether the users were sympathetic or not to the object labeled. 'Bandits' was a standard term employed by the Americans and their followers for what many popular domestic strata thought of as resistance movements and *guerrilleros* in the countries occupied by the United States around this time.

In another sense, however, the 'bandit' label acquires an analytical importance: when we start to think of Olivorio and his movement in terms of 'social' banditry in the sense of Eric Hobsbawm,[529] i.e. without the degrading connotations of the contemporary American use, the term being laden with positive ('social') values instead. In spite of the fact that Olivorio's movement was a religious one, it contains enough 'social bandit' features to allow us to put it in the Hobsbawm category.

In the first place, there are the obvious parallels between Olivorio and some of the traditional *caudillos* and *gavilleros*. Thus, social anthropologist Nancie González defines Desiderio Arias as a 'Hobsbawmian' social bandit[530] and Bruce Calder puts the *gavilleros* into a similar context:

> The condition of the uprooted Dominican peasantry corresponds closely to that which Eric Hobsbawm has found most favorable to social banditry. Upsurges of this phenomenon, he writes, often 'reflect the disruption of an entire society, the rise of new classes and social structures, the resistance of entire communities or peoples against the destruction of its way of life.'[531]

The quotation may be applied to Olivorio with as much right as to the *gavilleros*. Many of the features ascribed to him directly point towards his place in the category of 'social bandits'.[532]

529 Hobsbawm (1959), (1972).
530 González (1984), pp. 206–12.
531 Calder (1984), p. 119. The quotation is from Hobsbawm (1972), p. 23.
532 It should be noted that the notion of 'social bandits' has been questioned altogether. Hobsbawm's theory has thus become subject to intense debate, triggering research on bandits all over the world. See, for example, Crummey (1986), Slatta (1987), (1991), Joseph (1990), (1991), and Birkbeck (1991) to mention but a few works. 'Intermediate'

Like most other social bandits Olivorio never opted for becoming an outlaw. Society made him one. After his trial in Azua in 1910, Olivorio realized that he would not be tolerated by the authorities and therefore moved his quarters to a secluded area of the Cordillera Central, whereupon government troops followed him, attacked his supporters and burned his hideout. This corresponds well to the traditional beginning of a social bandit career: 'The State shows an interest in a peasant because of some minor infraction of the Law, and the man takes to the hills because how does he know what a system which does not know or understand peasants, and which peasants do not understand, will do to him?'[533]

Olivorio not only began his career in the standard social bandit way, he also finished it in accordance with traditional requirements, by being betrayed by members of his own band.

According to Hobsbawm, a social bandit is a peasant outlaw, regarded as a criminal by those who wield power in the society, i.e. landowners and authorities, but as a hero by folks of his own kind.[534] 'It is important that the incipient social bandit should be regarded as "honourable" or non-criminal by the population, for if he was regarded as a criminal against local convention, he could not enjoy the local protection on which he must rely completely.'[535]

A social bandit must not steal or rob from his own kind, and Olivorio apparently never did anything to upset the peasant population. He shared their values and was a part of their society. Thus he passes the test with flying colors, since not only was he 'honorable' but he actively helped the peasants through his thaumaturgical and religious activities. The American reports from the period clearly indicate his popularity among the peasantry: 'the inhabitants act as his spies and supply his band with provisions, even rum';[536] 'every countryman in this commune [San Juan de la Maguana] looks upon Olivorio as a saint'.[537]

Related to this is the 'Robin Hood criterion' of stealing from the rich to give to the poor, a quality which we know is attributed to Olivorio, who also came from the lower echelons of rural Dominican society, being a landless laborer. Also, to qualify as a Hobsbawmian social bandit 'the characteristic

views have been advanced as well, e.g. by Chandler (1987), pp. 99–100: 'Is Hobsbawm talking about bandits in the flesh or the legends about them? [...] It need not be argued that Hobsbawm is totally wrong. His work is provocative, and the force of many of his ideas has an almost irresistible appeal. Bandits, especially when they lived long ago and, more crucially, far away, strike our fancy. His thesis has some validity, no doubt, even if peripherally.'

533 Hobsbawm (1959), p. 16.
534 Hobsbawm (1972), p. 14.
535 Hobsbawm (1959), p. 16.
536 Feeley (1919).
537 Bales (1920).

victims' of the bandit's activities must be the 'quintessential enemies of the poor', among those 'foreigners and others who upset the traditional life of the peasant.'[538] Olivorio was wanted by the Americans and the traditional elite, the two groups who together tried to implant radical changes in the San Juan area and hence constituted a threat to the peasants and their time-honored ways. Olivorio was thus a social bandit in the sense that he represented traditional values in a non-revolutionary fashion: 'social banditry, though a protest, is a modest and unrevolutionary protest. It protests not against the fact that peasants are poor and oppressed. [...] The bandit's practical function is at best to impose certain limits to traditional oppression in a traditional society ...'[539]

A social bandit does not kill indiscriminately – only in self-defense or to avenge injustice.[540] With a single exception, contemporary reports regarding Olivorio's band unanimously state that his band never disturbed any rural inhabitants. Lieutenant Colonel Thorpe, who wrote the deviating report, appears to have been unfamiliar with the area and his statement about Olivorio's unpopularity is contradicted by the fact that he, as most other leaders of search parties that went after *El Maestro*, never received any substantial support from the peasants and accordingly did not accomplish much.[541] It was only when he was attacked by the police and the military that Olivorio resorted to violence, and then only if there was no other way out. Besides, participating in the struggle against the Americans was 'just', since the Americans were invaders both in Haiti and in the Dominican Republic.

Even if Olivorio could be considered as a bandit, at least in the Hobsbawmian sense of the word, it appears as if the Americans after a while became rather reluctant to label him as such. Even if, as mentioned above, US marine reports sometimes called him a bandit, they occasionally placed him in another category. Thus the first official US report mentioning Olivorio, refers to him as 'the well known revolutionist Olivorio'.[542] A report issued four months later mentions him as a 'religious and medical fanatic, seriously self-styled a Saint',[543] and in later reports he is routinely labeled 'religious fanatic'.[544] Even if Olivorio easily fits into the bandit category the Americans apparently considered him to be something more.

538 Hobsbawm (1959), p. 22.
539 Ibid., p. 24.
540 Hobsbawm (1972), p. 35.
541 'Certainly Olivorio is a great curse to the people of the whole part of Azua Province north of San Juan. Most of the people know it and would be glad to be rid of him but fear to oppose him or give information' (Thorpe (1918a)).
542 Ramsey (1917).
543 Chief of Staff (1917).
544 Cf. Breckenridge (1920) and McNamee (1921).

Olivorio's appeal

The fact that Olivorio shared a number of characteristics with the group defined as 'social bandits' is important when it comes to understanding his appeal among the Dominican peasants. Being fairly close to the archetype of one of the most important kinds of primitive rebels, one inevitably idealized and idolized by the local peasant population, goes a long way towards explaining his charisma.

It could be argued that charisma had nothing to do with Olivorio's success. According to Peter Worsley prophets appear all the time, but it is only in times of crisis that people listen to them, because then their message is attractive and that message is often the millenarian one: the outsiders will perish and the believers, the formerly oppressed, will rule the world.[545] We will soon discuss the importance of crisis, but first it should be stated that Worsley's argument may not fit Olivorio's (or Plinio and Romilio Ventura's) case. The *Olivorista* movement was strangely centered on its leaders and reflected the peasants' confidence in 'strong' men. As we will note in the discussion of Palma Sola in Chapter 8, to be a mediator between the spiritual and the terrestrial spheres requires extraordinary 'powers', some amount of charisma, and this charisma must be *demonstrated*, e.g. by thaumaturgical action. This Olivorio did. He healed the sick and thereby convinced the peasants that he was a leader with extraordinary powers.

Quite probably charismatic qualities were needed in another way as well. Gerrit Huizer has pointed out that this is a feature of the initial stages of the formation of peasant organization virtually everywhere in Latin America.[546] It is needed simply because the environment in which the organizers have to operate is a notoriously risky one that easily crushes the movement while it is still embryonic. In this environment, strong personal qualities are needed.

However, Olivorio's personal characteristics do not provide more than a partial explanation of his success, for a peasant hero, as Hobsbawm has pointed out, cannot be conceived of outside his social and economic environment, i.e. outside the peasant society that exists when he makes his appearance.[547] Thus, to complete the picture, we must make use of the socioeconomic information gathered in the present chapter.

During the period when Olivorio began his work, the San Juan Valley was in a state of social and economic change which threatened the already precarious positions of the type of people who were attracted to the new movement. Olivorio provided these people with an alternative to the new

545 Worsley (1970), p. 289.
546 Huizer (1973), pp. 120–2.
547 Hobsbawm (1972), p. 58.

economic and social conditions that were emerging. From the point of view of the *Olivoristas* this alternative had two clear advantages. In the first place it constituted an exit option in the sense of Albert Hirschman,[548] i.e. when the peasants perceived that their situation was deteriorating, they were given a possibility to enter a new society where the rules had not been made to their disadvantage. Michael Adas, in his investigations of Asia, has described the same phenomenon as 'avoidance protest', i.e. the sectarian withdrawal of the *Olivoristas* operated to minimize the possibility of a clash with the forces that were reshaping Dominican society.[549]

It is particularly important to note that the world in which these peasants were living was not a 'stable' world, but a world that was beginning to change, and these changes were perceived as threats to the economic and social order that had been established over a period of four centuries, and in particular to the place of the peasants in this order. In this situation there were three options. The first was to adapt to the changes, the second to try to change them (voice in Hirschman's terminology) and the third to opt out of the society in question (exit). Since the changes were perceived as unfavorable, adaption was not an alternative, and since the San Juan peasants were 'pre-political' people who had 'not yet found, or only begun to find, a specific language in which to express their aspirations about the world'[550] that was emerging among them, much against their will, voice was an inefficient option.

Second, *Olivorismo* offered an alternative that could be understood by the peasants. Religion and secular matters were closely intertwined in daily peasant life and, as was demonstrated in Chapter 6, it must be assumed that Olivorio was deeply rooted in the religious environment that existed when he had his vision and, vice versa, much of what he preached was an expression of what the peasants already felt.[551] *Olivorismo* was a movement that sprang from among the peasants themselves and which interpreted the world in terms that could be understood, not least supernatural ones.

The society that was emerging in the San Juan Valley did not offer any satisfactory choices for the peasants. Olivorio did. The sick were healed and a religious belief was provided. There was, however, more to it than that. In a system dominated by large landowners, the peasants would be highly dependent on these for incomes. Besides, the new intermediary

---

548 Hirschman (1970). Cf. also Hirschman (1981).
549 Adas (1981), p. 217.
550 Hobsbawm (1959), p. 2.
551 This is the characteristic situation in the type of societies where Olivorio appeared. Cf. ibid., p. 65: 'The kinds of community which produced millenarian heresies are not the ones in which clear distinctions between religious and secular things can be drawn. To argue about whether [...] a sect is religious *or* social is meaningless, for it will automatically and always be both in some manner.' (Cf. also Hobsbawm (1972), p. 31.)

class (which at times coincided with the landowner class) provided a threat to the traditional commerce carried on by the peasants with Haiti which, furthermore, was threatened by the control attempts carried out under the American customs receivership. In the *Olivorista* community, production and marketing was organized along completely different lines.

Garrido Puello reports that in El Naranjo the fields were cultivated with the aid of the *convite*, 'which permitted them to get products from the land without much muscular fatigue. The women and the children participated in these works.'[552] The output obtained was divided equally among the participants.[553] The *convite* (*konbit* in Haitian Creole)[554] constitutes a form of communal or cooperative work which is used on both sides of the border in Hispaniola for especially demanding tasks, in particular clearing and harvesting the fields.[555] The practice builds on reciprocity principles, the peasants taking part in clearing each other's fields in turn. On top of this it offers an opportunity for social activities and festivities for the participants.[556] This organization of production, which built on old peasant traditions, was a far cry from what the inhabitants of the San Juan Valley could look forward to in a system dominated by large landowners.[557] In addition, distribution was egalitarian. What Olivorio received from his devotees was redistributed among the members of his community.[558] According to one of his old followers, he 'was for the people and helped the poor. He would go around with a mule loaded with food that he was giving out.'[559]

Commerce was organized differently as well. Whereas the new commercial currents following the rise of the sugar industry in Barahona were concentrated on exchange of food from the San Juan area against imported goods and rum from Barahona and Azua, Olivorio and his people continued to trade with Haiti, apparently quite successfully. 'The flow of people, more numerous every day, favored the commerce of the place [El Palmar] and the establishment of a market with a nearby

552 Garrido Puello (1963), p. 34.
553 Blanco Fombona (1927), p. 28, claims that 'communism' existed among the *Olivoristas*.
554 Elsewhere in the Dominican Republic this form of cooperation was known under other names. Baud (1995), p. 59, refers to *juntas gratuitas* and *juntas de vecinos* in the Cibao.
555 The *convites* employed in the border areas frequently consisted of people from both Haiti and the Dominican Republic, up to the closure of the border in 1937 (Palmer (1976), p. 90).
556 For an analysis of the Haitian *konbit*, see Lundahl (1979), pp. 110–18 and (1983).
557 Possibly Olivorio took an anti-*latifundista* stance as well. It has been claimed by his later followers that Olivorio wanted to distribute land to the peasants. (Cf. Cordero Regalado (1981), p. 17-A.) Whether this was actually the case is, however, impossible to determine unless contemporary sources indicating this are uncovered.
558 Garrido Puello (1963), p. 27.
559 Interview with Julián Ramos, Higüerito, 16 January 1986.

cockfight arena in La Sigua, Hato Nuevo, in the same jurisdiction', writes Garrido Puello.[560] Olivorio was accused of smuggling Haitian rum and *kleren* across the border, which was probably true.[561] Again, in these commercial ventures, he provided a 'traditional' alternative to the new threatening economic and social order that was about to establish itself in the San Juan Valley.

Thus it is not difficult to explain why Olivorio received such an enthusiastic reception from the peasants of the valley. The social and economic balance there – 'the traditional way of life' – was threatened as the modern market economy was making its presence felt.[562] In the valley, as elsewhere in the Dominican Republic, 'resources pivotal to the reproduction of the peasant economy acquired an economic value that they had lacked in the past'.[563] The peasants were facing a very patent risk of being turned into paupers. In this situation, Olivorio, however 'radical' his movement may have appeared to outside observers, essentially represented a 'conservative' response to the new, unfamiliar and frightening society that was being constructed. He provided continuity rather than change, retaining the traditional social and economic life when this was about to undergo a change for the worse in the eyes of the peasants. His message was 'nativistic', i.e. it represented a 'conscious attempt ... to revive or perpetuate selected aspects' of the old peasant culture.[564]

Olivorio of course was aided by the apocalyptic circumstances under which he appeared, delivering his initial message to peasants who had just witnessed a natural catastrophe, followed later by an omen, Halley's Comet and an earthquake. Typically, Olivorio got most of his followers from the driest and poorest parts of the southwest, not only from the San Juan Valley, but also from dry areas further to the south.[565] He was also fortunate in that he appeared during a period of social and political chaos in the Dominican Republic. No government was strong enough to wipe the movement out, having its hands full with combating factions in the struggle over power. Instead, as we have seen several times, factions attempted to make Olivorio side with them.

---

560 Garrido Puello (1963), p. 27.
561 Ibid. Feeley (1919) contains a list of 'bandits, followers of "Olivorio"' and the offenses commited by them. In this list, two instances of 'smuggling rum' appear. The peasants of the San Juan Valley produced their own liquor, but the quality of the Haitian one was better (interview with Julián Ramos, Higüerito, 16 January 1986). The Dominican peasants took their molasses to Haiti to have it distilled there (Cano y Fortuna (n.d.), p. 57).
562 Cf. Baud (1986), p. 10.
563 San Miguel (1987), p. 359.
564 Linton (1943), p. 230.
565 Cf. e.g. the interview with Mayobanex Rodríguez, San Juan de la Maguana, 12 December 1985.

Who killed Olivorio?

Olivorismo had deep roots in the changes that took place in the San Juan Valley during the first two decades of the twentieth century. It is in these changes that its success as a popular movement must be sought. It is also here that we find the reasons why the movement was brutally crushed in 1922.

In the account in Chapter 2 of the events that took place between 1908 and 1922 we pointed to the fact that sometimes the *Olivoristas* were left in relative peace, whereas at other times they were subject to persecution. What finally decided their fate was that the American occupation authorities felt that the movement should be brought to an end. The question then becomes: 'Why?'

The main concern of the Americans was that of pacifying the Dominican Republic. Garrido Puello emphatically states that the American persecution of Olivorio had nothing to do with his religious or thaumaturgical activities, remarking sarcastically that 'Olivorio as a religious left the Yankee military cold and unfeeling, accustomed as they were to looking with humoristic tolerance upon the confessional restlessness in their [own] enormous country'.[566] On the other hand, Olivorio was acting at a time when the occupation forces already had a guerilla war on their hands in the eastern part of the country while at the same time Charlemagne Péralte was stirring the Haitians on the other side of the border, and, as we know, Olivorio's men quite probably took part in Péralte's fights against the marines.

The contacts across the border constituted a recurrent source of trouble for the Americans. Weapons and ammunition traveled from one side to the other and the insurgents were not restricted in their movements by the ill-defined line of demarcation between the two countries. In the last volume of his monumental study of the American occupation of Haiti, Roger Gaillard points to the elimination of the Dominican 'sanctuary' as one of the factors that made *caco* activities hopeless after 1921:

> One of the first military tasks of the Occupation was the sealing of the border, especially on both sides of the Massacre River. The peasants of Maribaroux, the traditional 'steamroller' of the cacoism, could thereafter not take refuge among their neighbors (who came from the same social situation and the same ethnic group), nor could they receive any money or weapons from them, nor dispose of nearby infirmaries or secret ammunition depots in their fields. With the exterior base thus destroyed, rebellion was easier to crush.[567]

566 Garrido Puello (1963), pp. 39–40.
567 Gaillard (1983), pp. 251–2.

Thus the Americans were eager to stamp out 'subversive' contacts across the Haitian-Dominican border. 'Bandits' from one side of the border often had to be pursued into the neighboring country.[568] This naturally made the occupation force alert to all reports regarding peasant bands that could possibly develop into guerilla units.

Nevertheless, it seems that for quite some time Olivorio was not considered any serious threat by the Americans. In particular, once the Haitian *caco* uprising had been put down in 1920, the American interest in him dwindled.[569] In his Christmas Day memorandum that year, the commanding officer of the *Guardia Nacional Dominicana* in San Juan, William Bales, had the following to say:

> I have been in this Province more than a year and during that time have never heard of Livorio or his followers molesting anyone. [...] I do not believe that the Comun of San Juan is suffering from Livorio or his group. [...] People from half the Republic come to him to get medicine. Due to the veneration in which he is held in this province it is hopeless to get definite information about him. His principal offense is harboring a few criminals.[570]

On 11 January 1921, James McLean, director of the *Departamento del Sur*, forwarded the information to the commandant of the *Guardia Nacional*, adding, among other things, the following:

> They are never hostile and invariably refuse to fight as a band even when attacked ... Olivorio Mateo would surrender if assured that he and his followers would not be prosecuted and be allowed to go free. It perhaps would be a good thing to have him surrender himself, but a number of his followers are accused of crimes for which they are wanted by Civil Courts. These cannot be offered immunity.[571]

Thus it appears as if the Americans considered Olivorio a minor nuisance only. But then, why persecute him? The answer to this question must be sought among those Dominicans who had a personal interest in putting an end to Olivorio's activities. Garrido Puello reports that when President Juan Isidro Jimenes had fallen from power in May 1916, *Olivorismo* had grown so strong that 'the population of San Juan de la Maguana' felt uneasy and frightened by the threat 'against property and family' represented

---

568 Cf. ibid., pp. 122–3, for a contemporary report of such an expedition.
569 Bales (1920), McLean and Pina Chevalier (1921), p. 174, McLean (1921).
570 Bales (1920).
571 McLean (1921).

by Olivorio and his followers. At that point, 'some merchants' asked the American military government for protection. A meeting consisting of 'merchants and respectable persons' from San Juan took place, and at the initiative of General Wenceslao Ramírez, i.e. the local *caudillo*, a deputation (which, however, failed), including among others Carmito Ramírez, was sent off to Olivorio to persuade him to put his weapons down.[572]

The Ramírezes, father and son, as we know, were also active when, in the following year, the marines, under Colonel Bearss, started to move against Olivorio.[573] Somewhat earlier the two generals had offered their assistance to the Americans when they were able to make Olivorio and his men hand over their weapons.

They were not alone in their views. For much of the urban bourgeoisie Olivorio became the symbol of the backwardness and the anarchism they held to be characteristic of the peasants that had earlier given the San Juan Valley its special features: peasants with freely roaming cattle herds, rudimentary agriculture, trade with Haiti and the openness to cultural influences from that country.

It is fairly clear that the opposition to Olivorio came from those who stood to lose in purely pecuniary terms if his movement became successful – landowners and merchants – and that these groups spread the rumor to the Americans that Olivorio was a dangerous criminal, in terms that appealed to the American fear of *cacos* and *gavilleros*, to further their own interests. It may thus be argued that Olivorio fell victim to a 'conspiracy of the rich'.[574] As was natural, the agents of economic change in the area, the agents of penetrating capitalism, if you will, regarded tradition-based peasant movements like the one led by Olivorio as an obstacle to change and thus united to form a powerful lobby. The existing set of property rights in particular had to change if the economy was to develop in the direction envisaged by these interests. The *Olivoristas*, on the other hand, represented the old times, a system based on communal ownership of land, coupled with communal worship and equality principles, and a hopelessly antiquated mode of production from the capitalist perspective.

This, and not primarily the American desire to stamp out 'bandits', is what sealed Olivorio's fate. It also explains why Olivorio has been portrayed as a madman with mainly criminals among his followers by Emigdio Garrido Puello and his brother Víctor Garrido, culturally the most prominent persons in the San Juan area during Olivorio's time. Together they edited *El Cable*, the newspaper of San Juan founded by Emigdio, that propagated liberal, capitalist ideas.

572 Garrido Puello (1963), pp. 34–6.
573 Garrido (1970), p. 104.
574 This phrase was coined by Thomas More (quoted by Hobsbawm (1959), p. 4).

Figure 7.14 Víctor Garrido.

   The brothers were intimately connected with the type of interests that wanted to modernize the San Juan Valley. They came from a family of merchants and military officers and were the sons of a local *caudillo*. Víctor Garrido was to become the son-in-law of General Wenceslao Ramírez. (Later, during the Trujillo era, he was to rise to political prominence, serving as minister in several of Trujillo's cabinets and as attorney general of the country.)[575] Emigdio, in turn, was married to Dulce María, the daughter of Carmito Ramírez, Wenceslao's son and successor as the most powerful *caudillo* of the San Juan Valley. Thus, the views of the Garrido brothers on Olivorio were the views of the strong landowner and merchant class that was being created in San Juan at the time. Their social background makes it clear why they sided with the interests that combated Olivorio.

575 Garrido's autobiography (1970) makes interesting reading. 'Another of the Dominican intellectuals who changed from being an adversary to becoming a staunch follower of Trujillo was Lic. Víctor Garrido. Endowed with a passionate temperament and being a man of radical sentiments, upright in his intentions, and loyal to the point of exaggeration in his political behavior, he adopted without reservations the Trujillista cause and served the dictator with devotion and sincerity, from the highest public positions' (Balaguer (1989), p. 239).

8 A new era

Economic change, politics and Palma Sola, 1922–63

The American heritage

The members of the San Juan elite in the 1920s were men with a view to the future. They wanted to develop the agriculture and the commerce of their *común*. Their goal was to adapt the 'outdated' economic life of the San Juan Valley to the demands of a rapidly changing market economy. This made some of them embark on an intense effort to modernize their 'backward' environment. Even if several acted as, and probably felt like, fierce Dominican patriots and took every opportunity to condemn the United States intervention, most accepted the American presence and tried to take advantage of the foreign presence, silently giving their consent to the stability and change it brought about.

The local population had grown considerably during the past fifty years. In 1920, according to the census taken that year, the province of Azua, which included the San Juan Valley, had a population of more than 100,000,[1] against less than 55,000 in 1914 and less than 60,000 in 1917,[2] and the *común* of San Juan alone more than 32,000,[3] against possibly less than 5,000 at the beginning of the 1870s.[4] Thus, both the size of the local market and the size of the local labor force had increased.

Also, transportation was improving. During the 1910s, the state of the roads had effectively precluded trade on a large scale. One of the main concerns of the American occupation forces had been the poor condition of the Dominican communication system. It was common that enlisted men and officers complained when they had to go on missions to remote places like the San Juan Valley. Not only did they find the isolation of the place depressing; the trip in itself was also very exhausting. A US marine

---

1 Moreta (1986), p. 102.
2 Boin and Serulle Ramia (1981), p. 251.
3 Moreta (1986), p. 102.
4 *Informe* (1960), p. 75.

Figure 8.1 Calle Trinitaria, San Juan de la Maguana, 1925.

report from 1918 laments the deplorable condition of most Dominican roads and stresses the fact that this had severely limited the marines' efforts to fight 'bandits'. The report mentions that it took at least '4 to 5 days for mounted troops and from 5 to 7 days for foot troops' to reach Azua from Santo Domingo. Azua could also be reached from the sea and the marines had two small vessels at their disposal, but the vessels were described as 'unseaworthy' with bottoms that could 'drop out any time'. The boats made about five knots an hour and could carry about fifteen to twenty-five men 'depending on weather'. In good conditions the boat trip from Santo Domingo to Azua could be made in fourteen hours, but it could also require thirty-five hours if the sea was rough.[5]

Thus a far-reaching program of road construction topped the list of priorities of the US military government, and already in 1917 work was begun on a network of roads intended to link the eastern, western and northern parts of the country with the capital. One road, the Carretera Duarte, was planned to go through Santiago to Monte Cristi in the north, a second one, the Carretera Mella, would pass through El Seibo and Higüey to La Romana, thus linking the east with the capital, and a third one, the Carretera Sánchez, was to be directed westward through Azua and San Juan de la Maguana to the Haitian frontier. However, World War I crippled the whole road-building program and at the time of the American withdrawal in 1924 Carretera Sánchez had not advanced beyond

5 Thorpe (1918e).

Figure 8.2 Road conditions in the Dominican Republic, 1917.

Azua.[6] Still, the construction of these roads resulted in a complete change of Dominican social life and economy. Trucks replaced the slow and awkward mule trails which earlier had transported all goods to and from the country's isolated parts, like the San Juan Valley.

The first motor vehicle came to San Juan de la Maguana in 1918. Upon this innovation, the authorities of San Juan and Azua decided to repair the road between the two cities, which at that point only had 15 kilometers in acceptable shape.[7] In May 1924 Collado & Marra, one of the trading houses in San Juan, could offer regular transport service with large trucks all the way to the capital.[8] Since the Americans were unable to promise its completion before their final withdrawal, it was the *ayuntamientos* of San Juan de la Maguana and Azua which, on the initiative of the energetic Domingo Rodríguez, completed and paved the road between their respective towns.[9] As soon as the road had been finished, the two *Sanjuaneros* who had provided most of the transports of goods between Azua and the San Juan Valley, Flor Marra and Liberato Marranzini, both sold their mules and bought trucks instead.[10]

Already in 1918 Carmito Ramírez and Domingo Rodríguez had bought the valley's first tractors and invited agricultural experts from Puerto Rico to advise the large landowners in the area about the efficient use of mechanical equipment and give instruction about other modern methods

---

6 Calder (1984), pp. 49–52. Cf. Moya Pons (1986), pp. 215–16. The section between Baní and Azua was officially inaugurated on 27 February, 1924 (*El Cable*, 1 January 1924).
7 Moreta (1986), p. 105.
8 *El Cable*, 3 May, 1924.
9 Garrido Puello (1981), p. 104.
10 Interview with Maximiliano Rodríguez Piña, Santo Domingo, 23 April 1986.

for efficient agriculture.[11] Soon Emigdio Garrido Puello could advertise in his newspaper, *El Cable*, that he had become the local agent of the Fordson tractors:

> The day does not appear to be far away, when the tractor will replace the ox in the toilsome task of plowing and pulling heavy burdens, a work through which the patient beast suffers great hardship, until its existence is finally ended in the slaughterhouse.[12]

> Increase your profits by cultivating with a Fordson.[13]

> Fordson, the universal tractor: buy your own today. Do not leave it until tomorrow.[14]

Garrido Puello was also the general agent for several other American companies which manufactured agricultural machinery and agricultural inputs.[15] Later on, in the mid-1920s, he established a garage and a repair shop. He sold trucks of the Diamond make, which came in pieces and were assembled in his workshop.[16]

The agricultural pattern of the San Juan Valley was undergoing a gradual change. Slowly but steadily, the cultivation of beans, plantains, rice, manioc, potatoes, coffee and peanuts gained importance in the valley.[17] The better communications opened up bigger markets for *Sanjuanero* products, and after 1920 the merchants of San Juan de la Maguana enhanced their influence in the rural *comunes* of the province, buying agricultural produce from the peasants to an increasing extent.[18] As shown in Chapter 7, at the time of the publication of the *Libro azul*, in 1920, the San Juan merchants had already established a regular trade network with the surrounding countryside, and this network was extended and strengthened during the next decade. Some of the products grown in the valley even left the country. Beans were exported to Puerto Rico,[19] to an extent which made Víctor Garrido, in 1922, refer to this trade as a 'flourishing export business'. At this time, in addition, rice, maize, pigeon peas

---

11 Interview with Mimicito Ramírez, San Juan de la Maguana, 14 December 1985.
12 *El Cable*, 9 February 1924.
13 *El Cable*, 5 February 1923.
14 *El Cable*, 21 July 1925.
15 Ibid.
16 Interview with Carlos Peguero Matos, San Juan de la Maguana, 4 July 1990.
17 Interview with Mimicito Ramírez, San Juan de la Maguana, 14 December 1985. Cf. Boin and Serulle (1981), pp. 252–3.
18 Moreta (1986), p. 87.
19 Ibid., pp. 79–80.

Figure 8.3 The public market-place of San Juan de la Maguana, 1925.

[*guandules*], chick-peas, (different types of) plantains [*plátanos, rulos*], yucca, sweet potatoes, sugar cane and tobacco were cultivated.[20]

During the 1920s, the conversion of the San Juan Valley from a cattle-raising area to a region dominated by agricultural production gained momentum. The Americans favored foreign investment and supported the expansion of agricultural enterprises, particularly within the sugar sector. The most important market for the Dominican sugar was the United States. In 1919 new customs tariffs were introduced which exempted a large number of American manufactured goods from taxes, thus favoring big foreign and local investors.[21] These policies stimulated the growth of agro-industries south of the San Juan Valley, notably the expansion of the sugar industry in Azua and the foundation of a huge American-owned *ingenio* in Barahona, which began production of refined sugar in 1921.[22] Since food-producing areas thus had been converted into

20 Garrido (1922), p. 227. Garrido maintained that the tobacco produced in San Juan de la Maguana, and especially in the *sección* of Yabonico, was as good as that of the Cibao, the tobacco region *par excellence* in the Dominican Republic, and that San Juan should be turned into a tobacco center, like Santiago de los Caballeros.
21 Moya Pons (1986), pp. 215, 217–18.
22 Organized in New York in 1916, the Barahona Company Inc. started to clear and prepare large areas around Barahona in 1917. Through the purchase of numerous *terrenos comuneros* and the acquisition of extensive water rights the company expanded rapidly. By 1925 it owned 49,400 acres. It was common knowledge that most of the land titles of the company were false, purchased from two men who were later indicted for title forgery. The company, however, had the best lawyers in the country and obtained all the land it wanted anyway, at the expense of several smallholders in the area (Calder (1984), p.104). The population in Barahona rose from 48,000 inhabitants in 1920 to 62,000 in 1935

sugar cane fields, food had to be obtained from further away and locally grown products had to meet a large part of the increased demand.

During the 1910s, commercial agriculture had not yet managed to drive out other activities in the San Juan Valley.[23] Cattle raising remained an important activity, and in agriculture, subsistence production dominated the scene,[24] but as food crops became increasingly profitable, commercialization was greatly aided by changes in the system of property rights. The modernizing forces in the San Juan Valley demanded that the land had to be properly surveyed and the old *terrenos comuneros* subdivided between the shareholders. As we found in Chapter 7, Carmito Ramírez began working as a surveyor in the valley already in 1902. However, even though various Dominican governments tried to find means to eradicate the system of *terrenos comuneros*, it was not until the American forces put weight behind the laws that the latter could be applied to their full extent. The law which the US military government passed in 1920 calling for compulsory registration of all land and the final 'demarcation, survey, and partition of the *terrenos comuneros*' paved the way for the end of the system of *terrenos comuneros*[25] and the transformation of an economy based on cattle breeding to one based on the cultivation of food and export crops. Still, many peasants refused to plant crops for the market because they could not pay the costs of having *terrenos comuneros* surveyed and divided, fifty cents to three dollars per hectare, depending on the quality of the land, or because they could not get a loan for cultivation purposes.[26]

The Americans also enforced the laws against free-straying cattle. With the spread of commercial agriculture these animals were increasingly conceived as a problem by crop growers. The marines often simply ordered free-roaming animals to be shot on the spot.[27] For some time the whole of the town of San Juan de la Maguana was surrounded by a fence of barbed wire, erected on the order of the US military and paid for by the cattle owners. Guarded gates permitted access to the town at its main entrances. The system proved to be very awkward and finally fell into neglect. The occupation force then attempted harsher measures by fining or imprisoning any owner whose cattle were straying in the streets of towns or villages, or found on the grounds of other landowners.[28]

(López Reyes (1983), p. 116). Not all the land around Barahona was dedicated to sugar production, however. Coffee was also of great importance (ibid. p.127). Together, these two export crops left insufficient land for food production.
23 Moreta (1986), pp. 58–9.
24 Ibid., p. 61.
25 Calder (1984), p. 107. Cf. Vargas-Lundius (1991), pp. 159–61.
26 Peynado (1919), pp. 2–3.
27 Jovine Soto (1965), p. 63.
28 Interview with Carlos Peguero Matos, San Juan de la Maguana, 4 July 1990.

The uncompromising attitude of the American military towards free-straying cattle contributed to switching the attention of the *Sanjuaneros* to other means of subsistence. The region was gradually transformed into an agricultural district and cattle breeding was increasingly carried out behind fences. However, several poor peasants who could not afford to fence their pastures were forced to sell their animals. The metamorphosis from the breeding of free-roaming cattle into fenced breeding and crop production was speeded up by successive droughts which hit the region at the beginning of the 1920s. The entire San Juan Valley fell victim to a state of destitution which lasted for several years. Poor people did not have a drop of milk to sell, not even a calf to slaughter for their own maintenance, or to sell in order to acquire a few pesos.[29]

It was mainly the wealthy landowners and large producers of food and export crops who benefited from the measures taken by the United States military government. In spite of their alleged fierce nationalism most influential *Sanjuaneros* thus finally came to share the opinion that the Americans after all had left a beneficial inheritance in the San Juan Valley. This was one of the reasons why they willingly lent the 'foreign invaders' a helping hand in the task of eradicating the *Olivorista* creed, a task which was pursued during the last months of the American occupation of the valley. Notwithstanding the hopes of his adversaries, however, the cult of *El Maestro* did not perish with him. It would continue to thrive because hardships continued to haunt his faithful followers among the poor inhabitants of the San Juan Valley.

In the present chapter we will examine the reasons why, in spite of considerable repression, the *Olivorista* movement managed to survive the period from the end of the American occupation until the fall of Trujillo in 1961, why it reemerged as a mass movement in the latter year and why it was put down violently for a second time at the end of 1962. This entails, in the first place, a continued analysis of economic change in the San Juan Valley from the early 1920s to the beginning of the 1960s, to demonstrate that *Olivorismo* in its Palma Sola shape appealed to people living under circumstances that resembled those that prevailed when Olivorio himself made his appearance or which had deteriorated even further. Thereafter we will examine the role played by politics, both on the local level and on the national one, in the destruction of Palma Sola and its inhabitants.

The Vásquez years: irrigation and colonization

In spite of the hardships referred to above, many *Sanjuaneros* still consider the Vásquez years of the 1920s (1924–30) as an era of hope and modest

---

29 Garrido Puello (1972), p. 122.

prosperity. The valley saw some progress and was spared the recurrent political turmoils which formerly had harassed its population. However, far from all its inhabitants prospered. In the 1920s the land concentration became more accelerated than before and many peasants lost their land, at the same time as they were forced to change their traditional livelihood.[30]

During this period the country as a whole benefited from a recuperating world economy. Agricultural production increased and the government launched extensive construction programs. The national road-net begun by the Americans was completed, the streets of most towns were paved and aqueducts and sewers were constructed. The most important ports were reconstructed and expanded. An automatic telephone system was introduced and direct lines were established with all parts of the country. The Dominican telephone directory of 1928 lists 130 numbers in the town of San Juan de la Maguana alone. Among them are numbers to car and bicycle dealers, local agents for sewing machines and electrical equipment, banks and insurance companies, as well as garages, hotels, cigar factories, print shops, dentists, pharmacies, ice factories and a movie theater. All these telephone numbers bear witness of the changes which during the 1920s had swept over the lazy little provincial town.[31]

The Vásquez government had declared that agriculture was its main concern and various initiatives stimulated the agricultural production in all parts of the Republic. Efforts were concentrated to the construction of irrigation canals, and during the six years the Vásquez government lasted more than 3,000 hectares were put under irrigation.[32] In 1924, an *Oficina Técnica de Riego* [technical irrigation office] was created in the Ministry of Agriculture and the same year, the United States agreed to a loan of US$2.5 million for roads and irrigation in Baní, Monte Cristi and Santiago de los Caballeros.[33] The San Juan Valley also received its due share of the new watering systems. During the 1910s and 1920s the water level had constantly diminished in the rivers of the San Juan Valley, probably due to the excessive felling of trees along the riverbeds and springs high up in the Cordillera.[34] Long periods of drought dried up many watercourses and wells and thousands of cattle died.[35] The rising desperation made the demands for proper irrigation of the valley more urgent than before:

30 Interview with Tala Cabral Ramírez, Santo Domingo, 21 November 1985.
31 *Directorio* (1928), p. 507.
32 Maríñez (1984), p. 75.
33 Inoa (1994), pp. 14–15.
34 *El Cable*, 19 August 1924, describes how a Cuban logging company, La Habanero Lumber Co., was clean-cutting dense pine forests along the mountain streams. Tens of thousands of huge tree trunks were left rotting on the slopes. Cf. *El Cable*, 25 July 1925 and 16 January 1926, Pérez (1972), pp. 232–7 and López Reyes (1983), p. 123.

The most serious problem, which at the present moment demands an urgent solution from San Juan, is, without doubt, the water problem. It is the most serious and significant problem, since the future of this region lies in agriculture, but the land does not produce water. Before it rained a lot. The nickname 'green bellies' applied to the *Sanjuaneros* derives from this fact. However, over the years the rains have become more infrequent. The emerald green of our pastures has, by the heat, been converted to the color of dead leaves, heralding ruin and misery. It is because of this that our fortune, which originated from free roaming cattle, has disappeared as soon as it stopped raining.[36]

In 1919 the US military government had issued a law regulating the distribution of water in dry regions. When the *ayuntamiento* of San Juan de la Maguana accordingly contacted the military government and applied for the help of an American engineer in order to make necessary studies for future irrigation projects, the US administrators simply answered that it was no use for the *Sanjuaneros* to plan for future irrigation with the help of the Río Yaque del Sur, because the Barahona Sugar Company had in 1919 been given permission to take a maximum of 21m³ per second from that river and when the Barahona Company started to irrigate its sugar lands there would be no water left for the San Juan farmers.[37]

The minds of the *Sanjuaneros* were ignited by this news and a *Comité de Defensa de las Aguas del Sur* [Committee for the Defense of the Waters of the South] was organized by the 'most prominent citizens' of San Juan de la Maguana. A fierce campaign, spearheaded by *El Cable*, whipped up support for the *Sanjuanero* cause all over the country.[38] The conflict was not solved until after the Vásquez government had assumed power, when the Barahona Company was finally forced to agree to limiting its use of the Yaque water and thorough land surveys could be carried out in the San Juan Valley to prepare for future irrigation works. Before the works on public canals could be initiated a thorough effort was made to establish, once and for all, the proprietorship to the land by cleaning up the mess of false titles and inadequate bookkeeping. The enthusiasm for irrigation was great after the battles over the water rights had been won by the *Sanjuaneros* and the surveys and preparations for the canal constructions were speeded up. After April 1922 a cadastral office was functioning in San Juan de la

---

35 Interview with Tala Cabral Ramírez, Santo Domingo, 21 November 1985. Cf. Jovine Soto (1965), pp. 11–12.
36 *El Cable*, 16 April 1921.
37 *El Cable*, 21 May and 4 June 1921.
38 *El Cable*, 11 June, 25 June, 15 July 1921 and 20 March 1923. Cf. Garrido (1970), pp. 111–13.

Maguana and by mid-1923 most properties in the *común* of San Juan de la Maguana had been surveyed, parceled and duly inscribed.[39]

In 1926 the long, government-financed Canal Juan de Herrera, using water from the Yaque del Sur, was completed. The principal branch of the canal was 32 kilometers long, its capacity was 1 m^3 per second and it irrigated most of the lands in the *común* of San Juan north and east of San Juan de la Maguana (approximately 3,000 hectares).[40] The construction of the big Yaque canal, and other irrigation systems all over the valley,[41] finally changed the traditional way of life of the *Sanjuaneros* by dealing a death blow to the traditional cattle breeding, based on free-roaming animals:

> The [canal] constructed by the government of President Vásquez, a work which was planned and executed scientifically and with an extraordinary capability, definitely shook Sanjuanero confidence and grazing was followed by the break-up of the ground by the plow and the tractor. As a consequence, agriculture, which hitherto only had a local market, is now expanding, and San Juan de la Maguana can offer to the national consumer not only beans but also rice, potatoes, onions, peanuts and other products that contribute to the flourishing economy (and continue to be the backbone of the progress of the valley).[42]

Efforts were made to turn cattle breeders into farmers. The state provided the valley with experimental cultivations and agricultural instructors. In San Juan de la Maguana a certain Señor Saurí was in charge of a state-owned 'model cultivation' and made excursions all over the province in order to promote new cultivation methods and alternative crops.[43]

The Vásquez government also promoted the establishment of various 'agricultural colonies'. In 1926 nine such colonies were created, five in the border area and the remaining four in the interior of the country.[44] By 1929 the colonies had a population of 3,611 inhabitants and covered 19,877 hectares.[45] The beneficiaries of this program were partly landless agricultural laborers, partly immigrants.

---

39 *El Cable*, 3 April 1923.
40 Garrido Puello (1972), pp. 37–8. Cf. González-Blanco (1953), pp. 120–1. As a matter of fact the Yaque canal was the first government-financed irrigation project ever and its success triggered off various similar projects in other parts of the country.
41 Among them the government financed two canals, Estebanía and Las Charcas, which watered 190 hectares, mainly rice fields. Several private canals were also constructed. In 1942, approximately 3,000 hectares in the district of San Juan were irrigated by privately constructed canals (González-Blanco (1953), pp. 121 and 129).
42 Garrido Puello (1981), p. 103.
43 SEA (1924), p. 28.
44 Inoa (1994), p. 15.
45 Maríñez (1984), p. 75. However, only 1,295 hectares were cultivated by that date (ibid.).

Around this time, the 'underdeveloped' state of the Dominican Republic was felt more acutely than before by the modernizing forces. Many Dominican intellectuals felt that their native country had been sinking steadily into progressive decay. According to certain social-Darwinistic beliefs propagated at the time this perceived decay was due to racial factors. The 'inertia' of the rural Dominican population was blamed on the 'African blood' which ran through their veins and Haiti, a country which population, taken as a whole, was darker than ordinary Dominicans was accordingly seen as a source of 'racial inferiority'.[46]

As we demonstrated in Chapter 7, the population of the San Juan Valley had always been in closer contact with Haiti and Port-au-Prince than with Santo Domingo and, for various historical reasons, the *Sanjuaneros* also displayed a number of 'African' elements in their racial composition and culture. This fact made some of its modernizing citizens agree with the many influential policy makers who considered that immigration by Europeans would bestow magnificent results on the country. Such claims were frequently discussed in the columns of *El Cable*.

> Very wisely our legislation perceives the ethnic, social and economic dangers that an immigration of inferior races entails, and their introduction is accordingly absolutely forbidden. [...] We need immigration. Our deserted plains need arms, but arms of healthy, industrious and strong people. Our race has to be regenerated: but this regeneration has to come from white people, because this, apart from the color, is an advantage which is scientifically proved. They will bring us honest customs and ... their acquired skills, the proverbial laboriousness of the European immigrant and, above all, a tradition which has shaped their individual consciousness and turned them into instruments for progress and civilization within the societies where they are assimilated. Not Cocolos and Haitians. Our country is plagued by these and the horrific scenes they frequently perform are too notorious; we are unable to passively watch them while they establish themselves in the country. We request that the law which limits the immigration of inferior races be obeyed.[47]

---

46 A more detailed discussion of this issue is presented in Chapter 9.
47 *El Cable*, 23 July 1921. The term *cocolos* refers to immigrants from the English West Indies. The racist implications inherent in the statement appear to have been commonplace by the time. The former United States ambassador to the Dominican Republic, Sumner Welles, wrote in 1928: 'It is one of the most noteworthy peculiarities of the Dominican people that among all classes and all shades, there is a universal desire that the black may be obliterated by the white. The stimulation of white immigration has become a general demand' (Welles (1928), p. 909).

All over the Dominican Republic groups were formed to stimulate immigration of Europeans. In San Juan de la Maguana various committees were established and petitions were sent to the government, pleading for the promotion of immigration of 'white people, healthy and laborious'.[48] Most of this, however, was in vain. Consequently the expectations ran high when any 'white' foreigner appeared in the valley and indicated that he wanted to establish himself as an agriculturist. When three Romanian peasants appeared in San Juan de la Maguana in 1927 an editorial in *El Cable* greeted them with the heading: 'Romanian workers. The salvaging stream has started to flow!' These three 'exotic foreigners' immediately struck a deal with Domingo Rodríguez, who gave them a piece of his land to cultivate and facilitated them with a tractor, because 'counting with the native element or with the Haitian, agriculture will not prosper efficiently in San Juan'.[49]

When the Vásquez government ceded state-owned land north of the San Juan Valley to 'real Nordic workers' – a group of Finnish peasants – the leading *Sanjuaneros* were eager that their part of the country should be benefited by the influx of such men. However, their applications came to nothing.[50] Few skilled foreign farmers were attracted to the valley in the 1920s, and of those who showed up the majority left after a short while, an insignificant exception being five Spaniards who came together with Carmito Ramírez after a visit he made to Cuba in 1928.[51]

The Dominican economy under Trujillo

Rafael Trujillo had made his career within the ranks of the *Policía Nacional Dominicana*, which had been set up and controlled by the US marines. During the occupation most Dominican members of this force were frowned upon and treated with disdain by their compatriots. It was considered that only unscrupulous, or extremely poor, individuals were ready to join a 'national' army entirely at the beck and call of a foreign invader. Trujillo was indeed a completely unscrupulous character. He came from humble origins and had several times, both before and after his entry into the military ranks, commited illegal acts.[52] However, he was cunning,

48 See for example 'Inmigración italiana. Proyecto para traerla a esta región', a proposal quoted in *El Cable*, 20 June 1925.
49 *El Cable*, 19 September 1925.
50 Agricultural colonies designed in order to attract foreigners were founded in Villa Vásquez, Pedernales, Agua Negra and Mencia. However, very few foreign workers came to the country and the Finns who settled in Villa Vásquez soon moved on to other countries, just like the three Romanians in San Juan (interview with Mimicito Ramírez, San Juan de la Maguana, 11 April 1986).
51 Ibid.
52 Vega (1995b).

intelligent and extremely ambitious, qualities which ultimately invested him with the Republic's highest office. Trujillo's deeds eclipsed, for over thirty years, all other activities carried out in the Dominican Republic.

Even though the Dominican Republic underwent a radical change during his authoritarian rule, Trujillo was no revolutionary. It was not his wish to overthrow either the system or the traditions of the government he encountered when he came to power. He never proposed any deep reforms of the social order and was never interested in pulling down or overturning the existing economic and social order. He just wanted to be on top of it himself. Trujillo was endowed with a manipulative character and preferred to extend and build upon what he found. He wanted to enrich himself and, above all, he wanted to dominate. 'Power was the great river of his being, flowing through every extremity of his life. Tributary to it were all the other qualities of his mind, spirit, and will.'[53]

Trujillo bided his time as commander of the army under Vásquez. While the traditional political elite, the *caudillos* and their clients, became more and more involved in their age-old power games, he was able to obtain a good general view of their machinations and discreetly back would-be presidents who believed they could easily control the poorly educated soldier. However, thanks to his cunning and ruthlessness, Trujillo was able to outwit them all in a very short time and soon stood as the sole and undisputed leader of the country.

Trujillo benefited from the thorough changes brought about by the Americans. The marines had almost broken the power of the *caudillos* and had left behind a well-organized army and an efficient transportation net. These achievements proved to be very helpful when Trujillo crushed all political and armed opposition his government faced at the beginning of his reign. The Americans had labeled their opponents 'bandits' and concentrated all power in their own hands; Trujillo followed suit. He killed or subjugated the remaining *caudillos*. With the use of terror he unified the country in a forced idolization of himself. The Fatherland and Trujillo became identical concepts in the minds of most Dominicans. In the words of a popular *Trujillista merengue*: '*Trujillo en la tierra, y en el cielo, Dios*' ['Trujillo on earth, and in heaven, God'].[54] By letting entire provinces, the capital and the highest mountain be named after himself Trujillo put his personal imprint on the Dominican landscape. Every town, every village were adorned with pictures, statues and busts of *El Benefactor*. Popular tunes, even prayers and hymns, sang his praise; every corner of the country felt his presence.

53 Crassweller (1966), p. 4.
54 *Najayo*, in: *Música, parte de nuestra historia*, RUHT, LP 14.

Figure 8.4 Trujillo and his son Ramfis at the Gulfstream Polo Fields, Delray Beach, Florida, in 1953.

Trujillo had no scruples. He was the 'Little Caesar of the Caribbean',[55] a mafia boss who ran his country like a *capo* runs his empire of crime, with the aid of the army, the *Servicio de Inteligencia Militar* (SIM) [Military Intelligence Service], the police and a number of other spy and intelligence agencies inside and outside the country. He was an extraordinarily greedy kleptocrat with a strong flair for business. According to a US observer, writing in 1940, the government during the *Era de Trujillo* could be summarized by the single word 'grab'.[56] Making systematic use of the state machinery, he proceeded to plunder the citizens and concentrate resources in his own hand by all available means. 'His commercial enterprises were of such inordinate magnitude that the government dwindled in importance to a sideline.'[57] When he was assassinated in 1961, his holdings had reached staggering proportions:

> Though exact figures will probably never be available, an estimate of Trujillo's holdings can be made. It is estimated, for example, that between 50 and 60 per cent of the arable land belonged to him or his family. This included roughly 700,000 acres of the best farming and grazing lands in the country.

55 Ornes (1958).
56 Sinks (1940), p. 169.
57 Krehm (1984), p. 182.

One tabulation concluded that the Trujillo family owned, in addition, 119 enterprises accounting for some 80 per cent of the volume of business in Ciudad Trujillo. At the time of Trujillo's assassination, it was discovered that he had an interest ranging from only a small percentage to total ownership in at least fifty-five corporations. The total assets of the fifty largest corporations were found to be $78 million, of which Trujillo's share was about $25 million. Trujillo, his family, and their associates controlled an estimated three-quarters of the country's means of production and probably an even greater share of the national income.[58]

His estimated fortune in 1961 was around US$800 million, obtained at the expense of the Dominican people:

> The Trujillo family fortune, in the relatively short span of thirty years, came to be ranked with the greatest fortunes in the world. He achieved this huge fortune by squeezing the population, cutting off almost all public consumption, and literally starving his people to death for the sake of building up his own private income.[59]

During the first years of Trujillo's reign the Dominican Republic was immersed in the worldwide economic crisis, aggravated furthermore by the San Zenón hurricane in 1930. The prices of Dominican primary export products had fallen drastically in the world market.[60] The crisis was felt very strongly until 1933 but thereafter, little by little, the economy started to recover. An extensive program was launched to reactivate agricultural production – e.g. rice, meat and dairy products – by means of import substitution.[61] Roads, irrigation systems and bridges were constructed and thousands of hectares of formerly uncultivated land were put under the plow.[62] In 1960, 11.6 million *tareas* were cultivated – against 7.3 million in 1935.[63] Agricultural production increased and after a few years the Dominican Republic became self-sufficient in rice, corn, beans and other primary products.[64]

However, much of this production was concentrated on big farms which mostly belonged to the Trujillo clan, while simultaneously the proletarianization of the peasants increased. In 1960, 0.8 percent of the farms

---

58 Wiarda (1968), p. 83.
59 Ibid., p. 86. For an economic analysis of this process, see Lundahl and Vedovato (1989). Cassá (1982) deals with the economic aspects of the Trujillo period in great detail.
60 Cassá (1982), p. 21, Inoa (1994), pp. 44, 64.
61 Inoa (1994), pp. 66–70.
62 Cassá (1982), pp. 87–91.
63 Ibid., p. 87.
64 Moya Pons (1980), pp. 518 and 516.

concentrated 41 percent of the land while the overwhelming majority – 88.5 percent – had to make do with 23.6 percent of the acreage.[65] Many small peasants had holdings expropriated and were forced to move or had to start working on the *latifundios*.[66] Howard Wiarda describes how Trujillo operated and the consequences this had for the victims:

> Trujillo ... swallowed up numerous small-holdings and lands previously held communally or by the government. The social ramifications of this tactic were enormous. Trujillo simply sent his strong-arm squads out into the countryside to tear down the houses of the subsistence farmers who had squatted on the unused land or whose claim to possession, if they had any at all, was lodged in an ancient and obscure communal land title which Trujillo – with his control of the government – could readily change. Many of the dispossessed peasants flocked to the cities, where the slums multiplied and a whole host of new social problems arose, brought on by rapid, unplanned urbanization. Others were forced to work on the Trujillo plantations under a system that amounted to slave labor. Still others were driven into the hillsides where they had to try to eke out a new susbsistence in the stony soils. Trujillo called this 'agrarian reform' and accompanied his dispossession of the rural peasantry with a flood of propaganda pointing out that the total land area under cultivation was being extended and that the peasant had become a new landowner with a new love for his country and a stake in its future! Soon, however, because of rapid deforestation and wasteful cultivation, the meagre soil in the mountainous areas had washed away and the Dominican Republic faced the prospect that in a few years it could become another Haiti, with its denuded hillsides and starving rural population.[67]

During the 1930s and 1940s access to land became restricted. The concentration of ownership in the hands of the Trujillo family coincided with rapid population growth. From 1935 to 1960 the Dominican population more than doubled – from 1,479,000 to 3,047,000.[68] Simultaneously, the state tightened its grip on the peasantry:

65 Cassá (1982), Cuadro II-2, Chapter 2.
66 ONAPLAN (1983a), p. 55.
67 Wiarda (1975), pp. 1509–10. The erosion process in Haiti is analyzed in Lundahl (1979), Chapter 5.
68 ONE (1983), p. 12. One of the reasons for this increase may have been the constant efforts of the Trujillo regime to stimulate immigration, but since these programs never were as successful as intended population growth was probably a result of improved health programs and the patronizing of big families.

One of the main tenets of the agrarian policy during the *trujillato* was the attachment of the peasantry to the land. To accomplish this goal, the State applied a dual policy which encompassed a peasantization program as well as repressive measures. Through the expansion of the agrarian frontier, the establishment of the *colonias agrarias*[69] and the selling of land, the State contributed to slow down the outright separation of the peasantry from the land. But as the State enhanced its position as arbiter of society, it was able to impose limits to the relationships between the peasantry and the land. In other words, one of the dominant features of the *Era* [*de Trujillo*] was the capacity of the State to enforce a given economic policy while being able to define the relations of property regarding land. This was a long-term tendency which had begun decades before and which had its legal expression in the land laws approved at the onset of the century. Economically and socially, this trend expressed itself in the increased constraints confronted by the peasantry to control and expand its resources. For instance, if until the early twentieth century the peasantry had settled the countryside in a sort of spontaneous movement, from the 1930s onwards this settlement was increasingly regulated by the State.[70]

As a result, contractual conditions changed and the incidence of sharecropping and tenant farming increased in the countryside.[71] The former, in particular, meant a loss of autonomy: 'As *medianeros* [sharecroppers working on a fifty-fifty basis], cultivators often had to accept interference in the actual agricultural process, but for landless peasant cultivators, these contracts were the only way they could obtain access to land', summarizes Michiel Baud.[72] As it seems, this process continued, and was possibly even speeded up, through the 1950s.[73]

The land concentration process also led to increased rural–urban migration. Pushed by the deteriorating conditions in the countryside and pulled by whatever improvements of communications, modernization of the towns and the creation of work opportunities that took place in urban areas, peasants were increasingly attracted to the growing urban centers,

---

69 Cf. below.
70 San Miguel (1987), p. 308.
71 Cassá (1982), pp. 100–1.
72 Baud (1995), p. 213.
73 Census data for 1950 and 1960 indicate that the number of farms working on regular cash tenancy contracts amounted to 4,594 in 1950 and 16,474 in 1960, with an increase in area from 353,761 *tareas* the former year to 1,471,532 *tareas* the latter year, and that the number of farms operating on sharecropping contracts had increased from 12,460 to 30,782, or from 540,643 *tareas* to 1,376,318 (Cassá (1982), Cuadros II-8A, II-8b, Chapter 2).

especiallyafter 1935 when the government began to use 'voluntary' peasant labor in the construction of infrastructure (roads and irrigation) and peasants who did not maintain at least 10 *tareas* in permanent cultivation risked to pay a fine either in cash or by working.[74] The migration process was accelerated both in the 1940s[75] and the1950s.[76]

To stem the migration flow, Trujillo distributed land to the landless peasant population, beginning in 1934, but hardly with altruistic motives in mind:

> Behind the charitable appearence of this measure was hidden a reality that did not square well with the assumed government interest in protecting the peasant. The first thing that we observe in the process of granting lands is that these were of very low quality and, yet worse, that they were located in marginalized agricultural zones. [...] A great deal of them were undistributed lands that, due to the legal condition in which they found themselves, could not be put into agriculture. On the other hand, many landowners agreed to surrender part of their idle lands because, when the contract with the installed peasant expired they received it [back] in optimal conditions: cleared and in many cases sown with coffee or grass. This was very attractive because frequently they were zones where labor was scarce or expensive. [...] The reason motivating the Trujillista state to begin this massive redistribution, except for the political effect that would be obtained, was the necessity to incorporate the peasant into the production of the foodstuffs that were indispensable for his existence, using the marginal soils.[77]

'There is no doubt that during the *trujillato* the State and the dominant classes became increasingly able to exploit the peasantry', concludes Pedro San Miguel.[78]

During World War II Trujillo started to invest the capital which had been accumulated through the increase in agricultural production in the establishment of new industries in the capital.[79] In the late 1940s, he also turned to the sugar sector, and resources which could have been directed to other agricultural activities were directed to sugar production and urban industrialization instead.[80] The production of food started to decline and

74 Inoa (1994), p. 218.
75 Ibid., p. 219.
76 ONAPLAN (1983b), pp. 6–7.
77 Inoa (1994), pp. 86, 88.
78 San Miguel (1987), p. 305.
79 Moya Pons (1980), pp. 515–18.
80 The land area under sugar production increased from 92,000 hectares in 1948 to 183,000 hectares in 1960 (Cassá (1982), Cuadro III-8, Chapter 3).

agricultural output per capita fell.[81] In 1960, 44 percent of the farms were smaller than 15 *tareas* [0.9 hectares] and occupied less than 4 percent of the total farmland.[82] These cultivators did not have sufficient incomes from their own land and were therefore forced to find temporal work on bigger farms or migrate to the growing towns.

The San Juan Valley under Trujillo

With some important exceptions developments in the San Juan Valley reflected what also took place in the rest of the country. Although the land concentration was less pronounced in the valley than in the Dominican Republic in general, most of the fertile land there belonged to big, private landowners and not to Trujillo personally or the state (which amounted to more or less the same thing). Trujillo was certainly the largest landowner in the San Juan Valley, with 1.1 million *tareas* in the *municipio* of San Juan – far more than anywhere else in the country – but what he owned was mostly pine-covered, mountainous and rather infertile land.[83]

As we found in Chapter 3, Trujillo initially tried to subdue the traditional power holders of San Juan with the same violent methods as he used in other parts in the country. However, after a while the San Juan *caudillos*, primarily the members of the Ramírez clan, realized that it was better to make some kind of truce with Trujillo if they wanted to keep some of their influence. The result was that the wealthy landowners in the valley were mostly left in peace if they did not interfere with Trujillo's brutal politics. The reasons for this tolerance may differ from case to case, but most important is probably the limited possibilities of Trujillo to exercise complete control over such a remote area, with a long and rather violent history of independence and lawlessness. From the viewpoint of the capital San Juan was also extremely close to the Haitian border, with everything that this meant in terms of clandestine business and political machinations with a people who traditionally had been considered as the archenemy of an independent Dominican Republic.

When Trujillo embarked on his 'Dominicanization' policy he had to rely on the support and knowhow of influential *Sanjuaneros*. By elevating San Juan de la Maguana to the provincial capital of a province named after himself – *Provincia del Benefactor* – Trujillo stressed the new and vital importance he gave this formerly so neglected part of the country. Everything was done to divert the *Sanjuaneros'* traditional contacts with Haiti and integrate them with the rest of the country. Several already wealthy *Sanjuaneros*

---

81 ONAPLAN (1968), p. 142.
82 Cassá (1982), Cuadro II-2, Chapter 2.
83 Cf. Chapter 4.

prospered, but for many poor peasants Trujillo's anti-Haitian politics meant decreasing incomes. During the Vásquez years the livestock trade with Haiti, which had suffered a setback during the American occupation, continued. Cattle, mules, donkeys, horses and fighting cocks were once more exported from the San Juan Valley.[84] However, Trujillo's strict border policy, which began to have an impact around 1935, put an end to most border trade:

> The immediate effects felt by Dominicans were that many lost herds which had been allowed to range in Haitian territory. In addition, with inexpensive Haitian products no longer available, the Dominicans' buying power was reduced by about 50 percent. [...] Of greater economic importance, the displacement of the Haitians and the closing of the border ended legal overland trade and reduced cattle exports to Haiti to a small amount of contraband.[85]

Many of the old links of the San Juan Valley peasants with Haiti were thus severed by the closure of the border.[86] Family unions between Haitians and Dominicans were made difficult and cooperative work efforts that had previously often involved people from both sides could no longer be carried out in the time-honored way.[87] There was nothing the peasants could do to reverse these changes. Trujillo's policy versus the peasantry served to hold the masses back. They were by law forbidden to organize and had no influence whatsoever on politics. In this, Trujillo was aided by the physical isolation of the San Juan area and of the general dismally low level of education, with 80 to 90 percent being illiterate in rural districts. The peasants constituted a very large, but also very inarticulate, group in society.

Already in the 1920s a few landowners in San Juan de la Maguana and Las Matas de Farfán had concentrated huge areas into their own

---

84 *El Cable* regularly published prices offered for cattle in the Haitian markets during the 1920s.

85 Palmer (1976), p. 89. By that time several of the large landowners had already sold what was left of their Haitian cattle herds. They had realized it was too complicated to keep animals on the other side of the border, especially because large numbers of cattle had been slaughtered by Haitian *cacos* during their war with the Americans. During the 1920s the Americans, who continued to control the Haitian government until 1934, demanded customs duties on cattle which several of the Dominicans considered to be too high. Thus, the large cattle owners directed their trade to the Dominican Republic instead, while the smaller ones continued their dealings with the Haitians (interview with Mimicito Ramírez, San Juan de la Maguana, 11 April 1986).

86 Note, however, that the border was never totally closed. Mimicito Ramírez (ibid.) claims that it was not until Balaguer's presidency in the 1960s that the border was effectively controlled.

87 Palmer (1976), p. 90.

hands,[88] a process which was continued and accelerated after 1930.[89] Frequently, the peasants were cheated out of their land. Angel Moreta quotes an old man (108 years) whom he interviewed in 1983:

> Many got it [the land] with intelligence; with the finger they said: 'This is mine, and that too' ... And like that they acquired it. In those days, it was with the finger that you acquired the land. You said: 'This is mine', and found and paid a surveyor well, measured the land, found a notary and you kept it and all that you wanted. In that way, the Mesas acquired the entire savanna of Solorín and the environs of the village; all that was theirs. The peasants? They were unhappy; they were thrown away. From them they bought sticks from some little fence they might have and for [what they paid for] that fence they then took the entire land. The land had no value in those days ...[90]

According to Moreta, the old man's view of how the land concentration process took place was shared by a majority:

> The majority of the elderly persons in the region that were interviewed coincide in pointing out how the process of appropriation and concentration of the best agricultural resources was produced through the ignorance of the peasants and the 'intelligence' of the buyers. The former transferred, 'sold' or parted with their means of production for 'a herring's head' or 'a cigar butt'. 'The land wasn't worth anything'; 'in the land of the blind the one-eyed is king.' The peasants were cheated by fraudulent measurement, by the legislation and the system of taking possession that this legislation, the 'Law Concerning Agrarian Concessions' [*ley de concesiones agrícolas*] – which the Americans passed in 1911, established on the basis of the new relations of production.[91]

Much of that land, the best in the valley,[92] is still controlled by children and grandchildren with surnames like de los Santos, Mesa, Paniagua and Caamaño.[93]

88 Interview with Leopoldo Figuereo, San Juan de la Maguana, 4 June 1989.
89 Moreta (1986), p. 113. According to Moreta, virtually all the merchants increased their landholdings: 'the Paniaguas, the Heyaimes, Octavio, Marranzini, Felipe Collado, Recio, the Marras, Rodríguez, etc.' (ibid., note, pp. 129–30).
90 A 'grandfather' of 108 years of age, interviewed by Angel Moreta, 26 February 1983 (Moreta (1986), pp. 113–14).
91 Ibid., p. 121. Presumably the law referred to is the *Ley sobre Franquicias Agrarias* (cf. Knight (1928), pp. 47, 181, Calder (1984), pp. 103–4, Baud (1995), p. 158). Moreta indicates that his source is Bosch (1984), pp. 358, 361, who in turn quotes Knight (1928), p. 47.
92 Moreta (1986), p. 149.
93 Interview with Leopoldo Figuereo, San Juan de la Maguana, 4 June 1989.

The peasants had to move elsewhere: into the foothills of the Cordillera Central in the north, into the dry tropical forest of the south and into the dry xerophytic forest in the east.[94] The number of *minifundios*, too small to provide the subsistence of a family, increased, until, in 1950, the Benefactor province had 15,000 farms that were smaller than 80 *tareas* [approximately 5 hectares],[95] and 1960, when 28,700 farms were smaller than 75 *tareas*.[96] However, it is difficult to argue that San Juan constituted a typical case of Latin American *latifundio-minifundio* polarization, since the former year less than 14 percent of the land was held in units of 800 *tareas* or more (none in units exceeding 8,000 *tareas*),[97] and the latter year only 16.3 percent of the total area was accounted for by farms of 1,000 tareas or more.[98]

The incidence of tenant farming [*arrendamiento*] and sharecropping [*aparcería*] also increased during the Trujillo period, albeit, it seems, not to any alarming proportions. The 1950 agricultural census revealed 95 cases (8,000 *tareas*) of tenant farming and 668 of sharecropping (26,000 *tareas*), i.e. a total of about 2,000 hectares, and in 1960, the former figure had increased to 422 (33,000 *tareas*) and the latter to 1,254 (45,000 *tareas*).[99]

Little was done to alleviate the situation of the poor in the countryside. The 171,000 *tareas* [10,800 hectares] of land distributed by Trujillo to the landless in San Juan de la Maguana in 1935 (and whatever may have been distributed thereafter) shared the general characteristics of such land elsewhere in the Dominican Republic: 'marginal plots, located in zones which lacked the elementary infrastructure to develop their agricultural potential and, besides, they had remained unproductive for centuries.' They were all located in the mountains.[100]

---

94 Moreta (1986), pp. 122–3.
95 Ibid., p. 144.
96 Martínez (1991), p. 114.
97 Moreta (1986), p. 145.
98 Martínez (1991), p. 114.
99 Cassá (1982), Cuadros II-10–II-12, Chapter 2.
100 Inoa (1994), p. 88. In the district of San Juan de la Maguana most smallholders today still complain that lack of land is their biggest problem, while those in the neighboring district of Las Matas de Farfán often state that lack of water is an even bigger problem (Eusebio Pol (1980), p. 119). (Both districts are part of the San Juan province.) This is due to the fact that the district of San Juan de la Maguana has more government-constructed irrigation canals than the district of Las Matas. Dominican law requires that *latifundistas* who own land where state-constructed canals are dug have to set aside 25 percent of their lands to smaller landowners (50 percent if the land is not under cultivation), which means that smallholders living in areas with state canals often have access to water. This is essential in a place like the San Juan Valley which receives less precipitation than any other important agricultural district in the Dominican Republic (interview with Mimicito Ramírez, San Juan de la Maguana, 11 April 1986). It is common that small peasants own a small piece of land along a canal and from there they bring up water to other fields which often are situated far away from any watercourse (interview

Rice was the most important crop of most of the 'agricultural colonies' Trujillo set up in the San Juan Valley. The first one was a colony close to San Juan de la Maguana, which was constructed on land which the state bought from the son of Ulises Heureaux.[101] There, houses were constructed, machinery installed, canals built and fields prepared. In 1939 and 1940, 120 Spaniards arrived to work the land together with Dominican peasants, who also were going to participate in the experiment.[102] However, most of the Spaniards had left after a few years, in spite of the fact that the colony functioned quite well.[103] They were Republican fugitives from the Spanish Civil War and had come as beneficiaries of a huge immigration project that Trujillo had launched after the massacres of Haitians that he had staged in 1937.

The colonies – forty-nine altogether in the entire country in 1952, with a total area of 1.7 million *tareas*[104] – formed part of Trujillo's 'Dominicanization' policies and he had several reasons to welcome foreigners into these areas, among them a wish to 'improve the race' through the influx of strong 'Caucasian' agriculturists. Another reason was that by granting Dominican visas to misplaced and persecuted groups in Europe, Trujillo and the people around him hoped to obtain some money from people eager to obtain visas and escape the insecure European environment. A third reason was the possibility of appearing as a great humanitarian by receiving Spanish Republicans and Jewish refugees.[105]

with Jorge Feliz, Santo Domingo, 5 January 1986). The law does not apply to *latifundistas* who have constructed their own irrigation canals, which several *latifundistas* in the valley began to do long before agriculturists in other parts of the country. The *latifundistas*' access to water has made the San Juan Valley one of the country's biggest producers of rice. Other important products of the valley are peanuts, beans, pigeon peas, meat, and tobacco, while the production of coffee, cocoa, sugar, bananas and other tropical fruits, which are important export crops in other parts of the Dominican Republic, are rather insignificant in the San Juan Valley (interview with Mimicito Ramírez, San Juan de la Maguana, 11 April 1986).

101 Interview with Mimicito Ramírez, San Juan de la Maguana, 11 April 1986.
102 Cf. Gardiner (1979), p. 80.
103 Interview with Mimicito Ramírez, San Juan de la Maguana, 11 April 1986.
104 Cassá (1982), p. 131. The acreage grew further up to 1960 (ibid.).
105 Vega (1984), p. 45. In 1940, the Dominican government had made an agreement with an American organization called Agro-Joint, which tried to arrange settlements for European Jews, to settle 100,000 individuals in the Dominican Republic. Agro-Joint founded an organization called DORSA (Association of Dominican Settlements) and by 1942, 571 Jewish settlers had been established in the colony of Sosúa on the north coast of the Dominican Republic. However, the war and problems related to agricultural practices, lack of experience, diseases and conflicts with the local population crippled the progress of the initially flourishing colony. No more settlers came, but the colony of Sosúa was still the only one of Trujillo's colonies of immigrants which can be called at least modestly successful, partly due to the international interest and support the colony received (Gardiner (1979), pp. 93–141).

The *Trujillista* propaganda boasted that at least 150,000 refugees found a new home in the Dominican Republic between 1940 and 1957.[106] The modest truth was that less than 1,500 refugees arrived during this period and most of them left as soon as they could.[107] Neither the Republican Spaniards, nor the 580 Hungarian refugees who came after the 1956 rebellion, nor the 781 Japanese peasants who came after 1957, could stand the oppression in Trujillo's strange state or the hard living conditions in wretched and isolated colonies along the Haitian border. Thus, most of the newcomers left after one or two years.[108]

Even though Trujillo's immigrant policies failed, he succeeded in attracting Dominican peasants to his colonies, although some had to be populated with prisoners, among these the Benefactor colony established in 1938 outside the border town Loma de Cabrera.[109] As mentioned above most colonies were situated close to the border with Haiti and it is striking how many were established in, or close to, old *Olivorista* strongholds. There may be several reasons for this. An obvious one is that some places, like Guayajayuco and Río Limpio, were villages which traditionally had had a strong Haitian population and had been centers of clandestine trade with the neighboring country.[110] It is also possible that people living there were perceived as particularly poor and in need of the incentives offered by the colonies.

Be that as it may. In 1952 we find colonies in Carrera de Yeguas, close to Palma Sola, in Mijo, the Ramírez farm outside San Juan de la Maguana, and in Juan de Herrera, just south of La Maguana. Biggest of these was the one in Carrera de Yeguas, where 12,500 *tareas* were dedicated to rice cultivation, watered by an irrigation canal which also provided water to several small farmers living close to the Yacahueque stream, although only fifty-three individuals benefited directly from the rice cultivation in 1952.[111] In comparison there were 294 colonists in El Mijo and 247 in Juan de Herrera.[112]

---

106 Gardiner (1979), p. 164.
107 Cf. ibid., pp. 176–7, for the real number of refugees entering the country between 1 July 1947 and 31 December 1951 (altogether 413 persons).
108 Ibid., pp. 203–5, 225–7, 234–6.
109 Vega (1984), p. 100, Inoa (1994), p. 179.
110 Most Haitians living in these areas had fled or been killed in 1937 (interview with Marcelina Ovando, Río Limpio, 1 May 1986).
111 *La frontera de la República Dominicana con Haití* (1958), pp. 96–7 and 101–2 and González-Blanco (1953), p. 127. Photos published in *El Caribe* 1962 show how pilgrims on their way to Palma Sola pass through the rice paddies of La Colonia in Carrera de Yeguas (Gómez Pepín (1962a)).
112 *La frontera de la República Dominicana con Haití* (1958), p. 101. In Guayajayuco there were twenty-four colonists cultivating 598 *tareas* and in Río Limpio eighty-nine individuals were tilling 10,000 *tareas* (ibid.). These are figures published under the Trujillo regime

Considering the impoverished state of most agriculturists in the San Juan Valley, the dry land and the unequal land distribution, next to nothing was done by the Trujillo regime to improve the lot of the small peasants. In the early 1960s the control of the larger local landowners was firm and the situation of the small farmers appeared to be as precarious as ever. John Bartlow Martin, the American ambassador at the time, describes the situation:

> We toured the *campo*, beautiful farms, and were told that Spaniards, Syrians and a few Dominican politicians controlled all the good land and all the water. Once again, seeing the misery in the *barrio* [presumably the poor quarters of San Juan de la Maguana] and the arid plains, seeing the lush fields where the river had been harnessed, I left the Southwest determined to develop the Yaque del Sur.[113]

Howard Wiarda, an American historian who toured rural areas in the Dominican Republic shortly after Trujillo's death, offers similar descriptions:

> I have been in some pretty squalid places in Central and South America, but in the Dominican Republic at this time the rural people were probably living as close to the animal level as anywhere in the Americas. Off the main roads life, to borrow … Hobbes' famous statement, is poor, nasty, brutish and short. There are no medical or health facilities. There is no available water (except that which comes from polluted streams) and no electricity. Illiteracy is almost universal and there is practically no contact with the outside world – few schools, few religious institutions (except perhaps for a local matriarch or seer), irregular mail service, few tertiary or farm-to-market roads, limited communications media, no government officials, little trade, little mobility. The people have no or inadequate clothes; inadequate and unhealthy houses are made of mud, sticks and leaves; inadequate food. Relatively few heads of families are able to obtain work – and then only seasonally. The children run naked, wallowing in the same grime as the unhappy-looking animals; all have bloated bellies that signify malnutrition; and the few that survive the early years are scarred, marked and frequently mal-formed. Perhaps, most important there is no hope of ever achieving anything better. Poverty, disease,

and are as such very unreliable, but we have seen the coffee plantations of the colony in Río Limpio, which are still in use, as well as the irrigation canals and rice paddies in Carrera de Yeguas.
113 Martin (1966), p. 319.

malnutrition, lack of ambition, un- and underemployment, lack of
dignity, hate, hopelessness – the sorry conditions of the Dominican
rural areas are simply unbelievable.[114]

In 1959, food consumption per capita in the Dominican Republic
amounted to a mere 2,100 calories per day and less than 50 grams of
proteins. In the best case the situation had not changed since 1950.[115] In
the entire country, the production of all primary food products except rice
and sugar grew slower than the population in the 1950s.[116] From his first-
hand observations, Wiarda concluded that most of the rural Dominicans
lived no better than the Haitians next door, and in Haiti, the worst living
conditions in the western hemisphere are to be found.[117] However, poverty
and squalor were not equally distributed across the Dominican countryside. Some areas stood out, in particular those 'off the highways [...] where
there are no passable roads at all', not least in the Cordillera Central and
in the mountains and desert-dry plains of the southwest.[118]

> It is in the vast Southwest that one finds people living under probably
> the most primitive conditions to be found anywhere in the Republic –
> or in the Americas. The shanties here are usually patched together
> from mud, leaves, and a few sticks. The people have inadequate food
> and clothing, no electricity, no educational facilities, no medical facil-
> ities, no readily-available water. Even the few elements with some
> incomes – shopkeepers, tenant farmers, canecutters, etc. – live under
> conditions that the poorest Mississippi sharecroppers could match.[119]

The lot of these people quite probably had become worse since the time
when Olivorio had made his appearance. They had less land, their traditional trade with Haiti had been cut off, and incomes were on their way
down. Towards the end of the 1950s, per capita income in the Dominican
Republic as a whole was falling at about 2 percent per annum.[120] In the
southwest, conditions were worse than elsewhere. The continuous growth
of the population ever since the 1920s had had an impact on farming in
the area. Around the turn of the century, subsistence farming had been
limited to the mountainsides bordering the San Juan Valley, but during the
1920s and 1930s, when possible, the subsistence plots began to spread into

114 Wiarda (1975), pp. 599–600.
115 ONAPLAN (1968), pp. 109–10.
116 Spitzer (1972), p. 421.
117 Cf. Lundahl (1979), for details.
118 Wiarda (1975), p. 602.
119 Ibid., pp. 603–4.
120 Ibid., p. 609.

the valley itself.[121] This exerted an upward pressure on land prices – as did increased land concentration and the advent of large-scale irrigation.

Finally, the upward pressure on land prices was reinforced by the activities of the so-called *Manicera, La Sociedad Industrial Dominicana,* a peanut-processing firm which from the beginning of the 1930s contracted farmers to grow peanuts. Landless people and peasants with too little land to meet their families' subsistence requirements found that the scarcity value of land was increasing.[122] This, in turn, meant that the pressure on the land already under food cultivation increased, and with that erosion, making for deteriorating production possibilities over time.[123] In addition, with the *Manicera,* the plow and the tractor became more common: labor-saving devices which allowed the farmers of the San Juan Valley to cultivate more hectares than hitherto with the aid of the given labor force.[124] In 1950, more than 40,000 *tareas* were dedicated to peanut production in the Benefactor province and ten years later, the figure had increased to over 75,000 *tareas.*[125]

Against this background, it does not come as a surprise to learn that in both 1950 and 1960, San Juan de la Maguana was the province of the southwest with the highest rate of net outmigration: 9,928 and 13,760 persons, respectively, with gross outflows of 16,447 and 24,500.[126] The strength of the push factor stands out once we take into account what the migrants usually met at their place of arrival:

> At the end of the Trujillo era, thus, the condition of life of the Dominican peasant was extremely bad. He continued to live in misery, squalor, and disease. Because the situation in the countryside was so hopeless, many *campesinos* migrated to the provincial capitals and to Santo Domingo itself, in the hope of finding employment and a better standard of living. But jobs in Santo Domingo, where the population had doubled between 1950 and 1960, became increasingly difficult to find. The unemployment rate soared to a whopping 40% of the total work force. Occasionally, these unskilled and illiterate peasants-in-the-city found work as stevedores, peddlers, bottle-collectors, housemaids, charcoal vendors, day-laborers, or prostitutes; but this employment

121 Palmer (1976), p. 103
122 Ibid., p. 111.
123 Cf. ibid., note, p. 129.
124 Ibid., p. 111. Of course it was only the larger landowners who used tractors, while oxen and plows could be rented by peasants with smaller plots. Also *minifundistas* grew peanuts for the *Manicera* which provided them with peanuts for seeding and bought up their harvests. León Romilio Ventura worked for several years as a local representative for *Manicera* in the region of Carrera de Yeguas (Martínez (1991), p. 131).
125 Moreta (1986), p. 156.
126 Martínez (1991), pp. 112–13.

was irregular and relatively few newcomers could be absorbed even into these occupations. The urbanized *campesinos* set up shacks much like they had lived in in the country in the city's teeming slums ... Crowded, filthy, without water, electricity, or sanitation; filled with naked, diseased, starving people; with rats and pigs competing for the meagre food, these shanty towns – made of strips of bark and old packing cases – presented a sorry spectacle. Crime and violence became a way of life – so much that the Police were reluctant to enter and usually did so only in groups and during daylight hours.[127]

The *sección* of Carrera de Yeguas at the beginning of the 1960s

In the early 1960s a particularly long period of drought struck the San Juan Valley. In 1961 and 1962 the *House Annals* of the parish of Santa Lucía in Las Matas de Farfán bear witness of increasing political chaos coupled with the signs of a threatening famine.[128] On the mountain slopes just north of the little town desperate peasants sought the consolation of religion and a new *Olivorista* cult was gaining force.

The Redemptorist priests in the San Juan Valley were quite familiar with such 'outbreaks' of religious enthusiasm among their rural parishioners and they regarded them as typical dry-season phenomena which occurred when the peasants had some spare time during periods of fallow. Poor peasants and landless workers also used to be short of cash and food during idle periods and sought help from their religion in the struggle against drought, famine and sickness.[129] Since the drought had been dragging on and was worse than usual it was not at all surprising that the peasants north of Las Matas de Farfán appeared to be more fervent than usual while carrying out their traditional rituals.

The landscape around Carrera de Yeguas always conveys a very dry impression. Most of the fields are arid, looking gray and desolate where they lie covered with small stones. Goats run around freely under thorny *bayahonda* trees, which together with different kinds of cacti constitute the main vegetation. However, in some spots a lush greenness may be found, particularly along the small Yacahueque River, which is shadowed by high leafy trees. Along its shores farms are found with rice, pigeon peas and sweet potatoes.

The Sección de Carrera de Yeguas, named after the village of Carrera de Yeguas situated 8 kilometers north of Las Matas de Farfán, is relatively densely populated, in spite of its dry and poor appearance. The small fields

127 Wiarda (1975), p. 607.
128 *House Annals* (1959–1962).
129 Interview with Bryan Kennedy, Las Matas de Farfán, 4 May 1986.

are all fenced with well-constructed enclosures, made of sprigs and thin poles. The dusty road that runs across undulating hills is lined with small, tidy houses, most of them built with whitewashed clay spread over a network of reeds and sprigs.[130]

The exodus to these mountainsides began in the 1930s when long droughts struck the San Juan Valley.[131] Peasants who owned cattle used to bring their starving herds up to the slopes in order to provide them with forage from *guásima* trees and *tinajos*.[132]

Life in this *común* has always been precarious. The isolation of its inhabitants has forced them to rely on mutual help and it has always been common to tend the fields using the *convite* system.[133] The peasants' close association with their neighbors is also reflected by the strong bonds which are maintained through their religious practices. Vigils for the dead, reunions in front of the altars of the saints, pilgrimages, feasts on great holidays, etc. are all carried out in community and many *Sanjuaneros* belong to a *cofradía*, like those dedicated to the Holy Spirit in Las Matas de Farfán and El Batey.

With the exception of the Trujillo-constructed irrigation canal which waters the northern parts of the section, few governmental efforts have been made to revive the barren Sección de Carrera de Yeguas. The irrigation problem has continued to be unresolved for the majority of the peasants. At the beginning of the 1960s the constant drought made the water problem an even more burning issue than before. Trujillo's limited canal project triggered widespread hopes of future irrigation, but petitions to the new government lay unattended.[134] The Redemptorist priests of Las Matas de Farfán occasionally provided the peasants with emergency

---

130 On a map of the district compiled by the US army map service in 1962 most of the vegetation within the district is designated as 'brushwood'. The majority of the houses are situated along the road. From Las Matas to Carrera de Yeguas around 500 houses are indicated (Sheet 58721, series E733, edition 1: Las Matas de Farfán, Dominican Republic).

131 Interview with Bryan Kennedy, Las Matas de Farfán, 4 May 1986.

132 Jovine Soto (1978), p. 12.

133 This is common practice all over the San Juan Valley and in an investigation published in 1980 it was found that 63 percent of the peasants organized in the valley's peasant associations still used to organize *convites*. Approximately 40 percent of the valley's rural population then belonged to some kind of association (Eusebio Pol (1980), pp. 101 and 70).

134 Interview with Zita Závala, Paraje El Ranchito, 10 April 1986. The canals are not shown on a map from 1962, but the rice paddies and canals below the barren hill of Palma Sola are seen on various newspaper photos from December 1962. A second map of the area compiled by the US army map service in 1968 clearly shows the canal and the rather extensive rice paddies of La Colonia. This map also indicates the cultivated areas along the Yacahueque River and shows a little village called Palma Sola just north of them (Sheet 58721, series E733, edition 2: Las Matas de Farfán, Dominican Republic).

provisions from CARITAS, the Catholic relief organization, and had launched a program in order to dig wells and try to organize the rural workers in peasant associations. Already before the death of Trujillo a priest named Pablo Delaere had started to organize the peasants around San Juan de la Maguana[135] and in Las Matas de Farfán, Father Tom Forrest tried to do the same.[136]

It was during these precarious times, after several decades of continuous deterioration of peasant living conditions in this desolate area, that *Olivorismo* once more grew into an important vehicle of the peasants' hopes which their leaders not only attempted to make a religious movement of national importance, but also a political factor which had to be reckoned with in the upcoming elections. To that end they attracted the interest of several political factions which were active in the San Juan Valley.

Local politics and Palma Sola

When Rafael Leonidas Trujillo Molina was killed on 30 May 1961, the Dominican Republic was thrown into a new world. The dictator's shadow had covered everything. His presence could be felt everywhere; the eyes and ears of the SIM, Trujillo's secret service, captured every signal of dissent and people huddled in their houses when they heard the distinctive sound of the *cepillos* ['brushes', popular name of Volkswagen cars] as the secret agents came in the dark of the night to pick up people for interrogation and torture. However, suddenly Trujillo was gone and the Dominicans had to adapt themselves to a completely new political reality. Politics was in the air in every corner of the country.

This was true also with respect to the peasantry. Trujillo had not paid more political attention to the *campesinos* than was necessary to ensure that they did not stir trouble. In fact, little had been required, because the peasants had always been a politically marginal group except in situations where their services were required by the local *caudillos* in the traditional fights for power. Already when he came to power they were unorganized. The dictator had an easy task:

> The peasantry remained, during the Trujillo period, the most atomized of all Dominican social sectors. In the case of the peasantry, however, this lack of solidarity or organization and of group self-consciousness was, by and large, not accomplished through a forced campaign of purposeful atomization on the part of the regime. The *campesinos* had historically been isolated and without much contact or

---

135 Eusebio Pol (1980), p. 78.
136 Interview with Bryan Kennedy, Las Matas de Farfán, 4 May 1986.

awareness of national politics. The Dominican peasantry was not a revolutionary force and posed no threat to the dictatorship. Trujillo, therefore, seldom bothered with it.[137]

This, of course, does not mean that the peasants were left in peace by the Trujillo regime, only that *El Benefactor* considered that most of the time no special measures or organizational solutions were called for:

> Trujillo's efforts to bring them under the control of his system were feeble and halfhearted. If their children went to school they received the same *trujillista* indoctrination as other schoolchildren; but few attended school. The official Dominican Party had a peasant branch, but this organization existed almost exclusively on paper. Some *campesinos* were appointed to minor government posts in the rural areas, but the number of these was insignificant. Under the Trujillo agrarian reform much of the less fertile land in the country was distributed to dispossessed and landless peasants and the entire program was accompanied by widespread propaganda, but this effort never reached the dimensions of a full-scale mass movement.[138]

The situation was to change quickly once Trujillo had been assassinated. Politics was no longer the monopoly of a single individual. Already before the Trujillo family had been forced to leave the country, the competition for the presidency was on. When Trujillo died he left his puppet president, Joaquín Balaguer, in power. Since no strong political organizations existed within the country, Balaguer believed he had every possibility to succeed in holding on to the presidential power. Almost every Dominican had been forced to register in the *Partido Dominicano*, which had been totally controlled by Trujillo. Politics had been out of reach for most Dominicans, and old *Trujillistas*, as well as members of the military and the small oligarchy spoke of a 'political immaturity' of the Dominican people, which made them 'unfit' for democracy.

Nevertheless, it quickly became clear that things were changing and that elections might become inevitable. Balaguer and Ramfis Trujillo were forced to allow opposition parties to organize themselves and the *Partido Dominicano* might have to compete with these. In this situation, Ramfis called for the first national congress of peasants in the history of the Dominican Republic, under the auspices of the official *Trujillista* party, to obtain support for continued *Trujillista* rule. However, as soon as the Trujillo family had been forced out of the country, the *Partido Dominicano*

137 Wiarda (1968), p. 92.
138 Ibid., p. 93.

crumbled.[139] This left the road open for other parties that lost little time before they began to court the peasants – for good reasons:

> Now, with the Trujillos gone and the definite prospect that there would be an honest election in which diverse groups could compete, interest in the *campesinos* was accelerated. The several newly-formed political parties sought to woo the peasant vote (numerically, of course, this was the largest bloc in the country) and enlist the peasants into their organizational ranks. The efforts of the parties to win *campesino* support represented the first real attempt to mobilize this social sector in all Dominican history.[140]

From 1 January 1962, the Dominican Republic was governed by a seven-member provisional state council [*consejo de estado*], charged with preparing elections at the end of the year, and,

> with elections upcoming in only a few months, the realization gradually dawned on all the party leaders that the peasant vote could well be decisive. If the concept of popularly-elected government was now to replace the traditional pattern of rule by largely self-appointed elites as the proper or legitimate way of achieving power and arranging for its transfer, then the so-called 'popular' forces would acquire an importance they had never had before. There ensued, then, a frantic scramble for the peasant vote.[141]

Two parties showed an interest in the Palma Sola movement: the *Unión Cívica Nacional* [National Civic Union] and the *Partido Nacionalista Revolucionario Democrático* [Nationalist Revolutionary Democratic Party].

La Unión Cívica Nacional

The rapidly emerging opposition against what was left of *Trujillismo* was initially organized by an entity called the *Unión Cívica Nacional* (UCN). In the beginning the UCN defined itself as an 'apolitical and patriotic' conglomerate of 'concerned citizens' and it surfaced during the tumultuous months just after the dictator's death, at the same time as Trujillo's son Ramfis, as chief of the army, was carrying out a murderous hunt for the killers of his father and President Balaguer tried to keep the crumbling state apparatus together. The UCN became a mouthpiece for the demands

---

139 Wiarda (1975), pp 610–12.
140 Ibid., p. 612.
141 Ibid.

of the majority of the Dominican people, at a moment when strikes and riots flared up almost every day.

While exercising its 'action diplomacy' the American embassy became involved in the formation and support of the UCN. In a country without any real political parties it was believed to be beneficial for all if a group of 'distinguished and honorable persons, who had demonstrated their faithfulness to democratic principles',[142] could clean up the political mess, get rid of both Balaguer and the remaining *Trujillistas*, while at the same time keeping the communists at bay. All over the country people wanted to prove their innocence by proclaiming they all had been 'honorable' citizens, denying that they had been involved in any way with a dictator who almost overnight had been transformed from *Benefactor* to monster. Several old, well-known *Trujillistas* rushed in under the banners of the UCN, declaring that they had been clandestine members of the opposition against the late dictator. When the UCN, on 8 February 1962, was converted into a political party it was mainly a conservative movement without any well-defined ideology, except a fierce 'anti-*Trujillismo*' and fear of everything which smelled of 'communism'.

In San Juan de la Maguana the UCN was headed by César (Salim) Heyaime, a member of the richest family in the San Juan Valley. His father, José Pedro Heyaime, owned at least a hundred houses in San Juan, as well as a rice mill and a cement factory. Pedro Heyaime had also constructed a luxurious theater named Anacaona, which was the principal movie theater and community hall in San Juan. Like most leading *Sanjuaneros* Pedro Heyaime had posed as a loyal *Trujillista* and in 1960 he was decorated with the *Orden de Caballero* for his services to the dictator.[143] Many other influential *Sanjuaneros* were UCN members, among them the province governor Alberto Dimaggio, who had been involved in the preliminary investigations concerning Palma Sola.[144]

The UCN was not late in perceiving the potential voting power of the people of Palma Sola and since it was a common belief that the *Mellizos* exercised 'a total control' over the peasants,[145] it was quite natural that Salim Heyaime and several other UCN leaders were making contact with the *Mellizos*, who were far from reluctant to enter politics:

> Of course they [the *Mellizos*] were in politics. In the beginning I think it was mostly on a local level. They wanted to know what the political parties had to offer. Principally they wanted to have a road constructed

142 Bosch (1964), p. 22.
143 *Santomé*, 12 January 1960, and interview with Mimicito Ramírez, San Juan de la Maguana, 11 April 1986.
144 García (1986), p. 338.
145 Gómez Pepín (1962a).

to Palma Sola, a school and water facilities. I believe that was how it all
began.[146]

On various occasions leaders of the UCN came to talk to the *Mellizos* and
asked for their support in the upcoming elections. The *Cívicos* [UCN
members] knew that 'we, the Ventura Rodríguez brothers, in those days
were supporting this party'.[147] It is possible that the *Mellizos*, in order to put
strength behind their words presented the UCN representatives with the
names in the book they kept at the entrance of Palma Sola.[148] It has been
indicated that before the *Mellizos* started to call the Palma Sola community
the *Unión Cristiana Mundial* (UCM) they had considered their community
to be a kind of political branch of the *Unión Cívica Nacional*. A Radhamés
Gómez article published on 20 November 1962, mentions that several
Palmasolistas had told District Attorney Miguel Tomás Suzaña that they
were living in Palma Sola with the 'authorization of the executives of the
Unión Cívica Nacional party in Santo Domingo',[149] and in an interview
León Romilio Ventura told the reporter that the UCN had nothing to do
with Palma Sola: 'I am inscribed in the Unión Cívica ... but I cannot say
which party I am going to vote for.'[150]

León Romilio was cautious in pointing out that Palma Sola was an apolitical organization:

> He denied vehemently that it [Palma Sola] had any contact whatsoever
> with the political parties and explained that the persons whose names
> are written in note books belong to an 'Unión Cristiana Mundial'. This
> 'Union', he explained, has as its objective that everyone shall know
> that he is the son of God and that no one can hurt his fellow man.[151]

It appears that the two principal leaders in Palma Sola differed in their
political beliefs. In early December León Romilio still stated that he was a
member of the UCN, while Plinio was believed to support another party,
the *Partido Nacionalista Revolucionario Democrático*, or to have alienated
himself completely from politics:

> In the beginning the UCN appeared as the most resourceful political
> party in the San Juan Valley. It was governed by the economically
> powerful people and they perceived the potential of Palma Sola where
> thousands and thousands gathered every week. People from the UCN

146 Interview with Patoño Bautista Mejía, Distrito de Haina, 5 March 1986.
147 León Romilio Ventura, quoted in Martínez (1980), p. 188.
148 García (1986), p.155.
149 Gómez Pepín (1962c).
150 Gómez Pepín (1962d).
151 Gómez Pepín (1962b).

were the first politicians who visited Palma Sola in search of political support. In the beginning they were supported by the *Mellizos* and the *Cívicos* received various benefits from the *Mellizos*. But after a while problems occurred when the *Mellizos* wanted to meet with their leader, Viriato, in the capital. They wanted to rest assured that the *Cívicos* would keep the promises they had made them. The local leaders did not want the *Mellizos* to go all the way to the capital. When the *Mellizos* realized that they knew they had been used just in order to deliver votes in the upcoming elections, from that date they cut all strings with the *Cívicos*.[152]

The UCN was an unlikely partner for the *Mellizos* in the first place, since it shared few, if any, of the traditional *Olivorista* values. Howard Wiarda provides an eloquent summary of the party's problems in the rural districts of the country:

> Its leadership was rather stuffy and old-hat, could not talk the peasants' language, and dealt with them in the traditional paternalistic way. The social gaps were simply too large for the UCN leaders to comprehend and identify with the peasants and their problems. Moreover, the UCN enjoyed the backing of the wealthier business and landed interests and soon came to be identified as the party of the rich, of the upper class *patrones*, and of the do-nothing Council of State. It became difficult for the Dominican peasants, who may be illiterate but who are by no means stupid, who recognize where their interests lie, to comprehend how they would benefit from the coming to power of a party led by the very men who had always kept them subjugated, who were white and aristocratic, and who were uncomfortable in dealing with the peasants on any other than a patronizing level. The UCN had ... promised agrarian reform; but it was likewise difficult for the *campesinos* to see how they could profit from the agrarian reform when some UCN leaders were urging that the former Trujillo-owned lands now held by the government and earmarked for redistribution to the peasants be sold back into private ownership.[153]

Several years later León Romilio Ventura stated that Plinio, who according to him was 'illiterate and very violent',[154] had an argument with the San Juan leader of the UCN:

---

152 Interview with Patoño Bautista Mejía, Distrito de Haina, 5 March 1986.
153 Wiarda (1975), pp. 613–14.
154 León Romilio Ventura, quoted in Martínez (1980), p. 183.

He met with Salim Heyaime in San Juan, with whom he had serious problems. Plinio told him that the people of Palma Sola were not any herd of cattle which could be sold at a given price and he also told Salim that the UCN would never come to power. They started a violent argument and Plinio left, shouting: 'You are finished.' After that he decided it was no use voting in the upcoming elections. He wanted to get rid of the UCN.[155]

At the beginning of October 1962 the reports from the authorities in the San Juan Valley stated that the leaders of Palma Sola and its various 'branches' had started to recommend their devotees not to vote in the upcoming elections.[156]

Plinio was illiterate and the people of the UCN thought they could fool him They went as far as promising him the vice-presidency of the Republic, if he could convince his followers to vote for the *Cívicos*. I remember that Plinio told us: 'The new vice president will be a man from the South, a man wearing *soletas*.' However, someone showed Plinio a list the UCN had prepared, enumerating the political positions they wanted to give their supporters in an upcoming government. Plinio's name did not appear in the document and he got very angry, feeling betrayed by the local UCN representatives.[157]

Since the most prominent leaders of the governing state council were known to be UCN supporters, Plinio's rupture with the local representatives of the UCN has by some people been seen as the initiation of the campaign against Palma Sola. The former reluctance of the government to 'act in time' according to these people was due to the fact that 'The State Council was complaisant because its members were interested in the votes of Palma Sola for the UCN.'[158]

After that particular moment [the quarrel between Salim and Plinio] things started to be pretty bad in Palma Sola. The criticism of the *Mellizos*, which had existed from the beginning, now started to appear in the newspapers. It came to the point that Palma Sola was accused of sheltering criminals and it was denounced that a day in the week was

155 Interview with León Romilio Ventura, Media Luna, 17 January 1986.
156 García (1986), pp. 59 and 63.
157 Interview with Mimicito Ramírez, San Juan de la Maguana, 14 December 1985. *Soletas* are a kind of sandals commonly worn by peasants in the San Juan Valley. The official candidates to the various posts in a future government was published by the UCN on 29 October 1962 (*Unión Cívica Nacional*, 31 October 1962).
158 Dr Julio Méndez Puello, quoted in Martínez (1980), p. 159.

dedicated to free love. Before the break with the *Cívicos* everything was a marvel in Palma Sola. You do not have to go too far in order to see what it was that motivated the most gruesome crime in this Republic.[159]

El Partido Nacionalista Revolucionario Democrático

Miguel Angel Ramírez Alcántara returned to the Dominican Republic in January 1962, after four decades abroad, three of which in exile, and was received by UCN's leader Viriato Fiallo.[160] However, shortly after his arrival in the San Juan Valley Miguel Angel founded a new party: the *Partido Nacionalista Revolucionario Democrático* (PNRD). This was a party of the old *Sanjuanero* mold, centered around a powerful *caudillo* from the Ramírez clan, which had served as a reliable producer of powerful, local leaders during the last hundred years. The United States ambassador was told that Miguel Angel Ramírez was just another successor of the traditional, somewhat rough, *caudillos*: 'General Ramírez is a good man but he is a soldier, he has not the culture of civilian government.'[161]

The party was described as being 'oriented along the lines of the "friends and neighbors" concept' in an area where 'the Ramírez family reigns supreme'.[162] Juan Bosch, leader of another of the twenty-six parties which hoped to run in the upcoming elections, the *Partido Revolucionario Dominicano* (PRD) (the eventual winner), characterized the PNRD as 'a small but very active party'. However, Bosch lumped the PNRD together with the other parties that opposed him, and considered that all of them thought and acted along 'conspirational terms and did not dedicate themselves to political struggle'.[163]

Like Viriato Fiallo, Miguel Angel Ramírez was neither a powerful ideologist nor a skillful politician, but he served as a symbol of uncompromising and brave resistance against the old tyranny. It was the people surrounding him that created his images and ran his campaign. Miguel Angel's backing came from the old political foxes of the San Juan Valley. Once more the *Sanjuaneros* had to prove their relative independence when facing the central government in the capital and the charismatic and irreproachable Miguel Angel, nephew of the legendary Carmito Ramírez, was a trump card in this struggle.

The shrewd supporters of Miguel Angel were familiar with the folkways of the *Sanjuaneros*; they knew every facet of the political game in the valley

159 Interview with Patoño Bautista Mejía, Distrito de Haina, 5 March 1986.
160 *¡Ahora!*, 19 October 1985, p. 28.
161 Pompilio Brouwer, quoted in Martin (1966), p. 249.
162 Wiarda (1975), p. 1022.
163 Bosch (1964), pp. 93–4.

and accordingly they also realized what had to be done in order to win over
the *Olivoristas*:

> We carried out the campaign for Miguel Angel. Compared with the
> UCN ours was a poor party, but we used our contacts. We were quite a
> few working for Miguel Angel, myself, Plutarco Caamaño, Neftalí
> Méndez Ramírez, Danilo Ramírez, Augusto Ramírez Piña and José
> Altagracia de los Santos, among others. We won over many *Olivoristas*
> for the election register. We copied the famous photo Suazo had made
> of the dead Olivorio and gave it to his followers. It is the same photo
> that you can see today on almost every *Olivorista* altar in this area.
> Plutarco [Caamaño] was very helpful in our campaign; he was a true
> believer in Olivorio and had a house up in Palma Sola.[164]

Some of the Ventura brothers became active supporters of Miguel Angel
Ramírez. It was particularly Hilario and Delanoy Ventura who identified
themselves with the people from the PNRD and helped them to spread
their political message among the *Olivoristas*. Many political parties were
active in Palma Sola, but due to the esteem Plutarco Caamaño enjoyed
within the community, only the PNRD was allowed to have an office inside
the compound and the party was even allowed to raise its own red
banner.[165] Even if Plinio knew and approved of the activities of the PNRD,
he seems to have been somewhat unwilling to participate openly in the
game of party politics – probably a result from his discord with Salim
Heyaime. He preferred to give a more general and prophetic tinge to his
preaching and talked more about Palma Sola's own 'party', the *Unión Cristiana Mundial*, which he imagined would have a more 'mystic' and universal appeal. It is possible that he thought of playing a big, important part
himself in a future society, since he told Mimicito Ramírez, who wanted to
inscribe him in PNRD: 'Today I am in command here [in Palma Sola].
Tomorrow I will lead the whole Dominican Republic and the day after
tomorrow I will lead the entire universe.'[166]

Once the election campaign began to gain momentum the political
parties proceeded to boost their membership. 'The full realization of the
importance of the peasant vote resulted in a sometimes mad scramble to
enlist as many as possible on the parties' membership rolls.'[167] The PNRD

164 Interview with Mimicito Ramírez, San Juan de la Maguana, 4 July 1990.
165 Félix Caamaño, quoted in García (1986), pp. 338–9. León Romilio Ventura has consis-
    tently stressed that no kind of political propaganda was allowed in Palma Sola and he has
    accordingly denied the existence of any PNRD office inside the compound (cf. Martínez
    (1991), pp. 236–7).
166 Interview with Mimicito Ramírez, San Juan de la Maguana, 14 December 1985.
167 Wiarda (1975), p. 615.

Figure 8.5 Olivorista prisoners after the Palma Sola massacre, displaying the *Olivorista* banner, a sheet containing the motto of the *Unión Cristiana Mundial:* '*Todo con Dios y María, El Cristo, La Unión Cristiana*' [Everybody with God, and Mary, Christ, *Unión Cristiana*], and a *Palmasolista* banner, with the letters P, S, M, J, indicating Palma Sola, María and Jesús.

made inscriptions to the party in Palma Sola and took these inscriptions to the *Junta Electoral* [electoral board], to have the party officially recognized. The PNRD even offered the Palma Sola leaders some money for their support, 'but very little. Because here there were no resources. It was a poor party.'[168]

> We made inscriptions in Arroyo Limón; both Plinio and Plutarco were there. It was through the help of the *Olivoristas* we got the party recognized. In the end we had 75,000 inscribed in the party, of them around 40,000 names came from Palma Sola. Still, we got only 37,000 votes in the elections.[169]

Already before the elections many members of the UCN had grudges against the PNRD, a newcomer in the political arena, directed by an exiled Dominican who had not been in the country for forty years. When the turn of the political scales in San Juan began to favor the PNRD the UCN supporters started to accuse the opponent of foul play and accuse the PNRD of the same thing they had tried to do, namely manipulate the

168 Félix Caamaño, quoted in García (1986), p. 338.
169 Interview with Mimicito Ramírez, San Juan de la Maguana, 4 July 1990.

Olivoristas. The mutual mistrust even exploded in open violence: 'I myself was attacked and at one occasion I was shot at, but the bullet hit another person who still sits in a wheelchair.'[170]

In spite of all the people who abstained from voting, many of them surely *Olivoristas,* Miguel Angel Ramírez won a landslide victory in the province of San Juan. There, the PNRD got 23,528 votes, while it obtained 35,764 in the entire country, where it finished in fourth place. In the San Juan province its closest competitor, the UCN, could count a mere 5,921 votes and the nationwide winner, Juan Bosch's PRD, even less: 5,373.[171]

Just after the elections, when the *Cívicos* faced an even worse defeat than they had expected, some of them turned their wrath towards the people of Palma Sola whom they accused of either not voting at all, or of casting their ballot in favor of the PNRD, which they accused of buying the *Olivorista* votes. As mentioned above, this disdain may have triggered off the incident of 21 December, the day after the elections, which in its turn alerted the authorities in Santo Domingo. The choleric Plinio had become fed up with the political machinations within and around Palma Sola. The more the elections approached, the more the circle around him started to promote him as a future leader on a national level. It is also possible that this agitation grew in importance when León Romilio was arrested and many of the people living in Palma Sola felt forsaken by their former political allies and beleaguered by hostile forces.

These feelings were reflected in several *salves,* particularly in one which was found in a written version when the police sacked Palma Sola. It is now in archives of the general attorney in Santo Domingo,[172] and parts of the text were after the massacre used as proof of the *Mellizos'* alleged intentions to overthrow the legal government and as an illustration of the threat Palma Sola was claimed to constitute for the surrounding communities:

Hoy estamos reunidos	Today we are united
en este santo corral,	in this holy corral,
no queremos que los judíos	we do not want that the Jews
nos vengan a perturbar.	come and disturb us.
El Señor Plinio Rodríguez	Mr Plinio Rodríguez
hombre que está preparado	a man who is prepared
por orden de Dios y María	by order of God and Mary
se adría [sic] *cargo del Estado*	would be in charge of the state

---

170 Félix Caamaño, quoted in García (1986), p. 179.
171 Campillo Pérez (1986), p. 478, Wiarda (1975), pp. 1022–3, García (1986), p. 131.
172 *Expediente* J-735-*Letra,* PRO.

Viva Cristo, el rey mesía,	Long live Christ, the Messiah king
viva la madre piadosa,	long live the pious mother,
viva liborio mateo [sic],	long live Liborio Mateo,
esto es todo lo que anhelo	this is all which I aspire to
de aquí saldrá un presidente	from here will come a president
que domine el mundo entero.	who will dominate the whole world.
Ya dos milliones tenemos	We already have two million
inscrito [sic] *en este corral*	inscribed in this corral
aunque perdamo [sic] *la vida*	even if we lose our life
de aquí no nos pueden sacar.	they can't take us out of here.
Vengan las fuerzas armadas	Let the armed forces come
con todas sus armetralladoras	with all their machine guns
que preferimos morir	we prefer dying
que abandonar a Palma Sola	to leaving Palma Sola
No mandará Viriato	Viriato will not govern
ni menos mandará Juan Bosch	even less Juan Bosch
mandará Plinio Rodríguez	Plinio Rodríguez will govern
por una obra de Dios.	due to an act of God.
El señor Plinio Rodríguez va para	Mister Plinio Rodríguez goes into
la presidencia	the presidency.
el cristo [sic] *lo designó*	Christ appointed him
por ser un hombre de conciencia	because he was a man with a conscience
Cuando este poder divino	When this divine power
a palma sola [sic] *bajó*	descended to Palma Sola
despreció a mucho hombre rico	it scorned many a rich man
y a Plinio se dirigó.[173]	and turned to Plinio.

National politics and Palma Sola

The Palma Sola episode was related to politics in yet another way. One of the unsolved mysteries is why General Miguel Rodríguez Reyes was killed the day of the massacre, why, in fact, he was the only casualty on the military side. Who killed him: the *Olivoristas* or his own troops? In the final part

---

173 This *salve* contains thirty-four verses and is quoted in Martínez (1991), pp. 175–9. The verses reproduced here are 2, 9 (part), 18, 20, 21, 26, 30 and 31.

of the present chapter we will examine the various hypotheses that have been advanced over the years and see what evidence is available to support each one of them. This we will do in the wider context of politics on the national level in the Dominican Republic. Rodríguez Reyes in different ways was a public, visible, figure and part of the answer to our questions may be related to this fact. Let us begin with a sketch of some of the most important political developments between the death of Trujillo and the beginning of the State Council government on 1 January 1962.

Tyrannicides and US diplomats

When Trujillo was killed the nominal president was Joaquín Balaguer. Like his predecessors, Balaguer had been completely controlled by Trujillo. After the death of *El Benefactor*, Balaguer had a difficult dual role to play: he was the inheritor of a hated dictatorship, but also the cautious instigator of a new political model. The growing opposition was well aware of Balaguer's difficulties, the army was controlled by Trujillo's family members and the United States considered Balaguer to be a *Trujillista*. The US government wanted to get rid of both the Trujillo family and Balaguer, but its greatest fear was a 'Communist takeover'. The Americans had been highly involved in the risky game of Dominican politics for a long time. The CIA had known about the plans for murdering Trujillo and US diplomats were fervently engaged in the search for and creation of future governors of the Dominican Republic. As long as no better alternative could be found they gave their support to Balaguer.

The Castro takeover in Cuba came as a complete shock for the United States whose Latin American politics came to be concentrated on the goal of eliminating the newly installed regime in that island. To this end, the Americans directed substantial interest to their old Dominican ally, Trujillo. President Eisenhower stated: 'we knew that until the American nations made some effective move together against Trujillo, they would do nothing against Castro – a far more menacing presence in the hemisphere.'[174]

The United States embassy in the Dominican Republic was looking for a group of people who would be able to stage some kind of coup and establish a provisional government: 'if such a government takes over we should recognize it quickly. Then, if necessary, we could move in troops at its request.'[175] The right people were very hard to find, however: 'Manifestly

---

174 Eisenhower (1965), p. 534. When the CIA built a powerful propaganda radio station off the coast of Honduras CIA head Allen Dulles stated it was his agency's intention that 'this station will first attack Trujillo and then Castro' (ibid.).
175 Ibid.

Figure 8.6 Joaquín Balaguer in the 1960s.

our hands were tied until we knew for certain that a Castro-type would not succeed Trujillo, and this was difficult to determine in a nation that had for so many years lived under absolute, ruthless dictatorship.'[176]

At a cocktail party in May 1960, in the house of the American ambassador, Joseph Farland, a Dominican 'dissident' introduced himself to the host and asked him directly if the US government would be favorably disposed towards a group planning to kill Trujillo and intending to establish a democratic government. Farland said his government would most likely be very interested and when he had been presented with the names of the members of the group and found out that there were obviously no 'Castro communists' among them, he directed the future tyrannicides to his successor, Henry Dearborn.[177] Dearborn enthusiastically supported the dissidents' request for rifles, hand grenades, explosives and antitank rockets and sent it further to the US State Department, writing to them that he personally considered it necessary to have Trujillo killed:

> If you recall Dracula you will remember it was necessary to drive a stake through his heart to prevent a continuation of his crimes. I believe sudden death would be more humane than the solution of the Nuncio who once told me he thought he should pray that Trujillo would have a long and lingering illness.[178]

176 Ibid., p. 535.
177 Powers (1979), p. 146.
178 Dearborn, quoted in ibid., pp. 340–1.

Still, when John F. Kennedy became president on 20 January 1961, no more than three revolvers and three carbines had been transferred to the 'dissidents' through a 'special group' at the US State Department. Kennedy was busy with his Cuban schemes, he detested Trujillo and supported the sanctions that the Organization of American States had imposed on the Dominican Republic. Still, he was reluctant to be more actively involved. He told his advisers that he felt that Trujillo was ripe: 'If Trujillo goes, he goes, but why are we pushing that?' Kennedy did not seek the dictator's overthrow until he knew what would come after.[179] He wanted to postpone moving against Trujillo and his supporters until 'the US military, the CIA and its cooperating organizations could penetrate the country's shattered infrastructure, create a conservative alternative regime, and thereby control events'.[180] President Kennedy explained his preferences in a cabinet session: 'There are three possibilities in descending order of preference: decent democratic order, a continuation of the Trujillo regime or a Castro regime. We ought to aim for the first, but we really can't renounce the second until we are sure one can avoid the third.'[181]

Ambassador Dearborn was advised not to give any more weapons to the 'dissidents', who were considered to be a bad stake since their political skills were highly questionable: 'The central actors in the attack upon Trujillo's life were men whom the dictator had favored with numerous benefits, while at the same time he had hurt their personal sentiments.'[182] Most of the conspirators occupied high positions in the Dominican society. They knew the dictator personally and it was later generally agreed that for the majority of them personal revenge, rather than principle, accounted for their role in the assassination. What was going to happen after the tyrannicide was not thoroughly planned:

> This was a plot in which *compadrazgo* (godfatherism), not ideology, would bind its members. Ideology was exactly what the conspirators lacked. Conservatives, they had no definite political theory. They feared communism and Castroism as much, if not more than Trujillism. All had personal scores to settle, or fears of Trujillo's wrath to come. Above all they wanted to beat the leftists to the punch.[183]

The conspirators succeeded in killing Trujillo in an ambush on 30 May 1961, but they failed completely to offer an alternative to the reign of the

179 Schlesinger (1978), p. 490.
180 Goff and Locker (1969), p. 262.
181 Kennedy, quoted in Schlesinger (1965), p. 769.
182 Balaguer (1985), p. 403.
183 Diederich (1978), p. 63.

tyrant. Instead most of them, and many other accomplices and innocents, fell victims to a killing spree initiated by Ramfis Trujillo, the dictator's oldest son, who came back from Paris on 3 June and put himself in charge of the armed forces.[184] Balaguer succeeded to hold on to power until the fall of 1961. On 17 November, Ramfis Trujillo brought the six surviving principal members of the conspiracy against Trujillo to his estate, Hacienda María, had them all gunned down and fled the country.

Chaos hit the Dominican Republic and the remaining members of the Trujillo family tried to seize power under the command of the deceased dictator's brothers, Héctor (Negro) and José Arismendi (Petán) Trujillo, who suddenly returned from a short exile in the Bahamas. This attempted *Trujillista* coup was, however, frustrated by General Pedro Rodríguez Echavarría who shelled the Trujillo headquarters, while American warships appeared along the Dominican coasts. The UCN proclaimed a national strike, pressed Balaguer to resign and proposed that the *Cívicos* form a state council. Through its actions the UCN proved to the Americans that it was the strongest political force in the country and that its leadership, recruited from the Dominican bourgeoisie, was able to work in collaboration with United States diplomats. The events forced Balaguer and Rodríguez Echavarría to yield to John Calvin Hill, who was in charge of the US diplomatic mission, and who made President Balaguer and his generals agree to share their powers with a state council, which was going to take care of the state affairs and prepare for elections in 1962.[185]

General Rodríguez Echavarría and the Dominican army demanded that Balaguer stay in power and serve as the head of the State Council, instead of UCN leader Viriato Fiallo. In addition to Balaguer, the most prominent members of the seven-member council were Rafael Bonnelly and the two surviving killers of Trujillo: Antonio Imbert Barrera and Luis Amiama Tió.

Bonnelly was a lawyer who had served Trujillo on various posts, for example as Dominican ambassador in Madrid and as state secretary for interior and police. He had even been mentioned as a likely candidate for the vice presidency when he suddenly fell out of favor.[186] After the death of Trujillo he was in close connection with various UCN leaders and even if he, as a member of the State Council, stressed his apolitical position, he was generally considered to be a *Cívico*. Amiama had been in charge of the plans for a coup attempt after the death of Trujillo while Imbert had taken

---

184 Diederich (1978) gives a detailed account of the machinations in connection with the murder of Trujillo and its bloody aftermath. Guerrero (1991) deals with the period between the murder and the installation of the State Council, 1 January 1962.

185 Balaguer (1989), pp. 166–8. The Americans were not opposed to keeping Balaguer in power, they considered him to be a stabilizing factor. They believed they controlled all the party leaders, but feared radical groups within the UCN (Cassá (1986), pp. 40–8).

186 Crassweller (1966), pp. 327–8.

direct part in the tyrannicide. Imbert had driven the car which intercepted the Chevrolet of *El Benefactor* and it was he who, together with Octavio de la Maza, had fired the deadly shots against the dictator.[187] While all other principal actors involved in the tyrannicide were rounded up, and most of them were either severely tortured or killed, Amiama and Imbert succeeded in hiding from the murderous squadrons of Ramfis Trujillo, Amiama in the house of a medical doctor and Imbert in the home of an Italian embassy secretary.[188] By the beginning of December 1961 both came out of hiding, were hailed as heroes and offered seats in the State Council which started to function on 1 January 1962.[189]

Antonio Imbert Barrera and John Bartlow Martin

Amiama and Imbert feared for their lives and were working very hard to secure a position for themselves where they could feel secure from the various forces, particularly within the military ranks, who were seeking bloody revenge for the murdered dictator:

> The other five members on the Consejo have nothing to lose [...] But after [the elections] what about us? [...] All political parties are scared of us. We know *we* are the only ones we can trust. We don't want to get mixed up in politics. But we have to. If we depend on the party that gets elected, that party can get rid of us. We don't want power and money ourselves. Just our lives.[190]

The most active of the two was Imbert, 'ubiquitous, pragmatic, and politically ambitious'.[191] He was feared by everyone, even by his fellow members in the State Council.[192] Imbert recognized from the beginning that he did not have many friends and followers and was therefore content to use his influence behind the scenes.[193] He was helped in his machinations by his excellent contacts with the Americans. As a matter of fact, some considered him to be the United States' man in the council. He spoke fluent

187 Diederich (1978), pp. 62–3 and 114–18.
188 Ibid., pp. 179 and 182.
189 Balaguer headed the State Council until 17 January when the military opened fire at demonstrators in the center of Santo Domingo. In the chaos that followed, General Rodríguez Echavarría staged another coup in favor of Balaguer, who stepped down anyway and let Rodríguez Echavarría form a state council of his own. Popular outcry, however, finally forced Rodríguez Echavarría and Balaguer into exile and left the power to the original state council, which then was headed by Bonnelly (see Guerrero (1988)).
190 Imbert quoted in Martin (1966), p. 167.
191 Atkins (1981), p. 145.
192 Martin (1966), p. 205.
193 Atkins (1981), p. 78.

Figure 8.7 Antonio Imbert Barrera and John Bartlow Martin.

English after spending some time of his youth working for the United Fruit Company as administrator of one of their banana plantations called *La Grenada*.[194] The American ambassador was fascinated by him and frequently 'acted to maximize Imbert's political power'.[195] In order to consolidate his power and safeguard himself against his enemies within the military, Imbert became a keen supporter of the US program which meant supporting the police as a counterbalance to the army. He was the State Council member in charge of the police and he appointed one of 'his' own men, General Belisario Peguero, as chief of the police and he was also active in putting Francisco Caamaño in charge of the White Helmets.[196]

> The strategists [...] supported the idea that the police forces of the Third World countries constituted 'the first line of defense' in the struggle against Communism. [...] The generals Antonio Imbert and Belisario Peguero, served as channels for the introduction of the concept of 'the first line of defense.' To be in the focus of the United States attention was something which was highly valued by them.[197]

Through Belisario Peguero the police was directly loyal to Imbert who proceeded to transform it into what several observers considered to be a

194 Diederich (1978), p. 74.
195 Slater (1978), p. 318.
196 Interview with Miguel Antonio Rodríguez Landestoy, Santo Domingo, 29 April 1986. 'In those days Caamaño was the *niño bonito* [favorite child] of Imbert' (ibid.).
197 Hermann (1983), p. 81.

Figure 8.8 Luis Amiama Tió.

private army: 'Before the year was out the police force had grown to an army of 12,000 men with modern equipment. Imbert even tried to obtain tanks for the police [...] but the military commanders flagged him down on that plan.'[198] Imbert also 'controlled' the attorney general, Antonio García Vásquez, and the head of the secret police, 'Pupito' Sánchez.[199]

In order to secure his and Amiama's lives and increase his own power, Imbert sought other means as well. He obtained a personal guard, which after a year counted some 2,000 men.[200] He wanted to force the military under his direct control and counted on General Miguel Atila Luna Pérez, the chief of the air force, 'one of the most corrupt of the old-time *trujillista* officers',[201] as his close associate, but the Dominican army still contained several other old *Trujillistas* who tried to put a check on Imbert's increasing power. With the consent of the United States embassy the State Council decided to purge the army of people it considered to be 'unreliable'. The action alarmed many officers and they got support for their concerns from several radical groups that did not approve of the government's measures and interpreted the purges as a means to control the army and change it

198 Szulc (1965), p. 88.
199 Martin (1966), p. 205. García Vásquez had also been active in the conspiracy against Trujillo and among other things he had written a speech which was planned to be read on radio after the tyrannicide had succeeded, demanding all Dominicans to rise against the oppressors, but nothing turned out as planned and the speech was never aired (Diederich (1978), p. 89).
200 Slater (1978), p. 318.
201 Wiarda (1975), p. 308.

into an obedient instrument for certain political factions: 'By meeting all the demands of the Trujillist plan made by the reactionary block of military men the Unión Cívica is trying to use these officers and enlisted men [the ones assigned by the State Council] as a means for staying in power, laying all scruples aside, obediently serving the perverse designs of the national and international reactionary forces.'[202]

For reasons of power and security Imbert and Amiama wanted to become members of the armed forces themselves and on 7 December both were made generals through a decree issued by the state council. This measure was met with fierce resistance from several army officers who were unable to understand how two civilians, with no military background whatsoever, suddenly could be promoted to generals.[203] Their military ranks gave Imbert and Amiama complete access to all military reunions. Amiama continued to dress and behave like a civilian. He had a gun but never showed it. Imbert, on the other hand, adapted himself completely to his new role as a general, wearing his general's uniform almost daily, displaying a .45 in a holster by the hip.

Ambassador Martin, and others around him, considered that Imbert and Amiama were the actual governors of the Republic and that the other members of the State Council acted on their behalf.[204] Some people talked about them as 'a new two-headed Trujillo'.[205] None of them were affiliated with any political party; they did not trust anyone besides themselves. Imbert told the American ambassador: 'These little parties, Mr. Martin, they are no good, you cannot trust them, the United States cannot trust them. You must have somebody you can trust, really trust.'[206]

However, John Bartlow Martin's version of the actions of Imbert and other Dominican politicians has to be taken with some caution. It was in the ambassador's interest to depict Dominican politics in a certain way in order to defend the intense US involvement in Dominican internal affairs:

> It is easy to legitimize acts of direct penetration if one constantly depicts Imbert and Amiama as dangerous assassins, sinister and ambitious, Donald Reid as a potential assassin, or Bonnelly as an adherent of witchcraft. The presence of the pro-consul [Ambassador Martin] would accordingly be inevitable to guarantee order.[207]

---

202 *El 14 de Junio,* 11 April 1962.
203 Martin (1966), p. 277.
204 Ibid., p. 217.
205 Ibid., p. 205.
206 Imbert, quoted in ibid., p. 220.
207 Cassá (1986), note, p. 53. Donald Reid Cabral was a member of the State Council who later became the head of a provisional government which was established after the coup against Juan Bosch's constitutional government in September 1963.

While discussing Imbert and Amiama, Ambassador Martin constantly re-iterates his task as a lion tamer: 'They [Imbert and Amiama] were reason-able men, realistic men, not hot-head patriots or melodramatic *poseurs* ready to fling themselves over the cliff. They would listen to me, at least up to a point, and they respected the power of the United States.'[208]

Imbert did not hesitate to try to eliminate any faction he considered to be a danger to his own position. His fear of communism led him in Novem-ber 1962 to close down the offices of *El 14 de Junio*, a political group that had organized the internal and clandestine struggle against Trujillo and later formed a radical branch of the UCN. When the State Council had been put in charge of the government *El 14 de Junio* was ousted from the UCN, which meant a further radicalization of its members. Imbert made up lists of members of both *El 14 de Junio* and the MPD (*Movimiento Popular Dominicano*), a party which referred to itself as *Marxista-Leninista-Fidelista*. These lists were later presented to the US embassy which provided the radi-cals with visas in order to have them quietly deported from the country.[209]

Overtaken by Events, the book US ambassador Martin wrote about his experiences in the Dominican Republic, is filled with descriptions of various coup attempts he accuses Imbert of staging before the upcoming elections in December 1962. Martin portraits Imbert as a man who constantly intrigues and plots in order to maximize his own powers, while he sees himself as some kind of a noble knight, who time after time quenches the gross appetites of a power-hungry general.

Martin attributes a key role to Imbert in the Palma Sola affair. As stated above, Imbert was in charge of the police and both General Belisario Peguero and Francisco Caamaño were considered to be controlled by him personally. From the very beginning Imbert was very well informed about Palma Sola and he visited the area several times. He even accompanied León Romilio Ventura when the *Mellizo*, in a helicopter, was flown over Palma Sola and tried to deliver his message to clear the area. García Vásquez continuously briefed Imbert about the situation in Palma Sola and, when visiting San Juan and Las Matas at the beginning of December, he revealed that 'the *consejero* [member of the State Council] Imbert Barrera has instructed the army commander of San Juan de la Maguana to cooperate with the police in planning the eradication of the activities in Palma Sola ...'[210]

When Ambassador Martin got the report of unnecessary bloodshed and 'wanton killing' in Palma Sola from his military observers, Lieutenant Colonel Bevan Cass and Colonel Luther Long, he immediately visited

208 Martin (1966), p. 205.
209 Ibid., p. 263.
210 García (1986), p.180. Italics ours.

President Bonnelly and asked for an explanation. Martin found an angry president, who accused the Americans of rude behavior stating that: 'Your attachés are proving embarrassing. ... Because this is an internal political matter.' Martin writes that he found Bonnelly's statement very confusing: 'what was political about [Palma Sola]?' He decided that Imbert must have had something to do with it all. The attorney general, García Vásquez, was after all 'an Imbert man'. However, Martin states that he 'got nothing' from his visit to Imbert and speculates further: 'Why had only Rodríguez Reyes been killed? How? Why was this a "political matter"?'[211]

Ambassador Martin leaves his questions suspended in the air, but some authors have interpreted his way of writing as a means to put the blame on Imbert:

> The government offered an official version of the events, which Martin makes use of in his book. The latter in turn went on with his investigations and the information he was given coincided in the statement that the death of Rodríguez Reyes had a political origin and that Imbert was responsible.[212]

The general

Who, then, was General Rodríguez Reyes?

> My father was a very obedient man. He never had any problems with military discipline. He used to say: 'I am a military man, I obey orders and I am never intimate with anyone.' I think he was like that. From the moment I was born he behaved like an officer with me. He was my father and commander. But he was always just and I believe everyone respected him.[213]

General Miguel Félix Rodríguez Reyes initiated his military career in 1929 and became a member of Trujillo's personal bodyguard in 1930. He was always obedient to Trujillo, but in the end the general was well aware of the fact that the dictator could not stay in power much longer.[214] In 1959 and 1960 Miguel Rodríguez Reyes was decorated for his contributions in putting an end to the anti-*Trujillista* invasions in Constanza, Maimón and Estero Hondo.[215] Many of the men who were taken prisoners at that

---

211 Martin (1966), p. 305.
212 Jimenes Grullón (1977), p. 493.
213 Interview with Ramón Jesús Rodríguez Landestoy, Boca Chica, 15 June 1989.
214 Ibid.
215 García (1986), p. 140.

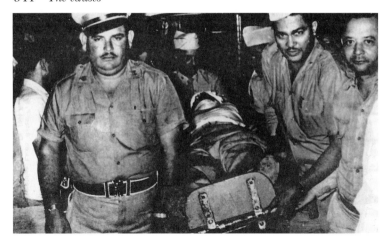

Figure 8.9 The body of Miguel Rodríguez Reyes, entering the military hospital
F. Lithgow Ceara, on the evening of 28 December 1962.

moment were shot in the aftermath of the invasions, but General
Rodríguez Reyes did not allow any executions within the district of his
jurisdiction and Trujillo accepted his general's position:

> Trujillo never dared to give my father any repulsive orders. He
> respected him too much. In those days I was already an officer and
> followed my father during the entire operation. We were forced to
> send some of the wounded and all prisoners to Santiago. We did not
> know what became of them there. At one moment I asked my father if
> he was not afraid and he answered me: 'My shame is much bigger than
> my fear.'[216]

The position of General Rodríguez Reyes was well known among his
fellow officers and when the conspiracy against Trujillo was being planned
some of the conspirators thought of him as a possible organizer of a coup
attempt and leader of a provisional government:

> When the plotters approached General Rodríguez Reyes with a care-
> fully disguised suggestion that he take over the government, he
> warned the conspirators angrily: 'I am Trujillo's man. I was formed by
> Trujillo. I don't know what you have in mind, but be careful … you
> could be hanged.' With the warning of the irate general ringing in
> their ears the conspirators dropped their plan.[217]

216 Interview with Ramón Jesús Rodríguez Landestoy, Boca Chica, 15 June 1989.
217 Diederich (1978), p. 49.

Figure 8.10 President Rafael Bonnelly, followed by Antonio Imbert Barrera and José A. Fernández Caminero, members of the State Council government at the funeral of Miguel Rodríguez Reyes.

He remained loyal to the Trujillos when General Rodríguez Echavarría frustrated their coup attempt in November 1961 and refused to join forces with Rodríguez Echavarría's troops.[218] However, he later joined Rodríguez Echavarría in the latter's second coup attempt in January 1962, when the general tried to overthrow the State Council in order to keep Balaguer in power. At that moment it was General Rodríguez Reyes who was in charge of the imprisonment of the members of the State Council,[219] but it was also the same general who, obeying the orders of the same State Council whose members he had imprisoned four days earlier, escorted his former chief, General Rodríguez Echavarría, to the plane which was going to bring him into a forced exile when the coup attempt had been quenched:[220]

> My father considered himself to be loyal to the Dominican constitution. At first he believed Balaguer was the rightful governor of the country and he supported him accordingly; later it was the State Council which had the legal support of our constitution and then he chose to obey them instead.[221]

It appears as if General Rodríguez Reyes was appreciated in all quarters, and in August 1962 he was promoted to inspector of the armed forces,

218 Interview with Ramón Jesús Rodríguez Landestoy, Boca Chica, 15 June 1989.
219 Guerrero (1988), p. 159.
220 Ibid., p. 213.
221 Interview with Ramón Jesús Rodríguez Landestoy, Boca Chica, 15 June 1989.

Figure 8.11 Monseñor Eliseo Sánchez, Luis Amiama Tió and Donald Reid Cabral, members of the State Council, at the funeral of Miguel Rodríguez Reyes.

which gave him access to all military conferences and station camps.[222] General Rodríguez Reyes became a key figure – 'he was a natural leader, people respected him'[223] – and it was therefore natural that he was initiated into the plans for a coup, which began to develop in October 1962. It was becoming clearer and clearer that the UCN was losing ground to the PRD, Juan Bosch's party. The PRD was a populist party with an elaborate program which advocated keeping a large part of the state property under direct governmental control as well as the immediate initiation of thorough land reforms.[224]

One who did not trust Bosch was Imbert and he has often been pointed to as the source of inspiration for the coup plans.[225] When General Rodríguez Reyes was informed about the plans by his *compadre*, José Miniño, he said:

222 García (1986), p. 140.
223 Interview with Ramón Jesús Rodríguez Landestoy, Boca Chica, 15 June 1989.
224 Ambassador Martin often expressed a certain mistrust concerning Bosch. This, however, did not preclude that one of Bosch's most intimate advisers (Sacha Volman) was a CIA agent (Jimenes Grullón, (1977), pp. 195, 287) and that many of the funds provided for PRD's campaign came from the CIA. The American policy was somewhat schizophrenic. At the same time as the PRD got considerable covert support, over US$50 million were committed to the UCN-supported State Council. When Bosch finally came to power his government received much less financial support than his predecessors, while the Kennedy administration trained and equipped the forces that eventually brought down his regime (Goff and Locker (1969), pp. 265 and 267–9).
225 Martin (1966), p. 404 and Atkins (1981), p. 78.

'*Compadre,* do not mention it any more.' Not all military men were in accordance with the plans. The idea was that Bosch would be made unable to govern. My father was a leader within the ranks, but he thought he could not lend himself to something like that. He became the sole obstacle, no one could govern him. He was loyal to Bosch. My father was a man of principles, all the rest were manageable. They had to kill him.[226]

General Rodríguez Reyes soon learned that someone was after his life. He was sent to Miches, south of the Samaná Bay, in order to investigate a 'disembarkation'. He did not like the environment up there, but felt something was wrong with his 'mission' and returned to the capital. Later he learned that the trip to Miches had been some sort of trap and that someone had planned to have him killed while he was in Miches.[227]

It is possible that Rodríguez Reyes' life was endangered because Juan Bosch trusted him and planned to put him in charge of the army if he won the elections, a scenario which was becoming more and more likely during the month of December. In those days Rodríguez Reyes and Bosch met frequently and Bosch often visited the general in order to have a chat and a cup of coffee around three o'clock in the afternoon.[228] In the middle of October Rodríguez Reyes came to Bosch's house and told him about the plans for a coup attempt:

> In those same days General Rodríguez Reyes came to see me one night. Rodríguez Reyes was Inspector of the Armed Forces and the only one among the generals who had the aptitude for leadership. He had entered the forces as a private and would die that year, by the end of December in the bloody episode of Palmasola [sic]. The general told me that strong internal pressures, divisions and tensions existed within the State Council. A group of councilors [members of the state council] wanted to prolong the life of the Council for one more year and one of the councilors had proposed a coup d'état. The armed forces, he [Rodríguez Reyes] assured me, were not going to lend themselves to any fiddling. He [Rodríguez Reyes] had said yes to the councilor who had proposed the coup to him and had then immediately informed the High Command of what was happening. Some days later three high ranking officers confirmed what General Rodríguez Reyes had told me.[229]

226 Interview with Miguel Antonio Rodríguez Landestoy, Santo Domingo, 29 April 1986.
227 Ibid.
228 Interview with Ramón Jesús Rodríguez Landestoy, Boca Chica, 15 June 1989.
229 Bosch (1964), pp. 105–6.

When Rodríguez Reyes left for Palma Sola, Bosch was in New York. He had gone there two days after the election victory of his party and nine days before he was officially proclaimed President of the Dominican Republic. Bosch's sudden departure came as a shock for his own party and Angel Miolán, secretary general of the PRD, later wrote that the trip of the party leader came as a total surprise even for the party's own directors and that it meant that a 'dangerous period of agitation' struck the country while Bosch was away. He stayed away until ten days before the inauguration of his government on 27 February 1963.[230] In the meantime General Rodríguez Reyes had gone to Palma Sola and been killed under mysterious circumstances. Bosch later stated:

> The tragedy of Palma Sola worried me a lot politically since a very important officer died there [...] The coup which was staged against me later was carried out on the orders from the US Military Mission. Rodríguez Reyes was a Dominican patriot who did not obey any orders from the US Mission. Rodríguez Reyes was a *Trujillista* general and the *Trujillistas* did not obey the North Americans. Had Rodríguez Reyes been in charge of the army in those days I do not think the coup would have come about.[231]

When the armed forces deposed Bosch on 25 September 1963, they were led by tank commander Elías Wessin y Wessin and Antonio Imbert Barrera.[232]

The political parties and Palma Sola

Juan Bosch had also been in contact with the Venturas:

> At the beginning of November [1962] one of the *Mellizos* came to the capital and went to see me in order to say that if I guaranteed that my party was going to help them they were going to preach in order to convince their people to vote for me. But I told him that if I had to write them the letter of promises they demanded in order to be president, I preferred not to be president at all. Then he threatened me with various misgivings which would happen to me if I did not accept his offer. He said that I would be unable to win any elections

---

230 Miolán (1984), pp. 391 and 393.
231 Interview with Juan Bosch, Santo Domingo, 11 October 1985.
232 'Others prominently involved in the conspiracy, apart from the armed forces, ministers and the chiefs of staff, included the chief of the National Police and the surviving assassins of Trujillo, Generals Imbert and Amiama Tió' (Black (1986), p. 34).

and told me that he was going to seek contact with Viriato Fiallo instead of me.[233]

In November it became apparent that neither the UCN nor Miguel Angel Ramírez' PNRD were going to win the elections and this was probably the reason why León Romilio sought the support of Juan Bosch's PRD instead:

A cousin of mine, Jesús Rodríguez, was a member of the PRD and he took me to meet Bosch in the capital. We wanted him to do something for Palma Sola. I also met Viriato Fiallo. It was in the palace, since he was close to the government. But they did not offer us anything. They were all beasts, like animals. How could they behave like that? It was these people who tore down the crosses. It was they who ordered people to be killed.[234]

It was the local politicians who were interested in using the votes from Palma Sola; the national politicians only felt disdain for the 'religious fanatics'. The politicians in the capital were entangled in their own power struggles and did not care so much about the votes of some strange religious sect somewhere in the backlands close to the Haitian border.

The UCN had emerged as the anti-*Trujillista* party of both the urbanites and the oligarchy and had found its acknowledged leader in Viriato Fiallo, who had succeeded in pursuing his career as a respected physician under Trujillo's reign without compromising himself. He had been steadfast in his opposition against the dictator and had suffered various imprisonments for his position. Fiallo was no intellectual and lacked political experience. He had some charisma and his often repeated phrase '*¡Basta ya!*' ['It's enough!'] proved to be effective during the early days of freedom from the dictatorship. However, soon the UCN proved to be inept in the field of political propaganda. Fiallo became little more than a bleak figurehead, surrounded by stout advisers who played upon his simple-minded faith that if all traces of *Trujillismo* could be wiped out the Republic's problems would be solved. In the meantime the wealthy and smart UCN supporters made plans for themselves. The UCN had very little of a political ideology and a very thin program.

Bosch's PRD, on the other hand, had a program and an ideology. Bosch depicted himself as the only politician in the political arena of the Dominican Republic and his advisers busied themselves building up efficient supporter groups all over the country, promising a just land distribution

233 Interview with Juan Bosch, Santo Domingo, 11 October 1985.
234 Interview with León Romilio Ventura, Media Luna, 17 January 1986.

Figure 8.12 Juan Bosch in the 1960s.

and a social welfare program. While the PRD concentrated its attacks on the right wing of the State Council – Archbishop Eliseo Pérez Sánchez and Antonio Imbert in particular – the UCN linked itself, more or less, to the governing State Council and concentrated its attacks on Bosch, depicting him as a *Trujillista*, a corrupt man and a communist who was opposed to the Christian faith. The gross exaggerations of the UCN propaganda led to its own defeat; the PRD appeared as more decent, more serious and was only helped by the unjustified invectives that the UCN showered on its leaders.[235]

The theme of Palma Sola was not part of the political struggle on the national level. The place was commonly viewed, both by left- and right-wing politicians, as a reminder of days gone by, characterized by witchcraft, ignorance and despotism, or as a den of communists. Most outsiders and city dwellers tended to view Palma Sola as a hideous projection of their own fears – a place imagined to be inhabited by various political monsters: *Trujillistas*, communists or plain evildoers in the form of devil worshipers and adulterers, all sunk into the lowest forms of debauchery, ignorance and superstition. Palma Sola was depicted as almost everything no one wanted to be associated with. It was not strange that León Romilio Ventura's offers were turned down in Santo Domingo. Even someone like Bosch, who saw himself as a politically mature and educated man, tended to view the *Olivoristas* from the outside, as an archaic survival which had to disappear in the name of progress:

235 Rodman (1964), p. 163.

The peasants search for some kind of heavenly protection. They do not search for it within the Catholic church, because the big landowners are protected by it. This is what explains Liborio, the *Mellizos* and the church of '*Bom Jesús*' in Brazil. The peasants feel supported by such leaders and instead of confronting themselves with the landowners they canalize their problems into that kind of faiths. Palma Sola was a tragedy, but it is easy to explain.[236]

It appears as if the politicians in Santo Domingo viewed Palma Sola as a place situated in another world with inhabitants as distant to them as creatures from outer space. Palma Sola constituted an integrated part of the local politics in the San Juan Valley, but it was totally alien to national politics, except, perhaps, as a useful instrument for certain politicians' shady plans and actions.

Speculations and accusations

What actually happened in Palma Sola and why did the massacre take place? Three speculations are usually aired when inquiries are made about the reasons behind the tragedy:

a)   the undisciplined Dominican army run amuck
b)   some political party wanted to cover up shady deals it had struck with leading men within the Palma Sola community
c)   the massacre was a cover-up for the murder of General Rodríguez Reyes.

Juan Bosch opted for the first theory:

It was logical. The State Council thought that Palma Sola constituted some kind of peasant rebellion directed against the wealthy landowners, who were supported by the council. But what the *Mellizos* had were only stones and they wounded Caamaño with one of them while Rodríguez Reyes was killed with blows. What happened there was a protest. It was the desperate situation of the poor peasants which created it all. They believed that the rich would perish after the elections and that they themselves would create a new government. The State Council was weak and ignorant, the situation got out of hand and the police and military could not handle it. That Rodríguez Reyes got murdered by his own is nothing but speculation.[237]

236 Interview with Juan Bosch, Santo Domingo, 11 October 1985.
237 Ibid.

The view of Bosch is echoed by, for example, Radhamés Gómez, the journalist who knew most about Palma Sola:

> They [the White Helmets] could not handle the situation, they were
> governed by their own fear. If someone wanted to kill the general it
> would have been easier to kill him in a more discrete way, in another
> place. He was the most serious military man around here. I think
> everything came about out of bad planning. It was a joint operation
> between the police and the military, but such arrangements tend to be
> worthless. The Dominican military is more violent than the police, but
> at the same time it is more reasonable. There exists a constant tension
> between the police and the military; it is hard for them to work
> together [...] I believe the general was killed by the *Olivoristas*, but
> when the police and the military heard about it the shock became too
> big to handle. A general is untouchable for the military and when news
> spread that Rodríguez Reyes had been killed the fury took hold of
> both soldiers and policemen [...] Palma Sola was not the first and not
> the last time things got out of hand for the military. They tend to
> overdo their operations. Remember the 'Battle of Avenida de las
> Americas', where five boys struggled during a whole day against the
> entire army, three generals, helicopters, attack planes, tanks and every-
> thing imaginable.[238]

District Attorney Suzaña, who was an eyewitness, agrees with Gómez and
states that he never understood why everything degenerated into chaos.
He suspected that the army and the police had not planned their actions
together and that both factions were caught up in a crossfire, shooting at
one another within a compact cloud of tear gas.[239]

The view that Palma Sola had in fact very little to do with politics became
widespread after the massacre and was reflected by the international press.
Time magazine wrote: 'Eight days after the elections there was a clash
between troops and members of a weird religious cult in the back country
that left at least 23 dead. But that had little to do with politics.'[240]

238 Interview with Radhamés Gómez Pepín, Santo Domingo, 18 March 1986. Gómez Pepín
    refers to an incident in January 1972 when four revolutionary youngsters were attacked
    at the outskirts of Santo Domingo by a force led by four generals and one admiral. The
    battle lasted for fifteen hours and the army used more than a thousand men with
    machine guns, bazookas, several MX-60 tanks and a Vampire attack plane which fired 81
    millimeter rockets at the fighting young men. While occupying themselves with these
    operations the military command later stated that they were unable to communicate with
    a group of civilians, led by the papal nuncio, who wanted to act as mediators and stop the
    bloodshed (*Listín Diario* (1972) and Franjul (1972)).
239 Interview with Miguel Tomás Suzaña, San Juan de la Maguana, 7 May 1986.
240 *Time*, 4 January 1963. No effective body count was carried out and the real number of the

However, too many questions still remain. Juan Isidro Jimenes Grullón, who was an old anti-*Trujillista* and very active in the politics of the day, agrees upon the fact that the army probably let everything get out of hand; after all 'Trujillo had accustomed his army to assassinations'. He also writes that he cannot understand why Attorney General García Vásquez, who had planned the action for a long time and who was the person who was ultimately responsible for the catastrophic results, could get away with the superficial report he wrote. Jimenes Grullón asks himself why the State Council did not demand the immediate separation of García Vásquez from his office and why it did not appoint an independent commission in order to investigate what had happened and indicate who were responsible for the bloodshed. Since the government never did so, all questions will remain. Was the massacre of Palma Sola a tragic incident, which came about through the mismanagement of the police and military, or was it the result of political machinations?[241]

The newspaper of Bosch's own PRD, *La Vanguardia*, seems to be unwilling to accept the explanations given by its party leader and suggests that 'We are able to find only one answer to all these questions: A political crime ... lies behind the Massacre of Palma Sola.'[242] *La Vanguardia* points to the huge influence that the United States embassy had on the State Council at the time of the massacre and suggests that it was in the interest of the Americans to have General Rodríguez Reyes killed: 'What powerful interests felt threatened by these two career army officers [Rodríguez Reyes and Caamaño]? Is it a coincidence that Colonel Caamaño after exactly two years and four months confronted 40,000 Yankee soldiers in the streets of Santo Domingo?'[243]

The role of the United States remains unclear. Ambassador Martin condemned the massacre and acted as if he had been, more or less, totally unaware of the details of the planned action. In *Overtaken by Events* he states that he began to suspect that something was wrong when members of the state council asked MAAG for military assistance in the form of sophisticated war equipment. His astonishment is strange, since he used to be well informed about all the subtleties of Dominican politics. Martin considered himself to be extremely influential and at times even viewed himself as the 'king in a doomed country'.[244] He regarded Rafael Bonnelly, the Dominican president, as something like his personal servant. Martin sometimes even wrote his speeches and later stated: 'Several times

---

dead will never be known. Surely more than 100 persons were killed and numbers between 500 and 1,000 have been mentioned (García (1986), pp. 233–5).

241 Jimenes Grullón (1977), pp. 492–3.
242 Cárdenas (1988).
243 Ibid.
244 Martin (1986), p. 207.

the Dominican Republic's fragile experiment in democracy depended upon my personal relationship with President Bonnelly.'[245] The American ambassador directed much of the council's policy: 'When people began to call the council a do-nothing government we devised a program of reforms, including agrarian reform, and I urged it on the council.'[246]

Martin also saw it as his duty to supervise the military: 'I lost no chance to make it clear to the Dominican military that we supported the civilian council.'[247] He influenced the political parties: 'My [...] job was to work with the twenty-six political parties from extremist left to extremist right. To the leaders of all I insisted on elections on schedule, encouraged them to participate fully and discouraged extremism [...] My political officers helped handle them.'[248]

The communists were kept under scrupulous surveillance:

> Soon I found myself urging the State Council to deport some Communist leaders and to harass others as Emil Smicklas and his Chicago robbery squad did. It was illegal detention, perhaps even police brutality, an invasion of constitutional rights ... Now trying to save a tottering democratic government, I found myself favoring it.[249]

In order to achieve all this, Martin had to rely on information both from his Dominican friends and from other sources, among them around 160 Peace Corps volunteers spread all over the country,[250] some of them working not far from Palma Sola.[251] Martin also worked closely with the CIA: 'Some ambassadors wanted nothing to do with the CIA, holding that CIA men were all a bunch of dirty spies – But I wanted to know everything the CIA was doing – I had to in the supercharged Dominican political atmosphere.'[252]

Considering all this, it appears strange if Ambassador Martin did not have more detailed information about Palma Sola than he claims to have had. Furthermore, two of his military attachés went into Palma Sola either together with the army or immediately after the massacre. One of them was Bevan Cass, a very well-informed person who later apparently had something to do with the toppling of Bosch in 1963. At that moment Martin stated:

245 Ibid., p. 229
246 Ibid., p. 217
247 Ibid., p. 346
248 Ibid., p. 218.
249 Ibid.
250 Ibid., p. 220.
251 *House Annals*, 25 January 1963.
252 Martin (1986), p. 221.

Cass was having problems of conscience about Bosch. As our naval
attaché, he was obliged to urge Dominican military officers to support
Bosch, but he himself had misgivings about Bosch's attitude toward
the Castro/Communists [...] and didn't know 'how much longer I can
go on supporting him like this' [...] he was probably our most influential attaché.[253]

The second person who went into Palma Sola was Luther ('Fritz') Long.
It has been suggested that Long was also involved in the planning of the
coup against Bosch:

Colonel Fritz Long, along with his colleague, a Colonel Cash [sic], had
reportedly been conspiring with representatives of the oligarchy and
the militantly anti-communist CEFA [*Centro de Enseñanza de las Fuerzas
Armadas*] group to topple the Bosch government. While the roles of
Colonels Long and Cash appear to be common knowledge among
Dominican political leaders, it is not known whether they were acting
on their own or on orders from superiors in the Pentagon.[254]

Martin raises a lot of questions but writes nothing about the results of the
investigations which his own people carried out in the area after the
massacre. They have however left a trace in the *House Annals* of the American Redemptorist priests in Las Matas de Farfán, which on 25 January
1963 mentions the visit of an American army captain: 'An "American"
supper served by the nuns in the Convent. Present were Frs. O'Hara and
May, the two Peace Corps Boys and an American Army Captain, attached
to the Dominican Army, and stationed here since the Palma Sola affair. A
pleasant time had by all.'[255]

A few days later the priests were visited by Ambassador Martin who also
shared dinner with them and 'drew comments from us on different aspects
of Las Matas, especially Palma Sola'.[256] Since Martin was so upset at the
news of the massacre it is strange that one perceives a note of anxiety when
he meets with former *consejero* Donald Reid, some months after Bosch had
taken over the presidency:

Business was virtually at a standstill [said Reid]. Businessmen feared
Bordas [Bosch's secretary of commerce and industry]. And they feared
that Bosch was handing over the country to the Castro/Communists.

253 Martin (1966), pp. 504–5.
254 Black (1986), p. 35.
255 *House Annals*, 25 January 1963.
256 Ibid., 6 February 1963.

Moreover, obscure young leftists, probably acting as a front for others, had gone to the Attorney General with complaints against President Bonnelly, Reid and Pichardo,[257] charging them with murder, torture, and misappropriation of public funds.

I [Ambassador Martin] said I couldn't believe it. Reid said it was true. What murder? The killings at Palma Sola, he said. But surely no formal charges would be filed? He said they would. And they were.[258]

We have not found any traces of any formal charges in any other source and Bosch himself denies that the case of Palma Sola was taken up for investigation under his presidency:

I was not in the country when the massacre took place. I left on 22 December [1962] and returned on 10 February, 1963. When I came back no prisoners were left. When I came to power it was a closed case [...] When I took possession of the presidency there was nothing pending and you did not hear anything more about Palma Sola.[259]

We have already seen that some members of the Palma Sola community believed that displeased members of the UCN let their wrath over Plinio's 'treachery' explode in a campaign against Palma Sola. There may be some truth behind such speculations, but going from that to an outright massacre in order to avenge themselves and cover up their former connections with Palma Sola seems like a far-fetched idea.

Then only the theory concerning the cover-up of a political murder remains. General Rodríguez Reyes was the only victim on the side of the army and the police. He was a highly controversial person whose life already had been threatened by politically ambitious groups. Was he murdered by his own men? Many witnesses coincide in stating that they saw him shot, or stabbed, by a man in uniform. However, it was hard to distinguish anything in the chaos and the clouds of tear gas that enveloped the area around the church in Palma Sola. After the massacre the police

257 Donald Reid Cabral and Nicolás Pichardo were both members of the State Council. Reid was later (1963–65) to become president of a civilian triumvirate which governed the Dominican Republic after the military coup against Bosch. He was seen as a representative of the oligarchy, and was ousted by a military revolt in April 1965, after introducing an austerity program which, among other things, built on wage freezes and prohibition of strikes, at a time when the prices of basic foodstuffs were rising. The revolt quickly grew into a full-scale social revolution and ended with the US intervention, after a mere five days (Wiarda (1975), pp. 251–5). Pichardo was the physician who had hidden Luis Amiama Tió after the murder of Trujillo. He had been instrumental, as a mediator, in the negotiations that led to the creation of the State Council (Guerrero (1988), p. 339).

258 Martin (1966), p. 359.

259 Interview with Juan Bosch, Santo Domingo, 11 October 1985.

presented a witness, who stated that he had seen the *Mellizos* killing the general:

> I saw General Rodríguez Reyes talking to Plinio, Eloy and Onilio Ventura. Then, when they saw that one of the military and the police approached them, Onilio struck at General Rodríguez Reyes with a knife, he fell to the ground, and at that moment Eloy took the knife and finished him off.[260]

However, if the *Mellizos* actually killed the general it is very strange that the officers in charge of the White Helmets did not let them live in order to be judged properly, instead of executing them summarily within Palma Sola, later burning their bodies. Were they acting in the heat of the moment, or were they obeying orders? No one knows. Tulio, who survived, witnessed to his friends and family that he had seen the general killed by a man in uniform, but he never presented his testimony to the authorities, who probably were unaware of his survival.

It is also strange that all prisoners from Palma Sola were suddenly released on 20 January 1963, just a few weeks after their capture.[261] No explanations were given and no kind of compensation has ever been offered to the survivors of the massacre. León Romilio Ventura was kept in custody until 13 February, when it was decided that he was to be brought to the prison in San Juan de la Maguana. However, the day after he arrived in that town he was released on the explicit orders of District Attorney Suzaña.

León Romilio was the only survivor from Palma Sola who was formally sentenced. He was accused of violating the Dominican laws concerning the exercise of witchcraft, private use of uniforms and abuse of ecclesiastical functions. León Romilio states that he got the news of the massacre when he was in solitary confinement in Santo Domingo. A lieutenant named Mendrano visited him in his cell and told him: 'You *Mellizos* have to watch out because someone has shot General Rodríguez in the head with a bullet No. 4.'[262]

---

260 Large parts of this testimony, given by a fourteen-year-old boy named Alcántara, reflects information given by Paulino (1962a) just before the massacre and may have been a fabrication. The boy is quoted in *El Caribe* on 30 December 1962, but the official interrogation document is marked 19 January 1963. Alcántara's testimony is the only one among the hundreds given by the Palma Sola survivors after their imprisonment which directly accuses the *Mellizos* of killing the general (see García (1986) pp. 255–7)).

261 Already on 10 January, 100 of the 723 prisoners from Palma Sola, detained at the main police quarters [*Cuartel General de la Policía Nacional*] in Santo Domingo, were released while the remaining prisoners were transferred to the lunatic asylum in Nigua, just outside San Cristóbal (*El Caribe*, 11 January 1963 and García (1986), p. 319).

262 Interview with León Romilio Ventura, Media Luna, 17 January 1986.

The mystery surrounding the general's death deepens further when it is taken into consideration that the body never underwent a proper autopsy. Members of his family were at least never presented with a proper death certificate, even though they had formally asked for one. Ramón Jesús Rodríguez, the general's son, remembers vividly what happened after the massacre:

> When we had to bring our dead father to the house and prepare every-thing for the *velorio* our mother told us not to be weaklings. While she prepared the house I was given the dead body of my father [...] He had various round holes in his chest and back, the skull was broken in the back, and so were his arms. It looked like he had been killed in an ambush by various persons. That was my impression. He was buried already the next day, without an autopsy, without any medical certifi-cate, something which differs completely from standard behavior in a case like this. This was in the morning of 29 December. In the after-noon, at 17.30, the secretary of the armed forces, Viñas Román, called me over the phone and told me that I had to be conscious of the fact that neither he, nor the government, nor the armed forces had anything to do with the death of my father. On the next day I went to the national police and met with General Imbert Barrera and General Belisario Peguero, chief of the police. I asked them for authorization to talk to the prisoners from Palma Sola, but they denied me such a permission. They told me later they did so because they were not sure how I would react when I was confronted with my father's murderers. Two days later I went to Fort Gulick in Panama, obeying superior orders. There I attended a basic course in infantry for one year and six months.[263]

The brother of Ramón Jesús, Miguel Antonio, did not rest quietly with the information the family had been given concerning the death of his father. He was preoccupied by all the rumors that continued to develop around the mysterious murder, like, for example, when an article about Palma Sola appeared in a Venezuelan magazine and its delivery was inter-cepted at the Santo Domingo airport. The annoying article was written by Florángel Cárdenas, the Chilean sociologist who in January 1963 had been put in charge of an investigation of the Palma Sola prisoners. Together with several university students she carried out extensive interviews, but the results were never published in the Dominican Republic. As a matter of fact, the article, which was published half a year after the events, accused both Imbert and García Vásquez of arranging the murder of the general

263 Interview with Ramón Jesús Rodríguez Landestoy, Boca Chica, 15 June 1989.

and of being the instigators of the massacre that followed.[264] Miguel Antonio never read the article, but various persons told him that his father had been murdered and that Imbert and Caamaño had planned the deed together. Someone even gave him the name of the presumed killer, a policeman named Erasme from Neiba who was killed in 1986.[265]

Still, no proofs exist which discredit Imbert and no one ever charged him, or anyone else for that matter, with the responsibility either for the massacre or the murder of the general. It is possible that Radhamés Gómez is right when he says that if someone wanted to kill the general he could always have had it done in a much more discreet way, and in another place. However, as long as most questions remain unanswered the crop of rumors will continue to grow.

264 Cárdenas Fontecha (1964).
265 Interview with Miguel Antonio Rodríguez Landestoy, Santo Domingo, 29 April 1986.

9 Justifying a massacre

Official religion and ideology in the Dominican Republic, 1492–1962

Could the persecution and death of Olivorio and the massacre of Palma Sola have been avoided? As should be clear by now, nothing seems to indicate that either Olivorio or the Ventura *Mellizos* constituted a real danger to public order or the established society in the San Juan Valley. The *Olivorista* movement was a peaceful and defensive one, a movement that catered to the have-nots – to people who had become the involuntary victims of exogenous changes in the economic and political situation of the Dominican Republic from the beginning of the present century until the death of Trujillo. Still, the *Olivoristas* were perceived in a completely different light by the outsiders: as a major threat to the society that the latter were trying to build in the 1910s and in the wake of the fall of the Trujillo regime.

In Chapter 5 we examined the hidden transcript of *Olivorismo*: the dreams of a society built on justice, cooperation and equality, and a better lot for the poor. Of course, the established society in the San Juan Valley also had its transcript, public as well as hidden, and that transcript differed substantially from that of the *Olivoristas*. This difference illuminates the question of why peaceful coexistence between the *Olivorista* insiders and the urban outsiders turned out to be impossible. In the present chapter we will examine how, over the centuries that elapsed since the partition of Hispaniola into one French and one Spanish part, a more-or-less official ideology developed that was at odds with a number of the real or imagined characteristics of the *Olivorista* religion.

In doing so, we will concentrate on the Palma Sola episode, and for two reasons. The first is the availability of contemporary data. The opinion of the outsiders at the very time when the movement was making an impact is far better documented for Palma Sola than for the original movement led by Olivorio himself. The second reason is that the 'official' ideology reached an apogee during the Trujillo period, i.e. just before the appearance of the *Mellizos*. During that period elements were added that had not been present in the 1910s and 1920s. These elements, however, represented continuity. They did not attempt to break the trend that had developed before 1930. Hence, with due caution, a great deal of what is being said about Palma Sola in this chapter, *mutatis mutandis*, applies to the original *Olivorismo* as well, and should be interpreted with that in mind. To set the stage, let us begin with a summary examination of the 'outsider' view of Palma Sola.

The condemnation of Palma Sola

The Dominican press described the people of Palma Sola as a horde of uneducated peasants. Frenzied and fanaticized by a barbaric religion, they were accused of violating every imaginable law of decency and civility:

> In the cult of Liborio virgins are violated. Women legally and honestly married are induced to adultery. And all this without remorse. Opposed to the Sacred are the sinfulness, the carnality and the diabolical, exactly the things that are done in the name of Holiness within the insane practices of Palma Sola [...]
>
> The authorities have now the last word whether this fetishist cult and immoral barbarism will be exterminated or not.[1]

Olivorismo was depicted as a primitive cult, and the vicinity to Haiti was stressed; it was repeatedly pointed out that Palma Sola was situated 'only approximately 30 kilometers from the border'.[2] For many Dominicans such a location conjured up strange notions connected with voodoo and 'African primitivism' and the *Olivoristas* were accordingly described as members of a savage tribe: 'The State Council tried on several occasions to disband the Liborista tribe by peaceful means. The results of these measures were always negative. Fanaticism does not respond to other reasons than its aberrant fetishistic cultic practice.'[3] *Santomé*, the local newspaper of San Juan de la Maguana, urged the authorities 'to finish off, once for all' the *Olivorista* religion which, according to the editorial writer, for more than fifty years had tried to change the region of San Juan de la Maguana into the '"CAFRE" of the Dominican Republic'.[4]

Reading the Dominican press of the time, it is hard to discern any individuals among the *Palmasolistas*; they are generally described as a faceless mass of illiterate wretches, manipulated by sinister charlatans:

---

1 Paniagua O. (1962), p. 23.
2 Bobea Bellini (1963).
3 *La Nación*, 7 December 1962. A cartoon published in *El Caribe*, 11 December 1962, depicts the *Mellizos* with necklaces, bracelets, fringes of leaves on their heads and a human skull at their feet.
4 *Santomé*, 30 November 1962, capital letters in the original. With *Cafre* the writer probably means *Kaffir*, a derogatory term for black Africans (from Arabic, *kafir* [infidel]).

The economy of a prosperous region in the heart of the south of the Republic is every day deteriorating in an alarming way due to the superstitious efforts of some clever individuals, who are met with absolute respect by thousands of peasants, the immense majority of them illiterate.[5]

In the south, some 16 kilometers from Las Matas de Farfán, are the mountains of Palma Sola. There the diabolical mind of Plinio, the Mellizo, while cunningly exploiting the credulity and illiteracy of our peasants, has established, protected by the isolation and shadows of these distant heights, a spectacle which is a mixture of savagery, super-stition, and fraud.[6]

Palma Sola was described as a den of vice and both divine and mundane laws were invoked to convince the authorities that something had to be done:

Mankind will be pardoned any sin or blasphemy; only blasphemy directed against the Holy Spirit will not be forgiven. Anyone who says a word against the Son of Man, will be forgiven; but he who speaks against the Holy Ghost will not be forgiven.[7]

We are facing an obvious case of flagrant violations of the national laws which chastise fraud, witchcraft and all other practices which the Melli-zos and their followers are accused of.[8]

There was no intent to view the affair from the perspective of the *Olivoris-tas*. During the whole campaign the people who had joined the movement were remarkably distant. They were seen from the outside and it appears as if both the press and the authorities, even the Catholic church, avoided any contact whatsoever with the devotees of Palma Sola. When solutions were proposed they were almost unanimously one-sided, aimed at the prompt disappearance of Palma Sola and the general impression is that a violent solution was advocated:

The moment to be judged came to the 'mellizos'. The bullets had already finished off 'Liborio'. We hope that now the action by the

---

5 Gómez Pepín (1962a).

6 Estrella Pimentel (1962). It is an exaggeration to call the hillocks around Palma Sola 'mountains'.

7 Paniagua O. (1962). The article begins with an illusion to *Matthew* 12:32: 'wherefore I say unto you, All manner of sin and blasphemy shall be forgiven unto men: but the blas-phemy against the Holy Ghost, it shall not be forgiven unto men.'

8 *El Caribe*, 9 December 1962.

authorities will put an end to the immoral practices of Liborian corruption.[9]

The situation created is so intolerable that San Juan de la Maguana and Las Matas de Farfán, through 42 of their representatives, have announced that if the government has not taken measures on the 12th of this month [December], they will be forced to act themselves to defend their respective collectives so that 'this state of primitivism' which has been inexplicably tolerated comes to an end'.[10]

With a feeling of alarm the South and the West live through moments of anxiety, and await with impatience that the State Council will order the destruction of the twins of Palma Sola.[11]

Which were the historical roots to this lack of communication between the government and the *Palmasolistas*? Why was Palma Sola so totally alienated from not only the policy makers, but also from the Catholic clergy and the members of the press? Why was the condemnation of Palma Sola so crude and why were images of sexual abuse, 'African primitivism' and 'witchcraft' constantly conjured up as instruments to spur the government into action?

As a matter of fact, the cult in Palma Sola did not have much to do with either promiscuity or witchcraft; it was a millenarian movement firmly rooted in genuine Dominican peasant religiosity. However, the government was alarmed by the concentration of thousands of poor peasants, who came together urged on by a presentiment of an imminent change and a deeply felt rootlessness after the murder of Trujillo, the ever-present and all-powerful dictator. Even though some indications exist that the massacre was planned and that the press campaign that preceded it was partly directed by people attached to certain political factions, hoping to gain political benefits in the upcoming elections, the question remains why the Catholic church, the press and public opinion were all so indifferent to the fate of thousands of individuals – men, women and children – who had gathered in Palma Sola. The silence after the massacre was appalling and the reaction of the church was extraordinarily meek; it offered few words of compassion for the victims. Instead its clergy accused the survivors of being 'victims of their own superstition'.[12]

The campaign against Palma Sola ultimately made the place and the cult rendered there synonymous with voodoo and 'African primitivism'. The

9 Paniagua O. (1962).
10 *El Caribe*, 8 December 1962.
11 Valenzuela (1962).
12 Pérez (1963). The article was published in the Catholic weekly *Fides*.

former president of the Dominican Republic, Joaquín Balaguer, repeated such views in his immensely popular book *La isla al revés*:

> Even though that taste for magic does not manifest itself in Santo Domingo to the same degree as in Haiti, it cannot be denied that there exists among the majority of the Dominicans a fund of superstition which cannot be explained as anything but the presence of characteristic traits of the primitivism of the African race in our blood.[13]

> In some frontier zones, such as in well-known sections of San Juan de la Maguana, centers are operating where magic is still openly practiced. In some cases, as in 1962, the cult of these 'Maitres Papa Loas' has caused mass concentrations which have disturbed the peace and created, in neighboring settlements, a state of exaltation close to paroxysm.[14]

> In December, 1962, thousands of persons gathered during several days in the place called Palma Sola in order to render cult to their god [Olivorio] with dances and songs of a typical African character [...] [In several villages] bohíos had been constructed for the Liboristic fanatics who had spread rapidly all over this region, close to the frontier with Haiti and who were beginning to be viewed among the authorities as a threat to the nation and to our traditional religious sentiments.[15]

Balaguer exposes views that surfaced during the last hundred years of Dominican history and in the following section we will present the formation of some ideas which may have influenced the actions and prejudiced the opinions that were expressed by the authorities, the press and the Catholic church while dealing with Palma Sola.

True Spaniards versus Ethiopian vices

We may take as our starting point the year 1697, the year of the Treaty of Ryswyick, following which the island of Hispaniola was divided into one French and one Spanish part. Surviving Spanish traditions in the French part soon merged with French and African customs, while the population

13 Balaguer (1983), p. 209.
14 Ibid., pp. 209–10. By using the French, and incorrect, term *Maitres Papa Loas*, for voodoo *hungans*, to describe the *Mellizos*, Balaguer is insinuating that Palma Sola was an offspring of Haitian voodoo.
15 Ibid., note, p. 210. The word 'bohío' is of Taino origin. The most common translation is 'house'. In the Dominican Republic it is mainly used for a rural dwelling. (Cf. Pané (1980), pp. 62 and 72.)

of the Spanish territories clung to a myth embellishing the early magnificence of their impoverished colony. Hispaniola, or La Española, was the first settlement of the mighty Spanish overseas empire and for some years the city of Santo Domingo was the busy center for the colonization of the New World. Here the New World's first cathedral was erected, and for a few decades Santo Domingo was also the administrative heart of the expanding empire. Before they embarked on their prosperous endeavors, men like Hernán Cortés and Francisco Pizarro lived and worked in Santo Domingo.

However, Spanish administration soon moved on to more thriving parts of the world, like Peru and Mexico. Santo Domingo found itself almost forgotten, in the backwater of the Spanish Main, witnessing from a distance how gold-ladened galleons passed by on their way to *La Madre Patria*. With envy the inhabitants of Santo Domingo looked westwards, to the French part of the island, which had started to prosper due to the establishment of huge sugar plantations. The 'Spanish' settlers, whose blood by now was mixed with that of Tainos, Africans and Canary Guanches, said to themselves: 'It does not matter if the French are richer than us, we are still the true inheritors of this island. In our veins runs the blood of the heroic *conquistadores* who won this island of ours with sword and blood.' The notion that Dominicans really are Spaniards has, for centuries, been a recurrent theme in the works of many Dominican authors and politicians. Joaquín Balaguer, for example, has always been a fervent defender of this thesis:

> Due to an instinct of preservation, Santo Domingo [i.e. the Dominican people] is the most Spanish and traditionalistic of the peoples of America [...] Without the cohesive power of its language and its customs, Santo Domingo would have disappeared under the pressure of what Menéndez y Pelayo called 'the savage Gallo-Ethiopian domination'.[16]

However, the people who called themselves 'Spaniards' were no longer peninsular Spaniards but had become a new and different entity: Dominican Creoles.[17]

---

16 Ibid., p. 63. Marcelino Menéndez y Pelayo is the author of *Historia de la poesía hispanoamericana* (1892), where he also states that the Spanish language is identical with the Fatherland, 'the pledge of nationality and the sign of the race' (cited in Rodríguez Demorizi (1975c), p. 18). With the 'Gallo-Ethiopian domination' he alludes to the Haitian rule of the entire island, 1822–44.

17 The word 'Creole' is probably of Portuguese origin, *crioulo*, meaning a slave born in one's household. In Latin America it has come to mean either a native-born person of European origin, or a native-born person of mixed European and African ancestry. *Cultura criolla* [Creole culture] in the Dominican Republic denotes everything considered to be

The Dominican church and the Spanish crown

The Catholic church became the foremost symbol of *La Hispanidad* [Spanish culture]. Its affinity with the interests of the Spanish crown created an identification of *Hispanidad* with Catholicism and made the Dominican Creoles feel that *Dominicanidad* [Dominicanism] meant the same thing as being white, being Spanish and being Catholic.[18]

The attachment of the Dominican church to the Spanish crown was established in the so-called *patronato*. In 1508 the Pope issued a bull granting the Spanish crown a coveted universal *patronato* over the Catholic church in the New World. This meant that the crown became absolute master of its colonies while the Pope declined any jurisdiction over all major ecclesiastical benefits in the areas conquered by Spaniards. The church became the ideological face of the state, a guardian of doctrine and morals, responsible for education and indoctrination.[19] The role of the church as guardian of 'Spanish' values was reinforced by the fact that through the centuries it was mainly ruled by men born in Spain. Since the establishment of the island's dioceses up to 1987 the Dominican church had been governed by seventy-five bishops; of these thirty-four resided in the country and only fifteen were born on the island.[20] Also, the majority of the members of religious orders who directed, and still direct, most seminars have been foreigners.[21]

The neglected state of the Santo Domingo colony was reflected by the sad condition of the Catholic church. In 1692 there were only forty-nine priests in the entire colony. To make things worse several members of the clergy were chronically ill: 'they are up and down', wrote a visiting bishop, who also described the divine worship as 'the most indecent I have ever seen'. He found no remedy for all this hopelessness and concluded his report with the following remark: 'I hold it would be better to remove all people from here and put them in a land where there is more income.'[22] Most priests lived in the capital, and in the godforsaken countryside poor peasants, ranchers and runaway slaves often practiced a religion of their own invention, mixing folk beliefs from southern Spain and the Canary Islands with the customs and creed of African slaves. In the towns the religious brotherhoods made it possible for people of African descent to

typically Dominican, mostly syncretistic religious traditions and other cultural expressions that have obtained a special 'Dominican flavor', like the *merengue* music and the *sancocho* stew.

18 Rodríguez Demorizi (1971), p. 6.
19 Elliot (1970), p. 102. Cf. Alfau Durán (1975).
20 Sáez (1987), p. 17.
21 Ibid., p. 18.
22 Archbishop Fray Fernando Carvajal y Rivera, quoted in Wipfler (1978), p. 36.

Figure 9.1 'Superstitious burial ceremony in the Rosario chapel'. Drawing by James E. Taylor, 1871.

guard their own traditions, and blend them with Catholic beliefs.[23] Dominicans continued to exercise their own rituals more or less independently from the official church; several religious brotherhoods had their own salaried clergy. A drawing by James E. Taylor (Figure 9.1), who visited the Dominican Republic in 1871, bears witness of this state of affairs; it depicts a 'Superstitious burial ceremony in the Rosario chapel' in Santo Domingo and clearly indicates that it is a syncretistic ritual.

During some decades of the eighteenth century Santo Domingo got a glimpse of prosperity. New priests arrived from Spain and several churches were renovated, but the liberation wars waged by the slaves in the neighboring French colony soon spread across the border into Santo Domingo. Settlers fled by the thousands and by the end of the century everything was back in a state of misery and neglect.

French, Spanish and Haitians ruled the Spanish-speaking population of the island successively: the French between 1801 and 1808, the Spaniards between 1808 and 1822 and the Haitians from 1822 to 1844. Even the English made incursions, attempting to conquer the spoils of the crumbling Spanish empire. This bewildering situation is reflected in a *quintilla* written at the time by a priest named Vásquez:

---

23 Larrazábal Blanco (1975), pp. 136–8.

Ayer español nací,	Yesterday I was born a Spaniard,
a la tarde fuí francés,	in the afternoon I was French,
a la noche etíope fuí,	at night I was Ethiopian,
hoy dicen que soy inglés:	today they say I am an Englishman:
No sé que será de mí![24]	I do not know what will become of me!

During these tumultuous times the Spanish-speaking clergy clung to the *patronato*, trying to maintain their status as exclusive subjects to the Spanish crown, defending their independence when various 'reform attempts' were initiated by French or Haitian authorities. Several priests came to nourish dreams about a return to the warm embrace of 'benevolent Mother Spain'.

In 1844 a resistance group composed of young idealists with a liberal outlook on life, the majority of them fervent Catholics, finally succeeded in triggering a rebellion that overthrew the Haitian government in the Spanish-speaking part of the island and proclaimed the independent Dominican Republic. These young idealists were, however, soon outmaneuvered by more conservative groups who wanted to turn the new Republic into a colony under the protection of some strong nation like Spain, France or the United States. Spain was favored by the majority of the Catholic clergy.[25]

In 1861 the government of Pedro Santana ceded the Dominican Republic to Spain. However, contrary to the hopes of many members of the Dominican clergy the annexation to the 'Mother Country' proved to be a humiliating experience:

> The Dominican priests, generally ignorant and poor, even though they had no power over their flock, that had gone astray and could not be brought back to its pen, had considerable influence which they demonstrated through fervent pleas for a reincorporation with Spain, maybe because they presumed that … [this] would increase their prestige and power […] they wanted to build a house beginning with the roof.[26]

The commander of the Spanish troops who wrote these lines suggested that the common people, neglected by the Catholic clergy, had created their own syncretistic cults. The commander describes the popular

---

24 Padre Vásquez quoted in Rodríguez Demorizi (1975c), p. 17. A *quintilla* is a five-line stanza.
25 Moya Pons (1978b), pp. 148 and 156. A noteworthy exception was the Dominican Archbishop Fernando Arturo de Meriño who opposed the annexation fervently and accordingly was sent into exile by the Spaniards, when they were invited to govern the country.
26 Gándara (1975), p. 223.

religion of the Dominicans as pure 'superstition', 'scandalous customs' and 'abusive practices' carried out during 'dances and nocturnal gatherings'.[27] He considered Dominican priests to be ignorant, and imbued with 'superstitious beliefs' themselves. Dominican clerics were accordingly forced to submit themselves to the authoritative rule of the Spanish church dignitaries, who arrived in the colony together with Spanish troops and magistrates. Spaniards viewed with amused disdain the 'peculiar' notions the Dominicans had about themselves:

> The foundation of the Dominican national character is a strange mixture of egotism, ferocity and capriciousness. The Dominican does not want to be Spanish; he does not want to be American; he does not want to be African or Haitian; he wants and yet does not want to be autonomous, independent, complete master of his actions. His individual vanity, his indisputable bravery, inspire him with noble ideas and energetic solutions, but he looks at his poverty, he measures his small stature among the civilized peoples, he looks at the [Dominican] faces that show every shade from olive to ebony, and he cannot stand the positivist instinct, showing him that only the stubborn toil of some generations will elevate him to a state of well being [...] of civilization, something he understands perfectly well in theory ...[28]

The growing disgust the Dominican population felt for Spanish rule led to a large-scale popular rebellion. Thirty thousand Dominicans, out of a population of barely more than 200,000, defeated the Spanish troops, who left the island in 1865,[29] leaving behind them more than 10,000 Spaniards and more than 7,000 Dominicans – perished in battles and epidemics.[30]

'Negroes' and 'Indians'

After the traumatic experience of the Spanish annexation some Dominicans engaged in a fervent search for a 'Dominican identity'. This was an occupation for the intellectual elite and the ideology which emerged from the quest was a hothouse plant, remote from the reality of the peasants, who were often viewed as a heterogeneous and ignorant mass, immersed in what a number of intellectuals viewed as 'Haitian superstitions'. Fed, no

---

27 Ibid., p. 226.
28 Ibid., pp. 79–80. One of the most important reasons for the following liberation war waged against Spain was the open racism of several Spanish authorities and soldiers: 'They stated that they despised all colored people; they were treating us like dogs' (Benito García, cited in *Informe* (1960), p. 417).
29 Gándara (1975), p. 506, Moya Pons (1974a), p. 21.
30 Moya Pons (1980), p. 352, Gándara (1975), p. 506.

doubt, by more than half a century of struggle against the neighboring nation, anti-Haitianism began to take root in official discourse:

> what was Dominican came to be defined with reference to what was Haitian. This dichotomy was established at practically all levels of society: Catholicism was opposed to Haitian voodoo; the Spanish language of the eastern part was held out against the *créole* spoken in the western part; Dominican mulattoness and whiteness was opposed to Haitian blackness. Even more, Haitian culture and society were seen basically as an extension of Africa, while for Santo Domingo a pure [*castizo*] Spanish origin was claimed.[31]

During the drawn-out warfare with various Haitian armies, race had become an important issue for the Dominicans.[32] In order to remove themselves from their Haitian enemies the Dominicans described themselves as 'Spaniards', while their enemies were labeled 'Ethiopians' or 'Africans'. Since the majority of the Dominican population was colored and some were just as black as most Haitians it was common to hear statements like: 'I am a Negro, but I am a white Negro. Even though I have a black skin my heart is white.'[33] The African heritage of the Dominican people was denied, but after their painful confrontations with prejudiced representatives of the Spanish government it became increasingly difficult for the Dominican Creoles to project themselves as 'unmixed' descendants of Spanish *conquistadores.*

One Dominican, who willingly had offered his services to the Spanish occupants, gave a possible solution to the intricate problem. Manuel de Jesús Galván had in his newspaper, *La Razón*, defended Spanish authorities against Dominican insurgents, whom he brandished as 'traitors without faith or opinion', unable to understand that 'Spanish dominion is the sane anchor of all social principles' and a true defense 'against noxious elements which threaten Santo Domingo'.[34] In 1882 he published his novel, *Enriquillo*, which soon became a minor classic in the Spanish-speaking parts of the world. *Enriquillo* is a historical novel about a Taino Indian who is brought up as a Spaniard. He becomes the victim of the insolence and unfairness of a Spanish plantation owner and in order to obtain justice he instigates a rebellion against the Spanish crown. His right is finally

---

31 San Miguel (1992), p. 77.
32 After the declaration of independence in 1844, the Dominicans fought three major wars against the Haitians: 1845 against invading armies sent by the Haitian president Pierrot, and in 1849 and 1855 against the armies of Soulouque (Rodríguez Demorizi (1957)).
33 A statement given in 1850 by a Dominican peasant to an American visitor named Benjamin Garden, cited in Pérez (1957), p. 96.
34 Quoted in Martínez (1971), p. 187.

acknowledged and the colonial authorities punish the man who caused the noble Enriquillo's decision to seek his rights through violent means. Enriquillo finally returns to a tranquil life among Spanish settlers, but is now treated with respect, acknowledged as a man of honor and bravery.[35]

Galván offered the Dominicans a possibility of identifying themselves with the noble savage Enriquillo. Like him they had been mistreated by the Spaniards, but they had kept their integrity and the true, dignified representatives of old, cultivated Spain would finally be forced to realize that the noble Dominicans had been badly treated by the empire's brutish underlings. Through their brave rebellion against the Spanish crown the Dominicans had in reality proved that they deserved to be honored as Latin American keepers of the true spirit of *Hispanidad*.[36] A regular cult of Enriquillo and his long ago extinct people took shape and it was not long before some Dominicans began to consider themselves as descendants of civilized Tainos.

The argument ran as follows: The Tainos had at an early stage mixed their blood with the Spaniards. The gentle and noble *Mestizos* who were a result of this mixture were forced to migrate to the eastern parts of the island, while Protestant riffraff from Europe occupied the western parts. These European wretches, buccaneers, indentured laborers and others who had been deported or had fled from Europe to escape punishment for their crimes could not mix with the Indians, since none of the latter were left. In order to get cheap labor they were forced to import African slaves, and the vile slave owners mixed their blood with their black servants.[37] It was these 'half-breeds' and 'Africans' who, according to this legend, butchered the white people of Haiti and finally occupied Santo Domingo in 1822:

> Let us not forget that this Spanish nation, Christian and Catholic as we Dominicans are, arose pure and homogeneous from the geographic unity of the island and like that it would have been conserved until today if it were not for the scion that was grafted to the original trunk in the 17th century, in order to infect its pure sap with elements profoundly and fatally alien to those that grew from the beginning on the island of Española.[38]

Conceptions like these have led to various absurdities; since the words *prieto* [very dark] or *negro* [black] are often interpreted as insults, dark-

35 Galván (1981).
36 Franco (1980), pp. 65–6.
37 Cf. Peña Batlle (1954), pp. 42–62.
38 Peña Batlle (1943a), p. 12.

skinned persons prefer to be called *morenos* [brownish people], or rather *indios* [Indians]. The denomination *indio* is even used by Dominican authorities in order to indicate the skin color on personal identity cards. Different complexions are determined as *indio claro* [light Indian], or *indio oscuro* [dark Indian].[39] Extensive blood tests have been carried out to trace the blood group O among the Dominican population, since this blood group is considered to be dominant among Indians.[40] Color vision, 'shovel-shaped teeth' and the ability to coil the tongue, have also been investigated among Dominican peasants in order to determine the Indian origin of Dominicans.[41]

The black 'menace' from the west

Spanish-American indigenism – the literary school which exalted the legendary exploits of long-extinguished Indians – had its heyday in the Dominican Republic during the 1870s and 1880s. In the limited world of the intellectuals it was followed by a period that glorified change and progress. In 1875 the Puerto Rican educator Eugenio María de Hostos came to the Dominican Republic, fleeing from the fierce battles against the Spaniards that took place in Cuba at the time. With the phrase 'civilization or death' as his device, he embarked on a mission whose aim was to guide Dominican youth into the 'modern world'. In Puerto Plata, on the north coast of the Dominican Republic, he taught a group of disciples who were going to spread his gospel all over Dominican territory.[42] Hostos stood for evolutionism in contrast to revelation, preferred experiments to dogma and rationalism to traditional oratory.

Through the teachings of Hostos the 'underdeveloped' condition of the Dominican Republic stood out in sharper relief than before. Many Dominican intellectuals felt that their native country was sinking steadily into a state of decay. According to some authors the Dominicans were going through a process of degeneration, 'losing their stature, their physical vigor and their mental potency'.[43] Starvation, political anarchy and constant warfare were given as reasons for this negative development. However, these were also times of vulgar scientific racism and social Darwinism. Human flaws were pinned to 'inferior races'; such authors blamed all problems afflicting the Dominican Republic on the presence of 'African blood' in Dominican veins. In the late nineteenth century and the

39 Castillo (1981), p. 148.
40 Alvarez Perelló (1973), pp. 67–87. On the use of blood groups as a basis for taxonomy of races, see Harris (1975), pp. 107–8.
41 Omos Cordones (1980), pp. 89–102.
42 Landolfi (1981), p. 137.
43 López (1975), p. 44.

beginning of the present one, Dominican discourse on racial issues and Haiti began to display new traits.[44] A newspaper article written in 1914 bluntly stated: 'The degree of civilization and general culture among the Ibero-American people can be measured by the size of the African population they lodge.'[45] The 'tropical' peasant, with his 'mixed blood' was described as not entirely human:

> be it because of flaw, or because of diseases, of which there are not few, he is a peculiar human variety. He is troublesome and idle, hardly of any good use. Sometimes he is a genuine nuisance and, moreover, a chest full of vices. Dancing, gambling, getting drunk and robbing other people are his characteristic qualities. He is still a primitive man, living without one single elevated idea, committed to very base passions [...] Nothing fills him with enthusiasm, nothing stimulates him. He is good only at fornication and petty thefts.
>
> He has many characteristics of the monkey, his most distinguished compatriot. His lack of patriotism is notorious.[46]

The closer to the disputed and vaguely defined border with Haiti, a country described as the source of 'damaging influences on the race', the more lugubrious became the descriptions of these racist fanatics. The following is a description of the alleged character of *castisos*, Dominican citizens of mixed Dominican and Haitian ancestry[47] living close to the Dominican frontier with Haiti:

> if [a Dominican] fecundates a Haitian Negress, our [i.e. the Dominican] ... offspring is totally incorporated with Haiti, as a demographic object and as a psychological subject. Because of this, I believe, a castiso is a man that does not have any civil standards of measurements, only zoological ones.[48]

These offensive views gained importance during the first decades of the present century and their murky influences still linger on in the minds of some so-called Dominican intellectuals. Not even Joaquín Balaguer felt any

---

44 San Miguel (1992), p. 97.

45 *Listín Diario*, 21 February 1914.

46 Moscoso Puello (1974), pp. 52–3, quoted by Franco (1981), p. 105.

47 The use of the term *castiso* in this connection is somewhat bewildering, since *castizo* (note the different spelling) in Spanish denotes a 'pure-blooded' person. Nevertheless, several Dominicans use the term, spelled *castiso*, to indicate a person of 'racially mixed' origin: 'The "castiso" is an international hybrid in whose veins the two bloods of the island are running; he is the fruit of the bed shared by a Dominican male with a Haitian female, or vice versa' (Prestol Castillo (1943), p. 20).

48 Ibid., p. 23.

restraint exposing views from the old horror chamber of 'scientific' racism. In a book from 1983, the former Dominican president writes:

> It is undeniable that secular commerce with Haiti not only has reduced the 'ethnic power' of the Dominican population by reducing its eugenic capacity, but it has also contributed to our depreciations of values and our decadent politics and morals.[49]

> The Ethiopian race is indolent by nature and does not apply its efforts to anything useful, if it does not experience the necessity to do so to gain its subsistence.[50]

> This population density [in Haiti] has a tendency to increase rapidly due to the influence of the following causes: a) the characteristic fecundity of the Negro; b) the primitive conditions that characterize the low social level of a considerable part of the Haitian population, and c) the resistance to diseases due to the Negro's physical strength.[51]

> The population excess of Haiti constitutes ... a growing threat to the Dominican Republic. This is due to a biological reason: the Negro, abandoned to his instincts and without the check that a relatively elevated living standard puts on reproduction in all countries, multiplies himself with a speed almost similar to that of certain vegetal species.[52]

49 Balaguer (1983), p. 57 . Eugenics is the study of methods of improving the quality of the human race, especially by selective breeding (from the Greek *eugenes*, wellborn).
50 Ibid., p. 52.
51 Ibid., p. 35.
52 Ibid., p. 36 (cf. p. 147). This last argument, which Balaguer presents twice in his book, is taken from John Roger Commons' *Races and Immigrants in America from 1907* (Commons (1907)). Commons, a sociologist from Wisconsin, opposed immigration and favored a racist and elitist view of human affairs, arguing against the egalitarian assumptions of the Declaration of Independence (Higham (1981), p. 117). We have been rather generous with quotations from Balaguer's book (almost every page of it contains some variant of race prejudices) due to his immense importance as policy maker in the Dominican Republic. He has been a highly influential politician and author since the 1920s. *La isla al revés* is in many parts an exact copy of his book *La realidad dominicana* (1947), first published in 1939. Needless to say, his sources are quite antiquated; of the sixty books mentioned in the bibliography, twenty-five were published in the nineteenth century, twenty-two before 1950 and only four after 1970. The book has seen various editions, the first and second ones in 1983 sold more than 10,000 copies during a few months. (The standard edition of Dominican books consists of 1,000 copies.) The whole book is characterized by malevolent use of facts and figures. For example, with respect to the last statement in the quotation it may be mentioned that the annual growth rate of the Dominican population in the 1970s was one of the highest in Latin America, 3.0 percent (Vargas-Lundius (1991), p. 27), while in Haiti it was 2.2 percent (Lundahl (1992), p. 8).

During much of the twentieth century members of various Dominican governments have been firm believers in such racial mishmash. Black people were permitted only on limited visas, issued in order to recruit them for work in the sugar fields. An immigration law from 1912 stated that only people of *pura raza blanca* [pure white race] could enter the Dominican Republic without previous permission from the secretary of state for agriculture and immigration.[53] At the same time, as we discussed in Chapter 8, efforts were made to attract white European settlers. The racist immigration laws were sharpened in 1933:

> Individuals of the Mongolian race and natives from the African continent, who are not of Caucasian race, are due to pay the following taxes: a) in order to obtain a permit to enter into Dominican territory ... \$300.00; b) for permission to stay within the territory of the Republic ... \$100.00.[54]

The efforts to attract white settlers continued during the Trujillo period.

Voodoo as the ultimate threat to *Hispanidad*

The majority of the Dominicans are mulattos or black, and a Dominican saying states that everyone has *el negro tras la oreja* [the Negro behind the ear]. Accordingly it is wrong to stress that the difference between Dominicans and Haitians is exclusively racial and it would be wrong to attribute the definition of Dominican identity in terms of a negation of things Haitian exclusively to racism:

> Anti-Haitianism [...] arose initially as consciousness of colonial difference, an identity marked first by language ... then by a series of derivative collective assertions of differences originating in colonial rivalries between the French and the Spanish. Anti-Haitianism's second layer of meaning stemmed from Saint-Domingue's ... former economic supremacy and colonial grandeur, in stark contrast to the poverty of the Spanish colony. The highly stratified hierarchy of class and color that developed in Haiti as a result of the sugar-plantation complex was very different from the social fluidity, minimal class differentiation, and maximal racial mixture of the open-range livestock economy of Santo Domingo. Finally, during the nineteenth century, the idea of Haiti derived from its status as an occupying force ... and thus as the traditional enemy of the Dominican Republic. As a form of social

---

53 *Memoria* (1924), p. 9.
54 Balaguer (1983), p. 73. The cost for permission to stay in the country was raised in 1940 to 500 pesos (ibid.). The Dominican peso was equivalent to the US dollar.

classification this meaning coincided with an emergent consciousness of national difference.[55]

That consciousness was all too easily exploited in vulgar propaganda. Dominican ideologists and politicians were quick to realize that their racial prejudices could be disguised behind a smoke screen of 'essential' cultural differences.

This was the case not least in the religious sphere. Since the Catholic church and *Hispanidad* have been so intimately entwined in the minds of Dominican hispanophiles, Roman Catholicism and culture have often been considered as synonyms. This view has led to the fact that popular beliefs among Dominican peasants, which are not wholly in accordance with established Catholic dogma, have almost unanimously been interpreted as influences from Haitian voodoo and as such brandished as alien elements.

When Américo Lugo in 1907, as a lawyer, defended a peasant living close to the border he stated that the poor man was not really to be blamed for his crime; it was his degrading environment which had destroyed him and it could destroy his wretched neighbors as well. They were all threatened by the terrible destiny of losing their Dominican character, thus ending up as 'Africans'. Most *rayanos* were 'totally Haitianized, nay, not even Haitianized, but Africanized through a process of fatal regression of the individual to his origins, as soon as he is left to himself'.[56]

As a part of their anti-Haitian politics and alleged safeguarding of 'Dominican values' several governments added fuel to this fear of 'Africa' and 'primitive religiosity'. It is still easy to find confused conceptions about 'Africa' and its religious traditions, as illustrated by the following quotation from a book published by a Dominican university in 1983:

> As we know, Africa has been the export continent of demonic religions in general [...] the religion [voodoo] that became most firmly rooted in this soil through the arrival of African slaves, was that of 'Lucumí'. The chroniclers of this pagan religion confess that the gods they worship are fond of rum and brandy; that they [the gods] have given themselves over to their sexual passions; they are considered to be jealous, unfaithful and incestuous. They also practice divination, witchcraft, sorcery and magic. Some have been cruel and tyrannical. All lived in an environment of jealousy, quarrels and wars. Some have even been compared to the devil.[57]

55 Derby (1994), p. 495.
56 Quoted in *La frontera de la República Dominicana con Haití* (1946), p. 82.
57 Mañón Rossi (1983), p. 39. In the Caribbean, Lucumí is the popular denomination of Yoruba descendants. Needless to say, the religious conceptions and way of life of real

The Catholic church considered itself as a bulwark against 'African superstitions', but for centuries reality made fun of its alleged intentions. The influential clergy were concentrated in the capital, where they often paid more attention to the perpetual political party strifes than to the attendance of their flock. The rural priests lived in a state of poverty and neglect. In 1923 the Dominican Republic had no more than 76 priests compared with the 770 priests who were active in neighboring Haiti at the same time. The standard of the clergy was considered to be extremely low. In 1925 the assistant to the Dominican archbishop, Luis Mera, publicly exhorted the priests of the Republic, demanding them to dedicate themselves to their pastoral work and abandon their concubines.[58] The contact that the rural clergy had with the peasants often limited itself to saying the mass on the days of the patron saints in the small *ermitas* that the peasants had erected themselves. The priest was paid for his service and then often joined in the nocturnal feasts, dancing to the drums, activities which had very little in common with Catholic dogma.[59]

In their search for signs of a unique Dominican culture, acceptable to their racist minds, some Dominicans embellished the Catholic church as the ultimate sign of the true Spanish heritage on Dominican soil. After all, Santo Domingo was the first place where the Christian cross had been planted in the New World and according to this view the Dominicans had stubbornly stuck to their god-given role as the original upholders of the Christian faith, in spite of all the hardship they had suffered under the yoke of 'African animists', such as the Haitians and other 'godless' peoples who had invaded their country: 'those Hispanic gentlemen [i.e. the Spanish conquerors] ... approached America in order to bless it [...] Catholicism is not a secondary or adjective factor in the Dominican nation, but it is substance, essence and life for our people.'[60]

In 1845, one year after the foundation of the Dominican Republic, the young country issued its first laws against various expressions of popular religion considered to be alien to Catholic dogma.[61] In 1862, the year after the Spanish annexation, another law was issued, explicitly mentioning voodoo: 'The dance called jodú [sic] is prohibited.'[62] A law issued in 1908 repeats the arguments of the one issued in 1845:

Yorubas have very little, if anything, in common with the fanciful descriptions of Mañón Rossi.

58 Belza (1976), pp. 44–5. The archbishop needed an assistant because he suffered from advanced arteriosclerosis (ibid.).

59 Cf. Wipfler (1978), p. 140.

60 Ruiz Tejada (1957), pp. 125–6.

61 *Un bando de policía de 1845* (1977), pp. 71–2.

62 Rodríguez Demorizi (1971), p. 95.

The non Christian cult was declared to be a pretext for vagrancy and different forms of corruption. 'The vigils, the *últimos rezos* [last prayers], the puberty rites and other acts [carried out as] non-authorized religious practices [...] are nothing but [examples of] extremely unreligious acts, acts of savagery that were occasions for getting drunk, diversions offending good customs', and, accordingly, they were to be strictly forbidden.[63]

In 1943 another law directed against voodoo and witchcraft was issued.[64] Even today, Dominicans may be prosecuted for practicing voodoo, or organizing similar acts.[65]

At the end of the 1870s the liberal teachings of Hostos began to make their presence felt in the Dominican Republic. In 1879 a law decreed the establishment of *escuelas normales* [teachers' training schools] all over the country. In public schools, a subject called *moral social* [social morality] was to be substituted for religion and sacred history.[66] The clerics raved over these *escuelas sin Dios* [schools without God], and pulled themselves together in order to meet the flagrant assault on the church carried out by the forces of 'impiety'. Catholic schools were founded and different holy orders entered the country, now declared to be *tierra de misión* [missionary territory]. The newcomers were assigned several parishes, both urban and rural. New churches were erected and old ones were restored. The preaching against voodoo and 'superstitions' was intensified, as well as the old fear of 'Haitian influences' on the popular religion. There were no doubts concerning the worst source of 'spiritual poison':

> Among the things which have come to us from the people of Louverture and Cristóbal [Henry Christophe], not less harmful than their barbaric hordes, we find the dance of cuyaya, cannibalism, voodoo, witchcraft and other sorceries and customs, some of which have introduced themselves into the simple customs of Dominicans, to such an extent that it now has proved to be impossible to eradicate their dark roots.[67]

---

63 Bryan (1979), p. 73.
64 'The spectacles known by the name "voudon" or "lua", or any others of the same, or similar, character, are considered to be a violation of good manners and as such they will be punished with correctional punishments', *Ley Núm.* 391, *G. O. Núm.* 5976, quoted in Cruz Díaz (1965), pp. 18–19.
65 Articles 258, 260 and 265 of the *Código Penal* [Penal Code] used to be applied in such cases. Article 258 concerns 'improper use of ecclesiastical jurisdictions or functions'. Article 260 deals with 'crimes against the free execution of Catholic cults' and Article 265 concerns 'associations of malefactors' (Rosell (1983), pp. 279–82, 287–92, 303–10 and 318–22).
66 Lluberes (1983), p. 9.

In 1929 the archbishop of Santo Domingo proposed the erection of a huge monument – *El Cristo de la Frontera* [Christ of the Frontier] – to commemorate a treaty which finally established the border between the two countries.[68] It was intended to be an ultimate sign that the Dominican Republic had been won for the True Church. It also appears that it was intended as a way to ward off the devil, who apparently had his abode across the border:

El blanco es hijo de Dios,	The white man is son of God
y el mulato de San Pedro;	and the mulatto of Saint Peter
y al negro lo engendra el diablo	and the Negro is begotten by the devil
para tizón del infierno.[69]	to be firebrand in Hell.

The church had a strong defender in Manuel Peña Batlle,[70] who as a firm believer in Spanish imperialism felt that the greatest tragedy of Latin American peoples was that they had broken the ties with their mother country. He attacked the liberal teachings of Hostos and sought his ideals in the Middle Ages, when the supreme and spiritual power of the church reigned over the 'material' world and the state was subdued to 'spiritual potencies' and 'Christian values', safeguarded by emperors with dictatorial powers.[71] Peña Batlle was not alone in believing that the 'degenerate' mass of the Dominican population was unable to govern itself; even well-known liberals and followers of Hostos had their doubt about the abilities of the Dominican population to rule through democratic means:

---

67 Rodríguez Demorizi (1945), p. 5. Of course Dominican voodoo has been influenced by Haitian variants, but influences have taken the other direction as well. Slaves often escaped from French plantations in order to live with Spanish *cimarrones* on the other side of the border. Some of these groups were led by Spanish-speaking runaway slaves, like Santyague (Santiago). The most violent variant of Haitian voodoo, the Pétro cult, appears to have been brought to the French part by a former slave from the Spanish part of the island, Don Pédre. Moreau de Saint-Méry writes that 'In 1768, a Negro of Petit-Goave, of Spanish origin, abused the Negroes' credibility in superstitious practices, and gave them the idea of a dance analogous with that of Vaudoux, but with much more rapid movements [...] even spectators get electrified by the spectacle of these convulsive exercises; they share the drunkenness of the actors, and by their singing, and an irresistible rhythm, they whip up some kind of common frenzy [*une crise commune*]' (Moreau de Saint-Méry (1958), p. 69).

68 García (1972), p. 12.

69 Popular Dominican *copla* [song], quoted in Nolasco (1956), p. 303.

70 Manuel Arturo Peña Batlle (1902–54) was a very prolific writer of important historical studies and one of the most influential intellectuals under Trujillo, whom he served as minister of the interior and police, minister of commerce and industry, as well as minister of foreign affairs. He was also ambassador to Haiti and wrote several of Trujillo's most important speeches (Balcácer (1989)).

71 García (1972), pp. 51–2.

Due to the fact that the people is incapable of ruling itself and, after fifty years of independence, does not want to be ruled by a foreign state, the enlightened minority, which constitutes its most noble element [...] ought to constitute itself as a political party [...] The political parties ... should prepare the Dominicans for the presently impossible task of exercising a republican, democratic and representative government.[72]

Peña Batlle regarded all kinds of 'superstition' as false paths, lethally dangerous because they led the Dominican people astray from their only security: the Catholic church. Worst of all the dangers was voodoo, which Peña Batlle imagined as a vile enemy constantly creeping across the border to poison the morals of Dominican peasants. During his entire life Peña Batlle was obsessed with Haiti which he described as the arch enemy of all values he believed to be holy and truly Dominican, i.e. in reality, Spanish:

No human feelings, neither political reason, nor occasional agreement, can induce us to contemplate the spectacle of Haitian penetration with indifference [...] the Haitian who approaches us lives infected by numerous and fatal vices, and he is nearly without exception deformed by diseases and physiological deficiencies, endemic among the base characters of that society.[73]

Finally, the Catholic church and Peña Batlle found their Caesar in the figure of Colonel Rafael Leonidas Trujillo, a man who, ruling the Dominican Republic with an iron hand for more than thirty years, willingly shouldered the role as benefactor of church and people. As his motto Trujillo chose *Dios y Trujillo* [God and Trujillo]. 'Trujillo is the Messiah [...] The flock was there under the eyes of God, waiting for God's decisive gift.'[74]

El Jefe and his crusade against voodoo

The beliefs of Peña Batlle were to have a formidable influence on the shaping of Trujillo's ideology. A study of Trujillo's speeches, mostly written by Peña Batlle or Joaquín Balaguer, reveals some recurrent themes: the Dominican Republic was the first Christian country of the New World, and since the days of Spanish conquerors Christianity had been the sole foundation and true essence of the Dominican national character. The divinely ordained mission of the Dominican people was to preserve the Spanish

---

72 Lugo (1949), p. 32, quoted in Cassá (1976), p. 70.
73 Peña Batlle (1943a), p. 13.
74 Pérez (1957), p. 321.

and Christian heritage and the only way to do so was by submitting oneself to the morals preached by the Catholic church and supporting Trujillo in his struggle to preserve the age-old values of *Hispanidad*. The union between state and church was the only guarantee for the survival of a Dominican national identity and all Dominican citizens had to be steadfast in the ongoing battle against evil forces which threatened to annihilate their society: communism and 'Haitian' superstitions.[75]

As soon as he came to power Trujillo proposed a partnership to the Catholic church; the church would serve as the legitimator of his absolute power and Trujillo would be its benevolent patron. In 1931 he greeted José Fietta, the first papal nuncio to the Dominican Republic, with the following words: 'I ... trust that your perseverance will achieve the greatest possible success with the support that will be cheerfully given by the government over which I preside.'[76]

Trujillo, however, experienced some initial difficulties with a newly ordained 'apostolic administrator',[77] Rafael Castellanos, who openly showed his disgust with Trujillo's limitless self-assertion.[78] Trujillo did everything in his power to get rid of the offensive priest, and backed by the congress he finally succeeded in having Castellanos removed from his post. The political skills and unscrupulous character of Trujillo were obvious to all observers and the Vatican was no exception. When the former Italian citizen Ricardo Pittini in 1935 was consecrated as archbishop in Santo Domingo, it was rumored that he had been suggested for that position by the dictator himself.[79]

Under the servile and flexible Pittini the Catholic church in the Dominican Republic apparently agreed upon and even contributed to the totally

---

75 Sáez (1988b).
76 Trujillo, quoted in Wipfler (1978), p. 123.
77 This title was given to Castellanos (a Dominican born in Puerto Plata) when he acted as archbishop instead of Adolfo Noel, who was unable to fulfill his duties due to poor health (Sáez (1987), p. 110).
78 The most famous clash between Trujillo and Castellanos took place in the cathedral of Santo Domingo, when Trujillo rose to deliver an obituary speech over one of his dead supporters. The dictator was greeted by a deafening applause from his retinue of flatterers, but this enthusiastic outburst was immediately interrupted by Castellanos who reprimanded the churchgoers by stating: 'In the house of God, no mortal is applauded.' When the stunned audience had calmed down, Castellanos turned to Trujillo and snapped: 'You may continue' (ibid., pp. 115–16).
79 Wipfler (1978), p. 126. Pittini had been sent to the Dominican Republic to administer the Salesians (who were founding several schools in the country). It was commonly believed that Trujillo asked the papal nuncio, Fietta, if he could not have Pittini ordained as archbishop. When the nuncio pointed out that Pittini was an Italian citizen Trujillo retorted: 'I arrange that in ten minutes.' The Vatican complied with the will of the strong-minded dictator and the recently arrived Pittini was installed as the head of the Dominican church (Rodríguez Grullón (1991), p. 120).

Figure 9.2 Archbishop Ricardo Pittini and Trujillo. With his back to the camera, the papal nuncio, Salvatore Siino.

absurd idolatry that Trujillo forced upon 'his' country. Trujillo's birthday became a national holiday, signs were posted on hospitals and asylums proclaiming 'Only Trujillo can cure us.' Village pumps carried inscriptions stating 'Only Trujillo gives us water'; at irrigation channels posters boasted 'Water runs here due to Trujillo'; and nearby fields were littered with signs which claimed that 'Crops are plentiful because Trujillo has given us all the water we need'.[80] Tourists were surprised to find not only a bible, but also an English edition of *Trujillo: The Biography of a Great Leader* in every hotel room in the country.[81] Every published book carried a dedication to *El Benefactor*, every home exposed his portrait in a prominent place and even the boxes of street shoeshiners bore inscriptions like 'Trujillo is my Protector' and 'God and Trujillo are my Faith'.[82]

An army of flatterers outwitted one another in shameless blarney; nothing was sacred in their quest to please *El Jefe*. Thus a rather commonplace article, '*La independencia, política en la cancelación de la deuda externa*' ['Independence, politics related to the cancelation of the foreign debt'] could contain this plagiarism of a well-known hymn (*Psalms* 23:1–4):

80 The fountains of the capital had plaques which announced 'This water comes to you through the benevolence of God and Trujillo.' However, *El Jefe* 'could not bear to share honors even with God. The plaques came down and were replaced with the ones reading: "Trujillo alone supplies the people with this water"' (Brown (1947), p. 136).
81 Nanita (1957). Tattered copies of this book are still easily available on streetcorners and in second-hand bookshops in Santo Domingo.
82 Examples could be multiplied; the absurdities were limitless. Cf. Ornes (1958), p. 229 and Brown (1947), p. 136.

Trujillo is my shepherd; I shall not want.
He maketh me to lie down in green pastures:
he leadeth me beside the still waters.
He restoreth my soul;
he leadeth me in the paths of righteousness for his name's sake.
Yea, though I walk through the valley of the shadow of death,
I will fear no evil:
for Trujillo is with me.[83]

Trujillo had extreme difficulties in accepting any other gods before himself and old *Olivoristas* state they were persecuted because Trujillo could not stand the divinity of Olivorio.[84] The name of *El Maestro* even crops up in a poem dedicated to Trujillo:

Oiga el colmo: en un velorio	Listen to the height of folly, during a vigil
Discutiendo muy fogosa	in an ardent discussion
la trujillista Forosa	the Trujillo supporter Forosa
le dijo al vale Liborio:	told buddy Liborio:
'Dejese de requilorio	'Stop beating around the bush,
eso e jablai poi jablai,	that is talking only for the sake of talking,
si Trujillo, ei generai,	if Trujillo, the general,
de la silla apiaise quiere,	intends to step down from the [presidential] chair
lo caigamo la mujere	the women will carry him
y lo voivamo a sentai.'[85]	and put him back again.'

Another part of the poem repeats the messianic terminology which so often was applied to Trujillo: 'With the heart filled with joy the country has put the same hopes in him as Israel when it waited for the Messiah.'[86] Trujillo was elevated to a position close to God; he even appeared to have superseded the other two parts of the Holy Trinity:

---

83 Quoted in Malek (1971), p. 341.
84 Interview with Julián Ramos, Higüerito, 16 January 1986.
85 Jiménez R. (1938), p. 10. This is part of a long poem which in 1937 won a contest intended to reward the best poem propagating the reelection of Trujillo. It is not explicitly stated that the Liborio of the poem is identical with Olivorio Mateo. However, the quite uncommon name of Liborio, the rural environment and the *velación*, which would be an appropriate moment for the spirit of Olivorio to appear, all indicate that the poet had *El Maestro* in mind, thus indicating for the *Olivoristas* that it was to no avail to oppose Trujillo.
86 Ibid., p. 9.

The most superficial analysis of the national history reveals that ... only after 1930, that is, four hundred and thirty-eight years after the Discovery, the Dominican people is no longer exclusively assisted by God, but also by a hand which seems to have been touched by some kind of Divine predestination: the providential hand of Trujillo.[87]

The Dominican church was amazingly indulgent towards all these conspicuous violations of the First Commandment. Instead it joined in the choir of ovations to this earthly God, who filled his prison cells with tortured victims and tossed his adversaries as food for the sharks of the Caribbean Sea: 'Without GOD the FATHERLAND sinks and LIBERTY disappears. This was the intuition of *Generalísimo* Trujillo. Making a stable FATHERLAND and guaranteeing its LIBERTY; to that end he insisted in the idea of GOD.'[88]

Reading an account of the religious acts celebrated in San Juan de la Maguana (or any other Dominican town for that matter) during 1937, one starts to wonder to whom religious devotion was rendered, God or Trujillo?

Solemn Te Deum as an act of thanksgiving to the Highest Lord and in honor of the Benefactor of the Fatherland, on 1 January. Te Deum for the precious life of our Renowned Chief, Generalísimo Trujillo Molina, 30 April. Solemn Death Mass dedicated to the memory of don José Trujillo Valdez, illustrious progenitor of the celebrated savior of the Republic, on 10 March. Solemn Mass for the precious health and felicity of the Benefactor of the Fatherland during his stay abroad, on 6 August. Solemn Mass for the happy return of the Idolized Chief; solemn Te Deum, on 19 August, on the occasion of his happy arrival in New York, on his way from Europe, of the immortal creator of our true nationality; Salve in our Holy Parish Church for the happy return to the soil of the Fatherland of our incomparable genius, on the 23th of the same month ...[89]

etc., etc., until the end of the year.

During the fall of 1937 Trujillo embarked on his most loathsome crime; thousands of Haitians living in Dominican territory – men, women and children – were butchered with knives, clubs and bayonets. The massacre was carried out by soldiers dressed in civilian clothes, and it is probable that firearms were not used because the dictator wanted it to look like a

---

87 Balaguer (1955), p. 61.
88 Robuster (1957) p. 11.
89 Cocco (1940), p. 139. The list continues for another full page. Every year the procedure was the same.

desperate act committed by peasants.⁹⁰ No member of the Catholic clergy raised his voice openly in defense of the victims of this vile crime. Instead the highest Catholic dignitaries hurried to pour oil on troubled waters when the news was leaked to the international press, causing a violent reaction. Archbishop Pittini figured on the front page of the country's largest newspaper, telling the whole world that all Haitians living in different parts of the Dominican territory enjoyed 'good health, peace and benevolent treatment'.⁹¹ When the international uproar did not diminish the papal nuncio convinced the Haitian government that it ought to accept an indemnity on behalf of the Dominican government, and in February 1938 Archbishop Pittini personally delivered a check for US$250,000 to the Haitian president.⁹²

The aftermath of this terrible incident was particularly distasteful since cadres of authors were whipped up in support of Trujillo and his bloody deed. Hundreds of books were published, the intention of which was apparent to every reader – to depict the Haitian in the vilest and most brutal way as possible. Here we find the black voodoo myth in its most extreme variety. Voodoo is depicted as nothing but cannibalism and promiscuity:

> el **vaudou** [sic] or Haitian popular cult, from times immemorial professed by the immense majority of our neighbors, constitutes a **psycho-neurosis** of a racial type. The **vaudouist** is a paranoiac of a most dangerous sort [...] If we consider the growing influence the monstrous practice of fetishism is acquiring among the lower half of our population, we realize that if we do not act with a firm hand and brave heart, the moment will come when the damage is irremediable among us, as well as it is on the other [Haitian] side. There does not exist any genuinely cultivated and civilized government in the world which would not take necessary steps against such a threat, so serious, so lethal.⁹³

The following is a typical example of Dominican descriptions of a voodoo ceremony:

90 Cf. Vega (1988c). The reasons for the carnage are still discussed. They were probably various – the old Haitiphobia, a desire to gain firm control over the border area where contraband commerce flourished and political opponents to the regime could easily slip away from the terror of the dictator, a personal grudge between Trujillo and Haiti's president – all these are possible reasons, besides the madness of the dictator. The order came directly from *El Benefactor* and he never told anyone about his reasons for giving it.
91 *Listín Diario*, 17 December 1937.
92 Cuello (1985), pp. 34 and 171–6.
93 Peña Batlle (1943a), pp. 13 and 15. This was a part of a speech delivered by Peña Batlle in the frontier town of Elías Piña in order to defend the horrible massacre. It was printed in the national newspapers and distributed as a booklet in several thousand copies.

The rhythm of the ceremonies, which initially is methodical and gloomy, gains strength as the consumption of alcohol increases a frantic and insane pulse that urges the fanatics to devour the intestines of the sacrificed animal, even more so if the latter, as may happen, is a child.[94]

The example could easily be multiplied since the theme of cannibalism appears in almost every Dominican book on voodoo published before the 1970s. Needless to say, the description has no relation to reality.

The Catholic church and its *Benefactor*

Archbishop Pittini has often been accused of submitting the Catholic church to the arbitrary rule of Trujillo, thereby offering the ideological support he needed to keep his terror regime going for so many years. The condemnation of Pittini has come from various quarters and it has often been very harsh. He has been described as an unscrupulous political lackey, a competent drinker and 'no stranger to off-color jokes'.[95] Exiled Dominicans were particularly harsh in their judgements, lamenting that the church had become a compliant servant of the 'satrap', stating that it 'celebrates more masses and processions for Trujillo than in honor of *La Virgen de la Altagracia*, the patron saint of the Republic'.[96] The worst broadside against Pittini was fired by an exiled Dominican named Félix Mejía:

> This individual, of Italian origin, recently arrived in the country as a simple priest, a private in the ecclesiastical hierarchy, without credentials or abilities – not only for Archbishop, but not even for canon; [...] became a perfect sucker [*mamón*] with more mobility than mercury in behalf of his Lord – who is not God but Trujillo [...] famous and insuperable are his discourses for their servility and exaggeration. Pittini will be recorded in the history of Santo Domingo as the prototype of the servile and easily bought Archbishop, and in the history of the Church as a sacrilegious and impious priest.[97]

---

94 Osorio Lizarazo (1947), p. 116.
95 Crassweller (1966), p. 97. In connection with Trujillo's brutal massacres of Haitians a Dominican journalist overheard Pittini telling an extraordinarily tasteless 'joke'. The archbishop said Haitian mothers 'nowadays' scared their children not by saying: '*Ahí viene el Cuco*' ['Here comes the Monster', a traditional way of playing with kids in Spanish-speaking countries], instead they said: '*Ahí viene Troillo.*' Pittini thus made fun of the Haitians alleged difficulty in pronouncing the 'j' in Trujillo (Javier García (1985), p. 298).
96 Landestoy (1946), p. 37.
97 Mejía (1951), p. 78, quoted in Wipfler (1978), pp. 130–1.

Pittini attracted the attention of the FBI during World War II. He was suspected of being pro-fascist, accused of preaching anti-democratic sermons and of mixing with Italian fascists and Spanish Falangist priests.[98] However, not all judgements are negative; some Dominican Catholics even want Pittini canonized,[99] considering him to be a martyr for his faith, a saintly priest who used his position in order to alleviate the burdens of Catholic devotees. They point to his telling in confidence that he would try to take as much as possible of the money Trujillo extracted from the miserable masses through his evil acts.[100]

Shortly after his ruthless massacres of the Haitians, which the church willingly helped him to cover up, Trujillo embarked on a huge project to 'Dominicanize' the frontier. By doing so he counted on and received the support of the Catholic church. Already one year before the massacres Jesuits had arrived in Dajabón, on the northern part of the border. They were soon engaged in missionary work among the peasants, and they built and administered a center for vocational training.[101] In 1935 the Redemptorists arrived in the San Juan Valley and started their missionary work and battle against superstition.[102]

During the 1950s anti-communism began to play an increasingly important role in Dominican politics, a preoccupation Trujillo shared with Pope Pius XII. This pope, when he served as papal nuncio under his 'civilian' name Eugenio Pacelli, had nearly been killed by communist Spartacists in 1919, a terrible memory which haunted him all his life.[103] The relative meekness and silence the Vatican maintained while dealing with the Nazis and fascists[104] has been contrasted to the Vatican's fierce condemnation of

---

98 Vega (1985b), pp. 340, 346, 363 and 373. Pittini was apparently a master in the art of flattery. An American visitor described him in the following way in 1944: 'His gracious voice, his well turned phrases and delicate compliments paid his listener the subtlest of all flattery by crediting the visitor with the perception to appreciate them' (Cooper (1947), p. 14).

99 'Perhaps our future generations will be able to read in the calendar of saints of our beloved Church: SAN RICARDO, MISSIONARY AND ARCHBISHOP. That is my most ardent desire' (Pou Henríquez (1976), p. 7). Luís Pou Henríquez served as parish priest of the cathedral in Santo Domingo under Pittini. When the Catholic church in the beginning of the 1960s opposed Trujillo his house was burned down by *Trujillista* thugs (Sáez (1988a), p. 203).

100 Ibid., p. 6.

101 López de Santa Anna (1957), pp. 19–21.

102 Balaguer (1983), pp. 86–7.

103 Falconi (1970), p. 86.

104 A heated discussion for and against the actions of the Vatican during World War II has been going on since that time. The fact remains that the Vatican did not do much to condemn Nazi terror officially. The Vatican excommunicated German Catholics who put in their wills that they wanted to be cremated, but no Catholic was forbidden to work in concentration or death camps and at the end of 1938, 22.7 percent of the SS were

Figure 9.3 Trujillo and Pope Pius XII, following the signature of the Concordat with the Dominican Republic, June 1954.

communism.[105] The Catholic attacks on communism became even more accentuated when country after country in eastern and central Europe were annexed by the Soviet Union and the Vatican lost contact with and control over huge Catholic congregations. This, in connection with the alarming growth of the communist parties in Italy and France, made the Vatican increasingly preoccupied with the atheist communist system. In 1949 the Pope decreed the excommunication of all Catholics who adhered

practicing Catholics (even though the organization did not approve of religious affiliation). The only official stand the Vatican took against the extermination of Jews was a meek statement in the Vatican newspaper, *L'Osservatore Romano*, that the treatment of Jews in the concentration camps and the confiscation of their property was 'too harsh' (Johnson (1980), pp. 488–92).

105 Pius XI had condemned communism in an Encyclical, *Divini Redemptoris: Concerning the Atheistic Communism*, published in 1937 (Márquez (1960)) and two weeks later Nazism came under attack in another Encyclical, *Mit brennender Sorge*, where, even though the Nazi attacks on Germany's Jews were not specifically mentioned, the Vatican is quite clear about its disapproval: 'Whoever gives the idea of race or people or state or form of government a value beyond that of the ordinary world and claims to make idols out of them, violates the divine order of things' (quoted in Falconi (1970), p. 95). There are some signs that Pius XI, just before his death in 1939, became more markedly anti-Nazi and prepared to move against both Nazism and fascism, but Pius XII's first decision when he came to power was to consign his predecessor's planned denunciations of Nazism to the secret archives of the Vatican and confine himself to a resounding silence about Nazi and fascist crimes (ibid.).

to the Communist Party, or approved of its politics,[106] and many Catholic clerics came to consider themselves as God's soldiers in a global battle against communist agents.

While learning about exiled Dominicans who tried to win the support of liberal and socialist groups around the Caribbean basin, and even practiced guerilla warfare in places like Costa Rica, Cuba and Guatemala, Trujillo began to thunder about the communist threat and openly sought the willing support of the Vatican in what he called his battle for the 'free world'. A Concordat between the Dominican Republic and the Vatican was signed in 1954, making, among other things, Catholicism the official religion of the Republic.[107] The years between 1954 and 1959 were characterized by a 'spectacular expenditure of funds' directed to the Catholic church, from both the Dominican government and Trujillo personally.[108] A personal triumph for Trujillo in his dealing with the Vatican was the organization of an international congress on 'Catholic culture' which convened in Ciudad Trujillo as a part of the sumptuous celebrations of *El Benefactor's* twenty-fifth year in power.[109] Cardinal Spellman of New York, intimate friend of Pius XII, attended the meeting and had an avenue named after him. When he left the country the cardinal thanked Trujillo for all the favors which had been bestowed upon him and 'praised the Dominican regime warmly for its religious and anti-Communist policies'.[110]

The Dominican clergy was actively supporting *El Benefactor* in his 'battle against communism'. Particularly active were the Jesuits, who organized fifty labor unions and more than 7,000 peasant cooperatives.[111] They have been accused of practicing sophisticated brain-washing in *retiros espirituales* [spiritual resorts] called *Casas Manresas*.[112] There the participants were subjected to

---

106 It was even prohibited to read books, periodicals, or leaflets which supported communist doctrines (*Decreto de la Sagrada Congregación del Santo Oficio sobre la cooperación al comunismo*, quoted in Márquez (1960), pp. 7–8).

107 The Concordat guaranteed the Catholic church extraordinary independence in a country like the Dominican Republic, were Trujillo's power penetrated everything. It was granted sole control over church property and all education within Catholic institutions. The Concordat also guaranteed special juridicial treatment of clerics. (The complete text of the Concordat is reproduced in Castillo de Aza (1961), pp. 238–57)

108 Wipfler (1978), p. 148.

109 Ibid., p. 149.

110 Crassweller (1966) p. 325. Cf. Ornes (1958), p. 9. Cardinal Spellman was very influential during the reign of Pius XII. However, he lost influence after the death of his friend and his fierce criticism of the Vatican's peace initiatives during the Vietnam War finally opened a rift between him and the Holy See (Bull (1982), p. 138).

111 Cordero Michel (1970), p. 42. Sáez (1988a), p. 150, states that the figures are exaggerated.

112 While asking for the support of Trujillo for their *retiros* the Jesuits mentioned the communist specter: 'as you know so well, Your Excellency, religious Catholic awareness is the best

Figure 9.4 Cardinal Francis Spellman bids farewell to Trujillo and the Dominican Republic on his departure from Ciudad Trujillo, 1959.

long sessions of religious and political indoctrination combined with prayers; during the night the participants are left to themselves in dark cells while a persuading voice talks for hours over an electrical transmission system, urging them to confess their sins, to fear death and the punishment of God and to obey the Church and the temporal institutions.[113]

Pope Pius XII died in 1958. On 1 January 1959 Fidel Castro entered Havana and 14 June the same year a small invasion of exiled Dominicans was launched from Cuba. Trujillo's loyal army repelled the invasions without difficulty, but with excessive cruelty. It was becoming evident that

bulwark against Communism, which, being completely antireligious, infiltrates, above all, among intellectuals and workers who lack a religious Catholic foundation' (from Luís González Posada's letter of request to Trujillo, quoted in Sáez (1988a), p. 148). González Posada, who headed the Jesuit seminary in Santo Domingo, was a Spanish Jesuit who had arrived from Cuba in 1946. The Casa Manresa was constructed in Haina, just outside of Santo Domingo and inaugurated in August 1954 (Sáez (1988a), pp. 100–1 and 149). Manresa is the place in Catalonia where Ignatius of Loyola spent a year of retirement before he started the mission which led to the foundation of the Society of Jesus.

113 Cordero Michel (1970), pp. 41–2. The *retiros* were organized by Spanish Jesuits, of whom several were known to have 'Fascist inclinations' (ibid., p. 42). Cordero Michel knew the *retiros* only from hearsay and probably 'added a certain drama' to his description (Sáez (1988a), p. 150).

the end of Trujillo's thirty years of dictatorial reign was approaching. In October 1959 a new papal nuncio arrived in Ciudad Trujillo. Argentina's exiled strongman, Juan Perón, who stayed as a guest with Trujillo, warned his host saying that Zanini, the new nuncio, was a messenger of bad tidings since he had arrived in Buenos Aires shortly before Perón's own down-fall.[114] Zanini earned Trujillo's unreserved hatred when only a few days after his arrival in Ciudad Trujillo he turned down an offer to inaugurate a huge cattle market presided over by *El Jefe* himself. He dryly remarked that his mission in the Dominican Republic was of an exclusively diplomatic nature and that the kind of favor he was asked for could surely be carried out by any member of the local clergy.[115]

Trujillo understood that he did not have the church in his pocket anymore. New winds had begun to blow when Angelo Roncalli succeeded Pius as Pope John XXIII. Vatican policy changed in almost all its aspects and in the Dominican Republic the Catholic church finally prepared itself for the unavoidable breach with *El Benefactor*. The worried Trujillo even sent an envoy to the Pope to find out the position of the new Vicar of Christ. Pope John XXIII listened silently to the homage of Trujillo that his envoy presented, but afterwards made it clear in a few words that the Vatican supported a change of Dominican politics and disapproved of the brutal methods of Trujillo. The fearful Dominican diplomats did not dare to reveal the whole truth about the 'unsatisfactory results' of the mission, but Trujillo suspected the failure anyway, gave Pope John the nickname *Juan Pendejo* [John the Jerk], expressed a desire for his immediate death, and sent the one-armed Rodolfo Paradas Veloz as ambassador to the Vatican, hoping that this man, who was known to cause *fucú* [bad luck] to everyone around him, would hurt the Pope by his presence.[116]

To his amazement Trujillo found that the Catholic church did not comment on his brutal extermination of the invaders and 'traitors' of 14 June 1959. He had probably expected the customary ovations and homages to the 'Father of the New Fatherland'. Instead he had to listen to new, irritating tunes. A month after the invasion the bishop of Santiago, Hugo Polanco Brito, made a speech, where, among other things, he stated: 'If the State is sovereign in the discharge of its purely civil functions, the

---

114 Crassweller (1966), p. 382. Either Crassweller or Perón was mistaken because the Lino Zanini who came to Santo Domingo was not the same person as Mario Zanino, who had been nuncio in Argentina. However, true or legendary, the alleged warning of Perón indicates the concern various Latin American politicians felt regarding the changing politics of the Vatican (Sáez (1988a), p. 187).

115 Balaguer (1985), p. 309.

116 Ibid., pp. 312–13. Trujillo rejoiced when he learned that the Pope became ill a few days after the arrival of the Dominican emissary. However, John XXIII survived *El Jefe* by two years (ibid., p. 313).

church is also in the spiritual realm; to such a degree that I, personally as Bishop of Santiago, have no other superiors than the Pope and God, to whom I must render accounting for my actions.'[117]

In their brutal hunt for relatives and sympathizers of the exterminated invaders Trujillo's *calieses* broke into Catholic schools and seminaries, arresting Catholic seminarians and interrogating priests.[118] This constituted an outright violation of several clauses in the Concordat.[119] The bishops of La Vega and San Juan de la Maguana, Francisco Panal and Thomas Reilly, took up the cudgels for the church. It is possible that they could do so since they both were foreigners, without any Dominican relatives. Threats to relatives of the Dominican clergy were a means of pressure of which Trujillo frequently made effective use.[120] The acolytes of *El Benefactor* hit where the church was weakest, namely the generosity *El Jefe* had shown the Catholic church. To test the obedience of the clergy a massive campaign was launched in the submissive Dominican press. The intention was to add another sumptuous title to all those Trujillo already possessed: 'I raise my voice to invite all Dominicans of good will and all foreigners who share the advantages of the New Era in the Republic, that being possessed of an historic and religious sense of justice you acclaim Trujillo to be BENEFACTOR OF THE CHURCH.'[121]

Bishop Reilly of San Juan de la Maguana was not late in valiantly denouncing this new claim of *El Benefactor*. In a letter thanking Trujillo for exonerating some trucks destined to his bishopric from certain charges, Monseñor Reilly added the following critique:

> As a Catholic Bishop, I wish to lay open before Your Excellency that I am still seriously preoccupied by the present situation. The total absence of the military at the hours when they should fulfill their sacred duty to attend the Sunday Mass, means much to me. Moreover the activities of the Security Police and the campaign dealing with the title of 'Benefactor of the Church', do not contribute, to say the least, to the calm and tranquility of the country in these moments of crisis.[122]

117 Polanco Brito, quoted in Wipfler (1978), p. 153.
118 Sáez (1988a), p. 188.
119 Particularly the ones under Article 11, where it was stated that the juridical authorities had no right to question the Catholic clergy about information given during confessions, and Article 23, where the Dominican government guaranteed the autonomy of Catholic schools (Castillo de Aza (1961), pp. 246 and 251–2).
120 Crassweller (1966), p. 385.
121 Castillo de Aza (1960), quoted by Wipfler (1978), pp. 173–4.
122 Quoted in *Una carta histórica* (1961), p. 6. This booklet reproducing the correspondence between Trujillo and Reilly (carried out in March and April 1960) was published by the *La Nación* newspaper.

Figure 9.5 Trujillo and Bishop Thomas Reilly.

This was a declaration of war; Trujillo answered Reilly, who was an American citizen, by citing Alejandro Nouel, bishop in Santiago during the American occupation, 1916–24:

> The Dominican people [...] never knew about torture by water, the burning alive of women and children, torture by the rope, the hunting down of men in the fields as if they were wild animals, the dragging of an old man of seventy by the tail of a horse in broad noon-day light, across the central square in Hato Mayor. We, I do not deny it, knew business frauds and small-scale stealing of public funds; but with the help and lessons from different foreigners, we are getting better in the art of fraud and wholesale squandering.[123]

Trujillo, or the person who wrote the letter for him, also evokes the *Hispanidad* of the Dominicans:

> The people of the Dominican Republic are of Spanish origin and their ideology, their customs, their traditions, their feelings and their ideas, correspond to those of a country of the Spanish race. The governmental methods cannot be identical for the two countries [the United States and the Dominican Republic] because their idiosyncrasies and their mentalities are not the same.[124]

123 *Una carta histórica* (1961), p. 14.
124 Ibid., pp. 12–13.

Therefore it is understandable that priests of North American nationality, influenced by sentiments and ideas proper to the environment of their origin, easily commit flagrant errors when judging a small and poor country as ours, which differs so much from their original fatherland when it comes to the evolution of institutions and the aptitude of every individual to exercise the rights and comply with the fundamental duties of the human being.[125]

With that letter Trujillo put an end to pleasant talk. While the Dominican press launched a massive campaign, listing every peso Trujillo had spent on the Catholic church through the years, an organized flood of public fury was let loose on Panal and Reilly, the bishops who had dared to doubt Trujillo's omnipotence. Long lists with persons who condemned the bishops and demanded their expulsion from the country were published and sent to the Catholic authorities. The radio announced a contest for the best slogan repudiating the 'conspiratorial traitor bishops'.[126]

In San Juan de la Maguana, the *Servicio de Inteligencia Militar* organized different kinds of disturbances. They brought in prostitutes during mass, copulated in the lateral aisles, and shouted abuses at the celebrating priests. When Reilly did not yield, SIM agents, acting as local residents, sacked the parochial archives and burned them in the street, and even sacked the cathedral.[127] Finally the mob marched on Reilly's house and hurled stones on it. Reilly gave absolution to the priests and nuns who were with him and they left the house while the surrounding mob shouted: 'To the rope with the Yankee priest!' When asked if he had not been afraid at that moment, Monseñor Reilly answered that he knew Trujillo had a 'superstitious fear of clerical robes' and that he would probably not dare to let his hooligans kill a bishop. Reilly was, however, not so sure when, six weeks later, he sat in the basement of the SIM headquarters in Santo Domingo and listened to the moans of tortured victims, coming from surrounding cells. Guards entered every hour telling him that he had to prepare himself to die. However, suddenly Reilly was released and brought in front of the puppet president, Joaquín Balaguer. From him Reilly

---

125 Ibid., p. 14–15. In his efforts to subdue the rebellious bishop, Trujillo cut down on the economic aid to the border parishes, closed several schools and 'centers of catechism' and expelled thirteen priests from Reilly's diocese (Reilly (1963)).
126 Crassweller (1966), p. 392.
127 Interview with José Saladino Figueroa O., San Juan de la Maguana, 4 July 1990. Saladino, a fervent Catholic and friend of Thomas Reilly, owns a photo atelier just in front of the cathedral and the bishop's offices in San Juan de la Maguana. Saladino witnessed all the commotion and even hid a huge crucifix which had been stolen from the cathedral. Several *Sanjuaneros* knew he kept the crucifix and he was interrogated by SIM agents, who wanted him to turn over the cross and the negatives of several photos he had taken. When Trujillo had been killed he returned the crucifix to Bishop Reilly.

learned that Trujillo had been shot to death on an abandoned highway, on the morning of 30 May 1961.[128]

The death of *El Jefe* produced an overheated political atmosphere, which culminated with the first free elections in thirty years, on 20 December 1962, one week before the massacre in Palma Sola. When it became clear that Juan Bosch, a 'radical liberal' who had been educated in the secular tradition of Eugenio María de Hostos, was going to win the elections, a number of Dominican clerics started to worry. They joined forces with the UCN, the main opponent of the PRD, which was a party that mainly appealed to the urban bourgeoisie, businessmen, and professionals. An article by a Cuban Jesuit[129] awakened the old communist specter and a fierce debate about whether Bosch and the leading members of his party were crypto-communists or not raged in mass media until a few days before the elections. Bosch was described as a communist and one priest did not hesitate to liken him to Hitler, Mussolini, and Castro.[130]

The temperature in this inflamed debate increased at the same time as inflated reports about what was happening in Palma Sola occupied more and more space in the domestic press. When only a few days were left before the elections on 20 December, Bosch threatened to withdraw his candidacy if he was not given time on national television to defend himself against the accusations. On the evening of 18 December more than a million Dominicans witnessed how Bosch for several hours defended himself in a very convincing way and how the Jesuit priest, Láutico García, finally had to admit that Juan Bosch was no communist.[131] The dispute was kept alive during the election day and probably contributed to Bosch's overwhelming victory. After the elections it was Christmas and Bosch departed for Europe and the United States. The general feeling in the country after the first free elections in thirty years was one of relief and exhaustion. It was during the days between Christmas and the New Year, when news is scarce and people relaxed, that the Dominican army and police wiped out Palma Sola in a storm of bullets, gas and fire.

The changing attitude of the church

Few people who had not been personally affected were shocked by the merciless massacre which had taken place in a distant corner of the Republic. It was as if all the stress and tensions of the past years had come to a fitting and violent end in Palma Sola. The press gave the impression that

128 Interview with Thomas Reilly, San Juan de la Maguana, 5 January 1986.
129 García (1962), p. 3.
130 Faustino García, quoted in Wipfler (1978), p. 256.
131 Bosch (1964), pp. 117–19.

what had happened had been inevitable. Palma Sola had become a symbol of everything the average Dominican had disliked in the old regime: ignorance, intolerance and overheated idolatry of Trujillo. The bloodbath in Palma Sola became something of a propitiatory sacrifice where everything old, scarred, and backward in the Dominican Republic had been burned to ashes. The *Mellizos* became scapegoats for the crimes of Trujillo and his acolytes:

> The cult of human beings cannot be revived again in the Dominican Republic. The fetishism is one of the most elementary stages of this type of cult. With this in mind it is necessary, as now has been done, to eradicate, once and for all, the superstitious myths which only lead to collective crimes against social security and public peace.
>
> The devastated Palma Sola ought to serve as an excellent example to the Dominicans.[132]

The interpretation of the reality in Palma Sola was badly biased by decades of officially sanctioned prejudice and a deep breach between urban and rural notions. No serious study and analysis of the phenomenon was ever carried out before the massacre and when an attempt was made after the tragedy had taken place it proved to be inopportune and was prematurely suppressed.

As seen above, the construction of a Dominican national character was conceived in negative terms. The Creole culture of the Dominicans was despised, particularly the 'African' traits of their popular religion. Official ideology stressed the Dominicans' Spanish character, barred their contacts with Haiti and persecuted all rural traditions that had been branded as superstitious. 'The Dominican Republic presents a very peculiar situation with respect to the problem of identity and the ethnic-racial discourse', summarizes Pedro San Miguel.[133]

Even if Bishop Reilly of San Juan came to the capital to visit the imprisoned survivors from Palma Sola and later aided them in their 'resettlement', he did not officially regret the government's bloody persecution of *Olivorismo*. In a letter where the bishop asks for economic support for church efforts to 'educate and reform the peasant masses', he also urges the government to wipe out all vestiges of 'witchcraft and Liborismo' within his ecclesiastical domains:

---

132 *La Nación*, 7 December 1962. *La Nación*, which was forced to close down in 1963, had been the most scandalous mouthpiece of Trujillo's politics and a fervent propagator of his cult (cf. Martínez Paulino (1984), p. 208). It is hard to avoid the impression that the newspaper's aggressive condemnation of the cult of Palma Sola was a way to cover up for all the exaggerated servility it had offered the deceased dictator.

133 San Miguel (1992), p. 75.

It is the opinion of everyone that the public forces have to maintain a strict vigilance to avoid any kind of resurgence of Liborismo. During the cleaning up of the symbols [of *Olivorismo*] the police have not touched the center of major importance, with the exception of Palma Sola itself; namely LA MAGUANA, where a witch doctor has constructed a voodoo temple bigger than the Catholic church in this section.[134]

The Catholic church acted as the state's foremost weapon in its battles against the traditional peasant culture which had been identified as one, if not *the*, cause of the 'backwardness' of Dominican society. Much of the fierce cultural warfare against popular culture was tinged by racial prejudices. The Dominicans had to 'be washed clean' from their 'blackness' and their African heritage. Since everything 'negative' was considered to be of either 'African' or 'Haitian' origin, other traditions as well, which were not approved, such as European fertility cults and similar beliefs, were described as 'African'. The Dominican state of underdevelopment was blamed on something called 'Africanism' and the 'black' blood which ran through the veins of most Dominicans. Accordingly the most propagated remedy for this perceived backwardness was to 'whiten' the Dominican population, something which could be accomplished through the promotion of 'Caucasian' immigration and a war against 'superstitions, Africanism and Haitian influences'.

Even though the goals of this campaign were never reached and the Dominicans stuck to their old traditions, its values and notions slipped into the minds of many Dominicans. Thus, Olivorio and the *Mellizos* of Palma Sola, who honored old traditions and taught a religion with roots deep in Dominican soil, were depicted as the vilest imaginable destroyers of the psychological and physical health of hapless Dominican peasants. Accordingly were considered as enemies of the Dominican government, which stated it honored everything the *Olivoristas* were 'opposed' to: '*Hispanidad*', modernization and progress.

Unfortunately the Catholic church participated in this alienation of much of the rural population. Its connection with Trujillo, who used the church as a legitimation for his own regime, resulted in its coming out as a defender of his cruel and dictatorial methods. Although the church at the end of Trujillo's long reign turned into one of his foremost and most effective critics, other things did not change overnight: voodoo and peasant 'superstitions' continued to be considered the worst foes of the Catholic church. Peasants had to be educated and education meant submission

134 Reilly (1963).

to Catholic dogma. This view made close understanding and cooperation between the *Olivoristas* and the Catholic clergy impossible.

In the San Juan Valley the problem was further complicated by all the hardships the clergy had suffered at the hands of the *Trujillistas* due to the fierce and brave opposition of its bishop, Thomas Reilly. When Trujillo was finally murdered a feeling of exhaustion took hold of the *Sanjuanero* clergy and its members were not prepared for, or interested in, taking an opposite stand to that of the government or the local authorities. Supporting the *Palmasolistas* was seen as a step towards weakening the position of the church at a very crucial stage of Dominican history. Furthermore, the Catholic church at the time considered it much more important to address the communist threat than to defend 'superstitious peasant cults' which it had anyway fought for centuries.

Before he had become a sworn enemy of the church Trujillo had acted as its benevolent guardian angel. If economic problems occured the clergy had been accustomed to trust in the generosity of *El Benefactor*.

> When I [Pittini] presented my propositions and conditions concerning a School of Arts and Crafts to him [Trujillo], and the need for an extensive piece of land in the Capital and a sum of money to begin the constructions with, he told me: 'Go and pick the piece of land you like the most. And, concerning the sum … Do you need much?' I answered: 'I will not decide it, Mr. President, put one hand above your heart and the other one in your pocket and listen to what they both have to say to you.' A light smile; the offering of a large sum and a signed declaration of a land donation from him to the Salesian Congregation had decided its foundation in five minutes.[135]

If they wanted help from the authorities while dealing with heretics or voodooists, the Catholic clergy could count on *El Jefe*, like, for example, when a plea was presented to Trujillo from Archbishop Pittini in 1948, where the latter asks *El Benefactor* if something can be done against the Protestants, arguing that

> He who becomes a Protestant not only renounces his Catholic faith, but with that comes implicitly a renunciation of the Dominicanism that impregnates the life of the country. They no longer look in the direction of Rome, they look towards the United States, from where the 'light' has come to them. Where these small groups are formed a deep religious discord is created between them and the Catholic environment that surrounds them. The national unity is disintegrated,

---

135 Pittini (1949), p. 81.

maybe more thoroughly and dangerously than was the case along the frontier with the penetration of buduism [voodoo].[136]

El Benefactor of the Fatherland finally grew so big that his menacing figure threatened to extinguish even the Catholic church. Its clerics had no other choice than to help getting rid of the fantastic idol, whose creation they had been actively involved in. However, when Trujillo was killed he left a terrible void behind him. His protecting shadow, scrutinizing eye and firm grip were all gone; anything could come in the place of *El Jefe*, even, the horrible specter of communism: 'The priests accused us of being both sorcerers and communists. We were nothing of the kind, but they refused to listen to us', summarizes León Romilio Ventura.[137]

In recent years several members of the Catholic clergy have changed their attitude and are now actively engaged in dialogue with rural cultists. Today Catholic priests, all over the country, participate in rural rituals and invite influential cult leaders to the church. The Jesuit priest Francisco Lemus has carried out impressive and unprejudiced field research on popular beliefs in several rural districts of the Dominican Republic and the vast material he has collected through the years is far from being thoroughly investigated.[138] Another Jesuit priest, Jorge Cela, has studied urban voodoo, and Orlando Espín del Prado has made several unprejudiced studies of several popular cults, among them *Olivorismo*.

Bryan Kennedy, the young Redemptorist pastor of the parish of Santa Lucia in Las Matas de Farfán, was actively working among several of the survivors from the massacre in the 1980s and he is a personal friend with many of them. He feels it is the duty of the church to engage itself in the everyday problems of the peasantry and has come to accept peasant religion as an integrated part of the life of most peasants. León Romilio Ventura, the surviving *Mellizo*, talks with affection of Padre Bryan and calls him a 'good servant' of Olivorio. It is the expressed feeling of Father Bryan that the church was shamefully incapable of understanding the *Olivoristas*,

136 Pittini (1948). The archbishop wrote several letters to Trujillo warning against Protestants, reminding *El Jefe* that 'Protestant imperialism infiltrates through three stages; the Bible, the dollar, the marines' (Pittini (1943). The dictator saw himself unable to act against the powerful American churches, though he forbade the Jehovah's Witnesses to practice in the country. Note the use of 'was' while writing about voodoo; the letter is written after the massacres of Haitians in 1937 and voodoo is accordingly considered to have disappeared from the border areas. However, the legislation against voodoo had been renovated in 1943: 'Law No. 391 which establishes correctional punishments of persons who practice the dances named "Voudou" or "Luá"' (Peña Batlle (1943b)).
137 Interview with León Romilio Ventura, Las Matas de Farfán, 14 May 1989.
138 Lemus and Marty (1975) and Lemus and Oleo (1977) The last reference is just an example of a 'working paper' on one particular zone of the Dominican Republic. Several others are filed in the palace of the archbishop in Santo Domingo.

stubbornly labeling it witchcraft and fighting it with missionary zeal. According to him, the priests ought to have listened to the *Olivoristas*, tried to understand them and accept their teaching as a vehicle for the religious feeling of most peasants in the area. What happened in Palma Sola was

> like a breakdown in communication. They [the Catholic clerics] were unable to apprehend the gifts and talents of the *Mellizo*. He is a very gifted preacher. It was more like seeing him as a witch doctor, or something like that. The only effort that was made was to tell people: 'Don't go! Stay away from that, it is dangerous! It will corrupt your faith!' The church was not in a position of being an intermediary. It was already against that kind of experience. When the time came, the conflicts had grown too big. The church could not sort them out. It did not understand. It is a shame.[139]

139 Interview with Bryan Kennedy, Las Matas de Farfán, 4 May 1986.

Part IV

The wider context

10 Prophets, messiahs and gods
Olivorismo in a universal context

We have seen how American reports mentioning Olivorio ran into difficulties trying to label him and his movement. To begin with he was simply described as a 'bandit', but in the end he was characterized as a 'religious fanatic'. Likewise, the Ventura brothers of Palma Sola were alternatively described as 'communists' and 'guerillas', or 'voodooists' and 'religious manipulators'. The mixture of the profane and the holy, politics and religion, within the movement caused perplexity among outsiders. Olivorio was both bandit and messiah. His religion was both political and devotional, spiritual and human. Few realized that *Olivorismo*, both in its original manifestation and in its Palma Sola variety, was a social phenomenon responding to the times and locality in which it occured. The harsh judgments passed on Olivorio and subsequently on his followers in Palma Sola, could probably have been softened, or even avoided, if the decision makers had been familiar with similar movements in other times and in different cultural settings.

As a matter of fact, Olivorio and his movement were far from unique. In times of anomie, when members of a society feel that social and moral standards are in a state of disarray and the future appears as bleak and threatening, men like Olivorio are likely to attract people ready to believe in their alleged powers. This has happened all over the world and still occurs. By comparing similar notions from different times and places, a certain pattern emerges: a universal one that may differ substantially in details, but which still may be related to a phenomenon like *Olivorismo*.

In the following pages, we will examine why leaders like Olivorio can be labeled 'charismatic' and how they tend to perceive their norms and actions as legitimized by a superhuman source. In the Christian tradition this source has often been identified with the Holy Spirit, a concept which easily merges with similar notions in other cultural settings, such as *El Gran Poder de Dios* in the San Juan Valley. We will see how the Holy Spirit gave rise to messianic and millenarian movements during the European Middle Ages and how similar concepts have stimulated religious movements up to the present day. We will also discern how feelings of superhuman guidance have stimulated messianic ideas not only within the religious sphere, but also in the political discourse formulated by very different, and even anti-religious, ideologies.[1] A messiah is often a religious reformer but he can also appear in the guise of a worldly politician. Messianic concepts are not limited to the Christian or 'western' world. They may appear within other religious and political settings as well.

While dealing with *Olivorismo*, we move around in a bewildering land-scape, where theoretical guidelines and adequate definitions are hard to find. This, however, has not deterred researchers from trying to cut a path through the bush by offering generalizing and universal theories. We will present an account of some of these theories and adapt them to *Olivorismo*. It is not our intention to force *Olivorismo* into a theoretical straitjacket. Our main purpose is to emphasize that it is a social movement and that *Olivorismo* responds to certain demands that developed in interaction with a particular environment. We will also stress that the strategy Olivorio employed to tackle the problems he met was neither unique nor precon-ditioned by some 'primitive' or 'pre-logical' state of mind. *Olivorismo* belongs to a kind of approach to, and perception of, the world that may develop in diverse cultural settings.

Was Olivorio a charismatic leader?

According to Eric Hobsbawm a social bandit shares the value systems of his neighbors. He partakes in the peasants' religious beliefs and rituals, and shares their suspicions of alien groups.[2] This view is also applicable to Olivorio. His religion probably contained certain innovations of his own, mingled with influences from an outsider like Juan Samuel. Still, it was thoroughly steeped in the rural piety of his traditional upbringing: communal dancing, the *cofradía* system, cults centered around the *ermitas*, ritual clothing, calvaries, *salves*, pilgrimages and processions, the venera-tion of the Virgin, the belief in *El Gran Poder de Dios*, etc. – traditions that had existed for centuries in his immediate environment.

What makes a peasant a likely bandit, or, for that matter, a religious leader, is his marginal position; for example, if he, for one reason or another, is not entirely bound to a piece of land. However, even though he may be an ex-soldier, a herdsman, an itinerant agricultural worker or a de-frocked priest, he still remains a member of the peasant community, but a member with greater mobility and a broader outlook than his neighbors.[3]

---

1 In that context, divine guidance may be replaced by concepts like 'destiny', 'historical necessity', 'science' or 'nature'.
2 Hobsbawm (1972), p. 38.
3 Ibid., pp. 30–40.

Olivorio fits well into this category of people. He owned a piece of land, but occasionally worked as an itinerant worker, erecting fences all over the San Juan Valley. Nevertheless, he was not unique in his mobility. Most rural inhabitants of the *sección* of San Juan were, as a rule, not entirely tied to their plots. Many made procurement trips into Haiti, some drove their cattle all the way to Port-au-Prince and several went regularly on pilgrimages to the eastern parts of the island. Furthermore, many *Sanjuanero* peasants had served as irregulars in various revolutionary armies, fighting their way to Santo Domingo, or to Port-au-Prince. Olivorio was not even unique in his quality as a man who believed himself to be a keeper of *El Gran Poder de Dios*, acting as an intermediary between 'this world' and the 'spiritual sphere'. Several such personalities may still be encountered in certain areas of the San Juan Valley, although these persons have seldom – the main exception being the Ventura brothers – obtained the following and renown of Olivorio. In that sense, he was unique.

Olivorio was undoubtedly endowed with a charismatic personality, even though several 'outsiders' who met him in person later denied that he had any particularly impressive traits, stating that they were unable to understand the attraction he emitted. Several members of the urban elite suspected that Olivorio was a genuine lunatic, maybe a manic depressive,[4] or simply an ignorant person who fooled both himself and others,[5] or just a cheap imposter who invented his coarse religion in order to quench his sexual appetites.[6] Other outsiders have stated that Olivorio was a special person, who appeared to have been illuminated by an inner light.[7] No one has denied the genuine hold he had over his followers, who after his 'calling' named him Dios Olivorio, or *El Maestro*.

Olivorio definitely had the kind of personality which is regularly denominated as charismatic, the term Max Weber coined when attempting to characterize exceptional leaders: 'a certain quality [...] by virtue of which he is set apart from ordinary men and treated as endowed with supernatural, superhuman, or at least specifically exceptional powers or qualities.'[8]

The word 'charisma' comes from the Greek word *kharis*, meaning grace or favor, and Weber's use of it is connected with 1 *Corinthians* 12–14, where the term is applied to the gifts of grace given by the Lord to his faithful.[9]

---

4 Interview with Víctor Garrido Ramírez, Jr, Santo Domingo, 22 April 1986. Manic depressiveness is not so uncommon among charismatic, religious leaders. A famous example is Shabbetai Zevi, a very influential Jewish messianic leader in the seventeenth century, who has been described as an extreme manic depressive (Scholem (1978), pp. 246–7).

5 Garrido Puello (1963), pp. 51–2.

6 Ibid., p. 29. Cf. Cruz Díaz (1965), p. 151.

7 Interview with Manuel Emilio Mesa, San Juan de la Maguana, 20 January 1989. Cf. Rodríguez Varona (1947).

8 Weber (1968b), p. 48.

606 *The wider context*

Charisma, then, is the quality which is imputed to persons, actions, roles, institutions, symbols and material objects because of their presumed connection with 'ultimate', 'fundamental', 'vital' order-determining powers. This presumed connection with the ultimately 'serious' elements in the universe and in human life is seen as a quality, or a state of being, manifested in the bearing or demeanor and in the actions of individual persons.[10]

Defined in such a way, the concept of charisma emits much of the flavor of a similar concept existing in the San Juan Valley, namely that of *El Gran Poder de Dios*, a force which, as we know, is often mentioned in connection with Olivorio.

El Gran Poder de Dios

The forces of nature are always close to an agriculturist and he or she might be inclined to imagine them as emanating from an impersonal, morally indifferent and omnipotent power. Peasants often believe that their environment has a sacred overlay. Special places for contacting the divine are known to most peasants.[11] An ever-present force may come forth in springs, groves or caves, and it may also manifest itself through chosen individuals, who then serve as receptacles for a power which enables them to transmit its energy to other people.[12]

The world of many peasants can be said to consist of two spheres: one which can be controlled and one which cannot. The latter is the realm of spiritual forces. In a peasant society, the forces of such an invisible world are often conceived of in 'analogy' with the visible world.[13] It then becomes natural to try to communicate with the beings believed to inhabit the invisible sphere and knowledge of this sphere may be used as a vehicle for power, not only within a community, but also as a weapon directed against outsiders. In a peasant society, which in a certain sense is controlled and subdued by outside forces with a different usage and pattern of behavior, the claim to powers from a transcendent source often constitutes 'the only claim that could hope to stand against constituted authority'.[14]

---

9 1 *Corinthians* 12:4–11, list nine *kharis*, spiritual gifts, and, even if this part of the New Testament probably was unknown to Olivorio's followers they nevertheless endowed their *Maestro* with several of them. The gifts are: prophecy, discernment, revelation, vision, speaking in unknown tongues, interpretation of tongues, healing, performing miracles and faith.

10 Shils (1968), p. 386.

11 Christian (1981), p. 176.

12 Cf. Pitt-Rivers (1971), p. 189.

13 Cf. Godelier (1975), pp. 202–3.

14 Wilson (1975), p. viii.

Several *Sanjuaneros* believe that behind all forces of the 'spiritual sphere' stands a supreme power, *El Gran Poder de Dios*, or, as it is sometimes called, *El Espíritu Santo.* This power germinates the force inherent in nature and certain individuals:

> Olivorio is God. God is the word. The word is hidden, but appeared in Olivorio.[15]

> I do not help. You are helping yourselves. Come to me with confidence and the help comes with my assistance. You have to have confidence in me. I do not need to have confidence in you. God brings grace. What I have is not mine; it belongs to everyone. It is mine and it is not mine. I cannot say: 'I am Olivorio', but like me he also came to display the force of the Spirit [*hacer la fuerza del Espíritu*]. Because there is only one grace, and it is for everyone, but it [the force] comes through with the help of particular persons who have to show it to others. His name was Olivorio, mine is Enrique. Those are only names – two names, but the same grace.[16]

The man quoted above, Enrique Figueroa, has several times been accused of calling himself a new Olivorio. He has even been charged with stating that he is 'identical with Dios Olivorio'. On account of such statements, he has been interrogated by the police and has spent short periods in custody. While trying to explain his special faculty, Enrique hints at something different than a shared identity with Dios Olivorio. He maintains instead that he has a 'spiritual' experience in common with *El Maestro.* Enrique stresses that he never knew Olivorio personally but that he is convinced they both serve as vehicles for an immense spiritual force that expresses itself through their persons. In order to bring home his argument, during an interview, Enrique reached for two leaves on a big tree behind him. He held them in front of him, one in each hand, explaining:

> This leaf is Olivorio; the other one is Enrique Figueroa. They are two different leaves, but they look alike, because they grow on the same tree and share the same power. It is hard to tell the difference between them.[17]

The experience of Enrique Figueroa is far from being unique in the San Juan Valley. Several other persons have stated they share similar feelings.

---

15 Interview with Julían Ramos, Higüerito, 16 January 1986.
16 Interview with Enrique Figueroa, Hato Nuevo, 18 January 1986.
17 Ibid. Various persons directed us to Enrique Figueroa, saying that he was 'one of those who have stated they are Olivorio'.

Not far from Enrique lives Ramón Mora, who also has been harassed by the authorities for stating that he 'is Olivorio'.[18] The phenomenon is not new in the valley: 'In the 1930s there lived a man here. People said he was Olivorio. When you asked him if that was true or not he used to answer that he: "*era y no era*" [was and was not] Olivorio. Because of that they called him Einoé, *es y no es* [is and isn't].'[19]

The former Catholic bishop of San Juan de la Maguana, Thomas Reilly, stated that the belief in an omnipotent power, present in the landscape and in certain human beings, is one of the most characteristic beliefs of the *Sanjuaneros*: 'The most typical features of popular religion here are an exaggerated belief in healing saints and a belief in *El Gran Poder de Dios*, which means that they seek force and power in different places. They did so in Palma Sola and in the end they felt they had been deceived.'[20]

This is the view of Reilly, who considered such ideas to be mere superstitions and not worthy of any support from the Catholic church. However, his colleagues do not all agree with his opinion.

Modern syncretism: the Catholic church and El Gran Poder de Dios

Notions of ever-present, more-or-less 'impersonal' forces are known to cultures all over the world.[21] The Melanesian concept of *mana* has long been in common use as an all-encompassing denomination for such powers.[22] The *Sanjuanero* notion of *El Gran Poder de Dios* is obviously related to similar beliefs. The concept of the Great Power of God, *Megália chárites toú theoú* in Greek, is part of Christian doctrine and is as such mainly connected with *Luke* 6:19, where it is mentioned as a healing force believed to emanate from Jesus of Nazareth.[23] This force became connected with the concept of the 'Holy Spirit', which constitutes the third entity in the Christian Trinity. The Christian notion of an ever-present 'Holy Spirit' has merged with several related notions found in other religions all over the world and has thus served as a convenient vehicle for syncretism.[24]

---

18 Ibid. and interview with Mayobanex Rodríguez, San Juan de la Maguana, 12 December 1985.
19 Interview with Mayobanex Rodríguez, San Juan de la Maguana,12 December 1985.
20 Interview with Thomas Reilly, San Juan de la Maguana, 12 December 1985.
21 Pettersson (1980), pp. 31–43.
22 It was the English anthropologist Robert Marett (1866–1943) who in 1902 popularized the term *mana* which has ever since been used as a label for beliefs in 'impersonal' natural forces, but as is the case with most concepts which have been isolated from their immediate environments, the original Melanesian notion of *mana* is more intricate than it first appeared to be. It is not even entirely impersonal: 'In no case, however, does this power operate, except under the direction and control of a person – a living man, a ghost, or a spirit' (Codrington (1915), p. 530, quoted in Sharpe (1975), p. 69).
23 Pettersson (1980), p. 37.

An Austrian Jesuit, Wilhelm Schmidt, even proposed that 'at the very dawn of time', before human beings had been separated into individual groups, the peoples of the world shared a common belief in a 'Supreme Being', which contained all the attributes of 'eternity, omniscience, beneficence, morality, omnipotence and creative power'.[25] Schmidt was severely criticized for his ideas, but they have nevertheless served as an important inspiration for several missionaries, who have been prone to search for something of a Schmidtian *Gottesidee* among the peoples they have attempted to bring into the Christian fold. Particularly after Vatican II,[26] various missionaries have tried to bring their teachings into harmony with local traditions connected with powerful, spiritual forces.[27] The Christian Holy Spirit has during the last decades played an important role in several missionary efforts. In Africa it has been connected with the Ashé [Àṣẹ] of the Yoruba,[28] or the Nzambi in the Congo basin and several African ecclesiastics have made use of the concept in their search for 'a psychological and cultural basis for planting the Christian message in the African mind, without betraying either the one or the other'.[29]

Similar attitudes are common among several priests active in the Dominican Republic. The Jesuit Orlando Espín, to name one, participated in *Olivorista* rituals while collecting material for a doctoral dissertation, in which he argued that a profound study of Dominican popular religion would facilitate missionary work among the peasants in the countryside. In his thesis Espín offers an analysis of the concept of *El Gran Poder de Dios*,

24 Several African peoples have shown a great interest in the Christian concept of the 'Holy Spirit'. As one example, of several, we may mention the cult of *Edisana Odudo*, the Holy Spirit, which during the 1930s spread among the Ibos of the Calabar province in Nigeria. The Holy Spirit merged with concepts related to Ata Abassi, the supreme god of the Ibo pantheon. The cult was characterized by possessions and thaumaturgical activities (Lanternari (1965), p. 62). Similar examples could be given from several other African areas, particularly the Congo basin and South Africa.

25 Sharpe (1975), p. 184.

26 The twenty-first ecumenical council of the Roman Catholic church (1962–65).

27 An example: Jesuits active among the Oglala Lakota Indians in South Dakota have shown a great interest in the concept of *Wakantanka*, the Great Spirit, which is related to *wakan*, a power manifested in extraordinary phenomena and strong personalities. After their violent clashes with the 'Whites', several Indians came to believe that the *Wakantanka* of their enemies was superior to their own (Steinmetz (1980), p. 43). Old shamans, like the world famous Black Elk, became Catholics even if they continued to follow their old religious traditions (Kehoe (1989), pp. 51–69). Jesuit missionaries have incorporated several 'pagan' elements in their teachings (Steinmetz (1980), p. 16), mixing the concepts of *Wakantanka* with those connected with the Christian Holy Spirit. The Pine Ridge area, where most Oglala Indians live, has been a hotbed of revitalistic activities. The Oglalas were deeply engaged in the Ghost Dance cult of the 1890s.

28 See Hallgren (1995).

29 Augé (1982), p. 85.

tracing its origins back to African concepts of power and depicting it as a powerful vehicle for solidarity and compassion.[30] Several Redemptorist priests working in the San Juan Valley state that they feel both impressed and enriched by the 'deep religiosity' they have encountered among those of their parishioners who practice *Olivorista* rituals and believe in *El Gran Poder de Dios.*

The preaching and ideas of the priests in Las Matas de Farfán may have influenced present-day *Olivoristas,* particularly the group around León Romilio Ventura. The 'secretary' of *El Mellizo,* Macario Lorenzo, an eloquent school teacher who lives in Las Matas de Farfán, is the personal friend of several Redemptorist priests. Lorenzo interprets the Palma Sola experience along specific lines, often in harmony with Catholic notions. León Romilio has a lot of confidence in Lorenzo and often allows him to do most of the talking when they are together. While the *Mellizo* tends to be rather 'down-to-earth' in his reasoning, Lorenzo is more abstract; he writes quite a lot and it is possible that his notebooks contain the seeds to a 'new' and reformed *Olivorista* doctrine.[31]

Charisma and El Gran Poder de Dios

Power concepts like the *Sanjuaneros' Gran Poder de Dios* are obviously related to Weberian charisma. According to Weber, believers in charisma assume that it originated in an 'other-worldly, divine nature'.[32] Alleged possessors of charisma believe that their norms and actions are legitimated by a 'source remote in time', a source which is 'timeless' and 'spaceless',[33] in the sense that it is always present and never changes.

Weber has been severely criticized from various quarters and his charisma theory has been called too vague to be useful in any serious analysis.[34] The concept has also been criticized as 'fundamentally circular', since a leader is considered to have charisma when he is perceived, by his followers, as having charismatic qualities.[35] Still, when discussing the

---

30 Espín del Prado (1984). He relates Dominican concepts of power to the Yoruban 'Ashé', a very controversial notion which is hard to define. Among many researchers 'Ashé' has turned into an all-embracing power concept similar to *mana.* The shaky base for such speculations has been examined by Hallgren (1995).
31 Interview with Macario Lorenzo, Las Matas de Farfán, 14 May 1989.
32 MacRae (1982), p. 82.
33 Shils (1968), p. 388.
34 'Popularizers have reduced it to a catch-all label for leaders who excite mass adulation. The term has been applied to persons as disparate as Jesus, Adolf Hitler and Leonard Bernstein' (Adas (1987), p. xxi). 'By rejecting historical analysis and concentrating on the construction of "ideal types", Weber only creates pigeon-holes into which fragments of social behavior can be fitted' (Worsley (1970), p. 280).
35 Worsley (1970), p. 280.

attraction Olivorio exercised over his followers, it is hard to ignore Weber's charisma concept and it appears that this has also been the case with other researchers who have studied the behavior of popular, religious leaders. For want of better tools, attempts have been made to save the charisma concept by tightening up Weber's definitions.[36]

Even if charisma appears as being linked to psychology, or even theology, it is fundamentally a sociological concept. No person is considered to be charismatic if his or her followers do not recognize that faculty in him or her:[37] 'If a man runs naked down the street proclaiming that he alone can save others from impending doom, and if he immediately wins a following, then he is a charismatic leader: a social relationship has come into being. If he does not win a following, he is simply a lunatic.'[38]

The experience of charisma is thus a communal event. Charismatic leaders invoke, for themselves and their followers, a 'unified view of the world derived from a consciously integrated and meaningful attitude toward life'.[39] By their personalities and teachings charismatic leaders expose the hidden order believed to be manifest in nature. In the case of Olivorio and his followers in the San Juan Valley, such an order is equivalent to *El Gran Poder de Dios*.[40]

Even though charismatic leaders have the backing of a 'spiritual sphere', they stand alone in the sense that their authority lacks a formal rational-legal foundation. The direct object of charismatic authority is the limited administrative staff that implements the will of the leader, what Weber calls the *Gemeinde*, a group of people who often live close to the cult leader and are bound to him or her in an emotional form of relationship. The members of this group are chosen not only for their technical skills, but also for the intensity of their devotion.[41] The charismatic leader thus has to keep this devotion alive. The followers are true to a charismatic leader because of the leader's strength and qualities rather than because of 'ideology' alone. True charismatic leaders demand that their followers' commitment is to them personally. Accordingly, a test of the believers' fidelity is that they will readily adapt themselves to their leader's current pronouncements, rather than to any particular body of doctrine.[42] Charisma exists

---

36 Cf. Wilson (1975).
37 Wilson (1973), p. 499.
38 Wilson (1975), p. 7.
39 Weber (1963), p. 59.
40 Charismatic leadership 'requires that we acknowledge the importance of *local* apprehension of supernatural power' (Wilson (1975), p. 18).
41 Wallis (1984), p. 108.
42 Ibid. Several charismatic leaders have been conscious of this fact and have realized that the ultimate test of their charisma has been that their followers have stayed with them even if they constantly changed their doctrine. An extreme example of this type of

solely in the recognition and devotion of the followers. These facts mean that charismatic groups or congregations tend to be limited by the number of devotees – closeness to the leader is essential. Furthermore, since the charismatic leader is the sole authority for his or her followers, charismatics tend to seal themselves off from the surrounding world. The process of institutionalization is a constant threat to all charismatic movements and many leaders pursue a strategy that maximizes the dependence of their followers.[43] All these traits indicate that the *Olivorista* movement, under Olivorio Mateo's leadership, was a genuine charismatic movement.

Hobsbawm has pointed out that 'peasant bandits' ought to be conceived in relation to their social and economic environment, i.e. the peasant society in which they made their first appearance.[44] Thus, Olivorio is a result of his own immediate environment and the charisma he is endowed with is accordingly connected to local notions related to *El Gran Poder de Dios*. The rural society of San Juan provided Olivorio with the framework needed for the exposure of his particular faculties. As practically minded agriculturists, his prospective followers demanded tangible signs of what Olivorio could achieve.

> The charismatic leader gains strength and maintains authority solely by proving his strength in life. If he wants to be a prophet, he must perform miracles; if he wants to be a war lord, he must perform heroic deeds. Above all, however, his divine mission must 'prove' itself in that those who faithfully surrender to him must fare well. If they do not fare well, he is obviously not the master sent by the gods.[45]

The *Sanjuaneros* wanted Olivorio to demonstrate his charisma. This need for physical evidence of charismatic qualities is common to rural societies all over the world and also forms an integral part of the Christian tradition. Jesus is quoted as saying: 'Except ye see signs and wonders, ye will not believe.'[46]

---

behavior was the notorious Jim Jones of the People's Temple, who required frequent proofs of faith and commitment. Jim Jones often repeated that his followers had to look to him for guidance, rather than to the Bible (ibid., pp. 105, 108 and 117).

43 Ibid., pp. 111–12.

44 Hobsbawm (1972), p. 38.

45 Weber (1968b), pp. 22–3.

46 *John* 4:48. Reports of healing miracles still play an important role in the canonization processes directed by the Vatican Sacred Congregation for the Causes of Saints. The present pope, John Paul II, has for example submitted two letters to the Congregation as a part of the process concerning the canonization of an Italian priest. As a cardinal the Pope once asked the miracle-working South Italian priest Francesco Forgione, 'Padre Pio', to pray for a friend dying of cancer. According to John Paul II the friend was cured. 'One can point to no other comparable example of direct papal intervention in a beatification process' (Hebblethwaite (1987), pp. 113–14).

Just as the Hebrew priests of the Old Testament endeavored to confound the devotees of Baal by challenging them publicly to perform supernatural acts, so the Apostles of the early Church attracted followers by working miracles and performing supernatural cures. Both the New Testament and the literature of the patristic period testify to the importance of these activities in the work of conversion; and the ability to perform miracles soon became an indispensable test of sanctity.[47]

Like Palestine in the time of Jesus, the San Juan Valley in the time of Olivorio was a society devoid of specialist therapists, and spiritual purification was thus associated with physical healing. The ultimate sign of the abilities of a charismatic leader like Olivorio is his power to heal.[48] Examples from rural Brazil are close at hand:

> Whenever a priest works a miracle, restores a blind person's sight, enables a victim of paralysis to walk, or offers the common people some tangible proof that he is in communication with the supernatural, crowds converge upon him, precipitate fanatical actions, he is worshipped as a thaumaturge or a saint. [...]
>
> But the proof of his charisma lies solely in his works, and if some lay anchorite performs miracles or if some prophet roams the *sertão* healing the sick, the black too will turn away from the priest and follow the more powerful layman because the object of his respect is not the servant of God but the bearer of charisma, whether he wears a habit or not.[49]

Economic considerations influence most of a peasant's daily decisions –

47 Thomas (1984), pp. 27–8.
48 Wilson (1973), p. 382. For some people no differences exist between religion and medical treatment. A church, a sanctuary or a medical clinic may all be equal in the sense that they are places for healing, in both a spiritual and physical sense. Furthermore, several individuals make no delimitation between body and soul. The 'Zionist' churches of South Africa, that center around charismatic 'prophets', are typical of such an approach and their adherents often consider their places of worship to be more hospitals than churches (Sundkler (1948), p. 220). Their stress on healing is connected with old Zulu beliefs, but is also a result of Christian evangelizing which advanced hand-in-hand with aid for the sick. At an early stage the Christian missionaries realized the connection between healing and religion. Without being related, the activities of the Zionist churches present stunning similarities with the *Olivorismo* of the San Juan Valley. It is the power of the Holy Ghost (*uMoya*) which cures diseases; the devotees dress in a particular way, the power of certain Holy Places is crucial, as well as water and St John the Baptist, the healing is done by charismatic 'prophets', who obtain their powers through dreams and visions, etc. (West (1975), pp. 91–125).
49 Bastide (1978), pp. 351 and 352.

also when it comes religious matters. They make businesslike 'deals' with the dwellers of the 'spiritual sphere', offering their objects of worship things that they believe will please them, in return for favors of different kinds. This 'business logic' is common among rural *Sanjuaneros*: 'I am indecisive since I do not know if religion works. There [in town] I bought a San Antonio [chromolithograph depicting St Anthony] and offered it a hen, but it did not work. I asked: "San Antonio why are you doing this to me?" No, that portrait did not work at all.'[50]

The Holy Spirit within the European tradition

The *Sanjuanero* concept of *El Gran Poder de Dios* may be compared with popular European concepts of the Holy Spirit. Particularly during medieval times, but also later, such notions continuously triggered heretical movements. We do not intend to point to the medieval movements as possible forerunners to *Olivorismo*, even though, as we discussed in Chapter 6, it is highly likely that medieval notions form part of the vast conglomerate of Dominican popular religion. The purpose is instead to illustrate how a notion similar to *El Gran Poder de Dios* could serve as a powerful source of inspiration to heretic movements like the *Olivorista* one. In this, we will recognize how the feelings of direct inspiration from suprahuman forces stimulate independent thinking, foster rebellious attitudes towards established doctrines and are likely to give rise to sectarian behavior.

Around 1015 a group of clerics in Orléans had begun to conduct a ceremony in which initiates, through an act which included 'laying-on of hands', became 'filled by the gift of the Holy Spirit'. The new state of mind that resulted from the ceremony was interpreted as an inner illumination, superior to all the official teachings of the church. Through their spiritual baptism the initiates became convinced that they had gained full understanding of the Scriptures. The validity of officially santioned sacraments and penance were denied since the initiates considered that they had entered another level of being where they 'fed on heavenly food and saw angelic visions'. An infiltrator exposed the group and after a trial, in 1022, the unrepentant heretics were burnt alive in a cottage outside the walls of Orléans. This was the first capital punishment meted out for heresy in the West since AD 383.[51]

---

50 Day laborer interviewed in Higüerito, 16 January 1986.
51 Lambert (1992), pp. 9–13. In 383 the executed heretic was a certain Priscillian of Avila who had been accused of being a Manichee (i.e. a follower of the Persian prophet Mani). Notions related to an omnipotent, ever-present Holy Spirit are part of the European cultural tradition. Already the Greco-Roman Stoic school of philosophy (ca 300 BC –AD 200) taught that *pneuma* [Greek: breath, spirit, wind] was the lifegiving, organic principle, an all-encompassing entity of which man was a part (cf. Rist (1969)). Stoic

The notion that the Holy Spirit was able to bless its devotees with direct knowledge of the meaning of true Christianity had come to stay. A second burning of heretics took place in Milan in 1028. The leader of that heretical sect was a certain Gerard who, when interrogated, answered that his sect was governed by direct experience of the Holy Spirit, an entity which he described in the following way: 'We do not have that Roman pontiff, but another who daily visits our brothers, scattered throughout the world, and when he brings God to us, pardon is granted.'[52] Gerard denied the validity of any sacrament administered by Catholic priests and scorned papal authority by stating: 'There is no other pontiff beside our Pontiff, though he is without tonsure of the head or any sacred mystery.'[53] The heretics were given the choice to recant or enter flaming pyres. Some confessed their sins and returned to the folds of the Church, while others 'covering their faces with their hands leaped into the flames'.[54]

The obsession with the Holy Spirit among European heretics grew even stronger in the thirteenth century when they found a firm foundation for their beliefs in a prophetic system invented by the Calabrian abbot and heretic Joachim of Fiore (1145–1202). Joachim was convinced that he had found a key to the concealed meaning of the Scriptures. He believed he had discovered a pattern in history and was thus enabled to prophesy the future in some detail. He taught that the entire history of humankind could be divided into three periods: the Age of the Father and the Law (proclaimed by the Old Testament), the Age of the Son and the Gospel (proclaimed by the New Testament), and the Age of the Holy Spirit, which in comparison with the other ages would be like high summer compared with winter and spring. The Age of the Spirit would be one of love, joy and freedom in which intimate knowledge of God would be revealed directly in the hearts of men. Joachim of Fiore calculated that each of these periods lasted for a thousand [*mille*] years and that the last one was imminent in his own time.[55]

notions of the *pneuma* formed part of the different gnostic doctrines of faith which were seen as heresies by the founding fathers of Christianity. Many gnostics saw *pneuma* as the source to all life and the entire existence (cf. Pagels (1979)). Manicheeism, which often is referred to as an Iranian variety of gnosticism, influenced elusive and tenacious heretical sects of the Middle Ages, like the Balkan Bogomils and the Cathars of southern France (cf. Stoyanov (1994)).

52 From Gerard's defense speech reported by a certain Landulf, a Milanese historian writing seventy-five years after the event, quoted in ibid., p. 18.

53 Ibid.

54 Lambert (1992), p. 19.

55 Cohn (1970), pp. 108–9. During medieval times and the renaissance it was very common that prophecy influenced the decisions of kings and emperors. New geographical discoveries and inventions used to be fitted into prophetic systems, like the one of Joachim. Reeves (1969) offers a thorough record of the reverberations of Joachimite prophecy in

Like many millenarians after him, Joachim preached a message which was not entirely spiritual, since it predicted radical changes within this world. As his message had universal claims, Joachim directed himself 'to all believers in Christ', stating that the times when 'the man of the flesh persecutes those who are born of the spirit' would soon be over.[56] He prophesied that a new order of monks would characterize the third age, its members acting as 'agents of the new spiritual understanding'.[57] Several heretic sects proclaimed themselves to be the true representatives of the this new order.

Joachim's teachings had a decisively strong impact on the recently founded Franciscan order, which from an early stage had been divided into two factions. The *Conventuals* wanted to adapt themselves to the demands of papal authority by favoring convents and fixed rules. They were opposed to the *Zelanti*, also called Spirituals or *Fraticelli*, who wanted to follow St Francis' own ideas. The saint had desired neither cloisters nor any authoritative rules, ordering his disciples to live without possessions and legal protection, thus hoping to foster a new kind of asceticism which would enable his followers to take an entirely different way of the world from that of the representatives of the established church. Many *Fraticelli* considered themselves to be members of the new order predicted by Joachim, whose teachings thus became very influential within their ranks. For decades the *Fraticelli* were opposed by the papal authorities and several of their own superiors, though they did not lose their influence entirely until 1466, when they disappeared from recorded history after the last self-proclaimed *Fraticelli* were put on trial in Rome.[58]

Since the Franciscans belonged to a preaching order whose members lived in direct contact with the people, it did not take long before

the later Middle Ages. Indirect influences of Joachim's speculations can be traced to the present day. His fantasy of the three ages has been reflected in theories dealing with historical evolution presented by philosophers like Lessing, Schelling, Fichte and Comte, as well as in Marxist dialectics where it appears as the stages of primitive communism, class society and final communism. The catchphrase 'the Third Reich' which the Nazis used for their 'New Order', which was believed to last for a thousand years, was first coined by the German publicist Moeller van den Bruck and was a result of the emotional significance Joachim's beliefs had gained over the centuries in the realm of European social mythology (Cohn (1970), p. 109).

56 Joachim of Fiore quoted in Heer (1974), p. 283. Inspired by Joachimite teachings several men tried to turn his 'spiritual' tidings of a 'new era' into practical politics. A well-known example is Cola di Rienzi (later made famous through an early Wagner opera). He saw himself as a second St Francis, 'called to continue and complete his work by giving it a political basis'. Rienzi (1313–54) acted as a radical reformer in Rome and made a bid to become master of that town as a 'tribune of the people' (ibid., p. 286).

57 Lambert (1992), p. 195. Ibid., pp. 196–7 reproduces Joachim of Fiore's own diagrams which in graphic form presented his teachings.

58 Ibid., p. 213.

Joachimite ideas filtered down to the masses. Accordingly, the bones of a certain Gugliema were dug up in 1300 and burned by the Inquisition[59] in Milan after it had been revealed that she, before and after her death in 1281, had been revered as a reincarnation of the Holy Spirit. A follower of Gugliema, Manfreda de Pirovano, later posed as a 'counter-pope', telling her followers that she was guided by the Holy Spirit. In Parma, in 1260, members of an unauthorized order, the Apostolic Brethren, proclaimed themselves to be the forerunners of the Joachimite era of the Holy Spirit. Its founder, Gerard Segarelli, was an uneducated man who had established his order after being refused admission to the Franciscans. He was captured and burned at the stake in 1300.

Segarelli's leadership was continued by Fra Dolcini, the bastard son of a priest. Like Segarelli, Dolcini also claimed to act upon direct inspiration from the Holy Spirit. Followed by a large group of local peasants, Dolcini took to the mountains carrying out plundering raids against groups who opposed him and his followers. They soon came under fierce attack from armed forces supported by the church. It took several expeditions to conquer their stronghold and Dolcini was finally captured and executed in 1307. However, his movement did not die with him, but persisted for several decades.[60]

Spiritualist movements were not limited to Italy. They were present in almost every European country. Many of these heretic movements were dedicated to a cult of the 'Free Spirit'.[61] The heresy of the Free Spirit has been regarded as a certain form of mysticism which makes its adepts prone to consider themselves, and their communities, as chosen vessels for the Holy Spirit. Most believers in the Free Spirit disregarded any kind of authority save their own experiences.[62] Similar trends existed within medieval Judaism, where 'extra-spirited men', called 'masters of a holy soul' in the *Zohar* [a mystical work composed around AD 200], were believed to live in continual communion with a spiritual realm. Beliefs such as these tend to constitute a base for sectarianism:

> One so favored [by the Spirit] was in certain respects no longer consid-
> ered to be subject to the laws of everyday reality, having realized within

---

59 The Inquisition properly speaking came into being in 1232 when Frederick II (Holy Roman Emperor and king of Sicily) issued an edict entrusting the hunting-out of heretics to state officials. After excommunicating Frederick II, Pope Gregory IX claimed the office for the church and appointed papal inquisitors. Through the years inquisitors were mainly chosen among the Dominicans and Franciscans. The Inquisition was finally suppressed in 1820 (Livingstone (1977), p. 261).

60 Lambert (1992), pp. 193–203.

61 Cohn (1970), p. 151, points to a possible connection between the doctrine of the Free Spirit and that of certain *Sufi* orders active in medieval Spain.

62 Ibid. p. 150.

himself the hidden world of divine light. Naturally, spiritualistic groups of this sort have always regarded themselves as forming a group apart [...] Here then we have all the prerequisites for the sectarian disposition, for the sects serve the illuminati as both a rallying point for their own kind and a refuge from the incomprehension of the carnal and unenlightened masses. These sectarians regard themselves as the vanguard of a new world, but they do not therefore need to renounce the parent religion which inspired them, for they can always reinterpret it in the light of the supreme reality to which they owe their newly discovered allegiance.[63]

The description fits well not only with the leaders of the Brethren of the Free Spirit, but also with Olivorio, who believed he stood above the laws of everyday reality, permitting himself to be addressed as 'God'. He and his followers actually formed 'a group apart', considering themselves to be the vanguard of a new world at the same time as they confessed to be 'true Catholics'.

The Brethren of the Free Spirit spread their doctrines all over Europe. They did not form a single church, but rather constituted

a number of like-minded groups, each with its own particular rites and articles of belief; and the links between the various groups were often strenuous. But these people did keep in touch with one another; and the Free Spirit was at all times clearly recognizable as a quasi-religion with a single basic *corpus* of doctrine which was handed down from generation to generation.[64]

This state of affairs reminds one of the structure of present-day *Olivorista* communities and it appears as if the outlook of medieval heretics had a great deal in common with that of the *Olivoristas*, mainly through their belief in the Holy Spirit as an omnipresent entity that grants extraordinary powers to its believers and turns them into experts in spiritual matters. Medieval heretics were convinced that their direct communication with the Holy Spirit was more authoritative than the adherence to doctrines and rituals sanctioned by the church. Likewise *Olivoristas* commonly believe their faith to be more original and true than the doctrines of the

---

63 Scholem (1971), pp. 89–90.
64 Cohn (1970), p. 172. Much of Norman Cohn's famous study of medieval heretics can be regarded as a description of beliefs related to the doctrine of the Free Spirit. For a somewhat divergent view, see Lambert (1992): '[The heresy of the Free Spirit] was no organized sect at all with a teaching programme hostile to the Church [...]. All that really existed were individual mystics in communication with like-minded friends and followers on an informal basis, some of whom wrote or said some dangerous or extravagant things' (ibid., p. 186).

church, and they claim to have a direct experience of *El Gran Poder de Dios*, thus considering themselves to be in no need of any mediation on the behalf of the Catholic clergy. However, like the medieval heretics, the *Olivoristas* may be ready to accept the teachings of a radical clergy, i.e. preachers of messages which can be easily adopted into their own world of ideas. *Olivoristas* also have in common with the heretics the feeling that they are forerunners of a new era of spiritual bliss.

Anomie and the Holy Spirit

Several researchers have pointed out that a belief in the 'universality of God', i.e. an assumption that a supreme being, or force, is the prime mover of existence, is far from being an exclusively Christian notion. Accordingly, such a creed does not necessarily indicate any Christian influences.

It is not uncommon that the Holy Spirit and similar divinities come to the fore in times of social stress and anomie. This may occur in culturally different societies all over the world. A socially stressful situation was prevalent in much of Europe during what has been called 'the waning of the Middle Ages', when heretic movements cropped up and the Brethren of the Free Spirit were present in almost every country. Traditional ways of life were in rural districts disrupted by plagues and wars, at the same time as socioeconomic changes reshaped traditions and values. Similar developments have harassed districts in Africa, Asia and Latin America.

In small, close-knit societies where most people are engaged in agriculture and much interaction takes place between the inhabitants, individuals often find themselves within a 'familiar' microcosm where they share most beliefs with their neighbors. Members of such communities often imagine the 'spiritual sphere' in 'analogy' with their everyday existence – a situation which may change due to thorough socioeconomic changes:

> If thousands of people find themselves outside the microcosms, and if even those left inside see the boundaries weakening, if not actually dissolving, they can interpret these changes by assuming that the lesser spirits (underpinners of the microcosms) are in retreat, and that the supreme being (underpinner of the macrocosm) is taking direct control of the everyday world. [...] As more and more people become directly involved in the social life beyond the confines of their various microcosms, they begin to evolve a moral code for the governance of this wider life. Since the supreme being is already defined as the arbiter of everthing that transcends the boundaries of the microcosms, he is seen as underpinning this universalistic moral code.[65]

---

65 Horton (1971), p. 102, quoted in Ray (1975), p. 214.

Among *Olivoristas* the concept of *El Gran Poder de Dios* tends to over-shadow the importance of saints, Indians and *misterios*. It is considered to be a more universal entity than all other 'spiritual beings'. In Palma Sola it was stressed that the force which imbued that particular place also had a universal character and intended to save all humankind. This notion was reflected in the name that the *Palmasolistas* gave to their 'party': *Unión Cristiana Mundial*, Worldwide Christian Union. Olivorio also stressed the universal character of his movement and repeatedly declared that his ranks were open to anyone who wanted to join his group.

The illiterate message

Olivorio's followers demanded tangible proofs of the presence of *El Gran Poder de Dios* and got them in the form of healing miracles and inspired speech. Olivorio was 'one of their own', a peasant and an illiterate man, a fact which made his 'miracles' appear as even more astounding. People asked themselves: 'If Olivorio cannot read and write, how can he then be able to perform miracles and prophesy in such an accurate way?'

> The Protestants are a difficult lot [*una línea jodona*]. They do not light any candles for the dead, they do not respect the cross and they baptize people in the river. [...] They say we have to repent, but I myself do not need any salvation. I, who have done so much in my life! I say: 'Do everything to the best of your capacity.' So passes life and you gain knowledge. It is time that makes man strong. Time is a powerful master.[66]

The old peasant who made this statement defined himself as both Catholic and *Olivorista*. He was a personal friend of Olivorio and became a fervent believer in the divinity of *El Maestro*. Like many other followers of charismatic religious leaders, he believed that the power which emanates from such a leader is proof enough of the validity of his claims. When revelation takes place in front of your eyes, it is not necessary to study the Bible.[67]

> The Protestants carry their bibles around. The Catholics do not need any book.[68]

66 Interview with Julián Ramos, Higüerito, 16 January 1986.
67 Likewise, the members of Father Divine Peace Mission (see below) imagined themselves to share a belief that was superior to the one expounded in the Bible. This is a conviction that is common to several messianic sects – if people believe they have God in their midst both scriptures and eschatology become superfluous.
68 Interview with Julián Ramos, Higüerito, 16 January 1986.

I know the Bible word by word, without ever having read it. I am a living proof of the power of this place and my knowledge comes directly to me. Knowledge gained from books just stays on the surface. My knowledge goes deeper.[69]

The knowledge of Christ is neither with the people who have read so much, nor with the ministers of the Church, but in the depth of the mountain. In the depth of the mountains is the natural secret of Christ, the essentials.[70]

The Bible has never been widely read among the Catholic peasants in the Dominican Republic. In the countryside it is still common to hear people stating that 'he who reads the Bible becomes crazy'.[71] Furthermore, in the times of Olivorio most rural dwellers were illiterate and very few Protestant missionaries had ever visited the San Juan Valley. If a Bible was found in a peasant dwelling it was probably kept there for magical reasons and most often used to manufacture certain remedies.[72] It was sometimes placed on altars and in rooms in order to sanctify them, since the words of God 'attract good luck and ward off evil-doers'.[73] Even today, when many Dominican peasants know how to read and write, it is still quite unusual to find Bible-readers among the great majority of Catholic peasants.

In the San Juan Valley, spiritual leaders and cult functionaries often deny that they have ever read the Bible, and they often confess their fear that such an activity would diminish the validity of their message. *El Gran Poder de Dios* must be experienced in a direct way and it is considered to be more authoritative than the words of the Bible.[74] The leaders of Palma Sola occasionally used a language which seemed to be derived from the Bible, but León Romilio Ventura later vehemently denied that he had read a single word in the Scriptures before he began his activities in Palma Sola: 'They

69 Interview with Bartolo de Jiménez, Maguana Arriba, 13 December 1985. Bartolo's inspired speeches are not easy to follow and many outsiders consider him to be demented. Still, the peasants who come to the Spring of St John in search for remedies used to sit and listen to him intently and many praise Bartolo as a 'holy man'.
70 León Romilio Ventura, quoted in Martínez (1991), p. 191.
71 Quoted in Lemus and Marty (1975), p. 162.
72 The pages may be burnt and mixed into baths and decoctions.
73 Lemus and Marty (1975), p. 162.
74 The notion that a real prophet has to receive his message directly from God without the mediation of written text is often considered as a prerequisite for the validity of the message: 'The unlettered nature of the Prophet [in this particular case, Muhammad] demonstrates how the human recipient is completely passive before the divine. Were the purity and virginity of the soul not to exist, the Divine Word would become in a sense tainted with purely human knowledge and not be presented to mankind in its pristine purity' (Nasr (1979), p. 44).

[the Redemptorist priests in Las Matas de Farfán] have instructed me and given me a Bible and by reading it I have now found out that we were not wrong in Palma Sola. We acted in accordance with the will of the Lord.'[75]

A common *Olivorista* notion thus is that the knowledge of 'simple people', the 'tillers of the earth', is far superior to that of 'outsiders', urbanites whose 'bookish' learning has alienated them from any direct experience of *El Gran Poder de Dios*.[76] In their daily communication with the earth's vital force peasants do not need the mediation offered by clergy or Bible. This has been the belief of several rural prophets. It was found among the Spiritualists of the Middle Ages and the notion surfaced again during the German peasant wars of the sixteenth century:

> True Christian belief was a rarity in Christendom, Müntzer taught. Light-hearted belief was no belief at all. The Bible was not necessary to acquire true belief; it could be attained by those who had never heard of Scripture or of other books. The Bible merely bore witness as to how belief had been achieved by men in other times, but it did not in itself create belief. The potency for the common man of a doctrine of direct infusion of the Holy Spirit, in contrast to Luther's 'Bibel Babel Bubel', will be witnessed time and again in the history of the revolutionary utopia. [...] peasants and prophets were exalted over the great ones of the earth. The bestial drinkers and gluttons who had never known suffering what could they understand of the Kingdom of Heaven?[77]

Similar beliefs appeared during the English revolution in the seventeenth century: 'The Scriptures, Winstanley argued, should be used to illustrate truths of which one is already convinced. A man subject to Reason "needs not that any man should teach him". "What the Lord opened in me", Fox put it, "I afterwards found was agreeable to the Bible"'.[78]

75 Interview with León Romilio Ventura, Media Luna, 5 May 1986.
76 A certain 'pride' in not having obtained their 'wisdom' from outsiders is discernible among several messianic leaders. An example is the South African 'Messiah' Isaiah Shembe (1875–1935), who once stated: 'If you [the European missionaries] had taught him [Shembe] in your schools, you would have had a chance of boasting over him. But God, in order to reveal His wisdom, sent this Shembe [...] that he may speak as a wise and educated man' (Isaiah Shembe, quoted in Sundkler (1948), p. 110). Shembe never attended a European school but knew how to read and write and had been a catechist in a separatist African Baptist church.
77 Manuel and Manuel (1979), p.189. Thomas Müntzer (1488/89–1525) was a priest and scholar turned into a fervent agitator and 'God-sent leader' of the poor. He was beheaded after an army of peasants and miners had been vanquished outside Frankenhausen (Cohn (1970), pp. 234–51).
78 Hill (1987), pp. 264–5. Gerrard Winstanley was originally a clothing tradesman who after bankruptcy became a day laborer and visionary writer of radical religious pamphlets

Thaumaturges

Olivorio was a thaumaturge, a faith healer. Thaumaturgy is not a strictly religious phenomenon; it has more to do with power than with God. Strong charismatic personalities are often believed to emit power. Even things which have been in contact with such personalities are often considered to be charged with power. Items like Hitler's Mercedeses, Elvis Presley's Cadillacs, or John Lennon's guitars fetch high prices in quality auctions. In an earlier age the charisma of powerful people was even considered as curative. For centuries the mere touch of several European kings was considered as a remedy for a kind of scrofula called 'Kings Evil'. The English king Charles II reportedly ministered to over 90,000 scrofulous persons in a period of twenty years.[79]

The power to heal was believed to be endowed to the kings through the coronation ceremony. Thus, Louis XIV was said to be unable to perform any thaumaturgic activities before he had been properly 'consecrated'.[80] Several powerful heads of state have become so overpowered by their own megalomania that they have ended up considering themselves able to carry out miraculous acts. To that end Trujillo once advertised in the local Dominican press and offered medical consultations to any person suffering from physical ailments. Needless to say the dictator's poor schooling had not left any room for medical studies.[81]

However, even though thaumaturgy may appear outside the religious sphere it is intimately connected with it. Brian Wilson has divided the response to the world offered by various religious leaders into different categories.[82] Among them we find the thaumaturges, who work within a limited locality and perform miracles as a proof of the existence of a spiritual realm, thus attempting to show that God has granted them certain dispensations.[83]

(ibid. 112). George Fox (1624–91) was the founder of the Society of Friends (the Quakers). He taught that truth is to be found in the inner voice of God speaking to the soul (Livingstone (1977), p. 198).

79 Thomas (1984), pp. 227–8. Scrofula is tuberculosis of the lymphatic glands.

80 Ibid., p. 230.

81 García (1986), p. 310.

82 Revolutionists who mean that God will overturn the world, introversionists who state that God calls us to abandon the world, reformists who preach that God wants us to amend the world and utopians who want to reconstruct it, conversionalists who want to change us instead of the world, and manipulationists who want us to change our perception of the world (Wilson (1973), p. 27).

83 Ibid. In the category of believers in thaumaturges Wilson includes what he calls 'spiritists'. Needless to say, his categories are generalizations, ideal-type constructions. Several religious leaders may fit into more than one division. Nevertheless, Wilson is right when he states that the sects which result from the teachings of a certain leader often have a pronounced character and may easily fit in to one of his particular categories.

A thaumaturge naturally attracts more followers in times of change and stress than under 'normal' conditions. When traditional lifestyles are threatened and social disruption leads to economic exploitation and alienation, people tend to seek authoritative interpretations which may explain the altered social circumstances. A search for cosmos behind chaos takes place. What could be more natural than looking for the missing order in the spiritual sphere which is believed to abide behind everything? In the case of the San Juan Valley that sphere is constituted by the realm of *El Gran Poder de Dios*.

When a fellow peasant is credited with wonder-workings it is often interpreted as a sign of direct communication with spiritual powers transcending everyday experience. By accepting the blessings and services of a powerful thaumaturge, a distressed peasant thus partakes in a wider and more meaningful universe. Through the powers of the thaumaturge a believer may be able to divine a balance and meaning behind a disturbed social system.[84]

Thaumaturgy constitutes a 'personal' and 'marginal' phenomenon in the sense that it usually affects only people in the vicinity of a charismatic personality. So-called world religions, with an established dogma and a cultic hierarchy, like Islam and Christianity, tend to limit or reject thaumaturgic activities and usually consider them to be anarchic threats to order and authority. Rural faith healers have no need of any official backing from an established church or controlling state bureaucracy. They are laymen who feel they receive sufficient support from the 'spiritual sphere' and the people who believe in them. They work their miracles unaided by scriptures or professional cult functionaries.

Thaumaturgy is a highly pragmatical activity. Thaumaturges cure diseases, communicate with the spiritual sphere and offer advice and consolation. They impress their surroundings by action, presenting tangible evidence of their powers.[85] For prospective believers direct experience is of more crucial importance than original faith. Believers are prepared to abandon their former convictions if such proofs convince them of the efficiency of the thaumaturge's miraculous powers.

The miracle worker within his environment

Thaumaturgy lives and thrives within limited localities and the 'sects' that develop from the activities of a certain thaumaturge seldom become universal or arrive at any solid organization.[86] They have instead the character

---

84 Ibid. pp. 60 and 73.
85 Wilson (1970), p. 168.
86 Still, several originally small thaumaturgic communities have been forged into powerful,

of an organism which thrives in harmony with its immediate environment and reacts to changes within the society where it subsists. Thus, several religious leaders in the San Juan Valley state that they are *Olivoristas*, but each cultic center presents its own particular blend of *Olivorista* faith and most *Olivoristas* acknowledge only the beliefs of their own cultic group, which tend to be inspired by the *tronco del lugar*, an old patriarch who often is related to most villagers and acts as an unofficial authority of the place.

Palma Sola, where *Olivoristas* from the whole area gathered, never obtained a uniform faith pattern. It was the 'power of the place' which worked the miracles and León Romilio Ventura always points to the fact that this force manifested itself through actions, and through actions alone. Palma Sola was certainly 'ruled' by the Ventura brothers, but they did so in collaboration with others and the Venturas were far from being the only cult functionaries who were active within the compound. Several other religious leaders were allowed, and even invited, to preach and act within the sanctuary.

When *Olivoristas* move to Santo Domingo they often drop their old faith, which is considered to be firmly planted in their former surroundings and thus impossible to uproot. In the capital they may seek out a substitute for the village community they left behind, often a voodoo group or a Protestant sect.[87]

In order to understand Olivorio's activities, teachings and attraction we must study him in the context which gave his message a distinct meaning. He has to be viewed in connection with the common culture of his believers, the code he shared with them.[88] Like his followers, Olivorio was a product of his environment. By most outsiders, such as the elite groups of San Juan de la Maguana, he was considered to be nothing else but a wretched, ignorant witch doctor, but the rural dwellers who gathered around him recognized his particular skills and even before he received his revelations they discerned a certain erudition in him.

When Olivorio began his mission he was a fairly old and experienced man, who had picked up considerable knowledge during his constant wanderings through the entire district and from the connections he had fostered with influential people like the Ramírez family and the flamboyant foreigner Juan Samuel. His knowledge was combined with a persuasive

---

hierarchically organized churches. An example is the spiritistic *Cao Dài* in Vietnam, which is endowed with a pope and an extremely complicated clerical hierarchy (Oliver (1976)). *Cao Dài* is still (even under communist rule) believed to have more than a million followers. It may also be argued that a world religion like Christianity originated from a small thaumaturgic sect in Roman-occupied Palestine.

87 Interview with Jorge Feliz, Santo Domingo, 5 January 1986. Jorge was born in Carrera de Yeguas, a village close to Palma Sola, with strong *Olivorista* traditions.

88 Cf. Pentikäinen (1978), p. 24.

character. In that sense he resembles other charismatic leaders who distinguish themselves from their fellow citizens by a slightly higher degree of learning and experience. They might have obtained their superior knowledge from missionary schools or governmental institutions, such as the army and the state bureaucracy, or from contacts with outsiders who were able to teach them how to perceive their environment in a new light. Charismatic leaders tend also to be well traveled.[89]

Like Olivorio, the Venturas were also somewhat different from their neighbors; several were 'twins' and they were all respected middle-holders, fervent *Olivoristas* and anti-*Trujillistas* and upheld close connections with their relatives in Haiti. León Romilio also had a veneer of learning and respectability due to his position as emergency school teacher.

When interpreting prophetic movements it is common that researchers explain their particular features by applying general information obtained from other, similar phenomena, trying to categorize their research objects with the help of catchphrases like 'relative deprivation' or 'revitalization',[90] ignoring an in-depth study of the environment in which they developed.[91]

Even if the prophet is something of a stranger in the midst of his followers, and his message may appear to be both new and innovative, it still has to be relevant to his listeners and thus steeped in the traditions of the place. In order to interpret and gain an understanding of the attractive-

89 Adas (1987), p. 119. Cf. Ljungdahl (1969), p. 229. The African prophets Simon Kimbangou and Isaiah Shembe received much of their education from Christian missionaries, just like the Chinese Taiping leader, Hung Hsiu-ch'üan. The Paiute visionary Jack Wilson worked with white people and the famous shamans Sitting Bull and Black Elk had been in Europe with Buffalo Bill's Wild West Show. The founder of the Vietnamese *Cao Dài* sect, Ngô Minh Chiêu, was a functionary within the French colonial administration, and the Brazilian Messiah Antonio Conselheiro was a restless wanderer. It must, however, be stressed that the relative learning of popular prophets must always be viewed in relation to that of their neighbors. Compared with outsiders prophets may appear poorly educated. Several have been entirely illiterate, but all of them have still had certain skills and knowledge which placed them apart from their companions.
90 More about these concepts below.
91 A well-known example of how an 'all-embracing' explanation can fail in the interpretation of a religious phenomenon is the one which traditionally was used to explain the Navaho rejection of the Ghost Dance of the 1890s. The Ghost Dance was believed to bring about a resurrection of the dead. Indian ancestors would return to their decimated descendants, get rid of the Whites, bring back the buffalo herds and restore the old order of life. Most tribes of the Great Plains were enthusiastic about these prospects, but the movement was entirely rejected by the Navaho. The relative wellbeing and economic prosperity of the Navaho were traditionally presented as the reason for the rejection. However, local studies later revealed that the Navaho also suffered from feelings of relative deprivation and would probably have joined the Ghost Dance if they had not been 'out of their wits' for fear that the dead would come back. Contrary to their neighbors' beliefs, the fear of the dead was always an 'underlaying and pervasive pattern in Navaho culture' (cf. Hill (1944)).

ness of the message of a charismatic leader, a profound knowledge of the area of his activities is of crucial importance.

Apart from being well rooted in his environment the message of a charismatic leader must have a relevant meaning for the believers as well. Not every person is ready to consider any prophet as a divine messenger. Whether an individual is ready to believe or not depends on his or her previous expectations and experiences. The people of Nazareth, who knew Jesus as the son of a simple carpenter, rejected him and Jesus was not able to perform many miracles in his home village.[92] Most members of the urban elite met Olivorio with disdain, laughed at his teachings and miracles, and considered him to be nothing other than the illiterate day laborer he always had been.[93] Also, several old *Olivoristas* dismissed the Ventura brothers as politicizing impostors and denied that any miracles ever took place in Palma Sola.[94]

In order to believe in a miracle you probably have to be positively predisposed. Both Olivorio and the Ventura brothers had their hecklers and disbelievers. The fact that children in the Dominican countryside for decades have been singing libelous songs about the prophet of La Maguana may be considered as an indication of a widespread popular rejection of the powers of the miracle worker:

Oliverio [sic] *tiene catarro*	Olivorio has a cold
se lo cura con un cigarro;	he cures it with a cigar;
Oliverio [sic] *tiene moquillo,*	Olivorio has a running nose
se lo cura con un palillo.[95]	he cures it with a stick.

Several visitors to Palma Sola saw only fanaticism and peculiar people. An individual perceives what he or she believes.[96] This is true regarding the

---

92 *Mark* 6:1–6. Cf. Ljungdahl (1969), p. 225.

93 Nevertheless, contrary to Jesus' experience Olivorio succeeded in being a prophet in his home village. Many of his closest friends and relatives became strong believers in his powers (interview with Arquímedes Valdez, Maguana Abajo, 31 May 1989). Even some members of the San Juan elite state they have seen 'miracles' performed by Olivorio (interview with Mimicito Ramírez, San Juan de la Maguana, 16 January 1986). An interesting feature in the life of many thaumaturges and prophets is that they are often able to convince their closest kin about their divine missions. In the case of Olivorio, his brother Carlitos became one of the most important leader of the *Olivorista* movement. Several of Olivorio's sons participated in his campaigns and his first wife, Eusebia, kept her faith in him, even though he later shared his life with other women (interview with Arquímedes Valdez, Maguana Abajo, 31 May 1989).

94 Interview with Julían Ramos, Higüerito, 16 January 1986.

95 Children's play song from Gaspar Hernández (Joba), recorded in 1946 and quoted by Cruz Brache (1975), p. 102.

96 'Followers expect signs of power, but the demand for absolute faith and obedience precludes their asking for such' (Wilson (1975), p. 6).

acts of other charismatic leaders as well and is excellently illustrated by a story about Jack Wilson (Wovoka), the famous Paiute prophet who initiated the Ghost Dance movement of the 1890s.

In talking with Tall Bull, one of the Cheyenne delegates and then captain of the Indian police, he said that before leaving they had asked Wovoka to give them some proof of his supernatural powers. Accordingly he had ranged them in front of him, seated on the ground, he sitting facing them, with his sombrero between and his eagle feathers in his hand. Then with a quick movement he had put his hand into the empty hat and drawn out from it 'something black'. Tall Bull would not admit that anything more had happened, and did not seem to be very profoundly impressed by the occurrence, saying that he thought there were medicine-men of equal capacity among the Cheyenne. In talking soon afterward with Black Coyote, one of the Arapho delegates and also police officer, the same incident came up, but with a very different sequel. Black Coyote told how they had seated themselves on the ground in front of Wovoka, as described by Tall Bull, and went on to tell how the messiah had waved his feathers over his hat, and then, when he withdrew his hand, Black Coyote looked into the hat and there 'saw the whole world'. The explanation is simple. Tall Bull [...] was a jovial, light-hearted fellow, fond of joking and playing tricks on his associates, but withal a man of good hard sense and disposed to be doubtful in regard to all medicine-men outside of his own tribe. Black Coyote, on the contrary, is a man of contemplative disposition, much given to speculation on the unseen world. His body and arms are covered with the scars of wounds which he has inflicted on himself in obedience to commands received in dreams. When the first news of the new religion came to the southern tribes, he had made a long journey, at his own expense, to his kindred in Wyoming, to learn the doctrine and the songs, and since his return had been drilling his people day and night in both. Now, on his visit to the fountain head of inspiration, he was prepared for great things, and when the messiah performed his hypnotic passes with the eagle feather, as I have so often witnessed in the Ghost dance, Black Coyote saw the whole spirit world where Tall Bull saw only an empty hat. From my knowledge of the men, I believe both were honest in their statements.[97]

97 Mooney (1965), pp. 17–18 (the book was originally published in 1896). The black sombrero of Jack Wilson was believed to be a powerful object and was desired by several of his followers. Occasionally he let his friend, the white storekeeper Dyer, mail one of his hats to some admirer together with a bill for twenty dollars. Like Olivorio, Jack Wilson was believed to be a mighty miracle worker, endowed with medical powers and able to cause earthquakes. Like his Dominican equivalent Jack Wilson lived most of his life as a peasant and day laborer.

In spite of his different perception, however, Tall Bull did not dismiss Wovoka as a simple charlatan. He listened to the prophet and respected the man. The statements of Tall Bull and Black Coyote may be contrasted to that of a white man and 'outsider', like C. C. Warner, the US Indian agent, within whose jurisdiction Wovoka lived:

> in regard to Jack Wilson, the 'Messiah' [...] I never saw him or a photo of him. He works among the whites about 40 miles from my Walker Lake reserve, and never comes near the agency when I visit it [...] I am pursuing the course with him of nonattention or a silent ignoring. He seems to think, so I hear, that I will arrest him should he come within my reach. I would give him no such notoriety. He, like all other prophets has but little honor in his own country. He has been visited by delegates from various and many Indian tribes, which I think should be discouraged all that is possible. Don't know what the 'Smoholler' religion, you speak of, is. He speaks English well, but is not educated. He got his doctrine in part from contact, living in and with a religious [Christian] family. There are neither ghost songs, dances, nor ceremonials among them [the Indians] about my agencies. Would not be allowed. I think they died out with 'Sitting Bull'.[98]

Warner's views may be compared with those held by several members of the San Juan elite, who likewise chose to ignore the *Olivoristas*, preferring to believe that mostly people from other parts of the country were attracted by Olivorio's cult and doctrine. Most of them believed that *Olivorismo* disappeared with the death of its leader. Like Agent Warner, the San Juan elite also ascribed the religious doctrines of their rural prophet to sources removed from traditional peasant beliefs and *Olivorismo* was accordingly interpreted as a blend of voodoo, Juan Samuel's 'exotic, evangelical' teachings and 'base' superstitions, when, as a matter of fact, it was firmly rooted in local traditions. On the other hand, several rural inhabitants of the valley are still eager for miracles and ready to believe in local prophets and miracle-workers: 'People here are extremely credulous and they are constantly looking for signs, for something to believe in.'[99]

---

98 Letter from C. C. Warner to James Mooney, quoted in ibid., p. 8. Several misconceptions are apparent in the letter. Wovoka spoke poor English, most of his religious doctrine was based on earlier Paiute traditions, and the Ghost Dance religion was still practiced about Warner's agencies.

99 Interview with Eugenio Fernández Durán, San Juan de la Maguana, 4 July 1990. It is important to point out that a thaumaturge is not identical with a *curandero*. Rural *curanderos* are constantly active in the San Juan Valley and several of them state that they act with the help of *El Gran Poder de Dios*. Olivorio, however, belongs to an entirely different category. He was far from being a simple *curandero*. His mandate contained several other aspects and this made him a religious personality of higher dignity than a *curandero*. (For

According to Peter Worsley, prophets appear constantly in all kinds of environments, but it is only in times of crisis that people are ready to listen to them, because it is only then that their message becomes attractive to the 'masses'.[100] Crisis nurtures hopes for better times and people search for signs that herald the arrival of such times. The worse the upheavals and changes get, the more desperate is the yearning for miracles, the readiness to believe.

When, in 1986, we interviewed Enrique Figueroa, who several times has been accused of trying to play the part of a reincarnated Olivorio, he stated that he was not alone in believing that *El Gran Poder de Dios* manifested itself in him, just as it had once done in the person of Olivorio. He even mentioned the names of two other persons in the vicinity who considered themselves to be vehicles of *El Gran Poder de Dios*.[101] León Romilio Ventura, in turn, declared several times that he would not hesitate 'if he was called upon' to reinitiate the movement. However, the times had not been auspicious yet.[102]

Prophet, messiah or god?

Prophets

A thaumaturge easily turns into a prophet.[103] His or her healing activities naturally lend themselves to an interpretation which considers the thaumaturge's personality to be the result of a divine will's incursions into everyday life. Superhuman powers are believed to *act* through a thaumaturge while they *speak* through a prophet. Both Olivorio and the Ventura brothers occasionally delivered inspired speeches, communicating the words of *El Gran Poder de Dios*, or other *misterios*, in a state of ecstasy or possession.[104] A fundamental criterion for a prophet is that an ecstatic element is involved in the exercise of his calling, combined with a strong conviction of spiritual or divine guidance, a feeling that he has been

the traditional activities of a Dominican *curandero*, see Avila Suero (1988), pp. 88–109.) Rural healers often present several similarities in their outlook and activities, even if they are active within the framework of peasant environments in entirely different parts of the world. (About Scandinavian healers, see Alver *et al.* (1980) and Gustafson (1981).)

100 Worsley (1970), pp. 289–90.
101 Interview with Enrique Figueroa, Hato Nuevo, 18 January 1986.
102 Interviews with León Romilio Ventura, Media Luna, 5 May 1986 and Las Matas de Farfán, 14 May 1989.
103 From Greek *prophetes* [one who declares the divine will] from *pro-* + *phanai* [to speak].
104 The word ecstasy comes from Greek *ekstasis* [to displace], and is like possession related to trance, an altered state of mind in which a person is considered to experience either a temporary absence of his soul (soul-loss) or an incursion (possession) by a supernatural being. (Lewis (1975), p. 29).

chosen for his task, not by human beings but by a supernatural power. The divine selection of a prophet usually takes the form of a personal meeting with spiritual forces, an encounter which in most cases takes in a state of altered consciousness. The often overwhelming experience of such a meeting may lead to the formation of an inner compulsion which forces the prophet to deliver the message he believes he has received from the 'spiritual' sphere.[105]

Thaumaturgical activities easily develop into full-fledged prophecy.[106] Like thaumaturges, prophets tend to be laymen practicing outside the bounds of established religion. Biblical prophets are often described as popular and 'democratic' in the sense that 'This gift of interpreting the mind of God granted to the prophets was something other than that of occult knowledge claimed by secluded spirits. They were essentially men of the world, practical men, concerned with the facts of daily life, but they saw these facts in relation to the Will of God.'[107]

This is true of several founders of world religions, like Moses, Jesus, Muhammad and Mani,[108] but also of agriculturists like Olivorio, Romilio and Plinio, who like their biblical counterparts experienced startling visions and thus became convinced of the fact that they were carrying out a heavenly ordained commission. With the biblical prophets the Ventura brothers also shared strong moral convictions, demands for social justice and an urge to right wrongs and change the world.[109]

The *Sanjuanero* prophets preached a religion which was down to earth and highly practical, just like those of their counterparts in other regions of the world. Prophets tend to inspire cults in which the sacred and the profane cannot be separated. Thus, a prophet, whether appearing in the Israel of biblical times, in the Brazilian backlands or the Dominican countryside, tends to be both a secular and a religious leader, eager to impress the world with his message, aspiring to take active part in the mundane government of his district, or even country.[110]

Prophetism is concerned with change and frequently preaches the coming of a 'new era' and a 'new world'. Movements which arise from such doctrines tend to be 'conservative' in the sense that they often try to rescue

---

105 Pettersson (1980), p. 281.
106 Lewis (1975), p. 128.
107 Epstein (1964), p. 55.
108 The divine inspiration of successful prophets often ends up as the institutionalized property of religious establishments, which mediate the inspired truth to the masses through rituals performed by duly accredited officers (Lewis (1975), p. 132).
109 With the old Israelite prophet Samuel, Olivorio even shared the ability of finding runaway donkeys (*1 Sam.* 9:20; cf. interview with Tala Cabral Ramírez, Santo Domingo, 21 November 1985).
110 Cf. Pereira de Queiroz (1965), pp. 66–7.

notions and traditions which have been neglected in times of chaos and disintegration. However, such a way of thinking is not conservative in the strict sense of the word. It intends rather to reform and modernize older customs. Accordingly, such movements have often been termed 'nativistic', i.e. they are considered as attempts of certain social groups to 'revive or perpetuate selected aspects' of their common culture.[111] This brings Jesus to mind, the prophet and thaumaturge who, firmly rooted in the Jewish tradition, declared that he was not only going to keep the law, but also wished to fulfill and sharpen it,[112] repeatedly stating that 'Ye have heard that it was said by them of old time [...] But I say unto you'.[113] Jesus furthermore claimed he was something more than just a prophet. He was the expected Messiah.

Messiahs

There is plenty of disagreement about how to characterize the kind of charismatic leaders we deal with here. Are they messiahs or prophets? In order to sort out the concepts we first have to establish who is really a messiah. The word originates from the Hebrew word *mashách* [to anoint], and was originally connected with the ritual of sanctifying an Israelite pretender to the throne by anointing him with holy oil, an act believed to transmit the spirit [*ruach*] of Yahweh to the future king, who after the ceremony was greeted as the 'son of Yahwheh'.[114]

When the Israelite state began its long political decline, popular imagination gave rise to hopes for a reestablishment of the Davidian monarchy, which was considered to have been the pinnacle of Israelite power. The Messiah was thus imagined to be a future, just and powerful monarch of Davidian descent – a mighty king who could restore the shattered Israelite nation to its former glory. As the situation grew worse, increasingly superhuman qualities were attached to the awaited Messiah. By the first century AD the Apocalypses of Baruch and Ezra depicted the Messiah as a fearsome warrior king, a 'roaring Lion of Judah', who would annihilate the heathen, gather the ten lost tribes from foreign lands and finally establish a kingdom which would afterwards flourish in peace and glory.[115]

This was, however, just one of many conceptions which arose around the longing for a future messiah. In later Judaism he was conceived as a less militant figure. Messianic speculation receded into the background while

---

111 Linton (1943), p. 415.
112 *Matthew* 5:17.
113 *Matthew* 5:21–48.
114 Albrektson and Ringgren (1969), p. 43.
115 Cohn (1970), p. 22.

practical aspects of personal growth and daily spirituality became paramount. Frequently the Messiah was imagined as a mere symbol of Israel's task as the Servant of Jahve, rather than a real person of royal lineage. However, he could also be imagined as the central and dominating figure in a future Kingdom of God, built on earth, by the hands of men under divine guidance, a fulfilment of man's striving towards righteousness. According to this view, the Messiah will be a mortal leader who will bring about the moral and spiritual regeneration of the whole of humanity.[116]

One of the most influential Jewish speculations concerning the awaited coming of the Messiah was offered by the Hispanic-Jewish philosopher Maimonides (1135–1204), who wrote that the Messiah would be a person of flesh and blood, renowned for his piety and scholarship. He would not perform any miracles, only compel all Israel to follow the Torah and observe its rules. If he acts in such a way, he may be presumed to be the Messiah and if he ultimately succeeds with his mission, the temple will be rebuilt, thus proving that he *is* the actual Messiah. Strife will end and the Jewish people will finally lead all nations in their peaceful recognition of their oneness as God's children.[117] This line of thought has been very influential in certain Hasidic circles, particularly among the Lubavitchers, who recently expected their *rebbe*, leader Menachem Mendel Schneerson, to proclaim himself as the Messiah.[118]

Christian concepts of the future Messiah are different from Jewish ones. They are all connected with Jesus of Nazareth, considered to be identical with the Trinity: the Father, the Son and the Holy Spirit. Jesus Christ[119] is either imagined to be a godhead who suffered and died in atonement for the sins of all humankind and is thus conceived as a celestial ruler of a purely spiritual kingdom, or he may be imagined to appear in the future as the returning Christ, who will establish a messianic kingdom on earth: 'For the Son of Man shall come in the Glory of his Father with his angels: and then he shall reward every man according to his works. Verily I say unto you, there be some standing here, which shall not taste death, till they see the Son of Man coming in his kingdom.'[120]

---

116 Epstein (1964), pp. 139–40.
117 Scholem (1971), pp. 24–7.
118 Hoffman (1991); cf. Beyer (1992) and Woodward and Brown (1992). The Lubavitchers staged huge advertisement campaigns, particularly in New York, where the subways often displayed their posters. On several occasions in 1991 the *New York Times* carried full-page advertisements hinting that Rabbi Schneerson was the Messiah, that the Temple would soon be rebuilt, and the Messiah would then stand upon its roof and cry out, and the messianic era would be upon us. Schneerson died on 16 June 1994.
119 Christ is derived from the Greek *khristos* [anointed], and a direct translation of the Hebrew *mashiach*.
120 *Matthew* 16:27–8; cf. *Matthew* 24:1–51.

Profane messiahs: returning heroes and other powerful men

Several *Olivoristas* believe that Olivorio will return in person some day and restore his order, not only in the San Juan Valley but in the whole of the Dominican Republic.[121] Notions of returning kings, or heroes, who will restore peace and prosperity are common in several different societies. Such hopes are nurtured by stress and suffering, probably answering to a basic human longing, irrespective of cultural background. Hopes for the resurrection of heroes are not reserved to a strictly religious sphere. In mundane folklore, popular rulers and heroes are frequently believed to bide their time for a triumphant return: Frederick Barbarossa is said to be asleep in a cave in the mountain of Kyffhäuser and all over Europe we find other alleged resting places for sleeping heroes, like King Arthur, Charlemagne, Robert Bruce and King Dan (Holger Danske), just to mention a few of them.[122]

During the Middle Ages interruptions of royal power, when popular rulers were suddenly killed or disappeared, often caused anguish and fear among poor people who were ready to follow popular leaders claiming that they were resurrected or returning princes; a pseudo-Baldwin, a pseudo-Frederick, a resurrected Charlemagne or a King Tafur.[123] However, the phenomenon has not been restricted to medieval times. While leading masses of peasants in a large-scale rebellion (1773–75), the Russian Cossack Emelian Pugachev impersonated a deceased tsar, telling his followers that he had come back in order to claim his throne from an usurper.[124] Hopes for the return of King Sebastião of Portugal, who was killed in North Africa in 1578, have until the present century caused several rebellions and messianic upheavals in Brazil.[125] Poverty-stricken *jagunços* of the Brazilian *sertão* have looked up towards the sky, awaiting the appearance of Sebastião at the head of huge celestial armies. Similarly, Mexican peasants are even today on the lookout for Emiliano Zapata who, wearing a big sombrero and riding a white horse, will return to take his place at the head of his men, ensuring that his given promise is kept: 'The land belongs to the one who works it.'[126]

Admiration for the high and mighty has always had the capacity to make

---

121 Interview with Niño Gómez, Restauración, 3 May 1986.
122 For a study of legends connected with 'hidden European kings', see Bercé (1990). The persistence of these myths as inspiration for nationalistic movements can be felt to this very day. The memory of the old Serbian hero Marko Kraljević (?1335–94), who is believed to sleep under a mountain in Montenegro, has for example been conjured up by Bosnian Serbs in the recent war in former Yugoslavia.
123 Cohn (1970), p. 283.
124 Bercé (1990), pp. 139–41.
125 About the myths which have developed around King Sebastião, see ibid., pp. 17–81.
126 Gruzinski (1989), pp. 187–8. Zapata was murdered in 1919.

people incredulous at reports of their untimely death. When Lord Kitchener, who from recruiting posters had told Englishmen that their country needed them in World War I, drowned in 1916, rumors quickly spread that he was alive and well in Russia, helping the Russian war effort. It also took a long time for Hitler to die. Persistent rumors insisted he had escaped the fall of Berlin and had been seen in various places all over the world, just as Elvis Presley is sometimes spotted at American supermarkets and, immediately after the death of Charlie Parker in 1955, graffiti with the text 'Bird Lives' appeared on the walls of New York.

Throughout the years, strange cults have grown up around both dead and living political leaders. An elaborate cult of Lenin went on for decades in the Soviet Union,[127] a cult whose dimensions would be surpassed by the deification of the living Stalin and later, in China, of Mao Zedong.[128] On a much more modest scale, a syncretistic cult in the Republic of the Congo worships Charles de Gaulle at altars decorated with the cross of Lorraine, while believers invoke *Ngolo*, which is a Bakongo word for power.[129] Other examples are closer at hand when discussing the cult of Olivorio. During the 1960s, Haitian schoolchildren read in unison a prayer to 'Papa Doc', François Duvalier:

> Our Doc, who art in the National Palace for life, hallowed be Thy name by present and future generations. Thy will be done in Port-au-Prince as it is in the provinces. Give us this day our new Haiti and forgive not the trespasses of the anti-patriots who daily spit upon our Fatherland. Let them succumb to temptation and under the weight of their evil doings. Do not deliver them from evil. Amen.[130]

A few decades earlier, religious hymns were composed to Rafael Trujillo in the Dominican Republic:

Es Trujillo pan bendito	Trujillo is the sanctified bread
que nos regala el Señor,	that the Lord gives us,

---

127 Tumarkin (1983).
128 The worship of Mao escalated during the 'Cultural Revolution' when members of the nationwide revolutionary committees found that 'the safest and most rewarding course of action was to do nothing, except promote the worship of Mao' (Chang (1991), p. 399). The citizens of several Chinese districts were forced to engage in strange activities, such as 'reporting to Chairman Mao', which meant that people had to come together at certain hours of the day, sometimes even at midnight, to pay homage to the country's leader: 'It involved gathering in front of a statue or portrait of Mao, chanting quotations from the Little Red Book, and shouting "Long live Chairman Mao, long live Chairman Mao and long long live Chairman Mao!" while waving the Little Red Book" (ibid.).
129 Paxton (1992), p. 18.
130 Fourcand (1964), p. 37. Cf. *Matthew* 6:9–13.

nuncio de paz y de amor	forerunner of peace and love
en este jardín marchito	in this withered garden
algo de fruto exquisito,	something like an exquisite fruit,
de – santa comunión,	of – the holy communion,
alientos de corazón	breath of the heart
esta hora soñada	in this hour that we dreamed of
por tanto tiempo esperada	expected for such a long time:
Redención y Reelección![131]	Redemption and Reelection!

It may be argued that it is not the man who is worshiped, but the power incarnated in him. Speculation about supernatural powers behind political decision makers are a common feature in different cultural settings and frequently crop up in Dominican politics as well. Joaquín Balaguer, who has served as his country's president for no less than seven periods, feels that, 'like Caesar or Napoleon' he is subjected to 'a superior force, which we have baptized with the name of destiny'. It is evident that Balaguer does not consider this destiny to be blind, since he states that he several times has experienced how its 'hand' has rescued him from violent death.[132] He believes that this hand of destiny is the ultimate director of his actions:

> I am, in a certain way, gentlemen, an instrument of destiny. I have not promoted the movement in favor of my candidacy; but it is an unforeseeable product of many circumstances which have been, and continue to be, out of reach of my personal will. At this moment I could not make any spontaneous decision and I am unable to opt freely for or against my own candidacy.[133]

The political discourse in the Dominican Republic is apt to be rather high-flown, and another influential politician, the PRD's José Peña Gómez, also liked to consider himself as governed by destiny, something which led another of the country's 'old political dinosaurs', Juan Bosch, to habitually refer to him as *El Predestinado* [the Predestined One]. When Jorge Blanco (Dominican president 1982–86) was jailed after his presidency for corruption,[134] he wrote lengthy articles in the country's largest newspaper where he compared himself with the suffering Christ, and a recurrent candidate

---

131 This poem was written by the pseudonym '*Cantor del Sur*' and is included in an anthology dedicated to poems urging *El Jefe* to let himself be reelected (León (1938), p. 32). Since the Dominican constitution forbade reelection it was common to stage 'popular campaigns' in order to have Trujillo reelected. These campaigns were organized from the presidential palace and people were more-or-less forced to participate.
132 Balaguer (1989), pp. 391–5.
133 Balaguer (1976), p. 10. For an analysis of Balaguer's ideology see, Franco (1981), pp. 232–53.
134 The process against him can be studied in González Canahuate (1992).

for the presidency, Jacobo Majluta, was in an advertisement campaign hailed as 'the Messiah of our future'.[135]

The belief in divine messiahs: a religion of the oppressed?

Even if messianism has been called an exclusively Judeo-Christian concept, similar phenomena are known to almost every culture in the world and they occur within the context of all established world religions. The reasons for this are varied, although a common factor underlying the emergence of such beliefs may be that every religion has a characteristic view of the future as well as specific ideas about past and present. We have already seen how the longing for just and virtuous monarchs has triggered far-reaching rebellions, while the legendary happiness of days gone by has turned reigns of deceased kings into myths about coming golden ages.

A myth complex which has had a vast influence on later myths and messianic speculation is that of Iranian Zoroastrianism. Central to Iranian eschatology is the concept of the *saosyant,* a savior whose name means 'incarnated truth and justice'. As the last of a succession of three *saosyants,* the savior Astvart-Arta would be born miraculously by a maiden. He would appear by the end of time and bodily resurrect all humans, purge mankind from sin and defeat all existing forces of evil and finally install an eternal reign of bliss and happiness.[136] In spite of his miraculous birth the *saosyant* is believed to be a fighting and triumphant savior, not a god, but a human endowed with extraordinary qualities.[137]

The Iranian concept of the *saosyant* may have given rise to Hindu beliefs around a future *cakravartin,* a divinely ordained, just and virtuous monarch. The coming *cakravartin,* Kalkin, will be the last *avatar* [incarnation] of Vishnu and he will appear by the end of the present age. Endowed with supernatural strength he will destroy all foreign invaders and raze the wicked cities inhabited by men of evil acts and thoughts. When Kalkin has succeeded with his mission and the end of this terrible and exhausted *Kali* Age approaches, the minds of the people will become pure as flawless crystal, and they will be as if awakened at the conclusion of a long night.[138] The children of this purified people will finally be governed by the righteous Kalkin, living in the wonderful *Krta* Age, a Golden Age which will be the best of all epochs.

For many Buddhists Asoka (?273–32 BC), the ruler who elevated Buddhism to the official state religion of his Indian kingdom came to be regarded as a model of a Buddhist *cakravartin.* Such speculations merged

---

135 *Amigo del Hogar,* No. 472, May 1986, p. 20.
136 Widengren (1965), pp. 106–7.
137 Ibid., p. 107.
138 O'Flaherty (1976), p. 237. *Avatar* is Sanskrit: *avatarati* [he descends].

with the hope of the coming of a future Buddha, called Maitreya. Maitreya (Mi-lo fo in China, Mi-reuk in Korea and Mirou in Japan) is a *bodhisattva* who has not yet arrived on earth. His abode is in the Tushita heaven[139] and he is supposed 'to be a future Buddha who is to come to this world to preach the dharma when the teaching delivered by Sakyamuni Buddha decays. Maitreya literally means benevolent, and he will come to the world as an incarnation of great benevolence, just as Sakyamuni Buddha did.'[140]

Even if Maitreya is recognized by every Buddhist group as the future Buddha, the needs and interests of his various devotees shape what they see in him. In China various sects have nurtured the hope for a descent of Mi-lo fo to the earth where he will establish *Kalpa*, a new cosmic era of peace and prosperity when the doctrine of Buddha will reign uncontested. From the sixth century onwards, Chinese non-canonical texts depict Mi-lo fo, and similar figures, as militant saviors cleansing the world of evil through their cosmic warfare with demonical forces. These texts, which are independent from official doctrines and praise lay piety, were probably written by groups in which literate laymen, rather than priests, were present. In these texts, Mi-lo fo becomes a *bodhisattva* who is very much concerned with life in this world. He is

> a symbol of universal and collective hope, beyond individual aspirations, beyond the history of the present age [...] [having] two bases of operation, one in heaven, one on earth, and [...] he moves easily between them. He is the future 'lord of history' but he can also be present now, as a preacher, sect leader or peasant boy. As such he promises to have a scope and depth beyond those of a *Sákyamuni* who is gone or an Amitabha who stays in Paradise.[141]

Such popular notions have, throughout Chinese history, served as an inspiration for several violent uprisings.[142] In other Buddhist countries, like Burma, Maitreya beliefs served as inspiration for attacks on colonial rulers.

139 The Tushita heaven is a place where an 'anointed' *bodhisattva* must be born before descending to earth in his final incarnation (Papmanabh S. (1988), p. 71). A *bodhisattva* (from Sanskrit *bodhi* [enlightenment] + *sattva* [essence]) is in *Mahayana* Buddhism a divine being worthy of nirvana who remains on the human plane to help humans reach salvation.
140 Yamaguchi (1956), p. 181. *Dharma* is the doctrine of the Buddha, the universal norms or laws which govern human existence. Sákyamuni, the wise man from the Sakya clan, is according to Buddhist beliefs the last in a succession of past Buddhas (enlightened ones) Siddhartha Gotama (?563–483 BC) is the 'rediscoverer of the path to enlightenment' and thus the founder of Buddhism.
141 Overmyer (1988), p. 131. Italics in the original.
142 Dunstheimer (1982), pp. 147–54. For more recent rebellions inspired by beliefs in Mi-lo fo, see Naquin (1976).

There the rebellions were often led by prophets who have claimed to be the *Sektya-Min,* i.e. a powerful and benevolent ruler who will prepare mankind for the benevolent reign of Maitreya:

> The totality of Burma's people shall be made happy through an abundance of gold and silver. [And the] people of the entire world shall equally become Buddhist [in] religion [...] the people of the land will practice the Law, and the ruler will have the ideal royal virtues [...] people will be pious, freed from illness and shall have peace of mind and body.[143]

Even within monotheistic Islam, the concept of a divine savior has developed among certain groups. Thus *Mahdism* denotes the hope for a future arrival of *al-Mahdi* [the rightly guided one], who according to most Shi'ites is identical with Muhammad al-Muntazar, the last of the *Imams,* who disappeared in 878. 'He is the *axis mundi,* the invisible ruler of universe. Before the end of time he will appear again on earth to bring equity and justice and to fill it with peace after it has been torn by war and injustice.'[144]

Several religious leaders have pretended to be the returning *Mahdi.* Most famous was Muhammad Ahmed ibn el-Sayyid 'Abdallah (1844–85) who in 1881 proclaimed himself as *al-Mahdi,* gathered a huge army and in constant fights with Anglo-Egyptian forces conquered most of what is present-day Sudan, establishing a theocratic state founded on fundamentalist Islam. He died five months after the capture of Khartoum.[145]

Common to all these 'messianic' beliefs is that forces from another realm of existence are thought to be able actively to produce a thorough change in the wretched conditions on earth. Divine entities occupy themselves not only with spiritual problems, but also with mundane matters, and in order to do so they appear in our midst, transformed into human beings. We have offered just a fraction of examples of what appears to be a universal longing for future saviors and golden ages. We have chosen them simply in order to demonstrate that such expectations are not limited to any

143 Sarkisyanz (1965), pp. 64, 153–4, quoted in Adas (1987), p. 101.
144 Nasr (1979), p. 166. *Imam* means 'leader' in Arabic (from *amma* [he guided]). The Shi'ites (*shi'at 'Ali* [the party of Ali]) constitute the largest minority group within Islam and believe that Ali, Muhammad's cousin and son-in-law, and a direct line of his descendants, were all divinely inspired and constituted a main source of religious instruction and guidance, as opposed to the *ijima* [consensus], of the Sunni Muslims. The Shi'ites are also divided among themselves. Most important are the Imamites who believe the twelfth Imam, al Muntazar, will be al-Mahdi and the Ismaelis, who believe that the succession of Imams ended with Isma'il, older brother of Muza-al Kazim who by the Imamites is counted as the seventh Imam (cf. Sachedina (1981)).
145 Cf. Moorehead (1963), pp. 205–88, for an account of the Sudanese Mahdist wars and the siege and fall of Khartoum.

particular religious doctrines. They occur across the entire spectrum of religious beliefs, not least within the folds of established 'world' religions.

The liberal use of the term 'messianism' finds itself under constant fire. Several researchers are of the opinion that the term is only applicable to Jewish-Christian concepts. Accordingly, the scientific use of the concept when studing other religions is described as an act of 'ethnocentric nominalism'.[146] Still, as we have seen above, Jewish and Christian messianism is not unique, as has been claimed. In a wider sense, this messianism may be seen as a different manifestation of a specific phenomenon found in societies all over the world.[147]

It appears as if messianic beliefs often surface outside the hierarchies of established religion. They are primarily developed within lay circles and may thus be considered as reactions to specific social conditions and to institutionalized, elite-dominated religions. If conditions are favorable for the appearance of such beliefs they easily adapt themselves to any religious system. However, it appears as if messianic expectations are most likely to emerge under conditions characterized by poverty and relative deprivation,[148] something which has lead Vittorio Lanternari to label them 'religions of the oppressed'.[149] He tries to demonstrate that a phenomenon like messianism tends to develop among people 'who live under colonial or semi-colonial conditions, or have recently liberated themselves from colonial oppression', in short – among people who experience an 'oppres-

---

146 Burridge (1969), p. 99. Cf. Adas (1987), p. 191 and Ljungdahl (1969). 'The term [messianism] is unfortunately frequently used for movements in which there is no specific promise of a Messiah. Worse, messianism is often confused with prophetism. The role of the prophet and the charismatic leader calls for further investigation' (Wilson (1973), p. 485).

147 Religious terms and concepts – like taboo, *mana* or messiah – used in religious studies, tend to be inadequate, since an exact meaning can seldom be established, not even within its own context, i.e. the cultural and social environment in which its original users are found. While using any word or concept, one has to keep in mind that they are all approximations, subject to change over time, and that their use and meaning may differ from person to person. At best they are inexact tools. Still, in spite of all their inadequacies they may help us in our search for a deeper understanding of different phenomena.

148 Relative deprivation may be defined as a condition in which 'significant numbers of individuals and whole groups [...] came to feel that a gap existed between what they felt they deserved in terms of status and material rewards and what they possessed or had the capacity to obtain' (Adas (1987), p. 44). Adas writes exclusively about colonialized peoples.

149 This view has been challenged from various quarters. For example, J. F. C. Harrison, who in a study of millenarianism in England during the seventeenth and eigteenth centuries states that 'the theory of relative deprivation (like the theory of stress and strain) is in danger of accounting for everything and nothing' (Harrison (1979), p. 222). According to him factors like the role of personalities, local traditions and timing must be studied very closely before general judgements can be passed.

sive condition executed, in their own environment, by groups or social classes upon other groups or subordinate classes'.[150]

In the case of *Olivorismo*, it may also be justified to talk about some degree of relative deprivation. When Olivorio embarked on his mission, the people of the San Juan Valley were just starting to perceive the first signs of a thorough-going social and economic change which threatened the already precarious position of several of the individuals who were attracted by his movement.[151] They began to experience how other groups and social classes tried to control their traditional way of living, relegating them to a marginal position within their own environment.

The traditional rural elite and the newly arrived immigrants, acting as merchants and intermediaries in the small towns of San Juan de la Maguana and Las Matas de Farfán, opted for a thorough 'modernization' of the agriculture of the valley. The most influential of these reformers considered that 'the idleness of so much land, labor, and resources in the Dominican Republic' was unacceptable.[152] They bought up land, introduced various kinds of machinery and tried to implement a more effective and intensive use of the land. At times they asserted that their efforts were counteracted by a 'backward' peasantry, who did 'not understand their own good': 'People lived satisfactorily in those days. Cultivators who owned a small plot of land, which they called *conuco* felt themselves to be rich, when in reality they were poor since they lacked aspirations and initiative towards progress and civilization.'[153]

Several members of the San Juan elite were furthermore adherents to racist ideologies, something of a universal fashion at the time. They were inclined to blame the peasantry for everything that they themselves perceived as being bad in the country. Reading the press and certain books which were published in the Dominican Republic during the first half of the twentieth century, it is easy to gain the impression that peasants belonged to an entirely different race than city dwellers and large landowners. The 'stagnation' of Dominican agriculture was depicted as an

---

150 Lanternari (1965), p. 15. 'American, like British millenarianism, has never been a product only of the poor' (Shepperson (1962), p. 52). Harrison (1979), pp. 221–3, affirms that a commitment to social change is essential for the movements and personalities he has examined, but he finds it difficult to pass a clear judgement about their motives, or social belonging: 'None of the millenarian movements we have looked at had any substantial following among the very poor. There is little to suggest that the disinherited and outcasts of society found solace or hope in millenarian belief. Such evidence as we have points to support from artisans, small farmers, shopkeepers, tradesmen, domestic servants and women, together with an important minority of merchants, businessmen, clergy and members of the professions' (ibid., p. 221).

151 Cf. Baud (1986), pp. 38–9.

152 Baud (1995), p. 148.

153 The governor of La Vega, Fermín Rodríguez 1906, quoted in ibid., p. 147.

inevitable result of 'race mixture' and 'atavistic rural superstitions'. Decision makers were encouraged to stimulate the immigration of able agriculturists of Caucasian stock and restrict the entrance of people of 'Ethiopian' and 'Mongolian' descent,[154] possibly combining such an initiative with efforts to raise the 'moral' standard of the local peasantry, through educational campaigns and the legal suppression of a wide range of rural customs and pastimes. Nevertheless, many authors considered the Dominican peasants to be incorrigible, particularly those who lived in the vicinity of the Haitian border.

The arrival of a class of wealthy newcomers successively changed the traditional patron-client pattern of the San Juan Valley and strengthened the old antagonism between peasants and urban dwellers, a development which became even more accentuated under US military rule. Several marine officers looked upon Dominican peasants as if they were members of some 'primitive' tribe who had to be bribed and lured into the pen of the modern market economy:

> The Dominican will not work unless he wants something which can be had only in exchange for money, which he must work to obtain, therefore we must create in him an appetite for things that he must purchase with money. We must get those who deal in such things to take them right into the country and show them to the bushmen and their families, who will first desire, then work, then buy; what they acquired through work they will doubtless stay home and guard; the more they own, the more liable they are to remain at home and behave themselves. We must do all we can to make them own things, the more and the heavier they are the better.[155]

Olivorio provided the rural dwellers with an alternative to the economic and social conditions that were emerging at the time. From the point of view of the *Olivoristas*, Olivorio's alternative had a clear advantage since it constituted an exit option in the sense of Albert Hirschman,[156] i.e. when the peasants perceived that their situation was deteriorating, they were given the possibility to enter a new society where the rules had not been made to their disadvantage. Michael Adas in his investigations of Asia has expressed the same phenomenon as 'avoidance protests'. In accordance with Adas' framework, the sectarian withdrawal of the *Olivoristas* can be interpreted as a means for minimizing the possibility of a clash with the forces that were reshaping Dominican society.[157]

154 *Memoria* (1924), p. 9.
155 Brigade Commander James C. Breckenridge quoted in Baud (1995), p. 165.
156 Hirschman (1970). Cf. also Hirschman (1981).
157 Adas (1981), p. 217.

The peasants of the San Juan Valley wanted to be free from the threatening encroachments of 'outsiders' like the old San Juan elite and newcomers like Italian and Lebanese businessmen. Several hoped they could find their freedom together with Dios Olivorio, who through miracles and sermons brought down the age-old *Sanjuanero* spiritual sphere to earth, making it real and almost tangible for his followers. By living within Olivorio's community the believers partook of a magnificent, magical world, ruled by entirely different and, according to them, more righteous laws than those of the rest of society. According to his followers Olivorio did not really die when he was killed, or crucified, as they prefer to describe his martyrdom. He simply withdrew to the spiritual realms where Indians and ancestors had gone before him and like them he now dwells and acts within the living landscape that surrounds the religiously inclined *Sanjuanero* peasant. Olivorio is now united with *El Gran Poder de Dios*. Like a messiah, Olivorio is thus a divine entity which roams within an ever-present divine sphere. Several *Olivoristas* also believe that *El Maestro* will return some day, either in the flesh, or – as in Palma Sola – in the spirit.

In the clash between the *Olivoristas* and the unified forces of the American marines and the *Sanjuanero* elite we witness how a vast, complicated 'magical' universe, firmly rooted in the local environment is confronted with another, perhaps more presumptuous, view of life. Several of Olivorio's adversaries shared a 'modern' and 'progressive' urban ideology, a way of thinking which was universal in its outlook, but also narrow minded compared with the magical-religious thinking of the *Olivoristas*. Olivorio and his followers considered themselves to be living within a community which was a tiny, integrated part of a vast universe which in itself incorporated two different spheres: one tangible and mundane, and another invisible and spiritual. In the opinion of several *Olivoristas* the adversaries of Olivorio were nothing other than profit-obsessed technocrats, totally unaware of the presence of *El Gran Poder de Dios* and the magnitude of all the other spiritual forces which *Olivoristas* believe to be present in the valley. A conflict with such connotations is almost insoluble, since the opposing concepts are so utterly different and may be apprehended, or accepted, only through profound understanding and unprejudiced tolerance, a state of mind which comes close to total identification.[158]

Can *Olivorismo* be considered as messianism? We have seen that it presents several features that fit rather well with such a concept. However, if the term 'messianism' is to be limited to a description of religious phenomena within a strictly Judeo-Christian tradition its application would

---

158 Taussig (1987) is a complex study which describes the confrontation of 'Western', capitalistic culture with the magical world views of South American Indians, particularly in the Peruvian and Colombian Amazon.

be improper, since *Olivorismo* is a faith which cannot be said to adhere completely to any Christian doctrine. It is extremely syncretistic, mixing several different kinds of religious notions which through the centuries have filtered into the San Juan Valley.

The term 'prophet' also originated within the Judeo-Christian tradition but has been more readily accepted since it has been considered to be a broader and less culture-bound term. Like the term 'millenarian' it has been in recurrent use in comparative studies of 'salvationist' leaders in diverse cultures.[159]

However, the terminology continues to be extremely confusing and many researchers stick to the term 'messianism', particularly while describing certain popular religious movements in Brazil, which have much in common with Dominican *Olivorismo*:

> The prophets do not organize anything permanent; they maintain nothing more than a momentary contact with the faithful; [...] they never monopolize the whole physical existence and morals of the faithful. The messiah, on the other hand, actively engages himself in resolving the practical problems of everyday life, as well as any other problems which may occur; he is an organizer par excellence; he creates a new group whose supreme authority rests with him; be it religious, social, political, economic.[160]

If such a definition is applied to Olivorio he was definitely more of a messiah than a prophet.

Some gods of the 1920s: messiahs in different environments

Olivorismo has much in common with messianic beliefs. However, one difference is noticeable: Olivorio never claimed he was a returning savior. Neither did the Ventura brothers of Palma Sola. Even if he was considered as some kind of incarnation of *El Gran Poder de Dios*, Olivorio considered himself to be unique. He did not consider himself to be a messiah, his pretension was greater than that. Olivorio Mateo called himself Dios Olivorio and his followers agreed upon the fact that he was divine. Such a delusion was not uncommon in other parts of the world at the same time. Human beings were proclaimed as gods in several different places, particularly within communities whose members felt they had lost all meaning and direction in life before they encountered their saviors.

Several prophets and 'gods' appeared after World War I in the defeated Germany. Individuals proclaimed themselves to be superior beings, giving

---

159 Particularly Adas (1987) and Ljungdahl (1969).
160 Pereira de Queiroz (1969), p. 238.

hopes and inspiration to their followers. It was a time when inner strength was called for. Feelings of exhaustion and personal worthlessness were combated by individuals who claimed they acted under divine inspiration. These so-called *Inflationsheilige* [holy men of the inflation] delivered a message of absolute self-reliance which could eventually lead to a sense of limitless strength and power. Men like Louis Haeusser declared:

> I am the great midday. I am the truth and the act and the way, the life and the resurrection and the New Time. I am also the A and the O, the beginning and the end, the way up and the destruction, which shines like the lightning, from beginning to end. Likewise I am the future which I predict today. I am the repose and the life, and the peace. But I am also the sword and the murderer of your false beliefs and the killer of your Gods. I am the superman, the lightning of the clear midday. [etc., etc.][161]

Another German 'God' of the 1920s, Leonhard Stark, mentioned his sources of inspiration:

> I am Power.
>
> Unimagined spiritual forces emanate from me. Everything that is written about Rabindranath Tagore, Graf Kaiserling, Dr. Steiner, and others, I am all that.
> A man of existence and truth.
> I am: The Christ (after Christ).
> I alone understand the spiritual meaning of the Bible.
> I am: Zarathustra (after Nietzsche).
> I put down new values on new tables of stone.
> I am: The guide (after Laotse).
> I make known the course and the right path.[162]

161 Louis Haeusser quoted in Linse (1983), p. 163.
162 Leonhard Stark quoted in ibid., p. 221. Friedrich Nietzsche (1844–1900) was the ulti-mate inspiration for these admirers of *Übermenschen* and willpower. However, Stark also points to other sources of inspiration – the religions of the mysterious east. Among his spiritual equivalents he mentions Laotse, who was considered to be the founder of Taoism. The Indian poet and philosopher Rabindranath Tagore (1861–1941) received the Nobel prize for literature in 1913 and served as an introducer of Indian philosophy in the west. Count Hermann Keyserling (1880–1947), 'the most influential guru of Central Europe between 1918 and 1933' (Webb (1991), p. 182) popularized eastern philosophies by spreading knowledge of Buddhism in Germany. Stark's mentioning of Rudolf Steiner (1861–1925) leads to the world of anthroposophy and theosophy, philo-sophical schools which were fashionable at the time. Many theosophists speculated about the inherent divinity in humans and of the possibility that a divine force would come forth in a chosen individual. Such speculations led the leader of the Theosophical

The social and economic insecurity of Germany between the wars, combined with extreme political turmoil, constituted an excellent hotbed not only for a wide range of religious speculations but also for an intense longing for political saviors.[163] National Socialism has been described as a kind of secular apocalyptic movement. Like medieval visionaries, several Germans developed a disaster syndrome characterized by confusion and hysterical fear of annihilation. Hitler offered a way out of this state of anomie by revealing that the 'suffering' of all true Germans was caused by 'incarnate devils', like Jews or Marxists, and that the members of the National Socialist Party were the chosen ones who were going to unmask and destroy these evildoers in order to establish an earthly paradise in which the Nazis would be the rulers.[164]

During his bohemian years in Vienna and Munich, Adolf Hitler tasted the strange brew of several mystical 'philosophers' who made intense use of the muddy springs of occult and quasi-religious speculations. The National Socialist movement incorporated much of the overheated religious usage of the time. Hitler, even if he was something of an outsider, perceived himself as a member of and representative for Germany's faceless masses. Acting as a man of humble origins, he impersonated the magnitude of power inherent in an inarticulate multitude:

> From among the host of millions of men, who as individuals more or less clearly and definitely sense these truths or even grasp them, *one man* must step forward in order with apodictic force to form granite principles from the wavering world of the imaginings of the broad masses and to take up the struggle for the sole correctness of those principles, until from the shifting waves of a free world of ideas there rises up a brazen cliff of a united commitment in faith and will alike.[165]

Several devout Nazis came to consider their *Führer* as something like a god, or Messiah himself.[166]

Society, Annie Besant, to proclaim her adopted son, Jiddu Krishnamurti, as the incarnation of Maitreya and a 'World Teacher'. In the 1920s Krishnamurti, hailed as a world savior and by the press sometimes ridiculed as a 'messiah in tennis flannels', attracted millions of followers until he in 1929 rejected the spiritual claims of all sects and organizations: 'I am not concerned, either with creating new cages, or new decorations for those cages. My only concern is to set men absolutely, unconditionally free' (Krishnamurti, quoted in Luytens (1990), p. 80).

163 Cf. Mosse (1981). Politics and religion often went hand in hand. Several *Inflationsheilige* dabbled in politics. The most notorious 'god' of the time, Louis Haeusser, a former champagne dealer, formed a party of his own and participated in the *Reichstag* elections (Linse (1983), pp. 38–47 and 179–88).

164 Rhodes (1980).

165 Adolf Hitler quoted in Stern (1984), p. 60. Here Hitler appears to express feelings and ideas which reflect Victor Turner's *communitas* concept, which will be discussed below.

In the Soviet Union the 'cult' of Lenin was at its strongest in the 1920s, when 'Lenin corners' were arranged in workplaces and private houses and people gathered on 'Lenin evenings' to recite poems and sing songs in his honor. The deification of Lenin had began already during his lifetime, when he repeatedly was hailed as some kind of communist Messiah.[167]

When Lenin died in 1924 the mourning ceremonies acquired monumental proportions and a flood of eulogies was released in the Soviet press. Several were of a character that makes one think of *Olivorista* beliefs which state that *El Maestro* after his corporeal death was united with *El Gran Poder de Dios*, the life-giving force behind everything: 'Lenin – like nature and the world surrounding us – lives outside of our subjective ideas.'[168]

The cult of Lenin was far from being unique; it had been preceded by

---

166 'My belief is that our Leader, Adolf Hitler, was given by fate to the German nation as our saviour, bringing light into darkness' (an entry from *Why Hitler Came into Power: An Answer Based on the Original Life Stories of Six Hundred of his Followers*, quoted in Stern (1984), p. 194). SS baptismal ceremonies took place in a room decorated with an altar containing a photograph of Hitler and a copy of *Mein Kampf* (Johnson (1980), p. 486). The 'character-building process' which took place in an organization like *Hitler Jugend* was often accompanied by deification of Hitler, as in this invocation children of Cologne were forced to recite before lunch:

Führer, my Führer, bequeathed to me by the Lord,
Protect and preserve me as long as I live!
Thou hast rescued Germany from deepest distress,
I thank thee today for my daily bread.
Abide thou long with me, forsake me not,
Führer, my Führer, my faith and my light.
Heil, my Führer! (Quoted in Toland (1987), p. 308.)

167 'He [Lenin] is really the chosen one of millions. He is the leader by the grace of God. He is the authentic figure of a leader such as is born in 500 years in the life of mankind' (G.E. Zinoviev, quoted in Tumarkin (1983), p. 81). This speech was given on 6 September 1918, when Zinoviev was chairman of the Petrograd Soviet. It was published in 200,000 copies (ibid.). Zinoviev, whose real name was Radomylsky, was an outstanding orator. He was very influential in the Bolshevik party and helped Stalin in his rise to power, but was purged and executed in 1936.

168 From an eulogy by D. Manuil'skii, published in 1924 and quoted in Tumarkin (1983), p. 166. Most famous of all homages to the dead Lenin was a poem by the revolutionary poet above all others, Vladimir Mayakovsky, *Komsomolskaia*, which later was to be repeated on countless official occasions:

'Lenin' and 'Death' –
    these words are enemies.
'Lenin' and 'Life' –
    are comrades ...
Lenin –
    lived
Lenin –
    lives
Lenin –
    will live. (Quoted in ibid.)

similar cults rendered to Napoleon and George Washington and would be followed by the one rendered to the living Mao Zedong, who like Lenin (as well as Ho Chi Minh in Vietnam and Dimitrov in Bulgaria) after his death was embalmed like an apotheosized pharaoh.

In the United States several migrant groups and oppressed, rootless blacks nourished similar cravings for a direction in life. Like the Germans and Russians mentioned above, they searched for security and inner force in a crumbling world. In the aftermath of the terrible earthquake in San Francisco in 1906 a spiritual revival of huge proportions began in Los Angeles, taking hold of people who found themselves in a state of anomie. People who lived anonymous lives in big cities, where they did not attain any of the alluring richness and, even worse, often lost the feeling of unity and concord they had experienced in their places of origin. In a run-down prayer house, a lame and one-eyed black preacher named William J. Seymour called down the healing force of the Spirit over a mixed and enthusiastic crowd.

Speaking in tongues, Seymour's congregation often spilled into the streets and their shouting, singing and crying could be heard blocks away. People who had been hindered in their upward climb on the social ladder by their lack of verbal expressiveness, or other social inabilities, like color and origin, experienced how a supernatural power descended upon them, loosening their tongues, encouraging free and unchecked feelings and made them feel like new and powerful beings. Glossolalia was not a new phenomenon, but the 'Azusa Street Revival' made it accepted as a significant religious experience and pastor Seymour is now regarded as the father of American Pentecostalism.[169]

A black man from Maryland, George Baker Jr, was overpowered by the Spirit of the Lord and joined in the speaking in tongues in Los Angeles.[170] Later, he combined this feeling of intense, divine presence with ideas he formed after an intense reading of 'New Thought' literature.[171] Most crucial to the thought of George Baker were the teachings of the real-estate agent Charles Fillmore, who taught that God was an impersonal deity existing in all things, including people. By positive thinking, human beings could be brought close to divinity and be able to bring heaven,

---

169 Cf. Linderholm (1924), pp. 238–71.
170 Watts (1992), p. 25.
171 'New Thought' originated in the 1840s from the teachings of an American hypnotist, who advocated the healing of illnesses through positive thinking alone. It has since exercised a profound influence in American religiosity, giving rise to Christian Science and several other sects and churches. The bestselling books of Norman Vincent Peale and his Catholic equivalent, Fulton Sheen, which can be found in drugstores and supermarkets in North and South America, are, with their advocacy for 'positive thinking', typical examples of 'New Thought' theology (cf. George (1993)).

which in reality is a state of mind, down to earth.[172] Baker came to believe
that by exercising mind power, and a feeling of oneness with God, anyone
had the potential to assert control over his own destiny and become truly
divine. Baker became convinced that he was 'the only true and pure
expression of God's spirit'. His followers sang 'God is here on earth today.
Father Divine is his name',[173] and he preached that he was 'an existing
Spirit unembodied [sic], until condescendingly putting MYSELF in a
Bodily Form in the likeness of men I came, that I might speak to them in
their own language'.[174]

Father Divine created an alternative lifestyle and organized his followers
in communities where they lived in celibacy. Food and income were
equally shared. He advocated 'self-reliance' and 'self-help' and organized
an employment agency, demanding that all his followers had to work for
the cause. Soon his 'Peace Mission Movement' grew into an economic
empire controlling several business enterprises like laundries, hotels and
grocery shops, as well as vast land holdings. Central to the cult was Father
Divine's Holy Communion Banquets, recreating Christ's Last Supper, on
which Father Divine himself served his followers sumptuous dishes. In
1933 it was calculated that his movement had attracted over 2 million
followers.[175] Through his network of collectives based on mutual aid he
offered security for thousands of believers.

While earnestly believing he was God, Father Divine's followers, who
were both black and white, enthusiastically imbued him with miraculous
powers, like pouring endless cups of coffee from one small pot, damaging
enemies with his divine wrath, and being able to heal blindness, sickness
and alcoholism.[176] Father Divine's teaching was highly practical: self-help,
aspiration for economic independence, etc., and it was down to earth, in
the sense that he did not believe in any other-worldly paradise.[177]

We have dwelt on the case of Father Divine since he presents several
resemblances with Olivorio in the sense that he, like his German equals,
claimed to be divine due to his experience of a divine presence within

---

172 Watts (1992), pp. 21–3.
173 Ibid., p. 48.
174 Father Divine quoted in ibid., pp. 178–9.
175 Ibid., p. 112.
176 Ibid., p. 82. Something that contributed to Father Divine's fame was a strange coincidence, when a judge who sentenced him to one year in jail on public nuisance charges
died of a heart attack three days later (ibid., p. 97). Father Divine's healing mostly
consisted in advising his patients to believe in his and their own powers to heal. His presence, in dreams or in reality, was often believed to be enough in order to cure afflicted
devotees.
177 However, he often preached that Paradise could be created and achieved here on earth
and that neither he nor his followers would die if they followed his optimistic teachings
(ibid., pp. 92 and 32).

himself. Furthermore he was a practical man who accepted everyone into his movement, grouped his followers around himself and tried to provide them with material, as well as spiritual, wellbeing.[178] He was inspired not only by 'New Thought' ideology, but also by Pentecostalism, and may thus have had something in common with Juan Samuel, who probably introduced Olivorio to similar beliefs. Furthermore, Father Divine was a black man from humble origins and something of an outsider as well. As was the case with Olivorio, Father Divine's fame grew due to the misgivings of his foes. His firm belief in his own divinity and healing powers strengthened the grip he had over his followers, who, like most of Olivorio's followers, probably had found themselves in an initial state of anomie.

Self-proclaimed gods may thus occur in widely different cultural contexts. However, they apparently share a belief in some kind of 'impersonal' spiritual power, which is able to 'possess' human beings, often in the form of the Christian Holy Spirit. Father Divine and the German *Inflationsheilige* appeared at the same time, but in places extremely remote from the cultural setting of the San Juan Valley. However, if we study other Caribbean peasant societies we soon discover several movements which are even more similar to the *Olivorista* creed. Here we confine ourselves to the *Mita* movement, which was founded in 1940 in Puerto Rico. It has now spread to Venezuela, Mexico, Haiti and Colombia. In the Dominican Republic the *Mita* sect has two temples and at least sixty congregations.[179] It is endowed with a well-structured organization, with priests and deacons. In Puerto Rico it owns large businesses, extensive properties, several schools and a health clinic.

The sect, which was founded by Juanita García Peraza, teaches that Jesus was an illiterate prophet and that doctrine is not as important as the actual presence of the Holy Spirit. After an illness of eight years and several revelations, Juanita Peraza came forth claiming that she was an incarnation of the Holy Spirit, the third one after the 'Old Testament' and Jesus.[180] She called herself 'Mita', said to mean 'Word of Life' and she was believed by her followers to possess healing powers. Juanita delivered her messages constantly inspired by dreams and visions. When she died in 1970 the Holy Spirit was believed to have entered the body of the sect's present leader, Teofile Vargas Sein, known as Aaron. 'Mita has the appearance of being a better established church than any other in Puerto Rico.'[181]

---

178 Alexis de Tocqueville noted in 1831 that when listening to American preachers 'it is often difficult to ascertain from their discourse whether the principal object of religion is to procure eternal felicity in the other world or prosperity in this' (quoted in Johnson (1980), p. 497).
179 Hurbon (1986), p. 164.
180 A strange echo of the Joachimite prophesies mentioned above.
181 Hurbon (1986), p. 165.

With the *Mita* sect, whose origins present some similarities with those of *Olivorismo*,[182] we are witnessing the establishment of routines for a local thaumaturgical movement which thus enters a stable state of beliefs and fixed organization that *Olivorismo* has not yet attained.[183]

The taxonomy problem

What kind of movement is *Olivorismo*? Any student of a phenomenon like the movement of Olivorio and Palma Sola inevitably runs into a definition problem. Serge Gruzinski, who has written about Mexican Indians claiming to be divine, expresses this typological dilemma:

> Must the man-gods be compared with the messianic phenomena of the Andes, Africa, and Melanesia, and related in greater detail to the movements of medieval Europe? But what typology should be used? The typology of Wallace, Wilson, or Lanternari? Or should I suggest a new taxonomy, more sophisticated or better adapted to the phenomena that we have seemingly discerned? I myself have neither the taste nor the ability for such an undertaking. Moreover, we would be well advised to compare the comparable, and not to mix up or – as happens more often – confuse direct observation with second- or even third-hand sources.[184]

Under what heading can we file *Olivorismo*? Is it a nativistic movement, or some other kind of movement, like reformatory, peasant, sectarian, charismatic, revivalistic, revitalistic, millenarian, social, revolutionary, apocalyptic, manipulative, pre-political, thaumaturgical, introversionistic or prophetic? Is it a 'religion of the poor', a kind of spiritualism, a crisis, or salvation cult? The list of possible labels is endless. The borderlines between all these different kinds of religious movements are blurred to say the least. New and different taxonomies are constantly created. Studies of related, often contemporary, religious phenomena are thriving. New documentation centers are opened almost every year and institutions for their study have been founded at several universities. The reason for this is quite obvious, considering that on the African continent some 8,000 to 10,000

---

182 The *Mita* sect may be interpreted as a regional, 'conservative' reaction to the increasing amount of control the United States has exercised in Puerto Rico. Like *Olivorismo* it draws inspiration from age-old Caribbean Indian- and African-type cult practices. It 'obtains' its power and attraction from its communication with the ancestral spirits of the local environment and the Holy Spirit, as opposed to the doctrines of the established church and the modernist beliefs of the 'authorities' (ibid., p. 166).
183 See our discussion of 'revitalization' presented below.
184 Gruzinski (1989), pp. 182–3.

'new religious movements' are believed to have arisen during this century. In South Africa alone, 3,000 have been created, and over 500 in Ghana.[185] The same pattern is repeated in different cultures all over the world, and the phenomenon is far from being limited to the Third World. By 1980 over 900 Christian sects and 600 alternative religious bodies competed for members in the United States.[186]

Comparisons between and efforts to delimit and define all these sects, religions and religious movements may prove to be both revealing and rewarding for someone who studies a local religious phenomenon. However, it is easy to get lost among various definitions and generalities. Thus we have chosen to present some revealing examples from different historical periods and from various areas of the world, compare them with similar traits found within *Olivorismo* and see whether such comparisons can shed some light on that particular movement.

Nevertheless, it may prove to be unavoidable to relate *Olivorismo* with at least two definitions of 'salvationist' movements which figure prominently, in one form of another, in recent studies of similar phenomena: 'millenarianism' and 'revitalization'.

Millenarianism?

Norman Cohn's definition of a millenarian movement is almost compulsory in any study dealing with the kind of movements we discuss. According to Cohn a millenarian movement has to be:

a) *collective*, in the sense that it is to be enjoyed by the faithful as a group
b) *terrestrial*, in the sense that it is to be realized on this earth and not in some otherworldly heaven
c) *imminent*, in the sense that it will come both soon and suddenly
d) *total*, in the sense that it is utterly to transform life on earth so that the new disposition will be no mere improvement on the present but perfection itself
e) *accomplished by agencies* which are consciously regarded as *supernatural*.[187]

All of these criteria seem to be valid in connection with Palma Sola. We do not know enough about the teachings of Olivorio to pass a definite judgement on whether his movement was millenarian or not. In the case of Palma Sola the only deviation may be point d). León Romilio Ventura

---

185 H. Turner (1985), p. 449.
186 Melton (1985), p. 459.
187 Cohn (1962), p. 31.

has sometimes expressed that a total change was expected, but he could also state that what he and his brothers wanted to achieve was of a limited nature, like a decent road to Palma Sola, running water, a school, etc.[188] It is, however, probable that the course of events has forced León Romilio to reinterpret the radical message which was presented to the believers before the massacre. Even if it is hard to reconstruct today what kind of hope for the future the people in Palma Sola nurtured, it is quite clear that many of them awaited some kind of drastic change and wished it would bring about the establishment of a terrestrial paradise. Hence the name that was given to Palma Sola: *La Bella Aurora.* Still, most of our interviewees stated that they confided in the power of the place and avoided any speculations about what was going to happen in the immediate future.

The collective and the union among believers were explicitly stressed in Palma Sola, and so was supernatural guidance. Cohn's description of the origin of a millenarian movement is also easily applied to the original manifestation of *Olivorismo*:

> It seems that there is in many perhaps in all human psyches a latent yearning for total salvation from suffering [...] Where a particular frustration or anxiety or humiliation [...] is experienced at the same time and in the same area by a number of individuals, the result is a collective emotional agitation which is peculiar not only in its intensity but also in the boundlessness of its aims.[189]

When discussing another act of ultimate despair, suicide, Émile Durkheim mentions religion as a possible haven for frustrated individuals. His discussion may shed some light on the feeling of liberation several people experienced when they participated in the rituals of Palma Sola and what Olivorio's disciples may have felt in La Maguana. According to Durkheim, the real strength of religion is not that it preaches respect for the individual, but that it offers a sense of belonging and participation in a collective way of life.[190] When a member of a certain society finds himself under stress and valid solutions are hard to find, he may feel as if the society is shaken to its very foundations and that the entire base for his existence is crumbling. When an individual has nothing to relate himself to, he can experience the sensation that his entire 'social man' is dissolving.[191] A road to deliverance from such a feeling could be to seek out the values and feelings which are most common among his equals, particularly if the

188 Interview with León Romilio Ventura, Media Luna, 5 May 1986.
189 Cohn (1962), p. 42.
190 Durkheim (1993), p. 170.
191 Ibid., p. 213.

affected individual has been brought up in a traditionally stable community. If a group is able to safeguard and make use of such traditions it tends to grow stronger, not only since they influence the mind of the individual, but since they have a retroactive effect on the group as well. The more lively the interaction, the more contacts which are established between group members, the more integrated does the group become and the more valid do their own beliefs appear to the group members themselves.[192] The member of such a close-knit community obtains a very strong sense of personal security, as 'social man' becomes like a shell around the 'physical man'.[193]

Most millenarian movements do not begin as revolutionary movements directed against the surrounding society. The founders are seldom preachers of revolution. They expect changes to happen more or less by themselves, through divine revelation or some other kind of miracle. The leaders urge their followers to come together, prepare themselves and watch for signs of upcoming calamities.[194] A kind of ideal society develops, in which all group members are considered to be brothers and sisters and individual yearnings are sacrificed for the common good. The crucial question asked by millenarians usually is: 'If such a miracle of social cohabitation is possible, why could it not take place everywhere?'[195] This sincere conviction makes them prone to believe that they have found an ideal solution to all problems afflicting humanity and they thus tend to view their message and appeal as universal, claiming they are alone in knowing the entire truth. Such fanaticism frightens non-believers and may lead to mounting misunderstandings, and frequently to violent clashes, which consequently may bring about the end of the millenarian community.

However, even if they may appear to have been totally annihilated, millenarian movements easily surface again if the economic and social conditions for revolution are endemic. If that is the case the millenarians merely retire and wait for the next crisis which may cause the destruction of the old order and carry the seeds of renewal.[196]

In the San Juan Valley we have witnessed how millenarian hopes gave rise to an extensive religious movement during the twentieth century and how the notions that formed the base for upheavals on two occasions were constantly aglow, only to be triggered by revolutionary events like the US intervention in 1916 and Trujillo's death in 1961. *Olivorismo* is far from dead yet and there is a possiblity that it will once more gain in importance and thus complete a process of revitalization.

192 Ibid., pp. 201–2.
193 Ibid., p. 213.
194 Hobsbawm (1959), p. 58.
195 Cf. ibid., pp. 61–2.
196 Ibid., p. 63.

Revitalization

The anthropologist Anthony Wallace has suggested that 'what religion is all about' is a struggle between entropy [here used in the sense of 'disorganization'] and organization.[197] In accordance with this view he has proposed that the impetus for a movement like *Olivorismo* may be a common feeling of anomie. People feel that the cultural system they share has become chaotic and obsolete. In order to change the prevailing structures they 'innovate not merely discrete items, but a new cultural system, specifying new relationships as well as, in some cases, new traits'.[198] If such a reinterpretation and transformation of a society is sudden, in contrast to other processes of cultural change,[199] Wallace characterizes it as a *revitalization movement*, defined as a 'deliberate, organized, conscious effort by members of a society to construct a more satisfying culture'.[200]

Wallace's revitalization concept is very broad:

> Revitalization movements are evidently not unusual phenomena, but are recurrent features in human history. Probably few men have lived who have not been involved in an instance of the revitalization process [...] Both Christianity and Mohammedanism, and possibly Buddhism as well, originated in revitalization movements. [...] One can ask whether a large proportion of religious phenomena have not originated in personality transformation dreams or visions characteristic of the revitalization process. [...] In fact, it can be argued that all organized religions are relics of old revitalization movements, surviving in routinized form in stabilized cultures, and that religious phenomena per se originated (if it is permissible still in this day and age to talk about the 'origins' of major elements of culture) in the revitalization process – i.e., in visions of a new way of life by individuals under extreme stress.[201]

Wallace suggests that all revitalization processes follow a certain pattern. Initially the vast majority of a population experiences a kind of stable state where communal and individual stress factors are checked by the sociocultural environment. In such a system, modifications and substitutions of techniques for satisfying the needs of the population may occur without

---

197 Wallace (1966), p. 38.
198 Wallace (1979), p. 422. Wallace's theory of 'revitalization' crystallized from his studies of Handsome Lake, in reality a title of leadership among the Seneca Iroquois but nowadays commonly applied to a chieftain named Gan-yo-die-yo (1735–1815). Handsome Lake was a prophet and reformer of the traditional Iroquois religion (Wallace and Steen (1970)).
199 Like evolution, drift diffusion, historical change and acculturation (Wallace (1979), p. 422).
200 Ibid.
201 Ibid., pp. 423–4.

disturbing the general balance. If a person deviates from mainstream behavior he or she may either be allotted a proper niche within the system, or simply be considered as a psychopath.

Over the years individuals, or whole sectors of a society, may experience increasingly severe stress due to decreased efficiency of certain stress-reduction techniques, combined with drastic changes in the cultural system, such as climatic changes, economic distress, political subordination and alien pressure towards acculturation.

After a while a period of cultural distortion sets in. People feel that the elements within their cultural system are not harmoniously related and alternatives are increasingly hard to find. Rigid individuals tend to tolerate high levels of stress before they attempt to change their lives, while more flexible and sensitive personalities may try out various ways of escaping from a situation that is becoming more and more intolerable.

Finally, the traditional way of life breaks down completely, or a period of revitalization begins. Most religious revitalization movements are initiated by the hallucinatory visions of a single individual. Abrupt and dramatic instances occur as moments of insights, leading to a realization of new opportunities and changed relationships. Supernatural beings reveal themselves to prospective prophets answering to their need of higher guidance. The visionaries believe that the present state of affairs is doomed to destruction and that it will be purged through recurrent catastrophes. Their intense longing for more satisfying and stable conditions urges them to preach the establishment of a future Utopia. In order to reach such an ambitious goal the prophets induce people to change their minds and leave the wicked ways of a corrupt and crumbling society behind.

Since a revitalization movement is a kind of revolutionary enterprise, it will almost inevitably encounter resistance from powerful factions within the society or come under attack by the agents of a dominant alien society. A revitalistic movement may use different strategies as countermoves to such attacks, mainly political maneuvres or force. Violent clashes can lead to the annihilation of the movement, but adaptive attempts may also result in a routinization of the movement and a final establishment of a new stable situation.[202]

This pattern of revitalization can easily be adapted to *Olivorismo*. The traditional life of the San Juan Valley by the beginning of the twentieth century was showing the first signs of upcoming drastic changes. Newcomers brought with them different ways of thinking, together with new trading patterns and modernized agricultural methods. The increased control of the Haitian border disrupted traditional trade, and the measuring and enclosure of land threatened traditional cattle breeding and

202 Ibid., pp. 424–7.

landholding patterns. In the beginning few individuals discerned the signs of the time, but an itinerant worker and outsider like Olivorio perceived that something was going wrong. Hallucinatory experiences gave him supernatural backing, and enforced by his new mandate as a messenger of spiritual powers he condemned the old society and predicted the catastrophes which would befall his hecklers and other unbelievers. The socioeconomic stress and social distortions in the valley worsened through the increased influence of a newly developed urbanite elite and the meddling of the United States authorities and the military. Several individuals escaped from their feelings of disillusion and vulnerability by joining Olivorio, who successively created an alternative society under the direct guidance of the traditional spiritual forces of the valley. The community of Olivorio came under attack from powerful factions within San Juan society and the agents of a dominant foreign society, the United States. After the political maneuvering of the *Olivoristas* had failed, violence gradually became the only option open to both them and their adversaries.

For several *Sanjuaneros* Olivorio's movement appeared to have perished with the death of its leader. However, since the socioeconomic conditions and cultural stress factors which gave rise to *Olivorismo* survived, the whole process of revitalization was repeated and accelerated with the decline and fall of the Trujillo regime. The Ventura brothers shared visions and prophecies that were similar to those of Olivorio. They founded an alternative society in Palma Sola; they found themselves immersed in a political maelstrom and they finally witnessed how their creation was destroyed by alien agents and how their followers were shattered, massacred or jailed. What now remains to be seen is whether *Olivorismo* will survive that almost fatal blow and finally become routinized in order to complete the full circle of Wallace's revitalization process.

The spirit of the place: La Maguana and Palma Sola as hierophany

The dwellers in the Dominican frontier areas close to Haiti had by the beginning of the present century much in common with their neighbors on the other side of the border. Like them, most *rayanos* received their income from the land, and the landscape on both sides of the border was dotted with holy sites. The Dominican peasant's belief in the holiness of the land did not differ much from his Haitian counterpart. Both in Haiti and the Dominican Republic rural cult functionaries were inextricably linked to specific geographical locations. A Haitian *ougan* and a Dominican cult functionary both represented their village, their region and their nation, in that order. For both Haitian and Dominican peasants the land was an extension of their personal identity.[203]

203 Glazier (1983), pp. 321–2.

Most peasants in the time of Olivorio owned the land they worked and buried their dead on that piece of land. Inheriting the land also meant inheriting the relationships with the spirits that were present there. In the San Juan Valley, as in Haiti, the land, the family and the spirits were, in a way, one and the same.[204]

Not only the homestead but the entire surrounding landscape was imbued with holiness and one of the most serious violations that could be imagined was the violation of holy places, something that occurred several times during the American occupation. In Haiti the occupying US troops cut down holy trees, burned voodoo paraphernalia and destroyed shrines. In the San Juan Valley they burned down Olivorio's sanctuary in Maguana Arriba several times, as well as other *Olivorista* shrines. Such brutal behavior often became the igniting spark to armed resistance.

Olivorio received his divine assignment somewhere in the heart of the Cordillera Central. León Romilio Ventura states that in the caves under the mountain of La Nalga del Maco one might come in contact with God, and hundreds of peasants have testified that they experienced a strong 'spiritual presence' in Olivorio's sanctuary in La Maguana, St John's spring close by, and in Palma Sola. According to Mircea Eliade every manifestation of the sacred takes shape within a specific historical situation: 'Even the most personal and transcendent mystical experiences are affected by the age in which they occur.'[205] They are all unique and all occur in a given place at a particular movement, facts which do not deprive them of their universality. Thorough religious experiences tend to be very much alike in both content and expression.[206]

Many human beings search for a kind of order and sense of belonging in their lives. While they search for cosmos they attempt to overcome the constant threat of chaos. Humans strive for the establishment of a personal center – a homestead, a clan or a family – wanting to adjust themselves to certain laws and rules, partake in beliefs and rituals which can be shared with fellow human beings. Many people relate themselves to something which they believe to be ever present, omnipotent and yet to a certain degree unknown – due to its immensity and unbound character, a presence, a force, which is believed to comprise everything and exercise the ultimate control of the universe and everything living in it. In the Judeo-Christian tradition one of the qualities of such a force is 'holiness'. In the Bible holiness is not only one of God's qualities, it is also applicable to all that is connected with God and thus separated from everything which is worldly and sinful. The Hebrew word for holy is *kadosh*, meaning good,

---

204 Cf. Brown (1991), p. 36.
205 Eliade (1976), p. 2.
206 Cf. ibid., p. 3.

elevated, different, zealous or eager, in the sense of being exclusive and dynamic.[207]

The best-known scientific treatise on holiness is *The Idea of the Holy*, by Rudolf Otto.[208] In this book Otto describes holiness as a category peculiar to religion, a concept which may be studied and discussed, even if it cannot be defined in any satisfactory way. In order to describe the idea of holiness Otto coined the word 'numinous', derived from the Latin *Numus*, which was a Roman deity believed to preside over a certain thing or place. To experience something which is numinous creates a sensation of partaking in a *mysterium tremendum et fascinosum*, i.e. to experience the presence of something which is wholly different from everyday existence, something awful, majestic and energetic. Even if the mystery is uncanny it also attracts and is thus *fascinosum*, at the same time as it is *tremendum*.[209]

People were attracted to Palma Sola through such a *mysterium*. It was a place of hierophany,[210] where holiness revealed itself:

> Every kratophany and hierophany whatsoever transforms the place where it occurs: hitherto profane, it is thenceforward a sacred area. [...] To put it more precisely, nature undergoes a transformation from the very fact of the kratophany or hierophany, and emerges from it charged with myth.[211]

According to Eliade, a holy place turns into a source of power. In order to have a share in its force and communicate with the sacred presence it is enough for a man to enter the sphere of holiness.

It is assumed that a holy site is not chosen by any man; it is merely discovered by him. The holiness of the place reveals itself through the healing and mind-altering qualities believed to be present there. The detection of a sacred area is not necessarily effected by means of anything striking or particularly venerable in the nature of the spot, the sanctification is rather a result of revelations or similar 'other-worldly' experiences by people who thus recognize that the place is powerful.

---

207 Albrektson and Ringgren (1969), p. 28. The interpretations of the word *kadosh* differ quite extensively. Other possible meanings of the word may be 'shining' or 'pure'. The Greek *hagios* is related to 'venerating', while the Latin *sacer* may mean both 'holy' and 'cursed', i.e. something out of the ordinary.

208 Otto (1950), originally written in 1917.

209 Ibid. *Tremendus* is Latin for terrible or dreadful, from *tremere* [to quake]. It is noteworthy that Otto in his treatise on holiness was inspired by the Christian doctrine of the Holy Spirit, which had been the subject of his doctoral dissertation (Sharpe (1975), p. 164).

210 The term was coined by Eliade and originates from the Greek, *hieros* [holy] and *phanein* [to show].

211 Eliade (1976), p. 367. *Kratophany* is also derived from the Greek and signifies a manifestation of power.

A common way to mark and limit a holy sphere is to enclose it, preferably with stone circles. The establishment of a borderline is essential since it is considered to be dangerous to approach the holy unprepared, i.e. the visitor has to undergo proper 'gestures of approach'.

Every sacred place contains a center: a focal point for contact with the divine. This may be an altar, a cross, a tree or a stone and such an object is usually interpreted as an *Axis Mundi*, center of the earth, from which the divine power emanates. To reach this central part of a holy compound the devotees often have to undertake some kind of symbolic journey, stopping at several 'stations', thus cleansing themselves from sin and gradually prepare themselves for the 'tremendous and fascinating' meeting with the holiest of the holy – the center of the sacred place, the *Axis Mundi*.[212]

Eliade's description of holy places coincides neatly with Palma Sola, and since Palma Sola was a place constructed with reference to common *Olivorista* notions it is highly plausible that it had much in common with the pilgrimage centers Olivorio constructed in places like La Maguana and El Palmar. In Palma Sola it was commonly believed that it was the place rather than the teachings, healings and rituals of the Ventura brothers which bestowed blessings on the visitors. The community of Palma Sola was clearly delimited from its surroundings and no one was allowed to enter before all weapons had been deposited outside and an oath of allegiance had been sworn. Inside the compound the pilgrim walked from station to station, as an act of penitence and preparation, before he or she reached the center where the three crosses, surrounded by stone circles, marked the spiritual focal point of Palma Sola, its *Axis Mundi*. Several visitors have testified about the awe and veneration they experienced in the place and how the sheer force of Palma Sola was able to strike down evildoers.

In the case of Olivorio, it may have been the other way around, i.e. the presence of a particular individual gave force to a place. Nevertheless, La Maguana had been a place for pilgrimage long before the appearance of Olivorio and it is possible that the penetrative power of his message was due to the fact that he was born close to the holy spring of St John. Just as in Palma Sola, the absolute center of La Maguana is constituted by three crosses surrounded by stone circles, the *Axis Mundi* of the place.

Communitas

Many of the people who gathered in Palma Sola have given evidence of the reciprocal kindness and generosity which governed the behavior of most visitors. The *Olivoristas* called one another brother or sister, food was

---

212 Ibid., pp. 367–85. Eliade offers a wealth of examples of various sacred places from different cultures all over the world.

shared equally, the rituals were carried out in common, all preaching stressed union and charity, and a certain dress code was introduced.[213] A totally different set of rules was applied in Palma Sola (and in La Maguana before that) than the one which governed the surrounding world. Most visitors felt they had entered another realm of existence.

Victor Turner considers millenarian movements to be 'striking examples of communitas'.[214] He makes use of the Latin term *communitas* to distinguish a certain social position from the more encompassing term of 'community'. According to Turner, 'community' means a structured state of social life, while a state of *communitas* is transitory and denotes a 'communion of equal individuals' who submit themselves to the authority of certain masters of ritual.[215] In coining the concept of *communitas* Turner was inspired by Arnold van Gennep and his classical study of *rites de passage*, transition rites whose characteristics are determined by their 'purpose to ensure a change of condition or a passage from one magico-religious or secular group to another'.[216] van Gennep pointed out that change of social status is the *raison d'être* for *rites de passage*.[217] It was not his intention to explain the rituals he studied, but his chief aim was to determine their structure, to discern the ritual pattern.[218] van Gennep demonstrated that all *rites de passage* are marked by three stages: separation, marginal status and reincorporation.[219] Of these Turner is mainly concerned with the marginal phase, which van Gennep denominated *liminal* (from Latin *limen* [threshold]). During the liminal period of an initiation ritual the subjects find themselves in an ambiguous realm, which has few attributes in common with past or future conditions.

> Liminal entities are neither here nor there; they are betwixt and between the positions assigned and arrayed by law, custom, convention, and ceremonial. [...] It is as though they are being reduced or ground down to a uniform condition to be fashioned anew and endowed with additional powers to enable them to cope with their new station in life. Among themselves, neophytes tend to develop an

213 Interview with Bolívar Ventura Rodríguez, Palma Sola, 5 May 1986.
214 V. Turner (1985), p. 111.
215 Ibid., p. 96 and Augé (1982), pp. 62–3.
216 van Gennep (1960), p. 11.
217 van Gennep disagreed with James Frazer, who considered *rites de passage* as merely a form of fertility ritual. However, he shared Frazer's conclusion that these particular rituals are often connected with fertility and physical maturity, but stated that these motives are of secondary importance. All ritual acts are symbolic. Sometimes they may express significant social ideas by associating the physical with the symbolic, but the symbolic meaning is always related to wider social significances (Fontaine (1985), p. 26).
218 Ibid.
219 V. Turner (1985), pp. 94–5.

intense comradeship and egalitarianism. Secular distinctions of rank and status disappear or are homogenized.[220]

Turner lets this liminal condition embrace not only neophytes but also other 'threshold people', who fall in the 'interstices of social structures', like hippies, court jesters, members of monastic orders, good samaritans, etc.[221] Writing about St Francis, Turner points to poverty as a tool for achieving a condition of *communitas* and he also observes that most millenarian movements try to abolish property, or hold things in common. This abolishment of property is often considered to last for a limited time. Even St Francis' holy mendicants considered themselves as living in a liminal state, since they saw life as a passage to the unchanging heavenly state of bliss. Likewise, millenarians wait for the coming of a new age of plenty. When prophecy fails, the movement disintegrates or is institutionalized while its members once more merge into the surrounding structured order,[222] modifying their former behavior, particularly their views of sharing and common ownership.

Turner writes about the 'power of the weak' and displays the rich mythology that has developed around the poor, downtrodden or marginal sections of society; like poor peasants, gypsies, beggars or the *Harijans* of Gandhi. The despised and rejected are assigned the symbolic function of representing humankind, since they are commonly believed to lack status qualifications or particular characteristics. The 'power of the weak' is set against the juridical-political power of the strong; it represents the undivided land against the segmented and hierarchical political system of rulers and conquerors.[223]

Shared poverty and a feeling of equality, which often have been presented as characteristics of communities of downtrodden people, may easily turn into a strength when the poor unite in order to face an external adversary. Their cause is considered to be simple and just, since they only demand what has been refused them. Furthermore, they are able to act as a uniform group, apparently unaware of selfish motives. Similar

---

220 Ibid., p. 95.
221 Ibid., p. 125.
222 Ibid., p. 129.
223 Turner (1987), p. 234. Compare Marxist notions of the proletariat which often is described as a class which is not a class and accordingly not subject to historical laws. The proletarian is an outsider, a representative of the 'natural man', one who is able to pass an unadulterated judgement on a society corrupted by age-old ideas and traditions. In something which appears to be an apocalyptic vision the unlimited, all encompassing, almost mystical force of the proletariat will bring about a transformation of the present society. When the proletariat comes to power, the other classes dissolve and a classless society will come into being.

notions are expressed in the stirring finale of *The Communist Manifesto*: 'The proletarians have nothing to lose but their chains. They have a world to win. Working men of all countries, unite!'[224] Such a display of a formerly slumbering strength and dedication often causes a great scare among outsiders, who already may have entertained unexpressed fears of the demands of the poor.

The undivided and 'impersonal' strength of the weak and poor has always been feared by outsiders, who furthermore have been apt to grant these groups magic powers. Michael Taussig has studied the fascination which emanates from the 'primitive' world of marginal social groups:

> The mythical and magical sphere fixed by the image of the New World Indian is one studied with political irony. In a country like Colombia where all the people classified by government censuses as Indian would fit into a few city blocks, the enormity of the magic attributed to those Indians is striking. [...] Indians are also among the poorest, most oppressed, and marginalized classes, and have furthermore a reputation for malice if not downright evil as well as ignorance and brutishness. Everyone knows that the *indio es malicioso*. Why they should also be credited with magical power is therefore an intriguing question and, moreover, an important political one since the magic of the Indian is intrinsic not only to their oppression, but also to the web of popular religion and magical curing of misfortune throughout the society as a whole, not to mention to the anthropologists (such as myself) who study it.[225]

Christians have often considered Jews to be alien and demonical magicians[226] and Swedish settlers of Northern Scandinavia feared the Sámi (Lapps) for similar reasons,[227] just as many Dominicans nowadays consider all Haitians to be powerful experts in black magic.[228]

Inhabitants of the realms of the unknown are considered to be both the cause and remedy for mystical attacks. Since they belong to a world different from what is considered as a structured state of social life, the poor and downtrodden have often been given liminal connotations by outsiders. Just as the Indians of the Amazon in the minds of 'white' peoples were connected with the apparent chaos, horror and savagery of the jungle, the

224 Marx and Engels (1992), p. 39.
225 Taussig (1987), p. 171.
226 Trachtenberg (1939), pp. 1–10.
227 Rooth (1969), p. 183.
228 Patín Veloz (1975), pp. 142–3. Among Dominican practicers of voodoo it is considered as particularly favorably to have been baptized as 'a servant of the *misterio*' by a Haitian *ougan* (ibid.).

poor in nineteenth-century England were often described as belonging to another world; brutal and, above all, unknown. In *Sybil, or the Two Nations*, Benjamin Disraeli described poor and rich as

> Two nations; between whom there is no intercourse and no sympathy; who are as ignorant of each other's habits, thoughts, and feelings, as if they were dwellers in different zones, or inhabitants of different planets; who are harmed by a different breeding, are fed by a different food, are ordered by different manners, and are not governed by the same laws.[229]

A similar ignorance characterized much of the treatment the American marines gave the *Olivoristas*, as well as the dealings between the Dominican political establishment and the representatives of Palma Sola.

Victor Turner finds several characteristics of liminal behavior and convictions among millenarian religious movements. Among typical features he lists homogeneity, equality, anonymity, absence of property, reduction of all to the same status level, the wearing of uniform apparel, sexual continence or its antithesis (since the liminal state liquidates marriage and family), minimization of sex distinctions (both men and women are 'equal in the sight of God'), abolition of rank, humility, disregard for personal appearance, unselfishness, obedience to the prophet, sacred institutions, maximization of religious attitudes and behavior, simplicity of speech and manners, sacred folly, acceptance of pain and suffering[230] – all of which appear as adequate descriptions of both Olivorio's community and Palma Sola.

The reaction of the outsiders also fits well within the picture. For them Olivorio and Palma Sola constituted 'magical' threats. The *Olivoristas* were considered to be poor and ignorant, but still in possession of demonic and manipulative powers emanating from a profound knowledge of black magic and other 'voodoo-related' skills.

Pilgrimages

One attraction of *Olivorismo*, which may be connected with Turner's *communitas* concept, was its relationship with the pilgrimage culture which is a dominant feature of popular religion in both Haiti and the Dominican Republic. We have already mentioned the importance attached to the land, how certain places are believed to expose a supernatural force and thus become focal points for human contacts with the divine. Since such

---

229 Disraeli (1981), p. 96. *Sybil* was written in 1845.
230 V. Turner (1985), pp. 111–12.

holy sites are governed by other rules than the ones which control daily life, the people who visit them tend to form certain kinds of communities, characterized by a high degree of *communitas*. The feeling of *communitas* may be described as a blissful condition which is eagerly coveted and often constitutes one of the main reasons why people are prepared to endure the hardships of a pilgrimage. In order to describe a state of *communitas* evoked by pilgrimage Victor Turner cites the autobiography of Malcolm X, where a *hadj* [pilgrimage] to Mecca is described:

> Love, humility, and true brotherhood was almost a physical feeling wherever I turned [...] All ate as One, and slept as One. Everything about the pilgrimage atmosphere accented the Oneness of Man under One God [...] Never have I witnessed such sincere hospitality and the overwhelming spirit of true brotherhood as it is practised by people of all colors and races, here in this Ancient, Holy Land.[231]

A similar feeling of *communitas* and personal bliss may be achieved at any of the pilgrimage sites spread over the island of Hispaniola, both in Haiti and the Dominican Republic. People go to these places, not only in search of remedies for various diseases and physical afflictions, but in order to carry out penitence, as an act of obedience to vows and promises they have given to supernatural powers, or to receive coveted benefits. Several pilgrims also arrive at these holy sites to partake in the general sensation of an intense communication with the 'other-worldly'. Just as *Olivoristas* may talk about the existence of 'two worlds in one', a 'daily' commonplace sphere and an invisible, spiritual realm, it is also possible to talk about two geographies of the island of Hispaniola, the well-known physical one, and an inner, spiritual one.

A galaxy of holy sites dots Hispaniola and they are all connected with one another through an intricate net of pilgrimage routes which crisscross the landscape. Some sites are 'national shrines', frequently visited by both Haitians and Dominicans, like Saut d'Eau in Haiti and Higüey, Bayaguana and Santo Cerro in the Dominican Republic. Several *hermandades* venerate the saints and divinities of these places and dedicate themselves to a complete circle of rituals which culminates with the yearly pilgrimage to the shrines.[232]

A more 'regionalized' holy geography exists in various parts of the island. In the San Juan Valley the most important pilgrimages are directed to El Batey de San Juan de la Maguana during Pentecost, to San Juan Bautista in Maguana Abajo and to the Agüita de Liborio in Maguana Arriba on 24

231 Malcolm X, quoted in Turner (1987), p. 204.
232 Davis (1987), p. 89.

June, to *La Virgen de los Remedios* in El Límon on 8 September and to Cerro de San Francisco in Bánica on 4 October. However, on other dates, several minor shrines, as well as various holy springs, caves, trees and calvaries, become destinations for smaller pilgrimages.

Going on a *romería*, as the people of San Juan call it, is to leave the ordinary world and enter a spiritual sphere. The road to the shrine is an important part of the act and its devotees often carry stones upon their heads to alleviate themselves from their weight when they finally reach their destination. The way to the pilgrimage site is a road on which you successively liberate yourself from 'things of this world'. You brace yourself in order to meet *lo sagrado*. When a pilgrim entered Palma Sola a similar, shorter but even more intense and significant 'spiritual' journey was repeated within the holy compound, until the devotee finally stood in front of the holy crosses of the calvary, the *Axis Mundi* of Palma Sola. As mentioned above, Palma Sola was a microcosm, a model which contained a rich assortment of different features of Dominican popular religion and within itself it constituted a holy geography. Like pilgrims to other holy places of the world most visitors to Palma Sola partook of a strong shared feeling of *communitas*, favored by the evident remoteness of the place, situated as it was in the dry bushland in an isolated corner of the Republic, far away from the main administrative centers of state and church[233] – a 'liminal' place outside ordinary time and space.

What Palma Sola also had in common with other pilgrimage sites was that the leaders of the cult were considered to be mere caretakers of the place. It was not their personal demands which were obeyed. They were rather considered as mouthpieces of the power of the place. The decision to come to Palma Sola was a voluntary act and the presence of the pilgrims in the place, as well as their submission to the rules which governed the life and behavior there, were based on voluntariness.[234] This may be one of the reasons as to why several of our interviewees stressed that they do not remember any politicizing in Palma Sola, that the *Mellizos* did not try to influence them, that 'all of that was not important at all':

> People stood around the tribune of Plinio while he talked about getting rid of corruption in order to create Christian Unity. After his preaching he delivered messages and gave advice. There would be no blacks [*prietos*] or whites, but a union for all. Palma Sola was to be the beginning of all that and the Dominican Republic would follow, maybe even the whole world. Not even the Haitians were rejected. This was a thing for everyone. There was something there [*tenía una cosa allá*].

---

233 Cf. Turner (1987), p. 195.
234 Cf. Ibid., p. 198.

They were not into politics [*no hicieron política*], that was not the main thing. People listened to Plinio, but he was no chief [*ningún jefe*].[235]

It was Olivorio who was in charge [*encabezando*] of the mystery [Palma Sola]. He could not be seen, but he was present. He was the real leader.[236]

The political influence surely came from other quarters. What interest could the peasants have in obtaining their political information from the *Mellizos?* What they were seeking was their religion, not politics. Religion is always with the peasants. They know what politics are, they are practical people. They separate their politics from religion. They listened to the *Mellizos,* but they did not submit to them. In those days the church told people all over the country not to vote for Bosch; he won anyway. That is only one proof that Dominicans do not let religion govern their politics.[237]

Contrary to the message given in most newspaper articles of the time, the people in Palma Sola were not a brainwashed herd of ignorant peasants and voodooists. They partook of something which they saw as a holy miracle, experiencing a sense of *communitas* and submitting themselves not to the authority of the Ventura brothers, but to the 'spiritual' presence which they believed manifested itself in Palma Sola, 'the Beautiful Dawn'.

Conclusions

We have established that it is extremely difficult to label a religious movement like *Olivorismo,* and it is doubtful whether we are in a great need of any exact definition. However, on the basis of the theories, comparisons and similarities that we have presented above we may establish that Olivorio was a charismatic leader, who by his followers was endowed with thaumaturgic powers.

Such leadership develops in close symbiosis with the traditions of the immediate environment of the leader, who in his teachings and behavior incorporates, and, to some extent, reforms or changes, older beliefs. This activity may take the form of a revitalization process. No charismatic leader can act as such if he does not receive the faith of the people who

---

235 Interview with Diego Cépeda, Jínova, 4 June 1989.
236 Interview with Arsidé Gardés, El Batey, 11 April 1986.
237 Interview with Radhamés Gómez Pepín, Santo Domingo, 18 March 1986. This view differs from the one Gómez Pepín expressed in his articles from 1962, where he depicted the *Mellizos* as sinister manipulators of their herd.

gather around him, and it is unlikely that a thaumaturge would be able to perform any 'miracles' if he were not surrounded by people who were ready to believe in his powers.

The readiness to believe in prophets and miracle workers may be fostered by sudden changes in people's living conditions, changes that often are caused by the introduction of new ideas and techniques. Difficulties in adapting to new ways of life, which, to make things worse, can be accompanied by climatological, economic and technical transitions, may cause intense feelings of anomie and relative deprivation, feelings which constitute an excellent breeding ground for religious revival.

When individuals come under stress they are eager to seek security and new directions in life. Many persons choose to do that within the folds of a certain community. Communal rituals and beliefs tend to strengthen individual convictions. Beliefs which in times of stress develop in close-knit communities tend to be intensified to such a degree that outsiders often perceive them as 'fanaticism', i.e. a state of mind in which believers are convinced that they act under the infallible guidance of a 'spiritual' force.

While studying various movements akin to *Olivorismo* we have found that the 'spiritual' force believed to be active on such occasions often has a character similar to Christian concepts regarding the Holy Spirit. The latter is usually perceived as an 'impersonal' and omnipotent force which manifests itself in human beings, who then are apt to consider themselves as divine beings, or even gods.

'Spiritual presence' may also be manifest in certain 'holy' places believed to be connected with supernatural forces. The behavior of people who accede to such places is universally similar and 'holy' places often develop into something of a microcosm, a kind of 'spiritual' map of the real world. The 'other-worldliness' that imbues such places transforms them into 'something out of the ordinary' and people who dwell in them often view themselves as being in a state of *communitas*, i.e. they feel like being 'outside' the 'real' world, as if they dwelt in a place and a time which are neither 'here nor there'. Such a state of mind is considered to be temporal in the sense that individuals who find themselves in a state of *communitas* often are waiting for something miraculous to happen. They find themselves within a 'liminal' sphere. Due to feelings of communal veneration of the inconceivable, previously conceived differences between individuals tend to lessen. The devotees feel sanctified and such a conviction makes them prone to believe they are the sole possessors of an ultimate truth. Everything is shared and all believers are considered as members of a great family. The more chaotic and inhospitable the surrounding world appears to be, the more attractive is the possible communication with a supernatural force and the expectations for something wonderful to happen. The attitudes of sectarians tend to alarm outsiders, particularly since the behavior of the 'chosen ones' appears to have changed in a drastic and incomprehensible way.

This is, in very broad terms, a description of the kind of religious communities we have studied in the present chapter. However, it is important to keep in mind that every religious activity is a specific social event and thus intimately related to its immediate environment. In order to be fully understood religious phenomena must be studied within their context and all features have to be related to the locality in which they originate. In order to understand cult origins and peculiarities, the changes and traditions of the limited area where they developed have to be studied in a multifaceted and interdisciplinary way. Concepts like social banditry, charisma, millenarianism, etc., have to be interpreted in relation not only to ideological changes, but must also be viewed as the outcome of changes, of climate, agricultural techniques, communications, migration, etc.

We have compared the particular phenomenon of *Olivorismo* with related movements from other places on the globe, with the aid of various theories that have evolved around them. Our comparisons have made us inclined to believe that *Olivorismo* is above all a social movement, which contains features from social banditry, messianism and millenarianism. Its leaders acted as charismatic thaumaturges, endowed with a prophetic view of the world, in the sense that they were practical and down to earth as well as visionary individuals. The charismatic inclination of the *Olivorista* leaders made them prone to consider themselves as vessels of a supernatural power, which manifested itself through them and in certain holy places. Their conviction made them able to attract several followers who left their everyday existence to enter a world of shared *communitas*, characterized by its liminal propensities.

The 'strange' and radically different behavior of the *Olivoristas* was perceived as dangerous fanaticism by outsiders, who either felt threatened by the attitudes of the sectarians or condemned the movement as a kind of outdated conservatism, paying homage to old, backward traditions considered as an obstacle to the wheel of progress.

In short, we have tried to highlight some outstanding features of *Olivorismo* in relation to their social context, i.e. the everyday life and the structural changes within the San Juan Valley. We have found that it is a practical religion which incorporates old beliefs but also adapts itself to an ever-changing situation. It is a living religion in the sense that it offers a constant reinterpretation related to socioeconomic changes – a living and dynamic faith immersed in an intense communication with both the forces inherent in nature and the necessities of the people within the community where it thrives. If a label has to be pinned on *Olivorismo*, perhaps the best is that of a 'regional, popular religion'.

11 Conclusions

The story of *Olivorismo* is a complex one – a story with many facets, one which may, and should, be studied from several different angles. As we have told it, it is a story about 'what actually happened', i.e. it represents an attempt at piecing together the available information about the main events in the rise and subsequent fate of the movement. Simultaneously, it focuses on the myths connected with the *Olivorista* movement, notably with Olivorio himself, and what these myths reveal about the possible hidden transcript of *Olivorismo*. It addresses the question of what made *Olivorismo* successful and also attempts to explain why the Dominican authorities on two occasions attempted to put a violent end to it. In doing so, it explores the economic history of the San Juan Valley, taking a local perspective, but one reflecting national and international events as the principal agents of change at the regional level. This causal analysis also focuses on political events and how these events are related to the history of the *Olivorista* movement.

The *Olivorista* story serves as a mirror of other events, and in a number of ways. First of all, it is impossible to arrive at an understanding of what happened unless the analysis proceeds against a backdrop containing elements of the microcosm – the local environment, physically, spiritually, socially, economically and politically – and the macrocosm – the world at large in terms of the geographical coordinates of the local scene, spiritual currents, social and economic change and political change on the national and international level. The story cannot be taken out of either its local or its global context. It was the interaction between these two contexts that determined the sequence of events, and it is in this interaction that the explanation of the events must be sought.

A third way of looking at the story of Olivorio and Palma Sola is as a story of the forces behind economic continuity and change. It is impossible to understand what happened without going into the questions of what determines production and trade patterns, how property rights are shaped, and what consequences such rights have for the generation and distribution of income. The answers to these questions turn out to be fundamental in the determination of social relations, and, in the end, of political action as well. The story of continuity and change is simultaneously a story about relations with neighboring Haiti and about the development of an economically integrated border area as well as about the destruction of these relations.

The story of Olivorio and Palma Sola can also be read as a story about antagonistic relations, between modernizers and resisters or between topdogs and underdogs. A new and powerful economic force was imposed on the San Juan Valley. Those who stood to gain from it gave it further momentum, but there were losers as well, among those the *Olivoristas* who were ill equipped to handle the new economic currents and who were bound to lose the struggle. Their rebellion was a primitive one which never stood any chance of success.

Finally, *Olivorismo* may be inserted into a wider picture. As a religious protest movement it is not unique, and similar movements can be found under similar circumstances in other places and at other points in time. It forms part of a recurrent pattern, a class of phenomena which lend themselves to some generalization.

Biography

On the most immediate level our story is about the life and death of Olivorio Mateo and about the fortunes and misfortunes of the Ventura family. For all we know of him, Olivorio remains a vague and enigmatic figure. The material at the disposal of the biographer is scarce. Separating real events from imagined or mythic ones is difficult and dates are hard to establish.

For example, we do not know with exactitude when Olivorio made his first appearance in his role as a founder of a religious movement. Those who were around and who could tell are dead. We have had the luck to meet a number of people with first-hand experience of the original *Olivorista* movement, but no one who was present from the very beginning. It has also proved impossible to trace Olivorio's movements in detail. Once he had been condemned by the powers that be, Olivorio was on the run, across a large territory, possibly extending into Haiti. The facts we have are mainly related to his appearances in or close to urban centers. These allow us to catch a few glimpses of his career, but not very much more. Olivorio made few public statements; those that he made were nebulous and the oral sources that would have allowed a fuller picture are gone forever.

Another reason behind the vagueness of the picture of Olivorio is the strong bias of some of the sources that must be consulted. This is already apparent in the descriptions of his physical features, and even more so in the often total incomprehension of his activities. Olivorio was seen as a stupid and backward illiterate by the modernizing forces in the San Juan Valley and was often treated as such when their path crossed his. The first biographic account (by Horacio Blanco Fombona)[1] borders on fiction and is unreliable in most aspects. The second account (by Emigdio Garrido Puello)[2] is better, but not very substantial, and, consciously or unconsciously, it is biased by the fact that the author was one of the leading modernizers among the *Sanjuaneros*, and was in addition closely related to those who stood to gain most from the changes that swept the San Juan Valley by the time Olivorio made his appearance.

The third source of vagueness comes from the myth surrounding Olivorio, a myth that sprang up after his death. The posthumous battle has been won by the *Olivoristas*, not by their adversaries. Seen in a mythological light, Olivorio appears as a man who did everything right and never committed any wrongs, a man who was unjustly persecuted by his enemies and killed by them for imaginary crimes that he never committed. Attributes and faculties that never existed and deeds that never took place have been added to the picture of Olivorio over time, but in a fashion that makes the contours gradually more difficult to discern. Taken together, the lack of sources, the bias of some of the contemporary ones, and the gradual mythification of the subject leave an elusive protagonist, but one who is presumably no more elusive than most other founders of religious movements.

In the case of Palma Sola and the Ventura family the task is easier from the biographic point of view. The events are closer in time and enough people survive to make it possible to reconstruct them with a great deal of accuracy. The main moot points concern what took place during the massacre itself and in particular who killed General Rodríguez Reyes. Other than that, it is much easier to disperse the clouds than in the case of Olivorio. The story of the Palma Sola movement can be told in a fair amount of detail.

Even the prehistory of the actual rise of the movement and the foundation of the holy place of Palma Sola is known and one of the protagonists, León Romilio Ventura, as well as other Ventura family members, are still around to tell the story of the *Olivorista* revival in Palma Sola. The movement has also been portrayed in two books, by Juan Manuel García[3] and Lusitania Martínez,[4] both based on the most important written sources as well as interviews with the survivors of the massacre and other protagonists of the one-and-a-half years that elapsed between the murder of Trujillo and the military attack on Palma Sola.

The relative closeness in time of the Palma Sola episode does not mean

---

1 Blanco Fombona (1927).
2 Garrido Puello (1963).
3 García (1986).
4 Martínez (1991).

that all the sources are reliable. On the contrary, as we have demonstrated earlier, most of the contemporary reporting about the events was severely biased, or even prejudiced, against the movement. Fortunately, however, the quarters from which some of the strongest attacks were delivered, notably the Catholic church and some of the mass media, have subsequently admitted that a severe mistake was committed. Besides, since so many of those involved in the events are still alive it is far easier to check the accuracy of the various accounts than in the case of Olivorio and his original movement. Thus, we have a good grasp of how the Palma Sola story unfolded, all the way up to the last chaotic days.

The emergence of a folk religion

The real significance of the *Olivorista* story does, however, not lie in the biographical findings, but in the interpretation of them. We set out to explain two facts: why both Olivorio and the Palma Sola movement led by the Ventura brothers were successful when it came to attracting followers, and why in both instances their movements were violently repressed by the authorities.

The story of *Olivorismo* is above all the story of the emergence of a religion and its subsequent fate. Olivorio managed to launch his movement and attract a following during a period of relatively few years. The explanations behind this success are found in the fact that everything Olivorio said and did was very well anchored in the local environment, i.e. – contrary to what one may think – none of it appeared as 'strange' or 'revolutionary' to those who eventually adhered to his doctrine.

The above is true in at least two senses. In the first place, Olivorio continued a tradition of local religion that had emerged over several centuries, connecting strands from many quarters. The first of these may go all the way back to the original inhabitants, the Tainos. At least it is connected with the common practice of conducting worship in places believed to be associated with them, notably springs. The association with the Tainos received further impetus through voodoo, where the Indians form part of the pantheon. All this was incorporated into *Olivorismo* as well – through the molding of Dominican folk religion in general – to the point where Olivorio was identified with Caonabo, the *cacique* of the 'kingdom' of Maguana when Columbus arrived in the island.

The second important strand was that of European – Spanish – down-to-earth folk religion, with fertility rituals as one of its main features, brought by the *conquistadores* and changed by local practice over the course of the centuries. The most important change agents were the African slaves imported into the island of Hispaniola, who brought their own faith with them and gradually made their impact on Christianity, as practiced in the Spanish colony, as well. It was particularly West African beliefs in certain fertility-preserving deities and concepts related to omnipresent, life-giving forces that mixed with similar ideas prevalent among Mediterranean peasants. The religious brotherhood (*cofradía*) tradition that stemmed from medieval Spain was adopted by the slaves and *cofradías* later became a common feature of popular religious life in general, serving as vehicles for a syncretism of European and African rural cults. To this as well the *Olivoristas* attuned, incorporating members in similar ways and sharing important beliefs and worship practices expressed by the brotherhoods.

The third, and least important, strand that merged into *Olivorismo* was that of voodoo. It is wrong to see Olivorio's movement as part of the voodoo religion, but this does not mean that *Olivorismo* has been unaffected by it. Voodoo is part of the panorama of folk religion in rural areas in the Dominican Republic even though it never came close to playing the role it has in Haiti. Olivorio is known to have had contacts with *ougan* and León Romilio Ventura is no stranger to voodoo. Still, the influence is minor and indirect. As in Haiti, voodoo in the Dominican Republic has demonstrated an amazing ability to exist alongside Catholicism in a symbiosis which on the popular level in various ways has turned into syncretism. Features like worship of the Indians, possession during ceremonies, and the use of *palos* in Dominican rural folk religion can be directly traced to contact with voodoo.

A number of details in the *Olivorista* ritual were inherited from the current popular religious practice around the time Olivorio appeared on the scene. Most notable is the central place given to the cross and to the groupings of three crosses known as *calvarios*. Other practices are the use of house altars, or altars in religiously important places, *promesas*, *velaciones* [vigils], *rosarios*, the playing of *palos*, and the singing of *salves*. All this made it easy for common people to identify with Olivorio and his teachings.

Another, related, factor which made *Olivorismo* palatable to the population in the San Juan Valley was that it was intimately connected with the local physical environment. Thinking of *Olivorismo* away from its local context is an impossible exercise. Its relation to the holy places of the valley is very close, as exemplified by the cases of La Agüita and La Nalga del Maco. *El Gran Poder de Dios* is present in the landscape of the valley and its surroundings, and acts within the context of the local geography. The creation of *Olivorista* centers in places like La Maguana and Palma Sola simply served to institutionalize the unfolding of the power and strengthen it in the battle against evil.

The creation of a myth

Olivorismo is not only a story of real events. In the minds of the faithful, mythical elements are often at least as important as facts. Frequently they do not even bother to make the distinction. More important, however, is that the myth that began to emerge during Olivorio's own lifetime has important clues to offer with respect to how his followers view and interpret the world they live in. This, in turn, makes it possible to contrast the *Olivorista Weltanschauung* with that of the outsiders and hence provides an additional valuable piece of information that may be used in the interpretation of the events that actually took place.

That real and imagined events should merge is no coincidence. This is entirely in the Dominican rural tradition. Events are frequently explained, not in terms of 'western' logic, but for many rural dwellers, the distinction between this world and that populated by spirits is an artificial one. The latter world regularly makes itself felt and interacts with the former, and it is often in the spiritual sphere that explanations of events and phenomena are sought.

These explanations are revealed above all in the *salves* that constitute the most important part of the myth about Olivorio and which make him as much a figure of the 'other', spiritual, world as of this one. They also constitute the main source of knowledge about the *Olivorista* religious, political and social message. From these it is possible to piece together the hidden transcript of the movement, the one dealing with how one day the faithful will be victorious when Olivorio returns to settle the scores with those who have done him and his adherents wrong and who will then be judged.

The economics of continuity and change

The story of *Olivorismo* is also a story that needs to be told with the aid of economics. It is a story of continuity over several centuries, but also a story of quick and brutal rupture with the past in a society that found it extremely difficult to adjust. The continuity tale begins with the arrival of the Spaniards in the San Juan Valley and the foundation of San Juan de la Maguana in 1503, and it extends all the way up to the beginning of the twentieth century when the arrival of the modern, capitalist sugar companies broke up the traditional economic and social order and threw the poor, small peasants into a situation they could not handle.

The economic history of the San Juan Valley is local economic history. Yet this history cannot be separated from world events, notably decisions made by the Spanish crown in the context of its overall imperial strategy. This global-local dimension was present from the very beginning of European colonization. Columbus was looking for gold, and the precious metal was found in Hispaniola. Once gold mining declined in the island, however, it proved exceedingly difficult for the Spanish authorities to retain a European population there. At the same time, the Indian population was dying out. What resembled a population vacuum installed itself – a vacuum that could not be satisfactorily filled with imports of slaves from Africa.

With the gold gone, the island held little economic attraction for the Spanish crown and the few remaining inhabitants were gradually left in a backwater. During the sixteenth and seventeenth centuries the island grew increasingly isolated. Legal trade could take place only with Spain, but few

Spanish ships arrived. The colonists were left to their own devices. The trade that developed was basically illegal. Without it the Spaniards would not have survived.

In the San Juan Valley an economic pattern that was to display an astonishing continuity developed. This continuity was due to at least two factors. The first was the sparse population. The valley was located in a peripheral area in a peripheral colony and was therefore never densely settled. On the contrary, from time to time the population was evacuated, for political reasons. The resulting factor endowment was eminently land-intensive, and in a situation where transportation to the capital, Santo Domingo, was difficult, the trading partners had to be sought in the west – on the French, and later Haitian, side. The political and military weakness of Spain during the seventeenth century opened the way for the French colonization of the western part of Hispaniola, and this colonization proved to be a blessing for the San Juan Valley. Cattle and products derived from cattle raising were traded for imported industrial goods that found their way into the French side and which could not be obtained from Spain. Transport difficulties and the simple non-availability of Spanish merchandise ensured this. Again, events outside the local economy decided the course that the latter would take.

This trade came under stress several times over the centuries. Political relations between the Spanish and French sides, before as well as after independence, were uneasy, and frequently degenerated into war. Nevertheless, the production and trade pattern survived and the border between the two sides remained an artificial construct. Occasional prohibitions of commerce with the adversary failed to have much effect. Output levels varied considerably, and from time to time trade was interrupted – only to be resurrected again, once normal conditions were reestablished. The basic pattern was never threatened. Cattle raising and trade with the western part of the island dominated the local economy of the San Juan Valley for four centuries.

The second factor making for economic continuity was the property rights system. From the end of the sixteenth century until the beginning of the nineteenth a system was established which in principle conferred equal rights to land on all heirs to a given property. The ranches (*hatos*) that the cattle economy had given rise to were not divided in terms of use, only in terms of ownership. In practice the land was held in a system of common ownership, which would have been very costly to break up and which, by and large, limited the use of the land to cattle raising.

Around 1900 the San Juan Valley was an economy dominated by the free breeding of animals on commonly held land. During the next few decades, however, this economy was subjected to a stress that it could not survive: that of one of the most powerful forces ever in the economic history of humankind – modern capitalism, in the form of large-scale sugar plantations. The valley did not have to suffer the direct onslaught of this force.

The San Juan area did not become a sugar-producing region, but it had to cope with the secondary consequences: an increasing demand for food in the sugar-producing regions which had to be satisfied by nearby areas. The pressure became irresistible. The San Juan Valley gradually was converted into an agricultural region instead of a cattle-raising one. Again, the local economy was feeling the consequences of changes at the global level.

This meant that the entire system of landownership had to change. It was no longer possible to operate a system based on what in practice amounted to common ownership. The land had to be surveyed and transferred into private (individual) hands, and in the process, the entire traditional way of life was jeopardized. Strong attempts were made to limit or end free breeding of animals. Land titles in general were in a confused state in the Dominican Republic at the turn of the century, and the inevitable result of this was that the poor and weak who had been protected by the vagueness of the common property system easily lost the land they were using to those who were better off and more fit to embrace the changes brought by the new times.

To this back side of the capitalist coin had to be added other economic changes that also contributed to upsetting the traditional way of life. One was the turning of the trade pattern from west to east, with the gradual improvement of transport to Santo Domingo and the increased availability of imported goods from Dominican sources. Corresponding to this was the closing of the border with Haiti and the prohibition of imports of goods that had simply been channeled from the outside through Haitian territory. To the attack on free breeding and communal land tenure was added the attack on the traditional routes of commerce.

It is obvious that economic factors are of supreme importance when it comes to explaining the success of Olivorio in attracting a following. *Olivorismo* offered a message that could hardly fail under the circumstances. The message praised the virtues of the economic order that was about to be dissolved, interpreted the changes as signs that the world was falling apart, stressed the necessity of cooperation and mutual aid, and forecasted that those who opposed Olivorio and his teachings would in the end be condemned and punished while those who believed in him would be saved.

The same economic factors were present behind the Palma Sola movement. During the years that elapsed from the death of Olivorio in 1922 to the death of Trujillo in 1961 and the subsequent rise of the *Mellizos*, the standard of living deteriorated for the poor in the San Juan Valley. The transition from an economy dominated by freely roaming cattle and *terrenos comuneros* to one dominated by agriculture and individual property rights was completed, communications with Santo Domingo were vastly improved and the border with Haiti was 'Dominicanized' by Trujillo. In the process, the poor were increasingly marginalized. In 1961 their situation was more desperate than it had been during Olivorio's times.

Once more they turned to *Olivorismo* for comfort. Now, the message was more radical. There was little time to waste. The world would come to an end as the year 1962 closed and there was a strong sense of urgency to join the Palma Sola movement. People left their homes and went to the holy place where the outside ugliness could be left at the gate, where money was banned, where a communal spirit reigned, where they could be healed, and where the teachings of the *Mellizos* inspired confidence that in the end the good forces would win the battle against the evil outside world.

The border: trade and prejudice

The story of *Olivorismo* can be read also as a story of a region and its relations with a neighboring country. The San Juan Valley is located close to the Haitian border and the contacts with Haiti were always intense – more so than the contacts with Santo Domingo until the beginning of the twentieth century. This was a natural state of affairs, since the San Juan Valley extends directly into the Plateau Central of Haiti. This offered easy communication and transport, while going to Santo Domingo across territory which presented numerous difficulties for the traveler was a complicated affair.

From the very beginning of European settlement in the San Juan Valley, trade took the westward route, in the form of contraband to European nationals other than Spaniards. The Spanish neglect of the hinterland of Hispaniola left no alternative. During the centuries to come this pattern was reinforced. The authorities proved completely unable to put an end to it, and once the French began their penetration of the western third of the island they were aided by the need of the border region population for an outlet for the few goods they produced and for a reliable source of imports of goods of European origin.

As the French colony grew in size and prosperity the volume of trade across the non-existent border grew as well, despite official Spanish prohibitions, and as the official position grew more liberal during the course of the eighteenth century it received a further boost. The damage caused by the Haitian wars of liberation and the subsequent invasion and occupation of Spanish territory, however, was severe. Cattle ranching came close to being extinct, but once the Haitian occupation (1822–44) was over, exports were resumed on a small scale and at the end of the 1870s old ties had been reestablished. Dominican cattle and related goods were again flowing west at a brisk pace.

This pattern was reinforced during the last decades of the nineteenth century. Haitian currency was circulating freely in the border areas and Haitian Creole was widely spoken there. Dominican landowners extended their holdings across the border and the local Dominican administration looked favorably on the contacts which increased the prosperity of the region. By the time Olivorio made his appearance the areas on both sides of the border constituted an economically well-integrated and well-functioning zone.

The *Sanjuanero* view of the close contacts with Haiti was, however, seldom shared by the Spanish and Dominican authorities in the capital. They were desperately pulling in the opposite direction, in favor of closer ties between the border area and Santo Domingo. Economic necessities, however, proved stronger. It was in the interest of the border dwellers to pursue their contacts with the neighboring country. The weakness of most administrations on the Spanish side and their notorious inability to supply the goods demanded by the population in such remote corners of the country as the San Juan Valley made cross-border contacts necessary for survival. Effective change in these relations could not take place until forces outside adminstrative control began to erode the old patterns – a process which coincided with Olivorio's appearance and activities.

The administrative prejudice against everything perceived as Haitian goes back to the French penetration of the western part of the island of Hispaniola during the seventeenth century and the subsequent importation of African slaves as the plantation society of Saint-Domingue was built up. Against these influences, the worldly and spiritual authorities on the Spanish side held out the Spanish and Catholic cultural and ethnic heritage. With time, a propaganda myth was established according to which Dominicans were basically 'European' while the Haitians were 'African'. To the extent that a mixture of the races had taken place among the Spaniards, it was with the Indians during the early years of European settlement.

The church had its own reasons for projecting a negative picture of Haiti: voodoo. The Haitian folk religion was portrayed as 'superstition', and those among the Dominicans who were suspected of adhering to it came dangerously close to being seen as heretics and savages. Voodoo was seen not only as a threat to the true Catholic religion but as a menace to the entire superior Spanish-derived culture inherited by the Dominicans. Consequently, it was outlawed.

This negative attitude towards things Haitian was exploited by unscrupulous politicians at more or less regular intervals, as the 'need' arose. The most obvious case is that of Trujillo, who made systematic use of it in his efforts at obtaining a close control of the border areas – efforts that culminated in the 1937 massacre of Haitian sugar-cane cutters. In this, until his last few years in power, he made explicit use of the services of the church, which he controlled and whose protector and *Benefactor* he was.

The anti-Haitian attitude was to play an important role both in the campaign against Palma Sola and in the efforts to cover up the massacre that took place during the years that followed it. The *Olivorista* religion was portrayed as being full of 'superstitions' of the kind that constituted Haitian voodoo and which were completely alien to the Dominican way of thinking, in a campaign with heavy racial overtones. These alleged religious traits were merged with accusations of *Trujillista* sympathies and political backwardness in general.

The political dimension

The unfolding of the *Olivorista* drama took place in a highly politicized setting: on the one hand the turbulent period of civil wars and foreign occupation in the 1910s and early 1920s, on the other hand the immediate aftermath of the murder of the worst ruler that the Dominican Republic ever had: Rafael Trujillo. Both these periods were critical ones for the country. Common people were experiencing considerable uncertainty and anxiety with respect to what the future would bring. In both instances national political currents had a strong impact on the local level as well. Neither Olivorio nor the Ventura brothers could avoid being drawn into the events.

The early years of *Olivorismo* were years of chaos and anarchy. *Caudillismo* and clientilism still dominated politics, and *caudillos* came and went as presidents. The fundament of *caudillismo* is the ability to raise sufficient armed forces and similar support. As a man with a following and with strong bonds with the most powerful man in the San Juan Valley, it was only natural that Olivorio would be approached for support by the Ramírez family when the 1912 revolution was being planned.

Times were also changing on the political level, however. The *caudillo* system was being undermined by economic events, notably the immigration of enterprising people from Italy and the Middle East. When the civil war of 1912 came to an end the political situation in the San Juan Valley was in a state of flux. The authority of the Ramírezes was disintegrating and the future looked uncertain. Under these circumstances, Olivorio could pursue his activities peacefully and with a fair amount of success.

Soon, however, politics would again cast a shadow over the life of the *Olivoristas*. The landing of the United States marines brought animosities to the forefront. Olivorio was a suspect from the very beginning. As a reputedly 'odd' figure who did not adhere to 'normal' behavior patterns and who made people believe wholeheartedly in strange doctrines, he was a potential troublemaker and had to be treated as such. The occupation was not a friendly affair. On the contrary, it triggered the *gavillero* guerilla war in the eastern part of the country – a war that could easily spread to other parts, not least those that were in contact with Haiti, where at the same time the *caco* uprising was going on. Consequently, Olivorio was labeled a 'bandit', and bandits were to be tracked down and destroyed.

Olivorio was killed in 1922. Eight years later, Rafael Trujillo assumed the presidency. Between 1930 and 1961, politics was a one-man affair in the Dominican Republic, and the political events that did take place were confined to the cities. Trujillo cared little for the peasants, and by the same token he did not involve them much in his political calculations, isolated and unorganized as they already were by the time he came into power. Once *El Benefactor* was gone, however, this picture quickly changed. The peasants were numerous and constituted an important group of voters – so important that it could tip the balance in favor of this or that candidate in the upcoming elections. Consequently, the emerging parties did what they could to enlist peasants and peasant leaders in their ranks.

Palma Sola did not escape the rapid politicization of the countryside. The *Mellizos* commanded a respectable number of votes and this made them vulnerable to outside attacks and rivalries. The Venturas came under pressure from the *Unión Cívica Nacional*, a party that had next to nothing in common with the peasants, but realized that with some luck the new religious movement could be used to its advantage. Its main contender for *Palmasolista* votes was the local *Partido Nacionalista Revolucionario Democrático*, headed by a member of the once powerful Ramírez family: Miguel Angel Ramírez, Carmito's nephew, who even managed to set up an office inside Palma Sola itself. It was inevitable that the religious movement would be entangled in politics, that real or imagined events in Palma Sola would be seen through a political lens and interpreted with the view to what it could bring in political terms, and that the eventual abstention from voting by many of the faithful would create resentment among the losers in the elections.

The 1962 elections were not the only episode that brought Palma Sola into the sphere of politics. The massacre itself may have had a 'political' background. General Miguel Rodríguez Reyes was a public figure, close to Juan Bosch, and the most probable choice as supreme commander of the armed forces in the likely event of a PRD victory in the elections. Nobody knows with certainty why the general was the only casualty on the army side on 28 December, or who killed him. Presumably the truth of these matters will never be fully revealed and by the same token the suspicion that his death was politically determined will never be dispelled.

Topdogs, underdogs and social bandits

Closely related to the story of economic change and the story of politics is the story of those outside the movement and those inside and the intolerance of the former against the latter. Economic and political change, especially if it is as strong as it was in the San Juan Valley, tends to redefine the social positions of the groups involved in it. When Olivorio made himself known large numbers of rural dwellers were already in economic distress and more were to suffer during the years to come. Economic change redistributes income, usually in favor of the agents of change and sweeps those who fail to adjust aside.

The result was a primitive rebellion. The circumstances, specified by Eric Hobsbawm, that produce such a rebellion were present. Primitive rebels do not by themselves embrace disruptive changes. The world of capitalism comes to them from outside insidiously by the operation of economic forces they do not understand and over which they have no control [...] They do not grow with or into modern society: they are broken into it ... Their problem is how to adapt themselves to its life and struggles ...[5]

Olivorismo was conditioned by change. Without the increased economic and social polarization that sprang out of the radical break with centuries of relative continuity there would not have been any *Olivorista* movement. The modernizing topdog group was constituted by the economically successful – the traditional elite and the newly arrived enterprising immigrants – who saw the possibilities of the new times heralded by the advent of the large sugar companies and the secondary shock waves these sent into the economic systems of even such remote areas as the San Juan Valley. They became the advocates of even further changes and began to exploit the economic upheaval to their own advantage. Many of them represented long-established interests but they understood that old positions would have to be reconsidered and compared with the emerging alternatives.

The underdog group differed radically from the topdogs. This group consisted of 'common', uneducated (most often illiterate) people: poor peasants and farmhands and their families, i.e. notorious underdogs in Dominican rural society. These people had little to gain from the changes that took place in the San Juan Valley and much to lose. Even worse, they completely lacked any influence on the course of events. There was no way to make things go even remotely their way. The new and dynamic economic force that penetrated the valley obeyed its own logic, and in that logic there was little room for the losers who hence had to seek comfort wherever they could find it.

It is hardly surprising that such a sequence of events would be perceived as unjust by the losers, as is clearly expressed in the hidden transcript of the *Olivorista* movement. Their humiliation, however, did not end there. In addition, they had to suffer the complete incomprehension and scorn of the outsiders – a disdain that was so serious as to lead to violent persecution and brutal repression of the manifestations of despair. Their defeat was total. What the victors asked for was unconditional surrender. There would be no negotiation of the terms.

When people are likely to suffer total defeat they usually resist this defeat to the best of their abilities. The *Olivorista* story is therefore also a story of resistance – an almost textbook example of conditions that breed primitive rebellion. Using the framework originated by Albert Hirschman,[6] it is a

5 Hobsbawm (1959), p. 3.
6 Hirschman (1970).

story about exit in a world where voice was inefficient or not even available. Both Olivorio and his followers and the *Mellizos* attempted exit, but in both cases the attempt failed. For voice to be effective it often has to be backed by a credible threat of exit, but in the *Olivorista* case exit itself was seen as threatening the established order. When recourse was made to it, the established order reacted and attempted to put an end to the movement.

The exit strategy backfired because it branded the *Olivoristas* as people who would have nothing to do with the social and economic order that was in the course of being established and who were hence likely to seek to undermine it. Possibly the strategy constituted an attempt at creating a platform for future voice, from a stronger position. If so, however, the strategy backfired since it converted the faithful into 'legitimate' targets for those who saw them as simple obstacles to progress and turned them into innocent victims of the repressive apparatus of the state. Their tragedy was the tragedy of the common man caught in circumstances that he lacked the adequate means to cope with.

The United States marines regarded Olivorio as a bandit – a common criminal and a rebel. A bandit he was, but not in the American sense. His variety of banditism was a social one. One of Olivorio's main attractions lay in the perceived contents of his teachings. His message was based on continuity, both in terms of folk religion and in terms of what he had to say about social and economic conditions. He was not a revolutionary or a radical who wanted to break with the past. If anything, he was a reactionary, in the literal sense of the word, since his gospel was a gospel of times gone by.

According to Hobsbawm, social bandits have no ideas that differ from those of the peasant population from which they come.[7] They are not prophets or visionaries who present new ideas about how society should be organized. They are reformers rather than revolutionaries, and their views of how society should be organized are based on some real or imagined past. Social bandits are not attempting to overturn the social order even though this order may be perceived as unjust. Social banditism attempts to curb excesses and manifest abuses but does not attack the underlying structure of traditional society. 'Its ambitions are modest: a traditional world in which men are justly dealt with, not a new and perfect world. It becomes epidemic rather than endemic when a peasant society which knows of no better means of self-defence is in a condition of abnormal tension or disruption.'[8] Nevertheless, the 'traditionalist' view of the world often coexists with millenarian dreams about a society where injustice has been abolished and all men are equal.

---

7 Hobsbawm (1972), p. 24.
8 Hobsbawm (1959), p. 3.

Olivorio in many respects conforms to the Hobsbawm prototype. His religion was a logical continuation of several of the strands that had merged into the current folk religion practiced in the rural areas of the Dominican Republic. As such, it could not fail to attract a listening, receptive and grateful audience. His view of society was one of the past, before the devastating changes that were besetting the Dominican Republic at the time had begun to upset the social equilibrium and undermine the position of the poor. It also, however, contained some utopian, millenarian, elements. Egalitarianism and cooperation were contrasted to unabashed individualism and competition. There was room for all the faithful in Olivorio's universe, not just for those who proved to be stronger and more fit for economic survival than others.

Olivorio thus comes close to being a social bandit. He never attacked anyone, but only defended himself when he had to. Olivorio was a representative of the poor. He was part of their culture and he gave them both immediate solace through his thaumaturgical activities and hope with respect to the future through his teachings. In the end, justice would reign and past wrongdoings would be avenged. The poor were the 'chosen' ones. Those who were against him were identified with the traditional elite and the American intruders, i.e. his cause was a 'just' one, and those opposing him will in the end have to pay their dues to Olivorio.

These were millenarian or apocalyptic visions, however. In the short run the goals were far more modest: a return to times and ways that were better than the contemporary ones, in a fashion typical of primitive rebels, '*pre-political* people who have not yet found or begun to find, a specific language in which to express their aspirations about the world'.[9]

The right time and the right place but the wrong men

The *Olivorista* story is also a story of historical coincidence. Olivorio was a primitive rebel – one who did not stand any chance of turning the sequence of events in a direction that was more favorable for the poor. The epoch when this – in the best case – would have been possible was over. Olivorio was doomed to fail since he lacked the understanding of the nature of the changes that were making themselves felt in the San Juan Valley.

Still, he, and the *Mellizos* after him, attracted large numbers of followers. There were no alternatives to *Olivorismo* for the simple people on the losing side in the battle against modern capitalism. The obvious counterfactual is that of a modernizing union or land reform movement that would have mitigated the inevitable impact of the intruding force on the

9 Ibid., p. 2.

poor rural dwellers. However, neither in the 1910s nor at the beginning of the 1960s had any peasant movements developed that were capable of going along with the inevitable economic changes and making the best of them. That this was the case when Olivorio appeared is perhaps not surprising, for in those days Dominican politics was personal politics. However, even in 1961–62, for example, Juan Bosch and his PRD, otherwise intent on social change, had not yet begun to make much of an inroad among the rural poor, and no other movement existed that could lead rural discontent into efficient channels of protest. Trujillo had seen to that and not enough time had elapsed after his death to allow such movements to constitute themselves.

Seen in this perspective, Olivorio was simply a product of the circumstances. He happened to be around with his message, and he was a charismatic leader, at a time when large numbers of people were under extraordinary stress and hence were extremely receptive to whatever alternatives were offered to the actual developments. The Palma Sola movement was the logical continuation of what Olivorio had begun but which had been forced to go into hiding during the more than thirty-year hiatus imposed by the Trujillo era, since the structural factors breeding rural discontent had not changed in the meantime. If anything, they had been reinforced. Neither Olivorio nor the Ventura brothers could possibly have handled the forces they were up against, but as the historical circumstances turned out, there were no alternatives to them.

The global context

The story about Olivorio Mateo and the Palma Sola movement is by no means a unique story. On the contrary, extending the perspective in space and time we find many parallels. This is what makes the story important. It does not simply deal with a local phenomenon that has sprung from local circumstances conditioned by national and international events. In addition, it has something to tell us about a recurrent pattern, one which tends to repeat itself in time and space.

Olivorio was a charismatic leader. Such leaders have appeared in many places over the centuries, under circumstances that both differed from each other and had important common characteristics. Olivorio sealed himself and his faithful off from the surrounding world and became their sole authority, having provided them with tangible demonstrations of his supernatural faculties, notably his ability to heal and foretell the future, common tests of charismatic qualities anywhere. He was inspired by *El Gran Poder de Dios*, a power mentioned in the Bible and connected with the Holy Spirit, which has inspired heretic prophets similar to Olivorio on many occasions over many centuries.

Another facet that unites Olivorio's movement with other, similar groupings is the circumstances under which it was created. *Olivorismo* is a product of extraordinary strain, a situation that called for extraordinary measures. Diseases, wars, drastic socioeconomic change, and whims of nature all serve to wreak havoc in societies like the one into which Olivorio was born. When anomie reigns people demand miracles both as a demonstration of the extraordinary faculties of those who aspire to lead them and as a sign that change may be possible after all.

The firm rooting in the local tradition of the message delivered is another recurrent characteristic of messianic prophets like Olivorio. Seemingly 'new' messages may contain a great deal of conventional folk wisdom. Otherwise they may not be perceived as relevant by the audience. Firm roots in the tradition are not enough, however, to ensure a receptive audience. For that a feeling of crisis is also needed. Only then will the listeners perceive messages that promise miraculous future change for the better as relevent to their situation, provided that these messages are delivered by someone who appears to be chosen by a supernatural power.

Olivorio doubtlessly met the latter criterion, as witnessed by his subsequent deification and the persistent belief that he is not really dead but will one day return to earth as a messiah and, in a manner reminiscent not only of Jesus Christ, but of a large number of folk heroes as well, separate the faithful and worthy from the skeptic and unworthy and establish a just society. It is also clear that the Palma Sola movement was millenarian, i.e. part of a worldwide and large class of movements in the sense that it predicted the sudden arrival on earth of a different and better order to be enjoyed by the adherents to the movement.[10] It was also revitalistic in that it predicted the coming of a Utopia through the intermediation of a prophet after a period of breakdown in society caused by the old order. Finally, both La Maguana and Palma Sola are examples of places where holiness appears, i.e. places of hierophany – another universal religious phenomenon. In such places the individuals often experience a sense of *communitas*, a sanctified feeling of equality while waiting for the millenium to be established.

The above concludes our analysis of *Olivorismo*. The book does not end here, however. The last chapter, which is an epilogue, sketches some of the developments from 1962–63 until the beginning of the 1990s. The *Olivorista* movement did not die with Olivorio, as we have seen in the foregoing. Nor did it come to an end with the Palma Sola massacre. *Olivorismo* continues to be a living and active force in the Dominican southwest. The economic structure of the San Juan Valley did not undergo any major

---

10 Much has been written about millenarian movements, and new studies appear every year. The following, pathbreaking works, however, still constitute the essential reading: Cohn (1970), Lanternari (1965), Worsley (1970), Thrupp (1970), Wilson (1973) and Adas (1987).

change during the three decades after 1962–63. Many of the circumstances that spurred the Palma Sola episode are still there. However, the relations between the faithful and the Catholic church have improved visibly. Also, León Romilio Ventura has become a political figure within the current party system – at a time when the political tension has lessened considerably in comparison with the situation during the first few years following the death of Trujillo. These changes have all brought a measure of 'normalcy' to *Olivorismo*. The movement has become an accepted feature of the local rural scene.

12 Epilogue
1963–90

Strictly speaking, our story ends in 1962 with the Palma Sola massacre. Our account of *Olivorismo* would not be complete without an epilogue, however. Most politicians, journalists and others involved in the massacre wanted to believe that Palma Sola was an isolated event, a negligible parenthesis in Dominican history, something that had been acted out in the desolate backlands of a remote corner of the Dominican Republic. They viewed it as an embarrassing incident which would soon be forgotten, when *Olivorismo*, once and for all, had been scorched from the surface of the earth and *El Maestro*'s superstitious followers finally had been convinced of their fatal errors. However, too many crucial questions remained unanswered, and, even if most people who had been involved in the tragic drama preferred to do nothing for its victims, they could not avoid the fact that the 'isolated incident' had made an imprint upon their lives and that Palma Sola thus came to exercise at least some influence upon the national events following the tragedy.

More important: their wishful thinking proved to be wrong. *Olivorismo* did not die in Palma Sola. It still thrives in its old heartland and it even shows signs of gaining importance. The lot of the peasantry from where the proselytes come has hardly improved since the massacre. When Angel Moreta carried out fieldwork in the San Juan Valley at the beginning of the 1980s, he found the peasants in the area involved in a difficult struggle against impoverishment and marginalization. The concentration of land had increased and the peasant smallholders had been forced out of the more fertile parts of the valley. They were found mainly on the outskirts, on low-quality lands where it was difficult to eke out a living, in the 'exceedingly hostile habitat' constituted by the xerophytic vegetation east of the valley,[1] in the dry, mountainous areas in the south, 'zones of generalized social pauperization and stagnant proletarianization'[2] towards the western

---

1 Moreta (1986), p. 201.
2 Ibid., p. 204.

Figure 12.1 Peasant dwellings in the San Juan Valley, early 1980s.

part of the valley where floods and salinization were pushing people out, and, finally, in the humid mountains to the north, where slash-and-burn agriculture was practiced and erosion made it necessary to clear a new *conuco* every year.

These patterns were not unique for the San Juan Valley. Michiel Baud paints the general picture:

> The irreversible consequences of the Trujillo period became apparent in the 1970s and 1980s. Indeed, they were rendered even more poignant by the fact that many landowners took advantage of the chaotic post-Trujillo period to usurp large tracts of land. The net closed around the peasant producers. The price that had to be paid to obtain access to land went up, undermining the viability of the peasant sector. Sharecropping contracts and unfavorable market conditions restricted peasant producers in the allocation of their produce. Many producers lost their land to creditors. Demographic growth aggravated pressures on agricultural resources. For the first time in Dominican history, land became a scarce commodity. Many landless cultivators now were unable to secure access to a piece of land which could maintain their families. Subsistence agriculture no longer functioned as a self-evident safety net for the peasant family. The enclosure of the peasant cultivators destroyed their economic independence.[3]

3 Baud (1995), p. 214.

The situation finally got so bad that, in 1972, the Balaguer government felt that a redistribution of land to the peasants was necessary. The project met with stern landowner resistance, however, and only some state lands were eventually redistributed. The results were meager:

> For the majority of the peasant producers ... poverty continued to increase dramatically in the 1980s. Some cultivators tried to get access to land via local networks or (illegal) squatting. Many people despaired, and the exodus of the younger generations out of the countryside intensified during the last two decades.[4]

It should come as no surprise then that the *Olivorista* religion is still alive. The conditions that created it are still present. The interest some politicians have in using it for their own ends has not disappeared either. *Olivorismo* continues to be a living religious and political force in the Dominican Republic.

In this final chapter we trace the fates of some of the most important religious and political actors involved in the Palma Sola affair up to the beginning of the 1990s. We then recount how the complicated and chaotic political situation that prevailed in the Dominican Republic at the time of the Palma Sola massacre developed over the following decades and how the protagonists in the massacre continued to play important parts. Thereafter, we follow the survivors of the massacre, notably León Romilio Ventura. Finally, we once more link national politics with the *Olivorista* movement, through the continued political career of Joaquín Balaguer.

Bosch, Imbert, Caamaño and the 1965 civil war

The murder of Rafael Trujillo continued to send its shock waves through Dominican politics during most of the 1960s and all the principal actors in the tragedy of Palma Sola were affected in one way or another. The country found itself in a state of both chaos and great expectation, and politicians and common people alike struggled to find their way out of the shambles the fallen dictator had left behind and to fill the power vacuum after the imposing tyrant.

Juan Bosch, a mostly self-educated intellectual of humble origins who had lived most of his life outside of the Dominican Republic, came to power carried by a wave of popular support. Still, he himself judged the prospects of his staying in power to be far from reassuring and just before he was elected he predicted that his regime would be a short-lived one.[5]

---

4 Ibid., p. 216.
5 Goff and Locker (1969), p. 264.

Bosch started very ambitiously by launching a new constitution, which was judged to be very radical. He thereby succeeded in irritating various groups which were extremely disappointed with his landslide victory. He annoyed the big landowners by prohibiting large landholdings; the Americans were irritated by restrictions on the right of foreigners to acquire Dominican land; and the Catholic church was appalled by such measures as legitimizing divorce and secularizing education.[6]

Actually, Bosch's constitution was not particularly radical, but it has to be kept in mind that it had been drafted after years of dictatorship and that it was launched in a time of extreme fear of communism, after the victory of the Cuban revolutionaries. Bosch was attacked from all directions, particularly by the church and the powerful, Ornes-owned *El Caribe*, which opened its pages to fierce campaigns against Bosch's legitimate government.[7] Unfortunately the new president did not make things easier himself. He proved to be a less than average administrator, surrounded himself with a mediocre cabinet, and furthermore allowed himself to be influenced by personal friends with strange business contacts, signing contracts for foreign loans on bad terms. He was an independent-minded president and often let himself be governed by his own theoretical, sometimes very impractical, convictions.[8]

The United States made a show of supporting Bosch, but it was clear that Ambassador Martin was not attracted by him. After all, Bosch was far from being as manageable as Bonnelly and the State Council had been. He did not want to have any speeches written for him by an American ambassador and Martin wrote with a shudder of horror that Bosch had told him that 'As a child [...] he had become anti-American and now he was determined to pursue a course independent of the United States'.[9] In his various writings the United States ambassador has offered a great variety of negative descriptions of the former Dominican president:

> I never developed the close, comfortable relationship with President Bosch that I had had with President Bonnelly. [...] His [Bosch's] was a dark and conspirational mind. To him everything had to be a plot. He was brilliant and intuitive, but unstable and reckless. He was moody and unpredictable. He was arrogant and vain and streaked with martyrdom.[10]

6 Ibid., p. 266.
7 Bosch (1964), pp. 132–3.
8 Szulc (1965), p. 14–15.
9 Martin (1986), p. 233.
10 Ibid.

However, Bosch was right in imagining himself surrounded by conspirators. They were everywhere: within the Catholic church, in the business community and among the journalists, within the ranks of the military and the police. The latter force was a constant preoccupation with Bosch. The growth of the police had been spectacular after the fall of Trujillo, when it counted 3,000 men. When Bosch came to power it numbered 9,000 and was equipped with heavy weapons, totally unnecessary for carrying out its normal functions.[11] Being under the protection of Antonio Imbert Barrera, the chief of police, Belisario Peguero, had been granted extraordinary power over his men. Bosch feared both Imbert and Peguero and one of the Dominican president's closest collaborators, Sacha Volman, who was in the service of the CIA,[12] told Ambassador Martin that Bosch was certain that both Imbert and Peguero were plotting with the military and members of the old UCN party to overthrow him and that he planned to imprison Imbert, Amiama, and Peguero.[13] When a coup d'état took place on 25 September 1963, Imbert Barrera and tank commander Elías Wessin y Wessin were in charge of it,[14] and Imbert personally escorted Bosch to his exile in Puerto Rico.[15]

The United States assured everyone about the loyalty it felt for Bosch, but many Dominicans suspected that the Americans had been in collusion with the perpetrators of the coup – an impression that was not contradicted by their unwillingness to support a reinstatement of Bosch in power. Ambassador Martin later wrote:

> When we saw President Kennedy, he looked at me and said 'I take it we don't want Bosch back?'
> 'No, Mr. President.'
> 'Why not?'
> 'Because he isn't a president.'[16]

One of the many reasons for the participation of Imbert and Peguero in the coup against Bosch was that some members of his cabinet had made efforts to limit the vast power of the police chief, arguing that the special laws concerning the independence of the police force were 'monstrous ... unconstitutional and dictatorial'.[17] Thanks to the coup Belisario Peguero

---

11 Cassá (1986), p. 110.
12 Goff and Locker (1969), pp. 267–8.
13 Martin (1966), p. 360.
14 Atkins (1981), p. 78.
15 Hermann (1983), pp. 102–3. Bosch believed that the company of Imbert would be his best protection against any attack on his and his family's security.
16 Martin (1986), p. 241.
17 Alcántara (1963).

was able to stay in charge of the police force with the same unlimited powers as before, but many members of the armed forces wanted to get rid of him and Imbert, both of whom they repeatedly accused of building up a private army.

The leaders who succeeded Bosch were faced with an anarchic situation and Belisario Peguero became a scapegoat both for the government and the people, as it was his police force that had to carry out the dirty job of the governing politicians, such as trying to repress recurrent and violent strikes. Peguero was in constant fear of being dismissed from his elevated position and therefore tried to use the funds he controlled to enrich himself as fast as possible. One illegal source of income for the police chief came from the so-called military canteens. In order to supplement the meager wages of his policemen Peguero had obtained permission to import tax-free goods and sell them at reduced prices to the members of his corps. These goods soon found their way onto the open market and Peguero personally pocketed a great deal of the gains from that trade.[18]

Francisco Caamaño, the man who had been in charge of the White Helmets in Palma Sola, had for some time been the protégé of both Peguero and Imbert, but after the coup against Bosch he started to feel increasingly troubled by his position. As the son of one of the most serious *Trujillista* generals he had been imbued with a code of honor which differed strongly from the one of the unscrupulous Peguero. His sense of loyalty came under increasing stress when he witnessed his boss' shameless handling of the military canteens. Caamaño, who had been promoted to the rank of colonel and put in charge of the police radio patrols, finally reacted violently when his former patron, Peguero, suddenly ordered his arrest for instigation. He entrenched himself with his loyal troops in the headquarters of the radio patrols. This amounted to open mutiny and the government reacted immediately, fearing that an internal quarrel within the armed forces would spread and worsen an already alarming situation.[19]

The army was already divided. Among the various factions was the San Cristóbal group, which opted for the return of Trujillo's last puppet president, Joaquín Balaguer. There were also the constitutionalists, mainly younger officers who had opposed the coup against Bosch, and, of course, the people of Imbert, among them Belisario Peguero. After the Caamaño mutiny, Donald Reid Cabral, the principal civilian leader of the government which succeeded Bosch, was ready to undertake a reorganization of the military. He appointed himself secretary of state for the armed forces, put the police directly under his personal jurisdiction and forced Imbert to let Peguero go, sending the latter off to a rather insignificant post as

18 Hermann (1983), p. 118.
19 Ibid., pp. 131–2.

Figure 12.2 Donald Reid Cabral.

vice-minister of the interior. Reid Cabral sided with the right-wing strong-man, General Elías Wessin y Wessin, who had advised Reid Cabral to relieve General Viñas Román of his post as secretary of state for the armed forces and give Francisco Caamaño a haven at CEPA, the center for educa-tion of the armed forces, which was headed by Wessin y Wessin himself.

It seems a bit strange that Reid Cabral, a businessman and a civilian, was able to amass so much power that he dared to make drastic changes within the military command, but behind Reid Cabral was the United States embassy and it has even been suggested that Caamaño's move was inspired by the Americans as a way of creating a crisis which would enable Reid Cabral to take action against the various military factions.[20] Antonio Imbert Barrera, always sensitive to signals from the United States, was ready to sacrifice his former aide, Belisario Peguero, without much ado, and Caamaño later stated that 'Imbert is not my enemy. He inspired me to rise against Belisario Peguero.'[21]

On 24 April 1965, Reid Cabral was deposed by a coup led by the consti-tutionalists, i.e. the radical army faction which had sided with Bosch. The constitutionalists were joined by thousands of civilians who, urged on by Bosch's *Partido Revolucionario Dominicano*, took to the streets in support of the perpetrators of the coup, demanding the quick return of Bosch. After a while General Wessin y Wessin, with strong American backing,[22] was able

---

20　Cassá (1986), 128–9.
21　Martin (1966), p. 688.
22　The same day the rebellion took place the Johnson administration had secretly decided that it would send in the marines if the rebels gained the upper hand (Goff and Locker (1969), p. 276).

Figure 12.3 Elías Wessin y Wessin.

to form a junta and take up arms against the constitutionalists who had taken over most of Santo Domingo and chosen José Rafael Molina Ureña as interim president while awaiting Bosch.[23] On 28 April it became clear that Wessin y Wessin's forces had been routed and US marines landed in Santo Domingo. By 30 April, some 23,000 United States troops had taken positions in the Dominican capital and throughout the country.[24] President Lyndon Johnson defended the move by stating that what had began as a democratic revolution now had got out of hand and was run by 'a band of communist conspirators'.[25]

The minister of the interior and highest commander of the constitutionalist troops was Francisco Caamaño. He soon turned out to be an able military commandant and a charismatic leader. When the fighting intensified and Bosch was unable to return, the exiled former president recommended the Dominican congress to vote for Caamaño as new interim president and on 3 May the latter was elected and sworn in as Dominican president.[26] The former United States ambassador, John Bartlow Martin,

23 It was Bosch himself who had advised the coup makers to install Molina Ureña as interim president. This was in accordance with the 1963 constitution which stated that the president of the *Cámara de Diputados* [Chamber of Deputies] would provisionally substitute for the president in his absence. When Bosch was overthrown, Molina Ureña served as president of the *Cámara de Diputados* (Grimaldi (1985), p. 46).
24 On 7 May the United States had 34,921 men under arms in the Dominican Republic and twenty-four ships around its coasts (Hermann (1983), p. 249).
25 Black (1986), p. 38. Cf. Goff and Locker (1969), p. 278.
26 58 percent of those who had been elected as members of the National Congress in 1962 were able to assemble and carry out the voting (Hermann (1983), p. 236).

Figure 12.4 Francisco Caamaño, 1965.

who was flown in to meddle in Dominican politics, warned in a telegram to Washington that Caamaño could become a 'Dominican Castro'[27] and later depicted him as an opportunist, with a reputation soiled by the massacre in Palma Sola, a weather cock who at every turn of his career had sided with people he later attacked, a man governed by a desire to avenge himself on his adversaries.[28] Other foreign commentators were puzzled by the sudden appearance of Caamaño on the side of the radicals and almost every commentator mentioned the black spot of Caamaño – Palma Sola:

> Caamaño's detractors say that he led the massacre after General Rodríguez Reyes was killed. Caamaño himself has said that he was knocked unconscious in the melee at the outset and was not responsible for the massacre.[29]

> Caamaño had been involved in the infamous Palma Sola massacre of 1962, in which members of a religious sect had been brutally murdered by a police unit.[30]

> In December 1962, Caamaño commanded the police and the troops which exterminated with bullets a rebellious religious sect in Palma Sola, close to the border with Haiti. Almost all members of this sect

27 Grimaldi (1985), p. 100.
28 Martin (1966), pp. 666–7.
29 Ibid., note, p. 666.
30 Slater (1970), p. 20.

seem to have been Haitians. In his book Crisis de la Democracia, Juan Bosch described what happened in Palma Sola as a 'genocide.' Caamaño participated in the overthrow of Bosch and later plotted for the overthrow of his boss, the commandant of the National Police, General Belisario Peguero.[31]

> Caamaño's role in the killings [in Palma Sola] is ambiguous. He claims that he was knocked out of the fight and therefore couldn't have directed the slaughter [...] But his association with an event that brought back searing memories of his father's great crimes intensified his feelings of guilt and his efforts to overcome them with toughness, bluster, and, sometimes, drink.[32]

It appears as if Caamaño struggled to overcome his past and he became appreciated by many of his countrymen as a good patriot, honestly dedicated to the constitutionalist cause. With him within the constitutionalist ranks were other military men who were unable to present a totally 'innocent' past: 'Perhaps such men were simply opportunists and adventurers; perhaps, as seems more persuasive in the case of Caamaño himself, they were seeking atonement for their past lives.'[33]

The Americans made every effort to whip up support for their side in the conflict. Their principal preoccupation was how to find a military leader with sufficient prestige and morale to enable him to gain public support and lead the US-backed troops opposed to the Dominican civilians and nationalistic officers, who were fighting to safeguard the Dominican constitution and arrange for Bosch's return. Ambassador Martin opted for his friend 'Tony' Imbert and convinced his government that Imbert was the right man to lead the country and the troops battling Caamaño's forces. 'Tony' willingly accepted Martin's offer.

When the rebellion exploded on 24 April, Imbert had been eager to find a place for himself in the rapid development of events. When the coup took place he had been hunting ducks together with the United States naval attaché and when he got back to Santo Domingo he first went to Reid Cabral and offered his support, on the condition that he himself would be named secretary of state of the armed forces. Reid Cabral had never been a friend of Imbert and had already in 1962 accused him, and some of his relatives, of enriching themselves at the expense of government. Even if Imbert had been crucial in the ousting of Bosch he never rose to prominence under the Reid Cabral regime that followed, although he was able

---

31 Mallín (1965), pp. 30–1.
32 Kurzman (1965), p. 164.
33 Slater (1978), pp. 305–6. Cf. Hermann (1983), pp. 160–1.

Figure 12.5 Antonio Imbert Barrera.

to maintain his power base and influence.[34] Reid Cabral consequently turned down Imbert's offer and the latter immediately went to the rebel leaders and, when he experienced their strength and resolution, told them he was ready to support their cause if they were willing to form a junta under his command and call for new elections. When he was informed that the insurgents already had decided to reinstall Bosch he ended up at the United States embassy and offered his services there instead.[35]

On Martin's initiative Imbert was put in charge of a provisional government backed by the United States. As was his wont when dealing with his 'presidential' friends in the Dominican Republic, Martin wrote Imbert's inaugural speech.[36] Martin's choice caused surprise and dismay among various Dominican specialists at the US State Department, where Imbert was known for his 'opportunism, predilection for power, and widespread unpopularity'[37] in the Dominican Republic:

> Moreover Martin ignored his instructions to make it clear that the new government would be only provisional and would not receive diplomatic recognition from the United States. Instead Martin promised Imbert a blank check and recognition within twenty-four hours. Predictably enough, Imbert immediately set out to form a military dictatorship and to destroy the constitutionalists and any other

34 Szulc (1965), pp. 88–9.
35 Lowenthal (1972), pp. 67–8, Hermann (1983), pp. 150–3.
36 Martin (1986), p. 254.
37 Slater (1978), pp. 321–2.

opposition, imprisoning, torturing and even murdering hundreds of Dominicans. Lyndon Johnson was furious – 'I'm not going down in history as the man responsible for putting another Trujillo in power.'[38]

Martin defended his choice of Imbert by stating that he was a man of action and pro-American, or as he told a Dominican friend: 'Tony will never go against us [the US].'[39]

Imbert immediately went to work. One of his first measures was to arrest and deport various high-ranking officers, mainly members of the San Cristóbal group, who had always been well-known opponents to Imbert.[40] Backed by a monthly support of more than 3 million dollars from USAID[41] and discreetly supported by the American military, Imbert, by the middle of May, let his troops loose on the constitutionalists. The international press noted their brutality and the OAS was presented with a report of 'Imbert atrocities'. The international commission which put the report together was not able to arrive at an exact number of persons killed through the terror, but mentioned as one example that a prison under Imbert's supervision 'once containing 3,000 now has been reduced to 500'.[42] Several summary executions took place in areas which had been conquered from the constitutionalists.[43] Imbert's 'Operation Clean-up' took a week and was a complete success. After heavy civilian and military casualties, the constitutionalist-held area became reduced to a stronghold in the southeastern corner of Santo Domingo.[44]

There are indications that the United States tried to limit the advance of Imbert's troops because the Americans feared that Imbert's increased power otherwise could be hard to cope with.[45] Imbert considered himself to be the administrator of the entire country. The slightest evidence of constitutionalist support was dealt harshly with wherever it occurred. A constitutionalist-inspired revolt in Santiago was easily and violently crushed and an 'arbitrary police rule' reigned in the whole country.[46] In support of Imbert's government the United States convinced some

---

38 Ibid., p. 322.
39 Slater (1970), p. 65.
40 Cassá (1986), p. 191. Imbert had to exile his old protégé Belisario Peguero, the controversial former chief of police.
41 Ibid., p. 212.
42 Goff and Locker (1969), p. 278.
43 Hermann (1983), p. 280.
44 It is possible that the attack was halted since the stronghold could not be taken without severe damage to the Republic's most famed historical monuments and enormous losses in human lives on both sides. The harbor and the principal banking and commercial centers were all in the hands of the constitutionalists.
45 Slater (1970), p. 93.
46 Wipfler (1978), pp. 345–6.

members of the OAS to send troops and an 'Inter-American Force' was formed to protect 'peace and order' in the Dominican Republic.[47]

After recurrent bombardments of the constitutionalist zone and drawn-out negotiations Caamaño ceded his powers to an interim president who finally was accepted by all parties that had taken active part in the fighting.[48] The departure from the country by all principal military leaders was seen as a prerequisite for the celebration of peaceful elections. Thirty-four officers were thus sent abroad on diplomatic missions or 'studies'.[49] First to go was Caamaño, who ended up in London. As a matter of fact, most of the exiled militaries belonged to the constitutionalist camp; such a highly controversial figure as Imbert was allowed to stay after he unwillingly had parted with his military command and dictatorial powers.

Imbert continued to be a major force in Dominican politics and proved himself to be a political survivor of significant aptitude. Under President Balaguer, who won the elections after the civil war, he was considered to be 'among the most adroit opportunists and enjoyed considerable influence with the president',[50] in spite of his initial opposition to Balaguer, who had been Trujillo's personally selected president at the time Imbert participated in the murder of the old dictator. In 1966, 1967 and 1978 Imbert survived attempts on his life by old, loyal *Trujillistas*. In 1971 Balaguer put him in charge of the construction of the huge and prestigious Sabaneta dam and after its completion he was in charge of another dam construction.[51] In 1973 he reentered active military service by accepting a post as general inspector of the armed forces, the position held by General Rodríguez Reyes when the latter was killed in Palma Sola.

Imbert was able to maintain his influence when Antonio Guzmán became president after defeating Balaguer in the elections of 1978, thereby putting an end to Balaguer's twelve years in power. Guzmán had been minister under Bosch when the latter was ousted by Imbert. Still he readily accepted the old coup maker. Under Guzmán Imbert kept himself out of the limelight; he accepted no official post and did not attend any

---

47 Apart from the US forces the OAS army included 1,170 soldiers from Brazil, 250 from Honduras, 159 from Nicaragua and 21 policemen from Costa Rica. The commander in chief was a Brazilian general, but in reality it was the United States that ran the show (Hermann (1983), p. 293). With the exception of Costa Rica and the United States, all the participating countries were ruled by dictators.

48 Héctor García-Godoy Cáceres, who was put in charge of a caretaker government until the upcoming elections, was presented as a 'neutral' choice, but in reality he was the vice-president of Balaguer's Reformist Party and the selection of this man was a clear indication of whom the United States would like to see as the future president of the Dominican Republic.

49 Hermann (1983), p. 346.

50 Atkins (1981), p. 78.

51 Balaguer (1989), p. 276.

Figure 12.6 The body of Francisco Caamaño, 1973.

ceremonies. Still, he concentrated a considerable amount of power in his hands. Under the auspices of Imbert two of his nephews rose to high positions within the military system of the Dominican Republic. One became chief of staff of the air force while the other one served as secretary of state of the armed forces. Together they formed what was called a 'family faction' and became the most influential group within the army.[52] When Balaguer, through the 1986 elections, once more came back in power Imbert proved his amazing ability in keeping his positions even within opposing political factions and in 1987 he was promoted to secretary of state of the armed forces. However, he left this position after just one year and became head of the state-owned mining company *Rosario Dominicano.*

While Imbert proved to be an extraordinary political survivor, the fate of Caamaño was totally different. Caamaño as well was a man who did not give up, but he stuck to the other side, choosing the revolutionary path he had initiated as his lifestyle and accordingly ended up as a revolutionary martyr in a pantheon where he, for the Dominican left, has come to equal Che Guevara.

The political violence continued uninterrupted after Balaguer had become president. Political assassinations were the order of the day. A high point appears to have been reached in 1971–72 and political activity grew intense in the country when in 1972 it became clear that Balaguer intended to run for a third term as president. Remnants of the constitutionalist movement and some scattered groups of the Dominican left

52 Atkins (1981), pp. 145–6.

started to plan for a revolution and in February 1973 Caamaño suddenly landed on a desolate beach in the southwest. Together with a small group of just ten men he made it for the mountains which they intended to make into a center for a campaign against the government of Balaguer. They were soon traced and hunted down by a party of 2,000 men, while 1,400 political, student and labor leaders were arrested all over the country. After two weeks Caamaño and his men were ambushed between Constanza and San José de Ocoa and there, where Olivorio Mateo had roamed fifty years before, the wounded and captured Francisco Alberto Caamaño Deñó was shot in the head by his captors.[53]

Some other actors

Caamaño was not the only man involved in the Palma Sola affair who met a violent death several years after the events. Attorney General Antonio García Vásquez in 1963 initiated a successful diplomatic career when he was appointed as ambassador to Madrid. By the beginning of the 1980s he served as ambassador to Colombia, where people who met him described him as 'an excellent diplomat, attentive to all who asked for his help and a very nice person altogether'.[54] Nevertheless, in 1981 he was shot down by one of his employees in a *crime de passion*. His colleague, Tomás Susaña, is still active as district attorney in San Juan de la Maguana.

Colonel Manuel Valentino Despradel Brache and Major Rafael Guillermo Guzmán Acosta, the two officers who served under Caamaño in Palma Sola, both pursued distinguished careers within the Dominican police. Despradel Brache had succeeded Caamaño in charge of the White Helmets. During the civil war in 1965 he was commanding the Ozama fort inside the constitutionalist zone and in spite of Caamaño's urgent pleas he refused to join forces with the constitutionalists, probably because his brother was chief of the national police and had sided with Imbert. When the constitutionalists finally attacked the fort, Despradel Brache was able to escape.[55] Under President Antonio Guzmán he was named subchief of the national police.[56]

53 There exist two well-informed, but somewhat hagiographic, accounts of the life of Caamaño. *Caamaño*, by Ricardo Sáenz Padrón and Hugo Rius Blein (1984), is a Cuban book, while the best one, *Francis Caamaño*, was written by Hamlet Hermann (1983), one of Caamaño's comrades-in-arms who was with him to the end. Caamaño launched his expedition from Cuba and a fascinating, but highly controversial, story about how Caamaño ended up with the Cubans and became a part of their revolutionary schemes is offered by Mañón (1989).
54 Interview with a Dominican who knew García Vásquez in Bogotá, Guatemala City, 25 May 1991.
55 Hermann (1983), pp. 221–2.
56 Atkins (1981), p. 144.

Guzmán Acosta was in 1972 promoted to brigadier general and named chief of the national police. He was later accused of various assassinations. Some of the victims were prominent journalists. The cases were never solved.[57] Later still he was put in charge of the military district of San Juan de la Maguana and before President Balaguer left power in 1978, he was made major general, together with Imbert Barrera.[58]

Miguel Angel Ramírez Alcántara was satisfied by winning a senatorial post after the elections in 1962, thus securing a voice for the Ramírez clan and the San Juan Valley during the Bosch regime.[59] In San Juan de la Maguana he continued the Ramírez tradition by acting as a local *caudillo*, regarding himself 'as the *patrón* of San Juan and the benevolent father of his followers'.[60] After the coup against Bosch, Miguel Angel joined the UCN party. When Balaguer was elected president he named Miguel Angel subsecretary of the ministry of agriculture. This position, which was 'mainly symbolic', Ramírez managed to retain also during the governments of Antonio Guzmán and Jorge Blanco that succeeded the twelve-year reign of Balaguer. Miguel Angel died in 1985.[61]

Bishop Thomas Reilly played a very active part in the campaign against Bosch, whom he accused of being a communist. He also wrote articles in the *New York Times* defending the politics of Donald Reid Cabral. At the same time he continued to be a colorful figure, liked and respected by most of his parishioners. After his retirement he stayed in San Juan de la Maguana, until cancer of the throat in 1989 forced him to go back to Boston for treatment. His illness hindered him from returning to the Dominican Republic.[62] He died in Boston on 21 July 1992 and his body was laid to rest in San Juan de la Maguana, in accordance with his own wish.

Ambassador John Bartlow Martin left the diplomatic service, wrote several books on United States politics in the Caribbean and a huge biography of Adlai Stevenson. He also taught journalism at a United States college. He died in 1987 after finishing his memoirs the year before.[63]

The survivors

After being released from prison the *Mellizo*, León Romilio Ventura, returned to till his soil in Media Luna, where he now lives as *el tronco del*

57 Ibid., pp. 81–2.
58 Ibid., p. 99.
59 *Bohemia Libre*, 20 January 1963, p. A-4.
60 Wiarda (1975), p. 1023.
61 Interview with Mimicito Ramírez, San Juan de la Maguana, 14 December 1985. Cf. García (1986), p. 132.
62 Based on various interviews with Thomas Reilly and some of his parishioners.
63 Martin (1986).

lugar, the center and patron of a large family group. Most of the inhabitants in the small village of Media Luna are members of the Ventura family and almost all of the older generation lived through the massacre, seeing parents and children killed in Palma Sola. Visitors are received with open arms and the Venturas freely tell them about their experiences. León Romilio still has intimate contacts with the spiritual sphere and receives messages from several spirits, among others Olivorio Mateo. He also has excellent contact with the priests of Las Matas de Farfán and exchanges his experiences with some of them:

> I have had several discussions with the priests and Father Bryan has participated in our ceremonies. They have instructed me and given me a Bible and by reading it I have found out that we were not wrong in Palma Sola. We acted in accordance with the will of the Lord.[64]

In Media Luna the *salves* from Palma Sola are still sung in unison and *El Mellizo* continues to preach the message of equality of all men and women and the importance of working in union to realize 'the work of Olivorio here on earth'. He states that he and his 'collaborators' are Catholics, *Olivoristas* and voodooists, and he does not find this contradictory, since 'truth is where real faith is'. Behind his house in Media Luna, León Romilio has a sanctuary akin to the one which is found by the dwellings of other *Olivorista* leaders in the region. However, at León Romilio's shrine the concentric stone circles are not laid out around three crosses. Instead they encircle a huge *ceiba* tree, which has a cross nailed to its trunk. Above the cross are written some incomprehensible words; their meaning is known only to God and León Romilio. By the side of the stone circles the three crosses of the calvary are erected. The traditional *ermita* is found a little further from the huge *ceiba*, by the shore of the small river Yacahueque which runs through León Romilio's lands. Inside, the familiar altar and oleographs of most *Olivorista* shrines are to be found and here traditional *Olivorista* ceremonies take place on Tuesdays and Fridays in the presence of the Venturas living around the place.[65]

'[T]he religion of the Mellizos has always been very politicized',[66] and León Romilio continues to be an active participant in the political life of the San Juan Valley. He is inscribed in the Reformist Party of Joaquín Balaguer and in his house he keeps a framed photograph which shows him swearing the oath of the party in front of Balaguer himself. If asked why he

---

64 Interview with León Romilio Ventura, Media Luna, 5 May 1986.
65 The description is based on several visits to Media Luna. Cf. Espín del Prado (1984), p. 695.
66 Espín del Prado (1984), p. 615.

Figure 12.7 León Romilio Ventura and Juana María Ventura, daughter of Delanoy Ventura, 1986.

supports Balaguer he answers: 'The work of Olivorio is made public by Balaguer.'[67] After eleven years as a member of the PRD he changed party and joined Balaguer's Reformists:

> I renounced my membership in the PRD because a general took me prisoner. I was taken to San Juan de la Maguana, without violence. I was unable to do anything. I told them: 'I am a member of the PRD and I have religious and political importance.' Nothing helped and I had to spend eight days in a prison cell. They jailed me only because I had an old knife in my possession and I had to pay 40 pesos to a lawyer. All in vain, everything was done in order to molest me. Then I was suddenly released and taken to the second floor by a member of the *Reformista* Party. He said to me: 'I want you to follow me. We are friends of yours.' Balaguer was there and he said he was my friend.[68]

After León Romilio became a party member he met Balaguer on several occasions, and at one of their meetings Balaguer even presented him with a revolver. Even if he is a firm supporter of Balaguer León Romilio stresses

---

67 Interview with León Romilio Ventura, Media Luna, 5 May 1986. Asked to explain better what he meant, León Romilio told us that Balaguer is the only Dominican president who has listened to the opinions of the *Olivoristas* and done something for the area. León Romilio often stresses that the message of Olivorio is 'to do something, to improve the wellbeing of people'.

68 Ibid.

that he is disappointed with all Dominican presidents: 'No one has ever done anything for the orphans of Palma Sola. They have not given me any apologies, not even five cents for cigarettes.'[69]

León Romilio says he has a personal commitment to Balaguer, not because the latter has done anything for the victims of the massacre, but because he has done some of the things predicted by Olivorio: 'He has done something to save the poor [*los infelices*]. He is the only president who has carried out Christian work in this area, building dams and roads, giving electric light and running water, food to the starving, etc.'[70]

During the last few years León Romilio has been given quite a lot of attention. He has been visited by various journalists and anthropologists and even appeared on national television on several occasions. He is well aware of his importance and often receives his guests together with Macario Lorenzo, a teacher who was in charge of the inscriptions in Palma Sola. Macario, who is very eloquent, now acts as León Romilio's 'secretary' and takes care of some of his contacts with the 'outer world'. León Romilio stresses that he does not carry out any 'mission' like the one he was 'called upon' to carry out in Palma Sola, but he states that 'if I receive the message once more I will not hesitate to do what it tells me to do. The power is constantly talking to me and I know it comes from God.'[71]

Opinion about León Romilio is very divided among the *Olivoristas*. Some are suspicious of him and say he is a false prophet and that they never approved of what happened in Palma Sola. Others mean that León Romilio had his moment. In Palma Sola he was chosen to act by the Great Power of God. Now he is just one among equals. Most *Olivoristas* work totally independently, although they are well acquainted with other cult functionaries and it happens that they carry out some ceremonies together. Still, they consider their own activity as exclusively concentrated in one area.

Diego Cépeda has been a faithful *Olivorista* all his life and was invited to Palma Sola by the *Mellizos* themselves. He lives in Jínova, just outside San Juan de la Maguana. He has a sanctuary with stone circles in his backyard and an elaborate altar in his bedroom; as a cult leader he serves the community around him. Diego, who is a very quiet and mild-mannered man, says he is convinced that Palma Sola was a thing of God. He does not have any contact with the *Mellizo* anymore but every year he celebrates a big feast which is an act of thanksgiving because all the twenty-eight people from Jínova who were with him in Palma Sola were saved from the massacre. He arranges the feast as a 'compromise with God and his

69 Ibid.
70 Ibid.
71 Ibid.

mother'. The arrangements are costly for a small farmer like Diego who spends almost 1,000 Dominican pesos out of his own pocket every year and slaughters a cow to feed his 500 guests:

> I am all alone with this. When I die, it ends with me. I do this for the people and in gratitude for what God has given to me. I give advice to people. I am a religious man and do not know anything about the voodoo spirits [*seres*] and all that. I believe you have to give to other people what God has given to you. Why do you have to give anything to God and the saints? They are not hungry, they have everything. No, we have to give to one another. The belief is for the humans.[72]

All over the San Juan Valley, in the Cordillera Central and along the Dominican-Haitian border, you meet people who have been in Palma Sola and most of them are prepared to talk about their experiences there. Most say they felt something there, something like the presence of the Great Power of God. They do not talk so much about the *Mellizos* or their teachings. What they usually speak about is the sense of unity and generosity they encountered there: 'Everyone ate out of one plate. Everything was divided equally.'[73] Still, the memories hurt and many people do not want to talk about their experiences, fearing persecution. In Santo Domingo live members of the Ventura family who have changed their names. What hurts is also the labels that were put on the *Olivoristas* by ignorant outsiders, who depicted them as idolaters and barbarians. Many feel that they still carry the stigma as the guilty party in the conflict and do not understand why all Dominican governments have been unwilling to investigate the matter further and why no indemnity has been paid to the survivors who were in fact never legally indicted for any crime. León Romilio himself told us: 'People come and go. They ask questions and leave us here. You come from far away and maybe know influential people. Could you maybe ask the President of the USA and the Pope of Rome to do something for the orphans of Palma Sola.'[74]

Bosch, Balaguer and the *Olivoristas*

The few comments Juan Bosch has made about the massacre have mostly been rather aloof and unengaged. When he heard about the massacre in New York he told the Dominican press it was a tragedy, but like most of the people of his day he also stressed that the ultimate reason for the massacre

---

72 Interview with Diego Cépeda, Jínova, 4 June, 1989.
73 Cf. Mateo Pérez and Mateo Comas (1980), p. 46 and Vásquez and Fermín (1980), p. 76.
74 Interview with León Romilio Ventura, Media Luna, 17 January, 1986.

Figure 12.8 Juan Bosch in the 1980s.

was the peasants' wretched and impoverished situation and their lack of education. *El Caribe* published an interview Bosch had given over the phone from New York. He said that he had sent a telegram to the armed forces where he

> pointed out that the outbreak of fanaticism and false religiosity in Palma Sola is the result of the social frustration of the Dominican peasantry. We are assured that when the Dominican peasant is treated like a human being he cannot be led astray, as has been the case in Palma Sola, where false religious leaders have occupied the place of those who ought to have been the real social leaders of the peasant.[75]

Before the elections Bosch had one encounter with León Romilio Ventura and did not like the man, as he felt that León Romilio had intended to blackmail him by threatening to withhold *Olivorista* votes if Bosch were not willing to offer them his support.[76] Something of this negative attitude towards the leaders of the movement is discernable in his book *Crisis de la democracia de América en la República Dominicana*, written in 1964, where they are compared with Haiti's dictator François Duvalier (Papa Doc):

> On the south side of the border, dividing the Dominican Republic from Haiti, one can, from time to time, see men of Duvalier's stamp, who were ordinary peasants until they felt themselves possessed with a

---

75 Juan Bosch quoted in *El Caribe*, 30 December 1962.
76 Interview with Juan Bosch, Santo Domingo, 11 October 1985.

power they call religious and began giving prescriptions, recommending cures, making up their own rites. They then took on the appearance of forest *caudillos*. They are mad with powers, as Hitler was on a much grander scale.[77]

Like Juan Bosch, Joaquín Balaguer is a prolific writer and his strong personality and personal opinions have loomed over the political and cultural life of the Republic to at least the same extent as those of Bosch.[78] For various reasons, Balaguer has been more pragmatic and attentive to *Olivorismo* than Bosch, who views the Palma Sola massacre as a rather marginal phenomenon, something that was due to the inexperience and clumsiness of the military. Balaguer, on the other hand, used the massacre in his political discourse, and in 1964, while he was exiled from the Republic, severely criticized the sitting government for its handling of the 'affair':

> The most important issue which the country now confronts is the reconstruction of the southern parts of the Republic. For several months the provinces of Azua, Barahona, San Juan, Baoruco, Independencia, and Elías Piña, experience a period of public calamity which is caused not only by the devastations which in these parts of the country are a result of natural phenomena, but it is also a result of the serious effects of the humiliating economic situation of the people in the South, for a long time victims of the indifference shown to them by the official institutions.[79]

> The actual government [the triumvirate which took power after the coup against Bosch] has contracted an unsettled moral and patriotic debt in the South. During the regime of the State Council, of which the Triumvirate is just a simple prolongation in the political and bureaucratic sphere, the village of Palma Sola was devastated. More than a thousand Dominicans were pulverized there in a genocidal act equal to the one, with exception of the proportions, committed in Hiroshima during the Second World War. That martyrized village is today a symbol of the region of the country which has been most severely punished by the cruelty of man and the harshness of the natural forces.[80]

---

77 Bosch (1964), p. 174. Italics ours.
78 It was not for nothing that *Time* magazine, 28 May 1990, gave the headline 'Battle of the Dinosaurs' to a commentary on the 1990 elections, when Bosch and Balaguer once more battled over the presidency. In these elections the blind and eighty-two-year-old Balaguer won his presidency in open elections for the fifth time in his life (Bosch is two years younger than Balaguer).
79 Balaguer (1964), p.129.
80 Ibid., p. 132.

Balaguer adequately compares the movement in Palma Sola with the messianic movement of Antonio Conselheiro in Brazil.[81] He recommends the excellent book on this theme by Euclides da Cunha and states that Palma Sola is a similar religious protest movement and that, in a Latin American context, it hardly constitutes any exception.[82] Balaguer mentions that no less than three huge military expeditions were necessary to vanquish Antonio Conselheiro and finally destroy his stronghold, Canudos.

> Against Palma Sola, on the other hand, there was only one expedition: the one which was necessary in order to carry out the definite massacre. In the history of America, maybe in the history of all mankind, no such abominable act of brutality is recorded in the present century as the one carried out in this martyrized village. Over its inhabitants fell a punishment worse than the fire that annihilated Sodom and more cruel than the rain of ashes which buried Herculaneum.
>
> May the Triumvirate reconstruct the South. If it does not do so out of patriotism, it has at least to do it in order to honor the debt which it has contracted with this vast region of the Republic; it has to wipe out and extenuate the crime committed in Palma Sola by making a restoring gesture [*gesto reparador*] and through constructive action.[83]

After firing such a broadside it seems a bit strange that Balaguer, when he finally came to power, did not make any attempt to follow up his accusations through legal action. As a matter of fact, after assuming the presidency Balaguer rarely mentioned the Palma Sola affair officially. In a book written twenty years after the events, he has changed his tune. He now calls the 'admirers of the god "Liborio"' 'fanatics' and relates *Olivorismo* to something he labels 'the animism of African tribes imported from the neighboring country' (i.e. Haitian voodoo).[84] He does not condemn the governmental actions. Instead he points out that the authorities regarded *Olivorismo* 'as a threat to the peace of the nation and to our traditional religious sentiments', a view he himself appears to share. He describes the actual massacre in the following way: 'On 29 December a military contingent was hurled against the so-called twins of Palma Sola, (Tulio and Plinio Rodríguez), whose adepts reacted against the intervention of the public forces and killed General Miguel Rodríguez Reyes.'[85]

---

81 Cunha (1944).
82 Balaguer (1964), p. 132.
83 Ibid., p. 133.
84 Balaguer (1983), note, p. 210.
85 Ibid. Balaguer mentions Tulio Ventura as one of the principal leaders, but he probably knows that it was the sole survivor, León Romilio Ventura, who shared the leadership with Plinio.

In a rather strange statement Balaguer writes that voodooistic beliefs have not yet been totally eradicated from the Republic and that 'Liborismo' still is active in the border regions, even though it seems to lose importance and adherents.[86] Balaguer must have been well aware of the fact that some of his most influential political allies in the San Juan Valley worked in union with some important *Olivorista* leaders and far from hindering the spreading of their teachings seemed to favor the growth of the *Olivorista* beliefs:

> It is Balaguer who finally has liberated the work of Olivorio. He gave the banners of Olivorio and the Republic to the Holy Queen Isabel who now guards the *ermita* in La Maguana. It was Balaguer who reconstructed the old *ermita* and the *calvario* up there, where the mystery was initiated. Now people come from all over the country in order to visit the place.[87]

> People come here from far away, even from the most distant place on earth, from Babylon. Even farther away, something which means that Babylon is not at the end of it all. In 1975, a general came here in order to hear about the miracles that have taken place here. He was sent by the president and he came together with several other officers. They all were impressed by our work and the next day they came back and gave me the Dominican banner. Flags have also been given to the *ermita* by the president.[88]

Many of the old community leaders and *caudillos* in the San Juan Valley, who earlier had been faithful to the Ramírez clan, people who had been active members of Trujillo's Dominican Party and who later campaigned for Miguel Angel Ramírez in the 1962 elections, followed Balaguer in the early 1970s and helped him with his campaigning in the valley. They considered Balaguer to be the politician on the national level who was best informed about the valley and the one who most likely would attend to its problems. Experienced as they were in the game of local politics, they were well aware of the political potential that lay concealed among the *Olivoristas* and they advised Balaguer to concentrate part of his campaigning on their leaders. Balaguer willingly followed their advice when he understood that *Olivorista* votes had already proved crucial for Miguel Angel Ramírez.

---

86 Ibid. Most anthropologists who have studied Dominican voodoo agree that it is alive and well and even shows signs of attracting more and more adherents every year.

87 Interview with León Romilio Ventura, Media Luna, 5 May 1986.

88 Interview with Bartolo de Jiménez, Maguana Arriba, 13 December 1985. Bartolo's inspired preaching is rather difficult to follow. His words come in a constant flow and their meaning is often not very clear to the listener.

Some of the *Olivoristas* are influential within their communities and we told Balaguer it would be a good thing to win these people over. We suggested to him that it would be a nice gesture to renovate the *ermita* in Maguana Arriba. It is an old religious center but many *Olivoristas* say that a stone close to the *ermita* once formed part of the foundations of the house of Olivorio's parents. When everything had been completed we sent up a truck with concrete in order to cement the floor. But they did not want to put any cement under the *enramada*, something which made some of us believe that Olivorio had been buried there after his disciples dug up his corpse from the churchyard here in San Juan.[89]

María Orfelia, also called Queen Isabel, who takes care of the *ermita* in Maguana Arriba, is clad mostly in red garments, the color of Balaguer's Reformist Party, and on her blouse she often wears a big button depicting a red cock, the Reformists' party symbol. Downhill, within the village of Maguana Arriba, lives Enemencio Mora, 'Evangelio', one of the 'grand old men' of *Olivorismo*. Evangelio keeps a huge *Olivorista* altar in a house in his backyard. There he also keeps a large portrait painted on commission from Balaguer by the artist Príamo Morel, who lives in faraway Santiago. It was presented to Evangelio by local *Reformistas*, who told him the painting was a personal gift from President Balaguer. Evangelio has red cocks painted on the four doors to the house of his altar and he is active within the Reformist Party.

It is interesting to note that most rural *ermitas* keeping *Olivorista* altars are painted white and blue, the colors of Olivorio, and that the tablecloths covering the altars as a rule are blue and white as well, while Evangelio has his *ermita* painted blue and red and keeps a red tablecloth on the altar, just as his colleague María Orfelia, who guards the *ermita* by Olivorio's calvary, does. Red is the color of the Holy Spirit, or Great Power of God, but it also, as mentioned above, happens to be the color of Balaguer's Reformist Party.[90] The local leaders meet once a week, usually on Saturdays, and Evangelio often has the meetings in his house. Both María Orfelia and Evangelio keep portraits of Balaguer close to their altars.[91]

---

89 Interview with Mimicito Ramírez, San Juan de la Maguana, 14 December 1985.
90 White and blue are the colors of the Virgen de la Altagracia, the patron of the Dominican Republic, to whom Olivorio, and accordingly all *Olivoristas*, was very devoted. Blue was the color preferred by Olivorio and all his male followers used to wear blue denim. In Palma Sola the men were asked to wear blue shirts and trousers and the women wore white dresses with long sleeves.
91 Descriptions based on various visits to Maguana Arriba. María Orfelia keeps a nicely framed color photograph of Balaguer on the wall just beside the altar, while Evangelio has a red and white sign saying 'Balaguer for President' among the framed pictures hanging and standing right above his altar.

Figure 12.9 María Orfelia outside the *ermita* at Maguana Arriba, 1986.

In Jínova, the influential *Olivorista* Diego Cépeda owns a huge crucifix, which he lends to people who carry out *Olivorista* ceremonies in the neighborhood. This crucifix, which is adorned with a ceramic image of Christ, was given to Diego by the wife of Senator Juan Mesa, the Reformists' most important representative in San Juan de la Maguana.[92] Juan Mesa, who is a respected medical doctor, has an *Olivorista* altar in his house and the Reformists support a peasants' collective in Jínova called Papá Liborio.[93] Mesa does not consider himself to be a believer in Olivorio's presumed divinity, but he is very well informed about the *Olivorista* beliefs and knows many stories about Olivorio and his alleged prophesies and miracles.[94]

Joaquín Balaguer has always shown a keen interest in the San Juan Valley and the Dominican border regions. His most ambitious novel, *Los carpinteros*, published in 1984, deals with *caudillo* fighting along the Haitian frontier at the turn of the century and it demonstrates a profound knowledge of the area.[95] Since the day he entered the world of Dominican politics Balaguer has seen it as his mission to safeguard the Dominican Republic from Haitian influences and one of the means to achieve that goal has been to 'Dominicanize' the areas under 'Haitian influence'. In 1927, when he was only twenty-one years old, Balaguer wrote: 'The work which demands most civil determination, after the creation of the Republic, is

92 Interview with Diego Cépeda, Jínova, 4 June 1989.
93 Interview with Leopoldo Figuereo, San Juan de la Maguana, 4 June 1989.
94 Interview with Juan José Medina Mesa, San Juan de la Maguana, 18 January 1989.
95 Balaguer (1984).

and will be the colonization of the border coastline [...] It is the work most predestined to guarantee our nationality eternal life.'[96]

All his life Balaguer has kept alive this fear of being overrun by Haitians. After becoming Dominican president for the fifth time he still warned of the Haitian danger:

> 'What do you want? [...] That we are going to Haitianize ourselves completely? That we lose our culture? That we lose the right to safeguard our country, so that it will once more be trampled underfoot during 22 years by a foreign nation?' These phrases by President Balaguer were received with strong and prolonged applause from the attending peasants. 'There, there in that applause, born in the heart of the people, is the answer to your question', concluded Balaguer.[97]

Race is an important ingredient in the conglomerate which forms Balaguer's ideological outlook. The black skin of the Haitians is the main danger to the Dominicans:

> Accordingly, the nearness of Haiti has been and continues to be the principal problem of the Dominican Republic [...] but while the race problem has an incalculable importance for all countries, for Santo Domingo it has [...] an enormous significance, since our ethnic and social shape depends on the very existence of the nationhood that for more than a century has been involved in a battle against a more prolific race ...[98]

> The immense wave of color that daily invaded the Dominican territory not only exposed Santo Domingo to the danger of losing its national character, but also to having its customs corrupted and to experiencing a decrease of its moral level.[99]

Considering this 'threat' it is the duty of every Dominican president to do his utmost in order to save the border regions from everything Haitian:

> To carry out this patriotic labor, dictated by a conservatory national instinct, it was necessary to create a community of aspirations between the population of the border zones and that of the rest of the country, and to propagate a feeling in these regions that the role which the

---

96 Balaguer, quoted in Vega (1988c), p. 18.
97 Ibid. pp. 415–16.
98 Balaguer (1947), p. 124. This argument is repeated word by word on p. 99 in his book *La isla al revés* from 1983. The quotation is from the latter work.
99 Balaguer (1983), p. 74.

men in the same nation are called upon to play loyally in the world: of the consciousness that the Fatherland is a sacred patrimony in which the common sufferings and hopes interact with ties to the earth and material richness.[100]

To achieve this Balaguer writes that not only material works, such as roads, dams, canals, and power plants, must be carried out; it is also necessary to 'conquer' the border territories 'morally' by creating a kind of ideological defense against the 'harmful' influences from the west, among them the 'animistic' beliefs of voodoo. To this end he created a National Council of the Borders, whose members shared an appalling degree of Haitianophobia. One of its members told Dominican newspapers that the Trujillo massacres of 1937, when thousands of Haitians, – men, women and children – were killed in cold blood was nothing less than a 'prophylaxis' for the Dominicans and if Trujillo had not ordered the murders 'we would not have been Dominicans [anymore]'.[101] Another member of the council, Carlos Corneille, wrote a book that is a shameless homage to Trujillo, 'the man history now calls a dictator', but who according to Corneille had the guts to treat the Haitians the way they ought to be treated; Trujillo was 'the man who finally put an end to Haitian vandalism'.[102] The author warns the Dominican youth who 'sleep, a deep and lethargic sleep, believing in the word "brother" when a Haitian speaks, without realizing that they [the Haitians] are descendants of cannibals dressed up as human beings'.[103]

However, these 'intellectual exercises' appear to be intended mainly for urban consumption. In the San Juan Valley Balaguer employed other techniques, already proven to be effective under Trujillo: construction of roads, irrigation canals and dams and the creation of an image that is easily accepted by some members of the rural population. Balaguer often posed as a 'peasant ruler' like the one depicted by Marx: 'Their representative must at the same time appear as their master, as an authority over them, as an unlimited power that protects them against the other classes and sends them rain and sunshine from above.'[104]

Balaguer fits well into this picture. In spite of his blindness and his advanced age he descended from the skies in his helicopter, or sped along the roads in impressive corteges, in order to inaugurate building projects or to give away land within the land reform program.

---

100 Ibid., p. 77.
101 Belliard Sarubbi quoted in Franco (1981), p. 234.
102 Corneille (1980), p. 155.
103 Ibid., p. 151.
104 Marx (1977), p. 481.

Figure 12.10 Joaquín Balaguer in the 1980s.

Every Saturday and Sunday the president roams around the rural back-waters of the Dominican Republic. He arrives by helicopter and listens to the complaints of smallholders and landless *campesinos* who sponta-neously and passionately air their grievances. When they have finished speaking into the microphone, they draw nearer to tell him their trou-bles, almost whispering into his ear as if in confession. They tell him about the overdue mortgage, the money they need for an operation, a sewing machine for the wife, a bicycle for a son, or a pregnant pig.

Balaguer grants their wishes with an immediate order or makes sure that they are given a pass to see him in the presidential palace in Santo Domingo. Then he begins to speak, publicly ridiculing his own minis-ters and administrators for their incompetence or berating some local landowner for monopolizing the irrigation scheme and leaving no water for the smallholders, 'with the complicity of the military' – who, standing by, listen impassively to the President's attack. The *campesinos* worship him like some sort of messiah. A woman in the village of Las Guáranas suddenly falls into epileptic convulsions.[105]

Balaguer is respected by most *Olivoristas*. Even if several of them do not approve of his politics and belong to other political parties, most of them tend to acknowledge that Balaguer appears to be imbued with divine power, maybe the same force which was inherent in *El Maestro* himself, namely the Great Power of God:

---

105 An article by José Comas in the Spanish daily *El País Internacional* (1 June 1987), trans-lated and quoted in Ferguson (1992), p. 41.

Figure 12.11 Olivorista Julián Ramos, aged 102, with his wife, 1986.

Many peasants still consider Olivorio to be a kind of community leader, able to solve problems of health and combat poverty. People feel his presence. He is a reality, just like Balaguer is real; a great, wise leader who lives far away in the Capital, but still able to make decisions that affect everybody. Just like Balaguer, Olivorio's presence can be felt everywhere.

Trujillo was a man of tremendous power and some people considered him to be a kind of incarnation of the Great Power of God, just like Olivorio was supposed to be, and you may still come across Trujillo's portrait on several altars in this area. Balaguer is considered to be a successor of Trujillo and I think he is conscious of it. For many people here he [Balaguer] seems to be animated by an internal force. He looks like an old and weak man and he is totally blind. Still he is an excellent orator and a born survivor with great powers.

Here in the valley his presence can be felt in various ways. He has a country estate on a mountainside overlooking the San Juan Valley. He is seldom there, but the white house can be seen from far away and it reminds the onlooker about Balaguer's presence.[106]

It should be kept in mind that *Olivorismo* is not an 'organized' religion. Every cult functionary has his own close-knit group of followers; he carries

106 Interview with Leopoldo Figuereo, San Juan de la Maguana, 4 June 1989.

out his own blend of rituals and the *salves* that are sung at the religious occasions are often composed within his particular group. The *Olivoristas* do not accept any higher authority in religious matters and the same goes for politics. *Olivorista* leaders may belong to the PRD or be members of Bosch's new *Partido de la Liberación Dominicana*, and there are even *Olivoristas* inscribed in the Communist Party. The cult leaders know several other *Olivorista* funcionaries and some of them often meet at the ceremonies carried out by religious brotherhoods, like the *cofradías* of the *Espíritu Santo* in El Batey and Las Matas de Farfán, the *Cofradía de San Juan Bautista* in Maguana Arriba, or the *Cofradía de San Francisco* in Bánica, just to mention the most important ones. They tend to respect each other, but it is not uncommon to hear disdainful commentaries about the others as well. León Romilio, the *Mellizo*, seems to be the most controversial one and some *Olivoristas* do not trust his political ambitions and his interest in publicity. Most *Olivoristas* are content with carrying out their rites among friends and neighbors within a rather limited area, while León Romilio is suspected of trying to spread his gospel across the whole country or even the whole world.

Even if most *Olivorista* groups act rather independently, some of them gather on certain occasions in order to carry out rituals together with other *Olivorista* cult leaders, particularly on 21 January, the day of *La Virgen de la Altagracia*, and 28 December, the day of the Palma Sola massacre.[107] In the actual place of the massacre no ceremonies are carried out. Many *Olivoristas* shun the place due to the painful memories it evokes and also because of all the bodies which still lie in unconsecrated ground there.

Conclusions

Palma Sola is still there, on a dry hillock covered by thorny bushes. It is a desolate and quite eerie place. Huge black crows hop along the spiny vegetation or fly by under the empty sky, emitting their hoarse shrieks. In a shallow mass grave under the hard and cracked earth rest the corpses of men, children and women who were slaughtered thirty-five years ago. No one really knows how many they are – their resting place has never been disturbed – but the peasants who live around the place know the dead are there and they all wait for justice, waiting for the 'authorities' to open up the graves and bring the dead to consecrated ground. They want the guilty

---

107 An *Olivorista* feast often follows the pattern of most other rural ceremonies in the Dominican Republic, like the *velas* in front of the saints. Common features are the ritual walks around a calvary, communal singing of *salves*, and communal feasting and dancing. In Chapter 6, pp. 363–5, we described what can be considered as the main features of a typical Olivorista ceremony.

Figure 12.12 The mass grave at Palma Sola, 1986.

ones to come forth and tell the whole truth and ask the *Olivoristas* for forgiveness, recompense them for all their suffering. As long as the dead are buried in Palma Sola it remains a holy place. The presence of the dead are there, like the presence of Olivorio's soul. Memories keep the myth alive:

> It was a strange place. Everyone was kind to one another. I was just a small boy back then, but I still remember it. Everything was shared. It is still as if the place is endowed with certain powers. Not even the storms get up there. All were like brothers and sisters. We said brother to one another. No one was deceived and it is still like that here in Palma Sola: *Aquí en este pueblo somos todos unidos* [here in this village we are all united].[108]

---

108 Interview with Bolívar Ventura Rodríguez, Palma Sola, 5 May 1986.

References

Abad, José Ramón (1888), *Reseña general geográfico-estadística*. Santo Domingo.

Abrahams, Roger D. (1976), 'Genre theory and folkloristics. Folk narrative research', in Tuula Juurika and Juha Pentikäinen (eds), *Some Papers Presented at the VI Congress of the International Society for Folk Narrative Research*. Helsinki.

Acevedo, Octavio A. (1918), *Viaje oficial por el interior de la República*. Santo Domingo.

Adam, André Georges (1982), *Une crise haïtienne 1867–1869: Sylvain Salnave*. Port-au-Prince.

Adas, Michael (1981), 'From advance to confrontation: peasant protest in precolonial and colonial Asia', *Comparative Studies in Society and History*, Vol. 23.

—— (1987), *Prophets of Rebellion: Millenarian Protest Movements against the European Colonial Order*. New York, NY.

Albert, [no first name given] (1979), 'Reseña topográfica de la isla de Santo Domingo habitada por los españoles', in Emilio Rodríguez Demorizi (ed.), *Viajeros de Francia en Santo Domingo*. Santo Domingo.

Albrektson, Bertil and Ringgren, Helmer (1969), *En bok om Gamla Testamentet*. Lund.

Alburquerque, Alcibíades (1961), *Títulos de los terrenos comuneros de la República Dominicana*. Ciudad Trujillo.

Alcántara, Virgilio (1963), 'Se impone la revisión de la ley de independencia total a los cuerpos policíacos, afirman varios senadores', *Bohemia Libre*, 11 August.

Alfau Durán, Vetilio (1940), 'El santo Liborio en Higüey', *La Nación*, 27 June.

—— (1975), *El derecho de patronato en la República Dominicana*. Santo Domingo.

Alvarez Castellanos, Federico and Atanay Cruz, Reginaldo (1962), 'Detienen cientos de personas. Las F. A. persiguen amotinados de Palma Sola', *La Nación*, 29 December.

Alvarez Perelló, José de Jesús (1973), 'La mezcla de razas en Santo Domingo y los factores sanguíneos', *Revista Eme Eme*, Vol. 2.

Alver, Bente Gullveg; Klintberg, Bengt af; Rørbye, Birgitte and Siikala, Anna-Leena (1980), *Botare: En bok om etnomedicin i Norden*. Stockholm.

Ameringer, Charles D. (1996), *The Caribbean Legion: Patriots, Politicians, Soldiers of Fortune, 1946–1950*. University Park, PA.

Andrade, Manuel José (1948), *Folklore de la República Dominicana*. Ciudad Trujillo.

Archambault, Pedro M. (1938), *Historia de la Restauración*. Paris.

Ariès, Philippe (1978), *Döden, föreställningar och seder i västerlandet från medeltiden till våra dagar.* Stockholm.
—— (1979), *Centuries of Childhood.* Harmondsworth.
Aristy, José R. (1919), 'Acerca de su viaje de inspección de la frontera dominico-haitiana', *Revista de Educación*, Vol. 1.
Arzeno Rodríguez, Luis (1980), *¿Enrique Blanco: Héroe o forajido?* Santo Domingo.
—— (n.d.), *Trujillo: Anécdotas de un dictador.* Santo Domingo.
Atkins, G. Pope (1981), *Arms and Politics in the Dominican Republic.* Boulder, CO.
Attwater, Donald (1965), *The Penguin Dictionary of Saints.* Harmondsworth.
Augé, Marc (1982), *The Anthropological Circle: Symbol, Function, History.* Cambridge.
Austen, Ralph A. (1986), 'Social bandits and other heroic criminals: western models of resistance and their relevance for Africa', in Donald Crummey (ed.), *Banditry, Rebellion and Social Protest in Africa.* London and Portsmouth, NH.
Avila Suero, Víctor (1988), *Barreras: Estudio etnográfico de una comunidad rural dominicana.* Santo Domingo.
Báez Evertsz, Frank (1986), *La formación del sistema agroexportador en el Caribe: República Dominicana y Cuba: 1515–1898.* Santo Domingo.
Bailey, F. G. (1966), 'The peasant view of the bad life', *Advancement of Science*, Vol. 23.
Bakhtin, Mikhail (1984), *Rabelais and His World.* Bloomington, IN.
Balaguer, Joaquín (1947), *La realidad dominicana.* Buenos Aires.
—— (1955), 'Dios y Trujillo: Una interpretación realista de la historia dominicana,' in Abelardo R. Nanita (ed.), *La Era de Trujillo. Tomo 1.* Ciudad Trujillo.
—— (1964), 'La consunción del Sur', in Joaquín Balaguer (1983), *Entre la sangre del 30 de mayo y la del 24 de abril.* Santo Domingo.
—— (1976), *Una jornada histórica.* Santo Domingo.
—— (1983), *La isla al revés: Haití y el destino dominicano.* Santo Domingo.
—— (1984), *Los carpinteros.* Santo Domingo.
—— (1985), *La palabra encadenada.* Second edition. Santo Domingo.
—— (1989), *Memorias de un cortesano de la 'Era de Trujillo'.* Santo Domingo.
Balcácer, Juan Daniel (1989), 'Peña Batlle y su marco histórico', in Manuel Arturo Peña Batlle, *Ensayos históricos.* Santo Domingo.
Bales, William T. (1920), Archivo General de la Nación: Gobierno Militar Interior/Policía Legajo No. 14, Oficina de la 9a Compañía, 5th Endorsement, San Juan R.D., 25 December. From Commanding Officer 9th Company, G.N.D. to Director, Department of the South, G.N.D.
Barskett, James (1818), *History of the Island of St. Domingo. From Its First Discovery by Columbus.* London.
Bastide, Roger (1978), *The African Religions of Brazil: Towards a Sociology of the Interaction of Civilizations.* Baltimore, MD.
Baud, Michiel (1986), 'Transformación capitalista y regionalización en la República Dominicana, 1875–1920', *Investigación y Ciencia*, Vol. 1.
—— (1987), 'The origins of capitalist agriculture in the Dominican Republic', *Latin American Research Review*, Vol. 22.
—— (1988a), 'The struggle for autonomy: peasant resistance to capitalism in the Dominican Republic, 1870–1924', in Malcolm Cross and Gad Heuman (eds), *Labour in the Caribbean: From Emancipation to Independence.* London and Houndmills, Basingstoke.
—— (1988b), 'Sugar and unfree labour: reflections on labour recruiting in the

Dominican Republic, 1870–1940'. Paper presented at the 46th International Congress of Americanists, Amsterdam, July 4–8, 1988. *Mimeo*, Erasmus University, Rotterdam.

—— (1993a), 'Una frontera-refugio: Dominicanos y haitianos contra el estado (1870–1930)', *Estudios Sociales*, Vol. 26.

—— (1993b), 'Una frontera para cruzar: La sociedad rural a través de la frontera dominico-haitiana (1870–1930)', *Estudios Sociales*, Vol. 26.

—— (1995), *Peasants and Tobacco in the Dominican Republic, 1870–1930*. Knoxville, TN.

Bautista Mejía, Domingo Antonio (1988), 'Si me permiten de hablar: La historia de Palma Sola', *Estudios Sociales*, Vol. 21.

Bearss, Hiram I. (1917), National Archives, Washington DC: RG 45. Naval Records. Collection of the Office of Naval Records and Library. Subject File, 1911-1927. WA-7, Allied Countries, Santo Domingo. Daily Reports. Box No. 756. Headquarters, Det. U.S. Marines and Guardia Republicana Operating in Azua Province, Monday 12:00, M. San Juan, D. R., April 9. From: Lieut. Colonel H. I. Bearss, M. C. To Brigade Commander. Subject: Report of Operations from April 2nd, to April 9th, 1917. 9 April.

Beeching, Jack (1969), 'Introduction', in Alexander O. Exquemelin, *The Buccaneers of America*. Harmondsworth.

Belza, Juan Esteban (1976), *El padre de los pobres y su mitra de plomo*. Santo Domingo.

Ben-Amos, D. (1982), *Folklore in Context: Essays*. New Delhi and Madras.

Bercé, Yves-Marie (1990), *Le roi caché. Sauveurs et imposteurs: Mythes politiques populaires dans l'Europe moderne*. Paris.

Berger, John (1979), *Pig Earth*. London.

Berman, Marshall (1983), *All That Is Solid Melts into Air: The Experience of Modernity*. London and New York, NY.

Bethell, Leslie (1984), 'A note on the American population on the eve of the European invasions', in Leslie Bethell (ed.), *The Cambridge History of Latin America, Volume I, Colonial Latin America*. Cambridge.

The Betrayal of Germán Ornes (no author given) (1956). Ciudad Trujillo.

Beyer, Lisa (1992), 'Expecting the Messiah: an ultra-orthodox sect says the redeemer is due any day now – and he might be an American', *Time*, 16 March.

Bianchi, Ugo (1975), *The History of Religions*. Leiden.

—— (1987), 'History of religions', in Mircea Eliade (ed.), *The Encyclopedia of Religion. Vol. 6*. New York, NY and London.

Birkbeck, Christopher (1991), 'Latin American banditry as peasant resistance: a dead-end trail?', *Latin American Research Review*, Vol. 26.

Black, Jan Knippers (1986), *The Dominican Republic: Politics and Development in an Unsovereign State*. Boston, MA.

Black, Max (1962), *Models and Metaphors*. Ithaca, NY.

Blanco, Leoncio (1930), Archivo del Palacio Nacional. Colección Leoncio Blanco, Las Matas de Farfán, 19 October. 'A Rafael L. Trujillo', in Bernardo Vega (ed.), *Los Estados Unidos y Trujillo 1930*. Santo Domingo, 1986.

Blanco Fombona, Horacio (1927), *Crímenes del imperialismo norteamericano*. México D.F.

Blassingame, John W. (1969), 'The press and American intervention in Haiti and the Dominican Republic', *Caribbean Studies*, Vol. 9.

Bloch, Marc (1953), *The Historian's Craft*. New York, NY.

Bobea Bellini, Mario (1963), '¿Fué Trujillo devoto del "Dios" Liborio?', *¡Ahora!*, No. 25, January.

Bodden, Julio C. (1962), 'Dan sepultura a 42 muertos en incidente', *El Caribe*, 30 December.

—— (1963), 'Gobierno encara solución de problema de hombres detenidos en Palma Sola. Funcionarios celebran reunión', *El Caribe*, 3 January.

Boin, Jacqueline and Serulle Ramia, José (1979), *El proceso de desarollo del capitalismo en la República Dominicana (1844–1930) Tomo primero: El proceso de transformación de la economía dominicana (1844 a 1875)*. Santo Domingo.

—— (1981), *El proceso de desarrollo del capitalismo en la República Dominicana (1844–1930). Tomo segundo: El desarrollo del capitalismo en la agricultura (1875–1930)*. Santo Domingo.

Bonnetti Burgos, Máximo (1938), Archivo Particular del Generalísimo. Palacio Nacional: 16 de Febrero. Núm. 03173. Del Subsecretario de Estado de la Presidencia al Señor Secretario de Estado de lo Interior y Policía. Asunto: Supresión de prácticas *liboristas*.

Bonó, Pedro F. (1980), 'Una súplica', in *Papeles de Pedro F. Bonó para la historia de las ideas políticas en Santo Domingo*. Second edition. Barcelona.

Booth, Wayne C. (1974), *Modern Dogma and the Rhetoric of Asssent*. Chicago, IL.

—— (1988), *The Company We Keep: An Ethics of Fiction*. Berkeley and Los Angeles, CA.

Bosch, Juan (1964), *Crisis de la democracia de América en la República Dominicana*. México, D.F.

—— (1984), *Composición social dominicana: Historia e interpretación*. Fourteenth edition. Santo Domingo.

Bossy, John (1970), 'The counter reformation and the people of Catholic Europe', *Past and Present*, No. 47, May.

—— (1985), *Christianity in the West, 1400–1700*. Oxford and New York, NY.

Braudel, Fernand (1980), *On History*. Chicago, IL.

Breault, Marc and King, Martin (1993), *Inside the Cult: A Member's Chilling Account of Madness and Depravity in David Koresh's Compound*. New York, NY.

Breckenridge, James C. (1920), National Archives, Washington DC: RG 38 (Chief of Naval Operations) Military Government of Santo Domingo, 1917–1924. General Correspondence, 1921. Miscellaneous: Copies of Reports and Documents for the Files of Headquarters, U.S. Marine Corps. Box No. 40. Santo Domingo City, 17 December. From: Guardia Intelligence Officer. To: The Brigade Intelligence Officer. Subject: Intelligence Information.

Bretón, Freddy and González Abercio (n.d.), 'El mito del Bacá en Valle de Neiba', *CEPAE Boletín*, No. 7.

Bronner, Simon J. (1986), *American Folklore Studies: An Intellectual History*. Lawrence, KS.

Brown, Jonathan (1837), *The History and Present Condition of St. Domingo. Volume II*. Philadelphia, PA.

Brown, Karen McCarthy (1991), *Mama Lola: A Vodou Priestess in Brooklyn*. Berkeley and Los Angeles, CA.

Brown, Wenzell (1947), *Angry Men – Laughing Men: The Caribbean Cauldron*. New York, NY.

Brutus, Edner (1969), *Révolution dans Saint-Domingue*. 2 vols. Bruxelles.

Bryan, Patrick E. (1979), 'La cuestión obrera en la industria azucarera de la República Dominicana a finales del siglo XIX y principios del XX', *Revista Eme Eme*, Vol. 7.

Bull, George (1982), *Inside the Vatican*. London.

Burke, William P. (1935), *Señor Burky: The Adventurous Life-story of William P. Burke*. New York, NY.

Burridge, Kenelm (1969), *New Heaven, New Earth: A Study of Millenarian Activities*. New York, NY.

Cabral, B. (1910), Archivo General de la Nación. Secretaría de Estado de Interior y Policía, Legajo No. 317. Azua, 29 de julio. De B. Cabral al Romá, Secretario de Interior.

Cabral, Manuel del (1943), *Compadre Mon*. Ciudad Trujillo.

Calder, Bruce J. (1984), *The Impact of Intervention: The Dominican Republic during the U.S. Occupation of 1916–1924*. Austin, TX.

Calderón, Telésforo R. (1948), Archivo Particular del Generalísimo. Palacio Nacional: 4 de julio. Num. 20294. Del Secretario de Estado de la Presidencia al Secretario de Estado de lo Interior y Policía.

Campillo Pérez, Julio G. (1986), *Historia electoral dominicana, 1848–1986*. Santo Domingo.

Candler, John (1842), *Brief Notice of Hayti with Its Conditions, Resources and Prospects*. London.

Cano y Fortuna, César Augusto (n.d.), *Las Matas de Farfán: Pasado y presente*. Santo Domingo.

Cárdenas, César (1988), 'La matanza de Palma Sola: ¿un crimen político?' *Vanguardia del Pueblo (Organo del Partido de la Liberación Dominicana)*, Vol. 15, No. 689, 28 December.

Cárdenas Fontecha, Florángel (1964), 'Masacre en Palma Sola: Brutal exterminio de una secta religiosa', *Bohemia Libre*, 7 June.

Caro, Nestor (1963), 'A propósito de Palma Sola: 'Brujería y curanderismo en amalgama intranscendente', *¡Ahora!*, No. 26, February.

Caro Baroja, Julio (1965), *El carnaval*. Madrid.

—— (1974), *Ritos y mitos equívocos*. Madrid.

Cassá, Roberto (1974), *Los taínos de La Española*. Santo Domingo.

—— (1976), 'El racismo en la ideología de la clase dominante dominicana', *Ciencia*, Vol. 3.

—— (1982), *Capitalismo y dictadura*. Santo Domingo.

—— (1983), *Historia social y económica de la República Dominicana, Tomo 2*. Santo Domingo.

—— (1985), *Historia social y económica de la República dominicana, Tomo 1*. Santo Domingo.

—— (1986), *Los doce años: Contrarevolución y desarollismo, Tomo I*. Santo Domingo.

—— (1993a), '1 – Persecución y muerte de Oliborio Mateo', *Isla Abierta, Suplemento de Hoy*, 9 October.

—— (1993b), '2 – Persecución y muerte de Oliborio Mateo', *Isla Abierta, Suplemento de Hoy*, 16 October.

—— (1994a), 'Olivorio se insurrecciona'. Unpublished article.

—— (1994b), 'Por las rutas de Popa', *Isla Abierta, Suplemento de Hoy*, 31 March.

—— (1994c), 'Orígenes remotos del gavillerismo', *Isla Abierta, Suplemento de Hoy*, 7 October.

—— (1994d), 'Antecedentes inmediatos del gavillerismo en el este', *Isla Abierta, Suplemento de Hoy*, 4 November.

—— (1994e), 'Gavillerismo, delito común y sector azucarero en el este', *Isla Abierta, Suplemento de Hoy*, 2 December.

Castillo, José del (1981), Ensayos de sociología dominicana. Santo Domingo.

Castillo, José del and Cordero, Walter (1982), 'La economía dominicana durante el primer cuarto del Siglo XX', in Tirso Mejía-Ricart (ed.), *La sociedad dominicana durante la segunda república 1865–1924*. Santo Domingo.

Castillo de Aza, Zenón (1960), 'Trujillo, Benefactor de la Iglesia Católica en la República', *El Caribe*, 14 March.

—— (1961), *Trujillo y otros benefactores de la iglesia*. Ciudad Trujillo.

Castor, Suzy (1971), *La ocupación norteamericana de Haití y sus consecuencias*. México, D.F.

—— (1987), *Migración y relaciones internacionales (El caso haitiano-dominicano)*. Santo Domingo.

Catlin, A. W. (1919), National Archives, Washington, DC: RG 38 (Chief of Naval Operations) Military Government of Santo Domingo, 1917–1924. General Correspondence, 1919. Box No. 16. April 24. From Brigade Commander. To: The Military Governor of Santo Domingo and the Military Representative of the United States in Haiti, Santo Domingo City, D.R. Subject: Authority to Cross Border.

Cela, Camilo José (1969), *Diccionario secreto, 1. Series coleo y afines*. Barcelona.

Celada, Gregorio (1993), 'La inculturación del evangelio en los primeros siglos', in Jesús Espeja (ed.), *Inculturación y teología indígena*. Salamanca.

Chadwick, Owen (1982), *The Reformation*. Harmondsworth.

Chandler, Billy Jaynes (1987), 'Brazilian cangaceiros as social bandits: a critical appraisal', in Richard W. Slatta (ed.), *Bandidos: The Varieties of Latin American Banditry*. Westport, CT.

Chang, Jung (1991), *Wild Swans: Three Daughters of China*. New York, NY.

Charlevoix, Pedro Francisco Javier (Pierre-François-Xavier) (1977), *Historia de la Isla Española o de Santo Domingo. Escrita particularmente sobre las memorias del Padre Juan Bautista Le Pers, jesuita, misionero en Santo Domingo y sobre los documentos originales que se conservan en el Depósito de la Marina, Tomo II*. Santo Domingo.

Chaunu, Huguette and Chaunu, Pierre (1955), *Séville et l'Atlantique (1504–1605) Première partie: partie statistique: Tome premier, Introduction méthodologique*. Paris.

—— (1956), *Séville et l'Atlantique (1504–1605) Première partie: partie statistique. Le mouvement des navires et de marchandises entre l'Espagne et l'Amérique de 1504 à 1560. Tome VI2, Tables statistiques (1504–1560)*. Paris.

Chief of Staff (1917), National Archives, Washington, DC; Naval Records. Collection of the Office of Naval Records and Library. Subject file 1911–1927. WA-7, Allied Countries, Santo Domingo. Daily Records. Box No. 758. H. M. 1988. Folder #11. Headquarters Second Provisional Brigade. U.S. Marine Corps. April 2. From: Chief of Staff (In absence of Brigadier General Pendleton) To: Head of Military Government. Subject: Estimate of Military Situation in Santo Domingo in Compliance with Direction of Head of Military Government.

Christian, William, A., Jr (1972), *Person and God in a Spanish Valley*. New York, NY and London.

—— (1981), *Local Religion in Sixteenth Century Spain*. Princeton, NJ.

—— (1987), 'Folk religion. An overview', in Mircea Eliade (ed.), *The Encyclopedia of Religion, Vol. 5.* New York, NY and London.

Clausner, Marlin David (1973), *Rural Santo Domingo. Settled, Unsettled and Resettled.* Philadelphia, PA.

Cocco, Salvador A. (1940), *Memoría que de sus actividades desarolladas durante el año 1939 rinde al hon. sr. Secretario de Estado de lo Interior y Polícia la Gobernación Provincial de Benefactor in Memoria que al honorable presidente de la república Dr. M. J. Troncoso de la Concha presenta el Mayor General José García, M.M. Secretario de Estado de lo Interior y Polícia relativa a las labores realizados en el departamento a su cargo durante el año de 1939.* Ciudad Trujillo.

Codrington, R.H. (1915), 'Melanesians', in *Encyclopedia of Religion and Ethics.* Edinburgh.

Cohn, Norman (1962), 'Medieval millenarianism: its bearing on the comparative study of millenarian movements', in Sylvia Thrupp (ed.), *Millenial Dreams in Action.* The Hague.

—— (1970), *The Pursuit of the Millennium: Revolutionary Millenarians and Mystical Anarchists of the Middle Ages,* revised and enlarged edition. New York, NY.

—— (1975), *Europe's Inner Demons: An Enquiry Inspired by the Great Witch-Hunt.* Bungay, Suffolk.

Colombino Perelló, Héctor (1972), *Baní en los años 20-30.* Santo Domingo.

Colón, Cristóbal (1988), *Diario de navegación y otros escritos.* Santo Domingo.

Commons, John Roger (1907), *Races and Immigrants in America.* New York, NY.

Conde Pausas, Alfredo (1983), *Liborio y 'El Caudillo de las Cinco Estrellas'.* Santo Domingo.

Cooke, Wythe (1983), 'Geografía', in T. W. Vaughan (ed.), *Un reconocimiento geológico de la República Dominicana.* Santo Domingo.

Cooper, Page (1947), *Sambumbia: A Discovery of the Dominican Republic, the Modern Hispaniola.* New York, NY.

Cordero Michel, José R. (1970), *Informe sobre la República Dominicana 1959.* Santo Domingo.

Cordero Regalado, R. A. (1981), 'Por San Juan de la Maguana sigue el culto al "Dios Liborio Mateo"', *¡Ahora!,* 5 April.

Corneille, Carlos (1980), *Proceso histórico dominico-haitiano: Una advertencia a la juventud dominicana.* Santo Domingo.

Courlander, Harold (1960), *The Drum and the Hoe: Life and Lore of the Haitian People.* Berkeley, CA.

—— (1966), 'Vodoun in Haitian culture', in Harold Courlander and Rémy Bastien, *Religion and Politics in Haiti.* Washington, DC.

Crapanzano, Vincent (1985), *Tuhami: Portrait of a Moroccan.* Chicago, IL and London.

Crassweller, Robert D. (1966), *Trujillo: The Life and Times of a Caribbean Dictator.* New York, NY.

Cross Beras, Julio A. (1984), *Sociedad y desarollo en República Dominicana, 1844–1899.* Santo Domingo.

Crouch, L. A. (ed.) (1979), 'Desarollo del capitalismo en el campo dominicano. Política agraria, pobreza rural y crecimiento agrícola (versión preliminar)'. *Mimeo,* Santiago de los Caballeros.

Crouse, Nellis M. (1940), *French Pioneers in the West Indies 1624–1664.* New York, NY.

—— (1943), *The French Struggle for the West Indies 1665–1713.* New York, NY.

Crummey, Donald (ed.) (1986), *Banditry, Rebellion and Social Protest in Africa.* London and Portsmouth, NH.

Cruz Brache, José Antonio (1975), 'Juego infantil: "La Magüita"', *Revista Dominicana de Folklore,* No. 1.

Cruz Díaz, M. R. (1965), *Supersticiones criminológicas y médicas: Apuntes folklóricos.* Santo Domingo.

Cuello, José Israel H. (ed.) (1985), *Documentos del conflicto dominico-haitiano de 1937.* Santo Domingo.

Cunha, Euclides da (1944), *Rebellion in the Backlands (Os Sertões).* Chicago, IL.

Dalton, George (1972), 'Peasantries in anthropology and history', *Current Anthropology,* Vol. 13.

Davidson, Basil (1980), *Black Mother: Africa and the Atlantic Slave Trade.* Harmondsworth.

Davis, Martha Ellen (1981), *Voces del purgatorio: Estudio de la salve dominicana.* Santo Domingo.

—— (1987), *La otra ciencia: El vodú dominicano como religión y medicina populares.* Santo Domingo.

Davis, Ralph (1973), *The Rise of the Atlantic Economies.* Ithaca, NY.

Deive, Carlos Esteban (1978), *El indio, el negro y la vida tradicional dominicana.* Santo Domingo.

—— (1979), *Vodú y magia en Santo Domingo.* Santo Domingo.

—— (1980), *La esclavitud del negro en Santo Domingo (1492–1844), tomos I–II.* Santo Domingo.

—— (1988), 'Fukú: Del negro boruco a Evtushenko', in Evgueni Evtushenko, *Fukú.* Santo Domingo.

—— (1989), *Las emigraciones dominicanas a Cuba (1795–1808).* Santo Domingo.

—— (1991), *Las emigraciones canarias a Santo Domingo (siglos XVII y XVIII).* Santo Domingo.

Derby, Lauren (1994), 'Haitians, magic, and money: *Raza* and society in the Haitian-Dominican borderlands, 1900 to 1937', *Comparative Studies in Society and History,* Vol. 36.

Deren, Maya (1953), *Divine Horsemen: The Living Gods of Haiti.* London and New York, NY.

Deschamps, Enrique (1908), *La República Dominicana: Directorio y guía general.* Santiago de los Caballeros.

Desmangles, Leslie G. (1992), *The Faces of the Gods: Vodou and Roman Catholicism in Haiti.* Chapel Hill, NC and London.

Díaz, J. (1909), Archivo General de la Nación. Secretaría de Estado de Interior y Policía, Legajo No. 273. Azua, 24 de septiembre. De J. Díaz, Gobernador de Azua, al Secretario de Interior.

—— (1910a), Archivo General de la Nación. Secretaría de Estado de Interior y Policía, Legajo No. 317. Azua, 22 de julio. De J. Díaz, Gobernador de Azua, al Secretario de Interior.

—— (1910b), Archivo General de la Nación. Secretaría de Estado de Interior y Policía, Legajo No. 317. Azua, 16 de julio. De J. Díaz, Gobernador de Azua, al Secretario de Interior.

—— (1910c), Archivo General de la Nación. Secretaría de Estado de Interior y Policía, Legajo No. 317. Azua, 23 de julio. De J. Díaz, Gobernador de Azua, al Secretario de Interior.

—— (1910d), Archivo General de la Nación. Secretaría de Estado de Interior y Policía, Legajo No. 317. Azua, 29 de julio. De J. Díaz, Gobernador de Azua, al Secretario de Interior.

Diccionario enciclopédico dominicano, Volumen I (1988). Santo Domingo.

Diederich, Bernard (1978), *Trujillo: The Death of the Goat*. London.

Diederich, Bernard and Burt, Al (1972), *Papa Doc: Haiti and Its Dictator*. Harmondsworth.

Dietrich, Albert (ed.) (1975), *Synkretismus im syrisch-persischen Kulturgebiet*. Göttingen.

Directorio (1928), Santo Domingo.

Disraeli, Benjamin (1981), *Sybil, or the Two Nations*. Harmondsworth.

Domínguez, Iván, Castillo, José and Tejeda Ortiz, Dagoberto (1978), *Almanaque folklórico dominicano*. Santo Domingo.

Domínguez, Jaime de Jesús (1979), *La anexión de Santo Domingo a España, 1861–1863*. Santo Domingo.

—— (1986), *La dictadura de Heureaux*. Santo Domingo.

—— (1994), *La sociedad dominicana a principios del siglo XX*. Santo Domingo.

Ducoudray h., Félix Servio (1976), *Los 'gavilleros' del este: Una epopeya calumniada*. Santo Domingo.

—— (1980), 'Los mercados de la frontera', *¡Ahora!*, No. 851, 17 March.

Dundes, Alan (1980), *Interpreting Folklore*. Bloomington, IN.

Dunstheimer, Guillaume H. (1982), 'Religión oficial, religión popular y sociedades secretas en la China posterior a los Han', in Henri-Charles Puech (ed.), *Historia de las religiones, siglo XXI. Volumen 10: Las religiones constituidas en Asia y sus contracorrientes, II*. México, D.F.

Durkheim, Emile (1993), *Suicide: A Study in Sociology*. London.

Edwards, Bryan (1797), *An Historical Survey of the French Colony in the Island of St. Domingo*. London.

Eisenhower, Dwight D. (1965), *The White House Years, a Personal Account, 1956–1961: Waging Peace*. New York, NY.

Ekman, Erik L. (1970), 'En busca del Monte Tina', in Emilio Rodríguez Demorizi (ed.), *Relaciones geográficas de Santo Domingo, Vol. 1*. Santo Domingo.

Eliade, Mircea (1976), *Patterns in Comparative Religion*. London.

Elliott, John H. (1970), *Imperial Spain 1469–1716*. Harmondsworth.

—— (1989), *Spain and Its World 1500–1700*. New Haven, CT and London.

Epstein, Isidore (1964), *Judaism: A Historical Presentation*. Harmondsworth.

Espeja, Jesús (1993), 'Introducción', in Jesús Espeja (ed.), *Inculturación y teología indígena*. Salamanca.

Espín del Prado, Orlando (1980), 'Hacia una "teología" de Palma Sola', *Estudios Sociales*, Vol. 13.

—— (1984), 'Evangelización y religiones negras: Propuesta de modelo de evangelización para el pastoral en la República Dominicana', PhD thesis. Pontifícia Universidade Católica de Rio de Janeiro.

Espinosa, Aurelio M. (1950), 'Spanish folklore', in Maria Leach (ed.), *Funk and Wagnall's Standard Dictionary of Folklore, Mythology and Legend, Vol. 2*. New York, NY.

Estrella Pimentel, Vicente (1962), 'Espectáculo que vive en lomas Palma Sola parece increíble', *La Nación*, 6 December.

Estrella Veloz, Santiago (1962a), 'Liboristas eran partidarios de Trujillo', *La Nación*, 31 December.

—— (1962b), 'Es necesario hacer campaña educativa en zona afectada: Procurador habla sobre Palma Sola', *La Nación*, 30 December.

—— (1963), 'Palma Sola: Víctima de la ignorancia', *La Nación*, 4 January.

Eusebio Pol, Noris (1980), 'Las asociaciones campesinas dominicanas y el caso de San Juan de la Maguana', MA thesis. Universidad Nacional Pedro Henríquez Ureña, Santo Domingo.

Eutasio L. (1962), 'Palma Sola ... Mellizos ... Liborio', *Santomé*, 30 November.

Exquemelin, Alexander O. (1969), *The Buccaneers of America*. Harmondsworth.

Fabian, Johannes (1983), *Time and the Other: How Anthropology Makes Its Object*. New York, NY.

Falconi, Carlo (1970), *The Silence of Pius XII*. London.

Feeley, Joseph W. (1919), Archivo General de la Nación: Gobierno Militar Interior/Policia Legajo No. 379. Azua, R.D. 20 January 1919. From the Inspector to the Director, Department of the South, G.N.D.

Ferguson, James (1992), *The Dominican Republic: Beyond the Lighthouse*. London.

Fernández-Armesto, Felipe (1988), *The Spanish Armada: The Experience of War in 1588*. Oxford.

Ferreras, Ramón Alberto (1983), *Negros. Media Isla (IV)*. Santo Domingo.

Figueres Ferrer, José (1987), *El espíritu del 48*. San José.

Fletcher, Richard A. (1989), *The Quest for El Cid*. London.

Fontaine, Jean S. (1985), *Initiation: Ritual Drama and Secret Knowledge across the World*. Harmondsworth.

Foster, George M. (1948), *Empire's Children: The People of Tzintzuntzán*. Washington, DC.

—— (1953a), '*Cofradía* and *Compadrazgo* in Spain and Spanish America', *Southwestern Journal of Anthropology*, Vol. 9.

—— (1953b), 'What is folklore?', *American Anthropologist*, Vol. 55.

—— (1960), *Culture and Conquest: America's Spanish Heritage*. New York, NY.

Fourcand, Jean M. (1964), *Catéchisme de la révolution*. Port-au-Prince.

Franck, Harry A. (1921), *Roaming through the West Indies*. New York, NY.

Franco, Franklin J. (1980), *Trujillismo: Génesis y rehabilitación*. Santo Domingo.

—— (1981), *Historia de las ideas políticas en la República Dominicana (contribución a su estudio) 1*. Santo Domingo.

Franco Pichardo, Franklin (1993), *Historia del pueblo dominicano*. Second edition. Santo Domingo.

Franjul, Miguel A. (1972), 'Combate dura 15 horas', *Listín Diario*, 13 January.

Franklin, James (1828), *The Present State of Hayti (Saint Domingo), with Remarks on Its Agriculture, Commerce, Laws, Religion, Finances and Population, etc. etc.* London.

Frazer, James G. (1919), *Folk-lore in the Old Testament: Studies in Comparative Religion, Legend and Law*. Vols. 1–3. New York, NY.

Freud, Sigmund (1938), *The Basic Writings of Sigmund Freud*. New York, NY.

Fromm, Erich (1951), *The Forgotten Language*. New York, NY.

La frontera de la República Dominicana con Haití (no author given) (1946). Ciudad Trujillo.

—— (no author given) (1958). Ciudad Trujillo.

Frye, Northrop (1982), *The Great Code: The Bible and Literature*. San Diego, CA.

Fuente, Santiago de la (1976), *Geografía dominicana*. Santo Domingo.

Fuller, Stephen M. and Cosmas, Graham A. (1974), *Marines in the Dominican Republic 1916–1924*. Washington, DC.

Funck-Brentano, Frantz (1979), *L'Île de la Tortue*. Paris.

Gaillard, Roger (1973), *Les blancs débarquent. Tome II. 1914–1915. Les cent-jours de Rosalvo Bobo ou un mise à mort politique*. Port-au-Prince.

—— (1981a), *Les blancs débarquent. Tome III. 1915–1916. Premier écrasement du cacoïsme*. Port-au-Prince.

—— (1981b), *Les blancs débarquent. Tome IV. 1916–1917. La république autoritaire*. Port-au-Prince.

—— (1982a), *Les blancs débarquent. Tome V. 1917–1918. Hinche mise en croix*. Port-au-Prince.

—— (1982b), *Les blancs débarquent. Tome VI. 1918–1919. Charlemagne Péralte le caco*. Port-au-Prince.

—— (1983), *Les blancs débarquent. Tome VII. 1919–1934. La guérilla de Batraville*. Port-au-Prince.

—— (1984), *Les blancs débarquent. Tome I. 1890–1896. La république exterminatrice. Première partie. Une modernisation manquée*. Port-au-Prince.

—— (1988), *La République exterminatrice. Deuxième partie. L'état vassal (1896–1902)*. Port-au-Prince.

—— (1992), *La république exterminatrice. Troisième partie: La déroute de l'intelligence (mai–juillet 1902)*. Port-au-Prince.

—— (1993), *La république exterminatrice. Quatrième partie: La guerre civile, une option dramatique (15 juillet–31 décembre 1902)*. Port-au-Prince.

—— (1995), *La république exterminatrice. Cinquième partie: Le grand fauve (1902–1908)*. Port-au-Prince.

Galíndez, Jesús de (1962), *La era de Trujillo*. Buenos Aires.

Gallego, Felipe P. (1943), 'Origen y principios de la misión fronteriza de Dajabón', in José Luis Sáez (1988), *Los Jesuitas en la República Dominicana. Volumen 1: Los primeros veinticinco años (1936–1961)*. Santo Domingo.

Galván, Manuel de Jésus (1981), *Enriquillo*. Santo Domingo.

Gándara, José de la (1975), *Anexión y guerra de Santo Domingo. Tomo I*. Santo Domingo.

García, José Gabriel (1982), *Compendio de la historia de Santo Domingo, Tomo II*. Fifth edition. Santo Domingo.

García, Juan Manuel (1983), *La matanza de los haitianos: Genocidio de Trujillo, 1937*. Santo Domingo.

—— (1986), *La masacre de Palma Sola (Partidos, lucha política y el asesinato del general: 1961–1963)*. Santo Domingo.

García, Láutico (1962), '¿Juan Bosch: Marxista-Leninista?' *La Nación*, 12 December.

—— (1972), *La Iglesia dominicana entre dos dictaduras*. Santo Domingo.

Gardiner, C. Harvey (1979), *La política de inmigración del dictador Trujillo: Estudio sobre la creación de una imagen humanitaria*. Santo Domingo.

Garrido, Víctor (1922), 'Común de San Juan; datos acerca de la situacion histórica, religión, fiestas, costumbres, industriales, lenguaje, etc.', in Emilio Rodríguez Demorizi (ed.), *Lengua y folklore de Santo Domingo*. Santiago de los Caballeros, 1975.

—— (1970), *En la ruta de mi vida, 1886–1966*. Santo Domingo.

—— (1972), *Espigas históricas*. Santo Domingo.

—— (1974), *Los Puello*. Santo Domingo.

Garrido de Boggs, Edna (1955), *Folklore infantil de Santo Domingo*. Madrid.

—— (1961), 'Panorama del folklore dominicano', *Folklore Americas*, Vol. 21.

Garrido Puello, Emigdio O. (1963), *Olivorio: un ensayo histórico*. Santo Domingo.

—— (1972), *Espejo del pasado*. Santo Domingo.

—— (1973), *Historia de un periódico*. Santo Domingo.

—— (1977), *En el camino de la historia, 1911–1967*. Santo Domingo.

—— (1981), *El Sur en la historia, las ciencias y la literatura*. Santo Domingo.

—— (n.d.), *Reflejos de ayer*. Santo Domingo.

Geggus, David (1987), *Slavery, War and Revolution: The British Occupation of Saint Domingue 1793–1798*. Oxford.

George, Carol V. R. (1993), *God's Salesman: Norman Vincent Peale and the Power of Positive Thinking*. New York, NY and Oxford.

Germán Ornes, a Self Portrait (no author given) (1958). Ciudad Trujillo.

Gibson, Reuben A. and Crocker, Thomas C. (1903), 'Anerkendelsesag, 16 Januar, 1903. No. 272, V. J. 1903', in Koloniernes Centralbestyrelse. Gruppordnede sager. Kirke og skole: Trossamfund udenfor folkekirken 1856–1917, F. 928. Rigsarkivet. København.

Gil-Bermejo García, Juana (1983), *La Española: Anotaciones históricas (1600–1650)*. Sevilla.

Glazier, Stephen D. (1983), 'Caribbean pilgrimages: a typology', *Journal for the Scientific Study of Religion*, Vol. 22.

Godelier, Maurice (1975), *Bas och överbyggnad: Studier i marxistisk antropologi*. Stockholm.

Goff, Fred and Locker, Michael (1969), 'The Violence of Domination: U.S. Power and the Dominican Republic', in Irving Louis Horowitz, Josué De Castro and John Gerassi (eds) (1969), *Latin American Radicalism: A Documentary Report on Left and Nationalist Movements*. New York, NY.

Gómez Pepín, Radhamés V. (1962a), 'La superchería afecta economía de región sur', *El Caribe*, 19 November.

—— (1962b), 'Comarca sureña afronta lastre de supersticiones', *El Caribe*, 20 November.

—— (1962c), 'Tratarán de terminar superchería en Palma Sola', *El Caribe*, 11 December.

—— (1962d), 'Terminará "Misión" en Palma Sola. Arrojan luz sobre caso', *El Caribe*, 13 December.

—— (1962e), 'Acusan jefe de culto de Palma Sola', *El Caribe*, 14 December.

—— (1962f) 'Desolación reina en Palma Sola; Informan 4 "Mellizos" murieron. Dos liboristas ofrecen versión de los sucesos', *El Caribe*, 30 December.

González, Antonio Camilo (1983), 'El Padre Esteban Rojas asediado por los coludos en Baní', *Revista Eme Eme*, Vol. 11.

González, Nancie L. (1984), 'Desiderio Arias: Caudillo y héroe cultural', in Ramón Alberto Ferreras (ed.), *Enfoques: De la intervención militar norteamericana a la R.D. (1916–1924)*. Santo Domingo.

González-Blanco, Pedro (1953), *Trujillo: The Rebirth of a Nation*. Ciudad Trujillo.

González Canahuate, Almanzor (ed.) (1992), *El juicio del siglo: Proceso Jorge Blanco-Cuervo Gómez*. Santo Domingo.

González Canalda, Filomena (1985a), 'Desiderio Arias y el caudillismo', *Estudios Sociales*, Vol. 17.

—— (1985b), *Línea Noroeste: Testimonio del patriotismo olvidado*. San Pedro de Macorís.

González-Wippler, Migene (1992), *Santería: African Magic in Latin America*. New York, NY.

Gray, Richard (1987), 'The papacy and the Atlantic slave trade: Lourenío Da Silva, the Capuchins and the decisions of the holy office', *Past and Present*, No. 115, May.

Grimaldi, Víctor (1985), *El diario secreto de la intervención norteamericana de 1965, basado en los archivos personales del presidente Johnson*. Santo Domingo.

Grullón, José Diego (1989), *Cayo Confites: La revolución traicionada*. Santo Domingo.

Gruzinski, Serge (1989), *Man-Gods in the Mexican Highlands: Indian Power and Colonial Society, 1520–1800*. Stanford, CA.

Guerrero, Miguel (1988), *Enero de 1962: ¡El despertar dominicano!* Santo Domingo.

—— (1991), *Los últimos días de la Era de Trujillo*. Santo Domingo.

Guerrero Cano, María Magdalenea (1986), *Santo Domingo (1795–1865)*. Cádiz.

Gunkel, Hermann (1901), *Genesis*. Göttingen.

—— (1906), *Die israelitische Literatur*. Berlin.

Gustafson, Jan (1981), *Åsumspågen: En folklig sjukdomsbotare under senare delen av 1800-talet*. Stockholm.

Gutiérrez Escudero, Antonio (1985), *Población y economía en Santo Domingo (1700–1746)*. Sevilla.

Hägerstrand, Torsten (1974), 'Tidsgeografisk beskrivning; syfte och postulat', *Svensk geografisk årsbok*, Vol. 50.

Haitian Creole-English-French Dictionary (1981). Bloomington, IN.

Hall, John R. (1990), 'The apocalypse at Jonestown (with afterword)', in Thomas Robbins and Dick Anthony (eds), *In Gods We Trust: New Patterns of Religious Pluralism in America*. Second edition, revised and expanded. New Brunswick, NJ and London.

Hallgren, Roland (1988), *The Good Things in Life: A Study of the Traditional Religious Culture of the Yoruba People*. Löberöd.

—— (1995), *The Vital Force: A Study of Àse in the Traditional and Neo-traditional Culture of the Yoruba People*. Stockholm.

Harris, J. Rendel (1906), *The Cult of the Heavenly Twins*. Cambridge.

Harris, Marvin (1975), *Culture, People, Nature: An Introduction to General Anthropolgy*. New York, NY.

—— (1980), *Cultural Materialism: The Struggle for a Science of Culture*. New York, NY.

Harrison, J. F. C. (1979), *The Second Coming: Popular Millenarianism, 1780–1850*. Ashford, Kent.

Harriss, John (1982), *Capitalism and Peasant Farming: Agrarian Structure and Ideology in Northern Tamil Nadu*. Bombay.

Hartman, Sven (ed.) (1969), *Syncretism*. Stockholm.

Hazard, Samuel (1873), *Santo Domingo. Past and Present: With a Glance at Haiti*. New York, NY.

Hebblethwaite, Peter (1987), *In the Vatican*. Oxford.

Heckscher, Eli F. (1944), 'Materialistisk och annan historieuppfattning', in *Historieuppfattning: materialistisk och annan*. Stockholm.

Hedlund, Stefan; Lundahl, Mats and Lyttkens, Carl-Hampus (1989), 'The attraction of extraction: three cases of state versus peasantry', *Scandia*, Vol. 55.

Heer, Friedrich (1974), *The Medieval World: Europe from 1100 to 1350*. London.

Heinl, Robert Debs, Jr and Heinl, Nancy Gordon (1978), *Written in Blood: The Story of the Haitian People 1492–1971*. Boston, MA.

Henríquez Ureña, Pedro (1978), *El español en Santo Domingo*. Santo Domingo.

Heredia y Mieses, D. José Fransisco (1955), 'Informe presentado al Muy Ilustrísimo Ayuntamiento de Santo Domingo, capital de la Isla Española, en 1812, por D. José Fransisco Heredia y Mieses', in Emilio Rodríguez Demorizi (ed.), *Invasiones haitianas de 1801, 1805 y 1822*. Ciudad Trujillo.

Hermann, Hamlet (1983), *Francis Caamaño*. Santo Domingo.

Herskovits, Melville J. and Herskovits, Frances S. (1933), 'An outline of Dahomean religious belief', *Memoirs of the American Anthropological Association*, No. 41.

Hicks, Albert C. (1946), *Blood in the Streets: The Life and Rule of Trujillo*. New York, NY.

Higham, John (1981), *Strangers in the Land: Patterns of American Nativism 1860–1925*. New York, NY.

Hilgers, Joseph (1912), 'Scapular', in *The Catholic Encyclopedia*, Vol. 13. New York, NY.

Hill, Cristopher (1987), *The World Turned Upside Down: Radical Ideas During the English Revolution*. Harmondsworth.

Hill, W. W. (1944), 'The Navaho Indians and the Ghost Dance of 1890', *American Anthropologist*, Vol. 46, reprinted in William A. Lessa and Evon Z. Vogt (eds) (1979), *Reader in Comparative Religion: An Anthropological Approach*. New York, NY.

Hirschman, Albert O. (1970), *Exit, Voice and Loyalty: Responses to Decline in Firms, Organizations, and States*. Cambridge, MA and London.

—— (1981), *Essays in Trespassing: Economics to Politics and Beyond*. Cambridge, MA and London.

Hobsbawm, Eric (1959), *Primitive Rebels: Studies in Archaic Forms of Social Movement in the 19th and 20th Centuries*. Manchester.

—— (1972), *Bandits*. Harmondsworth.

Hoepelman, Antonio (1909), 'El Brujo de San Juan', *La Voz del Sur*, 19 June.

—— (1910) 'Cometa Halley', *La Voz del Sur*, 29 January and 21 May.

Hoetink, Harmannus (1982), *The Dominican People, 1850–1900: Notes for a Historical Sociology*. Baltimore, MD and London.

Hoffman, Edward (1991), *Despite all Odds: The Story of Lubavitch*. New York, NY.

The Holy Bible: King James Version (1991), Ballantyne Books Edition. New York, NY and Toronto.

Honko, Lauri (1981), 'Traditionsekologi – en introduktion', in Lauri Honko and Orvar Löfgren (eds), *Tradition och miljö: Ett kulturekologiskt perspektiv*. Lund.

Hørlyk [No first name given] (1903), 'Fredriksteds Politikammer. St. Croix den 7 Februar 1903. Fortroligt. Ad. No. 272, V. J. 1903', in Koloniernes Central-bestyrelse. Gruppeornede sager. Kirke og skole: Trossamfund udenfor folke-kirken 1856–1917, F. 928. Rigsarkivet, København.

Horton, Robin (1971), 'African conversion', *Africa*, Vol. 41.

House Annals (1959–1962) Parroquia Santa Lucia. Las Matas de Farfán. Book #2. October 1959 – continued – 31 December 1962.

—— (1963) Parroquia Santa Lucia. Las Matas de Farfán. Book #3. January 1963 –.

Hue Tam, Ho Tai (1983), *Millenarianism and Peasant Politics in Vietnam*. Cambridge, MA.

Huizer, Gerrit (1973), *Peasant Rebellion in Latin America*. Harmondsworth.

Hultcrantz, Åke (1960), *General Ethnological Concepts. Vol. 1*. Copenhagen.

Hurbon, Laënnec (1986), 'New religious movements in the Caribbean', in James

A. Beckford (ed.), *New Religious Movements and Rapid Social Change*. London and Paris.

—— (1995), *Voodoo: Search for the Spirit*. New York, NY.

Incháustegui, J. Marino (1955), *Historia dominicana. Tomo I*. Ciudad Trujillo.

Informe de la comisión de investigación de los E.U.A. en Santo Domingo en 1871 (1960). Ciudad Trujillo.

Inoa, Orlando (1991), 'Los árabes en Santo Domingo', *Estudios Sociales*, Vol. 24.

—— (1994), *Estado y campesinos al inicio de la Era de Trujillo*. Santo Domingo.

Isa, Minerva (1985), 'Viejos ríos se han convertido hoy en puros pedregales', *Hoy*, 20 November.

Jahn, Janheinz (1960), *Muntu: Neoafrikansk kultur i vardande*. Stockholm.

James, Cyril L. R. (1963), *The Black Jacobins: Toussaint L'Ouverture and the San Domingo Revolution*. Second edition, revised. New York, NY.

Jasd, José (1973), *Beliná*. Santo Domingo.

Javier García, Manuel de Jesús (1985), *Mis 20 años en el Palacio Nacional junto a Trujillo y otros gobernantes dominicanos*. Santo Domingo.

—— (1986), *Mis 20 años en el Palacio Nacional junto a Trujillo y otros gobernantes dominicanos (segundo tomo)*. Santo Domingo.

Jimenes Grullón, Juan Isidro (1977), *John Bartlow Martin, un procónsul del Imperio Yanqui: Respuesta a su libro 'El destino dominicano'*. Mérida, Venezuela.

Jiménez, Ramón Emilio (1927), *Al amor del bohío. Tradiciones y costumbres dominicanas. Tomo I*. Santo Domingo.

—— (1929), *Al amor del bohío: Tradiciones y costumbres dominicanas. Tomo II*. Santo Domingo.

—— (1938), *Espigas sueltas*. Ciudad Trujillo.

Jiménez de León, Luis (1974), 'Adoran al Espíritu Santo en el Poblado El Batey', *El Caribe*, 15 June.

Jiménez Herrera, G. (1975), 'Informe acerca de psicología de los habitantes de este Distrito Escolar [San José de las Matas]', in Emilio Rodríguez Demorizi (ed.), *Lengua y folklore de Santo Domingo*. Santiago de los Caballeros.

Jiménez Lambertus, Abelardo (1980), 'Aspectos históricos y psicológicos del culto a los luases en República Dominicana', *Boletín del Museo del Hombre Dominicano*, Vol. 6.

Jiménez R., José Manuel (1938), 'El Caudillo Popular,' in Pedro M. de León (ed.), *La musa popular y Trujillo*. Santiago de los Caballeros.

Johnson, Paul (1980), *A History of Christianity*. Harmondsworth.

Joseph, Gilbert M. (1990), 'On the trail of Latin American bandits: a reexamination of peasant resistance', *Latin American Research Review*, Vol. 25.

—— (1991), '"Resocializing" Latin American banditry: a reply', *Latin American Research Review*, Vol. 26.

Jovine Soto, Rafael Silvio (1965), *Estampas de un pueblo del sur*. Santo Domingo.

—— (1978), *Del Sur y del Este*. Santo Domingo.

Jung, Carl Gustav and Kerényi, Károly (1993), *Essays on a Science of Mythology: The Myth of the Divine Child and the Mysteries of Eleusis*. Princeton, NJ.

Kahn, Joel S. (1985), 'Peasant ideologies in the Third World', *Annual Review of Anthropology*, Vol. 14.

Kamen, Henry (1980), *Spain in the Later Seventeenth Century 1665–1700*. London and New York, NY.

—— (1983), *Spain 1469–1714: A Society of Conflict*. London and New York, NY.

Kea, Ray A. (1986), '"I am here to plunder on the general road": bandits and banditry in the pre-nineteenth century Gold Coast', in Donald Crummey (ed.), *Banditry, Rebellion and Social Protest in Africa*. London and Portsmouth, NH.

Keeler, Mary Frear (1981), 'Introduction' to Mary Frear Keeler (ed.), *Sir Francis Drake's West Indian Voyage 1585–86*. London.

Kehoe, Alice Beck (1989), *The Ghost Dance: Ethnohistory and Revitalization*. Orlando, FL.

Keim, Randolph (1978), *Santo Domingo, pinceladas y apuntes de un viaje*. Santo Domingo.

Kelsey, Carl (1922), *The American Intervention in Haiti and the Dominican Republic*. Philadelphia, PA.

Kendrick, Thomas Downing (1960), *St. James in Spain*. London.

Kilduff, Marshall and Javers, Ron (1978), *The Suicide Cult: The Inside Story of the People's Temple Sect and the Massacre in Guyana*. New York, NY and Toronto.

Klintberg, Bengt af (1980), 'Hejnumkärringen', in Bente Gullveg Alver, Bengt af Klintberg, Birgitta Rørbye, and Anna-Leena Siikala, *Botare: En bok om etnomedicin i Norden*. Stockholm.

—— (1987), *Svenska folksägner*. Stockholm.

Knapp, Harry S. (1918), National Archives, Washington, DC: RG 38 (Chief of Naval Operations) Military Government of Santo Domingo, 1917–1924. General Correspondence, 1919. Box No. 16. From Military Governor of Santo Domingo to Commander, First Provisonal Brigade, 1 November. Reported Outrages upon Dominican Citizens.

Knight, Melvin M. (1928), *The Americans in Santo Domingo*. New York, NY.

Krehm, William (1984), *Democracies and Tyrannies of the Caribbean*. Westport, CT.

Kuper, Adam (1988), *The Invention of Primitive Society: Transformations of an Illusion*. London and New York, NY.

Kurath, Gertrude P. (1950a), 'Morisca', in Maria Leach (ed.), *Funk and Wagnall's Standard Dictionary of Folklore, Mythology and Legend, Vol. 2*. New York, NY.

—— (1950b), 'Stick dances', in Maria Leach (ed.), *Funk and Wagnall's Standard Dictionary of Folklore, Mythology and Legend, Vol. 2*. New York, NY.

Kurzman, Dan (1965), *Santo Domingo: Revolt of the Damned*. New York, NY.

La Barre, Weston (1971), 'Materials for a history of studies of crisis cults: a bibliographic essay', *Current Anthropology*, Vol. 12.

Labourt, José (1979), *Sana, sana, culito de rana … Santo Domingo.*

Lacroix, Pamhpile de (1819), *Mémoires de pour servir à l'histoire de la révolution de Saint-Domingue*. 2 volumes. Paris.

Laguerre, Michel (1987), *Afro-Caribbean Folk Medicine*. South Hadley, MA.

Lambert, Malcolm (1992), *Medieval Heresy: Popular Movements from the Gregorian Reform to the Reformation*. Oxford and Cambridge, MA.

Landestoy, Carmita (1946), *Yo también acuso*. New York, NY.

Landolfi, Ciricao (1981), *Evolución cultural dominicana, 1844–1899*. Santo Domingo.

Langley, Lester D. (1980), *The United States and the Caribbean, 1900–1970*. Athens, GA.

—— (1985), *The Banana Wars. United States Intervention in the Caribbean 1898–1934*. Revised edition. Lexington, KY.

Lanternari, Vittorio (1965), *Movimientos religiosos de libertad y salvación de los pueblos oprimidos*. Barcelona.

Larrazábal Blanco, Carlos (1975), *Los negros y la esclavitud en Santo Domingo*. Santo Domingo.

Larsen, Jens (1950), *Virgin Islands Story. A History of the Lutheran State Church, Other Churches, Slavery, Education, and Culture in the Danish West Indies, Now the Virgin Islands*. Philadelphia, PA.

Las Casas, Bartolomé de (1972), *The Tears of the Indians: Being an Historical and True Account of the Cruel Massacres and Slaughters Committed by the Spaniards in the Islands of the West Indies, Mexico, Peru, etc*. New York, NY.

Lash, Scott and Urry, John (1987), *The End of Organized Capitalism*. Cambridge.

Leach, Edmund (1985) *Lévi-Strauss*. Glasgow.

Lee, Harry (1922), National Archives, Washington, DC: RG 45. Naval Records Collection of the Office of Naval Records and Library. Subject File 1911–1927. W.A. Allied Countries, Santo Domingo. Operation of U.S. Marines. Box No. 757. August 24. From the Commanding General to the Major General Commandant of the Second Brigade, U.S. Marines, Dominican Republic, for the Year Ending June 30th, 1922.

Le Goff, Jaques (1980), *Time, Work and Culture in the Middle Ages*. Chicago, IL and London.

Lemus, Francisco Javier and Marty, Rolando (1975), 'Iniciación al estudio de la religiosidad popular en la República Dominicana', *Estudios Sociales*, Vol. 8.

—— (1976), 'Salud y enfermedad. Creencias populares', *Estudios Sociales*, Vol. 9.

Lemus, Francisco Javier and Oleo, Francisco de (1977), 'Estudio de la religiosidad popular en la República Dominicana. Zona: San Juan de la Maguana. Santo Domingo abril 1976–agosto 1977', *Mimeo*. Kept for consultation at the library of 'Instituto Nacional de Pastoral' in Santo Domingo.

León, Carlos V. de (1972), *Casos y cosas de ayer*. Santo Domingo.

León, Pedro M. de (ed.) (1938), *La musa popular y Trujillo*. Santiago de los Caballeros.

Lepkowski, Tadeusz (1968), *Haití. Tomo I*. La Habana.

—— (1969), *Haití. Tomo II*. La Habana.

Le Riverend, Julio (1985), *Historia económica de Cuba*. La Habana.

Le Roy Ladurie, Emmanuel (1979), *The Territory of the Historian*. Chicago, IL.

Lescallier, Daniel (1979), 'Nociones sobre los principales lugares de la colonia española por un ingeniero francés que la visitó en 1764', in Emilio Rodríguez Demorizi (ed.), *Viajeros de Francia en Santo Domingo*. Santo Domingo.

Levine, Robert M. (1992), *Vale of Tears: Revisiting the Canudos Massacre in Northeastern Brazil*. Berkeley, CA.

Lévi-Strauss, Claude (1972), *The Savage Mind (La Pensée Sauvage)*. London.

Lewis, Ioan M. (1975), *Ecstatic Religion: An Anthropological Study of Spirit Possession and Shamanism*. Harmondsworth.

Lewis, W. Arthur (1955), *The Theory of Economic Growth*. London.

Libro azul de Santo Domingo (1920). New York, NY.

Libros de bautismos de la Parroquia de Santa Lucía de las Matas de Farfán, Books Nos. 20, 23, 25 and 35.

Lieuwen, Edwin (1964), *Generals vs. Presidents: Neomilitarism in Latin America*. New York, NY.

Linderholm, Emanuel (1924), *Pingströrelsen: Dess förutsättningar och uppkomst*. Stockholm.

Linse, Ulrich (1983), *Barfüssige Propheten: Erlöser der zwanziger Jahre*. Berlin.

Linton, Ralph (1943), 'Nativistic movements', *American Anthropologist*, Vol. 45, reprinted in William A. Lessa and Evon Z. Vogt (eds) (1979), *Reader in Comparative Religion: An Anthropological Approach*. New York, NY.

Liogier, Alain Henri (1986), *La flora de la Española, Tomo IV*. San Pedro de Macorís.

Lipton, Michael (1968), 'The theory of the optimising peasant', *Journal of Development Studies*, Vol. 4.

Livingstone, Elizabeth A. (ed.) (1977), *The Concise Oxford Dictionary of the Christian Church*. Oxford and New York, NY.

Lizardo, Fradique (1975), *Danzas y bailes folklóricos dominicanos*. Santo Domingo.

—— (1982), *Apuntes: Investigación de campo para el montaje del espectáculo: Religiosidad popular dominicana*. Santo Domingo.

—— (1988), *Instrumentos musicales folklóricos dominicanos, Volumen I: Idiófonos y membranófonos*. Santo Domingo.

Ljungdahl, Axel (1969), *Profetrörelser, deras orsaker, innebörd och förutsättningar*. Stockholm.

Lluberes, Antonio (1973), 'La economía del tabaco en el Cibao en la segunda mitad del siglo XIX', *Revista Eme Eme*, Vol. 1.

—— (1983), 'Notas históricas sobre la enseñanza de la religión católica en las escuelas, 1795–1983', *Estudios Sociales*, Vol. 17.

—— (1990), 'La larga crisis azucarera, 1884–1902', *Estudios Sociales*, Vol. 23.

Lockward, George A. (1982), *El protestantismo en Dominicana*. Second edition. Santo Domingo.

Loederer, Richard A. (1935), *Voodoo Fire in Haiti*. New York, NY.

Long, Norman (1977), *An Introduction to the Sociology of Rural Development*. London.

López, Jacinto (1916), National Archives, Washington, DC: RG 45. Naval Records. Collection of the Office of Naval Records and Library. Subject File, 1911–1927. WA-7, Allied Countries, Santo Domingo. Daily Reports. Box No. 755. Subject: 'Paragraphs of a letter signed by 'Jacinto Lopez' (a Venezuelan) and published by the newspaper 'La Nación' of 'Havana' now reproduced here by the 'Listín Diario' of November 10, 1916'.

López, José Ramón (1975), *El gran pesimismo dominicano*. Santiago de los Caballeros.

López de Santa Anna, Antonio L. de (1957), *Misión fronteriza: Apuntes históricos, 1936–1957*. Dajabón.

López Reyes, Oscar (1983), *Historia del desarollo de Barahona: Narración e interpretación*. Santo Domingo.

Lovén, Sven (1935), *Origins of the Tainian Culture, West Indies*. Göteborg.

Lovering, John (1989), 'The restructuring debate', in Richard Peet and Nigel Thrift (eds), *New Models in Geography: The Political Economy Perspective*. London.

Lowenthal, Abraham F. (1972), *The Dominican Intervention*. Baltimore, MD and London.

Lugo, Américo (1949), 'El estado dominicano ante el derecho público', in Vetilio Alfau Durán (ed.), *Américo Lugo. Antología*. Ciudad Trujillo.

Lundahl, Mats (1979), *Peasants and Poverty: A Study of Haiti*. London.

—— (1983), 'Co-operative structures in the Haitian economy', in *The Haitian Economy: Man, Land and Markets*. London and Canberra.

—— (1984), 'Defense and distribution: agricultural policy in Haiti during the reign of Jean-Jaques Dessalines, 1804–1806', *Scandinavian Economic History Review*, Vol. 32.

—— (1985), 'Toussaint L'Ouverture and the war economy of Saint-Domingue, 1796–1802', *Slavery and Abolition*, Vol. 6.

—— (1992), 'The Haitian economy facing the 1990s', *Canadian Journal of Latin American and Caribbean Studies*, Vol. 17.

—— (1993), 'Spain and the conquest of America: profits, religion and forced labour in the fifteenth and sixteenth centuries', in Göte Hansson (ed.), *Trade, Growth and Development: The Role of Politics and Institutions*. London and New York, NY.

Lundahl, Mats and Vargas, Rosemary (1983), 'Haitian migration to the Dominican Republic', in Mats Lundahl, *The Haitian Economy: Man, Land and Markets*. London and Canberra.

Lundahl, Mats and Vedovato, Claudio (1989), 'The state and economic development in Haiti and the Dominican Republic', *Scandinavian Economic History Review*, Vol. 37.

—— (1991), 'The structure of landownership in Haiti and the Dominican Republic: causes and consequences', in Magnus Mörner and Thommy Svensson (eds), *The Transformation of Rural Societies in the Third World*. London and New York, NY.

Lundius, Jan (1990), *Voodoo, Hispanidad, and Noirisme: Popular Religion and the Search for Cultural Identity in Haiti and the Dominican Republic*. Minor Field Studies Series, No. 9, Department of Economics, Lund University, Lund.

—— (1993), 'Rural cofradías: a comparative study of syncretism, fertility beliefs and communal worship among peasants in medieval Europe, the Dominican Republic and the Mayan regions of Central America', *Ibero Americana, Nordic Journal of Latin American Studies*, Vol. 23.

Lundius, Jan and Lundahl, Mats (1989), 'Olivorio Mateo: Vida y muerte de un diós campesino', *Estudios Sociales*, Vol. 12.

Lundmark, Lennart (1985), *Protest och profetia: Korpela-rörelsen och drömmen om tidens ände*. Lund.

Lutyens, Mary (1990), *Krishnamurti: His Life and Death*. New York, NY.

McClellan, Edwin N. (1921), 'Operations ashore in the Dominican Republic', *United States Naval Institute: Proceedings*, Vol. 47.

McCloskey, Donald N. (1986), *The Rhetoric of Economics*. Brighton, Sussex.

—— (1990), *If You're So Smart: The Narrative of Economic Expertise*. Chicago, IL and London.

—— (1994), *Knowledge and Persuasion in Economics*. Cambridge.

Machado Báez, Manuel A. (1955), *La dominicanización fronteriza*. Cidudad Trujillo.

Machín, Jorge (1973), 'Orígenes del campesinado dominicano durante la ocupación haitiana', *Revista Eme Eme*, Vol. 1.

McLean, James J. (1918), '1st Endorsement, Guardia Nacional Dominicana, Office of the Inspector. From: Major James J. McLean, G.N.D. To: The Commandent. 12 December', reproduced on p. 24 in Ernesto Vega y Pagán (ed.) (1956), *Military Biography of Generalissimo Rafael Leonidas Trujillo Molina, Commander in Chief of the Armed Forces*. Ciudad Trujillo.

—— (1919), National Archives, Washington, DC: RG 38 (Chief of Naval Operations) Military Government of Santo Domingo, 1917–1924. General Correspondence, 1921. Box No. 40. Santo Domingo City, D. R., 6 August. 1919. From: Director. To: The Commandant, G.N.D. Subject: Report on Guardia, Department of the South, 1918.

——— (1921) Archivo General de la Nación: Gobierno Militar, Interior/Policía # [Legajo] 14, Departamento del Sur, Oficina del Director, Santo Domingo, D. R., 11 January 1921. From Director to Commandant, G.N.D..

McLean, James J. and Pina Chevalier, Teódulo (1921), *Datos históricos sobre la frontera haitiana*. Santo Domingo.

MacLeod, Murdo J. (1984), 'Spain and America: the Atlantic trade 1492–1720', in Leslie Bethell (ed.), *The Cambridge History of Latin America, Volume I. Colonial Latin America*. Cambridge.

McNamee, L. (1921), National Archives, Washington, DC: RG 45. Naval Records. Collection of the Office of Naval Records and Library. Subject File, 1911–1927. WA-7, Allied Countries, Santo Domingo. Daily Reports. Box No. 756. Summary of Intelligence, San Domingo. From November 1, 1921 to November 30, 1921.

MacRae, Donald G. (1982), *Weber*. Glasgow.

McWhirter, Norris (ed.) (1985), *Guinness 1985 Book of World Records*. New York, NY.

Maguire, James (1921), National Archives, Washington, DC: RG 38 (Chief of Naval Operations) Military Government of Santo Domingo, 1917–1924. General Correspondence, (Commandant General) Box No. 37. Brigade Intelligence Office, Second Brigade, U.S.M., Santo Domingo City, October 15. From: Brigade Intelligence Officer. To: The Secretary of State of the Department of Justice and Public Instruction. Subject: Records of Bandit Leaders.

Malek R., Michael (1971), 'Rafael Leonidas Trujillo Molina: the rise of a Caribbean dictator'. *Mimeo*, PhD thesis. University of California, Santa Barbara, CA.

Mallín, Jay (1965), *El Crisol Dominicano*. México, D.F.

Mañón, Melvin (1989), *Operación Estrella: Con Caamaño, la resistencia y la inteligencia cubana*. Santo Domingo.

Mañón Rossi, Wilfredo (1983), *La medicina folklórica en la República Dominicana*. Santo Domingo.

Manuel, Frank E. and Manuel, Fritzie P. (1979), *Utopian Thought in the Western World*. Cambridge, MA.

Marcano Fondeur, Eugenio de Jesús (1977), *Plantas venenosas en la República Dominicana. Santo Domingo*.

Maríñez, Pablo A. (1984), *Resistencia campesina, imperialismo y reforma agraria en República Dominicana*. Santo Domingo.

Márquez, Gabino (1960), *Las grandes encíclicas sociales III. Pío XI: Divini Redemptoris, sobre el comunismo ateo (19 de Marzo de 1937)*. Madrid.

Marrero Aristy, Ramón (1939), *Over*. Ciudad Trujillo.

Martin, John Bartlow (1966), *Overtaken by Events: The Dominican Crisis from the Fall of Trujillo to the Civil War*. New York, NY.

——— (1978), *U.S. Policy in the Caribbean*. Boulder, CO.

——— (1986), *It Seems Like Only Yesterday: Memoirs of Writing, Presidential Politics, and the Diplomatic Life*. New York, NY.

Martin, Malachi (1987), *The Jesuits: The Society of Jesus and the Betrayal of the Catholic Church*. New York, NY.

Martínez, Lusitania (1980), 'Un estudio preliminar acerca del movimiento de Palma Sola como movimiento mesiánico y social campesino', *Revista de Antropología e Historia de la Facultad de Humanidades, Universidad Autónoma de Santo Domingo*, Vol. 10.

——— (1991), *Palma Sola: opresión y esperanza (Su geografía mítica y social)*. Santo Domingo.

Martínez, Rufino (1971), *Diccionario biográfico-histórico dominicano, 1821–1930.* Santo Domingo.

Martínez García, Altagracia (1962), 'Al: Magistrado Procurador de la Corte de Apelación, San Juan de la Maguana. Asunto: Denuncia de perturbación social y exposición de la misma. Las Matas de Farfán, 8 de agosto.' Reproduced in *¡Ahora!*, No. 977, 12 August, 1982.

Martínez Paulino, Marcos Antonio (1984), *Publicaciones periódicas dominicanas desde la colonia.* San Pedro de Macorís.

Marvin, George (1917), 'Watchful acting in Santo Domingo', *The World's Work*, Vol. 34.

Marx, Karl (1954), *Capital: A Critique of Political Economy, Volume I.* London.

—— (1977) 'The Eighteenth Brumaire of Louis Bonaparte', in Karl Marx and Friedrich Engels, *Selected Works, Vol. 1.* Moscow.

Marx, Karl and Engels, Friedrich (1992), *The Communist Manifesto.* Oxford and New York, NY.

Mateo Pérez, Arnulfo V. and Mateo Comas, Ivelisse M. (1980), 'Psicopatologías de los pacientes ingresados en el Hospital Psiquiátrico Padre Billini procedentes de la Región IV de Salud', MD thesis, Universidad Autónoma de Santo Domingo.

Medina, Marta (1989), 'La Cueva de Mana: Centro de peregrinaciones', *Listín Diario*, 18 January.

Medina Benet, Víctor M. (1986), *Los responsables: Fracaso de la Tercera República.* Second edition. Santo Domingo.

Mejía, Félix A. (1951), *Vía Crucis de un pueblo.* México, D.F.

Mejía, Luis F. (1976), *De Lilís a Trujillo: Historia contemporánea de la República Dominicana.* Santo Domingo.

Mejía Ricart, Gustavo Adolfo (1951) *Historia de Santo Domingo (una interpretación objetiva), Volumen IV.* Ciudad Trujillo.

—— (1952), *Historia de Santo Domingo (una interpretación objetiva), Volumen V.* Ciudad Trujillo.

—— (1953), *Historia de Santo Domingo (una interpretación objetiva), Volumen VI.* Ciudad Trujillo.

—— (1954), *Historia de Santo Domingo (una interpretación objetiva), Volumen VII.* Ciudad Trujillo.

Melton, J. Gordon (1985), 'Modern alternative religions in the West', in John R. Hinnells (ed.), *A Handbook of Living Religions.* Harmondsworth.

Memoria de la Secretaría de Estado de Agricultura e Inmigración. Año 1923 (1924). Santo Domingo.

Méndez, Ana Marina (1986), *Palma Sola ... desde el sol hasta el ocaso.* Santo Domingo.

Menéndez y Pelayo, Marcelino (1892), *Historia de la poesía hispanoamericana.* Madrid.

Metcalf, Clyde H. (1939), *A History of the United States Marine Corps.* New York, NY.

Métraux, Alfred (1974), *Voodoo in Haiti.* London.

Miller, Edwin Haviland (1991), *Salem Is My Dwelling Place: A Life of Nathaniel Hawthorne.* Iowa City, IA.

Millspaugh, Arthur C. (1931), *Haiti under American Control 1915–1930.* Boston, MA.

Miniño, Manuel M. (1980), *Geo Ripley: Magical Environment.* Paris.

—— (1985), *¿Es el Vudú religión? El Vudú dominicano.* Santo Domingo.

Mintz, Sidney W. (1990) 'The peasantry as a sociohistorical category', in Mats

Lundahl and Thommy Svensson (eds), *Agrarian Society in History: Essays in Honour of Magnus Mörner*. London and New York, NY.

Miolán, Angel (1984), *El Perredé desde mi ángulo*. Santo Domingo.

Mish, John L. (1949), 'Folklore', in Maria Leach (ed.), *Funk and Wagnall's Standard Dictionary of Folklore, Mythology and Legend, Vol. 1*. New York, NY.

Montánd, Braullo (1986), '¡Hola Halley 1986! El trotamundos', Suplemento, *Listín Diario*, 1 March.

Mooney, James (1965), *The Ghost-Dance Religion and the Sioux Outbreak of 1890*. Edited and abridged, with an Introduction by Anthony F. C. Wallace. Chicago, IL and London.

Moorehead, Alan (1963), *The White Nile*. London.

Moral, Paul (1961), *Le paysan haïtien. Études sur la vie rurale en Haïti*. Paris.

Morales, Angel (1930), 'De Angel Morales a Sumner Welles, San Juan, P.R., 30 de julio de 1930', in Bernardo Vega (ed.), *Los Estados Unidos y Trujillo, 1930. Tomo II: Colección de documentos del Departamento de Estado, de las Fuerzas Armadas Norteamericanas y de los Archivos del Palacio Nacional Dominicano*. Santo Domingo, 1986.

Moreau de Saint-Méry, Médéric Louis Elie (1944), *Descripción de la parte española de Santo Domingo*. Ciudad Trujillo.

—— (1958), *Description topographique, physique, civile, politique et historique de la partie française de l'isle Saint-Domingue*. Paris.

Moreta, Angel (1986), 'Desarrollo de relaciones capitalistas en la agricultura del suroeste (SJM). Capitalismo y campesinado', tesis de postgrado para el título de Maestro en Sociología Rural. Universidad Autónoma de Santo Domingo. Consejo Latinoamericano de Ciencias Sociales (CLACSO). Santo Domingo.

Morse, George H., Jr (1922a), National Archives, Washington, DC: RG 38 (Chief of Naval Operations) Military Government of Santo Domingo, 1917–1924. General Correspondence, (Commandant General) Box No. 49. Oficina de la 9th [sic] compañía. San Juan, RD, 23 May. From: Commanding Officer. To: Colonel Commandant, PND. Subject: Report of Contact with Dios Olivorio.

—— (1922b), National Archives, Washington, DC: RG 38 (Chief of Naval Operations) Military Government of Santo Domingo, 1917–1924. General Correspondence, (Commendant General) Box No. 49. San Juan, RD, 20 June. From: Commanding Officer. To: Director, Department of South, PND.

Moscoso, Francisco (1993), 'Un señor de ingenios de Santo Domingo: Francisco Tostado (1520–1528)', *Ecos*, Vol. 1.

Moscoso Puello, Francisco (1936), *Cañas y bueyes*. Ciudad Trujillo.

Mosse, George L. (1981), *The Crisis of German Ideology: Intellectual Origins of the Third Reich*. New York, NY.

Mota, Ana Maritza de la (1980), 'Palma Sola: 1962', *Boletín del Museo del Hombre Dominicano*, Vol. 9.

Mota Acosta, Julio César (1977), *Los cocolos en Santo Domingo*. Santo Domingo.

Moya Pons, Frank (1973), 'Azúcar, negros y sociedad en la Española del siglo XVI', *Revista Eme Eme*, Vol. 1.

—— (1974a), 'Nuevas consideraciones sobre la historía de la población dominicana: Curvas, tasas y problemas', *Revista Eme Eme*, Vol. 3.

—— (1974b), 'La primera abolición de la esclavitud en Santo Domingo', *Revista Eme Eme*, Vol. 3.

—— (1977), *Historia colonial de Santo Domingo*. Santiago de los Caballeros.

—— (1978a), *La dominación haitiana, 1822–1844*. Santiago de los Caballeros.

—— (1978b), *La Española en el siglo XVI, 1493–1520: Trabajo, sociedad y política en la economía del oro*. Third edition. Santiago de los Caballeros.

—— (1980), *Manual de historia dominicana*. Fifth edition. Barcelona.

—— (1985), 'Haiti and Santo Domingo: 1790–c.1870', in Leslie Bethell (ed.), *The Cambridge History of Latin America. Volume III. From Independence to c.1870*. Cambridge.

—— (1986), *El pasado dominicano*. Santo Domingo.

Munro, Dana Gardner (1964), *Intervention and Dollar Diplomacy in the Caribbean, 1900–1921*. Princeton, NJ.

—— (1974), *The United States and the Caribbean Republics, 1921–1933*. Princeton, NJ.

Musicant, Ivan (1990), *The Banana Wars: A History of United States Military Intervention in Latin America from the Spanish-American War to the Invasion of Panama*. New York, NY.

Muto, M. Paul, Jr. (1976), 'The illusory promise: the Dominican Republic and the process of economic development, 1900–1930'. PhD thesis, University of Washington, Seattle, WA.

Naipaul, Shiva (1980), *Black and White*. London.

Nanita, Abelardo R. (1957), *Trujillo: The Biography of a Great Leader*. New York, NY.

Naquin, Susan (1976), *Millenarian Rebellion in China*. New Haven, CT.

Nasr, Seyyed Hossein (1979), *Ideals and Realities of Islam*. London and Boston.

Nicholls, David (1981), 'No hawkers and pedlars: Levantines in the Caribbean', *Ethnic and Racial Studies*, Vol. 4.

Nochlin, Linda (1971), *Realism*. Harmondsworth.

Nolasco, Flerida de (1956), *Santo Domingo en el folklore universal*. Ciudad Trujillo.

—— (1982), *Vibraciones en el tiempo. Días de la colonia*. Santo Domingo.

Nouel, Carlos (1970), 'Limites parroquiales, 1885', in Emilio Rodríguez Demorizi (ed.), *Relaciones geográficas de Santo Domingo, Vol. 1*. Santo Domingo.

Nygaard, Niels Peder (1903), 'Til Gouvernementet for de danske westindiske øer, d. 29 Januar, 1903. V.J. 1903', in Koloniernes Centralbestyrelse. Grupportdnede sager. Kirke og skole, F. 928: Trossamfund udenfor folkekirken 1856–1917. Rigsarkivet, København.

O'Flaherty, Wendy Doniger (ed.) (1976), *Hindu Myths: A Sourcebook Translated from the Sanskrit*. London.

Oliver, Victor L. (1976), 'Caodai spiritism: a study of religion in Vietnamese society', Supplements to *Studies in the History of Religions*, Vol. 34.

Omos Cordones, Hernán (1980), 'Tres rasgos genéticos en una población dominicana', *Boletín del Museo del Hombre Dominicano*, Vol. 9.

ONAPLAN (Oficina Nacional de Planificación) (1968), *Plataforma para el desarollo y crecimiento económico y social de la República Dominicana (1968–1985)*. Santo Domingo.

—— (1983a), *Estudio de base del sector agropecuario y forestal*. Santo Domingo.

—— (1983b), *El proceso de urbanización en la República Dominicana*. Santo Domingo.

ONE (Oficina Nacional de Estadísticas) (1983), *República Dominicana en cifras*. Santo Domingo.

Ornes, Germán E. (1958), *Trujillo: Little Caesar of the Caribbean*. New York, NY.

Ortiz, Sutti (1971), 'Reflections on the concept of "peasant culture" and "peasant cognitive systems"', in Teodor Shanin (ed.), *Peasants and Peasant Societies*. Harmondsworth.

Osorio Lizarazo, J.A. (1947), *La isla iluminada*. Santiago de los Caballeros.

Ott, Thomas O. (1973), *The Haitian Revolution 1789–1904.* Knoxville, TN.

Otto, Rudolf (1950), *The Idea of the Holy: An Inquiry into the Non-Rational Factor in the Idea of the Divine and its Relation to the Rational.* London.

Overmyer, Daniel L. (1988), 'Messenger, savior, and revolutionary: Maitreya in Chinese popular religious literature of the sixteenth and seventeenth centuries', in Alan Sponberg and Helen Hardacre (eds), *Maitreya: The Future Buddha.* Cambridge.

The Oxford English Dictionary, Vol. XII (1961). Oxford.

Pagán Perdomo, Dato (1982), 'Aspectos ergológicos en el arte rupestre de la Isla de Santo Domingo', *Boletín del Museo del Hombre Dominicano.* Vol. 10.

Pagels, Elaine (1979), *The Gnostic Gospels.* London and New York, NY.

Palmer, Ernest Charles (1976), 'Land use and landscape change along the Dominican-Haitian border', PhD thesis, University of Florida, Gainesville, FL.

Pané, Fray Ramón (1980), *Relación acerca de las antigüedades de los indios.* México, D.F.

Paniagua O., Alejandro (1962), 'La supersticion invade nuestro sur', *¡Ahora!,* No. 22, December.

Papmanabh S., Jain (1988), 'Stages in the bodhisattva career of the Tathagata Maitreya', in Alan Sponberg and Helen Hardacre (eds), *Maitreya: The Future Buddha.* Cambridge.

Parry, John H. (1966), *The Spanish Seaborne Empire.* London.

Patín Veloz, Enrique (1946), 'El luasismo en sus diferentes aspectos', *La Nación,* 4, 7, 14, 25, and 29 November.

—— (1975) 'El vudú y sus misterios (referencias y definiciones)', *Revista Dominicana de Folklore,* Vol. 1.

Paulino, Antonio (1962a), 'Se cree que en Palma Sola se refugian delincuentes', *El Caribe,* 23 December.

—— (1962b), 'Afirman que a Palma Sola llevaron armas de fuego', *El Caribe,* 28 December.

Paxton, Robert O. (1992), 'De Gaulle and His Myth', *New York Review of Books,* Vol. 39, No. 8, 23 April.

Peguero, Valentina and de los Santos, Danilo (1983), *Visión general de la historia dominicana.* Santo Domingo.

Peña Batlle, Manuel Arturo (1943a), *El sentido de una política.* Ciudad Trujillo.

—— (1943b), Archivo Particular del Generalísimo. Palacio Nacional: 23 de septiembre. Del Secretario de Estado de lo Interior y Policía. Asunto: Establecimiento de penas correccionables para las personas que practiquen los bailes conocidos con el nombre de "Voudou" o "Luá".

—— (1946), *Historia de la cuestión fronteriza dominico-haitiana, Tomo I.* Ciudad Trujillo.

—— (1951), *La Isla de la Tortuga: Plaza de armas, refugio y seminario de los enemigos de España en Indias.* Madrid.

—— (1954), *Orígenes del estado haitiano.* Ciudad Trujillo.

—— (1970), *La rebelión del Bahoruco.* Santo Domingo.

—— (1989), *Ensayos históricos.* Santo Domingo.

Peña Pérez, Frank (1980), *Antonio Osorio: Monopolio, contrabando y despoblación.* Santiago de los Caballeros.

—— (n.d.), *Cien años de miseria en Santo Domingo.* Santo Domingo.

Peñolguín, Santiago (1940), *Vodú: Tradiciones y costumbres haitianas.* Ciudad Trujillo.

Penson, César Nicolás (1951), *Cosas añejas*. Ciudad Trujillo.

Pentikäinen, Juha (1978), 'Oral repertoire and world view: an anthropological study of Marina Takalo's life history', *FF Communications*, Vol. 13, No. 219. Helsinki.

Pereira de Queiroz, Maria Isaura (1965), 'Messiahs in Brazil', *Past and Present.* No. 31, July.

—— (1969), *Historia y etnología de los movimientos mesiánicos*. México, D.F.

—— (1977), *O messianismo no Brazil e no mundo*. Second edition. São Paulo.

Pérez, A. (1963), 'Santa misión', *Fides*, 24 February.

Pérez, Angel S. del Rosario (1957), *La exterminación añorada*. Ciudad Trujillo.

Pérez, Juan B. (1972), *Geografía y sociedad*. Santo Domingo.

Pérez, Louis A., Jr (1987), '"La Chambelona": political protest, sugar and social banditry in Cuba, 1914–1917', in Richard W. Slatta (ed.), *Bandidos: The Varieties of Latin American Banditry*. Westport, CT.

Pérez, Rafael Leonidas, Jr (1985), *Minguilán o el jungan del Sur*. Santo Domingo.

Perkins, Whitney T. (1981), *Constraint of Empire: The United States and Caribbean Interventions*. Oxford.

Pettersson, Olof (1980), *Tro och rit: Religionsfenomenologisk översikt*. Stockholm.

Peynado, Fransisco J. (1909), *Por la inmigración: Estudio de las reformas que es necesario emprender para atraer inmigrantes a la República Dominicana*. Santo Domingo.

—— (1919), 'Deslinde, mensura y partición de terrenos', *Revista Jurídica*, No. 4.

Pieter, Heriberto (1972), *Autobiografía*. Santo Domingo.

Pittini, Ricardo (1943), Archivo Particular del Generalísimo. Palacio Nacional, No. 786: 23 de noviembre. Al: Generalísimo Doctor Don Rafael Leonidas Trujillo Molina, Honorable Presidente de la República, Benefactor de la Patria. De: Ricardo Pittini, Arzobispo de Santo Domingo.

—— (1948), Archivo Particular del Generalísimo. Palacio Nacional: 3 de abril. Memorandum del Arzobispo de Santo Domingo: Infiltración peligrosa.

—— (1949), *Memorias salesianas de un arzobispo ciego*. Buenos Aires.

Pitt-Rivers, Julian A. (1971), *The People of the Sierra*. Second edition. Chicago, IL and London.

—— (1977), *The Fate of Shechem, or the Politics of Sex: Essays in the Anthropology of the Mediterranean*. Cambridge.

Plummer, Brenda Gayle (1981), 'The Syrians in Haiti', *International History Review*, Vol. 3.

Popkin, Samuel L. (1979), *The Rational Peasant: The Political Economy of Rural Society in Vietnam*. Berkeley, CA.

Pou Henríquez, Luís E. (1976), 'Prólogo', in Juan Esteban Belza (ed.), *El padre de los pobres y su mitra de plomo*. Santo Domingo.

Powers, Thomas (1979), *The Man Who Kept the Secrets: Richard Helms and the CIA*. New York, NY.

Pratt, Mary Louise (1986), 'Fieldwork in common places', in James Clifford and George E. Marcus (eds), *Writing Culture: Twentieth-Century Ethnography, Literature, and Art*. Cambridge, MA and London.

Pred, Allan (1986), *Place, Practice and Structure: Social and Spatial Transformation in Southern Sweden: 1750–1850*. Cambridge.

—— (1990), *Making Histories and Constructing Human Geographies: The Local Transformation of Practice, Power Relations and Consciousness*. Boulder, CO.

Prestol Castillo, Freddy (1943), *Paisajes y meditaciones de una frontera.* Ciudad Trujillo.

Price, Thomas J., Jr (1955), 'Saints and spirits: a study of differential acculturation in Colombian Negro communities', PhD thesis, Northwestern University, Evanston, IL.

Price-Mars, Jean (1953), *La République d'Haïti et République Dominicaine. Les aspects divers d'une problème d'histoire, de géographie et d'éthnologie. Tome II.* Port-au-Prince.

Puig, Elisabeth de (1975), 'La Iglesia de la Maravilla: Un culto mágico religioso', *Revista Dominicana de Folklore*, Vol. 1.

Rahintel (1990), 'Somos así y así somos, Programas Nos. 38-48: "Palma Sola ... desde el sol hasta el ocaso"'. Ten television programs produced and presented by Cornelia Margarita, 11 August, 18 August, 25 August, 1 September, 8 September, 11 September, 15 September, 22 September, 29 September, 6 October and 13 October.

Ramírez, Wenceslao (1921), National Archives, Washington, DC: RG 38 (Chief of Naval Operations) Military Government of Santo Domingo, 1917–1924. General Correspondence (Commanding General) Box No. 35. From Military Governor of Santo Domingo to Commanding General, Second Brigade, USMC. Protest from W. Ramírez of Buena Vista, D.R. Regarding Disorder of Soldiers at Dance.

Ramsey, Frederick A. (1917), National Archives, Washington, DC; Naval Records. Collection of the Office of Naval Records and Library. Subject file 1911–1927. WA-7, Allied Countries, Santo Domingo. Daily Records. Box No. 756. H. M. 1980. Folder #3. Headquarters Second Provisional Brigade. U.S. Marine Corps. 2 January. From: Intelligence Officer. To: Chief of Staff. Subject: Information.

Ray, Benjamin C. (1975), *African Religions: Symbol, Ritual, and Community.* Englewood Cliffs, NJ.

Real Academia Española (1984), *Diccionario de la lengua española, Tomo I.* Twentieth edition. Madrid.

Redfield, Robert and Singer, Milton B. (1954), 'The cultural role of cities', *Economic Development and Cultural Change*, Vol. 3.

Reeves, Marjorie (1969), *The Influence of Prophecy in the Later Middle Ages: A Study of Joachism.* Oxford.

Rei, Dario (1974), 'Note sul concetto de "religione populare"', *Lares*, Vol. 40.

Reilly, Thomas F. (1963), 'Memorandum sobre el problema de la brujería y el vudú en el Sur de la República'. Prelatura de San Juan de la Maguana, 9 January.

Reyes, Leo (n.d.), *María de los jazmines: Los verdaderos orígenes del Dr. Peña Gómez.* Santo Domingo.

Rhodes, James M. (1980), *The Hitler Movement: A Modern Millenarian Revolution.* Stanford, CA.

Rigaud, Milo (1985), *Secrets of Voodoo.* San Francisco, CA.

Rines, Clarence C. (1921), National Archives, Washington, DC: RG 38 (Chief of Naval Operations) Military Government of Santo Domingo, 1917–1924. General Correspondence, 1921. Box No. 40. (Lake, F.U. Lt. Com. Personal) Telegrama múltiple, 21 June. From: C. C. Rine, Chief of Staff. P.N.D. To: Capitán Morse, P.N.D., San Juan, RD.

Ripley, Geo (1985), 'Vudú: Posesión ritual, cena ceremonial', *Revista Estudios Dominicanos*, Vol. 2.

Rist, John M. (1969), *Stoic Philosophy.* Cambridge.

Robuster, Julián León (1957), 'Introducción', in Antonio L. López de Santa Anna, *Misión fronteriza: Apuntes históricos, 1936–1957*. Dajabón.

Rodman, Selden (1964), *Quisqueya: A History of the Dominican Republic*. Seattle, WA.

Rodríguez, Alberto J. (1985), *El azúcar como hacedor de historia y de comunidades*. Santo Domingo.

Rodríguez, Domingo (1920), National Archives, Washington, DC: RG 38 (Chief of Naval Operations) Military Government of Santo Domingo, 1917–1924. General Correspondence, 1920 (Snowden, Rear Admiral (Personal)) Box No. 30. San Juan 19 January. Letter from Domingo Rodríguez, Importador y Exportador, Comisionista, San Juan de la Maguana.

Rodríguez, Manuel Tomás (1975), *Papá Legbá. (La crónica del voudú o pacto con el diablo y algo más ...)* Santo Domingo.

Rodríguez Demorizi, Emilio (ed.) (1942), *Relaciones históricas de Santo Domingo, Vol. 1*. Ciudad Trujillo.

—— (1945), 'Contra el Voudou', *La Nación*, 5 October.

—— (ed.) (1957), *Guerra dominico-haitiana: Documentos para su estudio*. Ciudad Trujillo.

—— (1971), 'Prefacio', in Antonio Sánchez Valverde, *Idea del valor de la isla Española y utilidades, que de ella puede sacar su Monarquía*. Barcelona.

—— (ed.) (1975a), *Lengua y folklore de Santo Domingo*. Santiago de los Caballeros.

—— (1975b), 'Del folklore en Santo Domingo', in Emilio Rodríguez Demorizi (ed.), *Lengua y folklore de Santo Domingo*. Santiago de los Caballeros.

—— (1975c), 'Vicisitudes de la lengua española en Santo Domingo', in Emilio Rodríguez Demorizi (ed.), *Lengua y folklore en Santo Domingo*. Santiago de los Caballeros.

Rodríguez Grullón, Julio (1991), *Trujillo y la iglesia*. Santo Domingo.

Rodríguez Jiménez, Julio César and Vélez Canelo, Rosajilda (1980), *El precapitalismo dominicano de la primera mitad del siglo XIX 1780–1850*. Santo Domingo.

Rodríguez Pereyra, Miguel Angel (1978), *Esbozos de mi patria. Conceptos históricos*. Santo Domingo.

Rodríguez Varona, Manuel de Jesús (1947), 'Para la historia: Olivorio Mateo (a) Papa Livorio', *Luz y Acción*, Vol. 4, No. 172, 27 February.

Rodríguez Vélez, Wendalina (1982), *El turbante blanco: Muertos, santos y vivos en lucha política*. Santo Domingo.

Rojas Lima, Flavio (1988), *La cofradía: Reducto cultural indígena*. Guatemala.

Rooth, Anna Birgitta (1969), *Lokalt och globalt II*. Lund.

Rosa, Antonio de la (Alexandre Richelieu Poujol) (1987) *Las finanzas de Santo Domingo y el control americano*. Santo Domingo.

Rosell, Pedro (1983), *Crímenes y delitos contra la cosa pública*. Santo Domingo.

Rosenberg, June C. (1979), *El gagá: Religión y sociedad de un culto dominicano. Un estudio comparativo*. Santo Domingo.

Rothkrug, Lionel (1979), 'Popular religion and holy shrines: their influence on the origins of the German reformation and their role in German cultural development', in James Obelkevich (ed.), *Religion and the People*. Chapel Hill, NC.

Roumasset, James A. (1976), *Rice and Risk: Decision Making among Low-Income Farmers*. Amsterdam.

Rueda, Manuel (1970), *Adivinanzas dominicanas*. Santo Domingo.

Ruiz Tejada (1957), 'La educación del ciudadano para la vida pública nacional e internacional', in *Memoria del Congreso Cultural Católico por la Paz del Mundo.* Ciudad Trujillo.

Sachedina, Abdulaziz Abdulhussein (1981), *Islamic Messianism: The Idea of the Mahdi in Twelver Shi'ism.* Albany, NY.

Sáenz Padrón, Ricardo and Rius Blein, Hugo (1984), *Caamaño.* La Habana.

Sáez, José Luis (1987), *Cinco siglos de iglesia dominicana.* Santo Domingo.

—— (1988a), *Los jesuitas en la República Dominicana.* Santo Domingo.

—— (1988b), 'Catolicismo e hispanidad en la oratoria de Trujillo', *Estudios Sociales,* Vol. 21.

Sagan, Carl and Druyan, Ann (1985), *Comet.* London.

Sallmann, Jean-Michel (1979), 'Image et fonction du saint dans la région de Naples à la fin du XVIIe siècle et au début du XVIIIe siècle', *Mélanges de l'École Française de Rome. Moyen Age – Temps Modernes,* Vol. 91.

Samuelsson, Kurt (1965), *Ekonomi och religion.* Stockholm.

Sánchez, Juan J. (1976), *La caña en Santo Domingo.* Santo Domingo.

Sánchez Valverde, Antonio (1988), *Ensayos.* Santo Domingo.

Sang, Mu-Kien A. (1987), *Ulises Heureaux: Biografía de un dictador.* Santo Domingo.

—— (1991), *Buenaventura Báez: El caudillo del sur (1844–1878).* Santo Domingo.

San Miguel, Pedro Luis (1987), 'The Dominican peasantry and the market economy: the peasants of the Cibao, 1880–1960', PhD thesis, Columbia University, New York.

—— (1992), 'Discurso racial e identidad nacional en la República Dominicana', *Op. Cit.,* No. 7.

Sarkisyanz, Emanuel (1965), *Buddhist Backgrounds of the Burmese Revolution.* The Hague.

Sauer, Carl Ortwin (1966), *The Early Spanish Main.* Berkeley and Los Angeles, CA.

Schiffino, José (1945), *Riqueza forestal dominicana.* Ciudad Trujillo.

Schlesinger, Arthur M., Jr (1965), *A Thousand Days: John F. Kennedy in the White House.* Boston, MA.

—— (1978), *Robert Kennedy and His Times.* Boston, MA.

Schmidt, Hans (1971), *The United States Occupation of Haiti 1915–1934.* New Brunswick, NJ.

Schoenrich, Otto (1977), *Santo Domingo, un país con futuro.* Santo Domingo.

Scholem, Gershom (1971), *The Messianic Idea in Judaism and Other Essays on Jewish Spirituality.* New York, NY.

—— (1978), *Kabbalah.* New York, NY.

Schultes, Richard E. and Hofmann, Albert (1987), *Pflanzen der Götter: Die magischen Kräfte der Rausch- und Giftgewächse.* Bern and Stuttgart.

Scott, James C. (1976), *The Moral Economy of the Peasant: Rebellion and Subsistence in Southeast Asia.* New Haven, CT and London.

—— (1985), *Weapons of the Weak: Everyday Forms of Peasant Resistance.* New Haven, CT and London.

—— (1990), *Domination and the Arts of Resistance: Hidden Transcripts.* New Haven, CT and London.

SEA (Secretaría de Estado de Agricultura) (1924), *Memoria de la Secretaría de Estado de Agricultura e Inmigración, Año 1923.* Santo Domingo.

—— (1977), *Aspectos del empleo rural en la República Dominicana.* Santo Domingo.

Seabrook, William B. (1929), *The Magic Island.* London.

Secretaría Particular del Presidente de la República (1948), Secretaría Particular del Presidente de la República: 10 November, 'Entrevista: Concha viuda de Juanico Ramírez, de esta ciudad', in Bernardo Vega (ed.), *Unos desafectos y otros en desgracia: Sufrimientos en la dictadura de Trujillo.* Santo Domingo, 1986.

Seligman, Edwin R. A (1907), *The Economic Interpretation of History.* Second edition, revised. New York, NY.

Serrano Mangas, Fernando (1992), *La crisis de la isla del oro. Ensayo sobre circulación y política monetaria en la Española (1530–1580).* Badajoz.

Sevilla Soler, María Rosario (1980), *Santo Domingo: Tierra de frontera (1750–1800).* Sevilla.

Seward, Desmond (1974), *The Monks of War.* Frogmore, St Albans.

Shanin, Teodor (1971), 'Peasantry: delineation of a sociological concept and a field of study', *Archives Européennes de Sociologie*, Vol. 12.

—— (1973), 'The nature and logic of the peasant economy – I: a generalization', *Journal of Peasant Studies*, Vol. 1.

—— (1974), 'The nature and logic of peasant economy – II: diversity and change, III: policy and intervention', *Journal of Peasant Studies*, Vol. 1.

—— (1990), *Defining Peasants.* Oxford.

Sharpe, Eric J. (1975), *Comparative Religion: A History.* London.

Shavit, David (1992), *The United States in Latin America: A Historical Dictionary.* New York, NY.

Shepperson, George (1962), 'The comparative study of millenarian movements', in Sylvia Thrupp (ed.), *Millenial Dreams in Action: Essays in Comparative Study.* The Hague.

Shils, Edward (1968), 'Charisma', in *International Encyclopedia of the Social Sciences*, Vol. 2. New York, NY.

Simpson, George Eaton (1971), 'The belief system of Haitian vodoun', in Michael M. Horowitz (ed.), *Peoples and Cultures of the Caribbean.* Garden City, NY.

Sinks, A. H. (1940), 'Trujillo: Caribbean dictator', *American Mercury*, Vol. 5.

Slater, Jerome (1970), *Intervention and Negotiation: The United States and the Dominican Revolution.* New York, NY.

—— (1978), 'The Dominican Republic, 1961–66', in Barry M. Blechman and Stephen S. Kaplan (eds), *Force without War. U.S. Armed Forces as a Political Instrument.* Washington, DC.

Slatta, Richard W. (ed.) (1987), *Bandidos: The Varieties of Latin American Banditry.* Westport, CT.

—— (1991), 'Bandits and rural social history: a comment on Joseph', *Latin American Research Review*, Vol. 26.

Smith, Grace Patridge (1949), 'Crossroads', in Maria Leach (ed.), *Funk and Wagnall's Standard Dictionary of Folklore, Mythology and Legend, Vol. 1.* New York, NY.

Snowden, Thomas (1919), National Archives, Washington, DC: RG 38 (Chief of Naval Operations) Military Government of Santo Domingo, 1917–1924. General Correspondence, Rear Admiral Snowden (personal). Box No. 16. 2 December. Letter to General Don Wenceslao Ramírez, San Juan, R.D..

Södersten, Bo and Reed, Geoffrey (1994), *International Economics.* Third edition. Houndmills, Basingstoke and London.

Soja, Edward W. (1989), *Postmodern Geographies: The Reassertion of Space in Critical Social Theory.* London and New York, NY.

Soler, Angel M. (1912), 'Memoria que al ciudadano Presidente de la República presenta el Secretario de Estado de Justicia e Instrucción Pública', *Gaceta Oficial,* Vol. 29, Nos. 23-24-25-26, 28 August.

Soler, Eduardo (1913), 'Memorias de la secretaría de estado de hacienda y comercio correspondiente al año 1912', *Gaceta Oficial,* No. 2453, Vol. 30, 19 November.

Sosa, Rafael (1982a), 'La tragedia de Palma Sola se inició en el mesianismo de "Papá Liborio"', *¡Ahora!,* No. 977, 12 August.

—— (1982b), 'En Palma Sola la masacre y el fetichismo danzaron la muerte hace 20 años', *¡Ahora!,* No. 977, 12 August.

Spitzer, Daniel Charles (1972), 'A contemporary political and socio-economic history of Haiti and the Dominican Republic', PhD thesis, University of Michigan, Ann Arbor, MI.

Steinmetz, Paul B. (1980), *Pipe, Bible and Peyote Among the Oglala Lakota.* Stockholm.

Stern, J. P. (1984), *Hitler: The Führer and the People.* Harmondsworh.

St John, Sir Spenser (1889), *Hayti, or the Black Republic.* Second edition. London.

Stoddard, T. Lothrop (1914), *The French Revolution in San Domingo.* Boston, MA.

Stoyanov, Yuri (1994), *The Hidden Tradition in Europe: The Secret History of Medieval Christian Heresy.* Harmondsworth.

Sturrock, John (ed.) (1982), *Structuralism and Since: From Lévi-Strauss to Derrida.* Oxford and New York, NY.

Sundkler, Bengt G. M. (1948), *Bantu Prophets in South Africa.* London.

Sutton, Paul (1990), *Cromwell's Jamaica Campaign: The Attack on the West Indies 1654–55.* Leigh-on-Sea, Essex.

Szulc, Tad (1965), *Dominican Diary.* New York, NY.

Taussig, Michael (1980), *The Devil and Commodity Fetishism in South America.* Chapel Hill, NC.

—— (1987), *Shamanism, Colonialism, and the Wild Man: A Study in Terror and Healing.* Chicago, IL.

Tawney, R. H. (1947), *Religion and the Rise of Capitalism.* New York, NY.

Tejeda Ortiz, Dagoberto (1978), *Mana: Monografía de un movimiento mesiánico abortado.* Santo Domingo.

Thomas, Hugh (1971), *Cuba: The Pursuit of Freedom.* New York, NY.

Thomas, Keith (1984), *Religion and the Decline of Magic: Studies in Popular Beliefs in Sixteenth- and Seventeenth-Century England.* Harmondsworth.

Thompson, P. R. (1985), Column in *Hoy,* 14 March.

Thompson, Robert Farris (1984), *Flash of the Spirit: Afro and Afro-American Art and Philosophy.* New York, NY.

Thoms, W. J. (1846), 'Folk-lore', *Athenæum,* No. 982.

Thorner, Daniel (1965), 'Peasant economy as a category in economic history', *Deuxième Conférence Internationale d'Histoire Économique, Aix-en-Provence, 1962, Volume II.* Paris and La Haye.

Thorpe, George C. (1918a), National Archives, Washington, DC; Naval Records. Collection of the Office of Naval Records and Library. Subject file 1911–1927. WA-7, Allied Countries, Santo Domingo. Daily Records. Box No. 756. H. M. 1988. Marine Barracks, San Juan, 23 January. From: Thorpe, George C., Lieut. Col., M.C., Commanding Expedition against Olivorio. To: Brigade Commander. Subject: Expedition against Dios Olivorio, alias Livorio.

—— (1918b), National Archives, Washington, DC; Naval Records. Collection of the Office of Naval Records and Library. Subject file 1911–1927. WA-7, Allied Countries, Santo Domingo. Daily Records. Box No. 756. H. M. 1988. Marine

Barracks, San Juan, 14 January. From: Thorpe, George C., Lieut. Col., M.C. To: Brigade Commander. Subject: Campaign.

—— (1918c), National Archives, Washington, DC; Naval Records. Collection of the Office of Naval Records and Library. Subject file 1911–1927. WA-7, Allied Countries, Santo Domingo. Daily Records. Box No. 756. H. M. 1988. (n.d.): Estimate of the Situation. Mission: To Capture or Destroy Dios Olivorio and his Band.

—— (1918d), National Archives, Washington, DC; Naval Records. Collection of the Office of Naval Records and Library. Subject file 1911–1927. WA-7, Allied Countries, Santo Domingo. Daily Records. Box No. 756. H. M. 1988. Headquarters, Expeditionary Force, San Juan, Dom. Rep., 15 January, 8:05 p.m.: Field Orders No. 1.

—— (1918e), National Archives, Washington, DC; Naval Records. Collection of the Office of Naval Records and Library. Subject file 1911–1927. WA-7, Allied Countries, Santo Domingo. Daily Records. Box No. 756. H. M. 1980. Headquarters, Second Provisional Brigade, US Marine Corps, 11 June. Mission: (I) Preserve Order in the Dominican Republic. (2) Contribute Maximum to Defeat of Teutons.

—— (1920), 'American achievements in Santo Domingo, Haiti, and Virgin Islands', *Journal of International Relations*, Vol. 2.

Thrupp, Sylvia L. (ed.) (1970), *Millennial Dreams in Action: Studies in Revolutionary Religious Movements*. New York, NY.

Toland, John (1987), *Adolf Hitler*. New York, NY.

Tolentino Rojas, Vicente (1944), *Historia de la división territorial, 1492–1943*. Ciudad Trujillo.

Trachtenberg, Joshua (1939), *Jewish Magic and Superstition: A Study in Folk Religion*. New York, NY.

—— (1945), *The Devil and the Jews: The Medieval Conception of the Jew and Its Relation to Modern Antisemitism*. New Haven, CT.

Troncoso Sánchez, Pedro (1964), *Ramón Cáceres*. Santo Domingo.

Trouillot, Michel-Rolph (1995), *Silencing the Past: Power and the Production of History*. Boston, MA.

Trujillo, Rafael L. (1930), Archivo del Palacio Nacional: Núm. 4540: 'Al Señor Leoncio Blanco, Mayor E.N.', Santo Domingo, 19 October, in Bernardo Vega (ed.), *Los Estados Unidos y Trujillo 1930*. Santo Domingo, 1986.

Tumarkin, Nina (1983), *Lenin Lives! The Lenin Cult in Soviet Russia*. Cambridge, MA.

Turner, Harold W. (1977), *Bibliography of New Religious Movements in Primal Societies. Vol 1. Black Africa*. Boston, MA.

—— (1979), *Bibliography of New Religious Movements in Primal Societies, Vol 2. North America*. Boston, MA.

—— (1985), 'New religious movements in primal societies', in John R. Hinnells (ed.), *A Handbook of Living Religions*. Harmondsworth.

Turner, Victor (1985), *The Ritual Process: Structure and Anti-Structure*. Ithaca, NY.

—— (1987), *Dramas, Fields, and Metaphors: Symbolic Action in Human Society*. Ithaca, NY.

Turner, Victor and Turner, Edith (1978), *Image and Pilgrimage in Christian Culture*. New York.

Un bando de policía de 1845 (1977), *Revista Eme Eme*, Vol. 5.

Una carta histórica al obispo de San Juan de la Maguana [No author given] (1961), Ciudad Trujillo.

Urbano Gilbert, Gregorio (1975), *Mi lucha contra el invasor Yanqui de 1916*. Santo Domingo.

Utrera, Cipriano de (1924), 'San Juan de la Maguana', *El Cable*, 5 February.

—— (1973), *Polémica de Enriquillo*. Santo Domingo.

—— (1978), *Santo Domingo: Dilucidaciones históricas*. Santo Domingo.

—— (1979), *Noticias históricas de Santo Domingo, Vol. III*. Santo Domingo.

—— (1982), *Noticias históricas de Santo Domingo, Vol. V*. Santo Domingo.

Valenzuela, Guillermo E. (1962), 'Rumoran: Los mellizos de Palma Sola bendicen y reparten puñales', *La Nación*, 11 December.

Valverde, Sebastián E. (1975), 'El Rosario', *Revista Dominicana de Folklore*, No. 2.

van Gennep, Arnold (1960), *The Rites of Passage*. London.

Vargas-Lundius, Rosemary (1991), *Peasants in Distress: Poverty and Unemployment in the Dominican Republic*. Boulder, CO.

Vásquez, Emilio and Fermín, María Felicia (1980), 'Creencias y prácticas religiosas populares y vigentes en El Granado. Provincia Bahoruco', *Revista Eme Eme*, Vol. 9.

Vásquez, Segundo (1986), 'En muchas personas una mezcla confusa de cábala y de fe lo hacen creer lo que es el fucú', *Hoy*, 7 February.

Vega, Bernardo (1981), *Imágenes del ayer*. Santo Domingo.

—— (ed.) (1982a), *Los Estados Unidos y Trujillo, año 1945*. Santo Domingo.

—— (ed.) (1982b), *Los Estados Unidos y Trujillo, año 1946*. Santo Domingo.

—— (ed.) (1984), *Los Estados Unidos y Trujillo, año 1947*. Santo Domingo.

—— (1985a), *La migracion española de 1939 y los inicios del marxismo-leninismo en la República Dominicana*. Santo Domingo.

—— (1985b), *Nazismo, fascismo y falangismo en la República Dominicana*. Santo Domingo.

—— (ed.) (1986a), *Los Estados Unidos y Trujillo, 1930*. Santo Domingo.

—— (ed.) (1986b), *Unos desafectos y otros en desgracia. Sufrimientos bajo la dictadura de Trujillo*. Santo Domingo.

—— (ed.) (1986c), *La vida cotidiana dominicana a través del Archivo Particular del Generalísimo*. Santo Domingo.

—— (1986d), *Los Trujillos se escriben*. Santo Domingo.

—— (1986e), *Control y represión en la dictadura trujillista*. Santo Domingo.

—— (1987), *Un interludio de tolerancia: El acuerdo con los comunistas en 1946*. Santo Domingo.

—— (1988a), *Más imágenes del ayer*. Santo Domingo.

—— (1988b), 'La herencia indígena en la cultura dominicana de hoy', in Bernardo Vega, Carlos Dobal, Carlos Esteban Deive, Rubén Silié, José del Castillo and Frank Moya Pons, *Ensayos sobre cultura dominicana*. Santo Domingo.

—— (1988c), *Trujillo y Haití, Volumen I (1930–1937)*. Santo Domingo.

—— (1989), *El 23 de febrero de 1930 o la más anunciada revolución de América*. Santo Domingo.

—— (1990), *Trujillo y el control financiero norteamericano*. Santo Domingo.

—— (1991a), *Eisenhower y Trujillo*. Santo Domingo.

—— (1991b), *Kennedy y los Trujillo*. Santo Domingo.

—— (1992), *Trujillo y las fuerzas armadas norteamericanas*. Santo Domingo.

—— (1993), *Kennedy y Bosch*. Santo Domingo.

—— (ed.) (1995a), *Trujillo y Haití, Volumen II (1937–1938)*. Santo Domingo.

—— (ed.) (1995b), *Trujillo ante una corte marcial por violación y extorsión en 1920*. Santo Domingo.

Vega y Pagán, Ernesto (1956), *Military Biography of Generalisimo Rafael Leonidas Trujillo Molina, Commander in Chief of the Armed Forces*. Ciudad Trujillo.

Verrill, A. Hyatt (1914), *Porto Rico, Past and Present and Santo Domingo of Today*. New York, NY.

Vicioso, Abelardo (1979), *Santo Domingo en las letras coloniales, 1492–1800*. Santo Domingo.

Vidal, Rafael (1972), 'Al margen de la frontera', in Juan B. Pérez (ed.), *Geografía y sociedad*. Santo Domingo.

Vidal de la Blache, Paul-Marie (1903), 'La géographie humaine. Ses rapports avec la géographie de la vie', *Revue de la Synthèse Historique*, Vol. 7.

von Franz, Marie Louise (1970), *Interpretation of Fairy Tales*. New York, NY.

Wagner, Roy (1981), *The Invention of Culture*. Chicago, IL and London.

Wallace, Anthony F. C. (1966), *Religion: An Anthropological View*. New York, NY.

—— (1979) 'Revitalization movements', in William A. Lessa and Evon Z. Vogt (eds), *Reader in Comparative Religion: An Anthropological Approach*. New York, NY.

Wallace, Anthony F. C. and Steen, S. C. (1970), *The Death and Rebirth of the Seneca*. New York, NY.

Wallis, Roy (1984), *The Elementary Forms of the New Religious Life*. London.

Ward, Henry P. (1960) 'Notas sobre la parte norte de la isla de Santo Domingo enclavada entre el Cabo Cabrón y Puerto Plata, una distancia de alrededor de doscientas millas, siguiendo el contorno de la costa', in *Informe de la comisión de investigación de los E.U.A. en Santo Domingo en 1871*. Ciudad Trujillo.

Warner, Marina (1983), *Alone of All Her Sex: The Myth and the Cult of the Virgin Mary*. New York, NY.

Watts, Jill (1992), *God, Harlem, USA: The Father Divine Story*. Berkeley, CA.

Webb, James (1991), *The Occult Establishment*. La Salle, IL.

Weber, Max (1930), *The Protestant Ethic and the Spirit of Capitalism*. London.

—— (1963), *The Sociology of Religion*. Boston, MA.

—— (1968a), 'Castes, Estates, Classes, and Religion', in S. N. Eisenstadt (ed.), *Max Weber on Charisma and Institution Building*. Chicago, IL and London.

—— (1968b), 'The Sociology of Charismatic Authority', in S. N. Eisenstadt (ed.), *Max Weber on Charisma and Institution Building*. Chicago, IL and London.

Welles, Sumner (1928), *Naboth's Vineyard: The Dominican Republic 1844-1924*. 2 Volumes. New York, NY.

Werbner, Richard P. (1977), 'Introduction', in Richard P. Werbner (ed.), *Regional Cults*. London.

West, Martin (1975), *Bishops and Prophets: African Independent Churches in Soweto, Johannesburg*. Cape Town.

Wheatley, Dennis (1974), 'Introduction', in Alfred Métraux, *Voodoo in Haiti*. London.

Wiarda, Howard J. (1968), *Dictatorship and Development: The Methods of Control in Trujillo's Dominican Republic*. Gainesville, FL.

—— (1975) *Dictatorship, Development and Disintegration: Politics and Social Change in the Dominican Republic*. Ann Arbor, MI.

Widengren, Geo (1965), *Die Religionen Irans*. Stuttgart.

Williams, G. A. (1922), National Archives, Washington, DC: Rg 38 (Chief of Naval Operations) Military Government of Santo Domingo, 1917–1924. General

Correspondence, 1922 (Corresponding General) Box No. 50. 31 July. From Company Commander to the Director, Dept of the South, P.N.D. Subject: Report of Contact with 'Dios' Olivorio.

Wilson, Bryan R. (1970), *Religösa sekter*. Stockholm.

—— (1973), *Magic and the Millennium: A Sociological Study of Religious Movements of Protests among Tribal and Third-World Peoples*. London.

—— (1975), *The Noble Savages: The Primitive Origins of Charisma and its Contemporay Survival*. Berkeley, CA.

Wilson, Stephen (1983), 'Introduction', in Stephen Wilson (ed.), *Saints and their Cults: Studies in Religious Sociology, Folklore and History*. Cambridge.

Wipfler, William Louis (1978), 'Power,influence and impotence: the church as a socio-political factor in the Dominican Republic', PhD thesis, Union Theological Seminary, New York, NY.

Wolf, Eric R. (1955), 'Types of Latin American peasantry: a preliminary discussion', *American Anthropologist*, Vol. 57.

—— (1957), 'Closed corporate peasant communities in Mesoamerica and Central Java', *Southwestern Journal of Anthropology*, Vol. 13.

—— (1966) *Peasants*. Englewood Cliffs, NJ.

Wolf, Eric R. and Hansen, Edward C. (1972), *The Human Condition in Latin America*. New York, NY.

Woodward, Kenneth L. and Brown, Hannah (1992), 'Doth my redeemer live? In Brooklyn Hasidim look for the Messiah', *Newsweek*, 27 April.

Worsley, Peter (1970), *The Trumpet Shall Sound: A Study of Cargo Cults in Melanesia*. London.

Wright, Lawrence (1993), 'A reporter at large: orphans of Jonestown', *The New Yorker*, 22 November.

Wright, Stuart A. (ed.) (1995), *Armageddon in Waco: Critical Perspectives on the Branch Davidian Conflict*. Chicago, IL and London.

Wuest, Joseph (1911), 'Redemptorists', in *The Catholic Encyclopedia, Volume XII*. New York, NY.

Yamaguchi, Susumu (1956) 'Development of Mahayana Buddhist beliefs', in Kenneth W. Morgan (ed.), *The Path of the Buddha: Buddhism Interpreted by Buddhists*. New York, NY.

Ziegler, Philip (1989), *The Black Death*. London.

Newspapers and magazines

¡Ahora!, Santo Domingo, 1962–1963, 1980, 1982 and 1985.

Amigo del Hogar, 'Las revista de la familia dominicana', Santo Domingo, 1986.

Blanco y Negro, Santo Domingo, 1909.

Bohemia Libre, Carácas, 1963–1964.

El 14 de Junio, Santo Domingo, 1962.

El Cable, Información, anuncios e intereses generales, San Juan de la Maguana, 1921–1930.

El Caribe, Santo Domingo,1962–1963.

El Diario, Periódico de información y de anuncios, Santiago de los Caballeros, 1910–1912.

Fides, Santo Domingo, 1963.

Gaceta Oficial, Santo Domingo, Vols. 28–30, 1911–13.

Hoy, Santo Domingo, 1985, 1993–1994.

El Imparcial, Higüey, 1914.

Listín Diario, Santo Domingo, 1910-1922, 1933, 1937, 1972, 1986.

Luz y Acción, Semanario de información e intereses generales, Las Matas de Farfán, 1947.

Le Monde, Paris, 1962.

La Nación, Santo Domingo, 1962–1963.

New York Times, New York, 1962.

Patria, Santo Domingo, 1965.

La Prensa, Santiago de los Caballeros, 1896.

El Radical, Santo Domingo, 1915.

Renacimiento, Santo Domingo, 1915.

Revista Judicial de la República Dominicana, Santo Domingo, 1909.

Revista Jurídica, Santo Domingo, 1919.

Santomé, Semanario informativo y de intereses generales. San Juan de la Maguana, 1960, 1962.

El Tiempo, Santo Domingo, 1910.

Time, New York, 1963.

The Times, London, 1962.

Unión Cívica Nacional, Santo Domingo, 1962.

Vanguardia del Pueblo (Organo del Partido de la Liberación Dominicana), Santo Domingo, 1988.

La Voz del Sur, Semanario político i de intereses generales, San Cristóbal, 1909–1910.

Interviews

Milita Alcántara. 45 years, widow, smallholder. Carrera de Yeguas, 17 January 1986.

Olimpia Almonte. 50 years, *pulpería* owner. Río Limpio, 30 April 1986.

'Aquilino'. Middleholder. Río Limpio, 1 May 1986.

Marina Bautista. 35 years, hairdresser, lived in Palma Sola with 'a woman of Plinio'. Las Matas de Farfán, 5 July 1990.

Domingo Antonio Bautista Mejía (Patoño). 58 years, former middleholder and intermediary salesman, former 'chief of the armed forces of Palma Sola'. Distrito de Haina, 5 March 1986.

Juan Bosch. Ex-president of the Dominican Republic. Santo Domingo, 11 October 1985.

Atala Cabral Ramírez (Doña Tala). 80 years, daughter of Alejandro Cabral, former physician in San Juan de la Maguana and married to Rosita Ramírez, daughter of Wenceslao Ramírez. Doña Tala was a teacher in San Juan de la Maguna for many years. Santo Domingo, 21 and 25 November 1985.

Diego Cépeda. 70 years, smallholder, *Olivorista*. Jínova, 4 June 1989.

Walter Cordero. Sociologist, lecturer at the Department of Sociology at Universidad Autónoma de Santo Domingo (UASD). Santo Domingo, 27 September 1985.

Lilian Corriveau. Canadian school sister of Notre Dame working for the Catholic church in Bánica. Bánica, 12 April 1986.

Day laborer. Higüerito, 16 January 1986.

A Dominican who knew Antonio García Vásquez in Bogotá. Guatemala City, 25 May 1991.

'Doña Blanca'. 60 years, *bruja*. Santo Domingo, 4 November 1985.

'Doña Nieves'. 30 years, *bruja* in the slum district of Buenos Aires, Santo Domingo. Santo Domingo, 6 January 1986.

Telma Odeida Dotel Matos. 53 years, pharmacist, daughter of Félix Dotel, former officer of the Guardia Nacional Dominicana (GND) in San Juan de la Maguana. Santo Domingo, 2 November, 1985.

Jorge Feliz. 25 years, school teacher, born in Carrera de Yeguas, but living in Barrio 27 Febrero in Santo Domingo. Santo Domingo, 5 January 1986.

Eugenio Fernández Durán. 54 years, schoolteacher in Las Zanjas, Mennonite. San Juan de la Maguana, 4 July 1990.

Leopoldo Figuereo. 32 years, correspondent of *Listín Diario* and *Ultima Hora* in San Juan de la Maguana. San Juan de la Maguana, 4 June 1989.

Enrique Figueroa. 53 years, smallholder, *brujo*. Hato Nuevo, 18 January 1986.

José Saladino Figueroa O. 52 years, photographer. San Juan de la Maguana. 4 July 1990.

Arsidé Gardés. 72 years, smallholder, vice treasurer of the *Cofradía del Espíritu Santo*. El Batey, 11 April 1986.

José Garrido Ramírez, Jr. 56 years, businessman, son of Emigdio O. Garrido Puello. Santo Domingo, 21 April 1986.

Víctor Garrido Ramírez, Jr. 70 years, lawyer, son of Víctor Garrido (brother of Emigdio O. Garrido Puello) and Tijides Ramírez, (daughter of Wenceslao Ramírez). Santo Domingo, 22 April 1986.

'Niño' Gómez. 45 years. *Camionero* [truck driver], middleholder. Restauración, 3 May 1986.

Radhamés Gómez Pepín. Former reporter of *El Caribe*, presently assistant editor-in-chief at *¡Ahora!*. Santo Domingo, 18 March 1986.

Bartolo de Jiménez. 'Missionary' by the Spring of San Juan Bautista, smallholder. Maguana Arriba, 13 December 1985.

Darío Jiménez Reynoso. 48 years, truck driver, former sergeant of the *Cascos Blancos*. Santo Domingo, 10 March 1986.

Javier Jovino. 76 years, smallholder. Río Limpio, 30 April 1986.

Bryan Kennedy. 37 years, six years in service as Redemptorist pastor in the parish of Santa Lucía in Las Matas de Farfán. Las Matas de Farfán, 4 May 1986.

Juana López. 24 years, domestic worker. Santo Domingo, 24 July 1983.

Macario Lorenzo. 52 years, teacher, former *secretario* of Palma Sola. Las Matas de Farfán, 14 May 1989.

Ana María Luciano (Pimpina). At least 84 years ('15 years when Olivorio was killed'). Mao, 22 January 1995. Ana María was interviewed by the Dominican historian Roberto Cassá, who generously gave us access to his tapes and transcripts.

Eugenio de Jesús Marcano Fondeur. Professor of Botany, Universidad Autónoma de Santo Domingo. Santo Domingo, 27 January 1989.

Americo Marra. 75 years, hotel owner (La Posada). Son of Flor Marra, retail dealer in San Juan de la Maguana. San Juan de la Maguana, 19 January 1989.

Lusitania Martínez. Teacher of philosophy and sociology at the Universidad Autónoma de Santo Domingo (UASD). Santo Domingo, 5 August 1985.

Juan José Medina Mesa. 60 years, medical doctor and senator. San Juan de la Maguana, 18 January 1989.

'Jamín' Medina Mora. 40 years, day laborer. Maguana Arriba, 13 December 1985.

Manuel Emilio Mesa. 98 years, former rancher. San Juan de la Maguana, 20 January 1989.

Angel Moreta. Director of the Faculty of Philosophy at the Universidad Autónoma de Santo Domingo (UASD). Moreta wrote a thesis on the San Juan area. Santo Domingo, 25 July 1985.

An *Olivorista* who wanted to remain anonymous, former member of 'the armed forces of Palma Sola'. Las Matas de Farfán, 5 July 1990.

María Orfelia, (*La Reina*). Keeper of the sanctuary in Maguana Arriba. Maguana Arriba, 13 December 1985 and 18 January 1986.

Marcelina Ovando. At least 87 years (born under Lilís), wife of Javier Jovino. Río Limpio, 1 May 1986.

Carlos Peguero Matos. 80 years, former retail dealer, son of José Peguero, former retail dealer and mayor in San Juan de la Maguana during the US occupation. San Juan de la Maguana, 4 July 1990.

José del Carmen Ramírez Fernández (Mimicito). 82 years (1985), son of José del Carmen Ramírez (Carmito). Three times province governor (*Provinicia El Benefactor*) San Juan de la Maguana, 14 December 1985, 15–18 January, 4 April, 11 April 1986, 1 June 1989 and 4 July 1990.

Leopoldo Ramírez (Sarni). 85 years, former member of the Dominican border patrol. Bánica, 2 June 1989.

Wenceslao Ramírez. Medical doctor, son of José del Carmen Ramírez (Carmito). Las Matas de Farfán, 17 January 1986.

Julián Ramos. 102 years, smallholder, *Olivorista*. Higüerito, Sección Maguana en Medio, 16 January 1986.

Thomas Reilly. 78 years, former bishop in San Juan de la Maguana, active in the San Juan Valley since 1948. San Juan de la Maguana, 12 December 1985, 5 January and 12 March 1986.

Mayobanex Rodríguez. 81 years (1985), twice mayor of San Juan de la Maguana. Son of Manuel de Jesús Rodríguez Varona, politician, author and for various periods chief of the police in San Juan de la Maguana. San Juan de la Maguana, 12 December 1985, 18 January 1989.

Miguel Antonio Rodríguez Landestoy. 44 years, agriculturist, son of General Miguel Rodríguez Reyes. Santo Domingo, 29 April 1986.

Ramón Jesús Rodríguez Landestoy. 49 years, retired major general, son of General Miguel Rodríguez Reyes. Boca Chica, 15 June 1989.

Maximiliano Rodríguez Piña. 88 years, son of Domingo Rodríguez, former businessman and hotel owner in San Juan de la Maguana. Santo Domingo, 23 April 1986.

Inés Rosario Alcántara. 50 years, former 'Virgin' of Palma Sola. Bánica, 2 June 1989.

Jesús Antonio Mario Santos (Maclín). 76 years, rice factory owner, son of Félix Valoy de los Santos Herrera, friend of Olivorio and McLean and former mayor in San Juan de la Maguana. San Juan de la Maguana, 19 January 1986.

Narciso Serrano. 40 years. His father served as guide to James McLean. Bánica, 3 May 1986.

Martín Solís (Pirindín). 73 years, smallholder. El Batey, 11 April 1986.

Miguel Tomás Suzaña. 62 years, *procurador* [district attorney] of the Court of Appeal in San Juan de la Maguana. San Juan de la Maguana, 7 May 1986.

Arquímedes Valdez. 91 years, smallholder, son of Olivorio Mateo. Maguana Abajo, 31 May 1989.

Juana María Ventura. 51 years, daughter of Delanoy Ventura. Media Luna, 17 January and 5 May 1986.

Bolívar Ventura Rodríguez. 35 years, smallholder. Palma Sola, 5 May 1986.

León Romilio Ventura Rodríguez (*El Mellizo*). 62 years (in 1986), smallholder, *Olivorista*, former leader of the cult in Palma Sola. Media Luna, 17 January and 5 May 1986, Las Matas de Farfán, 14 May 1989.

Ramón Závala (Zita). 66 years, smallholder and Mennonite. Paraje El Ranchito, Sección Carrera de Yeguas, 10 April 1986.

Index